COLLINS

WEBSTER'S

DICTIONARY

REVISED AND UPDATED

HARPER

An Imprint of HarperCollins*Publishers*

HARPER

An Imprint of HarperCollins*Publishers*
10 East 53rd Street
New York, New York 10022-5299

Copyright © 2002, 2003 HarperCollins Publishers
Bank of English® is a registered trademark of HarperCollins
Publishers Limited
ISBN: 978-0-06-055782-9
ISBN-10: 0-06-055782-6

First Harper paperback printing: June 2007
First HarperTorch paperback printing: July 2003

HarperCollins® and Harper® are registered trademarks of
HarperCollins Publishers.

Printed in the U.S.A.

20 19 18 17

CONTENTS

EDITORIAL STAFF

BANK *of* ENGLISH

This book has been compiled by referring to the Bank of English, a unique database of the English language with examples of over 520 million words taken from a very wide range of American and international books, newspapers, magazines, radio, TV, letters and talks, reflecting the whole spectrum of English today. This database enables Collins lexicographers to analyze how American English is actually used today and how it is changing.

The Bank of English was set up as a joint initiative by HarperCollins Publishers and Birmingham University to be a resourse for language research and lexicography. Its size and range make it an unequalled source of information and the purpose-built software for its analysis is unique to Collins English Dictionaries.

This ensures that Collins Dictionaries accurately reflect English as it is used today in a way that is most helpful to the user, as well as including the full range of rarer and historical meanings.

ARRANGEMENT OF ENTRIES

All main entries are arranged in a single alphabetical listing, including abbreviations, foreign words, and combining forms or prefixes. Each such entry consists of a paragraph, with a headword, that is, a main or core word, at the head of it in large bold blue type. Derived or related words, in smaller bold type, appear later in the paragraph in alphabetical order, with phrases included at the end. Thus, **"laborer"** and **"laborious"** will be found under **"labor,"** just as **"lends itself to"** will be found under **"lend"** and so on.

Alternative spellings are shown by placing the variants side by side (**amok, amuk**), but if the divergence in spelling is very great there is a separate entry.

Center dots, as in **"ab·sinthe"** and **"mol·lusk"**, are used to indicate divisions between syllables.

The part of speech is shown by an abbreviation placed after the pronunciation of the entry word (or after the entry word if it does not require pronouncing), for example, **"dog** (dawg) n." for noun. Words used as more than one part of speech are written out only once, the change being indicated by a new part of speech label, for example, **"rav·age** (RAV-ij) vt lay waste, plunder ▶ n destruction." In the case of very short, simple entries, parts of speech may be combined, for example, **"jest** n, vi joke."

The past tense and participles of verbs are shown in smaller bold type after the verb label when such information is considered helpful. The comparative and superlative forms of adjectives are also shown in smaller bold type after the adjective label when helpful to the reader. When it is considered helpful to readers to show the plural form or forms of a noun entry, this is also done after the noun label.

When a derived word is included within an entry, its meaning may be understood from the meaning of the headword or another derived word within the paragraph.

Field labels (such as *Radio*) and usage notes (such as *inf*) are added in italic type and abbreviated where there will be no confusion.

PRONUNCIATION

The pronunciation of some words is adequately shown by placing a mark (´) immediately after the syllable that carries the main stress, as in "**mon·soon´** *n*".

In most words, however, simple phonetic respelling is used to show pronunciation and stress. The respelled word appears in parentheses immediately after the headword, and the stressed syllable is given in capital letters.

Typical examples are: **cache** (kash); **ca·chet** (ka-SHAY); **cais·son** (KAY-son); **cap·puc·ci·no** (kap-ə-CHEE-noh); **cap·tious** (KAP-shəs).

Take note of the use of the schwa (ə), the neutral vowel sound typically occurring in unstressed syllables, as in the second syllable of **cap·puc·ci·no** and the second syllable of **cap·tious**.

The schwa and other special letters and letter combinations used in the phonetic respelling system are listed below. All letters that are not listed have their normal pronunciations.

a	sat	oh	rope	u	but
ah	calm	oi	boil	uu	book
ai	air	oo	food	ch	church
aw	law	yoo	sin*uo*us	ng	ring
ay	mate	or	four	sh	shin
e	met	ow	how	th	thin
ee	freeze	ə	*a*go	*th*	this
i	bit		em*e*r*a*ld	y	yes
ī	tight		penc*i*l	z	zebra
ī	del*i*ght		ven*o*m	*zh*	vis*i*on
o	hot		s*u*pport		

ABBREVIATIONS USED IN THE DICTIONARY

abbrev	abbreviation	m	meter(s)
adj	adjective	*masc*	masculine
adv	adverb	Math	Mathematics
Afr	Africa(n)	mm	millimeter(s)
Amer	America(n)	Mus	Music
Aust	Australia(n)	N	North
Brit	Britain, British	*n*	noun
Canad	Canada, Canadian	*n, pl*	plural noun
cent	century	N.Z.	New Zealand
Chem	Chemistry	*obs*	obsolete, obsolescent
cm	centimeter(s)	*offens*	offensive
comb	combining	oft	often
comp	comparative	orig	originally
conj	conjunction	*pers*	person
cu	cubic	pert	pertaining
dial	dialect	*pl*	plural
dim	diminutive	*poss*	possessive
e.g.	for example	*pp*	past participle
esp	especially	*prep*	preposition
fem	feminine	*pres t*	present tense
fig	figuratively	*pron*	pronoun
Fr	French	*pr p*	present participle
g	gram(s)	*pt*	past tense
Ger	German	R.C.	Roman Catholic
Gr	Greek	*refl*	reflexive
Hist	History	Russ	Russian
i.e.	that is	S	South
impers	impersonal	*sing*	singular
ind	indicative	*sl*	slang
inf	informal	Sp	Spanish
interj	interjection	sq	square
intr	intransitive	*sup*	superlative
It	Italian	*tr*	transitive
k	kilogram(s)	usu	usually
km	kilometer(s)	*v*	verb
l	liter(s)	*v aux*	auxiliary verb
Lat	Latin	*vi*	intransitive verb
lit	literally	*vt*	transitive verb

A a

a *adj* indefinite article, used before a noun being mentioned for the first time.

aard·vark [AHRD-vahrk] *n* S African mammal feeding on ants and termites.

a·back [ə-BAK] *adv* **taken aback** startled.

ab·a·cus [AB-ə-kəs] *n* counting device of beads on wire frame; flat tablet at top of architectural column.

ab·a·lo·ne [ab-ə-LOH-nee] *n* edible shellfish, yielding mother-of-pearl.

a·ban·don [ə-BAN-dən] *vt* desert; give up altogether. ▶ *n* freedom from inhibitions, etc. **a·ban'doned** *adj* deserted, forsaken; uninhibited; wicked.

a·base [ə-BAYS] *vt* **-based, -bas·ing.** humiliate, degrade. **a·base'ment** *n*

a·bash [ə-BASH] *vt* (usu. passive) confuse, make ashamed. **a·bash'ment** *n*

a·bate [ə-BAYT] *v* **-bat·ed, -bat·ing.** make or become less, diminish. **a·bate'ment** *n*

ab·at·toir [AB-ə-twahr] *n* slaughterhouse.

ab·bey [AB-ee] *n, pl* **-beys.** dwelling place of community of monks or nuns; church of an abbey.

ab·bot [AB-ət] *n (fem* **ab'bess)** head of abbey or monastery.

ab·bre·vi·ate [ə-BREE-vee-ayt] *vt* **-at·ed, -at·ing.** shorten, abridge. **ab·bre·vi·a'tion** *n* shortened form of word or phrase.

ab·di·cate [AB-di-kayt] *v* **-cat·ed, -cat·ing.** formally give up (throne, etc.). **ab·di·ca'tion** *n*

ab·do·men [AB-də-mən] *n* belly. **ab·dom'i·nal** *adj*

ab·duct [ab-DUKT] *vt* carry off, kidnap. **ab·duc'tion** *n*

ab·er·ra·tion [ab-ə-RAY-shən] *n* deviation from what is normal; flaw; lapse. **ab·er·rant** [ə-BER-ənt] *adj*

a·bet [ə-BET] *vt* **-bet·ted, -bet·ting.** assist, encourage, esp. in doing wrong. **a·bet'tor, -ter** *n*

a·bey·ance [ə-BAY-əns] *n* condition of not being in use or action.

ab·hor' *vt* **-horred, -hor·ring.** dislike strongly, loathe. **ab·hor'rent** *adj* hateful.

a·bide [ə-BID] *v* **a·bode'** or **a·bid'ed, a·bid'ing.** ▶ *vt* endure, put up with. ▶ *vi obs* stay, reside. **abide by** obey.

a·bil·i·ty [ə-BIL-i-tee] *n, pl* **-ties.** competence, power; talent.

ab·ject [AB-jekt] *adj* humiliated, wretched; despicable. **ab·ject'ness** *n*

ab·jure [ab-JOOR] *vt* **-jured, -jur·ing.** give up by oath, renounce. **ab·ju·ra'tion** *n*

a·blaze [ə-BLAYZ] *adj* burning.

a·ble [AY-bəl] *adj* capable, competent. **a'bled** *adj* having a range of physical powers as specified, e.g. *differently abled.* **a'bly** *adv* **a'ble-bod'ied** *adj*

ab·lu·tion [ə-BLOO-shən] *n* (usu. pl) act of washing (oneself).

ab·ne·gate [AB-ni-gayt] *vt* **-gat·ed, -gat·ing.** give up, renounce. **ab·ne·ga'tion** *n*

ab·nor·mal [ab-NOR-məl] *adj* irregular; not usual or typical; freakish, odd. **ab·nor·mal'i·ty** *n, pl* **-ties. ab·nor'mal·ly** *adv*

a·board [ə-BORD] *adv* on board, on ship, train, or aircraft.

a·bode [ə-BOHD] *n* home; dwelling; pt./pp. of ABIDE.

a·bol·ish [ə-BOL-ish] *vt* do away with. **ab·o·li'tion** *n* **ab·o·li'tion·ist** *n* one who wishes to do away with something, esp. slavery.

a·bom·i·nate [ə-BOM-ə-nayt] *vt* **-nat·ed, -nat·ing.** detest. **a·bom·i·na·ble** *adj* **a·bom·i·na'tion** *n* loathing; the object loathed. **abominable snowman** large legendary apelike creature said to inhabit the Himalayas.

ab·o·rig·i·nal [ab-ə-RIJ-ə-nl] *adj* (of people, etc.) original or earliest known in an area; of, relating to aborigines. **ab·o·rig'i·ne** [-ə-nee] *n* one of race of people inhabiting an area when European settlers arrived; original inhabitant of country, etc.; (**A-**) one of a race of people originally inhabiting Australia.

a·bort [ə-BORT] *v* (cause to) end prematurely (esp. pregnancy). ▶ *vi* give birth to dead fetus; fail. **a·bor'tion** *n* operation to terminate pregnancy; something deformed. **a·bor'tion·ist** *n* one who performs abortion, esp. illegally. **a·bor'tive** *adj* unsuccessful.

a·bound [ə-BOWND] *vi* be plentiful; overflow. **a·bound'ing** *adj*

a·bout [ə-BOWT] *adv* on all sides; nearly; up and down; out, on the move. ▶ *prep* around; near; concerning; ready to. **about turn** reversal, complete change.

a·bove [ə-BUV] *adv* higher up. ▶ *prep* over; higher than, more than; beyond.

a·brade [ə-BRAYD] *vt* **-brad·ed, -brad·ing.** rub off, scrape away.

a·bra·sion [ə-BRAY-zhən] *n* place scraped or worn by rubbing (e.g. on skin); scraping, rubbing. **a·bra'sive** [-siv] *n* substance for grinding, polishing, etc. ▶ *adj* causing abrasion; grating. **a·bra'sive·ness** *n* tendency to annoy.

a·breast [ə-BREST] *adv* side by side; keeping up with.

a·bridge [ə-BRIJ] *vt* cut short, abbreviate. **a·bridg'ment** *n*

a·broad [ə-BRAWD] *adv* to or in a foreign country; at large.

ab·ro·gate [AB-rə-gayt] *vt* cancel, repeal. **ab·ro·ga'tion** *n*

ab·rupt [ə-BRUPT] *adj* sudden; blunt; hasty; steep.

abs [ABZ] *pl n inf* abdominal muscles.

ab·scess [AB-ses] *n* gathering of pus in any part of the body.

ab·scis·sa [ab-SIS-ə] *n, pl* **-sae** [-see] *Math* distance of point from the axis of coordinates.

ab·scond [ab-SKOND] *vi* leave secretly, esp. having stolen something.

ab·sent [AB-sənt] *adj* away; not attentive. ▶ *vt* [ab-SENT] keep away. **ab'sence** *n* **ab·sen·tee'** *n* one who stays away esp. habitually. **ab·sen·tee'ism** *n* persistent absence from work, etc.

ab·sinthe [AB-sinth] *n* potent aniseed-flavored liqueur.

ab·so·lute [AB-sə-loot] *adj* complete; not limited, unconditional; pure, e.g. *absolute alcohol*. ▶ *n* **ab'so·lute·ly** *adv* completely. ▶ *interj* [-LOOT-lee] certainly.

ab·solve [ab-ZOLV] *vt* **-solved, -solv·ing.** free from, pardon, acquit. **ab·so·lu'tion** [-sə-LOO-shən] *n*

ab·sorb' *vt* suck up, drink in; engage, occupy (attention, etc.); receive impact. **ab·sorb'ent** *adj* **ab·sorp'tion** *n*

ab·stain [ab-STAYN] *vi* keep from, refrain from drinking alcohol, voting, etc. **ab·sten'tion** *n* **ab'sti·nence** *n*

ab·ste·mi·ous [ab-STEE-mee-əs] *adj* sparing in food or esp. drink, temperate. **ab·ste'mi·ous·ness** *n*

ab·stract [ab-STRAKT] *adj* existing only in the mind; not concrete; (of art) not representational. ▶ *n* [AB-strakt] summary, abridgment. ▶ *vt* [ab-STRAKT] draw from, remove; steal. **ab·stract'ed** *adj* preoccupied. **ab·strac'tion** *n*

ab·struse [ab-STROOS] *adj* obscure, difficult to understand, profound.

ab·surd' *adj* contrary to reason. **ab·surd'i·ty** *n*

a·bun·dance [ə-BUN-dəns] *n* great amount. **a·bun'dant** *adj* plentiful.

a·buse [ə-BYOOZ] *vt* **-bused, -bus·ing.** misuse; address rudely. ▶ *n* (ə-BYOOS). **a·bu'sive** [-siv] *adj* **a·bu'sive·ness** *n*

a·but [ə-BUT] *vi* **-but·ted, -but·ting.** adjoin, border on. **a·but'ment** *n* support, esp. of bridge or arch.

a·bys·mal [ə-BIZ-məl] *adj*
immeasurable, very great; *inf*
extremely bad. **a·bys'mal·ly** *adv*
a·byss [ə-BIS] *n* very deep gulf or
pit.
Ac *Chem* actinium.
a·cad·e·my [ə-KAD-ə-mee] *n, pl*
-mies. society to advance arts or
sciences; institution for specialized
training; secondary school.
ac·a·dem·ic [ak-ə-DEM-ik] *adj* of
academy, university, etc.;
theoretical.
ac·cede [ak-SEED] *vi* **-ced·ed,**
-ced·ing. agree, consent; attain
(office, right, etc.).
ac·cel·er·ate [ak-SEL-ə-rayt] *v*
-at·ed, -at·ing. (cause to) increase
speed, hasten. **ac·cel·er·a'tion** *n*
ac·cel'er·a·tor *n* mechanism to
increase speed, esp. in automobile.
ac·cent [AK-sent] *n* stress or pitch in
speaking; mark to show such stress;
local or national style of
pronunciation; particular attention
or emphasis. ▶ *vt*
ac·cen·tu·ate [ak-SEN-choo-ayt] *vt*
-at·ed, -at·ing. stress, emphasize.
ac·cept [ak-SEPT] *vt* take, receive;
admit, believe; agree to.
ac·cept'a·ble *adj* **ac·cept'ance** *n*
ac·cess [AK-ses] *n* act, right, or
means of entry. **ac·ces'si·ble** *adj*
easy to approach.
ac·ces·sion [ak-SESH-ən] *n*
attaining of office, right, etc.;
increase, addition.
ac·ces·so·ry [ak-SES-ə-ree] *n, pl*
-ries. additional or supplementary
part of automobile, woman's dress,
etc.; person inciting or assisting in
crime. ▶ *adj* contributory, assisting.
ac·ci·dent [AK-si-dənt] *n* event
happening by chance; misfortune
or mishap, esp. causing injury;
nonessential quality. **ac·ci·den'tal**
adj
ac·claim [ə-KLAYM] *vt* applaud,
praise. ▶ *n* applause.
ac·cla·ma'tion *n*
ac·cli·mate [AK-klə-mayt] *v*
-mat·ed, -mat·ing. acclimatize.
ac·cli·ma·tize [ə-KLĪ-mə-tīz] *v*
-tized, -tiz·ing. accustom to new

climate or environment.
ac·cli·ma·ti·za'tion *n*
ac·co·lade [AK-ə-layd] *n* praise,
public approval; award, honor;
token of award of knighthood, etc.
ac·com·mo·date [ə-KOM-ə-dayt]
vt **-dat·ed, -dat·ing.** supply, esp.
with board and lodging; oblige;
harmonize, adapt.
ac·com'mo·dat·ing *adj* obliging.
ac·com·mo·da'tions *pl n* lodgings.
ac·com·pa·ny [ə-KUM-pə-nee] *vt*
-nied, -ny·ing. go with;
supplement; occur with; provide a
musical accompaniment.
ac·com'pa·ni·ment *n* that which
accompanies, esp. in music, part
that goes with solos, etc.
ac·com'pa·nist *n*
ac·com·plice [ə-KOM-plis] *n* one
assisting another in criminal deed.
ac·com·plish [ə-KOM-plish] *vt* carry
out; finish. **ac·com'plished** *adj*
complete, perfect; proficient.
ac·com'plish·ment *n* completion;
personal ability.
ac·cord [ə-KORD] *n* agreement,
harmony. ▶ *v* (cause to) be in
accord with. ▶ *vt* grant.
ac·cord'ing·ly *adv* as the
circumstances suggest; therefore.
ac·cor·di·on [ə-KOR-dee-ən] *n*
portable musical instrument with
keys, metal reeds and a bellows.
ac·cost [ə-KAWST] *vi* approach and
speak to, often aggressively.
ac·count [ə-KOWNT] *n* report,
description; importance, value;
statement of moneys received,
paid, or owed; person's money
held in bank; credit available to
person at store, etc. ▶ *vt* reckon;
judge. ▶ *v* give reason, answer
(for). **ac·count'a·ble** *adj*
responsible. **ac·count'an·cy** *n*
keeping, preparation of business
accounts, financial records, etc.
ac·count'ant *n* one practicing
accountancy. **ac·count'ing** *n* skill
or practice of keeping and
preparing business accounts. ▶ *adj*
ac·cred·it·ed [ə-KRED-i-tid] *adj*
authorized, officially recognized.
ac·cre·tion [ə-KREE-shən] *n*

growth; something added on.
ac·crue [ə-KROO] *vi* **-crued,
-cru·ing.** be added; result.
ac·cu·mu·late [ə-KYOO-myə-layt] *v*
-lat·ed, -lat·ing. gather, become
gathered in increasing quantity;
collect. **ac·cu·mu·la'tion** *n*
ac·cu·rate [AK-yər-it] *adj* exact,
correct, without errors. **ac'cu·ra·cy**
n
ac·curs·ed [ə-KUR-sid] *adj* under a
curse; hateful, detestable.
ac·cuse [ə-KYOOZ] *vt* **-cused,
-cus·ing.** charge with wrongdoing;
blame. **ac·cu·sa·tion**
[ak-yə-ZAY-shən] *n* **ac·cu'sa·tive** *n*
grammatical case indicating the
direct object. **ac·cu'sa·to·ry** *adj*
ac·cus·tom [ə-KUS-təm] *vt* make
used to, familiarize. **ac·cus'tomed**
adj usual; used (to); in the habit
(of).
ace *n* the one at dice, cards,
dominoes; *Tennis* winning serve
untouched by opponent; very
successful fighter pilot. ▶ *vt* **aced,
ac·ing.** score an ace; *Golf* make
hole in one; *inf* make grade of A.
a·cer·bi·ty [ə-SUR-bi-tee] *n* severity,
sharpness; sour tasting. **a·cerb'** *adj*
ac·e·tate [AS-i-tayt] *n* salt or ester
of acetic acid; synthetic textile fiber.
a·ce·tic [ə-SEE-tik] *adj* derived from
or having the nature of vinegar.
ac·e·tone [AS-i-tohn] *n* colorless
liquid used as a solvent.
a·cet·y·lene [ə-SET-l-een] *n*
colorless, flammable gas used esp.
in welding metals.
ache [ayk] *n* continuous pain. ▶ *vi*
ached, ach·ing. to be in pain.
a·chieve [ə-CHEEV] *vt* **-chieved,
-chiev·ing.** accomplish, perform
successfully; gain. **a·chieve'ment** *n*
something accomplished.
ac·id [AS-id] *adj* sharp, sour. ▶ *n*
sour substance; *Chem* one of a class
of compounds that combine with
bases (alkalis, oxides, etc.) to form
salts. **a·cid'ic** *adj* **a·cid'i·fy** *vt* **-fied,
-fy·ing.** **a·cid'i·ty** *n* **a·cid'u·lous**
adj caustic. **acid rain** rain acidified
by atmospheric pollution. **acid
test** conclusive test of value.

ac·knowl·edge [ak-NOL-ij] *vt*
-edged, -edg·ing. admit, own to
knowing, recognize; say one has
received. **ac·knowl'edg·ment** *n*
ac·me [AK-mee] *n* highest point.
ac·ne [AK-nee] *n* pimply skin
disease.
ac·o·lyte [AK-ə-līt] *n* follower or
attendant, esp. of priest.
a·cous·tic [ə-KOO-stik] *adj* pert. to
sound and to hearing. **a·cous'tics**
n science of sounds. ▶ *pl* features of
room or building as regards sounds
heard within it.
ac·quaint [ə-KWAYNT] *vt* make
familiar, inform. **ac·quaint'ance** *n*
person known; personal knowledge.
ac·qui·esce [ak-wee-ES] *vi* **-esced,
-esc·ing.** agree, consent without
complaint. **ac·qui·es'cence** *n*
ac·quire [ə-KWIR] *vt* **-quired,
-quir·ing.** gain, get. **ac·qui·si·tion**
[ak-wə-ZISH-ən] *n* act of getting;
material gain. **ac·quis'i·tive** *adj*
desirous of gaining.
ac·quit [ə-KWIT] *vt* **-quit·ted,
-quit·ting.** declare innocent; settle,
discharge, as a debt; behave
(oneself). **ac·quit'tal** *n* declaration
of innocence in court.
a·cre [AY-kər] *n* measure of land,
43,560 square feet. ▶ *pl* lands,
estates; *inf* large area or plenty of.
a'cre·age *n* the extent of land in
acres.
ac·rid [AK-rid] *adj* pungent, sharp;
irritating.
ac·ri·mo·ny [AK-rə-moh-nee] *n*
bitterness of feeling or language.
ac·ri·mo'ni·ous *adj*
ac·ro·bat [AK-rə-bat] *n* one skilled
in gymnastic feats, esp. as
entertainer in circus, etc.
ac·ro·bat'ic *adj* **ac·ro·bat'ics** *pl n*
activities requiring agility.
ac·ro·nym [AK-rə-nim] *n* word
formed from initial letters of other
words, such as NATO.
a·crop·o·lis [ə-KROP-ə-lis] *n* citadel,
esp. in ancient Greece.
a·cross [ə-KRAWS] *adv, prep*
crosswise; from side to side; on or
to the other side. **get, put it across**
explain, make (something)

understood.

a·cros·tic [ə-KRAW-stik] n word puzzle (or verse) in which the first, middle, or last letters of each line spell a word or words.

a·cryl·ic [ə-KRIL-ik] n variety of synthetic materials, esp. paint and textiles.

act [akt] n thing done, deed; doing; law or decree; section of a play. ▶ v perform, as in a play. ▶ vi exert force, work, as mechanism; behave. **act'ing** n performance of a part. ▶ adj temporarily performing the duties of. **ac'tion** n operation; deed; gesture; expenditure of energy; battle; lawsuit. **ac'tion·a·ble** adj subject to lawsuit. **ac'ti·vate** vt -vat·ed, -vat·ing. to make active; make radioactive; make chemically active. **ac·ti·va'tion** n **ac'tive** adj moving, working; brisk, energetic. **ac'ti·vist** n one who takes (direct) action to achieve political or social ends. **ac·tiv'i·ty** n **ac'tor, ac'tress** n one who acts in a play, film, etc.

ac·tin·i·um [ak-TIN-ee-əm] n radioactive element occurring as decay product of uranium.

ac·tu·al [AK-choo-əl] adj existing in the present; real. **ac·tu·al'i·ty** n **ac'tu·al·ly** adv really, indeed.

ac·tu·ar·y [AK-choo-er-ee] n, pl -ar·ies. statistician who calculates insurance risks, premiums, etc. **ac·tu·ar'i·al** adj

ac·tu·ate [AK-choo-ayt] vt -at·ed, -at·ing. activate; motivate. **ac'tu·a·tor** n mechanism for controlling or moving something indirectly.

a·cu·i·ty [ə-KYOO-i-tee] n keenness, esp. in vision or thought.

a·cu·men [ə-KYOO-mən] n sharpness of wit, perception, penetration.

ac·u·punc·ture [AK-yə-pungk-chər] n medical treatment involving insertion of needles at various points on the body.

a·cute [ə-KYOOT] adj keen, shrewd; sharp; severe; of angle, less than 90°. ▶ n accent (´) over a letter to indicate the quality or length of its sound, as in café. **a·cute'ness** n

ad·age [AD-ij] n much used wise saying, proverb.

a·da·gio [ə-DAH-joh] adv, n, pl -gios. Mus leisurely, slow (passage).

ad·a·mant [AD-ə-mənt] adj very hard, unyielding. **ad·a·man'tine** [-MAN-teen] adj

Adam's apple [AD-əmz] projecting part at front of the throat, the thyroid cartilage.

a·dapt [ə-DAPT] vt alter for new use; fit, modify; change. **a·dapt'a·ble** adj **ad·ap·ta'tion** n **a·dapt'er, -tor** n device for connecting several electrical appliances to single socket.

add v join; increase by; say further. **ad·di·tion** [ə-DISH-ən] n **ad·di'tion·al** adj **ad'di·tive** n something added, esp. to food.

ad·den·dum [ə-DEN-dəm] n, pl -da [-də] thing to be added.

ad·der [AD-ər] n small poisonous snake.

ad·dict [AD-ikt] n one who has become dependent on something, esp. drugs. **ad·dict'ed** adj **ad·dic'tion** n **ad·dic'tive** adj causing addiction.

ad·dle [AD-l] v -dled, -dling. make or become rotten, muddled.

ad·dress [ə-DRES or AD-res] n direction on letter; place where one lives; Computers number giving the location of a piece of stored information; speech. ▶ vt mark destination, as on envelope; speak to; direct; dispatch. **address ball** Golf adjust club before striking ball. **ad·dress·ee'** n person addressed.

ad·duce [ə-DOOS] vt -duced, -duc·ing. offer as proof; cite. **ad·duc'i·ble** adj

ad·e·noids [AD-n-oidz] pl n tissue at back of nose and throat, sometimes obstructing breathing.

a·dept [ə-DEPT] adj skilled. ▶ n [AD-ept] expert.

ad·e·quate [AD-i-kwit] adj sufficient, enough, suitable; not outstanding. **ad'e·qua·cy** n

ad·here [ad-HEER] vi -hered,

-her·ing. stick to; be firm in opinion, etc. **ad·her'ent** n, adj
ad·he'sion [-HEE-zhən] n
ad·he'sive [-siv] adj, n
ad hoc [ad-HOK] adj, adv for a particular occasion only; improvised.
a·dieu [ə-DYOO] interj farewell. ▶ n, pl **a·dieus, a·dieux** [ə-DYOOZ] act of taking leave.
ad in·fi·ni·tum [in-fə-NĪ-təm] Lat endlessly.
ad·i·pose [AD-ə-pohs] adj of fat, fatty.
ad·ja·cent [ə-JAY-sənt] adj lying near, next (to).
ad·jec·tive [AJ-ik-tiv] n word that modifies or limits a noun.
ad·jec·ti'val [-TĪ-vəl] adj of adjective.
ad·join [ə-JOIN] v be next to; join.
ad·join'ing adj next to, near.
ad·journ [ə-JURN] v postpone temporarily, as meeting; inf move elsewhere.
ad·judge [ə-JUJ] vt **-judged, -judg·ing.** declare; decide; award.
ad·ju·di·cate [ə-JOO-di-kayt] v **-cat·ed, -cat·ing.** try, judge; sit in judgment. **ad·ju·di·ca'tion** n
ad·junct [AJ-ungkt] adj joined, added. ▶ n person or thing added or subordinate.
ad·jure [ə-JOOR] vt **-jured, -jur·ing.** beg, earnestly entreat. **ad·ju·ra'tion** [aj-ə-RAY-shən] n
ad·just [ə-JUST] vt make suitable, adapt; alter slightly, regulate. ▶ vi adapt or conform to new conditions, etc. **ad·just'a·ble** adj
ad·ju·tant [AJ-ə-tənt] n military officer who assists superiors. **ad'ju·tan·cy** n office, rank of adjutant.
ad-lib v **-libbed, -lib·bing.** improvise and speak spontaneously. **ad lib** n such speech, etc.
ad·min·is·ter [ad-MIN-ə-stər] vt manage, look after; dispense, as justice, etc.; apply. **ad·min·is·tra'tion** n **ad·min·is·tra·tive** adj
ad·mi·ral [AD-mər-əl] n naval

officer of highest sea rank.
ad'mi·ral·ty n Law court having jurisdiction over maritime matters.
ad·mire [ad-MĪR] vt **-mired, -mir·ing.** look on with wonder and pleasure; respect highly.
ad'mi·ra·ble adj **ad'mi·ra·bly** adv
ad·mi·ra'tion n **ad·mir'er** n
ad·mir'ing·ly adv
ad·mit [ad-MIT] vt **-mit·ted, -mit·ting.** confess; accept as true; allow; let in. **ad·mis'si·ble** adj
ad·mis'sion n permission to enter; entrance fee; confession.
ad·mit'tance n permission to enter.
ad·mit'ted·ly adv
ad·mix·ture [ad-MIKS-chər] n mixture; ingredient.
ad·mon·ish [ad-MON-ish] vt reprove; advise; warn; exhort.
ad·mo·ni'tion [-mə-NISH-ən] n
ad·mon'i·to·ry adj
ad nau·se·am [NAW-zee-əm] Lat to a boring or disgusting extent.
a·do [ə-DOO] n fuss.
a·do·be [ə-DOH-bee] n sun-dried brick.
ad·o·les·cence [ad-l-ES-ens] n period of life just before maturity.
ad·o·les'cent n a youth. ▶ adj
a·dopt [ə-DOPT] vt take into relationship, esp. as one's child; take up, as principle, resolution. **a·dop'tion** n **a·dop'tive** adj that which adopts or is adopted.
a·dore [ə-DOR] v **-dored, -dor·ing.** love intensely; worship.
a·dor'a·ble adj **ad·o·ra'tion** n
a·dorn [ə-DORN] vt beautify, embellish, deck. **a·dorn'ment** n ornament, decoration.
ad·re·nal [ə-DREEN-l] adj near the kidney. **adrenal glands** glands covering the top of the kidneys.
a·dren'a·line [-DREN-l-in] n hormone secreted by adrenal glands; this substance used as drug.
a·drift [ə-DRIFT] adj, adv drifting free; inf detached; inf off course.
a·droit [ə-DROIT] adj skillful, expert; clever. **a·droit'ness** n dexterity.
ad·sorb [ad-SORB] v (of gas, vapor) condense and form thin film on

surface. **ad·sorb'ent** *adj, n*
ad·sorp'tion *n*
ad·u·la·tion [aj-ə-LAY-shən] *n*
flattery. **ad'u·late** *vt* **-lat·ed,
-lat·ing.** flatter. **ad'u·la·to·ry** *adj*
a·dult [ə-DULT] *adj* grown-up,
mature. ▸ *n* grown-up person;
full-grown animal or plant.
a·dul·ter·ate [ə-DUL-tə-rayt] *vt*
-at·ed, -at·ing. make impure by
addition. **a·dul'ter·ant** *n*
a·dul·ter·y [ə-DUL-tə-ree] *n* sexual
unfaithfulness of a husband or wife.
a·dul'ter·er, a·dul'ter·ess *n*
a·dul'ter·ous *adj*
ad·vance [ad-VANS] *v* **-vanced,
-vanc·ing.** ▸ *vt* bring forward;
suggest; encourage; pay
beforehand; *Auto* to time spark
earlier in engine cycle. ▸ *vi* go
forward; improve in position or
value. ▸ *n* movement forward;
improvement; a loan. ▸ *pl* personal
approach(es) to gain favor, etc.
▸ *adj* ahead in time or position.
ad·vanced' *adj* at a late stage; not
elementary; ahead of the times.
ad·vance'ment *n* promotion.
ad·van·tage [ad-VAN-tij] *n*
superiority; more favorable position
or state; benefit. **ad·van·ta'geous**
[-vən-TAY-jəs] *adj*
ad·vent [AD-vent] *n* a coming,
arrival; (**A-**) the four weeks before
Christmas. **the Advent** the
coming of Christ. **Ad'vent·ist** *n*
one of number of Christian sects
believing in imminent return of
Christ.
ad·ven·ti·tious [ad-vən-TISH-əs]
adj added; accidental, casual.
ad·ven·ture [ad-VEN-chər] *n* risk;
bold exploit; remarkable
happening; enterprise; commercial
speculation. **ad·ven'tur·er,
ad·ven'tur·ess** *n* one who seeks
adventures; one who lives on his
wits. **ad·ven'tur·ous** *adj*
ad·verb [AD-vurb] *n* word used
with verb, adjective, or other
adverb to modify meaning.
ad·ver'bi·al *adj*
ad·verse [ad-VURS] *adj* opposed to;
hostile; unfavorable, bringing

harm. **ad'ver·sar·y** *n, pl* **-sar·ies.**
enemy. **ad·verse'ly** *adv*
ad·ver'si·ty *n* distress, misfortune.
ad·ver·tise [AD-vər-tīz] *v* **-tised,
-tis·ing.** ▸ *vt* publicize; make
known; give notice of, esp. in
newspapers, etc. ▸ *vi* make public
request (for). **ad·ver·tise'ment**
ad'ver·tis·ing *adj, n*
ad·vice [ad-VIS] *n* opinion given;
counsel; information; (formal)
notification.
ad·vise [ad-VĪZ] *vt* **-vised, -vis·ing.**
offer advice; recommend a line of
conduct; give notice (of).
ad·vis'a·ble *adj* expedient.
ad·vised' *adj* considered,
deliberate, e.g. *well-advised.*
ad·vis'ed·ly [-zid-lee] *adv* **ad·vi'ser**
n **ad·vi'so·ry** *adj*
ad·vo·cate [AD-və-kit] *n* one who
pleads the cause of another, esp. in
court of law; attorney. ▸ *vt* [-kayt]
uphold, recommend. **ad'vo·ca·cy**
[-kə-see] *n*
ae·gis [EE-jis] *n* sponsorship,
protection (orig. shield of Zeus).
aer·ate [AIR-ayt] *vt* **-at·ed, -at·ing.**
charge liquid with gas, as
effervescent drink; expose to air.
aer·a'tion *n* **aer'a·tor** *n* apparatus
for charging liquid with gas.
aer·i·al [AIR-ee-əl] *adj* of the air;
operating in the air; pertaining to
aircraft. ▸ *n* part of radio, etc.
receiving or sending radio waves.
aer·ie, aer·y *n* SEE EYRIE.
aero- *comb. form* air or aircraft, e.g.
aerodynamics.
aer·o·bat·ics [air-ə-BAT-iks] *pl n*
stunt flying.
aer·o·bics [air-OH-biks] *n* exercise
system designed to increase the
amount of oxygen in the blood.
aer·o·dy·nam·ics
[air-oh-dī-NAM-iks] *n* study of air
flow, esp. around moving solid
bodies.
aer·o·naut [AIR-ə-nawt] *n* pilot or
navigator of lighter-than-air craft.
aer·o·nau'tics *n* science of air
navigation and flying in general.
aer·o·nau'ti·cal *adj*
aer·o·sol [AIR-ə-sawl] *n* (substance

dispensed as fine spray from) pressurized can.

aer·o·space [AIR-oh-spays] *n* Earth's atmosphere and space beyond. ▸ *adj*

aes·thet·ic [es-THET-ik] *adj* relating to principles of beauty, taste and art. **aes·thet·ics** *n* study of art, taste, etc. **aes·thete** [ES-theet] *n* one who affects extravagant love of art.

a·far [ə-FAHR] *adv* from, at, or to, a great distance.

af·fa·ble [AF-ə-bəl] *adj* easy to speak to, polite and friendly. **af·fa·bil'i·ty** *n*

af·fair [ə-FAIR] *n* thing done or attended to; business; happening; sexual liaison. ▸ *pl* personal or business interests; matters of public interest.

af·fect [ə-FEKT] *vt* act on, influence; move feelings; make show of, make pretense; assume; have liking for. **affect** [AF-ekt] *n Psychology* emotion, feeling, desire. **af·fec·ta'tion** *n* show, pretense. **af·fect'ed** *adj* making a pretense; moved; acted upon. **af·fect'ing** *adj* moving the feelings. **af·fec'tion** *n* fondness, love. **af·fec'tion·ate** *adj*

af·fi·da·vit [af-i-DAY-vit] *n* written statement under oath.

af·fil·i·ate [ə-FIL-ee-ayt] *vt* **-at·ed, -at·ing.** connect, attach, as society to federation, etc.; adopt. ▸ *n* [-ee-it] affiliated organization.

af·fin·i·ty [ə-FIN-i-tee] *n, pl* **-ties.** natural liking; resemblance; relationship by marriage; chemical attraction.

af·firm [ə-FURM] *v* assert positively, declare; maintain statement; make solemn declaration. **af·fir·ma'tion** *n* **af·firm'a·tive** *adj* asserting. ▸ *n* word of assent.

af·fix [ə-FIKS] *vt* fasten (to); attach, append. ▸ *n* [AF-fiks] addition, esp. to word, as suffix, prefix.

af·flict [ə-FLIKT] *vt* give pain or grief to, distress; trouble, vex. **af·flic'tion** *n*

af·flu·ent [AF-loo-ənt] *adj* wealthy;

abundant. ▸ *n* tributary stream. **af'flu·ence** *n* wealth, abundance.

af·ford [ə-FORD] *vt* be able to buy; be able to spare the time, etc.; produce, yield, furnish.

af·front [ə-FRUNT] *vt* insult openly. ▸ *n* insult; offense.

a·field [ə-FEELD] *adv* away from home; in or on the field.

a·fire [ə-FĪR] *adv* on fire.

a·flame [ə-FLAYM] *adv* burning.

a·float [ə-FLOHT] *adv* floating; at sea; in circulation.

a·foot [ə-FUUT] *adv* astir; on foot.

a·fore [ə-FOR] *prep, adv* before, usually in compounds, e.g. *aforesaid; aforethought.*

a·foul [ə-FOWL] *adj, adv* into difficulty (with).

a·fraid [ə-FRAYD] *adj* frightened; regretful.

a·fresh [ə-FRESH] *adv* again, anew.

Af·ri·can [AF-ri-kən] *adj* belonging to Africa. ▸ *n* native of Africa. **African-American** *n* American of African descent. ▸ *adj* of African-Americans.

Af·ri·kaans [af-ri-KAHNS] *n* language used in S. Africa, derived from 17th cent. Dutch.

Af·ri·ka'ner *n* white native of S. Afr. with Afrikaans as mother tongue.

aft *adv* toward stern of ship or tail of aircraft.

af·ter [AF-tər] *adv* later; behind. ▸ *prep* behind; later than; on the model of; pursuing. ▸ *conj* at a later time than. ▸ *adj* behind; later; nearer stern of ship or tail of aircraft.

af·ter·birth [-burth] *n* membrane expelled after a birth.

af·ter·care [-kair] *n* care, esp. medical, bestowed on person after period of treatment.

af·ter·ef·fect [-ə-fekt] *n* subsequent effect of deed, event, etc.

af·ter·glow [-gloh] *n* light after sunset; reflection of past emotion.

af·ter·math *n* result, consequence.

af·ter·noon' *n* time from noon to evening.

af'ter·taste [-tayst] *n* taste

remaining or recurring after eating or drinking something.

af·ter·thought [-thawt] *n* idea occurring later.

af·ter·ward(s) [-wərd *or* -wərdz] *adv* later.

Ag *Chem* silver.

a·gain [ə-GEN] *adv* once more; in addition; back, in return; besides.

a·gainst [ə-GENST] *prep* in opposition to; in contact with; opposite; in readiness for.

a·gape [ə-GAYP] *adj, adv* open-mouthed as in wonder, etc.

ag·ate [AG-it] *n* colored, semiprecious, decorative form of quartz.

age [ayj] *n* length of time person or thing has existed; time of life; period of history; maturity; long time. ▶ *v* **aged, ag·ing.** make or grow old. **aged** [AY-jid *or* ayjd] *adj* old. ▶ *pl. n* [AY-jid] old people. **aging** *n, adj* **age'less** *adj* not growing old, not showing signs of age. **age-old** *adj* ancient.

a·gen·da [ə-JEN-də] *n* things to be done; program of business meeting.

a·gent [AY-jənt] *n* one authorized to carry on business or affairs for another; person or thing producing effect; cause; natural force. **a'gen·cy** *n* instrumentality; business, place of business, of agent.

agent pro·vo·ca·teur [prə-vok-ə-TUR] *n, pl* **agents pro·vo·ca·teur.** *Fr* police or secret service spy.

ag·glu·ti·nate [ə-GLOOT-n-ayt] *vt* **-nat·ed, -nat·ing.** unite with glue, etc.; form words into compounds. ▶ *adj* [-n-it] united, as by glue. **ag·glu·ti·na'tion** *n*

ag·gran·dize [ə-GRAN-dīz] *vt* **-dized, -diz·ing.** make greater in size, power, or rank. **ag·gran'dize·ment** [-diz-mənt] *n*

ag·gra·vate [AG-rə-vayt] *vt* **-vat·ed, -vat·ing.** make worse or more severe; *inf* annoy. **ag·gra·va'tion** *n*

ag·gre·gate [AG-ri-gayt] *vt* **-gat·ed, -gat·ing.** gather into mass. ▶ *adj* [-git] gathered thus. ▶ *n* [-git] mass, sum total; rock consisting of mixture of minerals; mixture of gravel, etc. for concrete. **ag·gre·ga'tion** *n*

ag·gres·sion [ə-GRESH-ən] *n* unprovoked attack; hostile activity. **ag·gres'sive** *adj* **ag·gres'sive·ness** *n* **ag·gres'sor** *n*

ag·grieve [ə-GREEV] *vt* **-grieved, -griev·ing.** pain, injure.

a·ghast [ə-GAST] *adj* struck, stupefied with horror or terror.

ag·ile [AJ-əl] *adj* nimble; active; quick. **a·gil'i·ty** *n*

ag·i·tate [AJ-i-tayt] *v* **-tat·ed, -tat·ing.** ▶ *vt* disturb, excite; to keep in motion, stir, shake up; trouble. ▶ *vi* stir up public opinion (for or against). **ag'i·ta·tor** *n*

a·glow [ə-GLOH] *adj* glowing.

ag·nos·tic [ag-NOS-tik] *n* person who believes that it is impossible to know whether God exists. ▶ *adj* of this theory. **ag·nos'ti·cism** *n*

a·go [ə-goh] *adv* in the past.

a·gog [ə-GOG] *adj, adv* eager, astir.

ag·o·ny [AG-ə-nee] *n, pl* **-nies.** extreme suffering of mind or body, violent struggle. **ag'o·nize** *vi* **-nized, -niz·ing.** suffer agony; worry greatly. **agony column** newspaper or magazine feature column containing advertisements relating to personal problems, esp. to missing friends or relatives.

ag·o·ra·pho·bi·a [ag-ər-ə-FOH-bee-ə] *n* abnormal fear of open spaces.

a·grar·i·an [ə-GRAIR-ee-ən] *adj* of agriculture, land or its management.

a·gree [ə-GREE] *v* **-greed, -gree·ing.** be of same opinion; consent; harmonize; settle suit. **a·gree'a·ble** *adj* willing; pleasant. **a·gree'ment** *n* concord; contract.

ag·ri·cul·ture [AG-ri-kul-chər] *n* art, practice of cultivating land. **ag·ri·cul'tur·al** *adj*

a·gron·o·my [ə-GRON-ə-mee] *n* the study of the management of the land and the scientific cultivation of crops. **a·gron'o·mist**

n

a·ground [ə-GROWND] *adv* (of boat) touching bottom.

a·head [ə-HED] *adv* in front; forward; in advance.

a·hoy [ə-HOI] *interj* shout used at sea for hailing.

aid [ayd] *vt* to help. ▶ *n* help, support, assistance.

aide [ayd] *n* person acting as an assistant.

aide-de-camp [AYD-də-KAMP] *n, pl* **aides-de-camp** [AYD-də-KAMP] military officer personally assisting superior.

AIDS acquired immune deficiency syndrome.

ail [ayl] *vt* trouble, afflict, disturb. ▶ *vi* be ill. **ail'ing** *adj* sickly. **ail'ment** *n* illness.

ai·ler·on [AY-lə-ron] *n* movable section of wing of aircraft that gives lateral control.

aim [aym] *v* give direction to weapon, etc.; direct effort toward, try to. ▶ *n* direction; object, purpose. **aim'less** *adj* without purpose.

ain't [aynt] *nonstandard* am not; is not; are not; has not; have not.

air *n* mixture of gases we breathe, the atmosphere; breeze; tune; manner. ▶ *pl* affected manners. ▶ *vt* expose to air to dry or ventilate. **air'i·ly** *adv* **air'i·ness** *n* **air'ing** *v* time spent in the open air; exposure to public view; radio or TV broadcast. **air'less** *adj* stuffy. **air'y** *adj* **air·i·er, air·i·est.** **air'borne** *adj* flying, in the air. **air'bag** *n* safety device in car which inflates automatically in an accident to protect the driver or passenger. **air brake** brake worked by compressed air; method of slowing down an aircraft. **air'brush** *n* atomizer spraying paint by compressed air. **air'-con·di·tion** *vt* maintain constant stream of clean fresh air in building at correct temperature. **air conditioner** *n* **air'craft** *n* collective name for flying machines; airplane. **aircraft carrier** warship with a long flat

deck for the launching and landing of aircraft. **air cushion** pocket of air supporting hovercraft. **air'field** *n* landing and takeoff area for aircraft. **air force** military organization of country for air warfare. **air gun** gun discharged by force of compressed air. **air'lift** *n* transport of goods, etc. by aircraft. **air'line** *n* company operating aircraft. **air'lock** *n* air bubble obstructing flow of liquid in pipe; airtight chamber. **air pocket** less dense air that causes airplane to drop suddenly. **air'port** *n* station for civilian aircraft. **air pump** machine to extract or supply air. **air raid** attack by aircraft. **air shaft** passage for air into a mine, etc. **air'ship** *n* lighter-than-air flying machine with means of propulsion and steering.

air'sick·ness *n* nausea caused by motion of aircraft in flight.

air'speed *n* speed of aircraft relative to air. **air'strip** *n* small airfield with only one runway.

air'tight *adj* not allowing passage of air. **air'way** *n* regular aircraft route. **air'wor·thy** *adj* fit for service in air. **air'wor·thi·ness** *n*

air'plane [-playn] *n* heavier-than-air flying machine.

aisle [īl] *n* passageway separating seating areas in church, theater, etc.

a·jar [ə-JAHR] *adv* partly open.

a·kim·bo [ə-KIM-boh] *adv* with hands on hips and elbows outward.

a·kin [ə-KIN] *adj* related by blood; alike, having like qualities.

Al *Chem* aluminum.

al·a·bas·ter [AL-ə-bas-tər] *n* soft, white, semitransparent stone. **al·a·bas'trine** [-BAS-trin] *adj* of, like this.

à la carte [ah lə KAHRT] selected freely from the menu.

a·lac·ri·ty [ə-LAK-ri-tee] *n* quickness, briskness, readiness.

à la mode [ah lə MOHD] in fashion; topped with ice cream.

a·larm [ə-LAHRM] *n* sudden fright; apprehension; notice of danger; bell, buzzer; call to arms. ▶ *vt* frighten; warn of danger.

a·larm·ist n one given to prophesying danger or exciting alarm esp. needlessly.

a·las [ə-LAS] interj cry of grief, pity, or concern.

al·ba·tross [AL-bə-traws] n large oceanic bird, of petrel family; someone or something thought to make accomplishment difficult.

al·be·it [awl-BEE-it] conj although.

al·bi·no [al-BĪ-noh] n, pl **-nos.** person or animal with white skin and hair, and pink eyes, due to lack of pigment. **al·bi·nism** [AL-bə-niz-əm] n

al·bum [AL-bəm] n book of blank leaves, for photographs, stamps, autographs, etc.; one or more long-playing phonograph records or tape recordings.

al·bu·men [al-BYOO-mən] n egg white.

al·bu·min [al-BYOO-mən] n constituent of animal and vegetable matter, found nearly pure in white of egg.

al·che·my [AL-kə-mee] n medieval chemistry, esp. attempts to turn base metals into gold and find elixir of life. **al'che·mist** n

al·co·hol [AL-kə-hawl] n intoxicating fermented liquor; class of organic chemical substances. **al·co·hol'ic** adj of alcohol. ▶ n one addicted to alcoholic drink. **al'co·hol·ism** n disease, alcohol poisoning.

al·cove [AL-kohv] n recessed section of a room.

ale [ayl] n fermented malt liquor, type of beer, orig. without hops.

a·lert [ə-LURT] adj watchful; brisk, active. ▶ n warning of sudden attack or surprise. ▶ vt warn, esp. of danger; draw attention to. **a·lert'ness** n **on the alert** watchful.

al·fal·fa [al-FAL-fə] n plant widely used as fodder.

al·fres·co [al-FRES-koh] adv, adj in the open air.

al·gae [AL-jee] pl. n, sing **-ga** [-gə] various water plants, including seaweed.

al·ge·bra [AL-jə-brə] n method of calculating, using symbols to represent quantities and to show relations between them, making a kind of abstract arithmetic. **al·ge·bra'ic** [-BRAY-ik] adj

ALGOL, Algol [AL-gol] Computers algorithmic oriented language.

al·go·rithm [AL-gə-rith-əm] n procedural model for complicated calculations.

a·li·as [AY-lee-əs] adv otherwise known as. ▶ n, pl **-as·es.** assumed name.

al·i·bi [AL-ə-bī] n plea of being somewhere else when crime was committed; inf excuse.

a·li·en [AY-lee-ən] adj foreign; different in nature; repugnant (to). ▶ n foreigner. **a'li·en·a·ble** adj able to be transferred to another owner. **a'li·en·ate** [-ə-nayt] vt **-at·ed, -at·ing.** estrange; transfer. **a·li·en·a'tion** n

a·light[1] [ə-LĪT] vi get down; land, settle.

a·light[2] adj lit up.

a·lign [ə-LĪN] vt bring into line or agreement.

a·like [ə-LĪK] adj like, similar. ▶ adv in the same way.

al·i·men·ta·ry [al-ə-MEN-tə-ree] adj of food. **alimentary canal** food passage in body.

al·i·mo·ny [AL-ə-moh-nee] n allowance paid under court order to separated or divorced spouse.

a·live [ə-LĪV] adj living; active; aware; swarming.

al·ka·li [AL-kə-lī] n, pl **-lis.** substance that combines with acid and neutralizes it, forming a salt. **al'ka·line** adj **al·ka·lin'i·ty** n

all [awl] adj the whole of, every one of. ▶ adv wholly, entirely. ▶ n the whole; everything, everyone. ▶ pron everything, everyone. **all fours** hands and feet. **all in** exhausted. **all'-a·round'** adj showing ability in many fields. **all right** satisfactory; well, safe; pleasing; very well; beyond doubt.

Al·lah [AH-lə] n Muslim name for the Supreme Being.

al·lay [ə-LAY] *vt* lighten, relieve, calm, soothe.

al·lege [ə-LEJ] *vt* **-leged, -leg·ing.** state without or before proof; produce as argument. **al·le·ga·tion** [al-i-GAY-shən] *n* **al·leged'** *adj* **al·leg·ed·ly** *adv*

al·le·giance [ə-LEE-jəns] *n* duty of a subject or citizen to sovereign or government; loyalty (to person or cause).

al·le·go·ry [AL-i-gor-ee] *n, pl* **-ries.** story with a meaning other than literal one; description of one thing under image of another. **al·le·gor'i·cal** *adj*

al·le·gret·to [al-i-GRET-oh] *adv, adj, n Mus* lively (passage) but not so quick as allegro.

al·le·gro [ə-LEG-roh] *adv, adj, n Mus* fast (passage).

al·ler·gy [AL-ər-jee] *n, pl* **-gies.** abnormal sensitivity to some food or substance harmless to most people. **al'ler·gen** *n* substance capable of inducing an allergy. **al·ler·gic** [ə-LUR-jik] *adj* having or caused by an allergy; *inf* having an aversion (to).

al·le·vi·ate [ə-LEE-vee-ayt] *vt* **-at·ed, -at·ing.** ease, lessen, mitigate; make light. **al·le·vi·a'tion** *n*

al·ley [AL-ee] *n, pl* **-leys.** narrow street esp. through the middle of a block; walk, path; hardwood lane for bowling; building housing bowling lanes.

al·li·ance [ə-LĪ-əns] *n* state of being allied; union between families by marriage, and states by treaty; confederation.

al·li·ga·tor [AL-i-gay-tər] *n* animal of crocodile family; leather made from its hide.

al·lit·er·a·tion [ə-lit-ə-RAY-shən] *n* beginning of two or more words in close succession with same sound, e.g *Sing a Song of Sixpence.* **al·lit'er·a·tive** *adj*

al·lo·cate [AL-ə-kayt] *vt* **-cat·ed, -cat·ing.** assign as a share; designate. **al·lo·ca'tion** *n*

al·lo·mor·phism [al-ə-MOR-fiz-əm] *n* variation of form without change in essential nature; variation of crystalline form of chemical compound. **al'lo·morph** *n* **al·lo·morph'ic** *adj*

al·lop·a·thy [ə-LOP-ə-thee] *n* orthodox practice of medicine; opposite of homeopathy.

al·lot [ə-LOT] *vt* **-lot·ted, -lot·ting.** distribute as shares; give out. **al·lot'ment** *n* distribution; portion of land rented for cultivation; portion of land, pay, etc. allotted.

al·low [ə-LOW] *vt* let happen; permit; acknowledge; set aside. ▶ *vi* (usu. with *for*) take into account. **al·low'a·ble** *adj* **al·low'ance** *n* portion or amount allowed, esp. at regular times.

al·loy [AL-oi] *n* mixture of two or more metals. ▶ *vt* [ə-LOI] mix metals, debase.

all right see **ALL**.

all·spice [AWL-spīs] *n* berry of West Indian tree; the tree; aromatic spice prepared from its berries.

al·lude [ə-LOOD] *vi* **-lud·ed, -lud·ing.** mention lightly, hint at, make indirect reference to; refer to. **al·lu'sion** [-LOO-zhən] *n* **al·lu'sive** [-siv] *adj*

al·lure [ə-LOOR] *vt* **-lured, -lur·ing.** entice, win over, fascinate. ▶ *n* attractiveness. **al·lur'ing** *adj* charming, seductive.

al·lu·vi·al [ə-LOO-vee-əl] *adj* deposited by rivers. **al·lu'vi·on** [-vee-ən] *n* land formed by washed-up deposit. **al·lu'vi·um** [-vee-əm] *n, pl* **-vi·a** [-vee-ə] water-borne matter deposited by rivers, floods, etc.

al·ly [ə-LĪ] *vt* **-lied, -ly·ing.** join in relationship by treaty, marriage, or friendship, etc. ▶ *n* [AL-ī] *pl* **-lies.** country or ruler bound to another by treaty; confederate.

al·ma ma·ter [AL-mə MAH-tər] one's school, college, or university; its song or hymn.

al·ma·nac [AWL-mə-nak] *n* yearly publication with detailed information on tides, events, etc.

al·might·y [awl-MĪ-tee] *adj* having

all power, omnipotent; *inf* very great. **The Almighty** God.

al·mond [AH-mənd] *n* kernel of the fruit of a tree related to the peach; tree that bears it.

al·most [AWL-mohst] *adv* very nearly, all but.

alms [ahmz] *pl n* gifts to the poor.

al·oe [AL-oh] *n* genus of plants of medicinal value. ▶ *pl* bitter drug made from plant.

a·loft [ə-LAWFT] *adv* on high; overhead; in ship's rigging.

a·lone [ə-LOHN] *adj* single, solitary. ▶ *adv* separately, only.

a·long [ə-LAWNG] *adv* lengthwise; together (with); forward. ▶ *prep* over the length of. **a·long'side'** *adv, prep* beside.

a·loof [ə-LOOF] *adv* withdrawn; at a distance; apart. ▶ *adj* uninvolved. **a·loof'ness** *n*

al·o·pe·ci·a [al-ə-PEESH-ə] *n* baldness.

a·loud [ə-LOWD] *adj* in a voice loud enough to be heard. ▶ *adv* loudly; audibly.

alp *n* high mountain. **Alps** *pl* esp. mountains of Switzerland. **al·pine** [AL-pīn] *adj* of, growing on, high mountains; (**A-**) of the Alps. ▶ *n* mountain plant. **al·pin·ist** [AL-pə-nist] *n* mountain climber. **al'pen·stock** [-pən-stok] *n* iron-tipped staff used by climbers.

al·pac·a [al-PAK-ə] *n* Peruvian llama; its wool; cloth made from this.

al·pha·bet [AL-fə-bet] *n* the set of letters used in writing a language. **al·pha·bet'i·cal** *adj* in the standard order of the letters.

al·read·y [awl-RED-ee] *adv* before, previously; sooner than expected.

al·so [AWL-soh] *adv* as well, too; besides, moreover.

al·tar [AWL-tər] *n* raised place, stone, etc., on which sacrifices are offered; in Christian church, table on which priest consecrates the eucharist elements. **al'tar·cloth** *n* **al'tar·piece** *n* **al'tar rails** *n* **altar boy** *n* acolyte.

al·ter [AWL-tər] *v* change, make or become different; castrate, spay

(animal). **al'ter·a·ble** *adj* **al'ter·a·bly** *adv* **al·ter·a'tion** *n*

al·ter·ca·tion [awl-tər-KAY-shən] *n* dispute, wrangling, noisy controversy.

al·ter e·go [AWL-tər EE-goh] second self; close friend.

al·ter·nate [AWL-tər-nayt] *v* **-nat·ed, -nat·ing.** occur or cause to occur by turns. **al'ter·nate** [-nit] *adj, n* (one) after the other, by turns. **al·ter·na·tive** [awl-TUR-nə-tiv] *n* one of two choices. ▶ *adj* offering or expressing a choice. **al'ter·na·tor** *n* electric generator for producing alternating current. **alternative medicine** treatment of disease by non-traditional methods such as homeopathy and acupuncture.

al·though [awl-THOH] *conj* despite the fact that.

al·tim·e·ter [al-TIM-i-tər] *n* instrument for measuring height.

al·ti·tude [AL-ti-tood] *n* height, eminence, elevation, loftiness.

al·to [AL-toh] *n, pl* **-tos.** *Mus* male singing voice or instrument above tenor; contralto.

al·to·geth·er [awl-tə-GETH-ər] *adv* entirely; on the whole; in total. **in the altogether** nude.

al·tru·ism [AL-troo-iz-əm] *n* principle of living and acting for good of others. **al'tru·ist** *n* **al·tru·is'tic** *adj*

a·lu·mi·num [ə-LOO-mə-nəm] *n* light nonrusting metal resembling silver. **a·lu'mi·na** *n* oxide of aluminum.

a·lum·na [ə-LUM-nə] *n, pl* **-nae** [-nee] girl or woman graduate of a particular school, college, or university.

a·lum·nus [ə-LUM-nəs] *n, pl* **-ni** [-nī] graduate of a particular school, college, or university.

al·ways [AWL-wayz] *adv* at all times; forever.

am first person sing. pres. ind. of BE.

Am *Chem* americium.

A.M., a.m. ante meridiem: before noon.

a·mal·gam [ə-MAL-gəm] *n*

compound of mercury and another metal; soft, plastic mixture; combination of elements.

a·mal·ga·mate [ə-MAL-gə-mayt] *v* **-mat·ed, -mat·ing.** mix, combine or cause to combine. **a·mal·ga·ma'tion** *n*

a·man·u·en·sis [ə-man-yoo-EN-sis] *n, pl* **-ses** [-seez] one who writes from dictation; copyist, secretary.

a·mass [ə-MAS] *v* collect in quantity.

am·a·teur [AM-ə-chuur] *n* one who carries on an art, study, game, etc. for the love of it, not for money; unskilled practitioner. **am·a·teur'ish** *adj* imperfect, untrained.

am·a·to·ry [AM-ə-tor-ee] *adj* relating to love.

a·maze [ə-MAYZ] *vt* **-mazed, -maz·ing.** surprise greatly, astound. **a·maze'ment** *n* **amazing** *adj*

Am·a·zon [AM-ə-zon] *n* female warrior of legend; tall, strong woman. **Am·a·zo'ni·an** [-ZOH-nee-ən] *adj*

am·bas·sa·dor [am-BAS-ə-dər] *n* senior diplomatic representative sent by one government to another. **am·bas·sa·do'ri·al** *adj*

am·ber [AM-bər] *n* yellowish, translucent fossil resin. ▶ *adj* made of, colored like amber.

am·ber·gris [AM-bər-gris] *n* waxy substance secreted by the sperm whale, used in making perfumes.

am·bi·dex·trous [am-bi-DEK-strəs] *adj* able to use both hands with equal ease. **am·bi·dex·ter'i·ty** *n*

am·bi·ence, -ance [AM-bee-əns] *n* atmosphere of a place.

am·bi·ent [AM-bee-ənt] *adj* surrounding.

am·big·u·ous [am-BIG-yoo-əs] *adj* having more than one meaning; obscure. **am·bi·gu'i·ty** *n*

am·bi·tion [am-BISH-ən] *n* desire for power, fame, honor; the object of that desire. **am·bi'tious** *adj*

am·biv·a·lence [am-BIV-ə-ləns] *n* simultaneous existence of two conflicting desires, opinions, etc. **am·biv'a·lent** *adj*

am·ble [AM-bəl] *vi* **-bled, -bling.** move along easily and gently; move at an easy pace. ▶ *n* this movement or pace.

am·bro·sia [am-BROH-zhə] *n* Mythology food of the gods; anything smelling, tasting particularly good.

am·bu·lance [AM-byə-ləns] *n* conveyance for sick or injured.

am·bush [AM-buush] *n* a lying in wait (for). ▶ *vt* waylay, attack from hiding, lie in wait for.

a·mel·io·rate [ə-MEEL-yə-rayt] *v* **-rat·ed, -rat·ing.** make better, improve. **a·mel·io·ra'tion** *n*

a·men [AY-MEN] *interj* surely; so let it be.

a·me·na·ble [ə-MEE-nə-bəl] *adj* easy to be led or controlled; subject to, liable. **a·me'na·bly** *adv*

a·mend [ə-MEND] *vi* grow better. ▶ *vt* correct; improve; alter in detail, as bill in legislature, etc. **a·mend'ment** *n* **a·mends'** *pl n* reparation.

a·men·i·ty [ə-MEN-i-tee] *n, pl* **-ties.** useful or pleasant facility or service.

A·mer·i·can [ə-MER-i-kən] *adj* of, relating to, the North American continent or the United States of America.

am·e·thyst [AM-ə-thist] *n* bluish-violet precious stone; its color.

a·mi·a·ble [AY-mee-ə-bəl] *adj* friendly, kindly. **a·mi·a·bil'i·ty** *n*

am·i·ca·ble [AM-i-kə-bəl] *adj* friendly. **am·i·ca·bil'i·ty** *n*

a·mid [ə-MID], **a·midst** [ə-MIDST] *prep* in the middle of, among; during.

a·mid·ships [ə-MID-ships] *adv* near, toward, middle of ship.

a·mi·no acid [ə-MEE-noh] organic compound found in protein.

a·miss [ə-MIS] *adj* wrong. ▶ *adv* faultily, badly. **take amiss** be offended (by).

am·i·ty [AM-i-tee] *n* friendship.

am·me·ter [AM-mee-tər] *n* instrument for measuring electric current.

am·mo·nia [ə-MOHN-yə] *n*

pungent alkaline gas containing hydrogen and nitrogen.

am·mo·nite [AM-ə-nīt] *n* whorled fossil shell like ram's horn.

am·mu·ni·tion [am-yə-NISH-ən] *n* any projectiles (bullets, rockets, etc.) that can be discharged from a weapon; facts that can be used in an argument.

am·ne·sia [am-NEE-zhə] *n* loss of memory.

am·nes·ty [AM-nə-stee] *n, pl* **-ties.** general pardon. ▸ *vt* **-tied, -ty·ing.** grant this.

am·ni·ot·ic fluid [am-nee-OT-ik] fluid surrounding fetus in womb.

a·moe·ba [ə-MEE-bə] *n, pl* **-bas.** microscopic single-celled animal found in ponds, etc. and able to change its shape.

a·mok, a·muck [ə-MUK] *adv* **run amok** rush about in murderous frenzy.

a·mong [ə-MUNG], **a·mongst** [ə-MUNGST] *prep* mixed with, in the midst of, of the number of, between.

a·mor·al [ay-MOR-əl] *adj* nonmoral, having no moral qualities.

a·mo·ral·i·ty [ay-mə-RAL-i-tee] *n*

am·o·rous [AM-ər-əs] *adj* inclined to love; in love. **am'o·rous·ness** *n*

a·mor·phous [ə-MOR-fəs] *adj* without distinct shape.

am·or·tize [AM-ər-tīz] *vt* pay off a debt by a sinking fund. **am'or·tiz·a·ble** *adj*

a·mount [ə-MOWNT] *vi* come, be equal (to). ▸ *n* quantity; sum total.

a·mour [ə-MOOR] *n* (illicit) love affair.

am·pere [AM-peer] *n* unit of electric current. **am·per·age** [AM-pə-rij] *n* strength of current in amperes.

am·per·sand [AM-pər-sand] *n* the character (&), meaning *and*.

am·phet·a·mine [am-FET-ə-meen] *n* synthetic liquid used medicinally as stimulant, a dangerous drug if misused.

am·phib·i·ous [am-FIB-ee-əs] *adj* living or operating both on land and in water. **am·phib'i·an** *n*

animal that lives first in water then on land; vehicle able to travel on land or water; aircraft that can alight on land or water.

am·phi·the·a·ter [AM-fə-thee-ə-tər] *n* building with tiers of seats rising around an arena; room with gallery above from which one can observe surgical operations, etc.

am·pho·ra [AM-fər-ə] *n, pl* **-rae** [-ree] two-handled vessel of ancient Greece and Rome.

am·ple [AM-pəl] *adj* big enough; large, spacious. **am'ply** *adv*

am·pli·fy [AM-plə-fī] *vt* **-fied, -fy·ing.** increase; make bigger, louder, etc. **am·pli·fi·ca'tion** *n* **am'pli·fi·er** *n*

am·pli·tude [AM-pli-tood] *n* spaciousness, width; maximum departure from average of alternating current, etc. **amplitude modulation** modulation of amplitude of radio carrier wave; broadcasting system using this.

am·pule [AM-pyool] *n* container for hypodermic dose.

am·pu·tate [AM-pyə-tayt] *vi* **-tat·ed, -tat·ing.** cut off (limb, etc.). **am·pu·ta'tion** *n*

amuck see AMOK.

am·u·let [AM-yə-lit] *n* something carried or worn as a charm.

a·muse [ə-MYOOZ] *vt* **-mused, -mus·ing.** divert; occupy pleasantly; cause to laugh or smile.

a·muse'ment *n* entertainment, pastime.

an *adj* form of **a** used before vowels, and sometimes before *h*, e.g. *an hour.*

an·a·bol·ic ster·oid [an-ə-BOL-ik STEER-oid] any of various hormones used by athletes to encourage muscle growth.

a·nach·ro·nism [ə-NAK-rə-niz-əm] *n* mistake of time, by which something is put in wrong historical period; something out-of-date.

an·a·con·da [an-ə-KON-də] *n* large semi-aquatic snake that kills by constriction.

an·a·gram [AN-ə-gram] *n* word or sentence made by reordering the letters of another word or sentence, such as *ant* from *tan*.

anal see ANUS.

an·al·ge·si·a [an-l-JEE-zee-ə] *n* absence of pain. **an·al·ge'sic** *adj, n* (drug) relieving pain.

a·na·log [AN-ə-log] *n* physical object or quantity used to measure or represent another quantity; something that is analogous to something else. ▶ *adj* displaying information by means of a dial.

a·nal·o·gy [ə-NAL-ə-jee] *n, pl* **-gies.** agreement or likeness in certain respects; correspondence. **a·nal'o·gize** *v* **-gized, -giz·ing.** explain by analogy. **a·nal'o·gous** [-ə-gəs] *adj* similar; parallel.

a·nal·y·sis [ə-NAL-ə-sis] *n, pl* **-ses** [-seez] separation into elements or components. **an·a·lyze** [AN-l-īz] *vt* **-lyzed, -lyz·ing.** examine critically; determine the constituent parts. **an·a·lyst** [AN-l-ist] *n* one skilled in analysis, esp. chemical analysis; psychoanalyst. **an·a·lyt·ic·al** [an-l-IT-i-kəl], **an·a·lyt·ic** [an-l-IT-ik] *adj*

an·ar·chy [AN-ər-kee] *n* lawlessness; lack of government in a country; confusion. **an·ar·chic** [an-AHR-kik] *adj* **an'ar·chism** *n* **an'ar·chist** *n* one who opposes all government.

a·nath·e·ma [ə-NATH-ə-mə] *n, pl* **-mas.** anything detested, hateful; ban of the church; curse. **a·nath'e·ma·tize** *vt* **-tized, -tiz·ing.**

a·nat·o·my [ə-NAT-ə-mee] *n* science of structure of the body; detailed analysis; the body. **an·a·tom'i·cal** *adj*

an·ces·tor [AN-ses-tər] *n* person from whom another is descended; early type of later form or product. **an·ces'tral** *adj* **an'ces·try** *n*

an·chor [ANG-kər] *n* heavy (usu. hooked) implement dropped on cable, chain, etc. to bottom of sea, etc. to secure vessel; *Radio and TV* principal announcer in program of news, sports, etc. ▶ *vt* fasten by or as with anchor; perform as anchor. **an'chor·age** *n* act of, place of anchoring.

an·cho·rite [ANG-kə-rīt] *n* hermit, recluse.

an·cho·vy [AN-choh-vee] *n, pl* **(-vies).** small fish of herring family.

an·cient [AYN-shənt] *adj* belonging to former age; old; timeworn. ▶ *n* one who lived in an earlier age. **ancient history** history of ancient times; common knowledge.

an·cil·lar·y [AN-sə-ler-ee] *adj, n, pl* **-ies.** subordinate, subservient, auxiliary.

and *conj* joins words, phrases, clauses, and sentences to introduce a consequence, etc.

an·dan·te [ahn-DAHN-tay] *adv, n* *Mus* moderately slow (passage).

and·i·ron [AND-ī-ərn] *n* steel bar or bracket for supporting logs in a fireplace.

an·drog·y·nous [an-DROJ-ə-nəs] *adj* having characteristics of both male and female.

an·ec·dote [AN-ik-doht] *n* very short story dealing with single incident. **an'ec·do·tal** *adj* **an·ec·do'tal·ist** *n* one given to recounting anecdotes.

a·ne·mi·a [ə-NEE-mee-ə] *n* deficiency in number of red blood cells. **a·ne'mic** *adj* suffering from anemia; pale, sickly.

an·e·mom·e·ter [an-ə-MOM-i-tər] *n* wind gauge.

a·nem·o·ne [ə-NEM-ə-nee] *n* flower related to buttercup. **sea anemone** plantlike sea animal.

an·er·oid [AN-ə-roid] *adj* denoting a barometer that measures atmospheric pressure without use of mercury or other liquid.

an·es·the·si·ol·o·gy [an-is-thee-zi-OL-ə-jee] *n* branch of medicine dealing with anesthetics.

an·es·thet·ic [an-əs-THET-ik] *n, adj* (drug) causing loss of sensation. **an·es·the·sia** [-THEE-zhə] *n* loss of sensation. **an·es·the·tist** [ə-NES-thi-tist] *n* expert in use of anesthetics. **an·es'the·tize** *vt* **-tized, -tiz·ing.**

an·eu·rysm, an·eu·rism [AN-yə-riz-əm] n swelling out of a part of an artery.

a·new [ə-NOO] adv afresh, again.

an·gel [AYN-jəl] n divine messenger; ministering or attendant spirit; person with the qualities of such a spirit, as gentleness, purity, etc. **an·gel'ic** adj

An·ge·lus [AN-jə-ləs] n devotional service in R.C. Church in memory of the Incarnation, said at morning, noon and sunset; bell announcing the time for this service.

an·ger [ANG-gər] n strong emotion excited by a real or supposed injury; wrath; rage. ▶ vt excite to wrath; enrage. **an'gri·ly** adv **an'gry** adj full of anger; inflamed.

an·gi·na (pec·to·ris) [an-JĪ-nə PEK-tər-is] n severe pain accompanying some heart diseases.

an·gle¹ [ANG-gəl] vi **-gled, -gling.** fish with hook and line. **an'gler** n

angle² n meeting of two lines or surfaces; corner; point of view; inf devious motive. ▶ vt bend at an angle.

An·gli·can [ANG-gli-kən] adj, n (member) of the Church of England. **An'gli·can·ism** n

An·gli·cize [ANG-glə-sīz] vt **-cized, -ciz·ing.** express in English; turn into English form. **An'gli·cism** n English idiom or peculiarity.

Anglo- comb. form English, e.g. Anglo-Scottish; British, e.g. Anglo-American.

an·glo·phil·ia [ang-glə-FIL-ee-ə] n excessive admiration for English. **an'glo·phile** [-fīl] n

An·glo·pho·bi·a [ang-glə-FOH-bee-ə] n dislike of England, etc. **an'glo·phobe** n

an·go·ra [ang-GOR-ə] n variety of goat, cat, or rabbit with long silky hair; hair of the angora goat or rabbit; cloth made from this hair.

an·gos·tu·ra bark [ang-gə-STOOR-ə] n bitter bark of certain S American trees, used as flavoring in alcoholic drinks.

angst [ankst] n feeling of anxiety.

ang·strom [ANG-strəm] n unit of length for measuring wavelengths of electromagnetic radiation.

an·guish [ANG-gwish] n great mental or bodily pain. ▶ v suffer this pain; cause to suffer it.

an·gu·lar [ANG-gyə-lər] adj (of people) bony, awkward; having angles; measured by an angle. **an·gu·lar'i·ty** n

an·hy·drous [an-HĪ-drəs] adj (of chemical substances) free from water.

an·i·line [AN-l-in] n product of coal tar or indigo that yields dyes.

an·i·mal [AN-ə-məl] n living creature, having sensation and power of voluntary motion; beast. ▶ adj of, pert. to animals; sensual.

an·i·mal·cule [an-ə-MAL-kyool] n very small animal, esp. one that cannot be seen by naked eye.

animal husbandry branch of agriculture concerned with raising domestic animals.

an·i·mate [AN-ə-mayt] vt **-mat·ed, -mat·ing.** give life to; enliven; inspire; actuate; make cartoon film of. **an'i·mat·ed** adj lively; in form of cartoons. **an·i·ma'tion** n life, vigor; cartoon film.

an·i·mism [AN-ə-miz-əm] n primitive religion, belief that natural effects are due to spirits, that inanimate things have spirits. **an'i·mist** n

an·i·mos·i·ty [an-ə-MOS-i-tee] n, pl **-ties.** hostility, enmity.

an·i·mus [AN-ə-məs] n hatred; animosity.

an·i·on [AN-ī-ən] n ion with negative charge.

an·ise [AN-is] n plant with aromatic seeds, which are used for flavoring.

an·i·seed [AN-ə-seed] n the licorice-flavored seed of anise.

an·kle [ANG-kəl] n joint between foot and leg. **an·klet** [ANG-klit] n ankle-ornament; short sock reaching just above the ankle.

an·nals [AN-lz] pl n historical records of events. **an'nal·ist** n

an·neal [ə-NEEL] vt toughen (metal or glass) by heating and slow cooling; temper.

an·ne·lid [AN-l-id] *n* one of class of invertebrate animals, including the earthworm, etc.

an·nex [ə-NEKS] *vt* add, append, attach; take possession of (esp. territory). **an·nex·a·tion** [an-ik-SAY-shən] *n* **annex** *n* [AN-eks] supplementary building; something added.

an·ni·hi·late [ə-NĪ-ə-layt] *vt* **-lat·ed, -lat·ing.** reduce to nothing, destroy utterly. **an·ni·hi·la'tion** *n*

an·ni·ver·sa·ry [an-ə-VUR-sə-ree] *n* yearly return of a date; celebration of this.

an·no Dom·i·ni [AN-oh DOM-ə-nee] *Lat* in the year of our Lord.

an·no·tate [AN-ə-tayt] *vt* **-tat·ed, -tat·ing.** make notes upon, comment. **an·no·ta'tion** *n*

an·nounce [ə-NOWNS] *vt* **-nounced, -nounc·ing.** make known, proclaim. **an·nounce'ment** *n* **an·nounc'er** *n* broadcaster who announces items in program, introduces speakers, etc.

an·noy [ə-NOI] *vt* vex; make slightly angry; tease. **an·noy'ance** *n*

an·nu·al [AN-yoo-əl] *adj* yearly; of, for a year. ▶ *n* plant that completes its life cycle in a year; book published each year. **an'nu·al·ly** *adv*

an·nu·i·ty [ə-NOO-i-tee] *n, pl* **-ties.** sum or grant paid every year. **an·nu'i·tant** [-tnt] *n* holder of annuity.

an·nul [ə-NUL] *vt* **-nulled, -nul·ling.** make void, cancel, abolish.

an·nu·lar [AN-yə-lər] *adj* ring-shaped. **an'nu·lat·ed** [-lay-tid] *adj* formed in rings. **an'nu·let** [-lit] *n* small ring or molding in shape of ring.

An·nun·ci·a·tion [ə-nun-see-AY-shən] *n* angel's announcement of Incarnation to the Virgin Mary; (**a-**) announcing; announcement. **an·nun'ci·ate** *vt* **-at·ed, -at·ing.** proclaim, announce.

an·ode [AN-ohd] *n Electricity* the positive electrode or terminal. **an·o·dize** [AN-ə-dīz] *vt* cover (metal object) with protective film by using it as an anode in electrolysis.

an·o·dyne [AN-ə-dīn] *adj* relieving pain, soothing. ▶ *n* pain-relieving drug; something that soothes.

a·noint [ə-NOINT] *vt* smear with oil or ointment; consecrate with oil. **a·noint'ment** *n* the Anointed; the Messiah.

a·nom·a·lous [ə-NOM-ə-ləs] *adj* irregular, abnormal. **a·nom'a·ly** *n, pl* **-lies.** irregularity; deviation from rule.

a·non [ə-NON] *adv obs* in a short time, soon; now and then.

a·non·y·mous [ə-NON-ə-məs] *adj* nameless, esp. without an author's name. **an·o·nym·i·ty** [an-ə-NIM-i-tee] *n*

an·o·rak [AN-ə-rak] *n* lightweight, warm, waterproof, usu. hooded jacket; parka.

an·o·rex·i·a ner·vo·sa [an-ə-REK-see-ə nur-VOH-sə] *n* psychological disorder characterized by fear of becoming fat and refusal to eat.

an·oth·er [ə-NU*TH*-ər] *pron, adj* one other; a different one; one more.

an·ser·ine [AN-sə-rīn] *adj* of or like a goose; silly.

an·swer [AN-sər] *v* reply (to); solve; reply correctly; pay; meet; be accountable (for, to); match; satisfy, suit. ▶ *n* reply; solution. **an'swer·a·ble** *adj* accountable. **answering machine** apparatus for answering a telephone automatically and recording messages.

ant *n* small social insect, proverbial for industry. **ant'eat·er** *n* animal that feeds on ants by means of a long, sticky tongue. **ant'hill** the mound raised by ants.

an·tag·o·nist [an-TAG-ə-nist] *n* opponent, adversary. **an·tag'o·nism** *n* **an·tag·o·nis'tic** *adj* **an·tag'o·nize** *vt* **-nized, -niz·ing.** arouse hostility in.

Ant·arc·tic [ant-AHRK-tik] *adj* south polar. ▶ *n* these regions.

an·te [AN-tee] *n* player's stake in poker. ▶ *vt* **-ted, -te·ing.** (often with *up*) stake.

ante- *prefix* before in time or position, e.g. *antedate; antechamber.*

an·te·ced·ent [an-tə-SEED-nt] *adj, n* (thing) going before.

an·te·di·lu·vi·an [an-tee-di-LOO-vee-ən] *adj* before the Flood; ancient.

an·te·lope [AN-tl-ohp] *n* deer-like ruminant animal, remarkable for grace and speed.

ante me·rid·i·em [AN-tee mə-RID-ee-əm] *Lat* before noon.

an·ten·na [an-TEN-ə] *n, pl* **-nae** [-nee] insect's feeler; aerial.

an·te·pe·nult [an-tee-PEE-nult] *n* last syllable but two in a word. **an·te·pe·nul'ti·mate** *adj, n*

an·te·ri·or [an-TEER-ee-ər] *adj* to the front; before.

an·them [AN-thəm] *n* song of loyalty, esp. to a country; Scripture passage set to music; piece of sacred music, originally sung in alternate parts by two choirs.

an·ther [AN-thər] *n* in flower, part at top of stamen containing pollen.

an·thol·o·gy [an-THOL-ə-jee] *n, pl* **-gies.** collection of poems, literary extracts, etc. **an·thol'o·gist** *n* maker of such. **an·thol'o·gize** *vt* **-gized, -giz·ing.** compile or publish in an anthology.

an·thra·cite [AN-thrə-sīt] *n* hard coal burning slowly almost without flame or smoke.

an·thrax [AN-thraks] *n* malignant disease in cattle, communicable to people; sore caused by this.

an·thro·poid [AN-thrə-poid] *adj* like man. ▶ *n* ape resembling human being.

an·thro·pol·o·gy [an-thrə-POL-ə-jee] *n* scientific study of origins, development of human race. **an·thro·po·log'i·cal** [-pə-LOJ-i-kəl] *adj* **an·thro·pol'o·gist** *n*

an·thro·po·mor·phize [an-thrə-pə-MOR-fīz] *vt* **-pized, -piz·ing.** ascribe human attributes

to God or an animal. **an·thro·po·mor'phic** *adj*

anti- *prefix* against, opposed to, e.g. *anti-war;* opposite to, e.g. *anticlimax;* counteracting, e.g. *antifreeze.*

an·ti·bi·ot·ic [an-ti-bī-OT-ik] *n* any of various chemical, fungal or synthetic substances, esp. penicillin, used against bacterial infection. ▶ *adj*

an·ti·bod·y [AN-ti-bod-ee] *n* substance in, or introduced into, blood serum that counteracts the growth and harmful action of bacteria.

an·tic·i·pate [an-TIS-ə-payt] *vt* **-pat·ed, -pat·ing.** expect; take or consider beforehand; foresee; enjoy in advance. **an·tic·i·pa'tion** *n* **an·tic'i·pa·to·ry** [-pə-tor-ee] *adj*

an·ti·cli·max [an-ti-KLĪ-maks] *n* sudden descent to the trivial or ludicrous. **an·ti·cli·mac'tic** *adj*

an·tics [AN-tiks] *pl n* absurd or grotesque movements or acts.

an·ti·cy·clone [an-tee-Sī-klohn] *n* system of winds moving around center of high barometric pressure.

an·ti·dote [AN-ti-doht] *n* counteracting remedy.

an·ti·freeze [AN-ti-freez] *n* liquid added to water to lower its freezing point, as in automobile radiators.

an·ti·gen [AN-ti-jən] *n* substance stimulating production of antibodies in the blood.

an·ti·his·ta·mine [an-ti-HIS-tə-meen] *n* drug used esp. to treat allergies.

an·ti·mo·ny [AN-tə-moh-nee] *n* brittle, bluish-white metal.

an·tip·a·thy [an-TIP-ə-thee] *n, pl* **-thies.** dislike, aversion.

an·ti·per·spi·rant [an-ti-PUR-spər-ənt] *n* substance used to reduce sweating.

an·ti·phon [AN-tə-fon] *n* composition in which verses, lines are sung alternately by two choirs; anthem. **an·tiph·o·nal** [an-TIF-ə-nl] *adj*

an·tip·o·des [an-TIP-ə-deez] *pl n* countries, peoples on opposite side of the globe (often refers to Aust. and N Zealand). **an·tip·o·de·an** *adj*

an·ti·pope [AN-ti-pohp] *n* pope elected in opposition to the one regularly chosen.

an·tique [an-TEEK] *n* relic of former times, usu. a piece of furniture, etc. that is collected. ▶ *adj* ancient; old-fashioned. **an·ti·quar·i·an** *n* student or collector of old things. **an·ti·quat·ed** *adj* out-of-date. **an·tiq·ui·ty** [an-TIK-wi-tee] *n* great age; former times.

an·ti·Se·mit·ic [an-tee-sə-MIT-ik] *adj* hostile to or discriminating against Jews. **an·ti·Sem·i·tism** *n* **an·ti·Sem·ite** *n*

an·ti·sep·tic [an-tə-SEPT-tik] *n, adj* (substance) preventing infection. ▶ *adj* free from infection.

an·tith·e·sis [an-TITH-ə-sis] *n, pl* **-ses** [-seez] direct opposite; contrast; opposition of ideas. **an·ti·thet·i·cal** *adj*

an·ti·tox·in [an-ti-TOK-sin] *n* serum used to neutralize disease poisons.

an·ti·trust [an-ti-TRUST] *adj* (of laws) opposing business monopolies.

an·ti·tus·sive [an-ti-TUS-iv] *n, adj* (substance) controlling or preventing coughing.

an·ti·ven·in [an-tee-VEN-in] *n* antitoxin to counteract specific venom, type of snake or spider.

ant·ler [ANT-lər] *n* branching horn of certain deer.

an·to·nym [AN-tə-nim] *n* word of opposite meaning to another, e.g. *cold* is an antonym of *hot.*

a·nus [AY-nəs] *n* the lower opening of the bowels. **a'nal** *adj*

an'vil *n* heavy iron block with steel face on which a blacksmith hammers metal into shape.

anx·ious [ANGK-shəs] *adj* troubled, uneasy; concerned. **anx·i·e·ty** [ang-Zİ·ə-tee] *n*

an·y [EN-ee] *adj* [pron.] one indefinitely; some; every. **an'y·bod·y** *n* **an'y·how** *adv* **an'y·one** *n* **an'y·thing** *n* **an'y·way** *adv* **an'y·where** *adv*

a·or·ta [ay-OR-tə] *n* great artery

rising from left ventricle of heart. **a·or·tal** *adj*

a·pace [ə-PAYS] *adv* swiftly.

a·part [ə-PAHRT] *adv* separately, aside; in pieces.

a·part·heid [ə-PAHRT-hayt] *n* former official government policy of racial segregation in S Africa.

a·part·ment [ə-PAHRT-mənt] *n* room or suite of rooms in larger building used for dwelling.

ap·a·thy [AP-ə-thee] *n, pl* **-thies.** indifference; lack of emotion. **ap·a·thet·ic** *adj*

ape [ayp] *n* tailless monkey such as the chimpanzee or gorilla; coarse, clumsy person; imitator. ▶ *vt* **aped, ap·ing.** imitate.

a·pe·ri·od·ic [ay-peer-ee-OD-ik] *adj Electricity* having no natural period or frequency.

a·pe·ri·tif [ə-per-i-TEEF] *n* alcoholic appetizer.

ap·er·ture [AP-ər-chər] *n* opening, hole.

a·pex [AY-peks] *n, pl* **a·pex·es.** top, peak; vertex.

a·pha·sia [ə-FAY-zhə] *n* dumbness, or loss of speech control, due to disease of the brain.

a·phe·li·on [ə-FEE-lee-ən] *n* point of planet's orbit farthest from the sun.

a·phid [AY-fid] *n* any of various sap-sucking insects.

a·phis [AY-fis] *n, pl* **a·phi·des** [AY-fi-deez] an aphid.

aph·o·rism [AF-ə-riz-əm] *n* maxim, pithy saying. **aph·o·ris·tic** [-RIS-tik] *adj*

aph·ro·dis·i·ac [af-rə-DEE-zee-ak] *adj* exciting sexual desire. ▶ *n* substance that so excites.

a·pi·ar·y [AY-pee-er-ee] *n, pl* **-ar·ies.** place where bees are kept. **a'pi·a·rist** *n* beekeeper. **a'pi·cul·ture** *n*

a·piece [ə-PEES] *adv* for each.

a·plomb [ə-PLOM] *n* self-possession, coolness, assurance.

a·poc·a·lypse [ə-POK-ə-lips] *n* prophetic revelation esp. of future of the world; **(A-)** revelation to St. John, recounted in last book of the New Testament. **a·poc·a·lyp·tic** *adj*

a·poc·ry·pha [ə-POK-rə-fə] *pl n* religious writing of doubtful authenticity; (**A-**) collective name for 14 books originally in the Old Testament. **a·poc'ry·phal** *adj* spurious.

ap·o·gee [AP-ə-jee] *n* point farthest from Earth in orbit of moon or satellite; climax; highest point.

a·pol·o·gy [ə-POL-ə-jee] *n*, *pl* **-gies.** acknowledgment of offense and expression of regret; written or spoken defense; (with *for*) poor substitute. **a·pol·o·get'ic** *adj* **a·pol·o·get'ics** *n* branch of theology charged with defense of Christianity. **a·pol'o·gist** *n* **a·pol'o·gize** *vi* **-gized, -giz·ing.**

ap·o·plex·y [AP-ə-plek-see] *n* loss of sense and often paralysis caused by broken or blocked blood vessel in the brain; a stroke. **ap·o·plec'tic** *adj*

a·pos·ta·sy [ə-POS-tə-see] *n*, *pl* **-sies.** abandonment of one's religious or other faith. **a·pos'tate** [-tayt] *n*, *adj*

a pos·te·ri·o·ri [ay po-steer-ee-OR-ī] *adj* denoting form of inductive reasoning that arrives at causes from effects; empirical.

a·pos·tle [ə-POS-əl] *n* ardent supporter; leader of reform; (**A-**) one sent to preach the Gospel, esp. one of the first disciples of Jesus; founder of Christian church in a country. **ap·os·tol'ic** *adj*

a·pos·tro·phe [ə-POS-trə-fee] *n* a mark (') showing the omission of a letter or letters in a word; digression to appeal to someone dead or absent.

ap·o·thegm [AP-ə-them] *n* terse saying, maxim.

a·poth·e·o·sis [ə-poth-ee-OH-sis] *n*, *pl* **-ses** [-seez] deification, act of raising any person or thing into a god.

ap·pall [ə-PAWL] *vt* dismay, terrify. **ap·pall'ing** *adj inf* dreadful, terrible.

ap·pa·ra·tus [ap-ə-RAT-əs] *n* equipment, tools, instruments, for performing any experiment, operation, etc.; means by which something operates.

ap·par·el [ə-PAR-əl] *n* clothing. ▶ *vt* **-eled, -el·ing.** clothe.

ap·par·ent [ə-PAR-ənt] *adj* seeming; obvious; acknowledged, e.g. *heir apparent.*

ap·pa·ri·tion [ap-ə-RISH-ən] *n* appearance, esp. of ghost.

ap·peal [ə-PEEL] *vi* (with *to*) call upon, make earnest request; be attractive; refer to, have recourse to; apply to higher court. ▶ *n* request, reference, supplication. **ap·peal'ing** *adj* making appeal; pleasant, attractive. **ap·pel'lant** [-PEL-ənt] *n* one who appeals to higher court. **ap·pel'late** [-it] *adj* of appeals.

ap·pear [ə-PEER] *vi* become visible or present; seem, be plain; be seen in public. **ap·pear'ance** *n* an appearing; aspect; pretense.

ap·pease [ə-PEEZ] *vt* **-peased, -peas·ing.** pacify, quiet, allay, satisfy. **ap·pease'ment** *n*

appellant see APPEAL.

ap·pel·la·tion [ap-ə-LAY-shən] *n* name.

ap·pend [ə-PEND] *vt* join on, add. **ap·pend'age** *n*

ap·pen·di·ci·tis [ə-pen-də-SĪ-tis] *n* inflammation of vermiform appendix.

ap·pen·dix [ə-PEN-diks] *n*, *pl* **-di·ces** [-də-seez] subsidiary addition to book, etc.; *Anatomy* projection, esp. the small worm-shaped part of the intestine.

ap·per·cep·tion [ap-ər-SEP-shən] *n* perception; apprehension; the mind's perception of itself as a conscious agent.

ap·per·tain [ap-ər-TAYN] *vi* belong, relate to, be appropriate.

ap·pe·tite [AP-i-tīt] *n* desire, inclination, esp. desire for food. **ap'pe·tiz·er** *n* something stimulating to appetite. **ap'pe·tiz·ing** *adj*

ap·plaud [ə-PLAWD] *vt* praise by handclapping; praise loudly. **ap·plause'** [-PLAWZ] *n* loud approval.

ap·ple [AP-əl] *n* round, firm, fleshy fruit; tree bearing it.

ap·plet [AP-lət] *n Computers* computing program that runs within a page on the World Wide Web.

ap·pli·ance [ə-PLĪ-əns] *n* piece of equipment esp. electrical.

ap·pli·qué [ap-li-KAY] *n* ornaments, embroidery, etc., secured to surface of material. ▶ *vt* **-quéd, -qué·ing.** ornament thus.

ap·ply [ə-PLĪ] *v* **-plied, -ply·ing.** ▶ *vt* utilize, employ; lay or place on; administer, devote. ▶ *vi* have reference (to); make request (to). **ap′pli·ca·ble** *adj* relevant. **ap′pli·cant** *n* **ap·pli·ca′tion** *n* applying something for a particular use; relevance; request for a job, etc.; concentration, diligence. **applied** *adj* (of skill, science, etc.) put to practical use.

ap·point [ə-POINT] *vt* name, assign to a job or position; fix, settle; equip. **ap·point′ment** *n* engagement to meet; (selection for a) position. ▶ *pl* equipment, furnishings.

ap·por·tion [ə-POR-shən] *vt* divide out in shares. **ap·por′tion·ment** *n*

ap·po·site [AP-ə-zit] *adj* suitable, apt. **ap′po·site·ness** *n*

ap·po·si′tion [-ZISH-ən] *n* proximity, the placing of one word beside another that it describes.

ap·praise [ə-PRAYZ] *vt* **-praised, -prais·ing.** set price on, estimate value of. **ap·prais′al** *n* **ap·prais′er** *n*

ap·pre·ci·ate [ə-PREE-shee-ayt] *v* **-at·ed, -at·ing.** ▶ *vt* value at true worth; be grateful for; understand; enjoy. ▶ *vi* rise in value. **ap·pre′ci·a·ble** [-shə-bəl] *adj* estimable; substantial. **ap·pre′ci·a·bly** *adv* **ap·pre′ci·a′tion** *n* **ap·pre′cia·tive** [-shə-tiv] *adj* capable of expressing pleasurable recognition.

ap·pre·hend [ap-ri-HEND] *vt* arrest, seize by authority; take hold of; recognize, understand; dread. **ap·pre·hen′si·ble** [-HEN-sə-bəl] *adj*

ap·pre·hen′sion [-shən] *n* dread, anxiety; arrest; conception; ability to understand. **ap·pre·hen′sive** [-siv] *adj* **ap·pre·hen′sive·ly** *adv*

ap·pren·tice [ə-PREN-tis] *n* person learning a trade under specified conditions; novice. ▶ *vt* **-ticed, -tic·ing.** bind, set to work, as apprentice. **ap·pren′tice·ship** *n*

ap·prise [ə-PRIZ] *vt* **-prised, -pris·ing.** inform.

ap·proach [ə-PROHCH] *v* draw near (to); set about; address request to; approximate to; make advances to. ▶ *n* a drawing near; means of reaching or doing; approximation; (oft. pl) friendly or amatory overture(s). **ap·proach′a·ble** *adj*

ap·pro·ba·tion [ap-rə-BAY-shən] *n* approval.

ap·pro·pri·ate [ə-PROH-pree-ayt] *vt* **-at·ed, -at·ing.** take for oneself; put aside for particular purpose. ▶ *adj* [-it] suitable, fitting. **ap·pro′pri·ate·ness** [-it-nis] *n* **ap·pro·pri·a′tion** *n* act of setting apart for purpose; legislative vote of money.

ap·prove [ə-PROOV] *vt* **-proved, -prov·ing.** think well of, commend; authorize, agree to. **ap·prov′al** *n* **ap·prov′ing·ly** *adv*

ap·prox·i·mate [ə-PROK-sə-mit] *adj* very near, nearly correct; inexact, imprecise. ▶ *v* [-mayt] **-mat·ed, -mat·ing.** ▶ *vt* bring close. ▶ *vi* come near; be almost the same as. **ap·prox′i·mate·ly** *adv*

ap·pur·te·nance [ə-PUR-tn-əns] *n* thing that appertains to; accessory.

après-ski [ah-pray-SKEE] *n* social activities after day's skiing.

ap·ri·cot [AP-ri-kot] *n* orange-colored fruit related to the plum. ▶ *adj* of the color of the fruit.

A·pril fool [AY-prəl] butt of a joke or trick played on April Fools' Day, April 1.

a pri·o·ri [ay-prī-OR-ī] *adj* denoting deductive reasoning from general principle to expected facts or effects; denoting knowledge gained independently of experience.

a·pron [AY-prən] n cloth, piece of leather, etc., worn in front to protect clothes, or as part of costume; in theater, strip of stage before curtain; on airfield, paved area where aircraft stand, are refueled, etc.; fig any of a variety of things resembling these.

ap·ro·pos [ap-rə-POH] adv to the purpose; with reference to. ▶ adj apt, appropriate. **apropos of** concerning.

apse [aps] n arched recess, esp. in a church.

apt adj suitable; likely; prompt, quick-witted; dexterous. **ap·ti·tude** [AP-ti-tood] n capacity, fitness. **apt'ly** adv **apt'ness** n

aq·ua·ma·rine [ak-wə-mə-REEN] n precious stone, a transparent beryl. ▶ adj greenish-blue, sea-colored.

aq·ua·plane [AK-wə-playn] n plank or boat towed by fast motorboat and ridden by person standing on it. ▶ vi **-planed, -plan·ing.** ride on aquaplane; (of automobile) be in contact with water on road, not with road surface. **aquaplaning** n

a·quar·i·um [ə-KWAIR-ee-əm] n, pl **-i·ums.** tank or pond for keeping water animals or plants.

a·quat·ic [ə-KWAT-ik] adj living, growing, done in or on water. **a·quat'ics** pl. n water sports.

aq·ua·vit [AH-kwə-veet] n Scandinavian liquor usu. flavored with caraway seeds.

aq·ue·duct [AK-wi-dukt] n artificial channel for water, esp. one like a bridge; conduit.

a·que·ous [AY-kwee-əs] adj of, like, containing water.

aq·ui·fer [AK-wə-fər] n geological formation containing or conveying ground water.

aq·ui·line [AK-wə-līn] adj relating to eagle; hooked like an eagle's beak.

Ar Chem argon.

Ar·ab [AR-əb] n general term for inhabitants of Middle Eastern countries; Arabian horse. **Ar'a·bic** n language of Arabs. ▶ adj

Ar'ab·ist n specialist in Arabic

language or in Arabic culture.

ar·a·besque [ar-ə-BESK] n classical ballet position; fanciful painted or carved ornament of Arabian origin. ▶ adj

ar·a·ble [AR-ə-bəl] adj suitable for plowing or planting crops.

a·rach·nid [ə-RAK-nid] n one of the Arachnida (spiders, scorpions, and mites). **a·rach'noid** adj

ar·bi·ter [AHR-bi-tər] n judge, umpire. **ar·bi·tra'i·ly** [-TRER-ə-lee] adv **ar'bi·trar·y** adj not bound by rules, despotic; random.

ar'bi·trate [-trayt] v decide dispute; submit to, settle by arbitration; act as an umpire. **ar·bi·tra'tion** n hearing, settling of disputes, esp. industrial and legal, by impartial referee. **ar'bi·tra·tor** n

ar·bor [AHR-bər] n leafy glade, etc., sheltered by trees.

ar·bo·re·al [ahr-BOR-ee-əl] adj relating to trees. **ar·bo·re'tum** [-bə-REE-təm] n, pl **-tums.** place for cultivating specimens of trees. **ar·bor·i·cul·ture** [AHR-bər-i-kul-chər] n forestry, cultivation of trees. **ar'bor·ist** n

ar·bor vi·tae [ahr-bər VĪ-tee] a kind of evergreen conifer.

arc [ahrk] n part of circumference of circle or similar curve; luminous electric discharge between two conductors. **arc lamp, light** light source in which an arc between two electrodes produces intense white illumination.

ar·cade [ahr-KAYD] n row of arches on pillars; covered walk or avenue, esp. lined by shops.

ar·cane [ahr-KAYN] adj mysterious; esoteric.

arch¹ [ahrch] n curved structure in building, supporting itself over open space by pressure of stones one against the other; any similar structure; a curved shape; curved part of sole of the foot. ▶ v form, make into, an arch. **arched** adj **arch'way** n

arch² adj chief; experienced; expert; superior, knowing, coyly playful. **arch'ly** adv **arch'ness** n

arch- *comb. form* chief, principal, e.g. *archenemy.*

ar·cha·ic [ahr-KAY-ik] *adj* old, primitive. **ar·cha·ism** [AHR-kee-iz-əm] *n* obsolete word or phrase.

arch·bish·op [ahrch-BISH-əp] *n* chief bishop. **arch·bish′op·ric** *n*

ar·che·ol·o·gy [ahr-kee-OL-ə-jee] *n* study of ancient times from remains of art, implements, etc. **ar·che·o·log′i·cal** *adj* **ar·che·ol′o·gist** *n*

ar·cher·y [AHR-chə-ree] *n* skill, sport of shooting with bow and arrow. **arch′er** *n*

ar·che·type [AHR-ki-tīp] *n* prototype; perfect specimen. **ar·che·ty′pal** [-TĪ-pəl] *adj*

ar·chi·pel·a·go [ahr-kə-PEL-ə-goh] *n, pl* **-goes, -gos.** group of islands; sea with many small islands, esp. Aegean.

ar·chi·tect [AHR-ki-tekt] *n* one qualified to design and supervise construction of buildings; contriver. **ar·chi·tec′tur·al** [-TEK-chər-əl] *adj* **ar′chi·tec·ture** *n*

ar·chive [AHR-kīv] *n* (oft. pl) collection of records, documents, etc. about an institution, family, etc.; place where these are kept; *Computers* data put on tape or disk for long-term storage. ▶ *vt* store in an archive. **ar·chi′val** *adj* **ar′chi·vist** [-kə-vist] *n*

Arc·tic [AHRK-tik] *adj* of northern polar regions; (a-) very cold. ▶ *n* region around north pole.

ar·dent [AHR-dnt] *adj* fiery; passionate. **ar′dent·ly** *adv* **ar′dor** [-dər] *n* enthusiasm; zeal.

ar·du·ous [AHR-joo-əs] *adj* laborious, hard to accomplish, difficult, strenuous.

are¹ [ahr] *pres. ind. pl.* of BE.

are² [air] *n* unit of measure, 100 square meters.

ar·e·a [AIR-ee-ə] *n* extent, expanse of any surface; two-dimensional expanse enclosed by boundary (area of square, circle, etc.); region; part, section; subject, field of activity.

a·re·na [ə-REE-nə] *n* enclosure for sports events, etc.; space in middle of amphitheater or stadium; sphere, scene of conflict.

ar·gon [AHR-gon] *n* a gas, inert constituent of air.

ar·go·sy [AHR-gə-see] *n, pl* **-sies.** *Poet* large richly-laden merchant ship.

ar·got [AHR-goh] *n* slang.

ar·gue [AHR-gyoo] *v* **-gued, -gu·ing.** ▶ *vi* quarrel, dispute; prove; offer reasons. ▶ *vt* prove by reasoning; discuss. **ar′gu·a·ble** *adj* **ar′gu·ment** *n* quarrel; reasoning; discussion; theme. **ar·gu·men·ta′tion** *n* **ar·gu·men′ta·tive** *adj*

a·ri·a [AHR-ee-ə] *n* air or rhythmical song in cantata, opera, etc.

ar′id *adj* parched with heat, dry; dull. **a·rid·i·ty** [ə-RID-i-tee] *n*

a·right [ə-RĪT] *adv* rightly.

a·rise [ə-RĪZ] *vi* **a·rose, a·ris·en** [ə-RIZ-ən], **a·ris·ing.** come about; get up; rise (up), ascend.

ar·is·toc·ra·cy [ar-ə-STOK-rə-see] *n, pl* **-cies.** government by the best in birth or fortune; nobility; upper classes. **a·ris·to·crat** [ə-RIS-tə-krat] *n* **a·ris·to·crat′ic** *adj* noble; elegant.

a·rith·me·tic [ə-RITH-mə-tik] *n* science of numbers; art of reckoning by figures. **ar·ith·met′ic** *adj* **ar·ith·met′i·cal·ly** *adv*

ark [ahrk] *n* Noah's vessel; (**A-**) coffer containing scrolls of the Torah.

arm¹ [ahrm] *n* limb extending from shoulder to wrist; anything projecting from main body, as branch of sea, supporting rail of chair, etc. **arm′chair** *n* **arm′ful** *n, pl* **-fuls.** **arm′hole** *n* **arm′pit** *n* hollow under arm at shoulder.

arm-twisting *n* use of personal pressure to achieve a desired result.

arm² *vt* supply with weapons, furnish; prepare bomb, etc. for use. ▶ *vi* take up arms. ▶ *n* weapon; branch of army. ▶ *pl* weapons; war, military exploits; official heraldic symbols. **ar′ma·ment** *n*

ar·ma·da [ahr-MAH-də] *n* large

number of ships or aircraft.

ar·ma·dil·lo [ahr-mə-DIL-oh] *n, pl* **-los.** small Amer. animal protected by bands of bony plates.

ar·ma·ture [AHR-mə-chər] *n* revolving structure in electric motor, generator; framework used by a sculptor to support modeling clay, etc.

ar·mi·stice [AHR-mə-stis] *n* truce, suspension of fighting.

ar·mor [AHR-mər] *n* defensive covering or dress; plating of tanks, warships, etc.; armored fighting vehicles, as tanks. **ar'mor·y** *n, pl* **-mor·ies.**

ar·my [AHR-mee] *n, pl* **-mies.** large body of soldiers armed for warfare and under military command; host; great number.

a·ro·ma [ə-ROH-mə] *n* sweet smell; fragrance; peculiar charm. **ar·o·mat·ic** [ar-ə-MAT-ik] *adj*

a·rose pt. of ARISE.

a·round [ə-ROWND] *prep* on all sides of; somewhere in or near; approximately (of time). ▶ *adv* on every side; in a circle; here and there, nowhere in particular; *inf* present in or at some place.

a·rouse [ə-ROWZ] *vt* **-roused, -rous·ing.** awaken, stimulate.

ar·peg·gi·o [ahr-PEJ-ee-oh] *n, pl* **-gi·os.** *Mus* notes sounded in quick succession, not together; chord so played.

ar·raign [ə-RAYN] *vt* accuse, indict, put on trial. **ar·raign'ment** *n*

ar·range [ə-RAYNJ] *v* **-ranged, -rang·ing.** set in order; make agreement; adjust; plan; adapt, as music; settle, as dispute. **ar·range'ment** *n*

ar·rant [AR-ənt] *adj* downright, notorious.

ar·ras [AR-əs] *n* tapestry.

ar·ray [ə-RAY] *n* order, esp. military order; dress; imposing show, splendor. ▶ *vt* set in order; dress, equip, adorn.

ar·rears [ə-REERZ] *pl n* amount unpaid or undone.

ar·rest [ə-REST] *vt* detain by legal authority; stop; catch attention. ▶ *n*

seizure by warrant; making prisoner. **ar·rest'ing** *adj* attracting attention, striking. **ar·rest'er** *n* person who arrests; mechanism to stop or slow moving object.

ar·rive [ə-RĪV] *vi* **-rived, -riv·ing.** reach destination; (with *at*) reach, attain; *inf* succeed. **ar·ri'val** *n*

ar·ro·gance [AR-ə-gəns] *n* aggressive conceit. **ar'ro·gant** *adj* proud; overbearing.

ar·ro·gate [AR-ə-gayt] *vt* **-gat·ed, -gat·ing.** seize or claim without right.

ar·row [AR-oh] *n* pointed shaft shot from bow. **ar'row·head** *n* head of arrow; any triangular shape.

ar·row·root [AR-oh-root] *n* nutritious starch from W Indian plant, used as a food.

ar·se·nal [AHR-sə-nl] *n* place for manufacture, storage weapons and ammunition; *fig* repertoire (of skills, skilled personnel, etc.).

ar·se·nic [AHR-sə-nik] *n* soft, gray, metallic element; its oxide, a powerful poison. **ar'se·nate** [-nayt] *n* **ar·sen'i·cal** *adj*

ar·son [AHR-sən] *n* crime of intentionally setting property on fire.

art [ahrt] *n* skill; human skill as opposed to nature; creative skill in painting, poetry, music, etc.; any of the works produced thus; profession, craft; knack; contrivance, cunning, trick; system of rules. ▶ *pl* certain branches of learning, languages, history, etc., as distinct from natural science; wiles. **art'ful** *adj* wily. **art'ful·ly** *adv* **art'ist** *n* one who practices fine art, esp. painting; one who makes a fine art of a craft. **ar·tiste'** [-TEEST] *n* professional entertainer, singer, dancer, etc. **ar·tis'tic** *adj* **art'ist·ry** *n* **art'less** *adj* natural, frank. **art'less·ness** *n* **art'y** *adj* **art·i·er, art·i·est.** ostentatiously artistic.

ar·te·ri·o·scle·ro·sis [ahr-teer-ee-oh-sklə-ROH-sis] *n* hardening of the arteries. **ar·te·ri·o·scle·rot'ic** *adj*

ar·ter·y [AHR-tə-ree] *n, pl* **-ter·ies.** one of the vessels carrying blood from heart; any main channel of communications. **ar·te'ri·al** [-TEER-ee-əl] *adj* pert. to an artery; (of a route) major.

ar·te·sian [ahr-TEE-zhən] *adj* describes deep well in which water rises by internal pressure.

ar·thri·tis [ahr-THRĪ-tis] *n* painful inflammation of joint(s). **ar·thrit'ic** [-THRIT-ik] *adj, n*

ar·thro·pod [AHR-thrə-pod] *n* invertebrate with jointed limbs and segmented body e.g.; insect, spider.

ar·ti·choke [AHR-ti-chohk] *n* thistle-like perennial, edible flower.

ar·ti·cle [AHR-ti-kəl] *n* item, object; short written piece; paragraph, section; *Grammar* any of the words *the, a,* or *an;* clause in a contract; rule, condition.

ar·tic·u·late [ahr-TIK-yə-lit] *adj* able to express oneself fluently; jointed; of speech, clear, distinct. ▶ *v* [-layt] **-lat·ed, -lat·ing.** ▶ *vt* joint; utter distinctly. ▶ *vi* speak. **ar·tic'u·late·ly** *adv* **ar·tic'u·la'tion** *n*

ar·ti·fact [AHR-tə-fakt] *n* something made by a person, esp. by hand.

ar·ti·fice [AHR-tə-fis] *n* contrivance, trick, cunning, skill. **ar·tif'i·cer** [-TIF-ə-sər] *n* craftsperson.

ar·ti·fi·cial [-FISH-əl] *adj* manufactured, synthetic; insincere. **ar·ti·fi'cial·ly** *adv* **artificial intelligence** ability of machines, esp. computers, to imitate intelligent human behavior.

artificial respiration method of restarting person's breathing after it has stopped.

ar·til·ler·y [ahr-TIL-ə-ree] *n* large guns on wheels; the troops that use them.

ar·ti·san [AHR-tə-zən] *n* craftsperson, skilled mechanic, manual worker.

ar·tiste see ART.

Ar·y·an [AIR-ee-ən] *adj* relating to Indo-European family of nations and languages.

As *Chem* arsenic.

as [az] *adv, conj* denoting: comparison; similarity; equality; identity; concurrence; reason.

as·bes·tos [as-BES-təs] *n* fibrous mineral that does not burn.

as·bes·to·sis [as-be-STOH-sis] *n* lung disease caused by inhalation of asbestos fiber.

as·cend [ə-SEND] *vi* climb, rise. ▶ *vt* walk up, climb, mount.

as·cend'an·cy *n* control, dominance. **as·cend'ant** *adj* rising. **as·cen'sion** [-shən] *n* **as·cent'** *n* rise.

as·cer·tain [as-ər-TAYN] *v* get to know, find out, determine. **as·cer·tain'a·ble** *adj*

as·cet·ic [ə-SET-ik] *n* one who practices severe self-denial. ▶ *adj* rigidly abstinent, austere. **as·cet'i·cism** [-ə-siz-əm] *n*

ASCII [ASS-kee] *n* a code for transmitting data between computers.

a·scor·bic acid [ə-SKOR-bik] vitamin C, present in green vegetables, citrus fruits, etc.

as·cribe [ə-SKRĪB] *vt* **-cribed, -crib·ing.** attribute, impute, assign. **a·scrib'a·ble** *adj*

a·sep·tic [ə-SEP-tik] *adj* germ-free. **a·sep'sis** *n*

a·sex·u·al [ay-SEK-shoo-əl] *adj* without sex.

ash¹ *n* dust or remains of anything burned. ▶ *pl* ruins; remains after burning, esp. of a human body after cremation. **ash'en** *adj* like ashes; pale.

ash² *n* deciduous timber tree; its wood. **ash'en** *adj*

a·shamed [ə-SHAYMD] *adj* affected with shame, abashed.

a·shore [ə-SHOR] *adv* on shore.

Ash Wednesday first day of Lent.

A·sian [AY-zhən] *adj* pert. to continent of Asia. ▶ *n* native of Asia or descendant of one. **A·si·at'ic** [-zhee-AT-ik] *adj*

a·side [ə-SĪD] *adv* to or on one side; privately. ▶ *n* words spoken in an undertone not to be heard by some person present.

as·i·nine [AS-ə-nīn] *adj* of or like an

ass, silly. **as·i·nin'i·ty** [-NIN-i-tee] *n*
ask *vt* request, require, question,
invite. ▶ *vi* make inquiry or request.
a·skance [ə-SKANS] *adv* sideways,
awry; with a side look or meaning.
look askance view with suspicion.
a·skew [ə-SKYOO] *adv* aside, awry.
a·sleep [ə-SLEEP] *adj, adv* sleeping,
at rest.
asp *n* small venomous snake.
as·par·a·gus [ə-SPA-rə-gəs] *n* plant
whose young shoots are a table
delicacy.
as·pect [AS-pekt] *n* look, view,
appearance, expression.
as·pen [AS-pən] *n* type of poplar
tree.
as·per·i·ty [ə-SPER-i-tee] *n, pl* **-ties.**
roughness; harshness; coldness.
as·per·sion [ə-SPUR-zhən] *n* **cast
aspersions on** make derogatory
remarks about.
as·phalt [AS-fawlt] *n* black, hard
bituminous substance used for
road surfaces, etc.
as·phyx·i·a [as-FIK-see-ə] *n*
suffocation. **as·phyx'i·ate** [-ayt] *v*
-at·ed, -at·ing. as·phyx·i·a'tion *n*
as·pic [AS-pik] *n* jelly used to coat
or make a mold of meat, eggs, fish,
etc.
as·pire [ə-SPĪR] *vi* **-pired, -pir·ing.**
desire eagerly; aim at high things;
rise to great height. **as·pi·rant**
[AS-pər-ənt] *n* one who aspires;
candidate. **as'pi·rate** [-pə-rayt] *vt*
pronounce with full breathing, as
h. **as·pir'ing** *adj*
as·pi·rin [AS-pər-in] *n* (a tablet of)
drug used to allay pain and fever.
ass *n* quadruped of horse family;
stupid person.
as·sail [ə-SAYL] *vt* attack, assault.
as·sail'a·ble *adj* **as·sail'ant** *n*
as·sas·sin [ə-SAS-in] *n* one who
kills, esp. prominent person, by
treacherous violence; murderer.
as·sas'si·nate *vt* **-nat·ed, -nat·ing.
as·sas·si·na'tion** *n*
as·sault [ə-SAWLT] *n* attack, esp.
sudden. ▶ *vt* attack.
as·say [ə-SAY] *vt* test, esp.
proportions of metals in alloy or
ore. ▶ *n* [AS-ay] analysis, esp. of

metals; trial, test.
as·sem·ble [ə-SEM-bəl] *v* **-bled,
-bling.** meet, bring together;
collect; put together (of machinery,
etc.). **as·sem'blage** [-blij] *n*
as·sem'bly *n, pl* **-blies.** gathering,
meeting; assembling. **assembly
line** sequence of machines, workers
in factory assembling product.
as·sent [ə-SENT] *vi* concur, agree.
▶ *n* acquiescence, agreement,
compliance.
as·sert [ə-SURT] *vt* declare strongly,
insist upon. **as·ser'tion** *n*
as·sert'ive *adj* **as·ser'tive·ly** *adv*
as·sess [ə-SES] *vt* fix value;
evaluate, estimate, esp. for
taxation; fix amount (of tax or
fine); tax or fine. **as·sess'ment** *n*
as·ses'sor *n*
as·set [AS-et] *n* valuable or useful
person, thing. ▶ *pl* property
available to pay debts, esp. of
insolvent debtor.
as·sid·u·ous [ə-SIJ-oo-əs] *adj*
persevering, attentive, diligent.
as·si·du·i·ty [as-i-DOO-i-tee] *n*
as·sign [ə-SĪN] *vt* appoint to job,
etc.; allot, apportion, fix; ascribe;
transfer. **as·sign'a·ble** *adj*
as·sig·na·tion [as-ig-NAY-shən] *n*
secret meeting; appointment to
meet. **as·sign'ment** *n* act of
assigning; allotted duty.
as·sim·i·late [ə-SIM-ə-layt] *vt*
-lat·ed, -lat·ing. learn and
understand; make similar; absorb
into the system. **as·sim·i·la'tion** *n*
as·sist [ə-SIST] *v* give help; aid.
as·sis'tance *n* **as·sis'tant** *n* helper.
as·so·ci·ate [ə-SOH-shee-ayt] *v*
-at·ed, -at·ing. ▶ *vt* link, connect,
esp. as ideas in mind; join. ▶ *vi*
formerly, keep company with;
combine, unite. ▶ *n* [-it]
companion, partner; friend, ally;
subordinate member of
association. ▶ *adj* affiliated.
as·so·ci·a'tion *n* society, club.
as·sort [ə-SORT] *vt* classify,
arrange. ▶ *vi* match, agree with,
harmonize. **as·sort'ed** *adj* mixed.
as·sort'ment *n*
as·suage [ə-SWAYJ] *vt* **-suaged,**

-suag·ing. soften, pacify; soothe.
as·sume [ə-SOOM] *vt* **-sumed,**
-sum·ing. take for granted;
pretend; take upon oneself; claim.
as·sump'tion [-SUMP-shən] *n*
as·sure [ə-SHOOR] *vt* **-sured,**
-sur·ing. tell positively, promise;
make sure; insure against loss, esp.
of life; affirm. **as·sured'** *adj* sure.
as·sur'ed·ly [-id-lee] *adv*
as·ter·isk [AS-tə-risk] *n* star (*) used
in printing. ▶ *vt* mark thus.
a·stern [ə-STURN] *adv* in, behind
the stern; backward in direction.
as·ter·oid [AS-tə-roid] *n* small
planet. ▶ *adj* star-shaped.
asth·ma [AZ-mə] *n* illness in which
one has difficulty in breathing.
asth·mat'ic *adj, n*
a·stig·ma·tism [ə-STIG-mə-tiz-əm]
n inability of lens (esp. of eye) to
focus properly. **as·tig·mat·ic**
[as-tig-MAT-ik] *adj*
a·stir [ə-STUR] *adv* on the move;
out of bed; in excitement.
as·ton·ish [ə-STON-ish] *vt* amaze,
surprise. **as·ton'ish·ing** *adj*
as·ton'ish·ment *n*
as·tound [ə-STOWND] *vt* astonish
greatly; stun with amazement.
as·tound'ing *adj* startling.
as·tra·khan [AS-trə-kən] *n* lambskin
with curled wool.
as·tral [AS-trəl] *adj* of the stars or
spirit world.
a·stray [ə-STRAY] *adv* off the right
path, wanderingly.
a·stride [ə-STRID] *adv* with the legs
apart, straddling.
as·trin·gent [ə-STRIN-jənt] *adj*
severe, harsh; sharp; constricting
(body tissues, blood vessels, etc.).
▶ *n* astringent substance.
as·trol·o·gy [ə-STROL-ə-jee] *n*
foretelling of events by stars;
medieval astronomy. **as·trol'o·ger**
n **as·tro·log'i·cal** *adj*
as·tro·naut [AS-trə-nawt] *n* one
trained for travel in space.
as·tron·o·my [ə-STRON-ə-mee] *n*
scientific study of heavenly bodies.
as·tron'o·mer *n* **as·tro·nom'i·cal**
[-trə-NOM-i-kəl] *adj* very large; of
astronomy. **astronomical unit** unit

of distance used in astronomy
equal to the mean distance
between Earth and the sun.
as·tro·phys·ics [as-troh-FIZ-iks] *n*
the science of the chemical and
physical characteristics of heavenly
bodies. **as·tro·phys'i·cist** *n*
as·tute [ə-STOOT] *adj* perceptive,
shrewd. **as·tute'ly** *adv*
as·tute'ness *n*
a·sun·der [ə-SUN-dər] *adv* apart; in
pieces.
a·sy·lum [ə-SĪ-ləm] *n* refuge,
sanctuary, place of safety; old
name for hospital for mentally ill.
a·sym·me·try [ay-SIM-i-tree] *n* lack
of symmetry. **a·sym·met'ric**
[-sə-MET-rik] *adj*
as·ymp·tote [AS-im-toht] *n* straight
line that continually approaches a
curve, but never meets it.
at *prep, adv* denoting: location in
space or time; rate; condition or
state; amount; direction; cause.
At *Chem* astatine.
at·a·vism [AT-ə-viz-əm] *n*
appearance of ancestral, not
parental, characteristics in human
beings, animals or plants.
at·a·vis'tic *adj*
a·tax·i·a [ə-TAK-see-ə] *n* lack of
muscular coordination.
ate [ayt] *pt.* of EAT.
at·el·ier [at-l-YAY] *n* workshop,
artist's studio.
a·the·ism [AY-thee-iz-əm] *n* belief
that there is no God. **a'the·ist** *n*
a·the·is'tic *adj*
ath·lete [ATH-leet] *n* one trained for
physical exercises, feats or contests
of strength; one good at sports.
ath·let'ic *adj* **ath·let'ics** *pl n* sports
such as running, jumping,
throwing, etc. **ath·let'i·cal·ly** *adv*
a·thwart [ə-THWORT] *prep* across.
▶ *adv* across, esp. obliquely.
at·las [AT-ləs] *n* volume of maps.
at·mos·phere [AT-məs-feer] *n* mass
of gas surrounding heavenly body,
esp. Earth; prevailing tone or mood
(of place, etc.); unit of pressure in
cgs system. **at·mos·pher'ic**
[-FER-ik] *adj* **at·mos·pher'ics** *pl n*
noises in radio reception due to

electrical disturbance in the atmosphere; *Politics* mood or atmosphere.

at·oll [AT-awl] *n* ring-shaped coral island enclosing lagoon.

at·om [AT-əm] *n* smallest unit of matter that can enter into chemical combination; any very small particle. **a·tom·ic** [ə-TOM-ik] *adj* of, arising from atoms. **a·to·mic·i·ty** [at-ə-MIS-i-tee] *n* number of atoms in molecule of an element. **at'om·ize** *vt* **-ized, -iz·ing.** reduce to atoms or small particles. **at'om·iz·er** *n* instrument for discharging liquids in a fine spray. **atom(ic) bomb** one whose immense power derives from nuclear fission or fusion, nuclear bomb. **atomic energy** nuclear energy. **atomic number** the number of protons in the nucleus of an atom. **atomic reactor** see also REACTOR. **atomic weight** the weight of an atom of an element relative to that of carbon 12.

a·tone [ə-TOHN] *vi* **-toned, -ton·ing.** make reparation, amends (for); expiate; give satisfaction. **a·tone'ment** *n*

a·ton·ic [ay-TON-ik] *adj* unaccented.

a·top [ə-TOP] *adv* at or on the top; above.

a·tro·cious [ə-TROH-shəs] *adj* extremely cruel or wicked; horrifying; very bad. **a·troc'i·ty** [-TROS-i-tee] *n, pl* **-ties.** wickedness.

at·ro·phy [A-trə-fee] *n* wasting away, emaciation. ▶ *vi* **-phied, -phy·ing.** waste away, become useless. **atrophied** *adj*

at·tach [ə-TACH] *v* (mainly tr) join, fasten; unite; be connected with; attribute; appoint; seize by law. **at·tached'** *adj* (with *to*) fond of. **at·tach'ment** *n*

at·ta·ché [a-ta-SHAY] *n, pl* **-chés.** specialist attached to diplomatic mission. **attaché case** small suitcase for papers.

at·tack [ə-TAK] *vt* take action against (in war, etc.); criticize; set about with vigor; affect adversely. ▶ *n* attacking action; bout of

sickness.

at·tain [ə-TAYN] *vt* arrive at; reach, gain by effort, accomplish. **at·tain'a·ble** *adj* **at·tain'ment** *n* esp. personal accomplishment.

at·tain·der [ə-TAYN-dər] *n Hist* loss of civil rights usu. through conviction of treason.

at·tar [AT-ər] *n* a fragrant oil made esp. from rose petals.

at·tempt [ə-TEMPT] *vt* try, endeavor. ▶ *n* trial, effort.

at·tend [ə-TEND] *vt* be present at; accompany. ▶ *vi* (with *to*) take care of; give the mind (to), pay attention to. **at·tend'ance** *n* an attending; presence; persons attending. **at·tend·ee** [ə-ten-DEE] *n* **at·tend'ant** *n, adj* **at·ten'tion** *n* notice; heed; act of attending; care; courtesy. **at·ten'tive** *adj* **at·ten'tive·ness** *n*

at·ten·u·ate [ə-TEN-yoo-ayt] *v* **-at·ed, -at·ing.** weaken or become weak; make or become thin. **at·ten'u·at·ed** *adj* **at·ten·u·a'tion** *n* reduction of intensity. **at·ten'u·a·tor** *n* device for attenuating, esp. for reducing the amplitude of an electrical signal.

at·test [ə-TEST] *vt* bear witness to, certify. **at·tes·ta·tion** [a-tes-TAY-shən] *n* formal confirmation by oath, etc.

at·tic [AT-ik] *n* space within roof where ceiling follows line of roof. **Attic** *adj* of Attica, Athens; (of literary or artistic style) pure, refined, elegant.

at·tire [ə-TIR] *vt* **-tired, -tir·ing.** dress, array. ▶ *n* dress, clothing.

at·ti·tude [AT-i-tood] *n* mental view, opinion; posture, pose; disposition, behavior. **at·ti·tu'di·nize** *vi* **-nized, -niz·ing.** assume affected attitudes.

at·tor·ney [ə-TUR-nee] *n, pl* **-neys.** one legally appointed to act for another, esp. a lawyer. **attorney-at-law** *n, pl* **-neys-at-law.** a lawyer.

at·tract [ə-TRAKT] *v* draw (attention, etc.); arouse interest of; cause to come closer (as magnet, etc.). **at·trac'tion** n power to attract; something offered so as to interest, please. **at·trac'tive** adj **at·trac'tive·ness** n

at·trib·ute [ə-TRIB-yoot] vt **-ut·ed, -ut·ing.** regard as belonging to or produced by. ▶ n [A-trə-byoot] quality, property or characteristic of anything. **at·trib'ut·a·ble** adj **at·tri·bu'tion** n

at·tri·tion [ə-TRISH-ən] n wearing away of strength, etc.; rubbing away, friction.

at·tune [ə-TOON] vt **-tuned, -tun·ing.** tune, harmonize; make accordant.

Au Chem gold.

au·burn [AW-bərn] adj reddish brown. ▶ n this color.

au cou·rant [oh koo-RAHN] up-to-date; acquainted with.

auc·tion [AWK-shən] n public sale in which bidder offers increase of price over another and what is sold goes to one who bids highest. ▶ v **auc·tion·eer'** n **auction bridge** card game. **Dutch auction** one in which price starts high and is reduced until purchaser is found.

au·da·cious [aw-DAY-shəs] adj bold; daring, impudent. **au·dac'i·ty** [-DAS-i-tee] n

au·di·ble [AW-də-bəl] adj able to be heard. **au'di·bly** adv

au·di·ence [AW-dee-əns] n assembly of spectators or listeners; act of hearing; judicial hearing; formal interview.

audio- comb. form relating to sound or hearing.

au·di·o·phile [AW-dee-ə-fīl] n one who is enthusiastic about sound reproduction, esp. of music.

au·di·o·vis·u·al [aw-dee-oh-VIZH-oo-əl] adj (esp. of teaching aids) involving both sight and hearing.

au·dit [AW-dit] n formal examination or settlement of financial accounts. ▶ vt examine such accounts. **au'di·tor** n

au·di·tion [aw-DISH-ən] n screen or other test of prospective performer; hearing. ▶ vt conduct such a test.

au·di·to'ri·um n, pl **-ri·ums.** hall; place where audience sits.

au'di·to·ry adj pert. to sense of hearing.

auf Wie·der·seh·en [owf VEE-dər-zay-ən] Ger goodbye.

au·ger [AW-gər] n carpenter's tool for boring holes, large gimlet.

aught [awt] pron obs anything whatever.

aug·ment [awg-MENT] v increase, enlarge. **aug·men·ta'tion** n **aug·ment'a·ble** adj able to increase in force or size.

au grat·in [oh GRAHT-n] cooked or baked to form light crust.

au·gur [AW-gər] n among the Romans, soothsayer. ▶ v be a sign of future events, foretell. **au'gu·ry** [-gyə-ree] n divination from omens, etc.; omen.

au·gust [aw-GUST] adj majestic, dignified. **au·gust'ly** adv

auk [awk] n northern web-footed seabird with short wings used only as paddles.

aunt [ant] n father's or mother's sister, uncle's wife.

au pair [oh PAIR] n young foreign person, usu. a girl, who receives free board and lodging and usu. an allowance in return for housework, etc.

au·ra [OR-ə] n, pl **-ras.** quality, air, atmosphere considered distinctive of person or thing; medical symptom warning of impending epileptic seizure, etc.

au·ral [OR-əl] adj of, by ear. **au'ral·ly** adv

au·re·ole [OR-ee-ohl] n gold disk around head in sacred pictures; halo.

au re·voir [oh rə-VWAHR] Fr goodbye.

au·ri·cle [OR-i-kəl] n outside ear; an upper cavity of heart. **au·ric·u·lar** [aw-RIK-yə-lər] adj of the auricle; aural.

au·rif·er·ous [aw-RIF-ər-əs] adj gold-bearing.

au·ro·ra [aw-ROR-ə] n, pl **-ras.** dawn; lights in the atmosphere seen radiating from regions of the

poles. **aurora bo·re·al·is**
[bor-ee-AL-is] the northern lights.
aurora aus·tra·lis [aw-STRAY-lis]
the southern lights.

aus·cul·ta·tion [aw-skəl-TAY-shən]
n listening to sounds of heart and
lungs with stethoscope.

aus·pice [AW-spiss-siz] *pl n* **under
the auspices of** with the support
and approval of.

aus·pi·cious [aw-SPISH-əs] *adj* of
good omen, favorable.

aus·tere [aw-STEER] *adj* harsh,
strict, severe; without luxury.
aus·tere'ly *adv* **aus·ter·i·ty**
[aw-STER-i-tee] *n*

aus·tral [AW-strəl] *adj* southern.
Austral *adj* Australian.

Aus·tral·a·sian [aw-strə-LAY-zhən]
adj, n (native or inhabitant) of
Australasia (Australia, N Zealand
and adjacent islands).

Aus·tral·ian [aw-STRAYL-yən] *n, adj*
(native or inhabitant) of Australia.

au·tar·chy [AW-tahr-kee] *n, pl*
-chies. despotism, absolute power,
dictatorship.

au·then·tic [aw-THEN-tik] *adj* real,
genuine, true; trustworthy.
au·then'ti·cal·ly *adv*
au·then'ti·cate [-ti-kayt] *vt* make
valid, confirm; establish truth,
authorship, etc. of. **au·then·tic'i·ty**
n

au·thor [AW-thər] *n* writer of book;
originator, constructor.

au·thor·i·ty [ə-THOR-i-tee] *n, pl*
-ties. legal power or right;
delegated power; influence;
permission; expert; body or board
in control, esp. in pl.
au·thor'i·ta·tive [-tay-tiv] *adj*
au·thor'i·ta·tive·ly *adv*
au·thor·i·za'tion *n* **au'thor·ize** *vt*
-ized, -iz·ing. empower; permit,
sanction.

au·tis·tic [aw-TIS-tik] *adj* withdrawn
and divorced from reality. **au'tism**
n this condition.

auto- *comb. form* self-, e.g.
autobiography.

au·to [AW-toh] *n* automobile.

au·to·bi·og·ra·phy
[aw-tə-bī-OG-rə-fee] *n, pl* **-phies.**

life of person written by that
person. **au·to·bi·o·graph'i·cal** *adj*

au·toch·thon [aw-TOK-thən] *n*
primitive or original inhabitant;
native plant or animal.
au·toch'tho·nous *adj* indigenous,
native.

au·to·crat [AW-tə-krat] *n* absolute
ruler; despotic person.
au·toc'ra·cy [-TOK-rə-see] *n, pl*
-cies. au·to·crat'ic *adj*

au·to·er·o·tism
[aw-toh-ER-ə-tiz-əm] *n*
self-produced sexual arousal.

au·to·gi·ro [aw-tə-JĪ-roh] *n, pl* **-ros.**
aircraft like helicopter using
horizontal airscrew for vertical
ascent and descent.

au·to·graph [AW-tə-graf] *n* a
signature; one's own handwriting.
▶ *vt* sign.

au·to·in·tox·i·ca·tion
[aw-toh-in-tok-si-KAY-shən] *n*
poisoning of tissues of the body as
a result of the absorption of bodily
waste.

au·to·mate [AW-tə-mayt] *vt*
-mat·ed, -mat·ing. make
manufacturing process, etc.;
automatic. **au·to·ma'tion** *n* use of
automatic devices in industrial
production.

au·to·mat·ic [aw-tə-MAT-ik] *adj*
operated or controlled
mechanically; done without
conscious thought. ▶ *adj, n*
self-loading (weapon).
au·to·mat'i·cal·ly *adv*

au·tom'a·ton *n, pl* **-ta** [-tə]
self-acting machine, esp.
simulating a human being.

au·to·mo·bile [aw-tə-mə-BEEL] *n*
motor car.

au·ton·o·my [aw-TON-ə-mee] *n, pl*
-mies. self-government.
au·ton'o·mous *adj*

au·top·sy [AW-top-see] *n, pl* **-sies.**
postmortem examination to
determine cause of death.

au·to·sug·ges·tion
[aw-toh-səg-JES-chən] *n* process of
influencing the mind (toward
health, etc., conducted by oneself).

au·tumn [AW-təm] *n, adj* (typical

of) the season after summer.

au·tum·nal [aw-TUM-nl] *adj* typical of the onset of winter.

aux·il·ia·ry [awg-ZIL-yə-ree] *adj* helping, subsidiary. ▶ *n, pl* **-ries.** helper; something subsidiary, as troops; verb used to form tenses of others.

a·vail [ə-VAYL] *v* be of use, advantage, value (to). ▶ *n* use or advantage, esp. in **to no avail.** **a·vail·a·bil'i·ty** *n* **a·vail'a·ble** *adj* obtainable; accessible. **avail oneself of** make use of.

av·a·lanche [AV-ə-lanch] *n* mass of snow, ice, sliding down mountain; a sudden overwhelming quantity of anything.

a·vant-garde [ah-vahnt-GAHRD] *adj* markedly experimental or in advance.

av·a·rice [AV-ər-is] *n* greed for wealth. **av·a·ri'cious** [-RISH-əs] *adj*

a·vast [ə-VAST] *interj Nautical* stop.

av·a·tar [AV-ə-tahr] *n Hinduism* descent of god to Earth in bodily form.

a·venge [ə-VENJ] *vt* **-venged, -veng·ing.** take vengeance on behalf of (person) or on account of (thing). **a·veng'er** *n*

av·e·nue [AV-ə-nyoo] *n* route; a way of approach, a channel.

a·ver [ə-VUR] *vt* **-verred, -ver·ring.** affirm, assert.

av·er·age [AV-rij] *n* the mean value or quantity of a number of values or quantities. ▶ *adj* calculated as an average; medium, ordinary. ▶ *v* **-aged, -ag·ing.** ▶ *vt* fix or calculate a mean. ▶ *vi* exist in or form a mean.

a·verse [ə-VURS] *adj* disinclined, unwilling. **a·ver'sion** [-zhən] *n* dislike; person or thing disliked.

a·vert [ə-VURT] *vt* turn away; ward off.

a·vi·ar·y [AY-vee-er-ee] *n, pl* **-ar·ies.** enclosure for birds. **a'vi·a·rist** *n*

a·vi·a·tion [ay-vee-AY-shən] *n* art of flying aircraft; transport by aircraft. **a'vi·a·tor** *n*

av·id [AV-id] *adj* keen, enthusiastic; greedy (for). **a·vid'i·ty** *n* **av'id·ly** *adv*

av·o·ca·do [av-ə-KAH-doh] *n* tropical tree; its green-skinned edible fruit, alligator pear.

av·o·ca·tion [av-ə-KAY-shən] *n* vocation; employment, business.

a·void [ə-VOID] *vt* keep away from; refrain from; not allow to happen. **a·void'a·ble** *adj* **a·void'ance** *n*

av·oir·du·pois [av-ər-də-POIZ] *n* system of weights used in many English-speaking countries based on pounds and ounces.

a·vow [ə-VOW] *vt* declare; admit. **a·vow'a·ble** *adj* **a·vow'al** *n* **a·vowed'** *adj* **a·vow'ed·ly** *adv*

a·vun·cu·lar [ə-VUNG-kyə-lər] *adj* like or of an uncle esp. in manner.

a·wait [ə-WAYT] *vt* wait or stay for; be in store for.

a·wake [ə-WAYK] *v* **a·wak·ing, a·woke, a·wok·en.** emerge or rouse from sleep; become or cause to become alert. **a·wak'en·ing** *n*

a·wak·en [ə-WAY-kən] *vt* arouse (feelings, etc.) or cause to remember (memories, etc.).

a·ward [ə-WORD] *vt* to give formally (esp. a prize or punishment). ▶ *n* prize; judicial decision, amount awarded.

a·ware [ə-WAIR] *adj* informed, conscious. **a·ware'ness** *n*

a·wash [ə-WOSH] *adv* level with the surface of water; filled or overflowing with water. **awash in** marked by an abundance of.

a·way [ə-WAY] *adv* absent, apart, at a distance, out of the way. ▶ *adj Sports* played on opponent's grounds.

awe [aw] *n* dread mingled with reverence. **awe'some** [-səm] *adj* **awe'some·ly** *adv* **awe'some·ness** *n* **awe'struck** *adj* filled with awe.

aw·ful [AW-fəl] *adj* very bad, unpleasant; inspiring awe; *inf* very great. **aw'ful·ly** *adv* in an unpleasant way; *inf* very much.

a·while [ə-HWIL] *adv* for a time.

awk·ward [AWK-wərd] *adj* clumsy, ungainly; difficult; inconvenient; embarrassed. **awk'ward·ly** *adv* **awk'ward·ness** *n*

awl *n* pointed tool for marking or

boring wood, leather, etc.

awn'ing n (canvas, etc.) roof or shelter, to protect from weather.

awoke pt./pp. of AWAKE.

a·wry [ə-RĪ] adv crookedly; amiss; at a slant. ▶ adj crooked, distorted; wrong.

ax, axe [aks] n tool with handle and heavy, sharp blade for chopping; inf dismissal from employment, etc. ▶ vt **axed, ax·ing.** inf dismiss, dispense with.

ax·iom [AK-see-əm] n received or accepted principle; self-evident truth. **ax·i·o·mat'ic** adj

ax·is [AK-sis] n, pl **ax·es** [AK-seez] (imaginary) line around which a body spins; line or column about which parts are arranged. **ax'i·al** adj **ax'i·al·ly** adv

Ax·is n coalition of Germany, Italy and Japan, 1936–45.

ax·le [AK-səl] n shaft on which wheel turns.

a·ya·tol·lah [ah-yə-TOH-lə] adj one of a class of Islamic religious leaders.

aye [ī] adv yes. ▶ n affirmative answer or vote. ▶ pl those voting for motion.

a·zal·ea [ə-ZAYL-yə] n any of group of shrubby plants of the rhododendron genus.

az·i·muth [AZ-ə-məth] n vertical arc from zenith to horizon; angular distance of this from meridian.

Az·tec [AZ-tek] adj, n (member) of people ruling Mexico before Spanish conquest.

az·ure [AZH-ər] n sky-blue color; clear sky. ▶ adj sky-blue.

B b

B *Chem* boron.

Ba *Chem* barium.

bab·ble [BAB-əl] *v* **-bled, -bling.** speak foolishly, incoherently, or childishly. ▶ *n* foolish, confused talk. **bab′bler** *n*

babe [bayb] *n* baby; guileless person.

ba·bel [BAY-bəl] *n* confused noise or scene, uproar.

ba·boon [ba-BOON] *n* large monkey of Africa and Asia.

ba·by [BAY-bee] *n, pl* **-bies.** very young child, infant. **ba′by·ish** *adj* **ba′by·sit** *v* **-sat, -sit·ting. ba′by·sit·ter** *n* one who cares for children when parents are out.

bac·ca·lau·re·ate [bak-ə-LOR-ee-it] *n* degree of bachelor; service held at college or university awarding degree; sermon delivered at this service.

bac·ca·rat [BAH-kə-rah] *n* gambling card game.

bach·e·lor [BACH-lər] *n* unmarried man; holder of lowest four-year college or university degree.

ba·cil·lus [bə-SIL-əs] *n, pl* **-cil·li** [-SIL-ī] minute organism sometimes causing disease.

back [bak] *n* hinder part of anything, e.g. human body; part opposite front; part or side of something farther away or less used; (position of) player in football and other games behind other (forward) players. ▶ *adj* situated behind; earlier. ▶ *adv* at, to the back; in, into the past; in return. ▶ *vi* move backward. ▶ *vt* support; put wager on; provide with back or backing. **back′er** *n* one supporting another, esp. in contest or election campaign; one betting on horse, etc. in race. **back′ing** *n* support; material to protect the back of something. **back′ward, back′wards** *adv* to the rear; to the past; to worse state. **back′ward** *adj* directed toward the rear; (of a country, region or people) retarded in economic development; behind in education; reluctant, bashful. **back′ward·ness** *n* **back′bite** *vt* **-bit, -bit·ten, -bit·ing.** slander absent person. **back′bit·er** *n* **back′biting** *n* **back′bone** *n* spinal column. **back′date** *vt* **-dat·ed, -dat·ing.** make effective from earlier date. **back′drop** *n* painted cloth at back of stage. **back′fire** *vi* **-fired, -fir·ing.** ignite at wrong time, as fuel in cylinder of internal-combustion engine; (of plan, scheme, etc.) fail to work, esp. to the detriment of the instigator; ignite wrongly, as gas burner, etc. **back′gam·mon** [-gam-ən] *n* game played with counters and dice. **back′ground** *n* space behind chief figures of picture, etc.; past history of person. **back′hand** *n* stroke with hand turned backward. **back′hand·ed** *adj* (of compliment, etc.) with second, uncomplimentary meaning. **back′lash** *n* sudden and adverse reaction. **back′log** *n* accumulation of work, etc. to be dealt with. **back′pack** *n* type of knapsack. ▶ *vi* **-packed, -pack·ing.** hike with this. **back′side** *n* buttocks. **back′slash** *n* backward-sloping diagonal mark (\ ). **back′slide** *vi* **-slid** or **-slid·den, -slid·ing.** fall back in faith or morals. **back′stroke** *n* swimming stroke performed on the back. **back′talk** *n* impudent or insolent answer. **back′up** *n* a support or reinforcement; a reserve or substitute. **back up** *v* support; *Computers* make a copy of (a data file), esp. as a security copy. **back′wash** *n* water thrown back by ship's propellers, etc.; a backward current; a reaction. **back′wa·ter** *n* still water fed by back flow of stream; backward or isolated place or condition. **back′woods′** *pl n* remote forest areas; remote or backward area.

ba·con [BAY-kən] n cured and smoked meat from side of pig.

bac·te·ri·a [bak-TEER-ee-ə] pl n, sing **-ri·um**. microscopic organisms, some causing disease. **bac·te·ri·al** adj **bac·te·ri·cide** [-TEER-ə-sīd] n substance that destroys bacteria. **bac·te·ri·ol·o·gist** [-OL-ə-jist] n **bac·te·ri·ol·o·gy** n study of bacteria.

bad adj **worse, worst.** of poor quality; faulty; evil; immoral; offensive; severe; rotten, decayed. **bad'ly** adv **bad'ness** n **bad-mouth** vt sl speak unfavourably about.

bade [bad] pt. of BID.

badge [baj] n distinguishing emblem or sign.

badg·er [BAJ-ər] n burrowing night animal, about the size of fox; its pelt or fur. ▶ vt pester, worry.

bad·i·nage [bad-n-AHZH] n playful talk, banter.

bad·min·ton [BAD-min-tn] n game like tennis, played with rackets and shuttlecocks over high net.

baf·fle [BAF-əl] vt **-fled, -fling.** check, frustrate, bewilder. **baffling** adj **baffle** n device to regulate or divert flow of liquid, gas, sound waves, etc.

bag n sack, pouch; measure of quantity; woman's handbag; offens unattractive woman. ▶ v **bagged, bag·ging.** ▶ vi swell out; bulge; sag. ▶ vt put in bag; kill as game, etc. **bag'gy** adj **-gi·er, -gi·est.** loose, drooping. **bag lady** homeless woman who carries her possessions in shopping bags, etc. **bag'man** n, pl **-men.** person who collects and distributes illicitly obtained money for another.

bag·a·telle [bag-ə-TEL] n trifle; game like billiards.

bag·gage [BAG-ij] n suitcases, etc., packed for journey; offens woman.

bag·pipe [BAG-pīp] n (oft. pl) musical wind instrument, of windbag and pipes. **bag'pip·er** n

bail¹ [bayl] n Law security given for person's reappearance in court;

one giving such security. ▶ vt release, or obtain release of, on security; inf help a person, firm, etc. out of trouble.

bail² vt empty out water from boat. **bail out** leave aircraft by parachute; give up on or abandon something.

bail·iff [BAY-lif] n minor court officer.

bail·i·wick [BAY-li-wik] n a person's domain or special area of competence.

bait [bayt] n food to entice fish; any lure or enticement. ▶ vt set a lure; annoy, persecute.

baize [bayz] n smooth woolen cloth.

bake [bayk] v **baked, bak·ing.** ▶ vt cook or harden by dry heat. ▶ vi make bread, cakes, etc.; be scorched or tanned. **bak'er** n **bak'er·y** n **baking** n **baking powder** leavening agent containing sodium bicarbonate, etc. used in making baked goods.

bal·a·cla·va [bal-ə-KLAH-və] n close-fitting woolen helmet, covering head and neck.

bal·a·lai·ka [bal-ə-LĪ-kə] n Russian musical instrument, like guitar.

bal·ance [BAL-əns] n pair of scales; equilibrium; surplus; sum due on an account; difference between two sums. ▶ vt **-anced, -anc·ing.** weigh; bring to equilibrium. **balance sheet** tabular statement of assets and liabilities. **balance wheel** regulating wheel of watch.

bal·co·ny [BAL-kə-nee] n, pl **-nies.** railed platform outside window; upper seats in theater.

bald [bawld] adj hairless; plain; bare. **bald'ing** adj becoming bald. **bald'ness** n

bale [bayl] n bundle or package. ▶ vt **baled, bal·ing.** make into bundles or pack into cartons. **bal'er** n machine that does this.

ba·leen [bə-LEEN] n whalebone.

bale·ful [BAYL-fəl] adj menacing. **bale'ful·ly** adv

balk [bawk] vi swerve, pull up; Baseball commit a balk. ▶ vt thwart, hinder; shirk. ▶ n hindrance; rafter, beam; Baseball illegal motion of pitcher before releasing ball to batter. **balk at** recoil; stop short.

ball¹ [bawl] *n* anything round; globe, sphere, esp. as used in games; a ball as pitched; bullet. ▶ *vi* clog, gather into a mass. **ball bearings** hardened steel balls used to lessen friction on bearings. **ball′park** *n* stadium used for baseball games; *inf* approximate range. ▶ *adj inf* approximate. **ball′point, ball′point pen** pen with tiny ball bearing as nib.

ball² *n* formal social gathering for dancing; *inf* a very good time. **ball′room** *n*

bal·lad [BAL-əd] *n* narrative poem; simple song.

bal·lade [bə-LAHD] *n* short poem with refrain and envoi; piece of music.

bal·last [BAL-əst] *n* heavy material put in ship to give steadiness; that which renders anything steady. ▶ *vt* load with ballast, steady.

bal·let [ba-LAY] *n* theatrical presentation of dancing and miming to musical accompaniment. **bal·le·ri·na** [bal-ə-REE-nə] *n*

bal·lis·tic [bə-LIS-tik] *adj* moving as, or pertaining to motion of, a projectile. **bal·lis′tics** *n* scientific study of ballistic motion.

bal·loon [bə-LOON] *n* large bag filled with air or gas to make it rise in the air. ▶ *vi* puff out; increase rapidly. **bal·loon′ing** *n* **bal·loon′ist** *n*

bal·lot [BAL-ət] *n* method of voting secretly, usually by marking ballot paper and putting it into box. ▶ *vi* vote or decide by ballot. **ballot box** box into which voting papers are dropped on completion.

bal·ly·hoo [BAL-ee-hoo] *n* noisy confusion or uproar; flamboyant, exaggerated publicity or advertising.

balm [bahm] *n* aromatic substance, healing or soothing ointment; anything soothing. **balm′y** *adj* **balm·i·er, balm·i·est.** soothing; (of climate) mild; (of a person) foolish.

balm′i·ness *n*

ba·lo·ney [bə-LOW-nee] *n inf* nonsense.

bal·sa [BAWL-sə] *n* Amer. tree with light but strong wood.

bal·sam [BAWL-səm] *n* resinous aromatic substance obtained from various trees and shrubs; soothing ointment. **bal·sam′ic** *adj*

Baltimore oriole oriole of eastern N Amer.

bal·us·ter [BAL-ə-stər] *n* short pillar used as support to rail of staircase, etc. **bal′us·trade** [-strayd] *n* row of short pillars topped by rail.

bam·boo′ *n, pl* **-boos.** large tropical treelike reed.

bam·boo·zle [bam-BOO-zəl] *vt* **-zled, -zling.** mystify, hoodwink.

ban *vt* **banned, ban·ning.** prohibit, forbid, outlaw. ▶ *n* prohibition; proclamation. **banns** *pl n* proclamation of marriage.

ba·nal [bə-NAL] *adj* commonplace, trivial, trite. **ba·nal′i·ty** *n*

ba·nan·a [bə-NAN-ə] *n* tropical treelike plant; its fruit.

band¹ *n* strip used to bind; range of values, frequencies, etc., between two limits. **band·age** [BAN-dij] *n* strip of cloth for binding wound.

band² *n* company, group; company of musicians. ▶ *v* bind together. **band′mas·ter** *n* **band′stand** *n*

ban·dan·na [ban-DAN-ə] *n* large decorated handkerchief.

band·box [BAND-boks] *n* light box of cardboard for hats, etc.; theater or other public structure of small interior dimensions.

ban·deau [ban-DOH] *n, pl* **-deaux** [-DOHZ] band, ribbon for the hair; narrow bra or top.

ban′dit *n* outlaw; robber, brigand.

ban·do·leer [ban-də-LEER] *n* shoulder belt for cartridges.

band·wag·on [BAND-wag-ən] *n* **climb, jump, get on the bandwagon** join something that seems sure of success.

ban·dy [BAN-dee] *vt* **-died, -dy·ing.** beat to and fro, toss from one to another. **ban′dy-leg·ged** [-leg-id] *adj* bowlegged, having legs curving outward.

bane [bayn] *n* poison; person or thing causing misery or distress. **bane'ful** *adj*

bang[1] *n* sudden loud noise, explosion; heavy blow. ▶ *vt* make loud noise; beat; strike violently, slam.

bang[2] *n* (usu pl) fringe of hair cut straight across forehead.

ban·gle [BANG-gəl] *n* ring worn on arm or leg.

ban'ish *vt* condemn to exile; drive away; dismiss. **ban'ish·ment** *n* exile.

ban·is·ter [BAN-ə-stər] *n* handrail held up by balusters.

ban·jo [BAN-joh] *n*, *pl* **-jos.** musical instrument like guitar, with circular body. **ban'jo·ist** *n*

bank[1] [bangk] *n* mound or ridge of earth; edge of river, lake, etc.; rising ground in sea. ▶ *v* enclose with ridge; pile up; (of aircraft) tilt inward in turning.

bank[2] *n* establishment for keeping, lending, exchanging, etc. money; any supply or store for future use, as a **blood bank**. ▶ *vt* put in bank. ▶ *vi* keep with bank. **bank'er** *n* **bank'ing** *n* **bank teller** bank cashier. **bank'note** *n* written promise of payment acceptable as money. **bank on** rely on.

bank[3] *n* arrangement of switches, keys, oars, etc. in a row or in tiers.

bank·rupt [BANGK-rupt] *n* one who fails in business, insolvent debtor. ▶ *adj* financially ruined; broken; destitute. ▶ *vt* make, cause to be, bankrupt. **bank'rupt·cy** *n*

ban·ner [BAN-ər] *n* long strip with slogan, etc.; placard; flag used as ensign.

banns *n* see BAN.

ban·quet [BANG-kwit] *n* feast. ▶ *vi* feast. ▶ *vt* treat with feast.

ban·quette [bang-KET] *n* upholstered bench usu. along a wall; raised firing step behind parapet.

ban'shee *n* (in Irish folklore) female spirit with a wail portending death.

ban·tam [BAN-təm] *n* dwarf variety of domestic fowl; person of diminutive stature.

ban'tam·weight *n* boxer weighing no more than 118 pounds.

ban·ter [BAN-tər] *vt* make fun of. ▶ *n* light, teasing language.

Ban·tu [BAN-too] *a* collective name for large group of related tribes in Africa; family of languages spoken by Bantu peoples.

ban·yan [BAN-yən] *n* Indian fig tree with spreading branches that take root.

ba·o·bab [BAY-oh-bab] *n* Afr. tree with thick trunk and angular branches.

Bap'tist *n* member of Protestant Christian denomination believing in necessity of baptism by immersion, esp. of adults. **baptist** *n* one who baptizes.

bap·tize [BAP-tīz] *vt* **-tized, -tiz·ing.** immerse in, sprinkle with water ceremonially; christen. **bap'tism** [-tiz-əm] *n* **bap·tis'mal** [-TIZ-məl] *adj* **bap'tist·ry** *n*, *pl* **-ries.** place where baptism is performed.

bar[1] [bahr] *n* rod or block of any substance; obstacle; bank of sand at mouth of river; rail in law court; body of lawyers; room or counter where drinks are served, esp. in hotel, etc.; unit of music. ▶ *vt* **barred, bar·ring.** fasten; obstruct; exclude. ▶ *prep* except. **barring** *prep* excepting. **bar code** arrangement of numbers and parallel lines on package, electronically scanned at checkout to give price, etc. **bar'maid** *n* **bar'ten·der** *n*

bar[2] *n* unit of pressure.

barb [bahrb] *n* sharp point curving backward behind main point of spear, fishhook, etc.; cutting remark. **barbed** *adj* **barbed wire** fencing wire with barbs at close intervals.

bar·ba·rous [BAHR-bər-əs] *adj* savage, brutal, uncivilized. **bar·bar'ian** [-BAIR-ee-ən] *n* **bar·bar'ic** *adj* **bar'ba·rism** *n* **bar·bar'i·ty** *n*

bar·be·cue [BAHR-bi-kyoo] *n* food

cooked outdoors over hot charcoal; fireplace, grill used for this. ▸ *vt* **-cued, cu·ing.** cook meat, etc. in this manner.

bar·ber [BAHR-bər] *n* one whose job is to cut hair and shave beards. ▸ *v* **-bered, -ber·ing.** perform this service.

bar·bi·tu·rate [bahr-BICH-ər-it] *n* derivative of barbituric acid used as sedative drug.

bar·ca·role [BAHR-kə-rohl] *n* gondolier's song; music imitative of this.

bard [bahrd] *n* Celtic poet; wandering minstrel; poet. **the Bard of Avon** Shakespeare.

bare [bair] *adj* **bar·er, bar·est.** uncovered; naked; plain; scanty. ▸ *vt* **bared, bar·ing.** make bare. **bare'ly** *adv* only just, scarcely. **bare'back, -backed** *adj* on unsaddled horse. **bare'faced** *adj* shameless.

barf *v sl* vomit.

bar·gain [BAHR-gən] *n* something bought at price favorable to purchaser; contract, agreement. ▸ *vi* haggle, negotiate; make bargain.

barge [bahrj] *n* flat-bottomed freight boat propelled by towing; roomy pleasure boat. ▸ *vi inf* **barged, barg·ing.** interrupt; *inf* bump (into), push.

bar·i·tone [BAR-i-tohn] *n* (singer with) second lowest adult male voice. ▸ *adj* written for or possessing this vocal range.

bar·i·um [BA-ree-əm] *n* white metallic element.

bark¹ [bahrk] *n* sharp loud cry of dog, etc. ▸ *v* make, utter with such sound. **bark'er** *n* one who stands outside entrance to a circus, etc. calling out its attractions. **bark up the wrong tree** misdirect one's efforts; pursue a wrong course.

bark² *n* outer layer of trunk, branches of tree. ▸ *vt* strip bark from; rub off (skin), graze (shins, etc.).

bark³ *n* sailing ship, esp. large, three-masted one.

bar·ley [BAHR-lee] *n* grain used for food and making malt. **bar'ley·corn** *n* a grain of barley. **John Barleycorn** personification of intoxicating liquor.

bar mitz·vah [bahr MITS-və] *n* Jewish boy at age 13 who participates in religious ceremony signifying entry into adulthood; the ceremony.

barn [bahrn] *n* building to store grain, hay, etc. **barn dance** (party with) country music and dancing. **barn'yard** *n* area adjoining barn. **barnyard humor** earthy or smutty humor.

bar·na·cle [BAHR-nə-kəl] *n* shellfish that adheres to rocks, logs, ships' bottoms, etc.

ba·rom·e·ter [bə-ROM-i-tər] *n* instrument to measure pressure of atmosphere. **bar·o·met·ric** [bar-ə-ME-trik] *adj* **bar·o·graph** [BA-rə-graf] *n* recording barometer.

bar·on [BA-rən] *n* member of lowest rank of peerage in Great Britain; powerful businessman. **bar·o'ness** *n* **bar'o·ny** *n* **ba·ro'ni·al** [-ROH-nee-əl] *adj*

bar·on·et [BA-rə-nit] *n* lowest British hereditary title, below baron but above knight. **bar'o·net·cy** *n*

ba·roque [bə-ROHK] *adj* extravagantly ornamented, esp. in architecture and music. **baroque pearl** one irregularly shaped.

bar·rack [BA-rək] *n* (usu. in pl) building for housing soldiers; bare, barnlike building. ▸ *vt* house in barracks.

bar·ra·cu·da [ba-rə-KOO-də] *n* type of large, elongated, predatory fish, mostly tropical.

bar·rage [bə-RAHZH] *n* heavy artillery fire; continuous and heavy delivery, esp. of questions, etc.

bar·rel [BA-rəl] *n* round wooden vessel, made of curved staves bound with hoops; its capacity; great amount or number; anything long and hollow, as tube of gun, etc. ▸ *v* **-reled, -rel·ing.** put in barrel; move at high speed. **bar'rel·ful** *n*, *pl* **-fuls.** as much, as many, as a barrel can hold; large amount or number. **over a barrel** helpless.

bar·ren [BA-rən] *adj* unfruitful, sterile; unprofitable; dull. **bar′ren·ness** *n*

bar·ri·cade [BA-ri-kayd] *n* improvised fortification, barrier. ▸ *vt* **-cad·ed, -cad·ing.** to protect by building barrier; block.

bar·ri·er [BAR-ee-ər] *n* fence, obstruction, obstacle, boundary. **barrier reef** coral reef lying parallel to shore.

bar·row[1] [BA-roh] *n* small wheeled handcart; wheelbarrow.

barrow[2] *n* castrated male swine.

barrow[3] *n* burial mound of earth or stones.

bar·ter [BAHR-tər] *v* trade by exchange of goods. ▸ *n* trade by the exchange of goods.

bar·y·on [BA-ree-on] *n Physics* elementary particle of matter.

ba·salt [bə-SAWLT] *n* dark-colored, hard, compact, igneous rock. **ba·sal′tic** *adj*

base[1] [bays] *n* bottom, foundation; starting point; center of operations; fixed point; *Chem* compound that combines with an acid to form a salt; medium into which other substances are mixed. ▸ *vt* **based, bas·ing.** found, establish. **base′less** *adj* **base′ment** *n* lowest floor of building, partly or entirely below ground.

base[2] *adj* **-er, -est.** low, mean; despicable. **base′ly** *adv* **base′ness** *n*

base·ball [BAYS-bawl] *n* game played with bat and ball between teams of 9 (sometimes 10) players; the ball they use.

ba·sen·ji [bə-SEN-jee] *n* small African hunting dog that seldom barks.

bash *v inf* strike violently. ▸ *n* blow; attempt; festive party.

bash·ful [BASH-fəl] *adj* shy, modest. **bash′ful·ly** *adv*

BASIC [BAY-sik] computer programing language that uses common English words.

ba·sic [BAY-sik] *adj* relating to, serving as base; fundamental; necessary. **ba′si·cal·ly** *adv*

ba·sil·i·ca [bə-SIL-i-kə] *n* type of church with long hall and pillars.

bas·i·lisk [BAS-ə-lisk] *n* legendary small fire-breathing dragon; type of tropical lizard related to iguanas.

ba·sin [BAY-sən] *n* deep circular dish; harbor; land drained by river.

basis [BAY-sis] *n, pl* **-ses** [-seez] foundation; principal constituent.

bask *vi* lie in warmth and sunshine.

bas·ket [BAS-kit] *n* vessel made of woven cane, straw, etc. **bas′ket·ry** [-ki-tree] **bas′ket·ball** *n* ball game played by two teams of 5 players who score points by throwing ball through baskets suspended above ends of playing area; the ball they use.

Basque [bask] *n* one of a people from W Pyrenees; their language.

bas·re·lief [bah-ri-LEEF] *n* sculpture with figures standing out slightly from background.

bass[1] [bays] *n* lowest part in music; bass singer or voice. ▸ *adj*

bass[2] [bas] *n* any of large variety of freshwater or seawater fishes.

bas·set hound [BAS-it] *n* type of smooth-haired short-legged dog.

bas·soon [bə-SOON] *n* woodwind instrument of low tone. **bas·soon′ist** *n*

bas·tard [BAS-tərd] *n* child born of unmarried parents; *sl* person, esp. a man, e.g. *a lucky bastard.* ▸ *adj* illegitimate; spurious.

baste[1] [bayst] *vt* **bast·ed, bast·ing.** moisten (meat) during cooking with hot fat; beat severely. **bast′er** *n*

baste[2] *vt* **bast·ed, bast·ing.** sew loosely, tack.

bas·ti·na·do [bas-tə-NAY-doh] *n, pl* **-does.** beating with stick, etc. esp. on soles of feet. ▸ *vt* **-doed, -do·ing.**

bas·tion [BAS-chən] *n* projecting part of fortification, tower; strong defense or bulwark.

bat[1] *n* any of various types of clubs used to hit ball in certain sports, e.g. baseball. ▸ *v* **bat·ted, bat·ting.**

strike with bat or use bat in sport. **batting** n performance with bat.

bat² n nocturnal mouselike flying animal.

bat³ vt **bat·ted, bat·ting.** flutter (one's eyelids).

batch [bach] n group or set of similar objects, esp. cakes, etc. baked together.

bat·ed [BAY-tid] adj **with bated breath** anxiously.

bath n vessel or place to bathe in; water for bathing; act of bathing. **bath'house** n building with dressing and washing facilities for bathers. **bath'room** n room with toilet and washing facilities. **take a bath** sl experience serious, esp. financial, losses in a venture.

bathe [bayth] v **bathed, bath'ing.** apply liquid; wash; immerse in water. ▶ n **bath'er** n

ba·thos [BAY-thos] n ludicrous descent from the elevated to the ordinary in writing or speech.

ba·tik [bə-TEEK] n dyeing process using wax.

ba·ton [bə-TON] n stick, esp. of conductor, marshal, member of relay team.

ba·tra·chi·an [bə-TRAY-kee-ən] n, adj (of) any amphibian, esp. frog or toad.

bat·tal·ion [bə-TAL-yən] n military unit consisting of three or more companies; fig a large group.

bat·ten¹ [BAT-n] n narrow piece of board, strip of wood. ▶ vt (esp. with down) fasten, make secure.

batten² vi (usu. with on) thrive, esp. at someone else's expense.

bat·ter [BAT-ər] vt strike continuously. ▶ n mixture of flour, eggs, liquid, used in cooking.

bat·ter·y [BAT-ə-ree] n, pl **-ter·ies.** connected group of electrical cells; any electrical cell; number of similar things occurring together; Law assault by beating; number of guns; place where they are mounted; unit of artillery; Baseball pitcher and catcher as a unit.

bat·ting [BAT-ing] n cotton or wool fiber as stuffing or lining.

bat·tle [BAT-l] n fight between armies, combat. ▶ vi **-tled, -tling.** fight, struggle. **battle-ax** n sl sharp-tempered, domineering woman.

bat·tle·ment [BAT-l-mənt] n wall, parapet on fortification with openings for cannon.

bat·tle·ship [BAT-l-ship] n heavily armed and armored fighting ship of the largest and heaviest class.

bat·ty [BAT-ee] adj inf **-ti·er, -ti·est.** crazy, silly.

bau·ble [BAW-bəl] n showy trinket.

baud [bawd] n unit of data transmission speed.

baux·ite [BAWK-sīt] n mineral yielding aluminum.

bawd n prostitute; brothel keeper. **bawd'y** adj **bawd·i·er, bawd·i·est.** obscene, lewd.

bawl vi cry; shout. ▶ n loud shout or cry. **bawl out** vt inf reprimand severely.

bay¹ n wide inlet of sea; space between two columns; recess. **bay window** window projecting from a wall.

bay² n bark; cry of hounds in pursuit. ▶ v bark (at). **at bay** cornered.

bay³ n laurel tree.

bay⁴ adj reddish-brown. ▶ n horse with body of this color and black mane.

bay·o·net [BAY-ə-nit] n stabbing weapon fixed to rifle. ▶ vt **-net·ed, -net·ing.** stab with this.

bay·ou [BĪ-oo] n, pl **-ous.** marshy inlet or outlet of lake, river, etc., usu. sluggish.

ba·zaar [bə-ZAHR] n market (esp. in Orient); sale of goods for charity.

ba·zoo·ka [bə-ZOO-kə] n antitank rocket launcher.

be v, present sing 1st person **am.** 2nd person **are.** 3rd person **is.** present pl **are.** past sing 1st person **was.** 2nd person **were.** 3rd person **was.** past pl **were.** present participle **being.** past participle **been.** exist or live; pay a visit, e.g. have you been to Spain?; take place, e.g. my birthday was last Monday; used as a linking between the subject of a sentence and its complement, e.g. *John is a musician;* forms the progressive present tense, e.g. *the man is running;* forms the passive voice of all transitive verbs, e.g. *a good movie is being shown on television tonight.*

Be *Chem* beryllium.

beach [beech] *n* shore of sea. ▶ *vt* run boat on shore. **beach'comb·er** [-koh-mər] *n* one who habitually searches shore debris for items of value; loafer spending days aimlessly on beach. **beach'head** *n* area on beach captured from enemy; base for operations; foothold.

bea·con [BEE-kən] *n* signal fire; lighthouse, buoy; (radio) signal used for navigation.

bead [beed] *n* little ball pierced for threading on string of necklace, rosary, etc.; drop of liquid; narrow molding. ▶ *vt* string together or furnish with beads. **bead'ing** *n* **bead'y** *adj* **bead·i·er, bead·i·est.** small and bright.

bea·gle [BEE-gəl] *n* small hound.

beak [beek] *n* projecting horny jaws of bird; anything pointed or projecting; *sl* nose.

beak·er [BEE-kər] *n* large drinking cup; glass vessel used by chemists.

beam [beem] *n* long squared piece of wood; ship's cross timber, side, or width; ray of light, etc.; broad smile; bar of a balance. ▶ *vt* aim light, radio waves, etc. (to). ▶ *vi* shine; smile benignly.

bean [been] *n* any of various leguminous plants or their seeds; head. **full of beans** *inf* lively. **bean sprout** edible sprout of newly germinated bean, esp. mung bean.

bear[1] [bair] *vt* **bore, borne** *or* **born, bear·ing.** carry; support; produce; endure; press (upon). **bear'er** *n*

bear[2] *n* heavy carnivorous quadruped; other bearlike animals, such as the koala. **bear'skin** *n* tall fur helmet.

beard [beerd] *n* hair on chin. ▶ *vt* oppose boldly.

bear·ing [BAIR-ing] *n* support or guide for mechanical part, esp. one reducing friction; relevance; behavior; direction; relative position.

beast [beest] *n* animal; four-footed animal; brutal man. **beast'li·ness** *n* **beast'ly** *adj*

beat [beet] *v* **beat, beat·en, beat·ing.** ▶ *vt* strike repeatedly; overcome; surpass; stir vigorously with striking action; flap (wings); make, wear (path). ▶ *vi* throb; sail against wind. ▶ *n* stroke; pulsation; appointed course; basic rhythmic unit in piece of music. ▶ *adj sl* exhausted. **beat'er** *n* instrument for beating; one who rouses game for shooters.

be·at·i·fy [bee-AT-ə-fī] *vt* **-fied, -fy·ing.** make happy; *R.C. Church* pronounce in eternal happiness (first step in canonization). **be·a·tif·ic** [bee-ə-TIF-ik] *adj* **be·at·i·fi·ca'tion** *n* **be·at'i·tude** *n* blessedness.

beau [boh] *n, pl* **beaux** [bohz] suitor.

Beau·fort scale [BOH-fərt] system of indicating wind strength (from 0, calm, to 17, hurricane).

beau·ty [BYOO-tee] *n, pl* **-ties.** loveliness, grace; beautiful person or thing. **beau·ti·cian** [byoo-TISH-ən] *n* one who gives treatment in beauty parlor. **beau'ti·ful** *adj* **beau'ti·fy** [-tə-fī] *vt* **-fied, -fy·ing. beauty parlor** establishment offering hairdressing, manicure, etc.

bea·ver [BEE-vər] *n* amphibious rodent; its fur; exceptionally hard-working person.

be·calmed [bi-KAHMD] *adj* (of ship) motionless through lack of wind.

became pt. OF BECOME.

be·cause [bi-KAWZ] *adv, conj* by reason of, since.

beck [bek] *n* **at someone's beck and call** subject to someone's slightest whim.

beck·on [BEK-ən] *v* summon or lure by silent signal.

be·come [bi-KUM] v **be·came, be·come, be·com·ing.** ▶ vi come to be. ▶ vt suit. **becoming** adj suitable to; proper.

bed n piece of furniture for sleeping on; garden plot; supporting structure; bottom of river; layer, stratum. ▶ vt **bed·ded, bed·ding.** lay in a bed; plant. **bedding** n **bed'bug** n wingless bug infesting beds and sucking blood. **bed'pan** n container used as toilet by bedridden person. **bed'rid·den** adj confined to bed by age or sickness. **bed'rock** n solid rock beneath the surface soil; basic facts or principles. **bed'room** n **bed'spread** [-spred] n cover for bed when not in use. **bed'stead** [-sted] n framework of a bed.

be·dev·il [bi-DEV-əl] vt **-iled, -il·ing.** confuse; torment. **be·dev'il·ment** n

bed·lam [BED-ləm] n noisy confused scene.

Bed·ou·in [BED-oo-in] n nomadic Arab of the desert; nomad.

be·drag·gle [bi-DRAG-əl] vt **-gled, -gling.** dirty by trailing in wet or mud.

bee n insect that makes honey. **bee'hive** n **bee'line** n shortest route. **bees'wax** n wax secreted by bees. **bee in one's bonnet** an obsession.

beech n tree with smooth grayish bark and small nuts; its wood.

beef n flesh of cattle raised and killed for eating; inf complaint. ▶ vi inf complain. **beef'y** adj **beef·i·er, beef·i·est.** fleshy, stolid. **beef'burg·er** n hamburger.

been pp. of BE.

beep n short, loud sound of automobile horn, etc. ▶ v make this sound. **beep'er** n small portable electronic signaling device.

beer n fermented alcoholic drink made from hops and malt. **beer'y** adj **beer·i·er, beer·i·est.** affected by, smelling of, beer.

beet n any of various plants with root used for food or extraction of sugar.

bee·tle [BEET-l] n class of insect

with hard upper-wing cases closed over the back for protection. **bee'tle-browed** [browd] adj with prominent brows.

be·fall [bi-FAWL] v **be·fell, be·fall·en, be·fall·ing.** happen (to).

be·fit [bi-FIT] vt **be·fit·ted, be·fit·ting.** be suitable to.

be·fog [bi-FOG] vt **-fogged, -fog·ging.** perplex, confuse.

be·fore [bi-FOR] prep in front of; in presence of; in preference to; earlier than. ▶ adv earlier; in front. ▶ conj sooner than. **be·fore'hand** adv previously.

be·foul [bi-FOWL] vt make filthy.

be·friend [bi-FREND] vt make friend of.

beg v **begged, beg·ging.** ▶ vt ask earnestly, beseech. ▶ vi ask for or live on charity. **beg·gar** [BEG-ər] n

began pt. of BEGIN.

be·get [bi-GET] vt **be·got** or **be·gat, be·got·ten** or **be·got, be·get·ting.** obs produce, generate.

be·gin [bi-GIN] v **be·gan, be·gun, be·gin·ning.** (cause to) start; initiate; originate. **be·gin'ner** n novice.

be·go·nia [bi-GOHN-yə] n genus of tropical plant.

be·got pt./pp. of BEGET.

be·grudge [bi-GRUJ] vt **-grudged, -grudg·ing.** grudge, envy anyone the possession of.

be·guile [bi-GĪL] vt **-guiled, -guil·ing.** charm, fascinate; amuse; deceive. **beguiling** adj

be·gun pp. of BEGIN.

be·half [bi-HAF] n **on behalf of** in the interest of or for the benefit of.

be·have [bi-HAYV] vi **-haved, -hav·ing.** act, function in particular way. **be·hav·ior** [bi-HAYV-yər] n conduct. **behave oneself** conduct oneself well.

be·head [bi-HED] vt cut off head.

be·held pt./pp. of BEHOLD.

be·hest [bi-HEST] n charge, command.

be·hind [bi-HĪND] prep farther back or earlier than; in support of. ▶ adv in the rear. **behind-the-scenes** kept or made in secret.

be·hold [bi-HOHLD] *vt* **be·held,**
be·hold·ing. watch, see.
be·hold'er *n*

be·hol·den [bi-HOHL-dən] *adj*
bound in gratitude.

be·hoove [bi-HOOV] *vi* **-hooved,**
-hoov·ing. be necessary or fitting
for.

beige [bay*zh*] *n* color of undyed
woolen cloth.

be·ing [BEE-ing] *n* existence; that
which exists; creature; pr. p. of BE.

bel *n* unit for comparing two power
levels.

be·la·bor [bi-LAY-bər] *vt* beat
soundly; discuss (a subject)
endlessly.

be·lat·ed [bi-LAY-tid] *adj* late; too
late.

be·lay [bi-LAY] *vt* fasten rope to
peg, pin, etc.

belch *vi* void gas by mouth. ▶ *vt*
eject violently; cast up. ▶ *n* emission
of gas, etc.

be·lea·guer [bi-LEE-gər] *vt* besiege.

bel·fry [BEL-free] *n, pl* **-fries.** bell
tower.

be·lie [bi-LĪ] *vt* **-lied, -ly·ing.**
contradict; misrepresent.

be·lieve [bi-LEEV] *v* **-lieved,**
-liev·ing. ▶ *vt* regard as true or real.
▶ *vi* have faith. **be·lief'** *n*
be·liev'a·ble *adj* credible.
be·liev'er *n* esp. one of same
religious faith.

be·lit·tle [bi-LIT-l] *vt* **-tled, -tling.**
regard, speak of, as having little
worth or value. **be·lit'tler** *n*

bell *n* hollow metal instrument
giving ringing sound when struck;
electrical device emitting ring or
buzz as signal. **bell'hop** *n* hotel
employee who carries luggage,
conducts guests to rooms, etc.

bel·la·don·na [bel-ə-DON-ə] *n*
deadly nightshade.

belle [bel] *n* beautiful woman,
reigning beauty.

bel·li·cose [BEL-i-kohs] *adj* warlike.

bel·lig·er·ent [bə-LIJ-ər-ənt] *adj*
hostile, aggressive; making war. ▶
n warring person or nation.

bel·low [BEL-oh] *vi* roar like bull;
shout. ▶ *n* roar of bull; any deep cry
or shout.

bel·lows [BEL-ohz] *pl n* instrument
for creating stream of air.

bel·ly [BEL-ee] *n, pl* **-lies.** part of
body that contains intestines;
stomach. ▶ *v* **-lied, -ly·ing.** swell
out. **belly laugh** *n* hearty laugh.

be·long [bi-LAWNG] *vi* be the
property or attribute of; be a
member or inhabitant of; have an
allotted place; pertain to.
be·long'ings *pl n* personal
possessions.

be·lov·ed [bi-LUV-id or bi-LUVD]
adj much loved. ▶ *n* dear one.

be·low [bi-LOH] *adv* beneath.
▶ *prep* lower than.

belt *n* band; girdle; zone or district.
▶ *vt* surround, fasten with belt;
mark with band; *inf* thrash.

be·moan [bi-MOHN] *vt* grieve over
(loss, etc.).

be·muse [bi-MYOOZ] *v* **-mused,**
-mus·ing. confuse, bewilder.

bench *n* long seat; seat or body of
judges, etc. ▶ *vt* provide with
benches. **bench'mark** *n* fixed
point, criterion.

bend *v* **bent, bend·ing.** (cause to)
form a curve. ▶ *n* curve. **the bends**
pl n decompression sickness. **bend**
over backward exert oneself to the
utmost.

be·neath [bi-NEETH] *prep* under,
lower than. ▶ *adv* below.

ben·e·dic·tion [ben-i-DIK-shən] *n*
invocation of divine blessing.

ben·e·fit [BEN-ə-fit] *n* advantage,
favor, profit, good; money paid by
a government or business, etc. to
unemployed, etc. ▶ *v* **-fit·ed,**
-fit·ing. do good to; receive good.
ben'e·fac·tor *n* one who helps or
does good to others; patron.
ben'e·fice [-ə-fis] *n* an ecclesiastical
livelihood. **be·nef'i·cence** *n*
be·nef'i·cent *adj* doing good; kind.
ben·e·fi·cial [-FISH-əl] *adj*
advantageous, helpful.
ben·e·fi·ci·ar·y *n, pl* **-ar·ies.**
benefit society organization
providing life insurance, sickness
benefit, etc., to its members, and
often also social activities.

be·nev·o·lent [bə-NEV-ə-lənt] *adj* kindly, charitable. **be·nev′o·lence** *n*

be·night·ed [bi-NĪ-tid] *adj* ignorant, uncultured.

be·nign [bi-NĪN] *adj* kindly, mild, favorable. **be·nign′ly** *adv*

bent pt./pp. of BEND. *adj* curved; resolved (on); determined. ▶ *n* inclination, personal propensity.

be·numb [bi-NUM] *vt* make numb, deaden.

ben·zene [BEN-zeen] *n* one of group of related flammable liquids used in chemistry and as solvents, cleaning agents, etc.

be·queath [bi-KWEETH] *vt* leave property, etc. by will. **be·quest** [bi-KWEST] *n* bequeathing; legacy.

be·rate [bi-RAYT] *vt* **-rat·ed, -rat·ing.** scold harshly.

be·reave [bi-REEV] *vt* **-reaved, -reft, -reav·ing.** deprive of, esp. by death. **be·reave′ment** *n* loss, esp. by death.

be·ret [bə-RAY] *n* round, close-fitting hat.

ber·i·ber·i [ber-ee-BER-ee] *n* tropical disease caused by vitamin B deficiency.

ber·ke·li·um [bər-KEE-lee-əm] *n* artificial radioactive metallic element.

ber·ry [BER-ee] *n, pl* **-ries.** small juicy stoneless fruit. ▶ *vi* **-ried, -ry·ing.** look for, pick, berries.

ber·serk [bər-SURK] *adj* frenzied.

berth [burth] *n* ship's mooring place; place to sleep on ship or train. ▶ *vt* to moor.

ber·yl [BER-əl] *n* variety of crystalline mineral including aquamarine and emerald.

be·ryl·li·um [bə-RIL-ee-əm] *n* strong brittle metallic element.

be·seech [bi-SEECH] *vt* **-sought** or **-seeched, -seech·ing.** entreat, implore.

be·set [bi-SET] *vt* **-set, -set·ting.** assail, surround with danger, problems.

be·side [bi-SĪD] *adv, prep* by the side of, near; distinct from. **be·sides′** *adv, prep* in addition (to).

be·siege [bi-SEEJ] *vt* **-sieged,**

-sieg·ing. surround (with armed forces, etc.).

be·sot·ted [bi-SOT-id] *adj* drunk; foolish; infatuated.

besought pt./pp. of BESEECH.

be·speak [bi-SPEEK] *vt* **-spoke, -spok·en,, -speak·ing.** engage beforehand.

best *adj, adv* sup. of GOOD or WELL. ▶ *vt* defeat. **best seller** book or other product sold in great numbers; author of one or more of these books.

bes·tial [BES-chəl] *adj* like a beast, brutish. **bes·ti·al′i·ty** [-chee-AL-i-tee] *n*

be·stir [bi-STUR] *vt* **-stirred, -stir·ring.** rouse (oneself) to activity.

be·stow [bi-STOH] *vt* give, confer. **be·stow′al** *n*

be·stride [bi-STRĪD] *vt* **-strode** or **-strid, -strid·den** or **-strid, -strid·ing.** sit or stand over with legs apart, mount horse.

bet *v* **bet** or **bet·ted, bet·ting.** agree to pay money, etc. if wrong (or win if right) in guessing result of contest, etc. ▶ *n* money risked in this way.

be·tel [BEET-l] *n* species of pepper. **betel nut** the nut of the betel palm.

bête noire [bet NWAHR] *n, pl* **bêtes noires.** *Fr* pet aversion.

be·tide [bi-TĪD] *v* **-tid·ed, -tid·ing.** happen (to).

be·to·ken [bi-TOH-kən] *vt* be a sign of.

be·tray [bi-TRAY] *vt* be disloyal to, esp. by assisting an enemy; reveal, divulge; show signs of. **be·tray′al** *n* **be·tray′er** *n*

be·troth [bi-TROH*TH*] *vt* promise to marry. **be·troth′al** *n* **be·trothed′** *n, adj*

bet·ter [BET-ər] *adj, adv* comp. of GOOD or WELL. ▶ *v* improve. **bet′ter·ment** *n*

be·tween [bi-TWEEN] *prep, adv* in the intermediate part in space or time; indicating reciprocal relation or comparison.

be·twixt [bi-TWIKST] *prep, adv obs* between.

bev·el [BEV-əl] *n* surface not at

right angle to another; slant. ▶ *v* **-eled, -el·ing.** slope, slant; cut on slant. **bev'eled** *adj* slanted.

bev·er·age [BEV-rij] *n* drink.

bev·y [BEV-ee] *n, pl* **bev·ies.** flock or group.

be·wail [bi-WAYL] *vt* lament.

be·ware [bi-WAIR] *vi* be on one's guard, take care.

be·wil·der [bi-WIL-dər] *vt* puzzle, confuse. **be·wil'der·ing** *adj* **be·wil'der·ment** *n*

be·witch [bi-WICH] *vt* cast spell over; charm, fascinate. **be·witch'ing** *adj*

be·yond [bee-OND] *adv* farther away; besides. ▶ *prep* on the farther side of; later than; surpassing, out of reach of.

Bh *Chem* bohrium.

Bi *Chem* bismuth.

bi·as [BĪ-əs] *n, pl* **-as·es.** personal slant; inclination or preference; onesided inclination. ▶ *vt* **-ased, -as·ing.** influence, affect. **bi'ased** *adj* prejudiced.

bib *n* cloth put under child's chin to protect clothes when eating; part of apron or overalls above waist.

Bi·ble [BĪ-bəl] *n* the sacred writings of Christianity and Judaism. **bible** *n fig* book or journal considered unchallengeably authoritative. **Bib·li·cal** [BIB-li-kəl] *adj*

bib·li·og·ra·phy [bib-lee-OG-rə-fee] *n, pl* **-phies.** list of books on a subject; history and description of books. **bib·li·og'ra·pher** *n*

bib·li·o·phile [BIB-lee-ə-fīl] *n* lover, collector of books.

bib·u·lous [BIB-yə-ləs] *adj* given to drinking.

bi·cam·er·al [bī-KAM-ər-əl] *adj* (of a legislature) having two chambers.

bi·car·bo·nate [bī-KAHR-bə-nit] *n* chemical compound releasing carbon dioxide when mixed with acid.

bi·cen·ten·ni·al [bī-sen-TEN-ee-əl] *n* two hundredth anniversary; its celebration. ▶ *adj* relating to this.

bi·ceps [BĪ-seps] *n* two-headed muscle, esp. muscle of upper arm.

bick·er [BIK-ər] *vi, n* quarrel over petty things. **bick'er·ing** *n*

bi·cy·cle [BĪ-si-kəl] *n* vehicle with two wheels, one in front of other, pedaled by rider. **bi'cy·clist** *n*

bid *vt* **bade, bid** *or* **bid·den, bid·ding.** offer; say; command; invite. ▶ *n* offer, esp. of price; try. **bid'der** *n*

bide [bīd] *v* **bid·ed, bid·ing.** ▶ *vi* remain; dwell. ▶ *vt* await. **bid'ing** *n*

bi·det [bi-DAY] *n* low basin for washing genital area.

bi·en·ni·al [bī-EN-ee-əl] *adj* happening every two years; lasting two years. ▶ *n* plant living two years. **bi·en'ni·um** [-əm] *n* period of two years.

bier [beer] *n* frame for bearing dead to grave; stand for holding dead; coffin and its stand.

bi·fo·cal [bī-FOH-kəl] *adj* having two different focal lengths. **bi·fo'cals** *pl n* eyeglasses having bifocal lenses for near and distant vision.

big *adj* **big·ger, big·gest.** of great or considerable size, height, number, power, etc. **big cheese** *inf* important person. **big'head** *n* *inf* conceit. **big'head'ed** *adj* **big shot** *inf* important or influential person. **big'-time** *adv inf* very much, to a great extent.

big·a·my [BIG-ə-mee] *n, pl* **-mies.** crime of marrying a person while one is still legally married to someone else. **big'a·mist** *n*

bight [bīt] *n* curve or loop in rope; long curved shoreline or water bounded by it.

big·ot [BIG-ət] *n* person intolerant or not receptive to ideas of others (esp. on religion, race, etc.). **big'ot·ed** *adj* **big'ot·ry** *n*

bike [bīk] *n* short for bicycle or motor bike.

bi·ki·ni [bi-KEE-nee] *n, pl* **-nis.** woman's brief two-piece swimming costume.

bi·lat·er·al [bī-LAT-ər-əl] *adj* two-sided.

bile [bīl] *n* fluid secreted by the liver; anger, ill temper. **bil·ious**

[BIL-yəs] *adj* nauseous, nauseating. **bil'ious·ness** *n*

bilge [bilj] *n* bottom of ship's hull; dirty water collecting there; *inf* nonsense.

bi·lin·gual [bī-LING-gwəl] *adj* speaking, or written in, two languages. **bi·lin'gual·ism** *n*

bill[1] *n* written account of charges; draft of legislative act; poster; commercial document; paper money. ▶ *vt* present account of charges; announce by advertisement. **bill'ing** *n* degree of importance (esp. in theater, etc.). **bill'board** *n* large panel for outdoor advertising.

bill[2] *n* bird's beak. ▶ *vi* touch bills, as doves; caress affectionately.

bil·let [BIL-it] *n* civilian quarters for troops; resting place. ▶ *vt* quarter, as troops.

bil·let-doux [bil-ee-DOO] *n, pl* **billets-doux** [bil-ee-DOOZ] love letter.

bil·liards [BIL-yərdz] *n* game played on table with balls and cues.

bil·lion [BIL-yən] *n* thousand millions.

bil·low [BIL-oh] *n* great swelling wave. ▶ *vi* surge; swell out.

bi·month·ly [bī-MUNTH-lee] *adv, adj* every two months; oft. twice a month.

bin *n* box, etc. used for storage.

bi·na·ry [BĪ-nə-ree] *adj* composed of, characterized by, two; dual.

bind [bīnd] *v* **bound, bind·ing.** ▶ *vt* tie fast; tie around, gird; tie together; oblige; seal; constrain; bandage; cohere; unite; put (book) into cover. **bind'er** *n* one who, or that which binds. **bind'er·y** *n, pl* **-er·ies.** **bind'ing** *n* cover of book; tape for hem, etc.

binge [binj] *n inf* excessive indulgence in eating or drinking; spree.

bin·go [BING-goh] *n* game of chance in which numbers drawn are matched with those on a card.

bin·na·cle [BIN-ə-kəl] *n* box holding ship's compass.

bin·oc·u·lar [bə-NOK-yə-lər] *adj* seeing with, made for, both eyes. **bin·oc'u·lars** *pl n* telescope made for both eyes.

bi·no·mi·al [bī-NOH-mee-əl] *adj, n* (denoting) algebraic expression consisting of two terms.

bio- *comb. form* life or living organisms, e.g. *biology.*

bi·o·de·grad·a·ble [bī-oh-di-GRAY-də-bəl] *adj* capable of decomposition by natural means.

bi·o·di·ver·si·ty [bī-oh-dī-VURZ-ə-tee] *n* existence of a wide variety of species in their natural environment.

bi·og·ra·phy [bī-OG-rə-fee] *n, pl* **-phies.** story of one person's life. **bi·og'ra·pher** *n* **bi·o·graph'i·cal** *adj*

bi·ol·o·gy [bī-OL-ə-jee] *n* study of living organisms. **bi·o·log'i·cal** *adj* **bi·ol'o·gist** *n*

bi·on·ics [bī-ON-iks] *n* study of relation of biological and electronic processes. **bionic** *adj* having physical functions controlled, augmented by electronic equipment.

bi·op·sy [BĪ-op-see] *n, pl* **-sies.** examination of tissue removed surgically from a living body.

bi·o·rhythm [BĪ-oh-ri*th*-əm] *n* cyclically recurring pattern of physiological states.

bi·o·ter·ror·ism [bī-oh-TER-ər-iz-əm] *n* use of viruses, bacteria, etc by terrorists. **bi·o·ter'ror·ist** *n*

bi·par·ti·san [bī-PAHR-tə-zən] *adj* consisting of or supported by two political parties.

bi·par·tite [bī-PAHR-tīt] *adj* consisting of two parts, parties.

bi·ped [BĪ-ped] *n* two-footed animal.

bi·plane [BĪ-playn] *n* airplane with two pairs of wings.

birch [burch] *n* tree with silvery bark; rod for punishment, made of birch twigs. ▶ *vt* flog. **birch'en** *adj*

bird [burd] *n* feathered animal. ▶ *vi* observe or identify wild birds as a hobby. **bird'brain** *n* stupid person.

bird·ie [BUR-dee] *n, v Golf* (make) score of one under par for a hole.

bi·ret·ta [bə-RET-ə] *n* square cap with three or four ridges worn usu. by Catholic clergy.

birth [burth] *n* bearing, or the being born, of offspring; parentage, origin. **birth control** limitation of childbearing usu. by artificial means. **birth'mark** *n* blemish, usu. dark, formed on skin before birth. **birth'right** *n* right one has by birth.

bis·cuit [BIS-kit] *n* quick bread made from spoonful of rolled dough.

bi·sect [bī-SEKT] *vt* divide into two equal parts.

bi·sex·ual [bī-SEK-shoo-əl] *adj* sexually attracted to both men and women; of both sexes.

bish·op [BISH-əp] *n* clergyman typically governing diocese; chess piece. **bish'op·ric** *n* diocese or office of a bishop.

bis·muth [BIZ-məth] *n* reddish-white metal used in medicine, etc.

bi·son [BĪ-sən] *n* large wild ox; N Amer. buffalo.

bis·tro [BIS-troh] *n, pl* **-tros.** small restaurant.

bit¹ *n* fragment, piece; biting, cutting part of tool; mouthpiece of horse's bridle.

bit² pt./pp. of BITE.

bit³ *n Computers* smallest unit of information.

bitch [bich] *n* female dog, fox or wolf; *offens* spiteful woman; *inf* complaint. ▶ *vi inf* complain. **bitch'y** *adj* **bitch·i·er, bitch·i·est. bitch'i·ness** *n*

bite [bīt] *vt* **bit, bit·ten, bit·ing.** cut into esp. with teeth; grip; rise to bait; etch with acid. ▶ *n* act of biting; wound so made; mouthful. **biting** *adj* having power to bite.

bit·ter [BIT-ər] *adj* **-er, -est.** sharp, sour tasting; unpleasant; (of person) angry, resentful; sarcastic. **bit'ter·ly** *adv* **bit'ter·ness** *n* **bit'ters** *pl n* essence of bitter usu. aromatic herbs. **bitter end** final extremity.

bi·tu·men [bi-TOO-mən] *n* viscous substance occurring in asphalt, tar, etc. **bi·tu'mi·nous coal** coal yielding much bitumen on burning.

bi·valve [BĪ-valv] *adj* having a double shell. ▶ *n* mollusk with such shell.

biv·ou·ac [BIV-oo-ak] *n* temporary encampment of soldiers, hikers, etc. ▶ *vi* **-acked, -ack·ing.** pass the night in temporary camp.

bi·zarre [bi-ZAHR] *adj* unusual, weird.

Bk *Chem* berkelium.

blab *v* **blabbed, blab·bing.** reveal secrets; chatter idly. ▶ *n* chatter. **blab·ber** *v* **-bered, -ber·ing.** blab.

black [blak] *adj* of the darkest color; without light; dark; evil; somber; dishonorable. ▶ *n* darkest color; black dye, clothing, etc.; (**B-**) person of dark-skinned race; African-American. **black'en** *v* **black'ing** *n* substance used for blacking and cleaning leather, etc. **black'ball** *vt* vote against, exclude. **black'bird** *n* common American black bird. **black'board** *n* dark-colored surface for writing on with chalk. **black box** *inf* name for FLIGHT RECORDER. **black economy** illegally undeclared income. **black'head** *n* dark, fatty plug blocking pore in skin. **black'list** *n* list of people, organizations considered suspicious, untrustworthy, etc. ▶ *vt* put on blacklist. **Black Ma·ri·a** [mə-RĪ-ə] police van for transporting prisoners. **black market** illegal buying and selling of goods. **black widow** highly poisonous N Amer. spider.

black·guard [BLAG-ahrd] *n* scoundrel.

black·mail [BLAK-mayl] *vt* extort money from (a person) by threats. ▶ *n* act of blackmailing; money extorted thus. **black'mail·er** *n*

black·out [BLAK-owt] *n* complete failure of electricity supply; sudden turning off of all stagelights; state of temporary unconsciousness; obscuring of all lights as precaution against night air attack. **black out**

vi lose consciousness, memory, or vision temporarily.

black·smith [BLAK-smith] *n* smith who works in iron.

blad·der [BLAD-ər] *n* membranous bag to contain liquid, esp. urinary bladder.

blade [blayd] *n* edge, cutting part of knife or tool; leaf of grass, etc.; sword; *obs* dashing fellow; flat of oar.

blame [blaym] *n* censure; culpability. ▶ *vt* **blamed, blam·ing.** find fault with; censure. **blame'less** *adj* **blame'wor·thy** [-wur-*thee*] *adj*

blanch *v* whiten, bleach, take color out of; (of foodstuffs) briefly boil or fry; turn pale.

bland *adj* **-er, -est.** devoid of distinctive characteristics; smooth in manner.

blan'dish *vt* coax; flatter. **bland'ish·ment** *n*

blank *adj* without marks or writing; empty; vacant, confused; (of verse) without rhyme. ▶ *n* empty space; void; cartridge containing no bullet.

blan·ket [BLANG-kit] *n* thick woven covering for bed, horse, etc.; concealing cover. ▶ *vt* cover with blanket; cover, stifle.

blare [blair] *v* **blared, blar·ing.** sound loudly and harshly. ▶ *n* such sound.

blar·ney [BLAHR-nee] *n* flattering talk.

blasé [blah-ZAY] *adj* indifferent through familiarity; bored.

blas·pheme [blas-FEEM] *v* show contempt for God or sacred things, esp. in speech. **blas·phem'er** *n* **blas'phe·mous** [-fə-məs] *adj* **blas'phe·my** *n*

blast *n* explosion; high-pressure wave of air coming from an explosion; current of air; gust of wind or air; loud sound; reprimand; *sl* riotous party. ▶ *vt* blow up; remove, open, etc. by explosion; blight; ruin. **blast furnace** furnace for smelting ore, using blast of heated air.

bla·tant [BLAYT-nt] *adj* obvious.

bla'tan·cy *n*

blaze¹ [blayz] *n* strong fire or flame; brightness; outburst. ▶ *vi* **blazed, blaz·ing.** burn strongly; be very angry.

blaze² *v* **blazed, blaz·ing.** (mark trees to) establish trail. ▶ *n* mark on tree; white mark on horse's face.

blaze³ *vt* **blazed, blaz·ing.** proclaim.

blaz·er [BLAY-zər] *n* type of sports jacket.

bla·zon [BLAY-zən] *vt* make public, proclaim.

bleach [bleech] *v* make or become white. ▶ *n* bleaching substance.

bleak [bleek] *adj* **-er, -est.** cold and cheerless; exposed. **bleak'ly** *adv* **bleak'ness** *n*

blear·y [BLEER-ee] *adj* **blear·i·er, blear·i·est.** (of the eyes) dimmed, as with tears, sleep.

bleat [bleet] *v* cry, as sheep; say, speak, plaintively. ▶ *n* sheep's cry.

bleed *v* **bled, bleed·ing.** lose blood; draw blood or liquid from; extort money from.

bleep *n* short high-pitched sound e.g. from electronic device. ▶ *vt* obscure sound e.g. of TV program by making bleep. **bleep·er** *n* small portable radio receiver that makes a bleeping signal.

blem'ish *n* defect; stain. ▶ *vt* make (something) defective, dirty, etc. **blem'ished** *adj*

blend *vt* mix. ▶ *n* mixture. **blend'er** *n* one who, that which blends, esp. electrical kitchen appliance for mixing food.

bless *vt* **blessed** or **blest, bless·ing.** consecrate; give thanks to; ask God's favor for; (usu. passive) endow (with); glorify; make happy. **bless'ed** [-id] *adj* **blessing** *n* (ceremony asking for) God's protection, aid; short prayer; approval; welcome event, benefit.

blew pt. of BLOW.

blight [blīt] *n* plant disease; harmful influence. ▶ *vt* injure as with blight.

blimp *n* small, nonrigid airship used for observing.

blind [blīnd] *adj* unable to see; heedless, random; dim; closed at one end; *sl* very drunk. ▶ *vt* deprive of sight. ▶ *n* something cutting off light; window screen; pretext; place of concealment for hunters. **blind'ly** *adv* **blind'ness** *n* **blind flying** navigation of aircraft by use of instruments alone. **blind'fold** *vt* cover the eyes of so as to prevent vision. ▶ *n, adj* **blind·man's buff** game in which one player is blindfolded.

blink [blingk] *vi* wink; twinkle; shine intermittently. ▶ *n* gleam. **blink'ers** *pl n* leather flaps to prevent horse from seeing to the side. **blink at** see, know about, but ignore. **on the blink** *inf* not working (properly).

blip *n* repetitive sound or visible pulse, e.g. on radar screen. ▶ *vt* **blipped, blip·ping.** bleep.

bliss *n* perfect happiness. **bliss'ful** *adj* **bliss'ful·ly** *adv*

blis·ter [BLIS-tər] *n* bubble on skin; surface swelling, e.g. on paint. ▶ *v* form blisters (on). **blis'ter·ing** *adj* (of verbal attack) bitter. **blister pack** package for goods with hard, raised, transparent cover.

blithe [blīth] *adj* happy, gay; heedless. **blithe'ly** *adv* **blithe'ness** *n*

blitz [blits] *n* sudden, concentrated attack. **blitz'krieg** [-kreeg] *n* sudden concentrated military attack; war conducted in this way.

bliz·zard [BLIZ-ərd] *n* blinding storm of wind and snow.

bloat [bloht] *v* puff or swell out. ▶ *n* distention of stomach of cow, etc. by gas. **bloat'ed** *adj* swollen.

blob *n* soft mass, esp. drop of liquid; shapeless form.

bloc [blok] *n* (political) grouping of people or countries.

block [blok] *n* solid piece of wood, stone, etc.; *Hist* rectangular piece of wood on which people were beheaded; obstacle; stoppage; pulley with frame; group of buildings; urban area enclosed by intersecting streets. ▶ *vt* obstruct, stop up; shape on block; sketch (in). **block'age** *n* obstruction. **block'head** *n* fool, simpleton.

block letters written capital letters.

block·ade [blo-KAYD] *n* physical prevention of access, esp. to port, etc. ▶ *vt* **-ad·ed, -ad·ing.**

blonde, (*masc*) **blond** *adj, n* fair-haired (person).

blood [blud] *n* red fluid in veins; race; kindred; good parentage; temperament; passion. ▶ *vt* initiate (into hunting, war, etc.). **blood'less** *adj* **blood'y** *adj* **-i·er, -i·est.** covered in blood; slaughterous. ▶ *adj, adv sl* a common intensifier. ▶ *v* make bloody. **blood bank** (institution managing) store of human blood preserved for transfusion. **blood'cur·dling** *adj* horrifying. **blood'hound** *n* breed of large hound noted for keen powers of scent. **blood'shed** *n* slaughter, killing. **blood'shot** *adj* inflamed (said of eyes). **blood sport** sport in which animals are killed, e.g. fox hunting. **blood'suck·er** *n* parasite (e.g. mosquito) living on host's blood; parasitic person. **blood test** examination of sample of blood. **blood'thirst·y** *adj* murderous, cruel. **blood transfusion** transfer of blood from one person into another.

bloom *n* flower of plant; blossoming; prime, perfection; glow; powdery deposit on fruit. ▶ *vi* be in flower; flourish.

bloom·er [BLOO-mər] *n inf* plant in bloom; person reaching full competence; person reaching puberty; ludicrous mistake.

bloo·mers [BLOO-mərz] *pl n* girls' or women's wide, baggy underpants.

blos·som [BLOS-əm] *n* flower; flower bud. ▶ *vi* flower; develop.

blot *n* spot, stain; disgrace. ▶ *vt* **-ted, -ting.** spot, stain; obliterate; detract from; soak up ink, etc. from. **blot'ter** *n* **blotting paper** soft absorbent paper for soaking up ink.

blotch [bloch] *n* dark spot on skin. ▶ *vt* make spotted. **blotch'y** *adj* **blotch·i·er, blotch·i·est.**

blouse [blows] n light, loose upper garment.

blow¹ [bloh] v **blew, blown, blow·ing.** ▶ vi make a current of air; pant; emit sound. ▶ vt drive air upon or into; drive by current of air; sound; spout (of whales); fan; sl squander. ▶ n blast; gale. **blow-dry** vt **-dried, -dry·ing.** style hair after washing using stream of hot air. **blow fly** fly that infects food, etc. **blow'pipe** n dart tube. **blow'out** n sudden puncture in tire; uncontrolled escape of oil, gas, from well; sl festive party. **blow up** explode; inflate; enlarge (photograph); inf lose one's temper.

blow² n stroke, knock; sudden misfortune, loss.

blown pp. of BLOW¹.

blows·y [BLOW-zee] adj **blows·i·er, blows·i·est.** slovenly, sluttish; red-faced.

blub·ber [BLUB-ər] vi weep. ▶ n fat of whales; weeping.

bludg·eon [BLUJ-ən] n short thick club. ▶ vt strike with one; coerce (someone into).

blue [bloo] adj **blu·er, blu·est.** of the color of sky or shades of that color; livid; depressed; indecent. ▶ n the color; dye or pigment. ▶ vt **blued, blu·ing.** make blue; dip in blue liquid. **blues** pl n inf depression; song in slow tempo originating with Amer. Blacks, employed in jazz music. **blu'ish** adj **blue baby** baby born with bluish skin caused by heart defect. **blue blood** (person of) royal or aristocratic descent. **blue-col·lar** adj denoting factory workers. **blue jeans** pants made usu. of blue denim. **blue-pen·cil** vt **-ciled, -cil·ing.** alter, delete parts of, esp. to censor. **blue'print** n copy of drawing; original plan. **blue'stock·ing** n scholarly, intellectual woman.

bluff¹ n cliff, steep bank. ▶ adj **-er, -est.** hearty; blunt; steep; abrupt.

bluff² vt deceive by pretense of strength. ▶ n pretense.

blu·ing [BLOO-ing] n indigo powder used in laundering.

blun·der [BLUN-dər] n clumsy mistake. ▶ vi make stupid mistake; act clumsily.

blun·der·buss [BLUN-dər-bus] n obsolete short gun with wide bore.

blunt adj **-er, -est.** not sharp; (of speech) abrupt. ▶ vt make blunt. **blunt'ly** adv **blunt'ness** n

blur v **blurred, blur·ring.** make, become less distinct. ▶ n something vague, indistinct. **blur'ry** adj **-ri·er, -ri·est.**

blurb n statement advertising, recommending book, etc.

blurt vt (usu. with out) utter suddenly or unadvisedly.

blush vi become red in face; be ashamed; redden. ▶ n this effect.

blus·ter [BLUS-tər] vi, n (indulge in) noisy, aggressive behavior. **blus'ter·ing, -ter·y** adj (of wind, etc.) noisy and gusty.

bo·a [BOH-ə] n, pl **bo·as.** large, nonvenomous snake, esp. boa constrictor; long scarf of fur or feathers.

boar [bor] n male pig; wild pig.

board [bord] n broad, flat piece of wood; sheet of rigid material for specific purpose; table; meals; group of people who administer company; governing body; thick, stiff paper. ▶ pl stage. ▶ vt cover with planks; supply food daily; enter ship, etc. ▶ vi take daily meals. **board'er** n **board·ing house** lodging house where meals may be had. **boarding school** school providing living accommodation for pupils. **board'room** n room where board of company or governing body meets. **above board** beyond suspicion. **on board** aboard.

boast [bohst] vi speak too much in praise of oneself, one's possessions. ▶ vt brag of; have to show. ▶ n something boasted (of). **boast'er** n **boast'ful** adj

boat [boht] n small open vessel; ship. ▶ vi sail about in boat. **boat'ing** n **boat'swain** [BOH-sən] n ship's petty officer in charge of maintenance.

bob v **bobbed, bob·bing.** ▶ vi move up and down. ▶ vt move jerkily; cut (women's) hair short. ▶ n short, jerking motion; short hair style; weight on pendulum, etc. **bobbed** adj

bob·bin [BOB-in] n cylinder on which thread is wound.

bob·ble [BOB-əl] v, n Baseball **-bled, -bling.** fumble. ▶ n fumbled ball.

bob·cat [BOB-kat] n N Amer. lynx.

bob·o·link [BOB-ə-lingk] n Amer. songbird.

bode [bohd] vt **bod·ed, bod·ing.** be an omen of.

bod·ice [BOD-is] n upper part of woman's dress.

bod·y [BOD-ee] n, pl **bod·ies.** entire frame of body or animal; main part of such frame; corpse; main part of anything; substance; mass; person; number of persons united or organized; matter, opposed to spirit. **bod'i·ly** adj, adv **bod'y·guard** n escort to protect important person. **body stocking** undergarment covering body, oft. including arms and legs. **bod'y·work** n body of motor vehicle; repair of this.

Boer [bor] n a S Afr. of Dutch or Huguenot descent.

bof·fo [BOF-oh] adj sl excellent; highly successful.

bog n wet, soft ground. **bog'gy** adj **-gi·er, -gi·est.** marshy. **bog down** stick as in a bog.

bo·gey [BOH-gee] n evil or mischievous spirit; source of fear; Golf one stroke over par on a hole. **bo'gey·man** n

bog·gle [BOG-əl] v **-gled, -gling.** ▶ vi be surprised; be baffled. ▶ vt overwhelm with wonder; bewilder.

bo·gus [BOH-gəs] adj sham, false.

bo·he·mi·an [boh-HEE-mee-ən] adj unconventional. ▶ n one who leads an unsettled life. **bo·he'mi·a** n district, social circles of bohemians.

boil[1] vi change from liquid to gas, esp. by heating; become cooked by boiling; bubble; be agitated;

seethe; inf be hot; inf be angry. ▶ vt cause to boil; cook by boiling. ▶ n boiling state. **boil'er** n vessel for boiling. **boil·er·mak·er** n repairman, worker on boilers; whiskey with beer chaser. **boiling point** temperature at which boiling occurs; point at which anger becomes uncontrollable.

boil[2] n inflamed suppurating swelling on skin.

bois·ter·ous [BOI-stər-əs] adj wild; noisy; turbulent. **bois'ter·ous·ness** n

bold [bohld] adj **-er, -est.** daring, fearless; presumptuous; striking, prominent. **bold'ly** adv **bold'ness** n **bold'face** n Printing heavy-faced type.

bole [bohl] n trunk of a tree.

bo·le·ro [bə-LAIR-oh] n, pl **-ros.** Spanish dance; short loose jacket.

boll [bohl] n seed capsule of cotton, flax, etc. **boll weevil** beetle infesting the cotton plant.

Bol·she·vik [BOHL-shə-vik] n violent revolutionary, esp. member of Russian group active in overthrow of czarist regime.

bol·ster [BOHL-stər] vt support, uphold. ▶ n long pillow; pad, support.

bolt [bohlt] n bar or pin (esp. with thread for nut); rush; discharge of lightning; roll of cloth. ▶ vt fasten with bolt; swallow hastily. ▶ vi rush away; break from control.

bomb [bom] n explosive projectile; any explosive device; a failure. ▶ vt attack with bombs. **the bomb** nuclear bomb. **bom·bard'** vt shell; attack (verbally). **bom·bar·dier'** [-bər-DEER] n person in military aircraft who aims and releases bombs. **bom·bard'ment** n **bomb'er** n aircraft capable of carrying bombs; person using bombs illegally. **bomb'shell** n shell of bomb; surprise; inf very attractive woman.

bom'bast n pompous language; pomposity. **bom·bas'tic** adj

bo·na fide [BOH-nə fīd] Lat genuine(ly); sincere(ly). **bona**

fi·des [FĪ-deez] good faith, sincerity.
bo·nan·za [bə-NAN-zə] n sudden good luck or wealth.
bond n that which binds; link, union; written promise to pay money or carry out contract. ▶ vt bind; store goods until duty is paid on them. **bond'ed** adj placed in bond; mortgaged. **bonds'man** [-mən] n Law one whose work is to enter into bonds as surety.
bond·age [BON-dij] n slavery.
bone [bohn] n hard substance forming animal's skeleton; piece of this. ▶ v **boned, bon·ing.** ▶ vt take out bone. ▶ vi inf (with up) study hard. **bone'less** adj **bon'y** adj **bon·i·er, bon·i·est. bone'head** n inf stupid person.
bon·fire [BON-fīr] n large outdoor fire.
bon·go [BONG-goh] n, pl **-gos, -goes.** small drum, usu. one of a pair, played with the fingers.
bon·net [BON-it] n hat (usu. with strings).
bon·sai [BON-sī] n (art of growing) dwarf trees, shrubs.
bo·nus [BOH-nəs] n, pl **-nus·es.** extra (oft. unexpected) payment or gift.
boob n fool; sl female breast.
boo·by [BOO-bee] n, pl **-bies.** fool; tropical marine bird. **booby hatch** inf insane asylum. **booby prize** mock prize for poor performance. **booby trap** harmless-looking object that explodes when disturbed; form of practical joke.
boog·ie-woog·ie [BUUG-ee-WUUG-ee] n kind of jazz piano playing, emphasizing a rolling bass in syncopated eighth notes.
book [buuk] n collection of sheets of paper bound together; literary work; main division of this. ▶ vt reserve (table, ticket, etc.); charge with legal offense; enter name in book; schedule engagements for. **book'ing** n scheduled performance for entertainer, etc.; reservation. **book'ie** n inf bookmaker. **book'ish** adj studious, fond of reading.

book'keep·ing n systematic recording of business transactions. **book'keep·er** n **book'let** n
book'mak·er n one whose work is taking bets (also **book'ie**).
book'mark n strip of some material put between the pages of a book to mark a place; Computers identifier put on a website that enables the user to return to it quickly and easily. ▶ vt Computers identify and store a website so that one can return to it quickly and easily. **book'worm** n great reader.
boom¹ n sudden commercial activity; prosperity. ▶ vi become active, prosperous.
boom² vi, n (make) loud, deep sound.
boom³ n long spar, as for stretching the bottom of a sail; barrier across harbor, river, etc.; pole carrying overhead microphone, etc.
boo·mer·ang [BOO-mə-rang] n curved wooden missile of Aust. Aborigines that returns to the thrower. ▶ vi recoil; return unexpectedly; backfire.
boon n something helpful, favor.
boon·docks [BOON-doks] pl n rural, backward area.
boon·dog·gle [BOON-dog-əl] n, vi **-gled, -gling.** (do) work of no practical value performed merely to appear busy.
boor n rude person. **boor'ish** adj **boor'ish·ness** n
boost n encouragement, help; upward push; increase. ▶ vt
boost'er n person or thing that supports, increases power, etc.
boot n covering for the foot and ankle; inf kick. ▶ vt inf kick; start up (a computer). **boot'ed** adj
booth n stall; cubicle.
boot'leg v **-legged, -leg·ging.** make, carry, sell illicit goods, esp. alcohol. ▶ adj **boot'leg·ger** n
boo·ty [BOO-tee] n, pl **-ties.** plunder, spoil.
booze [booz] n, vi inf **boozed, booz·ing.** (consume) alcoholic drink; drinking spree. **booz'er** n inf person fond of drinking.

bo·rax [BOR-aks] *n* white soluble substance, compound of boron. **bo·rac·ic** [bə-RAS-ik] *adj*

bor·der [BOR-dər] *n* margin; frontier; limit; strip of garden. ▶ *v* provide with border; adjoin.

bore¹ [bor] *vt* **bored, bor·ing.** pierce, making a hole. ▶ *n* hole; caliber of gun. **bor'er** *n* instrument for making holes; insect that bores holes.

bore² *vt* **bored, bor·ing.** make weary by repetition, etc. ▶ *n* tiresome person or thing. **bore'dom** [-dəm] *n*

bore³ pt. of BEAR.

borne, born pp. of BEAR.

bo·ron [BOR-on] *n* chemical element used in hardening steel, etc.

bor·ough [BUR-oh] *n* political subdivision in some states.

bor·row [BOR-oh] *vt* obtain on loan or trust; appropriate.

bor'zoi *n* breed of tall hound with long, silky coat.

bos·om [BUUZ-əm] *n* human breast; seat of passions and feelings.

boss¹ [baws] *n* person in charge of or employing others. ▶ *vt* be in charge of; be domineering over. **boss'y** *adj* **boss·i·er, boss·i·est.** overbearing.

boss² *n* knob or stud; raised ornament. ▶ *vt* emboss.

bo·sun [BOH-sən] *n* boatswain.

bot·a·ny [BOT-n-ee] *n* study of plants. **bo·tan·ic·al** [bə-TAN-ik-əl] *adj* **bot'a·nist** *n* **botanical garden** garden for exhibition and study of plants.

botch [boch] *vt* spoil by clumsiness.

both [bohth] *adj, pron* the two. ▶ *adv, conj* as well.

both·er [BO *TH*-ər] *vt* pester; perplex. ▶ *vi, n* fuss, trouble.

bot·tle [BOT-l] *n* vessel for holding liquid; its contents. ▶ *vt* **-tled, -tling.** put into bottle; restrain. **bot'tler** *n* **bot'tle·neck** *n* narrow outlet that impedes smooth flow of traffic or production of goods; person who hampers flow of work, information, etc.

bot·tom [BOT-əm] *n* lowest part of anything; bed of sea, river, etc.; buttocks. ▶ *vt* put bottom to; base (upon); get to bottom of. **bot'tom·less** *adj* **bottom line** last line of financial statement; crucial or deciding factor.

bot·u·lism [BOCH-ə-liz-əm] *n* kind of food poisoning.

bou·clé [boo-KLAY] *n* looped yarn giving knobby effect.

bou·doir [BOO-dwahr] *n* woman's bedroom, private sitting room.

bough [rhymes with **cow**] *n* branch of tree.

bought pt./pp. of BUY.

boul·der [BOHL-dər] *n* large weather-worn rounded stone.

boul·e·vard [BUUL-ə-vahrd] *n* broad street or promenade.

bounce [bowns] *v* **bounced, bounc·ing.** (cause to) rebound (repeatedly) on impact, as a ball. ▶ *n* rebounding; quality in object causing this; *inf* vitality, vigor. **bounc'er** *n* esp. one employed to evict undesirables (forcibly). **bounc'ing** *adj* vigorous, robust. **bounc'y** *adj* **bounc·i·er, bounc·i·est.** lively.

bound¹ [bownd] *n, vt* limit. **bound'a·ry** *n, pl* **-ries. bound'ed** *adj* **bound'less** *adj*

bound² *vi, n* spring, leap.

bound³ *adj* on a specified course, e.g. *homeward bound.*

bound⁴ pt./pp. of BIND. *adj* committed; certain; tied.

boun·ty [BOWN-tee] *n, pl* **-ties.** liberality; gift; premium. **boun'te·ous** [-tee-əs], **boun'ti·ful** *adj* liberal, generous.

bou·quet [boo-KAY] *n* bunch of flowers; perfume of wine; compliment.

bour·bon [BUR-bən] *n* whiskey made from corn, malt and rye.

bour·geois [buur-*ZH*WAH] *n, adj disparaging* middle class; smugly conventional (person).

bourgeoisie [buur-*zh*wah-ZEE] *n* middle classes.

bout [bowt] *n* contest, fight; period of time spent doing something.

bou·tique [boo-TEEK] *n* small shop, esp. one selling clothes.

bo·vine [BOH-vīn] *adj* of cattle; oxlike; stolid, dull.

bow[1] [boh] *n* weapon for shooting arrows; implement for playing violin, etc.; ornamental knot of ribbon, etc.; bend, bent line. ▶ *v* bend. **bow'leg·ged** [-leg-id] *adj* having legs curved outward. **bow window** one with outward curve.

bow[2] [rhymes with **cow**] *vi* bend body in respect, assent, etc.; submit. ▶ *vt* bend downward; cause to stoop; crush. ▶ *n*

bow[3] [rhymes with **cow**] *n* fore end of ship; prow; rower nearest bow.

bowd·ler·ize [BOHD-lə-rīz] *vt* -**ized, -iz·ing.** expurgate, censor.

bow·el [BOW-əl] *n* (oft. pl) part of intestine (esp. with reference to defecation); inside of anything.

bow·er [BOW-ər] *n* shady retreat, arbor.

bowl[1] [bohl] *n* round vessel, deep basin; drinking cup; hollow.

bowl[2] *n* wooden ball. ▶ *pl* outdoor game played with such balls. ▶ *v* roll or throw ball in various ways. **bowl'ing** *n* indoor game, played usu. with large, heavy balls. **bowling green** place where bowls is played. **bowling alley** place where bowling is played.

box[1] [boks] *n* (wooden) container, usu. rectangular with lid; its contents; small enclosure; any boxlike cubicle, shelter or receptacle. ▶ *vt* put in box; confine.

box[2] *v* fight with fists, esp. with padded gloves on. ▶ *vt* strike. ▶ *n* blow. **box'er** *n* one who boxes; breed of pug-faced large dog.

boy [boi] *n* male child; young man. **boy'hood** [-huud] *n*

boy·cott [BOI-kot] *vt* refuse to deal with or participate in. ▶ *n*

Br *Chem* bromine.

bra [brah] *n* brassiere.

brace [brays] *n* tool for boring; clasp, clamp; pair, couple; strut, support. ▶ *pl* dental appliance worn to help straighten teeth. ▶ *vt* **braced, brac·ing.** steady (oneself) as before a blow; support, make firm. **bracing** *adj* invigorating.

brace'let *n* ornament for the arm. ▶ *pl sl* handcuffs.

brack·et [BRAK-it] *n* support for shelf, etc.; group. ▶ *pl* marks [ ], used to enclose words, etc. ▶ *vt* enclose in brackets; connect.

brack·ish [BRAK-ish] *adj* (of water) slightly salty.

bract [brakt] *n* small scalelike leaf.

brad *n* small nail.

brag *vi* **bragged, brag·ging.** boast. ▶ *n* boastful talk. **brag'gart** [-ərt] *n*

Brah·man [BRAY-mən] *n* breed of beef cattle.

Brah·min [BRAH-min] *n* member of priestly Hindu caste; socially or intellectually aloof person.

braid [brayd] *vt* interweave (hair, thread, etc.); trim with braid. ▶ *n* length of anything interwoven or plaited; ornamental tape.

Braille [brayl] *n* system of printing for blind, with raised dots instead of letters.

brain [brayn] *n* mass of nerve tissue in head; intellect. ▶ *vt* kill by hitting on head. **brain'less** *adj* **brain'y** *adj* **brain·i·er, brain·i·est.** **brain'child** *n* invention.

brain'storm *n* sudden mental aberration; sudden clever idea. ▶ *v* practice, subject to, brainstorming. **brain'storm·ing** *n* technique for coming upon innovative ideas.

brain trust group of experts without official status who advise government officials. **brain'wash** *vt* change, distort a person's ideas or beliefs. **brain wave** electrical impulse in brain.

braise [brayz] *vt* **braised, brais·ing.** cook slowly in covered pan.

brake [brayk] *n* instrument for retarding motion of wheel on vehicle. ▶ *vt* **braked, brak·ing.** apply brake to.

bram·ble [BRAM-bəl] *n* prickly shrub. **bram'bly** *adj* -**bli·er, -bli·est.**

bran *n* sifted husks of cereal grain.

branch *n* limb of tree; offshoot or subsidiary part of something larger or primary. ▶ *vi* bear branches;

diverge; spread. **branched** *adj*
branch′less *adj*

brand *n* trademark; class of goods;
particular kind, sort; mark made by
hot iron; burning piece of wood;
sword; mark of disgrace. ▶ *vt* burn
with iron; mark; stigmatize.
brand-new *adj* absolutely new.

bran′dish *vt* flourish, wave
(weapon, etc.).

bran·dy [BRAN-dee] *n, pl* **-dies.**
alcoholic liquor distilled from wine
or fruit juice. ▶ *vt* **-died, -dy·ing.**
flavor or preserve with brandy.

brash *adj* **-er, -est.** bold, impudent.

brass *n* alloy of copper and zinc;
group of brass wind instruments
forming part of orchestra or band;
inf (military) officers. ▶ *adj* **brass′y**
adj **brass·i·er, brass·i·est.** showy;
harsh. **brass′i·ness** *n*

bras·siere [brə-ZEER] *n* woman's
undergarment, supporting breasts,
bra.

brat *n* contemptuous term for a
child.

bra·va·do [brə-VAH-doh] *n* showy
display of boldness.

brave [brayv] *adj* **brav·er, brav·est.**
bold, courageous; splendid, fine.
▶ *n* N Amer. Indian warrior. ▶ *vt*
braved, brav·ing. defy, meet
boldly. **brav′er·y** *n, pl* **-er·ies.**

bra·vo [BRAH-voh] *interj* well done!

brawl *vi* fight noisily. ▶ *n* **brawl′er** *n*

brawn *n* muscle; strength. **brawn′y**
adj **brawn·i·er, brawn·i·est.**
muscular.

bray *n* donkey's cry. ▶ *vi* utter this;
give out harsh or loud sounds.

braze [brayz] *vt* **brazed, braz·ing.**
solder with alloy of brass or zinc.

bra·zen [BRAY-zən] *adj* of, like
brass; impudent, shameless. ▶ *vt*
(usu. with *out* or *through*) face,
carry through with impudence.
bra′zen·ness *n* effrontery.

bra·zier [BRAY-zhər] *n* pan for
burning charcoal or coals;
brassworker.

breach [breech] *n* break, opening;
breaking of rule, duty, etc.; quarrel.
▶ *vt* make a gap in; break (rule,
etc.).

bread [bred] *n* food made of flour
or meal baked; food; *sl* money.
bread′fruit *n* breadlike fruit found
in Pacific islands. **bread′win·ner** *n*
person who works to support
family.

breadth [bredth] *n* extent across,
width; largeness of view, mind.

break [brayk] *v* **broke, bro·ken,
break·ing.** ▶ *vt* part by force;
shatter; burst, destroy; fail to
observe; disclose; interrupt;
surpass; make bankrupt; relax;
mitigate; accustom (horse) to
being ridden; decipher (code). ▶ *vi*
become broken, shattered, divided;
open, appear; come suddenly;
crack, give way; part, fall out; (of
voice) change in tone, pitch. ▶ *n*
fracture; gap; opening; separation;
interruption; respite; interval; *inf*
opportunity; dawn; *Pool* opening
shot in a game; *Boxing* separation
after a clinch. **break′a·ble** *adj*
break′age *n* **break′er** *n* person or
device that breaks, for example an
electrical circuit; wave beating on
rocks or shore. **break dance** *n*
acrobatic dance style associated
with hip-hop. ▶ *vi* **break′down** *n*
collapse, as nervous breakdown;
failure to function effectively;
analysis. **break·fast** [BREK-fəst] *n*
first meal of the day. **break′-in** *n*
illegal entering of building, esp. by
thieves. **break′neck** *adj*
dangerous. **break′through** *n*
important advance. **break′wa·ter**
n barrier to break force of waves.

breast [brest] *n* human chest;
milk-secreting gland on chest of
human female; seat of the
affections; any protuberance. ▶ *vt*
face, oppose; reach summit of.
breast′stroke *n* stroke in
swimming.

breath [breth] *n* air used by lungs;
life; respiration; slight breeze.
breathe [breeth] *v* **breathed,
breath·ing.** ▶ *vi* inhale and exhale
air from lungs; live; pause, rest. ▶ *vt*
inhale and exhale; utter softly,
whisper. **breath′er** [-thər] *n* short
rest. **breath·less** [BRETH-lis] *adj*

breath'tak·ing adj causing awe or excitement.

Breath·a·lyz·er [BRETH-ə-lī-zər] n ® device that estimates amount of alcohol in breath.

bred pt./pp. of BREED.

breech n buttocks; hinder part of anything, esp. gun. **breech'load·er** n

breed v **bred**, **breed·ing**. ▶ vt generate, bring forth, give rise to; rear. ▶ vi be produced; be with young. ▶ n offspring produced; race, kind. **breeding** n producing; manners; ancestry. **breeder reactor** nuclear reactor producing more fissionable material than it consumes.

breeze [breez] n gentle wind. **breez'i·ly** adv **breez'y** adj **breez·i·er**, **breez·i·est**. windy; jovial, lively; casual. **in a breeze** easily.

breth·ren [BRETH-rən] obs pl. of BROTHER.

breve [breev] n long musical note.

bre·vi·ar·y [BREE-vee-er-ee] n, pl **-ar·ies**. book of daily prayers, hymns, etc.

brev·i·ty [BREV-i-tee] n conciseness of expression; short duration.

brew [broo] vt prepare liquor, as beer from malt, etc.; make drink, as tea, by infusion; plot, contrive. ▶ vi be in preparation. ▶ n beverage produced by brewing. **brew'er** n **brew'er·y** n

bri·ar¹, **br·ier** [BRĪ-ər] n prickly shrub, esp. the wild rose.

briar², **brier** n European shrub. **briar pipe** pipe made from its root.

bribe [brīb] n anything offered or given to someone to gain favor, influence. ▶ vt **bribed**, **brib·ing**. influence by bribe. **brib'er·y** n, pl **-er·ies**.

bric-a-brac [BRIK-ə-brak] n miscellaneous small objects, used for ornament.

brick [brik] n oblong mass of hardened clay used in building; good-hearted person. ▶ vt build, block, etc. with bricks.

bride [brīd] n woman about to be,

or just, married. **brid'al** adj of, relating to, a bride or wedding. **bride'groom** n man about to be, or just, married. **brides'maid** n

bridge¹ [brij] n structure for crossing river, etc.; something joining or supporting other parts; raised narrow platform on ship; upper part of nose; part of violin supporting strings. ▶ vt **bridged**, **bridg·ing**. make bridge over, span.

bridge² n card game.

bri·dle [BRĪD-l] n headgear of horse harness; curb. ▶ v **-dled**, **-dling**. ▶ vt put on bridle; restrain. ▶ vi show resentment. **bridle path** path suitable for riding horses.

brief [breef] adj **-er**, **-est**. short in duration; concise; scanty. ▶ n summary of case for judge or lawyer's use; papal letter; instructions. ▶ pl underpants; panties. ▶ vt give instructions, information. **brief'ly** adv **brief'case** n hand case for carrying papers. **brief·ing book** one prepared to provide (participant) information on meeting, etc.

brier see BRIAR.

brig n two-masted, square-rigged ship; inf ship's jail, guardhouse.

bri·gade [bri-GAYD] n subdivision of army; organized band. **brig·a·dier' gen·er·al** [-ə-DEER] one-star general.

brig·an·tine [BRIG-ən-teen] n two-masted vessel, with square-rigged foremast and fore-and-aft mainmast.

bright [brīt] adj **-er**, **-est**. shining; full of light; cheerful; clever. **bright'en** v

bril·liant [BRIL-yənt] adj shining; sparkling; splendid; very intelligent or clever; distinguished. **bril'liance** n

brim n margin, edge, esp. of river, cup, hat. **brim·ful** adj **brim'less** adj **brim'ming** adj to the brim; until it can hold no more.

brim·stone [BRIM-stohn] n sulfur.

brin·dled [BRIN-dld] adj brownish with streaks of other color. **brin'dle** n this color; a brindled animal.

brine [brīn] *n* salt water. **brin'y** *adj* **brin·i·er, brin·i·est.** very salty. ▶ *n inf* the sea.

bring *vt* **brought, bring·ing.** fetch; carry with one; cause to come.

brink [bringk] *n* edge of steep place; verge, margin. **brink'man·ship** *n* technique of attempting to gain advantage through maneuvering dangerous situation to limit of tolerance.

bri·quette [bri-KET] *n* block of compressed coal dust.

brisk *adj* **-er, -est.** active, vigorous. **brisk'ly** *adv* **brisk'ness** *n*

bris·ket [BRIS-kit] *n* cut of meat from breast of animal.

bris·tle [BRIS-əl] *n* short stiff hair. ▶ *vi* **-tled, -tling.** stand erect; show temper. **bris'tly** *adj* **-tli·er, -tli·est.**

brit·tle [BRIT-l] *adj* easily broken, fragile; curt, irritable. **brit'tle·ness** *n*

broach [brohch] *vt* pierce (cask); open, begin.

broad [brawd] *adj* **-er, -est.** wide, spacious, open; plain, obvious; coarse; general; tolerant; (of pronunciation) dialectal. **broad'en** *vt* **broad'ly** *adv* **broad'ness** *n* **broad'cast** *vt* **-cast** *or* **-cast·ed, -cast·ing.** transmit by radio or television; make widely known; scatter, as seed. ▶ *n* radio or TV program. **broad'cast·er** *n* **broad'loom** *n, adj* (carpet) woven on wide loom. **broad'-mind·ed** [-MĪN-did] *adj* tolerant; generous. **broad'side** *n* discharge of all guns on one side; strong (verbal) attack.

bro·cade [broh-KAYD] *n* rich woven fabric with raised design.

broc·co·li [BROK-ə-lee] *n* type of cabbage.

bro·chette [broh-SHET] *n* small spit; skewer.

bro·chure [broh-SHUUR] *n* pamphlet, booklet.

brogue [brohg] *n* stout shoe; dialect, Irish accent.

broil *vt* cook over hot coals; grill. ▶ *vi* be heated.

broke see BREAK. *adj inf* penniless.

bro·ker [BROH-kər] *n* one employed to buy and sell for others; dealer. **bro'ker·age** *n* business of broker; payment to broker.

bro·mide [BROH-mīd] *n* chemical compound used in medicine and photography; hackneyed, commonplace statement. **bro·mid'ic** [-MID-ik] *adj* lacking in originality.

bro·mine [BROH-meen] *n* liquid element used in production of chemicals.

bron·chus [BRONG-kəs] *n, pl* **-chi** [-kee] branch of windpipe. **bron'chi·al** *adj* **bron·chi'tis** [-KĪ-tis] *n* inflammation of bronchi.

bron·co [BRONG-koh] *n, pl* **-cos.** N Amer. half-tamed horse.

bron·to·sau·rus [bron-tə-SOR-əs] *n* very large herbivorous dinosaur.

bronze [bronz] *n* alloy of copper and tin. ▶ *adj* made of, or colored like, bronze. ▶ *vt* **bronzed, bronz·ing.** give appearance of bronze to.

brooch [brohch] *n* ornamental pin or fastening.

brood *n* family of young, esp. of birds; tribe, race. ▶ *v* sit, as hen on eggs; meditate, fret over. **brood'y** *adj* **brood·i·er, brood·i·est.** moody, sullen.

brook¹ [bruuk] *n* small stream.

brook² *vt* put up with, endure, tolerate.

broom *n* brush for sweeping; yellow-flowered shrub. **broom'stick** *n* handle of broom.

broth [brawth] *n* thick soup; stock.

broth·el [BROTH-əl] *n* house of prostitution.

broth·er [BRU*TH*-ər] *n* son of same parents; one closely united with another. **broth'er·hood** [-huud] *n* relationship; fraternity, company. **broth'er·ly** *adj* **broth'er-in-law** *n* brother of husband or wife; husband of sister.

brought pt./pp. of BRING.

brow *n* ridge over eyes; forehead; eyebrow; edge of hill. **brow'beat** *vt* **-beat, -beat·en, -beat·ing.** bully.

brown *adj* **-er, -est.** of dark color inclining to red or yellow. ▶ *n* the color. ▶ *v* make, become brown.
browned off *sl* angry; fed up.
Brown·ie [BROW-nee] *n* Girl Scout 7 to 10 years old; **(b-)** small, nutted square of chocolate cake. **Brownie point** notional mark to one's credit for being seen to do the right thing.
browse [browz] *vi* **browsed, brows·ing.** look through (book, articles for sale, etc.) in a casual manner; feed on shoots and leaves; *Computers* read hypertext, esp. on the Internet. **brows'er** *n Computers* software package that enables a user to read hypertext, esp. on the Internet.
bruise [brooz] *vt* **bruised, bruis·ing.** injure without breaking skin. ▶ *n* contusion, discoloration caused by blow. **bruis'er** *n inf* strong, tough person.
brunch *n inf* breakfast and lunch combined.
bru·nette [broo-NET] *n* person of dark complexion and hair. ▶ *adj* dark brown.
brunt *n* shock of attack, chief stress; first blow.
brush *n* device with bristles, hairs, wires, etc. used for cleaning, painting, etc.; act, instance of brushing; brief contact; skirmish, fight; bushy tail, bushy haircut; dense growth of bushes, shrubs, etc.; (carbon) device taking electric current from moving to stationary parts of generator, etc. ▶ *v* apply, remove, clean, with brush; touch, discuss lightly. **brush'off** *n inf* dismissal; refusal; snub; rebuff.
brush'fire *n* fire in area of bushes, shrubs, etc. **brush'wood** *n* broken-off branches; land covered with scrub.
brusque [brusk] *adj* rough in manner, curt, blunt.
brute [broot] *n* any animal except man; crude, vicious person. ▶ *adj* animal; sensual, stupid; physical. **bru'tal** *adj* **bru·tal'i·ty** *n* **bru'tal·ize** *vt* **-ized, -iz·ing.** **brut'ish** *adj* bestial, gross.

Btu British thermal unit.
bub·ble [BUB-əl] *n* hollow globe of liquid, blown out with air; something insubstantial, not serious; transparent dome. ▶ *vi* **-bled, -bling.** rise in bubbles; make gurgling sound.
bu·bon·ic plague [byoo-BON-ik playg] *n* acute infectious disease characterized by swellings and fever.
buc·ca·neer [buk-ə-NEER] *n* pirate; unscrupulous adventurer. **buc·ca·neer'ing** *n*
buck [buk] *n* male deer, or other male animal; act of bucking; *sl* dollar. ▶ *v* of horse, attempt to throw rider by jumping upward, etc.; resist, oppose (something). **buck'shot** *n* lead shot in shotgun shell. **buck·teeth** *pl n* projecting upper teeth. **pass the buck** shift blame or responsibility to another person.
buck·et [BUK-it] *n* vessel, round with arched handle, for water, etc.; anything resembling this. **buck'et·ful** *n, pl* **-fuls.** **bucket seat** seat with back shaped to occupier's figure.
buck·le [BUK-əl] *n* metal clasp for fastening belt, strap, etc. ▶ *v* **-led, -ling.** ▶ *vt* fasten with buckle. ▶ *vi* warp, bend. **buckle down** start work.
bu·col·ic [byoo-KOL-ik] *adj* rustic.
bud *n* shoot or sprout on plant containing unopened leaf, flower, etc. ▶ *v* **bud·ded, bud·ding.** ▶ *vi* begin to grow. ▶ *vt* to graft.
Bud·dhism [BOO-diz-əm] *n* religion founded in India by Buddha. **Bud'dhist** *adj, n*
bud·dy [BUD-ee] *n inf pl* **-dies.** pal, chum.
budge [buj] *vi* **budged, budg·ing.** move, stir.
budg·et [BUJ-it] *n* annual financial statement; plan of systematic spending. ▶ *vi* prepare financial statement; plan financially.
buff¹ *n* light yellow color; bare skin; polishing pad. ▶ *vt* polish.
buff² *n inf* expert on some subject.

buf·fa·lo [BUF-ə-loh] *n, pl* **-los,**
-loes. any of several species of large
oxen.

buff·er [BUF-ər] *n* contrivance to
lessen shock of concussion; person,
country that shields another
against annoyance, etc.

buf·fet¹ [BUF-it] *n* blow, slap;
misfortune. ▶ *vt* strike with blows;
contend against. **buf'fet·ing** *n*

buf·fet² [bə-FAY] *n* refreshment bar;
meal at which guests serve
themselves; sideboard.

buf·foon [bə-FOON] *n* clown; fool.
buf·foon'er·y *n* clowning.

bug *n* any small insect; *inf* disease,
infection; concealed listening
device. ▶ *vt* **bugged, bug·ging.**
install secret microphone, etc.; *inf*
annoy.

bug·a·boo [BUG-ə-boo] *n, pl*
-boos. something that causes fear
or worry.

bug·bear [BUG-bair] *n* object of
needless terror; nuisance.

bug·ger [BUG-ər] *n vulg* sodomite;
inf worthless person; *inf* lad.

bu·gle [BYOO-gəl] *n* instrument like
trumpet. **bu'gler** *n*

build [bild] *v* **built, build·ing.** make,
construct, by putting together
parts or materials. ▶ *n* make, form;
physique. **build'ing** *n*

bulb *n* modified leaf bud emitting
roots from base, e.g. onion;
anything resembling this; globe
surrounding filament of electric
light. ▶ *vi* form bulbs. **bul'bous** *adj*

bulge [bulj] *n* swelling,
protuberance; temporary increase.
▶ *vi* **bulged, bulg·ing.** swell out.
bulg'i·ness *n*

bu·li·mi·a [byoo-LEE-mee-ə] *n*
disorder characterized by
compulsive overeating followed by
self-induced vomiting. **bu·li'mic**
[byoo-LEE-mik] *adj, n*

bulk *n* size; volume; greater part;
cargo. ▶ *vi* be of weight or
importance. **bulk'i·ness** *n* **bulk'y**
adj **bulk·i·er, bulk·i·est.**

bulk·head [BULK-hed] *n* partition in
interior of ship.

bull¹ [buul] *n* male of cattle; male of
various other animals. **bull'dog** *n*
thickset breed of dog. **bull'doze**
[-dohz] *v* **-dozed, -doz·ing.**

bull'doz·er *n* powerful tractor with
blade for excavating, etc. **bul'lock**
[-lək] *n* castrated bull. **bull's'-eye**
n, pl **-eyes.** middle part of target.

bull² *n* papal edict.

bull³ *n sl* nonsense. ▶ *v* talk
nonsense (to).

bul·let [BUUL-it] *n* projectile
discharged from rifle, pistol, etc.

bul·le·tin [BUUL-i-tn] *n* official
report.

bul·lion [BUUL-yən] *n* gold or silver
in mass.

bul·ly [BUUL-ee] *n, pl* **-lies.** one who
hurts, persecutes, or intimidates
weaker people. ▶ *vt* **-lied, -ly·ing.**
intimidate, overawe; ill-treat. ▶ *adj,
interj* first-rate.

bul·rush [BUUL-rush] *n* tall reedlike
marsh plant with brown velvety
spike.

bul·wark [BUUL-wərk] *n* rampart;
any defense or means of security;
raised side of ship; breakwater.

bum *n* loafer, scrounger. ▶ *vt inf*
bummed, bum·ming. get by
scrounging. ▶ *adj sl* worthless;
inferior; disabled.

bum·ble [BUM-bəl] *v* **-bled, -bling.**
perform clumsily. **bum'bler** *n*

bum·ble·bee [BUM-bəl-bee] *n*
large bee.

bump *n* heavy blow, dull in sound;
swelling caused by blow;
protuberance; sudden movement.
▶ *vt* strike or push against.

bump·er *n* horizontal bar at front
and rear of automobile to protect
against damage; full glass. ▶ *adj*
full, abundant. **bump off** *sl* murder.

bump·kin [BUMP-kin] *n* rustic.

bump·tious [BUMP-shəs] *adj*
offensively self-assertive.

bun *n* small, round bread or cake;
round knot of hair; *sl* enough liquor
to make one drunk.

bunch *n* number of things tied or
growing together; cluster; tuft,
knot; group, party. ▶ *vt* put
together in bunch. ▶ *vi* gather
together.

bun·dle [BUN-dl] n package; number of things tied together; sl lot of money. ▶ vt **-dled, -dling.** tie in bundle; send (off) without ceremony.

bung n stopper for cask; large cork. ▶ vt stop up, seal, close. **bung'hole** n

bun·ga·low [BUNG-gə-loh] n one-storied house.

bun·gle [BUNG-gəl] v **-gled, -gling.** ▶ vt do badly from lack of skill, botch. ▶ vi act clumsily, awkwardly. ▶ n blunder, muddle. **bun'gler** n

bun·ion [BUN-yən] n inflamed swelling on foot or toe.

bunk[1] [bungk] n narrow, shelflike bed. ▶ vi stay the night (with). **bunk bed** one of pair of beds constructed one above the other.

bunk[2] n bunkum.

bun·ker [BUNG-kər] n large storage container for oil, coal, etc.; sandy hollow on golf course; (military) underground defensive position.

bun·ko [BUNG-koh] n, pl **-kos.** swindling scheme or game.

bun·kum [BUNG-kəm] n nonsense.

bun·ny [BUN-ee] n inf pl **-nies.** rabbit.

Bun·sen burner [BUN-sən] gas burner, producing great heat, used for chemical experiments.

bun·ting[1] n material for flags.

bunting[2] n bird with short, stout bill.

bu·oy [BOO-ee] n floating marker anchored in sea; lifebuoy. ▶ vt mark with buoy; keep from sinking; support. **buoy·an·cy** [BOI-ən-see] n **buoy'ant** adj

bur·ble [BUR-bəl] vi **-bled, -bling.** gurgle, as stream or baby; talk idly.

bur·den [BUR-dn] n load; weight, cargo; anything difficult to bear. ▶ vt load, encumber. **burd'en·some** [-səm] adj

bu·reau [BYUUR-oh] n, pl **-reaus, -reaux** [-rohz] office; government department. **bu·reauc·ra·cy** [byuu-ROK-rə-see] n, pl **-cies.** government by officials; body of officials. **bu·reau·crat** [BYUUR-ə-krat] n

bur·geon [BUR-jən] vi bud; develop rapidly.

burg·er [BUR-gər] n hamburger.

bur·gess [BUR-jis] n member of colonial Maryland or Virginia legislature.

bur·glar [BUR-glər] n one who enters building to commit theft. **bur'gla·ry** [-glə-ree] n **bur'gle** [-gəl] vt **-gled, -gling.**

Bur·gun·dy [BUR-gən-dee] n, pl **-dies.** red or white wine produced in Burgundy, France; (b-) similar wine made elsewhere. **bur·gun·dy** adj dark-purplish red.

bur'lap n coarse canvas.

bur·lesque [bər-LESK] n (artistic) caricature; ludicrous imitation; provocative and humorous stage show. ▶ vt **-lesqued, -lesqu·ing.** caricature.

bur·ly [BUR-lee] adj **-li·er, -li·est.** sturdy, stout, robust.

burn v burned or burnt, **burn·ing.** ▶ vt destroy or injure by fire; record data on (a CD). ▶ vi be or feel hot; be consumed by fire. ▶ n injury, mark caused by fire.

bur'nish vt make bright by rubbing; polish. ▶ n gloss, luster.

burp v inf belch (esp. of baby). ▶ n

burr[1] n soft trilling sound given to letter r in some dialects.

burr[2] n rough edge left after cutting, drilling, etc.

burr[3] n head of plant with prickles or hooks.

bur·ro [BUR-oh] n, pl **-ros.** small donkey.

bur·row [BUR-oh] n hole dug by rabbit, etc. ▶ vt make holes in ground; bore; conceal oneself.

bur·sar [BUR-sər] n official managing finances of college, monastery, etc.

burst v burst, **burst·ing.** ▶ vi fly asunder; break into pieces; rend; break suddenly into some expression of feeling. ▶ vt shatter, break violently. ▶ n bursting; explosion; outbreak; spurt.

bur·y [BER-ee] vt **bur·ied, bur·y·ing.** put underground; inter; conceal. **bur'i·al** n, adj

bus n large motor vehicle for

passengers. ▶ *v* travel or transport by bus; work as busboy.
bus'man's holiday vacation spent in an activity closely resembling one's work.

bus·boy [BUS-boi] *n* waiter's helper in public dining room.

bush [buush] *n* shrub; woodland, thicket; uncleared country, backwoods, interior. **bushed** *adj inf* tired out. **bush'y** *adj* **bush·i·er, bush·i·est.** shaggy. **bush jacket** shirtlike jacket with patch pockets.

bush·el [BUUSH-əl] *n* dry measure of eight gallons.

busi·ness [BIZ-nis] *n* profession, occupation; commercial or industrial establishment; commerce, trade; responsibility, affair, matter; work.

bust¹ *n* sculpture of head and shoulders of human body; woman's breasts.

bust² *v inf* burst; make, become bankrupt. ▶ *vt sl* raid; arrest. ▶ *adj inf* broken; bankrupt. ▶ *n sl* police raid or arrest; *inf* punch.

bus·tle¹ [BUS-əl] *vi* **-tled, -tling.** be noisily busy, active. ▶ *n* fuss, commotion.

bustle² *n Hist* pad worn by ladies to support back of the skirt.

bus·y [BIZ-ee] *adj* **bus·i·er, bus·i·est.** actively employed; full of activity. ▶ *vt* **bus·ied, bus·y·ing.** occupy. **bus'y·bod·y** *n, pl* **-bod·ies.** meddler.

but *prep, conj* without; except; only; yet; still; besides.

bu·tane [BYOO-tayn] *n* gas used for fuel.

butch [buuch] *adj, n sl* markedly or aggressively masculine (person).

butch·er [BUUCH-ər] *n* one who kills, dresses animals for food, or sells meat; bloody, savage man. ▶ *vt* slaughter; murder; spoil work. **butch'er·y** *n*

but·ler [BUT-lər] *n* chief male servant.

butt¹ *n* the thick end; target; object of ridicule; bottom or unused end of anything. ▶ *v* lie, be placed end on to.

butt² *v* strike with head; push. ▶ *n* blow with head, as of sheep. **butt in** interfere, meddle. **butt·in'sky** *n, pl* **-skies.** *sl* meddler.

but·ter [BUT-ər] *n* fatty substance got from cream by churning. ▶ *vt* spread with or as if with butter; flatter.

but·ter·fly [BUT-ər-flī] *n, pl* **-flies.** insect with large wings; inconstant person; stroke in swimming. ▶ *vt* **-flied, -fly·ing.** split (foodstuff) into shape resembling butterfly.

but·ter·milk [BUT-ər-milk] *n* milk that remains after churning.

but·tock [BUT-ək] *n* (usu. pl) rump, protruding hinder part.

but·ton [BUT-n] *n* knob, stud for fastening dress; knob that operates doorbell, machine, etc. ▶ *vt* fasten with buttons. **but'ton·hole** *n* slit in garment to pass button through as fastening. ▶ *vt* **-holed, -hol·ing.** detain (unwilling) person in conversation.

but·tress [BU-tris] *n* structure to support wall; prop. ▶ *vt*

bux·om [BUK-səm] *adj* full of health, plump, gay; large-breasted.

buy [bī] *vt* **bought, buy·ing.** get by payment, purchase; bribe. **buy'er** *n*

buzz *vi* make humming sound. ▶ *n* humming sound of bees; *inf* telephone call. **buzz'er** *n* any apparatus that makes buzzing sound. **buzz word** *inf* word, oft. orig. jargon, that becomes fashionable.

buz·zard [BUZ-ərd] *n* bird of prey of hawk family.

by [bī] *prep* near; along; across; past; during; not later than; through use or agency of; in units of. ▶ *adv* near; away, aside; past. **by and by** soon, in the future. **by and large** on the whole; speaking generally. **come by** obtain.

bye [bī] *n Sports* in early round of a tournament, a situation in which player, team not paired with opponent advances to next round without playing.

by·gone [BĪ-gawn] *adj* past, former. ▶ *n* (oft. pl) past occurrence.

by-law [BĪ-law] *n* law, regulation made by an organization.

by·line [BĪ-līn] *n* printed line identifying author of news story, article, etc.

by·pass [BĪ-pas] *n* road for diversion of traffic from crowded centers; secondary channel carrying fluid around a part and back to the main stream. ▶ *vt*

by·play [BĪ-play] *n* diversion, action apart from main action of play.

byte [bīt] *n Computers* sequence of bits processed as single unit of information.

by·word [BĪ-wurd] *n* a well-known name, saying.

C c

C *Chem* Carbon; Celsius.

Ca *Chem* calcium.

cab *n* taxi; driver's enclosed compartment on locomotive, truck, etc. **cab'driv·er** *n* **cab'stand** *n* place where taxis may wait to be hired.

ca·bal [kə-BAL] *n* small group of intriguers; secret plot.

cab·a·ret [kab-ə-RAY] *n* night club.

cab·bage [KAB-ij] *n* green vegetable with usu. round head of leaves.

ca·ber [KAY-bər] *n* pole tossed as trial of strength at Scottish games.

cab·in [KAB-in] *n* hut, shed; small room esp. in ship. **cabin cruiser** power boat with cabin, bunks, etc.

cab·i·net [KAB-ə-nit] *n* piece of furniture with drawers or shelves; outer case of television, radio, etc.; body of advisers to head of state. **cab'i·net·mak·er** *n* artisan who makes fine furniture.

ca·ble [KAY-bəl] *n* strong rope; wire or bundle of wires conveying electric power, telegraph signals, etc.; message sent by this; cable TV. ▸ *v* **-bled, -bling.** telegraph by cable. **ca'ble·gram** *n* cabled message. **cable TV** TV service conveyed by cable to subscribers.

ca·boo·dle [kə-BOOD-l] *n inf* **the whole caboodle** the whole lot.

ca·boose [kə-BOOS] *n* (usu. last) car of freight train, for use by train crew.

ca·ca·o [kə-KAH-oh] *n* tropical tree from the seeds of which chocolate and cocoa are made.

cache [kash] *n* secret hiding place; store of food, arms, etc.

ca·chet [ka-SHAY] *n* mark, stamp; mark of authenticity; prestige, distinction.

cack·le [KAK-əl] *vi* **-led, -ling.** make chattering noise, as hen. ▸ *n* cackling noise or laughter; empty chatter.

ca·coph·o·ny [kə-KOF-ə-nee] *n, pl* **-nies.** disagreeable sound; discord of sounds. **ca·coph'o·nous** *adj*

cac·tus [KAK-təs] *n, pl* **-ti** [-tī] spiny succulent plant.

cad *n* dishonorable, ungentlemanly person.

ca·dav·er [kə-DAV-ər] *n* corpse. **ca·dav'er·ous** *adj* corpselike; sickly-looking; gaunt.

cad·die [KAD-ee] *n* person hired to carry golfer's clubs, find the ball, etc.

ca·dence [KAYD-ns] *n* fall or modulation of voice in music, speech, or verse.

ca·den·za [kə-DEN-zə] *n Mus* elaborate passage for solo instrument or singer.

ca·det [kə-DET] *n* youth in training, esp. for officer status in armed forces.

cadge [kaj] *v* **cadged, cadg·ing.** get (food, money, etc.) by begging. **cadg'er** *n* sponger.

cad·mi·um [KAD-mee-əm] *n* metallic element.

ca·dre [KAD-ree] *n* nucleus or framework, esp. skeleton of military unit.

Cae·sar·e·an section [si-ZAIR-ee-ən] surgical incision through abdominal wall to deliver a baby.

café [ka-FAY] *n* small or inexpensive restaurant serving light refreshments; bar. **caf·e·te·ri·a** [kaf-ə-TEE-ree-ə] *n* restaurant designed for self-service.

caf·feine [ka-FEEN] *n* stimulating alkaloid found in tea and coffee plants.

caf·tan [KAF-tan] *n* long coatlike Eastern garment; imitation of it, esp. as woman's long, loose dress with sleeves.

cage [kayj] *n* enclosure, box with bars or wires, esp. for keeping animals or birds; place of confinement; enclosed platform of elevator, esp. in mine. ▸ *vt* **caged,**

cag·ing. put in cage, confine.
cag'ey adj **cag·i·er, cag·i·est.**
wary, shrewd.

ca·hoots [kə-HOOTS] pl n sl
partnership, as **in cahoots with.**

cairn [kairn] n heap of stones, esp.
as monument or landmark.

cais·son [KAY-son] n chamber for
working under water; apparatus for
lifting vessel out of the water;
ammunition wagon. **caisson
disease** the bends.

ca·jole [kə-JOHL] vt **-joled, -jol·ing.**
persuade by flattery, wheedle.
ca·jol'er n

cake [kayk] n baked, sweetened,
bread-like food; compact mass. ▶ v
caked, cak·ing. make into a cake;
harden (as of mud).

cal·a·boose [KAL-ə-boos] n inf jail.

cal·a·mine [KAL-ə-mīn] n pink
powder used medicinally in
soothing ointment.

ca·lam·i·ty [kə-LAM-i-tee] n, pl
-ties. great misfortune; deep
distress, disaster. **ca·lam'i·tous** adj

cal·ci·um [KAL-see-əm] n metallic
element, the basis of lime.
cal·car'e·ous [-KAIR-ee-əs] adj
containing lime. **cal'ci·fy** v **-fied,
-fy·ing.** convert, be converted, to
lime.

cal·cu·late [KAL-kyə-layt] v **-lat·ed,
-lat·ing.** ▶ vt estimate; compute.
▶ vi make reckonings.
cal'cu·lat·ing adj able to perform
calculations; shrewd, designing,
scheming. **cal'cu·la·tor** n
electronic or mechanical device for
making calculations. **cal'cu·lus** n,
pl **-li** [-lī] branch of mathematics;
stone in body.

cal·en·dar [KAL-ən-dər] n table of
months and days in the year; list of
events, documents; register.

calf[1] [kaf] n, pl **calves** [kavz] young
of cow and of other animals;
leather made of calf's skin. **calve**
[kav] vi **calved, calv·ing.** give birth
to calf.

calf[2] n, pl **calves.** fleshy back part of
leg below knee.

cal·i·ber [KAL-ə-bər] n size of bore
of gun; capacity, character.

cal'i·brate [-brayt] vt **-brat·ed,
-brat·ing.** mark scale of measuring
instrument, etc. **cal·i·bra'tion** n

cal·i·co [KAL-i-koh] n, pl **-coes, -cos.**
printed cotton fabric.

cal·i·per [KAL-ə-pər] n instrument
for measuring diameters; thickness,
esp. of tree, paper.

cal·is·then·ics [kal-əs-THEN-iks] pl n
light gymnastic exercises.

call [kawl] vt speak loudly to attract
attention; summon; (oft. with up)
telephone; name. ▶ vi shout; pay
visit. ▶ n shout; animal's cry; visit;
inner urge, summons, as to be
minister, etc.; need, demand.
call'ing n vocation, profession. **call
box** outdoor telephone for calling
police or fire department. **call girl**
prostitute who accepts
appointments by telephone. **call
up** summon to serve in army;
imagine.

cal·lig·ra·phy [kə-LIG-rə-fee] n
handwriting, penmanship.
cal·li·graph'ic adj

cal·lous [KAL-əs] adj hardened,
unfeeling. **cal'lous·ness** n

cal·low [KAL-oh] adj inexperienced;
immature.

cal·lus [KAL-əs] n, pl **-lus·es.** area of
thick, hardened skin.

calm [kahm] adj **-er, -est.** still, quiet,
tranquil. ▶ n stillness; tranquility;
absence of wind. ▶ v become,
make, still or quiet. **calm'ly** adv

cal·o·rie [KAL-ə-ree] n unit of heat;
unit of energy obtained from
foods. **cal·o·rif'ic** adj heat-making.
cal·o·rim'e·ter n

cal·u·met [KAL-yə-met] n tobacco
pipe of N Amer. Indians; peace
pipe.

cal·um·ny [KAL-əm-nee] n, pl **-nies.**
slander, false accusation.
ca·lum'ni·ate vt **-at·ed, -at·ing.**
ca·lum·ni·a'tion n

ca·lyp·so [kə-LIP-soh] n, pl **-sos.**
(West Indies) improvised song on
topical subject.

ca·lyx [KAY-liks] n, pl **-lyx·es.**
covering of bud.

cam [kam] n device to change
rotary to reciprocating motion.

cam'shaft n in motor vehicles, rotating shaft to which cams are fixed to lift valves.

ca·ma·ra·de·rie [kah-mə-RAH-də-ree] n spirit of comradeship, trust.

cam·ber [KAM-bər] n convexity on upper surface of road, bridge, etc.; curvature of aircraft wing; setting of motor vehicle wheels closer together at bottom than at top.

cam·bric [KAYM-brik] n fine white linen or cotton cloth.

cam·cord·er [KAM-kor-dər] n combined portable video camera and recorder.

came pt. of COME.

cam·el [KAM-əl] n animal of Asia and Africa, with humped back, used as beast of burden.

cam·e·o [KAM-ee-oh] n, pl **-e·os.** medallion, brooch, etc. with profile head or design carved in relief; single brief scene or appearance in film, etc. by well-known performer.

cam·er·a [KAM-ər-ə] n apparatus used to make photographs. **cam'er·a·man** n photographer, esp. for TV or film. **camera ob·scu·ra** [ob-SKYUUR-ə] darkened chamber in which views of external objects are shown on sheet by means of lenses. **in camera** (of legal proceedings, etc.) conducted in private.

cam·i·sole [KAM-ə-sohl] n woman's short sleeveless undergarment.

cam·ou·flage [KAM-ə-flahzh] n disguise, means of deceiving enemy observation, e.g. by paint, screen. ▶ vt **-flaged, -flag·ing.** disguise.

camp [kamp] n (place for) tents of hikers, army, etc.; cabins, etc. for temporary accommodation; group supporting political party, etc. ▶ adj inf consciously artificial. ▶ vi form or lodge in a camp.

cam·paign [kam-PAYN] n series of coordinated activities for some purpose, e.g. political or military campaign. ▶ vi serve in campaign. **cam·paign'er** n

cam·pa·nol·o·gy [kam-pə-NOL-ə-jee] n art of ringing bells musically.

cam·phor [KAM-fər] n solid essential oil with aromatic taste and smell. **cam'phor·at·ed** adj

cam·pus [KAM-pəs] n, pl **-pus·es.** grounds of college or university.

can¹ [kan] vi **could.** pt be able; have the power; be allowed.

can² n container, usu. metal, for liquids, foods. ▶ v **canned, can·ning.** put in can; prepare (food) for canning. **canned** adj preserved in jar or can; (of music, TV or radio programs, etc.) previously recorded. **can'ner·y** n, pl **-ner·ies.** factory where food is canned.

Can·a·da Day [KAN-ə-də] July 1st, anniversary of establishment of Confederation in 1867.

Canada goose large grayish-brown N Amer. goose.

Ca·na·di·an [kə-NAY-dee-ən] n, adj (native) of Canada.

ca·nal [kə-NAL] n artificial watercourse; duct in body. **can·al·ize** [KAN-l-īz] vt **-ized, -iz·ing.** convert into canal; direct (thoughts, energies, etc.) into one channel.

can·a·pé [KAN-ə-pay] n small piece of toast, etc. with cheese, etc. topping.

ca·nar·y [kə-NAIR-ee] n, pl **-nar·ies.** yellow singing bird.

ca·nas·ta [kə-NAS-tə] n card game played with two packs.

can·can [KAN-kan] n high-kicking (orig. French music-hall) dance.

can·cel [KAN-səl] vt **-celed, -cel·ing.** cross out; annul; invalidate; call off. **can·cel·la'tion** n

can·cer [KAN-sər] n malignant growth or tumor. **can'cer·ous** adj

can·de·la [kan-DEE-lə] n basic unit of luminous intensity.

can·did [KAN-did] adj frank, open, impartial. **can'did·ly** adv **can'dor** [-dər] n frankness.

can·di·date [KAN-di-dayt] n one who seeks office, employment, etc.; person taking examination or test. **can'di·da·cy** [-də-see] n, pl

-cies.

can·dle [KAN-dl] *n* stick of wax with wick; light. **can·de·la'brum** [-AH-brəm] *pl* **-bra** [-brə] *n* large, branched candle holder. **can'dle·pow·er** *n* unit for measuring light. **can't hold a candle to** compare unfavorably with.

can·dy [KAN-dee] *n, pl* **-dies.** crystallized sugar; confectionery in general. ▸ *v* **-died, -dy·ing.** preserve with sugar; become encrusted with sugar.

cane [kayn] *n* stem of small palm or large grass; walking stick. ▸ *vt* **caned, can·ing.** beat with cane.

ca·nine [KAY-nīn] *adj* like, pert. to, dog. **canine tooth** one of four sharp, pointed teeth, two in each jaw.

can·is·ter [KAN-ə-stər] *n* container, oft. of metal, for storing dry food.

can·ker [KANG-kər] *n* spreading sore; thing that eats away, destroys, corrupts. **canker sore** painful ulcer esp. in mouth.

can·na·bis [KAN-ə-bis] *n* hemp plant; drug derived from this; marijuana; hashish.

can·nel·lo·ni [kan-l-OH-nee] *n* tubular pieces of pasta filled with meat, etc.

can·ni·bal [KAN-ə-bəl] *n* one who eats human flesh. ▸ *adj* relating to this practice. **can'ni·bal·ism** *n* **can'ni·bal·ize** *vt* **-ized, -iz·ing.** use parts from one machine, etc. to repair another.

can·non [KAN-ən] *n, pl* **-nons** or **-non.** large gun. **can'non·ball** *n*

can·not [KAN-ot] negative form of CAN[1].

can·ny [KAN-ee] *adj* **-ni·er, -ni·est.** shrewd; cautious; crafty. **can'ni·ly** *adv*

ca·noe [kə-NOO] *n, pl* **-noes.** very light boat propelled with paddle or paddles. **ca·noe'ist** *n*

can·on[1] [KAN-ən] *n* law or rule, esp. of church; standard; body of books accepted as genuine; list of saints. **can·on·i·za'tion** *n* **can'on·ize** *vt* **-ized, -iz·ing.** enroll in list of saints.

canon[2] *n* church dignitary, member of cathedral or collegiate chapter or staff. **ca·non'i·cal** *adj* **ca·non'i·cals** *pl n* canonical vestments.

can·o·py [KAN-ə-pee] *n, pl* **-pies.** covering over throne, bed, etc.; any overhanging shelter. ▸ *vt* **-pied, -py·ing.** cover with canopy.

cant[1] [kant] *n* hypocritical speech; whining; language of a sect; technical jargon; slang, esp. of thieves.

cant[2] *v* **cant·ed, cant·ing.** tilt, slope; bevel.

can·ta·loupe [KAN-tl-ohp] *n* variety of muskmelon.

can·tan·ker·ous [kan-TANG-kər-əs] *adj* ill-natured, quarrelsome.

can·ta·ta [kən-TAH-tə] *n* choral work like, but shorter than, oratorio.

can·teen [kan-TEEN] *n* flask for carrying water; place in factory, school, etc. where light meals are provided; post exchange.

can·ter [KAN-tər] *n* easy gallop. ▸ *v* move at, make to canter.

can·ti·le·ver *n* beam, girder, etc. fixed at one end only. ▸ *vi* project like a cantilever. ▸ *vt* build to project in this manner.

can·to [KAN-toh] *n, pl* **-tos.** division of a poem.

can·ton [KAN-tn] *n* division of country, esp. Swiss federal state.

can·ton·ment [kan-TON-mənt] *n* quarters for troops.

can·tor [KAN-tər] *n* chief singer of liturgy in synagogue.

can·vas [KAN-vəs] *n* coarse cloth used for sails, painting on, etc.; sails of ship; picture.

can·vass [KAN-vəs] *vt* solicit votes, contributions, etc.; discuss; examine. ▸ *n* solicitation.

can·yon [KAN-yən] *n* deep gorge.

cap [kap] *n* covering for head; lid, top, or other covering. ▸ *vt* **capped, cap·ping.** put a limit on; outdo; seal (a well).

ca·pa·ble [KAY-pə-bəl] *adj* able, gifted; competent; having the capacity, power. **ca·pa·bil'i·ty** *n*

ca·pac·i·ty [kə-PAS-i-tee] *n, pl* **-ties.**

power of holding or grasping; room; volume; character; ability, power of mind. **ca·pa′cious** [-PAY-shəs] *adj* roomy.

ca·pac′i·tance *n* (measure of) ability of system to store electric charge. **ca·pac′i·tor** *n*

cape¹ [kayp] *n* covering for shoulders.

cape² *n* point of land running into sea, headland. **Cape Cod** common type of cottage in Mass. and elsewhere in Northeast.

ca·per¹ [KAY-pər] *n* skip; frolic; escapade. ▶ *vi* skip, dance.

caper² *n* pickled flower bud of Sicilian shrub.

cap·il·lar·y [KAP-ə-ler-ee] *adj* hairlike. ▶ *n, pl* **-lar·ies.** tube with very small bore, esp. small blood vessel.

cap·i·tal [KAP-i-tl] *n* chief town; money, stock, funds; large-sized letter; headpiece of column. ▶ *adj* involving or punishable by death; serious; chief; leading; excellent. **cap′i·tal·ism** *n* economic system based on private ownership of industry. **cap′i·tal·ist** *n* owner of capital; supporter of capitalism. ▶ *adj* run by, possessing, capital, as capitalist state. **cap′i·tal·ize** *v* **-ized, -iz·ing.** convert into capital; (with **on**) turn to advantage.

Cap·i·tol [KAP-i-tl] *n* building in which US Congress meets; **(c-)** a state legislature building.

ca·pit·u·late [kə-PICH-ə-layt] *vi* **-lat·ed, -lat·ing.** surrender on terms, give in. **ca·pit·u·la′tion** *n*

ca·pon [KAY-pon] *n* castrated male fowl fattened for eating. **ca′pon·ize** *vt* **-ized, -iz·ing.**

cap·puc·ci·no [kap-ə-CHEE-noh] *n* espresso coffee with steamed milk.

ca·price [kə-PREES] *n* whim, freak. **ca·pri′cious** [-PRISH-əs] *adj*

cap·size [KAP-sīz] *v* **-sized, -siz·ing.** ▶ *vt* (of boat) upset. ▶ *vi* be overturned.

cap·stan [KAP-stən] *n* machine to wind cable, esp. to hoist anchor.

cap·sule [KAP-səl] *n* gelatin case for dose of medicine or drug; any

small enclosed area or container; seed vessel of plant. **cap′sul·ize** *vt* **-ized, -iz·ing.** enclose in a capsule; put (news or information) in concise form.

cap·tain [KAP-tən] *n* commander of ship or company of soldiers; leader, chief. ▶ *vt* be captain of.

cap·tion [KAP-shən] *n* heading, title of article, picture, etc.

cap·tious [KAP-shəs] *adj* ready to find fault; critical; peevish. **cap′tious·ness** *n*

cap·tive [KAP-tiv] *n* prisoner. ▶ *adj* taken, imprisoned. **cap′ti·vate** *vt* **-vat·ed, -vat·ing.** fascinate. **cap′ti·vat·ing** *adj* delightful. **cap·tiv′i·ty** *n*

cap·ture [KAP-chər] *vt* **-tured, -tur·ing.** seize, make prisoner. ▶ *n* seizure, taking. **cap′tor** *n*

car [kahr] *n* automobile; passenger compartment, as in cable car; vehicle running on rails. **car park** area, building where vehicles may be left for a time.

ca·rafe [kə-RAF] *n* glass water bottle for the table, decanter.

car·a·mel [KAR-ə-məl] *n* burned sugar or syrup for cooking; type of confectionery. **car′a·mel·ize** *v* **-ized, -iz·ing.** change (sugar, etc.) into caramel; become caramel.

car·at [KAR-ət] *n* small weight used for gold, diamonds, etc.; proportional measure of twenty-fourths used to state fineness of gold.

car·a·van [KAR-ə-van] *n* company of merchants traveling together for safety in the East.

car·a·way [KAR-ə-way] *n* plant whose seeds are used as a spice in bread, etc.

car·bide [KAHR-bīd] *n* compound of carbon with an element, esp. calcium carbide.

car·bine [KAHR-been] *n* light rifle.

car·bo·hy·drate [kahr-boh-HĪ-drayt] *n* any of large group of compounds containing carbon, hydrogen and oxygen, esp. sugars and starches as components of food.

car·bol·ic ac·id [kahr-BOL-ik] disinfectant derived from coal tar.

car·bon [KAHR-bən] *n* nonmetallic element, substance of pure charcoal, found in all organic matter. **car′bon·ate** *n* salt of carbonic acid. **car·bon′ic** *adj* **car′bon·ize** *vt* **-ized, -iz·ing. carbonic acid** carbon dioxide; compound formed by carbon dioxide and water. **carbon dioxide** colorless gas exhaled in respiration of animals. **carbon paper** paper coated with a dark, waxy pigment, used for duplicating written or typed matter, producing **carbon copy**.

car·bo·run·dum [kahr-bə-RUN-dəm] *n* artificial silicate of carbon.

car·bun·cle [KAHR-bung-kəl] *n* inflamed ulcer, boil or tumor.

car·bu·re·tor [KAHR-bə-ray-tər] *n* device for vaporizing and mixing gasoline with air in internal combustion engine.

car·cass [KAHR-kəs] *n* dead animal body; orig. skeleton.

car·cin·o·gen [kahr-SIN-ə-jən] *n* substance producing cancer.

car·ci·no·ma [kahr-sə-NOH-mə] *n, pl* **-mas.** a cancer.

card¹ [kahrd] *n* thick, stiff paper; piece of this giving identification, etc.; greeting card; one of the 48 or 52 playing cards making up a pack; *inf* a character, eccentric. ▶ *pl n* any card game. **card′board** *n* thin, stiff board made of paper pulp.

card² *n* instrument for combing wool, etc. ▶ *vt* comb.

car·di·ac [KAHR-dee-ak] *adj* pert. to the heart. ▶ *n* person with heart disease. **car′di·o·graph** [-ə-graf] *n* instrument that records movements of the heart. **car′di·o·gram** *n* graph of such.

car·di·gan [KAHR-di-gən] *n* knitted sweater opening in front.

car·di·nal [KAHR-dn-l] *adj* chief, principal. ▶ *n* highest rank, next to the Pope in Cath. church; N Amer. finch, male of which is bright red in summer. **cardinal numbers** 1, 2, 3, etc. **cardinal points** N, S, E, W.

care [kair] *vi* **cared, car·ing.** be anxious; have regard or liking (for); look after; be disposed to. ▶ *n* attention; pains, heed; charge; protection; anxiety; caution. **care′free** *adj* **care′ful** *adj* **care′less** *adj* **care′tak·er** *n* person in charge of premises. ▶ *adj* temporary, interim.

ca·reen [kə-REEN] *vt* cause ship to list; lay ship over on its side for cleaning and repair. ▶ *vi* keel over; sway dangerously.

ca·reer [kə-REER] *n* course through life; profession; rapid motion. ▶ *vi* run or move at full speed.

ca·ress [kə-RES] *vt* fondle, embrace, treat with affection. ▶ *n* act or expression of affection.

car·et [KAR-it] *n* mark (‸) showing where to insert something omitted.

car·go [KAHR-goh] *n, pl* **-goes.** load, freight, carried by ship, plane, etc.

car·i·bou [KAR-ə-boo] *n* N Amer. reindeer.

car·i·ca·ture [KAR-i-kə-chər] *n* likeness exaggerated or distorted to appear ridiculous. ▶ *vt* **-tured, -tur·ing.** portray in this way. **car′i·ca·tur·ist** *n*

car·ies [KAIR-eez] *n* tooth decay.

car·il·lon [KAR-ə-lon] *n* set of bells usu. hung in tower and played by set of keys, pedals, etc.; tune so played.

car·min·a·tive [kahr-MIN-ə-tiv] *n* medicine to remedy flatulence. ▶ *adj* acting as this.

car·mine [KAHR-min] *n* brilliant red color (prepared from cochineal). ▶ *adj* of this color.

car·nage [KAHR-nij] *n* slaughter.

car·nal [KAHR-nl] *adj* fleshly, sensual; worldly.

car·na·tion [kahr-NAY-shən] *n* cultivated flower; flesh color.

car·ni·val [KAHR-nə-vəl] *n* festive occasion; traveling fair; show or display for amusement.

car·niv·o·rous [kahr-NIV-ər-əs] *adj* flesh-eating. **car′ni·vore** [-nə-vor] *n*

car·ob [KAR-əb] n Mediterranean tree with edible pods.

car·ol [KAR-əl] n song or hymn of joy or praise (esp. Christmas carol). ▶ vi **-oled, -ol·ing.** sing (carols).

car·om [KAR-əm] n billiard stroke, hitting both object balls with one's own. ▶ vi make this stroke; rebound, collide.

ca·rouse [kə-ROWZ] vi **-roused, -rous·ing.** have merry drinking spree. ▶ n **ca·rous'er** n

car·ou·sel [kar-ə-SEL] n merry-go-round.

carp[1] [kahrp] n freshwater fish.

carp[2] vi complain about small faults or errors. **carp'ing** adj

car·pen·ter [KAHR-pən-tər] n worker in timber as in building, etc. **car'pen·try** [-tree] n this art.

car·pet [KAHR-pit] n heavy fabric for covering floor. ▶ vt cover floor. **car'pet·bag** n traveling bag. **car'pet·bag·ger** n political adventurer. **on the carpet** called up for censure.

car·riage [KA-rij] n bearing, conduct; horse-drawn vehicle; act, cost, of carrying.

car·ri·on [KA-ree-ən] n rotting dead flesh.

car·rot [KA-rət] n plant with orange-red edible root; inducement. **car'rot-top** n person with red hair.

car·ry [KA-ree] v **-ried, -ry·ing.** ▶ vt convey, transport; capture, win; effect; behave. ▶ vi (of projectile, sound) reach. ▶ n range. **car'ri·er** n one that carries goods; immune person who communicates a disease to others; aircraft carrier; kind of pigeon. **carry on** continue; inf fuss unnecessarily.

cart [kahrt] n open (two-wheeled) vehicle, esp. pulled by horse. ▶ vt convey in cart; carry with effort. **cart'er** n **cart'horse** n **cart'wheel** n large, spoked wheel; sideways somersault. **cart'wright** n maker of carts.

carte blanche [kahrt blanch] n, pl **cartes blanches** [kahrts blanch] complete discretion or authority.

car·tel [kahr-TEL] n commercial combination for the purpose of fixing prices, output, etc.; alliance of political parties, etc. to further common aims.

Car·te·sian [kahr-TEE-zhən] adj pert. to the French philosopher René Descartes (1596–1650) or his system of coordinates. ▶ n an adherent of his philosophy.

car·ti·lage [KAHR-tl-ij] n firm elastic tissue in the body; gristle. **car·ti·lag'i·nous** adj

car·tog·ra·phy [kahr-TOG-rə-fee] n map making. **car·tog'ra·pher** n

car·ton [KAHR-tn] n cardboard or plastic container.

car·toon [kahr-TOON] n drawing, esp. humorous or satirical; sequence of drawings telling story; animated cartoon.

car·tridge [KAHR-trij] n case containing charge for gun; container for film, magnetic tape, etc.; unit in head of phonograph pickup.

carve [kahrv] vt **carved, carv·ing.** cut; hew; sculpture; engrave; cut in pieces or slices (meat). **carv'er** n

car·y·at·id [kar-ee-AT-id] n supporting column in shape of female figure.

cas·cade [kas-KAYD] n waterfall; anything resembling this. ▶ vi **-cad·ed, -cad·ing.** fall in cascades.

case[1] [kays] n instance; event, circumstance; question at issue; state of affairs, condition; arguments supporting particular action, etc.; Med patient under treatment; law suit; grounds for suit; grammatical relation of words in sentence.

case[2] n box, sheath, covering; receptacle; box and contents. ▶ vt **cased, cas·ing.** put in a case. **case'hard·en** vt harden by carbonizing the surface of (esp. iron) by converting into steel; make hard, callous.

case·ment [KAYS-mənt] n window opening on hinges.

cash [kash] n money, bills and coin. ▶ vt turn into or exchange for

money. **cash·ier** [ka-SHEER] *n* one
in charge of receiving and paying
of money. **cash dispenser**
computerized device outside a
bank for supplying cash. **cash
register** till that records amount of
money put in.

cash·ier [ka-SHEER] *vt* dismiss from
office or service.

cash·mere [KAZH-meer] *n* fine soft
fabric; yarn made from goat's wool.

ca·si·no [kə-SEE-noh] *n, pl* **-nos.**
building, institution for gambling;
type of card game.

cask [kask] *n* barrel; container for
wine.

cas·ket [KAS-kit] *n* small case for
jewels, etc.; coffin.

Cas·san·dra [kə-SAN-drə] *n*
prophet of misfortune or disaster.

cas·se·role [KAS-ə-rohl] *n* fireproof
cooking and serving dish; food
cooked in this.

cas·sette [kə-SET] *n* plastic
container for film, magnetic tape,
etc.

cas·sock [KAS-ək] *n* long tunic
worn by clergymen.

cast [kast] *v* throw or fling; shed;
throw down; deposit (a vote); allot,
as parts in play; mold, as metal. ▶ *n*
throw; distance thrown; squint;
mold; that which is shed or
ejected; set of actors; type or
quality. **cast'ing** *n* **cast'a·way** *n*
shipwrecked person. **cast-iron** *adj*
made of a hard but brittle type of
iron; definite, unchallengeable.

cas·ta·nets [kas-tə-NETS] *pl n* (in
Spanish dancing) two small curved
pieces of wood, etc. clicked
together in hand.

caste [kast] *n* section of society in
India; social rank.

cast·er [KAS-tər] *n* container for
salt, etc. with perforated top; small
swiveled wheel on table leg, etc.

cas·ti·gate [KAS-ti-gayt] *vt* **-gat·ed,
-gat·ing.** punish, rebuke severely,
correct; chastise. **cas'ti·ga·tor** *n*

cas·tle [KAS-əl] *n* fortress; mansion;
chess piece. **castle in the air** pipe
dream.

cas·tor oil [KAS-tər] vegetable

medicinal oil.

cas·trate [KAS-trayt] *vt* **-trat·ed,
-trat·ing.** remove testicles, deprive
of power of generation; deprive of
vigor. **cas·tra'tion** *n*

cas·tra·to [ka-STRAH-toh] *n, pl* **-ti**
[-tee] singer castrated in boyhood
to preserve soprano or alto voice.

cas·u·al [KAZH-oo-əl] *adj*
accidental; unforeseen; occasional;
unconcerned; informal. **cas'u·al·ty**
n, pl **-ties.** person killed or injured
in accident, war, etc.; thing lost,
destroyed, in accident, etc.

cas·u·ist [KAZH-oo-ist] *n* one who
studies and solves moral problems;
quibbler. **cas'u·ist·ry** *n*

cat [kat] *n* any of various feline
animals, including, e.g. small
domesticated furred animal, and
lions, tigers, etc. **cat'ty** *adj* **-ti·er,
-ti·est.** spiteful. **cat'call** *n* derisive
cry. **cat'fish** *n* mainly freshwater
fish with catlike whiskers. **cat'kin** *n*
drooping flower spike. **cat'nap** *vi,
n* doze. **cat's'-eye** *n, pl* **-eyes.** glass
reflector set in road to reflect
beams from automobile headlights.
cat'walk *n* narrow, raised path or
plank.

ca·tab·o·lism [kə-TAB-ə-liz-əm] *n*
breaking down of complex
molecules, destructive metabolism.

cat·a·clysm [KAT-ə-kliz-əm] *n*
(disastrous) upheaval; deluge.
cat·a·clys'mic *adj*

cat·a·comb [KAT-ə-kohm] *n*
underground gallery for burial. ▶ *pl*
series of underground tunnels and
caves.

cat·a·lep·sy [KAT-l-ep-see] *n*
condition of unconsciousness with
rigidity of muscles. **cat·a·lep'tic** *adj*

cat·a·log [KAT-l-awg] *n* descriptive
list. ▶ *vt* make such list of; enter in
catalog.

cat·a·lyst [KAT-l-ist] *n* substance
causing or assisting a chemical
reaction without taking part in it;
person or thing that precipitates
event or change. **cat'a·lyze** [-l-īz]
vt **-lyzed, -lyz·ing. ca·tal'y·sis** *n*
cat·a·lyt'ic *adj* **catalytic converter**
type of antipollution device for

automotive exhaust system.

cat·a·ma·ran [kat-ə-mə-RAN] *n* type of sailing boat with twin hulls; raft of logs.

cat·a·pult [KAT-ə-pult] *n* small forked stick with elastic sling used for throwing stones; *Hist* engine of war for hurling arrows, stones, etc.; launching device. ▶ *vt*

cat·a·ract [KAT-ə-rakt] *n* waterfall; downpour; disease of eye.

ca·tas·tro·phe [kə-TAS-trə-fee] *n* great disaster, calamity; culmination of a tragedy. **cat·a·stroph'ic** *adj*

catch [kach] *v* **caught, catch·ing.** ▶ *vt* take hold of, seize, understand; hear; contract (disease); be in time for; surprise, detect. ▶ *vi* be contagious; get entangled; begin to burn. ▶ *n* seizure; thing that holds, stops, etc.; what is caught; *inf* snag, disadvantage; form of musical composition; thing, person worth catching, esp. as spouse. **catch'er** *n* **catching** *adj* **catch'y** *adj* **catch·i·er, catch·i·est.** pleasant, memorable; tricky. **catch'word** *n* popular phrase or idea. **catch 22** inescapable dilemma. **catch·ment area** drainage basin, area in which rainfall collects to form the supply of river, etc.; area from which people are allocated to a particular social service agency, hospital, etc. **catch-as-catch-can** *adj* using any method that can be applied.

cat·e·chize [KAT-i-kīz] *vt* **-chized, -chiz·ing.** instruct by question and answer; question. **cat'e·chism** *n* such instruction. **cat'e·chist** *n*

cat·e·go·ry [KAT-i-gohr-ee] *n, pl* **-ries.** class, order, division. **cat·e·gor'i·cal** *adj* positive; of category. **cat·e·gor'i·cal·ly** *adv* **cat'e·go·rize** *vt* **-ized, -iz·ing.**

ca·ter [KAY-tər] *vi* provide what is required or desired, esp. food, etc. **ca'ter·er** *n*

cat·er·pil·lar [KAT-ə-pil-ər] *n* hairy grub of moth or butterfly.

cat·er·waul [KAT-ər-wawl] *vi* wail, howl; argue noisily.

ca·the·dral [kə-THEE-drəl] *n*

principal church of diocese. ▶ *adj* pert. to, containing cathedral.

cath·ode [KATH-ohd] *n* negative electrode. **cathode rays** stream of electrons.

cath·o·lic [KATH-lik] *adj* universal; including whole body of Christians; (C-) relating to Catholic Church. ▶ *n* C-. adherent of Catholic Church. **Ca·thol·i·cism** [kə-THOL-ə-siz-əm] *n* **cath·o·lic·i·ty** [kath-ə-LIS-i-tee] *n*

CAT scan [kat skan] computerized axial tomography (also **CT scan**).

cat·tle [KAT-l] *pl n* beasts of pasture, esp. steers, cows. **cat'tle·man** *n* **cattle guard** heavy grid over ditch in road to prevent passage of livestock.

Cau·ca·sian [kaw-KAY-zhən] *adj, n* (of, pert. to) light-complexioned racial group of mankind. **Cau·ca·soid** [-kə-soid] *adj, n*

cau·cus [KAW-kəs] *n* group, meeting, esp. of members of political party, with power to decide policy, etc.

caught pt./pp. of CATCH.

caul·dron [KAWL-drən] *n* large pot used for boiling.

cau·li·flower [KAW-li-flow-ər] *n* variety of cabbage with edible white flowering head.

caulk [kawk] *vt* stop up cracks (orig. of ship) with waterproof filler. **caulk'er** *n* **caulk'ing** *n* **caulking compound** filler used in caulking.

cause [kawz] *n* that which produces an effect; reason, origin; motive, purpose; charity, movement; lawsuit. ▶ *vt* **caused, caus·ing.** bring about, make happen. **caus'al** *adj* **cau·sal'i·ty** *n* **cau·sa'tion** *n* **cause'less** *adj* groundless.

cause cé·lè·bre [kawz sə-LEB-rə] *n, pl* **causes cé·lè·bres** [kawz sə-LEB-rəz] great controversy e.g. famous legal case.

cause·way [KAWZ-way] *n* raised way over marsh, etc.; highway.

caus·tic [KAW-stik] *adj* burning; bitter, severe. ▶ *n* corrosive substance. **caus'ti·cal·ly** *adv*

cau·ter·ize [KAW-tə-rīz] *vt* **-ized,**

-iz·ing. burn with caustic or hot iron. **cau·ter·i·za'tion** n

cau·tion [KAW-shən] n heedfulness, care; warning. ▶ vt warn. **cau'tion·ary** adj containing warning or precept. **cau'tious** adj

cav·al·cade [KAV-əl-kayd] n column or procession of riders; series.

cav·a·lier [kav-ə-LEER] adj careless, disdainful. ▶ n courtly gentleman; obs horseman.

cav·al·ry [KAV-əl-ree] n, pl -ries. mounted troops.

cave [kayv] n hollow place in the earth; den. **cav·ern** [KAV-ərn] n deep cave. **cav'ern·ous** adj **cav'i·ty** n, pl -ties. hollow. **cave'man** n prehistoric cave dweller. **cave in** fall inward; submit; give in.

cav·i·ar [KAV-ee-ahr] n salted sturgeon roe.

cav·il [KAV-əl] vi -iled, -il·ing. find fault without sufficient reason, make trifling objections. **cav'il·ing** n **cav'il·er** n

cav·i·ta·tion [kav-i-TAY-shən] n rapid formation of cavities or bubbles. **cav'i·tate** vi -tat·ed, -tat·ing. undergo cavitation.

ca·vort [kə-VORT] vi prance, frisk.

caw [kaw] n crow's cry. ▶ vi cry so.

cay·enne pepper [kī-EN] n pungent red pepper.

Cd Chem cadmium.

CD compact disk; certificate of deposit. **CD-R** compact disk recordable. **CD-ROM** compact disk storing digitized read-only data. **CD-RW** compact disk read-write.

cease [sees] v **ceased, ceas·ing.** bring or come to an end. **cease'less** adj

ce·dar [SEE-dər] n large evergreen tree; its wood.

cede [seed] vt **ced·ed, ced·ing.** yield, give up, transfer, esp. of territory.

ce·dil·la [si-DIL-ə] n hooklike mark placed under a letter c to show the sound of s.

ceil·ing [SEE-ling] n inner, upper surface of a room; maximum price, wage, etc.; Aviation lower level of clouds; limit of height to which aircraft can climb.

cel·e·brate [SEL-ə-brayt] v **-brat·ed, -brat·ing.** rejoice or have festivities to mark (happy day, event, etc.). ▶ vt observe (birthday, etc.); perform (religious ceremony, etc.); praise publicly. **cel'e·brant** n **celebrated** adj famous. **cel·e·bra'tion** n **ce·leb'ri·ty** n, pl -ties. famous person; fame.

ce·ler·i·ty [sə-LER-i-tee] n swiftness.

cel·er·y [SEL-ə-ree] n vegetable with long juicy edible stalks.

ce·les·tial [sə-LES-chəl] adj heavenly, divine; of the sky.

cel·i·ba·cy [SEL-ə-bə-see] n sexual abstinence. **cel'i·bate** [-bit] n, adj

cell [sel] n small room, esp. in prison; small cavity; minute, basic unit of living matter; device converting chemical energy into electrical energy; small local group operating as nucleus of larger political or religious organization. **cel·lu·lar** [SEL-yə-lər] adj **cell phone, cellular phone** telephone, such as a car phone, operating by radio communication via a network of transmitters each serving a small area.

cel·lar [SEL-ər] n underground room or story; stock of wine; wine cellar.

cel·lo [CHEL-oh] n, pl -los. stringed instrument of violin family.

cel·lo·phane [SEL-ə-fayn] n transparent wrapping.

cel·lu·loid [SEL-yə-loid] n synthetic plastic substance with wide range of uses; motion-picture film.

cel·lu·lose [SEL-yə-lohs] n substance of vegetable cell wall; group of carbohydrates.

Cel·si·us [SEL-see-əs] adj, n (of) scale of temperature from 0° (melting point of ice) to 100° (boiling point of water).

Celt·ic [KEL-tik or SEL-] n branch of language including Gaelic and Welsh. ▶ adj of, or relating to the Celtic peoples or languages.

ce·ment [si-MENT] n fine mortar;

adhesive, glue. ▸ vt unite with cement; join firmly.

cem·e·ter·y [SEM-i-ter-ee] n, pl **-ter·ies.** burial ground.

cen·o·taph [SEN-ə-taf] n monument to one buried elsewhere.

cen·ser [SEN-sər] n pan in which incense is burned.

cen·sor [SEN-sər] n one authorized to examine films, books, etc. and suppress all or part if considered morally or otherwise unacceptable. ▸ vt **cen·so·ri·al** [sen-SOHR-ee-əl] adj of censor. **cen·so'ri·ous** adj faultfinding. **cen'sor·ship** n

cen·sure [SEN-shər] n blame; harsh criticism. ▸ vt **-sured, -sur·ing.** blame; criticize harshly.

cen·sus [SEN-səs] n, pl **-sus·es.** official counting of people, things, etc.

cent [sent] n hundredth part of dollar, etc.

cen·taur [SEN-tor] n mythical creature, half man, half horse.

cen·ten·ar·y [sen-TEN-ə-ree] n, adj centennial. **cen·te·nar·i·an** [sen-tn-AIR-ee-ən] n person a hundred years old.

cen·ten·ni·al [sen-TEN-ee-əl] adj lasting, happening every hundred years. ▸ n 100 years; celebration of hundredth anniversary.

cen·ter [SEN-tər] n midpoint; pivot; axis; point to or from which things move or are drawn; place for specific organization or activity. **cen'tral** [-trəl] adj **cen·tral'i·ty** n **cen'tral·ize** vt **-ized, -iz·ing.** bring to a center; concentrate under one control. **cen'tral·ly** adv

cen·trif'.u·gal [-TRIF-yə-gəl] adj tending away from center.

cen·trip'e·tal [-TRIP-i-tl] adj tending toward center. **central heating** method of heating building from one central source.

central processing unit Computers part of a computer that performs logical and arithmetical operations.

cen·ti·grade [SEN-ti-grayd] adj another name for Celsius; having one hundred degrees.

cen·ti·me·ter [SEN-tə-mee-tər] n hundredth part of meter.

cen·ti·pede [SEN-tə-peed] n small segmented animal with many legs.

cen·tu·ry [SEN-chə-ree] n, pl -ries. 100 years; any set of 100.

CEO chief executive officer.

ce·ram·ic [sə-RAM-ik] n hard brittle material of baked clay; object made of this. ▸ adj **ce·ram'ic** n hard brittle material made by heating clay to a very high temperature; object made of this. ▸ pl art of producing ceramic objects. ▸ adj made of ceramic.

ce·re·al [SEER-ee-əl] n any edible grain, such as wheat, rice, etc.; (breakfast) food made from grain. ▸ adj

ce·re·bral [sə-REE-brəl] adj pert. to brain or intellect.

cer·e·mo·ny [SER-ə-moh-nee] n, pl -nies. formal observance; sacred rite; courteous act. **cer·e·mo'ni·al** adj, n **cer·e·mo'ni·ous** adj

ce·rise [sə-REES] n, adj clear, pinkish red.

cer·tain [SUR-tn] adj sure; settled, inevitable; some, one; of moderate (quantity, degree, etc.). **cer'tain·ly** adv **cer'tain·ty** n, pl -ties. **cer'ti·tude** n confidence.

cer·ti·fy [SUR-tə-fī] vt -fied, -fy·ing. declare formally; endorse, guarantee; declare legally insane. **cer·tif'i·cate** [-kit] n written declaration. ▸ vt [-kayt] -cat·ed, -cat·ing. give written declaration. **cer·ti·fi·ca'tion** n

ce·ru·le·an [sə-ROO-lee-ən] adj sky blue; deep blue.

cer·vix [SUR-viks] n, pl -vix·es. neck, esp. of womb. **cer'vi·cal** adj

ces·sa·tion [se-SAY-shən] n ceasing or stopping, pause.

ces·sion [SESH-ən] n yielding up.

cess·pit [SES-pit] n pit for receiving sewage or other refuse.

cess·pool [SES-pool] n catch basin in which sewage collects; filthy place; place of moral filth.

Cf Chem californium.

cf. compare.

CFC chlorofluorocarbon.

cgs units metric system of units based on *centimeter, gram, second*.

chad *n* small pieces removed during the punching of holes in punch cards, printer paper, etc.

chafe [chayf] *vt* **chafed, chaf·ing.** make sore or worn by rubbing; make warm by rubbing; vex, irritate.

chaff *n* husks of corn; worthless matter; banter. ▸ *v* tease good-naturedly.

cha·grin [shə-GRIN] *n* vexation, disappointment. ▸ *vt* embarrass; annoy; disappoint.

chain [chayn] *n* series of connected links or rings; thing that binds; connected series of things or events; surveyor's measure. ▸ *vt* fasten with a chain; confine; restrain.

chair *n* movable seat, with back, for one person; seat of authority; professorship. ▸ *vt* preside over; carry in triumph. **chair'lift** *n* series of chairs fixed to cable for conveying people (esp. skiers) up mountain. **chair'per·son, -wom·an, -man** *n* one who presides over meeting. **chair'man·ship** *n*

chaise [shayz] *n* light horse-drawn carriage. **chaise longue** [lawng] sofa.

chal·ced·o·ny [kal-SED-n-ee] *n* whitish, bluish-white variety of quartz.

cha·let [sha-LAY] *n* Swiss wooden house; house in this style.

chal·ice [CHAL-is] *n* cup or bowl; communion cup.

chalk [chawk] *n* white substance, carbonate of lime; crayon. ▸ *v* rub, draw, mark with chalk. **chalk'y** *adj* **chalk·i·er, chalk·i·est.**

chal·lenge [CHAL-inj] *vt* **-lenged, -leng·ing.** call to fight or account; dispute; object to; claim. ▸ *n* **chal'lenged** *adj* disabled as specified, e.g. *physically challenged; mentally challenged.* **chal'leng·er** *n* **chal'leng·ing** *adj* difficult but stimulating.

cham·ber [CHAYM-bər] *n* room for assembly; assembly, body of legislators; compartment; cavity; *obs* room; chamber pot. ▸ *pl* office of lawyer or judge; lodgings.

cham'ber·lain [-lin] *n* official at court of a monarch having charge of domestic and ceremonial affairs. **cham'ber·maid** *n* female servant with care of bedrooms. **chamber music** music for performance by a few instruments. **chamber pot** vessel for urine.

cha·me·le·on [kə-MEEL-yən] *n* small lizard famous for its power of changing color.

cham·fer [CHAM-fər] *vt* groove; bevel; flute. ▸ *n* groove.

cham·ois [SHAM-ee] *n* goatlike mountain antelope; a soft pliable leather.

champ[1] *v* munch (food) noisily, as horse; be nervous, impatient.

champ[2] *n* short for CHAMPION.

cham·pagne [sham-PAYN] *n* light, sparkling white wine from Champagne region of France; similar wine made elsewhere.

cham·pi·on [CHAM-pee-ən] *n* one that excels all others; defender of a cause; one who fights for another; hero. ▸ *vt* fight for, maintain. **cham'pi·on·ship** *n*

chance [chans] *n* unpredictable course of events; fortune, luck; opportunity; possibility; risk; probability. ▸ *v* **chanced, chanc·ing.** ▸ *vt* risk. ▸ *vi* happen. ▸ *adj* casual, unexpected. **chanc'y** *adj* **chanc·i·er, chanc·i·est.** risky.

chan·cel [CHAN-səl] *n* part of a church where altar is.

chan·cel·lor [CHAN-sə-lər] *n* high officer of state; head of university; state educational system.

chan·cer·y [CHAN-sə-ree] *n, pl* **-ies.** court of equity.

chan·de·lier [shan-dl-EER] *n* hanging frame with branches for holding lights.

change [chaynj] *v* **changed, chang·ing.** alter, make or become different; put on (different clothes, fresh coverings). ▸ *vt* put or give for another; exchange, interchange. ▸ *n* alteration, variation; variety;

conversion of money; small money, coins; balance received on payment. **change'a·ble** adj **change'less** adj **change'ling** n child exchanged for another.

chan·nel [CHAN-l] n bed of stream; strait; deeper part of strait, bay, harbor; groove; means of passing or conveying; band of radio frequencies; TV broadcasting station. ▶ vt groove, furrow; guide, convey.

chant n simple song or melody; rhythmic or repetitious slogan. ▶ v sing or utter chant; speak monotonously or repetitiously.

chan·tey [SHAN-tee] n sailor's song with chorus.

chan·ti·cleer [CHAN-tə-kleer] n rooster.

cha·os [KAY-os] n disorder, confusion; state of universe before Creation. **cha·ot'ic** adj **cha·ot'i·cal·ly** adv

chap¹ v **chapped, chap·ping.** of skin, become dry, raw and cracked, esp. by exposure to cold and wind. **chapped** adj

chap² n inf fellow, man.

chap·el [CHAP-əl] n private church; subordinate place of worship; division of church with its own altar; place of worship used by a nonconforming Christian group; print shop.

chap·er·on, chaperone [SHAP-ə-rohn] n one who attends young unmarried woman in public as protector. ▶ vt **-oned, -on·ing.** attend in this way.

chap·lain [CHAP-lin] n clergyman attached to chapel, regiment, warship, institution, etc. **chap·lain·cy** n office or term of chaplain.

chaps pl n cowboy's leggings of thick leather.

chap·ter [CHAP-tər] n division of book; section, heading; assembly of clergy, bishop's council, etc.; organized branch of society, fraternity.

char [chahr] vt **charred, char·ring.** scorch, burn to charcoal. **charred**

adj

char·ac·ter [KAR-ik-tər] n nature; total of qualities making up individuality; moral qualities; reputation of possessing them; statement of qualities of person; an eccentric; personality in play or novel; letter, sign, or any distinctive mark; essential feature. **char·ac·ter·is'tic** adj, n **char·ac·ter·is'ti·cal·ly** adv **char·ac·ter·ize** vt **-ized, -iz·ing.** mark out, distinguish; describe by peculiar qualities.

char·ade [shə-RAYD] n absurd act; travesty. ▶ pl word-guessing parlor game with syllables of word acted.

char·coal [CHAHR-kohl] n black residue of wood, bones, etc., produced by smothered burning; charred wood.

charge [chahrj] v **charged, charg·ing.** ▶ vt ask as price; bring accusation against; lay task on; command; attack; deliver injunction; fill with electricity; fill, load. ▶ vi make onrush, attack. ▶ n cost, price; accusation; attack, onrush; command, exhortation; accumulation of electricity. ▶ pl expenses. **charge'a·ble** adj **charg'er** n strong, fast battle horse; that which charges, esp. electrically.

char·i·ot [CHAR-ee-ət] n two-wheeled vehicle used in ancient fighting. **char·i·ot·eer'** n

cha·ris·ma [kə-RIZ-mə] n special power of person to inspire fascination, loyalty, etc. **char·is·mat·ic** [kar-iz-MAT-ik] adj

char·i·ty [CHAR-i-tee] n, pl **-ties.** the giving of help, money, etc. to those in need; organization for doing this; the money, etc. given; love, kindness; disposition to think kindly of others. **char'i·ta·ble** adj

char·la·tan [SHAHR-lə-tn] n quack, impostor.

charm [chahrm] n attractiveness; anything that fascinates; amulet; magic spell. ▶ vt bewitch; delight, attract. **charmed** adj **charm'ing** adj

char·nel house [CHAHR-nl] n vault for bones of the dead.

chart 76 **cheep**

chart [chahrt] n map of sea; diagram or tabulated statement. ▶ vt map; represent on chart.

char·ter [CHAHR-tər] n document granting privileges, etc. ▶ vt let or hire; establish by charter.

char·wom·an [CHAHR-wuum-ən] n woman paid to clean office, house, etc.

char·y [CHAIR-ee] adj **char·i·er, char·i·est.** cautious, sparing. **char'i·ly** adv **char'i·ness** n caution.

chase¹ [chays] vt **chased, chas·ing.** hunt, pursue; drive from, away, into, etc. ▶ n pursuit, hunting; the hunted; hunting ground. **chas'er** n drink of beer, soda, etc., taken after straight whiskey.

chase² vt **chased, chas·ing.** ornament, engrave (metal). **chas'er** n **chas'ing** n

chasm [KAZ-əm] n deep cleft, fissure; abyss.

chas·sis [CHAS-ee] n, pl **chassis** [-eez] frame, wheels and machinery of motor vehicle on which body is supported.

chaste [chayst] adj virginal; pure; modest; virtuous. **chas·ti·ty** [CHAS-ti-tee] n

chas·ten [CHAY-sən] vt correct by punishment; restrain, subdue. **chas'tened** adj **chas·tise** [chas-TĪZ] vt **-tised, -tis·ing.** inflict punishment on.

chas·u·ble [CHAZ-yə-bəl] n priest's long sleeveless outer vestment.

chat vi **chat·ted, chat·ting.** talk idly, or familiarly. ▶ n familiar idle talk. **chat'room** n site on the Internet where users have group discussions by e-mail.

châ·teau [shat-TOH] n, pl **-teaus** or **-teaux** [-TOHZ] (esp. in France) castle, country house.

chat·tel [CHAT-l] n any movable property.

chat·ter [CHAT-ər] vi talk idly or rapidly; rattle teeth. ▶ n idle talk. **chat'ter·er** n **chat'terbox** n one who chatters incessantly.

chauf·feur [SHOH-fər] n paid driver of automobile. ▶ vt perform this work.

chau·vin·ism [SHOH-və-niz-əm] n aggressive patriotism. **male chauvinism** smug sense of male superiority over women. **chau'vin·ist** n

cheap [cheep] adj **-er, -est.** low in price; inexpensive; easily obtained; of little value or estimation; mean, inferior. **cheap'en** vt

cheat [cheet] vt deceive, defraud, swindle, impose upon. ▶ vi practice deceit to gain advantage; (oft. followed by on) be sexually unfaithful. **cheat, cheat'er** n one who cheats. **cheat'ers** pl n sl eyeglasses.

check [chek] vt stop; restrain; hinder; repress; control; examine for accuracy, quality, etc. ▶ n repulse; stoppage; restraint; brief examination for correctness or accuracy; pattern of squares on fabric; threat to king at chess; written order to banker to pay money from one's account; printed slip of paper used for this. **check'book** n book of checks. **check'mate** n Chess final winning move; any overthrow, defeat. ▶ vt **-mat·ed, -mat·ing.** Chess make game-ending move; defeat. **check'out** n counter in supermarket where customers pay. **check'up** n examination (esp. medical) to see if all is in order.

checked [chekt] adj having pattern of small squares.

check·er [CHEK-ər] n marking as on checkerboard; playing piece in game of checkers. ▶ vt mark in squares; variegate. **check'ered** adj marked in squares; uneven, varied. **check'ers** n game played on checkered board of 64 squares with flat round playing pieces. **check'er·board** n

Ched·dar [CHED-ər] n smooth hard cheese.

cheek n side of face below eye; impudence; buttock. ▶ vt inf address impudently. **cheek by jowl** in close intimacy.

cheep vi, n (utter) high-pitched cry, as of young bird.

cheer vt comfort; gladden; encourage by shouts. ▶ vi shout applause. ▶ n shout of approval; happiness, good spirits; mood. **cheer'ful** adj **cheer'i·ly** adv **cheer'less** adj

cheese [cheez] n curd of milk coagulated, separated from the whey and pressed. **chees'y** adj **chees·i·er, chees·i·est.** suggesting cheese in aroma, etc.; sl cheap, shabby. **cheese'cake** n cake made with cottage or cream cheese and oft. with fruit mixture; inf photograph of shapely, scantily clad woman. **cheese'cloth** n loosely woven cotton cloth.

chee·tah [CHEE-tə] n large, swift, spotted feline animal.

chef [shef] n head cook, esp. in restaurant.

chef-d'oeu·vre [shay-DUR-vr] Fr masterpiece.

chem·is·try [KEM-ə-stree] n science concerned with properties of substances and their combinations and reactions; interaction of one personality with another. **chem'i·cal** n, adj **chem'ist** n one trained in chemistry.

che·mo·ther·a·py [kee-moh-THER-ə-pee] n treatment of disease by chemical means.

che·nille [shə-NEEL] n soft yarn, fabric of silk, wool, etc.

cher'ish vt treat with affection; protect; foster.

che·root [shə-ROOT] n cigar with both ends open.

cher·ry [CHER-ee] n small red fruit with stone; tree bearing it. ▶ adj ruddy, bright red.

cher·ub [CHER-əb] n, pl **cher·u·bim, cher·ubs.** winged creature with human face; angel. **che·ru·bic** [chə-ROO-bik] adj

cher·vil [CHUR-vil] n an herb.

chess n game of skill played by two with 32 pieces on checkered board of 64 squares. **chess'board** n **chess'man** n, pl -men. piece used in chess.

chest n upper part of trunk of body; large, strong box. **chest of**

drawers piece of furniture containing drawers.

chest·nut [CHES-nut] n large reddish-brown nut growing in prickly husk; tree bearing it; horse of chestnut color; old joke. ▶ adj reddish-brown.

chev·ron [SHEV-rən] n Military V-shaped band of braid worn on sleeve to designate rank.

chew [choo] v grind with teeth. ▶ n **chew'y** adj **chew·i·er, chew·i·est.** firm, sticky when chewed.

chi·an·ti [kee-AHN-tee] n dry red Italian wine.

chic [sheek] adj -er, -est. stylish, elegant. ▶ n

chi·can·er·y [shi-KAY-nə-ree] n, pl -er·ies. quibbling; trick, artifice.

chick [chik], **chick·en** [CHIK-ən] n young of birds, esp. of hen; sl, oft offens girl, young woman. **chicken feed** trifling amount of money. **chick'en-heart·ed** adj cowardly. **chick'en·pox** n infectious disease, esp. of children. **chick'pea** n legume bearing pods containing pealike seeds; seed of this plant.

chic·o·ry [CHIK-ə-ree] n salad plant; ground root of the plant used with, or instead of, coffee.

chide [chīd] vt **chid·ed** or **chid, chid·ed** or **chid.** or **chid·den, chid·ing.** scold, reprove, censure.

chief [cheef] n head or principal person. ▶ adj principal, foremost, leading. **chief'ly** adv **chief'tain** [-tən] n leader, chief of clan or tribe.

chif·fon [shi-FON] n thin gauzy material.

chi·gnon [SHEEN-yon] n roll, knot, of hair worn at back of head.

chi·hua·hua [chi-WAH-wah] n breed of tiny dog, orig. from Mexico.

chil·blain [CHIL-blayn] n inflamed sore on hands, legs, etc., due to cold.

child [chīld] n, pl **chil·dren** [CHIL-drən] young human being; offspring. **child·ish** adj of or like a child; silly; trifling. **child'ish·ly** adv **child'less** adj **child'like** adj of or like a child; innocent; frank; docile. **child'birth** n **child'hood** n period between birth and puberty. **child's play** very easy task.

chil·i [CHIL-ee] *n, pl* **chil·ies.** small red hot-tasting seed pod; plant producing it; chili con carne. **chili con carne** [kon KAHR-nee] Mexican-style dish of chilies or chili powder, ground beef, onions, etc.

chill *n* coldness; cold with shivering; anything that damps, discourages. ▶ *v* make, become cold (esp. food, drink). **chill'i·ness** *n* **chill'y** *adj* **chill·i·er, chill·i·est.** **chill out** *sl* relax, calm down; spend time in trivial occupations; keep company (with).

chime [chīm] *n* sound of bell; harmonious, ringing sound. ▶ *v* **chimed, chim·ing.** ▶ *vi* ring harmoniously; agree. ▶ *vt* strike (bells). **chime in** break into a conversation to express an opinion.

chi·me·ra [ki-MEER-ə] *n* fabled monster, made up of parts of various animals; wild fancy. **chi·mer'i·cal** [-MER-i-kəl] *adj* fanciful.

chim·ney [CHIM-nee] *n, pl* **-neys.** a passage for smoke; narrow vertical cleft in rock.

chim·pan·zee [chim-pan-ZEE] *n* gregarious, intelligent ape of Africa.

chin *n* part of face below mouth.

chi·na [CHĪ-nə] *n* fine earthenware, porcelain; cups, saucers, etc. collectively.

chin·chil·la [chin-CHIL-ə] *n* S Amer. rodent with soft, gray fur; its fur.

chine [chīn] *n* backbone; cut of meat including backbone; ridge or crest of land; intersection of bottom and side of boat.

chink¹ [chingk] *n* cleft, crack.

chink² [chingk] *n* light metallic ring. ▶ *v* (cause to) make this sound.

chintz [chints] *n* cotton cloth printed in colored designs.

chip *n* splinter; place where piece has been broken off; tiny wafer of silicon forming integrated circuit in computer, etc. ▶ *v* **chipped, chip·ping.** ▶ *vt* chop into small pieces; break small pieces from; shape by cutting off pieces. ▶ *vi*

break off. **chip in** contribute; butt in.

chip·munk [CHIP-mungk] *n* small, striped N Amer. squirrel.

chi·rop·o·dist [ki-ROP-ə-dist] *n* one who treats disorders of feet. **chi·rop'o·dy** *n*

chi·ro·prac·tor [KĪ-rə-prak-tər] *n* one skilled in treating bodily disorders by manipulation, massage, etc. **chi·ro·prac'tic** *n*

chirp [churp] *n* short, sharp cry of bird. ▶ *vi* make this sound. **chirp'y** *adj inf* **chirp·i·er, chirp·i·est.** happy.

chis·el [CHIZ-əl] *n* cutting tool, usu. bar of steel with edge across main axis. ▶ *vt* **-eled, -el·ing.** cut, carve with chisel; *sl* cheat.

chit¹ *n* signed note for money owed; informal receipt.

chit² *n* child, esp. young girl.

chiv·al·ry [SHIV-əl-ree] *n* bravery and courtesy; medieval system of knighthood. **chiv'al·rous** *adj*

chive [chīv] *n* herb with mild onion flavor.

chlo·rine [KLOR-een] *n* nonmetallic element, yellowish-green poison gas, used as disinfectant. **chlo'rate** [-ayt] *n* salt of chloric acid. **chlo'ric** *adj* **chlo'ride** *n* compound of chlorine; bleaching agent.

chlo·ri·nate [KLOR-ə-nayt] *vt* **-nat·ed, -nat·ing.** disinfect; purify with chlorine.

chlo·ro·fluo·ro·car·bon [klor-ə-fluur-ə-KAHR-bən] *n* (also **CFC**) any of various gaseous compounds of carbon, hydrogen, chlorine, and fluorine, used in refrigerators and aerosol propellants, some of which break down the ozone in the atmosphere.

chlo·ro·form [KLOR-ə-form] *n* volatile liquid formerly used as anesthetic. ▶ *vt* render insensible with it.

chlo·ro·phyll [KLOR-ə-fil] *n* green coloring matter in plants.

chock [chok] *n* block or wedge to prevent heavy object from rolling or sliding. **chock'-full** *adj* packed full.

choc·o·late [CHAWK-lit] *n* paste

from ground cacao seeds; candy, drink made from this. ▶ *adj* dark brown.

choice [chois] *n* act or power of choosing; alternative; thing or person chosen. ▶ *adj* select, fine, worthy of being chosen.

choir [kwīr] *n* company of singers, esp. in church; part of church set aside for them.

choke [chohk] *v* **choked, chok·ing.** ▶ *vt* hinder, stop the breathing of; smother, stifle; obstruct. ▶ *vi* suffer choking. ▶ *n* act, noise of choking; device in carburetor to increase richness of fuel-air mixture.

chol·er [KOL-ər] *n* bile, anger. **chol'er·ic** *adj* irritable.

chol·er·a [KOL-ər-ə] *n* deadly infectious disease marked by vomiting and diarrhea.

cho·les·ter·ol [kə-LES-tə-rawl] *n* substance found in animal tissue and fat.

chomp *v* chew noisily.

choose [chooz] *v* **chose, cho·sen, choos·ing.** ▶ *vt* pick out, select; take by preference. ▶ *vi* decide, think fit. **choos'y** *adj* **choos·i·er, choos·i·est.** fussy.

chop *vt* **chopped, chop·ping.** cut with blow; hack. ▶ *n* hewing blow; slice of meat containing rib or other bone. **chop'per** *n* short axe; *inf* helicopter. **chop'py** *adj* **-pi·er, -pi·est.** (of sea) having short, broken waves.

chops *pl n* jaw, mouth.

chop·sticks [CHOP-stiks] *pl n* implements used by Chinese and others for eating food.

cho·ral [KOR-əl] *adj* of, for, sung by, a choir.

cho·rale [kə-RAL] *n* slow, stately hymn tune.

chord [kord] *n* emotional response, esp. of sympathy; simultaneous sounding of musical notes; straight line joining ends of arc.

chore [chor] *n* (unpleasant) task; odd job.

cho·re·og·ra·phy [kor-ee-OG-rə-fee] *n* art of arranging dances, esp. ballet; art,

notation of ballet dancing. **cho·re·og'ra·pher** *n* **cho·re·o·graph'ic** *adj*

chor·tle [CHOR-tl] *vi* **-tled, -tling.** chuckle happily. ▶ *n*

cho·rus [KOR-əs] *n* group of singers; combination of voices singing together; refrain. ▶ *vt* **-rused, -rus·ing.** sing or say together. **chor'is·ter** *n*

chose pt. of CHOOSE. **cho'sen** pp. of CHOOSE.

chow[1] *inf* ▶ *n* food. ▶ *vi* (oft. with *down*) eat heartily. **chow'hound** *n sl* glutton.

chow[2] *n* thick-coated dog with curled tail, orig. from China.

chow·der [CHOW-dər] *n* thick soup of seafood, vegetables, etc.; soup resembling it, such as corn chowder.

Christ [krīst] *n* Jesus of Nazareth, regarded by Christians as the Messiah.

Chris·tian [KRIS-chən] *n* follower of Christ. ▶ *adj* following Christ; relating to Christ or his religion. **chris'ten** [-ən] *vt* baptize, give name to. **Chris'ten·dom** [-ən-dəm] *n* all the Christian world. **Chris·ti·an'i·ty** [-chee-AN-i-tee] *n* religion of Christ. **Christian name** name given at baptism. **Christian Science** religious system founded by Mary Baker Eddy.

Christ·mas [KRIS-məs] *n* festival of birth of Christ.

chro·mat·ic [kroh-MAT-ik] *adj* of color; *Mus* of scale proceeding by semitones.

chro·ma·tin [KROH-mə-tin] *n* part of protoplasmic substance in nucleus of cells that takes color in staining tests.

chrome [krohm], **chro'mi·um** [-mee-əm] *n* metal used in alloys and for plating.

chro·mo·some [KROH-mə-sohm] *n* microscopic gene-carrying body in the tissue of a cell.

Chron. Chronicles.

chron·ic [KRON-ik] *adj* lasting a long time; habitual.

chron·i·cle [KRON-i-kəl] *n* record of

events in order of time; account.
▶ *vt* **-cled, -cling.** record.
chron'i·cler *n*
chro·nol·o·gy [krə-NOL-ə-jee] *n, pl*
-gies. determination of sequence of
past events; arrangement in order
of occurrence; account of events,
reference work arranged in order of
time. **chron·o·log·i·cal**
[kron-l-OJ-i-kəl] *adj* arranged in
order of time.
chro·nom·e·ter [krə-NOM-i-tər] *n*
instrument for measuring time
exactly; watch.
chrys·a·lis [KRIS-ə-lis] *n, pl*
chry·sal·i·des [kri-SAL-i-deez]
resting state of insect between
grub and butterfly, etc.; case
enclosing it.
chrys·an·the·mum
[kri-SAN-thə-məm] *n* garden
flower of various colors.
chub·by [CHUB-ee] *adj* **-bi·er,
-bi·est.** plump.
chuck¹ [chuk] *vt inf* throw; pat
affectionately (under chin); give
up, reject.
chuck² *n* cut of beef; device for
gripping, adjusting bit in power
drill, etc.
chuck·le [CHUK-əl] *vi* **-led, -ling.**
laugh softly. ▶ *n* such laugh.
chuk·ker [CHUK-ər] *n* period of
play in game of polo.
chum *n inf* close friend. **chum'my**
adj **-mi·er, -mi·est.**
chunk [chungk] *n* thick, solid piece.
chunk·y *adj* **chunk·i·er, chunk·i·est.**
church *n* building for Christian
worship; (**C-**) whole body or sect of
Christians; clergy. **church'ward·en**
n officer who represents interests of
Anglican parish; long clay pipe.
church'yard *n*
churl *n* rustic; rude, boorish person.
churl'ish *adj* **churl'ish·ness** *n*
churn *n* vessel for making butter. ▶ *v*
shake up, stir (liquid) violently;
make (butter) in churn; (of a
stockbroker) trade (stocks)
excessively to increase commissions.
chute [shoot] *n* slide for sending
down parcels, coal, etc.; channel;
narrow passageway, e.g. for

spraying, counting cattle, sheep,
etc.; *inf* short for PARACHUTE.
chut·ney [CHUT-nee] *n* condiment
of fruit, spices, etc.
chutz·pah [HUUT-spə] *n* shameless
audacity; gall.
ci·ca·da [si-KAY-də] *n* cricketlike
insect.
cic·a·trix [SIK-ə-triks] *n* scar of
healed wound.
cic·e·ro·ne [sis-ə-ROH-nee] *n* guide
for sightseers.
ci·der [SĪ-dər] *n* drink made from
apples. **hard cider** cider after
fermentation. **soft cider** cider
before fermentation.
ci·gar [si-GAHR] *n* roll of tobacco
leaves for smoking. **cig·a·rette**
[sig-ə-RET] *n* finely cut tobacco
rolled in paper for smoking.
ci·lan·tro [si-LAN-troh, -LAHN-] *n*
coriander.
cinch [sinch] *n inf* easy task,
certainty; strong girth used on
saddle.
cin·der [SIN-dər] *n* remains of
burned coal.
cin·e·ma [SIN-ə-mə] *n* building
used for showing of motion
pictures; these generally or
collectively.
cin·na·mon [SIN-ə-mən] *n* spice
got from bark of Asian tree; the
tree. ▶ *adj* light-brown color.
ci·pher [SĪ-fər] *n* secret writing;
arithmetical symbol; person of no
importance; monogram. ▶ *vt* write
in cipher.
cir·ca [SUR-kə] *Lat* about,
approximately.
cir·cle [SUR-kəl] *n* perfectly round
figure; ring; *Theater* balcony or tier
of seats above main level of
auditorium; group, society with
common interest; class of society.
▶ *v* **-cled, -cling.** ▶ *vt* surround. ▶ *vi*
move in circle. **cir·cu·lar** [-kyə-lər]
adj round; in a circle. ▶ *n* letter, etc.
intended for wide distribution.
cir·cu·late [-kyə-layt] *v* **-lat·ed,
-lat·ing.** ▶ *vi* move around; pass
from hand to hand or place to
place. ▶ *vt* send around.
cir·cu·la'tion *n* flow of blood from,

and back to, heart; act of moving around; extent of sale of newspaper, etc. **cir·cu·la·to·ry** *adj*

cir·cuit [SUR-kit] *n* complete round or course; area; path of electric current; round of visitation, esp. of judges; series of sporting events; district. **cir·cu·i·tous** [sər-KYOO-i-təs] *adj* roundabout, indirect. **cir·cuit·ry** *n* electrical circuit(s).

cir·cum·cise [SUR-kəm-sīz] *vt* **-cised, -cis·ing.** cut off foreskin of (penis). **cir·cum·ci·sion** [-SIZH-ən] *n*

cir·cum·fer·ence [sər-KUM-fər-əns] *n* boundary line, esp. of circle.

cir·cum·flex [SUR-kəm-fleks] *n* accent (^) over vowel to indicate length of its sound.

cir·cum·lo·cu·tion [sur-kəm-loh-KYOO-shən] *n* roundabout speech.

cir·cum·nav·i·gate [sur-kəm-NAV-i-gayt] *vt* **-gat·ed, -gat·ing.** sail or fly right around.

cir·cum·scribe [SUR-kəm-skrīb] *vt* **-scribed, -scrib·ing.** confine, bound, limit, hamper.

cir·cum·spect [SUR-kəm-spekt] *adj* watchful, cautious, prudent. **cir·cum·spec'tion** *n*

cir·cum·stance [SUR-kəm-stans] *n* detail; event; matter of fact. ▸ *pl* state of affairs; condition in life, esp. financial; surroundings or things accompanying an action. **cir·cum·stan'tial** *adj* depending on detail or circumstances; detailed, minute; incidental.

cir·cum·vent [sur-kəm-VENT] *vt* outwit, evade, get round. **cir·cum·ven'tion** *n*

cir·cus [SUR-kəs] *n, pl* **-cus·es.** (performance of) traveling group of acrobats, clowns, performing animals, etc.; circular structure for public shows.

cir·rho·sis [si-ROH-sis] *n* any of various chronic progressive diseases of liver. **cir·rhot'ic** [-ROT-ik] *adj*

cir·rus [SIR-əs] *n, pl* **cirrus.** high wispy cloud.

cis·tern [SIS-tərn] *n* water tank, esp. for rain water.

cit·a·del [SIT-ə-dl] *n* fortress in, near, or commanding a city.

cite [sīt] *vt* **cit·ed, cit·ing.** quote; bring forward as proof. **ci·ta·tion** [sī-TAY-shən] *n* quoting; commendation for bravery, etc.

cit·i·zen [SIT-ə-zən] *n* native, naturalized member of state, nation, etc.; inhabitant of city. **cit'i·zen·ship** *n*

cit·ron [SI-trən] *n* fruit like a lemon; the tree. **cit'ric** *adj* of the acid of lemon or citron. **cit·rus fruit** citrons, lemons, limes, oranges, etc.

cit·y [SIT-ee] *n, pl* **cit·ies.** a large town.

civ·et [SIV-it] *n* strong, musky perfume. **civet cat** catlike animal producing it.

civ·ic [SIV-ik] *adj* pert. to city or citizen. **civ'ics** *n* study of the responsibilities and rights of citizenship.

civ·il [SIV-əl] *adj* relating to citizens of state; not military; refined, polite; *Law* not criminal. **ci·vil·ian** [si-VIL-yən] *n* nonmilitary person. **ci·vil'i·ty** *n, pl* **-ties. civ'il·ly** *adv* **civil service** service responsible for the public administration of the government of a city, state, or country.

civ·i·lize [SIV-ə-līz] *vt* **-lized, -liz·ing.** bring out of barbarism; refine. **civ·i·li·za'tion** *n*

Cl *Chem* chlorine.

clack [klak] *n* sound, as of two pieces of wood striking together. ▸ *v*

clad pt./pp. of CLOTHE.

clad·ding [KLAD-ing] *n* metal bonded to inner core of another metal, as protection against corrosion.

claim [klaym] *vt* demand as right; assert; call for. ▸ *n* demand for thing supposed due; right; thing claimed; plot of mining land marked out by stakes as required by law. **claim'ant** [-mənt] *n*

clair·voy·ance [klair-VOI-əns] *n* power of seeing things not present to senses, second sight. **clair·voy'ant** *n, adj*

clam [klam] *n* edible mollusk.

clam·ber [KLAM-bər] vi to climb with difficulty or awkwardly.

clam·my [KLAM-ee] adj **-mi·er, -mi·est.** moist and sticky. **clam'mi·ness** n

clam·or [KLAM-ər] n loud shouting, outcry, noise. ▶ vi shout, call noisily (for). **clam'or·ous** adj

clamp [klamp] n tool for holding or compressing. ▶ vt fasten, strengthen with or as with clamp.

clan [klan] n tribe or collection of families under chief and of common ancestry; faction, group. **clan'nish** adj

clan·des·tine [klan-DES-tin] adj secret; sly.

clang [klang] v (cause to) make loud ringing sound. ▶ n loud ringing sound.

clank [klangk] n short sound as of pieces of metal struck together. ▶ v cause, move with, such sound.

clap¹ [klap] v **clapped, clap·ping.** (cause to) strike with noise; strike (hands) together; applaud. ▶ vt pat; place or put quickly. ▶ n hard, explosive sound; slap. **clap'per** n **clap'trap** n empty words.

clap² [klap] n sl gonorrhea.

clar·et [KLAR-it] n a dry dark red wine of Bordeaux; similar wine made elsewhere.

clar·i·fy [KLAR-ə-fī] v **-fied, -fy·ing.** make or become clear, pure, or more easily understood. **clar·i·fi·ca'tion** n **clar'i·ty** n clearness.

clar·i·net [klar-ə-NET] n woodwind musical instrument.

clar·i·on [KLAR-ee-ən] n clear-sounding trumpet; rousing sound.

clash [klash] n loud noise, as of weapons striking; conflict, collision. ▶ vi make clash; come into conflict; (of events) coincide; (of colors) look ugly together. ▶ vt strike together to make clash.

clasp [klasp] n hook or other means of fastening; embrace. ▶ vt fasten; embrace, grasp.

class [klas] n any division, order, kind, sort; rank; group of school pupils, etc. taught together; division by merit; quality; inf excellence or elegance. ▶ vt assign to proper division. **clas'si·fy** [-ə-fī] vt **-fied, -fy·ing.** arrange methodically in classes. **clas·si·fi·ca'tion** n **clas·si·fied** adj arranged in classes; secret; (of advertisements) arranged under headings in newspapers, etc. **class'y** adj **class·i·er, class·i·est.** inf stylish, elegant.

clas·sic [KLAS-ik] adj of first rank; of highest rank generally, but esp. of art; refined; typical; famous. ▶ n (literary) work of recognized excellence. ▶ pl ancient Latin and Greek literature. **clas·si·cal** adj of Greek and Roman literature, art, culture; of classic quality; Mus of established standards of form, complexity, etc. **clas·si·cism** n **clas·si·cist** n

clat·ter [KLAT-ər] n rattling noise; noisy conversation. ▶ v (cause to) make clatter.

clause [klawz] n part of sentence, containing verb; article in formal document as treaty, contract, etc.

claus·tro·pho·bia [klaw-strə-FOH-bee-ə] n abnormal fear of confined spaces.

clav·i·chord [KLAV-i-kord] n musical instrument with keyboard, forerunner of piano.

clav·i·cle [KLAV-i-kəl] n collarbone.

claw [klaw] n sharp hooked nail of bird or beast; foot of bird of prey; clawlike article. ▶ vt tear with claws; grip.

clay [klay] n fine-grained earth, plastic when wet, hardening when baked; earth.

clean [kleen] adj **-er, -est.** free from dirt, stain, or defilement; pure; guiltless; trim, shapely. ▶ adv **-er, -est.** so as to leave no dirt; entirely. ▶ vt free from dirt. **clean·li·ness** [KLEN-lee-nis] n **clean·ly** [KLEEN-lee] adv, adj **-li·er, -li·est.** clean. **cleanse** [klenz] vt **cleansed, cleans·ing.** make clean. **come clean** inf confess.

clear [kleer] adj **-er, -est.** pure,

undimmed, bright; free from cloud; transparent; plain, distinct; without defect or drawback; unimpeded. ▶ *adv* **-er, -est.** brightly; wholly, quite. ▶ *vt* make clear; acquit; pass over or through; make as profit; free from obstruction, debt, difficulty. ▶ *vi* become clear, bright, free, transparent. **clear′ance** *n* making clear; removal of obstructions, surplus stock, etc.; certificate that ship has been cleared at custom house; space for moving part, vehicle, to pass within, through or past something. **clear′ing** *n* land cleared of trees. **clear′ly** *adv* **clear′head·ed** [-hed-id] *adj* discerning.

cleat [kleet] *n* wedge; piece of wood or iron with two projecting ends round which ropes are made fast; (on shoes) projecting piece to furnish a grip. ▶ *pl* shoes equipped with cleats.

cleave¹ [kleev] *v* **cleft, cleaved** or **clove; cleft, cleaved** or **clo·ven; cleav·ing.** ▶ *vt* split asunder. ▶ *vi* crack, part asunder. **cleav′age** *n* space between a woman's breasts, as revealed by a low-cut dress, top, etc.; division, split. **cleav′er** *n* butcher's heavy knife with a square blade.

cleave² *vi* **cleaved, cleav·ing.** stick, adhere; be loyal.

clef *n Mus* mark showing pitch of music on staff.

cleft *n* crack, fissure, chasm; opening made by cleaving; pt./pp. of CLEAVE¹.

clem·ent [KLEM-ənt] *adj* merciful; gentle; mild. **clem′en·cy** *n*

clench *vt* set firmly together; grasp, close (fist).

cler·gy [KLUR-jee] *n* body of ordained ministers in a religion. **cler′gy·man** *n*

cler·ic [KLER-ik] *n* member of clergy. **cler·i·cal** [KLER-i-kəl] *adj* of clergy; of, connected with, office work.

clerk [klurk] *n* employee who keeps files, etc. in an office; officer in charge of records, correspondence,

etc. of court, government department, etc.; sales or service employee.

clev·er [KLEV-ər] *adj* quick to understand; able, skillful, adroit. **clev′er·ly** *adv* **clev′er·ness** *n*

cli·ché [klee-SHAY] *n, pl* **-chés.** stereotyped hackneyed phrase.

click¹ [klik] *n* short, sharp sound, as of latch in door; catch. ▶ *vi* make this sound. ▶ *v* (usu. foll. by *on*) *Computers* press and release (button on a mouse).

click² *vi sl* be a success; *inf* become clear; *inf* strike up friendship.

cli·ent [KLĪ-ənt] *n* customer; one who employs professional person; *Computers* program or work station that requests data from a server. **cli·en·tele′** [-ən-TEL] *n* body of clients.

cliff [klif] *n* steep rock face. **cliff′hang·er** *n* tense situation.

cli·mate [KLĪ-mit] *n* condition of region with regard to weather; prevailing feeling, atmosphere. **cli·mat′ic** *adj* of climate.

cli·max [KLĪ-maks] *n* highest point, culmination; point of greatest excitement, tension in story, etc. **cli·mac′tic** *adj*

climb [klīm] *v* go up or ascend; progress with difficulty; creep up; mount; slope upwards.

clinch [klinch] *vt* clench; settle, conclude (an agreement). ▶ *vi* (in boxing) hold opponent close with arm or arms; *sl* embrace, esp. passionately. ▶ *n* clinching; *sl* embrace. **clinch′er** *n inf* something decisive.

cling *vi* **clung, cling·ing.** adhere; be firmly attached to; be dependent.

clin·ic [KLIN-ik] *n* hospital facility for examination, treatment of outpatients; medical training session with hospital patients as subjects. **clin′i·cal** *adj* relating to clinic, care of sick, etc.; objective, unemotional; bare, plain. **clinical thermometer** used for taking body temperature.

clink¹ [klingk] *n* sharp metallic sound. ▶ *v* (cause to) make this sound.

clink² *n sl* prison.

clink·er [KLING-kər] *n* fused coal residues from fire or furnace; hard brick.

clip¹ *vt* **clipped, clip·ping.** cut with scissors; cut short; *sl* cheat. ▶ *n inf* sharp blow. **clip'per** *n*

clip² *n* device for gripping or holding together, esp. hair, clothing, etc.

clip·per [KLIP-ər] *n* fast commercial sailing ship.

clique [kleek] *n* small exclusive set; faction, group of people. **cli'quish** *adj* **cli'quish·ness** *n*

clit·o·ris [KLIT-ər-is] *n* small erectile part of female genitals.

cloak [klohk] *n* loose outer garment; disguise, pretext. ▶ *vt* cover with cloak; disguise, conceal.

clob·ber [KLOB-ər] *vt inf* beat, batter; defeat utterly.

clock [klok] *n* instrument for measuring time; device with dial for recording or measuring. **clock'wise** *adv, adj* in the direction that the hands of a clock rotate. **clock'work** *n* mechanism similar to that of a clock, as in a windup toy. **clock in** *or* **on, out** *or* **off** record arrival, or departure, on automatic time recorder.

clod [klod] *n* lump of earth; blockhead. **clod'dish** *adj*

clog [klog] *vt* **clogged, clog·ging.** hamper, impede, choke up. ▶ *n* obstruction, impediment; wooden-soled shoe.

cloi·son·né [kloi-zə-NAY] *n* enamel decoration in compartments formed by small strips of metal. ▶ *adj*

clois·ter [KLOI-stər] *n* covered pillared arcade; monastery or convent. **clois'tered** *adj* confined, secluded, sheltered.

clone [klohn] *n* group of organisms, cells of same genetic constitution as another, derived by asexual reproduction, as graft of plant, etc.; person closely resembling another in appearance, behavior, etc. ▶ *v* **cloned, clon·ing.**

clop [klop] *vi* **clopped, clop·ping.** move, sound, as horse's hooves.

close¹ [klohs] *adj* **clos·er, clos·est.** adjacent, near; compact; crowded; affectionate, intimate; almost equal; careful, searching; confined; secret; unventilated, stifling; reticent; niggardly; strict, restricted. ▶ *adv* nearly; tightly. **close'ly** *adv* **close'fist'ed** *adj* mean; avaricious. **close'up** *n* close view, esp. portion of motion picture.

close² [klohz] *v* **closed, clos·ing.** ▶ *vt* shut; stop up; prevent access to; finish. ▶ *vi* come together; grapple. ▶ *n* end. **closed season** when it is illegal to kill certain kinds of game and fish. **closed shop** place of work in which all workers must belong to a union.

clos·et [KLOZ-it] *n* small room, etc. for storing clothing; small private room. ▶ *vt* shut up in private room, esp. for conference. **clos'et·ful** *n, pl* **-fuls.**

clo·sure [KLOH-zhər] *n* act of closing; (sense of contentment experienced after) resolution of a significant event or relationship in a person's life; cloture.

clot [klot] *n* mass or lump; *Med* coagulated mass of blood. ▶ *v* **clot·ted, clot·ting.** form into lumps; coagulate.

cloth [klawth] *n* woven fabric. **clothes** [klohthz] *pl n* dress; bed coverings. **clothe** [klohth] *vt* **clothed** *or* **clad, cloth·ing.** put clothes on. **clo·thier** [KLOH-yər] *n* **cloth·ing** [KLOH-thing] *n*

clo·ture [KLOH-chər] *n* ending of debate by majority vote or other authority.

cloud [klowd] *n* condensed water vapor floating in air; state of gloom; multitude. ▶ *vt* overshadow, dim, darken. ▶ *vi* become cloudy. **cloud'less** *adj* **cloud'y** *adj* **cloud·i·er, cloud·i·est.**

clout [klowt] *n inf* blow; influence, power. ▶ *vt* strike.

clove¹ [klohv] *n* dried flower bud of tropical tree, used as spice; one of small bulbs making up compound bulb.

clove[2] pt. of CLEAVE[1]. **clo'ven** pp. of CLEAVE[1].

clo·ver [KLOH-vər] n low-growing forage plant. **be in clover** be in luxury.

clown [klown] n comic entertainer in circus; jester, fool.

cloy [kloi] vt weary by sweetness, sameness, etc.

club [klub] n thick stick; bat, stick used in some games; association for pursuance of common interest; building used by such association; one of the suits at cards. ▶ v **clubbed, club·bing.** strike with club; combine for a common object. **club foot** deformed foot.

cluck [kluk] vi, n (make) noise of hen.

clue [kloo] n indication, esp. of solution of mystery or puzzle. **not have a clue** be ignorant or incompetent.

clump[1] [klump] n cluster of trees or plants; compact mass.

clump[2] vi walk, tread heavily. ▶ n

clum·sy [KLUM-zee] adj **-si·er, -si·est.** awkward, unwieldy, ungainly; badly made or arranged. **clum'si·ly** adv **clum'si·ness** n

clung pt./pp. of CLING.

clunk [klungk] n (sound of) blow or something falling.

clus·ter [KLUS-tər] n group, bunch. ▶ v gather, grow in cluster.

clutch[1] [kluch] v grasp eagerly; snatch (at). ▶ n grasp, tight grip; device enabling two rotating shafts to be connected and disconnected at will.

clutch[2] n set of eggs hatched at one time; brood of chickens.

clut·ter [KLUT-ər] v strew; crowd together in disorder. ▶ n disordered, obstructive mass of objects.

Cm Chem curium.

Co Chem cobalt.

coach [kohch] n large four-wheeled carriage; railway carriage; class of airline travel; tutor, instructor. ▶ vt instruct.

co·ag·u·late [koh-AG-yə-layt] v **-lat·ed, -lat·ing.** curdle, clot, form into a mass; congeal, solidify. **co·ag·u·la'tion** n

coal [kohl] n mineral consisting of carbonized vegetable matter, used as fuel; glowing ember. ▶ v supply with or take in coal. **coal'field** n area in which coal is found.

co·a·lesce [koh-ə-LES] vi **-lesced, -lesc·ing.** unite, merge. **co·a·les'cence** n

co·a·li·tion [koh-ə-LISH-ən] n alliance, esp. of political parties.

coarse [kors] adj **coars·er, coars·est.** rough, harsh; unrefined; indecent. **coarse'ness** n

coast [kohst] n seashore. ▶ v move under momentum; proceed without making much effort; sail by the coast. **coast'er** n small ship; that which, one who, coasts; small table mat for glasses, etc.

coat [koht] n sleeved outer garment; animal's fur or feathers; covering layer. ▶ vt cover with layer; clothe. **coat of arms** armorial bearings.

coax [kohks] vt wheedle, cajole, persuade, force gently.

co·ax·i·al [koh-AK-see-əl] adj having the same axis. **co·ax'i·al·ly** adv

co·balt [KOH-bawlt] n metallic element; blue pigment from it.

cob·ble [KOB-əl] vt **-bled, -bling.** patch roughly; mend shoes. ▶ n round stone. **cob'bler** n shoe mender.

co·bra [KOH-brə] n venomous, hooded snake of Asia and Africa.

cob'web n spider's web.

co·caine [koh-KAYN] n addictive narcotic drug used medicinally as anesthetic.

coch·i·neal [koch-ə-NEEL] n scarlet dye from Mexican insect.

cock [kok] n male bird, esp. of domestic fowl; tap for liquids; hammer of gun; its position drawn back. ▶ vt draw back (gun hammer) to firing position; raise, turn in alert or jaunty manner. **cock'eyed** [-īd] adj crosseyed; with a squint; askew.

cock'fight *n* staged fight between roosters.

cock·a·trice [KOK-ə-tris] *n* fabulous animal similar to basilisk.

cock·chaf·er [KOK-chay-fər] *n* large, flying beetle.

cock·le [KOK-əl] *n* shellfish.

Cock·ney [KOK-nee] *n, pl* **-neys.** native of East End of London; urban dialect of London or its East End.

cock·pit [KOK-pit] *n* pilot's seat, compartment in small aircraft; driver's seat in racing car; orig. enclosure for cockfighting.

cock·roach [KOK-rohch] *n* kind of insect, household pest.

cock·tail [KOK-tayl] *n* short drink of whiskey, gin, etc. with flavorings, etc.

cock·y [KOK-ee] *adj* **cock·i·er, cock·i·est.** conceited, pert. **cock'i·ness** *n*

co·coa [KOH-koh] *n* powder made from seed of cacao (tropical) tree; drink made from the powder.

co·co·nut [KOH-kə-nut] *n* tropical palm; very large, hard nut from this palm.

co·coon [kə-KOON] *n* sheath of insect in chrysalis stage; any protective covering.

co·da [KOH-də] *n Mus* final part of musical composition.

cod·dle [KOD-l] *vt* **-dled, -dling.** overprotect, pamper; cook (eggs) lightly.

code [kohd] *n* system of letters, symbols and rules for their association to transmit messages secretly or briefly; scheme of conduct; collection of laws. **cod'i·fy** [KOD-] *vt* **-fied, - fy·ing. cod·i·fi·ca'tion** *n*

co·deine [KOH-deen] *n* alkaline sedative, analgesic drug.

co·de·pend·ent [koh-di-PEND-dənt] *adj* of a relationship involving an addict. ▸ *n* **co·de·pen'den·cy** *n*

co·dex [KOH-deks] *n, pl* **-di·ces** [-də-seez] ancient manuscript volume, esp. of Bible, etc.

codg·er [KOJ-ər] *n inf* man, esp. old.

cod·i·cil [KOD-ə-səl] *n* addition to will.

co·ed·u·ca·tion·al [koh-ej-ə-KAY-shə-nl] *adj* of education of boys and girls together in mixed classes. **co-ed** [koh-ed] *n* (female student at) coeducational school. ▸ *adj*

co·ef·fi·cient [koh-ə-FISH-ənt] *n Math* numerical or constant factor.

co·erce [koh-URS] *vt* **-erced, -erc·ing.** compel, force. **co·er'cion** [-UR-shən] *n* forcible compulsion or restraint.

co·ex·ist [koh-ig-ZIST] *vi* exist together. **co·ex·ist'ence** *n*

cof·fee [KAW-fee] *n* seeds of tropical shrub; drink made from roasting and grinding these.

cof·fer [KAW-fər] *n* chest for valuables; treasury, funds.

cof·fer·dam [KAW-fər-dam] *n* watertight structure enabling construction work to be done underwater.

cof·fin [KAW-fin] *n* box for corpse.

cog [kog] *n* one of series of teeth on rim of wheel; person, thing forming small part of big process, organization, etc.

co·gent [KOH-jənt] *adj* convincing, compelling, persuasive. **co'gen·cy** *n*

cog·i·tate [KOJ-i-tayt] *vi* **-tat·ed, -tat·ing.** think, reflect, ponder.

co·gnac [KOHN-yak] *n* French brandy.

cog·nate [KOG-nayt] *adj* of same stock, related, kindred.

cog·ni·tion [kog-NISH-ən] *n* act or faculty of knowing. **cog'ni·tive** *adj*

cog·ni·zance [KOG-nə-zəns] *n* knowledge, perception. **cog'ni·zant** *adj*

co·gno·scen·ti [kon-yə-SHEN-tee] *pl n* people with knowledge in particular field, esp. arts.

co·hab·it [koh-HAB-it] *vi* live together as husband and wife.

co·here [koh-HEER] *vi* **-hered, -her·ing.** stick together, be consistent. **co·her'ence** *n* **co·her'ent** *adj* capable of logical speech, thought; connected; making sense; sticking together.

co·he·sion [-HEE-zhən] *n* cohering. **co·he·sive** *adj*

co·hort [KOH-hort] *n* troop; associate.

coif·feur [kwah-FUUR] *n* hairdresser.

coif·fure [kwah-FYUUR] *n* hairstyle.

coil [koil] *vt* lay in rings; twist into winding shape. ▶ *vi* twist, take up a winding shape or spiral. ▶ *n* series of rings; device in vehicle, etc. to transform low-voltage direct current to higher voltage for ignition purposes; contraceptive device inserted in womb.

coin [koin] *n* piece of money; money. ▶ *vt* make into money, stamp; invent. **coin'age** *n* coining; coins collectively. **coin money** *inf* make money rapidly.

co·in·cide [koh-in-SID] *vi* **-cid·ed, -cid·ing.** happen together; agree exactly. **co·in'ci·dence** [-si-dəns] *n* **co·in'ci·dent** *adj* coinciding. **co·in·ci·den'tal** *adj*

co·i·tus [KOH-i-təs], **co·i·tion** [koh-ISH-ən] *n* sexual intercourse.

coke[1] [kohk] *n* residue left from distillation of coal, used as fuel.

coke[2] *n sl* cocaine.

Col. Colossians.

co·la [KOH-lə] *n* tropical tree; its nut, used to flavor drink.

col·an·der [KUL-ən-dər] *n* culinary strainer perforated with small holes.

cold [kohld] *adj* **-er, -est.** lacking heat; indifferent, unmoved, apathetic; dispiriting; reserved or unfriendly; (of colors) giving an impression of coldness. ▶ *n* lack of heat; illness, marked by runny nose, etc. **cold'ly** *adv* **cold'-blood·ed** *adj* lacking pity, mercy; having body temperature that varies with that of the surroundings. **cold chisel** toughened steel chisel. **cold feet** fear. **cold storage** method of preserving perishable foods, etc. by keeping them at artificially reduced temperature. **cold turkey** *sl* abrupt halt in use of addictive drug, etc. **cold war** economic, diplomatic but nonmilitary hostility.

cole·slaw [KOHL-slaw] *n* salad dish based on shredded cabbage.

col·ic [KOL-ik] *n* severe pains in the intestines. **co·li·tis** [kə-LI-tis] *n* inflammation of the colon.

col·lab·o·rate [kə-LAB-ə-rayt] *vi* **-rat·ed, -rat·ing.** work with another on a project. **col·lab'o·ra·tor** *n* one who works with another, esp. one who aids an enemy in occupation of his own country.

col·lage [kə-LAHZH] *n* (artistic) composition of bits and pieces stuck together on background.

col·lapse [kə-LAPS] *vi* **-lapsed, -laps·ing.** fall; give way; lose strength, fail. ▶ *n* act of collapsing; breakdown. **col·laps'i·ble** *adj*

col·lar [KOL-ər] *n* band, part of garment, worn round neck; *inf* police arrest. ▶ *vt* seize by collar; *inf* capture, seize. **col'lar·bone** *n* bone from shoulder to breastbone.

col·late [kə-LAYT] *vt* **-lat·ed, -lat·ing.** compare carefully; place in order (as printed sheets for binding). **col·la'tion** *n* collating; light meal.

col·lat·er·al [kə-LAT-ər-əl] *n* security pledged for repayment of loan. ▶ *adj* accompanying; side by side; of same stock but different line; subordinate. **collateral damage** unintentional civilian casualties or damage to civilian property caused by military action.

col·league [KOL-eeg] *n* associate, companion in office or employment, fellow worker.

col·lect [kə-LEKT] *vt* gather, bring together. ▶ *vi* come together; *inf* receive money. **col·lect'ed** *adj* calm; gathered. **col·lec'tion** *n* **col·lec'tive** *n* factory, farm, etc., run on principles of collectivism. ▶ *adj* **col·lec'tiv·ism** *n* theory that a government should own all means of production.

col·lege [KOL-ij] *n* place of higher education; society of scholars; association. **col·le·giate** [kə-LEE-jit] *adj* **col·le·gian** *n* student.

col·lide [kə-LID] *vi* **-lid·ed, -lid·ing.** strike or dash together; come into conflict. **col·li'sion** [-LIZH-ən] *n* colliding.

col·lo·di·on [kə-LOH-dee-ən] *n* chemical solution used in photography and medicine.

col·loid [KOL-oid] *n* suspension of particles in a solution.

col·lo·qui·al [kə-LOH-kwee-əl] *adj* pert. to or used in informal conversation. **col·lo'qui·al·ism** *n*

col·lo·quy [KOL-ə-kwee] *n, pl* **-quies.** conversation; dialogue.

col·lu·sion [kə-LOO-zhən] *n* secret agreement for a fraudulent purpose, esp. in legal proceedings. **col·lu'sive** [-siv] *adj*

co·logne [kə-LOHN] *n* perfumed liquid.

co·lon¹ [KOH-lən] *n* mark (:) indicating break in a sentence.

colon² *n* part of large intestine from cecum to rectum.

colo·nel [KUR-nl] *n* commander of regiment or battalion.

col·on·nade [kol-ə-NAYD] *n* row of columns.

col·o·ny [KOL-ə-nee] *n, pl* **-nies.** body of people who settle in new country but remain subject to parent country; country so settled; distinctive group living together. **co·lo·ni·al** [kə-LOH-nee-əl] *adj* of colony. **col'o·nist** *n* **col·o·ni·za'tion** *n* **col'o·nize** *vt* **-nized, -niz·ing.**

col·or [KUL-ər] *n* hue, tint; complexion; paint; pigment; *fig* semblance, pretext; timbre, quality; mood. ▸ *pl* flag; distinguishing symbol. ▸ *vt* stain, dye, paint, give color to; disguise; influence or distort. ▸ *vi* become colored; blush. **col·or·a'tion** *n* **col'or·ful** *adj* with bright or varied colors; distinctive.

co·los·sus [kə-LOS-əs] *n, pl* **-los·si** [-LOS-ī] huge statue; something, somebody very large. **co·los'sal** *adj* huge, gigantic.

colt [kohlt] *n* young male horse.

col·umn [KOL-əm] *n* long vertical cylinder, pillar; support; division of page; body of troops. **co·lum·nar** [kə-LUM-nər] *adj* **col'um·nist** *n* journalist writing regular feature for newspaper.

com-, con- *prefix* together, jointly, e.g. *commingle.*

co·ma [KOH-mə] *n* state of unconsciousness. **co'ma·tose** [-tohs] *adj*

comb [kohm] *n* toothed instrument for tidying, arranging, ornamenting hair; rooster's crest; mass of honey cells. ▸ *vt* use comb on; search with great care.

com·bat [KOM-bat] *n* fight or struggle. ▸ *vt* [kəm-BAT] fight, contest. **com·bat·ant** [kəm-BAT-nt] *n* **com·bat'ive** *adj*

com·bine [kəm-BĪN] *v* join together; ally. ▸ *n* [KOM-bīn] trust, syndicate, esp. of businesses, trade organizations, etc. **com·bi·na·tion** [kom-bə-NAY-shən] *n* **com'bine** machine to harvest and thresh grain in one operation.

com·bus·tion [kəm-BUS-chən] *n* process of burning. **com·bus'ti·ble** *adj*

come [kum] *vi* **came, come, com·ing.** approach, arrive, move toward; reach; happen to; occur; be available; originate (from); become; turn out to be. **come'back** *n inf* return to active life after retirement; retort. **come'down** *n* setback; descent in social status.

com·e·dy [KOM-i-dee] *n, pl* **-dies.** dramatic or other work of light, amusing character; humor. **co·me·di·an** [kə-MEE-dee-ən] *n* entertainer who tells jokes, etc.; actor in comedy.

come·ly [KUM-lee] *adj* fair, pretty, good-looking. **come'li·ness** *n*

co·mes·ti·bles [kə-MES-tə-bəlz] *n* food.

com·et [KOM-it] *n* luminous heavenly body consisting of diffuse head, nucleus and long tail.

com·fort [KUM-fərt] *n* well-being; ease; consolation; means of consolation or satisfaction. ▸ *vt* soothe; cheer, gladden, console. **com·fort·a·ble** [KUMF-tə-bəl] *adj* free from pain, etc.; *inf* financially secure. **com'fort·a·bly** *adv*

com′fort·er n one who comforts; woolen scarf; quilt.

com·ic [KOM-ik] adj relating to comedy; funny, laughable. ▶ n comedian; magazine consisting of strip cartoons. **com′i·cal** adj

com·ma [KOM-ə] n punctuation mark (,) separating parts of sentence.

com·mand [kə-MAND] vt order; rule; compel; have in one's power; overlook, dominate. ▶ vi exercise rule. ▶ n order; power of controlling, ruling, dominating, overlooking; knowledge, mastery; post of one commanding; district commanded, jurisdiction. **com′man·dant** [KOM-ən-dant] n **com·man·deer′** vt seize for military use, appropriate. **com·mand′er** n **com·mand′ing** adj in command; with air of authority. **com·mand′ment** n

com·man·do [kə-MAN-doh] n, pl **-dos.** (member of) special military unit trained for airborne, amphibious attack.

com·mem·o·rate [kə-MEM-ə-rayt] vt **-rat·ed, -rat·ing.** celebrate, keep in memory by ceremony; be a memorial of. **com·mem·o·ra′tion** n **com·mem′o·ra·tive** adj

com·mence [kə-MENS] v **-menced, -menc·ing.** begin. **com·mence′ment** n beginning; graduation of students.

com·mend [kə-MEND] vt praise; commit, entrust. **com·mend′a·ble** adj **com·men·da′tion** n

com·men·su·rate [kə-MEN-sər-it] adj equal in size or length of time; in proportion, adequate.

com·ment [KOM-ent] n remark, criticism; gossip; note, explanation. ▶ vi remark, note; annotate, criticize. **com′men·tar·y** n, pl **-tar·ies.** explanatory notes or comments; spoken accompaniment to film, etc. **com′men·ta·tor** n author, speaker of commentary.

com·merce [KOM-ərs] n buying and selling; dealings; trade.

com·mer·cial [kə-MUR-shəl] adj of, concerning, business, trade, profit, etc. ▶ n advertisement on radio or TV.

com·mis·er·ate [kə-MIZ-ə-rayt] vt **-at·ed, -at·ing.** pity, condole, sympathize with.

com·mis·sion [kə-MISH-ən] n something entrusted to be done; delegated authority; body entrusted with some special duty; payment by percentage for doing something; warrant, esp. presidential warrant, giving authority; document appointing person to officer's rank; doing, committing. ▶ vt charge with duty or task; Military confer a rank; give order for. **com·mis′sion·er** n one empowered to act by commission or warrant; member of commission or government board; administrative head of professional sport.

com·mit [kə-MIT] vt **-mit·ted, -mit·ting.** entrust, give in charge; perpetrate, be guilty of; pledge, promise; compromise, entangle; place in prison or mental institution. **com·mit′ment** n

com·mit·tee [kə-MIT-ee] n body appointed, elected for special business usu. from larger body.

com·mode [kə-MOHD] n chest of drawers; toilet.

com·mo·di·ous [kə-MOH-dee-əs] adj roomy.

com·mod·i·ty [kə-MOD-i-tee] n, pl **-ties.** article of trade; anything useful.

com·mon [KOM-ən] adj shared by or belonging to all, or to several; public, general; ordinary, usual, frequent; inferior; vulgar. ▶ n land belonging to community. ▶ pl ordinary people; (**C-**) lower house of British parliament. **com′mon·ly** adv **Common Market** former name for EUROPEAN UNION.

com′mon·place adj ordinary, everyday. ▶ n trite remark; anything occurring frequently. **common sense** sound, practical understanding. **com′mon·wealth** n republic; state of the US;

federation of self-governing countries.

com·mo·tion [kə-MOH-shən] *n* stir, disturbance, tumult.

com·mune[1] [kə-MYOON] *vi* **-muned, -mun·ing.** converse together intimately. **com·mun'ion** *n* sharing of thoughts, feelings, etc.; fellowship; body with common faith; (**C-**) participation in sacrament of the Lord's Supper; (**C-**) that sacrament, Eucharist.

com·mune[2] [KOM-yoon] *n* group of families, individuals living together and sharing property, responsibility, etc. **com·mu·nal** [kə-MYOON-l] *adj* for common use.

com·mu·ni·cate [kə-MYOO-ni-kayt] *v* **-cat·ed, -cat·ing.** ▶ *vt* impart, convey; reveal. ▶ *vi* give or exchange information; have connecting passage, door; receive Communion. **com·mu'ni·ca·ble** *adj* **com·mu'ni·cant** *n* one who receives Communion.

com·mu·ni·ca'tion *n* act of giving, esp. information; information, message; (usu pl) passage (road, railway, etc.), or means of exchanging messages (radio, mail, etc.) between places. ▶ *pl* connections between military base and front. **com·mu'ni·ca·tive** *adj* free with information.

com·mu·ni·qué [kə-myoo-ni-KAY] *n* official announcement.

com·mu·nism [KOM-yə-niz-əm] *n* doctrine that all goods, means of production, etc., should be property of community. **com'mu·nist** *n, adj*

com·mu·ni·ty [kə-MYOO-ni-tee] *n, pl* **-ties.** body of people with something in common, e.g. neighborhood, religion, etc.; society, the public; joint ownership; similarity, agreement.

com·mute [kə-MYOOT] *v* **-mut·ed, -mut·ing.** ▶ *vi* travel daily some distance to work. ▶ *vt* exchange; change (punishment, etc.) into something less severe; change (payment, etc.) into another form. ▶ *n* journey made by commuting.

com·mu·ta·tion [kom-yə-TAY-shən] *n* **com'mu·ta·tor** *n* device to change alternating electric current into direct current. **com·mut'er** *n* one who daily travels some distance to work.

com·pact[1] [kəm-PAKT] *adj* neatly arranged or packed; solid, concentrated; terse. ▶ *v* make, become compact; compress. **com·pact'ness** *n* **com·pact disk** [KOM-pakt] small disk on which sound is recorded as series of metallic pits enclosed in polyvinyl chloride and played back by optical scanning by laser.

com·pact[2] [KOM-pakt] *n* small case to hold face powder, powder puff and mirror.

com·pact[3] [KOM-pakt] *n* agreement, covenant, treaty, contract.

com·pan·ion[1] [kəm-PAN-yən] *n* chum, fellow, comrade, associate; person employed to live with another. **com·pan'ion·a·ble** *adj*

companion[2] *n* raised cover over staircase from deck to cabin of ship; deck skylight. **com·pan'ion·way** *n* staircase from deck to cabin.

com·pa·ny [KUM-pə-nee] *n, pl* **-nies.** gathering of persons; companionship, fellowship; guests; business firm; division of regiment under captain; crew of ship; actors in play.

com·pare [kəm-PAIR] *vt* **-pared, -par·ing.** notice or point out likenesses and differences of things; liken; make comparative and superlative of adjective or adverb. ▶ *vi* be like; compete with. **com·pa·ra·bil·i·ty** [kom-pər-ə-BIL-i-tee] *n* **com'pa·ra·ble** *adj* **com·par'a·tive** *adj* that may be compared; not absolute; relative, partial; *Grammar* denoting form of adjective, adverb, indicating "more". ▶ *n* **com·par'a·tive·ly** *adv* **com·par'i·son** *n* act of comparing.

com·part·ment [kəm-PAHRT-mənt] *n* division or part divided off;

section.

com·pass [KUM-pəs] *n* instrument for showing the north; instrument for drawing circles; circumference, measurement around; space, area; scope, reach. ▶ *vt* surround; comprehend; attain, accomplish.

com·pas·sion [kəm-PASH-ən] *n* pity, sympathy. **com·pas'sion·ate** [-it] *adj*

com·pat·i·ble [kəm-PAT-ə-bəl] *adj* capable of harmonious existence; consistent, agreeing with. **com·pat·i·bil'i·ty** *adv*

com·pa·tri·ot [kəm-PAY-tree-ət] *n* fellow countryman. ▶ *adj*

com·pel [kəm-PEL] *vt* **-pelled, -pel·ling.** force, oblige; bring about by force.

com·pen·di·um [kəm-PEN-dee-əm] *n, pl* **-di·ums.** abridgment, summary. **com·pen'di·ous** *adj* brief but inclusive.

com·pen·sate [KOM-pən-sayt] *vt* **-sat·ed, -sat·ing.** make up for; recompense suitably; reward. **com·pen·sa'tion** *n*

com·pete [kəm-PEET] *vi* **-pet·ed, -pet·ing.** (oft. with *with*) strive in rivalry, contend for, vie with. **com·pe·ti·tion** [kom-pi-TISH-ən] *n* **com·pet'i·tive** [kəm-] *adj* **com·pet'i·tor** *n*

com·pe·tent [KOM-pi-tənt] *adj* able, skillful; properly qualified; proper, due, legitimate; suitable, sufficient. **com'pe·tence** *n* efficiency.

com·pile [kəm-PĪL] *vt* **-piled, -pil·ing.** make up (e.g. book) from various sources or materials; gather, put together. **com·pi·la·tion** [kom-pə-LAY-shən] *n* **com·pil'er** *n*

com·pla·cent [kəm-PLAY-sənt] *adj* self-satisfied; pleased or gratified. **com·pla'cen·cy** *n*

com·plain [kəm-PLAYN] *vi* grumble; bring charge, make known a grievance; (with *of*) make known that one is suffering from. **com·plaint'** *n* statement of a wrong, grievance; ailment, illness. **com·plain'ant** *n*

com·ple·ment [KOM-plə-mənt] *n* something making up a whole; full allowance, equipment, etc. ▶ *vt* add to, make complete. **com·ple·men'ta·ry** *adj*

com·plete [kəm-PLEET] *adj* full, perfect; finished, ended; entire; thorough. ▶ *vt* **-plet·ed, -plet·ing.** make whole, perfect; finish. **com·plete'ly** *adv* **com·ple'tion** *n*

com·plex [kəm-PLEKS] *adj* intricate, compound, involved. ▶ *n* [KOM-pleks] complicated whole; group of related buildings; psychological abnormality, obsession. **com·plex'i·ty** *n*

com·plex·ion [kəm-PLEK-shən] *n* look, color, of skin, esp. of face; appearance; aspect, character; disposition.

compliant see COMPLY.

com·pli·cate [KOM-pli-kayt] *vt* **-cat·ed, -cat·ing.** make intricate, involved, difficult; mix up. **com·pli·ca'tion** *n*

com·plic·i·ty [kəm-PLIS-i-tee] *n, pl* **-ties.** partnership in wrongdoing.

com·pli·ment [KOM-plə-mənt] *n* expression of regard, praise; flattering speech. ▶ *pl* expression of courtesy, formal greetings. ▶ *vt* praise, congratulate. **com·pli·men'ta·ry** *adj* expressing praise; free of charge.

com·ply [kəm-PLĪ] *vi* **-plied, -ply·ing.** consent, yield, do as asked. **com·pli'ance** *n* **com·pli'ant** *adj*

com·po·nent [kəm-POH-nənt] *n* part, element, constituent of whole. ▶ *adj* composing, making up.

com·port [kəm-PORT] *v* agree; behave.

com·pose [kəm-POHZ] *vt* **-posed, -pos·ing.** arrange, put in order; write, invent; make up; calm; settle, adjust. **com·posed'** *adj* calm. **com·pos'er** *n* one who composes, esp. music. **com·po·site** [kəm-POZ-it] *adj* made up of distinct parts. **com·po·si·tion** [kom-pə-ZISH-ən] *n* **com·pos·i·tor** [kəm-POZ-i-tər] *n* typesetter, one who arranges type for printing. **com·po·sure** [kəm-POH-zhər] n calmness.

com·pos men·tis [KOM-pəs MEN-tis] Lat of sound mind.

com·post [KOM-pohst] n fertilizing mixture of decayed vegetable matter for soil.

com·pote [KOM-poht] n fruit stewed or preserved in syrup.

com·pound¹ [KOM-pownd] n mixture, joining; substance, word, made up of parts. ▶ adj not simple; composite, mixed. ▶ vt [kəm-POWND] mix, make up, put together; intensify, make worse; compromise, settle debt by partial payment.

com·pound² [KOM-pownd] n (fenced or walled) enclosure containing houses, etc.

com·pre·hend [kom-pri-HEND] vt understand, take in; include, comprise. **com·pre·hen·si·ble** adj **com·pre·hen·sion** n **com·pre·hen·sive** adj wide, full; taking in much.

com·press [kəm-PRES] vt squeeze together; make smaller in size, bulk. ▶ n [KOM-pres] pad of cloth applied to wound, inflamed part, etc. **com·press·i·ble** adj **com·pres·sion** [kəm-PRESH-ən] n in internal combustion engine, squeezing of explosive charge before ignition, to give additional force. **com·pres·sor** n esp. machine to compress air, gas.

com·prise [kəm-PRIZ] vt -prised, -pris·ing. include, contain.

com·pro·mise [KOM-prə-mīz] n meeting halfway, coming to terms by giving up part of claim; middle course. ▶ v -mised, -mis·ing. settle (dispute) by making concessions. ▶ vt expose to risk or suspicion.

comp·trol·ler [kən-TROH-lər] n controller (in some titles).

com·pul·sion [kəm-PUL-shən] n act of compelling; irresistible impulse. **com·pul·sive** adj **com·pul·so·ri·ly** [-sə-rə-lee] adv **com·pul·so·ry** adj not optional.

com·punc·tion [kəm-PUNGK-shən] n regret for wrongdoing.

com·pute [kəm-PYOOT] vt -put·ed, -put·ing. reckon, calculate, esp. using computer. **com·pu·ta·tion** [kom-pyə-TAY-shən] n reckoning, estimate. **com·put·er** n electronic device for storing, retrieving information and performing calculations. **com·put·er·ize** v -ized, -iz·ing. equip with, perform by computer.

com·rade [KOM-rad] n chum, companion, friend. **com·rade·ship** n **com·rade·ly** adj

con¹ [kon] v inf conned, con·ning. swindle, defraud; cajole.

con² vt conned, con·ning. direct steering (of ship).

con- prefix see COM-.

con·cat·e·nate [kon-KAT-n-ayt] vt -nat·ed, -nat·ing. link together. **con·cat·e·na·tion** n connected chain (as of circumstances).

con·cave [kon-KAYV] adj hollow, rounded inward. **con·cav·i·ty** n

con·ceal [kən-SEEL] vt hide, keep secret.

con·cede [kən-SEED] vt -ced·ed, -ced·ing. admit, admit truth of; grant, allow, yield.

con·ceit [kən-SEET] n vanity, overweening opinion of oneself; far-fetched comparison. **con·ceit·ed** adj

con·ceive [kən-SEEV] v -ceived, -ceiv·ing. think of, imagine; believe; form in the mind; become pregnant. **con·ceiv·a·ble** adj

con·cen·trate [KON-sən-trayt] v -trat·ed, -trat·ing. ▶ vt focus (one's efforts, etc.); increase in strength; reduce to small space. ▶ vi devote all attention; come together. ▶ n concentrated material or solution. **con·cen·tra·tion** n **concentration camp** prison camp, esp. one in Nazi Germany.

con·cen·tric [kən-SEN-trik] adj having the same center.

con·cept [KON-sept] n abstract idea; mental expression. **con·cep·tu·al** [kən-SEP-choo-əl] adj **con·cep·tion** [kən-SEP-shən] n idea, notion; act of conceiving.

con·cern [kən-SURN] *vt* relate, apply to; interest, affect, trouble; (with *in* or *with*) involve (oneself). ▶ *n* affair; regard; worry; importance; business, enterprise. **con·cerned'** *adj* connected with; interested; worried; involved. **con·cern'ing** *prep* respecting, about.

con·cert [KON-surt] *n* musical entertainment; harmony, agreement. ▶ *vt* [kən-SURT] arrange, plan together. **con·cert'ed** *adj* mutually arranged, planned; determined. **con·cer·ti·na** [kon-sər-TEE-nə] *n* musical instrument with bellows and keys. **con·cer·to** [kən-CHER-toh] *n*, *pl* **-tos**. musical composition for solo instrument and orchestra.

con·ces·sion [kən-SESH-ən] *n* act of conceding; thing conceded; grant; special privilege.

conch [kongk] *n* seashell. **con·chol·o·gy** [kong-KOL-ə-jee] *n* study, collection of shells and shellfish.

con·cierge [kon-see-AIRZH] *n* in France esp., caretaker, doorkeeper.

con·cil·i·ate [kən-SIL-ee-ayt] *vt* **-at·ed, -at·ing.** pacify, win over from hostility. **con·cil'i·a·tor** *n* **con·cil'i·a·to·ry** *adj*

con·cise [kən-SĪS] *adj* brief, terse. **con·cise'ly** *adv* **con·cise'ness** *n*

con·clave [KON-klayv] *n* private meeting; assembly for election of a pope.

con·clude [kən-KLOOD] *v* **-clud·ed, -clud·ing.** ▶ *vt* end, finish; deduce; settle. ▶ *vi* come to end; decide. **con·clu·sion** [-KLOO-*zh*ən] *n* **con·clu'sive** *adj* decisive, convincing.

con·coct [kən-KOKT] *vt* make mixture, prepare with various ingredients; make up; contrive, plan. **con·coc'tion** *n*

con·com·i·tant [kon-KOM-i-tənt] *adj* accompanying.

con·cord [KON-kord] *n* agreement; harmony. ▶ *vi* [kən-KORD] agree. **con·cord'ance** [-əns] *n* agreement;

index to words of book (esp. Bible).

con·course [KON-kors] *n* crowd; large, open place in public area; boulevard.

con·crete [KON-kreet] *n* mixture of sand, cement, etc., used in building. ▶ *adj* made of concrete; particular, specific; perceptible, actual; solid. **con·crete'ly** *adv*

con·cu·bine [KONG-kyə-bīn] *n* woman living with man as his wife, but not married to him; mistress. **con·cu·bi·nage** [kon-KYOO-bə-nij] *n*

con·cu·pis·cence [kon-KYOO-pi-səns] *n* lust.

con·cur [kən-KUR] *vi* **-curred, -cur·ring.** agree, express agreement; happen together; coincide. **con·cur'rence** *n* **con·cur'rent** *adj* **con·cur'rent·ly** *adv* at the same time.

con·cus·sion [kən-KUSH-ən] *n* brain injury; physical shock.

con·demn [kən-DEM] *vt* blame; find guilty; doom; find, declare unfit for use. **con·dem·na·tion** [kon-dem-NAY-shən] *n* **con·dem'na·to·ry** *adj*

con·dense [kən-DENS] *v* **-densed, -dens·ing.** ▶ *vt* concentrate, make more solid; turn from gas into liquid; pack into few words. ▶ *vi* turn from gas to liquid. **con·den·sa·tion** [kon-den-SAY-shən] *n* **con·dens'er** *n Electricity* apparatus for storing electrical energy, a capacitor; apparatus for reducing gas to liquid form; a lens or mirror for focusing light.

con·de·scend [kon-də-SEND] *vi* treat graciously one regarded as inferior; do something below one's dignity. **con·de·scend'ing** *adj* **con·de·scen'sion** *n*

con·di·ment [KON-də-mənt] *n* sauce, seasoning for food.

con·di·tion [kən-DISH-ən] *n* state or circumstances of anything; thing on which statement or happening or existing depends; stipulation, prerequisite; health, physical fitness; rank. ▶ *vt* accustom;

regulate; make fit, healthy; be essential to happening or existence of; stipulate. **con·di′tion·al** *adj* dependent on circumstances or events. ▶ *n Grammar* form of verbs.

con·do [KON-doh] *n, pl* **-dos.** condominium (building).

con·dole [kən-DOHL] *vi* **-doled, -dol·ing.** grieve with; offer sympathy; commiserate with. **con·do′lence** *n*

con·dom [KON-dəm] *n* sheathlike usu. rubber contraceptive device worn by man.

con·do·min·i·um [kon-də-MIN-ee-əm] *n* joint rule by two or more countries; building with apartments, offices, etc.; individually owned.

con·done [kən-DOHN] *vt* **-doned, don·ing.** overlook, forgive, treat as not existing.

con·duce [kən-DOOS] *vi* **-duced, -duc·ing.** help, promote; tend toward. **con·du′cive** *adj*

con·duct [KON-dukt] *n* behavior; management. ▶ *vt* [kən-DUKT] escort, guide; lead, direct; manage; transmit (heat, electricity). **con·duc′tion** *n* **con·duc′tive** *adj* **con·duc·tiv′i·ty** *n* **con·duc′tor** *n* employee on bus, train, etc. who collects fares; director of orchestra; one who leads, guides; substance capable of transmitting heat, electricity, etc.

con·du·it [KON-doo-it] *n* channel or pipe for conveying water, electric cables, etc.

cone [kohn] *n* solid figure with circular base, tapering to a point; fruit of pine, fir, etc. **con·ic** [KON-ik], **con′i·cal** *adj*

con·fab·u·late [kən-FAB-yə-layt] *vi* **-lat·ed, -lat·ing.** chat. **con·fab** [KON-fab] *n inf* shortened form of confabulation. **con·fab·u·la′tion** *n* confidential conversation.

con·fec·tion [kən-FEK-shən] *n* prepared delicacy, esp. something sweet; candy. **con·fec′tion·er** *n* dealer in candies, fancy cakes, etc. **con·fec′tion·er·y** *n* confectioner's shop; things confectioner sells.

con·fed·er·ate [kən-FED-ər-it] *n* ally; accomplice. ▶ *v* [-ə-rayt] **-at·ed, -at·ing.** unite. **con·fed′er·a·cy** *n* **con·fed·er·a′tion** *n* alliance of political units.

con·fer [kən-FUR] *v* **-ferred, -fer·ring.** ▶ *vt* grant, give; bestow; award. ▶ *vi* talk with, take advice. **con·fer·ence** [KON-fər-əns] *n* meeting for consultation or deliberation.

con·fess [kən-FES] *vt* admit, own; (of priest) hear sins of. ▶ *vi* acknowledge; declare one's sins orally to priest. **con·fes′sion** [-FESH-ən] *n* **con·fes′sion·al** *n* confessor's stall. **con·fes′sor** *n* priest who hears confessions.

con·fet·ti [kən-FET-ee] *n* small bits of colored paper for throwing at weddings.

con·fide [kən-FĪD] *v* **-fid·ed, -fid·ing.** ▶ *vi* (with *in*) tell secrets, trust. ▶ *vt* entrust. **con·fi·dant** [KON-fi-dant] *n* (*fem* **con·fi·dante**) one entrusted with secrets. **con′fi·dence** *n* trust; boldness, assurance; intimacy; something confided, secret. **con′fi·dent** *adj* **con·fi·den′tial** [-shəl] *adj* private; secret; entrusted with another's confidences. **con′fi·dent·ly** *adv* **confidence game** con game, swindle in which victim entrusts money, etc. to thief, believed honest.

con·fig·u·ra·tion [kən-fig-yə-RAY-shən] *n* shape, aspect, conformation, arrangement.

con·fine [kən-FĪN] *vt* **-fined, fin·ing.** keep within bounds; keep in house, bed, etc.; shut up, imprison. **con·fines** [KON-finz] *pl n* boundaries, limits. **confine′ment** *n* esp. childbirth; imprisonment.

con·firm [kən-FURM] *vt* make sure, verify; strengthen, settle; make valid, ratify; administer confirmation to. **con·fir·ma·tion** [kon-fər-MAY-shən] *n* making strong, certain; Christian rite administered to confirm vows made at baptism; Jewish ceremony

to admit boys, girls to adult status.
con·firm'a·to·ry *adj* tending to
confirm or establish; corroborative.
con·firmed' *adj* (of habit, etc.)
long-established.
con·fis·cate [KON-fə-skayt] *vt*
-cat·ed, -cat·ing. seize by
authority. **con·fis·ca'tion** *n*
con·fis·ca·to·ry [kən-FIS-kə-tor-ee]
adj
con·fla·gra·tion
[kon-flə-GRAY-shən] *n* great
destructive fire.
con·flict [KON-flikt] *n* struggle, trial
of strength; disagreement. ▶ *vi*
[kən-FLIKT] be at odds with, be
inconsistent with; clash.
con·flu·ence [KON-floo-əns] *n*
union of streams; meeting place.
con'flu·ent *adj*
con·form [kən-FORM] *v* comply
with accepted standards,
conventions, etc.; adapt to rule,
pattern, custom, etc.
con·for·ma·tion
[kon-for-MAY-shən] *n* structure,
adaptation. **con·form'ist** *n* one
who conforms, esp. excessively.
con·form'i·ty *n* compliance.
con·found [kon-FOWND] *vt* baffle,
perplex; confuse; defeat.
con·found'ed *adj old-fashioned*
damned.
con·front [kən-FRUNT] *vt* face;
bring face to face with.
con·fron·ta·tion
[kon-frən-TAY-shən] *n*
con·fuse [kən-FYOOZ] *vt* **-fused,
-fus·ing.** bewilder; jumble; make
unclear; mistake (one thing) for
another; disconcert. **con·fu'sion** *n*
con·geal [kən-JEEL] *v* solidify by
cooling or freezing.
con·gen·ial [kən-JEEN-yəl] *adj*
pleasant, to one's liking; of similar
disposition, tastes, etc.
con·ge·ni·al'i·ty *n*
con·gen·i·tal [kən-JEN-i-tl] *adj*
existing at birth; dating from birth.
con·ge·ries [KON-jə-reez] *n, sing
and pl* collection or mass of small
bodies, conglomeration.
con·gest [kən-JEST] *v* overcrowd or
clog. **con·ges'tion** *n* abnormal

accumulation, overcrowding.
con·gest'ed *adj*
con·glom·er·ate [kən-GLOM-ər-it]
n thing, substance (esp. rock)
composed of mixture of other,
smaller elements or pieces;
business organization comprising
many companies. ▶ *v* [-ə-rayt]
-at·ed, -at·ing. gather together.
▶ *adj* **con·glom·er·a'tion** *n*
con·grat·u·late
[kən-GRACH-ə-layt] *vt* **-lat·ed,
-lat·ing.** express pleasure at good
fortune, success, etc.
con·grat·u·la'tion *n*
con·grat'u·la·to·ry *adj*
con·gre·gate [KONG-gri-gayt] *v*
-gat·ed, -gat·ing. assemble;
collect, flock together.
con·gre·ga'tion *n* assembly, esp.
for worship. **con·gre·ga'tion·al** *adj*
con·gre·ga'tion·al·ism *n* form of
Protestant church organization in
which local churches are
self-governing.
con·gress [KONG-gris] *n* meeting;
sexual intercourse; formal assembly
for discussion; legislative body.
con·gres·sion·al [kən-GRESH-ə-nl]
adj **con'gress·man** *n* member of
US House of Representatives.
con·gru·ent [KONG-groo-ənt] *adj*
suitable, accordant; fitting
together, esp. triangles.
con'gru·ence *n* **con·gru'i·ty** *n*
con'gru·ous *adj*
conic see CONE.
con·i·fer [KON-ə-fər] *n*
cone-bearing tree, as fir, pine, etc.
co·nif'er·ous [koh-NIF-ər-əs] *adj*
con·jec·ture [kən-JEK-chər] *n*
guess, guesswork. ▶ *v* **-tured,
-tur·ing.** guess, surmise.
con·jec'tur·al *adj*
con·join·ed twins [kən-JOIND
twinz] *pl n* the technical name for
SIAMESE TWINS.
con·ju·gal [KON-jə-gəl] *adj* relating
to marriage; between married
persons. **con·ju·gal'i·ty** *n*
con·ju·gate [KON-jə-gayt] *v*
-gat·ed, -gat·ing. inflect verb in its
various forms (past, present, etc.).
con·ju·ga'tion *n*

con·junc·tion [kən-JUNGK-shən] *n* union; simultaneous happening; part of speech joining words, phrases, etc. **con·junc'tive** *adj*

con·junc·ti·va [kon-jungk-TĪ-və] *n* mucous membrane lining eyelid. **con·junc·ti·vi·tis** [kən-jungk-tə-VĪ-tis] *n* inflammation of this.

con·jure [KON-jər] *v* **-jured, -jur·ing.** produce magic effects; perform tricks by sleight of hand, etc.; invoke devils; [kən-JUUR] implore earnestly. **con·jur·a·tion** [kon-jə-RAY-shən] *n* **con'jur·er** *n*

conk [kongk] *vt inf* strike (esp. on head). **conk out** *vi inf* break down, stall; faint; fall asleep.

con·nect [kə-NEKT] *v* join together, unite; associate in the mind. **con·nec'tion** *n* association; train, etc. timed to enable passengers to transfer from another; family relation; social, commercial, etc. relationship. **con·nec'tive** *adj* **connecting rod** part of engine that transfers motion from piston to crankshaft.

con·ning tower [KON-ing] raised observation tower containing the periscope on a submarine.

con·nive [kə-NĪV] *vi* **-nived, -niv·ing.** plot, conspire; assent, refrain from preventing or forbidding. **con·niv'ance** *n*

con·nois·seur [kon-ə-SUR] *n* critical expert in matters of taste, esp. fine arts; competent judge.

con·note [kə-NOHT] *vt* **-not·ed, -not·ing.** imply, mean in addition to primary meaning. **con·no·ta·tion** [kon-ə-TAY-shən] *n*

con·nu·bi·al [kə-NOO-bee-əl] *adj* of marriage.

con·quer [KONG-kər] *vt* win by force of arms, overcome; defeat. ▶ *vi* be victorious. **con'quer·or** *n* **con'quest** [KON-kwest] *n*

con·san·guin·i·ty [kon-sang-GWIN-i-tee] *n* kinship. **con·san·guin'e·ous** *adj*

con·science [KON-shəns] *n* sense of right or wrong governing person's words and actions.

con·sci·en·tious [-shee-EN-shəs] *adj* scrupulous; obedient to the dictates of conscience. **con·sci·en'tious·ly** *adv* **conscientious objector** one who refuses military service on moral or religious grounds.

con·scious [KON-shəs] *adj* aware; awake to one's surroundings and identity; deliberate, intentional. **con'scious·ly** *adv* **con'scious·ness** *n* being conscious.

con·script [KON-skript] *n* one compulsorily enlisted for military service. ▶ *vt* [kən-SKRIPT] enrol (someone) for compulsory military service. **con·scrip'tion** *n*

con·se·crate [KON-si-krayt] *vt* **-crat·ed, -crat·ing.** make sacred. **con·se·cra'tion** *n*

con·sec·u·tive [kən-SEK-yə-tiv] *adj* in unbroken succession.

con·sen·sus [kən-SEN-səs] *n* widespread agreement, unanimity.

con·sent [kən-SENT] *vi* agree to, comply. ▶ *n* acquiescence; permission; agreement.

con·se·quence [KON-si-kwens] *n* result, effect, outcome; that which naturally follows; significance, importance. **con'se·quent** *adj* **con·se·quen'tial** *adj* important. **con'se·quent·ly** *adv* therefore, as a result.

con·serv·a·to·ry [kən-SUR-və-tor-ee] *n, pl* **-ries.** school for teaching music or painting, etc.; greenhouse.

con·serve [kən-SURV] *vt* **-served, -serv·ing.** keep from change or decay; preserve; maintain. ▶ *n* [KON-surv] jam, preserved fruit, etc. **con·ser·va·tion** [kon-sər-VAY-shən] *n* protection, careful management of natural resources and environment. **con·ser·va'tion·ist** *n, adj* **con·serv·a'tive** *adj* tending or wishing to conserve; moderate. ▶ *n Politics* one who desires to preserve institutions of country against change and innovation; one opposed to hasty changes or innovations. **con·serv'a·tism** *n*

con·sid·er [kən-SID-ər] *vt* think
over; examine; make allowance for;
be of opinion that; discuss.
con·sid′er·a·ble *adj* important;
somewhat large. **con·sid′er·ate**
[-it] *adj* thoughtful for others'
feelings, careful. **con·sid′er·ate·ly**
adv **con·sid·er·a′tion** *n*
deliberation; point of importance;
thoughtfulness; bribe, recompense.
con·sign [kən-SĪN] *vt* commit, hand
over; entrust to carrier.
con·sign·ee [kon-sī-NEE],
con·sign′or *n* **con·sign′ment** *n*
goods consigned.
con·sist [kən-SIST] *vi* be composed
of; (with *in*) have as basis; agree
with, be compatible.
con·sist′en·cy *n* agreement;
harmony; degree of firmness.
con·sist′ent *adj* unchanging,
constant; agreeing (with).
con·sis·to·ry [kən-SIS-tə-ree] *n, pl*
-ries. ecclesiastical court or council,
esp. of pope and cardinals.
con·sole¹ [kən-SOHL] *vt* **-soled,**
-sol·ing. comfort, cheer in distress.
con·so·la·tion [kon-sə-LAY-shən] *n*
con·sole² [KON-sohl] *n* bracket
supporting shelf; keyboard, stops,
etc., of organ; cabinet for TV,
radio, etc.
con·sol·i·date [kən-SOL-i-dayt] *vt*
-dat·ed, -dat·ing. combine into
connected whole; make firm,
secure. **con·sol·i·da′tion** *n*
con·som·mé [kon-sə-MAY] *n* clear
meat soup.
con·so·nant [KON-sə-nənt] *n*
sound making a syllable only with
vowel; non-vowel. ▶ *adj* agreeing
with, in accord. **con′so·nance** *n*
con·sort [kən-SORT] *vi* associate,
keep company with. ▶ *n* [KON-sort]
husband, wife, esp. of ruler; ship
sailing with another. **con·sor′ti·um**
[-SOR-shee-əm] *n, pl* **-ti·a** [-shee-ə]
▶ *n* association of banks,
companies, etc.
con·spic·u·ous [kən-SPIK-yoo-əs]
adj striking, noticeable,
outstanding; prominent; eminent.
con·spire [kən-SPĪR] *vi* **-spired,**
-spir·ing. combine for evil purpose;

plot, devise. **con·spir′a·cy**
[-SPIR-ə-see] *n, pl* **-cies.**
con·spir′a·tor *n* **con·spir·a·to′ri·al**
adj
con·stant [KON-stənt] *adj* fixed,
unchanging; steadfast; always duly
happening or continuing. ▶ *n*
quantity that does not vary.
con′stan·cy *n* steadfastness; loyalty.
con·stel·la·tion [kon-stə-LAY-shən]
n group of stars.
con·ster·na·tion
[kon-stər-NAY-shən] *n* alarm,
dismay, panic. **con′ster·nate** *v*
-nat·ed, -nat·ing.
con·sti·pa·tion [kon-stə-PAY-shən]
n difficulty in emptying bowels.
con′sti·pate *vt* **-pat·ed, -pat·ing.**
affect with this disorder.
con·stit·u·ent [kən-STICH-oo-ənt]
adj going toward making up
whole; having power to make, alter
constitution of a government. ▶ *n*
component part; element; voter.
con·stit′u·en·cy *n* body of
constituents, supporters.
con·sti·tute [KON-sti-toot] *vt*
-tut·ed, -tut·ing. compose, set up,
establish, form; make into, found,
give form to. **con·sti·tu′tion** *n*
structure, composition; health;
character, disposition; principles on
which country, state is governed.
con·sti·tu′tion·al *adj* pert. to
constitution; in harmony with
political constitution. ▶ *n* walk
taken for health's sake.
con·strain [kən-STRAYN] *vt* force,
compel. **con·straint′** *n*
compulsion; restraint;
embarrassment, tension.
con·stric·tion [kən-STRIK-shən] *n*
compression, squeezing together.
con·strict′ *vt* **con·stric′tive** *adj*
con·stric′tor *n* that which
constricts; see also BOA.
con·struct [kən-STRUKT] *vt* make,
build, form; put together;
compose. **con·struct** [KON-strukt]
n **con·struc′tion** *n* **con·struc′tive**
adj serving to improve; positive.
con·strue [kən-STROO] *vt* **-strued,**
-stru·ing. interpret; deduce;
analyze grammatically.

con·sul [KON-səl] *n* official appointed by a government to represent it in a foreign country; in ancient Rome, one of the chief magistrates. **con'su·lar** *adj* **con'su·late** [-lit] *n*

con·sult [kən-SULT] *v* seek counsel, advice, information from. **con·sult'ant** *n* specialist, expert. **con·sul·ta·tion** [kon-səl-TAY-shən] *n* consulting; appointment to seek professional advice, esp. of doctor, lawyer. **con·sul·ta·tive** [kən-SUL-tə-tiv] *adj* having privilege of consulting, but not of voting; advisory.

con·sume [kən-SOOM] *vt* **-sumed, -sum·ing.** eat or drink; engross, possess; use up; destroy. **con·sum'er** *n* buyer or user of commodity; one who consumes. **con·sump'tion** [-SUMP-shən] *n* using up; destruction; *old-fashioned* pulmonary tuberculosis. **con·sump'tive** *adj, n*

con·sum·mate [KON-sə-mayt] *vt* **-mat·ed, -mat·ing.** perfect; fulfill; complete (esp. marriage by sexual intercourse). ▸ *adj* [kən-SUM-it] of greatest perfection or completeness. **con·sum'mate·ly** *adv* **con·sum·ma'tion** *n*

con·tact [KON-takt] *n* touching; being in touch; junction of two or more electrical conductors; useful acquaintance. ▸ *vt* **contact lens** lens fitting over eyeball to correct defect of vision.

con·ta·gion [kən-TAY-jən] *n* passing on of disease by touch, contact; contagious disease; harmful physical or moral influence. **con·ta'gious** *adj* communicable by contact, catching.

con·tain [kən-TAYN] *vt* hold; have room for; include, comprise; restrain (oneself). **con·tain'er** *n* box, etc. for holding; large cargo-carrying standard-sized receptacle for various modes of transport.

con·tam·i·nate [kən-TAM-ə-nayt] *vt* **-nat·ed, -nat·ing.** stain, pollute, infect; make radioactive.

con·tam·i·na'tion *n* pollution.

con·tem·plate [KON-təm-playt] *vt* **-plat·ed, -plat·ing.** reflect, meditate on; gaze upon; intend. **con·tem·pla'tion** *n* thoughtful consideration; spiritual meditation. **con·tem·pla·tive** [kən-TEM-plə-tiv] *adj, n*

con·tem·po·rar·y [kən-TEM-pə-rer-ee] *adj* existing or lasting at same time; of same age; modern. ▸ *n, pl* **-rar·ies.** one existing at same time as another. **con·tem·po·ra'ne·ous** [-RAY-nee-əs] *adj*

con·tempt [kən-TEMPT] *n* feeling that something is worthless, despicable, etc.; expression of this feeling; state of being despised, disregarded; willful disrespect of authority.

con·tend [kən-TEND] *vi* strive, fight; dispute. ▸ *vt* maintain (that). **con·ten'tion** *n* strife; debate; subject matter of dispute. **con·ten'tious** *adj* quarrelsome; causing dispute.

con·tent[1] [KON-tent] *n* that contained; holding capacity. ▸ *pl* that contained; index of topics in book.

con·tent[2] [kən-TENT] *adj* satisfied; willing (to). ▸ *vt* satisfy. ▸ *n* satisfaction. **con·tent'ed** *adj*

con·ter·mi·nous [kən-TUR-mə-nəs] *adj* of the same extent (in time, etc.); meeting along a common boundary; meeting end to end. **co·ter'mi·nous** *adj*

con·test [KON-test] *n* competition; conflict. ▸ *vt* [kən-TEST] dispute, debate; fight or compete for. **con·test'a·ble** *adj* **con·test'ant** *n*

con·text [KON-tekst] *n* words coming before, after a word or passage; conditions and circumstances of event, fact, etc. **con·tex·tu·al** [kən-TEKS-choo-əl] *adj*

con·tig·u·ous [kən-TIG-yoo-əs] *adj* touching, near. **con·ti·gu'i·ty** *n*

con·ti·nent[1] [KON-tə-nənt] *n* large continuous mass of land. **con·ti·nen'tal** *adj*

continent² adj able to control one's urination and defecation; sexually chaste. **con'ti·nence** n

con·tin·gent [kən-TIN-jənt] adj depending (on); possible; accidental. ▶ n group (of troops, supporters, etc.); part of or representative of a larger group. **con·tin'gen·cy** n

con·tin·ue [kən-TIN-yoo] v -ued, -u·ing. remain, keep in existence; carry on, last, go on; resume; prolong. **con·tin'u·al** adj **con·tin·u·a'tion** n extension, extra part; resumption; constant succession, prolongation. **con·ti·nu'i·ty** n logical sequence; state of being continuous. **con·tin'u·ous** adj

con·tort [kən-TORT] vt twist out of normal shape. **con·tor'tion** n **con·tor'tion·ist** n one who contorts own body to entertain.

con·tour [KON-tuur] n outline, shape, esp. of mountains, coast, etc.; (also **contour line**) line on map drawn through places of same height.

contra- prefix against or contrasting, e.g. contradistinction; contrapuntal.

con·tra·band [KON-trə-band] n smuggled goods; illegal traffic in such goods. ▶ adj prohibited by law.

con·tra·cep·tion [kon-trə-SEP-shən] n prevention of conception usu. by artificial means, birth control. **con·tra·cep'tive** adj, n

con·tract [kən-TRAKT] v make or become smaller, shorter; enter into agreement; agree upon. ▶ vt incur, become affected by. ▶ n [KON-trakt] bargain, agreement; formal document recording agreement; agreement enforceable by law. **con·tract'ed** adj drawn together. **con·trac·tile** [kən-TRAK-tl] adj tending to contract. **con·trac'tion** n **con'trac·tor** n one making contract, esp. builder. **con·trac·tu·al** [-choo-əl] adj **con·tra·dict** [kon-trə-DIKT] vt deny;

be at variance or inconsistent with. **con·tra·dic'tion** n **con·tra·dic'to·ry** adj

con·tral·to [kən-TRAL-toh] n, pl **-tos.** lowest of female voices.

con·trap·tion [kən-TRAP-shən] n gadget; device; construction, device often overelaborate or eccentric.

con·tra·pun·tal [kon-trə-PUN-tl] adj Mus pert. to counterpoint.

con·trar·y [KON-trer-ee] adj opposed; opposite, other; [kən-TRAIR-ee] perverse, obstinate. ▶ n something the exact opposite of another. ▶ adv in opposition. **con'trar·i·ness** n

con·trast [kən-TRAST] vt bring out differences; set in opposition for comparison. ▶ vi show great difference. ▶ n [KON-trast] striking difference; TV sharpness of image.

con·tra·vene [kon-trə-VEEN] vt -vened, -ven·ing. transgress, infringe; conflict with; contradict. **con·tra·ven'tion** n

con·tre·temps [KON-trə-tahn] n unexpected and embarrassing event or mishap.

con·trib·ute [kən-TRIB-yoot] v -ut·ed, -ut·ing. give, pay to common fund; help to occur; write for the press. **con·tri·bu'tion** [kon-trə-BYOO-shən] n **con·trib'u·tive** adj **con·trib'u·tor** n one who writes articles for newspapers, etc.; one who donates. **con·trib'u·to·ry** adj partly responsible; giving to pension fund, etc.

con·trite [kən-TRĪT] adj remorseful for wrongdoing, penitent. **con·trite'ly** adv **con·tri'tion** [-TRISH-ən] n

con·trive [kən-TRĪV] vt -trived, -triv·ing. manage; devise, invent, design. **con·triv'ance** n artifice or device. **con·trived'** adj obviously planned, artificial.

con·trol [kən-TROHL] vt -trolled, -trol·ling. command, dominate; regulate; direct, check, test. ▶ n power to direct or determine; curb, check; standard of comparison in experiment. ▶ *pl* system of instruments to control automobile, aircraft, etc. **con·trol'la·ble** *adj* **con·trol'ler** *n* one who controls; official controlling expenditure. **control tower** tower in airport from which takeoffs and landings are directed.

con·tro·ver·sy [KON-trə-vur-see] *n*, *pl* **-sies.** dispute, debate, esp. over public issues. **con·tro·ver'sial** *adj* **con'tro·vert** *vt* deny; argue. **con·tro·vert'i·ble** *adj*

con·tu·ma·cy [KON-tuu-mə-see] *n*, *pl* **-cies.** stubborn disobedience. **con·tu·ma'cious** [-MAY-shəs] *adj*

con·tu·me·ly [kon-TUU-mə-lee] *n*, *pl* **-lies.** insulting language or treatment. **con·tu·me'li·ous** [-MEE-lee-əs] *adj* abusive, insolent.

con·tu·sion [kən-TOO-zhən] *n* bruise.

co·nun·drum [kə-NUN-drəm] *n* riddle, esp. with punning answer.

con·ur·ba·tion [kon-ər-BAY-shən] *n* densely populated urban sprawl formed by spreading of towns.

con·va·lesce [kon-və-LES] *vi* **-lesced, -lesc·ing.** recover health after illness, operation, etc. **con·va·les'cence** *n* **con·va·les'cent** *adj, n*

con·vec·tion [kən-VEK-shən] *n* transmission, esp. of heat, by currents in liquids or gases. **con·vec'tor** *n* **con·vec'tive** *adj*

con·vene [kən-VEEN] *vt* **-vened, -ven·ing.** call together, assemble, convoke. **con·ven'tion** *n* assembly; treaty, agreement; rule; practice based on agreement; accepted usage. **con·ven'tion·al** *adj* (slavishly) observing customs of society; customary; (of weapons, war, etc.) not nuclear.

con·ven·ient [kən-VEEN-yənt] *adj* handy; favorable to needs, comfort; well adapted to one's purpose. **con·ven'ience** *n* ease, comfort, suitability. ▶ *adj* (of food) quick to prepare.

con·vent [KON-vent] *n* religious community, esp. of nuns; their building.

con·verge [kən-VURJ] *vi* **-verged, -verg·ing.** approach, tend to meet. **con·ver'gence, -gen·cy** *n* **con·ver'gent** *adj*

con·ver·sant [kən-VUR-sənt] *adj* acquainted, familiar (with), versed in.

conversation see CONVERSE[1].

con·verse[1] [kən-VURS] *vi* **-versed, -vers·ing.** talk (with). **con·ver·sa'tion** *n* **con·ver·sa'tion·al** *adj*

con·verse[2] [KON-vurs] *adj* opposite, turned around, reversed. ▶ *n* the opposite, contrary.

con·vert [kən-VURT] *vt* apply to another purpose; change; transform; cause to adopt (another) religion, opinion; *Football* make a conversion. ▶ *n* [KON-vurt] converted person. **con·ver'sion** [-zhən] *n* change of state; unauthorized appropriation; change of opinion, religion, or party; *Football* extra point scored after a touchdown. **con·vert'er** *n* one who, that which converts; electrical device for changing alternating current into direct current; vessel in which molten metal is refined. **con·vert'i·ble** *n* car with folding roof. ▶ *adj*

con·vex [kon-VEKS] *adj* curved outward; of a rounded form. **con·vex'i·ty** *n*

con·vey [kən-VAY] *vt* carry, transport; impart; communicate; *Law* make over, transfer. **con·vey'ance** *n* carrying; vehicle; act by which title to property is transferred. **con·vey'or belt** continuous moving belt for transporting things, esp. in factory.

con·vict [kən-VIKT] *vt* prove or declare guilty. ▶ *n* [KON-vikt] person found guilty of crime; criminal serving prison sentence. **con·vic'tion** *n* verdict of guilty; being convinced, firm belief, state of being sure.

con·vince [kən-VINS] *vt* **-vinced, -vinc·ing.** firmly persuade, satisfy by evidence or argument. **con·vinc'ing** *adj* capable of

compelling belief, effective.
con·viv·i·al [kən-VIV-ee-əl] *adj*
sociable, festive, jovial.
con·viv·i·al'i·ty *n*
con·voke [kən-VOHK] *vt* **-voked,
-vok·ing.** call together.
con·vo·ca·tion [kon-və-KAY-shən]
n calling together, assembly, esp.
of clergy, college faculty, etc.
con·vo·lute [KON-və-loot] *vt*
-lut·ed, -lut·ing. twist, coil, tangle.
con'vo·lut·ed *adj* **con·vo·lu'tion** *n*
con·voy [KON-voi] *n* party (of
ships, troops, trucks, etc.) traveling
together for protection. ▶ *vt* escort
for protection.
con·vulse [kən-VULS] *vt* **-vulsed,
-vuls·ing.** shake violently; affect
with violent involuntary
contractions of muscles.
con·vul'sion *n* violent upheaval.
▶ *pl* spasms; fits of laughter or
hysteria. **con·vul'sive** *adj*
coo [koo] *n* cry of doves. ▶ *vi* **cooed,
coo·ing.** make such cry.
cook [kuuk] *vt* prepare (food) for
table, esp. by heat; *inf* falsify
(accounts, etc.). ▶ *vi* undergo
cooking; act as cook. ▶ *n* one who
prepares food for table. **cook'er** *n*
cooking apparatus. **cook'ie** *n* small
cake made from sweet dough.
cook'out *n* (party featuring) meal
cooked and served outdoors. **cook
up** *inf* invent, plan; prepare (meal).
cool [kool] *adj* moderately cold;
unexcited, calm; lacking
friendliness or interest; *inf* calmly
insolent; *inf* sophisticated, elegant.
▶ *v* make, become cool. ▶ *n* cool
time, place, etc.; *inf* calmness,
composure. **cool'ant** *n* fluid used
for cooling tool, machinery, etc.
cool'er *n* vessel in which liquids are
cooled; iced drink usu. with wine
or whiskey base; *sl* jail. **cool one's
heels** be kept waiting, esp. because
of deliberate discourtesy.
coon [koon] *n* raccoon.
coop [koop] *n* cage or pen for
pigeons, etc. ▶ *vt* shut up in a coop;
confine.
co-op [KOH-op] *n* cooperative
enterprise; apartment or business

run by one.
coop·er [KOO-pər] *n* one who
makes casks.
co·op·er·ate [koh-OP-ə-rayt] *vi*
-at·ed, -at·ing. work together.
co·op·er·a'tion *n* **co·op'er·a·tive**
adj willing to cooperate; (of an
enterprise) owned collectively and
managed for joint economic
benefit. ▶ *n* cooperative
organization.
co·opt [koh-OPT] *vt* preempt,
appropriate as one's own; elect by
votes of existing members.
co·or·di·nate [koh-OR-dn-ayt] *vt*
-nat·ed, -nat·ing. bring into order
as parts of whole; place in same
rank; put into harmony. ▶ *n* [-it]
Math any of set of numbers
defining location of point. ▶ *adj*
equal in degree, status, etc.
co·or·di·na'tion *n*
coot [koot] *n* small black water
fowl; *inf* silly (old) person.
cop [kop] *vt sl* **copped, cop·ping.**
catch. ▶ *n inf* policeman. **cop a
plea** *sl* plead guilty in return for
light sentence.
cope [kohp] *vi* **coped, cop·ing.** deal
successfully (with).
Co·per·ni·can [koh-PUR-ni-kən] *adj*
pert. to Copernicus, Polish
astronomer (1473–1543), or to his
system.
cop·ing [KOH-ping] *n* top course of
wall, usu. sloping to throw off rain.
co·pi·ous [KOH-pee-əs] *adj*
abundant; plentiful; full, ample.
cop·per[1] [KOP-ər] *n* reddish-brown
malleable ductile metal; bronze
money, coin. ▶ *vt* cover with
copper. **copper beech** tree with
reddish leaves. **cop'per·plate**
[-playt] *n* plate of copper for
engraving, etching; print from this;
copybook writing; first-class
handwriting.
copper[2] *n sl* policeman.
co·pra [KOH-prə] *n* dried coconut
kernels.
copse [kops] *n* a wood of small
trees.
cop·u·la [KOP-yə-lə] *n, pl* **-las.**
word, esp. verb acting as

connecting link in sentence; connection, tie.

cop·u·late [KOP-yə-layt] *vi* **-lat·ed, -lat·ing.** unite sexually. **cop·u·la'tion** *n*

cop·y [KOP-ee] *n, pl* **cop·ies.** imitation; single specimen of book; matter for printing. ▸ *vt* **cop·ied, cop·y·ing.** make copy of; imitate; transcribe; follow an example. **cop'y·right** *n* legal exclusive right to print and publish book, article, work of art, etc. ▸ *vt* protect by copyright. **cop'y·writ·er** *n* one who writes advertisements.

co·quette [koh-KET] *n* woman who flirts. **co·quet·ry** [KOH-ki-tree] *n* **co·quet'tish** *adj*

Cor. Corinthians.

cor·al [KOR-əl] *n* hard substance made by sea polyps and forming growths, islands, reefs; ornament of coral. ▸ *adj* made of coral; of deep pink color.

cord [kord] *n* thin rope or thick string; rib on cloth; ribbed fabric. ▸ *vt* fasten with cord. **cord'age** *n*

cor·date [KOR-dayt] *adj* heart-shaped.

cor·dial [KOR-jəl] *adj* hearty, sincere, warm. ▸ *n* sweet, fruit-flavored alcoholic drink; liqueur. **cor·di·al·i·ty** [kor-jee-AL-i-tee] *n* warmth.

cord·ite [KOR-dīt] *n* explosive compound.

cor·don [KOR-dn] *n* chain of troops or police; fruit tree grown as single stem. ▸ *vt* form cordon around.

cor·don bleu [kor-DAWN BLUU] *adj* (esp. of food preparation) of highest standard.

cor·du·roy [KOR-də-roi] *n* cotton fabric with velvety, ribbed surface.

core [kor] *n* horny seed case of apple and other fruits; central or innermost part of anything. ▸ *vt* **cored, cor·ing.** take out the core.

co·re·spond·ent [koh-ri-SPON-dənt] *n* one cited in divorce case, alleged to have committed adultery with the respondent.

cor·gi [KOR-gee] *n* short-legged

sturdy dog.

co·ri·an·der [KOR-ee-an-dər] *n* plant grown for its aromatic seeds and leaves.

Co·rin·thi·an [kə-RIN-thee-ən] *adj* of Corinth; of Corinthian order of architecture, ornate Greek. ▸ *pl* books in New Testament.

cork [kork] *n* bark of an evergreen Mediterranean oak tree; piece of it or other material, esp. used as stopper for bottle, etc. ▸ *vt* stop up with cork. **cork'age** *n* charge for opening wine bottles in restaurant. **cork'er** *n sl* something, someone outstanding. **cork'screw** *n* tool for pulling out corks.

corn¹ [korn] *n* (kernels of) sweet corn, corn on the cob; *inf* oversentimental, trite quality in play, film, etc. ▸ *vt* preserve (meat) with salt or brine. **corn'y** *adj* **corn·i·er, corn·i·est.** *inf* trite, oversentimental, hackneyed. **corn·cob** *n* ear of sweet corn. **corn'flour** *n* finely ground corn. **corn'flow·er** *n* blue flower, oft. growing in grainfields.

corn² *n* painful horny growth on foot or toe.

cor·ne·a [KOR-nee-ə] *n* transparent membrane covering front of eye.

cor·ner [KOR-nər] *n* part of room where two sides meet; remote or humble place; point where two walls, streets, etc. meet; angle; projection; *Business* buying up of whole existing stock of commodity, shares. ▸ *vt* drive into position of difficulty, or leaving no escape; establish monopoly. ▸ *vi* turn around corner. **cor'ner·stone** *n* indispensable part, basis. **corner kick** *Soccer* free kick from corner of field.

cor·net [kor-NET] *n* trumpet with valves.

cor·nice [KOR-nis] *n* projection near top of wall; ornamental, carved molding below ceiling.

cor·nu·co·pia [kor-nə-KOH-pee-ə] *n* symbol of plenty, consisting of goat's horn, overflowing with fruit and flowers.

co·rol·la [kə-ROL-ə] *n* flower's inner envelope of petals.

cor·ol·lar·y [KOR-ə-ler-ee] *n, pl* **-lar·ies.** inference from a preceding statement; deduction; result.

co·ro·na [kə-ROH-nə] *n, pl* **-nas.** halo around heavenly body; flat projecting part of cornice; top or crown.

cor·o·nar·y [KOR-ə-ner-ee] *adj* of blood vessels surrounding heart. ▶ *n, pl* **-nar·ies.** coronary thrombosis. **coronary thrombosis** disease of the heart.

cor·o·na·tion [kor-ə-NAY-shən] *n* ceremony of crowning a sovereign.

cor·o·ner [KOR-ə-nər] *n* officer who holds inquests on bodies of persons supposed killed by violence, accident, etc.

cor·o·net [KOR-ə-net] *n* small crown.

cor·po·ral[1] [KOR-pər-əl] *adj* of the body; material, not spiritual. **corporal punishment** (flogging, etc.) of physical nature.

corporal[2] *n* noncommissioned officer below sergeant.

cor·po·ra·tion [kor-pə-RAY-shən] *n* association, body of persons legally authorized to act as an individual; authorities of town or city. **cor'po·rate** [-rit] *adj*

cor·po·re·al [kor-POR-ee-əl] *adj* of the body; material; tangible.

corps [kor] *n, pl* **corps** [korz] military force, body of troops; any organized body of persons.

corpse [korps] *n* dead body.

cor·pu·lent [KOR-pyə-lənt] *adj* fat. **cor'pu·lence** *n*

cor·pus [KOR-pəs] *n* collection or body of works, esp. by single author; main part or body of something.

cor·pus·cle [KOR-pə-səl] *n* minute organism or particle, esp. red and white corpuscles of blood.

cor·ral [kə-RAL] *n* enclosure for cattle, or for defense. ▶ *vt* **-raled, -ral·ing.**

cor·rect [kə-REKT] *vt* set right; indicate errors in; rebuke, punish; counteract, rectify. ▶ *adj* right,

exact, accurate; in accordance with facts or standards. **cor·rec'tion** *n* **cor·rec'tive** *n, adj*

cor·re·late [KOR-ə-layt] *vt* **-lat·ed, -lat·ing.** bring into reciprocal relation. ▶ *n* [-lit] either of two things or words necessarily implying the other. **cor·re·la'tion** *n* **cor·rel·a·tive** [kə-REL-ə-tiv] *adj, n*

cor·re·spond [kor-ə-SPOND] *vi* be in agreement, be consistent with; be similar (to); exchange letters. **cor·re·spond'ence** *n* agreement, corresponding; similarity; exchange of letters; letters received. **cor·re·spond'ent** *n* writer of letters; one employed by newspaper, etc. to report on particular topic, country, etc.

cor·ri·dor [KOR-i-dər] *n* passage in building, etc.; strip of territory (or air route) not under control of country through which it passes; densely populated area incl. two or more major cities.

cor·ri·gen·dum [kor-i-JEN-dəm] *n, pl* **-da** [-də] thing to be corrected.

cor·rob·o·rate [kə-ROB-ə-rayt] *vt* **-rat·ed, -rat·ing.** confirm, support (statement, etc.). **cor·rob·o·ra'tion** *n* **cor·rob'o·ra·tive** *adj*

cor·rode [kə-ROHD] *vt* **-rod·ed, -rod·ing.** eat, wear away, eat into (by chemical action, disease, etc.). **cor·ro'sion** [-ROH-zhən] *n* **cor·ro'sive** *adj*

cor·ru·gate [KOR-ə-gayt] *v* **-gat·ed, -gat·ing.** wrinkle, bend into wavy ridges.

cor·rupt [kə-RUPT] *adj* lacking integrity; open to, or involving, bribery; wicked; spoiled by mistakes, altered for the worse (of words, literary passages, etc.). ▶ *vt* make evil, pervert; bribe; make rotten. **cor·rupt'i·ble** *adj* **cor·rup'tion** *n*

cor·sage [kor-SAH*ZH*] *n* (flower, spray, worn on) bodice of woman's dress.

cor·sair [KOR-sair] *n* pirate (ship).

cor·set [KOR-sit] *n* close-fitting undergarment stiffened to give

support or shape to the body.
cor·tege [kor-TEZH] *n* formal
(funeral) procession.
cor·tex [KOR-teks] *n, pl* **-ti·ces**
[-tə-seez] *Anatomy* outer layer;
bark; sheath. **cor'ti·cal** *adj*
cor·ti·sone [KOR-tə-zohn] *n*
synthetic hormone used in the
treatment of a variety of diseases.
cor·vette [kor-VET] *n* lightly armed
warship for escort and
antisubmarine duties.
co·sine [KOH-sīn] *n* in a right
triangle, the ratio of a side adjacent
to a given angle and the
hypotenuse.
cos·met·ic [koz-MET-ik] *n*
preparation to beautify or improve
skin, hair, etc. ▶ *adj* designed to
improve appearance only.
cos·mic [KOZ-mik] *adj* relating to
the universe; of the vastness of the
universe. **cos·mog'ra·pher** *n*
cos·mog'ra·phy *n* description or
mapping of the universe.
cos·mo·log·i·cal [koz-mə-LOJ-i-kəl]
adj **cos·mol'o·gy** *n* the science or
study of the universe.
cosmic rays high-energy
electromagnetic rays from space.
cos·mo·naut [KOZ-mə-nawt] *n* the
Russian name for an astronaut.
cos·mo·pol·i·tan [koz-mə-POL-i-tn]
n person who has lived and
traveled in many countries. ▶ *adj*
familiar with many countries;
sophisticated; free from national
prejudice.
cos·mos¹ [KOZ-məs] *n* the world or
universe considered as an ordered
system.
cosmos² *n, pl* **-mos.** plant cultivated
for brightly colored flowers.
cos·sack [KOS-ak] *n* member of
tribe in SE Russia.
cost [kawst] *n* price; cost price;
expenditure of time, labor, etc. ▶ *pl*
expenses of lawsuit. ▶ *vt* **cost,**
cost·ing. have as price; entail
payment, or loss, or sacrifice of.
costing *n* system of calculating
cost of production, sale.
cost'li·ness *n* **cost'ly** *adj* **-li·er,**
-li·est. valuable; expensive. **cost**

price price at which article is
bought by one intending to resell it.
cos·tal [KOS-tl] *adj* pert. to side of
body or ribs.
cos·tume [KOS-toom] *n* style of
dress of particular place or time, or
for particular activity; theatrical
clothes. **cos'tum·er** *n* dealer in
costumes. **costume jewelry**
inexpensive jewelry.
cot [kot] *n* narrow, usu. collapsible
bed.
cote [koht] *n* shelter, shed for
animals or birds, e.g. *dovecote.*
co·te·rie [KOH-tə-ree] *n* exclusive
group of people with common
interests; social clique.
coterminous see CONTERMINOUS.
cot·tage [KOT-ij] *n* small house.
cottage cheese mild, soft cheese.
cottage industry industry in which
workers work in their own homes.
cot·ter [KOT-ər] *n* pin, wedge, etc.
to prevent relative motion of two
parts of machine, etc.
cot·ton [KOT-n] *n* plant; white
downy fibrous covering of its
seeds; thread or cloth made of this.
cotton (on) to begin to like,
understand (idea, person, etc.).
cot·y·le·don [kot-l-EED-n] *n*
primary leaf of plant embryos.
couch [kowch] *n* piece of furniture
for sitting or reclining on by day,
sofa. ▶ *vt* put into (words), phrase;
cause to lie down. **couch potato**
inf lazy person whose only hobby is
watching television. **on the couch**
under psychiatric treatment.
cou·gar [KOO-gər] *n* mountain lion.
cough [kawf] *vi* expel air from lungs
with sudden effort and noise, often
to remove obstruction. ▶ *n* act of
coughing.
could pt. of CAN¹.
cou·lomb [KOO-lom] *n* unit of
quantity of electricity.
coun·cil [KOWN-səl] *n* deliberative
or administrative body; one of its
meetings; local governing authority
of town, etc. **coun'ci·lor** *n*
member of council.
coun·sel [KOWN-səl] *n* advice,
deliberation or debate; lawyer or

lawyers; plan, policy. ▶ *vt* advise, recommend. **coun·se·lor** *n* adviser; lawyer. **keep one's counsel** keep a secret.

count¹ [kownt] *vt* reckon, calculate, number; include; consider to be. ▶ *vi* be reckoned in; depend (on); be of importance. ▶ *n* reckoning; total number reached by counting; item in list of charges or indictment; act of counting. **count'less** *adj* too many to be counted.

count² *n* European nobleman of rank corresponding to that of British earl.

coun·te·nance [KOWN-tn-əns] *n* face, its expression; support, approval. ▶ *vt* **-nanced, -nanc·ing.** give support, approve.

count·er¹ [KOWN-tər] *n* horizontal surface in bank, store, etc., on which business is transacted; work surface in kitchen; disk, token used for counting or scoring, esp. in board games. **coun'ter·top** flat upper surface of counter, display case, etc.

coun·ter² *adv* in opposite direction; contrary. ▶ *vi* oppose, contradict; *Fencing* parry. ▶ *n* parry.

counter- *prefix* opposite, against, e.g. *counterattack;* complementary, corresponding, e.g. *counterpart.*

coun·ter·act [kown-tər-AKT] *vt* neutralize or hinder.

coun·ter·at·tack [KOWN-tər-ə-tak] *v, n* attack after enemy's advance.

coun·ter·bal·ance [KOWN-tər-bal-əns] *n* weight balancing or neutralizing another. ▶ *vt* **-anced, anc·ing.**

coun·ter·feit [KOWN-tər-fit] *adj* sham, forged. ▶ *n* imitation, forgery. ▶ *vt* imitate with intent to deceive; forge.

coun·ter·mand [kown-tər-MAND] *vt* cancel (previous order).

coun·ter·part [KOWN-tər-pahrt] *n* thing so like another as to be mistaken for it; something complementary to or correlative of another.

coun·ter·point [KOWN-tər-point] *n*

melody added as accompaniment to given melody; art of so adding melodies.

coun·ter·sign [KOWN-tər-sīn] *vt* sign document already signed by another; ratify. ▶ *n Military* secret sign.

coun·ter·sink [KOWN-tər-singk] *v* **-sunk, -sink·ing.** enlarge upper part of hole (drilled in wood, etc.) to take head of screw, bolt, etc. below surface.

count'ess *n* wife or widow of count or earl.

coun·try [KUN-tree] *n, pl* **-tries.** region, district; territory of nation; land of birth, residence, etc.; rural districts as opposed to city; nation. **coun'tri·fied** [-fid] *adj* rural in manner or appearance. **coun'try·man** *n* rustic; compatriot. **country music** popular music based on Amer. folk music. **coun'try·side** *n* rural district; its inhabitants.

coun·ty [KOWN-tee] *n, pl* **-ties.** division of a state.

coup [koo] *n, pl* **coups** [kooz] successful stroke, move or gamble; coup d'état. **coup d'é·tat** [koo-day-TAH] sudden, violent seizure of government.

cou·ple [KUP-əl] *n* two, pair; husband and wife; any two persons. ▶ *v* **-pled, -pling.** ▶ *vt* connect, fasten together; associate, connect in the mind. ▶ *vi* join, associate. **cou'plet** *n* two lines of verse, esp. rhyming and of equal length. **cou'pling** *n* connection.

cou·pon [KOO-pon] *n* ticket or voucher entitling holder to discount, gift, etc.; detachable slip used as order form.

cour·age [KUR-ij] *n* bravery, boldness. **cou·ra·geous** [kə-RAY-jəs] *adj*

cour·i·er [KUUR-ee-ər] *n* express messenger.

course [kors] *n* movement in space or time; direction of movement; successive development, sequence; line of conduct or action; series of lessons, exercises, etc.; any of successive parts of meal; continuous line of masonry at particular level in building; area where golf is played; track or ground on which a race is run. ▶ *v* **coursed, cours·ing.** ▶ *vt* hunt. ▶ *vi* run swiftly, gallop about; (of blood) circulate.

court [kort] *n* space enclosed by buildings, yard; area marked off or enclosed for playing various games; retinue and establishment of sovereign; body with judicial powers, place where it meets, one of its sittings; attention, homage, flattery. ▶ *vt* woo, try to win or attract; seek, invite. **cour·ti·er** [KOR-tee-ər] *n* one who frequents royal court. **court′li·ness** *n* **court′ly** *adj* **-li·er, -li·est.** ceremoniously polite; characteristic of a court. **court martial** *n, pl* **courts martial.** court of naval or military officers for trying naval or military offenses. **court′yard** *n* paved space enclosed by buildings or walls.

cour·te·san [KOR-tə-zən] *n* court mistress; high-class prostitute.

cour·te·sy [KUR-tə-see] *n, pl* **-sies.** politeness, good manners; act of civility. **cour′te·ous** *adj* polite.

court·ship [KORT-ship] *n* wooing.

cous·in [KUZ-ən] *n* son or daughter of uncle or aunt.

cove [kohv] *n* small inlet of coast, sheltered bay.

cov·en [KUV-ən] *n* gathering of witches.

cov·e·nant [KUV-ə-nənt] *n* contract, mutual agreement; compact. ▶ *v* agree to a covenant.

cov·er [KUV-ər] *vt* place or spread over; extend, spread; bring upon (oneself); screen, protect; travel over; include; be sufficient; point a gun at. ▶ *n* lid, wrapper, envelope, binding, screen, anything that covers. **cov′er·age** *n* amount, extent covered. **cov′er·let** *n* bedspread. **cover girl** attractive model whose picture appears on magazine cover.

co·vert [KOH-vərt] *adj* secret,

veiled, concealed, sly. ▶ *n* [KUV-ərt] thicket, place sheltering game.

cov·et [KUV-it] *vt* long to possess, esp. what belongs to another. **cov′et·ous** *adj* greedy.

cov·ey [KUV-ee] *n, pl* **-eys.** brood of partridges or quail.

cow[1] [kow] *n* mature female of cattle and of certain other mammals, such as the elephant or seal. **cow′boy** *n* ranch hand in charge of cattle on western plains of US; *inf* reckless driver, etc.

cow[2] *vt* frighten into submission, overawe, subdue.

cow·ard [KOW-ərd] *n* one who lacks courage, shrinks from danger. **cow′ard·ice** [-dis] *n* **cow′ard·ly** *adj*

cow·er [KOW-ər] *vi* crouch, shrink in fear.

cowl [kowl] *n* monk's hooded cloak; its hood; cowling.

cowl·ing [KOW-ling] *n* covering for aircraft engine.

cow·rie [KOW-ree] *n* brightly colored sea shell.

cox·swain [KOK-sən] *n* steersman of boat. **cox** *v inf* act as coxswain.

coy [koi] *adj* **-er, -est.** (pretending to be) shy, modest. **coy′ness** *n*

coy·o·te [kī-OH-tee] *n* N Amer. prairie wolf.

co·zy [KOH-zee] *adj* **-zi·er, -zi·est.** snug, comfortable, sheltered; suggesting conspiratorial intimacy. **co′zi·ly** *adv* **co′zi·ness** *n*

CPU *Computers* central processing unit.

Cr *Chem* chromium.

crab [krab] *n* edible crustacean with ten legs, noted for sidelong and backward walk; type of louse. ▶ *vi* **crabbed, crab·bing.** catch crabs; move sideways. **crab·bed** [KRAB-id] *adj* of handwriting, hard to read. **crab′by** *adj* **-bi·er, -bi·est.** irritable.

crack [krak] *vt* break, split partially; break with sharp noise; cause to make sharp noise, as of whip, rifle, etc.; break down, yield; *inf* tell (joke); solve, decipher. ▶ *vi* make sharp noise; split, fissure; of the voice, lose clearness when

changing from boy's to man's. ▶ *n*
sharp explosive noise; split, fissure;
flaw; *inf* joke, esp. sarcastic; chat; *sl*
pure, highly addictive form of
cocaine. ▶ *adj inf* special, smart, of
great reputation for skill or fashion.
crack'er *n* thin dry biscuit; (**C-**) *sl,
offens* native or inhabitant of
Georgia. **crack'le** [-əl] *n* sound of
repeated small cracks. ▶ *vi* **-led,
-ling.** make this sound. **crack'ling**
n crackle; crisp skin of roast pork,
etc.

cra·dle [KRAYD-l] *n* infant's bed (on
rockers); *fig* earliest resting place or
home; supporting framework. ▶ *vt*
-dled, -dling. hold or rock as in a
cradle; cherish.

craft[1] [kraft] *n* skill, ability, esp.
manual ability; cunning; skilled
trade; members of a trade.
craft'i·ly *adv* **craft'y** *adj* **craft·i·er,
craft·i·est.** cunning, shrewd.
crafts'man crafts'man·ship *n*
craft[2] *n* vessel; ship.

crag [krag] *n* steep rugged rock.
crag'gy *adj* **-gi·er, -gi·est.** rugged.

cram [kram] *vt* **crammed,
cram·ming.** fill quite full; stuff,
force; pack tightly. ▶ *vi* feed to
excess; prepare quickly for
examination.

cramp [kramp] *n* painful muscular
contraction; clamp for holding
masonry, wood, etc. together. ▶ *vt*
restrict or hamper; hem in, keep
within too narrow limits.

cram·pon [KRAM-pon] *n* spike in
shoe for mountain climbing esp. on
ice.

crane [krayn] *n* wading bird with
long legs, neck, and bill; machine
for moving heavy weights. ▶ *vi*
craned, cran·ing. stretch neck to
see.

cra·ni·um [KRAY-nee-əm] *n* skull.
cra'ni·al *adj*

crank [krangk] *n* arm at right angles
to axis, for turning main shaft,
changing reciprocal into rotary
motion, etc.; *inf* eccentric person,
faddist. ▶ *v* start (engine) by
turning crank. **crank'y** *adj*
crank·i·er, crank·i·est.

bad-tempered; eccentric.
crank'shaft *n* principal shaft of
engine.

cran·ny [KRAN-ee] *n, pl* **-nies.** small
opening, chink. **cran'nied** *adj*

crap [krap] *n* gambling game
played with two dice (also **craps**).

crape [krayp] *n* crepe, esp. when
used for mourning clothes.

crash [krash] *v* (cause to) make loud
noise; (cause to) fall with crash. ▶ *vi*
break, smash; collapse, fail, esp.
financially; cause (aircraft) to hit
land or water; collide with (another
car, etc.); move noisily or violently.
▶ *vi* (of computer system or
program) fail suddenly because of
malfunction. ▶ *n* loud, violent fall or
impact; collision, esp. between
vehicles; sudden, uncontrolled
descent of aircraft to land; sudden
collapse or downfall, esp. of
economy; bankruptcy. ▶ *adj*
requiring, using, great effort to
achieve results quickly. **crash
helmet** helmet worn by
motorcyclists, etc. to protect head.

crass [kras] *adj* **-er, -est.** grossly
stupid; insensitive. **crass'ness** *n*

crate [krayt] *n* large (usu. wooden)
container for packing goods.

cra·ter [KRAY-tər] *n* mouth of
volcano; bowl-shaped cavity, esp.
one made by explosion of large
shell, bomb, mine, etc.

cra·vat [krə-VAT] *n* man's neckband
or scarf.

crave [krayv] *v* **craved, crav·ing.**
have very strong desire for, long
for. ▶ *vt* ask humbly; beg. **craving** *n*

cra·ven [KRAY-vən] *adj* cowardly,
abject, spineless. ▶ *n* coward.
cra'ven·ness *n*

craw [kraw] *n* bird's or animal's
stomach; bird's crop.

crawl [krawl] *vi* move on belly or on
hands and knees; move very
slowly; ingratiate oneself, cringe;
swim with crawl stroke; be overrun
(with). ▶ *n* crawling motion; very
slow walk; racing stroke at
swimming.

cray·fish [KRAY-fish] *n* edible
freshwater crustacean like lobster

(also **craw'fish**).

cray·on [KRAY-on] n stick or pencil of colored chalk, wax, etc.

craze [krayz] n short-lived current fashion; strong desire or passion, mania; madness. **crazed** adj demented; (of porcelain) having fine cracks. **cra'zy** adj **-zi·er, -zi·est.** insane; very foolish; madly eager (for). **crazy quilt** patchwork quilt of irregular patches; jumble.

creak [kreek] n harsh grating noise. ▶ vi make creaking sound.

cream [kreem] n fatty part of milk; various foods, dishes, resembling cream; cosmetic, etc. with creamlike consistency; yellowish-white color; best part of anything. ▶ vt take cream from; take best part from; beat to creamy consistency. **cream'y** adj **cream·i·er, cream·i·est.**

crease [krees] n line made by folding; wrinkle; *Ice Hockey* marked rectangular area in front of goal cage; superficial bullet wound. ▶ v **creased, creas·ing.** make, develop creases.

cre·ate [kree-AYT] v **-at·ed, -at·ing.** ▶ vt bring into being; give rise to; make. ▶ vi inf make a fuss. **cre·a'tion** n **cre·a'tive** adj **cre·a'tor** n

crea·ture [KREE-chər] n living being; thing created; dependent, tool (of another). **creature comforts** bodily comforts.

crèche [kresh] n representation of the Nativity scene.

cre·dence [KREED-ns] n belief, credit; small table for bread and wine of the Eucharist.

cre·den·tials [kri-DEN-shəlz] pl n testimonials; letters of introduction, esp. those given to ambassador.

cred·i·ble [KRED-ə-bəl] adj worthy of belief; trustworthy. **cred·i·bil'i·ty** n

cred·it [KRED-it] n commendation, approval; source, cause, of honor; belief, trust; good name; influence, honor or power based on trust of others; system of allowing customers to take goods for later

payment; money at one's disposal in bank, etc.; side of ledger on which such sums are entered; reputation for financial reliability. ▶ pl list of those responsible for production of film, etc. ▶ vt attribute, believe that person has; believe; put on credit side of account. **cred'it·a·ble** adj bringing honor. **cred'i·tor** n one to whom debt is due.

cred·u·lous [KREJ-ə-ləs] adj too easy of belief, easily deceived or imposed on, gullible. **cre·du·li·ty** [krə-DOO-li-tee] n

creed [kreed] n formal statement of religious beliefs; statement, system of beliefs or principles.

creek [kreek] n narrow inlet on seacoast.

creel [kreel] n angler's fishing basket.

creep [kreep] vi **crept, creep·ing.** make way along ground, as snake; move with stealthy, slow movements; crawl; act in servile way; of skin or flesh, feel shrinking, shivering sensation, due to fear or repugnance. ▶ n creeping; sl repulsive person. ▶ pl feeling of fear or repugnance. **creep'er** n creeping or climbing plant, such as ivy. **creep'y** adj **creep·i·er, creep·i·est.** inf uncanny, unpleasant; causing flesh to creep.

cre·ma·tion [kri-MAY-shən] n burning as means of disposing of corpses. **cre·mate** [KREE-mayt] vt **-mat·ed, -mat·ing.** **cre·ma·to·ri·um** [kree-mə-TOR-ee-əm] n place for cremation.

cre·ole [KREE-ohl] n hybrid language; (**C-**) native born W Indian, Latin American, of European descent.

cre·o·sote [KREE-ə-soht] n oily antiseptic liquid distilled from coal or wood tar, used for preserving wood. ▶ vt **-sot·ed, -sot·ing.** coat or impregnate with creosote.

crepe [krayp] n fabric with crimped surface; crape; thin, light pancake. **crepe rubber** rough-surfaced rubber used for soles of shoes.

crept pt./pp. of CREEP.

cre·scen·do [kri-SHEN-doh] *n* gradual increase of loudness, esp. in music. ▶ *adj, adv*

cres·cent [KRES-ənt] *n* (shape of) moon as seen in first or last quarter; any figure of this shape; curved portion of a street.

crest [krest] *n* comb or tuft on bird's or animal's head; plume on top of helmet; top of mountain, ridge, wave, etc.; badge above shield of coat of arms, also used separately on seal, plate, etc. ▶ *vi* crown. ▶ *vt* reach top of.
crest'fall·en *adj* cast down by failure, dejected.

cre·ta·ceous [kri-TAY-shəs] *adj* chalky.

cre·tin [KREET-n] *n offens* stupid or mentally defective person; *obs* person afflicted with deficiency in thyroid gland causing physical and mental retardation.

cre·vasse [kri-VAS] *n* deep open chasm, esp. in glacier.

crev·ice [KREV-is] *n* cleft, fissure, chink.

crew [kroo] *n* ship's, boat's or aircraft's company, excluding passengers; *inf* gang or set. ▶ *v* serve as crew. **crew cut** closely cropped haircut.

crew·el [KROO-əl] *n* fine worsted yarn, used in needlework and embroidery.

crib [krib] *n* child's cot; barred rack used for fodder; plagiarism; translation used by students, sometimes illicitly. ▶ *vt* **cribbed, crib·bing.** confine in small space; copy unfairly.

crib·bage [KRIB-ij] *n* card game for two, three, or four players.

crick [krik] *n* spasm or cramp in muscles, esp. in neck.

crick·et¹ [KRIK-it] *n* chirping insect.

cricket² *n* outdoor game played with bats, ball and wickets by teams of eleven a side. **crick'et·er** *n*

crime [krīm] *n* violation of law (usu. a serious offense); wicked or forbidden act; *inf* something to be

regretted. **crim·i·nal** [KRIM-ə-nl] *adj, n* **crim·i·nal'i·ty** *n* **crim·i·nol'o·gy** *n* study of crime and criminals.

crimp [krimp] *vt* pinch into tiny parallel pleats; wrinkle.

crim·son [KRIM-zən] *adj, n* (of) rich deep red.

cringe [krinj] *vi* **cringed, cring·ing.** shrink, cower; behave obsequiously.

crin·kle [KRING-kəl] *v, n* **-kled, -kling.** wrinkle.

crin·o·line [KRIN-l-in] *n* hooped petticoat or skirt of stiff material.

crip·ple [KRIP-əl] *n offens* one not having normal use of limbs, disabled or deformed person. ▶ *vt* **-pled, -pling.** maim, disable, impair; weaken, lessen efficiency of.

cri·sis [KRĪ-sis] *n, pl* **-ses** [-seez] turning point or decisive moment, esp. in illness; time of acute danger or difficulty.

crisp [krisp] *adj* **-er, -est.** brittle but firm; brisk, decided; clear-cut; fresh, invigorating; crackling; of hair, curly. ▶ *n* dessert of fruit baked with a crunchy mixture. **crisp'er** *n* refrigerator compartment for storing salads, etc.

cri·te·ri·on [krī-TEER-ee-ən] *n, pl* **-ri·a** [-ree-ə] standard of judgment.

crit·i·cal [KRIT-i-kəl] *adj* faultfinding; discerning; skilled in or given to judging; of great importance, crucial, decisive. **crit'ic** *n* one who passes judgment; writer expert in judging works of literature, art, etc. **crit'i·cism** *n* **crit'i·cize** *vt* **-cized, ciz·ing.** **cri·tique** [kri-TEEK] *n* critical essay, carefully written criticism.

croak [krohk] *v* utter deep hoarse cry, as raven, frog; talk dismally. ▶ *vi sl* die. ▶ *n* deep hoarse cry.

cro·chet [kroh-SHAY] *n* kind of handicraft like knitting, done with small hooked needle. ▶ *v* do, make such work.

crock [krok] *n* earthenware jar or pot; broken piece of earthenware. **crock'er·y** *n* earthenware dishes, utensils, etc.

croc·o·dile [KROK-ə-dīl] *n* large

amphibious reptile. **crocodile tears** insincere grief.

crois·sant [krwah-SAHN] *n* buttery, crescent-shaped roll of leavened dough or puff pastry.

crone [krohn] *n* witchlike old woman.

cro·ny [KROH-nee] *n, pl* **-nies.** intimate friend.

crook [kruuk] *n* hooked staff; any hook, bend, sharp turn; *inf* swindler, criminal. **crook'ed** *adj* bent, twisted; deformed; dishonest.

croon [kroon] *v* hum, sing in soft, low tone. **croon'er** *n*

crop [krop] *n* produce of cultivation of any plant or plants; harvest; pouch in bird's gullet; stock of whip; hunting whip; short haircut. ▶ *v* **cropped, crop·ping.** cut short; raise, produce or occupy land with crop; (of animals) bite, eat down; poll or clip. **crop'-dust·ing** *n* spreading fungicide, etc. on crops from aircraft. **crop up** *inf* happen unexpectedly.

cro·quet [kroh-KAY] *n* lawn game played with balls, wooden mallets and hoops.

cro·quette [kroh-KET] *n* breaded, fried ball of minced meat, fish, etc.

cro·sier [KROH-zhər] *n* bishop's or abbot's staff.

cross [kraws] *n* structure or symbol of two intersecting lines or pieces (at right angles); such a structure of wood as means of execution by tying or nailing victim to it; symbol of Christian faith; any thing or mark in the shape of cross; misfortune, annoyance, affliction; intermixture of breeds, hybrid. ▶ *v* move or go across (something); intersect; meet and pass. ▶ *vt* mark with lines across; (with *out*) delete; place or put in form of cross; make sign of cross on or over; modify breed of animals or plants by intermixture; thwart; oppose. ▶ *adj* out of temper, angry; peevish; perverse; transverse; intersecting; contrary; adverse. **cross'ing** *n* intersection of roads, rails, etc.; part of street where pedestrians are

expected to cross. **cross'ly** *adv* **cross'wise** *adv, adj* **cross'bow** [-boh] *n* bow fixed across wooden shoulder stock. **cross'breed** *n* breed produced from parents of different breeds. **cross-country** *adj, n* (long race) held over open ground. **cross'-ex·am'ine** *vt* examine witness already examined by other side. **cross'-eyed** *adj* having eye(s) turning inward. **cross'-fer·ti·li·za·tion** *n* fertilization of one plant by pollen of another. **cross'-grained'** *adj* having fibers running diagonally, etc.; perverse. **cross'-ref'er·ence** *n* reference within text to another part of text. **cross section** transverse section; group of people fully representative of a nation, community, etc. **cross'word puzzle** puzzle built up of intersecting words, of which some letters are common, the words being indicated by clues.

crotch [kroch] *n* angle between legs, genital area; fork.

crotch·et [KROCH-it] *n* musical note, equal to half the length of a minim.

crotch·et·y [KROCH-i-tee] *adj* peevish; irritable.

crouch [krowch] *vi* bend low; huddle down close to ground; stoop servilely, cringe. ▶ *n*

croup [kroop] *n* throat disease of children, with cough.

crou·pi·er [KROO-pee-ər] *n* person dealing cards, collecting money, etc. at gambling table.

crow¹ [kroh] *n* large black scavenging bird. **crow's'-foot** *n* wrinkle at corner of eye. **crow's'-nest** *n* lookout platform high on ship's mast.

crow² *vi* utter rooster's cry; boast one's happiness or superiority. ▶ *n* rooster's cry.

crow·bar [KROH-bahr] *n* iron or steel bar, usu. wedge-shaped, for levering.

crowd [krowd] *n* throng, mass. ▶ *vi* flock together. ▶ *vt* cram, force, thrust, pack; fill with people. **crowd out** exclude by excess already in.

crown [krown] *n* monarch's headdress; wreath for head; monarch; monarchy; royal power; various foreign coins; top of head; summit, top; completion or perfection of thing. ▶ *vt* put crown on; confer title; occur as culmination of series of events; *inf* hit on head. **crown prince** heir to throne.

cru·cial [KROO-shəl] *adj* decisive, critical; *inf* very important.

cru·ci·ble [KROO-sə-bəl] *n* small melting pot.

cru·ci·fy [KROO-sə-fī] *vt* **-fied, -fy·ing.** put to death on cross; treat cruelly; *inf* ridicule. **cru'ci·fix** [-fiks] *n* cross; image of (Christ on the) Cross. **cru·ci·fix'ion** *n*

crude [krood] *adj* **crud·er, crud·est.** lacking taste, vulgar; in natural or raw state, unrefined; rough, unfinished. **cru'di·ty** *n, pl* **-ties.**

cru·el [KROO-əl] *adj* **-er, -est.** delighting in others' pain; causing pain or suffering. **cru'el·ly** *adv* **cru'el·ty** *n, pl* **-ties.**

cru·et [KROO-it] *n* small container for salt, pepper, vinegar, oil, etc.; stand holding such containers.

cruise [krooz] *vi* **cruised, cruis·ing.** travel about in a ship for pleasure, etc.; (of vehicle, aircraft) travel at safe, average speed. ▶ *n* cruising voyage. **cruis'er** *n* ship that cruises; warship lighter and faster than battleship. **cruise missile** subsonic missile guided throughout its flight.

crumb [krum] *n* small particle, fragment, esp. of bread. ▶ *vt* reduce to, break into, cover with crumbs.

crum·ble [KRUM-bəl] *v* **-bled, -bling.** break into small fragments, disintegrate, crush; perish, decay. ▶ *vi* fall apart or away. **crum'bly** *adj* **-bli·er, -bli·est.**

crum·my [KRUM-ee] *adj sl* **-mi·er, -mi·est.** inferior, contemptible.

crum·ple [KRUM-pəl] *v* **-pled, -pling.** (cause to) collapse; make or become crushed, wrinkled, creased.

crunch [krunch] *n* sound made by chewing crisp food, treading on gravel, hard snow, etc.; *inf* critical moment or situation. ▶ *v* make crunching sound.

cru·sade [kroo-SAYD] *n* medieval Christian war to recover Holy Land; campaign against something believed to be evil; concerted action to further a cause. ▶ *vi* **-sad·ed, -sad·ing. cru·sad'er** *n*

crush[1] [krush] *vt* compress so as to break, bruise, crumple; break to small pieces; defeat utterly, overthrow. ▶ *n* act of crushing; crowd of people, etc.

crush[2] *n inf* infatuation.

crust [krust] *n* hard outer part of bread; similar hard outer casing on anything. ▶ *v* cover with, form, crust. **crust'i·ly** *adv* **crust'y** *adj* **crust·i·er, crust·i·est.** having, or like, crust; harsh, surly; rude.

crus·ta·cean [kru-STAY-shən] *n* hard-shelled animal, e.g. crab, lobster. ▶ *adj*

crutch [kruch] *n* staff with crosspiece to go under armpit of lame person, device resembling this; support; groin, crotch.

crux [kruks] *n, pl* **-es.** that on which a decision turns; anything that puzzles very much.

cry [krī] *v* **cried, cry·ing.** ▶ *vi* weep; wail; utter call; shout; clamor or beg (for). ▶ *vt* utter loudly, proclaim. ▶ *n* loud utterance; scream, wail, shout; call of animal; fit of weeping; watchword.

cry·o·gen·ics [krī-ə-JEN-iks] *n* branch of physics concerned with phenomena at very low temperatures. **cry·o·gen'ic** *adj*

crypt [kript] *n* vault, esp. under church. **cryp'tic** *adj* secret, mysterious. **cryp'ti·cal·ly** *adv* **cryp'to·gram** *n* piece of writing in code. **cryp·tog'ra·phy** *n* art of writing, decoding ciphers.

crys·tal [KRIS-tl] *n* clear transparent mineral; very clear glass; cut-glass ware; characteristic form assumed by many substances, with definite internal structure and external shape of symmetrically arranged plane surfaces. **crys·tal·line** [-tl-in] *adj* **crys·tal·li·za'tion** *n*

crys'tal·lize *v* **-lized, -liz·ing.** form into crystals; become definite.

Cs *Chem* cesium.

Cu *Chem* copper.

cub [kub] *n* young of fox and other animals; cub scout. ▶ *v* **cubbed, cub·bing.** bring forth cubs. **cub scout** member of junior division of the Boy Scouts.

cub·by·hole [KUB-ee-hohl] *n* small, enclosed space or room; pigeonhole.

cube [kyoob] *n* regular solid figure contained by six equal square sides; cube-shaped block; product obtained by multiplying number by itself twice. ▶ *vt* **cubed, cub·ing.** multiply thus. **cu'bic** *adj* **cub'ism** *n* style of art in which objects are presented as assemblage of geometrical shapes. **cub'ist** *n, adj*

cu·bi·cle [KYOO-bi-kəl] *n* partially or totally enclosed section of room, as in study hall.

cu·bit [KYOO-bit] *n* old measure of length, about 18 inches.

cuck·old [KUK-əld] *n* man whose wife has committed adultery. ▶ *vt*

cuck·oo [KOO-koo] *n, pl* **-oos.** migratory bird that deposits its eggs in the nests of other birds; its call. ▶ *adj sl* crazy. ▶ *vi* **-ooed, -oo·ing.**

cu·cum·ber [KYOO-kum-bər] *n* plant with long fleshy green fruit; the fruit, used in salad.

cud [kud] *n* food that ruminant animal brings back into mouth to chew again. **chew the cud** reflect, meditate.

cud·dle [KUD-l] *v* **-dled, -dling.** ▶ *vt* hug. ▶ *vi* lie close and snug, nestle. ▶ *n*

cudg·el [KUJ-əl] *n* short thick stick. ▶ *vt* **-eled, -el·ing.** beat with cudgel.

cue¹ [kyoo] *n* last words of actor's speech, etc. as signal to another to act or speak; signal, hint, example for action.

cue² *n* long tapering rod used in pool, billiards, etc.

cuff¹ [kuf] *n* ending of sleeve;

wristband. **off the cuff** *inf* without preparation.

cuff² *vt* strike with open hand. ▶ *n* blow with hand.

cui·sine [kwi-ZEEN] *n* style of cooking; menu, food offered by restaurant, etc.

cul-de-sac [KUL-də-SAK] *n, pl* **culs-** [kulz-] street, lane open only at one end; blind alley.

cu·li·nar·y [KYOO-lə-ner-ee] *adj* of, for, suitable for, cooking or kitchen.

cull [kul] *vt* gather, select; take out selected animals from herd. ▶ *n* something culled.

cul·mi·nate [KUL-mə-nayt] *vi* **-nat·ed, -nat·ing.** reach highest point; come to climax, to a head. **cul·mi·na'tion** *n*

cul·pa·ble [KUL-pə-bəl] *adj* blameworthy. **cul·pa·bil'i·ty** *n*

cul·prit [KUL-prit] *n* one guilty of usu. minor offense.

cult [kult] *n* system of religious worship; pursuit of, devotion to, some person, thing, or activity. **cult'ism** *n* practices of a religious cult. **cult'ist** *n*

cul·ti·vate [KUL-tə-vayt] *vt* **-vat·ed, -vat·ing.** till and prepare (soil) to raise crops; develop, improve, refine; devote attention to, cherish; practice; foster. **cul·ti·va'tion** *n*

cul·ture [KUL-chər] *n* state of manners, taste, and intellectual development at a time or place; cultivating; artificial rearing; set of bacteria so reared. **cul'tur·al** *adj* **cul'tured** *adj* refined, showing culture. **cultured pearl** pearl artificially induced to grow in oyster shell.

cul·vert [KUL-vərt] *n* tunneled drain for passage of water under road, railroad, etc.

cum·ber·some [KUM-bər-səm] *adj* awkward, unwieldy.

cu·mu·la·tive [KYOO-myə-lə-tiv] *adj* becoming greater by successive additions; representing the sum of many items.

cu·mu·lus [KYOO-myə-ləs] *n, pl* **-li** [-lī] cloud shaped in rounded white woolly masses.

cu·ne·i·form [kyoo-NEE-ə-form] *adj* wedge-shaped, esp. of ancient Babylonian writing.

cun·ning [KUN-ing] *adj* crafty, sly; ingenious; cute. ▶ *n* skill in deceit or evasion; skill, ingenuity.

cup [kup] *n* small drinking vessel with handle at one side; any small drinking vessel; contents of cup; various cup-shaped formations, cavities, sockets, etc.; cup-shaped trophy as prize; portion or lot; iced drink of wine and other ingredients. ▶ *vt* **cupped, cup·ping.** shape as cup (hands, etc.). **cup·ful** *n, pl* **-fuls. cup·board** [KUB-ərd] *n* piece of furniture, recess in room, with door, for storage.

Cu·pid [KYOO-pid] *n* god of love.

cu·pid·i·ty [kyoo-PID-i-tee] *n* greed for possessions; covetousness.

cu·po·la [KYOO-pə-lə] *n* dome.

cu·pre·ous [KYOO-pree-əs] *adj* of, containing, copper.

cur [kur] *n* dog of mixed breed; surly, contemptible, or mean person.

cu·ra·re [kyuu-RAHR-ee] *n* poisonous resin of S Amer. tree, now used as muscle relaxant in medicine.

cu·rate [KYUUR-it] *n* parish priest. **cu'ra·cy** *n* office or term of office of curate.

cur·a·tive [KYUUR-ə-tiv] *adj* tending to cure disease. ▶ *n*

cu·ra·tor [kyuur-AY-tər] *n* person in charge, esp. of museum, library, etc.

curb [kurb] *n* check, restraint; chain or strap passing under horse's lower jaw and giving powerful control with reins; edging, esp. of stone or concrete, along street, path, etc. ▶ *vt* restrain; apply curb to.

curd [kurd] *n* coagulated milk. **cur·dle** [KUR-dl] *v* **-dled, -dling.** turn into curd, coagulate.

cure [kyuur] *vt* **cured, cur·ing.** heal, restore to health; remedy; preserve (fish, skins, etc.). ▶ *n* remedy; course of medical treatment; successful treatment, restoration to

health. **cur'a·ble** *adj*

cu·rette [kyuu-RET] *n* surgical instrument for removing dead tissue, etc. from some body cavities. **cu·ret·tage** [kyuur-i-TAHZH] *n*

cur·few [KUR-fyoo] *n* official regulation restricting or prohibiting movement of people, esp. at night; time set as deadline by such regulation.

cu·rie [KYUUR-ee] *n* standard unit of radium emanation.

cu·ri·o [KYUUR-ee-oh] *n, pl* **-ri·os.** rare or curious thing of the kind sought for collections.

cu·ri·ous [KYUUR-ee-əs] *adj* eager to know, inquisitive; prying; puzzling, strange, odd. **cu·ri·os·i·ty** *n, pl* **-ties.** eagerness to know; inquisitiveness; strange or rare thing.

cu·ri·um [KYUUR-ee-əm] *n* element produced from plutonium.

curl [kurl] *vi* take spiral or curved shape or path. ▶ *vt* bend into spiral or curved shape. ▶ *n* spiral lock of hair; spiral, curved state, form or motion. **curl·ing** *n* target game played with large rounded stones on ice. **curl'y** *adj* **curl·i·er, curl·i·est.**

cur·mudg·eon [kər-MUJ-ən] *n* surly or miserly person.

cur·rent [KUR-ənt] *adj* of immediate present, going on; up-to-date, not yet superseded; in circulation or general use. ▶ *n* body of water or air in motion; tendency, drift; transmission of electricity through conductor. **cur'ren·cy** *n* money in use; state of being in use; time during which this is current.

cur·ric·u·lum [kə-RIK-yə-ləm] *n, pl* **-la** [-lə] specified course of study.

cur·ry¹ [KUR-ee] *n, pl* **-ries.** highly-flavored, pungent condiment; meat, etc. dish flavored with curry. ▶ *vt* **-ried, -ry·ing.** prepare, flavor dish with curry.

cur·ry² *vt* **-ried, -ry·ing.** groom (horse) with comb; dress (leather). **curry favor** try to win favor unworthily, ingratiate oneself.

curse [kurs] *n* profane or obscene expression of anger, etc.; utterance expressing extreme ill will toward some person or thing; affliction, misfortune, scourge. ▶ *v* **cursed, curs·ing.** utter curse, swear (at); afflict. **curs·ed** [KUR-sid] *adj* hateful; wicked; deserving of, or under, a curse.

cur·sive [KUR-siv] *adj, n* (written in) running script, with letters joined.

cur·so·ry [KUR-sə-ree] *adj* rapid, hasty, not detailed, superficial. **cur'so·ri·ly** *adv*

curt [kurt] *adj* **-er, -est.** short, rudely brief, abrupt. **curt'ness** *n*

cur·tail [kər-TAYL] *vt* cut short, diminish.

cur·tain [KUR-tn] *n* hanging drapery at window, etc.; cloth hung as screen; screen separating audience and stage in theater; end to act or scene, etc. ▶ *pl sl* death. ▶ *vt* provide, cover with curtain. **curtain call** return to stage by performers to acknowledge applause.

curt·sy [KURT-see] *n, pl* **-sies.** woman's bow or respectful gesture made by bending knees and lowering body. ▶ *vi* **-sied, sy·ing.**

curve [kurv] *n* line of which no part is straight; bent line or part. ▶ *v* bend into curve. **cur·va'ceous** [-VAY-shəs] *adj* shapely. **cur'va·ture** [-və-chər] *n* a bending; bent shape.

cush·ion [KUUSH-ən] *n* bag filled with soft stuffing or air, to support or ease body; any soft pad or support; resilient rim of pool table. ▶ *vt* provide, protect with cushion; lessen effects of.

cush·y *adj* **cush·i·er, cush·i·est.** *inf* easy.

cusp [kusp] *n* pointed end, esp. of tooth; *Astrology* point marking the beginning of a house or sign. **cus'pid** *n* pointed tooth.

cus·pi·dor [KUS-pi-dor] *n* spittoon.

cus·tard [KUS-tərd] *n* dessert made of eggs, sugar and milk.

cus·to·dy [KUS-tə-dee] *n, pl* **-dies.** safekeeping, guardianship, imprisonment. **cus·to'di·an** *n* keeper, caretaker.

cus·tom [KUS-təm] *n* habit; practice; fashion, usage; business patronage; tax. ▶ *pl* duties levied on imports; government department that collects these; area in airport, etc. where customs officials examine baggage for dutiable goods. **cus·tom·ar'i·ly** *adv* **cus'tom·ar·y** *adj* usual, habitual. **cus'tom·er** *n* one who enters store to buy, esp. regularly; purchaser.

cut [kut] *vt* **cut, cut·ting.** sever, penetrate, wound, divide, or separate with pressure of edge or edged instrument; pare, detach, trim, or shape by cutting; divide; intersect; reduce, decrease; abridge; *inf* ignore (person); strike (with whip, etc.); *inf* deliberately stay away from. ▶ *n* act of cutting; stroke; blow, wound (of knife, whip, etc.); reduction, decrease; fashion, shape; incision; engraving; piece cut off; division; excavation (for road, canal, etc.) through high ground; *inf* share, esp. of profits. **cut'ter** *n* one who, that which, cuts; ship's boat for carrying stores, etc.; small armed government boat. **cut'ting** *n* act of cutting; thing cut off or out; shoot, twig of plant. ▶ *adj* sarcastic, unkind. **cut'throat** *adj* merciless. ▶ *n* murderer. **cut dead** refuse to recognize an acquaintance.

cu·ta·ne·ous [kyoo-TAY-nee-əs] *adj* of skin.

cute [kyoot] *adj* **cut·er, cut·est.** appealing, attractive, pretty.

cu·ti·cle [KYOO-ti-kəl] *n* dead skin, esp. at base of fingernail.

cut·lass [KUT-ləs] *n* short broad-bladed sword.

cut·ler·y [KUT-lə-ree] *n* knives, forks, spoons, etc.

cut·let [KUT-lit] *n* small piece of meat broiled or fried.

cy·a·nide [SĪ-ə-nīd] *n* extremely poisonous chemical compound.

cy·a·no·sis [sī-ə-NOH-sis] *n* blueness of the skin. **cy·a·not'ic** *adj*

cyber- [SĪ-bər] *comb. form*

indicating computers, e.g. *cyberspace*.

cy·ber·net·ics [sī-bər-NET-iks] *n* comparative study of control mechanisms of electronic and biological systems.

cy·ber·space [SĪ-bər-spays] *n* hypothetical environment containing all the data stored in computers.

cy·ber·squat·ting [SĪ-bər-skwot-ing] *n* registering an Internet domain name belonging to another person in the hope of selling it to them for a profit. **cy'ber·squat·ter** *n*

cy·cle [SĪ-kəl] *n* recurrent series or period; rotation of events; complete series or period; development following course of stages; series of poems, etc.; bicycle. ▶ *vi* **-cled, -cling.** move in cycles; ride bicycle. **cy'clist** *n* bicycle rider.

cy·clone [SĪ-klohn] *n* system of winds moving around center of low pressure; circular storm. **cy·clon'ic** [-KLON-ik] *adj*

cy·clo·tron [SĪ-klə-tron] *n* powerful apparatus that accelerates the circular movement of subatomic particles in a magnetic field, used for work in nuclear disintegration.

cyg·net [SIG-nit] *n* young swan.

cyl·in·der [SIL-in-dər] *n* roller-shaped solid or hollow body, of uniform diameter; piston chamber of engine. **cy·lin'dri·cal** *adj*

cym·bal [SIM-bəl] *n* one of pair of two brass plates struck together to produce ringing or clashing sound in music.

cyn·ic [SIN-ik] *n* one who expects, believes, the worst about people, their motives, or outcome of events. **cyn'i·cal** *adj* **cyn'i·cism** *n* being cynical.

cy·no·sure [SĪN-ə-shuur] *n* center of attraction.

cyst [sist] *n* sac containing liquid secretion or pus. **cys'tic** *adj* of cysts; of the bladder. **cys·ti'tis** *n* inflammation of bladder.

Czar [zahr] *n Hist* emperor of Russia. **Cza·ri·na** [zah-REE-nə] *n* wife of Czar.

D d

D *Chem* deuterium.

dab *vt* **dabbed, dab·bing.** apply with momentary pressure, esp. anything wet and soft; strike feebly. ▶ *n* smear; slight blow or tap; small mass.

dab·ble [DAB-əl] *vi* **-bled, -bling.** splash about; be desultory student or amateur (in). **dab'bler** *n*

dac·tyl [DAK-til] *n* metrical foot of one long followed by two short syllables.

dad·dy [DAD-ee] *n inf pl* **-dies.** father.

da·do [DAY-doh] *n, pl* **-dos.** lower part of room wall when lined or painted separately.

dag·ger [DAG-ər] *n* short, edged stabbing weapon.

da·guerre·o·type [də-GAIR-ə-tīp] *n* early photographic process; photograph by it.

dahl·ia [DAL-yə] *n* garden plant of various colors.

dai·ly [DAY-lee] *adj* done, occurring, published every day. ▶ *adv* every day. ▶ *n, pl* **-lies.** daily newspaper.

dain·ty [DAYN-tee] *adj* **daint·i·er, daint·i·est.** delicate; elegant, choice; pretty and neat; fastidious. ▶ *n, pl* **-ties.** delicacy. **dain'ti·ly** *adv* **dain'ti·ness** *n*

dair·y [DAIR-ee] *n, pl* **-ries.** place for processing milk and its products. **dair'y·ing** *n*

da·is [DAY-is] *n* raised platform, usually at end of hall.

dai·sy [DAY-zee] *n, pl* **-sies.** flower with yellow center and white petals.

Da·lai La·ma [DAH-lī-LAH-mə] *n* head of Buddhist hierarchy in Tibet.

dale [dayl] *n* valley.

dal·ly [DAL-ee] *vi* **-lied, -ly·ing.** trifle, spend time in idleness or amusement; loiter. **dal'li·ance** *n*

Dal·ma·tian [dal-MAY-shən] *n* large dog, white with black spots.

dam¹ *n* barrier to hold back flow of waters; water so collected. ▶ *vt* **dammed, dam'ming.** hold with or as with dam.

dam² *n* female parent (used of animals).

dam·age [DAM-ij] *n* injury, harm, loss. ▶ *pl* sum claimed or adjudged in compensation for injury. ▶ *vt* **-maged, -mag·ing.** harm.

dam·ask [DAM-əsk] *n* figured woven material of silk or linen, esp. white table linen with design shown up by light; color of damask rose, velvety red.

dame [daym] *n obs* lady; *sl* woman.

damn [dam] *v* **damned, damn·ing.** ▶ *vt* condemn to hell; be the ruin of; give hostile reception to. ▶ *vi* curse. ▶ *interj* expression of annoyance, impatience, etc. **dam'na·ble** *adj* deserving damnation; hateful, annoying. **dam·na'tion** *n*

damp *adj* moist; slightly moist. ▶ *n* diffused moisture; in coal mines, dangerous gas. ▶ *vt* make damp; (often with *down*) deaden, discourage. **damp'en** *v* make, become damp. ▶ *vt* stifle, deaden. **damp'er** *n* anything that discourages or depresses; plate in a flue to control draft.

Dan. Daniel.

dance [dans] *v* **danced, danc·ing.** ▶ *vi* move with measured rhythmic steps, usu. to music; be in lively movement; bob up and down. ▶ *vt* perform (dance); cause to dance. ▶ *n* lively, rhythmical movement; arrangement of such movements; tune for them; social gathering for the purpose of dancing. **danc'er** *n* **dan·seuse** [dahn-SUUZ] *n* female battle dancer.

dan·de·li·on [DAN-dl-ī-ən] *n* yellow-flowered wild plant.

dan·der [DAN-dər] *n inf* temper, fighting spirit.

dan·druff [DAN-drəf] *n* dead skin in small scales on the scalp, in hair.

dan·dy [DAN-dee] *n, pl* **-dies.** man excessively concerned with

smartness of dress. ▶ *adj inf* excellent.

dan·ger [DAYN-jər] *n* liability or exposure to harm; risk, peril. **dan′ger·ous** *adj*

dan·gle [DANG-gəl] *v* **-gled, -gling.** hang loosely and swaying; hold suspended; tempt with.

dank [dangk] *adj* **-er, -est.** unpleasantly damp and chilly. **dank′ness** *n*

dap·per [DAP-ər] *adj* neat and precise, esp. in dress, spruce.

dap·ple [DAP-əl] *v* **-pled, -pling.** mark with spots. **dappled** *adj* spotted; mottled; variegated. **dapple-gray** *adj* (of horse) gray marked with darker spots.

dare [dair] *vt* **dared, dar·ing.** venture, have courage (to); challenge. ▶ *n* challenge. **daring** *adj* bold. ▶ *n* adventurous courage. **dare′dev·il** *adj, n* reckless (person).

dark [dahrk] *adj* **-er, -est.** without light; gloomy; deep in tint; dim; secret; unenlightened; wicked. ▶ *n* absence of light or color or knowledge. **dark′en** *v* **dark′ness** *n* **dark horse** somebody, something, esp. competitor in race, about whom little is known. **dark′room** *n* darkened room for processing film.

dar·ling [DAHR-ling] *adj, n* much loved or very lovable (person).

darn¹ [dahrn] *vt* mend by filling (hole) with yarn. ▶ *n* place so mended. **darn′ing** *n*

darn² *interj* mild expletive.

dart [dahrt] *n* small light pointed missile; darting motion; small seam or intake in garment. ▶ *pl* indoor game played with numbered target and miniature darts. ▶ *vt* cast, throw rapidly (dart glance, etc.). ▶ *vi* go rapidly or abruptly.

dash *vt* smash, throw, thrust, send with violence; cast down; tinge, flavor, mix. ▶ *vi* move, go with great speed or violence. ▶ *n* rush; vigor; smartness; small quantity, tinge; stroke (–) between words. **dash′ing** *adj* spirited, showy. **dash′board** *n* in car, etc., instrument panel in front of driver.

da·shi·ki [də-SHEE-kee] *n, pl* **-kis.** loose pullover garment, orig. African.

das·tard [DAS-tərd] *n obs* contemptible, sneaking coward. **das′tard·ly** *adj*

da·ta [DAY-tə] *n* information consisting of observations, measurements, or facts; numbers, digits, etc., stored by a computer. **database** systematized collection of data that can be manipulated by data-processing system for specific purpose. **data processing** handling of data by computer.

date¹ [dayt] *n* day of the month; statement on document of its time of writing; time of occurrence; period of work of art, etc.; engagement, appointment. ▶ *v* **dat·ed, dat·ing.** ▶ *vt* mark with date; refer to date; reveal age of; *inf* accompany on social outing. ▶ *vi* exist (from); betray time or period of origin, become old-fashioned. **date′less** *adj* without date; immemorial.

date² *n* sweet, single-stone fruit of palm; the palm.

da·tive [DAY-tiv] *n* case indicating indirect object, etc.

da·tum *n, pl* **da·ta.** single piece of information in the form of a fact or statistic.

daub [dawb] *vt* coat, plaster, paint coarsely or roughly. ▶ *n* crude picture; smear. **daub′er** *n*

daugh·ter [DAW-tər] *n* one's female child. **daugh′ter-in-law** *n, pl* **daugh′ters-in-law.** son's wife.

daunt [dawnt] *vt* frighten, esp. into giving up purpose. **daunt′less** *adj* intrepid, fearless.

dav·en·port [DAV-ən-port] *n* small writing table with drawers; large couch or settee.

Da·vy Jones's locker [DAY-vee JOHN-ziz] bottom of sea, considered as sailors' grave.

daw·dle [DAWD-l] *vi* **-dled, -dling.** idle, waste time, loiter. **daw′dler** *n*

dawn *n* first light, daybreak; first gleam or beginning of anything. ▶ *vi* begin to grow light; appear,

begin; (begin to) be understood.

day n period of 24 hours; time when sun is above horizon; point or unit of time; daylight; part of day occupied by certain activity, time period; special or designated day. **day'break** n dawn. **day'-care center** place providing daytime care, meals, etc. for preschool children, etc. **day'dream** n idle fancy. ▶ vi **day'light** n natural light; dawn. ▶ pl consciousness, wits. **daylight saving** in summer, time set one hour ahead of local standard time, giving extra daylight in evenings. **day'time** n time between sunrise and sunset.

daze [dayz] vt **dazed, daz·ing.** stupefy, stun, bewilder. ▶ n stupefied or bewildered state.

daz·zle [DAZ-əl] vt **-zled, -zling.** blind, confuse or overpower with brightness, light, brilliant display or prospects. ▶ n brightness that dazzles the vision.

Db Chem dubnium.

D-day [DEE-day] day selected for start of something, orig. the Allied invasion of Europe on June 6th 1944.

de- prefix indicating: removal, e.g. dethrone; reversal, e.g. declassify; departure, e.g. decamp.

dea·con [DEE-kən] n in hierarchical churches, member of the clergy next below priest; in other churches, one who superintends secular affairs. **dea·con·ess** n, fem

dead [ded] adj **-er, -est.** no longer alive; obsolete; numb, without sensation; no longer functioning, extinguished; lacking luster or movement or vigor; sure, complete. ▶ adv utterly. **the dead** dead person or persons. **dead'en** vt **dead'ly** adj **-li·er, -li·est.** fatal; deathlike. ▶ adv as if dead.

dead'beat n inf one who avoids payment of debts; lazy, useless person. **dead'head** n log sticking out of water as hindrance to navigation; boring person; train, aircraft, etc. operating empty, as when returning to terminal. **dead**

heat race in which competitors finish exactly even. **dead letter** rule no longer observed; letter that post office cannot deliver.

dead'line n limit of time allowed. **dead'lock** n standstill. **dead'pan** adj expressionless. **dead reckoning** calculation of ship's position from log and compass, when observations cannot be taken. **dead set** absolutely; resolute attack. **dead of night** time of greatest stillness and darkness.

deaf [def] adj **-er, -est.** wholly or partly without hearing; unwilling to listen. **deaf'en** vt make deaf.

deal [deel] v **dealt, deal'ing.** ▶ vt distribute, give out; inflict. ▶ vi act; treat; do business (with, in). ▶ n agreement; treatment; share; business transaction. **deal'er** n one who deals (esp. cards); trader. **deal'ings** pl n transactions or relations with others. **deal with** handle, act toward (someone).

dean [deen] n university or college official; head of cathedral chapter.

dear [deer] adj beloved; precious; costly, expensive. ▶ n beloved one. ▶ adv at a high price. **dear'ly** adv

dearth [durth] n scarcity.

death [deth] n dying; end of life; end, extinction; annihilation; (D-) personification of death, as skeleton. **death'less** adj immortal. **death'ly** adj, adv like death. **death mask** cast of person's face taken after death. **death'watch** n vigil at dying person's bedside.

de·ba·cle [day-BAH-kəl] n utter collapse, rout, disaster.

de·bar [di-BAHR] vt **-barred, -bar'ring.** shut out from; stop; prohibit; preclude.

de·bark [di-BAHRK] v disembark.

de·base [di-BASE] vt **-based, -bas·ing.** lower in value, quality or character; adulterate coinage. **de·base'ment** n

de·bate [di-BAYT] v **-bat·ed, -bat·ing.** argue, discuss, esp. in a formal assembly; consider. ▶ n discussion; controversy.

de·bat'a·ble adj

de·bauch [di-BAWCH] vt lead into a life of depraved self-indulgence. ▶ n bout of sensual indulgence. **de·bauch·ee** [deb-aw-CHEE] n dissipated person. **de·bauch·er·y** n

de·ben·ture [di-BEN-chər] n bond of company or corporation.

de·bil·i·ty [di-BIL-i-tee] n, pl **-ties.** feebleness, esp. of health; languor. **de·bil'i·tate** vt weaken, enervate.

deb'it n Accounting entry in account of sum owed; side of ledger in which such sums are entered. ▶ vt charge, enter as due.

deb·o·nair [deb-ə-NAIR] adj suave, genial, affable.

de·brief [dee-BREEF] v of soldier, etc., report to superior on result of mission.

de·bris [də-BREE] n fragments, rubbish.

debt [det] n what is owed; state of owing. **debt'or** n

debug [dee-BUG] vt inf find and remove defects in (computer program); remove concealed microphones from (room or telephone).

de·bunk [di-BUNGK] vt expose falseness, pretentiousness of, esp. by ridicule.

de·but [day-BYOO] n first appearance in public. **deb·u·tante** [DEB-yuu-tahnt] n young woman making official debut into society.

deca- comb. form ten, e.g. decagon.

dec·ade [DEK-ayd] n period of ten years; set of ten.

dec·a·dent [DEK-ə-dənt] adj declining, deteriorating; morally corrupt. **dec'a·dence** n

de·caf·fein·at·ed [dee-KAF-ə-nay-tid] adj (of coffee) with the caffeine removed.

dec·a·gon [DEK-ə-gon] n figure of 10 angles.

dec·a·he·dron [dek-ə-HEE-drən] n solid of 10 faces.

de·cal·ci·fy [dee-KAL-si-fī] vt **-fied, -fy·ing.** deprive of lime, as bones or teeth.

Dec·a·logue [DEK-ə-lawg] n the Ten Commandments.

de·camp [di-KAMP] vi make off, break camp, abscond.

de·cant [di-KANT] vt pour off (liquid, as wine) to leave sediment. **de·cant'er** n stoppered bottle for wine or whiskey.

de·cap·i·tate [di-KAP-i-tayt] vt behead. **de·cap·i·ta'tion** n

de·cath·lon [di-KATH-lon] n athletic contest with ten events.

de·cay [di-KAY] v rot, decompose; fall off, decline. ▶ n rotting; a falling away, break up.

de·cease [di-SEES] n death. ▶ vi **-ceased, -ceas·ing.** die. **deceased** adj dead. ▶ n person lately dead.

de·ceive [di-SEEV] vt **-ceived, -ceiv·ing.** mislead, delude, cheat. **de·ceit'** n fraud; duplicity. **de·ceit'ful** adj

de·cel·er·ate [dee-SEL-ə-rayt] vi **-at·ed, -at·ing.** slow down.

de·cen·ni·al [di-SEN-ee-əl] adj of period of ten years.

de·cent [DEE-sənt] adj respectable; fitting, seemly; not obscene; adequate; inf kindly. **de'cen·cy** n

de·cen·tral·ize [dee-SEN-trə-līz] vt **-ized, -iz·ing.** divide (government, organization) among local centers.

de·cep·tion [di-SEP-shən] n deceiving; illusion; fraud; trick. **de·cep'tive** adj misleading; apt to mislead.

deci- comb. form one tenth, e.g. decimetre.

dec·i·bel [DES-ə-bəl] n unit for measuring intensity of a sound.

de·cide [di-SĪD] v **-cid·ed, -cid·ing.** ▶ vt settle, determine, bring to resolution; give judgment. ▶ vi come to a decision, conclusion. **de·cid'ed** adj unmistakable; settled; resolute. **de·cid'ed·ly** adv certainly, undoubtedly. **de·cis'ion** [-SIZH-ən] n **de·ci'sive** adj **de·ci'sive·ness** n

de·cid·u·ous [di-SIJ-oo-əs] adj of trees, losing leaves annually; of antlers, teeth, etc. being shed at the end of a period of growth.

dec·i·mal [DES-ə-məl] adj relating to tenths; proceeding by tens. ▶ n decimal fraction. **decimal system**

system of weights and measures, or coinage, in which value of each denomination is ten times the one below it.

dec·i·mate [DES-ə-mayt] *vt* **-mat·ed, -mat·ing.** destroy or kill a tenth of, large proportion of. **dec·i·ma'tion** *n*

de·ci·pher [di-SĪ-fər] *vt* make out meaning of; decode. **de·ci'pher·a·ble** *adj*

deck [dek] *n* platform or floor, esp. one covering whole or part of ship's hull; cassette deck; pack of playing cards; *sl* small packet of a narcotic. ▸ *vt* array, decorate. **deck chair** folding chair made of canvas suspended in wooden frame.

de·claim [di-KLAYM] *v* speak dramatically, rhetorically or passionately; protest loudly. **dec·la·ma·tion** [dek-lə-MAY-shən] *n* **de·clam'a·to·ry** *adj*

de·clare [di-KLAIR] *v* **-clared, -clar·ing.** ▸ *vt* announce formally; state emphatically; show; name (as liable to customs duty). ▸ *vi* take sides (for); *Bridge* bid (a suit or no trump). **dec·la·ra·tion** [dek-lə-RAY-shən] *n* **de·clar'a·tive** *adj* **de·clar'er** *n Bridge* person who plays the contract.

de·cline [di-KLĪN] *v* **-clined, -clin·ing.** refuse; slope, bend or sink downward; deteriorate gradually; grow smaller, diminish; list the case endings of nouns, pronouns, adjectives. ▸ *n* gradual deterioration; movement downward; diminution; downward slope. **de·clen'sion** *n* in grammar, set of nouns, pronouns, etc.; falling off; declining. **de·clin'a·ble** *adj* **dec·li·na'tion** *n* sloping away, deviation; angle.

de·cliv·i·ty [di-KLIV-i-tee] *n* downward slope.

de·code [dee-KOHD] *vt* **-cod·ed, -cod·ing.** put in intelligible terms a message in code or secret alphabet.

dé·col·le·té [day-kol-TAY] *adj* (of women's garment) having a low-cut neckline. **dé·col·le·tage'** [-TAHZH] *n* low-cut neckline.

de·com·mis·sion [dee-kə-MISH-ən] *vt* dismantle (nuclear reactor, industrial plant) sufficiently to abandon safely; remove (ship) from service.

de·com·pose [dee-kəm-POHZ] *v* **-posed, -pos·ing.** separate into elements; rot. **de·com·po·si·tion** [dee-kom-pə-ZISH-ən] *n* decay.

de·com·press [dee-kəm-PRES] *vt* free from pressure; return to condition of normal atmospheric pressure. **de·com·pres'sion** *n*

de·con·ges·tant [dee-kən-JES-tənt] *adj, n* (drug) relieving (esp. nasal) congestion.

de·con·tam·i·nate [dee-kən-TAM-ə-nayt] *vt* **-nat·ed, -nat·ing.** free from contamination e.g. from poisons, radioactive substances.

de·con·trol [dee-kən-TROHL] *vt* **-trolled, -trol·ling.** release from government control.

dé·cor [day-KOR] *n* decorative scheme of a room, etc.; stage decoration, scenery.

dec·o·rate [DEK-ə-rayt] *vt* **-rat·ed, -rat·ing.** beautify by additions; select paint, furniture, etc. for room, apartment, etc.; award (medal, etc.). **dec·o·ra'tion** *n* **dec'o·ra·tive** [-rə-tiv] *adj*

de·co·rum [di-KOR-əm] *n* seemly behavior, propriety, decency. **dec·o·rous** [DEK-ə-rəs] *adj*

de·coy [DEE-koi] *n* something used to entrap others or to distract their attention; bait, lure. ▸ *v* [di-KOI] lure, be lured as with decoy.

de·crease [di-KREES] *v* **-creased, -creas·ing.** diminish, lessen. ▸ *n* [DEE-krees] lessening.

de·cree [di-KREE] *n* order having the force of law; edict. ▸ *v* **-creed, -cree·ing.** determine judicially; order.

dec·re·ment [DEK-rə-mənt] *n* act or state of decreasing; quantity lost by decrease.

de·crep·it [di-KREP-it] *adj* old and feeble; broken down, worn out. **de·crep'i·tude** *n*

de·cry [di-KRĪ] *vt* **-cried, -cry·ing.**

disparage.

ded·i·cate [DED-i-kayt] vt -cat·ed, -cat·ing. commit wholly to special purpose or cause; inscribe or address (book, etc.); devote to God's service. **ded·i·ca'tion** n **ded'i·ca·to·ry** [-kə-tor-ee] adj

de·duce [di-DOOS] vt -duced, -duc·ing. draw as conclusion from facts. **de·duct** [di-DUKT] vt take away, subtract. **de·duct'i·ble** adj **de·duc'tion** n deducting; amount subtracted; conclusion deduced; inference from general to particular. **de·duc'tive** adj

deed n action or fact; exploit; legal document.

deem vt judge, consider, regard.

deep adj -er, -est. extending far down, in or back; at, of given depth; profound; heartfelt; hard to fathom; cunning; engrossed, immersed; of color, dark and rich; of sound, low and full. ▶ n deep place; the sea. ▶ adv far down, etc. **deep'en** vt **deep'ly** adv **deep freeze** condition or period of suspended activity.

deer n, pl **deer.** family of ruminant animals typically with antlers in male. **deer'stalk·er** n one who stalks deer; kind of cloth hat with visor in front and behind.

de·face [di-FAYS] vt -faced, -fac·ing. spoil or mar surface; disfigure. **de·face'ment** n

de fac·to [day FAK-toh] Lat existing in fact, whether legally recognized or not.

de·fal·ca·tion [dee-fal-KAY-shən] n misappropriation of money held by trustee, etc.; the money taken. **de·fal·cate** [di-FAL-kayt] vi -cat·ed, -cat·ing.

de·fame [di-FAYM] vt -famed, -fam·ing. speak ill of, dishonor by slander or rumor. **def·a·ma·tion** [def-ə-MAY-shən] n **de·fam'a·to·ry** adj

de·fault [di-FAWLT] n failure, neglect to act, appear or pay; Computers instruction to a computer to select a particular option unless the user specifies

otherwise. ▶ v fail (to pay). **de·fault'er** n one who defaults.

de·feat [di-FEET] vt overcome, vanquish; thwart. ▶ n overthrow; lose battle or encounter; frustration. **de·feat'ism** n attitude tending to accept defeat. **de·feat'ist** n, adj

def·e·cate [DEF-i-kayt] vt -cat·ed, -cat·ing. empty the bowels; clear of impurities. **def·e·ca'tion** n

de·fect [DEE-fekt] n lack, blemish, failing. ▶ vi [di-FEKT] desert one's country, cause, etc., esp. to join opponents. **de·fec'tion** n abandonment of duty or allegiance. **de·fec'tive** adj incomplete; faulty.

de·fend [di-FEND] vt protect, ward off attack; support by argument, evidence; (try to) maintain (title, etc.) against challenger. **de·fense'** n **de·fend'ant** n person accused in court. **de·fend'er** n **de·fen'si·ble** adj **de·fen'sive** adj serving for defense. ▶ n position or attitude of defense.

de·fer¹ [di-FUR] vt -ferred, -fer·ring. put off, postpone. **de·fer'ment, de·fer'ral** n

de·fer² vi -ferred, -fer·ring. submit to opinion or judgment of another. **def'er·ence** n respectful submission to views, etc. of another. **def·er·en'tial** [-shəl] adj

defiance, defiant see DEFY.

de·fi·cient [di-FISH-ənt] adj lacking or falling short in something, insufficient. **de·fi'cien·cy** n

def·i·cit [DEF-ə-sit] n amount by which sum of money is too small; lack, shortage.

de·file¹ [di-FIL] vt -filed, -fil·ing. make dirty, pollute, soil; sully; desecrate.

de·file² n narrow pass or valley. ▶ vi -filed, -fil·ing. march in file.

de·fine [di-FIN] vt -fined, -fin·ing. state contents or meaning of; show clearly the form; lay down clearly, fix; mark out. **de·fin'a·ble** adj **def·i·ni'tion** [-NISH-ən] n **def'i·nite** [-nit] adj exact, defined; clear, specific; certain, sure.

de·fin·i·tive *adj* conclusive, to be looked on as final.

de·flate [di-FLAYT] *v* **-flat·ed, -flat·ing.** (cause to) collapse by release of gas from; take away (person's) self-esteem; *Economics* cause deflation. **de·fla'tion** *n* deflating; *Economics* reduction of economic and industrial activity. **de·fla'tion·ar·y** *adj*

de·flect [di-FLEKT] *v* (cause to) turn from straight course. **de·flec'tion** *n*

de·flow·er [di-FLOW-ər] *vt* deprive of virginity, innocence, etc. **def·lo·ra'tion** *n*

de·fo·li·ate [dee-FOH-lee-ayt] *v* **-at·ed, -at·ing.** (cause to) lose leaves, esp. by action of chemicals. **defo'li·ant** *n* **de·fo·li·a'tion** *n*

de·form [di-FORM] *vt* spoil shape of; make ugly; disfigure. **de·formed'** *adj* **de·form'i·ty** *n, pl* **-ties.**

de·fraud [di-FRAWD] *vt* cheat, swindle.

de·fray [di-FRAY] *vt* provide money for (expenses, etc.).

de·frock [di-FROK] *vt* deprive (priest, minister) of ecclesiastical status.

de·frost [di-FRAWST] *v* make, become free of frost, ice; thaw.

deft *adj* **-er, -est.** skillful, adroit. **deft'ly** *adv* **deft'ness** *n*

de·funct [di-FUNGKT] *adj* dead, obsolete.

de·fuse [dee-FYOOZ] *vt* **-fused, -fus·ing.** remove fuse of bomb, etc.; remove tension (from situation, etc.).

de·fy [di-FĪ] *vt* **-fied, -fy·ing.** challenge, resist successfully; disregard. **de·fi'ance** *n* resistance. **de·fi'ant** *adj* openly and aggressively hostile; insolent.

de·gauss [dee-GOWS] *vt* neutralize magnetic field (of ship's hull, electronic apparatus, etc.).

de·gen·er·ate [di-JEN-ə-rayt] *vi* **-rat·ed, -rat·ing.** deteriorate to lower mental, moral, or physical level. ▶ *adj* [-rit] fallen away in quality. ▶ *n* [-rit] degenerate person. **de·gen'er·a·cy** *n*

de·grade [di-GRAYD] *v* **-grad·ed, -grad·ing.** ▶ *vt* dishonor; debase; reduce to lower rank. ▶ *vi* decompose chemically. **de·grad'a·ble** *adj* capable of chemical, biological decomposition. **de·grad'ed** *adj* shamed, humiliated. **deg·ra·da'tion** *n*

de·gree [di-GREE] *n* step, stage in process, scale, relative rank, order, condition, manner, way; academic title conferred by university or college; unit of measurement of temperature or angle. **third degree** severe, lengthy examination, esp. of accused person by police, to extract information, confession.

de·hu·mid·i·fy [dee-hyoo-MID-ə-fī] *vt* **-fied, -fy·ing.** extract moisture from.

de·hy·drate [dee-HĪ-drayt] *vt* **-drat·ed, -drat·ing.** remove moisture from. **de·hy·dra'tion** *n*

de·ice [dee-ĪS] *vt* **-iced, -ic·ing.** to dislodge ice from (e.g. windshield) or prevent its forming.

de·i·fy [DEE-ə-fī] *vt* **-fied, -fy·ing.** make god of; treat, worship as god. **de·i·fi·ca'tion** *n*

deign [dayn] *vt* condescend, stoop; think fit.

de·ism [DEE-iz-əm] *n* belief in god but not in revelation. **de'ist** *n*

de·i·ty [DEE-i-tee] *n, pl* **-ties.** divine status or attributes; a god.

dé·jà vu [DAY-*zh*ah VOO] *Fr* experience of perceiving new situation as if it had occurred before.

de·ject [di-JEKT] *vt* dishearten, cast down, depress. **de·ject'ed** *adj* **de·jec'tion** *n*

de ju·re [di JUUR-ee] *Lat* in law, by right.

de·lay [di-LAY] *vt* postpone, hold back. ▶ *vi* be tardy, linger. ▶ *n* act or instance of delaying; interval of time between events.

de·lec·ta·ble [di-LEK-tə-bəl] *adj* delightful delicious. **de·lec·ta·tion** [dee-lek-TAY-shən] *n* pleasure.

del·e·gate [DEL-i-git] *n* person

chosen to represent another. ▶ vt
[-gayt] **-gat·ed, -gat·ing.** send as
deputy; commit (authority,
business, etc.) to a deputy.
del·e·ga'tion n

de·lete [di-LEET] vt **-let·ed, -let·ing.**
remove, cancel, erase. **de·le'tion** n

del·e·te·ri·ous [del-i-TEER-ee-əs]
adj harmful, injurious.

de·lib·er·ate [di-LIB-ər-it] adj
intentional; well considered;
without haste, slow. ▶ v [-rayt]
-rat·ed, -rat·ing. consider, debate.
de·lib·er·a'tion n

del·i·cate [DEL-i-kit] adj exquisite;
not robust, fragile; sensitive;
requiring tact; deft. **del'i·ca·cy** n

del·i·ca·tes·sen [del-i-kə-TES-ən] n
store selling ready-to-eat foods; the
food sold.

de·li·cious [di-LISH-əs] adj
delightful, pleasing to senses, esp.
taste.

de·light [di-LĪT] vt please greatly.
▶ vi take great pleasure (in). ▶ n
great pleasure. **de·light'ful** adj
charming.

de·lin·e·ate [di-LIN-ee-ayt] vt
-at·ed, -at·ing. portray by drawing
or description; represent
accurately. **de·lin·e·a'tion** n

de·lin·quent [di-LING-kwənt] n
someone, esp. young person,
guilty of delinquency. ▶ adj
de·lin'quen·cy n, pl **-cies.** (minor)
offense or misdeed.

del·i·quesce [del-i-KWES] vi
-quesced, -quesc·ing. become
liquid. **del·i·ques'cence** n
del·i·ques'cent adj

de·lir·i·um [di-LEER-ee-əm] n
disorder of the mind, esp. in
feverish illness; violent excitement.
de·lir'i·ous adj raving;
light-headed, wildly excited.

de·liv·er [di-LIV-ər] vt carry (goods,
etc.) to destination; hand over;
release; give birth or assist in birth
(of); utter or present (speech, etc.).
de·liv'er·ance n rescue. **de·liv'er·y**
n

Del·phic [DEL-fik] adj pert. to
Delphi or to the oracle of Apollo.

del·ta [DEL-tə] n alluvial tract where

river at mouth breaks into several
streams; fourth letter in the Greek
alphabet; shape of this letter.

de·lude [di-LOOD] vt **-lud·ed,
-lud·ing.** deceive; mislead.
de·lu'sion [-zhən] n

del·uge [DEL-yooj] n flood, great
flow, rush, downpour, cloudburst.
▶ vt **-uged, -ug·ing.** flood,
overwhelm.

deluxe [də-LUKS] adj rich,
sumptuous; superior in quality.

delve [delv] v **delved, delv·ing.**
(with into) search intensively; dig.

de·mag·net·ize [dee-MAG-ni-tīz] vt
-tized, -tiz·ing. deprive of
magnetic polarity.

dem·a·gogue [DEM-ə-gog] n mob
leader or agitator. **dem·a·gog'ic**
[-GOJ-ik] adj **dem'a·go·gy**
[-goh-jee] n

de·mand [di-MAND] vt ask as
giving an order; ask as by right; call
for as due, right or necessary. ▶ n
urgent request, claim, requirement;
call for (specific commodity).
de·mand'ing adj requiring great
skill, patience, etc.

de·mar·cate [di-MAHR-kayt] vt
-cat·ed, -cat·ing. mark boundaries
or limits of. **de·mar·ca'tion** n

de·mean [di-MEEN] vt degrade,
lower, humiliate.

de·mean·or [di-MEEN-ər] n
conduct, bearing, behavior.

de·men·ted [di-MEN-tid] adj mad,
crazy; beside oneself. **de·men'tia**
[-shə] n form of insanity.

de·mer·it [di-MER-it] n bad mark;
undesirable quality.

demi- comb. form half, e.g. demigod.

de·mil·i·ta·rize [dee-MIL-i-tə-rīz] vt
-rized, -riz·ing. prohibit military
presence or function in (an area).

dem·i·monde [DEM-ee-mond] n
class of women of doubtful
reputation; group behaving with
doubtful legality, etc.

de·mise [di-MĪZ] n death;
conveyance by will or bequest;
transfer of sovereignty on death or
abdication.

dem·i·urge [DEM-ee-urj] n name
given in some philosophies (esp.

Platonic) to the creator of the world and man.

dem·o [DEM-oh] *n inf* short for DEMONSTRATION.

de·mo·bi·lize [dee-MOH-bə-līz] *vt* **-lized, -liz·ing.** disband (troops); discharge (soldier).

de·moc·ra·cy [di-MOK-rə-see] *n, pl* **-cies.** government by the people or their elected representatives; country so governed. **dem·o·crat** [DEM-ə-krat] *n* advocate of democracy. **dem·o·crat'ic** *adj* connected with democracy; favoring popular rights. **de·moc'ra·tize** *vt* **-tized, -tiz·ing.**

de·mog·ra·phy [di-MOG-rə-fee] *n* study of population statistics, as births, deaths, diseases. **dem·o·graph·ic** [dem-ə-GRAF-ik] *adj*

de·mol·ish [di-MOL-ish] *vt* knock to pieces; destroy utterly, raze. **dem·o·li·tion** [dem-ə-LISH-ən] *n*

de·mon [DEE-mən] *n* devil, evil spirit; very cruel or malignant person; person very good at or devoted to a given activity. **de·mo·ni·ac** [di-MOH-nee-ak] *n* one possessed with a devil. **de·mo·ni·a·cal** [dee-mə-NĪ-ə-kəl] *adj* **de·mon·ic** [di-MON-ik] *adj* of the nature of a devil. **de·mon·ol'o·gy** [dee-] *n* study of demons.

dem·on·strate [DEM-ən-strayt] *v* **-strat·ed, -strat·ing.** ▸ *vt* show by reasoning, prove; describe, explain by specimens or experiments. ▸ *vi* make exhibition of support, protest, etc. by public parade, demonstration; make show of armed force. **de·mon·stra·ble** [di-MON-strə-bəl] *adj* **dem·on·stra'tion** *n* making clear, proving by evidence; exhibition and description; organized public expression of opinion; display of armed force. **de·mon'stra·tive** *adj* expressing feelings, emotions easily and unreservedly; pointing out; conclusive. **dem'on·stra·tor** *n* one who demonstrates equipment, products, etc.; one who takes part

in a public demonstration.

de·mor·al·ize [di-MOR-ə-līz] *vt* **-ized, -iz·ing.** deprive of courage and discipline; undermine morally. **de·mor·al·i·za'tion** *n*

de·mote [di-MOHT] *vt* **-mot·ed, -mot·ing.** reduce in status or rank. **de·mo'tion** *n*

de·mur [di-MUR] *vi* **-murred, -mur·ring.** make difficulties, object. **de·mur'ral** *n* raising of objection; objection raised. **de·mur'rer** *n*

de·mure [di-MYUUR] *adj* **-mur·er, -mur·est.** reserved, quiet. **de·mure'ly** *adv*

den *n* cave or hole of wild beast; lair; small room, esp. study; site, haunt.

de·na·tion·a·lize [dee-NASH-ə-nl-īz] *vt* **-lized, -liz·ing.** return (an industry) from public to private ownership.

de·na·ture [dee-NAY-chər] *vt* **-tured, -tur·ing.** deprive of essential qualities, adulterate. **denatured alcohol** alcohol made undrinkable.

den·gue [DENG-gee] *n* an infectious tropical fever.

denial see DENY.

de·nier [DEN-yər] *n* unit of weight of silk and synthetic yarn.

den·i·grate [DEN-i-grayt] *vt* **-grat·ed, -grat·ing.** belittle or disparage character of.

den·im [DEN-əm] *n* strong twilled cotton fabric for trousers, overalls, etc. ▸ *pl* garment made of this.

den·i·zen [DEN-ə-zən] *n* inhabitant.

de·nom·i·nate [di-NOM-ə-nayt] *vt* **-nat·ed, -nat·ing.** give name to. **de·nom·i·na'tion** *n* distinctly named church or sect; name, esp. of class or group. **de·nom·i·na'tion·al** *adj* **de·nom'i·na·tor** *n* Arithmetic divisor in fraction.

de·note [di-NOHT] *vt* **-not·ed, -not·ing.** stand for, be the name of; mark, indicate, show. **de·no·ta·tion** [dee-noh-TAY-shən] *n* esp. explicit meaning of word or phrase.

de·noue·ment [day-noo-MAHN] *n*

unraveling of dramatic plot; final solution of mystery.

de·nounce [di-NOWNS] vt **-nounced, -nounc·ing.** speak violently against; accuse; terminate (treaty). **de·nun·ci·a'tion** n denouncing.

dense [dens] adj **dens·er, dens·est.** thick, compact; stupid. **den'si·ty** n, pl **-ties.** mass per unit of volume.

dent n hollow or mark left by blow or pressure. ▶ vt make dent in; mark with dent.

den·tal [DEN-tl] adj of, pert. to teeth or dentistry; pronounced by applying tongue to teeth. **den'ti·frice** [-fris] n powder, paste, or wash for cleaning teeth. **den'tist** n one skilled in care, repair of teeth. **den'tis·try** n art of dentist. **den·ti'tion** n teething; arrangement of teeth. **den'ture** [-chər] n (usu pl) set of false teeth. **dental floss** soft thread, oft. waxed, for cleaning between teeth.

den·tine [DEN-teen] n the hard bonelike part of a tooth.

de·nude [di-NOOD] vt **-nud·ed, -nud·ing.** strip, make bare; expose (rock) by erosion of plants, soil, etc. **denunciation** see DENOUNCE.

de·ny [di-NĪ] vt **-nied, -ny·ing.** declare untrue; contradict; reject; disown; refuse to give; refuse; (reflex) abstain from. **de·ni'a·ble** adj **de·ni'al** n

de·o·dor·ize [dee-OH-də-rīz] vt **-ized, -iz·ing.** rid of smell or mask smell of. **de·o'dor·ant** n **de·o'dor·iz·er** n

de·ox·i·dize [dee-OK-si-dīz] vt **-dized, -diz·ing.** deprive of oxygen.

de·part [di-PAHRT] vi go away; start out, set forth; deviate, vary; die. **de·par'ture** [-chər] n

de·part·ment [di-PAHRT-mənt] n division; branch; province. **de·part·men'tal** adj

de·pend [di-PEND] vi (usu. with on) rely entirely; live; be contingent, await settlement or decision. **de·pend'a·ble** adj reliable. **de·pend'ent** n one for whose maintenance another is responsible. ▶ adj depending on. **de·pend'ence** n **de·pend'en·cy** n dependence; subject territory.

de·pict [di-PIKT] vt give picture of; describe in words. **de·pic'tion** n

de·pil·a·to·ry [di-PIL-ə-tor-ee] n, pl **-ries.** substance that removes unwanted hair. ▶ adj

de·plete [di-PLEET] vt **-plet·ed, -plet·ing.** empty; reduce; exhaust. **de·ple'tion** n

de·plore [di-PLOR] vt **-plored, -plor·ing.** lament, regret; deprecate, complain of. **de·plor'a·ble** adj lamentable; disgraceful.

de·ploy [di-PLOI] v of troops, ships, aircraft (cause to) adopt battle formation; arrange. **de·ploy'ment** n

de·po·nent [di-POH-nənt] adj of verb, having passive form but active meaning. ▶ n deponent verb; one who makes statement under oath.

de·pop·u·late [di-POP-yə-layt] v **-lat·ed, -lat·ing.** (cause to) be reduced in population. **de·pop·u·la'tion** n

de·port [di-PORT] vt expel from foreign country, banish. **de·por·ta'tion** [dee-] n

de·port·ment [di-PORT-mənt] n behavior, conduct, bearing. **de·port'** v behave, carry (oneself).

de·pose [di-POHZ] v **-posed, -pos·ing.** ▶ vt remove from office, esp. of ruler. ▶ vi make statement under oath, give evidence. **de·pos'al** n removal from office.

de·pos·it [di-POZ-it] vt set down, esp. carefully; give into safekeeping, esp. in bank; let fall (as sediment). ▶ n thing deposited; money given in part payment or as security; sediment. **dep·o·si'tion** [dep-ə-ZISH-ən] n statement written and attested; act of deposing or depositing. **de·pos'i·tor** n **de·pos'i·to·ry** n, pl **-ries.** place for safekeeping.

dep·ot [DEE-poh] n storehouse; building for storage and servicing of buses, trains, etc.; railroad, bus station.

de·prave [di-PRAYV] vt **-praved, -prav·ing.** make bad, corrupt, pervert. **de·prav'i·ty** n, pl **-ties.** wickedness, viciousness.

dep·re·cate [DEP-ri-kayt] vt **-cat·ed, -cat·ing.** express disapproval of; advise against. **dep·re·ca'tion** n **dep're·ca·to·ry** adj

de·pre·ci·ate [di-PREE-shee-ayt] v **-at·ed, -at·ing.** ▶ vt lower price, value or purchasing power of; belittle. ▶ vi fall in value. **de·pre·ci·a'tion** n

dep·re·da·tion [dep-ri-DAY-shən] n plundering, pillage. **dep're·date** vt **-dat·ed, -dat·ing.** plunder, despoil.

de·press [di-PRES] vt affect with low spirits; lower, in level or activity. **de·pres'sion** [-PRESH-ən] n hollow; low spirits, dejection, despondency; poor condition of business, slump. **de·pres'sant** adj, n

de·prive [di-PRĪV] vt **-prived, -priv·ing.** strip, dispossess. **dep·ri·va·tion** [dep-rə-VAY-shən] n **deprived** adj lacking adequate food, care, amenities, etc.

depth n (degree of) deepness; deep place, abyss; intensity (of color, feeling); profundity (of mind). **depth charge** bomb for use against submarines.

de·pute [di-PYOOT] **-put·ed, -put·ing.** ▶ vt allot; appoint as an agent or substitute. **dep·u·ta·tion** [dep-yə-TAY-shən] n persons sent to speak for others. **dep'u·tize** vi **-tized, -tiz·ing.** act for another. ▶ vt depute. **dep'u·ty** n, pl **-ties.** assistant; substitute, delegate.

de·rail [dee-RAYL] v (cause to) go off the rails, as train, etc. **de·rail'ment** n

de·rail·leur [di-RAY-lər] n gear-changing mechanism for bicycles.

de·range [di-RAYNJ] vt **-ranged, -rang·ing.** put out of place, out of order; upset; make insane. **de·range'ment** n

der·by [DUR-bee] n horserace, esp.

Kentucky Derby, held at Churchill Downs, Kentucky; contest between teams of skaters, etc.; man's low-crowned stiff felt hat.

de·reg·u·late [dee-REG-yə-layt] vt **-lat·ed, -lat·ing.** remove regulations or controls from.

der·e·lict [DER-ə-likt] adj abandoned, forsaken; falling into ruins, dilapidated. ▶ n social outcast, vagrant; abandoned property, ship, etc. **der·e·lic'tion** n neglect (of duty); abandoning.

de·ride [di-RĪD] vt **-rid·ed, -rid·ing.** speak of or treat with contempt, ridicule. **de·ri'sion** [-RIZH-ən] n ridicule. **de·ri'sive** [-RĪ-siv] adj

de ri·gueur [də ri-GUR] Fr required by etiquette, fashion or custom.

de·rive [di-RĪV] vt **-rived, -riv·ing.** deduce, get from; show origin of. ▶ vi issue, be descended (from). **der·i·va·tion** [der-ə-VAY-shən] n **de·riv·a·tive** [di-RIV-ə-tiv] adj, n

der·ma·ti·tis [dur-mə-TĪ-tis] n inflammation of skin.

der·ma·tol·o·gy [dur-mə-TOL-ə-jee] n science of skin. **der·ma·tol'o·gist** n physician specializing in skin diseases.

de·rog·a·to·ry [di-ROG-ə-tor-ee] adj disparaging, belittling, intentionally offensive. **der·o·gate** [DER-ə-gayt] v **-gat·ed, -gat·ing.** ▶ vt disparage. ▶ vi detract.

der·rick [DER-ik] n hoisting machine; framework over oil well, etc.

der·ring-do [DER-ing DOO] n (act of) spirited bravery, boldness.

der·rin·ger [DER-in-jər] n short-barreled pocket pistol.

der·vish [DUR-vish] n member of Muslim ascetic order, noted for frenzied, whirling dance.

des·cant [DES-kant] n Mus decorative variation sung as accompaniment to basic melody. ▶ vi [des-KANT] Mus sing or play a descant; talk about in detail; dwell (on) at length.

de·scend [di-SEND] vi come or go down; slope down; stoop, condescend; spring from (ancestor, etc.); pass to heir, be transmitted; swoop on or attack. ▶ *vt* go or come down. **de·scend'ant** *n* person descended from an ancestor. **de·scent'** *n*

de·scribe [di-SKRĪB] *vt* **-scribed, -scrib·ing.** give detailed account of; pronounce or label; trace out (geometric figure, etc.). **de·scrip'tion** [-SKRIP-shən] *n* detailed account; marking out; kind, sort, species. **de·scrip'tive** *adj*

de·scry [di-SKRĪ] *vt* **-scried, -scry·ing.** make out, catch sight of, esp. at a distance espy.

des·e·crate [DES-i-krayt] *vt* **-crat·ed, -crat·ing.** violate sanctity of; profane; convert to evil use. **des·e·cra'tion** *n*

des·ert[1] [DEZ-ərt] *n* uninhabited and barren region. ▶ *adj* barren, uninhabited, desolate.

de·sert[2] [di-ZURT] *vt* abandon, forsake, leave. ▶ *vi* run away from service, esp. of soldiers, sailors, etc. **de·sert'er** *n* **de·ser'tion** *n*

de·sert[3] [di-ZURT] *n* (usu pl) what is due as reward or punishment; merit, virtue.

de·serve [di-ZURV] *vt* **-served, -serv·ing.** show oneself worthy of; have by conduct a claim to. **de·serv'ed·ly** *adv* **de·serv'ing** *adj* worthy (of reward, etc.).

deshabille *n* see DISHABILLE.

des·ic·cate [DES-i-kayt] *v* **-cat·ed, -cat·ing.** dry; dry up.

de·sid·er·a·tum [di-sid-ə-RAH-təm] *n, pl* **-ta** [-tə] something lacked and wanted.

de·sign [di-ZĪN] *vt* make working drawings for; sketch; plan out; intend, select for. ▶ *n* outline sketch; working plan; art of making decorative patterns, etc.; project, purpose, mental plan. **de·sign'ed·ly** *adv* on purpose. **de·sign'er** *n* esp. one who draws designs for manufacturers or selects typefaces, etc. for books, etc. **de·sign'ing** *adj* crafty, scheming.

des·ig·nate [DEZ-ig-nayt] *vt* **-nat·ed, -nat·ing.** name, pick out, appoint to office. ▶ *adj* [-nit]

appointed but not yet installed. **des·ig·na'tion** *n* name, appellation.

de·sire [di-ZĪR] *vt* **-sired, -sir·ing.** wish, long for; ask for, entreat. ▶ *n* longing, craving; expressed wish, request; sexual appetite; something wished for or requested. **de·sir'a·ble** *adj* worth desiring. **de·sir'ous** *adj* filled with desire.

de·sist [di-ZIST] *vi* cease, stop.

desk *n* table or other piece of furniture designed for reading or writing; counter; editorial section of newspaper, etc. covering specific subject; section of State Department having responsibility for particular operations.

des·o·late [DES-ə-lit] *adj* uninhabited; neglected, barren, ruinous; solitary; dreary, dismal, forlorn. ▶ *vt* [-layt] **-lat·ed, -lat·ing.** depopulate, lay waste; overwhelm with grief. **des·o·la'tion** *n*

de·spair [di-SPAIR] *vi* lose hope. ▶ *n* loss of all hope; cause of this; despondency.

despatch see DISPATCH.

des·pe·rate [DES-pər-it] *adj* reckless from despair; difficult or dangerous; frantic; hopelessly bad; leaving no room for hope. **des·per·a'do** [-pə-RAH-doh] *n, pl* **-dos.** reckless, lawless person. **des'per·ate·ly** *adv* **des·per·a'tion** *n*

de·spise [di-SPĪZ] *vt* **-spised, -spis·ing.** look down on as contemptible, inferior. **des·pi·ca·ble** [DES-pi-kə-bəl] *adj* base, contemptible, vile.

de·spite [di-SPĪT] *prep* in spite of.

de·spoil [di-SPOIL] *vt* plunder, rob, strip of. **de·spo·li·a·tion** [di-spoh-lee-AY-shən] *n*

de·spond·ent [di-SPON-dənt] *adj* dejected, depressed. **de·spond'en·cy** *n*

des·pot [DES-pət] *n* tyrant, oppressor. **des·pot·ic** [di-SPOT-ik] *adj* **des'pot·ism** *n* autocratic government, tyranny.

des·sert [di-ZURT] *n* course of pastry, fruit, etc. served at end of meal.

des·ti·na·tion [des-tə-NAY-shən] n place a person or thing is bound for; goal; purpose.

des·tine [DES-tin] vt **-tined, -tin·ing.** ordain or fix beforehand; set apart, devote.

des·ti·ny [DES-tə-nee] n, pl **-nies.** course of events or person's fate; the power that foreordains.

des·ti·tute [DES-ti-toot] adj in absolute want; in great need, devoid (of); penniless. **des·ti·tu'tion** n

de·stroy [di-STROI] vt ruin; pull to pieces; undo; put an end to; demolish; annihilate. **de·stroy'er** n one who destroys; small, swift, heavily armed warship. **de·struct** [di-STRUKT] v destroy (one's own missile, etc.) for safety; be destroyed. **de·struct'i·ble** adj **de·struc'tion** n ruin, overthrow; death. **de·struc'tive** adj destroying; negative, not constructive.

des·ue·tude [DES-wi-tood] n disuse, discontinuance.

des·ul·to·ry [DES-əl-tor-ee] adj passing, changing fitfully from one thing to another; aimless; unmethodical.

de·tach [di-TACH] vt unfasten, disconnect, separate. **de·tach'a·ble** adj **de·tached'** adj standing apart, isolated; impersonal, disinterested. **de·tach'ment** n aloofness; detaching; a body of troops detached for special duty.

de·tail [di-TAYL or DEE-tayl] n particular; small or unimportant part; treatment of anything item by item; party or personnel assigned for duty in military unit. ▶ vt relate in full; appoint for duty.

de·tain [di-TAYN] vt keep under restraint; hinder; keep waiting. **de·ten'tion** n confinement; arrest; detaining.

de·tect [di-TEKT] vt find out or discover existence, presence, nature or identity of. **de·tec'tion** n **de·tec'tive** n police officer or private agent employed in

detecting crime. ▶ adj employed in detection. **de·tec'tor** n esp. mechanical sensing device or device for detecting radio signals, etc.

dé·tente [day-TAHNT] n lessening of tension in political or international affairs.

detention n see DETAIN.

de·ter [di-TUR] vt **-terred, -ter·ring.** discourage, frighten; hinder; prevent. **de·ter'rent** adj, n

de·ter·gent [di-TUR-jənt] n cleansing, purifying substance. ▶ adj having cleansing power.

de·te·ri·o·rate [di-TEER-ee-ə-rayt] v **-rat·ed, -rat·ing.** become or make worse. **de·te·ri·o·ra'tion** n

de·ter·mine [di-TUR-min] v **-mined, -min·ing.** ▶ vt make up one's mind, decide; fix as known; bring to a decision; be deciding factor in; Law end. ▶ vi come to an end; come to a decision. **de·ter'mi·nant** adj, n **de·ter'mi·nate** [-nit] adj fixed in scope or nature. **de·ter·mi·na'tion** n determining; firm or resolute conduct or purpose; resolve. **determined** adj resolute. **de·ter'min·ism** n theory that human action is settled by forces independent of human will.

de·test [di-TEST] vt hate, loathe. **de·test'a·ble** adj **de·tes·ta'tion** [dee-te-STAY-shən] n

de·throne [dee-THROHN] vt **-throned, -thron·ing.** remove from throne, depose.

det·o·nate [DET-n-ayt] v of bomb, mine, explosives, etc., (cause to) explode. **det·o·na'tion** n **det'o·na·tor** n mechanical, electrical device, or small amount of explosive, used to set off main explosive charge.

de·tour [DEE-tuur] n course that leaves main route to rejoin it later; roundabout way. ▶ vi

de·tox [DEE-toks] inf ▶ n treatment to rid the body of poisonous substances. ▶ v [dee-TOKS] undergo or subject to such treatment.

de·tract [di-TRAKT] v take away (a

part) from, diminish. **de·trac'tor** n

det·ri·ment [DE-trə-mənt] n harm done, loss, damage. **det·ri·men'tal** adj damaging, injurious.

de·tri·tus [di-TRI-təs] n worn-down matter such as gravel, or rock debris; debris.

de trop [də TROH] Fr not wanted, superfluous.

deuce [doos] n two; playing card with two spots; Tennis forty all; in exclamatory phrases, the devil.

Deut. Deuteronomy.

deu·te·ri·um [doo-TEER-ee-əm] n isotope of hydrogen twice as heavy as the normal gas.

de·val·ue [dee-VAL-yoo] **-ued, -u·ing,** v (of currency) reduce or be reduced in value; reduce the value or worth of. **de·val·u·a'tion** n

dev·as·tate [DEV-ə-stayt] vt **-tat·ed, -tat·ing.** lay waste; ravage; inf overwhelm. **dev·as·ta'tion** n

de·vel·op [di-VEL-əp] vt bring to maturity; elaborate; bring forth, bring out; evolve; treat photographic plate or film to bring out image; improve value or change use of (land) by building, etc. ▶ vi grow to maturer state. **de·vel'op·er** n one who develops land; chemical for developing film. **de·vel'op·ment** n

de·vi·ate [DEE-vee-ayt] vi **-at·ed, -at·ing.** leave the way, turn aside, diverge. **de'vi·ant** n, adj (person) deviating from normal esp. in sexual practices. **de·vi·a'tion** n **de'vi·ous** adj deceitful, underhanded; roundabout; rambling; erring.

de·vice [di-VIS] n contrivance, invention; apparatus; stratagem; scheme, plot; heraldic or emblematic figure or design.

dev·il [DEV-əl] n personified spirit of evil; superhuman evil being; person of great wickedness, cruelty, etc.; inf fellow; inf something difficult or annoying; energy, dash, unconquerable spirit; inf rogue, rascal. ▶ vt **-iled, -il·ing.** prepare (eggs, etc.) with spicy seasoning. **dev'il·ish** adj like, of the devil; evil.

▶ adv inf very, extremely. **dev'il·try** n, pl **-tries.** wickedness; wild and reckless mischief, revelry, high spirits. **dev'il-may-care'** adj happy-go-lucky. **devil's advocate** one who advocates opposing, unpopular view, usu. for sake of argument; Catholic Church one appointed to state disqualifications of person who has been proposed for sainthood.

devious adj see DEVIATE.

de·vise [di-VIZ] vt **-vised, -vis·ing.** plan, contrive; invent; plot; leave by will.

de·void [di-VOID] adj (usu. with of) empty, lacking, free from.

de·volve [di-VOLV] vi **-volved, -volv·ing.** pass or fall (to, upon). ▶ vt throw (duty, etc.) on to another. **dev·o·lu·tion** [dev-ə-LOO-shən] n devolving, esp. transfer of authority from central to regional government.

de·vote [di-VOHT] vt **-vot·ed, -vot·ing.** set apart, give up exclusively (to person, purpose, etc.). **devoted** adj loving, attached. **dev·o·tee** [dev-ə-TEE] n ardent enthusiast; zealous worshiper. **de·vo'tion** n deep affection, loyalty; dedication; religious earnestness. ▶ pl prayers, religious exercises. **de·vo'tion·al** adj

de·vour [di-VOWR] vt eat greedily; consume, destroy; read, gaze at eagerly.

de·vout [di-VOWT] adj earnestly religious, pious; sincere, heartfelt.

dew [doo] n moisture from air deposited as small drops on cool surface between nightfall and morning; any beaded moisture. ▶ vt wet with or as with dew. **dew'y** adj **dew·i·er, dew·i·est.** **dew'claw** n partly developed inner toe of dogs. **dew'lap** n fold of loose skin hanging from neck.

dex·ter·i·ty [dek-STER-i-tee] n manual skill, neatness, deftness, adroitness. **dex'ter·ous** adj showing dexterity, skillful.

dex·trose [DEK-strohs] n white,

soluble, sweet-tasting crystalline solid, occurring naturally in fruit, honey, animal tissue.

dia- *prefix* through.

di·a·be·tes [dī-ə-BEE-tis] *n* various disorders characterized by excretion of abnormal amount of urine in which body fails to store and utilize glucose. **di·a·bet'ic** *n, adj*

di·a·bol·ic [dī-ə-BOL-ik], **di·a·bol'i·cal** *adj* devilish; *inf* very bad. **di·a·bol'i·cal·ly** *adv*

di·a·crit·ic [dī-ə-KRIT-ik] *n* sign above letter or character indicating special phonetic value, etc. **di·a·crit'i·cal** *adj* of a diacritic; showing a distinction.

di·a·dem [DĪ-ə-dem] *n* a crown.

di·ag·no·sis [dī-əg-NOH-sis] *n, pl* **-ses** [-seez] identification of disease from symptoms. **di'ag·nose** [-nohz] *vt* **-nosed, -nos·ing.** **di·ag·nos'tic** [-NOS-tik] *adj*

di·ag·o·nal [dī-AG-ə-nl] *adj* from corner to corner; oblique. ▶ *n* line from corner to corner. **di·ag'o·nal·ly** *adv*

di·a·gram [DĪ-ə-gram] *n* drawing, figure in lines, to illustrate something being expounded. **di·a·gram·mat'i·cal·ly** *adv*

di·al [DĪ-əl] *n* face of clock, etc.; plate marked with graduations on which a pointer moves (as on a meter, radio, scale, etc.); numbered disk on front of telephone. ▶ *vt* operate telephone; indicate on dial.

di·a·lect [DĪ-ə-lekt] *n* characteristic speech of region; local variety of a language. **di·a·lec'tal** *adj*

di·a·lec·tic [dī-ə-LEK-tik] *n* art of arguing. **di·a·lec'ti·cal** *adj* **di·a·lec·ti'cian** [-TISH-ən] *n* logician; reasoner.

di·a·logue [DĪ-ə-lawg] *n* conversation between two or more (persons); representation of such conversation in drama, novel, etc.; discussion between representatives of two governments, etc.

di·al·y·sis [dī-AL-ə-sis] *n, pl* **-ses** [-seez] *Med* filtering of blood

through membrane to remove waste products.

di·am·e·ter [dī-AM-i-tər] *n* (length of) straight line from side to side of figure or body (esp. circle) through center; thickness. **di·a·met'ri·cal** *adj* opposite. **di·a·met'ri·cal·ly** *adv*

di·a·mond [DĪ-mənd] *n* very hard and brilliant precious stone, also used in industry; rhomboid figure; suit at cards; playing field in baseball. **diamond jubilee** sixtieth anniversary of an event. **diamond wedding** sixtieth anniversary of a wedding.

di·a·pa·son [dī-ə-PAY-zən] *n* fundamental organ stop; compass of voice or instrument.

dia·per [DĪ-pər] *n* garment of absorbent material to absorb an infant's excrement. ▶ *vt* put a diaper on.

di·aph·a·nous [dī-AF-ə-nəs] *adj* transparent.

di·a·pho·ret·ic [dī-ə-fə-RET-ik] *n* drug promoting perspiration. ▶ *adj*

di·a·phragm [DĪ-ə-fram] *n* muscular partition dividing two cavities of body, midriff; plate or disk wholly or partly closing tube or opening; any thin dividing or covering membrane.

di·ar·rhe·a [dī-ə-REE-ə] *n* excessive looseness of the bowels.

di·a·ry [DĪ-ə-ree] *n, pl* **-ries.** daily record of events or thoughts; book for this; book for noting appointments, memoranda, etc. **di'a·rist** *n* writer of diary.

di·as·to·le [dī-AS-tl-ee] *n* dilatation of the chambers of the heart.

di·a·ther·my [DĪ-ə-thur-mee] *n* heating of body tissues with electric current for medical or surgical purposes.

di·a·tom [DĪ-ə-tom] *n* one of order of microscopic algae. **di·a·tom'ic** *adj* of two atoms.

di·a·ton·ic [dī-ə-TON-ik] *adj Mus* pert. to regular major and minor scales; (of melody) composed in such a scale.

di·a·tribe [DĪ-ə-trīb] *n* violently bitter verbal attack, invective, denunciation.

dice [dīs] *n, pl* **dice.** small cube each of whose sides has a different number of spots (1 to 6), used in games of chance. ▶ *v* **diced, dic·ing.** ▶ *vi* gamble with dice. ▶ *vt* Cookery cut vegetables into small cubes. **dic'er** *n* **dic'ey** *adj* **dic·i·er, dic·i·est.** *inf* dangerous, risky.

di·chot·o·my [dī-KOT-ə-mee] *n, pl* **-mies.** division into two parts.

dic·tate [DIK-tayt] *v* **-tat·ed, -tat·ing.** say or read for another to transcribe; prescribe, lay down; impose (as terms). ▶ *n* bidding. **dic·ta'tion** *n* **dic·ta·tor** *n* absolute ruler. **dic·ta·to'ri·al** *adj* despotic; overbearing. **dic·ta'tor·ship** *n*

dic·tion [DIK-shən] *n* choice and use of words; enunciation.

dic·tion·ar·y [DIK-shə-ner-ee] *n, pl* **-ar·ies.** book setting forth, alphabetically, words of language with meanings, etc.; reference book with items in alphabetical order.

dic·tum [DIK-təm] *n, pl* **-ta** [-tə] pronouncement, saying, maxim.

did pt. of DO:

di·dac·tic [dī-DAK-tik] *adj* designed to instruct; (of people) opinionated, dictatorial.

die¹ [dī] *vi* **died, dy·ing.** cease to live; come to an end; stop functioning; *inf* be nearly overcome (with laughter, etc.); *inf* look forward (to). **die'hard** *n* one who resists (reform, etc.) to the end.

die² see DICE.

die³ *n* shaped block of hard material to form metal in forge, press, etc.; tool for cutting thread on pipe, etc.

di·e·lec·tric [dī-i-LEK-trik] *n* substance through or across which electric induction takes place; nonconductor; insulator.

di·er·e·sis [dī-ER-ə-sis] *n, pl* **-ses** [-seez] mark (¨) placed over vowel to show that it is sounded separately from preceding one, for example in *Noël.*

die·sel [DEE-zəl] *adj* pert. to internal-combustion engine using oil as fuel. ▶ *n* this engine; vehicle

powered by it.

di·et¹ [DĪ-it] *n* restricted or regulated course of feeding; kind of food lived on; food. ▶ *vi* follow a dietary regimen, as to lose weight. **di·e·ta·ry** *adj* relating to diet. ▶ *n* a regulated diet. **di·e·tet'ic** *adj* **di·e·tet'ics** *n* science of diet. **di·e·ti'tian** [-TISH-ən] *n* one skilled in dietetics. **dietary fiber** fibrous substances in fruit and vegetables, consumption of which aids digestion.

diet² *n* parliament of some countries; formal assembly.

dif·fer [DIF-ər] *vi* be unlike; disagree. **dif'fer·ence** *n* unlikeness; degree or point of unlikeness; disagreement; remainder left after subtraction. **dif'fer·ent** *adj* unlike.

dif·fer·en·tial [dif-ə-REN-shəl] *adj* varying with circumstances; special; *Math* pert. to an infinitesimal change in variable quantity; *Physics* relating to difference between sets of motions acting in the same direction or between pressures, etc. ▶ *n Math* infinitesimal difference between two consecutive states of variable quantity; mechanism in automobile, etc. permitting back wheels to revolve at different speeds when rounding corner; difference between rates of pay for different types of labor.

dif·fer·en'ti·ate [-shee-ayt] *v* **-at·ed, -at·ing.** ▶ *vt* serve to distinguish between, make different. ▶ *vi* discriminate. **dif·fer·en·ti·a'tion** *n* **differential calculus** method of calculating relative rate of change for continuously varying quantities.

dif·fi·cult [DIF-i-kult] *adj* requiring effort, skill, etc. to do or understand, not easy; obscure. **dif'fi·cul·ty** *n, pl* **-ties.** being difficult; difficult task, problem; embarrassment; hindrance; obscurity; trouble.

dif·fi·dent [DIF-i-dənt] *adj* lacking confidence, timid, shy. **dif'fi·dence** *n* shyness.

dif·fract [di-FRAKT] *vi* break up, esp. of rays of light, sound waves. **dif·frac'tion** [-FRAK-shən] *n* deflection of ray of light, electromagnetic wave caused by an obstacle.

dif·fuse [di-FYOOZ] *vt* **-fused, -fus·ing.** spread abroad. ▶ *adj* [-FYOOS] widely spread; loose, verbose, wordy. **dif·fuse'ly** *adv* loosely; wordily. **dif·fu'sion** [-zhən] *n* **dif·fu'sive** *adj*

dig *v* **dug, dig·ging.** ▶ *vi* work with spade; search, investigate. ▶ *vt* turn up with spade; hollow out, make hole in; excavate; thrust into; discover by searching; *sl* understand. ▶ *n* archaeological excavation; thrust; gibe, taunt. **dig'ger** *n*

di·gest [di-JEST] *vt* prepare (food) in stomach, etc. for assimilation; bring into handy form by sorting, tabulating, summarizing; reflect on; absorb. ▶ *vi* of food, undergo digestion. ▶ *n* [DĪ-jest] methodical summary, of laws, research, etc.; magazine containing condensed version of articles, etc. already published elsewhere. **di·gest'i·ble** *adj* **di·ges'tion** *n* digesting.

dig·it [DIJ-it] *n* finger or toe; any of the numbers 0 to 9. **dig'it·al** *adj* of, resembling digits; performed with fingers; displaying information (time, etc.) by numbers rather than by pointer on dial; of, relating to device that can write, read, or store information represented in numerical form. **digital recording** sound recording process that converts audio signals into pulses corresponding to voltage level. **digital television** television in which the picture is transmitted in digital form and then decoded. **dig·i·tal·is** [dij-i-TAL-is] *n* drug made from foxglove.

dig·ni·ty [DIG-ni-tee] *n, pl* **-ties.** stateliness, gravity; worthiness, excellence, repute; honorable office or title. **dig'ni·fy** *vt* **-fied, -fy·ing.** give dignity to. **dignified** *adj* stately, majestic. **dig'ni·ta·ry**

[-ter-ee] *n, pl* **-tar·ies.** holder of high office.

di·gress [di-GRES] *vi* turn from main course, esp. to deviate from subject in speaking or writing. **di·gres'sion** *n*

di·he·dral [dī-HEE-drəl] *adj* having two plane faces or sides.

dike [dīk] *n* embankment to prevent flooding; ditch.

di·lap·i·dat·ed [di-LAP-i-day-tid] *adj* in ruins; decayed.

dil·a·ta·tion [dil-ə-TAY-shən] *n* widening of body aperture for medical treatment, for example for curettage.

di·late [dī-LAYT] *v* **-lat·ed, -lat·ing.** ▶ *vt* widen, expand. ▶ *vi* expand; talk or write at length (on). **di·la'tion** *n*

dil·a·to·ry [DIL-ə-tor-ee] *adj* tardy, slow, belated. **dil'a·to·ri·ness** *n* delay.

di·lem·ma [di-LEM-ə] *n* position in fact or argument offering choice only between unwelcome alternatives; predicament.

dil·et·tante [DIL-i-tahnt] *n* person with taste and knowledge of fine arts as pastime; dabbler. ▶ *adj* amateur, desultory. **dil'et·tant·ism** *n*

dil·i·gent [DIL-i-jənt] *adj* unremitting in effort, industrious, hardworking. **dil'i·gence** *n*

di·lute [di-LOOT] *vt* **-lut·ed, -lut·ing.** reduce (liquid) in strength, esp. by adding water; thin; reduce in force, effect, etc. ▶ *adj* weakened thus. **di·lu'tion** *n*

dim *adj* **dim·mer, dim·mest.** indistinct, faint, not bright; mentally dull; unfavorable. ▶ *v* **dimmed, dim·ming.** make, grow dim. **dim'ly** *adv* **dim'mer** *n* device for dimming electric lights. **dim'ness** *n*

dime [dīm] *n* 10-cent piece, coin of US and Canada.

di·men·sion [di-MEN-shən] *n* measurement, size; aspect. **fourth dimension** *Physics* time; supernatural, fictional dimension additional to those of length, breadth, thickness.

di·min·ish v lessen. **dim·i·nu·tion** [dim-ə-NOO-shən] n **di·min·u·tive** [di-MIN-yə-tiv] adj very small. ▶ n derivative word, affix implying smallness.

di·min·u·en·do [di-min-yoo-EN-doh] adj, adv Mus of sound, dying away.

dim·ple [DIM-pəl] n small hollow in surface of skin, esp. of cheek; any small hollow. ▶ v **-pled, -pling.** mark with, show dimples.

din n continuous roar of confused noises. ▶ vt **dinned, din·ning.** repeat to weariness, ram (fact, opinion, etc.) into.

dine [dīn] v **dined, din·ing.** ▶ vi eat esp. dinner. ▶ vt give dinner to. **din'er** n one who dines; informal usu. cheap restaurant. **dining room** room where meals are eaten.

din·ghy [DING-gee] n, pl **-ghies.** small open boat; inflatable life raft.

din·go [DING-goh] n, pl **-goes.** Aust. wild dog.

din·gy [DIN-jee] adj **-gi·er, -gi·est.** dirty-looking, shabby. **din'gi·ness** n

din·ner [DIN-ər] n chief meal of the day; official banquet.

di·no·saur [DĪ-nə-sor] n extinct reptile, often of gigantic size.

dint n force, power. **by dint of** by means of.

di·o·cese [DĪ-ə-sis] n ecclesiastical district under jurisdiction of bishop. **di·oc·e·san** [dī-OS-ə-sən] adj having jurisdiction over diocese.

di·ode [DĪ-ohd] n Electronics device for converting alternating current to direct current.

di·op·ter [dī-OP-tər] n unit for measuring refractive power of lens.

di·o·ram·a [dī-ə-RAM-ə] n miniature three-dimensional scene, esp. as museum exhibit.

di·ox·ide [dī-OK-sīd] n oxide with two parts of oxygen to one of the other constituents.

di·ox·in [dī-OK-sin] n extremely toxic byproduct of the manufacture of certain herbicides and bactericides.

dip v **dipped, dip·ping.** ▶ vt put partly or for a moment into liquid; immerse, involve; lower and raise again; take up in ladle, bucket, etc. ▶ vi plunge partially or temporarily; go down, sink; slope downward. ▶ n act of dipping; brief swim; liquid chemical in which livestock are immersed to treat insect pests, etc.; downward slope; hollow; creamy mixture in which cracker, etc. is dipped before being eaten. **dip into** glance at (book, etc.).

diph·the·ri·a [dif-THEER-ee-ə] n infectious disease of throat with membranous growth.

diph·thong [DIF-thawng] n union of two vowel sounds in single compound sound.

di·plo·ma [di-PLOH-mə] n, pl **-mas.** document vouching for person's proficiency; title to degree, honor, etc.

di·plo·ma·cy [di-PLOH-mə-see] n management of international relations; skill in negotiation; tactful, adroit dealing. **dip·lo·mat** [DIP-lə-mat] n one engaged in official diplomacy. **dip·lo·mat'ic** adj **di·plo'ma·tist** n tactful person.

di·plo·pi·a [di-PLOH-pee-ə] n double vision.

di·po·lar [dī-POH-lər] adj having two poles.

di·pole [DĪ-pohl] n type of radio and television antenna.

dip·per [DIP-ər] n ladle, bucket, scoop.

dip·so·ma·ni·a [dip-sə-MAY-nee-ə] n uncontrollable craving for alcohol. **dip·so·ma'ni·ac** n victim of this.

dip·tych [DIP-tik] n ancient tablet hinged in the middle, folding together like a book; painting, carving on two hinged panels.

dire [dīr] adj **dir·er, dir·est.** terrible; urgent.

di·rect [di-REKT] vt control, manage, order; point out the way; aim, point, turn; address (letter, etc.); supervise actors, etc. in play or film. ▶ adj frank, straightforward; straight; going straight to the point; immediate; lineal.

di·rec·tion n directing; aim, course of movement; address, instruction.

di·rec·tive adj, n **di·rec·tor** n one who directs, esp. a film; member of board of directors of company.

di·rec·to·rate [-tər-it] n body of directors; office of director.

di·rec·to·ry n, pl **-ries.** book of names, addresses, streets, etc.; *Computers* area of a disk containing the names and locations of the files it currently holds. **direction finder** radio receiver that determines the direction of incoming waves.

dirge [durj] n song of mourning.

dir·i·gi·ble [DIR-i-jə-bəl] adj steerable. ▶ n airship.

dirt [durt] n filth; soil, earth; obscene material; contamination. **dirt'i·ness** n **dirt'y** adj **-i·er, -i·est.** unclean, filthy; obscene; unfair; dishonest.

dis- prefix indicating: reversal, e.g. *disconnect;* negation or lack, e.g. *dissimilar; disgrace;* removal or release, e.g. *disembowel.*

dis·a·ble [dis-AY-bəl] vt **-bled, -bling.** make ineffective, unfit, or incapable. **dis·a'bled** adj lacking a physical power, such as the ability to walk. **dis·a·bil'i·ty** n, pl **-ties.** incapacity; drawback.

dis·a·buse [dis-ə-BYOOZ] vt **-bused, -bus·ing.** undeceive, disillusion; free from error.

dis·ad·van·tage [dis-əd-VAN-tij] n drawback; hindrance; detriment. ▶ vt **-taged, -tag·ing.** handicap. **disadvantaged** adj deprived, discriminated against, underprivileged.

dis·ad·van·ta·geous [-TAY-jəs] adj

dis·af·fect·ed [dis-ə-FEK-tid] adj ill-disposed, alienated, estranged. **dis·af·fec'tion** n

dis·a·gree [dis-ə-GREE] vt **-greed, -gree·ing.** be at variance; conflict; (of food, etc.) have bad effect on. **dis·a·gree'ment** n difference of opinion; discord; discrepancy. **dis·a·gree'a·ble** adj unpleasant.

dis·al·low [dis-ə-LOW] vt reject as untrue or invalid.

dis·ap·pear [dis-ə-PEER] vi vanish; cease to exist; be lost. **dis·ap·pear'ance** n

dis·ap·point [dis-ə-POINT] vt fail to fulfill (hope), frustrate. **dis·ap·point'ment** n

dis·ap·prove vi (foll. by *of*) consider wrong or bad. **dis·ap·prov'al** n

dis·arm [dis-AHRM] v deprive of arms or weapons; reduce country's war weapons; win over. **dis·ar'ma·ment** n **dis·arm'ing** adj removing hostility, suspicion.

dis·ar·range v throw into disorder.

dis·ar·ray [dis-ə-RAY] vt throw into disorder, derange. ▶ n disorderliness, esp. of clothing.

dis·as·ter [di-ZAS-tər] n calamity, sudden or great misfortune. **dis·as'trous** adj calamitous.

dis·band' v (cause to) cease to function as a group.

dis·bar [dis-BAHR] vt **-barred, -bar·ring.** *Law* expel from the bar.

dis·be·lieve' vt reject as false. ▶ vi (foll. by *in*) have no faith (in). **dis·be·lief'** n

dis·burse [dis-BURS] vt **-bursed, -burs·ing.** pay out (money). **dis·burse'ment** n

disc see DISK. **disc jockey** person who introduces and plays pop records on a radio program or at a disco.

dis·card [di-SKAHRD] v reject; give up; cast off, dismiss.

dis·cern [di-SURN] vt make out; distinguish. **dis·cern'i·ble** adj **dis·cern'ing** adj discriminating; penetrating. **dis·cern'ment** n insight.

dis·charge [dis-CHAHRJ] vt **-charged, -charg·ing.** release; dismiss; emit; perform (duties), fulfill (obligations); let go; fire off; unload; pay. ▶ n [DIS-chahrj] discharging; being discharged; release; matter emitted; document certifying release, payment, etc.

dis·ci·ple [di-SĪ-pəl] n follower, one who takes another as teacher and model.

dis·ci·pline [DIS-ə-plin] n training that produces orderliness, obedience, self-control; result of such training in order, conduct, etc.; system of rules, etc. ▶ vt **-plined, -plin·ing.** train; punish.

dis·ci·pli·nar·i·an n one who enforces rigid discipline.

dis'ci·pli·nar·y adj

dis·claim [dis-KLAYM] vt deny, renounce. **dis·claim'er** n repudiation, denial.

dis·close [di-SKLOHZ] vt **-closed, -clos·ing.** allow to be seen; make known. **dis·clo'sure** [-zhər] n revelation.

dis·col·or [dis-KUL-ər] vt alter color of, stain. **dis·col·or·a'tion** n

dis·com·fit [dis-KUM-fit] vt embarrass, disconcert, baffle. **dis·com'fi·ture** [-fi-chər] n

dis·com·pose' vt disturb, upset. **dis·com·po'sure** n

dis·con·cert [dis-kən-SURT] vt ruffle, confuse, upset, embarrass.

dis·con·nect' vt undo or break the connection between (two things); stop the supply of electricity or gas of.

dis·con·so·late [dis-KON-sə-lit] adj unhappy, downcast, forlorn.

dis·con·tent' n lack of contentment. **dis·con·tent'ed** adj **dis·con·tent'ment** n

dis·con·tin·ue v come or bring to an end. **dis·con·ti'nu·ous** adj characterized by interruptions. **dis·con·ti·nu'i·ty** n

dis·cord [DIS-kord] n strife; difference, dissension; disagreement of sounds. **dis·cord'ant** adj

dis·co·theque [DIS-kə-tek] n club, etc. for dancing to recorded music.

dis·count [dis-KOWNT] vt consider as possibility but reject as unsuitable, inappropriate, etc.; deduct (amount, percentage) from usual price; sell at reduced price. ▶ n [DIS-kownt] amount deducted from price, expressed as cash amount or percentage.

dis·coun·te·nance [dis-KOWN-tn-əns] vt **-nanced, -nanc·ing.** abash; discourage; frown upon.

dis·cour·age [di-SKUR-ij] vt **-aged, -ag·ing.** reduce confidence of; deter; show disapproval of.

dis·course [DIS-kors] n conversation; speech, treatise, sermon. ▶ vi [dis-KORS] **-coursed, -cours·ing.** speak, converse, lecture.

dis·cour·te·sy n showing bad manners. **dis·cour'teous·ly** adv

dis·cov·er [di-SKUV-ər] vt (be the first to) find out, light upon; make known. **dis·cov'er·a·ble** adj **dis·cov'er·er** n **dis·cov'er·y** n, pl **-er·ies.**

dis·cred·it [dis-KRED-it] vt damage reputation of; cast doubt on; reject as untrue. ▶ n disgrace; doubt. **dis·cred'it·a·ble** adj

dis·creet [di-SKREET] adj prudent, circumspect. **dis·creet'ness** n

dis·crep·an·cy [di-SKREP-ən-see] n, pl **-cies.** conflict, variation, as between figures. **dis·crep'ant** adj

dis·crete [di-SKREET] adj separate, disunited, discontinuous.

dis·cre·tion [di-SKRESH-ən] n quality of being discreet; prudence; freedom to act as one chooses. **dis·cre'tion·ar·y** adj

dis·crim·i·nate [di-SKRIM-ə-nayt] vi **-nat·ed, -nat·ing.** single out for special favor or disfavor; distinguish between; be discerning. **dis·crim·i·na'tion** n

dis·cur·sive [di-SKUR-siv] adj passing from subject to subject, rambling.

dis·cus [DIS-kəs] n disk-shaped object thrown in athletic competition.

dis·cuss [di-SKUS] vt exchange opinions about; debate. **dis·cus'sion** n

dis·dain [dis-DAYN] n scorn, contempt. ▶ vt scorn. **dis·dain'ful** adj

dis·ease [di-ZEEZ] n illness; disorder of health.

dis·em·bark' v get off a ship, aircraft, or bus. **dis·em·bar·ka'tion** n

dis·em·bod·ied [dis-em-BOD-eed] adj (of spirit) released from bodily form.

dis·em·bow·el [dis-em-BOW-əl] vt take out entrails of.

dis·en·chant·ed [dis-en-CHAN-tid] adj disillusioned.

dis·en·gage' v release from a connection. **dis·en·gage'ment** n

dis·en·tan·gle v release from entanglement or confusion.

dis·es·tab'lish vt remove state support from (a church etc.). **dis·es·tab'lish·ment** n

dis·fa'vor n disapproval or dislike.

dis·fig·ure [dis-FIG-yər] vt -ured, -ur·ing. mar appearance of. **dis·fig·ur·a'tion** n **dis·fig'ure·ment** n blemish, defect.

dis·gorge [dis-GORJ] vt -gorged, -gorg·ing. vomit; give up.

dis·grace [dis-GRAYS] n shame, loss of reputation, dishonor. ▶ vt -graced, -grac·ing. bring shame or discredit upon. **dis·grace'ful** adj shameful.

dis·grun·tled [dis-GRUN-tld] adj vexed; put out.

dis·guise [dis-GĪZ] vt -guised, -guis·ing. change appearance of, make unrecognizable; conceal, cloak; misrepresent. ▶ n false appearance; device to conceal identity.

dis·gust' n violent distaste, loathing, repugnance. ▶ vt affect with loathing.

dish n shallow vessel for food; portion or variety of food; contents of dish; sl attractive person. **dish out** inf put in dish; serve up; dispense (money, abuse, etc.).

dis·ha·bille [dis-ə-BEEL] n state of being partly or carelessly dressed.

dis·har'mo·ny n lack of agreement, discord.

dis·heart'en vt weaken or destroy the hope, courage, or enthusiasm of.

di·shev·eled [di-SHEV-əld] adj with disordered hair; ruffled, untidy, unkempt.

dis·hon'est adj not honest or fair. **dis·hon'est·ly** adv **dis·hon'es·ty** n

dis·hon'or vt treat with disrespect; refuse to cash (a check). ▶ n lack of respect; state of shame or disgrace;

something that causes a loss of honor. **dis·hon'or·a·ble** adj **dis·hon'or·a·bly** adv

dis·il·lu·sion [dis-i-LOO-zhən] vt destroy ideals, illusions, or false ideas of. ▶ n

dis·in·fect·ant [dis-in-FEK-tənt] n substance that prevents or removes infection. **dis·in·fect'** vt

dis·in·for·ma·tion [dis-in-fər-MAY-shən] n false information intended to deceive or mislead.

dis·in·gen·u·ous [dis-in-JEN-yoo-əs] adj not sincere or frank.

dis·in·her·it [dis-in-HE-rit] vt to deprive of inheritance.

dis·in·te·grate [dis-IN-tə-grayt] v -grat·ed, -grat·ing. break up, fall to pieces. **dis·in·te·gra'tion** n

dis·in·ter' vt -ter·ring, -terred. dig up; reveal, make known.

dis·in·ter·est [dis-IN-trist] n freedom from bias or involvement. **dis·in'ter·est·ed** adj

dis·joint' vt put out of joint; break the natural order or logical arrangement of. **dis·joint'ed** adj (of discourse) incoherent; disconnected.

disk n thin, flat, circular object like a coin; Computers storage device, consisting of a disk coated with a magnetic layer, used to record and retrieve data; a phonograph record. **disk drive** Computers controller and mechanism for reading and writing data on computer disks. **disk harrow** harrow that cuts the soil with inclined disks. **disk jockey, disc jockey** person who introduces and plays pop records on a radio program or at a disco.

dis·lo·cate [DIS-loh-kayt] vt -cat·ed, -cat·ing. put out of joint (e.g. dislocate shoulder); disrupt, displace. **dis·lo·ca'tion** n

dis·lodge [dis-LOJ] vt -lodged, -lodg·ing. drive out or remove from hiding place or previous position.

dis·loy'al adj not loyal, deserting

one's allegiance. **dis·loy'al·ty** n

dis·mal [DIZ-məl] adj depressing; depressed; cheerless, dreary, gloomy. **dis'mal·ly** adv

dis·man·tle [dis-MAN-tl] vt **-tled, -tling.** take apart. **dis·man'tle·ment** n

dis·may' vt dishearten, daunt. ▶ n consternation, horrified amazement; apprehension.

dis·mem·ber [dis-MEM-bər] vt tear or cut limb from limb; divide, partition. **dis·mem'ber·ment** n

dis·miss' vt remove, discharge from employment; send away; reject. **dis·miss'al** n

dis·mount' v get off a horse or bicycle.

dis·o·bey [dis-ə-BAY] v refuse or fail to obey. **dis·o·be'di·ence** [-BEE-dee-əns] n

dis·o·blige [dis-ə-BLĪJ] vt **-bliged, -blig·ing.** disregard the wishes, preferences of.

dis·or·der [dis-OR-dər] n disarray, confusion, disturbance; upset of health, ailment. ▶ vt upset order of; disturb health of. **dis·or'der·ly** adj untidy; unruly.

dis·or·gan·ize vt disrupt the arrangement or system of. **dis·or·gan·i·za'tion** n

dis·o·ri·ent [dis-OR-ee-ənt] vt cause to lose one's bearings, confuse.

dis·own [dis-OHN] vt refuse to acknowledge.

dis·par·age [di-SPAR-ij] vt **-aged, -ag·ing.** speak slightingly of; belittle. **dis·par'age·ment** n

dis·pa·rate [DIS-pər-it] adj essentially different, unrelated. **dis·par'i·ty** n, pl **-ties.** inequality; incongruity.

dis·pas·sion·ate [dis-PASH-ə-nit] adj unswayed by passion; calm, impartial. ·

dis·patch [di-SPACH] vt send off to destination or on an errand; send off; finish off, get done with speed; inf eat up; kill. ▶ n sending off; efficient speed; official message, report.

dis·pel [di-SPEL] vt **-pelled, -pel·ling.** clear, drive away, scatter.

dis·pense [di-SPENS] vt **-pensed, -pens·ing.** deal out; make up (medicine); administer (justice); grant exemption from. **dis·pen'sa·ble** adj **dis·pen'sa·ry** n, pl **-ries.** place where medical aid is given. **dis·pen·sa'tion** n act of dispensing; license or exemption; provision of nature or providence. **dis·pens'er** n dispense with do away with; manage without.

dis·perse [di-SPURS] vt **-persed, -pers·ing.** scatter. **dispersed** adj scattered; placed here and there. **dis·per'sal, dis·per'sion** [-zhən] n

dis·pir·it·ed [di-SPIR-i-tid] adj dejected, disheartened. **dis·pir'it·ing** adj

dis·place [dis-PLAYS] vt **-placed, -plac·ing.** move from its place; remove from office; take place of. **dis·place'ment** n displacing; weight of liquid displaced by a solid in it.

dis·play [di-SPLAY] vt spread out for show; show, expose to view. ▶ n displaying; parade; show, exhibition; ostentation.

dis·please [dis-PLEEZ] v **-pleased, -pleas·ing.** offend; annoy. **dis·pleas'ure** [-PLEZH-ər] n anger, vexation.

dis·port [di-SPORT] v refl gambol, amuse oneself, frolic.

dis·pose [di-SPOHZ] v **-posed, -pos·ing.** ▶ vt arrange; distribute; incline; adjust. ▶ vi determine. **dis·pos'a·ble** adj designed to be thrown away after use. **dis·pos'al** n **dis·po·si·tion** [dis-pə-ZISH-ən] n inclination; temperament; arrangement; plan. **dispose of** sell, get rid of; have authority over, deal with.

dis·pos·sess [dis-pə-ZES] vt cause to give up possession (of).

dis·pro·por·tion n lack of proportion or equality. **dis·pro·por'tion·ate** adj

dis·prove' vt show (an assertion or claim) to be incorrect.

dis·pute [di-SPYOOT] v **-put·ed, -put·ing.** ▶ vi debate, discuss. ▶ vt call in question; debate, argue;

oppose, contest. **dis·put'a·ble** adj
dis·pu'tant n **dis·pu·ta'tious** adj
argumentative; quarrelsome.
dis·qual·i·fy [dis-KWOL-ə-fī] vt
-fied, -fy·ing. make ineligible, unfit
for some special purpose.
dis·qui·et [dis-KWĪ-it] n anxiety,
uneasiness. ▶ vt cause (someone) to
feel this.
dis·qui·si·tion [dis-kwə-ZISH-ən] n
learned or elaborate treatise,
discourse or essay.
dis·re·pute' n loss or lack of good
reputation. **dis·rep'u·ta·ble** adj
having or causing a bad reputation.
dis·re·spect' n lack of respect.
dis·re·spect'ful adj
dis·rupt' vt interrupt; throw into
turmoil or disorder. **dis·rup'tion** n
dis·rup'tive adj
dis·sat·is·fied adj not pleased or
contented. **dis·sat·is·fac'tion** n
dis·sect [di-SEKT] vt cut up (body,
organism) for detailed
examination; examine or criticize in
detail. **dis·sec'tion** n
dis·sem·ble [di-SEM-bəl] v -bled,
-bling. conceal, disguise (feelings,
etc.); act the hypocrite.
dis·sem'bler n
dis·sem·i·nate [di-SEM-ə-nayt] vt
-nat·ed, -nat·ing. spread abroad,
scatter. **dis·sem·i·na'tion** n
dis·sent [di-SENT] vi differ in
opinion; express such difference;
disagree with doctrine, etc. of
established church, etc. ▶ n such
disagreement. **dis·sent'er** n
dis·ser·ta·tion [dis-ər-TAY-shən] n
written thesis; formal discourse.
dis·serv·ice [dis-SUR-vis] n ill turn,
wrong, injury.
dis·si·dent [DIS-i-dənt] n, adj (one)
not in agreement, esp. with
government. **dis'si·dence** n
dissent; disagreement.
dis·sim·i·lar adj not alike, different.
dis·sim·i·lar'i·ty n
dis·sim·u·late [di-SIM-yə-layt] v
-lat·ed, -lat·ing. pretend not to
have; practice deceit.
dis·sim·u·la'tion n
dis·si·pate [DIS-ə-payt] vt -pat·ed,
-pat·ing. scatter; waste, squander.

dis'si·pat·ed adj indulging in
pleasure without restraint,
dissolute; scattered, wasted.
dis·si·pa'tion n scattering;
frivolous, dissolute way of life.
dis·so·ci·ate [di-SOH-shee-ayt] v
-at·ed, -at·ing. separate, sever;
disconnect.
dis·so·lute [DIS-ə-loot] adj lacking
restraint, esp. lax in morals.
dis·so·lu·tion [dis-ə-LOO-shən] n
breakup; termination of legislature,
meeting or legal relationship;
destruction; death.
dis·solve [di-ZOLV] v -solved,
-solv·ing. ▶ vt absorb or melt in
fluid; break up, put an end to,
annul. ▶ vi melt in fluid; disappear,
vanish; break up, scatter.
dis·sol·u·ble [di-SOL-yə-bəl] adj
capable of being dissolved.
dis·so·nant [DIS-ə-nənt] adj jarring,
discordant. **dis'so·nance** n
dis·suade [di-SWAYD] vt -suad·ed,
-suad·ing. advise to refrain,
persuade not to. **dis·sua'sion**
[-zhən] n **dis·sua'sive** adj
dis·taff [DIS-taf] n cleft stick to hold
wool, etc., for spinning. **distaff
side** maternal side; female line.
dis·tance [DIS-təns] n amount of
space between two things;
remoteness; aloofness, reserve. ▶ vt
-tanced, -tanc·ing. hold or place at
distance. **dis'tant** adj far off,
remote; haughty, cold.
dis·taste [dis-TAYST] n dislike of
food or drink; aversion, disgust.
dis·taste'ful adj unpleasant,
displeasing to feelings.
dis·taste'ful·ness n
dis·tem·per [dis-TEM-pər] n
disease of dogs; method of
painting on plaster without oil;
paint used for this. ▶ vt paint with
distemper.
dis·tend [di-STEND] v swell out by
pressure from within, inflate.
dis·ten'sion n
dis·tich [DIS-tik] n couplet.
dis·till [di-STIL] vt vaporize and
recondense a liquid; purify,
separate, concentrate liquids by
this method; fig extract quality of.

▶ *vi* trickle down. **dis·til·late** [DIS-tə-lit] *n* distilled liquid, esp. as fuel for some engines. **dis·till'er** *n* one who distills, esp. manufacturer of whiskey.

dis·tinct [di-STINGKT] *adj* clear, easily seen; definite; separate, different. **dis·tinc'tion** *n* point of difference; act of distinguishing; eminence, repute, high honor, high quality. **dis·tinc'tive** *adj* characteristic. **dis·tinct'ly** *adv*

dis·tin·guish [di-STING-gwish] *vt* make difference in; recognize, make out; honor; (usu refl) make prominent or honored; classify. ▶ *vi* (usu with *between* or *among*) draw distinction, grasp difference. **dis·tin'guish·a·ble** *adj* **dis·tin'guished** *adj* dignified; famous, eminent.

dis·tort [di-STORT] *vt* put out of shape, deform; misrepresent; garble, falsify. **dis·tor'tion** *n*

dis·tract [di-STRAKT] *vt* draw attention of (someone) away from work, etc.; divert; perplex, bewilder, drive mad. **dis·trac'tion** *n*

dis·traught [di-STRAWT] *adj* bewildered, crazed with grief; frantic, distracted.

dis·tress [di-STRES] *n* severe trouble, mental pain; severe pressure of hunger, fatigue or want. ▶ *vt* afflict, give mental pain. **dis·tress'ful** *adj*

dis·trib·ute [di-STRIB-yoot] *vt* **-ut·ed, -ut·ing.** deal out, dispense; spread, dispose at intervals; classify. **dis·tri·bu'tion** *n* **dis·trib'u·tive** *adj* **dis·trib'u·tor** *n* rotary switch distributing electricity in automotive engine.

dis·trict [DIS-trikt] *n* region, locality; portion of territory.

dis·trust' *v* regard as untrustworthy. ▶ *n* feeling of suspicion or doubt. **dis·trust'ful** *adj*

dis·turb' *vt* trouble, agitate, unsettle, derange. **dis·turb'ance** *n*

dis·use [dis-YOOS] *n* state of being no longer used. **dis·used'** [-YOOZD] *adj*

ditch [dich] *n* long narrow hollow dug in ground for drainage, etc. ▶ *v* make, repair ditches; run car, etc. into ditch. ▶ *vt sl* abandon, discard.

dith·er [DITH-ər] *vi* be uncertain or indecisive. ▶ *n* this state.

dith·y·ramb [DITH-ə-ram] *n* ancient Greek hymn sung in honor of Dionysus.

dit·to [DIT-oh] *n, pl* **-tos.** same, aforesaid (used to avoid repetition in lists, etc.).

dit·ty [DIT-ee] *n, pl* **-ties.** simple song.

di·u·ret·ic [dī-ə-RET-ik] *adj* increasing the discharge of urine. ▶ *n* substance with this property.

di·ur·nal [dī-UR-nəl] *adj* daily; in or of daytime; taking a day.

di·va·lent [dī-VAY-lənt] *adj* capable of combining with two atoms of hydrogen or their equivalent.

di·van' *n* bed, couch without back or head.

dive [dīv] *vi* **dived** or **dove, div·ing.** plunge under surface of water; descend suddenly; disappear; go deep down into; reach quickly. ▶ *n* act of diving; *sl* disreputable bar, club, etc. **div'er** *n* one who descends into deep water. **dive bomber** aircraft that attacks after diving steeply.

di·verge [di-VURJ] *vi* **-verged, -verg·ing.** get farther apart; separate. **di·ver'gence** *n* **di·ver'gent** *adj*

di·vers [DĪ-vərz] *adj obs* some, various.

di·verse [di-VURS] *adj* different, varied. **di·ver'si·ty** *n, pl* **-ties.** quality of being different or varied; range of difference. **di·ver'si·fy** *vt* **-fied, -fy·ing.** make diverse or varied; give variety to. **di·ver·si·fi·ca'tion** *n*

di·vert [di-VURT] *vt* turn aside, ward off; amuse, entertain. **di·ver'sion** [-zhən] *n* a diverting; official detour for traffic when main route is closed; amusement.

di·vest' *vt* unclothe, strip; dispossess, deprive; sell off.

di·vide [di-VĪD] *v* **-vid·ed, -vid·ing.** ▶ *vt* make into two or more parts, split up, separate; distribute, share; diverge in opinion; classify. ▶ *vi* become separated; part into two groups for voting, etc. ▶ *n* division esp. between adjacent drainage areas. **div'i·dend** *n* share of profits, of money divided among shareholders, etc.; number to be divided by another. **di·vid'ers** *pl n* pair of compasses.

di·vine [di-VĪN] *adj* **-vin·er, -vin·est.** of, pert. to, proceeding from, God; sacred; heavenly. ▶ *n* theologian; clergyman. ▶ *v* **-vined, -vin·ing.** guess; predict, foresee, tell by inspiration or magic. **div·i·na·tion** [div-ə-NAY-shən] *n* divining. **di·vine'ly** *adv* **di·vin'er** *n* **di·vin'i·ty** *n* quality of being divine; god; theology. **divining rod** [forked] stick, etc. said to move when held over ground where water is present]

di·vi·sion [di-VIZH-ən] *n* act of dividing; part of whole; barrier; section; difference in opinion, etc.; *Math* method of finding how many times one number is contained in another; army unit; separation, disunion. **di·vis'i·ble** *adj* capable of division. **di·vi'sive** [-VĪ-siv] *adj* causing disagreement. **di·vi'sor** [-VĪ-zər] *n Math* number that divides dividend.

di·vorce [di-VORS] *n* legal dissolution of marriage; complete separation, disunion. ▶ *vt* **-vorced, -vorc·ing.** dissolve marriage; separate; sunder. **di·vor·cee'** [-SAY] *n*

div·ot [DIV-ət] *n* piece of turf.

di·vulge [di-VULJ] *vt* **-vulged, -vulg·ing.** reveal, let out (secret).

Dix·ie [DIK-see] *n* southern states of the US.

diz·zy [DIZ-ee] *adj* **-zi·er, -zi·est.** feeling dazed, unsteady, as if about to fall; causing or fit to cause dizziness, as speed, etc.; *inf* silly. ▶ *vt* **-zied, -zy·ing.** make dizzy. **diz'zi·ly** *adv* **diz'zi·ness** *n*

DJ *n* disc jockey. ▶ *v* **DJ'd, DJ'·ing.** act as DJ.

DNA *n* deoxyribonucleic acid, the main constituent of the chromosomes of all organisms.

do¹ [doo] *v* **did, done, do·ing.** ▶ *vt* perform, effect, transact, bring about, finish; work at; work out, solve; suit; cover (distance); provide, prepare; *inf* cheat, trick; frustrate; look after. ▶ *vi* act; manage; work; fare; serve, suffice; happen. ▶ *v aux* makes negative and interrogative sentences and expresses emphasis. ▶ *n inf* celebration, festivity. **do away with** destroy. **do up** fasten; renovate. **do with** need; make use of. **do without** deny oneself.

do² [doh] *n* first sol-fa note.

doc·ile [DOS-əl] *adj* willing to obey, submissive.

dock¹ [dok] *n* artificial enclosure near harbor for loading or repairing ships; platform for loading and unloading trucks. ▶ *v* of vessel, put or go into dock; (of spacecraft) link or be linked together in space. **dock'er** *n* longshoreman. **dock'yard** *n* enclosure with docks, for building or repairing ships.

dock² *n* solid part of animal's tail; cut end, stump. ▶ *vt* cut short, esp. tail; curtail, deduct (an amount) from.

dock³ *n* enclosure in criminal court for prisoner.

dock·et [DOK-it] *n* agenda; list of court cases to be heard. ▶ *vt* place on docket.

doc·tor [DOK-tər] *n* medical practitioner; one holding university's highest degree in any faculty. ▶ *vt* treat medically; repair, mend; falsify (accounts, etc.). **doc'tor·al** [-əl] *adj* **doc'tor·ate** [-it] *n*

doc·trine [DOK-trin] *n* what is taught; teaching of church, school, or person; belief, opinion, dogma. **doc·tri·naire'** [-trə-NAIR] *adj* stubbornly insistent on applying theory without regard for circumstances. ▶ *n* **doc'.tri·nal** *adj*

doc·u·ment [DOK-yə-mənt] *n* piece of paper, etc. providing information or evidence. ▶ *vt* furnish with proofs, illustrations, certificates. **doc·u·men·ta·ry** adj, n, pl **-ries.** (of) type of film, TV program dealing with real life, not fiction. **doc·u·men·ta'tion** n

dod·der [DOD-ər] vi totter or tremble, as with age.

dodge [doj] v avoid or attempt to avoid (blow, discovery, etc.) as by moving quickly; evade questions by cleverness. ▶ n trick, artifice; ingenious method; act of dodging. **dodg'er** n shifty person; evader.

do·do [DOH-doh] n, pl **-dos.** large extinct bird; person with old-fashioned ideas.

doe [doh] n female of deer, hare, rabbit.

Doe [doh] n **John** or **Jane Doe** unknown or unidentified person.

does [duz] third pers. sing., pres. ind. active of DO.

doff [dof] vt take off (hat, clothing); discard, lay aside.

dog [dawg] n domesticated carnivorous four-legged mammal; person (in contempt, abuse or playfully); name given to various mechanical contrivances for gripping, holding; device with tooth that penetrates or grips object and detains it; andiron or firedog; sl ugly person; sl thing of extremely poor quality; inf a fellow. ▶ vt **dogged, dog·ging.** follow steadily or closely. **dog'ged** [-gid] adj persistent, resolute, tenacious. **dog'gy** adj **-gi·er, -gi·est. dog days** hot season of the rising of Dog Star; period of inactivity. **dog'-ear** n turned-down corner of page in book. ▶ vt turn down corners of pages. **dog'-eat-dog'** n action based on complete cynicism, ruthless competition. **dog'fight** n skirmish between fighter planes; savage contest characterized by disregard of rules. **doggy bag** bag in which diner may take leftovers (ostensibly for dog). **dog'house** n kennel. **in the doghouse** inf in disfavor. **dog'leg** n sharp bend or angle. **dog's age** quite a long time. **Dog Star** star

Sirius. **go to the dogs** degenerate.

doge [dohj] n formerly, chief magistrate in Venice.

dog·ger·el [DAW-gər-əl] n slipshod, unpoetic or trivial verse.

do·gie [DOH-gee] n motherless calf.

dog·ma [DAWG-mə] n, pl **-mas.** article of belief, esp. one laid down authoritatively by church; body of beliefs. **dog·mat'ic** adj asserting opinions with arrogance; relating to dogma. **dog·mat'i·cal·ly** adv **dog'ma·tism** n arrogant assertion of opinion.

doi·ly [DOI-lee] n, pl **-lies.** small cloth, paper, piece of lace to place under cake, dish, etc.

Dol·by [DOHL-bee] n ® system used in tape recording to reduce unwanted noise.

dol·ce [DOHL-chay] adj Music sweet.

dol·drums [DOHL-drəmz] pl n state of depression, dumps; region of light winds and calms near the equator.

dole [dohl] n charitable allotment, gift. ▶ vt **doled, dol·ing.** (usu. with out) deal out sparingly.

dole·ful [DOHL-fəl] adj dreary, mournful. **dole'ful·ly** adv

doll [dol] n child's toy image of human being; sl attractive person. ▶ v dress (up) in latest fashion or smartly.

dol·lar [DOL-ər] n standard monetary unit of many countries, esp. US and Canada.

dol·lop [DOL-əp] n inf semisolid lump; unmeasured amount, a dash.

dol·ly [DOL-ee] n, pl **-lies.** doll; wheeled support for film, TV camera; platform on wheels for moving heavy objects; various metal devices used as aids in hammering, riveting.

dol·men [DOHL-mən] n prehistoric monument; stone table.

do·lo·mite [DOH-lə-mīt] n a type of limestone.

do·lor [DOH-lər] n grief, sadness, distress. **dol'or·ous** [DOL-] adj

dol·phin [DOL-fin] n sea mammal, smaller than whale, with beaklike snout.

dolt [dohlt] *n* stupid fellow.
 dolt'ish *adj*

do·main [doh-MAYN] *n* lands held or ruled over; sphere, field of influence; province; *Computers* group of computers with the same name on the Internet.

dome [dohm] *n* a rounded vault forming a roof; something of this shape.

Domes·day Book [DOOMZ-day] record of survey of England in 1086.

do·mes·tic [də-MES-tik] *adj* of, in the home; homeloving; (of animals) tamed, kept by man; of, in one's own country, not foreign. ▸ *n* household servant. **do·mes'ti·cate** [-kayt] *vt* **-cat·ed, -cat·ing.** tame (animals); accustom to home life; adapt to an environment. **do·mes·tic·i·ty** [doh-me-STIS-i-tee] *n*

dom·i·cile [DOM-ə-sīl] *n* person's regular place of abode. **dom'i·ciled** *adj* living.

dom·i·nate [DOM-ə-nayt] *vt* **-nat·ed, -nat·ing.** rule, control, sway; of heights, overlook. ▸ *vi* control, be the most powerful or influential member or part of something. **dom'i·nant** *adj* **dom·i·na'tion** *n* **dom·i·neer'** *v* act imperiously, tyrannize.

Do·min·i·can [də-MIN-i-kən] *n* priest or nun of the order of St. Dominic. ▸ *adj* pert. to this order.

do·min·ion [də-MIN-yən] *n* sovereignty, rule; territory of government.

dom·i·noes [DOM-ə-nohz] *n* game played with 28 oblong flat pieces marked on one side with 0 to 6 spots on each half of the face. **dom·i·no** *n* one of these pieces; cloak with eye mask for masquerading.

don¹ *vt* **donned, don·ning.** put on (clothes).

don² *n* in English universities, fellow or tutor of college; Spanish title, Sir; in Mafia, head of a family or syndicate.

do·nate [DOH-nayt] *vt* **-nat·ed,**
-nat·ing. give. **do·na'tion** *n* gift to fund. **do·nor** [DOH-nər] *n* **donor card** specifying organs that may be used for transplant after cardholder's death.

done pp. of DO.

don·key [DONG-kee] *n, pl* **-keys.** ass; stupid or obstinate person. **donkey engine** auxiliary engine. **don'key·work** *n* drudgery.

donned pt./pp. of DON.

doo·dle [DOOD-l] *vi* **-dled, -dling.** scribble absentmindedly. ▸ *n*

doom *n* fate, destiny; ruin; judicial sentence, condemnation; the Last Judgment. ▸ *vt* sentence, condemn; destine to destruction or suffering. **dooms'day** *n* the day of the Last Judgment.

door [dor] *n* hinged or sliding barrier to close any entrance. **door'way** *n* entrance with or without door.

dope [dohp] *n* kind of varnish; *sl* drug, esp. illegal, narcotic drug; *inf* information; *inf* stupid person. ▸ *vt* doped, dop·ing. drug (esp. of racehorses). **dop·ey** [DOH-pee] *adj* **dop·i·er, dop·i·est.** *inf* foolish; drugged; half-asleep.

Dop·pler effect [DOP-lər] shift in frequency of sound, light, other waves when emitting source moves closer or farther from the observer.

Dor·ic [DOR-ik] *n* dialect of Dorians; style of Greek architecture; rustic dialect. ▸ *adj* **Do·ri·an** [DOR-ee-ən] *adj, n* (member) of early Greek race.

dork [dork] *n* *vulg sl* penis; *sl* stupid or clumsy person. ▸ *adj* **dork·i·er, dork·i·est.**

dor·mant [DOR-mənt] *adj* not active, in state of suspension; sleeping. **dor'man·cy** *n*

dor·mer [DOR-mər] *n* upright window set in sloping roof; such a projecting structure.

dor·mi·to·ry [DOR-mi-tor-ee] *n, pl* **-ries.** sleeping room with many beds. **dormitory suburb** suburb whose inhabitants commute to work.

dor·mouse [DOR-mows] *n* small hibernating mouselike rodent.

dor·sal [DOR-səl] *adj* of, on back.

do·ry [DOR-ee] *n, pl* **-ries.** flat-bottomed boat with high bow and flaring sides.

dose [dohs] *n* amount (of drug, etc.) administered at one time; *inf* instance or period of something unpleasant, esp. disease. ▶ *vt* **dosed, dos·ing.** give doses to. **dos'age** *n*

dos·si·er [DOS-ee-ay] *n* set of papers on some particular subject or event.

dot *n* small spot, mark. ▶ *vt* **dot·ted, dot·ting.** mark with dot(s); sprinkle. **dot'ty** *adj inf* **-ti·er, -ti·est.** eccentric; crazy; (with *about*) *inf* extremely fond of.

dot·com, dot-com *n* company that conducts most of its business on the Internet.

dote [doht] *vi* **dot·ed, dot·ing.** (with *on* or *upon*) be passionately fond of; be silly or weak-minded. **dot'age** [-ij] *n* senility. **do'tard** [-tərd] *n* **dot'ing** *adj* blindly affectionate.

dotty see DOT.

dou·ble [DUB-əl] *adj* of two parts, layers, etc., folded; twice as much or many; of two kinds; designed for two users; ambiguous; deceitful. ▶ *adv* twice; to twice the amount or extent; in a pair. ▶ *n* person or thing exactly like, or mistakable for, another; quantity twice as much as another; sharp turn; running pace. ▶ *v* **-bled, -bling.** make, become double; increase twofold; fold in two; turn sharply; get around, sail around. **dou'bly** *adv* **double agent** spy employed simultaneously by two opposing sides. **double bass** largest and lowest-toned instrument in violin form. **dou'ble-cross'** *v* betray, swindle a colleague. **dou'ble-cross'er** *n* **dou'ble-deal'ing** *n* artifice, duplicity. **double Dutch** *sl* incomprehensible talk, gibberish. **double dutch** form of the game of jump rope. **double glazing** two panes of glass in a window to insulate against cold, sound, etc. **dou'ble·head'er** *n Sports* two games played consecutively on same day in same stadium. **dou'ble-quick'** *adj, adv* very fast. **double take** delayed reaction to a remark, situation, etc. **dou'ble-talk** *n, vt* (engage in) intentionally garbled speech.

dou·ble en·ten·dre [DUB-əl ahn-TAHN-drə] *n, pl* **-dres** [-drəz] word or phrase with two meanings, one usu. indelicate.

dou·blet [DUB-lit] *n* close-fitting body garment formerly worn by men.

dou·bloon [du-BLOON] *n* ancient Spanish gold coin.

doubt [dowt] *vt* hesitate to believe; call in question; suspect. ▶ *vi* be wavering or uncertain in belief or opinion. ▶ *n* uncertainty, wavering in belief; state of affairs giving cause for uncertainty. **doubt'ful** *adj* **doubt'less** *adv*

douche [doosh] *n* jet or spray of water applied to (part of) body; device for douching. ▶ *vt* **douched, douch·ing.** give douche to.

dough [doh] *n* flour or meal kneaded with water; *sl* money. **dough'nut** *n* sweetened and fried, usu. ring-shaped, piece of dough.

dough·ty [DOW-tee] *adj* **-ti·er, -ti·est.** valiant. **dough'ti·ness** *n* boldness.

dour [duur] *adj* grim, stubborn, severe.

douse [dows] *vt* **doused, dous·ing.** thrust into water; extinguish (light).

dove [duv] *n* bird of pigeon family; person opposed to war. **dove'cote** [-koht] *n* house for doves. **dove'tail** *n* joint made with fan-shaped tenon. ▶ *v* fit closely, neatly, firmly together.

dow·a·ger [DOW-ə-jər] *n* widow with title or property derived from deceased husband; dignified elderly woman, esp. with wealth or social prominence.

dow·dy [DOW-dee] *adj* **-di·er, -di·est.** unattractively or shabbily dressed. ▶ *n* woman so dressed.

dow·el [DOW-əl] *n* wooden, metal peg, esp. joining two adjacent parts.

dow·er [DOW-ər] *n* widow's share for life of husband's estate. ▶ *vt* endow. **dow'ry** *n* property wife brings to husband at marriage; any endowment.

down[1] *adv* to, in, or toward, lower position; below the horizon; (of payment) on the spot, immediate. ▶ *prep* from higher to lower part of; at lower part of; along. ▶ *adj* depressed, miserable. ▶ *vt* knock, pull, push down; *inf* drink, esp. quickly. **down'ward** *adj, adv* **down'wards** *adv* **down'cast** *adj* dejected; looking down. **down'er** *n sl* barbiturate, tranquillizer, or narcotic; state of depression. **down'load** *vt* transfer (data) from the memory of one computer to that of another. **down'pour** *n* heavy rainfall. **down'right** *adj* plain, straightforward. ▶ *adv* quite, thoroughly. **down·stage** *adj, adv* at, to front of stage. **down'-and-out'** finished, defeated. **down in the mouth** dejected, discouraged. **down East** New England, esp. the state of Maine. **down under** Australia and New Zealand.

down[2] *n* soft underfeathers, hair or fiber; fluff. **down'y** *adj* **down·i·er, down·i·est.**

Down syndrome genetic disorder characterized by degree of mental and physical retardation.

dowry see DOWER.

dowse [dowz] *v* **dowsed, dows·ing.** use divining rod. **dows'er** *n* water diviner.

dox·ol·o·gy [dok-SOL-ə-jee] *n* short hymn of praise to God.

doy·en [doi-EN] *n* senior member of a body or profession. **doyenne** *n, fem*

doze [dohz] *vi* **dozed, doz·ing.** sleep drowsily, be half-asleep. ▶ *n* nap.

doz·en [DUZ-ən] *n* (set of) twelve.

drab *adj* dull, monotonous; of a dingy brown color. ▶ *n* mud color; slut, prostitute.

drach·ma [DRAK-mə] *n, pl* **-mas.** former monetary unit of Greece.

Dra·co·ni·an [dray-KOH-nee-ən] *adj* like the laws of Draco; **(d-)** very harsh, cruel.

draft[1] *n* design, sketch; preliminary plan or layout for work to be executed; rough copy of document; order for money; current of air between apertures in room, etc.; act or action of drawing; act or action of drinking; amount drunk at once; inhaling; depth of ship in water. ▶ *vt* make sketch, plan, or rough design of; make rough copy (of writing, etc.). ▶ *adj* of beer, etc., for drawing; drawn. **draft'y** *adj* **draft·i·er, draft·i·est.** full of air currents. **draft horse** horse for vehicles carrying heavy loads. **drafts'man** *n, pl* **-men.** one who makes drawings, plans, etc. **drafts'man·ship** *n*

draft[2] *vt* select for compulsory military service; select (professional athlete) by draft; compel (person) to serve.

drag *v* **dragged, drag·ging.** ▶ *vt* pull along with difficulty or friction; trail, go heavily; sweep with net or grapnels; protract; *Computers* move (an image) on screen by use of the mouse. ▶ *vi* lag, trail; be tediously protracted. ▶ *n* check on progress; checked motion; sledge, net, grapnel, rake; *sl* influence; *sl* tedious person or thing; *sl* women's clothes worn by (transvestite) man. **drag'ster** *n* automobile designed, modified for drag racing; driver of such car. **drag'net** *n* fishing net to be dragged along sea floor; comprehensive search, esp. by police for criminal, etc. **drag race** automobile race where cars are timed over measured distance.

drag·on [DRAG-ən] *n* mythical fire-breathing monster, like winged crocodile; type of large lizard. **drag'on·fly** *n, pl* **-flies.** long-bodied insect with gauzy wings.

dra·goon [drə-GOON] *n* formerly, cavalryman of certain regiments. ▶ *vt* oppress; coerce.

drain [drayn] *vt* draw off (liquid) by pipes, ditches, etc.; dry; drink to dregs; empty, exhaust. ▶ *vi* flow off or away; become rid of liquid. ▶ *n* channel for removing liquid; sewer; depletion, strain. **drain'age** [-ij] *n*

drake [drayk] *n* male duck.

dram *n* small draft of strong drink; unit of weight, one eighth of fluid ounce, one sixteenth of avoirdupois ounce.

dra·ma [DRAH-mə] *n* stage play; art or literature of plays; playlike series of events. **dra·mat·ic** [drə-MAT-ik] *adj* pert. to drama; suitable for stage representation; with force and vividness of drama; striking; tense; exciting. **dram'a·tist** *n* writer of plays. **dram·a·ti·za'tion** *n* **dram'a·tize** *vt* **-tized, -tiz·ing.** adapt story, novel for acting.

dram·a·tur·gy [DRAM-ə-tur-jee] *n* the technique of writing and producing plays. **dram'a·tur·gist** *n* playwright.

drape [drayp] *vt* **draped, drap·ing.** cover, adorn with cloth; arrange in graceful folds. **dra·per·y** [DRAY-pə-ree] *n, pl* **-per·ies.** covering, curtain, etc. of cloth.

dras·tic [DRAS-tik] *adj* extreme, forceful; severe.

draw *v* **drew, drawn, draw·ing.** ▶ *vt* pull, pull along, haul; inhale; entice; delineate, portray with pencil, etc.; frame, compose, draft, write; attract; bring (upon, out, etc.); get by lot; of ship, require (depth of water); take from (well, barrel, etc.); receive (money); bend (bow). ▶ *vi* pull; shrink; attract; make, admit current of air; make pictures with pencil, etc.; finish game in tie; write orders for money; come, approach (near). ▶ *n* act of drawing; casting of lots; unfinished game, tie. **draw'er** *n* one who or that which draws; sliding box in table or chest. ▶ *pl* undergarment for the lower body. **draw'ing** *n* art of depicting in line;

sketch so done; action of verb. **draw'back** *n* anything that takes away from satisfaction; snag. **draw'bridge** *n* hinged bridge to pull up. **drawing room** living room, sitting room. **draw near** approach. **draw out** lengthen. **draw up** arrange; come to a halt.

drawl *v* speak slowly. ▶ *n* such speech.

drawn pp. of DRAW.

dread [dred] *vt* fear greatly. ▶ *n* awe, terror. ▶ *adj* feared, awful. **dread'ful** *adj* disagreeable, shocking or bad. **dread'locks** *pl n* Rastafarian hair style of long matted or tightly curled strands. **dread'nought** *n* large battleship mounting heavy guns.

dream [dreem] *n* vision during sleep; fancy, reverie, aspiration; very pleasant idea, person, thing. ▶ *v* **dreamed** or **dreamt, dream·ing.** ▶ *vi* have dreams. ▶ *vt* see, imagine in dreams; think of as possible. **dream'y** *adj* **dream·i·er, dream·i·est.** given to daydreams, impractical, vague; *inf* wonderful.

drear·y [DREER-ee] *adj* **drear·i·er, drear·i·est.** dismal, dull. **drear'i·ly** *adv* **drear'i·ness** *n* gloom.

dredge¹ [drej] *v* **dredged, dredg·ing.** bring up mud, etc., from sea bottom; deepen channel by dredge; search for, produce obscure, remote, unlikely material. ▶ *n* form of scoop or grab. **dredg'er** *n* ship for dredging.

dredge² *vt* sprinkle with flour, etc. **dredg'er** *n*

dregs [dregz] *pl n* sediment, grounds; worthless part.

drench *vt* wet thoroughly, soak; make (an animal) take dose of medicine. ▶ *n* soaking; dose for animal.

dress *vt* clothe; array for show; trim, smooth, prepare surface of; prepare (food) for market or table; put dressing on (wound); align (troops). ▶ *vi* put on one's clothes; form in proper line. ▶ *n* one-piece garment for woman; clothing; clothing for ceremonial evening wear. **dress'er** *n* one who dresses, esp. actors or actresses; chest of drawers, oft. with mirror.

dress'ing *n* something applied to something else, as sauce to food, ointment to wound, manure to land, etc. **dress'y** *adj* **dress·i·er, dress·i·est.** stylish; fond of dress. **dress circle** usu. first gallery in theater. **dressing down** *inf* scolding. **dressing gown** coat-shaped garment worn over pyjamas or nightdress. **dressing room** room used for changing clothes, esp. backstage in a theater. **dressing table** piece of bedroom furniture with a mirror and drawers. **dress'mak·er** *n*

dres·sage [drə-SAHZH] *n* method of training horse in special maneuvers to show obedience.

drew pt. of DRAW.

drib·ble [DRIB-əl] *v* **-bled, -bling.** flow in drops, trickle; run at the mouth; *Basketball* work ball forward with short bounces; *Soccer* work ball forward with short kicks. ▶ *n* trickle, drop. **drib'let** *n* small portion or installment.

drift *vi* be carried as by current of air, water; move aimlessly or passively. ▶ *n* process of being driven by current; slow current or course; deviation from course; tendency; speaker's, writer's meaning; wind-heaped mass of snow, sand, etc.; material driven or carried by water. **drift'er** *n* one who, that which drifts; *inf* aimless person with no fixed job, etc. **drift'wood** [-wuud] *n* wood washed ashore by sea.

drill[1] *n* boring tool or machine; exercise of soldiers or others in handling of arms and maneuvers; repeated routine in teaching. ▶ *vt* bore, pierce hole; exercise in military and other routine. ▶ *vi* practice routine.

drill[2] *n* machine for sowing seed; small furrow for seed; row of plants. ▶ *vt* sow seed in drills or furrows.

drill[3] *n* coarsely woven twilled fabric.

drink [dringk] *v* **drank, drunk, drink·ing.** swallow liquid; absorb; take intoxicating liquor, esp. to excess. ▶ *n* liquid for drinking; portion of this; act of drinking; intoxicating liquor; excessive use of it. **drink'a·ble** *adj* **drink to, drink the health of** express good wishes, etc. by drinking a toast to.

drip *v* **dripped, drip·ping.** fall or let fall in drops. ▶ *n* act of dripping; drop; *Med* intravenous administration of solution; *sl* dull, insipid person. **dripping** *n* melted fat that drips from roasting meat. ▶ *adj* very wet. **drip-dry** [-drī] *adj* (of fabric) drying free of creases if hung up while wet.

drive [drīv] *v* **drove, driv·en, driv·ing.** ▶ *vt* urge in some direction; make move and steer (vehicle, animal, etc.); urge, impel; fix by blows, as nail; chase; convey in vehicle; hit a ball with force as in golf, baseball. ▶ *vi* keep machine, animal, going; steer it; be conveyed in vehicle; rush, dash, drift fast. ▶ *n* act, action of driving; journey in vehicle; private road leading to house; capacity for getting things done; united effort, campaign; energy; forceful stroke in golf, baseball. **driv'er** *n* one that drives; golf club. **drive time** time in the morning or evening when people drive to and from work.

driv·el [DRIV-əl] *vi* run at the mouth or nose; talk nonsense. ▶ *n* silly nonsense.

driz·zle [DRIZ-əl] *vi* **-zled, -zling.** rain in fine drops. ▶ *n* fine, light rain.

drogue [drohg] *n* any funnel-like device, esp. of canvas, used as sea anchor; small parachute; wind indicator; windsock towed behind target aircraft; funnel-shaped device on end of refueling hose of tanker aircraft to receive probe of aircraft being refueled.

droll [drohl] *adj* **-er, -est.** funny, odd, comical. **droll'ness** *n* **drol'ly** *adv*

drone [drohn] *n* male of honey bee; lazy idler; deep humming; bass

pipe of bagpipe; its note. ▶ v
droned, dron·ing. hum; talk in
monotonous tone.

drool vi to slaver, drivel.

droop vi hang down; wilt, flag. ▶ vt
let hang down. ▶ n drooping
condition. **droop'y** adj **droop·i·er,
droop·i·est.**

drop n globule of liquid; very small
quantity; fall, descent; distance
through which thing falls; thing
that falls, as gallows platform. ▶ v
dropped, drop·ping. ▶ vt let fall;
let fall in drops; utter casually; set
down, unload; discontinue. ▶ vi fall;
fall in drops; lapse; come or go
casually. **drop'let** n **drop'pings** pl
n dung of birds, rabbits, etc.
drop'out n person who fails to
complete course of study or one
who rejects conventional society.

dross [draws] n scum of molten
metal; impurity, refuse; anything of
little or no value.

drought [drowt] n long spell of dry
weather.

drove[1] [drohv] pt. of DRIVE.

drove[2] n herd, flock, crowd, esp. in
motion. **drov'er** n driver of cattle.

drown v die or be killed by
immersion in liquid; get rid of as by
submerging in liquid; make sound
inaudible by louder sound.

drow·sy [DROW-zee] adj **-si·er,
-si·est.** half-asleep; lulling; dull.
drowse vi **drow'si·ly** adv
drow'si·ness n

drub vt **drubbed, drub·bing.**
thrash, beat. **drubbing** n beating.

drudge [druj] vi work at menial or
distasteful tasks, slave. ▶ n one who
drudges, hack. **drudg'er·y** n, pl
-er·ies.

drug n medical substance; narcotic;
merchandise that is unsalable
because of overproduction. ▶ vt
drugged, drug·ging. mix drugs
with; administer drug to, esp. one
inducing unconsciousness.
drug'store n pharmacy where
wide variety of goods is available.
drug·gist n

dru·id [DROO-id] n (**D-**) member of
ancient order of Celtic priests.

drum n percussion instrument of
skin stretched over round hollow
frame, played by beating with
sticks; various things shaped like
drum; part of ear. ▶ v **drummed,
drum·ming.** play drum; tap, thump
continuously. **drum'mer** n one
who plays drum; traveling
salesman. **drum'head** n part of
drum that is struck. **drumhead
court-martial** summary one held at
war front. **drum major** leader of
military band. **drum'stick** n stick
for beating drum; lower joint of
cooked fowl's leg. **drum out** expel
from military service, etc.

drunk [drungk] adj **-er, -est.**
overcome by strong drink; fig
under influence of strong emotion.
drunk'ard [-ərd] n one given to
excessive drinking. **drunk'en** adj
drunk; caused by, showing
intoxication. **drunk'en·ness** n

dry [drī] adj **dri·er, dri·est.** without
moisture; rainless; not yielding
milk, or other liquid; cold,
unfriendly; caustically witty; having
prohibition of alcoholic drink;
uninteresting; needing effort to
study; lacking sweetness (as wines).
▶ v **dried, dry·ing.** remove water,
moisture; become dry; evaporate.
dri'ly adv **dry'ness** n **dry'er** n
person or thing that dries;
apparatus for removing moisture.
dry battery electric battery
without liquid. **dry'-clean** v clean
clothes with solvent other than
water. **dry'-clean·er** n **dry ice**
solid carbon dioxide. **dry'point**
needle for engraving without acid;
engraving so made. **dry rot**
fungoid decay in wood. **dry run**
practice, rehearsal in simulated
conditions.

dry·ad [DRĪ-əd] n wood nymph.

du·al [DOO-əl] adj twofold; of two,
double, forming pair. **du'al·ism** n
recognition of two independent
powers or principles, e.g. good and
evil, mind and matter. **du·al'i·ty** n

dub vt **dubbed, dub·bing.** give title
to; confer knighthood on; provide
film with soundtrack not in original

language; smear with grease, dubbin. **dub'bin, dub'bing** n grease for making leather supple.

du·bi·ous [DOO-bee-əs] adj causing doubt, not clear or decided; of suspect character. **du·bi'e·ty** [-BĪ-i-tee] n **-ties.** uncertainty, doubt.

du·cal [DOO-kəl] adj of, like a duke.

duch·ess [DUCH-is] n duke's wife or widow.

duch·y [DUCH-ee] n, pl **duch·ies.** territory of duke, dukedom.

duck¹ [duk] n common swimming bird. ▶ v plunge (someone) under water; bob down. **duck'ling** n **duck'billed platypus** see PLATYPUS.

duck² n strong linen or cotton fabric. ▶ pl trousers of it.

duct [dukt] n channel, tube. **duc·tile** [DUK-tl] adj capable of being drawn into wire; flexible and tough; easily led. **duc·til'i·ty** n **duct'less** adj (of glands) secreting directly certain substances essential to health.

dud n futile, worthless person or thing; shell that fails to explode. ▶ adj worthless.

dude [dood] n city man, esp. Easterner in the West; sl fellow. **dude ranch** ranch operating as vacation resort.

dudg·eon [DUJ-ən] n anger, indignation, resentment.

duds [dudz] pl n inf clothes.

due [doo] adj owing; proper to be given, inflicted, etc.; adequate, fitting; under engagement to arrive, be present; timed for. ▶ adv (with points of compass) exactly. ▶ n person's right; (usu pl) charge, fee, etc. **du'ly** adv properly; fitly; rightly; punctually. **due to** attributable to; caused by.

du·el [DOO-əl] n arranged fight with deadly weapons, between two persons; keen two-sided contest. ▶ vi **-eled, -el·ing.** fight in duel. **du'el·ist** n

du·en·na [doo-EN-ə] n in Spain or Portugal, elderly governess, guardian, chaperone.

du·et [doo-ET] n piece of music for two performers.

duff n sl buttocks.

duf·fel [DUF-əl] n coarse woolen cloth; coat of this.

duff·er [DUF-ər] n inf stupid inefficient person; inept golfer.

dug¹ pt./pp. of DIG.

dug² n udder, teat of animal.

dug·out [DUG-owt] n covered excavation to provide shelter for troops, etc.; canoe of hollowed-out tree; Baseball roofed structure with bench for players when not on the field.

duke [dook] n in Great Britain, peer of rank next below prince; ruler of duchy. **duch'ess** n, fem **duke'dom** [-dəm] n

dukes [dooks] pl n sl fists.

dul·cet [DUL-sit] adj (of sounds) sweet, melodious.

dul·ci·mer [DUL-sə-mər] n stringed instrument played with light hammers, ancestor of piano.

dull adj **-er, -est.** stupid; insensible; sluggish; tedious; lacking liveliness or variety; gloomy, overcast. ▶ v make or become dull. **dull'ard** [-ərd] n

duly see DUE.

dumb [dum] adj **-er, -est.** incapable of speech; silent; inf stupid. **dumb'ly** adv **dumb'ness** n **dumb'bell** n weight for exercises; dolt. **dumb·found'** vt confound into silence.

dumb down vt make less intellectually demanding or sophisticated. **dumb show** gestures without speech.

dum'dum n soft-nosed bullet that expands on impact.

dum·my [DUM-ee] n, pl **-mies.** tailor's, dressmaker's model; imitation object; Cards hand exposed on table and played by partner. ▶ adj sham, bogus. **dummy up** inf to keep silent.

dump vt throw down in mass; deposit; unload; send (low-priced goods) for sale abroad. ▶ n place where garbage is dumped; inf dirty, unpleasant place; temporary depot of stores or munitions. ▶ pl low spirits, dejection. **dump'ling** *n* small round mass of boiled or steamed dough; dessert of fruit wrapped in dough and baked. **dump truck** truck for hauling and dumping sand, stone, etc. **dump'y** *adj* **dump·i·er, dump·i·est.** short, stout.

dun[1] *vt* **dunned, dun·ning.** persistently demand payment of debts. ▶ *n* one who duns; urgent request for payment.

dun[2] *adj* of dull grayish brown. ▶ *n* this color; dun horse.

dunce [duns] *n* slow learner, stupid pupil.

dune [doon] *n* sandhill on coast or desert.

dung *n* excrement of animals; manure. ▶ *vt* fertilize or spread with manure.

dun·ga·ree [dung-gə-REE] *n* blue denim. ▶ *pl* work clothes, etc. of this material.

dun·geon [DUN-jən] *n* underground cell or vault for prisoners; formerly, tower or keep of castle.

dunk [dungk] *vt* dip bread, etc. in liquid before eating it; submerge. **dunk shot** *Basketball* shot made by jumping high to thrust ball through basket.

dun·nage [DUN-ij] *n* padding, loose material for packing cargo.

du·o [DOO-oh] *n, pl* **du·os.** pair of performers, etc.

du·o·dec·i·mal [doo-ə-DES-ə-məl] *adj* computed by twelves; twelfth.

du·o·dec·i·mo [doo-ə-DES-ə-moh] *n, pl* **-mos.** size of book in which each sheet is folded into 12 leaves before cutting; book of this size. ▶ *adj* of this size.

du·o·de·num [doo-ə-DEE-nəm] *n* upper part of small intestine. **du·o·de'nal** *adj*

dupe [doop] *n* victim of delusion or sharp practice. ▶ *vt* **duped, dup·ing.** deceive for advantage, impose upon.

du·plex [DOO-pleks] *adj* twofold. ▶ *n* apartment with rooms on two floors; two-family house.

du·pli·cate [DOO-pli-kayt] *vt* **-cat·ed, -cat·ing.** make exact copy of; double. ▶ *adj* [-kit] double; exactly the same as something else. ▶ *n* exact copy. **du'pli·ca·tor** *n* machine for making copies (of typewritten matter, etc.). **du·plic'i·ty** [-PLIS-i-tee] *n, pl* **-ties.** deceitfulness, double-dealing, bad faith.

du·ra·ble [DUUR-ə-bəl] *adj* lasting, resisting wear. **du·ra·bil'i·ty** *n*

du·ra·tion [duu-RAY-shən] *n* time thing lasts.

du·ress [duu-RES] *n* compulsion by use of force or threats.

dur·ing [DUUR-ing] *prep* throughout, in the time of, in the course of.

dusk *n* darker stage of twilight; partial darkness. **dusk'y** *adj* **dusk·i·er, dusk·i·est.** dark; dark-colored.

dust *n* fine particles, powder of earth or other matter, lying on surface or blown along by wind; ashes of the dead. ▶ *vt* sprinkle with powder, fertilizer, etc.; rid of dust. **dust'er** *n* cloth for removing dust; housecoat. **dust'y** *adj* **dust·i·er, dust·i·est.** covered with dust. **dust'bowl** [-bohl] *n* area in which dust storms have carried away the top soil.

Dutch [duch] *adj* pert. to the Netherlands, its inhabitants, its language. **Dutch courage** drunken bravado. **Dutch treat** one where each person pays own share.

du·ty [DOO-tee] *n, pl* **-ties.** moral or legal obligation; that which is due; tax on goods; military service; one's proper employment. **du'te·ous** *adj* **du'ti·a·ble** *adj* liable to customs duty. **du'ti·ful** *adj*

du·vet [doo-VAY] *n* quilt filled with down or artificial fiber.

DVD Digital Versatile *or* Video Disk.

dwarf [dworf] *n, pl* **dwarfs** *or* **dwarves** [dworvz] very undersized person; mythological, small, manlike creature. ▶ *adj* unusually small, stunted. ▶ *vt* make seem small by contrast; make stunted.

dwell *vi* **dwelt** *or* **dwelled,**
dwell·ing. live, make one's abode
(in); fix one's attention, write or
speak at length (on). **dweller** *n*
dwell'ing *n* house.

dwin·dle [DWIN-dl] *vi* **-dled, -dling.**
grow less, waste away, decline.

Dy *Chem* dysprosium.

dye [dī] *vt* **dyed, dye·ing.**
impregnate (cloth, etc.) with
coloring matter; color thus. ▶ *n*
coloring matter in solution or that
can be dissolved for dyeing; tinge,
color. **dy'er** *n*

dyke[1] [dīk] *n* wall built to prevent
flooding.

dyke[2] *n sl, often offens* lesbian.

dy·nam·ics [dī-NAM-iks] *n* branch
of physics dealing with force as
producing or affecting motion. ▶ *pl*
forces that produce change in a
system. **dy·nam'ic** *adj* of, relating
to motive force, force in operation;
energetic and forceful.
dy·nam'i·cal·ly *adv*

dy·na·mite [DĪ-nə-mīt] *n* high
explosive mixture. ▶ *vt* **-mit·ed,**
-mit·ing. blow up with this. ▶ *adj inf*
topnotch.

dy·na·mo [DĪ-nə-moh] *n, pl* **-mos.**
machine to convert mechanical
into electrical energy, generator of
electricity. **dy·na·mom'e·ter** *n*
instrument to measure energy
expended.

dy·nas·ty [DĪ-nə-stee] *n, pl* **-ties.**
line, family, succession of
hereditary rulers. **dy'nast** *n* ruler.
dy·nas'tic *adj* of dynasty.

dyne [dīn] *n* cgs unit of force.

dys·en·ter·y [DIS-ən-ter-ee] *n*
infection of intestine causing severe
diarrhea.

dys·func·tion [dis-FUNGK-shən] *n*
abnormal, impaired functioning,
esp. of bodily organ.

dys·lex·ia [dis-LEK-see-ə] *n*
impaired ability to read, caused by
condition of the brain. **dys·lex'ic**
adj, n

dys·pep·sia [dis-PEP-see-ə] *n*
indigestion. **dys·pep'tic** *adj, n*

dys·tro·phy [DIS-trə-fee] *n* wasting
of body tissues, esp. muscles.

E e

e- *prefix* electronic, e.g. *e-mail; e-tail.*

each [eech] *adj, pron* every one taken separately.

ea·ger [EE-gər] *adj* having a strong wish (for something); keen, impatient. **ea'ger·ness** *n*

ea·gle [EE-gəl] *n* large bird with keen sight that preys on small birds and animals; *Golf* score of two strokes under par for a hole. **ea·glet** [EE-glit] *n* young eagle.

ear¹ [eer] *n* organ of hearing, esp. external part of it; sense of hearing; sensitiveness to sounds; attention. **ear'ache** *n* acute pain in ear. **ear'mark** *vt* assign, reserve for definite purpose. **ear'phone** *n* receiver for radio, etc. held to or put in ear. **ear'ring** *n* ornament for lobe of the ear. **ear'shot** *n* hearing distance.

ear² *n* spike, head of corn.

earl [url] *n* British nobleman ranking next below marquis.

ear·ly [UR-lee] *adj, adv* **-li·er, -li·est.** before expected or usual time; in first part, near or nearer beginning of some portion of time.

earn [urn] *vt* obtain by work or merit; gain. **earn'ings** *pl n*

ear·nest¹ [UR-nist] *adj* serious, ardent, sincere. **in earnest** serious, determined.

earnest² *n* money paid over in token to bind bargain, pledge; token, foretaste.

earth [urth] *n* (**E-**) planet or world we live on; ground; dry land; mold, soil, mineral. **earth'en** *adj* made of clay or earth. **earth'ly** *adj* possible, feasible. **earth'y** *adj* **earth·i·er, earth·i·est.** of earth; uninhibited; vulgar. **earth'en·ware** *n* (vessels of) baked clay. **earth'quake** *n* convulsion of Earth's surface.

ease [eez] *n* comfort; freedom from constraint, annoyance, awkwardness, pain or trouble; idleness. ▶ *v* **eased, eas·ing.** reduce burden; give bodily or mental ease to; slacken; (cause to) move carefully or gradually; relieve of pain. **ease'ment** *n Law* right of way, etc., over another's land.

eas·i·ly *adv* **eas'y** *adj* **eas·i·er, eas·i·est.** not difficult; free from pain, care, constraint or anxiety; compliant; characterized by low demand; fitting loosely; *inf* having no preference for any particular course of action. **easy-going** *adj* not fussy; indolent.

ea·sel [EE-zəl] *n* frame to support picture, etc.

east [eest] *n* part of horizon where sun rises; (**E-**) eastern lands, Orient. ▶ *adj* on, in, or near, east; coming from east. ▶ *adv* from, or to, east. **east'er·ly** *adj, adv* from, or to, east. **east'ern** *adj* of, dwelling in, east. **east'ern·er** *n* **east'ward** *adj, adv, n* **east'ward, east'wards** *adv*

Eas·ter [EE-stər] *n* annual festival of the resurrection of Christ.

easy see EASE.

eat [eet] *v* **ate, eat·en, eat·ing.** chew and swallow; consume, destroy; gnaw; wear away.

eaves [eevz] *pl n* overhanging edges of roof. **eaves'drop** *v* **-dropped, -drop·ping.** listen secretly. **eaves'drop·per** *n*

ebb *vi* flow back; decay. ▶ *n* flowing back of tide; decline, decay. **at a low ebb** in a state of weakness.

eb·on·y [EB-ə-nee] *n* **-on·ies.** hard black wood. ▶ *adj* made of, black as ebony.

e-book [EE-buuk] *n* book in the form of a file that can be downloaded to a computer via the Internet.

e·bul·lient [i-BUUL-yənt] *adj* exuberant; boiling. **e·bul'lience** *n* **eb·ul·li·tion** [eb-ə-LISH-ən] *n* boiling; effervescence; outburst.

ec·cen·tric [ik-SEN-trik] *adj* odd, unconventional; irregular; not placed, or not having axis placed, centrally; not circular (in orbit). ▶ *n* odd, unconventional person; mechanical device to change circular into to-and-fro movement. **ec·cen·tric'i·ty** n

Eccles. Ecclesiastes.

ec·cle·si·as·tic [i-klee-zee-AS-tik] n clergyman. ▶ adj of, relating to the Christian Church. **ec·cle·si·as'ti·cal** adj

ech·e·lon [ESH-ə-lon] n level, grade, of responsibility or command; formation of troops, planes, etc. in parallel divisions each slightly to left or right of the one in front.

ech·o [EK-oh] n, pl **ech·oes.** repetition of sounds by reflection; close imitation. ▶ v **ech·oed, ech·o·ing.** ▶ vt repeat as echo, send back the sound of; imitate closely. ▶ vi resound; be repeated. **echo sounding** system of ascertaining depth of water by measuring time required to receive an echo from sea bottom or submerged object.

éclair [ee-KLAIR] n finger-shaped, chocolate-frosted cake filled with whipped cream or custard.

éclat [ay-KLAH] n splendor, renown, acclamation.

e·clec·tic [i-KLEK-tik] adj selecting; borrowing one's philosophy from various sources; catholic in views or taste. ▶ n **e·clec'ti·cism** n

e·clipse [i-KLIPS] n blotting out of sun, moon, etc. by another heavenly body; obscurity. ▶ vt **-clipsed, -clips·ing.** obscure, hide; surpass. **e·clip'tic** adj of eclipse. ▶ n apparent path of sun.

e·col·o·gy [i-KOL-ə-jee] n science of plants and animals in relation to their environment. **ec·o·log'i·cal** adj **e·col'o·gist** n specialist in or advocate of ecological studies.

e·com·merce n business transactions conducted on the Internet.

e·con·o·my [i-KON-ə-mee] n, pl **-mies.** careful management of resources to avoid unnecessary expenditure or waste; sparing, restrained or efficient use; system of interrelationship of money,

industry and employment in a country. **ec·o·nom'ic** adj of economics; profitable; economical. **ec·o·nom'i·cal** adj not wasteful of money, time, effort, etc.; frugal. **ec·o·nom'ics** n study of economies of nations; financial aspects. **e·con'o·mist** n specialist in economics. **e·con'o·mize** v **-mized, -miz·ing.** limit or reduce expense, waste, etc.

ec·ru [EK-roo] n, adj (of) color of unbleached linen.

ec·sta·sy [EK-stə-see] n, pl **-sies.** exalted state of feeling, mystic trance; frenzy; (**E-**) sl powerful drug that can produce hallucinations. **ec·stat·ic** [ik-STAT-ik] adj **ec·stat'i·cal·ly** adv

ec·u·men·i·cal [ek-yuu-MEN-i-kəl] adj of the Christian Church throughout the world, esp. with regard to its unity; interdenominational; universal. **ec·u·men'i·cism** n

ec·ze·ma [EK-sə-mə] n skin disease.

ed·dy [ED-ee] n, pl **-dies.** small whirl in water, smoke, etc. ▶ vi **-died, -dy·ing.** move in whirls.

e·del·weiss [AY-dəl-vīs] n white-flowered alpine plant.

e·de·ma [i-DEE-mə] n an abnormal excess of fluid in tissues, organs; swelling due to this.

E·den [EE-dən] n garden in which Adam and Eve were placed at the Creation; any delightful, happy place or condition.

edge [ej] n border, boundary; cutting side of blade; sharpness; advantage; acrimony, bitterness. ▶ v **edged, edg·ing.** ▶ vt sharpen, give edge or border to; move gradually. ▶ vi advance sideways or gradually. **edge'ways, -wise** adv **edg'ing** n **edg'y** adj **edg·i·er, edg·i·est.** irritable, sharp or keen in temper. **on edge** nervous, irritable; excited.

ed·i·ble [ED-ə-bəl] adj eatable, fit for eating.

e·dict [EE-dikt] n order proclaimed by authority, decree.

ed·i·fice [ED-ə-fis] n building, esp.

big one.

ed·i·fy [ED-ə-fī] *vt* **-fied, -fy·ing.**
improve morally, instruct.
ed·i·fi·ca'tion *n* improvement of
the mind or morals.

ed'it *vt* prepare book, film, tape,
etc. for publication or broadcast.
e·di·tion [i-DISH-ən] *n* form in
which something is published;
number of copies of new
publication printed at one time.
ed·i·to'ri·al *adj* of editor. ▸ *n* article
stating opinion of newspaper, etc.

ed·u·cate [EJ-uu-kayt] *vt* **-cat·ed,
-cat·ing.** provide schooling for;
teach; train mentally and morally;
train; improve, develop.
ed·u·ca'tion *n* **ed·u·ca'tion·al** *adj*
ed'u·ca·tive *adj* **ed'u·ca·tor** *n*

e·duce [i-DOOS] *vt* **-duced,
-duc·ing.** bring out, elicit, develop;
infer, deduce.

ee·rie [EER-ee] *adj* **-ri·er, -ri·est.**
weird, uncanny; causing
superstitious fear.

ef·face [i-FAYS] *vt* **-faced, -fac·ing.**
wipe or rub out. **ef·face'a·ble** *adj*

ef·fect [i-FEKT] *n* result,
consequence; efficacy; impression;
condition of being operative. ▸ *pl*
movable property; lighting,
sounds, etc. to accompany film,
broadcast, etc. ▸ *vt* bring about,
accomplish. **ef·fec'tive** *adj* having
power to produce effects; in effect,
operative; serviceable; powerful;
striking. **ef·fec'tive·ly** *adv*
ef·fec'tu·al [-choo-əl] *adj*
successful in producing dous.
effect; satisfacto~ ~yt] *vt* **-at·ed,**
~out, effect.
ef·fec'tuate [i-FEM-ə-nit] *adj*
~an~anish, unmanly.
~f·fem'i·na·cy *n*

ef·fer·ent [EF-ər-ənt] *adj* conveying
outward or away.

ef·fer·vesce [ef-ər-VES] *vi* **-vesced,
-vesc·ing.** give off bubbles; be in
high spirits. **ef·fer·ves'cent** *adj*

ef·fete [i-FEET] *adj* worn out, feeble.

ef·fi·ca·cious [ef-i-KAY-shəs] *adj*
producing or sure to produce
desired effect; effective; powerful;

adequate. **ef'fi·ca·cy** [-kə-see] *n*
-cies. potency; force; efficiency.

ef·fi·cient [i-FISH-ənt] *adj* capable,
competent, producing effect.
ef·fi'cien·cy *n, pl* **-cies.**

ef·fi·gy [EF-i-jee] *n, pl* **-gies.** image,
likeness.

ef·flo·resce [ef-lə-RES] *vi* **-resced,
-res·cing.** burst into flower.
ef·flo·res'cence *n*

ef·flu·ent [EF-loo-ənt] *n* liquid
discharged as waste; stream
flowing from larger stream, lake,
etc. ▸ *adj* flowing out. **ef·flu·vi·um**
[i-FLOO-vee-əm] *n, pl* **-vi·a.**
something flowing out invisibly,
esp. affecting lungs or sense of
smell.

ef·fort [EF-ərt] *n* exertion,
endeavor, attempt or something
achieved. **ef'fort·less** *adj*

ef·fron·ter·y [i-FRUN-tə-ree] *n, pl*
-ter·ies. brazen impudence.

ef·ful·gent [i-FUL-jənt] *adj* radiant,
shining brightly. **ef·ful'gence** *n*

ef·fu·sion [i-FYOO-zhən] *n*
(unrestrained) outpouring. **ef·fuse**
[i-FYOOZ] *v* **-fused, -fus·ing.** pour
out, shed; radiate. **ef·fu'sive** [-siv]
adj gushing, demonstrative.

e.g. for example.

e·gal·i·tar·i·an [i-gal-i-TAIR-ee-ən]
adj believing that all people should
be equal; promoting this ideal. ▸ *n*

egg[1] *n* oval or round object
produced by female of bird, etc.,
from which young emerge, esp.
egg of domestic hen, used as food.
egg'~ant *n* egg-shaped dark
purple fruit; plant bearing it.

egg[2] *vt* **egg on** encourage, urge;
incite.

e·go [EE-goh] *n, pl* **e·gos.** the self;
the conscious thinking subject;
one's image of oneself; morale.
e'go·ism *n* systematic selfishness;
theory that bases morality on
self-interest. **e'go·tism** *n*
selfishness; self-conceit. **e'go·tist,**
eg'o·ist *n* **e·go·tis'tic, e·go·is'tic**
adj **e·go·cen'tric** *adj* self-centered;
egoistic; centered in the ego.

e·gre·gious [i-GREE-jəs] *adj*
outstandingly bad, blatant;

absurdly obvious, esp. of mistake, etc.

e·gress [EE-gres] *n* way out; departure.

e·gret [EE-grit] *n* one of several white herons.

ei·der [Ī-dər] *n* any of several northern sea ducks; eiderdown. **ei'der·down** *n* its breast feathers; quilt (stuffed with feathers).

eight [ayt] *n* cardinal number one above seven; crew of eight-oared shell. ▶ *adj* **eight·een'** *adj, n* eight more than ten. **eight·eenth'** *adj, n* **eighth** [ayth] *adj, n* ordinal number. **eight'i·eth** *adj, n* **eight'y** *adj, n, pl* **eight·ies.** ten times eight. **figure eight** a skating figure; any figure shaped as 8.

ei·ther [EE-*th*ər] *adj, pron* one or the other; one of two; each. ▶ *adv, conj* bringing in first of alternatives or strengthening an added negation.

e·jac·u·late [i-JAK-yə-layt] *v* **-lat·ed, -lat·ing.** eject (semen); exclaim, utter suddenly. **e·jac·u·la'tion** *n*

e·ject [i-JEKT] *vt* throw out; expel, drive out. **e·jec'tion** *n*

eke out [eek] *vt* make (supply) last, esp. by frugal use; supply deficiencies of; make with difficulty (a living, etc.).

e·lab·o·rate [i-LAB-ər-it] *adj* carefully worked out, detailed; complicated. ▶ *v* [-ayt] **-rat·ed, -rat·ing.** ▶ *vi* expand (upon). ▶ *vt* work out in detail; take pains with.

élan [ay-LAHN] *n* dash; ardor, impetuosity. **élan vi·tal** [vee-TAL] esp. in Bergsonian philosophy, the creative force within an organism that is responsible for growth, change, etc.

e·lapse [i-LAPS] *vi* **-lapsed, -laps·ing.** of time, pass.

e·las·tic [i-LAS-tik] *adj* resuming normal shape after distortion, springy; flexible. ▶ *n* tape, fabric, containing interwoven strands of flexible rubber, etc. **e·las'ti·cized** [-sīzd] *adj* **e·las·tic'i·ty** *n*

e·la·tion [i-LAY-shən] *n* high spirits; pride. **e·late** [i-LAYT] *vt* **-lat·ed,**

-lat·ing. (usu. passive) be elated, etc.; raise the spirits of; make happy; exhilarate.

el·bow [EL-boh] *n* joint between fore and upper parts of arm (esp. outer part of it); part of sleeve covering this; something resembling this, esp. angular pipe fitting. ▶ *vt* shove, strike with elbow. **elbow grease** hard work. **elbow room** *n* sufficient room.

eld·er¹ [EL-dər] *adj* older, senior; comp. of OLD. ▶ *n* person of greater age; old person; official of certain churches. **el'der·ly** *adj* growing old. **eld'est** *adj* oldest; sup. of OLD.

el·der² *n* white-flowered tree or shrub.

El Do·ra·do [el də-RAH-doh] *n* fictitious country rich in gold.

e·lect [i-LEKT] *vt* choose by vote; choose. ▶ *adj* appointed but not yet in office; chosen, select, choice. **e·lec'tion** *n* choosing, esp. by voting. **e·lec·tion·eer'** *vi* work in political campaign. **e·lec'tive** *adj* appointed, filled, or chosen by election. **e·lec'tor** *n* one who elects. **e·lec'tor·al** *adj* **electoral college** body of electors chosen by voters to elect President and Vice President. **e·lec'tor·ate** *n* body of persons entitled to vote.

e·lec·tric·i·ty [i-lek-TRIS-i-tee] *n* form of energy associated with stationary or moving electrons or other charged particles; electric current or charge; science dealing with electricity. **e·lec'tric** *adj* producing, produced by, powered by, transmitting or emotionally charged. **e·lec·tri'cian** *n* one cited, installation, etc. of electrical wal and devices. **e·lec·tri·fi·ca'tion** *n* **e·lec'tri·fy** *vt* **-fied, -fy·ing. electric chair** chair in which criminals sentenced to death are electrocuted. **electric organ** *Mus* organ in which sound is produced by electric devices instead of wind. **electro-** *comb. form* operated by or caused by electricity, e.g.

absurdly obvious, esp. of mistake, etc.

e·gress [EE-gres] *n* way out; departure.

e·gret [EE-grit] *n* one of several white herons.

ei·der [Ī-dər] *n* any of several northern sea ducks; eiderdown. **ei'der·down** *n* its breast feathers; quilt (stuffed with feathers).

eight [ayt] *n* cardinal number one above seven; crew of eight-oared shell. ▶ *adj* **eight·een'** *adj, n* eight more than ten. **eight·eenth'** *adj, n* **eighth** [ayth] *adj, n* ordinal number. **eight'i·eth** *adj, n* **eight'y** *adj, n, pl* **eight·ies.** ten times eight. **figure eight** a skating figure; any figure shaped as 8.

ei·ther [EE-thər] *adj, pron* one or the other; one of two; each. ▶ *adv, conj* bringing in first of alternatives or strengthening an added negation.

e·jac·u·late [i-JAK-yə-layt] *v* **-lat·ed, -lat·ing.** eject (semen); exclaim, utter suddenly. **e·jac·u·la'tion** *n*

e·ject [i-JEKT] *vt* throw out; expel, drive out. **e·jec'tion** *n*

eke out [eek] *vt* make (supply) last, esp. by frugal use; supply deficiencies of; make with difficulty (a living, etc.).

e·lab·o·rate [i-LAB-ər-it] *adj* carefully worked out, detailed; complicated. ▶ *v* [-ayt] **-rat·ed, -rat·ing.** ▶ *vi* expand (upon). ▶ *vt* work out in detail; take pains with.

élan [ay-LAHN] *n* dash; ardor; impetuosity. **élan vi·tal** [vee-TAL] esp. in Bergsonian philosophy, the creative force within an organism that is responsible for growth, change, etc.

e·lapse [i-LAPS] *vi* **-lapsed, -laps·ing.** of time, pass.

e·las·tic [i-LAS-tik] *adj* resuming normal shape after distortion; springy; flexible. ▶ *n* tape, fabric, containing interwoven strands of flexible rubber, etc. **e·las'ti·cized** [-sīzd] *adj* **e·las·tic'i·ty** *n*

e·la·tion [i-LAY-shən] *n* high spirits; pride. **e·late** [i-LAYT] *vt* **-lat·ed,**

-lat·ing. (usu. passive) be elated, etc.; raise the spirits of; make happy; exhilarate.

el·bow [EL-boh] *n* joint between fore and upper parts of arm (esp. outer part of it); part of sleeve covering this; something resembling this, esp. angular pipe fitting. ▶ *vt* shove, strike with elbow. **elbow grease** hard work. **elbow room** *n* sufficient room.

eld·er[1] [EL-dər] *adj* older, senior; comp. of OLD. ▶ *n* person of greater age; old person; official of certain churches. **el'der·ly** *adj* growing old. **eld'est** *adj* oldest; sup. of OLD.

el·der[2] *n* white-flowered tree or shrub.

El Do·ra·do [el də-RAH-doh] *n* fictitious country rich in gold.

e·lect [i-LEKT] *vt* choose by vote; choose. ▶ *adj* appointed but not yet in office; chosen, select, choice. **e·lec'tion** *n* choosing, esp. by voting. **e·lec·tion·eer'** *vi* work in political campaign. **e·lec'tive** *adj* appointed, filled, or chosen by election. **e·lec'tor** *n* one who elects. **e·lec'tor·al** *adj* **electoral college** body of electors chosen by voters to elect President and Vice President. **e·lec'tor·ate** *n* body of persons entitled to vote.

e·lec·tric·i·ty [i-lek-TRIS-i-tee] *n* form of energy associated with stationary or moving electrons or other charged particles; electric current or charge; science dealing with electricity. **e·lec'tric** *adj* derived from, produced by, producing, transmitting or powered by electricity; excited, emotionally charged. **e·lec'tri·cal** *adj* **e·lec·tri'cian** *n* one trained in installation, etc. of electrical wiring and devices. **e·lec·tri·fi·ca'tion** *n* **e·lec'tri·fy** *vt* **-fied, -fy·ing. electric chair** chair in which criminals sentenced to death are electrocuted. **electric organ** *Mus* organ in which sound is produced by electric devices instead of wind.

electro- *comb. form* operated by or caused by electricity, e.g.

big one.

ed·i·fy [ED-ə-fī] vt **-fied, -fy·ing.** improve morally, instruct. **ed·i·fi·ca'tion** n improvement of the mind or morals.

ed'it vt prepare book, film, tape, etc. for publication or broadcast. **e·di·tion** [i-DISH-ən] n form in which something is published; number of copies of new publication printed at one time. **ed·i·to'ri·al** adj of editor. ▸ n article stating opinion of newspaper, etc.

ed·u·cate [EJ-uu-kayt] vt **-cat·ed, -cat·ing.** provide schooling for; teach; train mentally and morally; train; improve, develop. **ed·u·ca'tion** n **ed·u·ca'tion·al** adj **ed'u·ca·tive** adj **ed'u·ca·tor** n

e·duce [i-DOOS] vt **-duced, -duc·ing.** bring out, elicit, develop; infer, deduce.

ee·rie [EER-ee] adj **-ri·er, -ri·est.** weird, uncanny; causing superstitious fear.

ef·face [i-FAYS] vt **-faced, -fac·ing.** wipe or rub out. **ef·face'a·ble** adj

ef·fect [i-FEKT] n result, consequence; efficacy; impression; condition of being operative. ▸ pl movable property; lighting, sounds, etc. to accompany film, broadcast, etc. ▸ vt bring about, accomplish. **ef·fec'tive** adj having power to produce effects; in effect, operative; serviceable; powerful; striking. **ef·fec'tive·ly** adv **ef·fec'tu·al** [-choo-əl] adj successful in producing desired effect; satisfactory; efficacious. **ef·fec'tu·ate** [-choo-ayt] vt **-at·ed, -at·ing.** bring about, effect.

ef·fem·i·nate [i-FEM-ə-nit] adj womanish, unmanly. **ef·fem'i·na·cy** n

ef·fer·ent [EF-ər-ənt] adj conveying outward or away.

ef·fer·vesce [ef-ər-VES] vi **-vesced, -vesc·ing.** give off bubbles; be in high spirits. **ef·fer·ves'cent** adj

ef·fete [i-FEET] adj worn out, feeble.

ef·fi·ca·cious [ef-i-KAY-shəs] adj producing or sure to produce desired effect; effective; powerful;

adequate. **ef'fi·ca·cy** [-kə-see] n **-cies.** potency; force; efficiency.

ef·fi·cient [i-FISH-ənt] adj capable, competent, producing effect. **ef·fi'cien·cy** n, pl **-cies.**

ef·fi·gy [EF-i-jee] n, pl **-gies.** image, likeness.

ef·flo·resce [ef-lə-RES] vi **-resced, -res·cing.** burst into flower. **ef·flo·res'cence** n

ef·flu·ent [EF-loo-ənt] n liquid discharged as waste; stream flowing from larger stream, lake, etc. ▸ adj flowing out. **ef·flu·vi·um** [i-FLOO-vee-əm] n, pl **-vi·a.** something flowing out invisibly, esp. affecting lungs or sense of smell.

ef·fort [EF-ərt] n exertion, endeavor, attempt or something achieved. **ef'fort·less** adj

ef·fron·ter·y [i-FRUN-tə-ree] n, pl **-ter·ies.** brazen impudence.

ef·ful·gent [i-FUL-jənt] adj radiant, shining brightly. **ef·ful'gence** n

ef·fu·sion [i-FYOO-zhən] n (unrestrained) outpouring. **ef·fuse** [i-FYOOZ] v **-fused, -fus·ing.** pour out, shed; radiate. **ef·fu'sive** [-siv] adj gushing, demonstrative.

e.g. for example.

e·gal·i·tar·i·an [i-gal-i-TAIR-ee-ən] adj believing that all people should be equal; promoting this ideal. ▸ n

egg[1] n oval or round object produced by female of bird, etc., from which young emerge, esp. egg of domestic hen, used as food. **egg'plant** n egg-shaped dark purple fruit; plant bearing it.

egg[2] vt **egg on** encourage, urge; incite.

e·go [EE-goh] n, pl **e·gos.** the self; the conscious thinking subject; one's image of oneself; morale. **e'go·ism** n systematic selfishness; theory that bases morality on self-interest. **e'go·tism** n selfishness; self-conceit. **e'go·tist, eg'o·ist** n **e·go·tis'tic, e·go·is'tic** adj **e·go·cen'tric** adj self-centered; egoistic; centered in the ego.

e·gre·gious [i-GREE-jəs] adj outstandingly bad, blatant;

electrocute.

e·lec·tro·car·di·o·graph [i-lek-troh-KAHR-dee-ə-graf] n instrument for recording electrical activity of heart. **e·lec·tro·car'di·o·gram** n tracing produced by this.

e·lec·tro·cute [i-LEK-trə-kyoot] vt -cut·ed, -cut·ing. execute, kill by electricity. **e·lec·tro·cu'tion** n

e·lec·trode [i-LEK-trohd] n conductor by which electric current enters or leaves battery, vacuum tube, etc.

e·lec·tro·en·ceph·a·lo·graph [i-lek-troh-en-SEF-ə-lə-graf] n instrument for recording electrical activity of brain. **e·lec·tro·en·ceph'a·lo·gram** n tracing produced by this.

e·lec·tro·lyte [i-LEK-trə-līt] n solution, molten substance that conducts electricity. **e·lec·tro·lyt'ic** [-LIT-ik] adj

e·lec·tro·lyze [i-LEK-trə-līz] vt -lyzed, -lyz·ing. decompose by electricity. **e·lec·trol'y·sis** [-TROL-ə-sis] n

e·lec·tro·mag·net [i-lek-troh-MAG-nit] n magnet containing coil of wire through which electric current is passed. **e·lec·tro·mag·net'ic** adj

e·lec·tron [i-LEK-tron] n one of fundamental particles of matter identified with unit of charge of negative electricity and essential component of the atom. **e·lec·tron'ic** adj of electrons or electronics; using devices, such as semiconductors, transistors or vacuum tubes, dependent on action of electrons. **electronic mail** see E-MAIL. **e·lec·tron'ics** n technology concerned with development of electronic devices and circuits; science of behavior and control of electrons. **electron volt** unit of energy used in nuclear physics.

e·lec·tro·plate [i-LEK-trə-playt] vt -plat·ed, -plat·ing. coat with silver, etc. by electrolysis. ▶ n articles electroplated.

el·e·gant [EL-ə-gənt] adj graceful, tasteful; refined. **el'e·gance** n

el·e·gy [EL-ə-jee] n, pl -gies. lament for the dead in poem or song. **el·e·gi·ac** [el-ə-JĪ-ək] adj suited to elegies; plaintive.

el·e·ment [EL-ə-mənt] n substance that cannot be separated into other substances by ordinary chemical techniques; component part; small amount, trace; heating wire in electric kettle, stove, etc.; proper abode or sphere. ▶ pl powers of atmosphere; rudiments, first principles. **el·e·men'tal** adj fundamental; of powers of nature. **el·e·men'ta·ry** adj rudimentary, simple.

el·e·phant [EL-ə-fənt] n huge four-footed, thick-skinned animal with ivory tusks and long trunk. **el·e·phan·ti·a·sis** n disease with hardening of skin and enlargement of legs, etc. **el·e·phan'tine** [-FAN-teen] adj unwieldy, clumsy, heavily big.

el·e·vate [EL-ə-vayt] vt -vat·ed, -vat·ing. raise, lift up, exalt. **el·e·va'tion** n raising; height, esp. above sea level; angle above horizon, as of gun; drawing of one side of building, etc. **el'e·va·tor** n cage raised and lowered in vertical shaft to transport people, etc.

e·lev·en [i-LEV-ən] n number next above 10; team of 11 persons. ▶ adj **e·lev'en·fold** adj, adv **e·lev'enth** adj the ordinal number. **eleventh hour** latest possible time.

elf n, pl **elves.** fairy; woodland sprite. **elf'in** adj roguish, mischievous.

e·lic·it [i-LIS-it] vt draw out, evoke; bring to light.

e·lide [i-LĪD] vt **e·lid·ed, e·lid·ing.** omit in pronunciation a vowel or syllable. **e·li·sion** [i-LIZH-ən] n

el·i·gi·ble [EL-ə-jə-bəl] adj fit or; qualified to be chosen; suitable, desirable. **el·i·gi·bil'i·ty** n

e·lim·i·nate [i-LIM-ə-nayt] vt -nat·ed, -nat·ing. remove, get rid of, set aside. **e·lim·i·na'tion** n

elision see ELIDE.

e·lite [i-LEET] *n* choice or select body; the pick or best part of society; typewriter type size (12 letters to inch). ▸ *adj* **e·lit'ism** *n* **e·lit'ist** *n*

e·lix·ir [i-LIK-sər] *n* preparation sought by alchemists to change base metals into gold, or to prolong life; panacea.

elk *n* large deer.

el·lipse [i-LIPS] *n* oval. **el·lip'ti·cal** *adj*

el·lip·sis [i-LIP-sis] *n, pl* **-ses** [-seez] omission of parts of word or sentence; mark (. . .) indicating this.

el·o·cu·tion [el-ə-KYOO-shən] *n* art of public speaking, voice management. **el·o·cu'tion·ist** *n* teacher of this.

e·lon·gate [i-LAWNG-gayt] *vt* **-gat·ed, -gat·ing.** lengthen, extend, prolong. **e·lon·ga'tion** *n*

e·lope [i-LOHP] *vi* **-loped, -lop·ing.** run away from home with lover; do this with intention of marrying. **e·lope'ment** *n*

el·o·quence [EL-ə-kwəns] *n* fluent, powerful use of language. **el'o·quent** *adj*

else [els] *adv* besides, instead; otherwise. **else·where** *adv* in or to some other place.

e·lu·ci·date [i-LOO-si-dayt] *vt* **-dat·ed, -dat·ing.** throw light upon, explain. **e·lu·ci·da'tion** *n*

e·lude [i-LOOD] *vt* **-lud·ed, -lud·ing.** escape, slip away from, dodge; baffle. **e·lu'sion** *n* act of eluding; evasion. **e·lu'sive** *adj* difficult to catch hold of, deceptive. **e·lu'sive·ness** *n*

elves, elvish see ELF.

em *n Printing* the square of any size of type.

em- *prefix* see EN-.

e·ma·ci·ate [i-MAY-see-ayt] *v* **-at·ed, -at·ing.** make or become abnormally thin. **e·ma·ci·a'tion** *n*

e-mail, e·mail *n* (also **electronic mail**) sending of messages between computer terminals or other electronic devices. ▸ *v* communicate in this way.

em·a·nate [EM-ə-nayt] *vi* **-nat·ed,** **-nat·ing.** issue, proceed from, originate. **em·a·na'tion** *n*

e·man·ci·pate [i-MAN-sə-payt] *vt* **-pat·ed, -pat·ing.** set free. **e·man·ci·pa'tion** *n* act of setting free, esp. from social, legal restraint; state of being set free. **e·man'ci·pa·tor** *n*

e·mas·cu·late [i-MAS--kyə-layt] *vt* **-lat·ed, -lat·ing.** castrate; enfeeble, weaken. **e·mas·cu·la'tion** *n*

em·balm [em-BAHM] *vt* preserve corpse from decay by use of chemicals, herbs, etc. **em·balm'er** *n*

em·bank·ment [em-BANGK-mənt] *n* artificial mound carrying road, railway, or serving to dam water.

em·bar·go [em-BAHR-goh] *n, pl* **-goes.** order stopping movement of ships; suspension of commerce; ban. ▸ *vt* **-goed, -go·ing.** put under embargo.

em·bark [em-BAHRK] *v* put, go, on board ship, aircraft, etc.; (with *on* or *upon*) commence new project, venture, etc. **em·bar·ka'tion** *n*

em·bar·rass [em-BAR-əs] *vt* perplex, disconcert; abash; confuse; encumber. **em·bar'rass·ment** *n*

em·bas·sy [EM-bə-see] *n, pl* **-sies.** office, work or official residence of ambassador; deputation.

em·bed' *vt* **-bed·ded, -bed·ding.** fix fast in something solid.

em·bel'lish *vt* adorn, enrich. **em·bel'lish·ment** *n*

em·ber [EM-bər] *n* glowing cinder. ▸ *pl* red-hot ashes.

em·bez·zle [em-BEZ-əl] *vt* **-zled, -zling.** divert fraudulently, misappropriate (money in trust, etc.). **em·bez'zle·ment** *n* **em·bez'zler** *n*

em·bit·ter [em-BIT-ər] *vt* make bitter. **em·bit'ter·ment** *n*

em·bla·zon [em-BLAY-zən] *vt* adorn richly, esp. heraldically.

em·blem [EM-bləm] *n* symbol; badge, device. **em·ble·mat'ic** *adj*

em·bod·y [em-BOD-ee] *vt* **-bod·ied, -bod·y·ing.** give body, concrete expression to; represent,

include, be expression of.
em·bod'i·ment n

em·bo·lism [EM-bə-liz-əm] n Med
obstruction of artery by blood clot
or air bubble.

em·boss [em-BAWS] vt mold,
stamp or carve in relief.

em·brace [em-BRAYS] vt **-braced,
-brac·ing.** clasp in arms, hug; seize,
avail oneself of, accept; comprise.
▶ n

em·bra·sure [em-BRAY-zhər] n
opening in wall for cannon;
beveling of wall at sides of window.

em·bro·ca·tion [em-brə-KAY-shən]
n lotion for rubbing limbs, etc. to
relieve pain. **em'bro·cate** vt
-cat·ed, -cat·ing. apply lotion, etc.

em·broi·der [em-BROI-dər] vt
ornament with needlework;
embellish, exaggerate (story).
em·broi'der·y n

em·broil' vt bring into confusion;
involve in hostility. **em·broil'ment**
n

em·bry·o [EM-bree-oh] n, pl **-os.**
unborn or undeveloped offspring,
germ; undeveloped thing.
em·bry·ol'o·gist n **em·bry·ol'o·gy**
n **em·bry·on'ic** adj

e·mend [i-MEND] vt remove errors
from, correct. **e·men·da'tion** n

em·er·ald [EM-ər-əld] n bright
green precious stone. ▶ adj of the
color of emerald.

e·merge [i-MURJ] vi **-merged,
-merg·ing.** come up, out; rise to
notice; come into view; come out
on inquiry. **e·mer'gence** n
e·mer'gent adj

e·mer·gen·cy [i-MUR-jən-see] n, pl
-cies. sudden unforeseen thing or
event needing prompt action;
difficult situation; exigency, crisis.

e·mer·i·tus [i-MER-i-təs] adj retired,
honorably discharged but retaining
one's title (e.g. professor) on
honorary basis.

em·er·y [EM-ər-ee] n hard mineral
used for polishing. **emery board**
cardboard coated with powdered
emery.

e·met·ic [i-MET-ik] n, adj (medicine
or agent) causing vomiting.

em·i·grate [EM-i-grayt] vt **-grat·ed,
-grat·ing.** go and settle in another
country. **em'i·grant** [-grənt] n
em·i·gra'tion n

é·mi·gré [EM-i-gray] n, pl **-grés.**
emigrant, esp. one forced to leave
native land for political reasons.

em·i·nent [EM-ə-nənt] adj
distinguished, notable. **em'i·nence**
n distinction; height; rank; fame;
rising ground; (**E-**) title of cardinal.
em'i·nent·ly adv **é·mi·nence grise**
[ay-mee-nahns GREEZ] Fr person
wielding unofficial power, oft.
surreptitiously.

em·is·sar·y [EM-ə-ser-ee] n, pl
-sar·ies. agent, representative (esp.
of government) sent on mission.

e·mit [i-MIT] vt **-mit·ted, -mit·ting.**
give out, put forth. **e·mis'sion** n
e·mit'ter n

e·mol·lient [i-MOL-yənt] adj
softening, soothing. ▶ n ointment
or other softening application.

e·mol·u·ment [i-MOL-yə-mənt] n
salary, pay, profit from work.

e·mot·i·con [i-MOH-ti-kon] n series
of keyed characters, used esp. in
e-mail, to indicate an emotion.

e·mo·tion [i-MOH-shən] n mental
agitation, excited state of feeling,
as joy, fear, etc. **e·mo'tion·al** adj
given to emotion; appealing to the
emotions. **e·mo'tive** adj tending
to arouse emotion.

em·pa·thy [EM-pə-thee] n power of
understanding, imaginatively
entering into, another's feelings.

em·per·or [EM-pər-ər] n ruler of an
empire. **em'press** [-pris] n, fem

em·pha·sis [EM-fə-sis] n, pl **-ses**
[-seez] importance attached; stress
on words; vigor of speech,
expression. **em'pha·size** vt **-sized,
-siz·ing. em·phat'ic** [-FAT-ik] adj
forceful, decided; stressed.

em·pire [EM-pīr] n large territory,
esp. aggregate of territories or
peoples under supreme ruler,
supreme control.

em·pir·i·cal [em-PIR-i-kəl] adj
relying on experiment or
experience, not on theory.
em·pir'i·cal·ly adv **em·pir'i·cist**

[-ə-sist] *n* one who relies solely on experience and observation. **em·pir'i·cism** *n*

em·place·ment [em-PLAYS-mənt] *n* putting in position; gun platform.

em·ploy [em-PLOI] *vt* provide work for (a person) in return for money, hire; keep busy; use. **em·ploy·ee'** *n* **em·ploy'er** *n* **em·ploy'ment** *n* an employing, being employed; work, trade; occupation.

em·po·ri·um [em-POHR-ee-əm] *n*, *pl* **-ri·ums.** large store, esp. one carrying general merchandise; center of commerce.

em·pow·er [em-POW-ər] *vt* enable, authorize. **em·pow·er·ment** *n*

empress see EMPEROR.

emp·ty [EM-tee] *adj* **-ti·er, -ti·est.** containing nothing; unoccupied; senseless; vain, foolish. ▶ *v* **-tied, -ty·ing.** make, become devoid of content; discharge (contents) into. **emp'ties** *pl n* empty boxes, bottles, etc. **emp'ti·ness** *n*

e·mu [EE-myoo] *n* large Aust. flightless bird like ostrich.

em·u·late [EM-yə-layt] *vt* **-lat·ed, -lat·ing.** strive to equal or excel; imitate. **em·u·la'tion** *n* rivalry; competition. **em'u·la·tive** *adj* **em'u·la·tor** *n*

e·mul·sion [i-MUL-shən] *n* light-sensitive coating of film; milky liquid with oily or resinous particles in suspension; paint, etc. in this form. **e·mul'si·fi·er** *n* **e·mul'si·fy** *vt* **-fied, -fy·ing.**

en *n* Printing unit of measurement, half an em.

en-, em- *prefix* put in, into, or on, e.g. enrage.

en·a·ble [en-AY-bəl] *vt* **-bled, -bling.** make able, authorize, empower, supply with means (to do something).

en·act [en-AKT] *vi* make law; act part. **en·act'ment** *n*

e·nam·el [i-NAM-əl] *n* glasslike coating applied to metal, etc. to preserve surface; coating of teeth; any hard outer coating. ▶ *vt* **-eled, -el·ing.**

e·nam·or [i-NAM-ər] *vt* inspire with

love; charm; bewitch.

en·camp [en-KAMP] *v* set up (in) camp. **en·camp'ment** *n* camp.

en·cap·su·late [en-KAP-sə-layt] *vt* **-lat·ed, -lat·ing.** enclose in capsule; put in concise or abridged form. **en·cap·su·la'tion** *n*

en·ceph·a·lo·gram [en-SEF-ə-lə-gram] *n* X-ray photograph of brain.

en·chant' *vt* bewitch, delight. **en·chant'er** *n* **en·chant'ress** *n, fem* **en·chant'ment** *n*

en·chi·la·da [en-chə-LAH-də] *n* rolled tortilla filled with sauce of meat, etc.

en·cir·cle [en-SUR-kəl] *vt* **-cled, -cling.** surround; enfold; go around so as to surround.

en·clave [EN-klayv] *n* portion of territory entirely surrounded by foreign land; distinct area or group isolated within larger one.

en·close [en-KLOHZ] *vt* **-closed, -clos·ing.** shut in; surround; envelop; place in with something else (in letter, etc.). **en·clo'sure** [-zhər] *n*

en·co·mi·um [en-KOH-mee-əm] *n* **-mi·ums.** formal praise; eulogy. **en·co'mi·ast** *n* one who composes encomiums.

en·com·pass [en-KUM-pəs] *vt* surround, encircle, contain.

en·core [ONG-kor] *interj* again, once more. ▶ *n* call for repetition of song, etc.; the repetition.

en·coun·ter [en-KOWN-tər] *vt* meet unexpectedly; meet in conflict; be faced with (difficulty, etc.). ▶ *n*

en·cour·age [en-KUR-ij] *vt* **-aged, -ag·ing.** hearten, animate, inspire with hope; embolden. **en·cour'age·ment** *n*

en·croach [en-KROHCH] *vi* intrude (on) as usurper; trespass. **en·croach'ment** *n*

en·crust [en-KRUST] *v* incrust. **en·crus·ta'tion** *n*

en·cum·ber [en-KUM-bər] *vt* hamper; burden. **en·cum'brance** *n* impediment, burden.

en·cyc·li·cal [en-SIK-li-kəl] *adj* sent

to many persons or places. ▶ *n* circular letter, esp. papal letter to all Catholic bishops.

en·cy·clo·pe·dia [en-sī-klə-PEE-dee-ə] *n* book, set of books of information on all subjects, or on every branch of subject, usu. arranged alphabetically. **en·cy·clo·pe'dic** *adj*

end *n* limit; extremity; conclusion, finishing; fragment; latter part; death; event, issue; purpose, aim; *Football* one of two linemen stationed farthest from the center. ▶ *v* put an end to; come to an end, finish. **end'ing** *n* **end'less** *adj* **end'pa·pers** *pl n* blank pages at beginning and end of book.

en·dear [en-DEER] *vt* to make dear or beloved. **en·dear'ing** *adj* **en·dear'ment** *n* loving word; tender affection.

en·deav·or [en-DEV-ər] *vi* try, strive after. ▶ *n* attempt, effort.

en·dem·ic [en-DEM-ik] *adj* found only among a particular people or in a particular place. ▶ *n* endemic disease.

en·dive [EN-dīv] *n* curly-leaved plant used in salad.

endo- *comb. form* within, e.g. *endocrine.*

en·do·car·di·um [en-doh-KAHR-dee-əm] *n* lining membrane of the heart. **en·do·car·di'tis** [-dī-tis] *n* inflammation of this.

en·do·crine [EN-də-krin] *adj* of those glands (thyroid, pituitary, etc.) that secrete hormones directly into bloodstream. **en·do·cri·nol'o·gy** *n* science dealing with endocrine glands.

en·dorse [en-DORS] *vt* **-dorsed, -dors·ing.** sanction; confirm; write (esp. sign name) on back of. **en·dorse'ment** *n*

en·dow' *vt* provide permanent income for; furnish (with). **en·dow'ment** *n*

en·dure [en-DUUR] *v* **-dured, -dur·ing.** undergo; tolerate; bear; last. **en·dur'a·ble** *adj* **en·dur'ance** *n* act or power of enduring.

en·e·ma [EN-ə-mə] *n* medicine, liquid injected into rectum.

en·e·my [EN-ə-mee] *n, pl* **-mies.** hostile person; opponent; armed foe; hostile force.

en·er·gy [EN-ər-jee] *n, pl* **-gies.** vigor, force, activity; source(s) of power, as oil, coal, etc.; capacity of machine, battery, etc. for work or output of power. **en·er·get'ic** *adj* **en'er·gize -gized, -giz·ing.** ▶ *vt* give vigor to.

en·er·vate [EN-ər-vayt] *vt* **-vat·ed, -vat·ing.** weaken, deprive of vigor. **en·er·va'tion** *n* lassitude, weakness.

en·fee·ble [en-FEE-bəl] *vt* **-bled, -bling.** weaken, debilitate.

en·fi·lade [EN-fi-layd] *n* fire from artillery, sweeping line from end to end.

en·force [en-FORS] *vt* compel obedience to; impose (action) upon; drive home. **en·force'a·ble** *adj*

en·fran·chise [en-FRAN-chīz] *vt* **-chised, -chis·ing.** give right of voting to; give legislative representation to; set free. **en·fran'chise·ment** [-chiz·mənt] *n*

en·gage [en-GAYJ] *v* **-gaged, -gag·ing.** ▶ *vt* employ; reserve, hire; bind by contract or promise; order; pledge oneself; betroth; undertake; attract; occupy; bring into conflict; interlock. ▶ *vi* employ oneself (in); promise; begin to fight. **en·gaged'** *adj* betrothed; in use; occupied, busy. **en·gage'ment** *n* **engaging** *adj* charming.

en·gen·der [en-JEN-dər] *vt* give rise to; beget; rouse.

en·gine [EN-jin] *n* any machine to convert energy into mechanical work, as steam or gasoline engine; railroad locomotive; fire engine. **en·gi·neer'** *n* one who is in charge of engines, machinery, etc. or construction work (e.g. roads, bridges); one who originates, organizes something; one trained and skilled in engineering. ▶ *vt* construct as engineer; contrive. **en·gi·neer'ing** *n*

Eng·lish [ING-glish] *n* the language

of the US, Britain, most parts of the British Commonwealth and certain other countries; the people of England. ▶ *adj* relating to England.

engrain *vt* see INGRAIN.

en·grave [en-GRAYV] *vt* **-graved, -grav·ing.** cut in lines on metal for printing; carve, incise; impress deeply. **en·grav'er** *n* **en·grav'ing** *n* copy of picture printed from engraved plate.

en·gross [en-GROHS] *vt* absorb (attention); occupy wholly; write out in large letters or in legal form; monopolize.

en·gulf' *vt* swallow up.

en·hance [en-HANS] *vt* **-hanced, -hanc·ing.** heighten, intensify, increase value or attractiveness. **en·hance'ment** *n*

e·nig·ma [ə-NIG-mə] *n, pl* **-mas.** puzzling thing or person; riddle. **en·ig·mat'ic** *adj*

en·join' *vt* command; impose, prescribe.

en·joy [en-JOI] *vt* delight in; take pleasure in; have use or benefit of. ▶ *v refl* be happy. **en·joy'a·ble** *adj*

en·large [en-LAHRJ] *v* **-larged, -larg·ing.** ▶ *vt* make bigger; reproduce on larger scale, as photograph. ▶ *vi* grow bigger; talk, write about, in greater detail. **en·large'a·ble** *adj* **en·large'ment** *n* **en·larg'er** *n* optical instrument for enlarging photographs.

en·light·en [en-LĪ-tən] *vt* give information to; instruct, inform, shed light on. **en·light'en·ment** *n*

en·list' *v* engage as soldier or helper. **en·list'ment** *n*

en·liv·en [en-LĪ-vən] *vt* brighten, make more lively, animate.

en masse [ahn MAS] *adv* in a group, body; all together.

en·mesh' *vt* entangle.

en·mi·ty [EN-mi-tee] *n, pl* **-ties.** ill will, hostility.

en·no·ble [en-NOH-bəl] *vt* **-bled, -bling.** make noble, elevate. **en·no'ble·ment** *n*

en·nui [ahn-WEE] *n* boredom.

e·nor·mous [i-NOR-məs] *adj* very big, vast. **e·nor'mi·ty** *n* a gross

offense; great wickedness; *inf* great size.

e·nough [i-NUF] *adj* as much or as many as need be; sufficient. ▶ *n* sufficient quantity. ▶ *adv* (just) sufficiently.

enquire see INQUIRE.

en·rap·ture [en-RAP-chər] *vt* **-tured, -tur·ing.** delight excessively; charm.

en·rich' *vt* make rich; add to. **en·rich'ment** *n*

en·roll [en-ROHL] *vt* write name of on roll or list; engage, enlist, take in as member; enter, record. ▶ *vi* become member. **en·roll'ment** *n*

en route [ahn ROOT] *Fr* on the way.

en·sconce [en-SKONS] *vt* **-sconced, -sconc·ing.** place snugly; establish in safety.

en·sem·ble [ahn-SAHM-bəl] *n* whole; all parts taken together; woman's complete outfit; company of actors, dancers, etc.; *Mus* group of soloists performing together; *Mus* concerted passage; general effect.

en·shrine [en-SHRĪN] *vt* **-shrined, -shrin·ing.** set in shrine, preserve with great care and sacred affection.

en·sign [EN-sin] *n* naval or military flag; badge; *Navy, Coast Guard* lowest commissioned officer.

ensilage see SILAGE.

en·slave [en-SLAYV] *vt* **-slaved, -slav·ing.** make into slave. **en·slave'ment** *n* bondage.

en·snare [en-SNAIR] *vt* **-snared, -snar·ing.** capture in snare or trap; trick into false position; entangle.

en·sue [en-SOO] *vi* **-sued, -su·ing.** follow, happen after.

en·sure [en-SHUUR] *vt* **-sured, -sur·ing.** make safe or sure; make certain to happen; secure.

en·tail [en-TAYL] *vt* involve as result, necessitate; *Law* restrict ownership of property to designated line of heirs. **en·tail'ment** *n*

en·tan·gle [en-TANG-gəl] *vt* **-gled, -gling.** ensnare; perplex. **en·tan'gle·ment** *n*

en·tente [ahn-TAHNT] *n* friendly

understanding between nations.

en·ter [EN-tər] *vt* go, come into; penetrate; join; write in, register. ▶ *vi* go, come in, join, begin. **en'trance** [-trəns] *n* going, coming in; door, passage to enter; right to enter; fee paid for this. **en'trant** *n* one who enters, esp. contest. **en'try** *n*, *pl* **-tries.** entrance; entering; item entered, e.g. in account, list.

en·ter·ic [en-TER-ik] *adj* of or relating to the intestines. **en·ter·i'tis** *n* inflammation of intestines.

en·ter·prise [EN-tər-prīz] *n* bold or difficult undertaking; bold spirit; force of character in launching out; business, company. **en'ter·pris·ing** *adj*

en·ter·tain [en-tər-TAYN] *vt* amuse, divert; receive as guest; maintain; consider favorable, take into consideration. **en·ter·tain'er** *n*

en·thrall [en-THRAWL] *vt* captivate, thrill, hold spellbound.

en·thu·si·asm [en-THOO-zee-az-əm] *n* ardent eagerness, zeal. **en·thuse'** *v* (cause to) show enthusiasm. **en·thu'si·ast** *n* ardent supporter of. **en·thu·si·as'tic** *adj*

en·tice [en-TĪS] *vt* **-ticed, -tic·ing.** allure, attract, inveigle, tempt. **en·tic'ing** *adj* alluring.

en·tire [en-TĪR] *adj* whole, complete, unbroken. **en·tire'ly** *adv* **en·tire'ty** *n*, *pl* **-ties.**

en·ti·tle [en-TĪ-təl] *vi* **-tled, -tling.** give claim to; qualify; give title to.

en·ti·ty [EN-ti-tee] *n*, *pl* **-ties.** thing's being or existence; reality; thing having real existence.

en·to·mol·o·gy [en-tə-MOL-ə-jee] *n* study of insects. **en·to·mol'o·gist** *n*

en·tou·rage [ahn-tuu-RAHZH] *n* associates, retinue; surroundings.

en·trails [EN-traylz] *pl n* bowels, intestines; inner parts.

en·trance¹ *n* see ENTER.

en·trance² [en-TRANS] *vt* **-tranced, -tranc·ing.** delight; throw into a trance.

en·treat [en-TREET] *vt* ask earnestly; beg, implore. **en·treat'y** *n*, *pl* **-treat·ies.** earnest request.

en·trée [AHN-tray] *n* main course of meal; right of access, admission.

en·trench' *vt* establish in fortified position with trenches; establish firmly.

en·tre·pre·neur [ahn-trə-prə-NUR] *n* person who attempts to profit by risk and initiative.

en·tro·py [EN-trə-pee] *n* unavailability of the heat energy of a system for mechanical work; measurement of this.

en·trust' *vt* commit, charge with; put into care or protection of.

en·twine [en-TWĪN] *vt* **-twined, -twin·ing.** interweave; wreathe with; embrace.

e·nu·mer·ate [i-NOO-mə-rayt] *vt* **-at·ed, -at·ing.** mention one by one; count. **e·nu·mer·a'tion** *n* **e·nu'mer·a·tor** *n*

e·nun·ci·ate [i-NUN-see-ayt] *vt* **-at·ed, -at·ing.** state clearly; proclaim; pronounce. **e·nun·ci·a'tion** *n*

en·vel·op [en-VEL-əp] *vt* wrap up, enclose, surround; encircle. **en·vel'op·ment** *n*

en·vel·ope [EN-və-lohp] *n* folded, gummed cover of letter; covering, wrapper.

en·ven·om [en-VEN-əm] *vt* put poison, venom in; embitter.

en·vi·ron [en-VĪ-rən] *vt* surround. **en·vi'ron·ment** *n* surroundings; conditions of life or growth. **en·vi·ron·men'tal** *adj* **en·vi·ron·men'tal·ist** *n* ecologist. **en·vi'rons** *pl n* districts around (town, etc.), outskirts.

en·vis·age [en-VIZ-ij] *vt* **-aged, -ag·ing.** conceive of as possibility; visualize.

en·voy [EN-voi] *n* messenger, representative; diplomatic agent of rank below ambassador.

en·vy [EN-vee] *n*, *pl* **-vies.** bitter contemplation of another's good fortune; object of this feeling. ▶ *vt* **-vied, -vy·ing.** grudge another's good fortune, success or qualities;

feel envy of. **en'vi·a·ble** *adj* arousing envy. **en'vi·ous** *adj* full of envy.

en·zyme [EN-zīm] *n* any of group of complex proteins produced by living cells and acting as catalysts in biochemical reactions.

e·on [EE-ən] *n* age, very long period of time.

ep·au·lette [EP-ə-let] *n* shoulder ornament on uniform.

Eph. Ephesians.

e·phem·er·al [i-FEM-ər-əl] *adj* short-lived, transient. **e·phem'er·a** [i-FEM-ər-ə] *pl n* items designed to last only for a short time, such as programmes or posters.

epi-, eph- (*or before a vowel*) **ep-** *prefix* upon, during, e.g. *epitaph; ephemeral; epoch.*

ep·ic [EP-ik] *n* long poem or story telling of achievements of hero or heroes; film, etc. about heroic deeds. ▶ *adj* of, like, an epic; impressive, grand.

ep·i·cene [EP-i-seen] *adj* common to both sexes; effeminate; weak. ▶ *n* epicene person or thing.

ep·i·cen·ter [EP-i-sen-tər] *n* focus of earthquake.

ep·i·cure [EP-i-kyuur] *n* one delighting in eating and drinking. **ep·i·cu·re'an** *adj* of Epicurus, who taught that pleasure, in the shape of practice of virtue, was highest good; given to refined sensuous enjoyment. ▶ *n* such person or philosopher. **ep·i·cu·re'an·ism** *n*

ep·i·dem·ic [ep-i-DEM-ik] *adj* (esp. of disease) prevalent and spreading rapidly; widespread. ▶ *n*

ep·i·der·mis [ep-i-DUR-mis] *n* outer skin.

ep·i·du·ral [ep-i-DUUR-əl] *n, adj* (of) spinal anesthetic used esp. for relief of pain during childbirth.

ep·i·glot'tis *n, pl* **-tis·es.** cartilage that covers opening of larynx in swallowing. **ep·i·glot'tal** [-GLOT-əl] *adj*

ep·i·gone [EP-i-gohn] *n* imitative follower.

ep'i·gram *n* concise, witty poem or saying. **ep·i·gram·mat'ic**

[-grə-MAT-ik] *adj* **ep·i·gram'ma·tist** [-GRAM-ə-tist] *n* **ep·i·graph** [EP-i-graf] *n* inscription.

ep·i·lep·sy [EP-ə-lep-see] *n* disorder of nervous system causing convulsions. **ep·i·lep'tic** *n* sufferer from this. ▶ *adj* of, subject to, this.

ep·i·logue [EP-ə-lawg] *n* short speech or poem at end, esp. of play.

E·piph·a·ny [i-PIF-ə-nee] *n, pl* **-nies.** festival of the announcement of Christ to the Magi, celebrated January 6; (**e-**) sudden intuitive perception or insight.

e·pis·co·pal [i-PIS-kə-pəl] *adj* of bishop; ruled by bishops. **e·pis'co·pa·cy** [-pə-see] *n* government by body of bishops. **E·pis·co·pa'li·an** [-PAYL-yən] *adj, n* (member, adherent) of Episcopalian church. **e·pis'co·pate** [-kə-pit] *n* bishop's office, see, or duration of office; body of bishops.

ep·i·sode [EP-ə-sohd] *n* incident; section of (serialized) book, TV program, etc. **ep·i·sod'ic** [-SOD-ik] *adj*

e·pis·te·mol·o·gy [i-pis-tə-MOL-ə-jee] *n* study of source, nature and limitations of knowledge. **e·pis·te·mo·log'i·cal** *adj*

e·pis·tle [i-PIS-əl] *n* letter, esp. of apostle; poem in letter form. **e·pis'to·lar·y** [-tə-ler-ee] *adj*

ep·i·taph [EP-i-taf] *n* memorial inscription on tomb.

ep·i·thet [EP-ə-thet] *n* additional, descriptive word or name.

e·pit·o·me [i-PIT-ə-mee] *n* embodiment, typical example; summary. **e·pit'o·mize** [-ə-mīz] *vt* **-mized, -miz·ing.** typify.

ep·och [EP-ək] *n* beginning of period; period, era, esp. one of notable events. **ep'o·chal** [-ə-kəl] *adj*

eq·ua·ble [EK-wə-bəl] *adj* even-tempered, placid; uniform, not easily disturbed. **eq'ua·bly** *adv* **eq·ua·bil'i·ty** *n*

e·qual [EE-kwəl] *adj* the same in number, size, merit, etc.; identical;

fit or qualified; evenly balanced. ▶ *n* one equal to another. ▶ *vt* be equal to. **e·qual·i·ty** [i-KWOL-i-tee] *n, pl* **-ties.** state of being equal; uniformity. **e'qual·ize** *v* **-ized, -iz·ing.** make, become, equal. **e'qual·ly** *adv* **equal opportunity** nondiscrimination as to sex, race, etc. in employment, pay, etc.

e·qua·nim·i·ty [ee-kwə-NIM-i-tee] *n* calmness, composure, steadiness.

e·quate [i-KWAYT] *vt* **-quat·ed, -quat·ing.** make equal; bring to a common standard. **e·qua'tion** [-zhən] *n* equating of two mathematical expressions; balancing.

e·qua·tor [i-KWAY-tər] *n* imaginary circle around Earth equidistant from the poles. **e·qua·to·ri·al** [ee-kwə-TOR-ee-əl] *adj*

e·ques·tri·an [i-KWES-tree-ən] *adj* of, skilled in, horseback riding; mounted on horse. ▶ *n* rider.

equi- *comb. form* equal, at equal, e.g. *equidistant.*

e·qui·an·gu·lar [ee-kwee-ANG-gyə-lər] *adj* having equal angles.

e·qui·lat·er·al [ee-kwə-LAT-ər-əl] *adj* having equal sides.

e·qui·lib·ri·um [ee-kwə-LIB-ree-əm] *n* state of steadiness, equipoise or stability.

e·quine [EE-kwīn] *adj* of, like a horse.

e·qui·nox [EE-kwə-noks] *n* time when sun crosses equator and day and night are equal; either point at which sun crosses equator.

e·quip [i-KWIP] *vt* **-quipped, -quip·ping.** supply, fit out, array. **e·quip'ment** *n*

eq·ui·poise [EK-wə-poiz] *n* perfect balance; counterpoise; equanimity.

eq·ui·ty [EK-wə-tee] *n, pl* **-ties.** fairness; use of principles of justice to supplement law; system of law so made. **eq'ui·ta·ble** *adj* fair, reasonable, just.

e·quiv·a·lent [i-KWIV-ə-lənt] *adj* equal in value; having the same meaning or result; tantamount; corresponding. **e·quiv'a·lence** *n*

e·quiv'a·len·cy *n*

e·quiv·o·cal [i-KWIV-ə-kəl] *adj* of double or doubtful meaning; questionable; liable to suspicion. **e·quiv'o·cate** *vi* **-cat·ed, -cat·ing.** use equivocal words to mislead. **e·quiv·o·ca'tion** *n*

Er *Chem* erbium.

e·ra [EER-ə] *n* system of time in which years are numbered from particular event; time of the event; memorable date, period.

e·rad·i·cate [i-RAD-i-kayt] *vt* **-cat·ed, -cat·ing.** wipe out, exterminate; root out. **e·rad'i·ca·ble** *adj* **e·rad·i·ca'tion** *n*

e·rase [i-RAYS] *vt* **-rased, -ras·ing.** rub out; remove, e.g. recording from magnetic tape. **e·ras'er** *n* **e·ra'sure** [-shər] *n*

ere [air] *prep, conj Poet* before; sooner than.

e·rect [i-REKT] *adj* upright. ▶ *vt* set up; build. **e·rec'tile** [-tl] *adj* **e·rec'tion** *n* esp. an erect penis. **e·rect'or** *n*

erg [urg] *n* cgs unit of work or energy.

er·go·nom·ics [ur-gə-NOM-iks] *n* study of relationship between workers and their environment.

er·got [UR-gət] *n* disease of grain; diseased seed used as drug. **er'got·ism** *n* disease caused by eating ergot-infested grain.

er·mine [UR-min] *n* weasel in northern regions, esp. in winter; its white winter fur.

e·rode [i-ROHD] *vt* **-rod·ed, -rod·ing.** wear away; eat into. **e·ro'sion** [-zhən] *n*

e·rog·e·nous [i-ROJ-ə-nəs] *adj* sensitive to sexual stimulation.

e·rot·ic [i-ROT-ik] *adj* relating to, or treating of, sexual pleasure. **e·rot'i·ca** [-ə-kə] *n* sexual literature or art. **e·rot'i·cism** [-ə-sizm] *n*

err [er] *vi* make mistakes; be wrong; sin. **er·rat·ic** [i-RAT-ik] *adj* irregular in movement, conduct, etc. **er·rat'i·cal·ly** *adv* **er·ra·tum** [i-RAH-təm] *n, pl* **-ta** [-tə] printing mistake noted for correction. **er·ro·ne·ous** [i-ROH-nee-əs] *adj* mistaken, wrong. **er'ror** *n* mistake; wrong opinion; sin.

er·rand [ER-ənd] *n* short journey for simple business; the business, mission of messenger; purpose.

er·rant [ER-ənt] *adj* wandering in search of adventure; erring. **er'ran·cy** *n, pl* **-cies.** erring state or conduct. **er'rant·ry** *n, pl* **-ries.** state or conduct of knight errant.

erst·while [URST-hwīl] *adj* of times past, former.

er·u·dite [ER-yə-dīt] *adj* learned. **er·u·di'tion** [-DISH-ən] *n* learning.

e·rupt [i-RUPT] *vi* burst out. **e·rup'tion** *n* bursting out, esp. volcanic outbreak; rash on the skin.

er·y·sip·e·las [er-ə-SIP-ə-ləs] *n* acute skin infection.

Es *Chem* einsteinium.

es·ca·late [ES-kə-layt] *v* **-lat·ed, -lat·ing.** increase, be increased, in extent, intensity, etc.

es·ca·la·tor [ES-kə-lay-tər] *n* moving staircase.

es·cape [i-SKAYP] *v* **-caped, -cap·ing.** ▶ *vi* get free; get off safely; go unpunished; find way out. ▶ *vt* elude; be forgotten by. ▶ *n* escaping. **es'ca·pade** *n* wild (mischievous) adventure.

es·cap'ism [-KAYP-izm] *n* taking refuge in fantasy to avoid facing disagreeable facts.

es·carp·ment [i-SKAHRP-mənt] *n* steep hillside.

es·cha·tol·o·gy [es-kə-TOL-ə-jee] *n* study of death, judgment and last things. **es·cha·to·log'i·cal** *adj*

es·chew [es-CHOO] *vt* avoid, abstain from, shun.

es·cort [ES-kort] *n* armed guard for traveler, etc.; person or persons accompanying another. **es·cort'** *vt*

es·cri·toire [es-kri-TWAHR] *n* type of writing desk.

es·cut·cheon [i-SKUCH-ən] *n* shield with coat of arms; ornamental plate around keyhole, etc.

Es·ki·mo [ES-kə-moh] *n, pl* **-mos.** member of the aboriginal race inhabiting N Canada, Greenland, Alaska, and E Siberia; their language. Note that many of the peoples traditionally called **Eskimos** prefer to call themselves **Inuit.**

e·so·phag·us [i-SOF-ə-gəs] *n, pl* **-gi** [-jī] canal from mouth to stomach; gullet. **e·soph·a·ge'al** [-JEE-əl] *adj*

es·o·ter·ic [es-ə-TER-ik] *adj* abstruse, obscure; secret; restricted to initiates.

ESP extrasensory perception.

es·pal·ier [i-SPAL-yər] *n* shrub, (fruit) tree trained to grow flat, as against wall, etc.; trellis for this.

es·pe·cial [i-SPESH-əl] *adj* preeminent, more than ordinary; particular. **es·pe'cial·ly** *adv*

Es·pe·ran·to [es-pə-RAHN-toh] *n* artificial language designed for universal use.

es·pi·o·nage [ES-pee-ə-nah*zh*] *n* spying; use of secret agents.

es·pla·nade [ES-plə-nahd] *n* level space, esp. one used as public promenade.

es·pouse [i-SPOWZ] *vt* **-poused, -pous·ing.** support, embrace (cause, etc.); marry. **es·pous'al** *n*

es·pres·so [e-SPRES-oh] *n* strong coffee made by forcing steam through ground coffee beans; cup of espresso.

es·prit [e-SPREE] *n* spirit; animation. **esprit de corps** [də kor] attachment, loyalty to the society, etc., one belongs to.

es·py [i-SPĪ] *vt* **-pied, -py·ing.** catch sight of.

es·quire [ES-kwīr] *n* gentleman's courtesy title used on letters; formerly, a squire.

es'say *n* prose composition; short treatise; attempt. **es·say'** *vt* **-sayed, -say'ing.** try, attempt; test. **es'say·ist** *n*

es·sence [ES-əns] *n* all that makes thing what it is; existence, being; entity, reality; extract got by distillation. **es·sen·tial** [ə-SEN-shəl] *adj* necessary, indispensable; inherent; of, constituting essence of thing. ▶ *n* indispensable element; chief point.

es·tab·lish [i-STAB-lish] *vt* make secure; set up; settle; prove.

es·tab'lish·ment n establishing; permanent organized body; place of business together with its employees, equipment, etc.; household; public institution. **established church** church officially recognized as national institution. **the Establishment** n group, class of people holding authority within a profession, society, etc.

es·tate [i-STAYT] n landed property; person's property; deceased person's property; class as part of nation; rank, state, condition of life.

es·teem [i-STEEM] vt think highly of; consider. ▶ n favorable opinion, regard, respect.

es·ter [ES-tər] n Chem organic compound produced by reaction between acid and alcohol.

es·ti·mate [ES-tə-mayt] vt **-mat·ed, -mat·ing.** form approximate idea of (amounts, measurements, etc.); form opinion of; quote probable price for. ▶ n [-mit] approximate judgment of amounts, etc.; amount, etc., arrived at; opinion; price quoted by contractor. **es·ti·ma·ble** adj worthy of regard. **es·ti·ma'tion** n opinion, judgment, esteem.

es·ti·vate [ES-tə-vayt] vi **-vat·ed, -vat·ing.** spend the summer.

es·trange [i-STRAYNJ] vt **-tranged, -trang·ing.** lose affection of; alienate. **es·trange'ment** n

es·tro·gen [ES-trə-jən] n hormone in females esp. controlling changes, cycles, in reproductive organs. **es·tro·gen'ic** adj

es·tu·ar·y [ES-choo-er-ee] n, pl **-ar·ies.** tidal mouth of river, inlet.

e·tail n selling of goods via the Internet.

etc. et cetera.

et cet·er·a [et SET-ər-ə] and the rest, and others; or the like. **etceteras** pl n miscellaneous extra things or people.

etch [ech] vt make engraving by eating away surface of metal plate with acids, etc.; imprint vividly. **etch'er** n **etch'ing** n

e·ter·nal [i-TUR-nəl] adj without beginning or end; everlasting; changeless. **e·ter'ni·ty** n, pl **-ties.**

e·ther [EE-thər] n colorless volatile liquid used as anesthetic; intangible fluid formerly supposed to fill all space; the clear sky, region above clouds. **e·the·re·al** [i-THEER-ee-əl] adj light, airy; heavenly, spirit-like.

eth·i·cal [ETH-i-kəl] adj relating to morals. **eth'i·cal·ly** adv **eth'ics** n science of morals; moral principles, rules of conduct.

eth·nic [ETH-nik] adj of race or relating to classification of humans into social, cultural, etc., groups. **eth·nog'ra·phy** [-NOG-rə-fee] n description of human races. **eth·nol'o·gy** n study of human races. **ethnic cleansing** expulsion or extermination of other ethnic groups by the dominant ethnic group in an area

e·thos [EE-thos] n distinctive character, spirit, etc. of people, culture, etc.

eth·yl [ETH-əl] n of, consisting of, or containing the hydrocarbon group C_2H_5. **eth'y·lene** [-leen] n poisonous gas used as anesthetic and fuel.

e·ti·ol·o·gy [ee-tee-OL-ə-jee] n, pl **-gies.** study of causes, esp. inquiry into origin of disease. **e·ti·o·log'i·cal** adj

et·i·quette [ET-i-kit] n conventional code of conduct or behavior.

é·tude [AY-tood] n short musical composition, study, intended often as technical exercise.

et·y·mol·o·gy [et-ə-MOL-ə-jee] n tracing, account of, formation of word's origin, development; study of this. **et·y·mo·log'i·cal** adj **et·y·mol'o·gist** n

eu-, ev- comb. form well, e.g. eugenic; euphony; evangelist.

Eu Chem europium.

eu·ca·lyp·tus [yoo-kə-LIP-təs] n mostly Aust. genus of tree, the gum tree, yielding timber and oil, used medicinally from leaves.

Eu·cha·rist [YOO-kə-rist] n Christian sacrament of the Lord's

Supper; the consecrated elements; (**e-**) thanksgiving.

eu·gen·ic [yoo-JEN-ik] *adj* relating to, or tending toward, production of fine offspring. **eu·gen'ics** *n* this science.

eu·lo·gy [YOO-lə-jee] *n, pl* **-gies.** speech or writing in praise of person esp. dead person; praise. **eu'lo·gist** *n* **eu'lo·gize** [-jīz] *vt* **-gized, -giz·ing.**

eu·nuch [YOO-nək] *n* castrated man, esp. formerly one employed in harem.

eu·phe·mism [YOO-fə-miz-əm] *n* substitution of mild term for offensive or hurtful one; instance of this. **eu·phe·mis'tic** *adj* **eu·phe·mis'ti·cal·ly** *adv*

eu·pho·ny [YOO-fə-nee] *n, pl* **-nies.** pleasantness of sound. **eu·phon'ic** [-FON-ik] *adj* **eu·pho'ni·ous** [-FOH-nee-əs] *adj* pleasing to ear.

eu·pho·ria [yoo-FOR-ee-ə] *n* sense of well-being or elation. **eu·phor'ic** *adj*

eu·phu·ism [YOO-fyoo-iz-əm] *n* affected high-flown manner of writing, esp. in imitation of Lyly's *Euphues* (1580). **eu·phu·is'tic** *adj*

Eu·ra·sian [yuu-RAY-zhən] *adj* of mixed European and Asiatic descent; of Europe and Asia. ▶ *n* one of this descent.

eu·re·ka [yuu-REE-kə] *interj* exclamation of triumph at finding something.

eu·ro *n, pl* **eu'ros.** unit of the single currency of the European Union.

Euro- *comb. form* Europe or European, e.g. *Euroland.*

Eu·ro·land *n* (also **Eurozone**) the countries within the European Union that have adopted the euro.

Eu·ro·pe·an [yuur-ə-PEE-ən] *n, adj* (native) of Europe. **European Union** (also **EU**) economic and political association of a number of European nations.

Eu·sta·chian tube [yoo-STAY-shən] passage leading from pharynx to middle ear.

eu·tha·na·sia [yoo-thə-NAY-zhə] *n* gentle, painless death; putting to

death in this way, esp. to relieve suffering.

e·vac·u·ate [i-VAK-yoo-ayt] *vt* **-at·ed, -at·ing.** empty; withdraw from; discharge. **e·vac·u·a'tion** *n* **e·vac·u·ee'** *n* person moved from dangerous area esp. in time of war.

e·vade [i-VAYD] *vt* **-vad·ed, -vad·ing.** avoid, escape from; elude. **e·va'sion** [-zhən] *n* subterfuge; excuse; equivocation. **e·va'sive** *adj* elusive, not straightforward.

e·val·u·ate [i-VAL-yoo-ayt] *vt* **-at·ed, -at·ing.** find or judge value of. **e·val·u·a'tion** *n*

ev·a·nesce [ev-ə-NES] *vi* **-nesced, -nesc·ing.** fade away. **ev·a·nes'cence** *n* **ev·a·nes'cent** *adj* fleeting, transient.

e·van·gel·i·cal [ee-van-JEL-i-kəl] *adj* of, or according to, gospel teaching; of Protestant sect that stresses salvation by faith. ▶ *n* member of evangelical sect. **e·van'ge·lism** *n* **e·van'ge·list** *n* writer of one of the four gospels; ardent, zealous preacher of the gospel; revivalist. **e·van'ge·lize** *vt* **-lized, -liz·ing.** preach gospel to; convert.

e·vap·o·rate [i-VAP-ə-rayt] *v* **-rat·ed, -rat·ing.** ▶ *vi* turn into, pass off in, vapor. ▶ *vt* turn into vapor. **e·vap·o·ra'tion** *n*

evasion see EVADE.

eve [eev] *n* evening before (holiday, etc.); time just before (event, etc.).

e·ven [EE-vən] *adj* flat, smooth; uniform in quality, equal in amount, balanced; divisible by two; impartial. ▶ *vt* make even; smooth; equalize. ▶ *adv* equally; simply; notwithstanding; (used to express emphasis).

eve·ning [EEV-ning] *n* the close of day or early part of night; decline, end.

e·vent [i-VENT] *n* happening; notable occurrence; issue, result; any one contest in series in sports program. **e·vent'ful** *adj* full of exciting events. **e·ven'tu·al** [-choo-əl] *adj* resulting in the end;

ultimate; final. **e·ven·tu·al'i·ty** [-AL-i-tee] *n* possible event.

e·ven'tu·ate *vi* **-at·ed, -at·ing.** turn out; happen; end.

ev·er [EV-ər] *adv* always; constantly; at any time. **ev'er·green** *n, adj* (tree or shrub) bearing foliage throughout year. **ev·er·more'** *adv*

eve·ry [EV-ree] *adj* each of all; all possible. **eve'ry·body** *pron* **eve'ry·day** *adj* usual, ordinary. **eve'ry·one** *pron* **eve'ry·thing** *pron, n* **eve'ry·where** *adv* in all places.

e·vict [i-VIKT] *vt* expel by legal process, turn out. **e·vic'tion** [-shən] *n*

ev·i·dent [EV-i-dənt] *adj* plain, obvious. **ev'i·dence** *n* ground of belief; sign, indication; testimony. ▶ *vt* **-denced, -denc·ing.** indicate, prove. **ev·i·den'tial** *adj* **ev'i·dent·ly** *adv* in evidence conspicuous.

e·vil [EE-vəl] *adj* bad, harmful. ▶ *n* what is bad or harmful; sin. **e'vil·ly** *adv* **e'vil·do·er** *n* sinner.

e·vince [i-VINS] *vt* **-vinced, -vinc·ing.** show, indicate.

e·voke [i-VOHK] *vt* **-voked, -vok·ing.** draw forth; call to mind. **ev·o·ca'tion** [ev-ə-KAY-shən] *n* **e·voc·a·tive** [i-VOK-ə-tiv] *adj*

e·volve [i-VOLV] *v* **-volved, -volv·ing.** develop or cause to develop gradually. ▶ *vi* undergo slow changes in process of growth. **ev·o·lu'tion** [ev-ə-LOO-shən] *n* evolving; development of species from earlier forms. **ev·o·lu'tion·ar·y** *adj* **ev·o·lu'tion·ist** *n* one who supports theory of evolution.

ewe [yoo] *n* female sheep.

ew·er [YOO-ər] *n* pitcher with wide spout.

Ex. Exodus.

ex-, e-, ef- *prefix* out from, from, out of, formerly, e.g. *exclaim; evade; effusive; exodus.*

ex·ac·er·bate [ig-ZAS-ər-bayt] *vt* **-bat·ed, -bat·ing.** aggravate, embitter, make worse. **ex·ac·er·ba'tion** *n*

ex·act [ig-ZAKT] *adj* precise, accurate, strictly correct. ▶ *vt* demand, extort; insist upon; enforce. **ex·act'ing** *adj* making rigorous or excessive demands. **ex·ac'tion** *n* act of exacting; that which is exacted, as excessive work, etc.; oppressive demand. **ex·act'ly** *adv* **ex·act'ness** *n* accuracy; precision.

ex·ag·ger·ate [ig-ZAJ-ə-rayt] *vt* **-at·ed, -at·ing.** magnify beyond truth, overstate; enlarge; overestimate. **ex·ag·ger·a'tion** *n*

ex·alt [ig-ZAWLT] *vt* raise up; praise; make noble, dignify. **ex·al·ta·tion** [eg-zawl-TAY-shən] *n* an exalting; elevation in rank, dignity or position; rapture.

ex·am·ine [ig-ZAM-in] *vt* **-ined, -in·ing.** investigate; look at closely; ask questions of; test knowledge or proficiency of; inquire into. **ex·am·i·na'tion** *n* **ex·am'in·er** *n*

ex·am·ple [ig-ZAM-pəl] *n* thing illustrating general rule; specimen; model; warning, precedent, instance.

ex·as·per·ate [ig-ZAS-pə-rayt] *vt* **-at·ed, -at·ing.** irritate, enrage; intensify, make worse. **ex·as·per·a'tion** *n*

ex·ca·vate [EKS-kə-vayt] *vt* **-vat·ed, -vat·ing.** hollow out; make hole by digging; unearth. **ex·ca·va'tion** *n*

ex·ceed [ik-SEED] *vt* be greater than; do more than authorized; go beyond; surpass. **ex·ceed'ing·ly** *adv* very; greatly.

ex·cel [ik-SEL] *v* **-celled, -cel·ling.** ▶ *vt* surpass, be better than. ▶ *vi* be very good, preeminent. **ex'cel·lence** *n* **ex'cel·len·cy** *n* title borne by certain high officials. **ex'cel·lent** *adj* very good.

ex·cept [ik-SEPT] *prep* not including; but. ▶ *vt* leave or take out; exclude. **ex·cept'ing** *prep* not including. **ex·cep'tion** *n* thing excepted, not included in a rule; objection. **ex·cep'tion·a·ble** *adj* open to objection. **ex·cep'tion·al** *adj* not ordinary, esp. much above average.

ex·cerpt [EK-surpt] *n* quoted or extracted passage from book, etc. **ex·cerpt'** *vt* extract, quote (passage from book, etc.).

ex·cess [EK-ses] *n* an exceeding; amount by which thing exceeds; too great amount; intemperance or immoderate conduct. **ex·ces'sive** [-siv] *adj*

ex·change [iks-CHAYNJ] *vt* **-changed, -chang·ing.** give (something) in return for something else; barter. ▶ *n* giving one thing and receiving another; giving or receiving currency of one country for that of another; thing given for another; building where merchants, dealers meet for business; central telephone office. **ex·change'a·ble** *adj*

ex·cheq·uer [eks-CHEK-ər] *n* treasury, e.g. of a government; *inf* personal funds.

ex·cise¹ [EK-sīz] *n* tax levied on domestic goods during manufacture or before sale.

ex·cise² [ik-SĪZ] *vt* **-cised, -cis·ing.** cut out, cut away. **ex·ci·sion** [ek-SIZH-ən] *n*

ex·cite [ik-SĪT] *vt* **-cit·ed, -cit·ing.** arouse to strong emotion, stimulate; rouse up, set in motion; *Electricity* energize to produce electric activity or a magnetic field. **ex·cit'a·ble** *adj* **ex·ci·ta·tion** [ek-si-TAY-shən] *n* **ex·cite'ment** *n* **ex·cit'ing** *adj* thrilling; rousing to action.

ex·claim [ik-SKLAYM] *v* speak suddenly, cry out. **ex·cla·ma·tion** [ek-sklə-MAY-shən] *n* **ex·clam·a·to·ry** [ik-SKLAM-ə-tor-ee] *adj*

ex·clude [ik-SKLOOD] *vt* **-clud·ed, -clud·ing.** shut out; debar from; reject, not consider. **ex·clu·sion** [-zhən] *n* **ex·clu'sive** *adj* excluding; inclined to keep out (from society, etc.); sole, only; select. ▶ *n* something exclusive, esp. story appearing only in one newspaper. **ex·clu'sive·ly** *adv*

ex·com·mu·ni·cate [eks-kə-MYOO-ni-kayt] *vt* **-cat·ed,** **-cat·ing.** to cut off from the sacraments of the Church. **ex·com·mu·ni·ca'tion** *n*

ex·cre·ment [EKS-krə-mənt] *n* waste matter from body, esp. from bowels; dung. **ex·cre·ta** [ik-SKREE-tə] *n* excrement.

ex·crete' *vi* **-cret·ed, -cret·ing.** discharge from the system. **ex·cre'tion** *n* **ex'cre·to·ry** *adj*

ex·cres·cent [ik-SKRES-ənt] *adj* growing out of; redundant. **ex·cres'cence** *n* unnatural outgrowth.

ex·cru·ci·ate [ik-SKROO-shee-ayt] *vt* **-at·ed, -at·ing.** torment acutely, torture in body or mind.

ex·cul·pate [EK-skul-payt] *vt* **-pat·ed, -pat·ing.** free from blame, acquit. **ex·cul·pa'tion** *n* **ex·cul'pa·to·ry** *adj*

ex·cur·sion [ik-SKUR-zhən] *n* journey, ramble, trip for pleasure; digression.

ex·cuse [ik-SKYOOZ] *vt* **-cused,** **-cus·ing.** forgive, overlook; try to clear from blame; gain exemption; set free, remit. ▶ *n* [-SKYOOS] that which serves to excuse; apology. **ex·cus·a·ble** [ik-SKYOO-zə-bəl] *adj*

ex·e·cra·ble [EK-si-krə-bəl] *adj* abominable, hatefully bad.

ex·e·cute [EK-si-kyoot] *vt* **-cut·ed,** **-cut·ing.** inflict capital punishment on, kill; carry out, perform; make, produce; sign (document). **ex·e·cu'tion** *n* **ex·e·cu'tion·er** *n* one employed to execute criminals. **ex·ec'u·tive** *n* person in administrative position; executive body; executive branch of government. ▶ *adj* carrying into effect, esp. of branch of government executing laws. **ex·ec·u·tor** [ig-ZEK-yə-tər] *n* person appointed to carry out provisions of a will. **-u·trix** *n, fem*

ex·e·ge·sis [ek-si-JEE-sis] *n, pl* **-ses** [-seez] explanation, esp. of Scripture. **ex'e·gete** [-jeet] one skilled in exegesis.

ex·em·plar [ig-ZEM-plər] *n* model type. **ex·em'pla·ry** [-plə-ree] *adj* fit to be imitated, serving as example;

commendable; typical.

ex·em·pli·fy [ig-ZEM-plə-fī] *vt*
-fied, -fy·ing. serve as example of;
illustrate; exhibit; make attested
copy of. **ex·em·pli·fi·ca'tion** *n*

ex·empt [ig-ZEMPT] *vt* free from;
excuse. ▸ *adj* freed from, not liable
for; not affected by. **ex·emp'tion** *n*

ex·e·quies [EK-si-kweez] *pl n*
funeral rites or procession.

ex·er·cise [EK-sər-sīz] *v* **-cised,
-cis·ing.** ▸ *vt* use, employ; give
exercise to; carry out, discharge;
trouble, harass. ▸ *vi* take exercise.
▸ *n* use of limbs for health; practice
for training; task for training;
lesson; employment; use (of limbs,
mind, etc.).

ex·ert [ig-ZURT] *vt* apply (oneself)
diligently, make effort; bring to
bear. **ex·er'tion** *n* effort, physical
activity.

ex·hale [eks-HAYL] *v* **-haled,
-hal·ing.** breathe out; give, pass off
as vapor.

ex·haust [ig-ZAWST] *vt* tire out; use
up; empty; draw off; treat, discuss
thoroughly. ▸ *n* used steam or fluid
from engine; waste gases from
internal combustion engine;
passage for, or coming out of this.
ex·haust'i·ble *adj* **ex·haus'tion**
[-chən] *n* state of extreme fatigue;
limit of endurance. **ex·haus'tive**
adj thorough; comprehensive.

ex·hib·it [ig-ZIB-it] *vt* show, display;
manifest; show publicly (often in
competition). ▸ *n* thing shown, esp.
in competition or as evidence in
court. **ex·hi·bi·tion**
[ek-sə-BISH-ən] *n* display, act of
displaying; public show (of works
of art, etc.). **ex·hi·bi'tion·ist** *n* one
with compulsive desire to draw
attention to self or to expose
genitals publicly. **ex·hib'i·tor** *n*
one who exhibits, esp. in show.

ex·hil·a·rate [ig-ZIL-ə-rayt] *vt*
-rat·ed, -rat·ing. enliven, gladden.
ex·hil·a·ra'tion *n* high spirits,
enlivenment.

ex·hort [ig-ZORT] *vt* urge,
admonish earnestly. **ex·hor·ta·tion**
[eg-zor-TAY-shən] *n* **ex·hort'er** *n*

ex·hume [ig-ZOOM] *vt* **-humed,
-hum·ing.** unearth what has been
buried, disinter. **ex·hu·ma·tion**
[eks-hyuu-MAY-shən] *n*

ex·i·gent [EK-si-jənt] *adj* exacting;
urgent, pressing. **ex'i·gen·cy** *n, pl*
-cies. pressing need; emergency.

ex·ig·u·ous [ig-ZIG-yoo-əs] *adj*
scanty, meager.

ex·ile [EG-zīl] *n* banishment,
expulsion from one's own country;
long absence abroad; one banished
or permanently living away from
own home or country. ▸ *vt* **-iled,
-il·ing.** banish, expel.

ex·ist [ig-ZIST] *vi* be, have being,
live. **ex·ist'ence** *n* **ex·ist'ent** *adj*

ex·is·ten·tial·ism
[eg-zi-STEN-shə-liz-əm] *n*
philosophy stressing importance of
personal responsibility and the free
agency of the individual in a
seemingly meaningless universe.

ex·it [EG-zit] *n* way out; going out;
death; actor's departure from
stage. ▸ *vi* go out.

ex li·bris [eks LEE-bris] *Lat* from the
library of.

ex·o·crine [EK-sə-krin] *adj* of gland
(e.g. salivary, sweat) secreting its
products through ducts.

ex·o·dus [EK-sə-dəs] *n* departure,
esp. of crowd; (**E-**) second book of
Old Testament. **the Exodus**
departure of Israelites from Egypt.

ex of·fi·ci·o [eks ə-FISH-ee-oh] *Lat*
by right of position or office.

ex·on·er·ate [ig-ZON-ə-rayt] *vt*
-at·ed, -at·ing. free, declare free,
from blame; exculpate; acquit.
ex·on·er·a'tion *n*

ex·or·bi·tant [ig-ZOR-bi-tənt] *adj*
very excessive, inordinate,
immoderate. **ex·or'bi·tance** *n*

ex·or·cise [EK-sor-sīz] *vt* **-cised,
-cis·ing.** cast out (evil spirits) by
invocation; free person of evil
spirits. **ex'or·cism** *n* **ex'or·cist** *n*

ex·ot·ic [ig-ZOT-ik] *adj* brought in
from abroad, foreign; rare,
unusual, having strange or bizarre
allure. ▸ *n* exotic plant, etc.
ex·ot·i·ca [-i-kə] *pl n* (collection of)
exotic objects. **ex·ot'i·cism** *n*

exotic dancer stripper.

ex·pand [ik-SPAND] *v* increase, spread out, dilate, develop. **ex·pand'a·ble, -i·ble** *adj* **ex·panse'** *n* wide space; open stretch of land. **ex·pan'si·ble** *adj* **ex·pan'sion** *n* **ex·pan'sive** *adj* wide; extensive; friendly, talkative.

ex·pa·ti·ate [ik-SPAY-shee-ayt] *vi* **-at·ed, -at·ing.** speak or write at great length (on); enlarge (upon). **ex·pa·ti·a'tion** *n*

ex·pa·tri·ate [eks-PAY-tree-ayt] *vt* **-at·ed, -at·ing.** banish; exile; withdraw (oneself) from one's native land. ▶ *adj, n* (-tree-it). **ex·pa·tri·a'tion** *n*

ex·pect [ik-SPEKT] *vt* regard as probable; look forward to; await, hope. **ex·pect'an·cy** *n* state or act of expecting; that which is expected; hope. **ex·pect'ant** *adj* looking or waiting for, esp. for birth of child. **ex·pect'ant·ly** *adv* **ex·pec·ta·tion** [ek-spek-TAY-shən] *n* act or state of expecting; prospect of future good; what is expected; promise; value of something expected. ▶ *pl* prospect of fortune or profit esp. by inheritance.

ex·pec·to·rate [ik-SPEK-tə-rayt] *v* **-rat·ed, -rat·ing.** spit out (phlegm, etc.). **ex·pec·to·ra'tion** *n*

ex·pe·di·ent [ik-SPEE-dee-ənt] *adj* fitting, advisable; politic; suitable; convenient. ▶ *n* something suitable, useful, esp. in emergency. **ex·pe'di·en·cy** *n*

ex·pe·dite [EK-spi-dīt] *vt* help on, hasten; dispatch. **ex·pe·di'tion** [-DISH-ən] *n* journey for definite (often scientific or military) purpose; people, equipment engaged in expedition; excursion; promptness. **ex·pe·di'tion·ar·y** *adj* **ex·pe·di'tious** *adj* prompt, speedy.

ex·pel [ik-SPEL] *vt* **-pelled, -pel·ling.** drive, cast out; exclude; discharge. **ex·pul'sion** *n*

ex·pend [ik-SPEND] *vt* spend, pay out; use up. **ex·pend'a·ble** *adj* likely, or meant, to be used up or destroyed. **ex·pend'i·ture** [-i-chər]

n **ex·pense'** *n* cost; (cause of) spending. ▶ *pl* charges, outlay incurred. **ex·pen'sive** *adj*

ex·pe·ri·ence [ik-SPEER-ee-əns] *n* observation of facts as source of knowledge; being affected consciously by event; the event; knowledge, skill, gained from life, by contact with facts and events. ▶ *vt* **-enced, -enc·ing.** undergo, suffer, meet with. **experienced** *adj* skilled, expert, capable.

ex·pe·ri·en·tial [ik-speer-ee-EN-shəl] *adj*

ex·per·i·ment [ik-SPER-ə-mənt] *n* test, trial, something done in the hope that it may succeed, or to test hypothesis, principle, etc. ▶ *vi* conduct experiment. **ex·per·i·men'tal** *adj*

ex·pert [EK-spurt] *n* one skillful, knowledgeable, in something; authority. ▶ *adj* practiced, skillful. **ex·per·tise** [ek-spər-TEEZ] *n* expertness; know-how.

ex·pi·ate [EK-spee-ayt] *vt* **-at·ed, -at·ing.** pay penalty for; make amends for. **ex·pi·a'tion** *n* **ex·pi'a·to·ry** [-ə-tor-ee] *adj*

ex·pire [ik-SPIR] *vi* **-pired, -pir·ing.** come to an end; give out breath; die. ▶ *vt* breathe out. **ex·pi·ra'tion** *n*

ex·plain [ik-SPLAYN] *vt* make clear, intelligible; interpret; elucidate; give details of; account for. **ex·pla·na·tion** [ek-splə-NAY-shən] *n* **ex·plan'a·to·ry** *adj*

ex·ple·tive [EK-spli-tiv] *n* exclamation; exclamatory oath. ▶ *adj* serving only to fill out sentence, etc.

ex·pli·ca·ble [EK-splik-ə-bəl] *adj* explainable. **ex'pli·cate** *vt* **-cat·ed, -cat·ing.** develop, explain. **ex'pli·ca·to·ry** *adj*

ex·plic·it [ik-SPLIS-it] *adj* stated in detail; stated, not merely implied; outspoken; clear, plain; unequivocal.

ex·plode [ik-SPLOHD] *v* **-plod·ed, -plod·ing.** ▶ *vi* go off with bang; burst violently; (of population) increase rapidly. ▶ *vt* make explode;

discredit, expose (a theory, etc.).
ex·plo'sion [-zhən] *n* **ex·plo'sive**
adj, n
ex·ploit [EK-sploit] *n* brilliant feat,
deed. ▸ *vt* [ik-SPLOIT] turn to
advantage; make use of for one's
own ends. **ex·ploi·ta'tion** [ek-] *n*
ex·plore [ik-SPLOHR] *vt* **-plored,
-plor·ing.** investigate; examine;
scrutinize; examine (country, etc.)
by going through it.
ex·plo·ra·tion [ek-splə-RAY-shən] *n*
ex·plor·a·to·ry [ik-SPLOR-ə-tor-ee]
adj **ex·plor'er** *n*
explosion see EXPLODE.
exponent see EXPOUND.
ex·port [ik-SPORT] *vt* send (goods)
out of the country. ▸ *n, adj*
[EK-sport] **ex·por·ta'tion**
[-TAY-shən] *n* **ex·port'er** *n*
ex·pose [ik-SPOHZ] *vt* **-posed,
-pos·ing.** exhibit; disclose; reveal;
lay open (to); leave unprotected;
expose photographic plate or film
to light. **ex·po·sure** [-zhər] *n*
ex·po·sé [ek-spoh-ZAY] *n*
newspaper article, etc., disclosing
scandal, crime, etc.
exposition see EXPOUND.
ex·pos·tu·late [ik-SPOS-chə-layt] *vi*
-lat·ed, -lat·ing. remonstrate;
reason with (in a kindly manner).
ex·pos·tu·la'tion *n*
ex·pound [ik-SPOWND] *vt* explain,
interpret. **ex·po·nent**
[ik-SPOH-nənt] *n* one who
expounds or promotes (idea,
cause, etc.); performer, executant;
Math small, raised number showing
the power of a factor.
ex·po·nen·tial [ek-spə-NEN-shəl]
adj **ex·po·si·tion** [-ZISH-ən] *n*
explanation, description; exhibition
of goods, etc. **ex·pos·i·tor**
[ik-SPOZ-i-tər] *n* one who explains,
interpreter. **ex·pos'i·to·ry** *adj*
explanatory.
ex·press [ik-SPRES] *vt* put into
words; make known or understood
by words, behavior, etc.; squeeze
out. ▸ *adj* definitely stated; specially
designed; clear; positive; speedy; of
train, fast and making few stops.
▸ *adv* by express; with speed. ▸ *n*

express train; rapid parcel delivery
service. **ex·press'i·ble** *adj*
ex·pres'sion [-shən] *n* expressing;
word, phrase; look, aspect; feeling;
utterance. **ex·pres'sion·ism** *n*
theory that art depends on
expression of artist's creative self,
not on mere reproduction.
ex·pres'sive *adj* **ex·press'ly** *adv*
ex·pres'sive·ness *n*
ex·pro·pri·ate [eks-PROH-pree-ayt]
vt **-at·ed, -at·ing.** dispossess; take
out of owner's hands.
ex·pro·pri·a'tion *n*
expulsion see EXPEL.
ex·punge [ik-SPUNJ] *vt* **-punged,
-pung·ing.** strike out, erase.
ex·pur·gate [EK-spər-gayt] *vt*
-gat·ed, -gat·ing. remove
objectionable parts (from book,
etc.), purge. **ex·pur·ga'tion** *n*
ex·quis·ite [EK-skwiz-it] *adj* of
extreme beauty or delicacy; keen,
acute; keenly sensitive.
ex·quis'ite·ly *adv*
ex·tant [EK-stənt] *adj* still existing.
ex·tem·po·re [ik-STEM-pə-ree] *adj,
adv* without previous thought or
preparation. **ex·tem·po·ra'ne·ous**
adj **ex·tem'po·rize** *vt* **-rized,
-riz·ing.** speak without preparation;
devise for the occasion.
ex·tend [ik-STEND] *vt* stretch out,
lengthen; prolong in duration;
widen in area, scope; accord,
grant. ▸ *vi* reach; cover area; have
range or scope; become larger or
wider. **ex·tend'i·ble** *or* **-a·ble,
ex·ten'si·ble** *or* **-sile**
[ik-STEN-səl] *adj* that can be
extended. **ex·ten'sion** *n* stretching
out, prolongation or enlargement;
expansion; continuation; additional
part, as of telephone, etc.
ex·ten'sive *adj* wide, large,
comprehensive. **ex·ten'sor** *n*
straightening muscle. **ex·tent'** *n*
space or degree to which thing is
extended; size; compass; volume.
ex·ten·u·ate [ik-STEN-yoo-ayt] *vt*
-at·ed, -at·ing. make less
blameworthy, lessen; mitigate.
ex·ten·u·a'tion *n*
ex·te·ri·or [ik-STEER-ee-ər] *n* the

outside; outward appearance. ▶ *adj* outer, outward, external.

ex·ter·mi·nate [ik-STUR-mə-nayt] *vt* **-nat·ed, -nat·ing.** destroy utterly, annihilate, root out, eliminate. **ex·ter·mi·na'tion** *n* **ex·ter'mi·na·tor** *n* destroyer.

ex·ter·nal [ik-STUR-nəl] *adj* outside, outward. **ex·ter·nal·ly** *adv*

ex·tinct [ik-STINGKT] *adj* having died out or come to an end; no longer existing; quenched; no longer burning. **ex·tinc'tion** *n*

ex·tin·guish [ik-STING-gwish] *vt* put out, quench; wipe out. **ex·tin'guish·er** *n* device, esp. spraying liquid or foam, used to put out fires.

ex·tir·pate [EK-stər-payt] *vt* **-pat·ed, -pat·ing.** root out, destroy utterly. **ex·tir·pa'tion** *n* **ex'tir·pa·tor** *n*

ex·tol [ik-STOHL] *vt* **-tolled, -tol·ling.** praise highly.

ex·tort [ik-STORT] *vt* get by force or threats; wring out; exact. **ex·tor'tion** *n*

ex·tra [EK-strə] *adj* additional; larger, better, than usual. ▶ *adv* additionally; more than usually. ▶ *n* extra thing; something charged as additional; *Films* actor hired for crowd scenes.

extra- *prefix* outside or beyond an area or scope, e.g. *extradition; extramural; extraterritorial.*

ex·tract [ik-STRAKT] *vt* take out, esp. by force; obtain against person's will; get by pressure, distillation, etc.; deduce, derive; copy out, quote. ▶ *n* [EK-strakt] passage from book, film, etc.; matter got by distillation; concentrated solution. **ex·trac'tion** *n* extracting, esp. of tooth; ancestry.

ex·tra·di·tion [ek-strə-DISH-ən] *n* delivery, under treaty, of foreign fugitive from justice to authorities concerned. **ex'tra·dite** [-dīt] *vt* **-dit·ed, -dit·ing.** give or obtain such delivery.

ex·tra·mur·al [ek-strə-MYUUR-əl] *adj* connected with but outside

normal courses, etc. of college or school; situated outside walls or boundaries of a place.

ex·tra·ne·ous [ik-STRAY-nee-əs] *adj* not essential; irrelevant; added from without, not belonging.

ex·tra·or·di·na·ry [ik-STROR-dn-er-ee] *adj* out of the usual course; additional; unusual, surprising, exceptional.

ex·trap·o·late [ik-STRAP-ə-layt] *vt* **-lat·ed, -lat·ing.** infer something not known from known facts; *Math* estimate a value beyond known values.

ex·tra·sen·so·ry [ek-strə-SEN-sə-ree] *adj* of perception apparently gained without use of known senses.

ex·tra·ter·res·tri·al [ek-strə-tə-RES-tree-əl] *adj* of, or from outside Earth's atmosphere.

ex·trav·a·gant [ik-STRAV-ə-gənt] *adj* wasteful; exorbitant; wild, absurd. **ex·trav'a·gance** *n* **ex·trav'a·gant·ly** *adv* **ex·trav·a·gan'za** [-GAN-zə] *n* elaborate, lavish, entertainment, display, etc.

extravert see EXTROVERT.

ex·treme [ik-STREEM] *adj* **-trem·er, -trem·est.** of high or highest degree; severe; going beyond moderation; at the end; outermost. ▶ *n* utmost degree; thing at one end or the other, first and last of series. **ex·trem'ist** *n* advocate of extreme measures. **ex·trem'i·ty** [-TREM-i-tee] *n*, *pl* **-ties.** farthest point. ▶ *pl* hands and feet; utmost distress; extreme measures.

extreme sport any of various sports with a high risk of injury or death.

ex·tri·cate [EK-stri-kayt] *vt* **-cat·ed, -cat·ing.** disentangle, unravel, set free. **ex·tri·ca'tion** *n*

ex·trin·sic [ik-STRIN-sik] *adj* accessory, not belonging, not intrinsic. **ex·trin'si·cal·ly** *adv*

ex·tro·vert [EK-strə-vurt] *n* one who is interested in other people and things rather than own feelings. **ex·tro·ver'sion**

[-VUR-zhən] n

ex·trude [ik-STROOD] vt **-trud·ed, -trud·ing.** squeeze, force out; (esp. of molten metal or plastic, etc.) shape by squeezing through suitable nozzle or die.

ex·u·ber·ant [ig-ZOO-bər-ənt] adj high-spirited, vivacious; prolific, abundant, luxurious. **ex·u·ber·ance** n

ex·ude [ig-ZOOD] v **-ud·ed, -ud·ing.** ▶ vi ooze out. ▶ vt give off (moisture).

ex·ult [ig-ZULT] vi rejoice, triumph. **exult'an·cy** n **ex·ult'ant** adj triumphant. **ex·ul·ta·tion** [eg-zul-TAY-shən] n

eye [ī] n organ of sight; look, glance; attention; aperture; view; judgment; watch, vigilance; thing, mark resembling eye; slit in needle for thread. ▶ vt **eyed, ey·ing.** look at; observe. **eye'less** adj **eye'ball** n ball of eye. **eye'brow** n fringe of hair above eye. **eye'glass** n glass to assist sight; monocle. **eye'lash** n hair fringing eyelid. **eye'let** n small hole for rope, etc. to pass through. **eye'lid** n lid or cover of eye. **eye'o·pen·er** n surprising news; revealing statement. **eye shadow** colored cosmetic put on around the eyes. **eye'sore** n ugly object; thing that annoys one to see. **eye'tooth** n canine tooth. **eye'wash** n inf deceptive talk, etc., nonsense. **eye'wit·ness** n one who actually sees something and can give firsthand account of it.

ey·rie [AIR-ee] n nest of bird of prey, esp. eagle; high dwelling place.

F f

F *Chem* fluorine.

fa [fah] *n* fourth sol-fa note.

fa·ble [FAY-bəl] *n* short story with moral, esp. one with animals as characters; tale; legend; fiction or lie. ▶ *vt* invent, tell fables about. **fab′u·list** *n* writer of fables.

fab′u·lous [-yə-ləs] *adj* amazing; *inf* extremely good; told of in fables; unhistorical.

fab·ric [FAB-rik] *n* cloth; texture; frame, structure. **fab′ri·cate** *vt* **-cat·ed, -cat·ing.** build; frame; construct; invent (lie, etc.); forge (document). **fab·ri·ca′tion** *n*

fa·cade [fə-SAHD] *n* front of building; *fig* outward appearance.

face [fays] *n* front of head; distorted expression; outward appearance; front, upper surface, or chief side of anything; dial of a clock, etc.; dignity. ▶ *v* **faced, fac·ing.** ▶ *vt* look or front toward; meet (boldly); give a covering surface. ▶ *vi* turn. **fac·et** [FAS-it] *n* one side of many-sided body, esp. cut gem; one aspect. **fa·cial** [FAY-shəl] *adj* pert. to face. ▶ *n* cosmetic treatment for face. **fac′ings** *pl n* lining for decoration or reinforcement, sewn on collar, cuff, etc. **face′less** *adj* without a face; anonymous. **face′lift·ing** *n* operation to tighten skin of face to remove wrinkles.

fa·ce·tious [fə-SEE-shəs] *adj* (sarcastically) witty; humorous; given to jesting, esp. at inappropriate time.

facia *n* see FASCIA.

fac·ile [FAS-il] *adj* easy; working easily; easygoing; superficial, silly. **fa·cil′i·tate** *vt* make easy, help. **fa·cil′i·ta·tor** *n* **fa·cil′i·ty** *n, pl* **-ties.** easiness, dexterity. ▶ *pl* good conditions; means, equipment for doing something.

fac·sim·i·le [fak-SIM-ə-lee] *n* an exact copy.

fact [fakt] *n* thing known to be true; deed; reality. **fac′tu·al** [-choo-əl]

adj

fac·tion [FAK-shən] *n* (dissenting) minority group within larger body; dissension. **fac′tious** *adj* of or producing factions.

fac·ti·tious [fak-TISH-əs] *adj* artificial; specially made up; unreal.

fac·tor [FAK-tər] *n* something contributing to a result; one of numbers that multiplied together give a given number; agent, dealer; business that provides money to finance commerce. **fac·to′tum** [-TOH-təm] *n* one performing all types of work.

fac·to·ry [FAK-tə-ree] *n* building in which things are manufactured.

fac·ul·ty [FAK-əl-tee] *n, pl* **-ties.** inherent power; power of the mind; ability, aptitude; staff of school, college or university; department of university.

fad *n* short-lived fashion; whim. **fad′dish** *adj* **fad′dism** *n* **fad′dist** *n*

fade [fayd] *v* **fad·ed, fad·ing.** ▶ *vi* lose color, strength; wither; grow dim; disappear gradually. ▶ *vt* cause to fade. **fade′-in, -out** *n Radio* variation in strength of signals; *TV, Film* gradual appearance and disappearance of picture.

fag *n sl, offens* short for FAGGOT (sense 2).

fag·got [FAG-ət] *n* bundle of sticks for fuel, etc.; *sl, offens* male homosexual.

Fahr·en·heit [FAR-ən-hīt] *adj* measured by thermometric scale with freezing point of water 32°, boiling point 212°.

fa·ience [FAY-ahns] *n* glazed earthenware or china.

fail [fayl] *vi* be unsuccessful; stop operating or working; be below the required standard; be insufficient; run short; be wanting when in need; lose power; die away; become bankrupt. ▶ *vt* disappoint, give no help to; neglect, forget to do; judge (student) to be below required standard. **fail'ing** n deficiency; fault. ▶ prep in default of. **fail'ure** n **fail'-safe** adj of device ensuring safety or remedy of malfunction in machine, weapon, etc. **without fail** in spite of every difficulty; certainly.

faint [faynt] adj **-er, -est.** feeble, dim, pale; weak; dizzy, about to lose consciousness. ▶ vi lose consciousness temporarily.

fair¹ adj **-er, -est.** just, impartial; according to rules, legitimate; blond; beautiful; ample; of moderate quality or amount; unblemished; plausible; middling; (of weather) favorable. ▶ adv honestly. **fair'ing** n Aviation streamlined structure, or any part so shaped that it provides streamlined form. **fair'ly** adv **fair'ness** n **fair'way** n Golf trimmed turf between tee and green; navigable channel.

fair² n traveling entertainment with sideshows, amusements, etc.; large exhibition of farm, commercial or industrial products; periodical market often with amusements. **fair'ground** n

fair·y [FAIR-ee] n, pl **fair·ies.** imaginary small creature with powers of magic; sl, offens male homosexual. ▶ adj of fairies; like fairy, beautiful and delicate, imaginary. **fair'y·land** n **fair'y-tale** adj of or like fairy tale. **fairy tale** story of imaginary beings and happenings, esp. as told to children.

fait ac·com·pli [fay ta-kawn-PLEE] n, pl **faits accomplis** [fe za-kawn-PLEE] Fr something already done that cannot be altered.

faith [fayth] n trust; belief; belief without proof; religion; promise; loyalty, constancy. **faith'ful** adj constant, true. **faith'ful·ly** adv **faith'less** adj

fa·ji·tas [fa-HEE-taz] pl n Mexican dish of soft tortillas wrapped around fried strips meat or vegetables.

fake [fayk] vt **faked, fak·ing.** conceal defects of by artifice; touch up; counterfeit. ▶ n fraudulent object, person, act. ▶ adj **fak'er** n one who deals in fakes; swindler.

fa·kir [fə-KEER] n member of Islamic religious order; Hindu ascetic.

fa·la·fel [fə-LAH-fəl] n seasoned croquette of flour or ground chick peas.

fal·con [FAL-kən] n small bird of prey, esp. trained in hawking for sport. **fal'con·er** n one who keeps, trains, or hunts with falcons. **fal'con·ry** n hawking.

fall [fawl] vi **fell, fall·en.** drop, come down freely; become lower; decrease; hang down; come to the ground, cease to stand; perish; collapse; be captured; revert; lapse; be uttered; become; happen. ▶ n falling; amount that falls; amount of descent; decrease; collapse, ruin; drop; (oft pl) cascade; cadence; yielding to temptation; autumn. **fall'out** n radioactive particles spread as result of nuclear explosion; incidental effect or outcome. **fall for** inf fall in love with; inf be taken in by.

fal·la·cy [FAL-ə-see] n, pl **-cies.** incorrect, misleading opinion or argument; flaw in logic; illusion. **fal·la·cious** [fə-LAY-shəs] adj **fal·li·bil'i·ty** n **fal'li·ble** adj liable to error.

fallen pp. of FALL.

Fal·lo·pi·an tube [fə-LOH-pee-ən] either of a pair of tubes through which egg cells pass from ovary to womb.

fal·low¹ [FAL-oh] adj plowed and harrowed but left without crop; uncultivated; neglected.

fallow² adj brown or reddish yellow. **fallow deer** deer of this color.

false [fawls] adj **fals·er, fals·est.** wrong, erroneous; deceptive; faithless; sham, artificial. **false'ly** adv **false'ness** n faithlessness. **fal·si·fi·ca'tion** n **fal'si·fy** vt **-fied, -fy·ing.** alter fraudulently; misrepresent. **fal'si·ty** n, pl **-ties.** **false'hood** n lie.

fal·set·to [fawl-SET-oh] *n, pl* **-tos.** forced voice above natural range.

Fal·staff·i·an [fawl-STAF-ee-ən] *adj* like Shakespeare's Falstaff; fat; convivial; boasting.

fal·ter [FAWL-tər] *vi* hesitate; waver; stumble. **fal'ter·ing·ly** *adv*

fame [faym] *n* reputation; renown. **famed** *adj* **fa'mous** *adj* widely known; excellent.

fa·mil·i·ar [fə-MIL-yər] *adj* well-known; frequent, customary; intimate; closely acquainted; unceremonious; impertinent, too friendly. ▶ *n* familiar friend; familiar demon. **fa·mil·i·ar'·i·ty** *n, pl* **-ties.** **fa·mil'iar·ize** *vt* **-ized, -iz·ing.**

fam·i·ly [FAM-ə-lee] *n, pl* **-lies.** group of parents and children, or near relatives; person's children; all descendants of common ancestor; household; group of allied objects. **fa·mil·ial** [fə-MIL-yəl] *adj* **family leave** unpaid work leave for family reasons.

fam·ine [FAM-in] *n* extreme scarcity of food; starvation. **fam'ished** *adj* very hungry.

famous see FAME.

fan[1] *n* instrument for producing current of air, esp. for ventilating or cooling; folding object of paper, etc., used, esp. formerly, for cooling the face; outspread feathers of a bird's tail. ▶ *v* **fanned, fan'ning.** spread out like fan. ▶ *vt* blow or cool with fan. **fan'light** *n* (fan-shaped) window over door.

fan[2] *n inf* devoted admirer; an enthusiast, particularly of a sport, etc.

fa·nat·ic [fə-NAT-ik] *adj* filled with abnormal enthusiasm, esp. in religion. ▶ *n* fanatic person. **fa·nat'ical** *adj* **fa·nat'i·cism** *n*

fan·cy [FAN-see] *adj* **-ci·er, -ci·est.** ornamental, not plain; of whimsical or arbitrary kind. ▶ *n, pl* **-cies.** whim, caprice; liking, inclination; imagination; mental image. ▶ *vt* **-cied, -cy·ing.** imagine; be inclined to believe; *inf* have a liking for. **fan'ci·er** *n* one with liking and expert knowledge (respecting some specific thing). **fan'ci·ful** *adj* **fan'ci·ful·ly** *adv*

fan·dan·go [fan-DANG-goh] *n, pl* **-goes.** lively Spanish dance with castanets; music for this dance.

fan·fare [FAN-fair] *n* a flourish of trumpets or bugles; ostentatious display.

fang *n* snake's poison tooth; long, pointed tooth.

fan·tail [FAN-tayl] *n* (kind of bird with) fan-shaped tail; projecting part of ship's stern.

fan·ta·sy [FAN-tə-see] *n, pl* **-sies.** power of imagination, esp. extravagant; mental image; fanciful invention or design. **fan·ta·sia** [-TAY-zhə] *n* fanciful musical composition. **fan'ta·size** *v* **-sized, -siz·ing.** **fan·tas'tic** *adj* quaint, grotesque, extremely fanciful, wild; *inf* very good; *inf* very large. **fan·tas'ti·cal·ly** *adv*

FAQ *Internet* frequently asked question *or* questions.

far [fahr] *adv* **far·ther** *or* **fur·ther, far·thest** *or* **fur·thest.** at or to a great distance, or advanced point; at or to a remote time; by very much. ▶ *adj* distant; more distant. **far'-fetched'** *adj* incredible.

far·ad [FA-rəd] *n* unit of electrical capacity.

farce [fahrs] *n* comedy of boisterous humor; absurd and futile proceeding. **far'ci·cal** *adj* ludicrous.

fare [fair] *n* charge for passenger's transport; passenger; food. ▶ *vi* **fared, far·ing.** get on; happen; travel, progress. **fare·well'** *interj* goodbye. ▶ *n* leave-taking.

far·i·na·ceous [far-ə-NAY-shəs] *adj* mealy, starchy; made of flour or meal.

farm [fahrm] *n* tract of land for cultivation or rearing livestock; unit of land, water, for growing or rearing a particular crop, animal, etc. ▶ *v* cultivate (land); rear livestock (on farm). **farm'er** *n* **farm'house** *n* **farm'yard** *n* **farm out** send (work) to be done by others; put into care of others.

far·o [FAIR-oh] *n* card game.

far·ra·go [fə-RAH-goh] *n, pl* **-gos.** medley, hodgepodge.

far·row [FA-roh] *n* litter of pigs. ▶ *v* produce this.

fart [fahrt] *n vulg* (audible) emission of gas from anus. ▶ *vi*

far·ther [FAHR-*thər*] *adv, adj* further; comp. of FAR. **far'thest** *adv, adj* furthest; sup. of FAR.

fas·ces [FAS-eez] *pl n* bundle of rods bound together around ax, forming Roman badge of authority; emblem of Italian fascists.

fas·cia [FAY-shə] *n, pl* **-cias.** *Architecture* long flat surface between moldings under eaves; face of wood or stone in a building.

fas·ci·nate [FAS-ə-nayt] *vt* **-nat·ed, -nat·ing.** attract and delight by arousing interest and curiosity; render motionless, as with a fixed stare. **fas·ci·na'tion** *n*

fas·cism [FASH-iz-əm] *n* authoritarian political system opposed to democracy and liberalism; behavior (esp. by those in authority) supposedly typical of this system. **fas'cist** *adj, n* **fa·scis'tic** [fə-SHIS-tik] *adj*

fash·ion [FASH-ən] *n* (latest) style, esp. of dress, etc.; manner, mode; form, type. ▶ *vt* shape, make. **fash'ion·a·ble** *adj* **fash'ion·a·bly** *adv*

fast¹ *adj* **-er, -est.** (capable of) moving quickly; permitting, providing, rapid progress; ahead of true time; firm, steady; permanent. ▶ *adv* rapidly; tightly. **fast'ness** *n* fast state; fortress, stronghold. **fast'back** *n* car with back forming continuous slope from roof to rear. **fast food** food, esp. hamburgers, etc., prepared and served very quickly.

fast² *vi* **fast·ed, fast·ing.** go without food, or some kinds of food. ▶ *n* **fasting** *n*

fas·ten [FAS-ən] *vt* attach, fix, secure. ▶ *vi* become joined; seize (upon).

fas·tid·i·ous [fa-STID-ee-əs] *adj* hard to please; discriminating; particular.

fat *n* oily animal substance; fat part. ▶ *adj* **fat·ter, fat·test.** having too much fat; containing fat, greasy; profitable; fertile. **fat'ten** *vt* feed (animals) for slaughter. ▶ *vi* become fat. **fat'ness** *n* **fat'ty** *adj* **-ti·er, -i·est.** containing fat. ▶ *n, pl* **-ties.** *inf* fat person. **fat'head** *n sl* dolt, fool. **fat farm** resort for helping people lose weight.

fate [fayt] *n* power supposed to predetermine events; goddess of destiny; destiny; person's appointed lot or condition; death or destruction. ▶ *vt* **fat·ed, fat·ing.** preordain. **fa'tal** *adj* deadly, ending in death; destructive; disastrous; inevitable. **fa'tal·ism** *n* belief that everything is predetermined; submission to fate. **fa'tal·ist** *n* **fa·tal·is'tic** *adj* **fa·tal'i·ty** *n, pl* **-ties.** accident resulting in death; person killed in war, accident. **fa'tal·ly** *adv* **fate'ful** *adj* fraught with destiny, prophetic.

fa·ther [FAH-*thər*] *n* male parent; forefather, ancestor; **(F-)** God; originator, early leader; priest, confessor; oldest member of a society. ▶ *vt* beget; originate; pass as father or author of; act as father to. **fa'ther·hood** *n* **fa'ther·less** *adj* **fa'ther·ly** *adj* **fa·ther·in·law** *n* husband's or wife's father.

fath·om [FATH-əm] *n* measure of six feet of water. ▶ *vt* sound (water); get to bottom of, understand. **fath'om·a·ble** *adj* **fath'om·less** *adj* too deep to fathom.

fa·tigue [fə-TEEG] *n* weariness; toil; weakness of metals, etc., subjected to stress; soldier's nonmilitary duty. ▶ *pl* clothing worn for such duty. ▶ *vt* **-tigued, -tigu·ing.** weary.

fat·u·ous [FACH-oo-əs] *adj* very silly, idiotic. **fat'u·ous·ness** *n*

fau·cet [FAW-sit] *n* device for controlling flow of liquid; tap.

fault [fawlt] *n* defect; flaw; misdeed; blame, culpability; blunder; mistake; *Tennis* ball wrongly served; *Geology* break in strata. ▶ *v* find fault in; (cause to) undergo or commit fault. **fault'i·ly** adv **fault'less** adj **fault'y** adj **fault·i·er, fault·i·est.**

faun [fawn] n mythological woodland being with tail and horns.

fau·na [FAW-nə] n, pl **-nas** or **-nae** [-nee] animals of region or period collectively.

faux pas [foh-PAH] n, pl **faux pas** [-PAHZ] social blunder or indiscretion.

fa·vor [FAY-vər] n goodwill; approval; special kindness; partiality. ▶ pl sexual intimacy granted by woman; small party gift for a guest. ▶ vt regard or treat with favor; oblige; treat with partiality; aid; support; resemble. **fa'vor·a·ble** adj **fa'vor·ite** [-it] n favored person or thing; horse, team, etc. expected to win race (or game). ▶ adj chosen, preferred. **fa'vor·it·ism** n practice of showing undue preference.

fawn¹ n young deer. ▶ adj light yellowish brown.

fawn² vi of person, cringe, court favor servilely; esp. of dog, show affection by wagging tail and groveling.

fax [faks] n facsimile. ▶ vt transmit facsimile of (printed matter, etc.) electronically.

faze [fayz] vt **fazed, faz·ing.** fluster; daunt.

Fe Chem iron.

fear [feer] n dread, alarm, anxiety, unpleasant emotion caused by coming evil or danger. ▶ vi have this feeling, be afraid. ▶ vt regard with fear; hesitate, shrink from; revere. **fear'ful** adj **fear'ful·ly** adv **fear'less** adj intrepid. **fear'some** adj terrifying.

fea·si·ble [FEE-zə-bəl] adj able to be done; likely. **fea·si·bil'i·ty** n

feast [feest] n banquet, lavish meal; religious anniversary; something very pleasant, sumptuous. ▶ vi partake of banquet, fare sumptuously. ▶ vt regale with feast; provide delight for.

feat [feet] n notable deed; surprising or striking trick.

feath·er [FETH-ər] n one of the barbed shafts that form covering of birds; anything resembling this. ▶ vt provide, line with feathers. ▶ vi grow feathers. ▶ v turn (oar, propeller) edgewise. **feath'er·y** adj **feath'er·weight** n very light person (esp. boxer) or thing; inf person of small consequence or ability. **feather one's nest** enrich oneself. **in fine feather** in good form.

fea·ture [FEE-chər] n (usu pl) part of face; characteristic or notable part of anything; main or special item. ▶ v **-tured, -tur·ing.** ▶ vt portray; present in leading role in a film; give prominence to. ▶ vi be prominent (in). **fea'ture·less** adj without striking features.

fe·brile [FEE-brəl] adj of fever; feverish.

fe·ces [FEE-seez] pl n excrement, waste matter. **fe'cal** [-kəl] adj

feck·less [FEK-lis] adj spiritless, weak, irresponsible. **feck'less·ness** n

fec·u·lent [FEK-yə-lənt] adj full of sediment, turbid, foul. **fec'u·lence** n

fe·cund [FEE-kund] adj fertile, fruitful, fertilizing. **fe'cun·date** vt **-dat·ed, -dat·ing.** fertilize, impregnate. **fe·cun·di·ty** [fi-KUN-di-tee] n

fed pt./pp. of FEED. **fed up** bored, dissatisfied.

fed·er·al [FED-ər-əl] adj of, or like, the government of countries that are united but retain internal independence of the separate states. **fed'er·al·ism** n **fed'er·ate** [-ə-rayt] v **-at·ed, -at·ing.** form into, become, a federation. **fed·er·a'tion** n league; federal union.

fee n payment for professional and other services.

fee·ble [FEE-bəl] adj **-bler, -blest.** weak; lacking strength or effectiveness, insipid. **fee'bly** adv

feed v **fed, feed·ing.** give food to; supply, support; take food. ▶ n feeding; fodder, pasturage; allowance of fodder; material supplied to machine; part of machine taking in material. **feed'er** *n* one who or that which feeds. **feed'back** *n* return of part of output of electrical circuit or loudspeakers; information received in response to inquiry, etc. **feed'lot** *n* area, building where cattle are fattened for market.

feel *v* **felt**, **feel·ing**. perceive, examine by touch; experience; proceed, find (one's way) cautiously; be sensitive to; show emotion (for); believe, consider. ▶ *n* act or instance of feeling; quality or impression of something perceived by feeling; sense of touch. **feel'er** *n* special organ of touch in some animals; proposal put forward to test others' opinions; that which feels. **feel'ing** *n* sense of touch; ability to feel; physical sensation; emotion; sympathy, tenderness; conviction or opinion not solely based on reason. ▶ *pl* susceptibilities. ▶ *adj* sensitive, sympathetic, heartfelt. **feel like** have an inclination for.

feet see FOOT. **feet of clay** hidden flaw in person's character.

feign [fayn] *v* pretend, sham.

feint [faynt] *n* sham attack or blow meant to deceive opponent; semblance, pretense. ▶ *vi* make feint.

feist·y [FĪ-stee] *adj* **feist·i·er**, **feist·i·est.** spirited, spunky, plucky; ill-tempered. **feist'i·ness** *n*

feld·spar [FELD-spahr] *n* crystalline mineral found in granite, etc.

fe·lic·i·ty [fi-LIS-i-tee] *n, pl* **-ties.** great happiness, bliss; appropriateness of wording. **fe·lic'i·tate** *vt* **-tat·ed**, **-tat·ing.** congratulate. **fe·lic·i·ta'tion** *pl n* congratulations. **fe·lic'i·tous** *adj* apt, well-chosen; happy.

fe·line [FEE-līn] *adj* of cats; catlike.

fell¹ pt. of FALL.

fell² *vt* knock down; cut down (tree).

fell³ *adj* fierce, terrible.

fell⁴ *n* skin or hide with hair.

fel·low [FEL-oh] *n inf* man, boy; person; comrade, associate; counterpart; like thing; member (of society); student granted university fellowship. ▶ *adj* of the same class, associated. **fel'low·ship** *n* fraternity; friendship; (in university, etc.) research post or special scholarship.

fel·on [FEL-ən] *n* one guilty of felony. **fe·lo·ni·ous** [fə-LOH-nee-əs] *adj* **fel'o·ny** *n, pl* **-nies.** serious crime.

felt¹ pt./pp. of FEEL.

felt² *n* soft, matted fabric made by bonding fibers chemically and by pressure; thing made of this. ▶ *vt* make into, or cover with, felt. ▶ *vi* become matted like felt. **felt'-tip pen** pen with writing point made of pressed fibers.

fe·male [FEE-mayl] *adj* of sex that bears offspring; relating to this sex. ▶ *n* one of this sex.

fem·i·nine [FEM-ə-nin] *adj* of women; womanly; class or type of grammatical inflection in some languages. **fem'i·nism** *n* advocacy of equal rights for women. **fem'i·nist** *n, adj* **fem·i·nin'i·ty** *n*

femme fa·tale [FAHM fat-TAHL] *n, pl* **femmes fa·tales.** *Fr* alluring woman who leads men into dangerous situations by her charm.

fem·o·ral [FEM-ər-əl] *adj* of the thigh.

fe·mur [FEE-mər] *n* thigh bone.

fen *n* tract of marshy land, swamp.

fence [fens] *n* structure of wire, wood, etc. enclosing an area; (machinery) guard, guide; *sl* dealer in stolen property. ▶ *v* **fenced**, **fenc·ing.** erect fence; enclose; fight (as sport) with swords; avoid question, etc.; *sl* deal in stolen property. **fencing** *n* art of swordplay.

fend *vt* ward off, repel. ▶ *vi* provide (for oneself, etc.). **fend'er** *n* low metal frame in front of fireplace; name for various protective devices; frame; edge; buffer; mudguard of car. **fender bender** *inf* collision between automobiles causing minor damage.

fen·es·tra·tion [fen-ə-STRAY-shən] *n* arrangement of windows in a building; (in medicine) perforation in a structure; operation to create this.

feng shui [FUNG SHWAY] *n* Chinese art of deciding the best design or position of a grave, building, furniture, etc., in order to bring good luck.

fe·ral¹ [FER-əl] *adj* wild, uncultivated.

feral² *adj* funereal, gloomy; causing death.

fer·ment [FUR-ment] *n* leaven, substance causing thing to ferment; excitement, tumult. ▶ *v* [fər-MENT] (cause to) undergo chemical change with effervescence, liberation of heat and alteration of properties, e.g. process set up in dough by yeast; (cause to) become excited. **fer·men·ta·tion** [fur-] *n*

fern [furn] *n* plant with feathery fronds.

fe·ro·cious [fə-ROH-shəs] *adj* fierce, savage, cruel. **fe·roc'i·ty** [-ROS'i·tee] *n*

fer·ret [FER-it] *n* tamed animal like weasel, used to catch rabbits, rats, etc. ▶ *vt* drive out with ferrets; search out. ▶ *vi* search about, rummage.

fer·ric [FER-ik], **fer·rous** [FER-əs] *adj* pert. to, containing, iron. **fer·ru·gi·nous** [fə-ROO-jə-nəs] *adj* containing iron; reddish-brown. **fer·ro·con'crete** *n* reinforced concrete (strengthened by framework of metal).

Fer·ris wheel [FER-is] in amusement park, large, vertical wheel with seats for riding.

fer·rule [FER-əl] *n* metal cap to strengthen end of stick, etc.

fer·ry [FER-ee] *n, pl* **-ries.** boat, etc. for transporting people, vehicles, across body of water, esp. as repeated or regular service. ▶ *v* **-ried, -ry·ing.** carry, travel, by ferry; deliver (airplanes, etc.) by air.

fer·tile [FUR-tl] *adj* (capable of) producing offspring, bearing crops, etc.; fruitful, producing abundantly; inventive. **fer·til·i·ty** [fər-TIL-i-tee] *n* **fer·ti·li·za'tion** *n* **fer'ti·lize** *vt* **-lized, -liz·ing.** make fertile. **fer'ti·liz·er** *n*

fer·vent [FUR-vənt], **fer·vid** [-vid] *adj* ardent, vehement, intense. **fer'ven·cy** *n* **fer'vent·ly** *adv* **fer'vor** [-vər] *n*

fes·cue [FES-kyoo] *n* grass for pasture or lawns, with stiff narrow leaves.

fes·tal [FES-tl] *adj* of feast or holiday; merry.

fes·ter [FES-tər] *v* (cause to) form pus. ▶ *vi* rankle; become embittered.

fes·ti·val [FES-tə-vəl] *n* day, period set aside for celebration, esp. of religious feast; organized series of events, performances, etc. usu. in one place. **fes·tive** [-tiv] *adj* joyous, merry; of feast. **fes·tiv'i·ty** *n* gaiety, mirth; rejoicing. ▶ *pl* celebrations.

fe·stoon' *n* chain of flowers, ribbons, etc. hung in curve between two points. ▶ *vt* form, adorn with festoons.

fetch [fech] *vt* go and bring; draw forth; be sold for; attract. ▶ *n* act of fetching. **fetch'ing** *adj* attractive.

fete [fayt] *n, pl* **fetes.** gala, bazaar, etc., esp. one held out of doors; festival, holiday, celebration. ▶ *vt* **fet·ed, fet·ing.** feast; honor with festive entertainment.

fet'id *adj* stinking.

fet'ish *n* (inanimate) object believed to have magical powers; excessive attention to something; object, activity, to which excessive devotion is paid; form of behaviour in which sexual pleasure is derived from looking at or handling an inanimate object. **fet'ish·ism** *n* **fet'ish·ist** *n*

fet·lock [FET-lok] *n* projection behind and above horse's hoof, or tuft of hair on this.

fet·ter [FET-ər] *n* chain or shackle for feet; check, restraint. ▶ *pl* captivity. ▶ *vt* chain up; restrain, hamper.

fet·tle [FET-l] *n* condition, state of health.

fe·tus [FEE-təs] *n, pl* **-tus·es.** fully developed young in womb or egg. **fe·tal** [FEET-l] *adj*

feud [fyood] *n* bitter, lasting, mutual hostility, esp. between two families or tribes; vendetta. ▸ *vi* carry on feud.

feu·dal [FYOOD-l] *adj* of, like, medieval social and economic system based on holding land from superior in return for service. **feu'dal·ism** *n*

fe·ver [FEE-vər] *n* condition of illness with high body temperature; intense nervous excitement. **fe'vered, fe'ver·ish** *adj* having fever; accompanied by, caused by, fever; in a state of restless excitement. **fe'ver·ish·ly** *adv* **fever pitch** very fast pace; intense excitement.

few [fyoo] *adj* **-er, -est.** not many. ▸ *n* small number. **quite a few** several.

fey [fay] *adj* supernatural, unreal; enchanted.

fez *n, pl* **fez·zes.** red, brimless, orig. Turkish tasseled cap.

fi·an·cé [fee-ahn-SAY] *n* man engaged to be married. **fi·an·cée** *n, fem*

fi·as·co [fee-AS-koh] *n, pl* **-cos.** breakdown, total failure.

fi·at [FEE-aht] *n* decree; official permission.

fib [fib] *n* trivial lie, falsehood. ▸ *vt* **fibbed, fib·bing.** tell fib. **fib'ber** *n*

fi·ber [FI-bər] *n* filament forming part of animal or plant tissue; substance that can be spun (e.g. wool, cotton). **fi'brous** *adj* made of fiber. **fi'ber·board** *n* building material of compressed plant fibers. **fi'ber·glass** *n* material made of fine glass fibers. **fiber optics** use of bundles of long transparent glass fibers in transmitting light.

fib·u·la [FIB-yə-lə] *n* slender outer bone of lower leg. **fib'u·lar** *adj*

fick·le [FIK-əl] *adj* changeable, inconstant. **fick'le·ness** *n*

fic·tion [FIK-shən] *n* prose, literary works of the imagination; invented statement or story. **fic'tion·al** *adj* **fic·ti·tious** [-TISH-əs] *adj* not genuine, false; imaginary; assumed.

fid·dle [FID-l] *n* violin. ▸ *v* **-dled, -dling.** ▸ *vi* play fiddle; make idle movements, fidget, trifle. **fid'dle·sticks** *interj* nonsense.

Fi·de·i De·fen·sor [FEE-de-ee de-FEN-sor] *Lat* defender of the faith.

fi·del·i·ty [fi-DEL-i-tee] *n, pl* **-ties.** (conjugal) faithfulness; quality of sound reproduction.

fidg·et [FIJ-it] *vi* move restlessly; be uneasy. ▸ *n* (oft pl) nervous restlessness, restless mood; one who fidgets. **fidg'et·y** *adj*

fi·du·ci·ar·y [fi-DOO-shee-er-ee] *adj* held, given in trust; relating to trustee. ▸ *n* trustee.

fief [feef] *n Hist* land held of a superior in return for service. **fief'dom** [-dəm] *n* estate of a feudal lord; *inf* organization, etc. owned by controlled by one person.

field [feeld] *n* area of (farming) land; enclosed piece of land; tract of land rich in specified product (e.g. gold field); players in a game or sport collectively; all competitors but the favorite; battlefield; area over which electric, gravitational, magnetic force can be exerted; sphere of knowledge; range, area of operation. ▸ *v Baseball* stop and return ball; send player, team, on to field. **field'er** *n* **field day** day of outdoor activities; important occasion. **field events** throwing and jumping events in athletics. **field glasses** binoculars. **field hockey** hockey played on field, as distinct from ice hockey. **field marshal** (in some countries) army officer of highest rank. **field'work** *n* research, practical work, conducted away from the classroom, laboratory, etc. **field of view** area covered in telescope, camera, etc.

fiend [feend] n demon, devil; wicked person; person very fond of or addicted to something, e.g. *fresh-air fiend; drug fiend.* **fiend'ish** adj wicked, difficult, unpleasant.

fierce [feers] adj **fierc·er, fierc·est.** savage, wild, violent; rough; severe; intense. **fierce'ly** adv **fierce'ness** n

fier·y [FĪ-ə-ree] adj **fier·i·er, fier·i·est.** consisting of fire; blazing, glowing, flashing; irritable; spirited. **fier'i·ness** n

fi·es·ta [fee-ES-tə] n (religious) celebration, carnival.

fife [fīf] n high-pitched flute. ▸ v play on fife. **fif'er** n

fifteen, fifth, fifty see FIVE.

fig n soft, pear-shaped fruit; tree bearing it.

fight [fīt] v **fought, fight·ing.** contend with in battle or in single combat; maintain against opponent; settle by combat. ▸ n **fight'er** n one who fights; prizefighter; aircraft designed for destroying other aircraft.

fig·ment [FIG-mənt] n invention, purely imaginary thing.

fig·ure [FIG-yər] n numerical symbol; amount, number; form, shape; bodily shape; appearance, esp. conspicuous appearance; space enclosed by lines, or surfaces; diagram, illustration; likeness; image; pattern; movement in dancing, skating, etc.; abnormal form of expression for effect in speech, e.g. metaphor. ▸ v **-ured, -ur·ing.** ▸ vt calculate, estimate; represent by picture or diagram; ornament. ▸ vi (oft. with *in*) show, appear, be conspicuous, be included. **fig'ur·a·tive** adj metaphorical; full of figures of speech. **fig'ur·a·tive·ly** adv **fig·ur·ine'** [-REEN] n statuette. **fig'ure·head** n nominal leader; ornamental figure under bowsprit of ship.

fil·a·ment [FIL-ə-mənt] n fine wire in electric light bulb and vacuum tube that is heated by electric current; threadlike body.

filch vt steal, pilfer.

file[1] [fīl] n box, folder, clip, etc. holding papers for reference; papers so kept; information about specific person, subject; orderly line, as of soldiers, one behind the other; *Computers* organized collection of related material. ▸ v **filed, fil·ing.** ▸ vt arrange (papers, etc.) and put them away for reference; transmit (e.g. tax return); *Law* place on records of a court; bring suit in law court. ▸ vi march in file. **filing** n **single file** single line of people one behind the other.

file[2] n roughened tool for smoothing or shaping. ▸ vt **filed, fil·ing.** apply file to, smooth, polish. **filing** n action of using file; scrap of metal removed by file.

filet see FILLET.

fil·i·al [FIL-ee-əl] adj of, befitting, son or daughter.

fil·i·bus·ter [FIL-ə-bus-tər] n process of obstructing legislation by using delaying tactics. ▸ vi

fil·i·gree [FIL-i-gree] n fine tracery or openwork of metal, usu. gold or silver wire.

fill vt make full; occupy completely; hold, discharge duties of; stop up; satisfy; fulfill. ▸ vi become full. ▸ n full supply; as much as desired; soil, etc., to bring area of ground up to required level. **fill'ing** n **filling station** business selling oil, gasoline, etc. **fill the bill** inf supply all that is wanted.

fil·let [fi-LAY] n boneless slice of meat, fish; narrow strip. ▸ vt cut into fillets, bone.

fil·lip [FIL-əp] n stimulus; sudden release of finger bent against thumb; snap so produced.

fil·ly [FIL-ee] n, pl **-lies.** young female horse; inf girl, young woman.

film n sequence of images projected on screen, creating illusion of movement; story, etc. presented thus, and shown in movie theater or on TV; sensitized celluloid roll used in photography, cinematography; thin skin or layer; dimness on eyes; slight haze. ▶ *adj* connected with movies. ▶ *vt* photograph with movie camera; make movie of (scene, story, etc.). ▶ *v* cover, become covered, with film. **film'y** *adj* **film·i·er, film·i·est.** membranous; gauzy. **film star** popular movie actor or actress.

fil·ter [FIL-tər] *n* cloth or other material, or a device, permitting fluid to pass but retaining solid particles; anything performing similar function. ▶ *vt* act as filter, or as if passing through filter. ▶ *vi* pass slowly (through). **fil·trate** [FIL-trayt] *n* filtered gas or liquid. **fil·tra'tion** *n*

filth *n* disgusting dirt; pollution; obscenity. **filth'i·ly** *adv* **filth'i·ness** *n* **filth'y** *adj* **filth·i·er, filth·i·est.** unclean; foul.

fin *n* propelling or steering organ of fish; vertical tailplane of an airplane; *sl* five-dollar bill.

fi·nal [FĪN-l] *adj* at the end; conclusive. ▶ *n* game, heat, examination, etc., coming at end of series or school term. **fi·na·le** [fi-NAL-ee] *n* closing part of musical composition, opera, etc.; termination. **fi·nal·i·ty** [fī-NAL-i-tee] *n* **fi'na·lize** *v* **-lized, -liz·ing. fi'nal·ly** *adv*

fi·nance [fi-NANS] *n* management of money. ▶ *pl* money resources. ▶ *vt* **-nanced, nanc·ing.** find capital for. **fi·nan'cial** [-shəl] *adj* of finance. **fin·an·cier'** [-SEER] *n*

finch *n* one of family of small songbirds.

find [fīnd] *vt* **found, find·ing.** come across; light upon, obtain; recognize; experience, discover; discover by searching; ascertain; supply (as funds); *Law* give a verdict. ▶ *n* finding; (valuable) thing found. **find'er** *n* **finding** *n* judicial verdict.

fine¹ [fīn] *adj* **fin·er, fin·est.** choice, of high quality; delicate, subtle; pure; in small particles; slender; excellent; handsome; showy; *inf* healthy, at ease, comfortable; free

of rain. ▶ *vt* **fined, fin·ing.** make clear or pure; refine; thin. **fine'ly** *adv* **fine'ness** *n* **fin'er·y** *n, pl* **-er·ies.** showy dress. **fi·nesse** [fi-NES] *n* elegant, skillful management. **fine art** produced for its aesthetic value. **fine-tune** *vt* make fine adjustments to for optimum performance.

fine² *n* sum fixed as penalty. ▶ *vt* **fined, fin·ing.** punish by fine. **in fine** in conclusion; in brief.

fin·ger [FING-gər] *n* one of the jointed branches of the hand; various things like this. ▶ *vt* touch or handle with fingers; *sl* inform against (a criminal). **fin'ger·ing** *n* manner or act of touching; choice of fingers, as in playing musical instrument; indication of this. **fin'ger·board** *n* part of violin, etc. against which fingers are placed. **fin'ger·print** *n* impression of tip of finger, esp. as used for identifying criminals.

fin·i·al [FIN-ee-əl] *n* ornament at apex of gable, spire, furniture, etc. **fin·ick·y** [FIN-i-kee] *adj* **-ick·i·er, -ick·i·est.** fastidious, fussy; too fine. **fin'is** *Lat* end, esp. of book. **fin'ish** *v* (mainly *tr*) bring, come to an end, conclude; complete; perfect; kill. ▶ *n* end; way in which thing is finished of furniture, e.g. *oak finish;* final appearance. **fi·nite** [FĪ-nīt] *adj* bounded, limited. **fiord** see FJORD. **fir** [fur] *n* kind of coniferous resinous tree; its wood.

fire [fīr] *n* state of burning, combustion, flame, glow; mass of burning fuel; destructive burning, conflagration; burning fuel for heating a room, etc.; ardor, keenness, spirit; shooting of firearms. ▶ *v* **fired, fir·ing.** ▶ *vt* discharge (firearm); propel from firearm; *inf* dismiss from employment; bake; make burn; supply with fuel; inspire; explode. ▶ *vi* discharge firearm; begin to burn; become excited. **fire'arm** *n* gun, rifle, pistol, etc. **fire'brand** *n* burning piece of wood; energetic (troublesome) person. **fire'break** [-brayk] *n* strip of cleared land to arrest progress of forest or grass fire. **fire'bug** *n inf* person who practices arson. **fire department** organized body of personnel and equipment to put out fires and rescue those in danger. **fire drill** rehearsal of procedures for escape from fire. **fire engine** vehicle with apparatus for extinguishing fires. **fire escape** means, esp. metal stairs, for escaping from burning buildings. **fire'fight·er** *n* member of fire department; person employed to fight forest fires. **fire'fly** *n, pl* **-flies.** insect giving off phosphorescent glow. **fire'guard** *n* protective grating in front of fire. **fire irons** tongs, poker and shovel. **fire'man** *n, pl* **fire'men.** firefighter; stoker; assistant to locomotive driver. **fire'place** *n* recess in room for fire. **fire house** building housing fire department equipment and personnel. **fire'work** *n* device to give spectacular effects by explosions and colored sparks. ▶ *pl* show of fireworks; outburst of temper, anger. **firing squad** group of soldiers ordered to execute an offender by shooting.

fir·kin [FUR-kin] *n* small cask.

firm [furm] *adj* **-er, -est.** solid, fixed, stable; steadfast; resolute; settled. ▶ *v* make, become firm. ▶ *n* commercial enterprise; partnership.

fir·ma·ment [FUR-mə-mənt] *n* expanse of sky, heavens.

first [furst] *adj* earliest in time or order; foremost in rank or position; most excellent; highest, chief. ▶ *n* beginning; first occurrence of something; *Baseball* first base. ▶ *adv* before others in time, order, etc. **first'ly** *adv* **first aid** help given to injured person before arrival of doctor. **first-hand** *adj* obtained directly from the first source. **first mate, first officer** officer of merchant vessel immediately below captain. **first-rate** *adj* of highest class or quality. **first-strike** *adj* (of

a nuclear missile) for use in an opening attack to destroy enemy nuclear weapons.

fis·cal [FIS-kəl] *adj* of (government) finances.

fish *n, pl* **fish** *or* **fish·es.** vertebrate cold-blooded animal with gills, living in water; its flesh as food. ▶ *v* (attempt to) catch fish; search (for); try to get information indirectly. **fish'er** *n* **fish'er·y** *n, pl* **-er·ies.** business of fishing; fishing ground. **fish'y** *adj* **fish·i·er, fish·i·est.** of, like, or full of fish; dubious, open to suspicion; unsafe. **fish'er·man** *n* one who catches fish for a living or for pleasure. **fish'plate** *n* piece of metal holding wooden beams, etc. together. **fish stick** small piece of fish covered in breadcrumbs.

fis·sure [FISH-ər] *n* cleft, split, cleavage. **fis'sile** [-əl] *adj* capable of splitting; tending to split. **fis·sion** [FISH-ən] *n* splitting; reproduction by division of living cells with two parts, each of which becomes complete organism; splitting of atomic nucleus with release of large amount of energy. **fis'sion·a·ble** *adj* capable of undergoing nuclear fission. **fis·sip·a·rous** [fi-SIP-ər-əs] *adj* reproducing by fission.

fist *n* clenched hand. **fist'i·cuffs** *pl n* fighting.

fis·tu·la [FIS-chuu-lə] *n, pl* **-las.** pipelike ulcer.

fit[1] *v* **fit·ted** *or* **fit, fit·ting.** ▶ *vt* be suited to; be properly adjusted to; arrange, adjust, apply, insert; supply, furnish. ▶ *vi* be correctly adjusted or adapted; be of right size. ▶ *adj* **fit·ter, fit·test.** well-suited, worthy; qualified; proper, becoming; ready; in good condition or health. ▶ *n* way anything fits, its style; adjustment. **fit'ly** *adv* **fit'ment** *n* piece of equipment. **fit'ness** *n* **fitter** *n* one who, that which, makes fit; one who supervises making and fitting of garments; mechanic skilled in fitting up metal work. **fitting** *adj* appropriate, suitable; proper. ▶ *n* fixture; apparatus; action of fitting.

fit² n seizure with convulsions, spasms, loss of consciousness, etc., as of epilepsy, hysteria, etc.; sudden passing attack of illness; passing state, mood. **fit'ful** adj spasmodic, capricious. **fit'ful·ly** adv

five [fīv] adj, n cardinal number after four. **fifth** adj, n ordinal number. **fifth'ly** adv **fif'teen** adj, n ten plus five. **fif'teenth** adj, n **fif'ti·eth** adj, n **fif'ty** adj, n, pl **-ties.** five tens. **fifth column** organization spying for enemy within country at war.

fix [fiks] vt fasten, make firm or stable; set, establish; appoint, assign, determine; make fast; repair; inf influence the outcome of unfairly or by deception; bribe; sl treat someone vengefully. ▶ vi become firm or solidify; determine. ▶ n difficult situation; position of ship, aircraft ascertained by radar, observation, etc.; sl dose of narcotic drug. **fix·a'tion** n act of fixing; preoccupation; obsession; situation of being set in some way of acting or thinking. **fix'a·tive** adj capable of, or tending to fix. ▶ n **fix'ed·ly** [-sid-lee] adv intently. **fix'ture** [-chər] n thing fixed in position; thing attached to house; sporting event that takes place regularly; person long-established in a place. **fix up** arrange. **fix (someone) up** attend to person's needs, esp. arrange date.

fizz vi hiss, splutter. ▶ n hissing noise; effervescent liquid such as champagne. **fiz'zle** [-əl] vi **-zled, -zling.** splutter weakly. ▶ n fizzling noise; fiasco. **fizzle out** inf come to nothing, fail.

fjord [fyord] n (esp. in Norway) long, narrow inlet of sea.

flab·ber·gast [FLAB-ər-gast] vt overwhelm with astonishment.

flab·by [FLAB-ee] adj **-bi·er, -bi·est.** hanging loose, limp; out of condition, too fat; feeble; yielding. **flab** n inf unsightly fat on the body. **flab'bi·ness** n

flac·cid [FLAK-sid] adj flabby, lacking firmness. **flac·cid'i·ty** n

flag¹ n banner, piece of bunting attached to staff or halyard as standard or signal. ▶ vt **flagged, flag·ging.** inform by flag signals. **Flag Day** June 14. **flag'ship** n admiral's ship; most important ship of fleet. **flag'staff** n pole for flag.

flag² n flat slab of stone. ▶ pl pavement of flags. ▶ vt **flagged, flag·ging.** pave with flags. **flag'stone** n

flag³ vi **flagged, flag·ging.** droop, fade; lose vigor.

flag·el·late [FLAJ-ə-layt] vt **-lat·ed, -lat·ing.** scourge, flog. **flag'el·lant** [-lənt] n one who scourges self, esp. in religious penance. **flag·el·la'tion** n **flag'el·la·tor** n

flag·eo·let [flaj-ə-LET] n small flutelike instrument.

flag·on [FLAG-ən] n large bottle of wine, etc.

fla·grant [FLAY-grənt] adj glaring, scandalous, blatant. **fla'gran·cy** n

flail [flayl] n instrument for threshing grain by hand. ▶ v beat with, move as, flail.

flair n natural ability; elegance.

flak n antiaircraft fire; inf adverse criticism.

flake [flayk] n small, thin piece, esp. particle of snow; piece chipped off. ▶ v **flaked, flak·ing.** (cause to) peel off in flakes. **flak'y** adj **flak·i·er, flak·i·est.** of or like flakes; sl eccentric. **flake out** inf collapse, sleep from exhaustion.

flam·boy·ant [flam-BOI-ənt] adj florid, gorgeous, showy; exuberant, ostentatious.

flame [flaym] n burning gas, esp. above fire; visible burning; passion, esp. love; inf sweetheart; inf an abusive message sent by e-mail. ▶ v **flamed, flam·ing.** give out flames, blaze; shine; burst out; inf to send an abusive message by e-mail.

fla·men·co [flə-MENG-koh] n Spanish dance to guitar; music for this.

fla·min·go [flə-MING-goh] n, pl **-gos** or **-goes.** large pink to scarlet bird with long neck and legs.

flam·ma·ble [FLAM-ə-bəl] *adj* liable to catch fire, inflammable.

flan *n* open sweet dessert with caramel topping; tartlike pastry.

flange [flanj] *n* projecting flat rim, collar, or rib. ▶ *v* **flanged, flang·ing.** provide with or take form of flange.

flank [flangk] *n* part of side between hips and ribs; side of anything, e.g. body of troops. ▶ *vt* guard or strengthen on flank; attack or take in flank; be at, move along either side of.

flan·nel [FLAN-l] *n* soft woolen fabric for clothing, esp. trousers. **flan'nel·mouth** *n* person of slow, thick speech or deceptively smooth speech.

flap *v* **flapped, flap·ping.** move (wings, arms, etc.) as bird flying; (cause to) sway; strike with flat object; *sl* be agitated, flustered. ▶ *n* act of flapping; broad piece of anything hanging from hinge or loosely from one side; movable part of aircraft wing; *inf* state of excitement or panic. **flap'pa·ble** *adj inf* easily confused, esp. under stress.

flare [flair] *vi* **flared, flar·ing.** blaze with unsteady flame; *inf* (with *up*) burst suddenly into anger; spread outward, as bottom of skirt. ▶ *n* instance of flaring; signal light.

flash *n* sudden burst of light or flame; sudden short blaze; very short time; brief news item; display. ▶ *vi* break into sudden flame; gleam; burst into view; move very fast; appear suddenly; *sl* expose oneself indecently. ▶ *vt* cause to gleam; emit (light, etc.) suddenly. **flash'er** *n* thing that flashes; *sl* one who indecently exposes self. **flash'back** *n* break in continuity of book, play or film, to introduce what has taken place previously. **flash'y** *adj* **flash·i·er, flash·i·est.** showy, sham. **flash point** temperature at which a vapor ignites; point at which violence or anger breaks out.

flask *n* long-necked bottle for scientific use; metal or glass pocket bottle.

flat¹ *adj* **flat·ter, flat·test.** level; spread out; at full length; smooth; downright; dull, lifeless; *Mus* below true pitch; (of vehicle tire) deflated, punctured. ▶ *n* what is flat; *Mus* note half tone below natural pitch. **flat'ly** *adv* **flat'ness** *n* **flat'ten** *vt* **flat feet** feet with abnormally flattened arches. **flat'foot** *n, pl* **-foots.** *sl* police officer. **flat race** horse race over level ground with no jumps. **flat rate** the same price in all cases. **flat out** at, with maximum speed or effort.

flat² *n* apartment.

flat·ter [FLAT-ər] *vt* fawn on; praise insincerely; inspire unfounded belief; gratify (senses); represent too favorably. **flat'ter·er** *n* **flat'ter·y** *n, pl* **-ter·ies.**

flat·u·lent [FLACH-ə-lənt] *adj* suffering from, generating (excess) gases in intestines; pretentious. **flat'u·lence** *n* flatulent condition; verbosity, emptiness.

flaunt [flawnt] *v* show off; wave proudly.

flautist *n* see FLUTE.

fla·vor [FLAY-vər] *n* mixed sensation of smell and taste; distinctive taste, savor; undefinable characteristic, quality of anything. ▶ *vt* give flavor to; season. **fla'vor·ing** *n* **fla'vor·ful** *adj*

flaw *n* crack; defect; blemish. ▶ *vt* make flaw in. **flaw'less** *adj* perfect.

flax [flaks] *n* plant grown for its textile fiber and seeds; its fibers, spun into linen thread. **flax'en** *adj* of flax; light yellow or straw-colored.

flay *vt* strip skin off; criticize severely.

flea [flee] *n* small, wingless, jumping, blood-sucking insect. **flea'bag** *n sl* worthless racehorse, unkempt dog, etc.; shabby hotel, etc. **flea'bite** *n* insect's bite; trifling injury; trifle. **flea'-bit·ten** *adj* bitten by flea; mean, worthless; scruffy. **flea market** market, usu. held outdoors, for used articles, cheap goods.

fleck [flek] n small mark, streak, or particle. ▶ vt mark with flecks.

fled pt./pp. of FLEE.

fledged [flejd] adj (of birds) able to fly; experienced, trained. **fledg'ling** n young bird; inexperienced person.

flee v **fled, flee·ing.** run away from.

fleece [flees] n sheep's wool. ▶ vt **fleeced, fleec·ing.** rob. **fleec'y** adj **fleec·i·er, fleec·i·est.** resembling wool.

fleet¹ n number of warships organized as unit; number of ships, automobiles, etc. operating together.

fleet² adj **-er, -est.** swift, nimble. **fleet'ing** adj passing, transient. **fleet'ing·ly** adv

flesh n soft part, muscular substance, between skin and bone; in plants, pulp; fat; person's family. **flesh'ly** adj **-li·er, -li·est.** carnal, material. **flesh'y** adj **flesh·i·er, flesh·i·est.** plump, pulpy. **flesh'pots** pl n (places catering to) self-indulgent living. **in the flesh** in person, actually present.

fleur-de-lis [flur-dl-EE] n, pl **fleurs-de-lis** [-dl-EEZ] heraldic lily with three petals.

flew pt. of FLY.

flex [fleks] n act of flexing. ▶ v bend, be bent. **flex·i·bil'i·ty** n **flex'i·ble** adj easily bent; manageable; adaptable. **flex'time** n system permitting variation in starting and finishing times of work, providing agreed total time is worked over a specified period.

flib·ber·ti·gib·bet [FLIB-ər-tee-jib-it] n flighty, chattering person.

flick [flik] vt strike lightly, jerk. ▶ n light blow; jerk; sl motion picture.

flick·er [FLIK-ər] vi burn, shine, unsteadily; waver, quiver. ▶ n unsteady light or movement.

flight [flīt] n act or manner of flying through air; number flying together, as birds; journey in aircraft; air force unit of command; power of flying; swift movement or passage; sally; distance flown; stairs between two landings; running away. **flight recorder** electronic device in aircraft storing information about its flight.

flight·y [FLĪ-tee] adj **flight·i·er, flight·i·est.** frivolous, erratic.

flim·sy [FLIM-zee] adj **-si·er, -si·est.** frail, weak, thin; easily destroyed. **flim'si·ness** n

flinch vi shrink, draw back, wince.

fling v **flung, fling·ing.** mainly tr throw, send, move, with force. ▶ n throw; hasty attempt; spell of indulgence; vigorous dance.

flint n hard steel-gray stone; piece of this; hard substance used (as flint) for striking fire. **flint'y** adj **flint·i·er, flint·i·est.** like or consisting of flint; hard, cruel.

flip v **flipped, flip·ping.** throw or flick lightly; turn over; sl react with astonishment, become irrational. ▶ n instance, act, of flipping; drink with beaten egg. **flip'pan·cy** n, pl **-cies. flip'pant** adj treating serious things lightly. **flip'per** n limb, fin for swimming. ▶ pl fin-shaped rubber devices worn on feet to help in swimming.

flirt [flurt] vi toy, play with another's affections; trifle, toy (with). ▶ n person who flirts. **flir·ta'tion** [-TAY-shən] n **flir·ta'tious** adj

flit vi **flit·ted, flit·ting.** pass lightly and rapidly; dart; inf go away hastily, secretly.

flitch [flich] n side of bacon.

float [floht] vi rest, drift on surface of liquid; be suspended freely; move aimlessly. ▶ vt of liquid, support, bear alone; in commerce, get (company) started; obtain loan. ▶ n light object used to help someone or something float; motor vehicle carrying tableau, etc., in parade; uncollected checks, etc. in process of transfer between banks, etc. **flo·ta'tion** n act of floating, esp. floating of business venture.

floc·cu·late [FLOK-yə-layt] vt **-lat·ed, -lat·ing.** form into masses of particles. **floc'cu·lant** [-lənt] n chemical for accomplishing this.

floc·cu·lent [FLOK-yə-lənt] *adj* like tufts of wool.

flock[1] [flok] *n* number of animals of one kind together; *fig* body of people; religious congregation. ▸ *vi* gather in a crowd.

flock[2] *n* lock, tuft of wool, etc.; wool refuse for stuffing cushions, etc.

floe [floh] *n* sheet of floating ice.

flog *vt* **flogged, flog·ging.** beat with whip, stick, etc.; *sl* sell, esp. vigorously.

flood [flud] *n* inundation, overflow of water; rising of tide; outpouring; flowing water. ▸ *vt* inundate; cover, fill with water; arrive, move, etc. in great numbers. **flood'gate** *n* gate, sluice for letting water in or out. **flood'light** *n* broad, intense beam of artificial light. **flood'lit** *adj* **flood tide** the rising tide.

floor [flor] *n* lower surface of room; set of rooms on one level, story; flat space; (right to speak in) meeting or legislative chamber; lower limit. ▸ *vt* supply with floor; knock down; confound. **floor'ing** *n* material for floors. **floor show** entertainment in nightclub, etc.

flop *vi* **flopped, flop·ping.** bend, fall, collapse loosely, carelessly; fall flat on floor, on water, etc.; *inf* go to sleep; *inf* fail. ▸ *n* flopping movement or sound; *inf* failure. **flop'pi·ness** *n* **flop'py** *adj* **-pi·er, -pi·est.** limp, unsteady. **flop'house** *n* run-down rooming house. **floppy disk** *Computers* flexible magnetic disk that stores information.

flo·ra [FLOR-ə] *n* plants of a region; list of them. **flor'al** *adj* of flowers. **flo·res'cence** [-əns] *n* state or time of flowering. **flo·ret** [FLOR-it] *n* small flower forming part of composite flower. **flo'ri·cul·ture** *n* cultivation of flowers. **flo·ri·cul'tur·ist** *n* **flo'rist** *n* dealer in flowers.

flor'id *adj* with red, flushed complexion; ornate.

floss [flaws] *n* mass of fine, silky fibers; fluff. **floss'y** *adj* **floss·i·er, floss·i·est.** light and downy; excessively fancy.

flotation see FLOAT.

flo·til·la [floh-TIL-ə] *n* fleet of small vessels, esp. naval vessels.

flot·sam [FLOT-səm] *n* floating wreckage; discarded waste objects; penniless population of city, etc.

flounce[1] [flowns] *vi* **flounced, flounc·ing.** go, move abruptly and impatiently. ▸ *n* fling, jerk of body or limb.

flounce[2] *n* ornamental gathered strip on woman's garment.

floun·der[1] [FLOWN-dər] *vi* plunge and struggle, esp. in water or mud; proceed in bungling, hesitating manner. ▸ *n* act of floundering.

flounder[2] *n* type of flatfish.

flour [FLOW-ər] *n* powder prepared by sifting and grinding wheat, etc.; fine soft powder. ▸ *vt* sprinkle with flour.

flour·ish [FLUR-ish] *vi* thrive; be in the prime. ▸ *vt* brandish, display; wave about. ▸ *n* ornamental curve; showy gesture in speech, etc.; waving (of hand, weapon, etc.); fanfare (of trumpets).

flout [flowt] *vt* show contempt for, mock; defy.

flow [floh] *vi* glide along as stream; circulate, as the blood; move easily; move in waves; hang loose; be present in abundance. ▸ *n* act, instance of flowing; quantity that flows; rise of tide; ample supply. **flow chart** diagram showing sequence of operations in industrial, etc. process.

flow·er [FLOW-ər] *n* colored (not green) part of plant from which fruit is developed; bloom, blossom; ornamentation; choicest part, pick. ▸ *vi* produce flowers; bloom; come to prime condition. ▸ *vt* ornament with flowers. **flow'er·et** *n* small flower. **flow'er·y** *adj* **-er·i·er, -er·i·est.** abounding in flowers; full of fine words, ornamented with figures of speech. **flower girl** girl selling flowers; young girl designated to attend bride at wedding ceremony.

flown pp. of FLY.

flu *n* short for INFLUENZA.

fluc·tu·ate [FLUK-choo-ayt] *v* **-at·ed, -at·ing.** vary, rise and fall, undulate. **fluc·tu·a'tion** *n*

flue [floo] *n* passage or pipe for smoke or hot air, chimney.

flu·ent [FLOO-ənt] *adj* speaking, writing a given language easily and well; easy, graceful.

fluff *n* soft, feathery stuff; down; *inf* mistake; *inf* anything insubstantial. ▶ *v* make or become soft, light; *inf* make mistake. **fluff'y** *adj* **fluff·i·er, fluff·i·est.**

flu·id [FLOO-id] *adj* flowing easily, not solid. ▶ *n* gas or liquid. **flu·id'i·ty** *n* **fluid ounce** one sixteenth of a pint.

fluke¹ [flook] *n* flat triangular point of anchor. ▶ *pl* whale's tail.

fluke² *n* stroke of luck, accident. **fluk'y** *adj* **fluk·i·er, fluk·i·est.** uncertain; got by luck.

fluke³ *n* type of flatfish; parasitic worm.

flume [floom] *n* narrow (artificial) channel for water.

flum·mer·y [FLUM-ə-ree] *n, pl* **-mer·ies.** nonsense, idle talk, humbug; dish of milk, flour, eggs, etc.

flum·mox [FLUM-əks] *vt inf* bewilder, perplex.

flung pt./pp. of FLING.

flun·ky [FLUNG-kee] *n, pl* **-kies.** servant, esp. liveried manservant; assistant doing menial work; servile person.

fluo·res·cence [fluu-RES-əns] *n* emission of light or other radiation from substance when bombarded by particles (electrons, etc. or other radiation, as in fluorescent lamp). **fluo·res'cent** *adj*

fluor·ide [FLUUR-īd] *n* salt containing fluorine, esp. as added to domestic water supply as protection against tooth decay. **fluor'i·date** *vt* **-dat·ed, -dat·ing.** treat with fluoride. **fluor·i·da'tion** *n* **fluor'ine** [-een] *n* nonmetallic element, yellowish gas.

flur·ry [FLUR-ee] *n, pl* **-ries.** squall, gust; bustle, commotion; fluttering (as of snowflakes). ▶ *vt* **-ried, -ry·ing.** agitate, bewilder, fluster.

flush¹ *vi* blush; of skin, redden; flow suddenly or violently; be excited. ▶ *vt* send water through (a toilet or pipe) so as to clean it; excite. ▶ *n* reddening, blush; rush of water; excitement; elation; glow of color; freshness, vigor. ▶ *adj* full, in flood; well supplied; level with surrounding surface.

flush² *v* (cause to) leave cover and take flight.

flush³ *n* set of cards all of one suit.

flus·ter [FLUS-tər] *v* make or become nervous, agitated. ▶ *n*

flute [floot] *n* wind instrument of tube with holes stopped by fingers or keys and blowhole in side; groove, channel. ▶ *v* **flut·ed, flut·ing.** ▶ *vi* play on flute. ▶ *vt* make grooves in. **flut'ist, flaut'ist** [FLOWT-] *n* flute player.

flut·ter [FLUT-ər] *v* flap (as wings) rapidly without flight or in short flights; quiver; be or make excited, agitated. ▶ *n* flapping movement; nervous agitation.

flu·vi·al [FLOO-vee-əl] *adj* of rivers.

flux [fluks] *n* discharge; constant succession of changes; substance mixed with metal to clean, aid adhesion in soldering, etc.; measure of strength in magnetic field.

fly¹ [flī] *v* **flew, flown, fly·ing.** move through air on wings or in aircraft; pass quickly (through air); float loosely; spring, rush; flee, run away. ▶ *vt* operate aircraft; cause to fly; set flying. ▶ *vi* run from. ▶ *n* (zipper or buttons fastening) opening in trousers; flap in garment or tent; flying. **flying** *adj* hurried, brief. **fly'fish** *v* fish with artificial fly as lure. **flying boat** airplane fitted with floats instead of landing wheels. **flying buttress** *Architecture* arched or slanting structure attached at only one point to a mass of masonry. **flying colors** conspicuous success. **flying fish** fish with winglike fins used for gliding above the sea. **flying**

saucer unidentified (disk-shaped) flying object, supposedly from outer space. **flying squad** special detachment of police, etc., ready to act quickly. **fly'leaf** n, pl **-leaves.** blank leaf at beginning or end of book. **fly'o·ver** n formation of aircraft in flight for observation from ground. **fly'wheel** n heavy wheel regulating speed of machine.

fly² n, pl **flies.** two-winged insect, esp. common housefly.

fly'catch·er n small insect-eating songbird.

Fm Chem fermium.

foal [fohl] n young of horse, ass, etc. ▶ v bear (foal).

foam [fohm] n collection of small bubbles on liquid; froth of saliva or sweat; light cellular solid used for insulation, packing, etc. ▶ v (cause to) produce foam; be very angry. **foam'y** adj **foam·i·er, foam·i·est.**

fob n short watch chain; small pocket in waistband of trousers or vest.

fob off v **fobbed, fob·bing.** ignore, dismiss someone or something in offhand (insulting) manner; dispose of.

foci pl. of FOCUS.

fo·cus [FOH-kəs] n, pl **-cus·es** or **-ci** [-sī] point at which rays meet after being reflected or refracted; state of optical image when it is clearly defined; state of instrument producing such image; point of convergence; point on which interest, activity is centered. ▶ v **-cused, -cus·ing.** ▶ vt bring to focus, adjust; concentrate. ▶ vi come to focus; converge. **fo'cal** [-kəl] adj of, at focus.

fod·der [FOD-ər] n bulk food for livestock.

foe [foh] n enemy.

fog n thick mist; dense watery vapor in lower atmosphere; cloud of anything reducing visibility; stupor. ▶ vt **fogged, fog·ging.** cover in fog; puzzle. **fog'gy** adj **-gi·er, -gi·est. fog'horn** n instrument to warn ships in fog.

fo·gy [FOH-gee] n, pl **-gies.**

old-fashioned person.

foi·ble [FOI-bəl] n minor weakness, idiosyncrasy.

foil¹ vt baffle, defeat, frustrate. ▶ n blunt sword, with button on point for fencing.

foil² n metal in thin sheet; anything or person that sets off another to advantage.

foist vt (usu. with on or upon) sell, pass off inferior or unwanted thing as valuable.

fold¹ [fohld] vt double up, bend part of; interlace (arms); wrap up; clasp (in arms); Cookery mix gently. ▶ vi become folded; admit of being folded; inf fail. ▶ n folding; coil; winding; line made by folding; crease; foldlike geological formation. **fold'er** n binder, file for loose papers.

fold² n enclosure for sheep; body of believers, church.

fo·li·age [FOH-lee-ij] n leaves collectively, leafage. **fo·li·a'ceous** [-AY-shəs] adj of or like leaf. **fo'li·ate** [-it] adj leaflike, having leaves.

fo·li·o [FOH-lee-oh] n, pl **-li·os.** sheet of paper folded in half to make two leaves of book; book of largest common size made up of such sheets; page numbered on one side only; page number.

folk [fohk] n people in general; family, relatives; race of people. **folk dance** traditional country dance. **folk'lore** n tradition, customs, beliefs popularly held. **folk song** music originating among a people.

fol·li·cle [FOL-i-kəl] n small cavity, sac; seed vessel.

fol·low [FOL-oh] v go or come after. ▶ vt accompany, attend on; keep to (path, etc.); take as guide, conform to; engage in; have a keen interest in; be consequent on; grasp meaning of. ▶ vi come next; result. **fol'low·er** n disciple, supporter. **fol'low·ing** adj about to be mentioned. ▶ n body of supporters. **fol'low-through** n in ball games, continuation of stroke after impact with ball. **fol′low-up** *n* something done to reinforce initial action.

fol·ly [FOL-ee] *n, pl* **-lies.** foolishness; foolish action, idea, etc.; useless, extravagant structure.

fo·ment [foh-MENT] *vt* foster, stir up; bathe with warm lotions.

fond *adj* **-er, -est.** tender, loving. **fond′ly** *adv* **fond′ness** *n* **fond of** having liking for.

fon·dant [FON-dənt] *n* soft sugar mixture for candies; candy made of this.

fon·dle [FON-dl] *vt* **-dled, -dling.** caress.

fon·due [fon-DOO] *n* Swiss dish of cheese and seasonings into which pieces of bread, etc. are dipped.

font *n* bowl for baptismal water usu. on pedestal; productive source; assortment of printing type of one size.

fon·ta·nel [fon-tn-EL] *n* soft, membraneous gap between bones of baby's skull.

food *n* solid nourishment; what one eats; mental or spiritual nourishment. **food additive** natural or synthetic substance added to commercially processed food as preservative or to add color, flavor, etc. **food processor** electric kitchen appliance for automatic chopping, blending, etc. of foodstuffs. **food′stuff** *n* food.

fool *n* silly, empty-headed person; dupe; simpleton; *Hist* jester, clown. ▶ *vt* delude; dupe. ▶ *vi* act as fool. **fool′er·y** *n, pl* **-er·ies.** habitual folly; act of playing the fool; absurdity. **fool′har·di·ness** *n* **fool′har·dy** *adj* **-di·er, -di·est.** foolishly adventurous. **fool′ish** *adj* ill-considered, silly, stupid. **fool′proof** *adj* proof against failure. **fool′s cap** jester's or dunce's cap. **fools′cap** *n* inexpensive paper, esp. legal-size (formerly with fool's cap as watermark).

foot [fuut] *n, pl* **feet.** lowest part of leg, from ankle down; lowest part of anything, base, stand; end of bed, etc.; measure of twelve inches; division of line of verse. ▶ *v* (usu. tr) dance. **foot it** *inf* walk. **foot the bill** pay the entire cost. **foot′age** *n* length in feet; length, extent, of film used. **foot′ing** *n* basis, foundation; firm standing, relations, conditions. ▶ *pl* (concrete) foundations for walls of buildings. **foot-and-mouth disease** infectious viral disease in sheep, cattle, etc. **foot′ball** *n* game played with inflated oval ball; the ball. **foot′ball pool** form of gambling on results of football games. **foot brake** brake operated by pressure on foot pedal. **foot fault** *Tennis* fault of overstepping baseline while serving. **foot′hold** *n* place affording secure grip for the foot; secure position from which progress may be made. **foot′lights** *pl n* lights across front of stage. **foot′loose** *adj* free of any ties. **foot′note** *n* note of reference or explanation printed at foot of page. **foot-pound** *n* unit of measurement of work in fps system. **foot′print** *n* mark left by foot. **playing foot′sie** flirting or sharing a surreptitious intimacy. **foot′slog** *vi* **-slogged, slogging.** walk, go on foot. **foot′slog·ger** *n*

fop *n* man excessively concerned with fashion. **fop′per·y** *n, pl* **-per·ies. fop′pish** *adj*

for *prep* intended to reach, directed or belonging to; because of; instead of; toward; on account of; in favor of; respecting; during; in search of; in payment of; in the character of; in spite of. ▶ *conj* because. **in for it** *inf* liable for punishment or blame.

for- *prefix* from, away, against, e.g. *forswear; forbid.*

for·age [FOR-ij] *n* food for cattle and horses. ▶ *vi* **-aged, -ag·ing.** collect forage; make roving search.

for′ay *n* raid, inroad. ▶ *vi* make one.

for·bear [for-BAIR] *v* **-bore, -borne, -bear·ing.** cease or refrain (from doing something). **for·bear′ance** *n* self-control, patience.

for·bid [fər-BID] *vt* **-bade** *or* **-bad,**

-bid or **-bid·den, -bid** or **-bid·ding.**
prohibit; refuse to allow.
forbidding adj uninviting,
threatening.
force [fors] n strength, power;
compulsion; that which tends to
produce a change in a physical
system; mental or moral strength;
body of troops, police, etc.; group
of people organized for particular
task or duty; effectiveness,
operative state; violence. ▸ vt
forced, forc·ing. constrain,
compel; produce by effort,
strength; break open; urge, strain;
drive; hasten maturity of. **forced**
adj accomplished by great effort;
compulsory; unnatural; strained;
excessive. **force'ful** adj powerful,
persuasive. **for'ci·ble** adj done by
force; efficacious, compelling,
impressive; strong. **for'ci·bly** adv
for·ceps [FOR-səps] pl n surgical
pincers.
ford n shallow place where river
may be crossed. ▸ vt **ford'a·ble** adj
fore¹ [for] adj in front. ▸ n front part.
fore² interj golfer's warning.
fore- prefix before in time or rank,
e.g. forefather; at the front, e.g.
forecourt.
fore-and-aft [FOR-ənd-AFT] adj
placed in line from bow to stern of
ship.
fore·arm [FOR-ahrm] n arm
between wrist and elbow. ▸ vt
[for-AHRM] arm beforehand.
fore·bear [FOR-bair] n ancestor.
fore·bode [for-BOHD] vt **-bod·ed,
-bod·ing.** indicate in advance.
foreboding n anticipation of evil.
fore·cast [FOR-kast] vt estimate
beforehand (esp. weather);
prophesy. ▸ n prediction.
fore·castle [FOHK-səl] n forward
raised part of ship; sailors' quarters.
fore·close [for-KLOHZ] vt **-closed,
-clos·ing.** take away power of
redeeming (mortgage); prevent,
shut out, bar. **fore·clo'sure** [-zhər]
n
fore·court [FOR-kort] n courtyard,
open space, in front of building;
Tennis part of court between

service line and net.
fore·fa·ther [FOR-fah-thər] n
ancestor.
fore·fin·ger [FOR-fing-gər] n finger
next to thumb, index finger.
foregather see FORGATHER.
fore·go [for-GOH] vt **-went, -gone,
-go·ing.** precede in time, place.
foregoing adj going before,
preceding. **foregone** adj
determined beforehand;
preceding. **foregone conclusion**
result that might have been
foreseen.
fore·ground [FOR-grownd] n part
of view, esp. in picture, nearest
observer.
fore·hand [FOR-hand] adj of stroke
in racquet games made with inner
side of wrist leading.
fore·head [FOR-id] n part of face
above eyebrows and between
temples.
for·eign [FOR-in] adj not of, or in,
one's own country; relating to, or
connected with other countries;
irrelevant; coming from outside;
unfamiliar, strange. **for'eign·er** n
fore·man [FOR-mən] n, pl **-men.**
one in charge of work; leader of
jury.
fore·mast [FOR-mast] n mast
nearest bow.
fore·most [FOR-mohst] adj, adv
first in time, place, importance, etc.
fore·noon [FOR-noon] n morning.
fo·ren·sic [fə-REN-sik] adj of courts
of law. **forensic medicine**
application of medical knowledge
in legal matters.
fore·play [FOR-play] n sexual
stimulation before intercourse.
fore·run·ner [FOR-run-ər] n one
that goes before, precursor.
fore·see [for-SEE] vt **-saw, -seen,
-see·ing.** see beforehand.
fore·shad·ow [for-SHAD-oh] vt
show, suggest beforehand, be a
type of.
fore·short·en [for-SHOR-tn] vt
draw (object) so that it appears
shortened; make shorter.
fore·sight [FOR-sīt] n foreseeing;
care for future.

fore·skin [FOR-skin] *n* skin that covers end of penis.

for·est [FOR-ist] *n* area with heavy growth of trees and plants; these trees; *fig* something resembling forest. ▶ *vt* plant, create forest (in an area). **for′est·er** *n* one skilled in forestry. **for′est·ry** *n* study, management of forest planting and maintenance.

fore·stall [for-STAWL] *vt* anticipate; prevent, guard against in advance.

fore·taste [FOR-tayst] *n* anticipation; taste beforehand.

fore·tell [for-TEL] *vt* **-told, -tel·ling.** prophesy.

fore·thought [FOR-thawt] *n* thoughtful consideration of future events.

for·ev·er [for-EV-ər] *adv* always; eternally; *inf* for a long time.

fore·warn [for-WORN] *vt* warn, caution in advance.

forewent see FOREGO.

fore·word [FOR-wurd] *n* preface.

for·feit [FOR-fit] *n* thing lost by crime or fault; penalty, fine. ▶ *adj* lost by crime or fault. ▶ *vt* lose by penalty. **for′fei·ture** [-fi-chər] *n*

for·gath·er [for-GATH-ər] *vi* meet together, assemble, associate.

forge¹ [forj] *n* place where metal is worked, smithy; furnace, workshop for melting or refining metal. ▶ *vt* **forged, forg·ing.** shape (metal) by heating in fire and hammering; make, shape, invent; make a fraudulent imitation of thing; counterfeit. **forg′er** *n* **for′ger·y** *n*, *pl* **-ger·ies.** forged artwork, document, currency, etc.; the making of it.

forge² *vi* **forged, forg·ing.** advance steadily.

for·get [fər-GET] *vt* **-got, -got·ten** *or* **-got, -get·ting.** lose memory of, neglect, overlook. **for·get′ful** *adj* liable to forget.

for·give [fər-GIV] *v* **-gave, -giv·en, -giv·ing.** cease to blame or hold resentment against; pardon. **for·give′ness** *n*

for·go [for-GOH] *vt* **-went, -gone, -go·ing.** go without; give up.

forgot, forgotten see FORGET.

fork *n* pronged instrument for eating food; pronged tool for digging or lifting; division into branches; point of this division; one of the branches. ▶ *vi* branch. ▶ *vt* dig, lift, throw, with fork; make fork-shaped. **fork out** *inf* pay (reluctantly).

for·lorn′ *adj* forsaken; desperate. **forlorn hope** anything undertaken with little hope of success.

form *n* shape, visible appearance; visible person or animal; structure; nature; species, kind; regularly drawn up document, esp. printed one with blanks for particulars; condition, good condition; customary way of doing things; set order of words; *Printing* frame for type. ▶ *vt* shape, mold, arrange, organize; train, shape in the mind, conceive; go to make up, make part of. ▶ *vi* come into existence or shape. **for·ma′tion** *n* forming; thing formed; structure, shape, arrangement; military order. **form′a·tive** *adj* of, relating to, development; serving or tending to form; used in forming. **form′less** *adj*

for·mal [FOR-məl] *adj* ceremonial, according to rule; of outward form or routine; of, for, formal occasions; according to rule that does not matter; precise; stiff. ▶ *n* formal dance. **for′mal·ism** *n* quality of being formal; exclusive concern for form, structure, technique in an activity. **for·mal′i·ty** *n*, *pl* **-ties.** observance required by custom or etiquette; condition or quality of being formal; conformity to custom; conventionality, mere form; in art, precision, stiffness, as opposed to originality.

for·mal·de·hyde [for-MAL-də-hīd] *n* colorless, poisonous, pungent gas, used in making antiseptics and in chemistry. **for′ma·lin** [-mə-lin] *n* solution of formaldehyde in water, used as disinfectant, preservative, etc.

for·mat *n* size and shape of book; organization of TV show, etc.

for·mer [FOR-mər] *adj* earlier in time; of past times; first named. ▶ *pron* first named thing or person or fact. **for′mer·ly** *adv* previously.

for·mi·da·ble [FOR-mi-də-bəl] *adj* to be feared; overwhelming; terrible, redoubtable; likely to be difficult, serious. **for′mi·da·bly** *adv*

for·mu·la [FOR-myə-lə] *n, pl* **-las** or **-lae** [-lee] set form of words setting forth principle, method or rule for doing, producing something; substance so prepared; specific category of racing car; recipe; group of numbers, letters, or symbols expressing a scientific or mathematical rule. **for′mu·late** [-layt] *vt* **-lat·ed, -lat·ing.** reduce to, express in formula, or in definite form; devise. **for·mu·la′tion** *n*

for·ni·ca·tion [for-ni-KAY-shən] *n* sexual intercourse outside marriage. **for′ni·cate** *vi* **-cat·ed, -cat·ing.**

for·sake [for-SAYK] *vt* **-sook, -sak·en, -sak·ing.** abandon, desert; give up.

for·sooth′ *adv obs* in truth.

for·swear [for-SWAIR] *vt* **-swore, -sworn, -swear·ing.** renounce, deny. ▶ *refl* perjure.

for·syth·i·a [for-SITH-ee-ə] *n* widely cultivated shrub with yellow flowers.

fort *n* fortified place, stronghold.

forte¹ [fort] *n* one's strong point, that in which one excels.

for·te² [FOR-tay] *adv Mus* loudly. **for·tis′si·mo** *adv Mus* very loudly.

forth *adv* onward, into view. **forth·com′ing** *adj* about to come; ready when wanted; willing to talk, communicative. **forth·with′** *adv* at once, immediately.

forth·right [FORTH-rīt] *adj* direct, outspoken.

fortieth see FOUR.

for·ti·fy [FOR-tə-fī] *vt* **-fied, -fy·ing.** strengthen; provide with defensive works. **for·ti·fi·ca′tion** *n*

for·ti·tude [FOR-ti-tood] *n* courage in adversity or pain, endurance.

fort·night [FORT-nīt] *n* two weeks. **fort′night·ly** *adv*

FORTRAN [FOR-tran] *Computers* a programming language for mathematical and scientific purposes.

for·tress [FOR-tris] *n* large fort or fortified town.

for·tu·i·tous [for-TOO-i-təs] *adj* accidental, by chance. **for·tu′i·tous·ly** *adv*

for·tune [FOR-chən] *n* good luck, prosperity; wealth; stock of wealth; chance, luck. **for′tu·nate** [-nit] *adj* **for′tu·nate·ly** *adv* **fortune hunter** person seeking fortune, esp. by marriage. **fortuneteller** *n* one who predicts a person's future.

forty see FOUR.

fo·rum [FOR-əm] *n* (place or medium for) meeting, assembly for open discussion or debate.

for·ward [FOR-wərd] *adj* lying in front of; onward; presumptuous, impudent; advanced, progressive; relating to the future. ▶ *n* player placed in forward position in various team games, e.g. basketball. ▶ *adv* toward the future; toward the front, to the front, into view; at, in fore part of ship; onward, so as to make progress. ▶ *vt* help forward; send, dispatch. **for′ward·ly** *adv* pertly. **for′ward·ness** *n* **for′wards** [-wərdz] *adv* **forward slash** forward-sloping diagonal mark (/).

forwent see FORGO.

fos·sil [FOS-əl] *n* remnant or impression of animal or plant, esp. prehistoric one, preserved in earth; *inf* person, idea, etc. that is outdated and incapable of change. **fos′sil·ize** *v* **-ized, -iz·ing.** turn into fossil; petrify.

fos·ter [FAW-stər] *vt* promote growth or development of; bring up child, esp. not one's own. ▶ *adj* of or involved in fostering a child, e.g. *foster parents.*

fought pt./pp. of FIGHT.

foul [fowl] *adj* **-er, -est.** loathsome, offensive; stinking; dirty; unfair; wet, rough; obscene, disgustingly abusive; charged with harmful matter, clogged, choked. ▶ *n* act of unfair play; the breaking of a rule. ▶ *adv* unfairly. ▶ *v* (mainly tr) make, become foul; jam; collide with. **foul'ly** *adv*

found¹ [fownd] pt./pp. of FIND.

found² *vt* establish, institute; lay base of; base, ground. **foun·da·tion** *n* basis; base, lowest part of building; founding; endowed institution, etc. **found'er** *n* **foundation stone** one of stones forming foundation of building, esp. stone laid with public ceremony.

found³ *vt* melt and run into mold; cast. **found'er** *n* **found'ry** *n, pl* **-ries.** place for casting; art of this.

found·er [FOWN-dər] *vi* collapse; sink; become stuck as in mud, etc.

found·ling [FOWND-ling] *n* deserted infant.

fount [fownt] *n* fountain.

foun·tain [FOWN-tn] *n* jet of water, esp. ornamental one; spring; source. **foun'tain·head** [-hed] *n* source. **fountain pen** pen with ink reservoir.

four [for] *n, adj* cardinal number next after three. **fourth** *adj* the ordinal number. **fourth'ly** *adv* **for'ti·eth** *adj* **for'ty** *adj, n, pl* **-ties.** four tens. **four'teen'** *n, adj* four plus ten. **four'teenth'** *adj* **four-stroke** *adj* describing an internal-combustion engine firing once every four strokes of piston. **four'post·er** *n* bed with four posts for curtains, etc. **four'some** *n* group of four people; game or dance for four people. **four'square** *adj* firm, steady. **on all fours** on hands and knees. **401K** employer-run savings plan for retirement.

fowl *n* domestic rooster or hen; bird, its flesh. ▶ *vi* hunt wild birds. **fowling piece** shotgun for fowling.

fox [foks] *n* red bushy-tailed animal; its fur; cunning person. ▶ *vt* perplex; discolor (paper) with brown spots; mislead. ▶ *vi* act craftily; sham. **fox'y** *adj* **fox·i·er,**

fox·i·est. foxlike; *sl* sexually appealing; attractive. **fox'hole** *n* in war, small trench giving protection. **fox'hound** *n* dog bred for hunting foxes. **fox terrier** small dog now mainly kept as a pet. **fox'trot** *n* (music for) ballroom dance. ▶ *v*

foy·er [FOI-ər] *n* entrance hall in theaters, hotels, etc.; vestibule.

Fr *Chem* francium.

fra·cas [FRAY-kəs] *n* noisy quarrel; uproar, brawl.

frac·tion [FRAK-shən] *n* numerical quantity not an integer; fragment, piece. **frac'tion·al** *adj* constituting a fraction; forming but a small part; insignificant.

frac·tious [FRAK-shəs] *adj* unruly, irritable.

frac·ture [FRAK-chər] *n* breakage, part broken; breaking of bone; breach, rupture. ▶ *v* **-tured, -tur·ing.** break.

frag·ile [FRAJ-əl] *adj* breakable; frail; delicate. **fra·gil'i·ty** *n*

frag·ment [FRAG-mənt] *n* piece broken off; small portion, incomplete part. ▶ *v* (-ment). **frag'men·tar·y** [-te-ree] *adj*

fra·grant [FRAY-grənt] *adj* sweet-smelling. **fra'grance** *n* scent.

frail [frayl] *adj* **-er, -est.** fragile, delicate; infirm; in weak health; morally weak. **frail'ly** *adv* **frail'ty** *n, pl* **-ties.**

frame [fraym] *n* that in which thing is set, as square of wood around picture, etc.; structure; build of body; constitution; mood; individual exposure on strip of film. ▶ *vt* put together, make; adapt; put into words; put into frame; bring false charge against. **frame-up** *n* *inf* plot, manufactured evidence. **frame'work** *n* structure into which completing parts can be fitted; supporting work.

franc [frangk] *n* monetary unit of Switzerland and (formerly) France.

fran·chise [FRAN-chīz] *n* right of voting; citizenship; privilege or right, esp. right to sell certain goods. ▶ *v* **-chised, -chis·ing.**

fran·gi·pane [FRAN-jə-payn] *n* type of pastry cake; its filling.

fran·gi·pan·i [fran-jə-PAN-ee] *n* tropical American shrub; perfume made of its flower.

frank [frangk] *adj* **-er, -est.** candid, outspoken; sincere. ▶ *n* official mark on letter either canceling stamp or ensuring delivery without stamp. ▶ *vt* mark letter thus. **frank'ly** *adv* candidly. **frank'ness** *n*

frank·furt·er [FRANGK-fər-tər] *n* smoked sausage, hot dog.

frank·in·cense [FRANG-kin-sens] *n* aromatic gum resin burned as incense.

fran·tic [FRAN-tik] *adj* distracted with rage, grief, joy, etc.; frenzied. **fran'ti·cal·ly** *adv*

fra·ter·nal [frə-TUR-nl] *adj* of brother, brotherly. **fra·ter'nal·ly** *adv* **fra·ter'ni·ty** *n, pl* **-ties.** brotherliness; brotherhood; college society. **frat·er·ni·za'tion** *n* **frat'er·nize** *vi* **-nized, -niz·ing.** to associate, make friends.

frat·ri·cid'al [-SĪD-əl] *adj* **frat'ri·cide** *n* killing, killer of brother or sister.

fraud [frawd] *n* criminal deception; swindle, imposture. **fraud·u·lence** [FRAW-jə-ləns] *n* **fraud'u·lent** *adj*

fraught [frawt] *adj* filled (with), involving.

fray¹ *n* fight; noisy quarrel.

fray² *v* wear through by rubbing; make, become ragged at edge.

fraz·zle [FRAZ-əl] *inf* ▶ *v* **-zled, -zling.** make or become exhausted; make or become irritated. ▶ *n* exhausted state.

freak [freek] *n* abnormal person, animal, thing. ▶ *adj* **freak'ish** *adj* **freak'y** *adj* **freak·i·er, freak·i·est.** **freak out** *sl* (cause to) hallucinate, be wildly excited, etc.

freck·le [FREK-əl] *n* light brown spot on skin, esp. caused by sun; any small spot. ▶ *v* **-led, -ling.** bring, come out in freckles.

free *adj* **fre·er, fre·est.** able to act at will, not under compulsion or restraint; not restricted or affected by; not subject to cost or tax;

independent; not exact or literal; generous; not in use; (of person) not occupied, having no appointment; loose, not fixed. ▶ *vt* **freed, free·ing.** set at liberty; remove (obstacles, pain, etc.); rid (of). **free'dom** *n* **free'ly** *adv* **free-for-all** *n* brawl. **free'hand** *adj* drawn without guiding instruments. **free'lance** [-lans] *adj, n* (of) self-employed, unattached person. **Free·ma·son** [-may-sən] *n* member of secret fraternity for mutual help. **freemasonry** *n* principles of Freemasons; fellowship, secret brotherhood. **free'-range** *adj* (of livestock and poultry) kept, produced in natural, nonintensive conditions. **free space** region that has no gravitational and electromagnetic fields. **free speech** right to express opinions publicly. **free-swinging** *adj* recklessly daring. **free-think'er** *n* skeptic who forms own opinions, esp. in religion. **free trade** international trade free of protective tariffs. **free'way** *n* express highway.

freeze [freez] *v* **froze, fro·zen, freez·ing.** change (by reduction of temperature) from liquid to solid, as water to ice. ▶ *vt* preserve (food, etc.) by extreme cold, as in freezer; fix (prices, etc.). ▶ *vi* feel very cold; become rigid as with fear; stop. **freez'er** *n* insulated cabinet for long-term storage of perishable foodstuffs. **frozen** *adj* of assets, etc., unrealizable. **freezing point** temperature at which liquid becomes solid.

freight [frayt] *n* commercial transport (esp. by rail, ship); cost of this; goods so carried. ▶ *vt* send as or by freight. **freight'er** *n*

French *n* language spoken by people of France. ▶ *adj* of, or pertaining to France. **French dressing** salad dressing. **French fries** deep-fried strips of potato. **French horn** musical wind instrument. **French leave** unauthorized leave. **French**

window window extended to floor level and used as door.

fre·net·ic [frə-NET-ik] *adj* frenzied.

fren·zy [FREN-zee] *n, pl* **-zies.** violent mental derangement; wild excitement. **fren'zied** *adj*

fre·quent [FREE-kwənt] *adj* happening often; common; numerous. ▶ *vt* [fri-KWENT] go often to. **fre'quen·cy** *n, pl* **-cies.** rate of occurrence; in radio, etc. cycles per second of alternating current. **fre·quen'ta·tive** [fri-KWEN-tə-tiv] *adj* expressing repetition.

fres·co [FRES-koh] *n, pl* **-coes.** method of painting in water color on plaster of wall before it dries; painting done thus.

fresh *adj* **-er, -est.** not stale; new; additional; different; recent; inexperienced; pure; not pickled, frozen, etc.; not faded or dimmed; not tired; of wind, strong; *inf* impudent; forward. **fresh'en** *v* **fresh'et** *n* rush of water at river mouth; flood of river water. **fresh'ly** *adv* **fresh'man** *n* first-year high school or college student.

fret[1] *v* **fret·ted, fret·ting.** be irritated, worry. ▶ *n* irritation. **fret'ful** *adj* irritable, (easily) upset.

fret[2] *n* repetitive geometrical pattern; small bar on fingerboard of guitar, etc. ▶ *vt* **fret·ted, fret·ting.** ornament with carved pattern. **fret saw** saw with narrow blade and fine teeth, used for fretwork. **fret'work** *n* carved or open woodwork in ornamental patterns and devices.

Freud·i·an [FROI-dee-ən] *adj* pert. to Austrian psychologist Sigmund Freud, or his theories.

fri·a·ble [FRĪ-ə-bəl] *adj* easily crumbled. **fri·a·bil'i·ty,** *n*

fri·ar [FRĪ-ər] *n* member of mendicant religious order. **fri'ar·y** *n* house of friars.

fric·as·see [frik-ə-SEE] *n* dish of pieces of chicken or meat, fried or stewed and served with rich sauce. ▶ *vt* **-seed, -see·ing.** cook thus.

fric·tion [FRIK-shən] *n* rubbing; resistance met with by body moving over another; clash of wills, etc., disagreement. **fric'tion·al** *adj*

fried pt./pp. of FRY.

friend [frend] *n* one well known to another and regarded with affection and loyalty; intimate associate; supporter; (**F-**) Quaker. **friend'less** *adj* **friend'li·ness** *n* **friend'ly** *adj* **-li·er, -li·est.** having disposition of a friend, kind; favorable. **friend'ship** *n* **friendly fire** *Military* shooting or bombing that injures or kills comrades or allies.

frieze [freez] *n* ornamental band, strip (on wall).

frig·ate [FRIG-it] *n* old (sailing) warship corresponding to modern cruiser; fast warship equipped for escort and antisubmarine duties.

fright [frīt] *n* sudden fear; shock; alarm; grotesque or ludicrous person or thing. **fright'en** *vt* cause fear, fright in. **fright'ful** *adj* terrible, calamitous; shocking; *inf* very great, very large. **fright'ful·ly** *adv inf* terribly; very.

frig·id [FRIJ-id] *adj* formal, dull; (sexually) unfeeling; cold. **fri·gid'i·ty** *n* **frig'id·ly** *adv*

frill *n* fluted strip of fabric gathered at one edge; ruff of hair, feathers around neck of dog, bird, etc.; fringe; unnecessary words, politeness; superfluous thing; adornment. ▶ *vt* make into, decorate with frill.

fringe [frinj] *n* ornamental edge of hanging threads, tassels, etc.; anything like this; edge, limit. ▶ *vt* **fringed, fring·ing.** adorn with, serve as, fringe. **fringe benefit** benefit provided in addition to regular pay.

frip·per·y [FRIP-ə-ree] *n, pl* **-per·ies.** finery; trivia.

fris·bee [FRIZ-bee] *n* ® disk-shaped object for throwing and catching as a sport or pastime.

frisk *vi* move, leap, playfully. ▶ *vt* wave briskly; search (person) for concealed weapons, etc. ▶ *n* **frisk'y** *adj* **frisk·i·er, frisk·i·est.**

frit·ter¹ [FRIT-ər] *vt* waste. **fritter away** throw away, waste.

fritter² *n* small deep-fried cake of batter oft. containing corn.

friv·o·lous [FRI-ə-ləs] *adj* not serious, unimportant; flippant. **fri·vol'i·ty** *n*

frizz *vt* curl into small crisp curls. ▶ *n* frizzed hair. **friz'zy** *adj* **-zi·er, -zi·est.**

fro [froh] *adv* away, only in *to and fro.*

frock [frok] *n* woman's dress; various similar garments. ▶ *vt* dress with frock; invest with office of priest.

frog¹ *n* tailless amphibian animal developed from tadpole. **frog'man** *n* swimmer equipped for swimming, working, underwater.

frog² *n* ornamental coat fastening of button and loop; (military) attachment to belt to carry sword.

frol·ic [FROL-ik] *n* merrymaking. ▶ *vi* **-icked, -ick·ing.** behave playfully. **frol'ic·some** *adj*

from [frum] *prep* expressing point of departure, source, distance, cause, change of state, etc.

frond *n* plant organ consisting of stem and foliage, usually with fruit forms, esp. in ferns.

front [frunt] *n* fore part; position directly before or ahead; battle line or area; *Meteorology* dividing line between two air masses of different characteristics; outward aspect, bearing; *inf* something serving as a respectable cover for another, usu. criminal, activity; field of activity; group with common goal. ▶ *v* look, face; *inf* be a cover for. ▶ *adj* of, at, the front. **front'age** [-ij] *n* front of building; property line along street, lake, etc. **fron'tal** [-əl] *adj* **fron'tier** [-TEER] *n* part of country that borders on another. **fron'tis·piece** *n* illustration facing title page of book.

frost [frawst] *n* frozen dew or mist; act or state of freezing; weather in which temperature falls below point at which water turns to ice. ▶ *v* cover, be covered with frost or something similar in appearance; give slightly roughened surface. **frost'i·ly** *adv* **frost'y** *adj* **frost·i·er, frost·i·est.** accompanied by frost; chilly; cold; unfriendly. **frost'bite** *n* destruction by cold of tissue, esp. of fingers, ears, etc.

froth [frawth] *n* collection of small bubbles, foam; scum; idle talk. ▶ *v* (cause to) foam. **froth'i·ly** *adv* **froth'y** *adj* **froth·i·er, froth·i·est.**

frown *vi* wrinkle brows. ▶ *n*

frowz·y [FROW-zee] *adj* **frowz·i·er, frowz·i·est.** dirty, unkempt.

froze pt. of FREEZE. **frozen** pp. of FREEZE.

fruc·ti·fy [FRUK-tə-fī] *v* **-fied, -fy·ing.** (cause to) bear fruit.

fru·gal [FROO-gəl] *adj* sparing; thrifty, economical; meager. **fru·gal'i·ty** *n*

fruit [froot] *n* seed and its envelope, esp. edible one; vegetable product; (usu in pl) result, benefit. ▶ *vi* bear fruit. **fruit'ful** [-fəl] *adj* **fru·i·tion** [froo-ISH-ən] *n* enjoyment; realization of hopes. **fruit'less** *adj* **fruit'y** *adj* **fruit·i·er, fruit·i·est.**

frump *n* dowdy woman. **frump'ish** *adj* **frump'y** *adj* **frump·i·er, frump·i·est.**

frus·trate [FRUS-trayt] *vt* **-trat·ed, -trat·ing.** thwart, balk; baffle, disappoint. **frus·tra'tion** *n*

fry¹ [frī] *v* **fried, fry·ing.** cook with fat; be cooked thus; *sl* be executed by electrocution.

fry² *n, pl* **fry.** young of fish. **small fry** young or insignificant beings.

fuch·sia [FYOO-shə] *n* ornamental shrub with purple-red flowers.

fud·dle [FUD-l] *v* **-dled, -dling.** (cause to) be intoxicated, confused. ▶ *n* this state.

fudge¹ [fuj] *n* soft, variously flavored candy.

fudge² *vt* **fudged, fudg·ing.** make, do carelessly or dishonestly; fake.

fuel [FYOO-əl] *n* material for burning as source of heat or power; something that nourishes. ▶ *vt* provide with fuel.

fu·gi·tive [FYOO-ji-tiv] *n* one who flees, esp. from arrest or pursuit.

▶ *adj* fleeing, elusive.

fugue [fyoog] *n* musical composition in which themes are repeated in different parts.

Füh·rer [FYUUR-ər] *n Ger* leader: title used by Hitler as Nazi dictator.

ful·crum [FUUL-krəm] *n, pl* **-crums.** point on which a lever is placed for support.

ful·fill [fuul-FIL] *vi* satisfy; carry out; obey; satisfy (desire, etc.). **ful·fill′ment** *n*

full [fuul] *adj* **-er, -est.** containing as much as possible; abundant; complete; ample; plump; (of garment) of ample cut. ▶ *adv* very; quite; exactly. **ful′ly** *adv* **full′ness** *n* **ful·some** [FUUL-səm] *adj* excessive. **full·blown′** [-BLOHN] *adj* fully developed.

ful·mi·nate [FUL-mə-nayt] *vi* **-nat·ed, -nat·ing.** (esp. with *against*) criticize harshly. ▶ *n* chemical compound exploding readily. **ful·mi·na′tion** *n*

fulsome see FULL.

fum·ble [FUM-bəl] *v* **-bled, -bling.** grope about; handle awkwardly; in football, etc., drop (ball). ▶ *n* awkward attempt.

fume [fyoom] *vi* be angry; emit smoke or vapor. ▶ *n* smoke; vapor. **fu′mi·gate** *vt* **-gat·ed, -gat·ing.** apply fumes or smoke to, esp. for disinfection. **fu′mi·ga·tor** *n*

fun *n* anything enjoyable, amusing, etc. **fun′ni·ly** *adv* **fun′ny** *adj* **-ni·er, -ni·est.** comical; odd; difficult to explain.

func·tion [FUNGK-shən] *n* work a thing is designed to do; (large) social event; duty; profession; *Math* quantity whose value depends on varying value of another. ▶ *vi* operate, work. **func′tion·al** *adj* having a special purpose; practical, necessary; capable of operating. **func′tion·ar·y** *n, pl* **-ar·ies.** official.

fund *n* stock or sum of money; supply, store. ▶ *pl* money resources. ▶ *vt* (in financial, business dealings) provide or obtain funds in various ways.

fun·da·men·tal [fun-də-MEN-tl] *adj*

of, affecting, or serving as, the base; essential, primary. ▶ *n* basic rule or fact. **fun′da·ment** [-mənt] *n* buttocks; foundation. **fun·da·men′tal·ism** *n* **fun·da·men′tal·ist** *n* one laying stress on belief in literal and verbal inspiration of Bible and other traditional creeds.

fu·ner·al [FYOO-nər-əl] *n* (ceremony associated with) burial or cremation of dead. **fu·ne′re·al** [-NEE-ree-əl] *adj* like a funeral; dark; gloomy.

fun·gi·ble [FUN-jə-bəl] *adj* (of assets) freely exchangeable.

fun·gus [FUNG-gəs] *n, pl* **-gi** [-jī] or **-gus·es.** plant without leaves, flowers, or roots, as mushroom, mold. **fun′gal** *adj* **fun′gous** *adj* **fun′gi·cide** [-jə-sīd] *n* fungus destroyer.

fu·nic·u·lar [fyoo-NIK-yə-lər] *n* cable railway on mountainside with two counterbalanced cars.

funk [fungk] *n* style of dance music with strong beat. **funk′y** *adj* **funk·i·er, funk·i·est.** (of music) having a strong beat; *sl* unconventional; *sl* fetid.

fun·nel [FUN-l] *n* cone-shaped vessel or tube; chimney of locomotive or ship; ventilating shaft. ▶ *v* **-neled, -nel·ing.** (cause to) move as through funnel; concentrate, focus.

funny see FUN.

fur *n* soft hair of animal; garment, etc.; of dressed skins with such hair; furlike coating. ▶ *vt* **furred, fur·ring.** cover with fur. **fur′ri·er** *n* dealer in furs; repairer, dresser of furs. **fur′ry** *adj* **-ri·er, -ri·est.** of, like fur.

fur′bish *vt* clean up.

fu·ri·ous [FYUUR-ee-əs] *adj* extremely angry; violent. **fu′ri·ous·ly** *adv*

furl *vt* roll up and bind (sail, umbrella, etc.).

fur·long [FUR-lawng] *n* eighth of mile.

fur·lough [FUR-loh] *n* leave of absence, esp. to soldier.

fur·nace [FUR-nis] *n* apparatus for applying great heat to metals; closed fireplace for heating boiler, etc.; hot place.

fur'nish *vt* fit up house with furniture; equip; supply, yield. **fur'ni·ture** [-chər] *n* movable contents of a house or room.

fu·ror [FYUUR-or] *n* public outburst, esp. of protest; sudden enthusiasm.

fur·row [FUR-oh] *n* trench as made by plow; groove. ▶ *vt* make furrows in.

fur·ther [FUR-*th*ər] *adv* more; in addition; at or to a greater distance or extent. ▶ *adj* additional; more distant; comp. of FAR. ▶ *vt* help forward; promote. **fur'ther·ance** *n* **fur'ther·more** *adv* besides. **fur'thest** *adj* sup. of FAR. ▶ *adv* **fur'ther·most** *adj*

fur·tive [FUR-tiv] *adj* stealthy, sly, secret. **fur'tive·ly** *adv*

fu·ry [FYUUR-ee] *n, pl* **-ries.** wild rage, violent anger; violence of storm, etc.; usu. snake-haired avenging deity.

fuse [fyooz] *v* **fused, fus·ing.** blend by melting; melt with heat; amalgamate. ▶ *n* (also **fuze**) soft wire, with low melting point, used as safety device in electrical systems; device (orig. combustible cord) for igniting bomb, etc. **fu'si·ble** [-zə-bəl] *adj* **fu·sion** [FYOO-zhən] *n* melting; state of being melted; union of things, as

atomic nuclei, as if melted together.

fu·se·lage [FYOO-sə-lah*zh*] *n* body of aircraft.

fu·sil·lade [FYOO-sə-layd] *n* continuous discharge of firearms.

fuss *n* needless bustle or concern; complaint; objection. ▶ *vi* make fuss. **fuss'i·ly** *adv* **fuss'i·ness** *n* **fuss'y** *adj* **fuss·i·er, fuss·i·est.** particular; hard to please; overmeticulous; overelaborate.

fus·tian [FUS-chən] *n* thick cotton cloth; inflated language.

fus·ty [FUS-tee] *adj* **-ti·er, -ti·est.** moldy; smelling of damp; old-fashioned. **fus'ti·ness** *n*

fu·tile [FYOOT-l] *adj* useless, ineffectual, trifling. **fu·til'i·ty** *n, pl* **-ties.**

fu·ton [FOO-ton] *n* Japanese padded quilt, laid on floor as bed.

fu·ture [FYOO-chər] *n* time to come; what will happen; tense of verb indicating this; likelihood of development. ▶ *adj* that will be; of, relating to, time to come. **fu'tur·ism** *n* movement in art marked by revolt against tradition. **fu'tur·ist** *n, adj* **fu·tur·ist'ic** *adj* ultramodern. **fu·tu'ri·ty** [-TUUR-i-tee] *n, pl* **-ties.** future time.

fuze see FUSE.

fuzz *n* fluff; fluffy or frizzed hair; blur; *sl* police (officer). **fuzz'y** *adj* **fuzz·i·er, fuzz·i·est.** fluffy, frizzy; blurred, indistinct.

G g

Ga *Chem* gallium.

gab·ar·dine, gab·er·dine [GAB-ər-deen] *n* fine twill cloth like serge; *Hist* loose outer garment worn by Orthodox Jews.

gab·ble [GAB-əl] *v* **-bled, -bling.** talk, utter inarticulately or too fast. ▶ *n* such talk. **gab** *n, v* **gabbed, gab·bing.** *inf* talk, chatter. **gab'by** *adj* **-bi·er, -bi·est.** *inf* talkative. **gift of gab** eloquence, loquacity.

ga·ble [GAY-bəl] *n* triangular upper part of wall at end of ridged roof.

gad *vi* **gad·ded, gad·ding. gad about, around** go around in search of pleasure. **gad'a·bout** *n* pleasure seeker.

gad·fly [GAD-flī] *n, pl* **-flies.** cattle-biting fly; worrying person.

gadg·et [GAJ-it] *n* small mechanical device; object valued for its novelty or ingenuity. **gadg'et·ry** *n*

Gael [gayl] *n* one who speaks Gaelic. **Gael'ic** *n* language of Ireland and Scottish Highlands. ▶ *adj* of Gaels, their language or customs.

gaff *n* stick with iron hook for landing fish; spar for top of fore-and-aft sail. ▶ *vt* seize (fish) with gaff.

gaffe [gaf] *n* blunder; tactless remark.

gaf·fer [GAF-ər] *n inf* old man; senior electrician on a TV or movie set.

gag¹ *v* **gagged, gag·ging.** stop up (person's mouth) with cloth, etc.; retch, choke. ▶ *n* cloth, etc. put into, tied across mouth.

gag² *n* joke, funny story.

ga·ga [GAH-gah] *adj inf* foolishly enthusiastic; infatuated.

gage¹ [gayj] *n* pledge, thing given as security; challenge, or something symbolizing one.

gage² see GAUGE.

gag·gle [GAG-əl] *n* flock of geese; *inf* disorderly crowd.

gaiety see GAY.

gain [gayn] *vt* obtain, secure; obtain as profit; win; earn; reach. ▶ *vi* increase, improve; get nearer; (of watch, clock) operate too fast. ▶ *n* profit; increase, improvement. **gain'ful·ly** *adv* profitably; for a wage, salary.

gain·say [GAYN-say] *vt* **-said, -say·ing.** deny, contradict.

gait [gayt] *n* manner of walking; pace.

Gal. Galatians.

ga·la [GAY-lə] *n* festive occasion; celebration; special entertainment. ▶ *adj* festive; showy.

gal·ax·y [GAL-ək-see] *n, pl* **-ax·ies.** system of stars bound by gravitational forces; splendid gathering, esp. of famous people. **ga·lac·tic** [gə-LAK-tik] *adj*

gale [gayl] *n* strong wind; *inf* loud outburst, esp. of laughter.

gall¹ [gawl] *n inf* impudence; bitterness. **gall'blad·der** *n* sac attached to liver, reservoir for bile. **gall'stone** *n* hard secretion in gallbladder or ducts leading from it.

gall² *n* painful swelling, esp. on horse; sore caused by chafing. ▶ *vt* make sore by rubbing; vex, irritate.

gall³ *n* abnormal growth or excrescence on trees, etc.

gal·lant [GAL-ənt] *adj* fine, stately, brave; [gə-LANT] chivalrous, very attentive to women. ▶ *n* [gə-LANT] lover, suitor; dashing, fashionable young man. **gal'lant·ly** *adv* **gal'lant·ry** *n, pl* **-ries.**

gal·le·on [GAL-ee-ən] *n* large, high-built sailing ship of war.

gal·ler·y [GAL-ə-ree] *n, pl* **-ler·ies.** covered walk with side openings, colonnade; platform or projecting upper floor in theater, etc.; group of spectators; long, narrow platform on outside of building; room or rooms for special purposes, e.g. showing works of art; passage in wall, open to interior of building.

gal·ley [GAL-ee] *n, pl* **-leys.** one-decked vessel with sails and oars, usu. rowed by slaves or criminals; kitchen of ship or aircraft; printer's tray for composed type. **galley proof** printer's proof before being made up into pages. **galley slave** one condemned to row in galley; drudge.

Gal·lic [GAL-ik] *adj* of ancient Gaul; French. **Gal'li·cism** *n* French word or idiom.

gal·li·um [GAL-ee-əm] *n* soft, gray metal of great fusibility.

gal·li·vant [GAL-ə-vant] *vi* gad about.

gal·lon [GAL-ən] *n* liquid measure of four quarts (3.7853 liters).

gal·lop [GAL-əp] *v* go, ride at gallop; move fast. ▶ *n* horse's fastest pace with all four feet off ground together in each stride; ride at this pace. **gal'lop·ing** *adj* at a gallop; speedy, swift.

gal·lows [GAL-ohz] *n* structure, usu. of two upright beams and crossbar, esp. for hanging criminals.

Gal·lup poll [GAL-əp] *n* method of finding out public opinion by questioning a cross section of the population.

ga·loot [gə-LOOT] *n inf* silly, clumsy person.

ga·lore [gə-LOR] *adv* in plenty.

ga·losh·es [gə-LOSH-əz] *pl n* waterproof overshoes.

gal·van·ic [gal-VAN-ik] *adj* of, producing, concerning electric current, esp. when produced chemically; *inf* resembling effect of electric shock, startling.

gal'va·nize [-və-nīz] *vt* **-nized, -niz·ing.** stimulate to action; excite, startle; cover (iron, etc.) with protective zinc coating.

gam'bit *n Chess* opening involving sacrifice of a piece; any opening maneuver, comment, etc. intended to secure an advantage.

gam·ble [GAM-bəl] *vi* **-bled, -bling.** play games of chance to win money; act on expectation of something. ▶ *n* risky undertaking; bet, wager. **gam'bler** *n*

gam·bol [GAM-bəl] *vi* **-boled, -bol·ing.** skip, jump playfully. ▶ *n* frolic.

game¹ [gaym] *n* diversion, pastime; jest; contest for amusement; scheme, strategy; animals or birds hunted; their flesh. ▶ *adj* **gam·er, gam·est.** brave; willing. **game'ster** *n* gambler. **game'cock** *n* rooster bred for fighting. **game'keep·er** *n* person employed to breed game, prevent poaching.

game² *adj* lame, crippled (leg).

gam·ete [GAM-eet] *n Biology* a sexual cell that unites with another for reproduction or the formation of a new individual.

gam·ma [GAM-ə] *n* third letter of the Greek alphabet. **gamma ray** a very penetrative electromagnetic ray.

gam·mon [GAM-ən] *n* cured or smoked ham; lower end of side of bacon.

gam·ut [GAM-ət] *n* whole range or scale (orig. of musical notes).

gan·der [GAN-dər] *n* male goose; *sl* a quick look.

gang *n* (criminal) group; organized group of persons working together. ▶ *vi* (esp. with *together*) form gang. **gang up** *vi* form an alliance (against).

gang'ling *adj* lanky, awkward in movement.

gan·gli·on [GANG-glee-ən] *n, pl* **-gli·a** [-glee-ə] nerve nucleus.

gang·plank [GANG-plangk] *n* portable bridge for boarding or leaving vessel.

gan·grene [GANG-green] *n* death or decay of body tissue as a result of disease or injury. **gan'gre·nous** [-grə-nəs] *adj*

gang·sta rap [GANG-sta] *n* a style of rap music featuring lyrics that are anti-authority and often derogatory to women.

gang·ster [GANG-stər] *n* member of criminal gang; notorious or hardened criminal.

gang'way *n* bridge from ship to shore; anything similar. ▶ *interj* make way!

gan·try [GAN-tree] *n, pl* **-tries.** structure to support crane, railway signals, etc.; framework beside rocket on launching pad.

gap *n* breach, opening, interval; cleft; empty space.

gape [gayp] *vi* **gaped, gap·ing.** stare in wonder; open mouth wide, as in yawning; be, become wide open.

ga·rage [gə-RAH*ZH*] *n* (part of) building to house automobiles; refueling and repair center for them. ▶ *vt* **-raged, -rag·ing.** leave automobile in garage.

garb [gahrb] *n* dress; fashion of dress. ▶ *vt* dress, clothe.

gar·bage [GAHR-bij] *n* rubbish; refuse. **garbage can** large, usu. cylindrical container for household rubbish.

gar·ble [GAHR-bəl] *vt* **-bled, -bling.** jumble or distort (story, account, etc.).

gar·den [GAHR-dn] *n* ground for growing flowers, fruit, or vegetables. ▶ *vi* cultivate garden. **gar·den·er** [GAHRD-nər] *n* **gar·den·ing** [GAHRD-ning] *n*

gar·de·nia [gahr-DEE-nyə] *n* (sub)tropical shrub, with fragrant white or yellow flowers.

gar·gan·tu·an [gahr-GAN-choo-ən] *adj* immense, enormous, huge.

gar·gle [GAHR-gəl] *v* **-gled, -gling.** ▶ *vi* wash throat with liquid kept moving by the breath. ▶ *vt* wash (throat) thus. ▶ *n* gargling; preparation for this purpose.

gar·goyle [GAHR-goil] *n* carved (grotesque) face on waterspout, esp. on Gothic church.

gar·ish [GAIR-ish] *adj* showy; gaudy.

gar·land [GAHR-lənd] *n* wreath of flowers worn or hung as decoration. ▶ *vt* decorate with garlands.

gar·lic [GAHR-lik] *n* (bulb of) plant with strong smell and taste, used in cooking and seasoning.

gar·ment [GAHR-mənt] *n* article of clothing. ▶ *pl* clothes.

gar·ner [GAHR-nər] *vt* store up, collect, as if in granary.

gar·net [GAHR-nit] *n* red semiprecious stone.

gar·nish [GAHR-nish] *vt* adorn, decorate (esp. food). ▶ *n* material for this.

gar·ret [GAR-it] *n* small (usu. wretched) room on top floor, attic.

gar·ri·son [GAR-ə-sən] *n* troops stationed in town, fort, etc.; fortified place. ▶ *vt* furnish or occupy with garrison.

gar·rote [gə-ROHT] *n* capital punishment by strangling; apparatus for this. ▶ *vt* **-rot·ed, -rot·ing.** execute, kill thus. **gar·rot'er** *n*

gar·ru·lous [GAR-ə-ləs] *adj* (frivolously) talkative. **gar·ru·li·ty** [gə-ROO-li-tee] *n* loquacity.

gar·ter [GAHR-tər] *n* band worn around leg to hold up sock or stocking. **garter snake** type of harmless snake.

gas *n, pl* **-es.** airlike substance, esp. one that does not liquefy or solidify at ordinary temperatures; fossil fuel in form of gas, used for heating or lighting; gaseous anesthetic; poisonous or irritant substance dispersed through atmosphere in warfare, etc.; gasoline; automobile accelerator; *sl* idle, boastful talk. ▶ *v* **gassed, gas·sing.** project gas over; poison with gas; fill with gas; *sl* talk idly, boastfully. **gas'e·ous** [-ee-əs] *adj* of, like gas. **gass'y** *adj* **-si·er, -si·est.** filled with gas. **gas'bag** *n sl* person who talks idly. **gas mask** mask with chemical filter to guard against poisoning by gas.

gash *n* gaping wound, slash. ▶ *vt* cut deeply.

gas·ket [GAS-kit] *n* rubber, neoprene, etc. used as seal between metal faces, esp. in engines.

gas·o·hol [GAS-ə-hawl] *n* mixture of gasoline and ethyl alcohol used as fuel for automobiles.

gas·o·line [gas-ə-LEEN] *n* refined petroleum used in automobiles, etc.

gasp *vi* catch breath with open mouth, as in exhaustion or surprise. ▶ *n* convulsive catching of breath.

gas·tric [GAS-trik] *adj* of stomach. **gas·tro·nom'i·cal** [-trə-NOM-ə-kəl] *adj* **gas·tron·o·my** [ga-STRON-ə-mee] *n* art of good eating.

gas·tro·en·ter·i·tis [gas-troh-en-tə-RĪ-tis] *n* inflammation of stomach and intestines.

gas·tro·pod [GAS-trə-pod] *n* mollusk, e.g. snail, with disklike organ of locomotion on ventral surface.

gate [gayt] *n* opening in wall, fence, etc.; barrier for closing it; sluice; any entrance or way out; (entrance money paid by) those attending sports event. **gate'-crash·er** *n inf* person who enters sports event, social function, etc. uninvited.

gath·er [GATH-ər] *v* (cause to) assemble; increase gradually; draw together. ▶ *vt* collect; learn, understand; draw material into small tucks or folds. **gath'er·ing** *n* assembly.

gauche [gohsh] *adj* tactless, blundering. **gau'che·rie** *n* awkwardness, clumsiness.

gau·cho [GOW-choh] *n, pl* **-chos.** cowboy of S Amer. pampas.

gaud [gawd] *n* showy ornament. **gaud'i·ly** *adv* **gaud'iness** *n* **gaud'y** *adj* **gaud·i·er, gaud·i·est.** showy in tasteless way.

gauge, gage [gayj] *n* standard measure, as of diameter of wire, thickness of sheet metal, etc.; distance between rails of railway; capacity, extent; instrument for measuring such things as wire, rainfall, height of water in boiler, etc. ▶ *vt* **gauged, gaug·ing.** measure; estimate.

gaunt [gawnt] *adj* **-er, -est.** extremely lean, haggard.

gaunt·let [GAWNT-lit] *n* armored glove; glove covering part of arm. **run the gauntlet** formerly, run as punishment between two lines of men striking at runner with sticks, etc.; be exposed to criticism or unpleasant treatment; undergo ordeal. **throw down the gauntlet** offer challenge.

gauss [gows] *n* unit of density of magnetic field.

gauze [gawz] *n* thin transparent fabric of silk, wire, etc.; this as surgical dressing.

gave pt. of GIVE.

gav·el [GAV-əl] *n* mallet of presiding officer or auctioneer.

ga·votte [gə-VOT] *n* lively dance; music for it.

gawk *vi* stare stupidly. **gawk'y** *adj* **gawk·i·er, gawk·i·est.** clumsy, awkward.

gay *adj* **-er, -est.** homosexual; merry; lively; cheerful; bright; lighthearted; showy; given to pleasure. ▶ *n* homosexual. **gai'e·ty** *n, pl* **-ties. gai'ly** *adv*

gaze [gayz] *vi* **gazed, gaz·ing.** look fixedly. ▶ *n*

ga·ze·bo [gə-ZEE-boh] *n* summerhouse, small roofed structure, with extensive view.

ga·zelle [gə-ZEL] *n* small graceful antelope.

ga·zette [gə-ZET] *n* name for newspaper. **gaz·et·teer'** *n* geographical dictionary.

ga·zil·lion [gə-ZIL-yən] *n inf* extremely large unspecified number.

Gd *Chem* gadolinium.

Ge *Chem* germanium.

gear [geer] *n* set of wheels working together, esp. by engaging cogs; connection by which engine, motor, etc. is brought into work; arrangement by which driving wheel of cycle, automobile, etc. performs more or fewer revolutions relative to pedals, pistons, etc.; equipment; clothing; goods, utensils; apparatus, tackle, tools; rigging; harness. ▶ *vt* adapt (one thing) so as to conform with another; provide with gear; put in gear. **gear'box** *n* case protecting gearing of bicycle, automobile, etc. **in gear** connected up and ready for work. **out of gear** disconnected.

geek n inf boring, unattractive person.

geese [gees] pl. of GOOSE.

gee·zer [GEE-zər] n sl (old, eccentric) man.

ge·fil·te fish [gə-FIL-tə] in Jewish cookery, a dish of various freshwater fish chopped and blended with eggs, matzo meal, etc.

Gei·ger count·er [GĪ-gər] n instrument for detecting radioactivity, cosmic radiation and charged atomic particles.

gei·sha [GAY-shə] n in Japan, professional female entertainer and companion for men.

gel [jel] n jelly-like substance. ▶ vi **gelled, gel·ling.** form a gel; jell.

gel·a·tin [JEL-ə-tn] n substance prepared from animal bones, etc., producing edible jelly; anything resembling this. **ge·lat·i·nous** [jə-LAT-n-əs] adj like gelatin or jelly.

geld vt castrate. **geld'ing** n castrated horse.

gel·id [JEL-id] adj very cold.

gem [jem] n precious stone, esp. when cut and polished; treasure. ▶ vt **gemmed, gem·ming.** adorn with gems.

Gen. Genesis.

gen·darme [ZHAHN-dahrm] n policeman in France.

gen·der [JEN-dər] n sex, male or female; grammatical classification of nouns, according to sex (actual or attributed).

gene [jeen] n biological factor determining inherited characteristics.

ge·ne·al·o·gy [jee-nee-AL-ə-jee] n, pl **-gies.** account of descent from ancestors; pedigree; study of pedigrees. **ge·ne·a·log'i·cal** [-LOJ'-ə-kəl] adj

genera pl. of GENUS.

gen·er·al [JEN-ər-əl] adj common, widespread; not particular or specific; applicable to all or most; usual, prevalent; miscellaneous; dealing with main element only; vague, indefinite. ▶ n army officer of rank above colonel.

gen·er·al'i·ty n, pl **-ties.** general principle; vague statement; indefiniteness. **gen·er·al·i·za'tion** n general conclusion from particular instance; inference. **gen'er·al·ize** v **-ized, -iz·ing.** ▶ vt reduce to general laws. ▶ vi draw general conclusions.

general practitioner physician with practice not restricted to particular branch of medicine.

gen·er·ate [JEN-ə-rayt] vt **-at·ed, -at·ing.** bring into being; produce. **gen·er·a'tion** n bringing into being; all persons born about same time; average time between two such generations (about 30 years). **gen'er·a·tor** n apparatus for producing (steam, electricity, etc.); begetter.

ge·ner·ic [ji-NER-ik] adj belonging to, characteristic of class or genus. **ge·ner'i·cal·ly** adv **generic drug** one sold without brand name.

gen·er·ous [JEN-ər-əs] adj liberal, free in giving; abundant. **gen·er·os'i·ty** n, pl **-ties.**

gen·e·sis [JEN-ə-sis] n, pl **-ses** [-seez] origin; mode of formation; (G-) first book of Bible.

ge·net·ics [jə-NET-iks] n scientific study of heredity and variation in organisms. **ge·net'ic** adj **ge·net'i·cist** n **genetic engineering** deliberate modification of heredity characteristics by treatment of DNA to transfer selected genes.

gen·ial [JEEN-yəl] adj cheerful, warm in behavior; mild, conducive to growth. **ge·ni·al'i·ty** n

ge·nie [JEE-nee] n in fairy tales, servant appearing by, and working, magic.

gen·i·tal [JEN-i-tl] adj relating to sexual organs or reproduction. **gen'i·tals** pl n the sexual organs.

gen·i·tive [JEN-i-tiv] adj, n possessive (case).

gen·ius [JEEN-yəs] n (person with) exceptional power or ability, esp. of mind; distinctive spirit or nature (of nation, etc.).

gen·o·cide [JEN-ə-sīd] n murder of a nationality or ethnic group.

gen·re [ZHAHN-rə] n kind; sort; style; painting of homely scene.

gen·teel [jen-TEEL] adj well-bred; stylish; affectedly proper.

gen·tile [JEN-tīl] adj, n non-Jewish (person).

gen·tle [JEN-tl] adj **-tler, -tlest.** mild, quiet, not rough or severe; soft and soothing; courteous; moderate; gradual; wellborn. **gen·til'i·ty** n respectability, (pretentious) politeness. **gen'tle·ness** n quality of being gentle; tenderness. **gent'ly** adv **gen·tri·fi·ca'tion** n buying of properties in run-down urban neighborhoods by affluent people, thus increasing property values but displacing less affluent residents and owners of small businesses. **gent'ry** n wellborn people. **gen'tle·man** n well-bred man; man of good social position; man (used as a mark of politeness). **gen'tle·man·ly** adj **gentlemen's agreement** agreement binding by honor but not valid in law; unwritten law in private club, etc. to discriminate against members of certain groups. **gen'tri·fy** v **-fied, -fy·ing.** change by gentrification, undergo this change.

gen·u·flect [JEN-yə-flekt] vi bend knee, esp. in worship. **gen·u·flec'tion** n

gen·u·ine [JEN-yoo-in] adj real, true, not sham, authentic; sincere; pure.

ge·nus [JEE-nəs] n, pl **gen·e·ra** [JEN-ər-ə] class, order, group (esp. of insects, animals, etc.) with common characteristics usu. comprising several species.

ge·o·cen·tric [jee-oh-SEN-trik] adj Astronomy measured, seen from Earth; having Earth as center.

ge·ode [JEE-ohd] n cavity lined with crystals; stone containing this.

ge·o·des·ic [jee-ə-DES-ik] adj of geometry of curved surfaces. **geodesic dome** light but strong hemispherical construction formed from set of polygons.

ge·og·ra·phy [jee-OG-rə-fee] n, pl -phies. science of Earth's form, physical features, climate, population, etc. **ge·og'ra·pher** n

ge·ol·o·gy [jee-OL-ə-jee] n science of Earth's crust, rocks, strata, etc. **ge·o·log'ic·al** adj

ge·om·e·try [jee-OM-i-tree] n science of properties and relations of lines, surfaces, etc. **ge·o·met'ric** adj

ge·o·phys·ics [jee-oh-FIZ-iks] n science dealing with physics of Earth. **ge·o·phys'i·cal** adj

ge·o·sta·tion·ar·y [jee-oh-STAY-shə-ner-ee] adj (of satellite) in orbit around Earth so satellite remains over same point on surface.

ger·bil [JUR-bəl] n burrowing, desert rodent of Asia and Africa.

ger·i·at·rics [jer-ee-A-triks] n branch of medicine dealing with old age and its diseases. **ger·i·at'ric** adj old. ▶ n sl old person.

germ [jurm] n microbe, esp. causing disease; elementary thing; rudiment of new organism, of animal or plant. **ger'mi·cide** [-mə-sīd] n substance for destroying disease germs.

Ger·man [JUR-mən] n, adj (language or native) of Germany. **German measles** rubella, mild disease with symptoms like measles. **german** adj of the same parents; closely akin, e.g. brother-german. **ger·mane** [jər-MAYN] adj relevant, pertinent.

ger·mi·nate [JUR-mə-nayt] v **-nat·ed, -nat·ing.** (cause to) sprout or begin to grow.

ger·ry·man·der [JER-i-man-dər] vt manipulate election districts so as to favor one side.

ger·und [JER-ənd] n noun formed from verb, such as living.

ges·ta·tion [je-STAY-shən] n carrying of young in womb between conception and birth; this period.

ges·tic·u·late [je-STIK-yə-layt] vi use expressive movements of hands and arms when speaking.

ges·ture [JES-chər] n movement to

convey meaning; indication of state of mind. ▸ vi **-tured, -tur·ing.** make such a movement.

get v **got** or **got·ten, get·ting.** ▸ vt obtain, procure; contract; catch; earn; cause to go or come; bring into position or state; induce; engender; be in possession of, have (to do); *inf* understand. ▸ vi succeed in coming or going; reach, attain; become. **get'a·way** n escape. **get across** be understood. **get at** gain access to; annoy; criticize; influence.

gey·ser [GI-zər] n hot spring throwing up spout of water from time to time.

ghast·ly [GAST-lee] adj *inf* **-li·er, -li·est.** unpleasant; deathlike, pallid; horrible. ▸ adv horribly.

gher·kin [GUR-kin] n small cucumber used in pickling.

ghet·to [GET-oh] n, pl **-tos.** densely populated (esp. by one racial or ethnic group) slum area. **ghet'to-blast·er** n *inf* large portable cassette or CD player and radio.

ghost [gohst] n spirit, dead person appearing again; specter; semblance; faint trace; one who writes work to appear under another's name, ghostwriter. ▸ v (also **ghost'write**) write another's work, speeches, etc. **ghost'ly** adj

ghoul [gool] n malevolent spirit; person with morbid interests; fiend. **ghoul'ish** adj of or like ghoul; horrible.

gi·ant [JI-ənt] n mythical being of superhuman size; very tall person, plant, etc. ▸ adj huge. **gi·gan'tic** adj enormous, huge.

gib·ber [JIB-ər] vi make meaningless sounds with mouth, jabber, chatter. **gib'ber·ish** n meaningless speech or words.

gib·bet [JIB-it] n gallows; post with arm on which executed criminal was hung; death by hanging. ▸ vt hang on gibbet; hold up to scorn.

gib·bon [GIB-ən] n type of ape.

gibe [jīb] v **gibed, gib·ing.** utter taunts; mock; jeer. ▸ n insulting remark.

gib·lets [JIB-lits] pl n internal edible parts of fowl, such as liver, gizzard, etc.

gid·dy [GID-ee] adj **-di·er, -di·est.** dizzy, feeling as if about to fall; liable to cause this feeling; flighty, frivolous. **gid'di·ness** n

gift n thing given, present; faculty, power. ▸ vt present (with); endow, bestow. **gift'ed** adj talented.

gig n light, two-wheeled carriage; *inf* single booking of musicians to play at club, etc.

giga- *prefix* denoting 10^9, e.g. *gigavolt*; *Computers* denoting 2^{30}, e.g. *gigabyte*.

gigantic see GIANT.

gig·gle [GIG-əl] vi **-gled, -gling.** laugh nervously, foolishly. ▸ n such a laugh.

gig·o·lo [JIG-ə-loh] n, pl **-los.** man kept, paid, by (older) woman to be her escort, lover.

gild vt **gilded** or **gilt, gild·ing.** put thin layer of gold on; make falsely attractive. **gilt** adj gilded. ▸ n thin layer of gold put on.

gill [jil] n liquid measure, quarter of pint.

gills [gillz] pl n breathing organs in fish and other water creatures.

gim·bals [JIM-bəlz] pl n pivoted rings, for keeping things, e.g. compass, horizontal at sea or in space.

gim·let [GIM-lit] n boring tool, usu. with screw point; drink of vodka or gin with lime juice.

gim·mick [GIM-ik] n clever device, stratagem, etc., esp. one designed to attract attention or publicity.

gimp n narrow fabric or braid used as edging or trimming; *sl* a limp; *sl* person who limps.

gin¹ [jin] n alcoholic liquor flavored with juniper berries.

gin² n primitive engine in which vertical shaft is turned to drive horizontal beam in a circle; machine for separating cotton from seeds.

gin·ger [JIN-jər] n plant with pungent spicy root used in cooking, etc.; the root; *inf* spirit,

mettle; light reddish-yellow color.
▶ vt stimulate. **gin′ger·y** adj of, like
ginger; spicy; high-spirited;
reddish. **ginger ale, beer**
ginger-flavored soft drink.
gin′ger·bread n cake, cookie
flavored with ginger.

gin·ger·ly [JIN-jər-lee] adv
cautiously, warily, reluctantly.

ging·ham [GING-əm] n cotton
cloth, usu. checked, woven from
dyed yarn.

gink·go [GING-koh] n, pl **-goes.**
large Chinese shade tree.

gin·seng [JIN-seng] n (root of)
plant believed to have tonic and
energy-giving properties.

gi·raffe [jə-RAF] n Afr. ruminant
animal, with spotted coat and very
long neck and legs.

gird [gurd] vt **gird·ed** or **girt,**
gird·ing. put belt around; fasten
clothes thus; equip with, or belt on,
a sword; prepare (oneself); encircle.
gird′er n large beam, esp. of steel.

gir·dle [GURD-l] n corset;
waistband; anything that
surrounds, encircles. ▶ vt **-dled,**
-dling. surround, encircle; remove
bark (of tree) from a band around
it.

girl [gurl] n female child; young
(formerly, an unmarried) woman.
girl′hood [-huud] n

girt pt./pp. of GIRD.

girth [gurth] n measurement
around thing; leather or cloth band
put around horse to hold saddle,
etc. ▶ vt surround, secure, with
girth; girdle.

gist [jist] n substance, main point
(of remarks, etc.).

give [giv] v **gave, giv·en, giv·ing.**
▶ vt bestow, confer ownership of,
make present of; deliver; impart;
assign; yield, supply; utter; emit; be
host of (party, etc.); make over;
cause to have. ▶ vi yield, give way,
move. ▶ n yielding, elasticity.
give′a·way n act of giving
something away; what is given
away; telltale sign. **give up**
acknowledge defeat; abandon.

giz·zard [GIZ-ərd] n part of bird's
stomach.

gla·brous [GLAY-brəs] adj smooth;
without hairs or any unevenness.

gla·cier [GLAY-shər] n river of ice,
slow-moving mass of ice formed by
accumulated snow in mountain
valleys. **gla′cial** adj of ice, or of
glaciers; very cold. **gla·ci·a′tion** n

glad adj **-der, -dest.** pleased;
happy, joyous; giving joy.
glad′den vt make glad. **glad′ly** adv
glad rags inf dressy clothes for
party, etc.

glade [glayd] n clear, grassy space
in wood or forest.

glad·i·a·tor [GLAD-ee-ay-tər] n
trained fighter in ancient Roman
arena.

glam·our [GLAM-ər] n alluring
charm, fascination. **glam′or·ize** vt
-ized, -iz·ing. make appear
glamorous. **glam′or·ous** adj

glance [glans] vi **glanced,**
glanc·ing. look rapidly or briefly;
allude, touch; glide off something
struck; pass quickly. ▶ n brief look;
flash; gleam; sudden (deflected)
blow.

gland n one of various small organs
controlling different bodily
functions by chemical means.
glan·du·lar [GLAN-jə-lər] adj

glare [glair] vi **glared, glar·ing.** look
fiercely; shine brightly, intensely;
be conspicuous. ▶ n

glass n hard transparent substance
made by fusing sand, soda, potash,
etc.; things made of it; tumbler; its
contents; lens; mirror; spyglass. ▶ pl
eyeglasses. **glass′i·ness** n **glass′y**
adj **glass·i·er, glass·i·est.** like glass;
expressionless. **glass wool**
insulating fabric of spun glass.

glau·co·ma [glow-KOH-mə] n eye
disease.

glaze [glayz] v **glazed, glaz·ing.**
▶ vt furnish with glass; cover with
glassy substance. ▶ vi become
glassy. ▶ n transparent coating;
substance used for this; glossy
surface. **gla·zier** [GLAY-zhər] n one
who glazes windows.

gleam [gleem] n slight or passing
beam of light; faint or momentary

show. ▶ *vi* give out gleams.
glean [gleen] *v* pick up (facts, etc.); gather, pick up, orig. after reapers in grainfields. **glean'er** *n*
glee *n* mirth, merriment; musical composition for three or more voices. **glee'ful** *adj* **glee club** chorus organized for singing choral music.
glen *n* narrow valley, usu. wooded and with a stream.
glib *adj* **-ber, -best.** fluent but insincere or superficial; plausible. **glib'ness** *n*
glide [glīd] *vi* **glid·ed, glid·ing.** pass smoothly and continuously; of airplane, move without use of engines. ▶ *n* smooth, silent movement; *Mus* sounds made in passing from tone to tone. **glid'er** *n* aircraft without engine that moves through the action of gravity and air currents; porch swing. **glid'ing** *n* sport of flying gliders.
glim·mer [GLIM-ər] *vi* shine faintly, flicker. ▶ *n* **glim'mer·ing** *n* faint gleam of light; faint idea, notion.
glimpse [glimps] *n* brief or incomplete view. ▶ *vt* **glimpsed, glimps·ing.** catch glimpse of.
glint *v* flash, glance, glitter; reflect. ▶ *n*
glis·ten [GLIS-ən] *vi* gleam by reflecting light.
glitch [glich] *n* small problem that stops something from working properly.
glit·ter [GLIT-ər] *vi* shine with bright quivering light, sparkle; be showy. ▶ *n* luster; sparkle.
gloam·ing [GLOH-ming] *n* evening twilight.
gloat [gloht] *vi* regard, dwell on with smugness or malicious satisfaction.
glob *n* soft lump or mass.
globe [glohb] *n* sphere with map of Earth or stars; heavenly sphere, esp. Earth; ball, sphere. **glob'al** *adj* of globe; relating to whole world. **glob·al·i·za'tion** [gloh-bəl-ī-ZAY-shən] *n* broadening the scope, application, influence,

or effect of something to the entire world. **glob'u·lar** [-yə-lər] *adj* globe-shaped. **glob'ule** [-yool] *n* small round particle; drop.
glob·u·lin *n* kind of simple protein.
global warming increase in overall temperature worldwide believed to be caused by pollutants.
globe'trot·ter *n* (habitual) world traveler.
glock·en·spiel [GLOK-ən-speel] *n* percussion instrument of metal bars struck with hammers.
gloom *n* darkness; melancholy, depression. **gloom'y** *adj* **gloom·i·er, gloom·i·est.**
glo·ry [GLOR-ee] *n* renown, honorable fame; splendor; exalted or prosperous state; heavenly bliss. ▶ *vi* **-ried, -ry·ing.** take pride (in). **glor'i·fy** *vt* **-fied, -fy·ing.** make glorious; invest with glory. **glo'ri·ous** *adj* illustrious; splendid; excellent; delightful.
gloss¹ *n* surface shine, luster. ▶ *vt* put gloss on; (esp. with *over*) (try to) cover up, pass over (fault, error). **gloss'i·ness** *n* **gloss'y** *adj* **gloss·i·er, gloss·i·est.** smooth, shiny. ▶ *n* photograph printed on shiny paper.
gloss² *n* marginal interpretation of word; comment, explanation. ▶ *vt* interpret; comment; explain away. **glos'sa·ry** *n, pl* **-ries.** dictionary, vocabulary of special words.
glot'tis *n* human vocal apparatus, larynx. **glot'tal** [GLOT-l] *adj*
glove [gluv] *n* covering for the hand. ▶ *vt* **gloved, glov·ing.** cover with, or as with glove. **glove compartment** storage area in dashboard of automobile. **the gloves** boxing gloves.
glow [gloh] *vi* give out light and heat without flames; shine; experience well-being or satisfaction; be or look hot; burn with emotion. ▶ *n* shining heat; warmth of color; feeling of well-being; ardor. **glow·worm** [GLOH-wurm] *n* female insect giving out green light.
glow·er [GLOW-ər] *vi* scowl.

glu·cose [GLOO-kohs] *n* type of sugar found in fruit, etc.

glue [gloo] *n* any natural or synthetic adhesive; any sticky substance. ▸ *vt* **glued, glu·ing.** fasten (as if) with glue. **glue sniffing** practice of inhaling fumes of glue for intoxicating or hallucinatory effects.

glum *adj* **glum·mer, glum·mest,** sullen, moody, gloomy.

glut *n* surfeit, excessive amount. ▸ *vt* **glut·ted, glut·ting.** feed, gratify to the full or to excess; overstock.

glu·ten [GLOOT-n] *n* protein present in cereal grain. **glu'ti·nous** *adj* sticky, gluey.

glut·ton [GLUT-n] *n* greedy person; one with great liking or capacity for something, esp. food and drink. **glut'ton·ous** *adj* like glutton, greedy. **glut'ton·y** *n*

glyc·er·in [GLIS-ər-in] *n* colorless sweet liquid with wide application in chemistry and industry.

GM genetically modified.

GMO genetically modified organism.

gnarled [nahrld] *adj* knobby, rugged, twisted.

gnash [nash] *v* grind (teeth) together as in anger or pain.

gnat [nat] *n* small, biting, two-winged fly.

gnaw [naw] *v* bite or chew steadily; (esp. with *at*) cause distress to.

gneiss [nīs] *n* coarse-grained metamorphic rock.

gnome [nohm] *n* legendary creature like small old man; international financier. **gnom'ish** *adj*

gno·mic [NOH-mik] *adj* of or like an aphorism.

gnos·tic [NOS-tik] *adj* of, relating to knowledge, esp. spiritual knowledge.

gnu [noo] *n* S Afr. antelope somewhat like ox.

go [goh] *vi* **went, gone, go·ing.** move along, make way; be moving; depart; function; make specified sound; fail, give way;

break down; elapse; be kept, put; be able to be put; result; contribute to result; tend to; be accepted, have force; become. ▸ *n* going; energy, vigor; attempt; turn.

go-go dancer dancer, usu. scantily dressed, who performs rhythmic and oft. erotic modern dance routines, esp. in nightclub.

goad [gohd] *n* spiked stick for driving cattle; anything that urges to action; incentive. ▸ *vt* urge on; torment.

goal [gohl] *n* end of race; object of effort; posts through which ball is to be driven in various games; the score so made.

goat [goht] *n* four-footed animal with long hair, horns and beard. **goat·ee'** *n* beard like goat's. **get someone's goat** *inf* annoy (someone).

gob *n* lump; *sl* sailor. **gob·ble** [GOB-əl] *vt* **-bled, -bling.** eat hastily, noisily or greedily.

gob·ble *n* throaty, gurgling cry of male turkey. ▸ *vi* **-bled, -bling.** make such a noise.

gob·ble·dy·gook, -de·gook [GOB-əl-dee-guuk] *n* pretentious, usu. incomprehensible language, esp. as used by officials.

gob·let [GOB-lit] *n* drinking cup.

gob'lin *n Folklore* small, usu. malevolent being.

god *n* superhuman being worshipped as having supernatural power; object of worship, idol; (**G-**) in monotheistic religions, the Supreme Being, creator and ruler of universe. **god'dess** *n, fem* **god'like** *adj* **god'li·ness** *n* **god'ly** *adj* **-li·er, -li·est.** devout, pious. **god'child** *n* child for whom a person stands as godparent. **god'father** *n* **god'mother** *n* **god'parent** *n* sponsor at baptism. **God-fearing** *adj* religious, good. **god'for·sak·en** [-fər-say-ken] *adj* hopeless, dismal. **God'head** *n* divine nature or deity. **god'send** *n* something unexpected but welcome.

gog·gle [GOG-əl] *vi* **-gled, -gling.**

(of eyes) bulge; stare. ▸ *pl n* protective eyeglasses.

goi·ter [GOI-tər] *n* neck swelling due to enlargement of thyroid gland.

go-kart, go-cart see KART.

gold [gohld] *n* yellow precious metal; coins of this; wealth; beautiful or precious thing; color of gold. ▸ *adj* of, like gold. **gold′en** *adj* **gold digger** *inf* woman skillful in extracting money from men. **golden mean** middle way between extremes. **gold′en·rod** *n* tall plant with golden flower spikes. **golden rule** important principle. **golden wedding** fiftieth wedding anniversary. **gold′field** *n* place where gold deposits are known to exist. **gold′finch** *n* bird with yellow feathers. **gold′fish** *n* any of various ornamental pond or aquarium fish. **gold standard** financial arrangement whereby currencies of countries accepting it are expressed in fixed terms of gold.

golf *n* outdoor game in which small hard ball is struck with clubs into a succession of holes. ▸ *vi* play this game.

go·nad [GOH-nad] *n* gland producing gametes.

gon·do·la [GON-dl-ə] *n* Venetian canal boat. **gon·do·lier′** *n* rower of gondola.

gone [gawn]. pp. of GO.

gong *n* metal plate with turned rim that resounds as bell when struck with soft mallet; anything used thus.

gon·or·rhea [gon-ə-REE-ə] *n* a venereal disease.

good [guud] *adj* **bet·ter, best.** commendable; right; proper; excellent; beneficial; well-behaved; virtuous; kind; safe; adequate; sound; valid. ▸ *n* benefit; well-being; profit. ▸ *pl* property; wares. **good′ly** *adj* large, considerable. **good′ness** *n* **good will** kindly feeling, heartiness; value of a business in reputation, etc. over and above its tangible assets.

good-bye [guud-BĪ] *interj, n* form of address on parting.

goof *n inf* mistake; stupid person. ▸ *vi* make mistake. **goof′y** *adj* **goof·i·er, goof·i·est.** silly.

goon *n sl* stupid, awkward fellow; *inf* hired thug, hoodlum.

goose [goos] *n, pl* **geese.** web-footed bird; its flesh; simpleton. **goose flesh** bristling of skin due to cold, fright. **goose step** formal parade step.

go·pher [GOH-fər] *n* various species of Amer. burrowing rodents. **gopher ball** *Baseball, sl* pitched ball hit for home run.

gore¹ [gor] *n* (dried) blood from wound. **gor′y** *adj* **gor·i·er, gor·i·est.**

gore² *vt* **gored, gor·ing.** pierce with horns.

gore³ *n* triangular piece inserted to shape garment. ▸ *vt* **gored, gor·ing.** shape thus.

gorge [gorj] *n* ravine; disgust, resentment. ▸ *vi* **gorged, gorg·ing.** feed greedily.

gor·geous [GOR-jəs] *adj* splendid, showy, dazzling; *inf* extremely pleasing.

gor·gon [GOR-gən] *n* terrifying or repulsive woman; (G-) in Greek mythology, any of three sisters whose appearance turned any viewer to stone.

go·ril·la [gə-RIL-ə] *n* largest anthropoid ape, found in Afr.

gor·mand·ize [GOR-mən-dīz] *vt* **-ized, -iz·ing.** eat hurriedly or like a glutton.

gory see GORE¹.

gos′hawk *n* large hawk.

gos·ling [GOZ-ling] *n* young goose.

gos·pel [GOS-pəl] *n* unquestionable truth; (G-) any of first four books of New Testament.

gos·sa·mer [GOS-ə-mər] *n* filmy substance like spider's web; thin gauze or silk fabric.

gos·sip [GOS-əp] *n* idle (malicious) talk about other persons, esp. regardless of fact; one who talks thus. ▸ *vi* **-siped, -sip·ing.** engage in gossip; chatter.

got see GET.

Goth·ic [GOTH-ik] *adj Architecture* of the pointed arch style common in Europe from twelfth to sixteenth century; of Goths; barbarous; gloomy; grotesque; (of type) German black letter.

gouge [gowj] *vt* **gouged, goug·ing.** scoop out; force out; extort from; overcharge. ▸ *n* chisel with curved cutting edge.

gou·lash [GOO-lahsh] *n* stew of meat and vegetables seasoned with paprika, etc.

gourd [gord] *n* trailing or climbing plant; its large fleshy fruit; its rind as vessel.

gour·mand [guur-MAHND] *n* glutton.

gour·met [guur-MAY] *n* connoisseur of wine, food; epicure.

gout [gowt] *n* disease with inflammation, esp. of joints.

gov·ern [GUV-ərn] *vt* rule, direct, guide, control; decide or determine; be followed by (grammatical case, etc.). **gov′ern·a·ble** *adj* **gov′ern·ess** *n* woman teacher in private household. **gov′ern·ment** *n* exercise of political authority in directing a people, country, etc.; system by which community is ruled; body of people in charge of government of country; executive power; control; direction; exercise of authority. **gov′ern·or** *n* one who governs, esp. one invested with supreme authority in a state, etc.; chief administrator of an institution; member of committee responsible for an organization or institution; regulator for speed of engine.

gown *n* loose flowing outer garment; woman's (long) dress; official robe, as in university, etc.

grab *vt* **grabbed, grab·bing.** grasp suddenly; snatch. ▸ *n* sudden clutch; quick attempt to seize; device or implement for clutching.

grace [grays] *n* charm, elegance; accomplishment; goodwill, favor; sense of propriety; postponement granted; short thanksgiving before or after meal. ▸ *vt* **graced, grac·ing.** add grace to, honor. **grace′ful** *adj* **grace′less** *adj* shameless, depraved. **gra′cious** [-shəs] *adj* favorable; kind; pleasing; indulgent, beneficent, condescending. **grace note** *Mus* melodic ornament.

grade [grayd] *n* step, stage; degree of rank, etc.; class; mark, rating; slope. ▸ *vt* **grad·ed, grad·ing.** arrange in classes; assign grade to; level ground, move earth with grader. **gra·da′tion** *n* series of degrees or steps; each of them; arrangement in steps; in painting, gradual passing from one shade, etc. to another. **grad′er** *n* esp. machine with wide blade used in road making. **make the grade** succeed.

gra·di·ent [GRAY-dee-ənt] *n* (degree of) slope.

grad·u·al [GRAJ-oo-əl] *adj* taking place by degrees; slow and steady; not steep. **grad′u·al·ly** *adv*

grad·u·ate [GRAJ-oo-ayt] *v* **-at·ed, -at·ing.** ▸ *vi* receive diploma or degree on completing course of study. ▸ *vt* divide into degrees; mark, arrange according to scale. ▸ *n* [-it] holder of diploma or degree. **grad·u·a′tion** *n*

graf·fi·ti [grə-FEE-tee] *pl n* words or drawings scribbled or sprayed on walls etc.

graft[1] *n* shoot of plant set in stalk of another; the process; surgical transplant of skin, tissue. ▸ *vt* insert (shoot) in another stalk; transplant (living tissue in surgery).

graft[2] *n inf* self-advancement, profit by unfair means, esp. through official or political privilege; bribe; swindle.

grail [grayl] *n* cup or dish used by Christ at the Last Supper (also **Holy Grail**).

grain [grayn] *n* seed, fruit of cereal plant; wheat and allied plants; small hard particle; unit of weight, 0.0648 gram; texture; arrangement of fibers; any very small amount; natural

temperament or disposition.
gram n unit of weight (equivalent to 0.035 ounce) in metric system, one thousandth of a kilogram.
gram·mar [GRAM-ər] n science of structure and usage of language; book on this; correct use of words. **gram·mar·i·an** [grə-MAIR-ee-ən] n **gram·mat'i·cal** adj according to grammar. **grammar school** elementary school.
gra·na·ry [GRAY-nə-ree] n, pl **-ries.** storehouse for grain; rich grain-growing region.
grand adj **-er, -est.** imposing; magnificent; majestic; noble; splendid; eminent; lofty; chief, of chief importance; final (total). **gran·deur** [GRAN-jər] n nobility; magnificence; dignity. **gran·dil'o·quence** n **gran·dil'o·quent** adj pompous in speech. **gran'di·ose** [-dee-ohs] adj imposing; affectedly grand; striking. **grand'child** n child of one's child. **grand'daugh·ter** n female grandchild. **grand'fa·ther** n male grandparent. **grand'moth·er** n female grandparent. **grand'par·ent** n parent of one's parent. **grand piano** large harp-shaped piano with horizontal strings. **grand'son** n male grandchild. **grand'stand** n structure with tiered seats for spectators.
grange [graynj] n farm with its farmhouse and farm buildings.
gran·ite [GRAN-it] n hard crystalline igneous rock. **gran'ite·like** adj
gran·ny [GRAN-ee] n, pl **-nies.** inf grandmother.
grant vt consent to fulfill (request); permit; bestow; admit. ▶ n sum of money provided by government or other source for specific purpose, as education; gift; allowance, concession.
gran·ule [GRAN-yool] n small grain; small particle. **gran'u·lar** [-yə-lər] adj of or like grains.
grape [grayp] n fruit of vine. **grape'shot** n bullets scattering

when fired. **grape'vine** [-vīn] n grape-bearing vine; inf unofficial means of conveying information.
grape·fruit [GRAYP-froot] n subtropical citrus fruit.
graph [graf] n drawing depicting relation of different numbers, quantities, etc. ▶ vt represent by graph.
graph·ic [GRAF-ik] adj vividly descriptive; of, in, relating to, writing, drawing, painting, etc. **graphics** pl n diagrams, graphs, etc., esp. as used on a TV programme or computer screen. **graph'i·cal·ly** adv **graph'ite** [-īt] n form of carbon (used in pencils). **graph·ol'o·gy** n study of handwriting.
grap·nel [GRAP-nl] n hooked iron instrument for seizing anything; small anchor with several flukes.
grap·ple [GRAP-əl] v **-pled, -pling.** come to grips with, wrestle; cope or contend. ▶ n grappling; grapnel.
grasp v (try, struggle to) seize hold; understand. ▶ n act of grasping; grip; comprehension. **grasp'ing** adj greedy, avaricious.
grass n common type of plant with jointed stems and long narrow leaves (including cereals, bamboo, etc.); such plants grown as lawn; pasture; sl marijuana. ▶ vt cover with grass. **grass'hop·per** n jumping, chirping insect. **grass roots** ordinary people; fundamentals. **grass-roots** adj coming from ordinary people, the rank and file.
grate[1] [grayt] n framework of metal bars for holding fuel in fireplace. **grat'ing** n framework of parallel or latticed bars covering opening.
grate[2] v **grat·ed, grat·ing.** ▶ vt rub into small bits on rough surface. ▶ vi rub with harsh noise; have irritating effect. **grat'er** n utensil with rough surface for reducing substance to small particles. **grating** adj harsh; irritating.
grate·ful [GRAYT-fəl] adj thankful; appreciative; pleasing. **grat·i·tude** [GRAT-ə-tood] n sense of being

thankful for favor.

grat·i·fy [GRAT-ə-fī] *vt* **-fied,
-fy·ing.** satisfy; please; indulge.
grat·i·fi·ca'tion *n*

gratin see AU GRATIN.

grat'is *adv, adj* free, for nothing.

gra·tu·i·tous [grə-TOO-i-təs] *adj*
given free; uncalled for.
gra·tu'i·tous·ly *adv* **gra·tu'i·ty** *n,
pl* **-ties.** a tip.

grave[1] [grayv] *n* hole dug to bury
corpse; death. **grave'stone** *n*
monument on grave. **grave'yard** *n*

grave[2] *adj* **grav·er, grav·est.**
serious, weighty; dignified, solemn;
plain, dark in color; deep in note.
grave'ly *adv*

grave[3] *n* accent (`) over vowel to
indicate special sound quality.

grav·el [GRAV-əl] *n* small stones;
coarse sand. ▶ *vt* **-eled, -el·ing.**
cover with gravel. **grav'el·ly** *adj*

grav·en [GRAY-vən] *adj* carved,
engraved.

grav·i·tate [GRAV-i-tayt] *vi* **-tat·ed,
-tat·ing.** move by gravity; tend
(toward) center of attraction; sink,
settle down. **grav·i·ta'tion** *n*

grav·i·ty [GRAV-i-tee] *n, pl* **-ties.**
force of attraction of one body for
another, esp. of objects to Earth;
heaviness; importance; seriousness;
staidness.

gra·vy [GRAY-vee] *n, pl* **-vies.** juices
from meat in cooking; sauce for
food made from these; thing of
value obtained unexpectedly.

gray *adj* between black and white,
as ashes or lead; clouded; dismal;
turning white; aged; intermediate,
indeterminate. ▶ *n* gray color; gray
or white horse.

graze[1] [grayz] *v* **grazed, graz·ing.**
feed on grass, pasture.

graze[2] *vt* **grazed, graz·ing.** touch
lightly in passing, scratch, scrape.
▶ *n* grazing; abrasion.

grease [grees] *n* soft melted fat of
animals; thick oil as lubricant. ▶ *vt*
greased, greas·ing. apply grease
to. **greas'i·ness** *n* **greas'y** *adj*
**greas·i·er, greas·i·est. grease
gun** appliance for injecting grease
into machinery. **grease monkey**

inf mechanic. **grease'paint** *n*
theatrical makeup.

great [grayt] *adj* **-er, -est.** large,
big; important; preeminent,
distinguished; *inf* excellent. **great-**
prefix one generation older or
younger than, e.g.
great-grandfather. **great'ly** *adv*
great'ness *n* **Great Dane** breed of
very large dog.

Gre·cian [GREE-shən] *adj* of
(ancient) Greece.

greed *n* excessive consumption of,
desire for, food, wealth. **greed'y**
adj **greed·i·er, greed·i·est.**
gluttonous; eagerly desirous;
voracious; covetous. **greed'i·ly** *adv*

Greek *n* native language of Greece.
▶ *adj* of Greece or Greek.

green *adj* **-er, -est.** of color
between blue and yellow;
grass-colored; emerald; unripe;
inexperienced; gullible; envious.
▶ *n* color; area of grass, esp. in golf,
for putting. ▶ *pl* green vegetables.
green'er·y *n, pl* **-er·ies.** vegetation.
green belt area of farms, open
country around a community.
green'horn *n* inexperienced
person; *sl* recent immigrant,
newcomer. **green'house** *n, pl*
-hous·es [-how-ziz] (usu.) glass
house for rearing plants.

greenhouse effect rise in the
temperature of the earth caused by
heat absorbed from the sun being
unable to leave the atmosphere.
green'room *n* room for actors, TV
performers, when offstage. **green
thumb** talent for gardening.

greet *vt* meet with expressions of
welcome; accost, salute; receive.
greet'ing *n*

gre·gar·i·ous [gri-GAIR-ee-əs] *adj*
fond of company, sociable; living in
flocks. **gre·gar'i·ous·ness** *n*

grem'lin *n* imaginary being blamed
for mechanical and other troubles.

gre·nade [gri-NAYD] *n* explosive
shell or bomb, thrown by hand or
shot from rifle.

gren·a·dine [gren-ə-DEEN] *n* syrup
made from pomegranate juice, for
sweetening and coloring drinks.

grew pt. of GROW.

grey·hound [GRAY-hownd] n swift slender dog used in racing.

grid n network of horizontal and vertical lines, bars, etc.; any interconnecting system of links; regional network of electricity supply.

grid·dle [GRID-l] n frying pan, flat iron plate for cooking. **grid·dle·cake** n pancake.

grid·i·ron [GRID-ī-ərn] n frame of metal bars for grilling; (field of play for) football.

grid·lock [GRID-lok] n situation where traffic is not moving; point in a dispute at which no agreement can be reached. **grid'locked** adj

grief [greef] n deep sorrow. **griev·ance** [GREE-vəns] n real or imaginary ground of complaint. **grieve** v **grieved, griev·ing.** ▶ vi feel grief. ▶ vt cause grief to. **griev'ous** adj painful, oppressive; very serious.

grif·fin, grif·fon [GRIF-in] n fabulous monster with eagle's head and wings and lion's body.

grill n grated utensil for broiling meat, etc.; food cooked on grill; grillroom. ▶ v cook (food) on grill; subject to severe questioning. **grill'ing** n severe cross-examination. **grill'room** n restaurant specializing in grilled food.

grille [gril] n grating, crosswork of bars over opening.

grim adj **grim·mer, grim·mest.** stern; of stern or forbidding aspect, relentless; joyless.

grim·ace [GRIM-əs] n wry face. ▶ vi **-aced, -ac·ing.** make wry face.

grime [grīm] n ingrained dirt, soot. ▶ vt **grimed, grim·ing.** soil; dirty; blacken. **grim'y** adj **grim·i·er, grim·i·est.**

grin vi **grinned, grin·ning.** show teeth, as in laughter. ▶ n grinning smile.

grind [grīnd] v **ground, grind·ing.** ▶ vt crush to powder; oppress; make sharp, smooth; grate. ▶ vi perform action of grinding; inf

(with *away*) work (esp. study) hard; grate. ▶ n inf hard work, excessively diligent student; action of grinding.

grin·go [GRING-goh] n, pl **-gos.** in Mexico, contemptuous name for foreigner, esp. American or Englishman.

grip n firm hold, grasp; grasping power; mastery; handle; suitcase or traveling bag. ▶ vt **gripped, grip·ping.** grasp or hold tightly; hold interest or attention of.

gripe [grīp] vi inf **griped, grip·ing.** complain (persistently). ▶ n inf complaint. ▶ pl intestinal pain.

gris·ly [GRIZ-lee] adj **-li·er, -li·est.** grim, causing terror, ghastly.

grist n grain to be ground. **grist for one's mill** something that can be turned to advantage.

gris·tle [GRIS-əl] n cartilage, tough flexible tissue.

grit n rough particles of sand; coarse sandstone; courage. ▶ pl hominy, etc. coarsely ground and cooked as breakfast food. ▶ vt **grit·ted, grit·ting.** clench, grind (teeth). **grit'ty** adj **-ti·er, -ti·est.**

griz·zle [GRIZ-əl] v **-zled, -zling.** make, become gray. **griz'zly** large Amer. bear (also **grizzly bear**).

groan [grohn] vi make low, deep sound of grief or pain; be in pain or overburdened. ▶ n

groats [grohts] n hulled grain or kernels of oats, wheat, etc. broken into fragments.

gro·cer [GROH-sər] n dealer in foodstuffs. **gro'cer·ies** pl n commodities sold by a grocer. **gro'cer·y** n, pl **-cer·ies.** trade, premises of grocer.

grog·gy [GROG-ee] adj inf **-gi·er, -gi·est.** unsteady, shaky, weak.

groin n fold where legs meet abdomen; euphemism for genitals.

groom n person caring for horses; bridegroom. ▶ vt tend or look after; brush or clean (esp. horse); train (someone for something). **well-groomed** adj neat, smart.

groove [groov] n narrow channel, hollow, esp. cut by tool; rut, routine. ▶ vt **grooved, groov·ing.**

cut groove in. **groov·y** adj sl
groov·i·er, groov·i·est. attractive,
exciting.

grope [grohp] vi **groped, grop·ing.**
feel about, search blindly.

gros·beak [GROHS-beek] n finch
with large powerful bill.

gross [grohs] adj **-er, -est.** very fat;
total, not net; coarse; indecent;
flagrant; thick, rank. ▶ n twelve
dozen. **gross out** sl disgust, sicken.

gro·tesque [groh-TESK] adj
(horribly) distorted; absurd. ▶ n
grotesque person, thing.

grot·to [GROT-oh] n, pl **-toes.** small
picturesque cave.

grouch [growch] n inf persistent
grumbler; discontented mood. ▶ vi
grumble, be peevish.

ground[1] [grownd] n surface of
Earth; soil, earth; reason, motive;
coating to work on with paint;
background, main surface worked
on in painting, embroidery, etc.;
special area; bottom of sea. ▶ pl
dregs; land around house and
belonging to it. ▶ vt establish;
instruct (in elements); place on
ground. ▶ vi run ashore; strike
ground. **ground'ed** adj of aircraft
or pilot, unable or not permitted to
fly; inf of child, punished by
restriction of activities. **ground'ing**
n basic general knowledge of a
subject. **ground'less** adj without
reason. **ground'speed** n aircraft's
speed in relation to ground.

ground[2] pt./pp. of GRIND.

group [groop] n number of persons
or things near together, or placed
or classified together; small musical
band of players or singers; class;
two or more figures forming one
artistic design. ▶ v place, fall into
group.

grouse[1] [grows] n, pl **grouse.** game
bird; its flesh.

grouse[2] vi **groused, grous·ing.**
grumble, complain. ▶ n complaint.
grous'er n grumbler.

grout [growt] n thin fluid mortar.
▶ vt fill up with grout.

grove [grohv] n small group of
trees.

grov·el [GRUV-əl] vi **-eled, -el·ing.**
abase oneself; lie or crawl
facedown.

grow [groh] v **grew, grown,
grow·ing.** ▶ vi develop naturally;
increase in size, height, etc.; be
produced; become by degrees. ▶ vt
produce by cultivation. **growth** n
growing; increase; what has grown
or is growing. **grown-up** adj
grownup n adult.

growl vi make low guttural sound
of anger; rumble; murmur,
complain. ▶ n

grub v **grubbed, grub·bing.** dig
superficially; root up; dig,
rummage; plod; drudge. ▶ n larva
of insect; sl food. **grub'by** adj
-bi·er, -bi·est. dirty.

grudge [gruj] vt **grudged,
grudg·ing.** be unwilling to give,
allow. ▶ n ill will.

gru·el [GROO-əl] n food of cereal
boiled in milk or water. **gru'el·ing**
adj, n exhausting, severe
(experience).

grue·some [GROO-səm] adj
fearful, horrible, grisly.
grue'some·ness n

gruff adj **-er, -est.** rough in manner
or voice, surly. **gruff'ness** n

grum·ble [GRUM-bəl] vi **-bled,
-bling.** complain; rumble, murmur;
make growling sounds. ▶ n
complaint; low growl.

grump·y [GRUM-pee] adj
grump·i·er, grump·i·est.
ill-tempered, surly. **grump'i·ness** n

grunge [grunj] n style of rock music
with a fuzzy guitar sound;
deliberately untidy and
uncoordinated fashion style.

grunt vi make sound characteristic
of pig. ▶ n pig's sound; gruff noise.

G-string [JEE-string] n very small
covering for genitals; Mus string
tuned to G.

gua·no [GWAH-noh] n manure of
seabird.

guar·an·tee [gar-ən-TEE] n formal
assurance (esp. in writing) that
product, etc. will meet certain
standards, last for given time, etc.
▶ vt **-teed, -tee'ing.** give guarantee

of, for something; secure (against risk, etc.). **guar′an·tor** n one who guarantees. **guar′an·ty** n, pl **-ties.**

guard [gahrd] vt protect, defend. ▶ vi be careful, take precautions (against). ▶ n person, group that protects, supervises, keeps watch; sentry; soldiers protecting anything; official in charge of train; protection; screen for enclosing anything dangerous; protector; posture of defense. **guard′i·an** [-ee-ən] n keeper, protector; person having custody of infant, etc. **guard′i·an·ship** n care. **guard′house** n place for stationing those on guard or for prisoners.

gua·va [GWAH-və] n tropical tree with fruit used to make jelly.

Guern·sey [GURN-zee] n, pl **-seys.** breed of cattle.

guer·ril·la [gə-RIL-ə] n member of irregular armed force, esp. fighting established force, government, etc. ▶ adj

guess [ges] vt estimate without calculation; conjecture, suppose; consider, think. ▶ vi form conjectures. ▶ n

guest [gest] n one entertained at another's house; one living in hotel. **guest′house** n small house for guests, separate from main house.

guff n inf silly talk; insolent talk.

guf·faw [gə-FAW] n crude noisy laugh. ▶ vi laugh in this way.

guide [gīd] n one who shows the way; adviser; book of instruction or information; contrivance for directing motion. ▶ vt **guid·ed, guid·ing.** lead, act as guide to; arrange. **guid′ance** [-əns] n **guided missile** missile whose flight path is controlled by radio signals or programmed homing mechanism.

guild [gild] n organization, club; society for mutual help, or with common object; Hist society of merchants or tradesmen.

guile [gīl] n cunning, deceit. **guile′ful** adj **guile′less** adj sincere, straightforward.

guil·lo·tine [GIL-ə-teen] n machine for beheading. ▶ vt **-tined, -tin·ing.** behead.

guilt [gilt] n fact, state of having done wrong; responsibility for criminal or moral offense. **guilt′less** adj innocent. **guilt′y** adj **guilt·i·er, guilt·i·est.** having committed an offense.

guin·ea pig [GIN-ee] n rodent originating in S Amer.; inf person used in experiments.

guise [gīz] n external appearance, esp. one assumed.

gui·tar [gi-TAHR] n usu. six-stringed instrument played by plucking or strumming. **gui·tar′ist** n

gulch n ravine; gully.

gulf n large inlet of the sea; chasm; large gap.

gull¹ n long-winged web-footed seabird.

gull² n dupe, fool. ▶ vt dupe, cheat. **gul·li·bil′i·ty** n **gul′li·ble** adj easily imposed on, credulous.

gul·let [GUL-it] n food passage from mouth to stomach.

gul·ly [GUL-ee] n, pl **-lies.** channel or ravine worn by water.

gulp vt swallow eagerly. ▶ vi gasp, choke. ▶ n

gum¹ n firm flesh in which teeth are set. ▶ vt **gummed, gum·ming.** chew with the gums.

gum² n sticky substance issuing from certain trees; an adhesive; chewing gum; gum tree, eucalyptus. ▶ vt **gummed, gum·ming.** stick with gum. **gum′my** adj **-mi·er, -mi·est. gum′shoe** n shoe of rubber; sl detective. **gum tree** any species of eucalyptus. **gum up the works** sl impede progress.

gump·tion [GUM-shən] n resourcefulness; shrewdness, sense.

gun n weapon with metal tube from which missiles are discharged by explosion; cannon, pistol, etc. ▶ v **gunned, gun·ning.** shoot; pursue, as with gun; race engine (of car). **gun′ner** n **gun′ner·y** n use or science of large guns. **gun′boat** n small warship. **gun dog** (breed of)

dog used to retrieve, etc. game.
gun′man *n* armed criminal.
gun′met·al *n* alloy of copper and tin or zinc, formerly used for guns.
gun′pow·der *n* explosive mixture of saltpeter, sulfur, charcoal.
gun′shot *n* shot or range of gun. ▶ *adj* caused by missile from gun.
gun′wale, gun′nel [GUN-l] *n* upper edge of ship's side.
gunk [gungk] *n inf* any sticky, oily matter.
gun·ny [GUN-ee] *n, pl* **-nies.** strong, coarse sacking made from jute.
gup·py [GUP-ee] *n, pl* **-pies.** small colorful aquarium fish.
gur·gle [GUR-gəl] *n* bubbling noise. ▶ *vi* **-gled, -gling.** utter, flow with gurgle.
gur·ney [GUR-nee] *n, pl* **-neys.** wheeled bed.
gu·ru [GUUR-oo] *n* a spiritual teacher, esp. in India.
gush *vi* flow out suddenly and copiously, spurt. ▶ *n* sudden and copious flow; effusiveness. **gush′er** *n* gushing person; oil well.
gus·set [GUS-it] *n* triangle or diamond-shaped piece of material let into garment. **gus′set·ed** *adj*
gust *n* sudden blast of wind; burst of rain, anger, passion, etc. **gust′y** *adj* **gust·i·er, gust·i·est.**
gus·to [GUS-toh] *n* enjoyment, zest.
gut *n* (oft. pl) entrails, intestines; material made from guts of animals, e.g. for violin strings, etc. ▶ *pl inf* essential, fundamental part; courage. ▶ *vt* **gut·ted, gut·ting.** remove guts from (fish, etc.); remove, destroy contents of (house). **guts′y** *adj inf* **guts·i·er, guts·i·est.** courageous; vigorous.
gut·ter [GUT-ər] *n* shallow trough for carrying off water from roof or side of street. ▶ *vt* make channels in. ▶ *vi* flow in streams; of candle, melt away by wax forming channels and running down.
gutter press journalism that relies on sensationalism. **gut′ter·snipe**

[-snīp] *n* neglected slum child.
gut·tur·al [GUT-ər-əl] *adj* of, relating to, or produced in, the throat. ▶ *n* guttural sound or letter.
guy¹ [gī] *n inf* person (usu. male). ▶ *vt* **guyed, guy·ing.** make fun of; ridicule. **wise guy** *inf, usu. disparaging* clever person.
guy² *n* rope, chain, etc. to steady, secure something, e.g. tent. ▶ *vt* **guyed, guy·ing.** keep in position by guy.
guz·zle [GUZ-əl] *v* **-zled, -zling.** eat or drink greedily. ▶ *n*
gym [jim] *n* short for GYMNASIUM or GYMNASTICS.
gym·kha·na [jim-KAH-nə] *n* competition or display of horse riding or gymnastics; place for this.
gym·na·si·um [jim-NAY-zee-əm] *n* place equipped for muscular exercises, athletic training.
gym′nast *n* expert in gymnastics.
gym·nas′tics *pl n* muscular exercises, with or without apparatus, e.g. parallel bars.
gy·ne·col·o·gy [gī-ni-KOL-ə-jee] *n* branch of medicine dealing with functions and diseases of women. **gy·ne·col′o·gist** *n*
gyp·sum [JIP-səm] *n* crystalline sulfate of lime, a source of plaster.
Gyp·sy [JIP-see] *n, pl* **-sies.** one of a wandering people originally from NW India, Romany.
gy·rate [JĪ-rayt] *vi* **-rat·ed, -rat·ing.** move in circle, spirally, revolve. **gy·ra′tion** *n*
gy·ro·com·pass [JĪ-roh-kum-pəs] *n* compass using gyroscope.
gy·ro·scope [JĪ-rə-skohp] *n* disk or wheel so mounted as to be able to rotate about any axis, esp. to keep disk (with compass, etc.) level despite movement of ship, etc. **gy·ro·scop′ic** [-SKOP-ik] *adj*
gy·ro·sta·bi·liz·er [jī-rə-STAY-bə-lī-zər] *n* gyroscopic device to prevent rolling of ship or airplane.

H h

H *Chem* hydrogen.

ha·be·as cor·pus [HAY-bee-əs KOR-pəs] *n* writ issued to produce prisoner in court.

hab·er·dash·er [HAB-ər-dash-ər] *n* dealer in articles of dress, ribbons, pins, needles, etc. **hab'er·dash·er·y** *n* **-er·ies.**

hab'it *n* settled tendency or practice; constitution; customary apparel esp. of nun or monk; woman's riding dress. **ha·bit·u·al** [hə-BICH-oo-əl] *adj* formed or acquired by habit; usual, customary. **ha·bit'u·ate** [-ayt] *vt* **-at·ed, -at·ing.** accustom. **ha·bit·u·a'tion** *n* **ha·bit'u·é** [-oo-ay] *n* constant visitor.

hab·it·a·ble [HAB-i-tə-bəl] *adj* fit to live in. **hab'i·tat** *n* natural home (of animal, etc.). **hab·i·ta'tion** [-TAY-shən] *n* dwelling place.

ha·ci·en·da [hah-see-EN-də] *n, pl* **-das.** ranch or large estate in Sp. Amer.

hack¹ [hak] *vt* cut, chop (at) violently; *inf* utter harsh, dry cough; *sl* deal or cope with. ▶ *n* **hack'er** *n sl* person who through personal computer breaks into computer system of company or government. **hack around** *sl* pass time idly.

hack² *n* drudge, esp. writer of inferior literary works; cabdriver. **hack'work** *n* dull, repetitive work.

hack·le [HAK-əl] *n* neck feathers of rooster, etc. ▶ *pl* hairs on back of neck of dog and other animals that are raised in anger.

hack·ney [HAK-nee] *n, pl* **-neys.** harness horse, carriage, coach kept for hire.

hack·neyed [HAK-need] *adj* (of words, etc.) stale, trite because of overuse.

hack·saw [HAK-saw] *n* handsaw for cutting metal.

had pt./pp. of HAVE.

Ha·des [HAY-deez] *n Greek myth* underworld home of the dead.

haft *n* handle (of knife, etc.). ▶ *vt* fit with one.

hag *n* ugly old woman; witch.

hag·gard [HAG-ərd] *adj* wild-looking; anxious, careworn.

hag'gis *n* Scottish dish made from sheep's heart, lungs, liver, chopped with oatmeal, suet, onion, etc., and boiled in the stomach.

hag·gle [HAG-əl] *vi* **-gled, -gling.** bargain, wrangle over price. ▶ *n*

hag·i·ol·o·gy [hag-ee-OL-ə-jee] *n, pl* **-gies.** literature of the lives of saints. **hag·i·og'ra·pher** [-rə-fər] *n* **hag·i·og'ra·phy** *n, pl* **-phies.** writing of this.

hail¹ [hayl] *n* (shower of) pellets of ice; intense shower, barrage. ▶ *v* pour down as shower of hail. **hail'stone** *n*

hail² *vt* greet (esp. enthusiastically); acclaim, acknowledge; call. ▶ *vi* come (from).

hair *n* filament growing from skin of animal, as covering of person's head; such filaments collectively. **hair'i·ness** *n* **hair'y** *adj* **hair·i·er, hair·i·est. hair'do** [-doo] *n, pl* **-dos.** way of styling hair. **hair'dress·er** *n* one who attends to and cuts hair, esp. women's hair. **hair'line** *adj, n* very fine (line); lower edge of human hair e.g. on forehead. **hair'pin** *n* pin for keeping hair in place. **hairpin bend** U-shaped turn in road. **hair'split·ting** *n* making of overly fine distinctions. **hair'spring** *n* very fine, delicate spring in timepiece. **hair trigger** trigger operated by light touch. **hair-trigger** *adj* easily set off, e.g. *a hair-trigger temper.*

hal·cy·on [HAL-see-ən] *n* bird fabled to calm the sea and to breed on floating nest. **halcyon days** time of peace and happiness.

hale [hayl] *adj* **hal·er, hal·est.** robust, healthy, e.g. *hale and hearty.*

half [haf] *n, pl* **halves** [havz] either

of two equal parts of thing. ▶ *adj* forming half. ▶ *adv* to the extent of half. **half'back** *n Football* one of two players lining up on each side of fullback. **half-baked** *adj* underdone; *inf* immature, silly. **half'-breed** *n offens* person with parents of different races. **half'-broth·er** *n* brother by one parent only. **half-cocked** *adj* ill-prepared. **half-heart·ed** *adj* unenthusiastic. **half'-life** *n, pl* **-lives.** time taken for half the atoms in radioactive material to decay. **half nel'son** hold in wrestling. **half'-sis·ter** *n* sister by one parent only. **half'time** *n Sports* rest period between two halves of a game. **half'tone** *n* illustration printed by photoengraving from plate, showing lights and shadows by means of minute dots. **half vol'ley** *Sport* striking of a ball the moment it bounces. **half'wit** *n* feeble-minded person; stupid person.

hal·i·but [HAL-ə-bət] *n* large edible flatfish.

hal·i·to·sis [hal-i-TOH-sis] *n* bad-smelling breath.

hall [hawl] *n* (entrance) passage; large room or building belonging to particular group or used for particular purpose esp. public assembly.

hal·le·lu·jah [hal-ə-LOO-yə] *n, interj* exclamation of praise to God.

hall·mark [HAWL-mahrk] *n* mark used to indicate standard of tested gold and silver; mark of excellence; distinguishing feature.

hal·low [HAL-oh] *vt* make, or honor as holy. **Hal·low·een** [hal-ə-WEEN] *n* the evening of Oct. 31st, the day before All Saints' Day.

hal·lu·ci·nate [hə-LOO-sə-nayt] *vi* **-nat·ed, -nat·ing.** suffers illusions. **hal·lu·ci·na'tion** *n* illusion. **hal·lu'ci·na·to·ry** *adj* **hal·lu'ci·no·gen** [-jən] *n* drug inducing hallucinations.

ha·lo [HAY-loh] *n, pl* **-los, -loes.** circle of light around moon, sun, etc.; disk of light around saint's head in picture; ideal glory attaching to person. ▶ *vt* **-loed, -lo·ing.** surround with halo.

halt¹ [hawlt] *n* interruption or end to progress, etc. (esp. as command to stop marching). ▶ *v* (cause to) stop.

halt² *vi* falter, fail. **halt'ing** *adj* hesitant, lame.

hal·ter [HAWL-tər] *n* rope or strap with headgear to fasten horses or cattle; low-cut dress style with strap passing behind neck. ▶ *vt* put halter on, fasten with one.

halve [hav] *vt* **halved, halv·ing.** cut in half; reduce to half; share.

hal·yard [HAL-yərd] *n* rope for raising sail, signal flags, etc.

ham *n* meat (esp. salted or smoked) from thigh of pig; actor adopting exaggerated, unconvincing style; amateur radio enthusiast. **ham it up** overact. **ham'string** *n* tendon at back of knee. ▶ *vt* **-strung, -string·ing.** cripple by cutting this; render useless; thwart.

ham·burg·er [HAM-burg-gər] *n* broiled, fried patty of ground beef, esp. served in bread roll.

ham·let [HAM-lit] *n* small village.

ham·mer [HAM-ər] *n* tool usu. with heavy head at end of handle, for beating, driving nails, etc.; machine for same purposes; contrivance for exploding charge of gun; auctioneer's mallet; heavy metal ball on wire thrown in sports. ▶ *v* strike with, or as with, hammer. **ham'mer·head** [-hed] *n* shark with wide, flattened head. **ham'mer·toe** *n* deformed toe. **hammer out** solve problem by painstaking work.

ham·mock [HAM-ək] *n* bed of canvas, etc., hung on cords.

ham·per¹ [HAM-pər] *n* large covered basket, such as for laundry; large parcel, box, etc. of food, wines, etc., esp. one sent as gift.

ham·per² *vt* impede, obstruct movements of.

ham·ster [HAM-stər] *n* type of rodent, sometimes kept as pet.

ham'strung *adj* crippled, thwarted;

see HAM.

hand *n* extremity of arm beyond wrist; side, quarter, direction; style of writing; cards dealt to player; measure of four inches; manual worker; sailor; help, aid; pointer on dial; applause. ▶ *vt* pass; deliver; hold out. **hand'ful** *n*, *pl* **-fuls.** small amount or number; *inf* person, thing causing problems. **hand'i·ly** *adv* **hand'i·ness** *n* dexterity; state of being near, available. **hand'y** *adj* **hand·i·er, hand·i·est.** convenient; clever with the hands. **hand'bag** *n* woman's bag for personal articles; bag for carrying in hand. **hand'bill** *n* small printed notice. **hand'book** *n* small reference or instruction book. **hand'cuff** *n* fetter for wrist, usu. joined in pair. ▶ *vt* secure thus. **hand'i·craft** *n* manual occupation or skill. **hand'i·work** *n* thing done by particular person. **hand·ker·chief** [HANG-kər-chif] *n* small square of fabric carried in pocket for wiping nose, etc. **hand'out** *n inf* money, food, etc. given free; pamphlet giving news, information, etc. **hands-on** *adj* involving practical experience of equipment. **hand'stand** *n* act of supporting body in upside-down position by hands alone. **hand'writ·ing** *n* way person writes. **hand'y·man** *n* one employed to do various tasks; one skilled in odd jobs. **hand in glove** very intimate.

hand·i·cap [HAN-dee-kap] *n* something that hampers or hinders; race, contest in which chances are equalized by weights carried, golf strokes, etc.; condition so imposed; any physical disability. ▶ *vt* **-capped, -cap·ping.** hamper; impose handicap on; attempt to predict winner of race, game. **handicapped** *dated* physically or mentally disabled.

han·dle [HAN-dl] *n* part of thing to hold it by. ▶ *vi* **-dled, -dling.** touch, feel with hands; manage; deal with; trade. **han'dle·bars** *pl n* curved metal bars used to steer bicycle, motorbike, etc. **handlebar mustache** one resembling handlebar.

hand·some [HAN-səm] *adj* of fine appearance; generous; ample.

hang *v* hung *or* hanged, hang·ing. ▶ *vt* suspend; kill by suspension by neck; attach, set up (wallpaper, doors, etc.). ▶ *vi* be suspended, cling. **hang'er** *n* frame on which clothes, etc. can be hung. **hang'dog** *adj* sullen, dejected. **hang glider** glider like large kite, with pilot hanging in frame below. **hang gliding** *n* **hang'man** *n* executioner. **hang'o·ver** *n* aftereffects of too much drinking. **hang out** *inf* reside, frequent. **hang-up** *n sl* persistent emotional problem; preoccupation.

hang·ar [HANG-ər] *n* large shed for aircraft.

hank [hangk] *n* coil, skein, length, esp. as measure of yarn.

hank·er [HANG-kər] *vi* (oft. with *after* or *for*) crave.

han·ky-pan·ky [HANG-kee-PANG-kee] *n inf* trickery; illicit sexual relations.

han·som [HAN-səm] *n* two-wheeled horse-drawn cab for two to ride inside with driver mounted up behind.

hap·haz·ard [hap-HAZ-ərd] *adj* random, careless.

hap·less [HAP-lis] *adj* unlucky.

hap·pen [HAP-ən] *vi* come about, occur; chance to do. **hap'pen·ing** *n* occurrence, event.

hap·py *adj* **-pi·er, -pi·est.** glad, content; lucky, fortunate; apt. **hap'pi·ly** *adv* **hap'pi·ness** *n* **hap'py-go-luck'y** *adj* casual, lighthearted.

ha·ra-ki·ri [HAHR-ə-KEER-ee] *n* in Japan, ritual suicide by disemboweling.

ha·rangue [hə-RANG] *n* vehement speech; tirade. ▶ *v* **-rangued, -rangu·ing.**

ha·rass [hə-RAS] *vt* worry, trouble, torment. **ha·rass'ment** *n*

har·bin·ger [HAHR-bin-jər] *n* one who announces another's approach; forerunner, herald.

har·bor [HAHR-bər] *n* shelter for ships; shelter. ▶ *v* give shelter, protection to; maintain (secretly) esp. grudge, etc.

hard [hahrd] *adj* **-er, -est.** firm, resisting pressure; solid; difficult to understand; harsh, unfeeling; difficult to bear; practical, shrewd; heavy; strenuous; of water, not making lather well with soap; of drugs, highly addictive. ▶ *adv* vigorously; with difficulty; close. **hard'en** *v* **hard'ly** *adv* unkindly, harshly; scarcely, not quite; only just. **hard'ship** *n* bad luck; severe toil, suffering; instance of this. **hard'ball** *n* baseball; *inf* forceful or ruthless methods of achieving a goal. **hard-boiled** *adj* boiled so long as to be hard; *inf* of person, unemotional, unsentimental. **hard copy** computer output printed on paper; original paper document. **hard disk** *Computers* rigid data-storage disk in a sealed container. **hard-hat** *n inf* construction worker. **hard'head'ed** *adj* shrewd. **hard-pressed** *adj* heavily burdened. **hard'ware** *n* tools, implements; necessary (parts of) machinery; *Computers* mechanical and electronic parts. **hard'wood** *n* wood from deciduous trees. **hard of hearing** rather deaf. **hard up** very short of money.

har·dy [HAHR-dee] *adj* **-di·er, -di·est.** robust, vigorous; bold; of plants, able to grow in the open all the year round. **har'di·hood** [-huud] *n* extreme boldness, audacity. **hard'i·ly** *adv* **har'di·ness** *n*

hare [hair] *n* animal like large rabbit, with longer legs and ears, noted for speed. **hare'brained** *adj* rash, wild. **hare'lip** *n* fissure of upper lip.

har·em [HAIR-əm] *n* women's part of Muslim dwelling; one man's wives and concubines.

hark [hahrk] *vi* listen. **hark back** return to previous subject of

discussion.

har·le·quin [HAHR-lə-kwin] *n* stock comic character, esp. masked clown in diamond-patterned costume. **har·le·quin·ade'** [-NAYD] *n* scene in pantomime; buffoonery.

har·lot [HAHR-lət] *n* whore, prostitute. **har'lot·ry** *n*

harm [hahrm] *n* damage, injury. ▶ *vt* cause harm to. **harm'ful** *adj* **harm'less** *adj* unable or unlikely to hurt.

har·mo·ny [HAHR-mə-nee] *n, pl* **-nies.** agreement; concord; peace; combination of notes to make chords; melodious sound. **har·mon'ic** *adj* of harmony. ▶ *n* tone or note whose frequency is a multiple of its pitch. **har·mon'ics** *n* science of musical sounds. **har·mon'i·ca** *n* various musical instruments, but esp. mouth organ. **har·mo'ni·ous** *adj* **har'mo·nize** [-mə-nīz] *v* **-nized, -niz·ing.** ▶ *vt* bring into harmony; cause to agree; reconcile. ▶ *vi* be in harmony.

har·ness [HAHR-nis] *n* equipment for attaching horse to cart, plow, etc.; any such equipment. ▶ *vt* put on, in harness; utilize energy or power of (waterfall, etc.).

harp [hahrp] *n* musical instrument of strings played by hand. ▶ *vi* play on harp; dwell (on) persistently. **harp'ist** *n* **harp'si·chord** [-si-kord] *n* stringed instrument like piano.

har·poon [hahr-POON] *n* barbed spear with rope attached for catching whales. ▶ *vt* catch, kill with this. **har·poon'er** *n* **harpoon gun** gun for firing harpoon in whaling.

Har·py [HAHR-pee] *n, pl* **-pies.** monster with body of woman and wings and claws of bird; **(h-)** cruel, grasping person.

har·ri·dan [HAHR-i-dn] *n* shrewish old woman, hag.

har·row [HAR-oh] *n* implement for smoothing, leveling or stirring up soil. ▶ *vt* draw harrow over; distress greatly. **har'row·ing** *adj* heartrending; distressful.

har·ry [HAR-ee] *vt* **-ried, -ry·ing.**

harass; ravage.

harsh [hahrsh] *adj* **-er, -est.** rough, discordant; severe; unfeeling. **harsh·ness** *n*

har·um-scar·um [HAIR-əm-SKAIR-əm] *adj* reckless, wild; disorganized.

har·vest [HAHR-vist] *n* (season for) gathering in grain; gathering; crop; product of action. ▶ *vt* reap and gather in.

has [haz] third person sing. pres. indicative of HAVE.

hash *n* dish of hashed meat, etc.; *inf* short for HASHISH; mess, jumble. ▶ *vt* cut up small, chop; mix up.

hash·ish [hash-EESH] *n* resinous extract of Indian hemp, esp. used as hallucinogen.

hasp *n* clasp passing over a staple for fastening door, etc. ▶ *vt* fasten, secure with hasp.

has·sle [HAS-əl] *n inf* quarrel; a lot of bother, trouble. ▶ *v* **-sled, -sling.**

has·sock [HAS-ək] *n* cushion used as footstool, ottoman; tuft of grass.

haste [hayst] *n* speed, quickness, hurry. ▶ *v* **hast·ed, hast·ing.** ▶ *vi* hasten. **has·ten** [HAY-sən] *v* (cause to) hurry, increase speed. **hast'i·ly** *adv* **hast'y** *adj* **hast·i·er, hast·i·est.**

hat *n* head covering, usu. with brim. **hat'ter** *n* dealer in, maker of hats. **hat trick** any three successive achievements, esp. in sports.

hatch¹ [hach] *v* of young, esp. of birds, (cause to) emerge from egg; contrive, devise. **hatch'er·y** *n*, *pl* **-er·ies.**

hatch² *n* hatchway; trapdoor over it; lower half of divided door. **hatch'back** *n* automobile with single lifting door in rear. **hatch'way** *n* opening in deck of ship, etc.

hatch³ *vt* engrave or draw lines on for shading; shade with parallel lines.

hatch·et [HACH-it] *n* small ax. **hatchet job** malicious verbal attack. **hatchet man** person carrying out unpleasant assignments for another; professional assassin. **bury the**

hatchet make peace.

hate [hayt] *vt* **hat·ed, hat·ing.** dislike strongly; bear malice toward. ▶ *n* this feeling; that which is hated. **hate'ful** *adj* detestable. **ha·tred** [HAY-trid] *n* extreme dislike, active ill will.

haugh·ty [HAW-tee] *adj* **-ti·er, -ti·est.** proud, arrogant. **haugh'ti·ness** *n*

haul [hawl] *vt* pull, drag with effort. ▶ *vi* of wind, shift in direction. ▶ *n* hauling; what is hauled; catch of fish; acquisition; distance (to be) covered. **haul·age** [HAW-lij] *n* carrying of loads; charge for this. **haul'er** *n* firm, person that transports goods by road.

haunch [hawnch] *n* human hip or fleshy hindquarter of animal; leg and loin of animal as food.

haunt [hawnt] *vt* visit regularly; visit in form of ghost; recur to. ▶ *n* esp. place frequently visited. **haunt'ed** *adj* frequented by ghosts; worried.

hau·teur [hoh-TUR] *n* haughty spirit; arrogance.

have [hav] *vt* **had, hav·ing.** hold, possess; be possessed, affected with; be obliged (to do); cheat, outwit; engage in, obtain; contain; allow; cause to be done; give birth to; used to form past tenses (with a past participle), e.g. *we have looked; she had done enough.*

ha·ven [HAY-vən] *n* place of safety.

hav·er·sack [HAV-ər-sak] *n* canvas bag for provisions, etc. carried on back or shoulder when hiking, etc.

hav·oc [HAV-ək] *n* devastation, ruin; *inf* confusion, chaos.

hawk¹ *n* bird of prey smaller than eagle; supporter, advocate, of warlike policies. ▶ *vi* hunt with hawks; attack like hawk.

hawk² *vt* offer (goods) for sale, as in street. **hawk'er** *n*

hawk³ *vi* clear throat noisily.

haw·ser [HAW-zər] *n* large rope or cable.

hay *n* grass mown and dried. **hay'cock** *n* conical pile of hay for drying. **hay fever** allergic reaction to pollen, dust, etc. **hay'stack** *n* large pile of hay. **hay'wire** *adj* crazy; disorganized.

haz·ard [HAZ-ərd] *n* chance; risk, danger. ▸ *vt* expose to risk; run risk of. **haz'ard·ous** *adj* risky.

haze [hayz] *n* mist, often due to heat; obscurity. **ha'zy** *adj* **-zi·er, -zi·est.** misty; obscured; vague.

ha·zel [HAY-zəl] *n* bush or small tree bearing nuts; yellowish-brown color of the nuts. ▸ *adj* light brown.

He *Chem* helium.

he [hee] *pron* third person masculine pronoun; person, animal already referred to. ▸ *comb. form* male, e.g. *he-goat*.

head [hed] *n* upper part of person's or animal's body, containing mouth, sense organs and brain; upper part of anything; chief of organization, school, etc.; chief part; aptitude, capacity; crisis; leader; title; headland; person, animal considered as unit; white froth on beer, etc.; *inf* headache; *sl* addict, habitual user of drug. ▸ *adj* chief, principal; of wind, contrary. ▸ *vt* be at the top, head of; lead, direct; provide with head; hit (ball) with head. ▸ *vi* make for; form a head. **head'er** *n* headfirst plunge; brick laid with end in face of wall; action of striking ball with head. **head'ing** *n* title. **heads** *adv inf* with obverse side (of coin) uppermost. **head'y** *adj* **head·i·er, head·i·est.** apt to intoxicate or excite. **head'ache** [-ayk] *n* continuous pain in head; worrying circumstance. **head'board** *n* vertical board at head of bed. **head'land** [-lənd] *n* promontory. **head'light** *n* powerful lamp carried on front of locomotive, motor vehicle, etc. **head'line** *n* news summary, in large type in newspaper. **head'long** *adv* head foremost, in rush. **head'quar·ters** *pl n* residence of commander-in-chief; center of operations. **head'stone** *n* gravestone. **head'strong** *adj* self-willed. **head'way** *n* advance, progress.

heal [heel] *v* make or become well.

health [helth] *n* soundness of body; condition of body; toast drunk in person's honor. **health'i·ly** *adv* **health'y** *adj* **health·i·er, health·i·est.** of strong constitution; of or producing good health, well-being, etc.; vigorous. **health food** vegetarian food, organically grown, eaten for dietary value.

heap [heep] *n* pile of things lying one on another; great quantity. ▸ *vt* pile, load with.

hear [heer] *v* **heard** [hurd], **hear·ing.** perceive by ear; listen to; *Law* try (case); heed; perceive sound; learn. **hear'ing** *n* ability to hear; earshot; judicial examination. **hear'say** *n* rumor. ▸ *adj*

heark·en [HAHR-kən] *vi* listen.

hearse [hurs] *n* funeral carriage for coffin.

heart [hahrt] *n* organ that makes blood circulate; seat of emotions and affections; mind, soul, courage; central part; playing card marked with figure of heart; one of these marks. **heart'en** *v* make, become cheerful. **heart'i·ly** *adv* **heart'less** [-lis] *adj* unfeeling. **heart'y** *adj* **heart·i·er, heart·i·est.** friendly; vigorous; in good health; satisfying the appetite. **heart attack** sudden severe malfunction of heart. **heart'burn** *n* pain in upper intestine. **heart'rend·ing** *adj* overwhelming with grief; agonizing. **heart'throb** *n* object of infatuation. **heart'-to-heart'** *adj* frank, sincere. **by heart** by memory.

hearth [hahrth] *n* floor of fireplace; part of room where fire is made; home.

heat [heet] *n* hotness; sensation of this; hot weather or climate; warmth of feeling, anger, etc.; sexual excitement caused by readiness to mate in female animals; one of many races, etc. to decide persons to compete in finals. ▸ *v* make, become hot. **heat'ed** *adj* esp. angry.

heath [heeth] *n* tract of wasteland; low-growing evergreen shrub.

hea·then [HEE-thən] *adj* not adhering to a religious system; pagan; barbarous; unenlightened. ▶ *n* heathen person. **hea'then·ish** *adj* of or like heathen; rough; barbarous.

heath·er [HE*th*-ər] *n* shrub growing on heaths and mountains.

heave [heev] *v* **heaved, heav·ing.** ▶ *vt* lift with effort; throw (something heavy); utter (sigh). ▶ *vi* swell, rise; vomit. ▶ *n*

heav·en [HEV-ən] *n* abode of God; place of bliss; (also pl) sky. **heav'en·ly** *adj* lovely, delightful, divine; beautiful; of or like heaven.

heav·y [HEV-ee] *adj* **heav·i·er, heav·i·est.** weighty, striking, falling with force; dense; sluggish; difficult, severe; sorrowful; serious; dull; *sl* serious, excellent. **heav'i·ly** *adv* **heav'i·ness** *n* **heavy industry** basic, large-scale industry producing metal, machinery, etc. **heavy metal** rock music with strong beat and amplified instrumental effects. **heavy water** deuterium oxide, water in which normal hydrogen content has been replaced by deuterium.

Heb. Hebrews.

He·brew [HEE-broo] *n* member of an ancient Semitic people; their language; its modern form, used in Israel.

heck·le [HEK-əl] *v* **-led, -ling.** interrupt or try to annoy (speaker) by questions, taunts, etc.

hect-, hecto- *comb. form* one hundred, e.g. *hectoliter; hectometer.*

hec·tare [HEK-tahr] *n* one hundred ares (10,000 square meters, 2.471 acres).

hec·tic [HEK-tik] *adj* rushed, busy.

hec·tor [HEK-tər] *v* bully, bluster. ▶ *n* bully.

hedge [hej] *n* fence of bushes. ▶ *v* **hedged, hedg·ing.** ▶ *vt* surround with hedge; obstruct; hem in; bet on both sides. ▶ *vi* make hedge; be evasive; secure against loss. **hedge'hog** *n* small animal covered with spines.

he·don·ism [HEED-n-iz-əm] *n*

doctrine that pleasure is the chief good. **he'don·ist** *n*

heed *vt* take notice of, care for. **heed'ful** *adj* **heed'less** *adj* careless.

heel[1] *n* hinder part of foot; part of shoe supporting this; undesirable person. ▶ *vt* supply with heel; touch ground with heel. ▶ *vi* of dog, follow at one's heels.

heel[2] *v* of ship, (cause to) lean to one side. ▶ *n* heeling, list.

heft·y [HEF-tee] *adj* **heft·i·er, heft·i·est.** bulky; weighty; strong.

he·gem·o·ny [hi-JEM-ə-nee] *n, pl* **-nies.** leadership, political domination.

heif·er [HEF-ər] *n* young cow.

height [hīt] *n* measure from base to top; quality of being high; elevation; highest degree; (oft. pl) area of high ground. **heights** extremes, e.g. *dizzy heights of success.* **height'en** *vt* make higher; intensify.

hei·nous [HAY-nəs] *adj* atrocious, extremely wicked, detestable.

heir [air] *n* person entitled to inherit property or rank. **heir'ess** *n, fem* **heir'loom** *n* thing that has been in family for generations.

held pt./pp. of HOLD.

hel·i·cal [HEL-i-kəl] *adj* spiral.

hel·i·cop·ter [HEL-i-kop-tər] *n* aircraft made to rise vertically by pull of rotating blades turning horizontally. **hel'i·port** *n* airport for helicopters.

helio- *comb. form* sun, e.g. *heliograph.*

he·li·o·graph [HEE-lee-ə-graf] *n* signaling apparatus employing a mirror to reflect sun's rays.

he·li·o·ther·a·py [hee-lee-oh-THER-ə-pee] *n* therapeutic use of sunlight.

he·li·o·trope [HEE-lee-ə-trohp] *n* plant with purple flowers; color of the flowers. **he·li·o·trop'ic** [-TROP-ik] *adj* growing, turning toward source of light.

he·li·um [HEE-lee-əm] *n* very light, nonflammable gaseous element.

he·lix [HEE-liks] *n* spiral.

hell *n* abode of the damned; abode

of the dead generally; place or state of wickedness, or misery, or torture. **hell'ish** adj

Hel·len·ic [he-LEN-ik] adj pert. to inhabitants of Greece.

hel·lo [he-LOH] interj expression of greeting or surprise.

helm n tiller, wheel for turning ship's rudder.

hel·met [HEL-mit] n defensive or protective covering for head.

help vt aid, assist; support; succor; remedy, prevent. ▶ n assistance or support. **help'ful** adj **help'ing** n single portion of food taken at a meal. **help'less** [-lis] adj useless, incompetent; unaided; unable to help. **help'mate, -meet** n helpful companion; husband or wife.

hel·ter-skel·ter [HEL-tər-SKEL-tər] adv, adj, n (in) hurry and confusion.

hem n border of cloth, esp. one made by turning over edge and sewing it down. ▶ vt **hemmed, hem·ming.** sew thus; confine, shut in. **hem'stitch** n ornamental stitch. ▶ vt

hemi- comb. form half, e.g. hemisphere.

hem·i·ple·gi·a [hem-i-PLEE-jə] n paralysis of one side of body. **hem·i·ple'gic** adj, n

hem·i·sphere [HEM-i-sfeer] n half sphere; half of celestial sphere; half of Earth. **hem·i·spher'i·cal** [-sfe-rə-kəl] adj

hem·lock [HEM-lok] n poisonous plant; poison extracted from it; evergreen of pine family.

hemo-, hema- comb. form blood, e.g. hemophilia.

he·mo·glo·bin [HEE-mə-gloh-bin] n coloring and oxygen-bearing matter of red blood corpuscles.

he·mo·phil·i·a [hee-mə-FIL-ee-ə] n hereditary tendency to intensive bleeding as blood fails to clot. **he·mo·phil'i·ac** n

hem·or·rhage [HEM-ər-ij] n profuse bleeding. ▶ vi **-rhaged, -rhag·ing.** bleed profusely; lose assets, esp. in large amounts.

hem·or·rhoids [HEM-ə-roidz] pl n swollen veins in rectum (also **piles**).

hemp n Indian plant; its fiber used for rope, etc.; any of several narcotic drugs made from varieties of hemp. **hemp'en** [-pən] adj made of hemp or rope.

hen n female of domestic fowl and others. **hen'peck** vt (of a woman) harass (a man, esp. husband) by nagging.

hence [hens] adv from this point; for this reason. **hence·for'ward, hence'forth** adv from now onward.

hench·man [HENCH-mən] n trusty follower; unscrupulous supporter.

hen·na [HEN-ə] n flowering shrub; reddish dye made from it.

hen·o·the·ism [HEN-ə-thee-iz-əm] n belief in one god (of several) as special god of one's family, tribe, etc.

hen·ry [HEN-ree] n, pl **-ries.** SI unit of electrical inductance.

he·pat·ic [hi-PAT-ik] adj pert. to the liver. **hep·a·ti·tis** [hep-ə-TĪ-tis] n inflammation of the liver.

hepta- comb. form seven, e.g. heptagon.

hep·ta·gon [HEP-tə-gon] n figure with seven angles. **hep·tag'o·nal** adj

her [hur] adj objective and possessive case of SHE. **hers** pron of her. **her·self'** pron emphatic form of SHE.

her·ald [HER-əld] n messenger, envoy; officer who makes royal proclamations, arranges ceremonies, etc. ▶ vt announce; proclaim approach of. **he·ral·dic** [hi-RAL-dik] adj **her'ald·ry** n study of (right to have) heraldic bearings.

herb [urb] n plant with soft stem that dies down after flowering; plant of which parts are used in cookery or medicine. **her·ba·ceous** [hur-BAY-shəs] adj of, like herbs; perennially flowering. **herb·al** [HUR-bəl] adj of herbs. ▶ n book on herbs. **herb'al·ist** n writer on herbs; collector, dealer in medicinal herbs. **herb'i·cide** [-sīd] n chemical that destroys plants. **her·biv·o·rous** [-ə-rəs] adj feeding on plants.

Her·cu·les [HUR-kyə-leez] *n*
mythical hero noted for strength.
her·cu·le·an [-kyə-LEE-ən] *adj*
requiring great strength, courage;
hard to perform.

herd [hurd] *n* company of animals,
usu. of same species, feeding or
traveling together. ▶ *v* crowd
together. ▶ *vt* tend (herd).
herds·man [HURDZ-mən] *n*

here [heer] *adv* in this place; at or
to this point. **here·af·ter** *adv* in
time to come. ▶ *n* future existence
after death. **here·to·fore′**
[-tə-FOR] *adv* before.

he·red·i·ty [hə-RED-i-tee] *n*
tendency of organism to transmit
its nature to its descendants.
he·red′i·tar·y [-ter-ee] *adj*
descending by inheritance; holding
office by inheritance; that can be
transmitted from one generation to
another.

her·e·sy [HER-ə-see] *n, pl* **-sies**
[-seez] opinion contrary to
orthodox opinion or belief.
her′e·tic *n* one holding opinions
contrary to orthodox faith.
he·ret′i·cal [-kəl] *adj*

her·it·age [HER-i-tij] *n* what may be
or is inherited; anything from past,
esp. owned or handed down by
tradition. **her′it·a·ble** *adj* that can
be inherited.

her·maph·ro·dite [hur-MAF-rə-dīt]
n person, animal with
characteristics or reproductive
organs of both sexes.

her·met·ic [hur-MET-ik] *adj* sealed
so as to be airtight.
her·met′i·cal·ly *adv*

her·mit [HUR-mit] *n* one living in
solitude, esp. from religious
motives. **her′mit·age** [-tij] *n* this
person's abode.

her·ni·a [HUR-nee-ə] *n* projection of
(part of) organ through lining
encasing it.

he·ro [HEER-oh] *n, pl* **-roes**. one
greatly regarded for achievements
or qualities; principal character in
poem, play, story; illustrious
warrior; demigod. **her·o·ine**
[HER-oh-in] *n, fem* **he·ro′ic**

[hi-ROH-ik] *adj* of, like hero;
courageous, daring. **he·ro′i·cal·ly**
adv **he·ro′ics** *pl n* extravagant
behavior. **her′o·ism** *n* qualities of
hero; courage, boldness. **hero
sandwich** large sandwich of meats,
etc. on loaf of Italian bread. **hero
worship** admiration of heroes or of
great men; excessive admiration of
others.

her·o·in [HER-oh-in] *n* white
crystalline derivative of morphine, a
highly addictive narcotic.

her·on [HER-ən] *n* long-legged
wading bird.

her·pes [HUR-peez] *n* any of several
diseases, including shingles and
cold sores.

her′ring *n* important food fish of
northern hemisphere.

hertz [hurts] *n, pl* **hertz**. SI unit of
frequency.

hes·i·tate [HEZ-i-tayt] *vi* **-tat·ed**,
-tat·ing. hold back; feel, or show
indecision; be reluctant.
hes′i·tan·cy [-tən-see] *n*
hes·i·ta′tion *n* wavering; doubt;
stammering. **hes′i·tant** *adj*
undecided, pausing.

hetero- *comb. form* other or
different, e.g. *heterosexual*.

het·er·o·dox [HET-ər-ə-doks] *adj*
not orthodox. **het′er·o·dox·y** *n, pl*
-dox·ies.

het·er·o·ge·ne·ous
[het-ər-ə-JEE-nee-əs] *adj* composed
of diverse elements.
het·er·o·ge·ne′i·ty [-jə-NEE-i-tee] *n*

het·er·o·sex·u·al
[het-ər-ə-SEK-shoo-əl] *n* person
sexually attracted to members of
the opposite sex.

heu·ris·tic [hyuu-RIS-tik] *adj* serving
to find out or to stimulate
investigation.

hew [hyoo] *v* **hewed** *or* **hewn**,
hew·ing. chop, cut with axe.
hew′er *n*

hex [heks] *n* magic spell. ▶ *v*
bewitch.

hex-, hexa- *comb. form* six, e.g.
hexagon.

hex·a·gon [HEK-sə-gon] *n* figure
with six angles. **hex·ag′o·nal** *adj*

hex·am·e·ter [hek-SAM-i-tər] *n* line of verse of six feet.

hey·day [HAY-day] *n* bloom, prime.

Hf *Chem* hafnium.

Hg *Chem* mercury.

hi·a·tus [hī-AY-təs] *n, pl* **-tus·es.** break or gap where something is missing.

hi·ber·nate [HĪ-bər-nayt] *vi* **-nat·ed, -nat·ing.** pass the winter, esp. in a torpid state. **hi·ber·na'tion** *n*

hi·bis·cus [hī-BIS-kəs] *n* flowering (sub)tropical shrub.

hic·cup [HIK-up] *n* spasm of the breathing organs with an abrupt cough-like sound. ▶ *vi* **-cupped, -cup·ping.** have this.

hick [hik] *adj inf* rustic; unsophisticated. ▶ *n* person, place like this.

hick·o·ry [HIK-ə-ree] *n, pl* **-o·ries.** N Amer. nut-bearing tree; its tough wood.

hide[1] [hīd] *v* **hid, hid·den** or **hid, hid·ing.** ▶ *vt* put, keep out of sight; conceal, keep secret. ▶ *vi* conceal oneself. **hide'out** *n* hiding place.

hide[2] *n* skin of animal. **hid'ing** *n sl* thrashing. **hide'bound** *adj* restricted, esp. by petty rules, etc.; narrow-minded.

hid·e·ous [HID-ee-əs] *adj* repulsive, revolting.

hi·er·ar·chy [HĪ-ə-rahr-kee] *n, pl* **-chies.** system of persons or things arranged in graded order. **hi·er·ar'chi·cal** *adj*

hi·er·o·glyph·ic [hī-ər-ə-GLIF-ik] *adj* of a system of picture writing, as used in ancient Egypt. ▶ *n* symbol representing object, concept or sound; symbol, picture, difficult to decipher. **hi'er·o·glyph** *n*

hi-fi [HĪ-FĪ] *adj* short for HIGH-FIDELITY. ▶ *n* high-fidelity equipment.

high [hī] *adj* **-er, -est.** tall, lofty; far up; of roads, main; of meat, tainted; of sound, acute in pitch; expensive; of great importance, quality, or rank; *inf* in state of euphoria, esp. induced by alcohol or drugs. ▶ *adv* far up; strongly, to a great extent; at, to a high pitch; at a high rate. **high'ly** *adv* **high'ness** *n* quality of being high; **(H-)** title of prince and princess. **high'brow** *n* intellectual, esp. intellectual snob. ▶ *adj* intellectual; difficult; serious. **high'-fi·del'i·ty** *adj* of high-quality sound-reproducing equipment. **high-flown** *adj* extravagant, bombastic. **high'-hand'ed** *adj* domineering, dogmatic. **high'land** [-lənd] *n* relatively high ground. **High'land** *adj* of, from the highlands of Scotland. **high'light** *n* lightest or brightest area in painting, photograph, etc.; outstanding feature. ▶ *vt* bring into prominence. **high'-rise** *adj, n* (of) building that has many stories and elevators. **high'-sound'ing** *adj* pompous, imposing. **high-strung** *adj* excitable, nervous.

high-tech *adj* same as HI-TECH. **high time** latest possible time. **high'way** *n* main road. **highway robbery** *inf* exorbitant fee or charge. **high'way·man** [-mən] *n* (formerly) robber on road, esp. mounted.

hi·jack [HĪ-jak] *vt* divert or wrongfully take command of a vehicle (esp. aircraft) or its contents or passengers; rob. **hi'jack·er** *n*

hike [hīk] *v* **hiked, hik·ing.** ▶ *vi* walk a long way (for pleasure) in country. ▶ *vt* pull (up), hitch. ▶ *n* **hik'er** *n*

hi·lar·i·ty [hi-LAR-i-tee] *n* cheerfulness, gaiety. **hi·lar'i·ous** *adj*

hill *n* natural elevation, small mountain; mound. **hill'ock** [-ək] *n* little hill. **hill'y** *adj* **hill·i·er, hill·i·est.** **hill'bil·ly** *n, pl* **-lies.** *offens* unsophisticated country person.

hilt *n* handle of sword, etc. **up to the hilt** completely.

him *pron* objective case of pronoun HE. **him·self'** *pron* emphatic form of HE.

hind[1] [hīnd] *n* female of deer.

hind[2] *adj* at the back, posterior; (also **hind·er**) [HĪN-dər]

hin·der [HIN-dər] *vt* obstruct, impede, delay. **hin'drance** [-drəns] *n*

Hin·di [HIN-dee] *n* language of N central India. **Hin'du** [-doo] *n* person who adheres to Hinduism. **Hin'du·ism** the dominant religion of India.

hinge [hinj] *n* movable joint, as that on which door hangs. ▶ *v* **hinged, hing·ing.** ▶ *vt* attach with, or as with, hinge. ▶ *vi* turn, depend on.

hint *n* slight indication or suggestion. ▶ *v* give hint of.

hin·ter·land [HIN-tər-land] *n* district lying behind coast, or near city, port, etc.

hip *n* either side of body below waist and above thigh; angle formed where sloping sides of roof meet; fruit of rose, esp. wild.

hip-hop [HIP-hop] *n* pop-culture movement involving rap music, graffiti, and break dancing.

hip·pie [HIP-ee] *n* (formerly) (young) person whose behavior, dress, etc. implies rejection of conventional values.

hip·po·pot·a·mus [hip-ə-POT-ə-məs] *n, pl* **-mus·es** or **-mi** [-mī] large Afr. animal living in and near rivers.

hire [hīr] *vt* **hired, hir·ing.** obtain temporary use of by payment; engage for wage. ▶ *n* hiring or being hired; payment for use of thing. **hire'ling** *n* one who works for wages.

hir·sute [HUR-soot] *adj* hairy.

his [hiz] *pron, adj* belonging to him.

His·pan·ic [hi-SPAN-ik] *adj* relating to Spain or to Spanish-speaking Central and S. America. ▶ *n* Spanish-speaking person; U.S. resident of Hispanic descent.

his'pid *adj* rough with bristles or minute spines; bristly, shaggy.

hiss *vi* make sharp sound of letter S, esp. in disapproval. ▶ *vt* express disapproval, deride thus. ▶ *n*

his·ta·mine [HIS-tə-meen] *n* substance released by body tissues, sometimes creating allergic reactions.

his·tol·o·gy [hi-STOL-ə-jee] *n* science that treats of minute

structure of organic tissues.

his·to·ry [HIS-tə-ree] *n, pl* **-ries.** record of past events; study of these; past events; train of events, public or private; course of life or existence; systematic account of phenomena. **his·to'ri·an** *n* writer of history. **his·tor'ic** *adj* noted in history. **his·tor'i·cal** *adj* of, based on, history; belonging to past. **his·tor·ic'i·ty** [-tə-RIS-i-tee] *n* historical authenticity. **his·to·ri·og'ra·pher** *n* official historian; one who studies historical method. **his·to·ri·og'ra·phy** *n* methods of historical research.

his·tri·on·ic [his-tree-ON-ik] *adj* excessively theatrical, insincere, artificial in manner. **his·tri·on'ics** *n* behavior like this.

hit *v* **hit, hit·ting.** ▶ *vt* strike with blow or missile; affect injuriously; find. ▶ *vi* strike; light (upon). ▶ *n* blow; success; *Computers* single visit to a website or single result of a search. **hit'ter** *n* **hit man** *sl* hired assassin. **hit it off** *inf* get along with (person). **hit or miss** haphazard(ly). **hit the hay** *inf* go to bed. **hit the road** *inf* proceed on journey; depart.

hitch [hich] *vt* fasten with loop, etc.; raise, move with jerk. ▶ *vi* be caught or fastened. ▶ *n* difficulty; knot, fastening; jerk. **hitch'hike** *vi* **-hiked, -hik·ing.** travel by begging free rides.

hi-tech *n* technology requiring sophisticated scientific equipment and engineering techniques; interior design using features of industrial equipment. ▶ *adj*

hith·er [HITH-ər] *adv* to or toward this place. **hith'er·to** *adv* up to now or to this time.

hive [hīv] *n* structure in which bees live or are housed; *fig* place swarming with busy occupants. ▶ *v* **hived, hiv·ing.** gather, place bees, in hive.

hives [hīvz] *pl n* eruptive skin disease.

Ho *Chem* holmium.

hoard [hord] *n* stock, store, esp. hidden away. ▶ *vt* amass and hide away; store.

hoarse [hors] *adj* **hoars·er, hoars·est.** rough, harsh sounding, husky.

hoar·y [HOR-ee] *adj* **hoar·i·er, hoar·i·est.** gray with age; grayish-white; of great antiquity; venerable. **hoar'frost** *n* frozen dew.

hoax [hohks] *n* practical joke; deceptive trick. ▶ *vt* play trick on; deceive. **hoax'er** *n*

hob *n* projection or shelf at side or back of fireplace, used for keeping food warm; tool for cutting gear teeth, etc. **hob'nail** [-nayl] *n* large-headed nail for boot soles.

hob·ble [HOB-əl] *v* **-bled, -bling.** ▶ *vi* walk lamely. ▶ *vt* tie legs together (of horse, etc.); impede, hamper. ▶ *n* straps or ropes put on an animal's legs to prevent it from straying; limping gait.

hob·by [HOB-ee] *n, pl* **-bies.** favorite occupation as pastime. **hob'by·horse** *n* toy horse; favorite topic, preoccupation.

hob'gob·lin *n* mischievous fairy.

hob'nob *vi* **-nobbed, -nob·bing.** associate, be familiar (with).

ho·bo [HOH-boh] *n, pl* **-boes.** shiftless, wandering person.

hock [hok] *n* backward-pointing joint on leg of horse, etc., corresponding to human ankle. ▶ *vt* disable by cutting tendons of hock, hamstring.

hock·ey [HOK-ee] *n* team game played on a field with ball and curved sticks; ice hockey.

ho·cus-po·cus [HOH-kəs-POH-kəs] *n* trickery; mystifying jargon.

hod *n* small trough on a pole for carrying mortar, bricks, etc.

hoe [hoh] *n* tool for weeding, breaking ground, etc. ▶ *vt* **hoed, hoe·ing.**

hog [hawg] *n* pig, esp. castrated male for fattening; greedy, dirty person. ▶ *vt* **hogged, hog·ging.** *inf* eat, use (something) selfishly.

hogs·head [HAWGZ-hed] *n* large cask; liquid measure of 63 to 140 gallons (238 to 530 liters). **hog'tie** *vt* **-tied, -ty·ing.** hobble; hamper.

hog'wash *n* nonsense; pig food.

ho·gan [HOH-gən] *n* Navajo Indian dwelling of earth, branches, etc.

hoi pol·loi [HOI pə-LOI] *n* the common mass of people; the masses.

hoist *vt* raise aloft, raise with tackle, etc.

ho·key·po·key [HO-kee-PO-kee] *n* kind of playful dance or its music.

hold[1] [hohld] *v* **held, hold·ing.** ▶ *vt* keep fast, grasp; support in or with hands, etc.; maintain in position; have capacity for; own, occupy; carry on; detain; celebrate; keep back; believe. ▶ *vi* cling; not to give away; abide (by); keep (to); last, proceed, be in force; occur. ▶ *n* grasp; influence. **hold'ing** *n* (oft pl) property, as land or stocks and bonds. **hold'up** *n* armed robbery; delay.

hold[2] *n* space in ship or aircraft for cargo.

hole [hohl] *n* hollow place, cavity; perforation; opening; *inf* unattractive place; *inf* difficult situation. ▶ *v* **holed, hol·ing.** make holes in; go into a hole; drive into a hole.

hol'i·day *n* day or other period of rest from work, etc., esp. spent away from home.

hol·low [HOL-oh] *adj* **-er, -est.** having a cavity, not solid; empty; false; insincere; not full-toned. ▶ *n* cavity, hole, valley. ▶ *vt* make hollow, make hole in; excavate.

hol·ly [HOL-ee] *n, pl* **-lies** [-leez] evergreen shrub usu. with prickly leaves and red berries.

hol·o·caust [HOL-ə-kawst] *n* great destruction of life, esp. by fire; (**H-**) mass slaughter of Jews in Nazi concentration camps during World War II.

hol'o·gram [HOL-ə-gram] *n* a three-dimensional photographic image.

hol·o·graph [HOL-ə-graf] *n* document wholly written by the signer.

ho·log·ra·phy [hə-LOG-rə-fee] *n* science of using lasers to produce a photographic record that can reproduce a three-dimensional image.

hol·ster [HOHL-stər] *n* case for pistol, hung from belt, etc.

ho·ly [HOH-lee] *adj* **-li·er, -li·est.** belonging, devoted to God; free from sin; divine; consecrated. **ho′li·ness** *n* sanctity; **(H-)** Pope's title. **holy day** day of religious festival. **Holy Communion** service of the Eucharist. **Holy Week** that before Easter Sunday.

hom·age [HOM-ij] *n* tribute, respect, reverence; formal acknowledgment of allegiance.

home [hohm] *n* dwelling place; residence; native place; institution for the elderly, infirm, etc. ▶ *adj* of, connected with, home; native. ▶ *adv* to, at one's home; to the point. ▶ *v* **homed, hom·ing.** direct or be directed onto a point or target. **home′boy** *n sl* close friend. **home fries** boiled potatoes, sliced and fried in butter, etc. **home′less** *adj* **home′ly** *adj* **-li·er, -li·est.** unpretentious; warm and domesticated; plain. **home′ward** [-wərd] *adj, adv* **home′wards** *adv* **home-brew** *n* alcoholic drink made at home, esp. beer. **home′sick** *adj* depressed by absence from home. **home′spun** *adj* domestic; simple. ▶ *n* cloth made of homespun yarn. **home′stead** [-sted] *n* house with outbuildings, esp. on farm. **home′stead·er** *n* **home′work** *n* school work done usu. at home. **bring home to** impress deeply upon. **home free** sure of success. **home page** *n Internet* introductory information about a website with links to the information or services provided.

ho·me·op·a·thy [hoh-mee-OP-ə-thee] *n* treatment of disease by small doses of what would produce symptoms in healthy person. **ho·me·o·path′ic** *adj*

hom·i·cide [HOM-ə-sīd] *n* killing of human being; killer. **hom·i·cid′al** *adj*

hom·i·ly [HOM-ə-lee] *n, pl* **-lies** [-leez] sermon; religious discourse. **hom·i·let′ic** *adj* of sermons. **hom·i·let′ics** *n* art of preaching.

Ho·mo [HOH-moh] *n* genus to which modern man belongs.

homo- *comb. form* same, like, e.g. *homophone; homosexual.*

ho·mo·ge·ne·ous [hoh-mə-JEE-nee-əs] *adj* formed of uniform parts; similar, uniform; of the same nature. **ho·mo·ge·ne′i·ty** *n* **ho·mog·e·nize** [hə-MOJ-ə-nīz] *vt* **-nized, -niz·ing.** break up fat globules in milk and cream to distribute them evenly; make uniform or similar.

ho·mol·o·gous [hə-MOL-ə-gəs] *adj* having the same relation, relative position, etc. **ho·mo·logue** [HOH-mə-lawg] *n* homologous thing.

hom·o·nym [HOM-ə-nim] *n* word of same form as another, but of different sense.

ho·mo·sex·u·al [hoh-mə-SEK-shoo-əl] *n* person sexually attracted to members of the same sex. ▶ *adj* **ho·mo·sex·u·al′i·ty** *n* **ho·mo·pho′bi·a** [-PHOH-bee-ə] *n* hate or fear of homosexuals and homosexuality.

hone [hohn] *n* whetstone for sharpening razors, etc. ▶ *vt* **honed, hon·ing.** sharpen on one.

hon·est [ON-ist] *adj* not cheating, lying, stealing, etc.; genuine; without pretension. **hon′est·y** *n* quality of being honest.

hon·ey [HUN-ee] *n, pl* **-eys.** sweet fluid made by bees. **hon′ey·comb** [-kohm] *n* wax structure in hexagonal cells in which bees place honey, eggs, etc. ▶ *vt* fill with cells or perforations. **hon′ey·dew** [-doo] *n* sweet sticky substance found on plants; type of sweet melon. **hon′ey·moon** *n* holiday taken by newly wedded couple; any new relationship with initial period of harmony. ▶ *vi* spend one's honeymoon.

honk [hongk] *n* call of goose; any sound like this, esp. sound of automobile horn. ▶ *vi* make this sound. ▶ *vt* cause (automobile horn) to sound.

hon·or [ON-ər] *n* personal integrity; renown; reputation; sense of what is right or due; chastity; high rank or position; source, cause of honor; pleasure, privilege. ▶ *pl* mark of respect; distinction in examination. ▶ *vt* respect highly; confer honor on; accept or pay (bill, etc.) when due. **hon'or·a·ble** *adj* **hon·o·rar'i·um** *n, pl* **-rar·i·a**. a fee. **hon'or·ar·y** *adj* conferred for the sake of honor only; holding position without pay or usual requirements; giving services without pay. **hon·or·if'ic** *adj* conferring, indicating honor. ▶ *n* in certain languages, form used to show respect, esp. in direct address.

hood[1] [huud] *n* covering for head and neck, often part of cloak or gown; hoodlike thing, as covering of engine compartment of automobile, etc. **hood'ed** *adj* covered with or shaped like a hood. **hood'wink** *vt* deceive.

hood[2] *n sl* hoodlum.

hood·lum [HUUD-ləm] *n* gangster; street ruffian.

hoo'doo *n* cause of bad luck.

hoof [huuf] *n, pl* **hoofs** or **hooves**. horny casing of foot of horse, etc. **on the hoof** [of livestock] alive]

hoo-ha [HOO-hah] *n* uproar. ▶ *interj* exclamation expressing excitement or surprise.

hook [huuk] *n* bent piece of metal, etc., for catching hold, hanging up, etc.; something resembling hook in shape or function; curved cutting tool; enticement; *Boxing* blow delivered with elbow bent. ▶ *vt* grasp, catch, hold, as with hook; fasten with hook; *Golf* drive (ball) widely to the left (of right-handed golfer, and vice versa). **hooked** *adj* shaped like hook; caught; *inf* addicted to; *sl* married. **hook'er** *n sl* prostitute. **hook'up** *n* linking of

radio, television stations.

hook'worm [-wurm] *n* parasitic worm infesting humans and animals.

hook·ah [HUUK-ə] *n* oriental pipe in which smoke is drawn through cooling water and long tube.

hoo·li·gan [HOO-li-gən] *n* violent, irresponsible (young) person; ruffian. **hoo'li·gan·ism** *n*

hoop *n* rigid circular band of metal, wood, etc. such a band used for binding barrel, etc., for use as a toy, or for jumping through as in circus acts. ▶ *vt* bind with hoops; encircle. **put through the hoops** *inf* subject to ordeal or test.

hoop·la [HOOP-lah] *n inf* excitement; hullabaloo.

hoot *n* owl's cry or similar sound; cry of disapproval or derision; *sl* funny person or thing. ▶ *vi* utter hoot (esp. in derision). ▶ *vt* assail (someone) with derisive cries; drive (someone) away by hooting.

hop[1] *vi* **hopped, hop·ping.** spring on one foot; *inf* move quickly. ▶ *n* leap, skip; one stage of journey. **hop'scotch** [-skoch] *n* children's game of hopping in pattern drawn on ground.

hop[2] *n* climbing plant with bitter cones used to flavor beer, etc. ▶ *pl* the cones.

hope [hohp] *n* expectation of something desired; thing that gives, or object of, this feeling. ▶ *v* **hoped, hop·ing.** feel hope (for). **hope'ful** *adj* **hope'less** *adj* **young hopeful** promising boy or girl.

hop·per [HOP-ər] *n* one who hops; device for feeding material into mill or machine or grain into truck, etc. **hopper car** railroad freight car, usu. open at top and containing one or more hoppers, for transport and discharge of grain, etc.

horde [hord] *n* large crowd (esp. moving together).

ho·ri·zon [hə-RĪ-zən] *n* boundary of part of Earth seen from any given point; lines where Earth and sky seem to meet; boundary of mental outlook. **hor·i·zon·tal**

[hor-ə-ZON-tl] *adj* parallel with horizon, level.

hor·mone [HOR-mohn] *n* substance secreted by certain glands that stimulates organs of the body; synthetic substance with same effect.

horn *n* hard projection on heads of certain animals, e.g. cattle; substance of it; various things made of, or resembling it; *Music* wind instrument orig. made of a horn; device (esp. in car) emitting sound as alarm, warning, etc. **horned** *adj* having horns. **horn'y** *adj* **horn·i·er, horn·i·est.** hornlike; *sl* lustful. **horn'pipe** *n* lively dance, esp. associated with sailors.

hor·net [HOR-nit] *n* large insect of wasp family. **hornet's nest** much opposition, animosity.

hor·o·scope [HOR-ə-skohp] *n* observation of, or scheme showing disposition of planets, etc. at given moment, esp. birth, by which character and abilities of individual are predicted; telling of person's fortune by this method.

hor·ren·dous [haw-REN-dəs] *adj* horrific.

hor·ror [HOR-ər] *n* terror; loathing, fear of; its cause. **hor'ri·ble** *adj* exciting horror, hideous, shocking. **hor'ri·bly** *adv* **hor'rid** *adj* unpleasant, repulsive; *inf* unkind. **hor'ri·fy** *vt* **-fied, -fy·ing.** move to horror. **hor·rif'ic** *adj* particularly horrible.

hors d'oeu·vre [or-DURV] *n, pl* **-vres** [-DURVZ] small appetizer served before main meal.

horse [hors] *n* four-legged animal used for riding and work; cavalry; vaulting horse; frame for support; *sl* heroin. ▶ *vt* **horsed, hors·ing.** provide with horse or horses. **hors'y** *adj* **hors·i·er, hors·i·est.** having to do with horses; devoted to horses or horse racing. **horse'fly** *n, pl* **-flies.** large bloodsucking fly. **horse laugh** harsh boisterous laugh usu. expressing derision. **horse'man** [-mən], **-wom·an** *n* rider on horse.

horse'play *n* rough, boisterous play. **horse'pow·er** *n* unit of power of engine, etc., 550 foot-pounds per second. **horse'shoe** [-shoo] *n* protective U-shaped piece of iron nailed to horse's hoof; thing so shaped. **horse around** *sl* play roughly, boisterously.

hor·ti·cul·ture [HOR-ti-kul-chər] *n* art or science of gardening. **hor·ti·cul'tur·al** *adj*

Hos. Hosea.

ho·san·na [hoh-ZAN-ə] *n, pl* **-nas.** cry of praise, adoration.

hose [hohz] *n* flexible tube for conveying liquid or gas; stockings. ▶ *vt* **hosed, hos·ing.** water with hose. **ho'sier·y** *n* stockings or socks.

hos·pice [HOS-pis] *n* traveler's house of rest kept by religious order; residence for care of terminally ill.

hos·pi·tal [HOS-pi-tl] *n* institution for care of sick. **hos·pi·tal·i·za'tion** *n* **hos'pi·tal·ize** *vt* **-ized, -iz·ing.** to place for care in a hospital.

hos·pi·tal·i·ty [hos-pi-TAL-i-tee] *n, pl* **-ties.** friendly and liberal reception of strangers or guests. **hos'pi·ta·ble** *adj* welcoming, kindly.

host¹ [hohst] *n* one who entertains another; master of ceremonies of show; animal, plant on which parasite lives; *Computers* computer that provides data or connectivity to others on a network. ▶ *vt* act as a host. **-ess** *n, fem*

host² *n* large number.

Host *n* consecrated bread of the Eucharist.

hos·tage [HOS-tij] *n* person taken or given as pledge or security.

hos·tel [HOS-tl] *n* building providing accommodation at low cost for particular category of people, as students, or the homeless.

hos·tile [HOS-tl] *adj* opposed, antagonistic; warlike; of an enemy; unfriendly. **hos·til'i·ty** *n* enmity. **hos·til'i·ties** *pl n* acts of warfare.

hot *adj* **hot·ter, hot·test.** of high

temperature, very warm, giving or feeling heat; angry; severe; recent, new; much favored; spicy; *sl* good, quick, smart, lucky, successful; *sl* stolen. **hot'ly** *adv* **hot'ness** *n* **hot air** *inf* boastful, empty talk.

hot'bed *n* bed of earth heated by manure and grass for young plants; any place encouraging growth; center of activity. **hot'-blood-ed** [-blud-id] *adj* passionate, excitable. **hot dog** frankfurter (in split bread roll). **hot'foot** [-fuut] *v, adv* (go) quickly. **hot'head** [-hed] *n* hasty, intemperate person. **hot'house** *n* forcing house for plants; heated building for cultivating tropical plants in cold or temperate climates. **hot line** direct communication link between heads of governments, etc. **hot pants** extremely brief and close-fitting pants for women; *sl* strong sexual desire. **hot'plate** *n* heated plate on electric cooker; portable device for keeping food warm.

ho-tel [hoh-TEL] *n* commercial establishment providing lodging.

hound [hownd] *n* hunting dog. ▶ *vt* chase, urge, pursue.

hour [owr] *n* twenty-fourth part of day; sixty minutes; time of day; appointed time. ▶ *pl* fixed periods for work, prayers, etc.; book of prayers. **hour'ly** *adv* every hour; frequently. ▶ *adj* frequent; happening every hour. **hour'glass** *n* instrument using dropping sand or mercury to indicate passage of an hour.

hou-ri [HUUR-ee] *n, pl* **-ris.** beautiful virgin provided in the Muslim paradise.

house [hows] *n, pl* **hous-es** [HOW-ziz] building for human habitation; building for other specified purpose; legislative or other assembly; family; business firm; theater audience, performance. ▶ *vt* [howz] **housed, hous-ing.** give or receive shelter, lodging or storage; cover or contain. **housing** *n* (providing of) houses; part or structure designed

to cover, protect, contain.

house'boat *n* boat for living in on river, etc. **house'break-er** [-brayk-ər] *n* burglar. **house'coat** *n* woman's long loose garment for casual wear at home. **house'hold** *n* inmates of house collectively. **house'hold-er** *n* occupier of house as own dwelling; head of household. **house'-hus-band** *n* man who runs a household. **house'keep-er** *n* person managing affairs of household. **house'keep-ing** *n* running household. **house'warm-ing** *n* party to celebrate entry into new house. **house'wife** *n* woman who runs a household.

hov-el [HUV-əl] *n* mean dwelling.

hov-er [HUV-ər] *vi* hang in the air (of bird, etc.); loiter; be in state of indecision. **hov'er-craft** *n* type of craft that can travel over land and sea on a cushion of air.

how *adv* in what way; by what means; in what condition; to what degree; (in direct or dependent question). **how-ev'er** *conj* nevertheless. ▶ *adv* in whatever way, degree; all the same.

how-dah [HOW-də] *n* (canopied) seat on elephant's back.

how-itz-er [HOW-it-sər] *n* short gun firing shells at high elevation.

howl *vi* utter long loud cry. ▶ *n* such cry. **howl'er** *n* one that howls; embarrassing mistake.

hoy-den [HOID-n] *n* wild, boisterous girl, tomboy.

Hs *Chem* hassium.

HTML *Computers* hypertext markup language: text description language that is used on the World Wide Web.

hub *n* middle part of wheel, from which spokes radiate; central point of activity.

hub'bub *n* confused noise of many voices; uproar.

huck-ster [HUK-stər] *n* retailer, peddler; person using aggressive or questionable methods of selling. ▶ *vt* sell goods thus.

hud-dle [HUD-l] *n* crowded mass;

inf impromptu conference, esp. of offensive football team during game. ▶ *v* **-dled, -dling.** heap, crowd together; hunch; confer.

hue [hyoo] *n* color, complexion.

hue and cry public uproar, outcry; loud outcry usually in pursuit of wrongdoer.

huff *n* passing mood of anger. ▶ *v* make or become angry, resentful. ▶ *vi* blow, puff heavily. **huff'i·ly** *adv* **huff'y** *adj* **huff·i·er, huff·i·est.**

hug *vt* **hugged, hug·ging.** clasp tightly in the arms; cling; keep close to. ▶ *n* fond embrace.

huge [hyooj] *adj* very big. **huge'ly** *adv* very much.

hu·la [HOO-lə] *n* native dance of Hawaii.

hulk *n* body of abandoned vessel; large, unwieldy thing. **hulk'ing** *adj* unwieldy, bulky.

hull *n* frame, body of ship; calyx of strawberry, raspberry, or similar fruit; shell, husk. ▶ *vt* remove shell, hull.

hul·la·ba·loo [HUL-ə-bə-loo] *n, pl* **-loos.** uproar, clamor, row.

hum *v* **hummed, hum·ming.** ▶ *vi* make low continuous sound as bee; be very active. ▶ *vt* sing with closed lips. ▶ *n* humming sound; smell; great activity; in radio, disturbance affecting reception. **hum'ming·bird** *n* very small bird whose wings make humming noise.

hu·man [HYOO-mən] *adj* of people; relating to, characteristic of, people's nature. **hu·mane'** [-MAYN] *adj* benevolent, kind; merciful. **hu'man·ism** *n* belief in human effort rather than religion; interest in human welfare and affairs; classical literary culture. **hu'man·ist** *n* **hu·man·i·tar'i·an** *n* philanthropist. ▶ *adj* **hu·man'i·ty** *n, pl* **-ties** [-teez] human nature; human race; kindliness. ▶ *pl* study of literature, philosophy, the arts. **hu'man·ize** *vt* **-ized, -iz·ing.** make human; civilize. **hu'man·ly** *adv* **hu'man·kind** [-kīnd] *n* human race as a whole.

hum·ble [HUM-bəl] *adj* **-bler,**

-blest. lowly, modest. ▶ *vt* **-bled, -bling.** bring low, abase, humiliate. **hum'bly** *adv*

hum'bug *n* impostor; sham, nonsense, deception. ▶ *vt* **-bugged, -bug·ging.** deceive; defraud.

hum·ding·er [HUM-DING-ər] *n inf* excellent person or thing.

hum'drum *adj* commonplace, dull, monotonous.

hu·mer·us [HYOO-mər-əs] *n, pl* **-mer·i** [-mə-rī] long bone of upper arm.

hu·mid [HYOO-mid] *adj* moist, damp. **hu·mid'i·fi·er** *n* device for increasing amount of water vapor in air in room, etc. **hu·mid'i·fy** *vt* **-fied, -fy·ing. hu·mid'i·ty** *n*

hu·mil·i·ate [hyoo-MIL-ee-ayt] *vt* **-at·ed, -at·ing.** lower dignity of, abase, mortify.

hu·mil·i·ty [hyoo-MIL-i-tee] *n* state of being humble; meekness.

hum·mock [HUM-ək] *n* low knoll, hillock; ridge of ice.

hum·mus [HEW-mus] *n* creamy dip of Middle East origin, made from puréed chickpeas.

hu·mor [HYOO-mər] *n* faculty of saying or perceiving what excites amusement; state of mind, mood; temperament; *obs* one of four chief fluids of body. ▶ *vt* gratify, indulge. **hu'mor·ist** *n* person who acts, speaks, writes humorously. **hu'mor·ous** *adj* funny; amusing.

hump *n* normal or deforming lump, esp. on back; hillock. ▶ *vt* make hump-shaped; *inf* exert (oneself), hurry; *sl* carry or heave. **hump'back** *n* person with hump. **hump'backed** *adj* having a hump.

hu·mus [HYOO-məs] *n* decayed vegetable and animal mold.

hunch *n inf* intuition or premonition; hump. ▶ *vt* thrust, bend into hump. **hunch'back** *n* humpback.

hun·dred [HUN-drid] *n, adj* cardinal number, ten times ten. **hun'dredth** [-dridth] *adj* the ordinal number. **hun'dred·fold** *adj, adv* **hun'dred·weight** *n* weight of 100 lbs. (45.359 kg).

hung pt./pp. of HANG. adj (of jury, etc.) unable to decide; not having majority. **hung'o'ver** adj inf experiencing a hangover. **hung up** inf delayed; stymied; baffled. **hung up on** sl obsessed by.

hun·ger [HUNG-gər] n discomfort, exhaustion from lack of food; strong desire. ▶ vi **hun'gri·ly** adv **hun'gry** adj **-gri·er, -gri·est.** having keen appetite. **hunger strike** refusal of all food, as a protest.

hunk [hungk] n thick piece; sl attractive man with excellent physique.

hunt v seek out to kill or capture for sport or food; search (for). ▶ n chase, search; track of country hunted over; (party organized for) hunting; pack of hounds; hunting club. **hunt'er** n one who hunts; horse, dog bred for hunting. **-ress** n, fem

hur·dle [HUR-dl] n portable frame of bars for temporary fences or for jumping over; obstacle. ▶ vi **-dled, -dling.** race over hurdles. **hurdles** n a race over hurdles. **hurd'ler** n

hurl vt throw violently. **hurl·y-burl·y** [HUR-lee-BUR-lee] n, pl **-burl·ies.** loud confusion.

hur·rah [hə-RAH], **hur·ray** [-RAY] interj exclamation of joy or applause. **last hurrah** final occasion of achievement.

hur·ri·cane [HUR-i-kayn] n very strong, potentially destructive wind or storm. **hurricane lamp** lamp with glass chimney around flame.

hur·ry [HUR-ee] v **-ried, -ry·ing.** (cause to) move or act in great haste. ▶ n, pl **-ries.** undue haste; eagerness. **hur'ried·ly** adv

hurt v hurt, hurt·ing. ▶ vt injure, damage, give pain to, wound feelings of; distress. ▶ vi inf feel pain. ▶ n wound, injury, harm. **hurt'ful** adj

hur·tle [HUR-tl] vi **-tled, -tling.** move rapidly; rush violently; whirl.

hus·band [HUZ-bənd] n married man. ▶ vt economize; use to best advantage. **hus'ban·dry** [-dree] n farming; economy.

hush v make or be silent. ▶ n stillness; quietness. **hush-hush** adj inf secret. **hush up** suppress rumors, information; make secret.

husk n dry covering of certain seeds and fruits; worthless outside part. ▶ vt remove husk from. **husk'y** adj **husk·i·er, husk·i·est.** rough in tone; hoarse; dry as husk, dry in the throat; of, full of, husks; big and strong.

husk·y [HUS-kee] n, pl **husk·ies.** Arctic sledge dog with thick hair and curled tail.

hus·sy [HUS-ee] n, pl **-sies.** brazen or immoral woman; impudent girl or young woman.

hus·tings [HUS-tingz] pl n any place from which political campaign speeches are made; political campaigning.

hus·tle [HUS-əl] v **-tled, -tling.** push about, jostle, hurry. ▶ vi sl solicit clients esp. for prostitution. ▶ n **hus·tler** [HUS-lər] industrious person; sl prostitute.

hut n any small house or shelter, usu. of wood or metal.

hutch [huch] n boxlike pen for rabbits, etc.

hy·brid [HĪ-brid] n offspring of two plants or animals of different species; mongrel. ▶ adj crossbred. **hy'brid·ism** n **hy'brid·ize** v **-ized, -iz·ing.** make hybrid; crossbreed.

hy·dra [HĪ-drə] n, pl **-dras** [-drəz] fabulous many-headed water serpent; any persistent problem; freshwater polyp. **hy'dra-head·ed** adj hard to understand, root out.

hy·dran·gea [hī-DRAYN-jə] n ornamental shrub with pink, blue, or white flowers.

hy·drant [HĪ-drənt] n water pipe with nozzle for hose.

hy·drau·lic [hī-DRAW-lik] adj concerned with, operated by, pressure transmitted through liquid in pipe. **hy·drau'lics** n science of mechanical properties of liquid in motion.

hydro- comb. form water, e.g. hydroelectric; presence of hydrogen, e.g. hydrocarbon.

hy·dro·car·bon [hī-drə-KAHR-bən] *n* compound of hydrogen and carbon.

hy·dro·chlor·ic ac·id [hī-drə-KLOR-ik] strong colorless acid used in many industrial and laboratory processes.

hy·dro·dy·nam·ics [hī-droh-dī-NAM-iks] *n* science of the motions of system wholly or partly fluid.

hy·dro·e·lec·tric [hī-droh-i-LEK-trik] *adj* pert. to generation of electricity by use of water.

hy·dro·foil [HĪ-drə-foil] *n* fast, light vessel with hull raised out of water at speed by action of vanes in water.

hy·dro·gen [HĪ-drə-jən] *n* colorless gas that combines with oxygen to form water. **hydrogen bomb** atom bomb of enormous power in which hydrogen nuclei are converted into helium nuclei. **hydrogen peroxide** colorless liquid used as antiseptic and bleach.

hy·drog·ra·phy [hī-DROG-rə-fee] *n* description of waters of the earth. **hy·dro·graph·ic** *adj*

hy·drol·y·sis [hī-DROL-ə-sis] *n* decomposition of chemical compound reacting with water.

hy·drom·e·ter [hī-DROM-i-tər] *n* device for measuring relative density of liquid.

hy·dro·pho·bi·a [hī-drə-FOH-bee-ə] *n* aversion to water, esp. as symptom of rabies; rabies.

hy·dro·plane [HĪ-drə-playn] *n* light skimming motorboat; seaplane; vane controlling motion of submarine, etc.

hy·dro·pon·ics [hī-drə-PON-iks] *n* science of cultivating plants in water without using soil.

hy·dro·ther·a·py [hī-drə-THER-ə-pee] *n Med* treatment of disease by external application of water.

hy·drous [HĪ-drəs] *adj* containing water.

hy·e·na [hī-EE-nə] *n* wild animal related to dog.

hy·giene [HĪ-jeen] *n* principles and practice of health and cleanliness; study of these principles. **hy·gi·en·ic** [hī-jee-EN-ik] *adj* **hy·gien'ist** [-JEE-nist] *n*

hy·grom·e·ter [hī-GROM-i-tər] *n* instrument for measuring humidity of air.

hy·gro·scop·ic [hī-grə-SKOP-ik] *adj* readily absorbing moisture from the atmosphere.

hy·men [HĪ-mən] *n* membrane partly covering vagina of virgin; **(H-)** Greek god of marriage.

hymn [him] *n* song of praise, esp. to God. ▶ *vt* praise in song. **hym·nal** [HIM-nl] *adj* of hymns. ▶ *n* book of hymns (also **hymn book**).

hype[1] [hīp] *n sl* hypodermic syringe; drug addict.

hype[2] *n inf* deception, racket; intensive publicity. ▶ *v* **hyped**, **hyp·ing.** *inf* promote (a product) using intensive publicity.

hyper- *comb. form* over, above, excessively, e.g. *hyperactive.*

hy·per·bo·la [hī-PUR-bə-lə] *n* curve produced when cone is cut by plane making larger angle with the base than the side makes.

hy·per·bo·le [hī-PUR-bə-lee] *n* rhetorical exaggeration. **hy·per·bol·ic** *adj*

hy·per·bo·re·an [hī-pər-BOR-ee-ən] *adj, n* (inhabitant) of extreme north.

hy·per·crit·i·cal [hī-pər-KRIT-i-kəl] *adj* too critical.

hy·per·link [HĪ-pər-lingk] *n Computers* link from a hypertext file that gives users instant access to related material in another file.

hy·per·sen·si·tive [hī-pər-SEN-si-tiv] *adj* unduly vulnerable emotionally or physically.

hy·per·ten·sion [hī-pər-TEN-shən] *n* abnormally high blood pressure.

hy·per·text [HĪ-pər-tekst] *n* computer software and hardware that allows users to store and view text and move between related items easily.

hy·phen [HĪ-fən] *n* short line (-)

indicating that two words or syllables are to be connected. **hy·phen·ate** [-nayt] *vt* **-at·ed, -at·ing.** join by a hyphen.

hyp·no·sis [HIP-noh-sis] *n, pl* **-ses** [-seez] induced state like deep sleep in which subject acts on external suggestion. **hyp·not'ic** *adj* of hypnosis or of the person or thing producing it; like something that induces hypnosis. **hyp·no·tism** [HIP-nə-tiz-əm] *n* **hyp·no·tist** *n* **hyp·no·tize** *vt* **-tized, -tiz·ing.** affect with hypnosis; affect in way resembling hypnotic state.

hy·po [HĪ-poh] *n* short for hyposulfite (sodium thiosulfate), used as fixer in developing photographs.

hypo-, hyph-, hyp- *comb. forms* under, below, less, e.g. *hypothermia.*

hy·po·al·ler·gen·ic [hī-poh-al-ər-JEN-ik] *adj* (of cosmetics, etc.) not likely to cause allergic reaction.

hy·po·chon·dri·a [hī-pə-KON-dree-ə] *n* morbid depression, without cause, about one's own health. **hy·po·chon'dri·ac** *adj, n*

hy·poc·ri·sy [hi-POK-rə-see] *n, pl* **-sies** [-seez] assuming of false appearance of virtue; insincerity. **hyp·o·crite** [HIP-ə-krit] *n* **hyp·o·crit'i·cal** *adj*

hy·po·der·mic [hī-pə-DUR-mik] *adj* introduced, injected beneath the skin. ▶ *n* hypodermic syringe or needle.

hy·po·gas·tric [hī-pə-GAS-trik] *adj* relating to, situated in, lower part of abdomen.

hy·pot·e·nuse [hī-POT-n-oos] *n* side of a right triangle opposite the right angle.

hy·po·ther·mi·a [hī-pə-THUR-mee-ə] *n* condition of having body temperature reduced to dangerously low level.

hy·poth·e·sis [hī-POTH-ə-sis] *n, pl* **-ses** [-seez] suggested explanation of something; assumption as basis of reasoning. **hy·po·thet'i·cal** *adj* **hy·poth'e·size** [-POTH-ə-sīz] *v* **-sized, -siz·ing.**

hypso- *comb. form* height, e.g. *hypsometry.*

hyp·sog·ra·phy [hip-SOG-rə-fee] *n* branch of geography dealing with altitudes.

hyp·som·e·ter [hip-SOM-i-tər] *n* instrument for measuring altitudes. **hyp·som'e·try** [-tree] *n* science of measuring altitudes.

hys·ter·ec·to·my [his-tə-REK-tə-mee] *n, pl* **-mies.** surgical operation for removing the uterus.

hys·ter·e·sis [his-tə-REE-sis] *n Physics* lag or delay in changes in variable property of a system.

hys·te·ri·a [hi-STER-ee-ə] *n* mental disorder with emotional outbursts; any frenzied emotional state; fit of crying or laughing. **hys·ter'i·cal** *adj* **hys·ter'ics** *pl n* fits of hysteria; *inf* uncontrollable laughter.

Hz hertz.

I i

I *Chem* iodine.

I *pron* the pronoun of the first person singular.

i·amb [Ī-amb] *n* metrical foot of short and long syllable. **i·am'bic** *adj*

i·bex [Ī-beks] *n, pl* **-bex·es.** wild goat with large horns.

ibid. [IB-id] (referring to a book, page, or passage already mentioned) in the same place.

i·bis [Ī-bis] *n* storklike bird.

ice [īs] *n* frozen water; frozen dessert made of sweetened water and fruit flavoring. ▶ *v* **iced, ic·ing.** cover, become covered with ice; cool with ice; cover with icing. **i'ci·cle** [-sə-kəl] *n* tapering spike of ice hanging where water has dripped. **i'ci·ly** *adv* in icy manner. **i'ci·ness** *n* **i'cing** *n* mixture of sugar and water, etc. used to decorate cakes. **i'cy** *adj* **i·ci·er, i·ci·est.** covered with ice; cold; chilling. **ice'berg** [-burg] *n* large floating mass of ice. **ice cream** sweetened frozen dessert made from cream, eggs, etc. **ice floe** [-floh] *n* sheet of floating ice. **ice hockey** team game played on ice with puck.

ich·thy·ol·o·gy [ik-thee-OL-ə-jee] *n* scientific study of fish.

icicle see ICE.

i·con [Ī-kon] *n* image, representation, esp. of religious figure; graphic representing a function, activated by clicking on. **i·con'o·clast** *n* one who attacks established principles, etc.; breaker of icons. **i·con·o·clas'tic** *adj* **i·co·nog'ra·phy** *n* icons collectively; study of icons.

id *n Psychoanalysis* the mind's instinctive energies.

i·de·a [ī-DEE-ə] *n* notion in the mind; conception; vague belief; plan, aim. **i·de'al** *n* conception of something that is perfect; perfect person or thing. ▶ *adj* perfect; visionary; existing only in idea.

i·de'al·ism *n* tendency to seek perfection in everything; philosophy that mind is the only reality. **i·de'al·ist** *n* one who holds doctrine of idealism; one who strives after the ideal; impractical person. **i·de·al·is'tic** *adj* **i·de'al·ize** *vt* **-ized, -iz·ing.** portray as ideal.

i·dem [Ī-dem] *Lat* the same.

i·den·ti·ty [ī-DEN-ti-tee] *n, pl* **-ties.** individuality; being the same, exactly alike. **i·den'ti·cal** *adj* very same. **i·den'ti·fi·a·ble** *adj* **i·den'ti·fy** *v* **-fied, -fy·ing.** establish identity of; associate (oneself) with; treat as identical.

id·e·o·graph [ID-ee-ə-graf] *n* picture, symbol, figure, etc., suggesting an object without naming it (also **id'e·o·gram**).

i·de·ol·o·gy [ī-dee-OL-ə-jee] *n, pl* **-gies.** body of ideas, beliefs of group, nation, etc. **i·de·o·log'i·cal** *adj* **i'de·o·logue** [-lawg] *n* zealous advocate of an ideology.

ides [īdz] *n* (in the Ancient Roman calendar) the 15th of March, May, July, or October, or the 13th of other months.

idiocy see IDIOT.

id·i·om [ID-ee-əm] *n* way of expression natural or peculiar to a language or group; characteristic style of expression. **id·i·o·mat'ic** *adj* using idioms; colloquial.

id·i·o·syn·cra·sy [id-ee-ə-SING-krə-see] *n* peculiarity of mind, temper or disposition in a person. **id·i·o·syn·crat'ic** [-oh-sing-KRAT-ik] *adj*

id·i·ot [ID-ee-ət] *n* foolish, senseless person. **id·i·o·cy** [-ə-see] *n* **id·i·ot'ic** *adj* utterly senseless or stupid.

i·dle [ĪD-l] *adj* **-dler, -dlest.** unemployed; lazy; useless, vain, groundless. ▶ *vi* **-dled, -dling.** be idle; (of engine) run slowly with gears disengaged. ▶ *vt* (esp. with *away*) waste. **i'dle·ness** *n* **i'dler** *n*

i'dly adv

i·dol [ĪD-l] n image of deity as object of worship; object of excessive devotion. **i·dol'a·ter** n worshiper of idols. **i·dol'a·trous** [-trəs] adj **i·dol'a·try** n **i'dol·ize** vt **-ized, -iz·ing.** love or venerate to excess; make an idol of.

i·dyll [ĪD-l] n short descriptive poem of picturesque or charming scene or episode, esp. of rustic life. **i·dyl·lic** [ī-DIL-ik] adj of, like, idyll; delightful.

i.e. that is to say.

if conj on condition or supposition that; whether; although. ▶ n uncertainty or doubt, e.g. no ifs, ands, or buts. **if'fy** [-ee] adj inf **-fi·er, -fi·est.** dubious.

ig'loo n dome-shaped Inuit house of snow and ice.

ig·ne·ous [IG-nee-əs] adj esp. of rocks, formed as molten rock cools and hardens.

ig·nite [ig-NĪT] v **-nit·ed, -nit·ing.** (cause to) burn. **ig·ni'tion** [-NISH-ən] n act of kindling or setting on fire; in internal combustion engine, means of firing explosive mixture, usu. electric spark.

ig·no·ble [ig-NOH-bəl] adj mean, base; of low birth. **ig·no'bly** adv

ig·no·min·y [IG-nə-min-ee] n, pl **-min·ies.** dishonor, disgrace; shameful act. **ig·no·min'i·ous** [-ee-əs] adj

ig·nore [ig-NOR] vt **-nored, -nor·ing.** disregard, leave out of account. **ig·no·ra'mus** [-RA-məs] n, pl **-mus·es.** ignorant person. **ig'no·rance** [-rəns] n lack of knowledge. **ig'no·rant** adj lacking knowledge; uneducated; unaware.

i·gua·na [i-GWAH-nə] n large tropical American lizard.

il- prefix same as IN-¹ or IN-².

il·e·um [IL-ee-əm] n lower part of small intestine. **il'e·ac** adj

ilk adj same. **of that ilk** of the same type or class.

ill adj not in good health; bad, evil; faulty; unfavorable. ▶ n evil, harm; mild disease. ▶ adv badly; hardly;

with difficulty. **ill'ness** n

ill'-ad·vised' adj imprudent; injudicious. **ill'-fat'ed** [-FAY-tid] adj unfortunate. **ill'-fa'vored** [-FAY-vərd] adj ugly, deformed; offensive. **ill'-got·ten** adj obtained dishonestly. **ill'-man'nered** adj boorish, uncivil. **ill-timed** adj inopportune. **ill-treat** vt treat cruelly. **ill will** unkind feeling, hostility.

il·le·gal adj against the law. **il·le'gal·ly** adv **il·le·gal'i·ty** n, pl **-ties.**

il·leg'i·ble adj unable to be read or deciphered. **il·leg·i·bil'i·ty** n

il·le·git·i·mate [il-i-JIT-ə-mit] adj born out of wedlock; unlawful; not regular. ▶ n bastard.

il·lic·it [i-LIS-it] adj illegal; prohibited, forbidden.

il·lit·er·ate [i-LIT-ər-it] adj not literate; unable to read or write. ▶ n illiterate person. **il·lit'er·a·cy** n

il·log'i·cal adj unreasonable; not logical.

il·lu·mi·nate [i-LOO-mə-nayt] vt **-nat·ed, -nat·ing.** light up; clarify; decorate with lights; decorate with gold and colors. **il·lu·mi·na'tion** n **il·lu'mine** vt **-mined, -min·ing.** illuminate.

il·lu·sion [i-LOO-zhən] n deceptive appearance or belief. **il·lu'sion·ist** n conjurer. **il·lu'so·ry** [-LOO-sə-ree] adj deceptive.

il·lus·trate [IL-ə-strayt] vt **-trat·ed, -trat·ing.** provide with pictures or examples; exemplify. **il·lus·tra'tion** n picture, diagram; example; act of illustrating. **il·lus'tra·tive** adj providing explanation.

il·lus·tri·ous [i-LUS-tree-əs] adj famous; distinguished; exalted.

im- prefix same as IN-¹ or IN-².

im·age [IM-ij] n representation or likeness of person or thing; optical counterpart, as in mirror; double, copy; general impression; mental picture created by words, esp. in literature. ▶ vt **-aged, -mag·ing.** make image of; reflect. **im'age·ry** n images collectively, esp. in literature.

im·ag·ine [i-MAJ-in] *vt* picture to oneself; think; conjecture. **im·ag'i·na·ble** *adj* **im·ag'i·nar·y** *adj* existing only in fancy. **im·ag·i·na'tion** *n* faculty of making mental images of things not present; fancy; resourcefulness. **im·ag'i·na·tive** *adj*

i·mam [i-MAHM] *n* Islamic minister or priest.

im·bal·ance [im-BAL-əns] *n* lack of balance, proportion.

im·be·cile [IM-bə-sil] *n* idiot. ▶ *adj* idiotic. **im·be·cil'i·ty** *n*

im·bibe [im-BĪB] *v* **-bibed, -bib·ing.** ▶ *vt* drink in; absorb. ▶ *vi* drink.

im·bri·cate [IM-brə-kit] *adj* lying over each other in regular order, like tiles or shingles on roof. **im·bri·ca'tion** *n*

im·bro·glio [im-BROHL-yoh] *n, pl* **-glios.** disagreement; complicated situation, plot.

im·bue [im-BYOO] *vt* **-bued, -bu·ing.** inspire; saturate.

im·i·tate [IM-i-tayt] *vt* **-tat·ed, -tat·ing.** take as model; mimic; copy. **im'i·ta·ble** *adj* **im·i·ta'tion** *n* act of imitating; copy of original; likeness; counterfeit. **im'i·ta·tive** *adj* **im'i·ta·tor** *n*

im·mac·u·late [im-AK-yə-lit] *adj* spotless; pure; unsullied.

im·ma·nent [IM-mə-nənt] *adj* abiding in, inherent. **im'ma·nence** *n*

im·ma·te·ri·al [im-ə-TEER-ee-əl] *adj* unimportant, trifling; not consisting of matter; spiritual.

im·ma·ture' *adj* not fully developed; lacking wisdom or stability because of youth. **im·ma·tu'ri·ty** *n*

im·me·di·ate [i-MEE-dee-it] *adj* occurring at once; direct, not separated by others. **im·me'di·a·cy** *n*

im·me·mo·ri·al [im-ə-MOR-ee-əl] *adj* beyond memory.

im·mense [i-MENS] *adj* huge, vast. **im·men'si·ty** *n* vastness.

im·merse [i-MURS] *vt* **-mersed, -mers·ing.** dip, plunge, into liquid; involve; engross. **im·mer'sion**

[-*zhən*] *n* immersing. **immersion heater** *n* electric appliance for heating liquid in which it is immersed.

im·mi·grate [IM-i-grayt] *vi* **-grat·ed, -grat·ing.** come into country as settler. **im'mi·grant** [-grənt] *n, adj* **im·mi·gra'tion** *n*

im·mi·nent [IM-ə-nənt] *adj* liable to happen soon; close at hand. **im'mi·nence** *n*

im·mo'bile *adj* not moving; unable to move. **im·mo·bil'i·ty** *n* **im·mo'bi·lize** *vt* make unable to move or work.

im·mod'er·ate *adj* excessive or unreasonable.

im·mod'est *adj* behaving in an indecent or improper manner; behaving in a boastful or conceited manner. **im·mod'es·ty** *n*

im·mo·late [IM-ə-layt] *vt* **-lat·ed, -lat·ing.** kill, sacrifice. **im·mo·la'tion** *n*

im·mor·al [i-MOR-əl] *adj* corrupt; promiscuous; indecent; unethical. **im·mo·ral'i·ty** *n, pl* **-ties.**

im·mor·tal [i-MOR-tl] *adj* deathless; famed for all time. ▶ *n* immortal being; god; one whose fame will last. **im·mor·tal'i·ty** *n* **im·mor'tal·ize** *vt* **-ized, -iz·ing.**

im·mov'a·ble *adj* unable to be moved; unwilling to change one's opinions or beliefs; not affected by feeling, emotionless.

im·mune [i-MYOON] *adj* proof (against a disease, etc.); secure, exempt. **im·mu'ni·ty** *n* state of being immune; freedom from prosecution, etc. **im·mu·ni·za'tion** *n* process of making immune to disease. **im'mu·nize** *vt* **-nized, -niz·ing.** make immune. **im·mu·nol'o·gy** *n* branch of biology concerned with study of immunity.

im·mu·ta·ble [i-MYOO-tə-bəl] *adj* unchangeable.

imp *n* little devil; mischievous child.

im·pact [IM-pakt] *n* collision; profound effect. **impact** [im-PAKT] *vt* drive, press.

im·pair' *vt* weaken, damage.

im·pair′ment

im·pal·a [im-PAL-ə] *n, pl* **-pal·as.** antelope of Africa.

im·pale [im-PAYL] *vt* **-paled, -pal·ing.** pierce with sharp instrument; make helpless as if pierced through.

im·part [im-PAHRT] *vt* communicate (information, etc.); give.

im·par·tial [im-PAHR-shəl] *adj* not biased or prejudiced; fair. **im·par·ti·al′i·ty** *n*

im·passe [IM-pas] *n* deadlock; place, situation, from which there is no outlet.

im·pas·sioned [im-PASH-ənd] *adj* deeply moved, ardent.

im·pas·sive [im-PAS-iv] *adj* showing no emotion; calm. **im·pas·siv′i·ty** *n*

im·pa′tient *adj* irritable at any delay or difficulty; restless (to have or do something). **im·pa′tience** *n*

im·peach [im-PEECH] *vt* charge with crime; call to account; *Law* challenge credibility of (a witness). **im·peach′a·ble** *adj*

im·pec·ca·ble [im-PEK-ə-bəl] *adj* without flaw or error.

im·pe·cu·ni·ous [im-pi-KYOO-nee-əs] *adj* poor. **im·pe·cu′ni·ous·ness** *n* **im·pe·cu·ni·os′i·ty** *n*

im·pede [im-PEED] *vt* **-ped·ed, -ped·ing.** hinder. **im·ped′ance** *n Electricity* measure of opposition offered to flow of alternating current. **im·ped′i·ment** [-PED-ə-mənt] *n* obstruction; defect.

im·pel′ *vt* **-pelled, -pel·ling.** induce, incite; drive, force. **im·pel′ler** *n*

im·pend′ *vi* threaten; be imminent; hang over. **im·pend′ing** *adj*

im·per·a·tive [im-PER-ə-tiv] *adj* necessary; peremptory; expressing command. ▶ *n* imperative mood.

im·per·cep′ti·ble *adj* too slight or gradual to be noticed.

im·per′fect *adj* having faults or mistakes; not complete; *Grammar* denoting a tense of verbs describing continuous, incomplete, or repeated past actions. ▶ *n*

Grammar imperfect tense. **im·per·fec′tion** *n*

im·pe·ri·al [im-PEER-ee-əl] *adj* of empire, or emperor; majestic. **im·pe′ri·al·ism** *n* extension of empire; belief in colonial empire. **im·pe′ri·al·ist** *n*

im·per·il [im-PER-əl] *vt* **-iled, -il·ing.** bring into peril, endanger.

im·pe·ri·ous [im-PEER-ee-əs] *adj* domineering; haughty; dictatorial. **im·pe′ri·ous·ness** *n*

im·per·son·al [im-PUR-sə-nl] *adj* objective, having no personal significance; devoid of human warmth, personality, etc.; (of verb) without personal subject. **im·per·son·al′i·ty** *n*

im·per·son·ate [im-PUR-sə-nayt] *vt* **-at·ed, -at·ing.** pretend to be (another person); play the part of. **im·per·son·a′tion** *n*

im·per·ti·nent [im-PUR-tn-ənt] *adj* insolent, rude. **im·per′ti·nence** *n*

im·per·turb·a·ble [im-pər-TUR-bə-bəl] *adj* calm, not excitable.

im·per·vi·ous [im-PUR-vee-əs] *adj* not affording passage; impenetrable (to feeling, argument, etc.).

im·pe·ti·go [im-pi-TĪ-goh] *n* contagious skin disease.

im·pet·u·ous [im-PECH-oo-əs] *adj* likely to act without consideration, rash. **im·pet·u·os′i·ty** *n*

im·pe·tus [IM-pi-təs] *n* force with which body moves; impulse.

im·pinge [im-PINJ] *vi* **pinged, -ping·ing.** encroach (upon); collide (with). **im·pinge′ment** *n*

im·pi·ous [IM-pee-əs] *adj* irreverent, profane, wicked. **im·pi·e·ty** [-PĪ-i-tee] *n*

im·plac·a·ble [im-PLAK-ə-bəl] *adj* not to be appeased; unyielding. **im·plac·a·bil′i·ty** *n*

im·plant′ *vt* insert, fix. **im′plant** *n Dentistry* artificial tooth implanted permanently in jaw; implanted breast enhancement.

im·ple·ment [IM-plə-mənt] *n* tool, instrument, utensil. ▶ *vt* [-ment] carry out (instructions, etc.); put into effect.

im·pli·cate [IM-pli-kayt] *vt* **-cat·ed,
-cat·ing.** involve, include; entangle;
imply. **im·pli·ca'tion** *n* something
implied. **im·plic'it** [-PLIS-it] *adj*
implied but not expressed;
absolute and unreserved.

im·plore [im-PLOR] *vt* **-plored,
-plor·ing.** entreat earnestly.

im·ply [im-PLĪ] *vt* **-plied, -ply·ing.**
indicate by hint, suggest; mean.

im·po·lite' *adj* showing bad
manners.

im·port' *vt* bring in, introduce (esp.
goods from foreign country);
imply. **im'port** *n* thing imported;
meaning; importance. **im·port'er** *n*

im·por·tant [im-POR-tnt] *adj* of
great consequence; momentous;
pompous. **im·por'tance** *n*

im·por·tune [im-por-TOON] *vt*
-tuned, -tun·ing. request, demand
persistently. **im·por'tu·nate**
[-POR-chə-nit] *adj* persistent.
im·por·tu'ni·ty *n*

im·pose [im-POHZ] *vt* **-posed,
-pos·ing.** levy (tax, duty, etc.,
upon). ▶ *vi* take advantage (of),
practice deceit on. **im·pos'ing** *adj*
impressive. **im·po·si'tion** *n* that
which is imposed; tax; burden;
deception. **im'post** *n* duty, tax on
imports.

im·pos·si·ble [im-POS-ə-bəl] *adj*
incapable of being done or
experienced; absurd; unreasonable.
im·pos·si·bil'i·ty *n, pl* **-ties.**

im·pos·tor [im-POS-tər] *n* deceiver,
one who assumes false identity.

im·po·tent [IM-pə-tənt] *adj*
powerless; (of males) incapable of
sexual intercourse. **im'po·tence** *n*

im·pound [im-POWND] *vt* take
legal possession of and, often,
place in a pound (automobile,
animal, etc.); confiscate.

im·pov·er·ish [im-POV-ər-ish] *vt*
make poor or weak.
im·pov'er·ish·ment *n*

im·prac·ti·ca·ble *adj* incapable of
being put into practice.

im·prac'ti·cal *adj* not sensible.

im·pre·ca·tion [im-pri-KAY-shən] *n*
invoking of evil; curse. **im'pre·cate**

vt **-cat·ed, -cat·ing.**

im·preg·na·ble [im-PREG-nə-bəl]
adj proof against attack;
unassailable; unable to be broken
into. **im·preg·na·bil'i·ty** *n*

im·preg·nate [im-PREG-nayt] *vt*
-nat·ed, -nat·ing. saturate, infuse;
make pregnant. **im·preg·na'tion** *n*

im·pre·sa·ri·o [im-prə-SAHR-ee-oh]
n, pl **-ri·os.** organizer of public
entertainment; manager of opera,
ballet, etc.

im·press'¹ *vt* affect deeply, usu.
favorably; imprint, stamp; fix. ▶ *n*
[IM-pres] act of impressing; mark
impressed. **im·pres'sion** *n* effect
produced, esp. on mind; notion,
belief; imprint; a printing; total of
copies printed at once; printed
copy. **im·pres'sion·a·ble** *adj*
susceptible to external influences.
im·pres'sion·ism *n* art style that
renders general effect without
detail. **im·pres'sion·ist** *n*
im·pres'sive *adj* making deep
impression.

im·press'² *vt* press into service.

im·pri·ma·tur [im-pri-MAH-tər] *n*
license to print book, etc.;
sanction, approval.

im'print *n* mark made by pressure;
characteristic mark. ▶ *vt* [im-PRINT]
produce mark; stamp; fix in mind.

im·pris·on [im-PRIZ-ən] *vt* put in
prison. **im·pris'on·ment** *n*

im·prob'a·ble *adj* not likely to be
true or to happen.
im·prob·a·bil'i·ty *n, pl* **-ties.**

im·promp·tu [im-PROMP-too] *adv,
adj* on the spur of the moment;
unrehearsed.

im·prop'er *adj* indecent; incorrect
or irregular. **improper fraction**
fraction in which the numerator is
larger than the denominator, as in
$\frac{5}{3}$.

im·pro·pri'e·ty *n, pl* **-ties.**
unsuitable or slightly improper
behaviour.

im·prove [im-PROOV] *v* **-proved,
-prov·ing.** make or become better
in quality, standard, value, etc.
im·prove'ment *n*

im·prov·i·dent [im-PROV-i-dənt]

adj thriftless; negligent; imprudent. **im·prov′i·dence** *n*

im·pro·vise [IM-prə-vīz] *v* **-vised, -vis·ing.** make use of materials at hand; compose, utter without preparation. **im·prov·i·sa′tion** [-ZAY-shən] *n*

im·pu·dent [IM-pyə-dənt] *adj* disrespectful, impertinent. **im′pu·dence** *n*

im·pugn [im-PYOON] *vt* **-pugned, -pugn·ing.** call in question, challenge as false.

im·pulse [IM-puls] *n* sudden inclination to act; sudden application of force; motion caused by it; stimulation of nerve moving muscle. **im·pul′sion** *n* impulse, usu. in its first sense. **im·pul′sive** *adj* given to acting without reflection, rash.

im·pu·ni·ty [im-PYOO-ni-tee] *n* freedom, exemption from injurious consequences or punishment.

im·pure′ *adj* having dirty or unwanted substances mixed in; immoral, obscene. **im·pu′ri·ty** *n, pl* **-ties.**

im·pute [im-PYOOT] *vt* **-put·ed, -put·ing.** ascribe, attribute to. **im·pu·ta′tion** *n* that which is imputed as a charge or fault; reproach, censure.

in *prep* expresses inclusion within limits of space, time, circumstance, sphere, etc. ▸ *adv* in or into some state, place, etc.; *inf* in vogue, etc. ▸ *adj inf* fashionable.

In *Chem* indium.

in-¹, il-, im-, ir- *prefix* not, non, e.g. *incredible;* lack of, e.g. *inexperience.*

in-², il-, im-, ir- *prefix* in, into, towards, within, on, e.g. *infiltrate.*

in·a·bil′i·ty *n* lack of means or skill to do something.

in·ac′cu·rate *adj* not correct. **in·ac′cu·ra·cy** *n, pl* **-cies.**

in·ad′e·quate *adj* not enough; not good enough. **in·ad′e·qua·cy** *n, pl* **-cies.**

in·ad·vert·ent [in-əd-VUR-tnt] *adj* not attentive; negligent; unintentional. **in·ad·vert′ence** *n*

in·ane [i-NAYN] *adj* foolish, silly, vacant. **in·a·ni′tion** [-NISH-ən] *n* exhaustion; silliness. **in·an′i·ty** *n*

in·an·i·mate [in-AN-ə-mit] *adj* lacking qualities of living beings; appearing dead; lacking vitality.

in·ap·pro′pri·ate *adj* not suitable.

in·as·much as [in-əz-MUCH] *conj* because or in so far as.

in·au·gu·rate [in-AW-gyə-rayt] *vt* **-rat·ed, -rat·ing.** begin, initiate the use of, esp. with ceremony; admit to office. **in·au′gu·ral** *adj* **in·au·gu·ra′tion** *n* act of inaugurating; ceremony to celebrate the initiation or admittance of.

in·aus·pi·cious [in-aw-SPISH-əs] *adj* not auspicious; unlucky; unfavorable. **in·aus·pi′cious·ly** *adv*

in·board [IN-bord] *adj* inside hull or bulwarks.

in′born *adj* existing from birth; inherent.

in′breed *vt* **-bred, -breed·ing.** breed from union of closely related individuals. **in′bred** *adj* produced as result of inbreeding; inborn, ingrained.

in·cal·cu·la·ble [in-KAL-kyə-lə-bəl] *adj* beyond calculation; very great.

in cam·er·a [KAM-ə-rə] in secret or private session.

in·can·des·cent [in-kən-DES-ənt] *adj* glowing with heat, shining; of artificial light, produced by glowing filament. **in·can·des′cence** *n*

in·can·ta·tion [in-kan-TAY-shən] *n* magic spell or formula, charm.

in·ca′pa·ble *adj* (foll. by *of*) unable (to do something); incompetent.

in·ca·pac·i·tate [in-kə-PAS-i-tayt] *vt* **-tat·ed, -tat·ing.** disable; make unfit; disqualify. **in·ca·pac′i·ty** *n*

in·car·cer·ate [in-KAHR-sə-rayt] *vt* **-at·ed, -at·ing.** imprison. **in·car·cer·a′tion** *n*

in·car·nate [in-KAR-nayt] *vt* **-nat·ed, -nat·ing.** embody in flesh, esp. in human form. ▸ *adj* [-nit] embodied in flesh, in human form; typified. **in·car·na′tion** *n*

in·cen·di·ar·y [in-SEN-dee-er-ee] *adj* of malicious setting on fire of property; creating strife, violence, etc.; designed to cause fires. ▶ *n* arsonist; agitator; bomb, etc. filled with inflammatory substance.

in·cense¹ [in-SENS] *vt* **-censed, -cens·ing.** enrage.

in·cense² [IN-sens] *n* gum, spice giving perfume when burned; its smoke. ▶ *vt* **-censed, -cens·ing.** burn incense to; perfume with it.

in·cen·tive [in-SEN-tiv] *n* something that arouses to effort or action; stimulus.

in·cep·tion [in-SEP-shən] *n* beginning. **in·cep'tive** [-tiv] *adj*

in·ces·sant [in-SES-ənt] *adj* unceasing.

in·cest [IN-sest] *n* sexual intercourse between two people too closely related to marry. **in·ces'tu·ous** [-SES-choo-əs] *adj*

inch *n* one twelfth of foot, or 2.54 centimeters. ▶ *v* move very slowly.

in·cho·ate [in-KOH-it] *adj* just begun; undeveloped.

in·ci·dent [IN-si-dənt] *n* event, occurrence. ▶ *adj* naturally attaching to; striking, falling (upon). **in'ci·dence** *n* degree, extent or frequency of occurrence; a falling on, or affecting. **in·ci·den'tal** *adj* occurring as a minor part or an inevitable accompaniment or by chance. **in·ci·den'tal·ly** *adv* by chance; by the way. **in·ci·den'tals** *pl. n* accompanying items.

in·cin·er·ate [in-SIN-ə-rayt] *vt* **-at·ed, -at·ing.** burn up completely; reduce to ashes. **in·cin'er·a·tor** *n*

in·cip·i·ent [in-SIP-ee-ənt] *adj* beginning.

in·cise [in-SĪZ] *vt* **-cised, -cis·ing.** cut into; engrave. **in·ci'sion** [in-SIZH-ən] *n* **in·ci'sive** *adj* keen or biting (of remark, etc.); sharp. **in·ci'sor** *n* cutting tooth.

in·cite [in-SĪT] *vt* **-cit·ed, -cit·ing.** urge, stir up. **in·cite'ment** *n*

in·clem·ent [in-KLEM-ənt] *adj* of weather, stormy, severe, cold. **in·clem'en·cy** *n*

in·cline [in-KLĪN] *v* **-clined, -clin·ing.**

lean, slope; (cause to) be disposed; bend or lower (the head, etc.). ▶ *n* [IN-klīn] slope. **in·cli·na'tion** *n* liking, tendency or preference; sloping surface; degree of deviation.

in·clude [in-KLOOD] *vt* **-clud·ed, -clud·ing.** have as (part of) contents; comprise; add in; take in. **in·clu'sion** [-zhən] *n* **in·clu'sive** *adj* including (everything).

in·cog·ni·to [in-kog-NEE-toh] *adv, adj* under assumed identity. ▶ *n, pl* **-tos.** assumed identity.

in·co·her·ent [in-koh-HEER-ənt] *adj* lacking clarity, disorganized; inarticulate. **in·co·her'ence** *n*

in·come [IN-kum] *n* amount of money, esp. annual, from salary, investments, etc.; receipts. **income tax** personal, corporate tax levied on annual income.

in·com·ing [IN-kum-ing] *adj* coming in; about to come into office; next.

in·com·mode [in-kə-MOHD] *vt* **-mod·ed, -mod·ing.** trouble, inconvenience; disturb. **in·com·mo'di·ous** *adj* cramped; inconvenient.

in·com·mu·ni·ca·do [in-kə-MYOO-ni-kah-doh] *adj, adv* deprived (by force or by choice) of communication with others.

in·com'pa·ra·ble *adj* beyond comparison, unequalled.

in·com·pat'i·ble *adj* inconsistent or conflicting. **in·com·pat·i·bil'i·ty** *n*

in·com'pe·tent *adj* not having the necessary ability or skill to do something. **in·com'pe·tence** *n*

in·con·gru·ous [in-KONG-groo-əs] *adj* not appropriate; inconsistent, absurd. **in·con·gru'i·ty** *n*

in·con·se·quen·tial [in-kon-si-KWEN-shəl] *adj* illogical; irrelevant, trivial.

in·con·sid'er·ate *adj* not considering other people.

in·con·sist'ent *adj* changeable in behaviour or mood; containing contradictory elements; not in accordance. **in·con·sist'en·cy** *n, pl* **-cies.**

in·con·tro·vert·i·ble

[in-kon-trə-VUR-tə-bəl] *adj*
undeniable; indisputable.

in·con·ven·ience *n* trouble or
difficulty. ▶ *v* cause trouble or
difficulty to. **in·con·ven'ient** *adj*

in·cor·po·rate [in-KOR-pə-rayt] *vt*
-rat·ed, -rat·ing. include; unite into
one body; form into corporation.

in·cor·ri·gi·ble [in-KOR-i-jə-bəl] *adj*
beyond correction or reform; firmly
rooted.

in·crease [in-KREES] *v* **-creased,
-creas·ing.** make or become
greater in size, number, etc. ▶ *n*
[IN-krees] growth, enlargement,
profit. **in·creas'ing·ly** *adv* more
and more.

in·cred·i·ble [in-KRED-ə-bəl] *adj*
unbelievable; *inf* marvelous,
amazing.

in·cred·u·lous [in-KREJ-ə-ləs] *adj*
unbelieving. **in·cre·du'li·ty**
[-krə-DOO-lə-tee] *n*

in·cre·ment [IN-krə-mənt] *n*
increase, esp. one of a series.
in·cre·men'tal *adj*

in·crim·i·nate [in-KRIM-ə-nayt] *vt*
-nat·ed, -nat·ing. imply guilt of;
accuse of crime. **in·crim'i·na·to·ry**
adj

in·crust [in-KRUST] *v* cover with or
form a crust or hard covering.

in·cu·bate [IN-kyə-bayt] *vt* **-bat·ed,
-bat·ing.** provide (eggs, embryos,
bacteria, etc.) with heat or other
favorable condition for
development. ▶ *vi* develop in this
way. **in·cu·ba'tion** *n* **in'cu·ba·tor**
n apparatus for artificially hatching
eggs, for rearing premature babies.

in·cu·bus [IN-kyə-bəs] *n, pl* **-bi** [-bī]
nightmare or obsession; *orig.*
demon believed to afflict sleeping
person.

in·cul·cate [in-KUL-kayt] *vt* **-cat·ed,
-cat·ing.** impress on the mind.
in·cul·ca'tion *n*

in·cum·bent [in-KUM-bənt] *adj*
lying, resting (on). ▶ *n* holder of
office, esp. elective office in
government. **in·cum'ben·cy** *n*
obligation; office or tenure of
incumbent. **it is incumbent on** it is
the duty of.

in·cur [in-KUR] *vt* **-curred, -cur·ring.**
fall into, bring upon oneself.

in·cur'sion [-zhən] *n* invasion,
penetration.

in·cur·a·ble *adj* not able to be
cured; not willing or able to
change. **in·cur'a·bly** *adv*

in·debt·ed [in-DET-id] *adj* owing
gratitude for help, favors, etc.;
owing money. **in·debt'ed·ness** *n*

in·de·cent *adj* morally or sexually
offensive; unsuitable or unseemly.
in·de'cen·cy *n*

in·de·ci·sive *adj* unable to make
decisions. **in·de·cis'ion** *n*

in·deed' *adv* in truth; really; in fact;
certainly. ▶ *interj* denoting surprise,
doubt, etc.

in·de·fat·i·ga·ble
[in-di-FAT-i-gə-bəl] *adj* untiring.
in·de·fat'i·ga·bly *adv*

in·de·fen·si·ble [in-di-FEN-sə-bəl]
adj not justifiable or defensible.

in·def'i·nite *adj* without exact
limits; vague, unclear. **indefinite
article** *Grammar* the word *a* or *an*.

in·del·i·ble [in-DEL-ə-bəl] *adj* that
cannot be blotted out, effaced or
erased; producing such a mark.
in·del'i·bly *adv*

in·del·i·cate [in-DEL-i-kit] *adj*
coarse, embarrassing, tasteless.

in·dem·ni·ty [in-DEM-ni-tee] *n, pl*
-ties. compensation; security
against loss. **in·dem·ni·fi·ca'tion** *n*
in·dem'ni·fy [-fī] *vt* **-fied, -fy·ing.**
give indemnity to; compensate.

in·dent' *v* set in (from margin, etc.);
make notches in. ▶ *n* [IN-dent]
indentation; notch. **in·den·ta'tion**
n **in·den'ture** *n* contract, esp. one
binding apprentice to master;
indentation. ▶ *vt* **-tured, -tur·ing.**
bind by indenture.

in·de·pend·ent [in-di-PEN-dənt]
adj not subject to others;
self-reliant; free; valid in itself;
politically of no party.
in·de·pend'ence *n* being
independent; self-reliance;
self-support.

in·de·scrib·a·ble
[in-di-SKRĪ-bə-bəl] *adj* beyond
description; too intense, etc. for

words. **in·de·scrib′a·bly** *adv*

in·de·ter·mi·nate
[in-di-TUR-mə-nit] *adj* uncertain;
inconclusive; incalculable.

in·dex [IN-deks] *n, pl* **-dex·es,
-di·ces** [-də-seez] alphabetical list
of references, usu. at end of book;
pointer, indicator; *Math* exponent;
Economics quantity indicating
relative level of wages, prices, etc.
compared with date established as
standard. ▸ *vt* provide book with
index; insert in index; adjust
wages, prices, etc. to reflect
change in some economic
indicator.

In·di·an [IN-dee-ən] *n* native of
India; *oft offens* person descended
from indigenous peoples of N
America. ▸ *adj*

in·di·cate [IN-di-kayt] *vt* **-cat·ed,
-cat·ing.** point out; state briefly;
signify. **in·di·ca′tion** *n* sign;
token; explanation. **in·dic′a·tive** *adj*
pointing to; *Grammar* stating fact.
in′di·ca·tor *n* one who, that which,
indicates; on vehicle, flashing light
showing driver's intention to turn.

in·dict [in-DIT] *vt* accuse, esp. by
legal process. **in·dict′ment** [-mənt]
n

in·dif·fer·ent [in-DIF-ər-ənt] *adj*
uninterested; unimportant; neither
good nor bad; inferior; neutral.
in·dif′fer·ence *n*

in·dig·e·nous [in-DIJ-ə-nəs] *adj*
born in or natural to a country.

in·di·gent [IN-di-jənt] *adj* poor,
needy. **in′di·gence** *n* poverty.

in·di·ges·tion [in-di-JES-chən] *n*
(discomfort, pain caused by)
difficulty in digesting food.
in·di·gest′i·ble *adj*

in·dig·nant [in-DIG-nənt] *adj*
moved by anger and scorn;
angered by sense of injury or
injustice. **in·dig·na′tion** *n*
in·dig′ni·ty *n* humiliation, insult,
slight.

in·di·go [IN-də-goh] *n, pl* **-gos.** blue
dye obtained from plant; the plant.
▸ *adj* deep blue.

in·di·rect′ *adj* done or caused by
someone or something else; not by

a straight route.

in·dis·creet′ *adj* incautious or
tactless in revealing secrets.
in·dis·cre′tion *n*

in·dis·crim·i·nate
[in-di-SKRIM-ə-nit] *adj* lacking
discrimination; jumbled.

in·dis·pen·sa·ble
[in-di-SPEN-sə-bəl] *adj* necessary;
essential.

in·dis·po·si·tion
[in-dis-pə-ZISH-ən] *n* sickness;
disinclination. **in·dis·posed′**
[-POHZD] *adj* unwell, not fit;
disinclined.

in·dis·sol·u·ble [in-di-SOL-yə-bəl]
adj permanent.

in·di·um [IN-dee-əm] *n* soft
silver-white metallic element.

in·di·vid·u·al [in-də-VIJ-oo-əl] *adj*
single; characteristic of single
person or thing; distinctive. ▸ *n*
single person or thing.
in·di·vid·u·al·ism *n* principle of
asserting one's independence.
in·di·vid·u·al·ist *n*
in·di·vid·u·al′i·ty *n* distinctive
character; personality.
in·di·vid·u·al·ize *vt* **-ized, -iz·ing.**
make (or treat as) individual.
in·di·vid·u·al·ly *adv* singly.

in·doc·tri·nate [in-DOK-trə-nayt] *vt*
-nat·ed, -nat·ing. implant beliefs in
the mind of.

in·do·lent [IN-dl-ənt] *adj* lazy.
in′do·lence *n*

in·dom·i·ta·ble [in-DOM-i-tə-bəl]
adj unyielding.

in·door [IN-dor] *adj* within doors;
under cover. **in·doors** [in-DORZ]
adv

in·du·bi·ta·ble [in-DOO-bi-tə-bəl]
adj beyond doubt; certain.
in·du′bi·ta·bly *adv*

in·duce [in-DOOS] *vt* **-duced,
-duc·ing.** persuade; bring on;
cause; produce by induction.
in·duce′ment *n* incentive,
attraction.

in·duct [in-DUKT] *vt* install in office.
in·duc′tion *n* an inducting; general
inference from particular instances;
production of electric or magnetic
state in body by its being near (not

touching) electrified or magnetized body. **in·duc'tance** [-təns] *n*
in·duc'tive *adj*

in·dulge [in-DULJ] *vt* **-dulged, -dulg·ing.** gratify; give free course to; pamper; spoil. **in·dul'gence** [-jəns] *n* an indulging; extravagance; something granted as a favor or privilege; *R.C. Church* remission of temporal punishment due after absolution. **in·dul'gent** [-jənt] *adj*

in·dus·try [IN-də-stree] *n* manufacture, processing, etc. of goods; branch of this; diligence; habitual hard work. **in·dus'tri·al** *adj* of industries, trades. **in·dus'tri·al·ize** *vt* **-ized, -iz·ing. in·dus'tri·ous** [-tree-əs] *adj* diligent.

in·e·bri·ate [in-EE-bree-ayt] *vt* **-at·ed, -at·ing.** make drunk; intoxicate. ▶ *adj* [-bree-it] drunken. ▶ *n* habitual drunkard. **in·e·bri·a'tion** *n* drunkenness.

in·ed·i·ble [in-ED-ə-bəl] *adj* not eatable; unfit for food.

in·ed·u·ca·ble [in-EJ-uu-kə-bəl] *adj* incapable of being educated, e.g. through mental retardation.

in·ef·fa·ble [in-EF-ə-bəl] *adj* too great or sacred for words; unutterable. **in·ef·fa·bil'i·ty** *n*

in·ef·fi'cient *adj* unable to perform a task or function to the best advantage. **in·ef·fi'cien·cy** *n*

in·el·i·gi·ble [in-EL-i-jə-bəl] *adj* not fit or qualified (for something). **in·el·i·gi·bil'i·ty** *n*

in·ept' *adj* absurd; out of place; clumsy. **in·ept'i·tude** *n*

in·ert [in-URT] *adj* without power of action or resistance; slow, sluggish; chemically unreactive. **in·er'tia** [-UR-shə] *n* inactivity; property by which matter continues in its existing state of rest or motion in straight line, unless that state is changed by external force.

in·es·ti·ma·ble [in-ES-tə-mə-bəl] *adj* too good, too great, to be estimated.

in·ev·i·ta·ble [in-EV-i-tə-bəl] *adj* unavoidable; sure to happen. **in·ev·i·ta·bil'i·ty** *n*

in·ex·o·ra·ble [in-EK-sər-ə-bəl] *adj* relentless. **in·ex'o·ra·bly** *adv*

in·ex·pe'ri·enced *adj* having no knowledge or experience of a particular situation, activity, etc. **in·ex·pe'ri·ence** *n*

in·ex·pli·ca·ble [in-EK-spli-kə-bəl] *adj* impossible to explain.

in ex·tre·mis [eks-TREE-mis] *Lat* at the point of death.

in·fal·li·ble [in-FAL-ə-bəl] *adj* unerring; not liable to fail; certain, sure. **in·fal·li·bil'i·ty** *n*

in·fa·mous [IN-fə-məs] *adj* notorious; shocking. **in'fa·my** [-mee] *n, pl* **-mies.**

in·fant [IN-fənt] *n* very young child. **in'fan·cy** *n* **in·fan'ti·cide** [-FAN-tə-sīd] *n* murder of newborn child; person guilty of this. **in'fan·tile** [-fən-tīl] *adj* childish.

in·fan·try [IN-fən-tree] *n, pl* **-tries.** foot soldiers.

in·fat·u·ate [in-FACH-oo-ayt] *vt* **-at·ed, -at·ing.** inspire with folly or foolish passion. **in·fat'u·at·ed** *adj* foolishly enamored. **in·fat·u·a'tion** *n*

in·fect [in-FEKT] *vt* affect (with disease); contaminate. **in·fec'tion** [-shən] *n* **in·fec'tious** [-shəs] *adj* catching, spreading, pestilential.

in·fer [in-FUR] *vt* **-ferred, -fer·ring.** deduce, conclude. **in·fer'ence** [-fər-əns] *n* **in·fer·en'tial** [-fər-EN-shəl] *adj* deduced.

in·fe·ri·or [in-FEER-ee-ər] *adj* of poor quality; lower. ▶ *n* one lower (in rank, etc.). **in·fe·ri·or'i·ty** *n* **inferiority complex** *Psychoanalysis* intense sense of inferiority.

in·fer·nal [in-FUR-nl] *adj* devilish; hellish; *inf* irritating, confounded. **in·fer·no** [in-FUR-noh] *n* region of hell; great destructive fire.

in·fer'tile *adj* unable to produce offspring; (of soil) barren, not productive. **in·fer·tile** *n*

in·fest' *vt* inhabit or overrun in dangerously or unpleasantly large numbers. **in·fes·ta'tion** *n*

in·fi·del·i·ty [in-fi-DEL-i-tee] *n* unfaithfulness; religious disbelief; disloyalty; treachery. **in'fi·del** [-dl] *n* unbeliever. ▶ *adj*

in·fil·trate [in-FIL-trayt] *v* **-trat·ed, -trat·ing.** trickle through; cause to pass through pores; gain access surreptitiously. **in·fil·tra'tion** *n*

in·fi·nite [IN-fə-nit] *adj* boundless. **in'fi·nite·ly** *adv* exceedingly. **in·fin·i·tes'i·mal** [-TES-ə-məl] *adj* extremely, infinitely small. **in·fin'i·ty** *n* unlimited and endless extent.

in·fin·i·tive [in-FIN-i-tiv] *adj Grammar* in form expressing notion of verb without limitation of tense, person, or number. ▶ *n* verb in this form; the form.

in·firm [in-FURM] *adj* physically weak; mentally weak; irresolute. **in·fir'ma·ry** [-mə-ree] *n* hospital; dispensary. **in·fir'mi·ty** *n, pl* **-ties.**

in·flame [in-FLAYM] *v* **-flamed, -flam·ing.** rouse to anger, excitement; cause inflammation in; become inflamed. **in·flam·ma·bil'i·ty** *n* **in·flam'ma·ble** *adj* easily set on fire; excitable. **in·flam·ma'tion** *n* infection of part of the body, with pain, heat, swelling, and redness.

in·flate [in-FLAYT] *v* **-flat·ed, -flat·ing.** blow up with air, gas; swell; cause economic inflation; raise price, esp. artificially. **in·fla'tion** *n* increase in prices and fall in value of money. **in·fla'tion·ar·y** *adj*

in·flect [in-FLEKT] *vt* modify (words) to show grammatical relationships; bend inward. **in·flec'tion** *n* modification of word; modulation of voice.

in·flex·i·ble [in-FLEK-sə-bəl] *adj* incapable of being bent; stern. **in·flex·i·bil'i·ty** *n*

in·flict [in-FLIKT] *vt* impose, deliver forcibly. **in·flic'tion** *n* inflicting; punishment.

in·flu·ence [IN-floo-əns] *n* effect of one person or thing on another; power of person or thing having an effect; thing, person exercising this. ▶ *vt* **-enced, -enc·ing.** sway; induce; affect. **in·flu·en'tial** *adj*

in·flu·en·za [in-floo-EN-zə] *n* contagious feverish respiratory virus disease.

in·flux [IN-fluks] *n* a flowing in; inflow.

in·form' *vt* tell; animate. ▶ *vi* give information (about). **in·form'ant** [-ənt] *n* one who tells. **in·for·ma'tion** *n* what is told, knowledge. **in·form'a·tive** *adj* **in·fo·mer'cial** [in-foh-MUR-shəl] *n* TV commercial advertising something in an informative way. **information superhighway** worldwide network of computers sharing information at high speed. **information technology** use of computers and electronic technology to store and communicate information. **in·for'mal** *adj* relaxed and friendly; appropriate for everyday life or use. **in·for·mal'i·ty** *n*

infraction *n* see INFRINGE.

in·fra·red [in-frə-RED] *adj* denoting rays below red end of visible spectrum.

in·fra·struc·ture [IN-frə-struk-chər] *n* basic structure or fixed capital items of an organization or economic system.

in·fre'quent *adj* not happening often.

in·fringe [in-FRINJ] *vt* **-fringed, -fring·ing.** transgress, break. **in·fringe'ment** *n* **in·frac'tion** *n* breach; violation.

in·fu·ri·ate [in-FYUUR-ee-ayt] *vt* **-at·ed, -at·ing.** enrage.

in·fuse [in-FYOOZ] *v* **-fused, -fus·ing.** soak to extract flavor, etc.; instill, charge. **in·fu'sion** [-FYOO-zhən] *n* an infusing; liquid extract obtained.

in·gen·ious [in-JEEN-yəs] *adj* clever at contriving; cleverly contrived. **in·ge·nu'i·ty** [-jə-NOO-ə-tee] *n*

in·gé·nue [AN-zhə-noo] *adj* artless girl or young woman; actress playing such a part.

in·gen·u·ous [in-JEN-yoo-əs] *adj* frank; naive, innocent. **in·gen'u·ous·ness** *n*

in·ges·tion [in-JES-chən] *n* act of introducing food into the body.

in·got [ING-gət] *n* brick of cast metal, esp. gold.

in·grain [in-GRAYN] *vt* implant deeply. **in·grained'** *adj* deep-rooted; inveterate.

in·gra·ti·ate [in-GRAY-shee-ayt] *v refl* get (oneself) into favor. **in·gra'ti·at·ing·ly** *adv*

in·grat'i·tude *n* lack of gratitude or thanks.

in·gre·di·ent [in-GREE-dee-ənt] *n* component part of a mixture.

in'gress *n* entry, means, right of entrance.

in·hab'it *vt* dwell in. **in·hab'it·a·ble** *adj* **in·hab'it·ant** [-i-tənt] *n*

in·hale [in-HAYL] *v* **-haled, -hal·ing.** breathe in (air, etc.). **in·ha·la'tion** *n* esp. medical preparation for inhaling. **in·ha'ler** *n* person who inhales; (also **in'ha·la·tor**) device producing, and assisting inhalation of therapeutic vapors.

in·here [in-HEER] *vi* **-hered, -her·ing.** of qualities, exist (in); of rights, be vested (in person). **in·her'ent** [-HEER-ənt] *adj* existing as an inseparable part.

in·her'it *vt* receive as heir; derive from parents. ▶ *vi* succeed as heir. **in·her'it·ance** [-əns] *n*

in·hib'it *vt* restrain (impulse, desire, etc.); hinder (action); forbid. **in·hi·bi'tion** *n* repression of emotion, instinct; a stopping or retarding. **in·hib'i·to·ry** *adj*

in·hos·pi'ta·ble *adj* not welcoming, unfriendly; difficult to live in, harsh.

in·hu·man [in-HYOO-mən] *adj* cruel, brutal; not human. **in·hu·man'i·ty** *n*

in·im·i·cal [i-NIM-i-kəl] *adj* unfavorable (to); unfriendly; hostile.

in·im·i·ta·ble [i-NIM-i-tə-bəl] *adj* defying imitation. **in·im'i·ta·bly** *adv*

in·iq·ui·ty [i-NIK-wi-tee] *n, pl* **-ties.** gross injustice; wickedness, sin. **in·iq'ui·tous** *adj* unfair, sinful, unjust.

in·i·tial [i-NISH-əl] *adj* of, occurring at the beginning. ▶ *n* initial letter, esp. of person's name. ▶ *vt* **-tialed, -tial·ing.** mark, sign with one's initials.

in·i·ti·ate [i-NISH-ee-ayt] *vt* **-at·ed, -at·ing.** originate; begin; admit into closed society; instruct in elements (of). ▶ *n* [-ee-it] initiated person. **in·i·ti·a'tion** *n* **in·i'ti·a·tive** *n* first step, lead; ability to act independently. ▶ *adj* originating.

in·ject [in-JEKT] *vt* introduce (esp. fluid, medicine, etc. with syringe). **in·jec'tion** *n*

in·junc·tion [in-JUNGK-shən] *n* judicial order to restrain; authoritative order.

in·ju·ry [IN-jə-ree] *n, pl* **-ries.** physical damage or harm; wrong. **in·jure** [IN-jər] *vt* **-jured, -jur·ing.** do harm or damage to. **in·ju'ri·ous** [-JUU-ree-əs] *adj*

in·jus·tice [in-JUS-tis] *n* want of justice; wrong; injury; unjust act.

ink *n* fluid used for writing or printing. ▶ *vt* mark with ink; cover, smear with it.

ink·ling [INGK-ling] *n* hint, slight knowledge or suspicion.

inlaid see INLAY.

in'land *n* interior of country. ▶ *adj* [IN-lənd] in this; away from the sea; within a country. ▶ *adv* [IN-land] in or toward the inland.

in'-law *n* relative by marriage esp. mother-in-law and father-in-law.

in'lay *vt* **-laid, -lay·ing.** embed; decorate with inset pattern. ▶ *n* inlaid piece or pattern.

in'let *n* entrance; small arm of sea, lake, etc.; piece inserted.

in lo·co pa·ren·tis [LOH-koh pə-REN-tis] *Lat* in place of a parent.

in·mate [IN-mayt] *n* occupant, esp. of prison, hospital, etc.

in·most [IN-mohst] *adj* most inward, deepest; most secret.

inn *n* restaurant or tavern; country hotel. **inn'keep·er** *n*

in·nards [IN-ərdz] *pl n* internal organs or working parts.

in·nate [i-NAYT] *adj* inborn; inherent.

in·ner [IN-ər] *adj* lying within. **in'ner·most** *adj* **inner tube** rubber air tube of pneumatic tire.

in'ning *n Sports* side's turn at bat; spell, turn.

in·no·cent [IN-ə-sənt] *adj* pure;
guiltless; harmless. ▶ *n* innocent
person, esp. young child.
in·'no·cence *n*

in·noc·u·ous [i-NOK-yoo-əs] *adj*
harmless.

in·no·vate [IN-ə-vayt] *vt* **-vat·ed,
-vat·ing.** introduce changes, new
things. **in·no·va'tion** *n*

in·nu·en·do [in-yoo-EN-doh] *n, pl*
-dos. allusive remark, hint; indirect
accusation.

in·nu·mer·a·ble [i-NOO-mər-ə-bəl]
adj countless; very numerous.

in·oc·u·late [i-NOK-yə-layt] *vt*
-lat·ed, -lat·ing. immunize by
injecting vaccine. **in·oc·u·la'tion** *n*

in·of·fen·sive *adj* causing no harm.

in·op·er·a·ble [in-OP-ər-ə-bəl] *adj*
unworkable; *Med* that cannot be
operated on. **in·op'er·a·tive** *adj*
not operative; ineffective.

in·op·por·tune [in-op-ər-TOON]
adj badly timed.

in·or·di·nate [in-OR-dn-it] *adj*
excessive.

in·or·gan·ic [in-or-GAN-ik] *adj* not
having structure or characteristics
of living organisms; of substances
without carbon.

in·pa·tient [IN-pay-shənt] *n* patient
who stays in hospital.

in·put [IN-puut] *n* act of putting in;
that which is put in, as resource
needed for industrial production,
etc.; data, etc. fed into a computer.

in·quest [IN-kwest] *n* legal or
judicial inquiry presided over by a
coroner; detailed inquiry or
discussion.

in·quire [in-KWIR] *vi* **-quired,
-quir·ing.** seek information.
in·quir'er *n* **in·quir'y** *n, pl*
-quir·ies. question; investigation.

in·qui·si·tion [in-kwə-ZISH-ən] *n*
searching investigation, official
inquiry; (**I-**) *Hist* organization within
the Catholic Church for
suppressing heresy. **in·quis'i·tor**
[-KWIZ-ə-tər] *n*

in·quis·i·tive [in-KWIZ-i-tiv] *adj*
curious; prying.

in·road [IN-rohd] *n* incursion;
encroachment.

in·sane [in-SAYN] *adj* mentally
deranged; crazy, senseless.
in·sane'ly *adv* like a lunatic, madly;
excessively. **in·san'i·ty** *n*

in·san·i·tar·y *adj* dirty or unhealthy.

in·sa·tia·ble [in-SAY-shə-bəl] *adj*
incapable of being satisfied.

in·scribe [in-SKRIB] *vt* **-scribed,
-scrib·ing.** write, engrave (in or on
something); mark; dedicate; trace
(figure) within another.
in·scrip'tion *n* inscribing; words
inscribed on monument, etc.

in·scru·ta·ble [in-SKROO-tə-bəl]
adj mysterious, impenetrable;
affording no explanation.
in·scru·ta·bil'i·ty *n*

in·sect [IN-sekt] *n* small
invertebrate animal with six legs,
usu. segmented body and two or
four wings. **in·sec'ti·cide** [-sīd] *n*
preparation for killing insects.
in·sec·tiv'o·rous *adj* insect-eating.

in·se·cure [in-si-KYUUR] *adj* not safe
or firm; anxious, not confident.

in·sem·i·nate [in-SEM-ə-nayt] *vt*
-nat·ed, -nat·ing. implant semen
into. **artificial insemination**
impregnation of the female by
artificial means.

in·sen·sate [in-SEN-sayt] *adj*
without sensation, unconscious;
unfeeling.

in·sen·si·ble [in-SEN-sə-bəl] *adj*
unconscious; without feeling; not
aware; not perceptible.
in·sen'si·bly *adv* imperceptibly.

in·sen'si·tive *adj* unaware of or
ignoring other people's feelings.
in·sen·si·tiv'i·ty *n*

in·sert [in-SURT] *vt* introduce; place
or put (in, into, between). ▶ *n*
[IN-surt] something inserted.
in·ser'tion [-shən] *n*

in'set *n* something extra inserted
esp. as decoration. **in·set'** *vt* **-set,
-set·ting.**

in·shore [IN-shor] *adj* near shore.
▶ *adv* toward shore.

in·side [IN-sīd] *n* inner side, surface,
or part; inner circle of influence; *sl*
confidential information. ▶ *pl inf*
internal parts of body. ▶ *adj* of, in,
or on, inside. ▶ *adv* [in-SĪD] in or

into the inside; *sl* in prison. ▶ *prep* within, on inner side.

in·sid·i·ous [in-SID-ee-əs] *adj* stealthy, treacherous; unseen but deadly.

in·sight [IN-sīt] *n* deep understanding.

in·sig·ni·a [in-SIG-nee-ə] *n, pl* **-ni·as, -ni·a.** badge or emblem of honor or office.

in·sig·nif·i·cant *adj* not important. **in·sig·nif′i·cance** *n*

in·sin·cere′ *adj* showing false feelings, not genuine. **in·sin·cer′i·ty** *n, pl* **-ties.**

in·sin·u·ate [in-SIN-yoo-ayt] *vt* **-at·ed, -at·ing.** hint; work oneself into favor; introduce gradually or subtly. **in·sin·u·a′tion** *n*

in·sip′id *adj* dull, tasteless, spiritless.

in·sist′ *vi* demand persistently; maintain; emphasize. **in·sist′ence** *n* **in·sist′ent** *adj*

in si·tu [SI-too] *Lat* in its original place or position.

in·so·lent [IN-sə-lənt] *adj* arrogantly impudent. **in′so·lence** *n*

in·sol′vent *adj* unable to pay one's debts. **in·sol′ven·cy** *n*

in·som·ni·a [in-SOM-nee-ə] *n* sleeplessness. **in·som′ni·ac** [-nee-ak] *adj, n*

in·so·much [in-sə-MUCH] *adv* to such an extent.

in·sou·ci·ant [in-SOO-see-ənt] *adj* indifferent, careless, unconcerned. **in·sou′ci·ance** *n*

in·spect [in-SPEKT] *vt* examine closely or officially. **in·spec′tion** *n* **in·spec′tor** *n* one who inspects; high-ranking police or fire officer.

in·spire [in-SPIR] *vt* **-spired, -spir·ing.** animate, invigorate, arouse, create feeling, thought; give rise to; breathe in, inhale. **in·spi·ra′tion** *n* good idea; creative influence or stimulus.

in·stall [in-STAWL] *vt* have (apparatus) put in; establish; place (person in office, etc.) with ceremony. **in·stal·la′tion** *n* act of installing; that which is installed.

in·stall·ment [in-STAWL-mənt] *n* payment of part of debt; any of parts of a whole delivered in succession.

in·stance [IN-stəns] *n* example; particular case; request. ▶ *vt* **-stanced, -stanc·ing.** cite.

in·stant [IN-stənt] *n* moment, point of time. ▶ *adj* immediate; urgent; (of foods) requiring little preparation. **in·stan·ta′ne·ous** *adj* happening in an instant. **in·stan′ter** *adv* at once. **in′stant·ly** *adv* at once.

in·stead [in-STED] *adv* in place (of); as a substitute.

in′step *n* top of foot between toes and ankle.

in·sti·gate [IN-sti-gayt] *vt* **-gat·ed, -gat·ing.** incite, urge; bring about. **in·sti·ga′tion** *n*

in·still′ *vt* implant; inculcate. **in·still′ment** *n*

in·stinct [IN-stingkt] *n* inborn impulse or propensity; unconscious skill; intuition. **in·stinc′tive** *adj*

in·sti·tute [IN-sti-toot] *vt* **-tut·ed, -tut·ing.** establish, found; appoint; set in motion. ▶ *n* society for promoting some public goal, esp. scientific; its building. **in·sti·tu′tion** *n* an instituting; establishment for care or education, hospital, college, etc.; an established custom or law; *inf* a well-established person. **in·sti·tu′tion·al** *adj* of institutions; routine. **in·sti·tu′tion·al·ize** *vt* **-ized, -iz·ing.** place in an institution esp. for care of mentally ill; make or become an institution.

in·struct [in-STRUKT] *vt* teach; inform; order; brief (jury, lawyer). **in·struc′tion** *n* teaching; order. ▶ *pl* directions. **in·struc′tive** *adj* informative; useful.

in·stru·ment [IN-strə-mənt] *n* tool, implement, means, person, thing used to make, do, measure, etc.; mechanism for producing musical sound; legal document. **in·stru·men′tal** *adj* acting as instrument or means; helpful; belonging to, produced by musical instruments. **in·stru·men′tal·ist** *n* player of musical instrument. **in·stru·men·tal′i·ty** *n, pl* **-ties.**

agency, means.

in·stru·men·ta'tion n arrangement of music for instruments.

in·sub·or·di·nate [in-sə-BOR-dn-it] adj not submissive; mutinous, rebellious. **in·sub·or·di·na'tion** n

in·su·lar [IN-sə-lər] adj of an island; remote, detached; narrow-minded or prejudiced. **in·su·lar'i·ty** n

in·su·late [IN-sə-layt] vt **-lat·ed, -lat·ing.** prevent or reduce transfer of electricity, heat, sound, etc.; isolate, detach. **in·su·la'tion** n

in·su·lin [IN-sə-lin] n pancreatic hormone, used in treating diabetes.

in·sult' vt behave rudely to; offend. ▶ n [IN-sult] offensive remark; affront. **in·sult'ing** adj

in·su·per·a·ble [in-SOO-pər-ə-bəl] adj that cannot be overcome or surmounted; unconquerable.

in·sure [in-SHUUR] v **-sured, -sur·ing.** contract for payment in event of loss, death, etc., by payment of premiums; make such contract about; make safe (against). **in·sur'a·ble** adj **in·sur'ance** n **in·sur'er** n insurance policy; contract of insurance.

in·sur·gent [in-SUR-jənt] adj in revolt. ▶ n rebel. **in·sur'gence, in·sur·rec'tion** n revolt.

in·tact [in-TAKT] adj untouched; uninjured.

in·tagl·io [in-TAL-yoh] n, pl **-tagl·ios.** engraved design; gem so cut.

in·take [IN-tayk] n what is taken in; quantity taken in; opening for taking in; in car, air passage into carburetor.

in·tan'gi·ble adj not clear or definite enough to be seen or felt easily.

in·te·ger [IN-ti-jər] n whole number; whole of anything.

in·te·gral [IN-ti-grəl] adj constituting an essential part of a whole. **in'te·grate** vt **-grat·ed, -grat·ing.** combine into one whole; unify diverse elements (of community, etc.). **in·te·gra'tion** n **integral calculus** branch of mathematics of changing

quantities that calculates total effects of the change. **integrated circuit** tiny electronic circuit, usu. on silicon chip.

in·teg·ri·ty [in-TEG-ri-tee] n honesty; original perfect state.

in·teg·u·ment [in-TEG-yə-mənt] n natural covering, skin, rind, husk.

in·tel·lect [IN-tl-ekt] n power of thinking and reasoning.

in·tel·lec'tu·al adj of, appealing to intellect; having good intellect. ▶ n one endowed with intellect and attracted to intellectual things.

in·tel·li·gent [in-TEL-i-jənt] adj having, showing good intellect; quick at understanding; informed. **in·tel'li·gence** n quickness of understanding; mental power or ability; intellect; information, news, esp. military information. **in·tel·li·gent'si·a** [-JENT-see-ə] n intellectual or cultured classes. **in·tel'li·gi·ble** [-jə-bəl] adj understandable.

in·tem·per·ate [in-TEM-pər-it] adj drinking alcohol to excess; immoderate; unrestrained. **in·tem'per·ance** [-əns] n

in·tend' vt propose, mean (to do, say, etc.). **in·tend'ed** adj planned, future. ▶ n inf proposed spouse.

in·tense [in-TENS] adj very strong or acute; emotional. **in·ten·si·fi·ca'tion** n **in·ten'si·fy** v **-fied, -fy·ing.** make or become stronger; increase. **in·ten'si·ty** n intense quality; strength. **in·ten'sive** adj characterized by intensity or emphasis on specified factor.

in·tent' n purpose. ▶ adj concentrating (on); resolved, bent; preoccupied, absorbed. **in·ten'tion** n purpose, aim. **in·ten'tion·al** adj

in·ter [in-TUR] vt **-terred, -ter·ring.** bury. **in·ter'ment** n

inter- prefix between, among, mutually, e.g. interglacial; interrelation.

in·ter·act [in-tər-AKT] vi act on each other. **in·ter·ac'tion** n

in·ter·cede [in-tər-SEED] vi

-ced·ed, -ced·ing. plead in favor of; mediate. **in·ter·ces'sion** n

in·ter·cept [in-tər-SEPT] vt cut off; seize, stop in transit.
in·ter·cep'tion n **in·ter·cept'or, -er** n one who, that which intercepts; fast fighter plane, missile, etc.

in·ter·change [in-tər-CHAYNJ] v **-changed, -chang·ing.** (cause to) exchange places. ▶ n [IN-tər-chaynj] interchanging; highway intersection.
in·ter·change'a·ble adj able to be exchanged in position or use.

in·ter·con·ti·nen·tal [in-tər-kon-tn-EN-təl] adj connecting continents; (of missile) able to reach one continent from another.

in·ter·course [IN-tər-kors] n mutual dealings; communication; sexual joining of two people; copulation.

in·ter·dict [IN-tər-dikt] n in Catholic church, decree restraining faithful from receiving certain sacraments; formal prohibition.
in·ter·dict' vt prohibit, forbid; restrain. **in·ter·dic'tion** n

in·ter·est [IN-tər-ist] n concern, curiosity; thing exciting this; sum paid for use of borrowed money; legal concern; right, advantage, share. ▶ vt excite, cause to feel interest. **in'ter·est·ing** adj

in·ter·face [IN-tər-fays] n area, surface, boundary linking two systems.

in·ter·fere [in-tər-FEER] vi **-fered, -fer·ing.** meddle, intervene; clash.
in·ter·fer'ence n act of interfering; *Radio* interruption of reception by atmospherics or by unwanted signals.

in·ter·fer·on [in-tər-FEER-on] n a cellular protein that stops development of an invading virus.

in·ter·im [IN-tər-əm] n meantime. ▶ adj temporary, intervening.

in·te·ri·or [in-TEER-ee-ər] adj inner; inland; indoors. ▶ n inside; inland region.

in·ter·ject [in-tər-JEKT] vt interpose (remark, etc.). **in·ter·jec'tion** n

exclamation; interjected remark.

in·ter·lard [in-tər-LAHRD] v intersperse.

in·ter·loc·u·tor [in-tər-LOK-yə-tər] n one who takes part in conversation; middle man in line of minstrel performers.
in·ter·loc·u·to·ry adj of a court decree, issued before the final decision in an action.

in·ter·lop·er [IN-tər-lohp-ər] n one intruding upon another's affairs; intruder.

in·ter·lude [IN-tər-lood] n interval (in play, etc.); something filling an interval.

in·ter·mar·ry [in-tər-MAR-ee] vi **-ried, -ry·ing.** (of families, races, religions) become linked by marriage; marry within one's family. **in·ter·mar'riage** n

in·ter·me·di·ate [in-tər-MEE-dee-it] adj coming between; interposed.
in·ter·me'di·ar·y n

in·ter·mez·zo [in-tər-MET-soh] n, pl **-zos.** short performance between acts of play or opera.

in·ter·mi·na·ble [in-TUR-mə-nə-bəl] adj endless.
in·ter'mi·na·bly adv

in·ter·mis·sion [in-tər-MISH-ən] n short interval between parts of a concert, play, etc. **in·ter·mit'tent** adj occurring at intervals.

in·tern¹ [in-TURN] vt confine to special area or camp. **in·tern'ment** n **in·tern·ee'** n

in·tern², in·terne [IN-turn] n recent medical school graduate residing in hospital and working under supervision as member of staff; trainee in occupation or profession.
in'tern·ship n

in·ter·nal [in-TUR-nl] adj inward; interior; within (a country, organization). **internal combustion** process of exploding mixture of air and fuel within engine cylinder.

in·ter·na·tion·al [in-tər-NASH-ə-nl] adj of relations between nations. ▶ n labor union, etc. with units, members, in more than one country.

in·ter·ne·cine [in-tər-NEE-seen] *adj* mutually destructive; deadly.

In·ter·net, in·ter·net [IN-tər-net] *n* large international public access computer network.

in·ter·po·late [in-TUR-pə-layt] *vt* **-lat·ed, -lat·ing.** insert new (esp. misleading) matter (in book, etc.); interject (remark); *Math* estimate a value between known values. **in·ter·po·la'tion** *n*

in·ter·pose [in-tər-POHZ] *v* **-posed, -pos·ing.** ▶ *vt* insert; say as interruption; put in the way. ▶ *vi* intervene; obstruct. **in·ter·po·si'tion** [-pə-ZISH-ən] *n*

in·ter·pret [in-TUR-prit] *v* explain; translate, esp. orally; *Art* render, represent. **in·ter·pre·ta'tion** *n*

in·ter·reg·num [in-tər-REG-nəm] *n*, *pl* **-nums.** interval between reigns; gap in continuity.

in·ter·ro·gate [in-TER-ə-gayt] *vt* **-gat·ed, -gat·ing.** question, esp. closely or officially. **in·ter·ro·ga'tion** *n* **in·ter·rog'a·tive** *adj* questioning. ▶ *n* word used in asking question. **in·ter·rog'a·to·ry** *adj* of inquiry. ▶ *n* question, set of questions.

in·ter·rupt [in-tə-RUPT] *v* break in (upon); stop the course of; block. **in·ter·rup'tion** *n*

in·ter·sect [in-tər-SEKT] *vt* divide by passing across or through. ▶ *vi* meet and cross. **in·ter·sec'tion** *n* point where lines, roads cross.

in·ter·sperse [in-tər-SPURS] *vt* **-spersed, -spers·ing.** sprinkle (something with or something among or in).

in·ter·stel·lar [in-tər-STEL-ər] *adj* (of the space) between stars.

in·ter·stice [in-TUR-stis] *n*, *pl* **-stic·es** [-stə-seez] chink, gap, crevice. **in·ter·sti'tial** [-STISH-əl] *adj*

in·ter·val [IN-tər-vəl] *n* intervening time or space; pause, break; short period between parts of play, concert, etc.; difference (of pitch).

in·ter·vene [in-tər-VEEN] *vi* **-vened, -ven·ing.** come into a situation in order to change it; be, come between or among; occur in meantime; interpose.

in·ter·ven'tion *n*

in·tes·tate [in-TES-tayt] *adj* not having made a will. ▶ *n* person dying intestate. **in·tes'ta·cy** [-tə-see] *n*

in·tes·tine [in-TES-tin] *n* (usu pl) lower part of alimentary canal between stomach and anus. **in·tes'ti·nal** *adj* of bowels.

in·ti·mate¹ [IN-tə-mit] *adj* closely acquainted, familiar; private; extensive; having sexual relations (with). ▶ *n* intimate friend. **in'ti·ma·cy** [-mə-see] *n*

in·ti·mate² [IN-tə-mayt] *vt* **-mat·ed, -mat·ing.** imply; announce. **in·ti·ma'tion** *n* notice.

in·tim·i·date [in-TIM-i-dayt] *vt* **-dat·ed, -dat·ing.** frighten into submission; deter by threats. **in·tim·i·da'tion** *n*

in·to [IN-too] *prep* expresses motion to a point within; indicates change of state; indicates coming up against, encountering; indicates arithmetical division.

in·tol'er·a·ble *adj* more than can be endured.

in·tone [in-TOHN] *vt* **-toned, -ton·ing.** chant; recite in monotone. **in·to·na'tion** *n* modulation of voice; intoning; accent.

in·tox·i·cate [in-TOK-si-kayt] *vt* **-cat·ed, -cat·ing.** make drunk; excite to excess. **in·tox'i·cant** [-kənt] *adj, n* intoxicating (liquor).

intr. intransitive.

intra- *prefix* within, e.g. *intravenous*.

in·trac·ta·ble [in-TRAK-tə-bəl] *adj* difficult to influence; hard to control.

in·tra·net [IN-trə-net] *n Computers* local network that makes use of Internet technology.

in·tran·si·gent [in-TRAN-si-jənt] *adj* uncompromising, obstinate.

in·tra·u·ter·ine [in-trə-YOO-tər-in] *adj* within the womb.

in·tra·ve·nous [in-trə-VEE-nəs] *adj* into a vein.

in·trep'id *adj* fearless, undaunted.

in·tre·pid·i·ty *n*

in·tri·cate [IN-tri-kit] *adj* involved, puzzlingly entangled. **in'tri·ca·cy** *n, pl* **-cies.**

in·trigue [in-TREEG] *n* underhanded plot; secret love affair. ▶ *v* **-trigued, -tri·guing.** ▶ *vi* carry on intrigue. ▶ *vt* interest, puzzle.

in·trin·sic [in-TRIN-sik] *adj* inherent, essential. **in·trin'si·cal·ly** *adv*

intro- *prefix* into, within, e.g. *introduce; introvert.*

in·tro·duce [in-trə-DOOS] *vt* **-duced, -duc·ing.** make acquainted; present; bring in; bring forward; bring into practice; insert. **in·tro·duc'tion** *n* an introducing; presentation of one person to another; preliminary section or treatment. **in·tro·duc'to·ry** *adj* preliminary.

in·tro·spec·tion *n* [in-trə-SPEK-shən] examination of one's own thoughts. **in·tro·spec'tive** *adj*

in·tro·vert [IN-trə-vurt] *n Psychoanalysis* one who looks inward rather than at the external world. **in·tro·ver'sion** [-zhən] *n* **in'tro·vert·ed** *adj*

in·trude [in-TROOD] *v* **-trud·ed, -trud·ing.** thrust (oneself) in uninvited. **in·tru'sion** [-zhən] *n* **in·tru'sive** *adj*

in·tu·i·tion [in-too-ISH-ən] *n* immediate mental apprehension without reasoning; immediate insight. **in·tu'it** *v* **in·tu'i·tive** *adj*

In·u·it [IN-oo-it] *n* one of race of indigenous people of Alaska, N Canada, and Greenland. ▶ *adj*

in·un·date [IN-ən-dayt] *vt* **-dat·ed, -dat·ing.** flood; overwhelm. **in·un·da'tion** *n*

in·ure [in-YUUR] *vt* **-ured, -ur·ing.** accustom, esp. to hardship, danger, etc.

in·vade [in-VAYD] *vt* **-vad·ed, -vad·ing.** enter by force with hostile intent; overrun; pervade. **in·va'sion** [-zhən] *n*

in·va·lid[1] [IN-və-lid] *n* one suffering from chronic ill health. ▶ *adj* ill, suffering from sickness or injury. ▶ *v* become an invalid; retire from active service because of illness, etc.

in·val·id[2] [in-VAL-id] *adj* not valid.

in·val·u·a·ble [in-VAL-yoo-ə-bəl] *adj* priceless.

invasion see INVADE.

in·veigh [in-VAY] *vi* speak violently (against). **in·vec'tive** *n* abusive speech or writing, vituperation.

in·vei·gle [in-VAY-gəl] *vt* **-gled, -gling.** entice, seduce, wheedle.

in·vent' *vt* devise, originate; fabricate (falsehoods, etc.). **in·ven'tion** *n* that which is invented; ability to invent; contrivance; deceit; lie. **in·vent'ive** *adj* resourceful; creative. **in·ven'tor** *n*

in·ven·to·ry [IN-vən-tor-ee] *n, pl* **-ries.** detailed list of goods, etc. ▶ *vt* **-ried, -ry·ing.** make list of.

in·vert [in-VURT] *vt* turn upside down; reverse position, relations of. **in·verse'** *adj* inverted; opposite. ▶ *n* **in·verse'ly** *adv* **in·ver'sion** [-zhən] *n*

in·ver·te·brate [in-VUR-tə-brit] *n* animal having no vertebral column. ▶ *adj* spineless.

in·vest' *vt* lay out (money, time, effort, etc.) for profit or advantage; install; endow; *Poet* cover as with garment. **in·ves'ti·ture** [-chər] *n* formal installation of person in office or rank. **in·vest'ment** *n* investing; money invested; stocks, bonds, etc. bought.

in·ves·ti·gate [in-VES-ti-gayt] *v* inquire into; examine. **in·ves·ti·ga'tion** *n*

in·vet·er·ate [in-VET-ər-it] *adj* deep-rooted; long established, confirmed.

in·vid·i·ous [in-VID-ee-əs] *adj* likely to cause ill will or envy.

in·vig·or·ate [in-VIG-ə-rayt] *vt* **-at·ed, -at·ing.** give vigor to, strengthen.

in·vin·ci·ble [in-VIN-sə-bəl] *adj* unconquerable. **in·vin·ci·bil'i·ty** *n*

in·vi·o·la·ble [in-VĪ-ə-lə-bəl] *adj* not to be profaned; sacred; unalterable. **in·vi'o·late** [-ə-lit] *adj* unhurt;

unprofaned; unbroken.

in·vis·i·ble adj not able to be seen. **in·vis·i·bil'i·ty** n

in·vite [in-VĪT] vt **-vit·ed, -vit·ing.** request the company of; ask courteously; ask for; attract, call forth. ▶ n [IN-vīt] inf an invitation. **in·vi·ta'tion** n

in·voice [IN-vois] n itemized bill for goods or services sold. ▶ vt **-voiced, -voic·ing.** make or present an invoice.

in·voke [in-VOHK] vt **-voked, -vok·ing.** call on; appeal to; ask earnestly for; summon. **in·vo·ca'tion** n

in·vol·un·tar·y [in-VOL-ən-ter-ee] adj not done willingly; unintentional; instinctive.

in·vo·lute [IN-və-loot] adj complex; coiled spirally; (also **in·vo·lut'ed**) rolled inward.

in·volve [in-VOLV] vt **-volved, -volv·ing.** include; entail; implicate (person); concern; entangle. **involved** adj complicated; concerned (in).

in·vul'ner·a·ble adj not able to be wounded or harmed.

in·ward [IN-wərd] adj internal; situated within; spiritual, mental. ▶ adv (also **in'wards**) toward the inside; into the mind. **in'ward·ly** adv in the mind; internally.

i·o·dine [Ī-ə-dīn] n nonmetallic element found in seaweed and used in antiseptic solution, photography, etc. **i'o·dize** vt **-dized, -diz·ing.** treat or react with iodine.

i·on [Ī-ən] n electrically charged atom or group of atoms. **i·on'ic** adj **i·on·i·za'tion** n **i'on·ize** vt **-ized, -iz·ing.** change into ions. **i·on'o·sphere** n region of atmosphere about 50 to 250 miles (80 to 400 km) above Earth.

I·on·ic [ī-ON-ik] adj Architecture distinguished by scroll-like decoration on columns.

i·o·ta [ī-OH-tə] n the Greek letter i; (usu. with not) very small amount.

ip·so fac·to [IP-soh FAK-toh] Lat by that very fact.

Ir Chem iridium.

ir- prefix same as IN-[1] or IN-[2].

ire [īr] n anger, wrath. **i·ras·ci·ble** [i-RAS-ə-bəl] adj hot-tempered. **i·ras'ci·bly** adv **i·rate** [ī-RAYT] adj angry.

ir·i·des·cent [ir-i-DES-ənt] adj exhibiting changing colors like those of the rainbow. **ir·i·des'cence** n

i·rid·i·um [i-RID-ee-əm] n very hard, corrosion-resistant metallic element.

i·ris [Ī-ris] n circular membrane of eye containing pupil; plant with sword-shaped leaves and showy flowers.

irk [urk] vt irritate, vex. **irk'some** [-sum] adj tiresome.

i·ron [Ī-ərn] n metallic element, much used for tools, etc., and the raw material of steel; tool, etc., of this metal; appliance used, when heated, to smooth cloth; metal-headed golf club. ▶ pl fetters. ▶ adj of, like, iron; inflexible, unyielding; robust. ▶ v smooth, cover, fetter, etc., with iron or an iron. **i'ron·clad** adj protected with or as with iron. **iron curtain** any barrier that separates communities or ideologies. **iron lung** apparatus for administering artificial respiration.

i·ro·ny [Ī-rə-nee] n, pl **-nies.** (usu. humorous or mildly sarcastic) use of words to mean the opposite of what is said; event, situation opposite of that expected. **i·ron'ic** adj of, using, irony.

ir·ra·di·ate [i-RAY-dee-ayt] vt **-at·ed, -at·ing.** treat by irradiation; shine upon, throw light upon, light up. **ir·ra·di·a'tion** n impregnation by X-rays, light rays.

ir·ra'tion·al adj not based on or not using logical reasoning.

ir·re·fran·gi·ble [ir-i-FRAN-jə-bəl] adj inviolable; in optics, not susceptible to refraction.

ir·ref·u·ta·ble [i-REF-yə-tə-bəl] adj that cannot be refuted, disproved.

ir·reg'u·lar adj not regular or even; not conforming to accepted practice; (of a word) not following the typical pattern of formation in a language. **ir·reg·u·lar′i·ty** n, pl -ties.

ir·rel′e·vant adj not connected with the matter in hand. **ir·rel′e·vance** n

ir·rep·a·ra·ble [i-REP-ər-ə-bəl] adj not able to be repaired or remedied.

ir·re·place′a·ble adj impossible to replace.

ir·re·sist′i·ble adj too attractive or strong to resist.

ir·res′o·lute adj unable to make decisions.

ir·re·spec·tive [ir-i-SPEK-tiv] adj without taking account (of).

ir·re·spon·si·ble adj not showing or not done with due care for the consequences of one's actions or attitudes.

ir·rev·o·ca·ble [i-REV-ə-kə-bəl] adj not able to be changed, undone, altered.

ir·ri·gate [IR-i-gayt] vt -gat·ed, -gat·ing. water by artificial channels, pipes, etc. **ir·ri·ga′tion** n

ir·ri·tate [IR-i-tayt] vt -tat·ed, -tat·ing. annoy; inflame; stimulate. **ir′ri·ta·ble** adj easily annoyed. **ir′ri·tant** adj, n (person or thing) causing irritation. **ir·ri·ta′tion** n

Is. Isaiah.

is [iz] third person singular, present indicative of BE.

Is·lam [iz-LAHM] n Muslim faith or world. **Is·lam′ic** adj

is·land [Ī-lənd] n piece of land surrounded by water; raised area for pedestrians in middle of road. **isle** [īl] n island. **is·let** [Ī-lit] n little island.

i·so·bar [Ī-sə-bahr] n line on map connecting places of equal mean barometric pressure.

i·so·late [Ī-sə-layt] vt -lat·ed, -lat·ing. place apart or alone. **i·so·la′tion** n **i·so·la′tion·ism** n policy of not participating in international affairs.

i·so·mer [Ī-sə-mər] n substance with same molecules as another but different atomic arrangement. **i·so·mer′ic** adj

i·so·met·ric [ī-sə-ME-trik] adj having equal dimensions; relating to muscular contraction without movement. **i·so·met′rics** pl n system of isometric exercises.

i·sos·ce·les [ī-SOS-ə-leez] adj of triangle, having two sides equal.

i·so·therm [Ī-sə-thurm] n line on map connecting points of equal mean temperature.

i·so·tope [Ī-sə-tohp] n atom of element having a different nuclear mass and atomic weight from other atoms in same element. **i·so·top′ic** adj

ISP Internet service provider: business providing its customers with connection to the Internet.

is·sue [ISH-oo] n sending or giving out officially or publicly; number or amount so given out; discharge; offspring, children; topic of discussion; question, dispute; outcome, result. ▶ v -sued, -su·ing. ▶ vi go out; result in; arise (from). ▶ vt emit, give out, send out; distribute, publish.

isth·mus [IS-məs] n neck of land between two seas.

it pron neuter pronoun of the third person. **its** adj belonging to it. **it's** it is; it has. **it·self′** pron emphatic form of IT.

i·tal·ic [i-TAL-ik] adj of type, sloping. **i·tal′ics** pl n this type, now used for emphasis, etc. **i·tal′i·cize** [-sīz] vt put in italics.

itch [ich] vi, n (feel) irritation in the skin. **itch′y** adj **itch·i·er, itch·i·est.**

i·tem [Ī-təm] n single thing in list, collection, etc.; piece of information; entry in account, etc. **i′tem·ize** vt -ized, -iz·ing.

it·er·ate [IT-ə-rayt] vt -at·ed, -at·ing. repeat. **it·er·a′tion** n **it′er·a·tive** adj

i·tin·er·ant [ī-TIN-ər-ənt] adj traveling from place to place; working for a short time in various places; traveling on circuit. **i·tin′er·ar·y** n, pl -ar·ies. record, line of travel; route; guidebook.

i·vo·ry [Ī-və-ree] n, pl -ries. hard white substance of the tusks of elephants, etc. **ivory tower**

seclusion, remoteness.
i·vy [Ī-vee] *n, pl* **-vies.** climbing evergreen plant. **i'vied** *adj* covered with ivy.

J j

jab *vt* **jabbed, jab·bing.** poke roughly; thrust, stab abruptly. ▶ *n* poke; punch.

jab·ber [JAB-ər] *v* chatter; utter, talk rapidly, incoherently. **Jab'ber·wock·y** *n* nonsense, esp. in verse.

jack [jak] *n* fellow, man; *inf* sailor; male of some animals; device for lifting heavy weight, esp. automobile; playing card with picture of soldier or servant; socket and plug connection for electrical equipment; small flag, esp. national, at sea. ▶ *vt* (usu. with *up*) lift (an object) with a jack. **jack-of-all-trades** *pl* **jacks.** person adept at many kinds of work.

jack·al [JAK-əl] *n* wild, gregarious animal of Asia and Africa closely allied to dog.

jack·ass [JAK-as] *n* male donkey; blockhead.

jack·et [JAK-it] *n* outer garment, short coat; outer casing, cover.

jack·knife [JAK-nīf] *n, pl* **-knives.** clasp knife; dive with sharp bend at waist in midair. ▶ *v* **-knifed, -knif·ing.** bend sharply, e.g. an articulated truck forming a sharp angle with its trailer.

jack·pot [JAK-pot] *n* large prize; accumulated stakes, as in poker.

jac·quard [JAK-ahrd] *n* fabric in which design is incorporated into the weave.

Ja·cuz·zi [jə-KOO-zee] *n* ® device that swirls water in a bath; bath with this device.

jade[1] [jayd] *n* ornamental semiprecious stone, usu. dark green; this color.

jade[2] *n* sorry or worn-out horse; disreputable woman. **jad'ed** *adj* tired and unenthusiastic.

jag *n* sharp or ragged projection; spree. **jag'ged** [-id] *adj*

jag·uar [JAG-wahr] *n* large S Amer. spotted cat.

jail [jayl] *n* building for confinement of criminals or suspects. ▶ *vt* send to, confine in prison. **jail'bait** [-bayt] *n sl* underage girl with whom sexual intercourse is considered a crime. **jail'er** *n* **jail'bird** *n* hardened criminal.

ja·lop·y [jə-LOP-ee] *n, pl* **-lop·ies.** *inf* old car.

jam *vt* **jammed, jam·ming.** pack together; (cause to) stick together and become unworkable; apply fiercely; squeeze; *Radio* block (another station) with impulses of equal wavelength. ▶ *n* fruit preserved by boiling with sugar; crush; delay of traffic; awkward situation. **jam-packed** *adj* filled to capacity. **jam session** [improvised] jazz session]

jamb [jam] *n* side post of arch, door, etc.

jam·bo·ree [jam-bə-REE] *n* large gathering or rally of scouts; spree, celebration.

jan·gle [JANG-gəl] *v* **-gled, -gling.** (cause to) sound harshly, as bell; (of nerves) irritate. ▶ *n* harsh sound.

jan·i·tor [JAN-i-tər] *n* custodian, cleaner.

jar[1] [jahr] *n* round vessel of glass, earthenware, etc.; *inf* drink of beer, whiskey, etc.

jar[2] *v* **jarred, jar·ring.** (cause to) vibrate suddenly, violently; have disturbing, painful effect on. ▶ *n* jarring sound; shock, etc.

jar·gon [JAHR-gən] *n* specialized language concerned with particular subject; pretentious or nonsensical language.

jas·per [JAS-pər] *n* red, yellow, dark green or brown quartz.

jaun·dice [JAWN-dis] *n* disease marked by yellowness of skin; bitterness, ill humor; prejudice. ▶ *v* **-diced, -dic·ing.** make, become prejudiced, bitter, etc.

jaunt [jawnt] *n* short pleasure trip. ▶ *vi* make one.

jaun·ty [JAWN-tee] *adj* **-ti·er, -ti·est.**

sprightly; brisk; smart, trim.
jaun'ti·ly adv
Java [JAH-və] n ® computer programming language that is widely used on the Internet.
jave·lin [JAV-lin] n spear, esp. for throwing in sporting events.
jaw n one of bones in which teeth are set. ▶ pl mouth; fig narrow opening of a gorge or valley; gripping part of vise, etc. ▶ vi sl talk lengthily.
jay n noisy bird of brilliant plumage. **jay'walk·er** n careless pedestrian. **jay'walk** vi
jazz n syncopated music and dance. **jazz'y** adj **-jazz·i·er, jazz·i·est.** flashy, showy. **jazz up** play as jazz; make more lively, appealing.
jeal·ous [JEL-əs] adj distrustful of the faithfulness (of); envious; suspiciously watchful.
jeans [jeenz] pl n casual trousers, esp. of denim.
jeer v scoff, deride. ▶ n scoff, taunt, gibe.
Je·ho·vah [ji-HO-və] n God.
je·june [ji-JOON] adj simple, naive; meager.
jell v congeal; assume definite form.
jel·ly [JEL-ee] n, pl **-lies.** semitransparent food made with gelatin, becoming softly stiff as it cools; anything of the consistency of this. **jel'ly·fish** n jellylike small sea animal.
jeop·ard·y [JEP-ər-dee] n danger. **jeop'ard·ize** vt **-ized, -iz·ing.** endanger.
Jer. Jeremiah.
jerk [jurk] n sharp, abruptly stopped movement; twitch; sharp pull; sl stupid person, inconsequential person. ▶ v move or throw with a jerk. **jerk'i·ly** adv **jerk'y** adj **jerk·i·er, jerk·i·est.** uneven, spasmodic.
jer·sey [JUR-zee] n, pl **-seys.** knitted sweater; machine-knitted fabric; (J-) breed of cow.
jest n, vi joke. **jest'er** n Hist professional clown at court.
Jes·u·it [JEZH-oo-it] n member of Society of Jesus, order founded by

Ignatius Loyola in 1534.
Jes·u·it'i·cal adj of Jesuits; (j-) crafty, using overly subtle reasoning.
jet¹ n stream of liquid, gas, etc., esp. shot from small hole; the small hole; spout, nozzle; aircraft driven by jet propulsion. ▶ v **jet·ted, -jet·ting.** throw out; shoot forth.
jet-black adj deep black. **jet lag** fatigue caused by crossing time zones in jet aircraft. **jet propulsion** propulsion by thrust provided by jet of gas or liquid. **jet ski** small self-propelled vehicle resembling a scooter, which skims across water on a flat keel.
jet² n hard black mineral capable of brilliant polish.
jet·sam [JET-səm] n goods thrown out to lighten ship and later washed ashore. **jet'ti·son** [-tə-sən] vt abandon; throw overboard.
jet·ty [JET-ee] n **-ties.** small pier, wharf.
Jew [joo] n one of Hebrew ancestry; one who practices Judaism. **Jew'ish** adj **Jew'ry** n the Jews. **jew's harp** n small musical instrument held between teeth and played by finger.
jew·el [JOO-əl] n precious stone; ornament containing one; precious thing. **jew'el·er** n dealer in jewels. **jew'el·ry** n
jib n triangular sail set forward of mast; projecting arm of crane or derrick.
jibe see GIBE.
jif·fy [JIF-ee] n, pl **-fies.** inf very short period of time.
jig n lively dance; music for it; small mechanical device; guide for cutting, etc.; Angling any of various lures. ▶ vi **jigged, jig·ging.** dance jig; make jerky up-and-down movements. **jig'saw** n machine-mounted saw for cutting curves, etc. **jigsaw puzzle** picture stuck on board and cut into interlocking pieces with jigsaw.
jig·ger [JIG-ər] n small glass holding and pouring measure of whiskey, etc.

jig·gle [JIG-əl] v -**gled, -gling.** move (up and down, etc.) with short jerky movements.

jilt vt cast off (lover).

jim·my [JIM-ee] n, pl -**mies.** short steel crowbar. ▶ vt -**mied, -my·ing.** force open with a jimmy, etc.

jin·gle [JING-gəl] n mixed metallic noise, as of shaken chain; catchy, rhythmic verse, song, etc. ▶ v -**gled, -gling.** (cause to) make jingling sound.

jin·go·ism [JING-goh-iz-əm] n chauvinism. **jin·go·is'tic** adj

jinks [jingks] pl n **high jinks** boisterous merrymaking.

jinx [jingks] n force, person, thing bringing bad luck. ▶ v be or put a jinx on.

jit·ters [JIT-ərz] pl n worried nervousness, anxiety. **jit'ter·y** adj -**ter·i·er, -ter·i·est.** nervous.

jiujitsu n see JUJITSU.

jive [jīv] n (dance performed to) swing music, esp. of 1950's. ▶ v **jived, jiv·ing.** play, dance to, swing music; sl tease; fool.

job n piece of work, task; position, office; inf difficult task; sl a crime, esp. robbery. **job'ber** n wholesale merchant. **job'less** [-lis] adj, pl. n unemployed (people).

jock·ey [JOK-ee] n, pl -**eys.** professional rider in horse races. ▶ v -**eyed, -ey·ing.** (esp. with for) maneuver.

jo·cose [joh-KOHS] adj waggish, humorous. **jo·cos'i·ty** [-KOS-i-tee] n **joc'u·lar** [-yə-lər] adj joking; given to joking. **joc·u·lar'i·ty** n

joc·und [JOK-ənd] adj merry, cheerful. **jo·cun·di·ty** [joh-KUN-di-tee] n, pl -**ties.**

jodh·purs [JOD-pərz] pl n tight-legged riding breeches.

jog v **jogged, jog·ging.** ▶ vi run slowly or move at trot, esp. for physical exercise. ▶ vt jar, nudge; remind, stimulate. ▶ n jogging. **jog'ger** n **jogging** n

jog·gle [JOG-əl] v -**gled, -gling.** move to and fro in jerks; shake.

John [jon] n name; (j-) sl toilet; sl prostitute's customer.

joie de vi·vre [zhwad VEE-vrə] Fr enjoyment of life, ebullience.

join vt put together, fasten, unite; become a member (of). ▶ vi become united, connected; (with up) enlist; take part (in). ▶ n joining; place of joining, seam. **join'er** n maker of finished woodwork; one who joins.

joint n arrangement by which two things fit together, rigidly or loosely; place of this; sl house, place, etc.; sl disreputable bar or nightclub; sl marijuana cigarette. ▶ adj common; shared by two or more. ▶ vt connect by joints; divide at the joints. **joint'ly** adv **out of joint** dislocated; disorganized.

joist n one of the parallel beams stretched from wall to wall on which to fix floor or ceiling.

joke [johk] n thing said or done to cause laughter; something not in earnest, or ridiculous. ▶ v **joked, jok·ing.** make jokes. **jok'er** n one who jokes; inf fellow; extra card in pack, counting as highest card in some games.

jol·ly [JOL-ee] adj -**li·er, -li·est.** jovial; festive, merry. ▶ vt -**lied, -ly·ing.** (esp. with along) (try to) make person, occasion, etc. happier.

jolt [johlt] n sudden jerk; bump; shock; inf a strong drink. ▶ v move, shake with jolts.

joss [jos] n Chinese idol. **joss house** Chinese temple. **joss stick** stick of Chinese incense.

jos·tle [JOS-əl] v -**tled, -tling.** knock or push against.

jot n small amount, whit. ▶ vt **jot·ted, jot·ting.** write briefly; make note of. **jot'ting** n quick note; memorandum.

joule [jool] n Electricity unit of work or energy.

jour·nal [JUR-nl] n daily newspaper or other periodical; daily record; logbook; part of axle or shaft resting on the bearings. **jour·nal·ese'** [-EEZ] n journalist's jargon; style full of clichés. **jour'nal·ism** n editing, writing in periodicals.

jour·ney [JUR-nee] *n, pl* **-neys.** going to a place, excursion; distance traveled. ▶ *vi* **-neyed, -ney·ing.** travel.

joust [jowst] *n Hist* encounter with lances between two mounted knights. ▶ *vi* engage in joust.

jo·vi·al [JOH-vee-əl] *adj* convivial, merry, gay. **jo·vi·al′i·ty** *n*

jowl *n* cheek, jaw; outside of throat when prominent.

joy [joi] *n* gladness, pleasure, delight; cause of this. **joy′ful** [-fuul] *adj* **joy′less** [-lis] *adj* **joy′ride** *n* (high-speed) automobile trip. **joy′stick** *n inf* control stick of aircraft or computer device.

ju′bi·lant [JOO-bə-lənt] *adj* exultant. **ju·bi·la′tion** *n*

ju·bi·lee [JOO-bə-lee] *n* time of rejoicing, esp. 25th (silver) or 50th (golden) anniversary.

Jud. Judges.

Ju·da·ic [joo-DAY-ik] *adj* Jewish. **Ju′da·ism** *n*

judge [juj] *n* officer appointed to try cases in law courts; one who decides in a dispute, contest, etc.; one able to form a reliable opinion, arbiter; umpire; in Jewish history, ruler. ▶ *v* **judged, judg·ing.** ▶ *vi* act as judge. ▶ *vt* act as judge of; try, estimate; decide. **judg′ment** *n* faculty of judging; sentence of court; opinion; misfortune regarded as sign of divine displeasure.

ju·di·ca·ture [JOO-di-kə-chər] *n* administration of justice; body of judges. **ju·di′cial** [-DISH-əl] *adj* of or by a court or judge; proper to a judge; discriminating. **ju·di′ci·ar·y** [-shee-er-ee] *n, pl* **-ar·ies.** system of courts and judges. **ju·di′cious** [-shəs] *adj* well-judged, sensible, prudent.

ju·do [JOO-doh] *n* modern sport derived from jujitsu.

jug *n* vessel for liquids, with handle and small spout; its contents; *sl* prison. ▶ *vt* **jugged, jug·ging.** stew (esp. hare) in jug.

jug·ger·naut [JUG-ər-nawt] *n* large

overpowering, destructive force.

jug·gle [JUG-əl] *v* **-gled, -gling.** throw and catch (several objects) so most are in the air simultaneously; manage, manipulate (accounts, etc.) to deceive. ▶ *n* **jug′gler** *n*

jug·u·lar vein [JUG-yə-lər] one of three large veins of the neck returning blood from the head.

juice [joos] *n* liquid part of vegetable, fruit, or meat; *sl* electric current; *sl* fuel used to run engine; vigor, vitality. **juic′y** *adj* **juic·i·er, juic·i·est.** succulent; scandalous, improper.

ju·jit·su [joo-JIT-soo] *n* the Japanese art of wrestling and self-defense.

ju·jube [JOO-joo-bee] *n* lozenge of gelatin, sugar, etc.; a fruit.

ju·lep [JOO-lip] *n* sweet drink; medicated drink.

Jul·ian [JOOL-yən] *adj* of Julius Caesar. **Julian calendar** calendar as adjusted by Julius Caesar in 46 B.C., in which the year was made to consist of 365 days, 6 hours, instead of 365 days.

ju·li·enne [joo-lee-EN] *n* kind of clear soup. ▶ *adj* of food, cut into thin strips or small pieces. ▶ *vt*

jum·ble [JUM-bəl] *vt* **-bled, -bling.** mingle, mix in confusion. ▶ *n* confused heap, muddle.

jum·bo [JUM-boh] *n inf* elephant; anything very large.

jump *v* (cause to) spring, leap (over); move hastily; pass or skip (over). ▶ *vi* move hastily; rise steeply; parachute from aircraft; start, jerk (with astonishment, etc.); of faulty film, etc., make abrupt movements. ▶ *vt* come off (tracks, rails, etc.); attack without warning. ▶ *n* act of jumping; obstacle to be jumped; distance, height jumped; sudden nervous jerk or start; sudden rise in prices. **jump′er** *n* one who, that which jumps; sleeveless dress; electric cable to connect discharged car battery to external battery to aid starting of engine. **jump′y** *adj* **jump·i·er, jump·i·est.** nervous. **jump′suit** *n* one-piece garment of trousers and top.

junc·tion [JUNGK-shən] *n* railroad station, etc. where lines, routes join; place of joining; joining.

junc·ture [JUNGK-chər] *n* state of affairs.

jun·gle [JUNG-gəl] *n* tangled vegetation of equatorial forest; land covered with it; tangled mass; condition of intense competition, struggle for survival.

jun·ior [JOON-yər] *adj* younger; of lower standing. ▶ *n* junior person.

ju·ni·per [JOON-ə-pər] *n* evergreen shrub with berries yielding oil of juniper, used for medicine and gin making.

junk¹ [jungk] *n* discarded, useless objects; *inf* nonsense; *sl* narcotic drug esp. heroin. **junk'ie** *n, pl* **-junk·ies.** *inf* drug addict. **junk food** food, oft. of low nutritional value, eaten in addition to or instead of regular meals. **junk mail** unsolicited mail advertising goods or services.

junk² *n* Chinese sailing vessel.

jun·ket [JUNG-kit] *n* curdled milk flavored and sweetened; pleasure trip esp. one paid for by others. ▶ *vi* go on a junket.

jun·ta [HUUN-tə] *n* group of military officers holding power in a country.

Ju·pi·ter [JOO-pi-tər] *n* Roman chief of gods; largest of the planets.

ju·ris·dic·tion [juur-is-DIK-shən] *n* administration of justice; authority; territory covered by it.

ju·ris·pru·dence [-PROO-dəns] *n* science of, skill in, law. **ju'rist** *n* one skilled in law.

ju·ry [JUUR-ee] *n, pl* **-ries.** body of persons sworn to render verdict in court of law; body of judges of competition. **ju'ror** *n* member of jury.

just *adj* fair; upright, honest; proper, right, equitable. ▶ *adv* exactly; barely; at this instant; merely, only; really. **jus'tice** *n* quality of being just; fairness; judicial proceedings; judge, magistrate. **jus'ti·fy** *vt* **-fied, -fy·ing.** prove right, true or innocent; vindicate; excuse. **jus'ti·fi·a·ble** *adj*

jut *vi* **jut·ted, jut·ting.** project, stick out. ▶ *n* projection.

jute [joot] *n* fiber of certain plants, used for rope, canvas, etc.

ju·ve·nile [JOO-və-nl] *adj* young; of, for young children; immature. ▶ *n* young person, child, male actor. **ju·ve·nil'i·a** *pl n* works produced in author's youth. **juvenile court** court dealing with young offenders or children in need of care. **juvenile delinquent** young person guilty of some offense, antisocial behavior, etc.

jux·ta·pose [JUK-stə-pohz] *vt* **-posed, -pos·ing.** put side by side. **jux·ta·po·si'tion** *n* contiguity, being side by side.

K k

K Kelvin; *Chem* potassium.

ka·bob [kə-BOB], **ke·bab** [kə-BAB] *n* dish of small pieces of meat, tomatoes, etc. grilled on skewers.

kale [kayl] *n* type of cabbage.

ka·lei·do·scope [kə-LĪ-də-skohp] *n* optical toy for producing changing symmetrical patterns by multiple reflections of colored glass chips, etc., in inclined mirrors enclosed in tube; any complex, frequently changing pattern. **ka·lei·do·scop·ic** [-SKOP-ik] *adj* swiftly changing.

ka·mi·ka·ze [kah-mi-KAH-zə] *n* suicidal attack, esp. as in World War II, by Japanese pilots.

kan·ga·roo [kang-gə-ROO] *n, pl* **-roos.** Aust. marsupial with very strongly developed hind legs for jumping. **kangaroo court** irregular, illegal court.

ka·pok [KAY-pok] *n* tropical tree; fiber from its seed pods used to stuff cushions, etc.

ka·put [kah-PUUT] *adj sl* ruined, out of order, no good.

ka·ra·te [kə-RAH-tee] *n* Japanese system of unarmed combat using feet, hands, elbows, etc. as weapons in a variety of ways.

kar·ma [KAHR-mə] *n Buddhism, Hinduism* one's actions seen as affecting fate for next reincarnation.

kart [kahrt] *n* miniature low-powered racing car (also **go-kart**).

kay·ak [KĪ-ak] *n* Inuit canoe made of sealskins stretched over frame; any canoe of this design.

ka·zoo [kə-ZOO] *n, pl* **-zoos.** cigar-shaped musical instrument producing nasal sound.

kbyte *Computers* kilobyte.

kebab, kebob see KABOB.

ked·ger·ee [KEJ-ə-ree] *n* East Indian dish of fish cooked with rice, eggs, etc.

keel *n* lowest longitudinal support on which ship is built. **keel'haul** *vt*

formerly, punish by hauling under keel of ship; rebuke severely. **keel over** turn upside down; collapse suddenly.

keen[1] *adj* **-er, -est.** sharp; acute; eager; shrewd, strong. **keen'ly** *adv* **keen'ness** *n*

keen[2] *n* funeral lament. ▸ *vi* wail over the dead.

keep *v* **kept, keep·ing.** retain possession of, not lose; store; cause to continue; take charge of; maintain, detain; provide upkeep; reserve; remain good; remain; continue. ▸ *n* living or support; charge or care; central tower of castle, stronghold. **keep'er** *n* **keep'ing** *n* harmony, agreement; care, charge, possession. **keep'sake** *n* thing treasured for sake of giver.

keg *n* small barrel usu. holding 5 to 10 gallons (19 to 38 liters).

kelp *n* large seaweed; its ashes, yielding iodine.

Kel'vin *adj* of thermometric scale starting at absolute zero (-273.15° Celsius). ▸ *n* SI unit of temperature.

ken *n* range of knowledge. ▸ *vt* **kenned** *or* **kent, ken·ning.** *Scot* know.

ken·do [KEN-doh] *n* Japanese sport of fencing, using bamboo staves.

ken·nel [KEN-l] *n* house, shelter for dog; (oft. pl) place for breeding, boarding dogs. ▸ *vt* **-neled, -nel·ing.** put into kennel.

kept pt./pp. of KEEP.

ker·chief [KUR-chif] *n* square scarf used as head covering; handkerchief.

ker·nel [KUR-nl] *n* inner seed of nut or fruit stone; central, essential part.

ker·o·sene [KER-ə-seen] *n* fuel distilled from petroleum or coal and shale.

ketch [kech] *n* two-masted sailing vessel.

ketch·up [KECH-əp] *n* condiment of vinegar, tomatoes, etc.

ket·tle [KET-l] n metal vessel with spout and handle, esp. for boiling water. **ket'tle·drum** n musical instrument made of membrane stretched over copper, brass, etc. hemisphere. **a fine kettle of fish** awkward situation, mess.

key [kee] n instrument for operating lock, winding clock, etc.; something providing control, explanation, means of achieving an end, etc.; Mus set of related notes; operating lever of typewriter, piano, computer, etc.; mode of thought. ▸ vt (also **key in**) enter (text) using a keyboard; provide symbols on map, etc. to assist identification of positions on it. ▸ adj vital; most important. **key'board** [-bord] n set of keys on piano, computer, etc. **key'hole** n hole for inserting key into lock; any shape resembling this. **key'note** [-noht] n dominant idea; basic note of musical key. **key'pad** n small keyboard with push buttons. **key'stone** n central stone of arch that locks all in position.

khak·i [KAK-ee] adj dull yellowish-brown. ▸ n, pl **khakis.** khaki cloth; (usu. pl) military uniform.

Khmer [kmair] n member of a people of Cambodia.

Ki. Kings.

kib·ble [KIB-əl] vt **-bled, -bling.** grind into small pieces. ▸ n dry dog food prepared in this way.

kib·butz [ki-BUUTS] n in Israel, Jewish communal agricultural settlement. **kib·butz'nik** n member of kibbutz.

ki·bosh [KĪ-bosh] n inf nonsense. **to put the kibosh on** silence; check; defeat.

kick [kik] vi strike out with foot; score with a kick; be recalcitrant; recoil. ▸ vt strike or hit with foot; sl free oneself of (drug habit, etc.). ▸ n foot blow; recoil; excitement, thrill. **kick'back** n strong reaction; money paid illegally for favors done, etc. **kick off** v start game of football; begin (discussion, etc.).

kick-start v start motorcycle engine, etc. by pedal that is kicked downward.

kid n young goat; leather of its skin; inf child. ▸ v **kid·ded, kid·ding.** (of a goat) give birth; inf tease, deceive; inf behave, speak in fun.

kid'nap vt **-napped, -nap·ping.** seize and hold for ransom. **kid'nap·per** n

kid·ney [KID-nee] n, pl **-neys.** either of the pair of organs that secrete urine; animal kidney used as food; nature, kind. **kidney bean** common bean, kidney-shaped at maturity.

kill vt deprive of life; destroy; neutralize; pass (time); weaken or dilute; inf tire, exhaust; inf cause to suffer pain; inf quash, defeat, veto. ▸ n act of killing; animals, etc. killed in hunt; enemy troops, aircraft, etc. killed or destroyed in combat. **kill'er** n one who, that which, kills. **kill'ing** adj inf very tiring; very funny. ▸ n sudden success, esp. on stock market.

kiln n furnace, oven.

kil·o [KEE-loh] n short for KILOGRAM.

kilo- comb. form one thousand, e.g. kiloliter; kilometer.

kil·o·byte [KIL-ə-bīt] n Computers 1,024 bytes; (loosely) one thousand bytes.

kil·o·gram [KIL-ə-gram] n weight of one thousand grams.

kil·o·hertz [KIL-ə-hurts] n one thousand cycles per second.

kil·o·watt [KIL-ə-wot] n Electricity one thousand watts.

kilt n short, usu. tartan, skirt, deeply pleated, worn orig. by Scottish Highlanders. **kilt'ed** adj

ki·mo·no [kə-MOH-nə] n, pl **-nos.** loose, wide-sleeved Japanese robe, fastened with sash; woman's garment like this.

kin n family, relatives. ▸ adj related by blood. **kin'dred** [-drid] n relationship; relatives. ▸ adj similar; related. **kin'folk** [-fohk] n **kin'ship** n

kind [kīnd] n genus, sort, class. ▸ adj **-er, -est.** sympathetic, considerate;

good, benevolent; gentle.
kind′li·ness n **kind′ly** adj **-li·er,
-li·est.** kind, genial. ▶ adv
kind′ness n **kind′heart·ed** adj **in
kind** (of payment) in goods rather
than money; with something
similar.

kin·der·gar·ten [KIN-dər-gahr-tn]
n class, school for children of about
four to six years old.

kin·dle [KIN-dl] v **-dled, -dling.** ▶ vt
set on fire; inspire, excite. ▶ vi catch
fire. **kind′ling** n small wood to
kindle fires.

ki·net·ic [ki-NET-ik] adj of motion in
relation to force. **ki·net′ics** n the
branch of mechanics concerned
with the study of bodies in motion.

king n male sovereign ruler of
independent country; monarch;
piece in game of chess; playing
card with picture of a king;
Checkers two pieces on top of one
another, allowed freedom of
movement. **king′ly** adj **-li·er,
-li·est.** royal; appropriate to a king.
king′dom [-dəm] n country ruled
by king; realm; sphere. **king′fish** n
any of several types of fish; inf
person in position of authority.
king′pin n swivel pin; central or
front pin in bowling; inf chief thing
or person. **king-size, king-sized**
adj inf large; larger than standard
size.

kink [kingk] n tight twist in rope,
wire, hair, etc.; crick, as of neck; inf
eccentricity. ▶ v make, become
kinked; put, make kink in; twist.
kink′y adj **kink·i·er, kink·i·est.** full
of kinks; inf eccentric, esp. given to
deviant (sexual) practices.

ki·osk [KEE-osk] n small, sometimes
movable booth selling soft drinks,
cigarettes, newspapers, etc.

kip·per [KIP-ər] vt cure (fish) by
splitting open, rubbing with salt,
and drying or smoking. ▶ n
kippered fish.

kirsch [keersh] n brandy made from
cherries.

kis·met [KIZ-mit] n fate, destiny.

kiss n touch or caress with lips; light
touch. ▶ v **kiss′er** n one who kisses;

sl mouth or face. **kissing kin**
relative(s) familiar enough to greet
with polite kiss. **kiss of death**
apparently friendly ruinous act.

kit n outfit, equipment; personal
effects, esp. of traveler; set of
pieces of equipment sold ready to
be assembled. **kit bag** small bag
for holding soldier's or traveler's kit.

kitch·en [KICH-ən] n room used for
cooking. **kitch·en·ette′** n small
compact kitchen. **kitchen garden**
garden for raising vegetables,
herbs, etc. **kitchen sink** sink in
kitchen; final item imaginable.

kite [kīt] n light papered frame
flown in wind; large hawk; check
drawn against nonexistent funds.
▶ vt **kit·ed, kit·ing.** use check in
this way; cash or pass such a check.

kith n **kith and kin** friends and
relatives.

kitsch [kich] n vulgarized,
pretentious art, literature, etc., usu.
with popular, sentimental appeal.

kit·ten [KIT-n] n young cat.

kit·ty [KIT-ee] n, pl **-ties.** short for
KITTEN; in some card games, pool of
money; communal fund.

ki·wi [KEE-wee] n, pl **-wis.** any N.Z.
flightless bird of the genus Apteryx;
inf New Zealander. **kiwi fruit** fuzzy
fruit of Asian climbing plant, the
Chinese gooseberry.

klax·on [KLAK-sən] n powerful
electric horn, used as warning
signal.

klep·to·ma·ni·a
[klep-tə-MAY-nee-ə] n compulsive
tendency to steal for the sake of
theft. **klep·to·ma′ni·ac** n

knack [nak] n acquired facility or
dexterity; trick; habit.

knap·sack [NAP-sak] n soldier's or
traveler's bag to strap to the back,
rucksack.

knave [nayv] n jack at cards; obs
rogue. **knav′er·y** n villainy.
knav′ish adj

knead [need] vt work (flour) into
dough; work, massage.

knee [nee] n joint between thigh
and lower leg; part of garment
covering knee. ▶ vt **kneed,**

knee·ing. strike, push with knee.
knee'cap n bone in front of knee.
kneel [neel] vi **knelt** or **kneeled,**
kneel·ing. fall, rest on knees.
knell [nel] n sound of a bell, esp. at
funeral or death; portent of doom.
knew pt. of KNOW.
knick·ers [NIK-ərz] pl n loose-fitting
short trousers gathered in at knee.
knick-knack [NIK-nak] n small
ornament or toy.
knife [nīf] n, pl **knives.** cutting
blade, esp. one in handle, used as
implement or weapon. ▶ vt **knifed,**
knif·ing. cut or stab with knife.
knife edge critical, possibly
dangerous situation.
knight [nīt] n Brit man of rank
below baronet, having right to
prefix Sir to his name; member of
medieval order of chivalry;
champion; piece in chess. ▶ vt
confer knighthood on.
knight'hood [-huud] n
knish n turnover filled with potato,
meat, etc. and fried or baked.
knit [nit] v **knit'ted** or **knit,**
knit·ting. form (garment, etc.) by
putting together series of loops in
wool or other yarn; draw together;
unite. **knit'ting** n knitted work; act
of knitting.
knob [nob] n rounded lump, esp. at
end or on surface of anything.
knob·by adj **-bi·er, -bi·est.**
knock [nok] vt strike, hit; inf
disparage; rap audibly; (of engine)
make metallic noise, ping. ▶ n
blow, rap. **knock'er** n metal
appliance for knocking on door;
who or what knocks. **knock-kneed**
adj having incurved legs. **knocked
out** exhausted, tired, worn out.
knock off inf cease work; inf copy,
plagiarize; sl kill; sl steal. **knock out**
inf render (opponent) unconscious;
overwhelm, amaze; make
(something) hurriedly. **knock'out**
n blow, etc. that renders
unconscious; inf person or thing
overwhelmingly attractive. **knock
up** sl make pregnant.
knoll [nohl] n small rounded hill,
mound.

knot [not] n fastening of strands by
looping and pulling tight; cluster;
small closely knit group; tie, bond;
hard lump, esp. of wood where
branch joins or has joined in; unit
of speed used by ships, equal to
one nautical mile per hour;
difficulty. ▶ vt **knot·ted, knot·ting.**
tie with knot, in knots. **knot'ty** adj
-ti·er, -ti·est. full of knots; puzzling,
difficult. **knot'hole** [-hohl] n hole
in wood where knot has been.
know [noh] v **knew, known,**
know·ing. ▶ vt be aware of, have
information about, be acquainted
with, recognize, have experience,
understand. ▶ vi have information
or understanding. **know'ing** adj
cunning, shrewd. **know'ing·ly** adv
shrewdly; deliberately.
knowl·edge [NOL-ij] n knowing;
what one knows; learning.
knowl'edge·a·ble adj intelligent,
well-informed. **know-how** n
practical knowledge, experience,
aptitude. **in the know** informed.
knuck·le [nuk-əl] n bone at finger
joint; knee joint of calf or pig. ▶ vt
-led, -ling. strike with knuckles.
knuckle ball Baseball pitch
delivered by holding ball by thumb
and first joints or tips of first two or
three fingers. **knuckle-dust·er** n
metal appliances worn on knuckles
to add force to blow, brass
knuckles. **knuckle down** get down
(to work). **knuckle under** yield,
submit.
knurled [nurld] adj serrated;
gnarled.
ko·a·la [koh-AH-lə] n marsupial
Aust. animal, native bear.
kohl n powdered antimony used
orig. in Eastern countries for
darkening the eyelids.
kohl·ra·bi [kohl-RAH-bee] n, pl
-bies. type of cabbage with edible
stem.
ko·peck [KOH-pek] n monetary
unit of Russia and Belarus, one
hundredth of ruble.
Ko·ran [kə-RAN] n sacred book of
Muslims.
ko·sher [KOH-shər] adj permitted,

clean, good, as of food, etc., conforming to the Jewish dietary law; *inf* legitimate, authentic. ▶ *n inf* kosher food. ▶ *vt* make (food, etc.) kosher.

kow·tow *n* former Chinese custom of touching ground with head in respect; submission. ▶ *vi* (esp. with *to*) prostrate oneself; be obsequious, fawn on.

Kr *Chem* krypton.

Krem'lin *n* central government of Russia and, formerly, the Soviet Union.

krill [kril] *n, pl* **krill.** small shrimplike marine animal.

kryp·ton [KRIP-ton] *n* rare gaseous element, present in atmosphere.

ku·dos [KOO-dohz] *n* honor; acclaim.

ku·du [KOO-doo] *n* Afr. antelope with spiral horns.

ku·lak [kuu-LAHK] *n* independent well-to-do Russian peasant of Czarist times.

kum·quat [KUM-kwot] *n* small Chinese tree; its round orange fruit.

kung fu [kung foo] Chinese martial art combining techniques of judo and karate.

Kwan·zaa [KWAHN-zə *or* -zah] *n* African-American festival held from December 26 through January 1.

L l

la see LAH.

La *Chem* lanthanum.

la·bel [LAY-bəl] *n* slip of paper, metal, etc., fixed to object to give information about it; brief, descriptive phrase or term. ▶ *vt* **-beled, -bel·ing.**

la·bi·al [LAY-bee-əl] *adj* of the lips; pronounced with the lips. ▶ *n* labial consonant.

la·bor [LAY-bər] *n* exertion of body or mind; task; workers collectively; effort, pain, of childbirth or time taken for this. ▶ *vi* work hard; strive; maintain normal motion with difficulty; (esp. of ship) be tossed heavily. ▶ *vt* elaborate; stress to excess. **la'bored** *adj* uttered, done, with difficulty. **la'bor·er** *n* one who labors, esp. person doing manual work for wages. **la·bo·ri·ous** [lə-BOR-ee-əs] *adj* tedious.

lab·o·ra·to·ry [LAB-rə-tor-ee] *n* place for scientific investigations or for manufacture of chemicals.

lab·ra·dor [LAB-rə-dor] *n* breed of large, smooth-coated retriever dog.

lab·y·rinth [LAB-ə-rinth] *n* network of tortuous passages, maze; inexplicable difficulty; perplexity. **lab·y·rin'thine** [-RIN-thin] *adj*

lace [lays] *n* fine patterned openwork fabric; cord, usu. one of pair, to draw edges together, e.g. to tighten shoes, etc.; ornamental braid. ▶ *vt* **laced, lac·ing.** fasten with laces; flavor with whiskey, etc. **lac'y** *adj* **lac·i·er, lac·i·est.** fine, like lace.

lac·er·ate [LAS-ə-rayt] *vt* **-at·ed, -at·ing.** tear, mangle; distress. **lac·er·a'tion** *n*

lach·ry·mal [LAK-rə-məl] *adj* of tears. **lach'ry·ma·to·ry** [-mə-tor·ee] *adj* causing tears or inflammation of eyes. **lach'ry·mose** [-mohs] *adj* tearful.

lack [lak] *n* deficiency, need. ▶ *vt* need, be short of. **lack'lus·ter** *adj* lacking brilliance or vitality.

lack·a·dai·si·cal [lak-ə-DAY-zi-kəl] *adj* languid, listless; lazy, careless.

lack·ey [LAK-ee] *n, pl* **-eys.** servile follower; footman. ▶ *v* **-eyed, -ey·ing.** be, or play, the lackey; wait upon.

la·con·ic [lə-KON-ik] *adj* using, expressed in few words; brief, terse; offhand, not caring. **la·con'i·cal·ly** *adv*

lac·quer [LAK-ər] *n* hard varnish. ▶ *vt* coat with this.

la·crosse [lə-KRAWS] *n* ball game played with long-handled racket, or crosse.

lac·tic [LAK-tik] *adj* of milk. **lac'tate** *vi* **-tat·ed, -tat·ing.** secrete milk. **lac·ta'tion** *n* **lac'tose** [-tohs] *n* white crystalline substance occurring in milk.

la·cu·na [lə-KYOO-nə] *n, pl* **-nae** [-nee] gap, missing part, esp. in document or series.

lad *n* boy, young fellow.

lad·der [LAD-ər] *n* frame of two poles connected by crossbars called rungs, used for climbing; flaw in stockings, caused by running of torn stitch.

lade [layd] *vt* **lad·ed** *or* **lad·en, lad·ing.** load; ship; burden, weigh down. **lad'ing** *n* cargo, freight.

la·dle [LAYD-l] *n* spoon with long handle for large bowl. ▶ *vt* **-dled, -dling.** serve out liquid with a ladle.

la·dy [LAY-dee] *n, pl* **-dies.** female counterpart of gentleman; polite term for a woman; title of some women of rank. **la'dy·like** *adj* gracious; well-mannered. **Our Lady** the Virgin Mary. **la'dy·fin·ger** *n* small sponge cake in shape of finger. **lady-of-the-night** *n, pl* **ladies-.** prostitute.

lag¹ *vi* **lagged, lag·ging.** go too slowly, fall behind. ▶ *n* lagging, interval of time between events. **lag'gard** [-ərd] *n* one who lags.

lagging *adj* loitering, slow.
lag² *vt* **lagged, lag·ging.** wrap
boiler, pipes, etc. with insulating
material. **lagging** *n* this material.
la·ger [LAH-gər] *n* a light-bodied
type of beer. ▶ *vt* age (beer) by
storing in tanks.
la·goon [lə-GOON] *n* saltwater
lake, enclosed by atoll, or separated
by sandbank from sea.
lah, la *n* sixth sol-fa note.
la·ic [LAY-ik] *adj* secular, lay.
la'i·cize [-sīz] *vt* **-cized, -ciz·ing.**
render secular or lay.
laid [layd] pt./pp. of LAY. **laid-back**
adj inf relaxed.
lain [layn] pp. of LIE.
lair *n* resting place, den of animal.
lais·sez faire [les-ay FAIR] *n*
principle of nonintervention, esp.
by government in commercial
affairs; indifference.
la·i·ty [LAY-i-tee] *n* lay worshipers,
the people as opposed to clergy.
lake [layk] *n* expanse of inland
water.
lam *n sl* hasty escape. ▶ *vi sl*
lammed, lam·ming. run away fast;
escape. **on the lam** *sl* escaping;
hiding esp. from police.
Lam. Lamentations.
la·ma [LAH-mə] *n* Buddhist priest in
Tibet or Mongolia. **la'ma·ser·y** *n*
monastery of lamas.
lamb [lam] *n* young of the sheep; its
meat; innocent or helpless
creature. ▶ *vi* (of sheep); give birth
to lamb. **lamb'like** *adj* meek,
gentle.
lam·baste [lam-BAYST] *vt* **-bast·ed,
-bast·ing.** beat, reprimand.
lam·bent [LAM-bənt] *adj* (of flame)
flickering softly; glowing.
lame [laym] *adj* **lam·er, lam·est.**
crippled in a limb, esp. leg;
limping; (of excuse, etc.)
unconvincing. ▶ *vt* **lamed, lam·ing.**
cripple. **lame duck** official serving
out term of office while waiting for
elected successor to assume office;
disabled, weak person or thing.
la·mé [la-MAY] *n, adj* (fabric)
interwoven with gold or silver
thread.

la·ment [lə-MENT] *v* feel, express
sorrow (for). ▶ *n* passionate
expression of grief; song of grief.
lam'en·ta·ble [LAM-] *adj*
deplorable. **lam·en·ta'tion** *n*
lam·i·na [LAM-ə-nə] *n, pl* **-nas.** thin
plate, scale, flake. **lam'i·nate**
[-nayt] *v* **-nat·ed, -nat·ing.** make
(sheet of material) by bonding
together two or more thin sheets;
split, beat, form into thin sheets;
cover with thin sheet of material.
▶ *n* [-nit] laminated sheet.
lam·i·na'tion *n*
lamp *n* any of various; appliances
(esp. electrical) that produce light,
heat, radiation, etc.; formerly,
vessel holding oil burned by wick
for lighting. **lamp'black** *n* pigment
made from soot. **lamp'light** *n*
lamp'post *n* post supporting lamp
in street.
lam·poon' *n* satire ridiculing
person, literary work, etc. ▶ *vt*
satirize, ridicule. **lam·poon'ist** *n*
lam·prey [LAM-pree] *n, pl* **-preys.**
fish like an eel with a round sucking
mouth.
lance [lans] *n* horseman's spear. ▶ *vt*
lanced, lanc·ing. pierce with lance
or lancet. **lan'ce·o·late**
[-see-ə-layt] *adj* lance-shaped,
tapering. **lanc'er** *n* formerly,
cavalry soldier armed with lance.
lan'cet [-sit] *n* pointed two-edged
surgical knife.
land *n* solid part of Earth's surface;
ground, soil; country; property
consisting of land. ▶ *pl* estates. ▶ *vi*
come to land, disembark; bring an
aircraft from air to land or water;
alight, step down; arrive on
ground. ▶ *vt* bring to land; come or
bring to some point or condition;
inf obtain; catch. **land'ed** *adj*
possessing, consisting of lands.
land'ing *n* act of landing; platform
between flights of stairs. **land'fall** *n*
ship's approach to land at end of
voyage. **land'locked** *adj* enclosed
by land. **land'lord, -la·dy** *n* person
who lets land or houses, etc.;
owner of apartment house, etc.
land'lub·ber *n* person ignorant of

the sea and ships. **land'mark** *n* boundary mark, conspicuous object, as guide for direction, etc.; event, decision, etc. considered as important stage in development of something. **land'scape** *n* piece of inland scenery; picture of it; prospect. ▶ *v* **-scaped, -scap·ing.** create, arrange, garden, park, etc. **landscape gardener** *n* person who designs gardens or parks so that they look attractive. **land'slide** *n* falling of soil, rock, etc. down mountainside; overwhelming electoral victory.

lane [layn] *n* narrow road or street; specified route followed by shipping or aircraft; area of road for one stream of traffic.

lan·guage [LANG-gwij] *n* system of sounds, symbols, etc. for communicating thought; specialized vocabulary used by a particular group; style of speech or expression; system of words and symbols for computer programming.

lan·guish [LANG-gwish] *vi* be or become weak or faint; be in depressing or painful conditions; droop, pine. **lan'guid** *adj* lacking energy, interest; spiritless, dull. **lan'guor** [-gər] *n* want of energy or interest; faintness; tender mood; softness of atmosphere. **lan'guor·ous** *adj*

lank [langk] *adj* lean and tall; straight and limp. **lank'y** *adj* **lank·i·er, lank·i·est.**

lan·o·lin [LAN-l-in] *n* grease from wool used in ointments, etc.

lan·tern [LAN-tərn] *n* transparent case for lamp or candle; erection on dome or roof to let out smoke, admit light.

lan·tha·num [LAN-thə-nəm] *n* silvery-white ductile metallic element.

lan·yard [LAN-yərd] *n* short cord for securing knife or whistle; short nautical rope; cord for firing cannon.

lap¹ *n* the part between waist and knees of a person when sitting; *fig*

place where anything lies securely; single circuit of racetrack, track; stage or part of journey; single turn of wound thread, etc. ▶ *vt* **lapped, lap·ping.** enfold, wrap around; overtake opponent to be one or more circuits ahead. **lap dog** *n* small pet dog. **lap'top** *adj* (of a computer) small and light enough to be held on the user's lap. ▶ *n* such a computer

lap² *vt* **lapped, lap·ping.** drink by scooping up with tongue; (of waves, etc.) beat softly.

la·pel [lə-PEL] *n* part of front of a jacket or coat folded back toward shoulders.

lap·i·dar·y [LAP-i-der-ee] *adj* of stones; engraved on stone; exhibiting extreme refinement; concise and dignified. ▶ *n, pl* **-dar·ies.** cutter, engraver of stones.

lap·is laz·u·li [LAP-is LAZ-uu-lee] bright blue stone or pigment.

lapse [laps] *n* fall (in standard, condition, virtue, etc.); slip; mistake; passing (of time, etc.). ▶ *vi* **lapsed, laps·ing.** fall away; end, esp. through disuse.

lar·board [LAHR-bord] *n, adj* old term for port (side of ship).

lar·ce·ny [LAHR-sə-nee] *n, pl* **-nies.** theft.

lard [lahrd] *n* prepared pig fat. ▶ *vt* insert strips of bacon in (meat); intersperse, decorate (speech with strange words, etc.).

lar·der [LAHR-dər] *n* storeroom for food.

large [lahrj] *adj* **larg·er, larg·est.** broad in range or area; great in size, number, etc.; liberal; generous. ▶ *adv* in a big way. **large'ly** *adv* **lar·gess', lar·gesse'** *n* bounty; gift; donation.. **at large** free, not confined; in general; fully.

lar·go [LAHR-goh] *adv Mus* slow and dignified.

lar·i·at [LAR-ee-ət] *n* lasso.

lark¹ [lahrk] *n* small brown songbird, skylark.

lark² *n* frolic, spree. ▶ *vi* indulge in lark.

lar·va [LAHR-və] *n, pl* **-vae** [-vee]

insect in immature but active stage.
lar'val *adj*

lar·ynx [LAR-ingks] *n, pl* **-es.** part of throat containing vocal cords. **lar·yn·gi·tis** [-jī-tis] *n* inflammation of this.

la·sa·gne [lə-ZAHN-yə] *n* pasta formed in wide, flat sheets; baked dish of this with meat, cheese, tomato sauce, etc.

las·civ'i·ous [lə-SIV-ee-əs] *adj* lustful.

la·ser [LAY-zər] *n* device for concentrating electromagnetic radiation or light of mixed frequencies into an intense, narrow, concentrated beam.

lash[1] *n* stroke with whip; flexible part of whip; eyelash. ▶ *vt* strike with whip, thong, etc.; dash against (as waves); attack verbally, ridicule; flick, wave sharply to and fro. ▶ *vi* (with *out*) hit, kick.

lash[2] *vt* fasten or bind tightly with cord, etc.

las·si·tude [LAS-i-tood] *n* weariness.

las·so [LAS-oh] *n, pl* **-sos** *or* **-soes.** rope with noose for catching cattle, etc. ▶ *vt* **-soed, -so·ing.**

last[1] *adj, adv* after all others, coming at the end; most recent(ly). ▶ *adj* only remaining; sup. of LATE. ▶ *n* last person or thing. **last'ly** *adv* finally.

last[2] *vi* continue, hold out, remain alive or unexhausted, endure.

last[3] *n* model of foot on which shoes are made, repaired.

latch [lach] *n* fastening for door, consisting of bar, catch for it, and lever to lift it; small lock with spring action. ▶ *vt* fasten with latch. **latch'key** [-kee] *n*

late [layt] *adj* **lat·er** *or* **lat·ter, lat·est** *or* **last.** coming after the appointed time; delayed; that was recently but now is not; recently dead; recent in date; of late stage of development. ▶ *adv* **lat·er, lat·est.** after proper time; recently; at, till late hour. **late'ly** *adv* not long since.

la·tent [LAYT-nt] *adj* existing but not developed; hidden.

lat·er·al [LAT-ər-əl] *adj* of, at, from the side. **lat'er·al·ly** *adv*

la·tex [LAY-teks] *n* sap or fluid of plants, esp. of rubber tree.

lath *n, pl* **laths** [la*th*z] thin strip of wood, or wire mesh. **lath'ing** *n*

lathe [lay*th*] *n* machine for turning object while it is being shaped.

lath·er [LA*TH*-ər] *n* froth of soap and water; frothy sweat. ▶ *v* make frothy; *inf* beat.

Lat·in [LAT-n] *n* language of ancient Romans. ▶ *adj* of ancient Romans, of, in their language; denoting people speaking a language descended from Latin esp. Spanish. **La·ti·no** [lə-TEE-noh] *n, pl* **-nos.** person of Central or S Amer. descent.

lat·i·tude [LAT-i-tood] *n* angular distance on meridian reckoned N or S from equator; deviation from a standard; freedom from restriction; scope. ▶ *pl* regions.

la·trine [lə-TREEN] *n* in army, etc., toilet.

lat·ter [LAT-ər] *adj* second of two; later; more recent. **lat'ter·ly** *adv*

lat·tice [LAT-is] *n* structure of strips of wood, metal, etc. crossing with spaces between; window, gate, so made. **lat'ticed** *adj*

laud [lawd] *n* hymn, song, of praise. ▶ *vt* **laud'a·ble** *adj* praiseworthy. **laud'a·bly** *adv* **laud'a·to·ry** [-tor-ee] *adj* expressing, containing, praise.

lau·da·num [LAWD-n-əm] *n* tincture of opium.

laugh [laf] *vi* make sounds instinctively expressing amusement, merriment, or scorn. ▶ *n* **laugh'a·ble** *adj* ludicrous. **laugh'a·bly** *adv* **laugh'ter** *n* **laughing gas** nitrous oxide as anesthetic. **laughing stock** object of general derision.

launch[1] [lawnch] *vt* set afloat; set in motion; start; propel (missile, spacecraft) into space; hurl, send. ▶ *vi* enter on course. **launch'er** *n* installation, vehicle, device for launching rockets, missiles, etc.

launch[2] *n* large engine-driven boat.

laun·dry [LAWN-dree] *n, pl* **-dries.**

place for washing clothes, esp. as a business; clothes, etc. for washing.

laun'der vt wash and iron.

laun·der·ette' n self-service laundry with coin-operated washing, drying machines.

lau·re·ate [LOR-ee-ət] adj crowned with laurels. ▶ n person honored for achievements. **poet laureate** poet honored as most eminent of country or region.

lau·rel [LOR-əl] n glossy-leaved shrub, bay tree. ▶ pl its leaves, emblem of victory or merit.

la·va [LAH-və] n molten matter thrown out by volcanoes, solidifying as it cools.

lav·a·to·ry [LAV-ə-tor-ee] n -ries. washroom; toilet.

lave [layv] vt **laved, lav·ing.** wash, bathe.

lav·en·der [LAV-ən-dər] n shrub with fragrant flowers; color of the flowers, pale lilac.

lav'ish adj giving or spending profusely; very; too abundant. ▶ vt spend, bestow, profusely.

law n rule binding on community; system of such rules; legal science; knowledge, administration of it; inf (member of) police force; general principle deduced from facts; invariable sequence of events in nature. **law'ful** [-fəl] adj allowed by law. **law'ful·ly** adv **law'less** [-lis] adj ignoring laws; violent. **law'yer** n professional expert in law. **law'·a·bid·ing** [-bid-ing] adj obedient to laws; well-behaved. **law'giv·er** n one who makes laws. **law'suit** [-soot] n prosecution of claim in court.

lawn¹ n stretch of carefully tended turf in garden, etc. **lawn tennis** tennis played on grass court.

lawn² n fine linen.

lawyer see LAW.

lax [laks] adj not strict; lacking precision; loose, slack. **lax'a·tive** adj having loosening effect on bowels. ▶ n **lax'i·ty, lax'ness** n slackness; looseness of (moral) standards.

lay¹ pt. of LIE¹.

lay² vt **laid, lay·ing.** deposit, set, cause to lie. **lay'er** n single thickness of some substance, as stratum or coating on surface; laying hen; shoot of plant pegged down or partly covered with soil or plastic to encourage root growth. ▶ vt propagate plants by making layers. **lay'down** n in bridge, unbeatable hand held by declarer who plays with all cards exposed to view. **lay'out** n arrangement, esp. of matter for printing. **lay off** dismiss employees during slack period. **lay'off** n **lay on** provide, supply; apply; strike. **lay on hands** of healer, place hands on person to be cured. **lay out** display; expend; prepare for burial; plan copy for printing, etc.; sl knock out; sl criticize severely. **lay waste** devastate.

lay³ n minstrel's song.

lay⁴ adj not clerical or professional; of, or done, by persons not clergymen. **lay'man, lay'per·son** n ordinary person.

lay·ette [lay-ET] n clothes, etc. for newborn child.

laz·ar [LAZ-ər] n leper.

la·zy [LAY-zee] adj **-zi·er, -zi·est.** averse to work, indolent. **laze** vi **lazed, laz·ing.** indulge in laziness. **la'zi·ly** adv **la'zi·ness** n

lead¹ [leed] v **led, lead·ing.** ▶ vt guide, conduct; persuade; direct; conduct people. ▶ vi be, go, play first; result; give access to. ▶ n leading; that which leads or is used to lead; example; front or principal place, role, etc.; cable bringing current to electric instrument. **lead'er** n one who leads; most important or prominent article in newspaper (also **leading article**). **lead'er·ship** n **leading question** question worded to prompt answer desired. **lead time** time between design of product and its production.

lead² [led] n soft heavy gray metal; plummet, used for sounding depths of water; graphite. ▶ vt **-ed, -ing.** cover, weight or space with

lead. lead'en *adj* of, like lead; heavy; dull. **go over like a lead balloon** *sl* fail to arouse interest or support.

leaf [leef] *n, pl* **leaves**. organ of photosynthesis in plants, consisting of a flat, usu. green blade on stem; two pages of book, etc.; thin sheet; flap, movable part of table, etc. ▶ *vt* turn through (pages, etc.) cursorily. **leaf'less** [-lis] *adj* **leaf'let** [-lit] *n* small leaf; single sheet, often folded, of printed matter for distribution as e.g. notice or advertisement. **leaf'y** *adj* **leaf·i·er, leaf·i·est**.

league¹ [leeg] *n* agreement for mutual help; parties to it; federation of teams, etc.; *inf* class, level. ▶ *vi* **leagued, lea·guing**. unite in a league; combine in an association. **lea'guer** *n* member of league.

league² *n obs* measure of distance, about three miles.

leak [leek] *n* hole, defect, that allows escape or entrance of liquid, gas, radiation, etc.; disclosure. ▶ *vi* let fluid, etc. in or out; (of fluid, etc.) find its way through leak. ▶ *vt* let escape. ▶ *v* (allow to) become known little by little. **leak'age** [-ij] *n* leaking; gradual escape or loss. **leak'y** *adj* **leak·i·er, leak·i·est**.

lean¹ [leen] *adj* **-er, -est**. lacking fat; thin; meager; (of mixture of fuel and air) with too little fuel. ▶ *n* lean part of meat, mainly muscular tissue.

lean² *v* **leaned, lean·ing**. rest against; bend, incline; tend (toward); depend, rely (on). **leaning** *n* tendency. **lean-to** *n, pl* **-tos**. shed built against tree or post.

leap [leep] *v* **leaped** or **leapt, leap·ing**. spring, jump; spring over. ▶ *n* jump. **leap'frog** *n* game in which player vaults over another bending down. **leap year** year with February 29th as extra day, occurring every fourth year.

learn [lurn] *v* **learned** or **learnt, learn·ing**. gain skill, knowledge by study, practice or teaching; gain knowledge; be taught; find out. **learn'ed** [LUR-nid] *adj* erudite, deeply read; showing much learning. **learn'er** *n* **learn'ing** *n* knowledge acquired by study.

lease [lees] *n* contract by which land or property is rented for stated time by owner to tenant. ▶ *vt* **leased, leas·ing**. let, rent by, take on lease.

leash [leesh] *n* thong for holding a dog; curb. ▶ *vt* hold on leash; restrain.

least [leest] *adj* smallest; sup. of LITTLE. ▶ *n* smallest one. ▶ *adv* in smallest degree.

leath·er [LE*TH*-ər] *n* prepared skin of animal. **leath'er·y** *adj* like leather, tough.

leave¹ [leev] *v* **left, leav·ing**. go away from; deposit; allow to remain; depart from; entrust; bequeath; go away, set out.

leave² *n* permission; permission to be absent from work, duty; period of such absence; formal parting.

leav·en [LEV-ən] *n* yeast; *fig* transforming influence. ▶ *vt* raise with leaven; influence; modify.

lech·er [LECH-ər] *n* man given to lewdness. **lech'er·ous** *adj* lewd; provoking lust; lascivious. **lech'er·ous·ly** *adv* **lech'er·ous·ness** *n* **lech'er·y** *n, pl* **-er·ies**.

lec·tern [LEK-tərn] *n* reading desk, esp. in church; stand with slanted top to hold book, notes, etc.

lec·ture [LEK-chər] *n* instructive discourse; speech of reproof. ▶ *v* **-tured, -tur·ing**. ▶ *vi* deliver discourse. ▶ *vt* reprove. **lec'tur·er** *n*

ledge [lej] *n* narrow shelf sticking out from wall, cliff, etc.; ridge, rock below surface of sea.

ledg·er [LEJ-ər] *n* book of debit and credit accounts, chief account book of firm; flat stone. **ledger line** *Mus* short line, above or below stave.

lee *n* shelter; side of anything, esp. ship, away from wind. **lee'ward** [-wərd] *adj, n* (on) lee side. ▶ *adv* toward this side. **lee'way** *n* leeward drift of ship; room for free movement within limits.

leech *n* species of bloodsucking worm.

leek *n* plant like onion with long bulb and thick stem.

leer *vi* glance with malign, sly, or lascivious expression. ▶ *n* such glance.

lees [leez] *pl n* sediment of wine, etc.; dregs.

left¹ *adj* denotes the side that faces west when the front faces north; opposite to the right. ▶ *n* the left hand or part; *Politics* reforming or radical party (also **left wing**) ▶ *adv* on or toward the left. **left'ist** *n, adj* (person) of the political left.

left² pt./pp. of LEAVE.

leg *n* one of limbs on which person or animal walks, runs, stands; part of garment covering leg; anything that supports, as leg of table; stage of journey. **leg'gings** *pl n* covering of leather or other material for legs. **leg'gy** *adj* **-gi·er, -gi·est.** long-legged; (of plants) straggling. **leg'warm·er** *n* one of pair of long knitted footless socks worn over tights when exercising.

leg·a·cy [LEG-ə-see] *n, pl* **-cies.** anything left by will, bequest; thing handed down to successor.

le·gal [LEE-gəl] *adj* of, appointed or permitted by, or based on, law. **le·gal'i·ty** *n* **le·gal·ize** *vt* **-ized, -iz·ing.** make legal.

leg·ate [LEG-it] *n* ambassador, esp. papal. **le·ga'tion** *n* diplomatic minister and staff; headquarters for these.

leg·a·tee [leg-ə-TEE] *n* recipient of legacy.

le·ga·to [lə-GAH-toh] *adv Mus* smoothly.

leg·end [LEJ-ənd] *n* traditional story or myth; traditional literature; famous, renowned, person or event; inscription. **leg'end·ar·y** *adj*

leg·er·de·main [lej-ər-də-MAYN] *n* juggling, conjuring, sleight of hand, trickery.

leg·i·ble [LEJ-ə-bəl] *adj* easily read. **leg·i·bil'i·ty** *n*

le·gion [LEE-jən] *n* body of infantry in Roman army; various modern military bodies; association of veterans; large number. **le'gion·ar·y** *adj, n* **le·gion·naires' disease** [-NAIRZ] serious bacterial disease similar to pneumonia.

leg·is·la·tor [LEJ-is-lay-tər] *n* maker of laws. **leg'is·late** *vi* **-lat·ed, -lat·ing.** make laws. **leg·is·la'tion** *n* act of legislating; law or laws that are made. **leg'is·la·tive** *adj* **leg'is·la·ture** [-chər] *n* body that makes laws of a country or state.

le·git·i·mate [lə-JIT-ə-mit] *adj* born in wedlock; lawful, regular; fairly deduced. **le·git'i·ma·cy** [-mə-see] *n* **le·git'i·mize** *vt* **-mized, -miz·ing.** make legitimate.

le·gu·mi·nous [li-GYOO-mə-nəs] *adj* (of plants) pod-bearing. **leg·ume** [LEG-yoom] *n* leguminous plant.

lei [lay] *n* garland of flowers.

lei·sure [LEE-zhər] *n* freedom from occupation; spare time. **lei'sure·ly** *adj* deliberate, unhurried. ▶ *adv* slowly. **lei'sured** *adj* with plenty of spare time.

leit·mo·tif [LIT-moh-teef] *n Mus* recurring theme associated with some person, situation, thought.

lem·ming [LEM-ing] *n* rodent of northern regions.

lem·on [LEM-ən] *n* pale yellow acid fruit; tree bearing it; its color; *inf* useless or defective person or thing. **lem·on·ade'** [-AYD] *n* drink made from lemon juice.

le·mur [LEE-mər] *n* nocturnal animal like monkey.

lend *vt* **lent, lend·ing.** give temporary use of; let out for hire or interest; give, bestow. **lends itself to** is suitable for.

length [lengkth] *n* quality of being long; measurement from end to end; duration; extent; piece of a certain length. **length'en** *v* make, become, longer; draw out. **length'i·ly** *adv* **length'wise** *adj, adv* **length'y** *adj* **length·i·er, length·i·est.** (over)long. **at length** in full detail; at last.

le·ni·ent [LEE-nee-ənt] *adj* mild,

tolerant, not strict. **le′ni·en·cy** n

len·i·ty [LEN-i-tee] n, pl **-ties.** mercy; clemency.

lens [lenz] n, pl **-es.** piece of glass or similar material with one or both sides curved, used to converge or diverge light rays in cameras, eyeglasses, telescopes, etc.

lent pt./pp. of LEND.

Lent n period of fasting from Ash Wednesday to Easter. **Lent′en** adj of, in, or suitable to Lent.

len′til n edible seed of leguminous plant. **len·tic′u·lar** adj like lentil.

len·to [LEN-toh] adv Mus slowly.

le·o·nine [LEE-ə-nīn] adj like a lion.

leop·ard [LEP-ərd] n large, spotted, carnivorous animal of cat family, like panther.

le·o·tard [LEE-ə-tahrd] n tight-fitting garment covering most of body, worn by acrobats, dancers, etc.

lep·er [LEP-ər] n one suffering from leprosy; person ignored or despised. **lep′ro·sy** [-rə-see] n disease attacking nerves and skin resulting in loss of feeling in affected parts. **lep′rous** [-rəs] adj

lep·re·chaun [LEP-rə-kawn] n mischievous elf of Irish folklore.

les·bi·an [LEZ-bee-ən] n a homosexual woman. **les′bi·an·ism** n

lese maj·es·ty [LEEZ] n treason; taking of liberties.

le·sion [LEE-zhən] n injury, injurious change in texture or action of an organ of the body.

less adj comp. of LITTLE; not so much. ▶ n smaller part, quantity; a lesser amount. ▶ adv to a smaller extent or degree. ▶ prep after deducting, minus. **less′en** vt diminish; reduce. **less′er** adj less; smaller; minor.

les·see [le-SEE] n one to whom lease is granted.

les·son [LES-ən] n installment of course of instruction; content of this; experience that teaches; portion of Scripture read in church.

les·sor [LES-or] n grantor of a lease.

lest conj in order that not; for fear

that.

let¹ v let, let·ting. ▶ vt allow, enable, cause; allow to escape; grant use of for rent, lease. ▶ vi be leased. ▶ v aux used to express a proposal, command, threat, assumption.

let² n in law, obstacle or hindrance; in tennis, etc., minor infringement, esp. obstruction of ball by net on service, requiring replaying of point.

le·thal [LEE-thəl] adj deadly.

leth·ar·gy [LETH-ər-jee] n, pl **-gies.** apathy, want of energy or interest; unnatural drowsiness. **le·thar′gic** adj **le·thar′gi·cal·ly** adv

let·ter [LET-ər] n alphabetical symbol; written message; strict meaning, interpretation. ▶ vt literature, knowledge of books. ▶ vt mark with, in, letters. **let′tered** adj learned. **let′ter·press** n process of printing from raised type; matter printed in this way.

let·tuce [LET-is] n plant grown for use in salad.

leu·co·cyte [LOO-kə-sīt] n one of white blood corpuscles.

leu·ke·mi·a [loo-KEE-mee-ə] n a progressive blood disease.

Lev. Leviticus.

lev′ee¹ n Hist reception held by sovereign on rising; reception in someone's honor.

levee² n river embankment, natural or artificial.

lev·el [LEV-əl] adj horizontal; even in surface; consistent in style, quality, etc. ▶ n horizontal line or surface; instrument for showing, testing horizontal plane; position on scale; standard, grade; horizontal passage in mine. ▶ v **-eled, -el·ing.** make level; bring to same level; knock down; aim (gun, or, fig accusation, etc.); inf (esp. with with) be honest, frank. **le′vel·head′ed** [-HED-id] adj not apt to be carried away by emotion.

lev·er [LEV-ər] n rigid bar pivoted about a fulcrum to transfer a force with mechanical advantage; handle pressed, pulled, etc.; to operate something. ▶ vt pry, move with

lever. **lev′er·age** [-ij] *n* action, power of lever; influence; power to accomplish something; advantage.

le·vi·a·than [lə-VĪ-ə-thən] *n* sea monster; anything huge or formidable.

lev·i·ta·tion [lev-i-TAY-shən] *n* the power of raising a solid body into the air supernaturally. **lev′i·tate** *v* **-tat·ed, -tat·ing.** (cause to) do this.

lev·i·ty [LEV-i-tee] *n, pl* **-ties.** inclination to make a joke of serious matters, frivolity; facetiousness.

lev·y [LEV-ee] *vt* **lev·ied, lev·y·ing.** impose (tax); raise (troops). ▶ *n, pl* **lev·ies.** imposition or collection of taxes; enrolling of troops; amount, number levied.

lewd [lood] *adj* **-er, -est.** lustful; indecent. **lewd′ly** *adv* **lewd′ness** *n*

lex·i·con [LEK-si-kon] *n* dictionary. **lex·i·cog′ra·pher** [-rə-fər] *n* writer of dictionaries. **lex·i·cog′ra·phy** *n*

Li *Chem* lithium.

li·a·ble [LĪ-ə-bəl] *adj* answerable; exposed (to); subject (to); likely (to). **li·a·bil′i·ty** *n* state of being liable, obligation; hindrance, disadvantage; (*pl* **-ties**) debts.

li·ai·son [lee-AY-zon] *n* union; connection; intimacy, esp. secret; person who keeps others in touch with one another.

li·ar [LĪ-ər] *n* one who tells lies.

li·ba·tion [lī-BAY-shən] *n* drink poured as offering to the gods; *facetious* drink of whiskey.

li·bel [LĪ-bəl] *n* published statement falsely damaging person's reputation. ▶ *vt* **-beled, -bel·ing.** defame falsely. **li′bel·ous** *adj* defamatory.

lib·er·al [LIB-ər-əl] *adj* of political party favoring democratic reforms or favoring individual freedom; generous; tolerant; abundant; (of education) designed to develop general cultural interests. ▶ *n* one who has liberal ideas or opinions. **lib′er·al·ism** *n* **lib·er·al′i·ty** *n, pl* **-ties.** munificence. **lib′er·al·ize** *vt* **-ized, -iz·ing.**

lib·er·ate [LIB-ə-rayt] *vt* **-at·ed, -at·ing.** set free. **lib·er·a′tion** *n*

lib·er·tar·i·an [lib-ər-TAIR-ee-ən] *n* believer in freedom of thought, etc., or in free will. ▶ *adj*

lib·er·tine [LIB-ər-teen] *n* morally dissolute person. ▶ *adj* dissolute.

lib·er·ty [LIB-ər-tee] *n* freedom; (*pl* **-ties**) rights, privileges. **at liberty** free; having the right; out of work. **take liberties (with)** be presumptuous.

li·bi·do [li-BEE-doh] *n, pl* **-dos.** life force; emotional craving, esp. of sexual origin. **li·bid′i·nous** *adj* lustful.

li·brar·y [LĪ-brer-ee] *n, pl* **-brar·ies.** room, building where books are kept; collection of books, phonograph records, etc.; reading, writing room in house. **li·brar′i·an** *n* keeper of library.

li·bret·to [li-BRET-oh] *n, pl* **-tos** or **-ti** [-tee] words of an opera. **li·bret′tist** *n*

lice *n* see LOUSE.

li·cense [LĪ-səns] *n* (document, certificate, giving) leave, permission; excessive liberty; dissoluteness; writer's, artist's intentional transgression of rules of art (also **poetic license**). **li′cense** *vt* **-censed, -cens·ing.** grant license to. **li·cen·see′** *n* holder of license.

li·cen·tious [lī-SEN-shəs] *adj* dissolute; sexually immoral.

li·chen [LĪ-kən] *n* small flowerless plants forming crust on rocks, trees, etc.

lick [lik] *vt* pass the tongue over; touch lightly; *inf* defeat; *inf* flog, beat. ▶ *n* act of licking; small amount (esp. of work, etc.); block or natural deposit of salt or other chemical licked by cattle, etc. **lick′ing** *n* beating; defeat.

lic·o·rice [LIK-ər-ish] *n* black substance used in medicine and as a candy; plant, its root from which it is obtained.

lid *n* movable cover; cover of the eye; *sl* hat.

lie¹ [lī] *vi* **lay, lain, ly·ing.** be horizontal, at rest; be situated; remain, be in certain state or position; exist, be found; recline.

▶ *n* manner, direction, position in which thing lies; of a golf ball, its position relative to difficulty of hitting it.

lie² *vi* **lied, ly·ing.** make false statement knowingly. ▶ *n* deliberate falsehood. **li'ar** [-ər] *n* **white lie** untruth said without evil intent. **give the lie to** disprove.

lien [leen] *n* right to hold another's property until claim is met.

lieu [loo] *n* place. **in lieu of** instead of.

lieu·ten·ant [loo-TEN-ənt] *n* deputy; *Army, Marines* rank below captain; *Navy* rank below lieutenant commander; police, fire department officer.

life [līf] *n, pl* **lives.** active principle of existence of animals and plants, animate existence; time of its lasting; history of such existence; way of living; vigor, vivacity. **life'less** [-lis] *adj* dead; inert; dull. **life'long** *adj* lasting a lifetime. **life belt, life jacket** buoyant device to keep afloat person in danger of drowning. **life style** particular attitudes, habits, etc. of person or group. **life-support** *adj* of equipment or treatment necessary to keep a person alive. **life'time** *n* length of time person, animal, or object lives or functions.

lift *vt* raise in position, status, mood, volume, etc.; take up and remove; exalt spiritually; *inf* steal. ▶ *vi* rise. ▶ *n* raising apparatus; ride in car, etc., as passenger; force of air acting at right angles on aircraft wing, so lifting it; *inf* feeling of cheerfulness, uplift.

lig·a·ment [LIG-ə-mənt] *n* band of tissue joining bones. **lig'a·ture** [-chər] *n* anything that binds; thread for tying up blood vessels or for removing tumors.

light¹ [līt] *adj* **-er, -est.** of, or bearing, little weight; not severe; gentle; easy, requiring little effort; trivial; (of industry) producing small, usu. consumer goods, using light machinery. ▶ *adv* in light manner. ▶ *v* **light·ed** or **lit,**

light·ing. ▶ *vi* alight (from vehicle, etc.); come by chance (upon). **light'en** *vt* reduce, remove (load, etc.). **lights** *pl n* lungs of animals as food. **light'head·ed** *adj* dizzy, inclined to faint; delirious. **light'heart·ed** *adj* carefree. **light'weight** *n, adj* (person) of little weight or importance; boxer weighing between 126 and 135 pounds (56.7 to 61 kg).

light² *n* electromagnetic radiation by which things are visible; source of this, lamp; window; light part of anything; means or act of setting fire to; understanding. ▶ *pl* traffic lights. ▶ *adj* **-er, -est.** bright; pale, not dark. ▶ *v* **light·ed** or **lit, light·ing.** set burning; give light to; take fire; brighten. **light'en** *vt* make light. **light'ing** *n* apparatus for supplying artificial light. **light'ning** *n* visible discharge of electricity in atmosphere. **light'house** *n* tower with a light to guide ships. **light-year** *n Astronomy* distance light travels in one year, about six trillion miles.

light·er [LĪ-tər] *n* device for lighting cigarettes, etc.; flat-bottomed boat for unloading ships.

like¹ [līk] *adj* resembling; similar; characteristic of. ▶ *adv* in the manner of. ▶ *pron* similar thing. **like'li·hood** [-huud] *n* probability. **like'ly** *adj* **-li·er, -li·est.** probable; hopeful, promising. ▶ *adv* probably. **lik'en** *vt* compare. **like'ness** *n* resemblance; portrait. **like'wise** *adv* in like manner.

like² *vt* **liked, lik·ing.** find agreeable, enjoy, love. **lik'a·ble** *adj* **liking** *n* fondness; inclination, taste.

li·lac [LĪ-lək] *n* shrub bearing purple or white flowers; pale reddish purple. ▶ *adj* of this color.

Lil·li·pu·tian [lil-i-PYOO-shən] *adj* diminutive. ▶ *n* very small person.

lilt *v* sing merrily; move lightly. ▶ *n* rhythmical effect in music, swing. **lilt'ing** *adj*

lil·y [LIL-ee] *n, pl* **lil·ies.** bulbous flowering plant. **lil·y-white** *adj* white; pure, above reproach; of an organization or community, forbidding admission to blacks.

limb¹ [lim] *n* arm or leg; wing; branch of tree.

limb² *n* edge of sun or moon; edge of sextant.

lim·ber¹ [LIM-bər] *n* detachable front of gun carriage.

lim·ber² *adj* pliant, lithe. **limber up** loosen stiff muscles by exercises.

lim·bo¹ [LIM-boh] *n, pl* **-bos.** supposed region intermediate between heaven and hell for the unbaptized; intermediate, indeterminate place or state.

lim·bo² *n, pl* **-bos.** West Indian dance in which dancers pass under a bar.

lime¹ [līm] *n* any of certain calcium compounds used in making fertilizer, cement. ▶ *vt* **limed, lim·ing.** treat (land) with lime. **lime'light** *n* formerly, intense white light obtained by heating lime; glare of publicity. **lime'stone** *n* sedimentary rock used in building.

lime² *n* small acid fruit like lemon.

lim·er·ick [LIM-ər-ik] *n* self-contained, nonsensical, humorous verse of five lines.

lim'it *n* utmost extent or duration; boundary. ▶ *vt* restrict, restrain, bound. **lim·i·ta'tion** *n* **lim'it·less** *adj*

lim·ou·sine [LIM-ə-zeen] *n* large, luxurious car.

limp¹ *adj* **-er, -est.** without firmness or stiffness. **limp'ly** *adv*

limp² *vi* walk lamely. ▶ *n* limping gait.

lim'pid *adj* clear; translucent. **lim·pid'i·ty** *n*

linch'pin *n* pin to hold wheel on its axle; essential person or thing.

line [līn] *n* long narrow mark; stroke made with pen, etc.; continuous length without breadth; row; series, course; telephone connection; progeny; province of activity; shipping company; railroad track; any class of goods; cord; string; wire; advice, guidance. ▶ *vt* **lined, lin·ing.** cover inside; mark with lines; bring into

line; be, form border, edge.

lin'e·age [-ee-ij] *n* descent from, descendants of an ancestor.

lin'e·al *adj* of lines; in direct line of descent. **lin'e·a·ment** *n* feature of face. **lin'e·ar** *adj* of, in lines. **lin·er** [LĪN-ər] *n* large ship or aircraft of passenger line. **line dancing** form of social dancing performed by rows of people to popular music. **lines'man** [-mən] *n Sports* official who helps referee, umpire. **get a line on** obtain all relevant information about.

lin·en [LIN-ən] *adj* made of flax. ▶ *n* cloth made of flax; linen articles collectively; sheets, tablecloths, etc., or shirts (orig. made of linen).

lin·ger [LING-gər] *vi* delay, loiter; remain long.

lin·ge·rie [LAHN-zhə-ree] *n* women's underwear or nightwear.

lin·go [LING-goh] *n inf* language; speech esp. applied to jargon and slang.

lin·gua fran·ca [LING-gwə FRANG-kə] *n, pl* **-fran·cas.** language used for communication between people of different mother tongues.

lin·gual [LING-gwəl] *adj* of the tongue or language. ▶ *n* sound made by the tongue, as *d, l, t*. **lin'guist** *n* one skilled in languages or language study. **lin·guis'tic** *adj* of languages or their study. **lin·guis'tics** *n* study, science of language.

lin·i·ment [LIN-ə-mənt] *n* lotion for rubbing on limbs, etc. for relieving pain.

lin·ing [LĪ-ning] *n* covering for the inside of garment, etc.

link [lingk] *n* ring of a chain; connection; measure, one hundredth part of surveyor's chain. ▶ *vt* join with, as with, link; intertwine. ▶ *vi* be so joined. **link'age** [-ij] *n*

links [lingks] *pl n* golf course, esp. one by the sea.

li·no·le·um [li-NOH-lee-əm] *n* floor covering of burlap or canvas with smooth, hard, decorative coating of powdered cork, etc.

lin'seed n seed of flax plant.

lint n tiny shreds of yarn; bits of thread; soft material for dressing wounds.

lin·tel [LIN-tl] n top piece of door or window.

li·on [LĪ-ən] n large animal of cat family. **li'on·ess** n, fem **li'on·ize** vt **-ized, -iz·ing.** treat as celebrity. **li'on·heart·ed** adj exceptionally brave.

lip n upper or lower edge of the mouth; edge or margin; sl impudence. **lip gloss** cosmetic to give lips sheen. **lip'read·ing** n method of understanding spoken words by interpreting movements of speaker's lips. **lip service** insincere tribute or respect. **lip'stick** n cosmetic preparation, usu. in stick form, for coloring lips. **lip·o·suc·tion** [LIP-oh-suk-shən, LĪP-oh-] n cosmetic operation removing fat from the body by suction.

li·queur [li-KUR] n alcoholic liquor flavored and sweetened.

liq·uid [LIK-wid] adj fluid, not solid or gaseous; flowing smoothly; (of assets) in form of money or easily converted into money. ▶ n substance in liquid form. **liq'ue·fy** [-wə-fī] v **-fied, -fy·ing.** make or become liquid. **li·quid'i·ty** n state of being able to meet financial obligations. **liquid air, liquefied gas** air, gas reduced to liquid state on application of increased pressure at low temperature.

liq·ui·date [LIK-wi-dayt] vt **-dat·ed, -dat·ing.** pay (debt); arrange affairs of, and dissolve (company); wipe out, kill. **liq·ui·da'tion** n process of clearing up financial affairs; state of being bankrupt. **liq'ui·da·tor** n official appointed to liquidate business.

liq·uor [LIK-ər] n liquid, esp. an alcoholic one.

li·ra [LEER-ə] n, pl **-ras.** monetary unit of Turkey and (formerly) Italy.

lisle [līl] n fine hard-twisted cotton thread.

lisp v speech defect in which s and z are pronounced th; speak falteringly. ▶ n

lis·some [LIS-əm] adj supple, agile.

list[1] n inventory, register; catalog; edge of cloth, selvage. ▶ pl field for combat. ▶ vt place on list.

list[2] vi (of ship) lean to one side. ▶ n inclination of ship.

lis·ten [LIS-ən] vi try to hear, attend to. **lis'ten·er** n

list·less [LIST-lis] adj indifferent, languid.

lit pt./pp. of LIGHT.

lit·a·ny [LIT-n-ee] n, pl **-nies.** prayer with responses from congregation; tedious account.

li·ter [LEE-tər] n measure of volume of fluid, one cubic decimeter, about 1.05 quarts.

lit·er·al [LIT-ər-əl] adj according to sense of actual words, not figurative; exact in wording; of letters.

lit·er·ate [LIT-ər-it] adj able to read and write; educated. ▶ n literate person. **lit'er·a·cy** n **lit·e·ra'ti** [-RAH-tee] pl n scholarly, literary people.

lit·er·a·ture [LIT-ər-ə-chər] n books and writings of a country, period or subject. **lit'er·ar·y** adj of or learned in literature.

lithe [līth] adj **lith·er, lith·est.** supple, pliant. **lithe'some** [-səm] adj lissome, supple.

lith·i·um [LITH-ee-əm] n one of the lightest alkaline metallic elements; this substance used in treatment of depression, etc.

li·thog·ra·phy [li-THOG-rə-fee] n method of printing from metal or stone block using the antipathy of grease and water. **lith'o·graph** n print so produced. ▶ vt print thus. **li·thog'ra·pher** n

lit·i·gant [LIT-i-gənt] n, adj (person) conducting a lawsuit. **lit·i·ga'tion** n lawsuit.

lit·i·gate [LIT-i-gayt] v **-gat·ed, -gat·ing.** ▶ vt contest in law. ▶ vi carry on a lawsuit. **li·ti'gious** [-jəs] adj given to engaging in lawsuits; disputatious. **li·ti'gious·ness** n

lit·mus [LIT-məs] *n* blue dye turned red by acids and restored to blue by alkali. **litmus paper** paper impregnated with litmus. **litmus test** use of litmus paper to test acidity or alkalinity of a solution; any crucial test based on only one factor.

lit·ter [LIT-ər] *n* untidy refuse; odds and ends; young of animal produced at one birth; straw, etc. as bedding for animals; portable couch; kind of stretcher for wounded. ▶ *vt* strew with litter; bring forth.

lit·tle [LIT-l] *adj* small, not much. ▶ *n* small quantity. ▶ *adv* slightly.

lit·to·ral [LIT-ər-əl] *adj* pert. to the shore of sea, lake, ocean. ▶ *n* littoral region.

lit·ur·gy [LIT-ər-jee] *n, pl* **-gies.** prescribed form of public worship. **li·tur′gi·cal** *adj*

live¹ [liv] *v* **lived, liv·ing.** have life; pass one's life; continue in life; continue, last; dwell; feed. **liv′a·ble** *adj* suitable for living in; tolerable. **living** *n* action of being in life; people now alive; way of life; means of living; church benefice.

live² [līv] *adj* **liv·er, liv·est.** living, alive, active, vital; flaming; (of transmission line, etc.) carrying electric current; (of broadcast) transmitted during the actual performance. **live′ly** *adj* **-li·er, -li·est.** brisk, active, vivid. **live′li·ness** *n* **liv′en** *vt* (esp. with *up*) make (more) lively. **live′stock** *n* domestic animals. **live wire** wire carrying electric current; able, very energetic person.

live·li·hood [LĪV-lee-huud] *n* means of living; subsistence; support.

live·long [LIV-lawng] *adj* of a period of time, lasting throughout, esp. as though forever.

liv·er [LIV-ər] *n* organ secreting bile; animal liver as food. **liv′er·ish** *adj* unwell, as from liver upset; cross, touchy, irritable.

liv·er·y [LIV-ə-ree] *n, pl* **-er·ies.** distinctive dress of person or group, esp. servant(s); care, feeding of horses; a livery stable. **livery stable** where horses are kept at a charge or hired out.

liv′id *adj* of a bluish pale color; discolored, as by bruising; of reddish color; *inf* angry, furious.

liz·ard [LIZ-ərd] *n* four-footed reptile.

Lk. Luke.

lla·ma [LAH-mə] *n* woolly-haired animal used as beast of burden in S Amer.

load [lohd] *n* burden; amount usu. carried at once; actual load carried by vehicle; resistance against which engine has to work; amount of electrical energy drawn from a source. ▶ *vt* put load on or into; charge (gun); weigh down. **load′ed** *adj* carrying a load; (of dice) dishonestly weighted; biased; (of question) containing hidden trap or implication; *sl* wealthy; *sl* drunk.

loadstar, -stone *n* see LODE.

loaf¹ [lohf] *n, pl* **loaves.** mass of bread as baked; shaped mass of food.

loaf² *vi* idle, loiter. **loaf′er** *n* idler.

loam [lohm] *n* fertile soil.

loan [lohn] *n* act of lending; thing lent; money borrowed at interest; permission to use. ▶ *vt* grant loan of.

loath, loth [lohth] *adj* unwilling, reluctant (to). **loathe** [loh*th*] *vt* **loathed, loath·ing.** hate, abhor. **loathing** [LOH*TH*-ing] *n* disgust; repulsion. **loath·some** [LOH*TH*-səm] *adj* disgusting.

lob *n* **lobbed, lob·bing.** in tennis, artillery, etc., ball, shell, sent high in air. ▶ *v* hit, fire, thus.

lob·by [LOB-ee] *n, pl* **-bies.** corridor into which rooms open; passage or room adjacent to legislative chamber; group of people who try to influence members of legislature. **lob′by·ing** *n* activity of this group. **lob′by·ist** *n*

lobe [lohb] *n* any rounded projection; subdivision of body organ; soft, hanging part of ear. **lobed** *adj* **lo·bot·o·my** [lə-BOT-ə-mee] *n, pl* **-mies.** surgical incision into lobe of organ, esp. brain.

lob·ster [LOB-stər] *n* shellfish with long tail and claws, turning red when boiled.

lo·cal [LOH-kəl] *adj* of, existing in particular place; confined to a definite spot, district or part of the body; of place; (of train) making many stops. ▶ *n* person belonging to a district; local branch of labor union; local train. **lo·cale** [loh-KAL] *n* scene of event. **lo·cal'i·ty** *n* place, situation; district. **lo'cal·ize** *vt* **-ized, -iz·ing.** assign, restrict to definite place. **local anesthetic** one that produces insensibility in one part of body.

lo·cate [loh-KAYT] *vt* **-cat·ed, -cat·ing.** attribute to a place; find the place of; situate. **lo·ca'tion** *n* placing; situation; site of film production away from studio.

lock[1] [lok] *n* appliance for fastening door, lid, etc.; mechanism for firing gun; enclosure in river or canal for moving boats from one level to another; air lock; appliance to check the motion of a mechanism; interlocking; block, jam. ▶ *vt* fasten, make secure with lock; place in locked container; join firmly; cause to become immovable; embrace closely. ▶ *vi* become fixed or united; become immovable. **lock'er** *n* small closet with lock. **lock'jaw** *n* tetanus. **lock'out** *n* exclusion of workmen by employers as means of coercion. **lock'smith** *n* one who makes and mends locks. **lock'up** *n* prison.

lock[2] *n* tress of hair.

lock·et [LOK-it] *n* small hinged pendant for portrait, etc.

lo·co·mo·tive [loh-kə-MOH-tiv] *n* engine for pulling train on railway tracks. ▶ *adj* having power of moving from place to place. **lo·co·mo'tion** *n* action, power of moving.

lo·cus [LOH-kəs] *n, pl* **-ci** [-sī] exact place or locality; curve made by all points satisfying certain mathematical condition, or by

point, line or surface moving under such condition.

lo·cust [LOH-kəst] *n* destructive winged insect; N Amer. tree; wood of this tree.

lo·cu·tion [loh-KYOO-shən] *n* a phrase; speech; mode or style of speaking.

lode [lohd] *n* vein of ore. **lode'star** *n* star that shows the way; any guide on which attention is fixed; Polaris. **lode'stone** *n* magnetic iron ore.

lodge [loj] *n* house, cabin used seasonally or occasionally, e.g. for hunting, skiing; gatekeeper's house; meeting place of branch of certain fraternal organizations; the branch. ▶ *v* **lodged, lodg·ing.** ▶ *vt* house; deposit; bring (a charge, etc.) against someone. ▶ *vi* live in another's house at fixed rent; come to rest (in, on). **lodg'er** *n* **lodgings** *pl n* rented room(s) in another person's house.

loft [lawft] *n* space between top story and roof; upper story of warehouse, factory, etc. typically with large unpartitioned space; gallery in church, etc. ▶ *vt* send (golf ball, etc.) high. **loft building** building in which all stories have large unobstructed space once used for manufacturing but now usu. are converted to residences. **loft'i·ly** *adv* haughtily. **loft'i·ness** *n* **loft'y** *adj* **loft·i·er, loft·i·est.** of great height; elevated; haughty.

log[1] [lawg] *n* portion of felled tree stripped of branches; detailed record of voyages, time traveled, etc., of ship, aircraft, etc.; apparatus used formerly for measuring ship's speed. ▶ *vt* **logged, log·ging.** keep a record of; travel (specified distance, time). **log'ging** *n* cutting and transporting logs to river. **log in, out** *v* gain entrance to *or* leave a computer system by keying in a special command.

log[2] *n* logarithm.

log·a·rithm [LAW-gə-*rith*-əm] *n* one of series of arithmetical functions tabulated for use in calculation.

log·ger·head [LAW-gər-hed] *n* **at loggerheads** quarreling, disputing.

log·ic [LOJ-ik] *n* art or philosophy of reasoning; reasoned thought or argument; coherence of various facts, events, etc. **log'i·cal** *adj* of logic; according to reason; reasonable; apt to reason correctly. **lo·gi·cian** [loh-JISH-ən] *n*

lo·gis·tics [loh-JIS-tiks] *n* the transport, housing and feeding of troops; organization of any project, operation. **lo·gis'ti·cal** *adj*

lo·go [LOH-goh] *n, pl* **-gos.** company emblem or similar device.

loin *n* part of body between ribs and hip; cut of meat from this. ▶ *pl* hips and lower abdomen. **loin'cloth** *n* garment covering loins only.

loi·ter [LOI-tər] *vi* dawdle, hang about; idle. **loi'ter·er** *n*

loll [lol] *vi* sit, lie lazily; hang out. ▶ *vt* allow to hang out.

lone [lohn] *adj* solitary. **lone'ly** *adj* **-li·er, -li·est.** sad because alone; unfrequented; solitary, alone. **lone'li·ness** *n* **lon'er** *n* one who prefers to be alone. **lone'some** [-səm] *adj*

long¹ [lawng] *adj* **-er, -est.** having length, esp. great length, in space or time; extensive; protracted. ▶ *adv* for a long time. **long'hand** *n* writing in which words are written out in full by hand rather than on typewriter, etc. **long'-play'ing** *adj* (of record) lasting for 10 to 30 minutes because of its fine grooves. **long-range** *adj* of the future; able to travel long distances without refueling; (of weapons) designed to hit distant target. **long shot** competitor, undertaking, bet, etc. with small chance of success. **long ton** 2240 lbs. **long'-wind'ed** *adj* tediously loquacious.

long² *vi* have keen desire, yearn (for). **long'ing** *n* yearning.

lon·gev·i·ty [lon-JEV-i-tee] *n* long existence or life; length of existence or life; tenure.

lon·gi·tude [LON-ji-tood] *n* distance east or west from prime meridian. **lon·gi·tu'di·nal** *adj* of length or longitude; lengthwise.

long·shore·man [LAWNG-SHOR-mən] *n* dock laborer.

look [luuk] *vi* direct, use eyes; face; seem; search (for); hope (for); (with *after*) take care of. ▶ *n* looking; view; search. ▶ *pl* appearance. **good looks** beauty. **look'a·like** *n* person who is double of another. **look'out** *n* guard; place for watching; watchman; object of worry, concern. **look after** tend. **look down on** despise.

loom¹ *n* machine for weaving; middle part of oar.

loom² *vi* appear dimly; seem ominously close; assume great importance.

loon¹ *n* Amer. fish-eating diving bird.

loon² *n* stupid, foolish person. **loon'y** *adj* **loon·i·er, loon·i·est,** *n, pl* **-nies. loony bin** *inf* mental hospital or ward.

loop *n* figure made by curved line crossing itself; similar rounded shape in cord or rope, etc. crossed on itself; contraceptive coil; aerial maneuver in which aircraft describes complete circle. ▶ *v* form loop.

loop·hole [LOOP-hohl] *n* means of evading rule without infringing it; vertical slit in building wall, esp. for defense.

loose [loos] *adj* **loos·er, loos·est.** not tight, fastened, fixed, or tense; slack; vague; dissolute. ▶ *v* **loosed, loos·ing.** ▶ *vt* free; unfasten; slacken. ▶ *vi* (with *off*) shoot, let fly. **loose'ly** *adv* **loos'en** *vt* make loose. **loose'ness** *n* **on the loose** free; on a spree.

loot *n, vt* plunder.

lop¹ *vt* **lopped, lop·ping.** cut away twigs and branches; chop off.

lop² *vi* **lopped, lop·ping.** hang limply. **lop'-eared** *adj* having drooping ears. **lop'sid·ed** *adj* with one side lower than the other;

badly balanced.

lope [lohp] *vi* **loped, lop·ing.** run with long, easy strides.

lo·qua·cious [loh-KWAY-shəs] *adj* talkative. **lo·quac'i·ty** [-KWAS-ə-tee] *n*

lord *n* British nobleman, peer of the realm; feudal superior; one ruling others; owner; (**L-**) God. ▶ *vi* domineer. **lord'li·ness** *n* **lord'ly** *adj* **-li·er, -li·est.** imperious, proud; fit for a lord. **lord'ship** *n* rule, ownership; domain; title of some noblemen.

lore [lòr] *n* learning; body of facts and traditions.

lor·gnette [lorn-YET] *n* pair of eyeglasses mounted on long handle.

lorn *adj poet* abandoned; desolate.

lose [looz] *v* **lost, los·ing.** ▶ *vt* be deprived of, fail to retain or use; let slip; fail to get; (of clock, etc.) run slow (by specified amount); be defeated in. ▶ *vi* suffer loss. **loss** [laws] *n* a losing; what is lost; harm or damage resulting from losing. **lost** *adj* unable to be found; unable to find one's way; bewildered; not won; not utilized.

lot *n* great number; collection; large quantity; share; fate; destiny; item at auction; one of a set of objects used to decide something by chance, as in **to cast lots**; area of land. ▶ *pl* great numbers or quantity. ▶ *adv* a great deal.

loth see LOATH.

lo·tion [LOH-shən] *n* liquid for washing to reduce itching, etc., improving skin, etc.

lot·ter·y [LOT-ə-ree] *n, pl* **-ter·ies.** method of raising funds by selling tickets and prizes by chance; any gamble.

lot·to [LOT-oh] *n* game of chance like bingo.

lo·tus [LOH-təs] *n, pl* **-tus·es.** legendary plant whose fruits induce forgetfulness when eaten; Egyptian water lily. **lotus position** seated cross-legged position used in yoga, etc.

loud [lowd] *adj* **-er, -est.** strongly

audible; noisy; obtrusive. **loud'ly** *adv* **loud'speak·er** *n* instrument for converting electrical signals into sound audible at a distance.

lounge [lownj] *vi* **lounged, loung·ing.** sit, lie, walk, or stand in a relaxed manner. ▶ *n* general waiting, relaxing area in airport, hotel, etc.; bar. **loung'er** *n* loafer.

louse [lows] *n, pl* **lice.** a parasitic insect. **lous'y** *adj inf* **lous·i·er, lous·i·est.** nasty, unpleasant; *sl* (too) generously provided, thickly populated (with); bad, poor; having lice.

lout [lowt] *n* crude, oafish person. **lout'ish** *adj*

lou·ver [LOO-vər] *n* one of a set of boards or slats set parallel and slanted to admit air but not rain or sunlight; ventilating structure of these.

love [luv] *n* warm affection; benevolence; charity; sweetheart; *Tennis, etc.* score of zero. ▶ *v* **loved, lov·ing.** ▶ *vt* admire passionately; delight in. ▶ *vi* be in love. **lov'a·ble** *adj* **love'less** [-lis] *adj* **love'lorn** *adj* forsaken by, pining for a lover. **love'li·ness** *n* **love'ly** *adj* **-li·er, -li·est.** beautiful, delightful. **loving** *adj* affectionate; tender. **lov'ing·ly** *adv* **loving cup** bowl formerly passed around at banquet; large cup given as prize. **make love** (to) have sexual intercourse (with).

low¹ [loh] *adj* **-er, -est.** not tall, high or elevated; humble; commonplace; coarse, vulgar; dejected; ill; not loud; moderate; cheap. **low'er** *vt* cause, allow to descend; move down; diminish, degrade. ▶ *adj* below in position or rank; at an early stage, period of development. **low'li·ness** *n* **low'ly** *adj* **-li·er, -li·est.** modest, humble. **low'brow** *n* person with no intellectual or cultural interests. ▶ *adj* **low'down** *n inf* inside information. ▶ *adj* mean, shabby, dishonorable. **low frequency** in electricity any frequency of alternating current from about 30 to 300 kilohertz; frequency within audible range. **low-key** [-kee] *adj* subdued, restrained, not intense. **low·land** *n* low-lying land. **low-ten·sion** *adj* carrying, operating at low voltage.

low² *vi* of cattle, utter their cry, bellow. ▶ *n* cry of cattle, bellow.

low·er [LOW-ər] *vi* look gloomy or threatening, as sky; scowl. ▶ *n* scowl, frown.

loy·al [LOI-əl] *adj* faithful, true to allegiance. **loy'al·ly** *adv* **loy'al·ty** *n*

loz·enge [LOZ-inj] *n* small candy or tablet of medicine; rhombus, diamond figure.

Lr *Chem* lawrencium.

LSD lysergic acid diethylamide (hallucinogenic drug).

Lu *Chem* lutetium.

lub·ber [LUB-ər] *n* clumsy fellow; unskilled seaman.

lu·bri·cate [LOO-bri-kayt] *vt* **-cat·ed, -cat·ing.** oil, grease; make slippery. **lu'bri·cant** [-kənt] *n* substance used for this. **lu·bri·ca'tion** [-KAY-shən] *n* **lu·bric'i·ty** [-BRIS-i-tee] *n, pl* **-ties.** slipperiness, smoothness; lewdness.

lu·cid [LOO-sid] *adj* clear; easily understood; sane. **lu·cid'i·ty** *n*

Lu·ci·fer [LOO-sə-fər] *n* Satan.

luck [luk] *n* fortune, good or bad; good fortune; chance. **luck'i·ly** *adv* fortunately. **luck'less** *adj* having bad luck. **luck'y** *adj* **luck·i·er, luck·i·est.** having good luck.

lu·cre [LOO-kər] *n* money, wealth. **lu'cra·tive** [-krə-tiv] *adj* very profitable. **filthy lucre** *inf* money.

lu·di·crous [LOO-di-krəs] *adj* absurd, laughable, ridiculous.

lug¹ *v* **lugged, lug·ging.** ▶ *vt* drag with effort. ▶ *vi* pull hard.

lug² *n* projection, tag serving as handle or support; *sl* fellow, blockhead.

lug·gage [LUG-ij] *n* traveler's suitcases and other baggage.

lu·gu·bri·ous [luu-GOO-bree-əs] *adj* mournful, doleful, gloomy. **lu·gu'bri·ous·ly** *adv*

luke·warm [look-worm] *adj* moderately warm, tepid;

indifferent.

lull *vt* soothe, sing to sleep; make quiet. ▶ *vi* become quiet, subside. ▶ *n* brief time of quiet in storm, etc. **lull'a·by** *n, pl* **-bies.** lulling song, esp. for children.

lum·bar [LUM-bahr] *adj* relating to body between lower ribs and hips.

lum·ba'go [-BAY-goh] *n* rheumatism in lower part of the back.

lum·ber [LUM-bər] *n* sawn timber; disused articles, useless rubbish. ▶ *vi* move heavily. ▶ *vt* convert (a number of trees) into lumber; burden with something unpleasant. **lum'ber·jack** *n* logger.

lu·men [LOO-mən] *n, pl* **-mi·na** [-mə-nə] SI unit of luminous flux.

lu·mi·nous [LOO-mə-nəs] *adj* bright; shedding light; glowing; lucid. **lu'mi·nar·y** [-ner-ee] *n* learned person; prominent person; heavenly body giving light. **lu·mi·nes'cence** [-NES-əns] *n* emission of light at low temperatures by process (e.g. chemical) not involving burning. **lu·mi·nos'i·ty** *n*

lump *n* shapeless piece or mass; swelling; large sum. ▶ *vt* throw together in one mass or sum. ▶ *vi* move heavily. **lump'ish** *adj* clumsy; stupid. **lump'y** *adj* **lump·i·er, lump·i·est.** full of lumps; uneven. **lump it** *inf* put up with; accept and endure.

lu·nar [LOO-nər] *adj* relating to the moon.

lu·na·tic [LOO-nə-tik] *adj* insane. ▶ *n* insane person. **lu'na·cy** *n, pl* **-cies. lunatic fringe** extreme, radical section of group, etc.

lunch *n* meal taken in the middle of the day. ▶ *v* eat, entertain at lunch. **lunch'eon** [-ən] *n* a lunch.

lung *n* one of the two organs of respiration in vertebrates. **lung'fish** *n* type of fish with air-breathing lung.

lunge [lunj] *vi* **lunged, lung·ing.** thrust with sword, etc. ▶ *n* such thrust; sudden movement of body, plunge.

lu·pine[1] [LOO-pin] *n* leguminous plant with tall spikes of flowers.

lu·pine[2] [LOO-pin] *adj* like a wolf.

lu·pus [LOO-pəs] *n* skin disease.

lurch *n* sudden roll to one side. ▶ *vi* stagger. **leave in the lurch** leave in difficulties.

lure [luur] *n* something that entices; bait; power to attract. ▶ *vt* **lured, lur·ing.** entice; attract.

lu·rid [LUUR-id] *adj* vivid in shocking detail, sensational; pale, wan; lit with unnatural glare.

lurk *vi* lie hidden. **lurk'ing** *adj* (of suspicion) not definite.

lus·cious [LUSH-əs] *adj* sweet, juicy; extremely pleasurable or attractive.

lush[1] *adj* **-er, -est.** (of grass, etc.) luxuriant and juicy; fresh.

lush[2] *n sl* heavy drinker; alcoholic.

lust *n* strong desire for sexual gratification; any strong desire. ▶ *vi* have passionate desire. **lust'ful** [-fəl] *adj* **lust'i·ly** *adv* **lust'y** *adj* **lust·i·er, lust·i·est.** vigorous, healthy.

lus·ter [LUST-ər] *n* gloss, sheen; splendor; renown; glory; glossy material; metallic pottery glaze. **lus'trous** [-trəs] *adj* shining, luminous.

lute [loot] *n* old stringed musical instrument played with the fingers. **lu'te·nist** *n*

lux [luks] *n, pl* **lu·ces** [LOO-seez] SI unit of illumination.

lux·u·ry [LUK-shə-ree] *n, pl* **-ries.** possession and use of costly, choice things for enjoyment; enjoyable but not necessary thing; comfortable surroundings. **lux·u·ri·ance** [lug-ZHUUR-ee-əns] *n* abundance, proliferation. **lux·u·ri·ant** *adj* growing thickly; abundant. **lux·u·ri·ate** [-ayt] *vi* **-at·ed, -at·ing.** indulge in luxury; flourish profusely; take delight (in). **lux·u·ri·ous** *adj* fond of luxury; self-indulgent; sumptuous.

ly·ce·um [lī-SEE-əm] *n* institution for popular education e.g. concerts, lectures; public building for this purpose.

lye [lī] *n* water made alkaline with wood ashes, etc. for washing.

lying pr. p. of LIE.

lymph [limf] *n* colorless bodily fluid, mainly of white blood cells. **lym·phat'ic** *adj* of lymph; flabby, sluggish. ▶ *n* vessel in the body conveying lymph.

lynch [linch] *vt* put to death without trial. **lynch law** procedure of self-appointed court trying and punishing esp. executing accused.

lynx [lingks] *n* animal of cat family.

lyre [līr] *n* instrument like harp. **lyr·ic** [LIR-ik], **lyr'i·cal** *adj* of short personal poems expressing emotion; of lyre; meant to be sung. **lyric** *n* lyric poem. ▶ *pl* words of popular song. **lyr'i·cist** [-sist] *n* writer of lyrics; lyric poet. **wax lyrical** express great enthusiasm.

M m

ma·ca·bre [mə-KAH-brə] *adj* gruesome, ghastly.

mac·ad·am [mə-KAD-əm] *n* road surface made of pressed layers of small broken stones; this stone.

mac·a·roon [mak-ə-ROON] *n* small cookie made of egg whites, almond paste, etc.

ma·caw [mə-KAW] *n* kind of parrot.

mace [mays] *n* spice made of the husk of the nutmeg.

Mace [mays] *n* ® liquid causing tears and nausea, used as spray for riot control.

mac·er·ate [MAS-ə-rayt] *vt* **-at·ed, -at·ing.** soften by soaking; cause to waste away.

mach (number) [mahk] *n* the ratio of the air speed of an aircraft to the velocity of sound under given conditions.

ma·chet·e [mə-SHET-ee] *n* broad, heavy knife used for cutting or as a weapon.

Mach·i·a·vel·li·an [mak-ee-ə-VEL-ə-ən] *adj* politically unprincipled, crafty, perfidious, subtle.

mach·i·na·tion [mak-ə-NAY-shən] *n* (usu pl) plotting, intrigue.

ma·chine [mə-SHEEN] *n* apparatus combining action of several parts to apply mechanical force; controlling organization; mechanical appliance; vehicle. ▶ *vt* **-chined, -chin·ing.** sew, print, shape, etc. with machine. **ma·chin·er·y** *n, pl* **-er·ies.** parts of machine collectively; machines. **ma·chin·ist** *n* one who makes or operates machines.

ma·chis·mo [mah-CHEEZ-moh] *n* strong or exaggerated masculine pride or masculinity. **ma′cho** [-choh] *adj* denoting or exhibiting such pride in masculinity. ▶ *n, pl* **-chos.** person exhibiting this.

mack·er·el [MAK-ər-əl] *n* edible sea fish with blue and silver stripes.

mac·ra·mé [MAK-rə-may] *n* ornamental webbing of knotted cord.

mac·ro·bi·ot·ics [mak-roh-bī-OT-iks] *n* (with sing v) dietary system advocating grain and vegetables grown without chemical additives. **mac·ro·bi·ot′ic** *adj, n* (relating to the diet of) person practicing macrobiotics.

mac·ro·cosm [MAK-rə-koz-əm] *n* the universe; any large, complete system.

mad *adj* **-der, -dest.** suffering from mental disease, insane; wildly foolish; very enthusiastic (about); excited; furious, angry. **mad′den** *vt* make mad. **mad′ly** *adv* **mad′man** *n* **mad′ness** *n* insanity; folly.

mad·am [MAD-əm] *n* polite form of address to a woman; woman in charge of house; woman in charge of house of prostitution.

made pt./pp. of MAKE.

Ma·don·na [mə-DON-ə] *n* the Virgin Mary; picture or statue of her.

mad·ri·gal [MAD-ri-gəl] *n* unaccompanied part song; short love poem or song.

mael·strom [MAYL-strəm] *n* great whirlpool; turmoil.

ma·es·to·so [mī-STOH-soh] *adv* *Mus* grandly, in majestic manner.

maes·tro [MĪ-stroh] *n* outstanding musician, conductor; man regarded as master of any art.

Ma·fi·a [MAH-fee-ə] *n* international secret organization engaging in crime, orig. Italian.

mag·a·zine [mag-ə-ZEEN] *n* periodical publication with stories and articles by different writers; appliance for supplying cartridges automatically to gun; storehouse for explosives or arms.

ma·gen·ta [mə-JEN-tə] *adj, n* (of) purplish-red color.

mag·got [MAG-ət] *n* grub, larva of certain flies. **mag′got·y** *adj* infested with maggots.

Ma·gi [MAY-jī] *pl n* priests of ancient Persia; the wise men from the East at the Nativity.

mag·ic [MAJ-ik] *n* art of supposedly invoking supernatural powers to influence events, etc.; any mysterious agency or power; witchcraft, conjuring. ▶ *adj* **mag'i·cal** *adj* **ma·gi'cian** *n* one skilled in magic, wizard, conjurer, enchanter.

mag·is·trate [MAJ-ə-strayt] *n* civil officer administering law; justice of the peace. **mag·is·te'ri·al** [-STEER-ee-əl] *adj* of, referring to magistrate; authoritative; weighty. **mag'is·tra·cy** [-strə-see] *n, pl* **-cies.** office of magistrate; magistrates collectively.

mag·ma [MAG-mə] *n* paste, suspension; molten rock inside Earth's crust.

mag·nan·i·mous [mag-NAN-ə-məs] *adj* noble, generous, not petty. **mag·na·nim'i·ty** *n*

mag·nate [MAG-nayt] *n* influential or wealthy person.

mag·ne·si·um [mag-NEE-zee-əm] *n* metallic element. **mag·ne'sia** [-zhə] *n* white powder compound of this used in medicine.

mag·net [MAG-nit] *n* piece of iron, steel having properties of attracting iron, steel and pointing north and south when suspended; lodestone. **mag·net'ic** *adj* with properties of magnet; exerting powerful attraction. **mag·net'i·cal·ly** *adv* **mag'net·ism** [-ni-tiz-əm] *n* magnetic phenomena; science of this; personal charm or power of attracting others. **mag'net·ize** *vt* **-ized, -iz·ing.** make into a magnet; attract as if by magnet; fascinate. **mag·ne'to** [-NEE-toh] *n, pl* **-tos.** apparatus for ignition in internal combustion engine.

mag·nif·i·cent [mag-NIF-ə-sənt] *adj* splendid; stately, imposing; excellent. **mag·nif'i·cence** *n*

mag·ni·fy [MAG-nə-fī] *v* **-fied, -fy·ing.** increase apparent size of,

as with lens; exaggerate; make greater. **mag·ni·fi·ca'tion** [-KAY-shən] *n*

mag·nil·o·quent [mag-NIL-ə-kwənt] *adj* speaking pompously; grandiose. **mag·nil'o·quence** *n*

mag·ni·tude [MAG-ni-tood] *n* importance; greatness, size.

mag·num [MAG-nəm] *n* large wine bottle (approx. 1.6 quarts, 1.5 liters).

mag·pie [MAG-pī] *n* black-and-white bird; incessantly talkative person.

ma·ha·ra·jah [mah-hə-RAH-jə] *n* former title of some Indian princes.

ma·ha·ri·shi [mah-hə-REE-shee] *n* Hindu religious teacher or mystic.

ma·hat·ma [mə-HAHT-mə] *n Hinduism* man of saintly life with supernatural powers; one endowed with great wisdom and power.

mahl·stick [MAHL-stik] *n* light stick with ball at one end, held in other hand to support working hand while painting.

maid·en [MAYD-n] *n lit* young unmarried woman. ▶ *adj* unmarried; of, suited to maiden; first; having blank record. **maid** *n* woman servant; *lit* young unmarried woman. **maid'en·ly** *adj* modest. **maid'en·hair** *n* fern with delicate stalks and fronds. **maid'en·head** *n* virginity. **maiden name** woman's surname before marriage.

mail¹ [mayl] *n* letters, etc. transported and delivered by the post office; letters, etc. conveyed at one time; the postal system; train, ship, etc. carrying mail. ▶ *vt* send by mail. **electronic mail** sending of messages between computer terminals (also **e-mail**).

mail² *n* armor of interlaced rings or overlapping plates. **mailed** *adj* covered with mail.

maim [maym] *vt* cripple, mutilate.

main [mayn] *adj* chief, principal, leading. ▶ *n* principal pipe, line carrying water, gas, etc.; chief part; strength, power; *obs* open sea.

main·ly *adv* for the most part, chiefly. **main'frame** *Computers* ▶ *adj* denoting a high-speed general-purpose computer. ▶ *n* such a computer. **main'land** *n* stretch of land that forms main part of a country. **main'mast** *n* chief mast in ship. **main'sail** *n* lowest sail of mainmast. **main'spring** *n* chief spring of watch or clock; chief cause or motive. **main'stay** *n* rope from mainmast; chief support.

main·tain [mayn-TAYN] *vt* carry on; preserve; support; sustain; keep up; keep supplied; affirm; support by argument; defend. **main'te·nance** [-tə-nəns] *n* maintaining; means of support; upkeep of buildings, etc.; provision of money for separated or divorced spouse.

maî·tre d'hô·tel [may-tər doh-TEL] *n, pl* **maî·tres** [-tərz] headwaiter, owner, or manager of hotel.

maize [mayz] *n* primitive corn with kernels of various colors, Indian corn.

maj·es·ty [MAJ-ə-stee] *n* stateliness; sovereignty; grandeur. **ma·jes'tic** [mə-] *adj* splendid; regal. **ma·jes'ti·cal·ly** *adv*

ma·jor [MAY-jər] *n* military officer ranking next above captain; scale in music; principal field of study at college; person engaged in this. ▶ *adj* greater in number, quality, extent; significant, serious. **ma·jor'i·ty** *n* greater number; larger party voting together; more than half of votes cast in election; coming of age; rank of major. **major-do·mo** [-DOH-moh] *n, pl* **-mos.** male servant in charge of large household.

make [mayk] *v* **made, mak·ing.** construct; produce; create; establish; appoint; amount to; cause to do something; accomplish; reach; earn; tend; contribute. ▶ *n* brand, type, or style. **making** *n* creation. ▶ *pl* necessary requirements or qualities. **make allowance for** take mitigating circumstance into consideration. **make'shift** *n*

temporary expedient. **make'up** *n* cosmetics; characteristics; layout. **make up** compose; compile; complete; compensate; apply cosmetics; invent. **on the make** *inf* intent on gain; *sl* seeking sexual relations.

mal- *comb. form* ill, badly, e.g. *malformation; malevolent.*

ma·lac·ca [mə-LAK-ə] *n* brown cane used for walking stick.

mal·a·droit [mal-ə-DROIT] *adj* clumsy, awkward.

mal·a·dy [MAL-ə-dee] *n, pl* **-dies.** disease.

ma·laise [ma-LAYZ] *n* vague, unlocated feeling of bodily discomfort.

mal·a·prop·ism [MAL-ə-prop-iz-əm] *n* ludicrous misuse of word.

ma·lar·i·a [mə-LAIR-ee-ə] *n* infectious disease caused by parasite transmitted by bite of some mosquitoes. **ma·lar'i·al** *adj*

mal·con·tent [mal-kən-TENT] *adj* actively discontented. ▶ *n* malcontent person.

male [mayl] *adj* of sex producing gametes that fertilize female gametes; of men or male animals; of machine part, made to fit inside corresponding recessed female part. ▶ *n* male person or animal.

mal·e·dic·tion [mal-i-DIK-shən] *n* curse.

mal·e·fac·tor [MAL-ə-fak-tər] *n* criminal.

ma·lev·o·lent [mə-LEV-ə-lənt] *adj* full of ill will. **ma·lev'o·lence** *n*

mal·fea·sance [mal-FEE-zəns] *n* illegal action; official misconduct.

mal·ice [MAL-is] *n* ill will; spite. **ma·li·cious** [mə-LISH-əs] *adj* intending evil or unkindness; spiteful; moved by hatred.

ma·lign [mə-LĪn] *adj* evil in influence or effect. ▶ *vt* slander, misrepresent. **ma·lig'nan·cy** [-LIG-nən-see] *n* **ma·lig'nant** *adj* feeling extreme ill will; (of disease) resistant to therapy; tending to produce death. **ma·lig'ni·ty** *n* malignant disposition.

ma·lin·ger [mə-LING-gər] *vi* feign illness to escape duty. **ma·lin'ger·er** *n*

mall [mawl] *n* level, shaded walk; street, shopping area closed to vehicles.

mal·le·a·ble [MAL-ee-ə-bəl] *adj* capable of being hammered into shape; adaptable.

mal·let [MAL-it] *n* (wooden, etc.) hammer; croquet or polo stick.

mal·nu·tri·tion [mal-noo-TRISH-ən] *n* inadequate nutrition.

mal·o·dor·ous [mal-OH-dər-əs] *adj* evil-smelling.

mal·prac·tice [mal-PRAK-tis] *n* immoral, careless illegal or unethical conduct.

malt [mawlt] *n* grain used for brewing or distilling. ▶ *vt* make into malt.

mam·bo [MAHM-boh] *n, pl* **-bos.** Latin Amer. dance like rumba.

mam·mal [MAM-əl] *n* animal of type that suckles its young. **mam·ma'li·an** [-MAY-lee-ən] *adj*

mam·ma·ry [MAM-er-ee] *adj* of, relating to breast or milk-producing gland.

mam·mon [MAM-ən] *n* wealth regarded as source of evil; (**M-**) false god of covetousness.

mam·moth [MAM-əth] *n* extinct animal like an elephant. ▶ *adj* colossal.

man *n, pl* **men.** human being; person; human race; adult male; manservant; piece used in chess, etc. ▶ *vt* **manned, man·ning.** supply (ship, artillery, etc.) with necessary crew; fortify. **man'ful** *adj* brave, vigorous. **man'li·ness** *n* **man'ly** *adj* **-li·er, -li·est. man'nish** *adj* like a man. **man'han·dle** *vt* **-dled, -dling.** treat roughly. **man'hole** *n* opening through which person can pass to a drain, sewer, etc. **man'hood** [-huud] *n* **man'kind'** [-KĪND] *n* human beings in general. **man'pow·er** *n* power of human effort; available number of workers. **man'slaugh·ter** [-slaw-tər] *n* culpable homicide without malice aforethought.

man·a·cle [MAN-ə-kəl] *n* fetter, handcuff. ▶ *vt* **-cled, -cling.** shackle.

man·age [MAN-ij] *vt* **-aged, -ag·ing.** be in charge of, administer; succeed in doing; control; handle, cope with; conduct, carry on; persuade. **man'age·a·ble** *adj* **man'age·ment** *n* those who manage, as board of directors, etc.; administration; skillful use of means; conduct. **man'ag·er** *n* one in charge of business, institution, actor, etc.; one who manages efficiently. **man·a·ge'ri·al** *adj*

man·a·tee [MAN-ə-tee] *n* large, plant-eating aquatic mammal.

man·da·rin [MAN-də-rin] *n Hist* Chinese high-ranking bureaucrat; *fig* any high government official; Chinese variety of orange.

man·date [MAN-dayt] *n* command of, or commission to act for, another; commission from United Nations to govern a territory; instruction from electorate to representative or government. **man'dat·ed** *adj* committed to a mandate. **man'da·tor·y** [-də-tor-ee] *n* holder of a mandate. **man'da·to·ry** *adj* compulsory.

man·di·ble [MAN-də-bəl] *n* lower jawbone; either part of bird's beak. **man·dib'u·lar** *adj* of, like mandible.

man·do·lin [MAN-dl-in] *n* stringed musical instrument.

man·drel [MAN-drəl] *n* axis on which material is supported in a lathe; spindle around which metal is forged.

man'drill *n* large blue-faced baboon.

mane [mayn] *n* long hair on neck of horse, lion, etc.

ma·neu·ver [mə-NOO-vər] *n* contrived, complicated, perhaps deceptive plan or action; skillful management. ▶ *v* employ stratagems, work adroitly; (cause to) perform maneuvers.

man·ga·nese [MANG-gə-neez] *n* metallic element; black oxide of this.

mange [maynj] *n* skin disease of dogs, etc. **man'gy** *adj* **-gi·er,**

-gi·est. scruffy, shabby.

man·ger [MAYN-jər] *n* eating trough in stable.

man·gle¹ [MANG-gəl] *n* machine for pressing clothes, etc. to remove water. ▶ *vt* **-gled, -gling.** press in mangle.

man·gle² *vt* **-gled, -gling.** mutilate, spoil, hack.

man·go [MANG-goh] *n, pl* **-goes.** tropical fruit; tree bearing it.

man·grove [MANG-grohv] *n* tropical tree that grows on muddy banks of estuaries.

ma·ni·a [MAY-nee-ə] *n* madness; prevailing craze. **ma'ni·ac, ma·ni'a·cal, man'ic** *adj* affected by mania. **maniac** *n inf* mad person; wild enthusiast.

man·i·cure [MAN-i-kyuur] *n* treatment and care of fingernails and hands. ▶ *vt* **-cured, -cur·ing.** apply such treatment. **man'i·cur·ist** *n* one who does this professionally.

man·i·fest [MAN-ə-fest] *adj* clearly revealed, visible, undoubted. ▶ *vt* make manifest. ▶ *n* list of cargo for customs. **man·i·fes·ta'tion** *n* **man'i·fest·ly** *adv* clearly. **man·i·fes'to** *n, pl* **-toes.** declaration of policy by political party, government, or movement.

man·i·fold [MAN-ə-fohld] *adj* numerous and varied. ▶ *n* in internal combustion engine, pipe with several outlets.

ma·nip·u·late [mə-NIP-yə-layt] *vt* **-lat·ed, -lat·ing.** handle; deal with skillfully; manage; falsify. **ma·nip·u·la'tion** *n* act of manipulating, working by hand; skilled use of hands. **ma·nip'u·la·tive** *adj*

man·na [MAN-ə] *n* food of Israelites in the wilderness; unexpected benefit.

man·ne·quin [MAN-i-kin] *n* person who models clothes, esp. at fashion shows; clothing dummy.

man·ner [MAN-ər] *n* way thing happens or is done; sort, kind; custom; style. ▶ *pl* social behavior. **man'ner·ism** *n* person's distinctive

habit, trait. **man'ner·ly** *adj* polite.

man·or [MAN-ər] *n* main house of estate or plantation. **ma·no'ri·al** *adj*

man·sard [MAN-sahrd] *n* roof with break in its slope, lower part being steeper than upper.

man·sion [MAN-shən] *n* large house.

man·tel [MAN-tl] *n* structure around fireplace; mantelpiece. **man'tel·piece, -shelf** *n* shelf at top of mantel.

man·til·la [man-TIL-ə] *n* in Spain, (lace) scarf worn as headdress.

man'tis *n, pl* **-tis·es.** genus of insects including the stick insects and leaf insects.

man·tle [MAN-tl] *n* loose cloak; covering; incandescent fireproof network hood around gas jet. ▶ *vt* **-tled, -tling.** cover; conceal. **man·tle·piece** *n* mantel.

man·tra [MAN-trə] *n* word or phrase repeated as object of concentration in meditation.

man·u·al [MAN-yoo-əl] *adj* of, or done with, the hands; by human labor, not automatic. ▶ *n* handbook; textbook; organ keyboard.

man·u·fac·ture [man-yə-FAK-chər] *vt* **-tured, -tur·ing.** process, make (materials) into finished articles; produce (articles); invent, concoct. ▶ *n* making of articles, materials, esp. in large quantities; anything produced from raw materials. **man·u·fac'tur·er** *n*

ma·nure [mə-NUUR] *vt* **-nured, -nur·ing.** enrich land. ▶ *n* dung, chemical fertilizer (used to enrich land).

man·u·script [MAN-yə-skript] *n* book, document, written by hand; copy for printing. ▶ *adj* handwritten or typed.

man·y [MEN-ee] *adj* **more, most.** numerous. ▶ *n, pron* large number.

Ma·o·ri [MAH-aw-ree] *n* member of New Zealand aboriginal population; their language.

map *n* flat representation of Earth or some part of it, or of the heavens. ▶ *vt* **mapped, map·ping.** make a map of; (with *out*) plan.

ma·ple [MAY-pəl] *n* tree with broad leaves, a variety of which (**sugar maple**) yields sugar.

ma·quis [mah-KEE] *n* scrubby undergrowth of Mediterranean countries; name adopted by French resistance movement in WWII.

mar [mahr] *vt* **marred, mar·ring.** spoil, impair.

mar·a·bou [MAR-ə-boo] *n* kind of stork; its soft white lower tail feathers, formerly used to trim hats, etc.; kind of silk.

ma·rac·a [mə-RAH-kə] *n* percussion instrument of gourd containing dried seeds, etc.

mar·a·schi·no [mar-ə-SKEE-noh] *n* liqueur made from cherries.

mar·a·thon [MAR-ə-thon] *n* long-distance race; endurance contest.

ma·raud [mə-RAWD] *v* make raid for plunder; pillage. **ma·raud′er** *n*

mar·ble [MAHR-bəl] *n* kind of limestone capable of taking polish; slab of, sculpture in this; small ball used in children's game. **mar′bled** *adj* having mottled appearance, like marble; (of beef) streaked with fat.

march [mahrch] *vi* walk with military step; go, progress. ▸ *vt* cause to march. ▸ *n* action of marching; distance marched in day; tune to accompany marching.

mar·chion·ess [MAHR-shə-nis] *n* wife, widow of marquis.

Mar·di Gras [MAHR-dee grah] *n* festival of Shrove Tuesday; revelry celebrating this.

mare [mair] *n* female horse. **mare's-nest** *n* supposed discovery that proves worthless.

mar·ga·rine [MAHR-jər-in] *n* butter substitute made from vegetable fats.

mar·gin [MAHR-jin] *n* border, edge; space around printed page; amount allowed beyond what is necessary. **mar′gin·al** *adj*

mar·i·gold [MAR-i-gohld] *n* plant with yellow flowers.

ma·ri·jua·na [mar-ə-WAH-nə] *n*

dried flowers and leaves of hemp plant, used as narcotic.

ma·ri·na [mə-REE-nə] *n* mooring facility for yachts and pleasure boats.

mar·i·nade [mar-ə-NAYD] *n* seasoned, flavored liquid used to soak fish, meat, etc. before cooking. **mar′i·nate** *vt* **-nat·ed, -nat·ing.**

ma·rine [mə-REEN] *adj* of the sea or shipping; used at, found in sea. ▸ *n* shipping, fleet; soldier trained for land or sea combat. **mar′i·ner** *n* sailor.

mar·i·on·ette [mar-ee-ə-NET] *n* puppet worked with strings.

mar·i·tal [MAR-i-tl] *adj* relating to marriage.

mar·i·time [MAR-i-tīm] *adj* connected with seafaring; naval; bordering on the sea.

mar·jo·ram [MAHR-jər-əm] *n* aromatic herb.

mark[1] [mahrk] *n* line, dot, scar, etc.; sign, token; inscription; letter, number showing evaluation of schoolwork, etc.; indication; target. ▸ *vt* make a mark on; be distinguishing mark of; indicate; notice; watch; assess, e.g. examination paper. ▸ *vi* take notice. **mark′er** *n* one who, that which marks; counter used at card playing, etc.; *sl* an IOU. **marks′man** *n* skilled shot.

mark[2] *n* former German monetary unit.

mar·ket [MAHR-kit] *n* assembly, place for buying and selling; demand for goods; center for trade. ▸ *vt* offer or produce for sale. **mar′ket·a·ble** *adj*

mar·ma·lade [MAHR-mə-layd] *n* preserve usually made of oranges, lemons, etc.

mar·mo·re·al [mahr-MOR-ee-əl] *adj* of or like marble.

ma·roon[1] [mə-ROON] *n* brownish-red; firework. ▸ *adj* of the color.

ma·roon[2] *vt* leave (person) on deserted island or coast; isolate, cut off by any means.

mar·quee [mahr-KEE] *n* rooflike shelter with open sides; rooflike projection above theater, etc. displaying name of play, etc. being performed.

mar·quis [MAHR-kwis] *n* nobleman of rank below duke.

mar·row [MAR-oh] *n* fatty substance inside bones; vital part.

mar·ry [MAR-ee] *v* **-ried, -ry·ing.** join as husband and wife; unite closely. **mar·riage** [MAR-ij] *n* state of being married; wedding. **mar'riage·a·ble** *adj*

Mars [mahrz] *n* Roman god of war; planet nearest but one to Earth. **Mar·tian** [MAHR-shən] *n* supposed inhabitant of Mars. ▸ *adj* of Mars.

marsh [mahrsh] *n* low-lying wet land. **marsh'y** *adj* **marsh·i·er, marsh·i·est.**

mar·shal [MAHR-shəl] *n* high officer of state; law enforcement officer. ▸ *vt* **-shaled, -shal·ing.** arrange in due order; conduct with ceremony. **field marshal** in some nations, military officer of the highest rank.

marsh'mal·low [MAHRSH-mal-oh] *n* spongy candy orig. made from root of **marsh mallow,** shrubby plant growing near marshes.

mar·su·pi·al [mahr-SOO-pee-əl] *n* animal that carries its young in pouch, e.g. kangaroo. ▸ *adj*

mar·ten [MAHR-tn] *n* weasel-like animal; its fur.

mar·tial [MAHR-shəl] *adj* relating to war; warlike, brave. **court martial** see COURT. **martial law** law enforced by military authorities in times of danger or emergency.

mar'tin *n* species of swallow.

mar·ti·net [mahr-tn-ET] *n* strict disciplinarian.

mar·ti·ni [mahr-TEE-nee] *n, pl* **-nis.** cocktail containing gin and vermouth.

mar·tyr [MAHR-tər] *n* one put to death for not renouncing beliefs; one who suffers in some cause; one in constant suffering. ▸ *vt* make martyr of. **mar'tyr·dom** [-dəm] *n*

mar·vel [MAHR-vəl] *vi* **-veled, -vel·ing.** wonder. ▸ *n* wonderful

thing. **mar'vel·ous** *adj* amazing; wonderful.

mar·zi·pan [MAHR-zə-pan] *n* paste of almonds, sugar, etc. used in candies, cakes, etc.

mas·car·a [ma-SKAIR-ə] *n* cosmetic for darkening eyelashes and eyebrows.

mas·cot [MAS-kot] *n* animal, person or thing supposed to bring luck.

mas·cu·line [MAS-kyə-lin] *adj* relating to males; manly; of the grammatical gender to which names of males belong.

mash *n* grain, meal mixed with warm water; warm food for horses, etc. ▸ *vt* make into a mash; crush into soft mass or pulp.

mask *n* covering for face; *Surgery* covering for nose and mouth; disguise, pretense. ▸ *vt* cover with mask; hide, disguise.

mas·och·ism [MAS-ə-kiz-əm] *n* abnormal condition in which pleasure (esp. sexual) is derived from pain, humiliation, etc. **mas'och·ist** *n* **mas·och·is'tic** *adj*

ma·son [MAY-sən] *n* worker in stone; (M-) Freemason. **Ma·son'ic** *adj* of Freemasonry. **ma'son·ry** *n* stonework; (M-) Freemasonry.

masque [mask] *n Hist* form of theatrical performance.

mas·quer·ade' *n* masked ball. ▸ *vi* **-ad·ed, -ad·ing.** appear in disguise.

Mass *n* service of the Eucharist.

mass *n* quantity of matter; dense collection of this; large quantity or number. ▸ *v* form into a mass. **mas'sive** *adj* large and heavy. **mass-pro·duce'** *vt* **-duced, -duc·ing.** produce standardized articles in large quantities. **mass production** manufacturing of standardized goods in large quantities. **the masses** the common people.

mas·sa·cre [MAS-ə-kər] *n* indiscriminate, large-scale killing, esp. of unresisting people. ▸ *vt* **-cred, -cring.** kill indiscriminately.

mas·sage [mə-SAHZH] *n* rubbing and kneading of muscles, etc. as

curative treatment. ▶ *vt* **-saged,
-sag·ing.** apply this treatment to.
mas·seur' [-SUR], *(fem)* **-seuse**
[-SOOS] *n* one who practices
massage.

mast *n* pole for supporting ship's
sails; tall upright support for aerial,
etc.

mas·tec·to·my [ma-STEK-tə-mee]
n, pl **-mies.** surgical removal of a
breast.

mas·ter [MAS-tər] *n* one in control;
employer; head of household;
owner; document, etc. from which
copies are made; captain of
merchant ship; expert; great artist;
teacher. ▶ *vt* overcome; acquire
knowledge of or skill in.
mas'ter·ful *adj* imperious,
domineering. **mas'ter·ly** *adj*
showing great competence.
mas'ter·y *n* full understanding (of);
expertise; authority; victory.
master key one that opens many
different locks. **mas'ter·mind** *vt*
plan, direct. ▶ *n* **mas'ter·piece** *n*
outstanding work.

mas·tic [MAS-tik] *n* gum obtained
from certain trees; pasty substance.

mas·ti·cate [MAS-ti-kayt] *vt*
-cat·ed, -cat·ing. chew.
mas·ti·ca'tion *n*

mas'tiff *n* large dog.

mas'toid *adj* nipple-shaped. ▶ *n*
prominence on bone behind
human ear. **mas·toid·i'tis** *n*
inflammation of this area.

mas·tur·bate [MAS-tər-bayt] *v*
-bat·ed, -bat·ing. stimulate (one's
own) genital organs.
mas·tur·ba'tion *n*

mat¹ *n* small rug; piece of fabric to
protect another surface or to wipe
feet on, etc.; thick tangled mass.
▶ *v* **mat·ted, mat·ting.** form into
such mass. **go to the mat** struggle
unyieldingly.

mat² see MATTE.

mat·a·dor [MAT-ə-dor] *n* bullfighter
who slays bulls in bullfights.

match¹ [mach] *n* contest, game;
equal; person, thing exactly
corresponding to another;
marriage; person regarded as

eligible for marriage. ▶ *vt* get
something corresponding to (color,
pattern, etc.); oppose, put in
competition (with); arrange
marriage for; join (in marriage). ▶ *vi*
correspond. **match'less** *adj*
unequaled. **match'mak·er** *n* one
who schemes to bring about a
marriage.

match² *n* small stick with head that
ignites when rubbed; fuse.
match'box *n*

mate¹ [mayt] *n* husband, wife; one
of pair; officer in merchant ship. ▶ *v*
mat·ed, mat·ing. marry; pair.

mate² *n, vt Chess* **mat·ed, mat·ing.**
checkmate.

ma·te·ri·al [mə-TEER-ee-əl] *n*
substance from which thing is
made; cloth, fabric. ▶ *adj* of matter
or body; affecting physical
well-being; unspiritual; important,
essential. **ma·te'ri·al·ism** *n*
excessive interest in, desire for
money and possessions; doctrine
that nothing but matter exists,
denying independent existence of
spirit. **ma·te·ri·al·is'tic** *adj*
ma·te'ri·al·ize *v* **-ized, -iz·ing.** ▶ *vi*
come into existence or view. ▶ *vt*
make material. **ma·te'ri·al·ly** *adv*
appreciably.

ma·ter·nal [mə-TUR-nl] *adj*
motherly; of a mother; related
through mother. **ma·ter'ni·ty** *n*
motherhood.

math·e·mat·ics [math-ə-MAT-iks] *n*
science of numbers, quantities and
shapes. **math·e·mat'i·cal** *adj*
math·e·ma·ti'cian [-TI-shən] *n*

mat·i·née [mat-n-AY] *n* afternoon
performance in theater.

ma·tri·arch [MAY-tree-ahrk] *n*
mother as head and ruler of family.
ma'tri·ar·chy *n, pl* **-chies.** society
with government by women and
descent reckoned in female line.

mat·ri·cide [MA-tri-sīd] *n* the crime
of killing one's mother; one who
does this.

ma·tric·u·late [mə-TRIK-yə-layt] *v*
-lat·ed, -lat·ing. enroll, be enrolled
as degree candidate in a college or
university. **ma·tric·u·la'tion** *n*

mat·ri·mo·ny [MA-trə-moh-nee] n marriage. **mat·ri·mo·ni·al** adj

ma·trix [MAY-triks] n, pl **-tri·ces** [-tri-seez] substance, situation in which something originates, takes form, or is enclosed; mold for casting; Math rectangular array of elements set out in rows and columns.

ma·tron [MAY-trən] n married woman esp. of established social position; woman who superintends domestic arrangements of public institution, boarding school, etc.; woman guard in prison, etc. **ma′tron·ly** adj sedate.

Matt. Matthew.

matte [mat] adj of photographic print, dull, lusterless, not shiny.

mat·ter [MAT-ər] n substance of which thing is made; physical or bodily substance; affair, business; cause of trouble; substance of book, etc. ▶ vi be of importance, signify.

mat·tock [MAT-ək] n tool like pick with ends of blades flattened for cutting, hoeing.

mat·tress [MA-tris] n stuffed flat case, often with springs, or foam rubber pad, used as part of bed. **air mattress** inflatable mattress usu. of rubbery material.

ma·ture [mə-CHUUR] adj **-tur·er, -tur·est.** ripe, completely developed; grown-up. ▶ v **-tured, -tur·ing.** bring, come to maturity. ▶ vi (of bond, etc.) come due. **mat·u·ra′tion** n process of maturing. **ma·tu′ri·ty** n state of being mature.

maud·lin [MAWD-lin] adj weakly or tearfully sentimental.

maul [mawl] vt handle roughly; beat or bruise. ▶ n heavy wooden hammer.

maulstick n see MAHLSTICK.

mau·so·le·um [maw-sə-LEE-əm] n stately building as a tomb.

mauve [mawv] adj, n (of) pale purple color.

mav·er·ick [MAV-ər-ik] n unbranded steer, strayed cow; independent, unorthodox person.

maw n stomach, crop.

mawk·ish [MAW-kish] adj weakly sentimental, maudlin; sickening.

max·im [MAK-sim] n general truth, proverb; rule of conduct, principle.

max·i·mum [MAK-sə-məm] n greatest size or number; highest point. ▶ adj greatest. **max′i·mize** vt **-mized, -miz·ing.**

may v, pt **might**. used as an auxiliary to express possibility, permission, opportunity, etc. **may′be** adv perhaps; possibly.

May′day n international radiotelephone distress signal.

may·fly [MAY-flī] n short-lived flying insect, found near water.

may′hem n in law, depriving person by violence of limb, member or organ, or causing mutilation of body; any violent destruction; confusion.

may·on·naise [may-ə-NAYZ] n creamy sauce of egg yolks, etc., esp. for salads.

may·or [MAY-ər] n head of municipality. **may′or·al** adj **may′or·al·ty** [-əl-tee] n (time of) office of mayor.

may·pole [MAY-pohl] n pole set up for dancing around on **May Day** to celebrate spring.

maze [mayz] n labyrinth; network of paths, lines; state of confusion.

ma·zur·ka [mə-ZUR-kə] n lively Polish dance like polka; music for it.

MC n master of ceremonies.

me [mee] pron objective case singular of first personal pronoun I.

me·a cul·pa [ME-ah KUUL-pah] Lat my fault.

mead·ow [MED-oh] n tract of grassland.

mea·ger [MEE-gər] adj lean, thin, scanty, insufficient.

meal¹ [meel] n occasion when food is served and eaten; the food.

meal² n grain ground to powder. **meal′y** adj **meal·i·er, meal·i·est. mealy-mouthed** [-mowthd] adj euphemistic, insincere in what one says.

mean¹ [meen] v **meant** [ment], **mean·ing.** intend; signify; have a meaning; have the intention of behaving. **mean'ing** n sense, significance. ▶ adj expressive. **mean'ing·ful** [-fəl] adj of great meaning or significance. **mean'ing·less** adj

mean² adj **-er, -est.** ungenerous, petty; miserly, niggardly; unpleasant; callous; shabby; ashamed. **mean'ness** n

mean³ n thing that is intermediate; middle point. ▶ pl that by which thing is done; money; resources. ▶ adj intermediate in time, quality, etc.; average. **means test** inquiry into person's means to decide eligibility for pension, grant, etc. **mean'time, -while** adv, n (during) time between one happening and another. **by all means** certainly. **by no means** not at all.

me·an·der [mee-AN-dər] vi flow windingly; wander aimlessly.

mea·sles [MEE-zəlz] n infectious disease producing rash of red spots. **mea'sly** adj **-sli·er, -sli·est.** inf poor, wretched, stingy; of measles.

meas·ure [MEZH-ər] n size, quantity; vessel, rod, line, etc. for ascertaining size or quantity; unit of size or quantity; course, plan of action; law; poetical rhythm; musical time; Poet tune; obs dance. ▶ vt **-ured, -ur·ing.** ascertain size, quantity of; be (so much) in size or quantity; indicate measurement of; estimate; bring into competition (against). **meas'ur·a·ble** adj **meas'ured** adj determined by measure; steady; rhythmical; carefully considered. **meas'ure·ment** n measuring; size. ▶ pl dimensions.

meat [meet] n animal flesh as food; food. **meat'y** adj **meat·i·er, meat·i·est.** (tasting) of, like meat; brawny; full of import or interest.

Mec·ca [MEK-ə] n holy city of Islam; (m-) place that attracts visitors.

me·chan·ic [mə-KAN-ik] n one employed in working with machinery; skilled worker. ▶ pl scientific theory of motion.

me·chan'i·cal adj concerned with machines or operation of them; worked, produced (as though) by machine; acting without thought. **me·chan'i·cal·ly** adv

mech·an·ism [MEK-ə-niz-əm] n structure of machine; piece of machinery. **mech'a·nize** vt **-nized, -niz·ing.** equip with machinery; make mechanical, automatic; Military equip with armored vehicles.

med·al [MED-l] n piece of metal with inscription, etc. used as reward or memento. **me·dal'lion** [mə-DAL-yən] n large medal; various things like this in decorative work. **med'al·ist** n winner of a medal; maker of medals.

med·dle [MED-l] vi **-dled, -dling.** interfere, busy oneself with unnecessarily. **med'dle·some** [-səm] adj

me·di·a [MEE-dee-ə] n pl. of MEDIUM; used esp. of the mass media, radio, TV, etc. **media event** event staged for or exploited by mass media.

mediaeval see MEDIEVAL.

me·di·al [MEE-dee-əl] adj in the middle; pert. to a mean or average. **me'di·an** adj, n middle (point or line).

me·di·ate [MEE-dee-ayt] v **-at·ed, -at·ing.** ▶ vi intervene to reconcile. ▶ vt bring about by mediation. ▶ adj depending on mediation. **me·di·a'tion** n intervention on behalf of another; act of going between.

med·i·cine [MED-i-sin] n drug or remedy for treating disease; science of preventing, diagnosing, alleviating, or curing disease. **med'i·cal** [-kəl] adj **me·dic'a·ment** n remedy. **med'i·cate** [-kayt] vt **-cat·ed, -cat·ing.** treat, impregnate with medicinal substances. **med·i·ca'tion** n **me·dic'i·nal** [-DIS-ə-nəl] adj curative.

me·di·e·val [mee-dee-EE-vəl] adj of Middle Ages. **me·di·e'val·ist** n student of the Middle Ages.

me·di·o·cre [mee-dee-OH-kər] adj

neither bad nor good, ordinary, middling; second-rate.

me·di·oc·ri·ty [-OK-rə-tee] *n*

med·i·tate [MED-i-tayt] *v* **-tat·ed, -tat·ing.** ▶ *vi* be occupied in thought; reflect deeply on spiritual matters; engage in transcendental meditation. ▶ *vt* think about; plan. **med·i·ta'tion** [-TAY-shən] *n* thought; absorption in thought; religious contemplation. **med'i·ta·tive** *adj* thoughtful; reflective.

me·di·um [MEE-dee-əm] *adj* between two qualities, degrees, etc., average. ▶ *n, pl* **-di·a** or **-di·ums.** middle quality, degree; intermediate substance conveying force; means, agency of communicating news, etc. to public, as radio, newspapers, etc.; person through whom communication can supposedly be held with spirit world; surroundings; environment.

med·ley [MED-lee] *n, pl* **-leys.** miscellaneous mixture.

Me·du·sa [mə-DOO-sə] *n, pl* **-sas.** *Mythology* Gorgon whose head turned beholders into stone.

meek *adj* **-er, -est.** submissive, humble. **meek'ly** *adv* **meek'ness** *n*

meer·schaum [MEER-shəm] *n* white substance like clay; tobacco pipe bowl of this.

meet *vt* **met, meet·ing.** come face to face come face to face with; encounter; satisfy; pay; converge at specified point; assemble; come into contact. ▶ *n* meeting, esp. for sports. **meeting** *n* assembly; encounter.

meg·a·bit [MEG-ə-bit] *n Computers* 1,048,576 bits; (loosely) one million bits.

meg·a·byte [MEG-ə-bīt] *n Computers* 1,048,576 bytes; (loosely) one million bytes.

meg·a·lith [MEG-ə-lith] *n* great stone. **meg·a·lith'ic** *adj*

meg·a·lo·ma'ni·a [meg-ə-loh-MAY-nee-ə] *n* desire for, delusions of grandeur, power, etc.

meg·a·ton [MEG-ə-tun] *n* one million tons; explosive power equal to that of million tons of TNT.

meg'ohm *n Electricity* one million ohms.

mel·an·chol·y [MEL-ən-kol-ee] *n* sadness, dejection, gloom. ▶ *adj* gloomy, dejected. **mel·an·cho'li·a** [-KOH-lee-ə] *n* former name for DEPRESSION.

mé·lange [may-LAHN*ZH*] *n* mixture.

mel·a·nin [MEL-ə-nin] *n* dark pigment found in hair, skin, etc. of man.

me·lee [MAY-lay] *n* confused fight among several people; confusion; turmoil.

mel·io·rate [MEEL-yə-rayt] *v* **-rat·ed, -rat·ing.** improve. **mel·io·ra'tion** *n* **mel'io·rism** *n* doctrine that the world can be improved by human effort.

mel·lif·lu·ous [mə-LIF-loo-əs] *adj* (of sound, voice) smooth, sweet.

mel·low [MEL-oh] *adj* **-er, -est.** ripe; softened by age, experience; soft, not harsh; genial, gay. ▶ *v* make, become mellow.

mel·o·dra·ma [MEL-ə-dram-ə] *n* play full of sensational and startling situations, often highly emotional; overly dramatic behavior, emotion. **mel·o·dra·mat'ic** [-drə-MAT-ik] *adj*

mel·o·dy [MEL-ə-dee] *n, pl* **-dies.** series of musical notes that make tune; sweet sound. **me·lo·di·ous** [mə-LOH-dee-əs] *adj* pleasing to the ear; tuneful.

mel·on [MEL-ən] *n* large, fleshy, juicy fruit.

melt *v* **melt·ed** or **mol·ten, melt·ing.** (cause to) become liquid by heat; dissolve; soften; waste away; blend (into); disappear. **melting** *adj* softening; languishing; tender. **melt'down** *n* in nuclear reactor, melting of fuel rods, with possible release of radiation.

mem·ber [MEM-bər] *n* any of individuals making up body or society; limb; any part of complex whole.

mem·brane [MEM-brayn] *n* thin flexible tissue in plant or animal body.

me·men·to [mə-MEN-toh] *n, pl*
-tos *or* **-toes.** thing serving to
remind, souvenir.

mem·oir [MEM-wahr] *n*
autobiography, personal history,
biography; record of events.

mem·o·ry [MEM-ə-ree] *n, pl* **-ries.**
faculty of recollecting, recalling to
mind; recollection; thing
remembered; length of time one
can remember; commemoration;
part or faculty of computer that
stores information. **me·mo′ri·al** *adj*
of, preserving memory. ▶ *n* thing,
esp. a monument, that serves to
keep in memory. **mem′or·a·ble** *adj*
worthy of remembrance,
noteworthy. **mem·o·ran′dum** *n, pl*
-dums *or* **-da.** note to help the
memory, etc.; informal letter; note
of contract. **me·mo′ri·al·ize** *vt*
-ized, -iz·ing. commemorate.
mem′o·rize *vt* **-ized, -iz·ing.**
commit to memory.

men·ace [MEN-is] *n* threat. ▶ *vt*
-aced, -ac·ing. threaten, endanger.

mé·nage [may-NAHZH] *n* persons
of a household. **ménage à trois**
[ah TWAH] arrangement in which
three persons, e.g. two men and
one woman, share sexual relations
while occupying same household.

me·nag·er·ie [mə-NAJ-ə-ree] *n*
exhibition, collection of wild
animals.

mend *vt* repair, patch; reform,
correct, put right; of household
esp. in health. ▶ *vi* improve,
breakage, hole. **on the mend**
regaining health.

men·da·cious [men-DAY-shəs] *adj*
untruthful. **men·dac′i·ty**
[-DAS-i-tee] *n* (tendency to)
untruthfulness.

men·di·cant [MEN-di-kənt] *adj*
begging. ▶ *n* beggar.
men′di·can·cy *n* begging.

me·ni·al [MEE-nee-əl] *adj* of work
requiring little skill; of household
duties or servants; servile. ▶ *n*
servant; servile person.

men·in·gi·tis [men-in-JĪ-tis] *n*
inflammation of the membranes of

the brain.

me·nis·cus [mə-NIS-kəs] *n* curved
surface of liquid; curved lens.

men·o·pause [MEN-ə-pawz] *n* final
cessation of menstruation.

men·stru·a·tion
[men-stroo-AY-shən] *n*
approximately monthly discharge
of blood and cellular debris from
womb of nonpregnant woman.
men′stru·al *adj* **men′stru·ate** *vi*
-at·ed, -at·ing.

men·su·ra·tion
[men-shə-RAY-shən] *n* measuring,
esp. of areas.

men·tal [MEN-təl] *adj* of, done by
the mind; *inf* slightly mad.
men·tal′i·ty *n* state or quality of
mind.

men·thol [MEN-thawl] *n* organic
compound found in peppermint,
used medicinally.

men·tion [MEN-shən] *vt* refer to
briefly, speak of. ▶ *n*
acknowledgment; reference to or
remark about (person or thing).
men′tion·a·ble *adj* fit or suitable to
be mentioned.

men′tor *n* wise, trusted adviser,
guide, teacher.

men·u [MEN-yoo] *n* list of dishes to
be served, or from which to order;
Computers list of options available
to user.

mer·can·tile [MUR-kən-tīl] *adj* of,
engaged in trade, commerce.

mer·ce·nar·y [MUR-sə-ner-ee] *adj*
influenced by greed; working
merely for reward. ▶ *n* **-nar·ies.**
hired soldier.

mer·chant [MUR-chənt] *n* one
engaged in trade; storekeeper.
mer′chan·dise *n* merchant's wares.
mer′chant·man [-mən] *n* trading
ship. **merchant navy** ships
engaged in a nation's commerce.

mer·cu·ry [MUR-kyə-ree] *n* silvery
metal, liquid at ordinary
temperature, quicksilver; **(M-)**
Roman god of eloquence,
messenger of the gods, etc.; planet
nearest to sun. **mer·cu′ri·al**
[-KYOO-ree-əl] *adj* relating to,
containing mercury; lively,

changeable.

mer·cy [MUR-see] *n, pl* **-cies.** refraining from infliction of suffering by one who has right, power to inflict it, compassion. **mer'ci·ful** [-fəl] *adj* **mer'ci·less** [-lis] *adj*

mere [meer] *adj, sup* **mer·est.** only; not more than; nothing but. **mere'ly** *adv*

mer·e·tri·cious [mer-i-TRISH-əs] *adj* superficially or garishly attractive; insincere.

merge [murj] *v* **merged, merg·ing.** (cause to) lose identity or be absorbed. **mer'ger** *n* combination of business firms into one; absorption into something greater.

me·rid·i·an [mə-RID-ee-ən] *n* circle of Earth passing through poles; imaginary circle in sky passing through celestial poles; highest point reached by star, etc.; period of greatest splendor. ▶ *adj* of meridian; at peak of something.

me·ringue [mə-RANG] *n* baked mixture of white of eggs and sugar; cake of this.

mer·it *n* excellence, worth; quality of deserving reward. ▶ *pl* excellence. ▶ *vt* deserve. **mer·i·to'ri·ous** *adj* deserving praise.

mer·maid [MUR-mayd] *n* imaginary sea creature with upper part of woman and lower part of fish.

mer·ry [MER-ee] *adj* **-ri·er, -ri·est.** joyous, cheerful. **mer'ri·ly** *adv* **mer'ri·ment** *n*

mesh *n* (one of the open spaces of, or wires, etc. forming) network, net. ▶ *v* entangle, become entangled; (of gears) engage. ▶ *vi* coordinate (with).

mes·mer·ism [MEZ-mə-riz-əm] *n* former term for HYPNOTISM. **mes'mer·ize** *vt* **-ized, -iz·ing.** hypnotize; fascinate, hold spellbound.

me·son [MEE-zon] *n* elementary atomic particle.

mess *n* untidy confusion; trouble, difficulty; place where military personnel group regularly eat together. ▶ *vi* make mess; putter

(about); *Military* eat in a mess. **mess up** make dirty; botch; spoil. **mess'y** *adj* **mess·i·er, mess·i·est.**

mes·sage [MES-ij] *n* communication sent; meaning, moral. **mes'sen·ger** *n* bearer of message.

Mes·si·ah [mi-SĪ-ə] *n* Jews' promised deliverer; Christ. **mes·si·an'ic** [mes-ee-AN-ik] *adj*

Messrs [MES-ərz] pl. of MR.

met pt./pp. of MEET.

meta- *comb. form* change, e.g. *metamorphose; metathesis.*

me·tab·o·lism [mə-TAB-ə-liz-əm] *n* chemical process of living body. **met·a·bol'ic** *adj* **me·tab'o·lize** *vt* **-lized, -liz·ing.**

met·al [MET-l] *n* mineral substance, opaque, fusible and malleable, capable of conducting heat and electricity; object made of metal. **me·tal'lic** *adj* **met'al·lur·gist** *n* **met'al·lur·gy** *n* scientific study of extracting, refining metals, and their structure and properties.

met·a·mor·pho·sis [met-ə-MOR-fə-sis] *n, pl* **-ses.** change of shape, character, etc. **met·a·mor'phic** *adj* (esp. of rocks) changed in texture, structure by heat, pressure, etc. **met·a·mor'phose** [-fohz] *vt* **-phosed, -phos·ing.** transform.

met·a·phor [MET-ə-for] *n* figure of speech in which term is transferred to something it does not literally apply to; instance of this. **met·a·phor'i·cal** *adj* figurative.

met·a·phys·ics [met-ə-FIZ-iks] *n* branch of philosophy concerned with being and knowing.

me·tath·e·sis [mə-TATH-ə-sis] *n, pl* **-ses** [-seez] transposition, esp. of letters in word, e.g. Old English *bridd* gives modern *bird.*

mete [meet] *vt* **met·ed, met·ing.** measure. **mete out** distribute; allot as punishment.

me·te·or [MEE-tee-ər] *n* small, fast-moving celestial body, visible as streak of incandescence if it enters Earth's atmosphere. **me·te·or'ic** *adj* of, like meteor;

brilliant but short-lived.

me′te·or·ite *n* fallen meteor.

me·te·or·ol·o·gy
[mee-tee-ə-ROL-ə-jee] *n* study of Earth's atmosphere, esp. for weather forecasting.

me·ter[1] [MEE-tər] *n* unit of length in decimal system; SI unit of length; rhythm of poem. **met′ric** *adj* of system of weights and measures in which meter is a unit. **met′ri·cal** *adj* of measurement of poetic meter.

meter[2] *n* that which measures; instrument for recording consumption of gas, electricity, etc.

meth·ane [METH-ayn] *n* inflammable gas, compound of carbon and hydrogen.

meth·od [METH-əd] *n* way, manner; technique; orderliness, system. **me·thod′i·cal** *adj* orderly. **meth·od·ol·o·gy** *n, pl* **-gies.** particular method or procedure.

Meth·od·ist [METH-ə-dist] *n* member of any of the churches originated by Wesley and his followers. ▶ *adj* **Meth′od·ism** *n*

me·tic·u·lous [mə-TIK-yə-ləs] *adj* (over)particular about details.

mé·tier [MAY-tyay] *n* profession, vocation; one's forte.

me·ton·y·my [mi-TON-ə-mee] *n* figure of speech in which thing is replaced by another associated with it, e.g. *the Oval Office* for *the president*.

met·ro·nome [ME-trə-nohm] *n* instrument that marks musical time by means of ticking pendulum.

me·trop·o·lis [mi-TROP-ə-lis] *n, pl* **-lis·es.** chief city of a country, region. **met·ro·pol′i·tan** *adj* of metropolis. ▶ *n* bishop with authority over other bishops of an ecclesiastical province.

met·tle [MET-l] *n* courage, spirit. **met′tle·some** [-səm] *adj* high-spirited.

mew [myoo] *n* cry of cat. ▶ *vi* utter this cry.

mez·za·nine [MEZ-ə-neen] *n* in a theater, lowest balcony or forward part of balcony; in a building, low

story between two other stories, esp. between first and second stories.

mez·zo·so·pran·o
[MET-soh-sə-PRAN-oh] *n, pl* **-pran·os.** voice, singer between soprano and contralto.

Mg *Chem* magnesium.

mi [mee] *n* third sol-fa note.

mi·as·ma [mī-AZ-mə] *n, pl* **-mas.** unwholesome or foreboding atmosphere.

mi·ca [MĪ-kə] *n* mineral found as glittering scales, plates.

mi·crobe [MĪ-krohb] *n* minute organism; disease germ. **mi·cro′bi·al** *adj*

mi·cro·chip [MĪ-kroh-chip] *n* small wafer of silicon, etc. containing electronic circuits, chip.

mi·cro·com·put·er
[MĪ-kroh-kəm-pyoo-tər] *n* computer having a central processing unit contained in one or more silicon chips.

mi·cro·cosm [MĪ-krə-koz-əm] *n* miniature representation, model, etc. of some larger system; human beings, society as epitome of universe.

mi·cro·fi·ber [MĪ-krə-fī-bər] *n* very fine synthetic yarn.

mi·cro·fiche [MĪ-krə-feesh] *n* microfilm in sheet form.

mi·cro·film [MĪ-krə-film] *n* miniaturized recording of manuscript, book on roll of film.

mi·crom·e·ter [mī-KROM-i-tər] *n* instrument for measuring very small distances or angles.

mi·cron [MĪ-kron] *n* unit of length, one millionth of a meter.

mi·cro·or·gan·ism
[mī-kroh-OR-gə-niz-əm] *n* organism of microscopic size.

mi·cro·phone [MĪ-krə-fohn] *n* instrument for amplifying, transmitting sounds.

mi·cro·proc·es·sor
[MĪ-kroh-pros-es-ər] *n* integrated circuit acting as central processing unit in small computer.

mi·cro·scope [MĪ-krə-skohp] *n* instrument by which very small body is magnified and made visible. **mi·cro·scop'ic** [-SKOP-ik] *adj* of microscope; very small. **mi·cros'co·py** [-KROS-kə-pee] *n* use of microscope.

mi·cro·wave [MĪ-kroh-wayv] *n* electromagnetic wave with wavelength of a few centimeters, used in radar, cooking, etc.; microwave oven.

mid *adj* intermediate, in the middle of. **mid'day** *n* noon. **mid'night** *n* twelve o'clock at night. **mid'ship·man** [-mən] *n* student, e.g. at US Naval Academy, training for commission as naval officer. **mid'sum'mer** *n* middle of summer; summer solstice. **mid'way** *adj, adv* halfway. **mid'win'ter** *n*

mid·dle [MID-l] *adj* equidistant from two extremes; medium, intermediate. ▶ *n* middle point or part. **mid'dling** *adj* mediocre; moderate. ▶ *adv* **Middle Ages** period from about 1000 AD to the 15th century. **middle class** social class of business, professional people, etc.; middle economic class. **mid'dle-class** *adj* **mid'dle·man** *n* business person between producer and consumer.

midge [mij] *n* gnat or similar insect. **midg·et** [MIJ-it] *n* very small person or thing.

mid'riff *n* middle part of body.

midst *prep* in the middle of. ▶ *n* middle. **in the midst of** surrounded by, among.

mid·wife [MID-wīf] *n* trained person who assists at childbirth. **mid·wife'ry** [-WĪF-ə-ree] *n* art, practice of this.

mien [meen] *n* person's bearing, demeanor or appearance.

might[1] [mīt] see MAY.

might[2] *n* power, strength. **might'i·ly** *adv* strongly; powerfully. **might'y** *adj* **might·i·er, might·i·est.** of great power; strong; valiant; important. ▶ *adv inf* very.

mi·graine [MĪ-grayn] *n* severe headache, oft. with nausea and other symptoms.

mi·grate [MĪ-grayt] *vi* **-grat·ed,**

-grat·ing. move from one place to another. **mi'grant** [-grənt] *n, adj* **mi·gra'tion** *n* act of passing from one place, condition to another; number migrating together. **mi'gra·to·ry** [-grə-TOR-ee] *adj* of, capable of migration; (of animals) changing from one place to another according to season.

mild [mīld] *adj* **-er, -est.** not strongly flavored; gentle, merciful; calm or temperate. **mild'ly** *adv* **mild'ness** *n*

mil·dew [MIL-doo] *n* destructive fungus on plants or things exposed to damp. ▶ *v* become tainted, affect with mildew.

mile [mīl] *n* measure of length, 1760 yards (1.609 km). **mile'age** *n* distance in miles; traveling expenses per mile; miles traveled (per gallon of gasoline). **mile'stone** *n* stone marker showing distance; significant event, achievement.

mi·lieu [mil-YUU] *n* environment, condition in life.

mil·i·tar·y [MIL-i-ter-ee] *adj* of, for, soldiers, armies or war. ▶ *n* armed services. **mil'i·tan·cy** [-tən-see] *n* **mil'i·tant** *adj* aggressive, vigorous in support of cause; prepared; willing to fight. **mil'i·ta·rism** [-tə-riz-əm] *n* enthusiasm for military force and methods. **mil'i·ta·rize** *vt* **-rized, -riz·ing.** convert to military use. **mi·li'tia** [-LISH-ə] *n* military force of citizens serving full time only in emergencies.

mil·i·tate [MIL-i-tayt] *vi* **-tat·ed, -tat·ing.** (esp. with *against*) have strong influence, effect on.

milk *n* white fluid with which mammals feed their young; fluid in some plants. ▶ *vt* draw milk from. **milk'y** *adj* **milk·i·er, milk·i·est.** containing, like milk; (of liquids) opaque, clouded. **milk'sop** *n* weak, effeminate fellow; milquetoast. **milk teeth** first set of teeth in young mammals. **Milky Way** luminous band of stars, etc. stretching across sky, the galaxy.

mill *n* factory; machine for grinding, pulverizing grain, paper, etc. ▸ *vt* put through mill; cut fine grooves across edges of (e.g. coins). ▸ *vi* move in confused manner, as cattle or crowds of people. **mill′er** *n* **mill′stone** *n* flat circular stone for grinding; heavy emotional or mental burden.

mil·len·ni·um [mi-LEN-ee-əm] *n, pl* **-ni·a** [-nee-ə] period of a thousand years during which some claim Christ is to reign on earth; period of a thousand years; period of peace, happiness. **millennium bug** *n Computers* software problem arising from the change in date at the start of the 21st century.

mil·let [MIL-it] *n* a cereal grass.

milli- *comb. form* thousandth, e.g. *milligram;* thousandth part of a gram.

mil·li·bar [MIL-ə-bahr] *n* unit of atmospheric pressure.

mil·li·ner [MIL-ə-nər] *n* maker of, dealer in women's hats, ribbons, etc. **mil′li·ner·y** *n* milliner's goods or work.

mil·lion [MIL-yən] *n* 1000 thousands. **mil·lion·aire′** *n* owner of a million dollars, etc. or more; very rich person. **mil′lionth** *adj, n*

mil·li·pede [MIL-ə-peed] *n* small arthropod, like centipede, with jointed body and many pairs of legs.

milque·toast [MILK-tohst] *n* ineffectual person esp. one easily dominated.

milt *n* spawn of male fish.

mime [mīm] *n* acting without the use of words; actor who does this. ▸ *v* **mimed, mim·ing.** act in mime.

mim·ic [MIM-ik] *vt* **-icked, -ick·ing.** imitate (person, manner, etc.) esp. for satirical effect. ▸ *n* one who, or animal that does this, or is adept at it. ▸ *adj* **mim′ic·ry** *n, pl* **-ries.** mimicking.

min·a·ret [min-ə-RET] *n* tall slender tower of mosque.

mince [mins] *v* **minced, minc·ing.** ▸ *vt* cut, chop very small; soften or moderate (words, etc.). ▸ *vi* walk, speak in affected manner. ▸ *n* something minced; mincemeat. **minc′ing** *adj* affected in manner. **mince′meat** *n* mixture of minced apples, currants, spices, sometimes meat, etc. **mince pie** pie containing mincemeat or mince.

mind [mīnd] *n* thinking faculties as distinguished from the body, intellectual faculties; memory, attention; intention; taste; sanity. ▸ *vt* take offense at; care for; attend to; be cautious, careful about (something); be concerned, troubled about. ▸ *vi* be careful; heed. **mind′ful** [fəl] *adj* heedful; keeping in memory. **mind′less** [-lis] *adj* stupid, careless.

mine¹ [mīn] *pron* belonging to me.

mine² *n* deep hole for digging out coal, metals, etc.; in war, hidden deposit of explosive to blow up ship, etc.; land mine; profitable source. ▸ *v* **mined, min·ing.** ▸ *vt* dig from mine; make mine in or under; place explosive mines in, on. ▸ *vi* make, work in mine. **mi′ner** *n* one who works in a mine. **mine′field** *n* area of land or sea containing mines. **mine′lay·er** *n* ship for laying mines. **mine′sweep·er** *n* ship, helicopter for clearing away mines.

min·er·al [MIN-ər-əl] *n* naturally occurring inorganic substance, esp. as obtained by mining. ▸ *adj* of, containing, or like minerals. **min·er·al′o·gy** *n* science of minerals. **mineral water** water containing some mineral, esp. natural or artificial kinds for drinking.

min·e·stro·ne [min-ə-STROH-nee] *n* type of vegetable soup containing pasta.

min·gle [MING-gəl] *v* **-gled, -gling.** mix, blend, unite, merge.

min·i [MIN-ee] *n* something small or miniature; short skirt; small computer. ▸ *adj*

min·i·a·ture [MIN-ee-ə-chər] *n* small painted portrait; anything on small scale. ▸ *adj* small-scale, minute.

min·i·bus [MIN-ee-bus] *n* small bus for about fifteen passengers.

min·im [MIN-əm] *n* unit of fluid measure, one-sixtieth of a dram; *Mus* note half the length of semibreve.

min·i·mize [MIN-ə-mīz] *vt* **-mized, -miz·ing.** bring to, estimate at smallest possible amount.

min'i·mal [-məl] *adj* **min'i·mum** [-məm] *n, pl* **-mums.** lowest size or quantity. ▶ *adj* least possible.

min·ion [MIN-yən] *n* favorite; servile follower.

min·is·ter [MIN-ə-stər] *n* person in charge of government department; diplomatic representative; clergyman. ▶ *vi* attend to needs of, take care of. **min·is·te'ri·al** [-STEER-ee-əl] *adj* **min·is·tra'tion** *n* rendering help, esp. to sick. **min'is·try** *n, pl* **-tries.** office of clergyman; body of ministers forming government; act of ministering. **minister without portfolio** minister of state not in charge of specific department.

mink [mingk] *n* variety of weasel; its (brown) fur.

min·now [MIN-oh] *n* small freshwater fish.

mi·nor [MĪ-nər] *adj* lesser; under age. ▶ *n* person below age of legal majority; scale in music. **mi·nor·i·ty** [mi-NOR-i-tee] *n* lesser number; smaller party voting together; ethical or religious group in a minority in any country; state of being a minor.

Min·o·taur [MIN-ə-tor] *n* fabled monster, half bull, half man.

min·strel [MIN-strəl] *n* medieval singer, musician, poet. ▶ *pl* performers in minstrel show. **minstrel show** formerly, an entertainment of songs and jokes provided by white performers with blackened faces.

mint¹ *n* place where money is coined. ▶ *vt* coin, invent.

mint² *n* aromatic plant.

min·u·et [min-yoo-ET] *n* stately dance; music for it.

mi·nus [MĪ-nəs] *prep, adj* less, with the deduction of, deprived of; lacking; negative. ▶ *n* the sign (-) denoting subtraction.

mi·nus·cule [MIN-iss-skyool] *adj* very small.

mi·nute¹ [mī-NOOT] *adj* **-nut·er, -nut·est.** very small; precise. **mi·nute'ly** *adv* **mi·nu·ti·ae** [mi-NOO-shee-ee] *pl n* trifles, precise details.

min·ute² [MIN-it] *n* 60th part of hour or degree; moment; memorandum. ▶ *pl* record of proceedings of meeting, etc.

minx [mingks] *n* bold, flirtatious girl.

mir·a·cle [MIR-ə-kəl] *n* supernatural event; marvel. **mi·rac'u·lous** *adj* **miracle play** drama (esp. medieval) based on sacred subject.

mi·rage [mi-RAH*ZH*] *n* deceptive image in atmosphere, e.g. of lake in desert.

mire [mīr] *n* swampy ground, mud. ▶ *vt* **mired, mir·ing.** stick in, dirty with mud; entangle, involve.

mir·ror [MIR-ər] *n* glass or polished surface reflecting images. ▶ *vt* reflect.

mirth [murth] *n* merriment, gaiety. **mirth'ful** *adj*

MIS management information system(s).

mis- *prefix* wrong(ly), bad(ly).

mis·an·thrope [MIS-ən-throhp] *n* hater of mankind. **mis·an·throp'ic** *adj*

mis·ap·pro·pri·ate [mis-ə-PROH-pree-ayt] *vt* **-at·ed, -at·ing.** put to dishonest use; embezzle.

mis·be·have' *v* behave badly. **mis·be·hav'iour** *n*

mis·cal'cu·late *vt* calculate or judge wrongly. **mis·cal·cu·la'tion** *n*

mis·car·ry [mis-KA-ree] *vi* **-ried, -ry·ing.** bring forth young prematurely; go wrong, fail. **mis·car'riage** [-KA-rij] *n*

mis·cast' *v* **-cast, -cast·ing.** distribute acting parts wrongly; assign to unsuitable role.

mis·cel·la·ne·ous [mis-ə-LAY-nee-əs] *adj* mixed, assorted. **mis'cel·la·ny** *n, pl* **-nies.**

collection of assorted writings in one book; medley.

mis·chief [MIS-chif] n annoying behavior; inclination to tease, disturb; harm; source of harm or annoyance. **mis'chie·vous** [-chi-vəs] adj of a child, full of pranks; disposed to mischief; having harmful effect.

mis·ci·ble [MIS-ə-bəl] adj capable of mixing.

mis·con·cep·tion [mis-kən-SEP-shən] n wrong idea, belief.

mis·con'duct n immoral or unethical behaviour.

mis·cre·ant [MIS-kree-ənt] n wicked person, evildoer, villain.

mis'deed n wrongful act.

mis·de·mean·or [mis-di-MEE-nər] n in law, offense less grave than a felony; minor offense.

mi·ser [MĪ-zər] n hoarder of money; stingy person. **mi'ser·ly** adj avaricious; niggardly.

mis·er·a·ble [MIZ-ər-ə-bəl] adj very unhappy, wretched; causing misery; worthless; squalid. **mis·er·y** n, pl **-er·ies.** great unhappiness; distress; poverty.

mis'fit n esp. person not suited to surroundings or work.

mis·for'tune n (piece of) bad luck.

mis·giv'ing n (oft pl) feeling of fear, doubt, etc.

mis·guid·ed [mis-GĪ-did] adj foolish, unreasonable.

mis'hap n minor accident.

mis·in·form' vt give incorrect information to. **mis·in·for·ma'tion** n

mis·judge' v judge wrongly or unfairly. **mis·judg'ment** n

mis·lay' vt **-laid, -lay·ing.** put in place that cannot later be remembered; place wrongly.

mis·lead [mis-LEED] vt **-led, -lead·ing.** give false information to; lead astray. **misleading** adj deceptive.

mis·man'age vt organize or run (something) badly. **mis·man'age·ment** n

mis·no·mer [mis-NOH-mər] n wrong name or term; use of this.

mi·sog·y·ny [mi-SOJ-ə-nee] n hatred of women. **mi·sog'y·nist** n

mis·place' vt mislay; put in the wrong place; give (trust or affection) inappropriately.

mis'print n printing error. ▶ vt

mis·pro·nounce' v pronounce (a word) wrongly. **mis·pro·nun·ci·a'tion** n

miss vt fail to hit, reach, find, catch, or notice; be late for; omit; notice or regret absence of; avoid. ▶ vi (of engine) misfire. ▶ n fact, instance of missing. **miss'ing** adj lost; absent.

mis·sal [MIS-əl] n book containing prayers, etc. of the Mass.

mis·shap·en [mis-SHAY-pən] adj badly shaped, deformed.

mis·sile [MIS-əl] n that which may be thrown, shot, homed to damage, destroy. **guided missile** see also GUIDE.

mis·sion [MISH-ən] n specific task or duty; calling in life; delegation; sending or being sent on some service; those sent. **mis'sion·ar·y** n, pl **-ar·ies.** one sent to a place, society to spread religion. ▶ adj

mis·sive [MIS-iv] n letter.

mis·spell' v spell (a word) wrongly.

mis·spent' adj wasted or misused.

mist n water vapor in fine drops. **mist'y** adj **mist·i·er, mist·i·est.** full of mist; dim; obscure.

mis·take [mi-STAYK] n error, blunder. ▶ v **-took** [-TUUK], **-tak·en, -tak·ing.** ▶ vt fail to understand; form wrong opinion about; take (person or thing) for another. ▶ vi be in error.

mis·ter [MIS-tər] n the full form of MR.

mis·tle·toe [MIS-əl-toh] n evergreen parasitic plant with white berries that grows on trees.

mis·tress [MIS-tris] n object of man's illicit love; woman with mastery or control; woman owner; woman teacher; obs title given to married woman.

mis·un·der·stand' v fail to understand properly. **mis·un·der·stand'ing** n

mis·use' n incorrect, improper, or careless use. ▶ vt use wrongly; treat badly.

mite [mīt] n very small insect; anything very small; small contribution but all one can afford.

mi·ter [MĪ-tər] n bishop's headdress; joint between two pieces of wood, etc. meeting at right angles. ▶ vt join with, shape for a miter joint; put miter on.

mit·i·gate [MIT-i-gayt] vt **-gat·ed, -gat·ing.** make less severe. **mit·i·ga'tion** n

mitt n baseball player's glove esp. for catcher, first baseman; sl hand.

mit·ten [MIT-n] n glove with two compartments, one for thumb and one for fingers.

mix [miks] vt put together, combine, blend, mingle. ▶ vi be mixed; associate. **mixed** adj composed of different elements, races, sexes, etc. **mix'er** n one who, that which mixes; informal party intended to help guests meet one another. **mix'ture** [-chər] n **mixed-up** adj confused; emotionally unstable. **mix-up** n confused situation; a fight.

mks units metric system of units based on the meter, kilogram and second.

Mn Chem manganese.

mne·mon·ic [ni-MON-ik] adj helping the memory. ▶ n something intended to help the memory.

Mo Chem molybdenum.

moan [mohn] n low murmur, usually of pain. ▶ v utter with moan, lament.

moat [moht] n deep wide ditch esp. around castle. ▶ vt surround with moat.

mob n disorderly crowd of people; mixed assembly. ▶ vt **mobbed, mob·bing.** attack in mob; crowd around boisterously.

mo·bile [MOH-bəl] adj capable of movement; easily moved or changed. ▶ n [moh-BEEL] hanging structure of card, plastic, etc. designed to move in air currents.

mo·bil'i·ty n **mobile home** large trailer, connected to utilities at a trailer park, etc., used as a residence. **mobile phone** portable phone powered by batteries.

mo·bi·lize [MOH-bə-līz] v **-lized, -liz·ing.** (of armed services) prepare for military service. ▶ vt organize for a purpose. **mo·bi·li·za'tion** [-ZAY-shən] n in war time, calling up of men and women for active service.

moc·ca·sin [MOK-ə-sin] n Amer. Indian soft shoe, usu. of deerskin.

mo·cha [MOH-kə] n type of strong, dark coffee; this flavor.

mock [mok] vt make fun of, ridicule; mimic. ▶ vi scoff. ▶ n act of mocking; laughingstock. ▶ adj sham, imitation. **mock'er·y** n, pl **-er·ies.** derision; travesty. **mocking bird** N Amer. bird that imitates songs of others. **mock-up** n scale model.

mode [mohd] n method, manner; prevailing fashion.

mod·el [MOD-l] n miniature representation; pattern; person or thing worthy of imitation; person employed by artist to pose, or by dress designer to display clothing. ▶ vt **-eled, -el·ing.** make model of; mold; display (clothing) for dress designer.

mo·dem [MOH-dem] n device for connecting two computers via a telephone line.

mod·er·ate [MOD-ər-it] adj not going to extremes, temperate, medium. ▶ n person of moderate views. ▶ v [-ayt] make, become less violent or excessive; preside over meeting, etc. **mod'er·a·tor** n mediator; president of Presbyterian body; arbitrator; person presiding over panel discussion.

mod·ern [MOD-ərn] adj of present or recent times; in, of current fashion. ▶ n person living in modern times. **mod'ern·ism** n (support of) modern tendencies, thoughts, etc. **mod·ern·i·za'tion** [-ZAY-shən] n **mod'ern·ize** [-īz] vt **-ized, -iz·ing.** bring up to date.

mod·est [MOD-ist] *adj* not overrating one's qualities or achievements; shy; moderate, not excessive; decorous, decent. **mod'es·ty** *n*

mod·i·cum [MOD-i-kəm] *n* small quantity.

mod·i·fy [MOD-ə-fī] *v* (mainly tr) **-fied, -fy·ing.** change slightly; tone down. **mod·i·fi·ca'tion** *n* **mod'i·fi·er** [-fī-ər] *n* esp. word qualifying another.

mod·u·late [MOJ-ə-layt] *v* **-lat·ed, -lat·ing.** *vt* regulate; vary in tone. ▶ *vi* change key of music. **mod·u·la'tion** *n* modulating; *Electronics* superimposing signals onto high-frequency carrier.

mod·ule [MOJ-ool] *n* (detachable) unit, section, component with specific function.

mo·dus op·e·ran·di [MOH-dəs op-ə-RAN-dee] *Lat* method of operating, tackling task.

mo·gul [MOH-gəl] *n* important or powerful person; bump in ski slope.

mo·hair [MOH-hair] *n* fine cloth of goat hair; hair of Angora goat.

mo·hel [MOH-əl] *n* in Jewish tradition, person who performs rite of circumcision.

moi·e·ty [MOI-i-tee] *n, pl* **-ties.** a half.

moist *adj* **-er, -est.** damp, slightly wet. **moist'en** [MOI-sən] *v* **mois'ture** [-chər] *n* liquid, esp. diffused or in drops.

mo·lar [MOH-lər] *adj* (of teeth) for grinding. ▶ *n* molar tooth.

mo·las·ses [mə-LAS-iz] *n* thick brown syrup, byproduct of process of sugar refining.

mold¹ [mohld] *n* hollow object in which metal, etc. is cast; pattern for shaping; character; shape, form. ▶ *vt* shape or pattern. **mold'ing** *n* molded object; ornamental edging; decoration.

mold² *n* fungoid growth caused by dampness. **mold'y** *adj* **mold·i·er, mold·i·est.** stale, musty.

mold³ *n* loose soil rich in organic matter. **mold'er** *vi* decay or cause to decay into dust.

mole¹ [mohl] *n* small dark protuberant spot on the skin.

mole² *n* small burrowing animal; spy, informer.

mole³ *n* SI unit of amount of substance.

mol·e·cule [MOL-ə-kyool] *n* simplest freely existing chemical unit, composed of two or more atoms; very small particle. **mo·lec'u·lar** *adj* of, inherent in molecules.

mo·lest [mə-LEST] *vt* pester, interfere with so as to annoy or injure; make indecent sexual advances esp. to a child.

mol·li·fy [MOL-ə-fī] *vt* **-fied, -fy·ing.** calm down, placate, soften. **mol·li·fi·ca'tion** *n*

mol·lusk [MOL-əsk] *n* soft-bodied, usu. hard-shelled animal, e.g. snail, oyster.

molt [mohlt] *v* cast or shed fur, feathers, etc. ▶ *n* molting.

molten see MELT.

mo·lyb·de·num [mə-LIB-də-nəm] *n* silver-white metallic element.

mo·ment [MOH-mənt] *n* very short space of time; (present) point in time. **mo·men·tar'i·ly** *adv* **mo'men·tar·y** *adj* lasting only a moment.

mo·men·tous [moh-MEN-təs] *adj* of great importance.

mo·men·tum [moh-MEN-təm] *n* force of a moving body; impetus gained from motion.

mon·arch [MON-ərk] *n* sovereign ruler of a country. **mo·nar'chi·cal** *adj* **mon'ar·chist** *n* supporter of monarchy. **mon'ar·chy** *n, pl* **-chies.** nation ruled by sovereign; monarch's rule.

mon·as·ter·y [MON-ə-ster-ee] *n, pl* **-ter·ies.** house occupied by members of religious order. **mo·nas·tic** [mə-NAS-tik] *adj* relating to monks, nuns, or monasteries. ▶ *n* monk, recluse.

mon·ey [MUN-ee] *n, pl* **-eys** or **-ies.** banknotes, coin, etc., used as medium of exchange.

mon·e·ta·rism [MON-ə-tə-riz-əm] *n* theory that inflation is caused by

increase in money supply.
mon·e·ta·rist n, adj **mon·e·tar·y** adj **mon·eyed, -ied** [MUN-eed] adj rich.

mon·gol·ism [MONG-gə-liz-əm] n a former and non-medical name for DOWN SYNDROME.

mon·goose [MON-goos] n, pl **-goos·es.** small animal of Asia and Africa noted for killing snakes.

mon·grel [MONG-grəl] n animal, esp. dog, of mixed breed; hybrid. ▶ adj

mon·i·tor [MON-i-tər] n person or device that checks, controls, warns or keeps record of something; pupil assisting teacher with conduct of class; television set used in a studio for checking program being transmitted; *Computers* cathode ray tube with screen for viewing data; type of large lizard. ▶ vt watch, check on. **mon'i·to·ry** [-tor-ee] adj giving warning.

monk [munk] n one of a religious community of men living apart under vows. **monk'ish** adj

mon·key [MUN-kee] n, pl **-keys.** long-tailed primate; mischievous child. ▶ vi **-keyed, -key·ing.** meddle, fool (with). **monkey wrench** one with adjustable jaw.

mono- comb. form single, e.g. monosyllabic.

mon·o·chrome [MON-ə-krohm] n representation in one color. ▶ adj of one color. **mon·o·chro·mat'ic** adj

mon·o·cle [MON-ə-kəl] n single eyeglass.

mo·noc·u·lar [mə-NOK-yə-lər] adj one-eyed.

mo·nog·a·my [mə-NOG-ə-mee] n custom of being married to one person at a time. **mo·nog'a·mous** adj

mon·o·gram [MON-ə-gram] n design of one or more letters interwoven.

mon·o·graph [MON-ə-graf] n short scholarly book on single subject.

mon·o·lith [MON-ə-lith] n monument consisting of single standing stone. **mon·o·lith'ic** adj of or like a monolith; massive,

inflexible.

mon·o·logue [MON-ə-lawg] n dramatic composition with only one speaker; long speech by one person.

mon·o·ma·ni·a [mon-ə-MAY-nee-ə] n excessive preoccupation with one thing.

mo·nop·o·ly [mə-NOP-ə-lee] n, pl **-lies.** exclusive control of commerce, privilege, etc. **mo·nop'o·lize** vt **-lized, -liz·ing.** claim, take exclusive possession of.

mon·o·rail [MON-ə-rayl] n railway with cars running on or suspended from single rail.

mon·o·the·ism [MON-ə-thee-iz-əm] n belief in only one God.

mon·o·tone [MON-ə-tohn] n continuing on one note. **mo·not·o·nous** [mə-NOT-n-əs] adj lacking in variety, dull, wearisome. **mo·not'o·ny** n

mon·soon' n seasonal wind of SE Asia; very heavy rainfall season.

mon·ster [MON-stər] n fantastic imaginary beast; misshapen animal or plant; very wicked person; huge person, animal or thing. ▶ adj huge. **mon·stros'i·ty** n monstrous being; deformity; distortion. **mon'strous** [-strəs] adj of, like monster; unnatural; enormous; horrible.

mon·tage [mon-TAHZH] n elements of two or more pictures imposed upon a single background to give a unified effect; method of editing a film.

month [munth] n one of twelve periods into which the year is divided; period of moon's revolution around Earth. **month'ly** adj happening or payable once a month. ▶ adv once a month. ▶ n magazine published every month.

mon·u·ment [MON-yə-mənt] n anything that commemorates, esp. a building or statue. **mon·u·ment'al** [-MEN-tl] adj vast, lasting; of or serving as monument.

mooch vi sl borrow without intending to repay; beg.

mood[1] *n* state of mind and feelings. **mood'y** *adj* **mood·i·er, mood·i·est.** gloomy, pensive; changeable in mood.

mood[2] *n Grammar* form indicating function of verb.

moon *n* satellite that takes lunar month to revolve around Earth; any secondary planet. ▶ *vi* go about dreamily. **moon'light** *n* **moon'shine** *n inf* whiskey, esp. corn liquor, illicitly distilled; nonsense; moonlight. **moon'stone** *n* transparent semiprecious stone.

moor[1] *n* tract of open uncultivated land, often hilly and overgrown with heath.

moor[2] *v* secure (ship) with chains or ropes. **moor'ings** *pl n* ropes, etc. for mooring; something providing stability, security.

moose [moos] *n* N Amer. deer with large antlers.

moot *adj* that is open to argument, debatable; purely academic.

mop *n* bundle of yarn, cloth, etc. on end of stick, used for cleaning; tangle (of hair, etc.). ▶ *vt* **mopped, mop·ping.** clean, wipe with mop or other absorbent material.

mope [mohp] *vi* **moped, mop·ing.** be gloomy, apathetic.

mo·ped [MOH-ped] *n* light motorized bicycle.

mo·raine [mə-RAYN] *n* accumulated mass of debris, earth, stones, etc., deposited by glacier.

mor·al [MOR-əl] *adj* pert. to right and wrong conduct; of good conduct. ▶ *n* practical lesson, e.g. of fable. ▶ *pl* habits with respect to right and wrong, esp. in matters of sex. **mor'al·ist** *n* teacher of morality. **mo·ral·i·ty** [mə-RAL-ə-tee] *n* good moral conduct; moral goodness or badness; kind of medieval drama, containing moral lesson. **mor'al·ize** *v* **-ized, -iz·ing.** ▶ *vi* write, think about moral aspect of things. ▶ *vt* interpret morally. **moral victory** triumph that is psychological rather than practical.

mo·rale [mə-RAL] *n* degree of confidence, hope of person or group.

mo·rass [mə-RAS] *n* marsh; mess.

mor·a·to·ri·um [mor-ə-TOR-ee-əm] *n, pl* **-ri·ums.** act authorizing postponement of payments, etc.; delay.

mor'bid *adj* unduly interested in death; gruesome; diseased.

mor·dant [MOR-dnt] *adj* biting; corrosive; scathing. ▶ *n* substance that fixes dyes.

more [mor] *adj* greater in quantity or number; comp. of MANY or MUCH. ▶ *adv* to a greater extent; in addition. ▶ *pron* greater or additional amount or number. **more·o'ver** *adv* besides, further.

mor·ga·nat·ic marriage [mor-gə-NAT-ik] marriage of king or prince in which wife does not share husband's rank or possessions and children do not inherit from father.

morgue [morg] *n* mortuary; newspaper reference file or file room.

mor·i·bund [MOR-ə-bund] *adj* dying; stagnant.

Mor·mon [MOR-mən] *n* member of religious sect founded in US.

morn'ing *n* early part of day until noon. **morning-after pill** woman's contraceptive pill for use within hours after sexual intercourse. **morning glory** plant with trumpet-shaped flowers that close in late afternoon.

mo·roc·co [mə-ROK-oh] *n* goatskin leather.

mo·ron [MOR-on] *n* (formerly) person with low intelligence quotient; *inf* fool. **mo·ron'ic** *adj*

mo·rose [mə-ROHS] *adj* sullen, moody.

morph [morf] *v* cause or undergo change of shape or appearance via computer graphic effects.

mor·phine [MOR-feen] *n* narcotic extract of opium used to induce sleep and relieve pain.

mor·phol·o·gy [mor-FOL-ə-jee] *n* science of structure of organisms; form and structure of words of a language.

Morse [mors] *n* system of telegraphic signaling in which letters of alphabet are represented by combinations of dots and dashes, or short and long flashes.

mor·sel [MOR-səl] *n* fragment, small piece.

mor·tal [MOR-tl] *adj* subject to death; causing death. ▶ *n* mortal creature. **mor·tal'i·ty** *n* state of being mortal; great loss of life; death rate. **mor'tal·ly** *adv* fatally; deeply, intensely.

mor·tar [MOR-tər] *n* mixture of lime, sand and water for holding bricks and stones together; small cannon firing over short range; vessel in which substances are pounded. **mor'tar·board** [-bord] *n* square academic cap.

mort·gage [MOR-gij] *n* conveyance of property as security for debt with provision that property be reconveyed on payment within agreed time. ▶ *vt* **-gaged, -gag·ing.** convey by mortgage; pledge as security. **mort·ga·gee'** *n* person to whom property is mortgaged. **mort'ga·gor, -ger** *n* person who mortgages property.

mor·ti·fy [MOR-tə-fī] *v* **-fied, -fy·ing.** humiliate; subdue by self-denial; (of flesh) be affected with gangrene. **mor·ti·fi·ca'tion** [-fi-KAY-shən] *n*

mor·tise [MOR-tis] *n* hole in piece of wood, etc. to receive the tongue (tenon) and end of another piece. ▶ *vt* **-tised, -tis·ing.** make mortise in; fasten by mortise and tenon.

mor·tu·ar·y [MOR-choo-er-ee] *n, pl* **-ar·ies.** funeral parlor. ▶ *adj* of, for burial; pert. to death.

mo·sa·ic [moh-ZAY-ik] *n* picture or pattern of small bits of colored stone, glass, etc.; this process of decoration.

Mo·sa·ic [moh-ZAY-ik] *adj* of Moses.

mosh *vi* dance violently and frantically with others in group at rock concert. ▶ *n*

Moslem *n* see MUSLIM.

mosque [mosk] *n* Muslim temple.

mos·qui·to [mə-SKEE-toh] *n, pl* **-toes** *or* **-tos.** any of various kinds of flying, biting insects.

moss [maws] *n* small plant growing in masses on moist surfaces. **moss'y** *adj* **moss·i·er, moss·i·est.** covered with moss.

most [mohst] *adj* greatest in size, number, or degree; sup. OF MUCH or MANY. ▶ *n* greatest number, amount, or degree. ▶ *adv* in the greatest degree; abbrev. OF ALMOST. **most'ly** *adv* for the most part, generally, on the whole.

mo·tel [moh-TEL] *n* roadside hotel with accommodation for motorists and their vehicles.

mo·tet [moh-TET] *n* short sacred vocal composition.

moth [mawth] *n* usu. nocturnal insect like butterfly; its grub. **moth'ball** *n* small ball of camphor or naphthalene to repel moths from stored clothing, etc. ▶ *vt* put in mothballs; store, postpone, etc. **moth'eat·en** *adj* eaten, damaged by grub of moth; decayed, scruffy.

moth·er [MUTH-ər] *n* female parent; head of religious community of women. ▶ *adj* natural, native, inborn. ▶ *vt* act as mother to. **moth'er·hood** [-huud] *n* **moth'er·ly** *adj* **mother-in-law** *n* mother of one's wife or husband. **mother of pearl** iridescent lining of certain shells.

mo·tif [moh-TEEF] *n* dominating theme; recurring design.

mo·tion [MOH-shən] *n* process or action or way of moving; proposal in meeting; application to judge. ▶ *vt* direct by sign. **mo'tion·less** [-lis] *adj* still, immobile.

mo·tive [MOH-tiv] *n* that which makes person act in particular way; inner impulse. ▶ *adj* causing motion. **mo'ti·vate** *vt* **-vat·ed, -vat·ing.** instigate; incite. **mo·ti·va'tion** [-VAY-shən] *n*

mot·ley [MOT-lee] *adj* miscellaneous, varied; multicolored.

mo·to·cross [MOH-toh-kraws] *n* motorcycle race over rough course.

mo·tor [MOH-tər] *n* that which

imparts movement; machine to supply motive power; automobile. ▶ vi travel by automobile.

mo′tor·ist n user of automobile.

mo′tor·ize vt **-ized, -iz·ing.** equip with motor. **motor home** large motor vehicle with living quarters, used for recreational travel.

mot·tle [MOT-l] vt **-tled, -tling.** mark with blotches, variegate. ▶ n arrangement of blotches; blotch on surface.

mot·to [MOT-oh] n, pl **-toes.** saying adopted as rule of conduct; short inscribed sentence; word or sentence on badge or banner.

mound [mownd] n heap of earth or stones; small hill.

mount [mownt] vi rise; increase; get on horseback. ▶ vt get up on; frame (picture); fix, set up; provide with horse. ▶ n that on which thing is supported or fitted; horse; hill.

moun·tain [MOWN-tn] n hill of great size; surplus. **moun·tain·eer′** n one who lives among or climbs mountains. **moun′tain·ous** adj very high, rugged. **mountain bike** bicycle with straight handlebars and broad, thick tires, for cycling over rough terrain.

moun·te·bank [MOWN-tə-bangk] n charlatan, fake.

Moun·tie [MOWN-tee] n inf member of Royal Canadian Mounted Police.

mourn [morn] v feel, show sorrow (for). **mourn′er** n **mourn′ful** [-fəl] adj sad; dismal. **mourn′ful·ly** adv **mourn′ing** n grieving; conventional signs of grief for death; clothes of mourner.

mouse [mows] n, pl **mice** [mīs] small rodent; Computers hand-operated device for moving the cursor, clicking on icons, etc. without keying. ▶ vi catch, hunt mice; prowl. **mous′er** n cat used for catching mice. **mous′y** adj **mous·i·er, mous·i·est.** like mouse, esp. in color; meek, shy.

mousse [moos] n sweet dessert of flavored cream whipped and frozen.

moustache see MUSTACHE.

mouth [mowth] n opening in head for eating, speaking, etc.; opening into anything hollow; outfall of river; entrance to harbor, etc. ▶ vt [mow*th*] declaim, esp. in public; form (words) with lips without speaking; take, move in mouth.

mouth′piece n end of anything placed between lips, e.g. pipe; spokesman.

move [moov] v **moved, mov·ing.** ▶ vt change position of; stir emotions; incite; propose for consideration. ▶ vi change places; change one's dwelling, etc.; take action. ▶ n a moving; motion toward some goal. **mov′a·ble** adj, n **move′ment** n process, action of moving; moving parts of machine; division of piece of music.

mov·ie [MOO-vee] n inf cinema film.

mow [moh] v **mowed** or **mown, mow·ing.** cut (grass, etc.). **mow′er** n person or machine that mows.

MP3, Mpeg-1 la·yer3 n Computers digital compression format used to reduce audio files to a fraction of their original size without loss of sound quality.

Mr mister.

Mrs title of married woman.

Ms title used instead of Miss or Mrs.

Mt Chem meitnerium.

much adj **more, most.** existing in quantity. ▶ n large amount; a great deal; important matter. ▶ adv in a great degree; nearly.

mu·ci·lage [MYOO-sə-lij] n gum, glue.

muck [muk] n horse, cattle dung; unclean refuse; insulting remarks. ▶ vt make dirty. **muck′y** adj **muck·i·er, muck·i·est.** dirty; messy; unpleasant. **muck out** v remove muck from. **muck up** v inf ruin, bungle, confuse.

mu·cus [MYOO-kəs] n viscid fluid secreted by mucous membrane. **mu′cous** [-kəs] adj resembling mucus; secreting mucus; slimy. **mucous membrane** lining of canals and cavities of the body.

mud n wet and soft earth; inf

slander. **mud·dy** adj **-di·er, -di·est.**
mud·dle [MUD-əl] vt **-dled, -dling.**
(esp. with up) confuse; bewilder;
mismanage. ▶ n confusion; tangle.
mu·ez·zin [myoo-EZ-in] n crier who
summons Muslims to prayer.
muff¹ n tube-shaped covering to
keep the hands warm.
muff² vt miss, bungle, fail in.
muf·fin n cup-shaped quick bread.
muf·fle [MUF-əl] vt **-fled, -fling.**
wrap up, esp. to deaden sound.
muf·fler [-lər] n on motor vehicles,
device for accomplishing this; scarf.
muf·ti [MUF-tee] n plain clothes as
distinguished from uniform, e.g. of
soldier.
mug¹ n drinking cup.
mug² n sl face; sl ruffian, criminal.
▶ vt **mugged, mug·ging.** rob
violently. **mug·ger** [-ər] n
mug·gy [MUG-ee] adj **-gi·er,
-gi·est.** damp and stifling.
Mu·ham·mad, Mo·ham·med
[muu-HAM-əd] n prophet and
founder of Islam. **Mu·ham·mad·an**
adj, n Muslim.
mu·lat·to [mə-LAT-oh] adj, n, pl
-oes. (child) of one white and one
black parent.
mul·ber·ry [MUL-ber-ee] n, pl **-ries.**
tree whose leaves are used to feed
silkworms; its purplish fruit.
mulch n straw, leaves, etc., spread
as protection for roots of plants.
▶ vt protect thus.
mule [myool] n animal that is cross
between female horse and male
donkey; hybrid; spinning machine;
small locomotive; slipper. **mul·ish**
adj obstinate.
mull vt heat (wine) with sugar and
spices; think (over), ponder.
mul·lah [MUL-ə] n Muslim
theologian.
mul·let¹ [MUL-it] n edible sea fish.
mul·let² n haircut in which the hair
is short at the top and sides and
long at the back.
mul·lion [MUL-yən] n upright
dividing bar in window.
multi-, mult- comb. form many, e.g.
multiracial; multistory.
mul·ti·far·i·ous [mul-tə-FAIR-ee-əs]

adj of various kinds or parts.
mul·ti·ple [MUL-tə-pəl] adj having
many parts. ▶ n quantity that
contains another an exact number
of times. **mul·ti·pli·cand'** n Math
number to be multiplied.
mul·ti·pli·ca'tion n **mul·ti·plic'i·ty**
[-PLIS-i-tee] n variety, greatness in
number. **mul'ti·ply** [-plī] v **-plied,
-ply·ing.** (cause to) increase in
number, quantity, or degree. ▶ vt
combine (two numbers or
quantities) by multiplication;
increase in number by
reproduction.
mul·ti·plex [MUL-tə-pleks] adj
Telecommunications capable of
transmitting numerous messages
over same wire or channel.
mul·ti·tude [MUL-ti-tood] n great
number; great crowd; populace.
mul·ti·tu'di·nous adj very
numerous.
mum adj silent. **mum's the word**
keep silent.
mum·ble [MUM-bəl] v **-bled,
-bling.** speak indistinctly, mutter.
mum·my [MUM-ee] n, pl **-mies.**
embalmed body. **mum'mi·fy** vt
-fied, -fy·ing.
mumps n infectious disease marked
by swelling in the glands of the
neck.
munch v chew noisily and
vigorously; crunch.
mun·dane [mun-DAYN] adj
ordinary, everyday; belonging to
this world, earthly.
mu·nic·i·pal [myuu-NIS-ə-pəl] adj
belonging to affairs of city or town.
mu·nic·i·pal'i·ty n, pl **-ties.** city or
town with local self-government;
its governing body.
mu·nif·i·cent [myoo-NIF-ə-sənt]
adj very generous. **mu·nif'i·cence**
n bounty.
mu·ni·tions [myoo-NISH-ənz] pl n
military stores.
mu·ral [MYUUR-əl] n painting on a
wall. ▶ adj of or on a wall.
mur·der [MUR-dər] n unlawful
premeditated killing of human
being. ▶ vt kill thus. **mur'der·ous**
adj

murk n thick darkness. **murk'y** adj **murk·i·er, murk·i·est.** gloomy.

mur·mur [MUR-mər] n low, indistinct sound. ▶ vi make such a sound; complain. ▶ vt utter in a low voice.

mus·cle [MUS-əl] n part of body that produces movement by contracting; system of muscles. **mus'cu·lar** [-kyə-lər] adj with well-developed muscles; strong; of, like muscle. **mus'cle·bound** adj with muscles stiff through overdevelopment. **muscular dystrophy** disease with wasting of muscles. **muscle in** inf force one's way into. **muscle shirt** inf shirt that leaves full arm exposed.

muse [myooz] vi **mused, mus·ing.** ponder; consider meditatively; be lost in thought.

Muse [myooz] n one of the nine goddesses inspiring learning and the arts.

mu·seum [myoo-ZEE-əm] n place housing collection of natural, artistic, historical or scientific objects.

mush¹ n soft pulpy mass; cloying sentimentality. **mush'y** adj **mush·i·er, mush·i·est.**

mush² vi travel over snow with dog team and sled. ▶ vt spur on (sled) dogs. ▶ interj go!

mush'room n fungoid growth, typically with stem and cap structure, some species edible. ▶ vi shoot up rapidly; expand. **mushroom cloud** large cloud resembling mushroom, esp. from nuclear explosion.

mu·sic [MYOO-zik] n art form using melodious and harmonious combination of notes; laws of this; composition in this art. **mu'si·cal** adj of, like music; interested in, or with instinct for, music; pleasant to ear. ▶ n play, motion picture in which music plays essential part. **mu·si'cian** n **mu·si·col'o·gist** [-jist] n **mu·si·col'o·gy** n scientific study of music. **musical comedy** light dramatic entertainment of songs, dances, etc.

musk n scent obtained from gland of **musk deer;** various plants with similar scent. **musk'y** adj **musk·i·er, musk·i·est. musk ox** ox of Arctic Amer. **musk'rat** n N Amer. rodent found near water; its fur.

mus·ket [MUS-kit] n Hist infantryman's gun. **mus·ket·eer'** n

Mus·lim [MUZ-lim] n follower of religion of Islam. ▶ adj of religion, culture, etc. of Islam.

mus·lin [MUZ-lin] n fine cotton fabric.

mus·sel [MUS-əl] n bivalve shellfish.

must¹ v aux be obliged to, or certain to. ▶ n something one must do.

must² n newly-pressed grape juice; unfermented wine.

mus·tache, mous·tache [MUS-tash] n hair on the upper lip.

mus'tang n wild horse.

mus·tard [MUS-tərd] n powder made from the seeds of a plant, used in paste as a condiment; the plant. **mustard gas** poisonous gas causing blistering, lung damage, etc.

mus·ter [MUS-tər] v assemble. ▶ n assembly, esp. for exercise, inspection.

mus·ty [MUS-tee] adj **-ti·er, -ti·est.** moldy, stale. **must** n **mus'ti·ness** n

mu·tate [MYOO-tayt] v **-tat·ed, -tat·ing.** (cause to) undergo mutation. **mu'ta·ble** [-tə-bəl] adj liable to change. **mu'tant** [-tənt] n mutated animal, plant, etc. **mu·ta'tion** [-TAY-shən] n change, esp. genetic change causing divergence from kind or racial type. **mu·ta'tive** adj

mute [myoot] adj **mut·er, mut·est.** dumb; silent. ▶ n person incapable of speech; Mus contrivance to soften tone of instruments. **mut'ed** adj (of sound) muffled; (of light) subdued.

mu·ti·late [MYOOT-l-ayt] vt **-lat·ed, -lat·ing.** deprive of a limb or other part; damage; deface. **mu·ti·la'tion** n

mu·ti·ny [MYOOT-n-ee] n, pl **-nies.**

rebellion against authority, esp. against officers of disciplined body. ▶ *vi* **-nied, -ny·ing.** commit mutiny. **mu·ti·neer'** *n* **mu'tin·ous** *adj* rebellious.

mutt *n inf* (mongrel) dog.

mut·ter [MUT-ər] *vi* speak with mouth nearly closed, indistinctly; grumble. ▶ *vt* utter in such tones. ▶ *n* (act of) muttering.

mut·ton [MUT-ən] *n* flesh of sheep used as food. **mut·ton·chops** *pl n* side whiskers broad at jaw, narrow at temples. **mut'ton·head** [-hed] *n inf* slow-witted person.

mu·tu·al [MYOO-choo-əl] *adj* done, possessed, etc., by each of two with respect to the other; reciprocal; common to both or all. **mu·tu·al'i·ty** *n* **mutual fund** investment company selling shares to public with repurchase on request.

muz·zle [MUZ-əl] *n* mouth and nose of animal; cover for these to prevent biting; open end of gun. ▶ *vt* **-zled, -zling.** put muzzle on; silence, gag.

my [mī] *adj* belonging to me. **my·self'** *pron* emphatic or reflexive form of I or ME.

my·col·o·gy [mī-KOL-ə-jee] *n* science of fungi.

my·o·pi·a [mī-OH-pee-ə] *n* nearsightedness; obtuseness. **my·op'ic** *adj*

myr·i·ad [MIR-ee-əd] *adj* innumerable. ▶ *n* large indefinite number.

myrrh [mur] *n* aromatic gum, formerly used as incense.

mys·ter·y [MIS-tə-ree] *n, pl* **-teries.** obscure or secret thing; anything strange or inexplicable; religious rite; in Middle Ages, biblical play. **mys·te'ri·ous** [-TEER-ree-əs] *adj*

mys·tic [MIS-tik] *n* one who seeks divine, spiritual knowledge, esp. by prayer, contemplation, etc. ▶ *adj* of hidden meaning, esp. in religious sense. **mys'ti·cal** *adj* **mys'ti·cism** [-siz-əm] *n*

mys·ti·fy [MIS-tə-fī] *vt* **-fied, -fy·ing.** bewilder, puzzle. **mys·ti·fi·ca'tion** [-KAY-shən] *n*

mys·tique [mi-STEEK] *n* aura of mystery, power, etc.

myth [mith] *n* tale with supernatural characters or events; invented story; imaginary person or object. **myth'i·cal** *adj* **myth·o·log'i·cal** [-LOJ-ə-kəl] *adj* **my·thol'o·gy** *n, pl* **-gies.** myths collectively; study of them.

N n

N *Chem* nitrogen; *Physics* newton.
Na *Chem* sodium.
na·bob [NAY-bob] *n* wealthy, powerful person.
na·cre [NAY-kər] *n* mother-of-pearl.
na·dir [NAY-dər] *n* point opposite the zenith; lowest point.
nag¹ *v* **nagged, nag·ging.** scold or annoy constantly; cause pain to constantly. ▶ *n* nagging; one who nags.
nag² *n* old horse; *sl* any horse; small horse for riding.
nai·ad [NAY-ad] *n* water nymph.
nail [nayl] *n* horny shield at ends of fingers, toes; claw; small metal spike for fastening wood, etc. ▶ *vt* fasten with nails; *inf* catch. **hit the nail on the head** do or say the right thing.
na·ive [nah-EEV] *adj* simple, unaffected, ingenuous. **na·ive·té** [-eev-TAY] *n*
nak·ed [NAY-kid] *adj* without clothes; exposed; bare; undisguised. **naked eye** the eye unassisted by any optical instrument.
name [naym] *n* word by which person, thing, etc. is denoted; reputation; title; credit; family; famous person. ▶ *vt* **named, nam·ing.** give name to; call by name; entitle; appoint; mention; specify. **name'less** [-lis] *adj* without a name; indescribable; too dreadful to be mentioned; obscure. **name'ly** *adv* that is to say. **name'sake** *n* person named after another; person with same name as another. **name and shame** make public the name of (a wrongdoer) in order to bring public condemnation on him or her.
nap¹ *vi* **napped, nap·ping.** take short sleep, esp. in daytime. ▶ *n* short sleep.
nap² *n* downy surface on cloth made by projecting fibers.
na·palm [NAY-pahm] *n* jellied

gasoline, highly incendiary, used in bombs, etc.
nape [nayp] *n* back of neck.
naph·tha [NAF-thə] *n* inflammable oil distilled from coal, etc. **naph'tha·lene** [-leen] *n* white crystalline product distilled from coal tar, used in disinfectants, mothballs, etc.
nap'kin *n* cloth, paper for wiping fingers or lips at table.
nar·cis·sus [nahr-SIS-əs] *n, pl* **nar·cis·sus.** genus of bulbous plants including daffodil, jonquil, esp. one with white flowers. **nar'cis·sism** *n* abnormal love and admiration of oneself. **nar'cis·sist** *n*
nar·cot·ic [nahr-KOT-ik] *n* any of a group of drugs, including morphine and opium, producing numbness and stupor, used medicinally but addictive. ▶ *adj*
nar·rate [NAR-ayt] *vt* **-rat·ed, -rat·ing.** relate, recount, tell (story). **nar·ra'tion** *n* **nar'ra·tive** [-rə-tiv] *n* account, story. ▶ *adj* relating. **nar'ra·tor** [-ray-tər] *n*
nar·row [NAR-oh] *adj* **-er, -est.** of little breadth, or width esp. in comparison to length; limited; barely adequate or successful. ▶ *v* make, become narrow. **nar'rows** *pl n* narrow part of straits. **nar'row·ness** *n* **narrow-minded** *adj* illiberal; bigoted. **narrow-mindedness** *n* prejudice, bigotry.
na·sal [NAY-zəl] *adj* of nose. ▶ *n* sound partly produced in nose. **na'sal·ly** *adv*
nas·cent [NAYS-ənt] *adj* just coming into existence; springing up.
nas·tur·tium [nə-STUR-shəm] *n* garden plant with red or orange flowers.
nas·ty [NAS-tee] *adj* **-ti·er, -ti·est.** foul, disagreeable, unpleasant. **nas'ti·ly** *adv* **nas'ti·ness** *n*
na·tal [NAYT-l] *adj* of birth.

na·tion [NAY-shən] *n* people or race organized as a country. **na'tion·al** [NASH-ə-nl] *adj* belonging or pert. to a nation; public, general. ▶ *n* member of a nation.

na'tion·al·ism *n* loyalty, devotion to one's country; movement for independence of country, people, ruled by another. **na·tion·al'i·ty** *n*, *pl* **-ties.** national quality or feeling; fact of belonging to particular nation; member of this.

na'tion·al·ize *vt* **-ized, -iz·ing.** convert (private industry, resources, etc.) to government control.

na·tive [NAY-tiv] *adj* inborn; born in particular place; found in pure state; that was place of one's birth. ▶ *n* one born in a place; member of indigenous people of a country; species of plant, animal, etc. originating in a place. **Native American** *n* person descended from the original inhabitants of the American continent. ▶ *adj* of Native Americans.

na·tiv·i·ty [nə-TIV-i-tee] *n*, *pl* **-ties.** birth; time, circumstances of birth; (**N-**) birth of Christ.

nat·ter [NAT-ər] *vi* talk idly.

nat·ty [NAT-ee] *adj* **ti·er, -ti·est.** neat and smart; spruce. **nat'ti·ly** *adv*

na·ture [NAY-chər] *n* innate or essential qualities of person or thing; class, sort; life force; (**N-**) power underlying all phenomena in material world; material world as a whole; natural unspoiled scenery or countryside, and plants and animals in it; disposition; temperament. **nat·u·ral** [NACH-ər-əl] *adj* of, according to, occurring in, provided by, nature; inborn; normal; unaffected; illegitimate. ▶ *n* something, somebody well suited for something; *Mus* symbol used to remove effect of sharp or flat preceding it. **nat'u·ral·ist** *n* student of natural history. **nat·u·ral·is'tic** *adj* of or imitating nature in effect or characteristics.

nat'u·ral·ize *vt* **-ized, -iz·ing.** admit to citizenship; accustom to different climate or environment.

nat'u·ral·ly *adv* of or according to nature; by nature; of course.

natural history study of animals and plants.

naught [nawt] *n* nothing; nought.

naugh·ty [NAW-tee] *adj* **-ti·er, -ti·est.** disobedient, not behaving well; mildly indecent, tasteless. **naugh'ti·ly** *adv*

nau·se·a [NAW-zee-ə] *n* feeling that precedes vomiting. **nau'se·ate** *vt* **-at·ed, -at·ing.** sicken. **nau'seous** [NAW-shəs], **nau'se·at·ing** *adj* disgusting; causing nausea.

nau·ti·cal [NAW-ti-kəl] *adj* of seamen or ships; marine. **nautical mile** 6080.20 feet (1853.25 meters).

nau·ti·lus [NAWT-l-əs] *n*, *pl* **-lus·es.** univalvular shellfish.

naval see NAVY.

nave [nayv] *n* main part of church.

na·vel [NAY-vəl] *n* umbilicus, small scar, depression in middle of abdomen where umbilical cord was attached.

nav·i·gate [NAV-i-gayt] *v* **-gat·ed, -gat·ing.** plan, direct, plot path or position of ship, etc.; travel. **nav'i·ga·ble** *adj* **nav·i·ga'tion** *n* science of directing course of seagoing vessel, or of aircraft in flight; shipping. **nav'i·ga·tor** *n* one who navigates.

na·vy [NAY-vee] *n*, *pl* **-vies.** fleet; warships of country with their crews and organization. ▶ *adj* navy-blue. **na'val** *adj* of the navy. **navy-blue** *adj* very dark blue.

Na·zi [NAHT-see] *n* member of the National Socialist political party in Germany, 1919–45; one who thinks, acts, like a Nazi. ▶ *adj*

Nb *Chem* niobium.

Nd *Chem* neodymium.

Ne *Chem* neon.

Ne·an·der·thal [nee-AN-dər-thawl] *adj* of a type of primitive man; (**n-**) primitive.

neap [neep] *adj* low. **neap tide** the low tide at the first and third quarters of the moon.

near [neer] *prep* close to. ▶ *adv* **-er, -est.** at or to a short distance. ▶ *adj* **-er, -est.** close at hand; closely related; narrow, so as barely to escape; stingy; (of vehicles, horses, etc.) at driver's left. ▶ *v* approach. **near'by** *adj* adjacent. **near'ly** *adv* closely; almost.

neat [neet] *adj* **-er, -est.** tidy, orderly; efficient; precise, deft; cleverly worded; undiluted; simple and elegant. **neat'ly** *adv*

neb·u·la [NEB-yə-lə] *n, pl* **-lae** [-lee] *Astronomy* diffuse cloud of particles, gases. **neb'u·lous** *adj* cloudy; vague, indistinct.

nec·es·sar·y [NES-ə-ser-ee] *adj* needful, requisite, that must be done; unavoidable, inevitable. **nec'es·sar·i·ly** *adv* **ne·ces'si·tate** *vt* **-tat·ed, -tat·ing.** make necessary. **ne·ces'si·tous** *adj* poor, needy, destitute. **ne·ces'si·ty** *n, pl* **-ties.** something needed, requisite; constraining power or state of affairs; compulsion; poverty.

neck [nek] *n* part of body joining head to shoulders; narrower part of a bottle, etc.; narrow piece of anything between wider parts. ▶ *vi inf* embrace, cuddle. **neck'lace** [-lis] *n* ornament around the neck.

nec·ro·man·cy [NEK-rə-man-see] *n* magic, esp. by communication with dead. **nec'ro·man·cer** *n* wizard.

ne·crop·o·lis [nə-KROP-ə-lis] *n, pl* **-lis·es.** cemetery.

nec·tar [NEK-tər] *n* honey of flowers; drink of the gods.

nec·tar·ine [nek-tə-REEN] *n* variety of peach.

nee [nay] *adj* indicating maiden name of married woman.

need *vt* want, require. ▶ *n* (state, instance of) want; requirement; necessity; poverty. **need'ful** *adj* necessary, requisite. **need'less** *adj* unnecessary. **needs** *adv* (preceded or foll. by *must*) necessarily. **need'y** *adj* **need·i·er, need·i·est.** poor, in want.

nee·dle [NEE-dl] *n* **-dled, -dling.**

pointed pin with an eye and no head, for sewing; long, pointed pin for knitting; pointer of gauge, dial; magnetized bar of compass; stylus for record player; leaf of fir, pine, etc.; obelisk; hypodermic syringe. ▶ *vt inf* goad, provoke. **nee·dle·craft, -work** *n* embroidery, sewing.

ne·far·i·ous [ni-FAIR-ee-əs] *adj* wicked. **ne·far'i·ous·ness** *n*

ne·gate [ni-GAYT] *vt* **-gat·ed, -gat·ing.** deny, nullify. **ne·ga'tion** *n* contradiction, denial.

neg·a·tive [NEG-ə-tiv] *adj* expressing denial or refusal; lacking enthusiasm, energy, interest; not positive; of electrical charge having the same polarity as the charge of an electron. ▶ *n* negative word or statement; *Photography* picture made by action of light on chemicals in which lights and shades are reversed.

ne·glect [ni-GLEKT] *vt* disregard, take no care of; fail to do; omit through carelessness. ▶ *n* fact of neglecting or being neglected. **ne·glect'ful** *adj*

neg·li·gee [NEG-li-zhay] *n* woman's light, gauzy nightgown or dressing gown.

neg·li·gence [NEG-li-jəns] *n* neglect; carelessness. **neg'li·gent** *adj* **neg'li·gi·ble** *adj* able to be disregarded; very small or unimportant.

ne·go·ti·ate [ni-GOH-shee-ayt] *v* **-at·ed, -at·ing.** ▶ *vi* discuss with view to mutual settlement. ▶ *vt* arrange by conference; transfer (bill, check, etc.); get over, past, around (obstacle). **ne·go'ti·a·ble** [-shə-bəl] *adj* **ne·go·ti·a'tion** [-shee-AY-shən] *n* dealing with another on business; discussion; transference (of bill, check, etc.).

Ne·gro [NEE-groh] *n, pl* **-groes.** *oft offens* dark-skinned person of African ancestry. ▶ *adj*

neigh [nay] *n* cry of horse. ▶ *vi* utter this cry.

neigh·bor [NAY-bər] *n* one who lives near another.

neigh'bor·hood n district; people of a district; region around about.

neigh'bor·ing adj situated nearby.

neigh'bor·ly adj as or befitting a good or friendly neighbor; friendly; helpful.

nei·ther [NEE-*th*ər] adj, pron not the one or the other. ▶ adv not on the one hand; not either. ▶ conj nor yet.

nem·e·sis [NEM-ə-sis] n, pl **-ses** [-seez] retribution; (**N-**) the goddess of vengeance.

neo- comb. form new, later, revived in modified form, based upon, e.g. neoclassicism.

Ne·o·lith·ic [nee-ə-LITH-ik] adj of the later Stone Age.

ne·ol·o·gism [nee-OL-ə-jiz-əm] n newly coined word or phrase.

ne·on [NEE-on] n one of the inert constituent gases of the atmosphere, used in illuminated signs and lights.

ne·o·phyte [NEE-ə-fīt] n new convert; beginner, novice.

neph·ew [NEF-yoo] n brother's or sister's son.

ne·phri·tis [nə-FRĪ-tis] n inflammation of kidneys. **ne·phro·sis** [-FROH-sis] n degenerative disease of kidneys.

nep·o·tism [NEP-ə-tiz-əm] n undue favoritism toward one's relations.

Nep·tune [NEP-toon] n god of the sea; planet second farthest from sun.

nep·tu·ni·um [nep-TOO-nee-əm] n synthetic metallic element.

nerd [nurd] n sl boring person obsessed with a particular subject.

nerve [nurv] n sinew, tendon; fiber or bundle of fibers conveying feeling, impulses to motion, etc. to and from brain and other parts of body; assurance; coolness in danger; audacity. ▶ pl irritability, unusual sensitiveness to fear, annoyance, etc. **nerve'less** [-lis] adj without nerves; useless; weak; paralyzed. **nerv'ous** [-əs] adj excitable; timid, apprehensive, worried; of the nerves. **nerv'y** [-ee] adj **nerv·i·er, nerv·i·est.** nervous,

jumpy, irritable; on edge. **nervous breakdown** condition of mental, emotional disturbance, disability.

nest n place in which bird lays and hatches its eggs; animal's breeding place; snug retreat. ▶ vi make, have a nest. **nest egg** (fund of) money in reserve.

nes·tle [NES-əl] vi **-tled, -tling.** settle comfortably, usu. pressing in or close to something.

nest'ling n bird too young to leave nest.

net¹ n openwork fabric of meshes of cord, etc.; piece of it used to catch fish, etc.; (**N-**) short for INTERNET. ▶ vt **net·ted, net·ting.** cover with, or catch in, net; catch, ensnare. **netting** n string or wire net.

net'ball n Tennis return shot that hits top of net and remains in play.

net·i·quette [NET-i-kit] n informal code of behaviour on the Internet.

net² adj left after all deductions; free from deduction. ▶ vt **net·ted, net·ting.** gain, yield as clear profit.

neth·er [NE*TH*-ər] adj lower.

ne·tsu·ke [NET-skee] n carved wooden or ivory toggle or button worn in Japan.

net·tle [NET-l] n plant with stinging hairs on the leaves. ▶ vt **-tled, -tling.** irritate, provoke.

net·work [NET-wurk] n system of intersecting lines, roads, etc.; interconnecting group of people or things; in broadcasting, group of stations connected to transmit same programs simultaneously; Computers system of interconnected computers.

neu·ral [NUUR-əl] adj of the nerves.

neu·ral·gia [nuu-RAL-jə] n pain in, along nerves, esp. of face and head. **neu·ral'gic** [-jik] adj

neu·ri·tis [nuu-RĪ-tis] n inflammation of nerves.

neu·rol·o·gy [nuu-ROL-ə-jee] n science, study of nerves. **neu·rol'o·gist** n

neu·ro·sis [nuu-ROH-sis] n, pl **-ses** [-seez] relatively mild mental disorder. **neu·rot'ic** adj suffering from nervous disorder; abnormally

sensitive. ▶ *n* neurotic person.
neu·ter [NOO-tər] *adj* neither
masculine nor feminine. ▶ *n* neuter
word; neuter gender. ▶ *vt* castrate,
spay (domestic animals).
neu·tral [NOO-trəl] *adj* taking
neither side in war, dispute, etc.;
without marked qualities;
belonging to neither of two classes.
▶ *n* neutral nation or a citizen of
one; neutral gear. **neu·tral'i·ty** *n*
neu'tral·ize *vt* **-ized, -iz·ing.** make
ineffective; counterbalance.
neutral gear in vehicle, position of
gears that leaves transmission
disengaged.
neu·tron [NOO-tron] *n* electrically
neutral particle of the nucleus of an
atom. **neutron bomb** nuclear
bomb designed to destroy people
but not buildings.
nev·er [NEV-ər] *adv* at no time.
nev'er·the·less' *adv* for all that,
notwithstanding.
ne·vus [NEE-vəs] *n* congenital mark
on skin; birthmark, mole.
new [noo] *adj* **-er, -est.** not existing
before, fresh; that has lately come
into some state or existence;
unfamiliar, strange. ▶ *adv* newly.
new'ly *adv* recently, fresh.
new'ness *n* **New Age** cultural
movement originating in the
1980s, characterized by such
things as alternative medicine,
astrology, and meditation.
new'com·er *n* recent arrival.
new'fang'led [-FANG-əld] *adj* of
new fashion.
new·el [NOO-əl] *n* central pillar of
winding staircase; post at top or
bottom of staircase rail.
news [nooz] *n* report of recent
happenings; tidings; interesting
fact not previously known.
news'cast *n* news broadcast.
news'deal·er *n* shopkeeper who
sells newspapers and magazines.
news'flash *n* brief news item, oft.
interrupting radio, TV program.
news'group *n* Computers forum
where subscribers exchange
information about a specific subject
by e-mail. **news'pa·per** *n*

periodical publication containing
news, advertisements, etc.
news'print *n* paper of the kind
used for newspapers, etc.
news'reel *n* motion picture giving
news. **news'room** *n* room where
news is received and prepared for
publication or broadcast.
news'wor·thy [-wur-*thee*] *adj*
-thi·er, -thi·est. sufficiently
interesting or important to be
reported as news.
newt [noot] *n* small, tailed
amphibious creature.
new·ton [NOOT-n] *n* SI unit of
force.
next [nekst] *adj, adv* nearest;
immediately following. **next of kin**
nearest relative(s).
nex·us [NEK-səs] *n, pl* **nexus.** tie;
connection, link.
Ni *Chem* nickel.
nib·ble [NIB-əl] *v* **-bled, -bling.** take
little bites of. ▶ *n* little bite.
nice [nīs] *adj* **nic·er, nic·est.**
pleasant; friendly, kind; attractive;
subtle, fine; careful, exact; difficult
to decide. **nice'ly** *adv* **ni'ce·ty** *n, pl*
-ties. minute distinction or detail;
subtlety; precision.
niche [nich] *n* recess in wall;
suitable place in life, public
estimation, etc.
nick [nik] *vt* make notch in, indent;
sl steal. ▶ *n* notch; exact point of
time. **in the nick of time** at the last
possible moment.
nick·el [NIK-əl] *n* silver-white metal
much used in alloys and plating;
five-cent piece.
nick·name [NIK-naym] *n* familiar
name added to or replacing an
ordinary name.
nic·o·tine [NIK-ə-teen] *n* poisonous
oily liquid in tobacco.
niece [nees] *n* brother's or sister's
daughter.
nif·ty [NIFT-ee] *adj* **-tier, -tiest.** *inf*
neat or smart.
nig·gard [NIG-ərd] *n* mean, stingy
person. **nig'gard·ly** *adj, adv*
nig'gard·li·ness *n*
nig·gle [NIG-əl] *vi* **-gled, -gling.**
find fault continually; annoy.

niggling adj petty; irritating and persistent.

nigh [nī] adj, adv, prep lit near.

night [nīt] n time of darkness between sunset and sunrise; end of daylight; dark. **night'ie** n inf nightgown. **night'ly** adj happening, done every night; of the night. ▶ adv every night; by night. **night'cap** n cap worn in bed; inf late-night (alcoholic) drink. **night'club** n establishment for dancing, music, etc. open until early morning. **night'gown** n woman's or child's loose gown worn in bed. **night'in·gale** n small Old World bird that sings usu. at night. **night'mare** [-mair] n very bad dream; terrifying experience. **night'time** n

ni·hil·ism [NĪ-ə-liz-əm] n rejection of all religious and moral principles; opposition to all constituted authority, or government. **ni'hil·ist** n **ni·hil·ist'ic** adj

nim·ble [NIM-bəl] adj **-bler, -blest.** agile, active, quick, dexterous. **nim'bly** adv

nim·bus [NIM-bəs] n, pl **-bi** [-bī] or **-bus·es.** rain or storm cloud; cloud of glory, halo.

nine [nīn] adj, n cardinal number next above eight. **ninth** adj **ninth'ly** adv **nine·teen'** adj, n nine more than ten. **nine·teenth'** adj **nine'ty** adj, n nine tens. **nine'ti·eth** adj **nine'pins** n game where wooden pins are set up to be knocked down by rolling ball, skittles.

nip v **nipped, nip·ping.** pinch sharply; detach by pinching, bite; check growth (of plants) thus; inf steal; inf beat (opponent) by close margin hurry. ▶ n pinch; check to growth; sharp coldness of weather; small alcoholic drink. **nip'per** n thing (e.g. crab's claw) that nips; inf small boy. ▶ pl pincers. **nip'py** adj **-pi·er, -pi·est.** inf cold; quick.

nip·ple [NIP-əl] n point of a breast, teat; anything like this.

nir·va·na [nir-VAH-nə] n Buddhism absolute blessedness; Hinduism merging of individual in supreme spirit.

nit n egg of louse or other parasite. **nit'pick·ing** adj inf overconcerned with detail, esp. to find fault. **nit'pick** v show such overconcern; criticize over petty faults. **nit'wit** n inf fool. **nit·ty-grit·ty** n sl basic facts, details.

ni·tro·gen [NĪ-trə-jən] n one of the gases making up the air. **ni'trate** n compound of nitric acid and an alkali. **ni'tric** adj **ni'trous** adj **ni·trog'e·nous** [-TROJ-ə-nəs] adj of, containing nitrogen. **ni·tro·glyc'er·in** [-troh-GLIS-ə-rin] n explosive liquid.

No Chem nobelium.

no [noh] adj not any, not a; not at all. ▶ adv expresses negative reply to question or request. ▶ n, pl **noes.** refusal; denial; negative vote or voter. **no one** nobody. **no-go** adj sl not operating; canceled. **no man's land** waste or unclaimed land; contested land between two opposing forces. **no way** inf absolutely not.

no·bel·i·um [noh-BEL-ee-əm] n synthetic element produced from curium.

no·ble [NOH-bəl] adj **-bler, -blest.** of the nobility; showing, having high moral qualities; impressive, excellent. ▶ n member of the nobility. **no·bil'i·ty** n in some countries, class holding special rank, usu. hereditary; being noble. **no'bly** adv

no·bod·y [NOH-bod-ee] pron no person; no one. ▶ n, pl **-bod·ies.** person of no importance.

noc·tur·nal [nok-TUR-nl] adj of, in, by, night; active by night.

noc·turne [NOK-turn] n dreamy piece of music.

nod v **nod·ded, nod·ding.** bow head slightly and quickly in assent, command, etc.; let head droop with sleep. ▶ n act of nodding. **nodding acquaintance** slight knowledge of person or subject. **give the nod to** inf express approval of. **nod off** fall asleep.

node [nohd] *n* knot or knob; point at which curve crosses itself. **no′dal** [-əl] *adj*

nod·ule [NOJ-ool] *n* little knot; rounded irregular mineral mass.

No·el [noh-EL] *n* Christmas; (**n-**) Christmas carol.

nog *n* drink made with beaten eggs; eggnog; peg, block.

nog·gin [NOG-ən] *n* small amount of liquor; small mug; *inf* head.

noise [noyz] *n* any sound, esp. disturbing one; clamor, din; loud outcry; talk or interest. ▶ *vt* rumor. **noise′less** [-lis] *adj* without noise, quiet, silent. **nois′i·ly** *adv* **nois′y** *adj* **nois·i·er, nois·i·est.** making much noise; clamorous.

noi·some [NOI-səm] *adj* disgusting; noxious.

no·mad [NOH-mad] *n* member of tribe with no fixed dwelling place; wanderer. **no·mad′ic** *adj*

nom de plume [nom də PLOOM] *Fr* writer's assumed name; pen name; pseudonym.

no·men·cla·ture [NOH-mən-klay-chər] *n* terminology of particular science, etc.

nom·i·nal [NOM-ə-nəl] *adj* in name only; (of fee, etc.) small, insignificant; of a name or names. **nom′i·nal·ly** *adv* in name only; not really.

nom·i·nate [NOM-ə-nayt] *vt* **-nat·ed, -nat·ing.** propose as candidate; appoint to office. **nom·i·na′tion** *n* **nom′i·na·tive** [-nə-tiv] *adj, n* (of) case of nouns, pronouns when subject of verb. **nom·i·nee′** *n* candidate.

non- *prefix* indicating: negation, e.g. *nonexistent;* refusal or failure, e.g. *noncooperation;* exclusion from a specified class, e.g. *nonfiction;* lack or absence, e.g. *nonevent.*

non·a·ge·nar·i·an [non-ə-jə-NAIR-ee-ən] *adj* aged between ninety and ninety-nine. ▶ *n* person of such age.

non·ag·gres′sion *n* policy of not attacking other countries.

non·al·co·hol′ic *adj* containing no alcohol.

nonce [nons] *n* **for the nonce** for the occasion only; for the present.

non·cha·lant [non-shə-LAHNT] *adj* casually unconcerned, indifferent, cool. **non′cha·lance** *n*

non·com·bat·ant [non-kəm-BAT-nt] *n* civilian during war; member of army who does not fight, e.g. chaplain.

non·com·mit·tal [non-kə-MIT-l] *adj* avoiding definite preference or pledge.

non com·pos men·tis [NON KOM-pohs MEN-tis] *Lat* of unsound mind.

non·con·duc′tor *n* substance that is a poor conductor of heat, electricity, or sound.

non·con·trib′u·to·ry *adj* denoting a pension scheme for employees, the premiums of which are paid entirely by the employer.

non·de·script [non-di-SKRIPT] *adj* lacking distinctive characteristics, indeterminate.

none [nun] *pron* no one, not any. ▶ *adj* no. ▶ *adv* in no way. **none·the·less′** *adv* despite that, however.

non·en·ti·ty [non-EN-ti-tee] *n, pl* **-ties.** insignificant person, thing; nonexistent thing.

non·e·vent′ *n* disappointing or insignificant occurrence.

non·exist′ent *adj* not existing, imaginary. **nonexistence** *n*

non·fic′tion *n* writing that deals with facts or real events.

non·in·ter·ven′tion *n* refusal to intervene in the affairs of others.

non·pa·reil [non-pə-REL] *adj* unequaled, matchless. ▶ *n* person or thing unequaled or unrivaled; small bead of colored sugar used to decorate cakes, etc.; flat round piece of chocolate covered with this sugar.

non·pay′ment *n* failure to pay money owed.

non·plus′ *vt* **-plussed, -plus·sing.** disconcert, confound, or bewilder completely.

non·prof·it *adj* not run with the

intention of making a profit.

non·sense [NON-sens] *n* lack of sense; absurd language; absurdity; silly conduct. **non·sen'si·cal** *adj* ridiculous; meaningless; without sense.

non se·qui·tur [non SEK-wi-tər] *Lat* statement with little or no relation to what preceded it.

non-smok'er *n* person who does not smoke. **non-smok'ing, no-smok'ing** *adj* denoting an area in which smoking is forbidden.

non-stand'ard *adj* denoting language that is not regarded as correct by educated native speakers.

non-start'er *n* person or idea that has little chance of success.

non-stick' *adj* coated with a substance that food will not stick to when cooked.

non-stop' *adj, adv* without a stop.

non-tox'ic *adj* not poisonous.

non-vi'o·lent *adj* using peaceful methods to bring about change. **non·vi·o·lence** *n*

noo·dle¹ [NOOD-l] *n* strip of pasta served in soup, etc.

noodle² *n* simpleton, fool; *sl* the head.

nook [nuuk] *n* sheltered corner, retreat.

noon *n* midday, twelve o'clock. **noon'day** *n* noon. **noon'tide** *n* the time about noon.

noose [noos] *n* running loop; snare. ▶ *vt* **noosed, noos·ing.** catch, ensnare in noose, lasso.

nor *conj* and not.

Nor·dic [NOR-dik] *adj* pert. to peoples of Germanic stock, e.g. Scandinavians.

norm *n* average level of achievement; rule or authoritative standard; model; standard type or pattern. **nor'mal** *adj* ordinary; usual; conforming to type. ▶ *n* Geom perpendicular. **nor'mal·ly** *adv*

north *n* direction to the right of person facing the sunset; part of the world, of country, etc. toward this point. ▶ *adv* toward or in the

north. ▶ *adj* to, from, or in the north. **north·er·ly** [NOR-thər-lee] *adj* (of wind) from the north. ▶ *n* a wind from the north. **north'ern** *adj* **north'ern·er** *n* person from the north. **north·ward** [NORTH-wərd] *adj* **north'ward(s)** *adv*

nose [nohz] *n* organ of smell, used also in breathing; any projection resembling a nose, as prow of ship, aircraft, etc. ▶ *v* **nosed, nos·ing.** (cause to) move forward slowly and carefully. ▶ *vt* touch with nose; smell, sniff. ▶ *vi* smell; pry. **nos·y** *adj* **nos·i·er, nos·i·est.** inquisitive.

nose'dive *n* downward sweep of aircraft; any sudden sharp fall.

nose'gay *n* bunch of flowers.

nos·tal·gia [no-STAL-jə] *n* longing for return of past events; homesickness. **nos·tal'gic** *adj*

nos·tril [NOS-trəl] *n* one of the two external openings of the nose.

nos·trum [NOS-trəm] *n* quack medicine; secret remedy.

not *adv* expressing negation, refusal, denial.

no·ta be·ne [NOH-tah BE-ne] *Lat* note well.

no·ta·ble [NOH-tə-bəl] *adj* worthy of note, remarkable. ▶ *n* person of distinction. **no·ta·bil'i·ty** *n, pl* **-ties.** prominence; an eminent person. **no'ta·bly** *adv*

no·ta·tion [noh-TAY-shən] *n* representation of numbers, quantities, by symbols; set of such symbols.

notch [noch] *n* V-shaped cut or indentation; *inf* step, grade. ▶ *vt* make notches in.

note [noht] *n* brief comment or record; short letter; promissory note; symbol for musical sound; single tone; sign; indication, hint; fame; notice; regard. ▶ *pl* brief jottings written down for future reference. ▶ *vt* **not·ed, not·ing.** observe, record; heed. **noted** *adj* well-known; celebrated.

note'book *n* small book with blank pages for writing. **note'wor·thy** [-wur-thee] *adj* worth noting, remarkable.

noth·ing [NUTH-ing] *n* no thing, not anything, nought. ▶ *adv* not at all, in no way.

no·tice [NOH-tis] *n* observation; attention, consideration; warning, intimation, announcement; advance notification of intention to end a contract, etc., as of employment; review. ▶ *vt* **-ticed, -tic·ing.** observe, mention; give attention to. **no′tice·a·ble** *adj* conspicuous; attracting attention; appreciable.

no·ti·fy [NOH-tə-fī] *vt* **-fied, -fy·ing.** report; give notice of or to. **no·ti·fi·ca′tion** [-KAY-shən] *n*

no·tion [NOH-shən] *n* concept; opinion; whim. ▶ *pl* small items e.g. buttons, thread for sale in store. **no′tion·al** *adj* speculative, imaginary, abstract.

no·to·ri·ous [noh-TOR-ee-əs] *adj* known for something bad; well-known. **no·to·ri′e·ty** [-tə-RĪ-i-tee] *n* discreditable publicity.

not·with·stand′ing *prep* in spite of. ▶ *adv* all the same. ▶ *conj* although.

nou·gat [NOO-gət] *n* chewy candy containing nuts, fruit, etc.

nought [nawt] *n* nothing; figure 0.

noun [nown] *n* word used as name of person, idea, or thing, substantive.

nour·ish [NUR-ish] *vt* feed; nurture; tend; encourage.

nou·velle cui·sine [noo-vel kwee-ZEEN] *Fr* style of preparing and presenting food with light sauces and unusual combinations of flavors.

no·va [NOH-və] *n, pl* **-vas.** star that suddenly becomes brighter then loses brightness through months or years.

nov·el[1] [NOV-əl] *n* fictitious tale in book form. **nov′el·ist** *n* writer of novels.

novel[2] *adj* new, recent; strange. **nov′el·ty** *n, pl* **-ties.** newness; something new or unusual; small ornament, trinket.

no·ve·na [noh-VEE-nə] *n R.C. Church* prayers, services usu.

extending over nine consecutive days.

nov·ice [NOV-is] *n* one new to anything; beginner; candidate for admission to religious order. **no·vi·ti·ate** [noh-VISH-ee-it] *n* probationary period; part of religious house for novices; novice.

now *adv* at the present time; immediately; (oft. with *just*) recently. ▶ *conj* seeing that, since. **now′a·days** *adv* in these times, at present.

no·where [NOH-hwair] *adv* not in any place or state.

no·wise [NOH-wīz] *adv* not in any manner or degree.

nox·ious [NOK-shəs] *adj* poisonous, harmful.

noz·zle [NOZ-əl] *n* pointed spout, esp. at end of hose.

Np *Chem* neptunium.

NT New Testament.

nu·ance [NOO-ahns] *n* delicate shade of difference, in color, tone of voice, etc.

nub *n* small lump; main point (of story, etc.).

nu·bile [NOO-bil] *adj* marriageable. **nu·bil′i·ty** *n*

nu·cle·us [NOO-klee-əs] *n, pl* **-cle·i** [-klee-ī] center, kernel; beginning meant to receive additions; core of the atom. **nu′cle·ar** [-klee-ər] *adj* of, pert. to atomic nucleus. **nuclear energy** energy released by nuclear fission. **nuclear fission** disintegration of the atom. **nuclear reaction** change in structure and energy content of atomic nucleus by interaction with another nucleus, particle. **nuclear reactor** SEE REACTOR. **nuclear winter** period of extremely low temperatures and little light after nuclear war.

nude [nood] *n* state of being naked; (picture, statue, etc. of) naked person. ▶ *adj* naked. **nud′ism** *n* practice of nudity. **nud′ist** *n* **nu′di·ty** *n*

nudge [nuj] *vt* **nudged, nudg·ing.** touch slightly esp. with elbow to gain someone's attention, prod someone into action. ▶ *n* such touch.

nu·ga·to·ry [NOO-gə-tor-ee] *adj* trifling; futile.

nug·get [NUG-it] *n* rough lump of native gold; anything of significance, value.

nui·sance [NOO-səns] *n* something or someone harmful, offensive, annoying or disagreeable.

null *adj* of no effect, void. **nul'li·fy** [-fī] *vt* **-fied, -fy·ing.** cancel; make useless or ineffective. **nul'li·ty** *n* state of being null and void.

Num. Numbers.

numb [num] *adj* **-er, -est.** deprived of feeling, esp. by cold. ▶ *vt* make numb; deaden.

num·ber [NUM-bər] *n* sum or aggregate; word or symbol saying how many; single issue of a journal, etc., issued in regular series; classification as to singular or plural; song, piece of music; performance; company, collection; identifying number, as of particular house, telephone, etc.; *inf* measure, correct estimation of. ▶ *vt* count; class, reckon; give a number to; amount to. **num'ber·less** *adj* countless. **number crunching** *inf* large-scale processing of numerical data.

nu·mer·al [NOO-mər-əl] *n* sign or word denoting a number. **nu'mer·ate** *vt* **-at·ed, -at·ing.** count. **nu·mer·a'tion** *n* **nu'mer·a·tor** *n* top part of fraction, figure showing how many of the fractional units are taken. **nu·mer·i·cal** *adj* of, in respect of, number or numbers. **nu'mer·ous** [-əs] *adj* many.

nu·mis·mat·ic [noo-miz-MAT-ik] *adj* of coins. **nu·mis·mat'ics** *n* the study of coins. **nu·mis'ma·tist** [-mə-tist] *n*

nun *n* woman living (in convent) under religious vows. **nun'ner·y** *n*, *pl* **-ies.** convent of nuns.

nun·cu·pa·tive [NUNG-kyə-pay-tiv] *adj* of a will, oral; not written.

nup·tial [NUP-shəl] *adj* of, relating to marriage. **nup'tials** *pl. n* marriage; wedding ceremony.

nurse [nurs] *n* person trained for care of sick or injured; woman tending another's child. ▶ *vt* **nursed, nurs·ing.** act as nurse to; suckle; pay special attention to; harbor (grudge, etc.). **nurs'er·y** *n*, *pl* **-er·ies.** room for children; rearing place for plants. **nurs'er·y·man** [-mən] *n* one who raises plants for sale. **nursing home** institution for housing and caring for the aged or chronically ill.

nur·ture [NUR-chər] *n* bringing up; education; rearing; nourishment. ▶ *vt* **-tured, -tur·ing.** bring up; educate.

nut *n* fruit consisting of hard shell and kernel; hollow metal collar into which a screw fits; *sl* the head; *sl* eccentric or crazy person. ▶ *vi* **nut·ted, nut·ting.** gather nuts. **nut'ty** *adj* **-ti·er, -ti·est.** of, like nut; pleasant to taste and bite; *sl* insane, crazy; eccentric. **nuts** *adj sl* insane. **nut'hatch** *n* small songbird. **nut'meg** *n* aromatic seed of Indian tree.

nu·tri·ent [NOO-tree-ənt] *adj* nourishing. ▶ *n* something nutritious.

nu·tri·ment [NOO-trə-mənt] *n* nourishing food. **nu·tri'tion** [-TRISH-ən] *n* food; act of nourishing; study of this process. **nu·tri'tion·ist** *n* one trained in nutrition. **nu·tri'tious, nu'tri·tive** *adj* nourishing; promoting growth.

nuz·zle [NUZ-əl] *vi* **-zled, -zling.** burrow, press with nose; nestle.

ny·lon [NĪ-lon] *n* synthetic material used for fabrics, bristles, ropes, etc. ▶ *pl* stockings made of this.

nymph [nimf] *n* legendary semidivine maiden of sea, woods, mountains, etc.

nym·pho·ma·ni·a [nim-fə-MAY-nee-ə] *n* abnormally intense sexual desire in women. **nym·pho·ma'ni·ac** *n*

O o

O *Chem* oxygen.

oaf [ohf] *n* lout; dolt.

oak [ohk] *n* common, deciduous forest tree. **oak·en** [-in] *adj* of oak.

oa·kum [OH-kəm] *n* loose fiber, used for caulking, got by unraveling old rope.

oar [or] *n* wooden lever with broad blade worked by the hands to propel boat; oarsman. ▶ *v* row. **oars·man** [ORZ-mən] *n*, *pl* **-men.** **oars'manship** *n* skill in rowing.

o·a·sis [oh-AY-sis] *n*, *pl* **-ses** [-seez] fertile spot in desert; place serving as pleasant change from routine.

oat [oht] *n* (usu. *pl*) grain of cereal grass; the plant. **oat·en** [-in] *adj* **oat'meal** [-meel] *n*

oath [ohth] *n*, *pl* **oaths** [oh*thz*] confirmation of truth of statement by naming something sacred; curse.

ob·bli·ga·to [ob-li-GAH-toh] *adj, n, pl* **-tos** *or* **-ti** [-tee] (in musical score) essential; essential part of a musical score.

ob·du·rate [OB-duu-rit] *adj* stubborn, unyielding. **ob'du·ra·cy** [-rə-see] *n*

o·be·di·ence [oh-BEE-dee-əns] *n* submission to authority. **o·be'di·ent** *adj* willing to obey; compliant; dutiful.

o·bei·sance [oh-BAY-səns] *n* deference; a bow or curtsy.

ob·e·lisk [OB-ə-lisk] *n* tapering rectangular stone column, with pyramidal apex.

o·bese [oh-BEES] *adj* very fat, corpulent. **o·be'si·ty** *n*

o·bey [oh-BAY] *vt* do the bidding of; act in accordance with. ▶ *vi* do as ordered; submit to authority.

ob·fus·cate [OB-fə-skayt] *vt* **-cat·ed, -cat·ing.** perplex; darken; make obscure.

o·bit·u·ar·y [oh-BICH-oo-er-ee] *n*, *pl* **-ar·ies.** notice, record of death; biographical sketch of deceased person, esp. in newspaper (also **ob'it**).

ob·ject[1] [OB-jikt] *n* material thing; that to which feeling or action is directed; end or aim; *Grammar* word dependent on verb or preposition. **object lesson** lesson with practical and concrete illustration. **no object** not an obstacle or hindrance.

ob·ject[2] [əb-JEKT] *vt* state in opposition. ▶ *vi* feel dislike or reluctance to something. **ob·jec'tion** *n* **ob·jec'tion·a·ble** *adj* disagreeable; justly liable to objection.

ob·jec·tive [əb-JEK-tiv] *adj* external to the mind; impartial. ▶ *n* thing or place aimed at. **ob·jec·tiv'i·ty** [ob-jek-TIV-] *n*

ob·jur·gate [OB-jər-gayt] *vt* **-gat·ed, -gat·ing.** scold, reprove. **ob·jur·ga'tion** *n*

ob·late [OB-layt] *adj* of a sphere, flattened at the poles.

o·blige [ə-BLĪJ] *vt* **o·bliged, o·blig·ing.** bind morally or legally to do service to; compel. **ob'li·gate** *vt* **-gat·ed, -gat·ing.** bind esp. by legal contract; put under obligation. **ob·li·ga'tion** *n* binding duty, promise; debt of gratitude. **o·blig'a·to·ry** *adj* required; binding. **o·blig'ing** *adj* ready to serve others, civil, helpful, courteous.

o·blique [ə-BLEEK] *adj* slanting; indirect. **o·blique'ly** *adv* **o·bliq'ui·ty** [-BLIK-wi-tee] *n*, *pl* **-ties.** slant; dishonesty. **oblique angle** one not a right angle.

ob·lit·er·ate [ə-BLIT-ə-rayt] *vt* **-at·ed, -at·ing.** blot out, efface, destroy completely.

ob·liv·i·on [ə-BLIV-ee-ən] *n* forgetting or being forgotten. **ob·liv'i·ous** *adj* forgetful; unaware.

ob·long [OB-lawng] *adj* rectangular, with adjacent sides unequal. ▶ *n* oblong figure.

ob·lo·quy [OB-lə-kwee] *n, pl* **-quies.** reproach, abuse; disgrace;

detraction.

ob·nox·ious [əb-NOK-shəs] *adj* offensive, disliked, odious.

o·boe [OH-boh] *n* woodwind instrument. **o'bo·ist** *n*

ob·scene [əb-SEEN] *adj* indecent, lewd, repulsive. **ob·scen'i·ty** [-SEN-i-tee] *n*

ob·scure [əb-SKYUUR] *adj* **-scur·er, -scur·est.** unclear, indistinct; unexplained; dark, dim; humble. ▶ *vt* **-scured, -scur·ing.** make unintelligible; dim; conceal. **ob·scu'rant** [-SKYUUR-ənt] *n* one who opposes enlightenment or reform. **ob·scu'rant·ism** *n* **ob·scu'ri·ty** *n* indistinctness; lack of intelligibility; darkness; obscure, esp. unrecognized, place or position.

ob·se·quies [OB-si-kweez] *pl n* funeral rites.

ob·se·qui·ous [əb-SEE-kwee-əs] *adj* servile, fawning.

ob·serve [əb-ZURV] *v* **-served, -serv·ing.** ▶ *vt* notice, remark; watch; note systematically; keep, follow. ▶ *vi* make a remark. **ob·serv'a·ble** *adj* **ob·serv'ance** [-əns] *n* paying attention; keeping. **ob·serv'ant** *adj* quick to notice; careful in observing. **ob·ser·va'tion** *n* action, habit of observing; noticing; remark. **ob·serv'a·to·ry** [-və-tor-ee] *n, pl* **-ries.** place for watching stars, etc.

ob·sess [əb-SES] *vt* haunt, fill the mind. **ob·ses'sion** [-SESH-ən] *n* fixed idea; domination of the mind by one idea. **ob·ses'sive** *adj*

ob·sid·i·an [əb-SID-ee-ən] *n* fused volcanic rock, forming hard, dark, natural glass.

ob·so·lete [ob-sə-LEET] *adj* disused, out of date. **ob·so·les'cent** [-LES-ənt] *adj* going out of use.

ob·sta·cle [OB-stə-kəl] *n* hindrance; impediment, barrier, obstruction.

ob·stet·rics [əb-STE-triks] *n* branch of medicine concerned with childbirth and care of women before and after childbirth. **ob·stet'ric** *adj* **ob·ste·tri'cian**

[-shən] *n*

ob·sti·nate [OB-stə-nit] *adj* stubborn; self-willed; unyielding; hard to overcome or cure. **ob'sti·na·cy** *n*

ob·strep·er·ous [əb-STREP-ər-əs] *adj* unruly, noisy, boisterous.

ob·struct [əb-STRUKT] *vt* block up; hinder; impede. **ob·struc'tion** *n* **ob·struc'tion·ist** *n* one who deliberately opposes transaction of business.

ob·tain [əb-TAYN] *vt* get; acquire; procure by effort. ▶ *vi* be customary. **ob·tain'a·ble** *adj* procurable.

ob·trude [əb-TROOD] *vt* **-trud·ed, -trud·ing.** thrust forward unduly. **ob·tru'sion** [-TROO-zhən] *n* **ob·tru'sive** *adj* forward, pushing.

ob·tuse [əb-TOOS] *adj* dull of perception; stupid; greater than right angle; not pointed.

ob·verse [OB-vurs] *n* a fact, idea, etc. that is the complement of another; side of coin, medal, etc. that has the principal design. ▶ *adj* [ob-VURS]

ob·vi·ate [OB-vee-ayt] *vt* **-at·ed, -at·ing.** remove, make unnecessary.

ob·vi·ous [OB-vee-əs] *adj* clear, evident; wanting in subtlety.

oc·ca·sion [ə-KAY-zhən] *n* time when thing happens; reason, need; opportunity; special event. ▶ *vt* cause. **oc·ca'sion·al** *adj* happening, found now and then; produced for some special event, e.g. *occasional music.* **oc·ca'sion·al·ly** *adv* sometimes, now and then.

Oc·ci·dent [OK-si-dənt] *n* the West. **oc·ci·dent'al** *adj*

oc·ci·put [OK-sə-put] *n* back of head. **oc·cip'i·tal** *adj*

oc·clude [ə-KLOOD] *vt* **-clud·ed, -clud·ing.** shut in or out. **oc·clu'sion** [-zhən] *n* **oc·clu'sive** *adj* serving to occlude.

oc·cult [ə-KULT] *adj* secret, mysterious; supernatural. ▶ *n* esoteric knowledge. ▶ *vt* hide from view. **oc·cul·ta·tion** [ok-əl-TAY-shən] *n* eclipse.

oc'cult·ism n study of supernatural.

oc·cu·py [OK-yə-pī] vt **-pied,
-py·ing.** inhabit, fill; employ; take
possession of. **oc'cu·pan·cy** n fact
of occupying; residing. **oc'cu·pant**
n tenant. **oc·cu·pa'tion** n
employment; pursuit; fact of
occupying; seizure.
oc·cu·pa'tion·al adj pert. to
occupation, esp. of diseases arising
from a particular occupation; pert.
to use of occupations, e.g. craft,
hobbies, etc. as means of
rehabilitation.

oc·cur [ə-KUR] vi **-curred, -cur·ring.**
happen; come to mind.
oc·cur'rence n happening.

o·cean [OH-shən] n great body of
water; large division of this; the
sea. **o·ce·an'ic** [-shee-AN-ik] adj
o·cea·nol·o·gy [oh-shə-NOL-ə-jee]
n branch of science that relates to
ocean.

oc·e·lot [OS-ə-lot] n Amer.
leopardlike cat.

o·cher [OH-kər] n various earths
used as yellow or brown pigments;
this color, from yellow to brown.

o'clock [ə-KLOK] adv by the clock.

oct-, octa-, octo- comb. form eight,
e.g. octagon; octopus.

oc·ta·gon [OK-tə-gon] n plane
figure with eight angles.
oc·tag'o·nal adj

oc·tane [OK-tayn] n ingredient of
gasoline. **octane number** measure
of ability of gasoline to reduce
engine knock.

oc·tave [OK-tiv] n Mus eighth note
above or below given note; this
space.

oc·ta·vo [ok-TAY-voh] n, pl **-vos.**
book in which each sheet is folded
three times forming eight leaves.

oc·tet [ok-TET] n group of eight;
music for eight instruments or
singers.

oc·to·ge·nar·i·an
[ok-tə-jə-NAIR-ee-ən] n person
aged between eighty and ninety.
▶ adj

oc·to·pus [OK-tə-pəs] n mollusk
with eight arms covered with
suckers. **oc'to·pod** n, adj (mollusk)

with eight feet.

oc·tu·ple [ok-TUU-pəl] adj eight
times as many or as much;
eightfold.

oc·u·lar [OK-yə-lər] adj of eye or
sight.

OD [oh-DEE] n overdose esp. of
dangerous drug; person who has
taken overdose. ▶ v **-ed, -ing.** take,
die of, overdose.

odd adj **-er, -est.** strange, queer;
incidental, random; that is one in
addition when the rest have been
divided into equal groups; not
even; not part of a set. **odds** pl n
advantage conceded in betting;
likelihood. **odd'i·ty** n, pl **-ties.** odd
person or thing; quality of being
odd. **odd'ments** [-mənts] pl n
remnants; trifles. **odds and ends**
odd fragments or scraps.

ode [ohd] n lyric poem on
particular subject.

o·di·um [OH-dee-əm] n hatred,
widespread dislike. **o'di·ous** adj
hateful, repulsive, obnoxious.

o·dor [OH-dər] n smell.
o·dor·if·er·ous [oh-də-RIF-ər-əs]
adj spreading an odor. **o'dor·ize** vt
-ized, -iz·ing. fill with scent.
o'dor·ous adj fragrant; scented.
o'dor·less [-lis] adj

od·ys·sey [OD-ə-see] n, pl **-seys.**
any long adventurous journey.

of [əv] prep denotes removal,
separation, ownership, attribute,
material, quality.

off [awf] adv away. ▶ prep away
from. ▶ adj not operative; canceled
or postponed; bad, sour, etc.;
distant; of horses, vehicles, etc., to
driver's right. **off-color** adj slightly
ill; risqué. **off·hand'** adj, adv
without previous thought; curt.
off·line' adj (of a computer) not
directly controlled by a central
processor; not connected to or
done via the Internet. ▶ adv
off·mes'sage adj not following the
official line, not saying what is
expected. **off-road** adj (of a motor
vehicle) designed for use away
from public roads. **off'set** n that
which counterbalances,

compensates; method of printing.
off·set' vt **off'spring** n children,
issue. **in the offing** likely to
happen soon.

of·fal [AW-fəl] n edible entrails of
animal; refuse.

of·fend [ə-FEND] vt hurt feelings
of, displease. ▶ vi do wrong.

of·fense' n wrong; crime; insult;
Sports, military attacking team,
force. **of·fen'sive** adj causing
displeasure; aggressive. ▶ n position
or movement of attack.

of·fer [AW-fər] vt present for
acceptance or refusal; tender;
propose; attempt. ▶ vi present
itself. ▶ n offering, bid. **of'fer·er,
-or** n **of'fer·to·ry** n, pl **-ies.**
offering of the bread and wine at
the Eucharist; collection in church
service.

of·fice [AW-fis] n room(s), building,
in which business, clerical work,
etc. is done; commercial or
professional organization; official
position; service; duty; form of
worship. ▶ pl task; service. **of'fi·cer**
n one in command in army, navy,
etc.; official.

of·fi·cial [ə-FISH-əl] adj with, by,
authority. ▶ n one holding office,
esp. in public body. **of·fi'cial·dom**
[-dəm] n officials collectively, or
their attitudes, work, usu. in
contemptuous sense.

of·fi·ci·ate [ə-FISH-ee-ayt] vi **-at·ed,
-at·ing.** perform duties of office;
perform ceremony.

of·fi·cious [ə-FISH-əs] adj
objectionably persistent in offering
service; interfering.

of·ten [AW-fən] adv many times,
frequently. **oft** adv poet often.

o·gle [OH-gəl] v **o·gled, o·gling.**
stare, look (at) amorously. ▶ n this
look. **o'gler** n

o·gre [OH-gər] n Folklore
man-eating giant; monster.

ohm n unit of electrical resistance.
ohm'me·ter [-ee-tər] n

oil n any of a number of viscous
liquids with smooth, sticky feel and
wide variety of uses; petroleum;
any of variety of petroleum

derivatives, esp. as fuel or lubricant.
▶ vt lubricate with oil; apply oil to.
oil'y adj **oil·i·er, oil·i·est. oil'skin** n
cloth treated with oil to make it
waterproof. **oiled** sl drunk.

oint·ment [OINT-mənt] n greasy
preparation for healing or
beautifying the skin.

OK, o·kay [oh-kay] adj, adv inf all
right. ▶ n, pl **OK's.** approval. ▶ vt
OK'd, OK'ing. approve.

o·ka·pi [oh-KAH-pee] n, pl **-pis.** Afr.
animal like short-necked giraffe.

old [ohld] adj **old·er, old·est** or
eld·er. or **eld·est.** aged, having
lived or existed long; belonging to
earlier period. **old-fash'ioned**
[-FASH-ənd] adj in style of earlier
period, out of date; fond of old
ways. **old maid** offens elderly
spinster; fussy person.

o·le·ag·i·nous [oh-lee-AJ-ə-nəs] adj
oily, producing oil; unctuous,
fawning.

ol·fac·to·ry [ohl-FAK-tə-ree] adj of
smelling.

ol·i·gar·chy [OL-i-gahr-kee] n, pl
-chies. government by a few.
ol·i·gar'chic adj

ol·ive [OL-iv] n evergreen tree; its
oil-yielding fruit; its wood, color.
▶ adj grayish-green.

O·lym·pi·ad [ə-LIM-pee-ad] n
four-year period between Olympic
games; celebration of modern
Olympic games.

om·buds·man [OM-bədz-mən] n,
pl **-men.** official who investigates
citizens' complaints against
government; person appointed to
perform analogous function in a
business.

o·me·ga [oh-MAY-gə] n last letter
of Greek alphabet; end.

om·e·let [OM-lit] n dish of eggs
beaten up and cooked in melted
butter with other ingredients and
seasoning.

o·men [OH-mən] n prophetic
object or happening. **om·i·nous**
[OM-ə-nəs] adj boding evil,
threatening.

o·mit [oh-MIT] vt **o·mit·ted,
o·mit·ting.** leave out, neglect;

leave undone. **o·mis'sion** [-MISH-ən] *n*

omni- *comb. form* all, e.g. *omnipresent.*

om·ni·bus [OM-nə-bəs] *n* bus; book containing several works. ▶ *adj* serving, containing several objects or subjects.

om·ni·di·rec·tion·al *adj* [om-nə-di-REK-shə-nl] in radio, denotes transmission, reception in all directions.

om·nip·o·tent [om-NIP-ə-tənt] *adj* all-powerful. **om·nip'o·tence** *n*

om·ni·pres·ent [om-nə-PREZ-ənt] *adj* present everywhere. **om·ni·pres'ence** *n*

om·nis·cient [om-NISH-ənt] *adj* knowing everything. **om·nis'cience** *n*

om·niv·o·rous [om-NIV-ər-əs] *adj* devouring all foods; not selective e.g. in reading.

on *prep* above and touching, at, near, toward, etc.; attached to; concerning; performed upon; during; taking regularly. ▶ *adj* operating; taking place. ▶ *adv* so as to be on; forward; continuously, etc.; in progress. **on·line'** *adj* (of a computer) directly controlled by a central processor; connected to, or done via, the Internet. ▶ *adv* **on·mes'sage** *adj* following the official line, saying what is expected.

o·nan·ism [OH-nə-niz-əm] *n* masturbation.

once [wuns] *adv* one time; formerly; ever. **once'-o·ver** *n inf* quick examination. **at once** immediately; simultaneously.

on·co·gene [ONG-kə-jeen] *n* any of several genes that when abnormally activated can cause cancer. **on·co·gen'ic** *adj*

on·col·o·gy [ong-KOL-ə-jee] *n* branch of medicine dealing with tumors; study of cancer.

one [wun] *adj* lowest cardinal number; single; united; only, without others; identical. ▶ *n* number or figure 1; unity; single specimen. ▶ *pron* particular but not stated person; any person. **one'ness** *n* unity; uniformity; singleness. **one·self'** *pron*

one'-sid'ed *adj* partial; uneven.

one-way *adj* denotes system of traffic circulation in one direction only.

on·er·ous [ON-ər-əs] *adj* burdensome.

on·ion [UN-yən] *n* edible bulb of pungent flavor. **know one's onions** *sl* know one's field, etc. thoroughly.

on·ly [OHN-lee] *adj* being the one specimen. ▶ *adv* solely, merely, exclusively. ▶ *conj* but then, excepting that.

on·o·mas·tics [on-ə-MAS-tiks] *n* study of proper names.

on·o·mat·o·poe·ia [on-ə-mat-ə-PEE-ə] *n* formation of a word by using sounds that resemble or suggest the object or action to be named. **on·o·mat·o·poe'ic**, **on·o·mat·o·po·et'ic** *adj*

on·set *n* violent attack; assault; beginning.

on·slaught [ON-slawt] *n* attack.

on·to [ON-too] *prep* on top of; aware of.

on·tog·e·ny [on-TOJ-ə-nee] *n* development of an individual organism.

on·tol·o·gy [on-TOL-ə-jee] *n* science of being or reality.

o·nus [OH-nəs] *n, pl* **-nus·es.** responsibility, burden.

on·ward [ON-wərd] *adj* advanced or advancing. ▶ *adv* in advance, ahead, forward. **on'wards** *adv*

on·yx [ON-iks] *n* variety of chalcedony.

ooze [ooz] *vi* **oozed, ooz·ing.** pass slowly out, exude (moisture). ▶ *n* sluggish flow; wet mud, slime.

o·pal [OH-pəl] *n* glassy gemstone displaying variegated colors. **o·pal·es'cent** *adj*

o·paque [oh-PAYK] *adj* not allowing the passage of light, not transparent. **o·pac'i·ty** [-PAS-i-tee] *n*

op. cit. [op sit] in the work cited.

o·pen [OH-pən] *adj* not shut or blocked up; without lid or door; bare; undisguised; not enclosed, covered or exclusive; spread out, accessible; frank, sincere. ▶ *vt* set open, uncover, give access to; disclose, lay bare; begin; make a hole in. ▶ *vi* become open; begin. ▶ *n* clear space, unenclosed country; *Sports* competition in which all may enter. **o'pen·ing** *n* hole, gap; beginning; opportunity. ▶ *adj* first; initial. **o'pen·ly** *adv* without concealment.
o'pen·hand·ed *adj* generous.
o'pen-heart'ed *adj* frank, magnanimous. **o'pen-mind'ed** *adj* unprejudiced. **o'pen·work** *n* pattern with interstices.
op·er·a [OP-ər-ə] *n* musical drama. **op·er·at'ic** *adj* of opera. **op·er·et·ta** *n* light, comic opera.
op·er·a·tion [op-ə-RAY-shən] *n* working, way things work; scope; act of surgery; military action. **op'er·ate** *v* **-at·ed, -at·ing.** ▶ *vt* cause to function; effect. ▶ *vi* work; produce an effect; perform act of surgery; exert power.
op·er·a'tion·al *adj* of operation(s); working. **op'er·a·tive** [-ə-tiv] *adj* working. ▶ *n* worker, esp. with a special skill; secret agent.
o·phid·i·an [oh-FID-ee-ən] *adj, n* (reptile) of the order including snakes.
oph·thal·mic [of-THAL-mik] *adj* of eyes. **oph·thal·mol'o·gist** [-jist] *n* **oph·thal·mol'o·gy** *n* study of eye and its diseases.
oph·thal'mo·scope [-skohp] *n* instrument for examining interior of eye.
opiate see OPIUM.
o·pin·ion [ə-PIN-yən] *n* what one thinks about something; belief, judgment. **o·pine** [oh-PIN] *vt* **o·pined, o·pin·ing.** think; utter opinion. **o·pin'ion·at·ed** *adj* stubborn in one's opinions; dogmatic.
o·pi·um [OH-pee-əm] *n* sedative-narcotic drug made from poppy. **o'pi·ate** [-it] *n* drug containing opium; narcotic. ▶ *adj* inducing sleep; soothing.
o·pos·sum [ə-POS-əm] *n* small Amer. marsupial animal, possum.
op·po·nent [ə-POH-nənt] *n* adversary, antagonist.
op·por·tune [op-ər-TOON] *adj* seasonable, well-timed.
op·por·tun'ism *n* policy of doing what is expedient at the time regardless of principle.
op·por·tun'ist *n, adj*
op·por·tu'ni·ty *n, pl* **-ties.** favorable time or condition; good chance.
op·pose [ə-POHZ] *vt* **-posed, -pos·ing.** resist, withstand; contrast; set against. **op·po·site** [OP-ə-zit] *adj* contrary; facing; diametrically different; adverse. ▶ *n* the contrary. ▶ *prep, adv* facing; on the other side. **op·po·si'tion** [-ZISH-ən] *n* antithesis; resistance; obstruction; hostility; group opposing another; party opposing that in power.
op·press [ə-PRES] *vt* govern with tyranny; weigh down.
op·pres'sion [-PRESH-ən] *n* act of oppressing; severity; misery.
op·pres'sive *adj* tyrannical; hard to bear; heavy; hot and tiring (of weather). **op·pres'sor** [-ər] *n*
op·pro·bri·um [ə-PROH-bree-əm] *n* disgrace. **op·pro'bri·ous** *adj* reproachful; shameful; abusive.
opt *vi* make a choice. **op'ta·tive** [OP-tə-tiv] *adj* expressing wish or desire.
op·tic [OP-tik] *adj* of eye or sight. ▶ *n* eye. **optics** *n* science of sight and light. **op'ti·cal** *adj* **optical character reader** device for scanning magnetically coded data on labels, cans, etc. **op·ti'cian** [-TISH-ən] *n* maker of, dealer in eyeglasses, contact lenses.
op·ti·mism [OP-tə-miz-əm] *n* disposition to look on the bright side; doctrine that good must prevail in the end; belief that the world is the best possible world. **op'ti·mist** *n* **op·ti·mis'tic** *adj*
op·ti·mum [OP-tə-məm] *adj, n* the best, the most favorable.

op·tion [OP-shən] *n* choice; preference; thing chosen; in business, purchased privilege of either buying or selling things at specified price within specified time. **op'tion·al** *adj* leaving to choice.

op·tom·e·trist [op-TOM-i-trist] *n* person qualified in testing eyesight, prescribing corrective lenses, etc. **op·tom'e·try** *n*

op·u·lent [OP-yə-lənt] *adj* rich; copious. **op'u·lence** *n* riches, wealth.

o·pus [OH-pəs] *n, pl* **o·pus·es** or **op·er·a** [OHP-ə-rə] work; musical composition, e.g. *Grieg's opus 53.*

or *conj* introduces alternatives; if not.

or·a·cle [OR-ə-kəl] *n* divine utterance, prophecy, oft. ambiguous, given at shrine of god; the shrine; wise or mysterious adviser. **o·rac·u·lar** [aw-RAK-yə-lər] *adj* of oracle; prophetic; authoritative; ambiguous.

o·ral [OR-əl] *adj* spoken; by mouth. ▶ *n* spoken examination. **o'ral·ly** *adv*

or·ange [OR-inj] *n* bright reddish-yellow round fruit; tree bearing it; fruit's color.

o·rang·u·tan [aw-RANG-uu-tan] *n* large E. Indian ape.

or·a·tor [OR-ə-tər] *n* maker of speech; skillful speaker. **o·ra'tion** [aw-RAY-shən] *n* formal speech. **or·a·tor'i·cal** *adj* of orator or oration. **or'a·to·ry** *n* speeches; eloquence; small private chapel.

or·a·to·ri·o [or-ə-TOR-ee-oh] *n, pl* **-ri·os.** semidramatic composition of sacred music.

orb *n* globe, sphere; eye, eyeball.

or'bit *n* track of planet, satellite, comet, etc., around another heavenly body; field of influence, sphere; eye socket. ▶ *v* move in, or put into, an orbit.

or·chard [OR-chərd] *n* area for cultivation of fruit trees; the trees.

or·ches·tra [OR-kə-strə] *n* band of musicians; place for such band in theater, etc. **or·ches'tral** *adj*

or'ches·trate *vt* **-trat·ed, -trat·ing.** compose or arrange music for orchestra; organize, arrange.

or·chid [OR-kid] *n* genus of various flowering plants.

or·dain [or-DAYN] *vt* admit to religious ministry; confer holy orders upon; decree, enact; destine. **or·di·na'tion** *n*

or·deal [or-DEEL] *n* severe, trying experience; *Hist* form of trial by which accused underwent severe physical test.

or·der [OR-dər] *n* regular or proper arrangement or condition; sequence; peaceful condition of society; rank, class; group; command; request for something to be supplied; mode of procedure; instruction; monastic society. ▶ *vt* command; request (something) to be supplied or made; arrange. **or'der·li·ness** *n* **or'der·ly** *adj* tidy; methodical; well-behaved. ▶ *n* hospital attendant; soldier performing chores for officer.

or·di·nal [OR-dn-əl] *adj* showing position in a series. ▶ *n* ordinal number.

or·di·nance [OR-dn-əns] *n* decree, rule; rite, ceremony.

or·di·nar·y [OR-dn-er-ee] *adj* usual, normal; common; plain; commonplace. ▶ *n* average condition. **or'di·nar·i·ly** *adv*

ord·nance [ORD-nəns] *n* big guns, artillery; military stores.

or·dure [OR-jər] *n* dung; filth.

ore [or] *n* naturally occurring mineral that yields metal.

o·reg·a·no [ə-REG-ə-noh] *n* herb, variety of marjoram.

or·gan [OR-gən] *n* musical wind instrument of pipes and stops, played by keys; member of animal or plant carrying out particular function; means of action; medium of information, esp. newspaper. **or·gan'ic** *adj* of, derived from, living organisms; of bodily organs; affecting bodily organs; having vital organs; *Chem* of compounds formed from carbon; grown with fertilizers derived from animal or vegetable matter; organized, systematic. **or·gan·i·cal·ly** adv

or'gan·ist n organ player.

or·gan·ize [OR-gə-nīz] vt **-nized, -niz·ing.** give definite structure; get up, arrange; put into working order; unite in a society.

or'gan·ism n organized body or system; plant, animal.

or·gan·i·za'tion n act of organizing; body of people; society.

or·gasm [OR-gaz-əm] n sexual climax.

or·gy [OR-jee] n, pl **-gies.** drunken or licentious revel, debauch; act of immoderation, overindulgence.

o·ri·el [OR-ee-əl] n projecting part of an upper room with a window; the window.

o·ri·ent [OR-ee-ənt] n (**O-**) East; luster of best pearls. ▶ adj rising; (**O-**) Eastern. ▶ vt [OR-ee-ent] place so as to face east or other known direction; take bearings; determine one's position. **o·ri·en'tal** adj of, or from, the East. ▶ n oft offens person from the East or of Eastern descent. **o·ri·en'tal·ist** n expert in Eastern languages and history. **o·ri·en·ta'tion** n

or·i·fice [OR-ə-fis] n opening, mouth of a cavity, e.g. pipe.

o·ri·ga·mi [or-i-GAH-mee] n Japanese art of paper folding.

or·i·gin [OR-i-jin] n beginning; source; parentage.

o·rig·i·nal [ə-RIJ-ə-nl] adj primitive, earliest; new, not copied or derived; thinking or acting for oneself; eccentric. ▶ n pattern, thing from which another is copied; unconventional or strange person. **o·rig·i·nal'i·ty** n power of producing something individual to oneself. **o·rig'i·nal·ly** adv at first; in the beginning.

o·rig·i·nate [ə-RIJ-ə-nayt] v **-nat·ed, -nat·ing.** come or bring into existence, begin. **o·rig'i·na·tor** [-tər] n

o·ri·ole [OR-ee-ohl] n any of several thrushlike birds.

O·ri·on [ə-RĪ-ən] n bright constellation.

or·i·son [OR-ə-zən] n prayer.

or·mo·lu [OR-mə-loo] n gilded bronze; gold-colored alloy; articles of these.

or·na·ment [OR-nə-mənt] n any object used to adorn or decorate; decoration. ▶ vt [-ment] adorn. **or·na·ment'al** adj **or·na·men·ta'tion** n

or·nate [or-NAYT] adj highly decorated or elaborate.

or·ni·thol·o·gy [or-nə-THOL-ə-jee] n science of birds. **or·ni·thol'o·gist** n

o·ro·tund [OR-ə-tund] adj full, clear, and musical; pompous.

or·phan [OR-fən] n child bereaved of one or both parents. **or'phan·age** [-fə-nij] n institution for care of orphans.

ortho- comb. form right, correct.

or·tho·dox [OR-thə-doks] adj holding accepted views; conventional. **or'tho·dox·y** n

or·thog·ra·phy [or-THOG-rə-fee] n correct spelling.

or·tho·pe·dic [or-thə-PEE-dik] adj for curing deformity, disorder of bones. **or·tho·pe'dics** n medical specialty dealing with this. **or·tho·pe'dist** n

Os Chem osmium.

os·cil·late [OS-ə-layt] vi **-lat·ed, -lat·ing.** swing to and fro; waver; fluctuate (regularly). **os·cil·la'tion** n **os·cil·la·tor** n **os·cil·la·to·ry** adj **os·cil'lo·scope** n electronic instrument producing visible representation of rapidly changing quantity.

os·mi·um [OZ-mee-əm] n heaviest known of metallic elements.

os·mo·sis [oz-MOH-sis] n percolation of fluids through porous partitions. **os·mot'ic** adj

os·se·ous [OS-ee-əs] adj of, like bone; bony. **os·si·fi·ca'tion** n **os'si·fy** [-fī] v **-fied, -fy·ing.** turn into bone; grow rigid.

os·ten·si·ble [o-STEN-sə-bəl] adj apparent; professed. **os·ten'si·bly** adv

os·ten·ta·tion [os-ten-TAY-shən] n show, pretentious display.

os·ten·ta'tious *adj* given to display; showing off.

os·te·op·a·thy [os-tee-OP-ə-thee] *n* art of treating disease by removing structural derangement by manipulation, esp. of spine. **os'te·o·path** *n* one skilled in this art.

os·tra·cize [OS-trə-sīz] *vt* **-cized, -ciz·ing.** exclude, banish from society, exile. **os'tra·cism** [-siz-əm] *n* social boycotting.

os'trich *n* large swift-running flightless Afr. bird.

oth·er [UTH-ər] *adj* not this; not the same; alternative, different. ▶ *pron* other person or thing. **oth'er·wise** *adv* differently; in another way. ▶ *conj* else, if not.

o·ti·ose [OH-shee-ohs *or* OH-tee-ohs] *adj* superfluous; useless.

o·ti·tis [oh-TĪ-tis] *n* inflammation of the ear.

ot·ter [OT-ər] *n* furry aquatic fish-eating animal.

Ot·to·man [OT-ə-mən] *adj* Turkish. ▶ *n* Turk; (**o-**) cushioned, backless seat; (**o-**) cushioned footstool.

ought [awt] *v aux* expressing duty or obligation or advisability; be bound.

Oui·ja [WEE-jə] *n* ® board with letters and symbols used to obtain messages at seances.

ounce [owns] *n* a weight, sixteenth of avoirdupois pound (28.349 grams), twelfth of troy pound (31.103 grams).

our [OW-ər] *adj* belonging to us. **ours** *pron* thing(s) belonging to us. **our·selves'** *pron* emphatic or reflexive form of WE.

oust [owst] *vt* put out, expel.

out [owt] *adv* from within, away; wrong; on strike. ▶ *adj* not worth considering; not allowed; unfashionable; unconscious; not in use, operation, etc.; at an end; not burning; *Baseball* failed to get on base. ▶ *vt inf* name (public figure) as being homosexual. **out'er** *adj* away from the inside. **out'er·most** [-mohst] *adj* on extreme outside. **out'ing** *n* pleasure excursion.

out'ward [-wurd] *adj, adv* **out'wards** [-wurdz] *adv*

out- *prefix* beyond, in excess, e.g. *outclass; outdistance; outsize.*

out·bal·ance [owt-BAL-əns] *vt* **-anced, -anc·ing.** outweigh; exceed in weight.

out·board [OWT-bord] *adj* of boat's engine, mounted on, outside stern.

out·break [OWT-brayk] *n* sudden occurrence, esp. of disease or strife.

out·burst [OWT-burst] *n* bursting out, esp. of violent emotion.

out·cast [OWT-kast] *n* someone rejected. ▶ *adj*

out·class [owt-KLAS] *vt* excel, surpass.

out·come [OWT-kum] *n* result.

out·crop [OWT-krop] *n Geology* rock coming out of stratum to the surface. ▶ *vi* [owt-KROP] **-cropped, -crop·ping.** come out to the surface.

out·doors [owt-DORZ] *adv* in the open air. **out'door** *adj*

out·fit [OWT-fit] *n* equipment; clothes and accessories; *inf* group or association regarded as a unit. **out'fit·ter** *n* one who supplies clothing and accessories.

out·flank [owt-FLANGK] *vt* to get beyond the flank (of enemy army); circumvent; outmaneuver.

out·go·ing [OWT-goh-ing] *adj* departing; friendly, sociable.

out·grow [owt-GROH] *vt* **-grew, -grown, -grow·ing.** become too large or too old for; surpass in growth.

out·house [OWT-hows] *n* outdoor toilet; shed, etc. near main building.

out·land·ish [owt-LAN-dish] *adj* queer, extravagantly strange.

out·law [OWT-law] *n* one beyond protection of the law; exile, bandit. ▶ *vt* make (someone) an outlaw; ban.

out·lay [OWT-lay] *n* expenditure.

out·let [OWT-let] *n* opening, vent; means of release or escape; market for product or service.

out·line [OWT-līn] *n* rough sketch; general plan; lines enclosing visible figure. ▶ *vt* **-lined, lin·ing.** sketch;

summarize.

out·look [OWT-luuk] *n* point of view; probable outcome; view.

out·ly·ing [OWT-lī-ing] *adj* distant, remote.

out·mod·ed [owt-MOH-did] *adj* no longer fashionable or accepted.

out·pa·tient [OWT-pay-shənt] *n* patient treated but not kept at hospital.

out·put [OWT-puut] *n* quantity produced; *Computers* data produced. ▶ *vt Computers* produce (data) at the end of a process.

out·rage [OWT-rayj] *n* violation of others' rights; gross or violent offense or indignity; anger arising from this. ▶ *vt* **-raged, rag·ing.** offend grossly; insult; injure, violate. **out·ra·geous** [-RAY-jəs] *adj*

ou·tré [oo-TRAY] *adj* extravagantly odd; bizarre.

out·rig·ger [OWT-rig-ər] *n* frame, esp. with float attached, outside boat's gunwale; frame on rowing boat's side with rowlock; boat with one.

out·right [OWT-rīt] *adj* undisputed; downright; positive. ▶ *adv* [owt-rīt] completely; once for all; openly.

out·set [OWT-set] *n* beginning.

out·side [OWT-sīd] *n* exterior. ▶ *adv* [owt-SĪD] not inside; in the open air. ▶ *adj* [owt-SĪD] on exterior; remote, unlikely; greatest possible, probable. **out·sid'er** *n* person outside specific group; contestant thought unlikely to win.

out·skirts [OWT-skurts] *pl n* outer areas, districts, esp. of city.

out·spok·en [OWT-SPOH-kən] *adj* frank, candid.

out·stand·ing [owt-STAN-ding] *adj* excellent; remarkable; unsettled, unpaid.

out·strip [owt-STRIP] *vt* **-stripped, -strip·ping.** outrun, surpass.

out·wit [owt-WIT] *vt* **-wit·ted, -wit·ting.** get the better of by cunning.

o·val [OH-vəl] *adj* egg-shaped, elliptical. ▶ *n* something of this shape.

o·va·ry [OH-və-ree] *n, pl* **-ries.**

female egg-producing organ.

o·var'i·an [-VAIR-ee-ən] *adj*

o·va·tion [oh-VAY-shən] *n* enthusiastic burst of applause.

ov·en [UV-ən] *n* heated chamber for baking in.

o·ver [OH-vər] *adv* above, above and beyond, going beyond, in excess, too much, past, finished, in repetition, across, downward, etc. ▶ *prep* above; on, upon; more than, in excess of, along, etc. ▶ *adj* upper, outer.

over- *prefix* too much, e.g. *overeat;* above, e.g. *overlord;* on top, e.g. *overshoe.*

o·ver·all [OH-vər-awl] *adj, adv* in total. ▶ *n* coat-shaped protective garment. ▶ *pl* protective garment consisting of trousers with a part extending up over the chest.

o·ver·awe' *vt* affect (someone) with an overpowering sense of awe.

o·ver·bal'ance *v* lose balance.

o·ver·bear·ing [oh-vər-BAIR-ing] *adj* domineering.

o·ver·blown [OH-vər-BLOHN] *adj* excessive, bombastic.

o·ver·board [OH-vər-bord] *adv* from a vessel into the water.

o·ver·cast [OH-vər-KAST] *adj* covered over, esp. by clouds.

o'ver·coat *n* heavy coat.

o·ver·come [oh-vər-KUM] *vt* **-came, -come, -com·ing.** conquer; surmount; make powerless.

o·ver·crowd' *vt* fill with more people or things than is desirable. **ov·er·crowd'ing** *n*

o·ver·do' *vt* do to excess; exaggerate (something).

o'ver·dose *n* excessive dose of a drug. ▶ *v* take an overdose.

o·ver·draft [OH-vər-draft] *n* withdrawal of money in excess of credit balance on bank account.

o·ver·due' *adj* still due after the time allowed.

o·ver·flow' *v* flow over; be filled beyond capacity. ▶ *n* something that overflows; outlet for excess liquid; excess amount.

o·ver·haul [oh-vər-HAWL] *vt* examine and set in order, repair;

overtake. ▶ n [OH-vər-hawl] thorough examination, esp. for repairs.

o·ver·head [OH-vər-hed] *adj* over one's head, above. ▶ n expense of running a business, over and above cost of manufacturing and of raw materials. ▶ *adv* [OH-vər-HED] aloft, above.

o·ver·kill [OH-vər-kil] n capacity, advantage greater than required.

o·ver·lap v share part of the same space or period of time (as). ▶ n area overlapping.

o·ver·look [oh-vər-LUUK] vt fail to notice; disregard; look over.

o·ver·pow·er v subdue or overcome (someone); make helpless or ineffective. **o·ver·pow·er·ing** *adj*

o·ver·re·act' vi react more strongly than is necessary.

o·ver·ride [oh-vər-RĪD] vt **-rode, -rid·den, -rid·ing.** set aside, disregard; cancel; trample down.

o·ver·rule' vt reverse the decision of (a person with less power); reverse (someone else's decision).

o·ver·run' v conquer rapidly; spread over (a place) rapidly; extend beyond a set limit.

o·ver·seas [OH-vər-SEEZ] *adj* foreign. ▶ *adj, adv* [oh-vər-SEEZ] to, from place over the sea.

o·ver·se·er [OH-vər-see-ər] n supervisor. **o·ver·see'** vt **-saw, -seen, -see·ing.** supervise.

o·ver·shoot' v go beyond (a mark or target).

o·ver·sight [OH-vər-sīt] n failure to notice; mistake; supervision.

o·vert [oh-VURT] *adj* open, unconcealed. **o·vert'ly** *adv*

o·ver·take [oh-vər-TAYK] vt **-took, -tak·en, -tak·ing.** move past (vehicle, person) traveling in same direction; come up with in pursuit; catch up.

o·ver·tax [oh-vər-TAKS] vt tax too heavily; impose too great a strain on.

o·ver·throw [oh-vər-THROH] vt **-threw, -thrown, -throw·ing.** upset, overturn; defeat. ▶ n

[OH-vər-throh] ruin; defeat; fall.

o·ver·tone [OH-vər-tohn] n additional meaning, nuance.

o·ver·ture [OH-vər-chər] n *Mus* orchestral introduction; opening of negotiations; formal offer.

o·ver·ween·ing [OH-vər-WEE-ning] *adj* thinking too much of oneself.

o·ver·whelm [oh-vər-HWELM] vt crush; submerge, engulf. **o·ver·whelm'ing** *adj* decisive; irresistible.

o·ver·wrought [OH-vər-RAWT] *adj* overexcited; too elaborate.

o·vip·a·rous [oh-VIP-ər-əs] *adj* laying eggs.

ov·ule [OV-yool] n unfertilized seed. **ov'u·late** [-yə-layt] vi **-lat·ed, -lat·ing.** produce, discharge (egg) from ovary.

o·vum [OH-vəm] n, pl **o·va** [OH-və] female egg cell, in which development of fetus takes place.

owe [oh] vt **owed, ow·ing.** be bound to repay, be indebted for. **owing** *adj* owed, due. **owing to** caused by, as result of.

owl n night bird of prey. **owl'ish** *adj* resembling an owl.

own [ohn] *adj* emphasizes possession. ▶ vt possess; acknowledge. ▶ vi to confess. **own'er·ship** n possession.

ox [oks] n, pl **ox·en.** large cloven-footed and usu. horned farm animal; bull or cow. **ox'bow** [-boh] n U-shaped harness collar of ox; bow-shaped bend in river.

ox·ide [OK-sīd] n compound of oxygen and another element. **ox'i·dize** v **-dized, -diz·ing.** (cause to) combine with oxide, rust.

ox·y·gen [OK-si-jən] n gas in atmosphere essential to life, combustion, etc. **ox'y·gen·ate** vt **-at·ed, -at·ing.** combine or treat with oxygen.

ox·y·mo·ron [ok-si-MOR-on] n figure of speech in which two ideas of opposite meaning are combined to form an expressive phrase or epithet, such as *cruel kindness*.

oys·ter [OI-stər] n edible bivalve

mollusk or shellfish.
o·zone [OH-zohn] *n* form of
oxygen with pungent odor. **ozone**
layer layer of upper atmosphere
with concentration of ozone.

P p

P *Chem* phosphorus.

Pa *Chem* protactinium.

pace [pays] *n* step; its length; rate of movement; walk, gait. ▶ *v* **paced, pac·ing.** ▶ *vi* step. ▶ *vt* set speed for; cross, measure with steps. **pac'er** *n* one who sets the pace for another; horse used for pacing in harness racing. **pace'mak·er** *n* esp. electronic device surgically implanted in those with heart disease.

pa·chin·ko [pə-CHING-koh] *n* Japanese pinball machine.

pach·y·derm [PAK-i-durm] *n* thick-skinned animal, such as an elephant. **pach·y·der'ma·tous** [-mə-təs] *adj* thick-skinned, stolid.

pac·i·fy [PAS-ə-fī] *vt* **-fied, -fy·ing.** calm; establish peace. **pa·cif'ic** *adj* peaceable; calm, tranquil. **pa'ci·fi·er** *n* ring or nipple for baby to suck or chew. **pac'i·fism** *n* **pac'i·fist** *n* advocate of abolition of war; one who refuses to help in war.

pack [pak] *n* bundle; band of animals; large set of people or things; set of, container for, retail commodities; set of playing cards; mass of floating ice. ▶ *vt* put together in suitcase, etc.; make into a bundle; press tightly together, cram; fill with things; fill (meeting, etc.) with one's own supporters; order off. **pack'age** [-ij] *n* parcel; set of items offered together. ▶ *vt* **-aged, -ag·ing. pack'et** [-it] *n* small parcel; small container (and contents); *inf* large sum of money; small mail, passenger, freight boat. **pack'horse** *n* horse for carrying goods. **pack ice** loose floating ice that has been compacted together.

pact [pakt] *n* covenant, agreement, compact.

pad¹ *n* piece of soft material used as a cushion, protection, etc.; block of sheets of paper; foot or sole of various animals; place for launching rockets; *sl* residence. ▶ *vt* **pad·ded, pad·ding.** make soft, fill in, protect, etc., with pad or padding; add to dishonestly. **padding** *n* material used for stuffing; literary matter put in simply to increase quantity.

pad² *vi* **pad·ded, pad·ding.** walk with soft step; travel slowly. ▶ *n* sound of soft footstep.

pad·dle¹ [PAD-əl] *n* short oar with broad blade at one or each end. ▶ *v* **-dled, -dling.** move by, as with, paddles; row gently. **paddle wheel** wheel with crosswise blades striking water successively to propel ship.

paddle² *vt* **-dled, -dling.** walk with bare feet in shallow water. ▶ *n* such a walk.

pad·dock [PAD-ək] *n* small grass field or enclosure.

pad·dy [PAD-ee] *n, pl* **-dies.** rice growing or in the husk. **paddy field** field where rice is grown.

pad·lock [PAD-lok] *n* detachable lock with hinged hoop to go through staple or ring. ▶ *vt* fasten thus.

pae·an [PEE-ən] *n* song of triumph or thanksgiving.

pa·gan [PAY-gən] *adj, n* heathen. **pa'gan·ism** *n*

page¹ [payj] *n* one side of leaf of book, etc.; screenful of information from a website or teletext service.

page² *n* boy servant; attendant. ▶ *vt* **paged, pag·ing.** summon (a person), by bleeper or loudspeaker, in order to pass on a message. **page'boy** *n* hair style with hair rolled under usu. at shoulder length.

pag·eant [PAJ-ənt] *n* show of persons in costume in procession, dramatic scenes, etc., usu. illustrating history; brilliant show. **pag'eant·ry** *n, pl* **-ies.**

pag·i·nate [PAJ-ə-nate] *vt* **-nat·ed, -nat·ing.** number pages of.

pag·i·na'tion n

pa·go·da [pə-GOH-də] n pyramidal temple or tower of Chinese or Indian type.

paid [payd] pt. of PAY. **paid-up** adj paid in full.

pail [payl] n bucket. **pail'ful** [-fəl] n, pl **-fuls.**

pain [payn] n bodily or mental suffering; penalty or punishment. ▶ pl trouble, exertion. ▶ vt inflict pain upon. **pain'ful** [-fəl] adj **pain'less** [-lis] adj **pain'kill·er** n drug, as aspirin, that reduces pain. **pains'tak·ing** adj diligent, careful.

paint [paynt] n coloring matter spread on a surface with brushes, roller, spray gun, etc. ▶ vt portray, color, coat, or make picture of, with paint; apply makeup; describe. **paint'er** n **paint'ing** n picture in paint.

paint·er [PAYN-tər] n line at bow of boat for tying it up.

pair n set of two, esp. existing or generally used together. ▶ v arrange in twos; group or be grouped in twos.

pais·ley [PAYZ-lee] n, pl **-leys.** pattern of small curving shapes.

pa·ja·mas [pə-JAH-məz] pl n sleeping suit of loose-fitting trousers and jacket.

pal n inf friend.

pal·ace [PAL-is] n residence of king, bishop, etc.; stately mansion. **pa·la·tial** [pə-LAY-shəl] adj like a palace; magnificent. **pal·a·tine** [PAL-ə-tīn] adj with royal privileges. **pal·ate** [PAL-it] n roof of mouth; sense of taste. **pal'at·a·ble** adj agreeable to eat. **pal'a·tal** [-təl] adj of the palate; made by placing tongue against palate.

palatial, palatine see PALACE.

pa·lav·er [pə-LAV-ər] n fuss; conference, discussion.

pale¹ [payl] adj **pal·er, pal·est.** wan, dim, whitish. ▶ vi **paled, pal·ing.** whiten; lose superiority or importance.

pale² n stake, boundary. **pal'ing** n upright stakes making up fence. **beyond the pale** beyond limits of propriety, safety, etc.

pa·le·o·lith·ic [pay-lee-ə-LITH-ik] adj of the old Stone Age.

pa·le·on·tol·o·gy [pay-lee-ən-TOL-ə-jee] n study of past geological periods and fossils.

pal·ette [PAL-it] n artist's flat board for mixing colors on.

pal·i·mo·ny [PAL-ə-moh-nee] n alimony awarded to partner in broken romantic relationship.

pal·in·drome [PAL-in-drohm] n word, verse or sentence that is the same when read backward or forward.

pal·i·sade [pal-ə-SAYD] n fence of stakes. ▶ pl line of cliffs. ▶ vt **-sad·ed, -sad·ing.** to enclose or protect with one.

pall¹ [pawl] n cloth spread over a coffin; depressing, oppressive atmosphere. **pall'bear·er** n one carrying, attending coffin at funeral.

pall² vi become tasteless or tiresome; cloy.

pal·let¹ [PAL-it] n straw mattress; small bed.

pallet² n portable platform for storing and moving goods.

pal·li·ate [PAL-ee-ayt] vt **-at·ed, -at·ing.** relieve without curing; excuse. **pal'li·a·tive** [-ə-tiv] adj giving temporary or partial relief. ▶ n that which excuses, mitigates or alleviates.

pal·lid [PAL-id] adj pale, wan, colorless. **pal'lor** [-ər] n paleness.

palm [pahm] n inner surface of hand; tropical tree; leaf of the tree as symbol of victory. ▶ vt conceal in palm of hand; pass off by trickery. **palm'is·try** n fortune telling from lines on palm of hand. **palm'y** adj **palm·i·er, palm·i·est.** flourishing, successful. **Palm Sunday** Sunday before Easter. **palm'top** adj (of a computer) small enough to be held in the hand. ▶ n such a computer.

pal·o·mi·no [pal-ə-MEE-noh] n, pl **-nos.** golden horse with white mane and tail.

pal·pa·ble [PAL-pə-bəl] adj obvious; certain; that can be touched or felt. **pal'pa·bly** adv

pal·pate [PAL-payt] *vt* **-pat·ed, -pat·ing.** *Med* examine by touch.

pal·pi·tate [PAL-pi-tayt] *vi* **-tat·ed, -tat·ing.** throb; pulsate violently. **pal·pi·ta'tion** *n* throbbing; violent, irregular beating of heart.

pal·sy [PAWL-zee] *n, pl* **-sies.** paralysis, esp. with tremors. **pal'sied** *adj* affected with palsy.

pal·try [PAWL-tree] *adj* **-tri·er, -tri·est.** worthless, contemptible, trifling.

pam·pas [PAM-pəz] *pl n* vast grassy treeless plains in S Amer.

pam·per [PAM-pər] *vt* overindulge, spoil by coddling.

pam·phlet [PAM-flit] *n* thin unbound book usu. on some topical subject. **pam·phlet·eer'** *n* writer of these.

pan¹ *n* broad, shallow vessel; depression in ground, esp. where salt forms. ▶ *vt* **panned, pan·ning.** wash gold ore in pan; *inf* criticize harshly. **pan out** *vi inf* result, esp. successfully.

pan² *v* **panned, pan·ning.** move motion picture or TV camera slowly while shooting to cover scene, follow moving object, etc.

pan-, pant-, panto- *comb. form* all, e.g. *panacea; pan-American.*

pan·a·ce·a [pan-ə-SEE-ə] *n* universal remedy, cure for all ills.

pa·nache [pə-NASH] *n* dashing style.

pan·cake [PAN-kayk] *n* thin cake of batter fried in pan; flat cake or stick of compressed makeup. ▶ *vi* **-caked, -cak·ing.** *Aviation* make flat landing by dropping in a level position.

pan·chro·mat·ic [pan-kroh-MAT-ik] *adj Photography* sensitive to light of all colors.

pan·cre·as [PAN-kree-əs] *n* digestive gland behind stomach. **pan·cre·at'ic** *adj*

pan·da [PAN-də] *n* large black and white bearlike mammal of China.

pan·dem·ic [pan-DEM-ik] *adj* (of disease) occurring over wide area.

pan·de·mo·ni·um [pan-də-MOH-nee-əm] *n* scene of din and uproar.

pan·der [PAN-dər] *v* (esp. with *to*) give gratification to (weakness or desires). ▶ *n* pimp.

pane [payn] *n* single piece of glass in a window or door.

pan·e·gyr·ic [pan-ə-JIR-ik] *n* speech of praise. **pan·e·gyr'i·cal** *adj* laudatory. **pan·e·gyr'ist** *n*

pan·el [PAN-l] *n* compartment of surface, usu. raised or sunk, for example in a door; any distinct section of something; strip of material inserted in garment; group of persons as team in quiz game, etc.; list of jurors, doctors, etc.; thin board with picture on it. ▶ *vt* **-eled, -el·ing.** adorn with panels. **paneling** *n* paneled work. **pan·el·ist** *n* member of panel.

pang *n* sudden pain, sharp twinge; compunction.

pan·ic [PAN-ik] *n* sudden and infectious fear; extreme fright; unreasoning terror. ▶ *adj* of fear, etc. ▶ *v* **-icked, -ick·ing.** feel or cause to feel panic. **pan'ick·y** *adj* inclined to panic; nervous. **panic button** button or switch that operates safety device, for use in emergency. **panic-stricken, -struck** *adj* panicky.

pan·o·ply [PAN-ə-plee] *n, pl* **-plies.** complete, magnificent array. **pan'o·plied** *adj*

pan·o·ram·a [pan-ə-RAM-ə] *n* wide or complete view; picture arranged around spectators or unrolled before them. **pan·o·ram'ic** *adj*

pan·sy [PAN-zee] *n, pl* **-sies.** flower, species of violet; *sl, offens* effeminate man.

pant *vi* gasp for breath; yearn; long; throb. ▶ *n* gasp.

pan·ta·loon [PAN-tl-oon] *n* in pantomime, foolish old man who is the butt of clown. ▶ *pl obs* baggy trousers.

pan·the·ism [PAN-thee-iz-əm] *n* identification of God with the universe. **pan·the·is'tic** *adj* **pan'the·on** [-thee-ən] *n* temple of all gods.

pan·ther [PAN-thər] *n* cougar;

puma; variety of leopard.

pant·ies [PAN-teez] *pl n* women's undergarment.

pan·to·mime [PAN-tə-mīm] *n* dramatic entertainment without speech.

pan·try [PAN-tree] *n, pl* **-tries** [-treez] room for storing food or utensils.

pants *pl n* trousers; undergarment for lower trunk.

pant·y·hose [PAN-tee-hohz] *pl n* women's one-piece garment combining stockings and panties.

pant·y·waist [PAN-tee-wayst] *n inf, offens* effeminate man.

pap *n* soft food for infants, invalids, etc.; pulp, mash; idea, book, etc. lacking substance.

pa·pa·cy [PAY-pə-see] *n, pl* **-cies.** office of Pope; papal system. **pa'pal** *adj* of, relating to, the Pope. **pa'pist** *n, adj offens* Roman Catholic.

pa·pa·raz·zo [pah-pə-RAHT-soh] *n, pl* **-raz·zi** [-RAHT-see] freelance photographer specializing in candid shots of celebrities.

pa·pa·ya [pə-PAH-yə] *n* tree bearing melon-shaped fruit; its fruit.

pa·per [PAY-pər] *n* material made by pressing pulp of rags, straw, wood, etc., into thin, flat sheets; printed sheet of paper; newspaper; article, essay. ▸ *pl* documents, etc. ▸ *vt* cover, decorate with paper. **paper over** (try to) conceal (differences, etc.) in order to preserve friendship, etc.

pa·pier-mâ·ché [PAY-pər mə-SHAY] *n* pulp from rags or paper mixed with size, shaped by molding and dried hard.

pa·poose [pa-POOS] *n* N Amer. Indian child.

pap·ri·ka [pa-PREE-kə] *n* (powdered seasoning prepared from) type of red pepper.

pa·py·rus [pə-PĪ-rəs] *n, pl* **-py·ri** [-PĪ-rī] species of reed; (manuscript written on) kind of paper made from this plant.

par [pahr] *n* equality of value or standing; face value (of stocks and bonds); *Golf* estimated standard score. ▸ *vt* **parred, par·ring.** *Golf* make par on hole or round.

par'i·ty *n* equality; analogy.

para-, par-, pa- *comb. form* beside, beyond, e.g. *paradigm; parallel; parody.*

par·a·ble [PA-rə-bəl] *n* allegory, story with a moral lesson.

pa·rab·o·la [pə-RAB-ə-lə] *n* section of cone cut by plane parallel to the cone's side.

par·a·chute [PA-rə-shoot] *n* apparatus extending like umbrella used to retard the descent of a falling body. ▸ *v* **-chut·ed, -chut·ing.** land or cause to land by parachute. **par'a·chut·ist** *n* **golden parachute** employment contract for key employee of company guaranteeing substantial severance pay, etc. if company is sold.

pa·rade [pə-RAYD] *n* display; muster of troops; parade ground. ▸ *v* **-rad·ed, -rad·ing.** march; display.

par·a·digm [PA-rə-dīm] *n* example; model. **par·a·dig·mat·ic** [-dig-MAT-ik] *adj*

par·a·dise [PA-rə-dīs] *n* heaven; state of bliss; (**P-**) Garden of Eden.

par·a·dox [PA-rə-doks] *n* statement that seems absurd or self-contradictory but may be true. **par·a·dox·i·cal** *adj*

par·af·fin [PA-rə-fin] *n* waxlike or liquid hydrocarbon mixture used as fuel, solvent, in candles, etc.

par·a·gon [PA-rə-gon] *n* pattern or model of excellence.

par·a·graph [PA-rə-graf] *n* section of chapter or book; short notice, as in newspaper. ▸ *vt* arrange in paragraphs.

par·a·keet [PA-rə-keet] *n* small kind of parrot.

par·al·lax [PA-rə-laks] *n* apparent difference in object's position or direction as viewed from different points.

par·al·lel [PA-rə-lel] *adj* continuously at equal distances; precisely corresponding. ▸ *n* line equidistant from another at all points; thing exactly like another; comparison; line of latitude. ▶ vt **-leled, -lel·ing.** represent as similar, compare. **par'al·lel·ism** n

par·al·lel'o·gram [-ə-gram] n four-sided plane figure with opposite sides parallel.

pa·ral·y·sis [pə-RAL-ə-sis] n, pl **-ses** [-seez] incapacity to move or feel, due to damage to nervous system.

par·a·lyze [PA-rə-līz] vt **-lyzed, -lyz·ing.** affect with paralysis; cripple; make useless or ineffectual.

par·a·lyt'ic [-LIT-ik] adj, n (person) affected with paralysis. **infantile paralysis** poliomyelitis.

par·a·med·i·cal [pa-rə-MED-i-kəl] adj of persons working in various capacities in support of medical profession. **par·a·med'ic** n

pa·ram·e·ter [pə-RAM-i-tər] n measurable characteristic; any constant limiting factor.

par·a·mil·i·tar·y [pa-rə-MIL-i-ter-ee] adj of civilian group organized on military lines or in support of the military.

par·a·mount [PA-rə-mownt] adj supreme, eminent, preeminent, chief.

par·a·mour [PA-rə-moor] n old-fashioned lover, esp. of a person married to someone else.

par·a·noi·a [pa-rə-NOI-ə] n mental disease with delusions of fame, grandeur, persecution.

par·a·noi'ac adj, n **par'a·noid** adj of paranoia; inf exhibiting fear of persecution, etc. ▶ n

par·a·pet [PA-rə-pit] n low wall, railing along edge of balcony, bridge, etc.

par·a·pher·na·lia [pa-rə-fər-NAYL-yə] pl n personal belongings; odds and ends of equipment.

par·a·phrase [PA-rə-frayz] n expression of meaning of passage in other words; free translation. ▶ vt **-phrased, -phras·ing.** put into other words.

par·a·ple·gi·a [pa-rə-PLEE-jee-ə] n paralysis of lower half of body.

par·a·ple'gic n, adj

par·a·psy·chol·o·gy [pa-rə-sī-KOL-ə-jee] n study of subjects pert. to extrasensory perception, e.g. telepathy.

par·a·site [PA-rə-sīt] n animal or plant living in or on another; self-interested hanger-on.

par·a·sit'ic [-SIT-ik] adj of the nature of, living as, parasite.

par'a·sit·ism [-si-tiz-əm] n

par·a·si·tol'o·gy n study of animal and vegetable parasites, esp. as causes of disease.

par·a·sol [PA-rə-sawl] n lightweight umbrella used as sunshade.

par·a·troop·er [PA-rə-troo-pər] n soldier trained to descend from airplane by parachute.

par·a·ty·phoid [pa-rə-TĪ-foid] n an infectious disease similar to but distinct from typhoid fever.

par·boil [PAHR-boil] vt boil until partly cooked.

par·cel [PAHR-səl] n packet of goods, esp. one enclosed in paper; quantity dealt with at one time; tract of land. ▶ vt **-celed, -cel·ing.** wrap up; divide into, distribute in, parts.

parch [pahrch] v dry by heating; make, become hot and dry; scorch; roast slightly.

parch·ment [PAHRCH-mənt] n sheep, goat, calf skin prepared for writing; manuscript of this.

par·don [PAHR-dn] vt forgive, excuse. ▶ n forgiveness; release from punishment. **par'don·a·ble** adj

pare [pair] vt **pared, par·ing.** trim, cut edge or surface of; decrease bit by bit. **par'ing** n piece pared off, rind.

par·e·gor·ic [pa-ri-GOR-ik] n tincture of opium used to stop diarrhea.

par·ent [PAIR-ənt] n father or mother. **par'ent·age** n descent, extraction. **pa·rent·al** [pə-REN-tl] adj **par'ent·hood** [-huud] n

pa·ren·the·sis [pə-REN-thə-sis] n word, phrase, etc. inserted in passage independently of grammatical sequence and usu. marked off by brackets, dashes, or commas. **pa·ren'the·ses** [-seez] *pl n* round brackets, ( ). **par·en·thet'ic·al** *adj*

pa·ri·ah [pə-RĪ-ə] *n* social outcast.

par·ish [PA-rish] *n* district under one clergyman; subdivision of county. **pa·rish'ion·er** *n* member, inhabitant of parish.

parity see PAR.

park [pahrk] *n* large area of land in natural state preserved for recreational use; field or stadium for sporting events; large enclosed piece of ground, usu. with grass or woodland, attached to country house or for public use; space in camp for military supplies. ▶ *vt* leave for a short time; maneuver (automobile, etc) into a suitable space; *inf* engage in caressing and kissing in parked automobile.

par·ka [PAHR-kə] *n* warm waterproof coat with hood.

par·lance [PAHR-ləns] *n* way of speaking, conversation; idiom.

par·ley [PAHR-lee] *n, pl* **-leys.** meeting between leaders or representatives of opposing forces to discuss terms. ▶ *vi* **-leyed, -ley·ing.** hold discussion about terms.

par·lia·ment [PAHR-lə-mənt] *n* legislature of some countries. **par·lia·men·tar'i·an** [-TAIR-ee-ən] *n* expert in rules and procedures of a legislature or other formal organization.

par·lor [PAHR-lər] *n* sitting room, room for receiving company in small house; place for milking cows; room or building as business premises, esp. undertaker, hairdresser, etc.

Par·me·san [PAHR-mə-zahn] *n* hard dry Italian cheese for grating.

pa·ro·chi·al [pə-ROH-kee-əl] *adj* narrow, provincial; of a parish. **pa·ro'chi·al·ism** *n*

par·o·dy [PA-rə-dee] *n, pl* **-dies.** composition in which author's style is made fun of by imitation; travesty. ▶ *vt* **-died, -dy·ing.** write parody of. **par'o·dist** *n*

pa·role [pə-ROHL] *n* early freeing of prisoner on condition of good behavior; word of honor. ▶ *vt* **-roled, rol·ing.** place on parole.

par·ox·ysm [PA-rək-siz-əm] *n* sudden violent attack of pain, rage, laughter.

par·quet [pahr-KAY] *n* flooring of wooden blocks arranged in pattern. ▶ *vt* **-queted** [-KAYD], **-quet·ing** [-KAY-ing] lay a parquet.

par·ri·cide [PA-rə-sid] *n* murder or murderer of a parent.

par·rot [PA-rət] *n* bird with short hooked beak, some varieties of which can imitate speaking; unintelligent imitator. ▶ *vt* imitate or repeat without understanding.

par·ry [PA-ree] *vt* **-ried, -ry·ing.** ward off, turn aside. ▶ *n, pl* **-ries.** act of parrying, esp. in fencing.

parse [pahrs] *vt* **parsed, pars·ing.** describe (word), analyze (sentence) in terms of grammar.

par·si·mo·ny [PAHR-sə-moh-nee] *n* stinginess; undue economy. **par·si·mo'ni·ous** *adj* sparing.

pars·ley [PAHR-slee] *n* herb used for seasoning, garnish, etc.

pars·nip [PAHR-snip] *n* edible whitish root vegetable.

par·son [PAHR-sən] *n* clergyman of parish or church; clergyman. **par'son·age** *n* parson's house.

part [pahrt] *n* portion, section, share; division; actor's role; duty. ▶ *v* region. ▶ *v* divide; separate. **part'ing** *n* division between sections of hair on head; separation; leave-taking. **part'ly** *adv* in part. **part song** song for several voices singing in harmony.

par·take [pahr-TAYK] *v* **-took, -tak·en, -tak·ing.** take or have share in; take food or drink.

par·tial [PAHR-shəl] *adj* not general or complete; prejudiced; fond of. **par'tial·ly** *adv* partly. **par·ti·al·i·ty** [pahr-shee-AL-i-tee] *n* favoritism; fondness for.

par·tic·i·pate [pahr-TIS-ə-payt] *v* **-pat·ed, -pat·ing.** share in; take part in. **par·tic'i·pant** *n*

par·tic′i·pa·to·ry *adj*

par·ti·ci·ple [PAHR-tə-sip-əl] *n* adjective made by inflection from verb and keeping verb's relation to dependent words. **par·ti·cip′i·al** *adj*

par·ti·cle [PAHR-ti-kəl] *n* minute portion of matter; least possible amount; minor part of speech in grammar, prefix, suffix.

par·ti-col·ored [PAHR-tee-kul-ərd] *adj* differently colored in different parts, variegated.

par·tic·u·lar [pahr-TIK-yə-lər] *adj* relating to one, not general; distinct; minute; very exact; fastidious. ▶ *n* detail, item. ▶ *pl* detailed account; items of information. **par·tic′u·lar·ize** *vt* **-ized, -iz·ing.** mention in detail. **par·tic′u·lar·ly** *adv*

par·ti·san [PAHR-tə-zən] *n* adherent of a party; guerrilla, member of resistance movement. ▶ *adj* adhering to faction; prejudiced.

par·ti·tion [pahr-TISH-ən] *n* division; interior dividing wall. ▶ *vt* divide, cut into sections.

part·ner [PAHRT-nər] *n* ally or companion; member of a partnership; one who dances with another; a husband or wife; *Sport* one who plays with another against opponents. ▶ *vt* be a partner of. **part′ner·ship** *n* association of persons for business, etc.

par·tridge [PAHR-trij] *n, pl* **-tridg·es.** game bird of the grouse family.

par·tu·ri·tion [pahr-tyuu-RISH-ən] *n* act of bringing forth young; childbirth.

par·ty [PAHR-tee] *n, pl* **-ties.** social assembly; group of persons traveling or working together; group of persons united in opinion; side; person. ▶ *adj* of, belonging to, a party or faction. **party line** telephone line serving two or more subscribers; policies of political party. **party wall** common wall separating adjoining premises.

par·ve·nu [PAHR-və-noo] *n* one newly risen into position of notice,

power, wealth; upstart.

Pas·cal [PAS-kal] *n* high-level computer programming language developed as a teaching language.

pas·chal [PAS-kəl] *adj* of Passover or Easter.

pass *vt* go by, beyond, through, etc.; exceed; be accepted by; undergo successfully; spend; transfer; exchange; disregard; bring into force, sanction a legislative bill, etc. ▶ *vi* go; be transferred from one state or person to another; elapse; undergo examination successfully; be taken as member of religious or racial group other than one's own. ▶ *n* way, esp. a narrow and difficult way; permit, license, authorization; successful result from test; condition; *Sports* transfer of ball by kick or throw. **pass′a·ble** *adj* (just) acceptable. **pass′ing** *adj* transitory; cursory, casual. **pass off** present (something) under false pretenses. **pass up** ignore, neglect, reject.

pas·sage [PAS-ij] *n* channel, opening; way through, corridor; part of book, etc.; journey, voyage, fare; enactment of rule, law by legislature, etc.; conversation, dispute; incident.

pas·sé [pa-SAY] *adj* out-of-date; past the prime.

pas·sen·ger [PAS-ən-jər] *n* traveler, esp. by public conveyance.

pas·ser·ine [PAS-ər-in] *adj* of the order of perching birds.

pas′sim *Lat* everywhere, throughout.

pas·sion [PASH-ən] *n* ardent desire, esp. sexual; any strongly felt emotion; suffering (esp. that of Christ). **pas′sion·ate** [-it] *adj* (easily) moved by strong emotions.

pas·sive [PAS-iv] *adj* unresisting; submissive; inactive; denoting grammatical voice of verb in which the subject receives the action. **pas·siv′i·ty** *n* **passive smoking** involuntary inhalation of smoke from other's cigarettes by nonsmoker.

Pass·o·ver [PAS-oh-vər] *n* Jewish

spring festival commemorating exodus of Jews from Egypt.

pass'port n official document granting permission to pass, travel abroad, etc.

pass·word [PAS-wurd] n word, phrase, to distinguish friend from enemy; countersign.

past adj ended; gone by; elapsed. ▶ n bygone times. ▶ adv by; along. ▶ prep beyond; after.

pas·ta [PAH-stə] n type of food, such as spaghetti, that is made in different shapes from flour and water.

paste [payst] n soft composition, as toothpaste; soft plastic mixture or adhesive; fine glass to imitate gems. ▶ vt past·ed, past·ing. fasten with paste. **past·y** adj **past·i·er, past·i·est.** like paste; white; sickly.

pas·tel [pa-STEL] n colored crayon; art of drawing with crayons; pale, delicate color. ▶ adj delicately tinted.

pas·teur·ize [PAS-chə-rīz] vt **-ized, -iz·ing.** sterilize by heat. **pas·teur·i·za'tion** n

pas·tiche [pa-STEESH] n literary, musical, artistic work composed of parts borrowed from other works and loosely connected together; work imitating another's style.

pas·tille [pa-STEEL] n lozenge; aromatic substance burned as deodorant or fumigator.

pas·time [PAS-tīm] n that which makes time pass agreeably; recreation.

pas·tor [PAS-tər] n priest or minister in charge of a church. **pas'to·ral** adj of, or like, shepherd's or rural life; of office of pastor. ▶ n poem describing rural life.

pas·try [PAY-stree] n, pl **-tries.** article of food made chiefly of flour, shortening and water.

pas·ture [PAS-chər] n grass for food of cattle; ground on which cattle graze. ▶ v **-tured, -tur·ing.** (cause to) graze. **pas'tur·age** n (right to) pasture.

pat¹ vt **pat·ted, pat·ting.** tap. ▶ n light, quick blow; small mass, as of

butter, beaten into shape.

pat² adv exactly; fluently; opportunely; glib; exactly right.

patch [pach] n piece of cloth sewn on garment; spot; plot of ground; protecting pad for the eye; small contrasting area; short period. ▶ vt mend; repair clumsily. **patch'y** adj **patch·i·er, patch·i·est.** of uneven quality; full of patches. **patch'work** n work composed of pieces sewn together; jumble.

patch·ou·li [pə-CHOO-lee] n Indian herb; perfume from it.

pate [payt] n head; top of head.

pâ·té [pah-TAY] n spread of finely chopped liver, etc. **pâté de foie gras** [də-fwah-GRAH] one made of goose liver.

pa·tel·la [pə-TEL-ə] n, pl **-las.** kneecap. **pa·tel'lar** adj

pat·ent [PAT-nt] n document securing to person or organization exclusive right to invention. ▶ adj open; evident; manifest; open to public perusal, e.g. letters patent. ▶ vt secure a patent. **pat·ent·ee'** n one who has a patent. **pat'ent·ly** adv obviously. **patent leather** (imitation) leather processed to give hard, glossy surface.

pa·ter·fa·mil·i·as [pah-tər-fə-MIL-ee-əs] n, pl **-ases.** father of a family.

pa·ter·nal [pə-TUR-nl] adj fatherly; of a father; related through a father. **pa·ter'nal·ism** n authority exercised in a way that limits individual responsibility. **pa·ter·nal·is'tic** adj **pa·ter·ni·ty** n relation of a father to his offspring; fatherhood.

pa·ter·nos·ter [PAY-tər-NOS-tər] n Lord's Prayer; beads of rosary.

path n, pl **paths** [pathz] way or track; course of action.

pa·thet·ic [pə-THET-ik] adj affecting or moving tender emotions; distressingly inadequate. **pa·thet'i·cal·ly** adv

path·o·gen·ic [path-ə-JEN-ik] adj producing disease. **path'o·gen** n disease-producing agent, e.g. virus.

pa·thol·o·gy [pə-THOL-ə-jee] n

science of diseases.

path·o·log·i·cal [-LOJ-i-kəl] *adj* of the science of disease; due to disease; compulsively motivated. **pa·thol'o·gist** *n*

pa·thos [PAY-thos] *n* power of exciting tender emotions.

pa·tient [PAY-shənt] *adj* bearing trials calmly. ▸ *n* person under medical treatment. **pa'tience** *n* quality of enduring; card game for one player.

pat·i·na [pə-TEE-nə] *n* fine layer on a surface; sheen of age on woodwork.

pat·i·o [PAT-ee-oh] *n, pl* **-ios.** (usu. paved) area adjoining house for lounging, etc.

pat·ois [PA-twah] *n* regional dialect.

pa·tri·arch [PAY-tree-ahrk] *n* father and founder of family, esp. Biblical. **pa·tri·ar'chal** *adj* venerable.

pa·tri·cian [pə-TRISH-ən] *n* noble of ancient Rome; one of noble birth. ▸ *adj* of noble birth.

pat·ri·cide [PA-trə-sīd] *n* murder or murderer of father.

pat·ri·mo·ny [PA-trə-moh-nee] *n, pl* **-nies.** property inherited from ancestors.

pa·tri·ot [PAY-tree-ət] *n* one who loves own country and maintains its interests. **pa'tri·ot·ism** *n* [-ə-tiz-əm] love of, loyalty to one's country. **pa·tri·ot'ic** [-OT-ik] *adj* inspired by love of one's country.

pa·trol [pə-TROHL] *n* regular circuit by guard; person, small group patrolling; unit of Boy Scouts or Girl Scouts. ▸ *v* **-trolled, -trol·ling.** go around on guard, or reconnoitering.

pa·tron [PAY-trən] *n* one who sponsors or aids artists, charities, etc.; protector; regular customer; guardian saint; one who has disposition of benefice, etc. **pa'tron·age** *n* support given by, or position of, a patron. **pa'tron·ize** *vt* **-ized, -iz·ing.** assume air of superiority toward; frequent as customer; encourage.

pat·ro·nym·ic [pa-trə-NIM-ik] *n* name derived from that of parent

or an ancestor.

pat·ter [PAT-ər] *vi* make noise, as sound of quick, short steps; tap in quick succession; pray, talk rapidly. ▸ *n* quick succession of taps; *inf* glib, rapid speech.

pat·tern [PAT-ərn] *n* arrangement of repeated parts; design; shape to direct cutting of cloth, etc.; model; specimen. ▸ *vt* (with *on* or *after*) model; decorate with pattern.

pat·ty [PAT-ee] *n, pl* **-ties.** a little pie; thin round piece of meat, candy, etc.

pau·ci·ty [PAW-si-tee] *n* scarcity; smallness of quantity; fewness.

paunch [pawnch] *n* belly; potbelly.

pau·per [PAW-pər] *n* poor person, esp. formerly, one supported by the public. **pau'per·ism** *n* destitution; extreme poverty. **pau'per·ize** *vt* **-ized, -iz·ing.** reduce to pauperism.

pause [pawz] *vi* **paused, paus·ing.** cease for a time. ▸ *n* stop or rest.

pave [payv] *vt* **paved, pav·ing.** form surface with stone or brick. **pave'ment** [-mənt] *n* paved floor, footpath; material for paving. **pave the way for** lead up to; facilitate entrance of.

pa·vil·ion [pə-VIL-yən] *n* clubhouse on playing field, etc.; building for housing exhibition, etc.; large ornate tent.

paw *n* foot of animal. ▸ *v* scrape with forefoot; handle roughly; stroke with the hands.

pawn[1] *vt* deposit (article) as security for money borrowed. ▸ *n* article deposited. **pawn'bro·ker** *n* lender of money on goods pledged.

pawn[2] *n* piece in chess; *fig* person used as mere tool.

pay *v* **paid, pay·ing.** ▸ *vt* give money, etc., for goods or services rendered; compensate; give or bestow; (with *out*) release bit by bit, as rope. ▸ *vi* be remunerative; be profitable; (with *out*) spend. ▸ *n* wages; paid employment. **pay'a·ble** *adj* justly due; profitable. **pay·ee'** *n* person to whom money is paid or due.

pay'ment [-mənt] n discharge of debt. **pay'load** n part of cargo earning revenue; explosive power of missile, etc. **paying guest** boarder, lodger, esp. in private house. **pay television** programs provided for viewers who pay monthly or per-program fees.

Pb Chem lead.

pc politically correct; personal computer.

Pd Chem palladium.

pea [pee] n fruit, growing in pods, of climbing plant; the plant. **pea-green** adj of shade of green like color of green peas. **pea green** this color. **pea soup** thick soup made of green peas; inf thick fog.

peace [pees] n freedom from war; harmony; quietness of mind; calm; repose. **peace'a·ble** adj disposed to peace. **peace'a·bly** adv **peace'ful** adj free from war, tumult; mild; undisturbed.

peach [peech] n stone fruit of delicate flavor; inf person or thing very pleasant; pinkish-yellow color. **peach'y** adj **peach·i·er**, **peach·i·est**. like peach; inf fine, excellent.

pea·cock [PEE-kok] n male of bird with fanlike tail, brilliantly colored. **pea'hen** n, fem **pea'fowl** n peacock or peahen.

peak [peek] n pointed end of anything, esp. hill's sharp top; point of greatest development, etc.; sharp increase; projecting piece on front of cap. ▶ v (cause to) form, reach peaks. **peaked** adj like, having a peak. **peak·ed** [PEE-kid] sickly, wan, drawn.

peal [peel] n loud sound or succession of loud sounds; changes rung on set of bells; chime. ▶ vi sound loudly.

pea·nut [PEE-nut] n pea-shaped nut that ripens underground; the plant. ▶ pl inf trifling amount of money.

pear [pair] n tree yielding sweet, juicy fruit; the fruit. **pear-shaped** adj shaped like a pear, heavier at the bottom than the top.

pearl [purl] n hard, lustrous structure found in several mollusks, esp. pearl oyster and used as jewel. **pearl'y** adj **pearl·i·er**, **pearl·i·est**. like pearls.

peas·ant [PEZ-ənt] n in certain countries, member of low social class, esp. in rural district; boorish person. **peas'ant·ry** n peasants collectively.

peat [peet] n decomposed vegetable substance found in bogs; turf of it used for fuel. **peat moss** dried peat, used as mulch, etc.

peb·ble [PEB-əl] n small roundish stone; pale, transparent rock crystal; grainy, irregular surface. ▶ vt **-bled**, **-bling**. pave, cover with pebbles.

pe·can [pi-KAHN] n N Amer. tree, species of hickory, allied to walnut; its edible nut.

pec·ca·dil·lo [pek-ə-DIL-oh] n, pl **-loes**. slight offense; petty crime.

pec·ca·ry [PEK-ə-ree] n, pl **-ries**. vicious Amer. animal allied to pig.

peck¹ [pek] n fourth part of bushel, equal to 8.81 liters; great deal.

peck² v pick, strike with or as with beak; nibble. ▶ n quick kiss. **peck'ish** adj inf irritable.

pecs [peks] pl n inf pectoral muscles.

pec·tin [PEK-tin] n gelatinizing substance obtained from ripe fruits. **pec'tic** adj congealing; denoting pectin.

pec·to·ral [PEK-tər-əl] adj of the breast. ▶ n pectoral part of organ; breastplate.

pec·u·late [PEK-yə-layt] v **-lat·ed**, **-lat·ing**. embezzle; steal. **pec·ula'tion** n

pe·cu·liar [pi-KYOOL-yər] adj strange; particular; belonging to. **pe·cu·li·ar'i·ty** n oddity; characteristic; distinguishing feature.

pe·cu·ni·ar·y [pi-KYOO-nee-er-ee] adj relating to, or consisting of, money.

ped·a·gogue [PED-ə-gog] n schoolmaster; pedant. **ped·a·gog'ic** [-GOJ-ik] adj

ped·al [PED-l] n something to transmit motion from foot; foot lever to modify tone or swell of musical instrument; *Mus* note, usu. bass, held through successive harmonies. ▶ *adj* of a foot. ▶ *v* **-daled, -dal·ing.** propel bicycle, etc. by using its pedals; use pedal.

ped·ant [PED-ənt] *n* one who overvalues, or insists on, petty details of book learning, grammatical rules, etc. **pe·dan'tic** *adj* **ped'ant·ry** *n, pl* **-tries.**

ped·dle [PED-l] *vt* **-dled, -dling.** go around selling goods. **ped'dler, ped'lar** *n*

ped·er·ast [PED-ə-rast] *n* man who has homosexual relations with boy. **ped'er·as·ty** *n*

ped·es·tal [PED-ə-stl] *n* base of column, pillar. **put on a pedestal** idealize.

pe·des·tri·an [pə-DES-tree-ən] *n* one who goes on foot; walker. ▶ *adj* going on foot; commonplace; dull, uninspiring.

pe·di·at·rics [pee-dee-A-triks] *n* branch of medicine dealing with diseases and disorders of children. **pe·di·a·tri'cian** [-ə-TRISH-ən] *n*

ped·i·cel [PED-ə-səl] *n* small, short stalk of leaf, flower or fruit.

ped·i·cure [PED-i-kyoor] *n* medical or cosmetic treatment of feet.

ped·i·gree *n* register of ancestors; genealogy.

ped·i·ment [PED-ə-mənt] *n* triangular part over Greek portico, etc. **ped·i·men'tal** [-MEN-tl] *adj*

pedlar see PEDDLE.

pe·dom·e·ter [pə-DOM-i-tər] *n* instrument that measures the distance walked.

pe·dun·cle [pi-DUNG-kəl] *n* flower stalk; stalklike structure.

peek *vi, n* peep, glance.

peel *vt* strip off skin, rind or any form of covering. ▶ *vi* come off, as skin, rind. ▶ *n* rind, skin. **peeled** *adj inf* of eyes, watchful. **peel'ings** *pl n* parings.

peep[1] *vi* look slyly or quickly. ▶ *n* such a look.

peep[2] *vi* cry, as chick; chirp. ▶ *n* such a cry.

peer[1] *n* nobleman; one of the same

rank, ability, etc. **peer'age** [-ij] *n* body of peers; rank of peer. **peer'ess** *n, fem* **peer'less** [-lis] *adj* without match or equal.

peer[2] *vi* look closely and intently.

peeved [peevd] *adj* sulky, irritated. **peeve** *vt* **peeved, peev·ing.** annoy; vex.

pee'vish *adj* fretful; irritable. **pee'vish·ly** *adv* **pee'vish·ness** [-nis] *n* annoyance.

peg *n* nail or pin for joining, fastening, marking, etc.; (mark of) level, standard, etc. ▶ *v* **pegged, peg·ging.** fasten with pegs; stabilize (prices); *inf* throw; (with *away*) persevere. **take down a peg** humble (someone).

peign·oir [pain-WAHR] *n* woman's dressing gown, jacket, wrapper.

pe·jo·ra·tive [pi-JOR-ə-tiv] *adj* (of words, etc.) with unpleasant, disparaging connotation.

Pe·king·ese [pee-kə-NEEZ] *n* small Chinese dog.

pe·lag·ic [pə-LAJ-ik] *adj* of the deep sea.

pel·i·can [PEL-i-kən] *n* large, fish-eating waterfowl with large pouch beneath its bill.

pel·let [PEL-it] *n* little ball, pill.

pell-mell *adv* in utter confusion, headlong.

pel·lu·cid [pə-LOO-sid] *adj* translucent; clear.

pelt[1] *vt* strike with missiles. ▶ *vi* throw missiles; rush; fall persistently, as rain.

pelt[2] *n* raw hide or skin.

pel·vis *n, pl* **-vis·es.** bony cavity at base of human trunk. **pel'vic** *adj* pert. to pelvis.

pen[1] *n* instrument for writing. ▶ *vt* **penned, pen·ning.** compose; write. **pen name** author's pseudonym. **pen pal** person with whom one corresponds, usu. someone whom one has never met.

pen[2] *n* small enclosure, as for sheep. ▶ *vt* **penned, pen·ning.** put, keep in enclosure.

pen[3] *n* female swan.

pe·nal [PEEN-l] *adj* of, incurring, inflicting, punishment. **pe'nal·ize**

vt **-ized, -iz·ing.** impose penalty on; handicap. **pen′al·ty** n, pl **-ties.** punishment for crime or offense; forfeit; Sports handicap or disadvantage imposed for infringement of rule, etc.

pen·ance [PEN-əns] n suffering submitted to as expression of penitence; repentance.

pen·chant [PEN-chənt] n inclination, decided taste.

pen·cil [PEN-səl] n instrument as of graphite, for writing, etc.; Optics narrow beam of light. ▸ vt **-ciled, -cil·ing.** paint or draw; mark with pencil.

pend·ant [PEN-dənt] n hanging ornament. **pend′ent** adj suspended; hanging; projecting.

pend′ing prep during, until. ▸ adj awaiting settlement; undecided; imminent.

pen·du·lous [PEN-jə-ləs] adj hanging, swinging. **pen′du·lum** [-ləm] n suspended weight swinging to and fro, esp. as regulator for clock.

pen·e·trate [PEN-i-trayt] vt **-trat·ed, trat·ing.** enter into; pierce; arrive at the meaning of. **pen·e·tra·bil′i·ty** n quality of being penetrable. **pen′e·tra·ble** [-trə-bəl] adj capable of being entered or pierced. **penetrating** adj sharp; easily heard; subtle; quick to understand. **pen·e·tra′tion** n insight, acuteness. **pen′e·tra·tive** [-tray-tiv] adj piercing; discerning.

pen·guin [PENG-gwin] n flightless, short-legged swimming bird.

pen·i·cil·lin [pen-ə-SIL-in] n antibiotic drug effective against a wide range of diseases, infections.

pen·in·su·la [pə-NINS-yə-lə] n portion of land nearly surrounded by water. **pen·in′su·lar** adj

pe·nis [PEE-nis] n, pl **-nis·es.** male organ of copulation (and of urination) in man and many mammals.

pen·i·tent [PEN-i-tənt] adj affected by sense of guilt. ▸ n one that repents of sin. **pen′i·tence** n

sorrow for sin; repentance. **pen·i·ten′tial** [-TEN-shəl] adj of, or expressing, penitence. **pen·i·ten′tia·ry** [-TEN-shə-ree] adj relating to penance, or to the rules of penance. ▸ n, pl **-ries.** prison.

pen·nant [PEN-ənt] n long narrow flag.

pen·non [PEN-ən] n small pointed or swallow-tailed flag.

pen·ny [PEN-ee] n, pl **-nies.** coin, 100th part of dollar; similar coin of other countries. **pen′ni·less** [-lis] adj having no money; poor. **a pretty penny** inf considerable amount of money.

pe·nol·o·gy [pee-NOL-ə-jee] n study of punishment and prevention of crime.

pen·sion [PEN-shən] n regular payment to old people, retired public officials, workers, etc. ▸ vt grant pension to. **pen′sion·er** n

pen·sive [PEN-siv] adj thoughtful with sadness; wistful.

pent adj shut up, kept in. **pent-up** adj not released, repressed.

pen·ta·gon [PEN-tə-gon] n plane figure having five angles. **pen·tag′o·nal** [-TAG-ə-nl] adj

pen·tam·e·ter [pen-TAM-i-tər] n verse of five metrical feet.

Pen·ta·teuch [PEN-tə-tyook] n first five books of Old Testament.

pen·tath·lon [pen-TATH-lən] n athletic contest of five events.

Pen·te·cost [PEN-ti-kawst] n Christian festival of seventh Sunday after Easter.

pent·house [PENT-hows] n, pl **-hous·es** [-howz-iz] apartment or other structure on top, or top floor, of building.

pen·tode [PEN-tohd] n Electronics five-electrode vacuum tube, having anode, cathode and three grids.

pe·nult [PEE-nult] n last syllable but one of word. **pen·ul·ti·mate** [pi-NUL-tə-mit] adj next before the last.

pe·num·bra [pi-NUM-brə] n imperfect shadow; in an eclipse, the partially shadowed region that surrounds the full shadow.

pen·u·ry [PEN-yə-ree] *n* extreme poverty; extreme scarcity.

pe·nu·ri·ous [pə-NUUR-ee-əs] *adj* niggardly, stingy; poor, scanty.

peo·ple [PEE-pəl] *pl n* persons generally; community, nation; race; family. ▶ *vt* **-pled, -pling.** stock with inhabitants; populate.

pep *n inf* vigor; energy; enthusiasm. ▶ *vt* **pepped, pep·ping.** impart energy to; speed up.

pep·per [PEP-ər] *n* fruit of climbing plant that yields pungent aromatic spice; various slightly pungent vegetables, e.g. capsicum. ▶ *vt* season with pepper; sprinkle, dot; pelt with missiles. **pep'per·y** *adj* having the qualities of pepper; irritable. **pep'per·corn** *n* dried pepper berry; something trifling. **pep'per·mint** *n* plant noted for aromatic pungent liquor distilled from it; a candy flavored with this.

pep·tic [PEP-tik] *adj* relating to digestion or digestive juices.

per [pər] *prep* for each; by; in manner of.

per-, par-, pel-, pil- *prefix* through, thoroughly, e.g. *perfect; pellucid.*

per·am·bu·late [pər-AM-byə-layt] *v* **-lat·ed, -lat·ing.** ▶ *vt* walk through or over; traverse. ▶ *vi* walk about. **per·am'bu·la·tor** *n* baby carriage.

per an·num [pər AN-əm] *Lat* by the year.

per·cale [pər-KAYL] *n* woven cotton used esp. for sheets.

per cap·i·ta [pər KAP-i-tə] *Lat* for each person.

per·ceive [pər-SEEV] *vt* **-ceived, -ceiv·ing.** obtain knowledge of through senses; observe; understand. **per·ceiv'a·ble** *adj* **per·cep'ti·ble** *adj* discernible, recognizable. **per·cep'tion** *n* faculty of perceiving; intuitive judgment. **per·cep'tive** *adj*

per·cent·age [pər-SEN-tij] *n* proportion or rate per hundred. **per cent** in each hundred.

perception *n see* PERCEIVE.

perch¹ [purch] *n* freshwater fish.

perch² *n* resting place, as for bird. ▶ *vt* place, as on perch. ▶ *vi* alight,
settle on fixed body; roost; balance on.

per·cip·i·ent [pər-SIP-ee-ənt] *adj* having faculty of perception; perceiving. ▶ *n* one who perceives.

per·co·late [PUR-kə-layt] *v* **-lat·ed, -lat·ing.** pass through fine mesh as liquid; permeate; filter. **per'co·la·tor** *n* coffeepot with filter.

per·cus·sion [pər-KUSH-ən] *n* collision; impact; vibratory shock. **percussion instrument** musical instrument played by being struck, such as drums or cymbals.

per di·em [pər DEE-əm] *Lat* by the day; for each day.

per·di·tion [pər-DISH-ən] *n* spiritual ruin.

per·e·gri·nate [PER-i-grə-nayt] *vi* **-nat·ed, -nat·ing.** travel about; roam.

per·e·grine [PER-i-grin] *n* type of falcon.

per·emp·to·ry [pə-REMP-tə-ree] *adj* authoritative, imperious; forbidding debate; decisive.

per·en·ni·al [pə-REN-ee-əl] *adj* lasting through the years; perpetual, unfailing. ▶ *n* plant lasting more than two years.

per·fect [PUR-fikt] *adj* complete; finished; whole; unspoiled; faultless; correct, precise; excellent; of highest quality. ▶ *n* tense denoting a complete act. ▶ *vt* [pər-FEKT] improve; finish; make skillful. **per·fect'i·ble** *adj* capable of becoming perfect. **per·fec'tion** [-FEK-shən] *n* state of being perfect; faultlessness. **per'fect·ly** *adv*

per·fi·dy [PUR-fi-dee] *n, pl* **-dies.** treachery, disloyalty. **per·fid'i·ous** *adj*

per·fo·rate [PUR-fə-rayt] *vt* **-rat·ed, -rat·ing.** make hole(s) in, penetrate. **per·fo·ra'tion** *n* hole(s) made through thing.

per·force [pər-FORS] *adv* of necessity.

per·form [pər-FORM] *vt* bring to completion; accomplish; fulfill; represent on stage. ▶ *vi* function; act part; play, as on musical instrument. **per·for'mance** [-məns] *n*

per·fume [PUR-fyoom] *n* agreeable scent; fragrance. ▶ *vt* **-fumed, -fum·ing.** imbue with an agreeable odor; scent. **per·fum'er** *n*

per·func·to·ry [pər-FUNGK-tə-ree] *adj* superficial; hasty; done indifferently.

per·go·la [PUR-gə-lə] *n* area covered by plants growing on trellis; the trellis.

per·haps [pər-HAPS] *adv* possibly.

peri- *prefix* round, e.g. *perimeter; period; periphrasis.*

per·i·car·di·um [per-i-KAHR-dee-əm] *n, pl* **-di·a** [-dee-ə] membrane enclosing the heart. **per·i·car·di'tis** *n* inflammation of this.

per·i·he·li·on [per-ə-HEE-lee-ən] *n, pl* **-li·a** [-lee-ə] point in orbit of planet or comet nearest to sun.

per·il [PER-əl] *n* danger; exposure to injury. **per'il·ous** *adj* full of peril, hazardous.

pe·rim·e·ter [pə-RIM-i-tər] *n* outer boundary of an area; length of this.

pe·ri·od [PEER-ee-əd] *n* particular portion of time; a series of years; single occurrence of menstruation; cycle; conclusion; full stop (.) at the end of a sentence; complete sentence. ▶ *adj* of furniture, dress, play, etc., belonging to particular time in history. **pe·ri·od'ic** *adj* recurring at regular intervals. **pe·ri·od'i·cal** *adj, n* (of) publication issued at regular intervals. ▶ *adj* of a period; periodic. **pe·ri·o·dic'i·ty** [-DIS-i-tee] *n*

per·i·pa·tet·ic [per-ə-pə-TET-ik] *adj* itinerant; walking, traveling about.

pe·riph·er·y [pə-RIF-ə-ree] *n, pl* **-er·ies.** circumference; surface, outside. **pe·riph'er·al** [-ə-rəl] *adj* minor, unimportant; of periphery.

pe·riph·ra·sis [pə-RIF-rə-sis] *n, pl* **-ses** [-seez] roundabout speech or phrase; circumlocution. **per·i·phras'tic** *adj*

per·i·scope [PER-ə-skohp] *n* instrument used esp. in submarines, for giving view of objects on different level.

per·ish [PER-ish] *vi* die, waste away; decay, rot. **per'ish·a·ble** *adj* that will not last long. ▶ *pl n* perishable food.

per·i·to·ne·um [per-i-tn-EE-əm] *n, pl* **-ne·ums** or **-to·ne·a** [-EE-ə] membrane lining internal surface of abdomen. **per·i·to·ni'tis** [-NĪ-tis] *n* inflammation of it.

per·i·win·kle [PER-i-wing-kəl] *n* myrtle; small edible shellfish.

per·jure [PUR-jər] *vt* **-jured, -jur·ing.** be guilty of perjury. **per'ju·ry** *n, pl* **-ries.** crime of false testimony under oath; false swearing.

perk·y [PUR-kee] *adj* **perk·i·er, perk·i·est.** lively, cheerful, jaunty, gay. **perk up** make, become cheerful.

per·ma·frost [PUR-mə-frawst] *n* permanently frozen ground.

per·ma·nent [PUR-mə-nənt] *adj* continuing in same state; lasting. **per'ma·nence, per'ma·nen·cy** *n* fixedness. **permanent wave** *n* (treatment of hair producing) long-lasting style.

per·me·ate [PUR-mee-ayt] *vt* **-at·ed, -at·ing.** pervade, saturate; pass through pores of. **per'me·a·ble** [-ə-bəl] *adj* admitting of passage of fluids.

per·mit [pər-MIT] *vt* **-mit·ted, -mit·ting.** allow; give leave to. ▶ *n* [PUR-mit] license to do something; written permission. **permis'si·ble** *adj* allowable. **per·mis'sion** *n* authorization; leave, liberty. **per·mis'sive** *adj* (too) tolerant, lenient, esp. as parent.

per·mute [pər-MYOOT] *vt* **-mut·ed, -mut·ing.** interchange. **per·mu·ta·tion** [pur-myuu-TAY-shən] *n* mutual transference; *Math* arrangement of a number of quantities in every possible order.

per·ni·cious [pər-NISH-əs] *adj* wicked or mischievous; extremely hurtful; having quality of destroying or injuring.

per·o·ra·tion [per-ə-RAY-shən] *n* concluding part of oration.

per·ox·ide [pə-ROK-sīd] *n* oxide of a given base containing greatest quantity of oxygen; short for HYDROGEN PEROXIDE.

per·pen·di·cu·lar [pur-pən-DIK-yə-lər] *adj* at right angles to the plane of the horizon; at right angles to given line or surface; exactly upright. ▶ *n* line falling at right angles on another line or plane.

per·pe·trate [PUR-pi-trayt] *vt* -trat·ed, -trat·ing. perform or be responsible for (something bad).

per·pet·u·al [pər-PECH-oo-əl] *adj* continuous; lasting for ever. **per·pet'u·ate** *vt* at·ed, -at·ing. make perpetual; not to allow to be forgotten. **per·pet·u·a'tion** *n* **per·pe·tu·i·ty** [pur-pi-TOO-i-tee] *n*

per·plex [pər-PLEKS] *vt* puzzle; bewilder; make difficult to understand. **per·plex'i·ty** *n, pl* -ties. puzzled or tangled state.

per·qui·site [PUR-kwi-zit] *n* any incidental benefit from a certain type of employment; casual payment in addition to salary; something due as a privilege.

per se [pur SAY] *Lat* by or in itself.

per·se·cute [PUR-si-kyoot] *vt* -cut·ed, -cut·ing. oppress because of race, religion, etc.; subject to persistent ill-treatment. **per·se·cu'tion** *n*

per·se·vere [pur-sə-VEER] *vi* -vered, -ver·ing. persist, maintain effort. **per·se·ver'ance** [-əns] *n* persistence.

per·si·flage [PUR-sə-flah*zh*] *n* idle talk; frivolous style of treating subject.

per·sim·mon [pər-SIM-ən] *n* Amer. tree; its hard wood; its fruit.

per·sist [pər-SIST] *vi* continue in spite of obstacles or objections. **per·sist'ence** [-əns] *n* **per·sist'en·cy** *n* **per·sist'ent** *adj* persisting; steady; persevering; lasting.

per·snick·et·y [pər-SNIK-i-tee] *adj* *inf* fussy; fastidious about trifles; snobbishly aloof; requiring great care.

per·son [PUR-sən] *n* individual (human) being; body of human being; *Grammar* classification, or one of the classes, of pronouns and verb forms according to the person speaking, spoken to, or spoken of. **per·so·na** [pər-SOH-nə] *n, pl* -nas. assumed character. **per'son·a·ble** *adj* good-looking. **per'son·age** [-ij] *n* notable person. **per'son·al** *adj* individual, private, or one's own; of, relating to grammatical person. **per·son·al'i·ty** *n, pl* -ties. distinctive character; a celebrity. **per'son·al·ly** *adv* in person. **per'son·ate** *vt* -at·ed, -at·ing. pass oneself off as. **personal computer** small computer used for word processing, e-mail, computer games, etc. **personal property** *Law* all property except land and interests in land that pass to heir. **personal stereo** very small portable cassette player with headphones.

per·son·i·fy [pər-SON-ə-fī] *vt* -fied, -fy·ing. represent as person; typify. **per·son·i·fi·ca'tion** *n*

per·son·nel [pur-sə-NEL] *n* staff employed in a service or institution.

per·spec·tive [pər-SPEK-tiv] *n* mental view; art of drawing on flat surface to give effect of solidity and relative distances and sizes; drawing in perspective.

per·spi·ca·cious [pur-spi-KAY-shəs] *adj* having quick mental insight. **per·spi·cac'i·ty** [-KAS-i-tee] *n*

per·spic·u·ous [pər-SPIK-yoo-əs] *adj* clearly expressed; lucid; plain; obvious. **per·spi·cu'i·ty** *n*

per·spire [pər-SPĪR] *v* -spired, -spir·ing. sweat. **per·spi·ra'tion** [-spi-RAY-shən] *n* sweating; sweat.

per·suade [pər-SWAYD] *vt* -suad·ed, -suad·ing. bring (one to do something) by argument, charm, etc.; convince. **per·sua'sion** [-SWAY-*zh*ən] *n* art, act of persuading; way of thinking or belief. **per·sua'sive** *adj*

pert *adj* -er, -est. forward, saucy.

per·tain [pər-TAYN] *vi* belong, relate, have reference (to); concern.

per·ti·na·cious [pur-tn-AY-shəs] *adj*
obstinate, persistent.
per·ti·nac'i·ty [-AS-i-tee] *n*
doggedness, resolution.
per·ti·nent [PUR-tn-ənt] *adj* to the
point. **per'ti·nence** *n* relevance.
per·turb [pər-TURB] *vt* disturb
greatly; alarm. **per·tur·ba'tion** *n*
disturbance; agitation of mind.
pe·ruse [pə-ROOZ] *vt* **-rused,**
-rus·ing. examine, read, esp. in
slow and careful, or leisurely,
manner. **pe·rus'al** *n*
per·vade [pər-VAYD] *vt* **-vad·ed,**
-vad·ing. spread through; be rife
among. **per·va'sive** *adj*
per·vert [pər-VURT] *vt* turn to
wrong use; lead astray. ▸ *n*
[PUR-vərt] one who shows
unhealthy abnormality, esp. in
sexual matters. **per·verse**
[pər-VURS] *adj* obstinately or
unreasonably wrong; self-willed;
headstrong; wayward.
per·ver'sion [-VUR-zhən] *n*
pes·sa·ry [PES-ə-ree] *n, pl* **-ries.**
instrument used to support mouth
and neck of uterus; appliance to
prevent conception; medicated
suppository.
pes·si·mism [PES-ə-miz-əm] *n*
tendency to see the worst side of
things; theory that everything turns
to evil. **pes'si·mist** *n* **pes·si·mis'tic**
adj
pest *n* troublesome or harmful
thing, person or insect; plague.
pest'i·cide [-sīd] *n* chemical for
killing pests, esp. insects.
pes·tif'er·ous [-ər-əs] *adj*
troublesome; bringing plague.
pes·ter [PES-tər] *vt* trouble or vex
persistently; harass.
pes·ti·lence [PES-tl-əns] *n* epidemic
disease, esp. bubonic plague.
pes'ti·lent *adj* troublesome;
deadly. **pes·ti·len'tial** [-LEN-shəl]
adj
pes·tle [PES-əl] *n* instrument with
which things are pounded in a
mortar.
Pet. Peter.
pet *n* animal or person kept or
regarded with affection. ▸ *vt*

pet·ted, pet·ting. make pet of; *inf*
hug, embrace, fondle.
pet·al [PET-l] *n* white or colored
leaflike part of flower. **pet'aled** *adj*
pe·tard [pi-TAHRD] *n* formerly, an
explosive device. **hoist by one's**
own petard ruined, destroyed by
plot one intended for another.
pe·ter [PEE-tər] *vi* **peter out** *inf*
disappear, lose power gradually.
pe·tit [PET-ee] *adj Law* small, petty.
pe·tite [pə-TEET] *adj* small, dainty.
pe·ti·tion [pə-TISH-ən] *n* entreaty,
request, esp. one presented to a
governing body or person. ▸ *vt*
present petition to. **pe·ti'tion·er** *n*
pet·rel [PE-trəl] *n* sea bird.
pet·ri·fy [PE-trə-fī] *vt* **-fied, -fy·ing.**
turn to stone; *fig* make motionless
with fear; make dumb with
amazement. **pet·ri·fac'tion** *n*
pe·tro·le·um [pə-TROH-lee-əm] *n*
unrefined oil.
pet·ti·coat [PET-ee-koht] *n*
women's undergarment worn
under skirts, dresses, etc.
pet·ti·fog·ger [PET-ee-fog-ər] *n*
quibbler; unethical lawyer; one
given to mean dealing in small
matters.
pet·ty [PET-ee] *adj* **-ti·er, -ti·est.**
unimportant, trivial; small-minded,
mean; on a small scale. **petty cash**
cash kept by firm to pay minor
incidental expenses. **petty officer**
noncommissioned officer in Navy.
pet·u·lant [PECH-ə-lənt] *adj* given
to small fits of temper; peevish.
pet'u·lance *n* peevishness.
pe·tu·nia [pi-TOON-yə] *n* plant
with funnel-shaped purple or white
flowers.
pew [pyoo] *n* fixed seat in church;
inf chair, seat.
pew·ter [PYOO-tər] *n* alloy of tin
and lead; utensil of this.
pha·lanx [FAY-langks] *n, pl* **-lanx·es.**
body of soldiers, etc. formed in
close array.
phal·lus [FAL-əs] *n, pl* **-lus·es.** penis;
symbol of it used in primitive rites.
phal'lic *adj*
phan·tas·ma·go'ri·a
[fan-taz-mə-GOR-ee-ə] *n* crowd of

dim or unreal figures; exhibition of illusions.

phan·tom [FAN-təm] n apparition; specter, ghost; fancied vision.

Phar·aoh [FAIR-oh] n title of ancient Egyptian kings.

phar·i·see [FĀ-rə-see] n sanctimonious person; hypocrite. **phar·i·sa'ic** [-SAY-ik] adj

phar·ma·ceu·tic [fahr-mə-SOO-tik] adj of pharmacy. **phar·ma·ceu'ti·cal** adj **phar'ma·cist** n person qualified to dispense drugs. **phar·ma·col'o·gy** [-KOL-ə-jee] n study of drugs. **phar·ma·co·poe'ia** [-kə-PEE-ə] n official book with list and directions for use of drugs. **phar'ma·cy** [-mə-see] n preparation and dispensing of drugs; drugstore.

phar·ynx [FA-ringks] n, pl **pha·ryn·ges** [fə-RIN-jeez] cavity forming back part of mouth and terminating in gullet. **pha·ryn'ge·al** adj

phase [fayz] n any distinct or characteristic period or stage in a development or chain of events. ▶ vt **phased, phas·ing.** arrange, execute in stages or to coincide with something else.

pheas·ant [FEZ-ənt] n game bird with bright plumage.

phe·no·bar·bi·tal [fee-noh-BAHR-bi-tawl] n drug inducing sleep.

phe·nom·e·non [fi-NOM-ə-non] n, pl **-na** [-nə] anything appearing or observed; remarkable person or thing. **phe·nom'e·nal** adj relating to phenomena; remarkable; recognizable or evidenced by senses.

Phil. Philippians.

phil- comb. form loving, e.g. philanthropy; philosophy.

phi·lan·der [fi-LAN-dər] vi (of man) flirt with, make love to, women, esp. with no intention of marrying them. **phi·lan'der·er** n

phi·lan·thro·py [fi-LAN-thrə-pee] n, pl **-pies.** practice of doing good to people; love of mankind; a philanthropic organization.

phi·lan·throp'ic adj loving mankind; benevolent. **phi·lan'thro·pist** n

phi·lat·e·ly [fi-LAT-l-ee] n stamp collecting. **phi·lat'e·list** n

phil·is·tine [FIL-ə-steen] n ignorant, smug person. ▶ adj

phi·lol·o·gy [fi-LOL-ə-jee] n science of structure and development of languages. **phi·lol'o·gist** n

phi·los·o·phy [fi-LOS-ə-fee] n pursuit of wisdom; study of realities and general principles; system of theories on nature of things or on conduct; calmness of mind. **phi·los'o·pher** n one who studies, possesses, or originates philosophy. **phil·o·soph'i·cal** adj of, like philosophy; wise, learned; calm, stoical. **phi·los'o·phize** [-fīz] vi **-phized, -phiz·ing.** reason like philosopher; theorize; moralize.

phle·bi·tis [flə-BĪ-tis] n inflammation of a vein.

phlegm [flem] n viscid substance formed; by mucous membrane and ejected by coughing, etc.; apathy, sluggishness. **phleg·mat·ic** [fleg-MAT-ik] adj not easily agitated; composed.

pho·bi·a [FOH-bee-ə] n fear or aversion; unreasoning dislike.

phoe·nix [FEE-niks] n legendary bird; unique thing.

phone [fohn] n, v inf telephone. **phone card** prepaid card used to pay for telephone calls. **phone tag** repeated unsuccessful attempts to contact by telephone.

pho·net·ic [fə-NET-ik] adj of, or relating to, vocal sounds. **pho·net'ics** n science of vocal sounds. **pho·ne·ti·cian** [foh-ni-TISH-ən] n

phono- comb. form sound, e.g. phonology.

pho·no·graph [FOH-nə-graf] n instrument recording and reproducing sounds, record player.

pho·ny [FOH-nee] inf ▶ adj **-ni·er, -ni·est.** not genuine; insincere. ▶ n, pl **pho'nies.** phony person or thing.

phos·pho·rus [FOS-fər-əs] n toxic, flammable, nonmetallic element

photo 354 **pick**

that appears luminous in the dark.
phos·phate [FOS-fayt] *n*
compound of phosphorus.
phos·pho·res'cence *n* faint glow in
the dark.
pho·to [FOH-toh] *n inf* short for
PHOTOGRAPH. **photo finish** photo
taken at end of race to show
placing of contestants.
photo- *comb. form* light, e.g.
photometer; photosynthesis.
pho·to·cop·y [FOH-toh-kop-ee] *n,
pl* **-cop·ies.** photographic
reproduction. ▶ *vt* **-cop·ied,
-cop·y·ing.**
pho·to·e·lec·tron
[foh-toh-i-LEK-tron] *n* electron
liberated from metallic surface by
action of beam of light.
pho·to·gen·ic [foh-tə-JEN-ik] *adj*
capable of being photographed
attractively.
pho·to·graph [FOH-tə-graf] *n*
picture made by chemical action of
light on sensitive film. ▶ *vt* take
photograph of. **pho·tog'ra·pher**
[-rə-fər] *n*
pho·to·syn·the·sis
[foh-tə-SIN-thə-sis] *n* process by
which green plant uses sun's
energy to build up carbohydrate
reserves.
phrase [frayz] *n* group of words;
pithy expression; mode of
expression. ▶ *vt* **phrased,
phras·ing.** express in words.
phra·se·ol·o·gy [fray-zee-OL-ə-jee]
n manner of expression, choice of
words. **phras·al verb** [-əl] phrase
consisting of verb and preposition,
often with meaning different to the
parts, such as *take in* meaning
deceive.
phre·nol·o·gy [frə-NOL-ə-jee] *n*
(formerly) study of skull's shape;
theory that character and mental
powers are indicated by shape of
skull. **phre·nol'o·gist** *n*
phy·lac·ter·y [fi-LAK-tə-ree] *n, pl*
-ter·ies. leather case containing
religious texts worn by Jewish men
during weekday morning prayers.
phys·ic [FIZ-ik] *n* medicine, esp.
cathartic. ▶ *pl* science of properties

of matter and energy. **phys'i·cal**
adj bodily, as opposed to mental or
moral; material; of physics of body.
phy·si'cian *n* medical doctor.
phys'i·cist *n* one skilled in, or
student of, physics.
phys·i·og·no·my
[fiz-ee-OG-nə-mee] *n, pl* **-mies.**
judging character by face; face;
outward appearance of something.
phys·i·ol·o·gy [fiz-ee-OL-ə-jee] *n*
science of normal function of living
things. **phy·si·ol'o·gist** *n*
phys·i·o·ther·a·py
[fiz-ee-oh-THER-ə-pee] *n*
therapeutic use of physical means,
as massage, etc.
phys·i·o·ther'a·pist *n*
phy·sique [fi-ZEEK] *n* bodily
structure, constitution and
development.
pi [pī] *n Math* ratio of circumference
of circle to its diameter, approx.
3.141592.
pi·an·o [pee-AN-oh] *n, pl* **-an·os.**
musical instrument with strings
that are struck by hammers worked
by keyboard (also **pianofor'te**).
pi·an·ist [pee-AN-ist] *n* performer
on piano.
pi·az·za [pee-AZ-ə] *n* square,
marketplace; veranda.
pi·ca [PĪ-kə] *n* printing type of 6
lines to the inch; size of type, 12
point; typewriter type size (10
letters to inch).
pi·ca·dor [PIK-ə-dor] *n* mounted
bullfighter with lance.
pic·a·resque [pik-ə-RESK] *adj* of
fiction, esp. episodic and dealing
with the adventures of rogues.
pic·co·lo [PIK-ə-loh] *n, pl* **-los.** small
flute.
pick[1] [pik] *vt* choose, select
carefully; pluck, gather; peck at;
pierce with something pointed;
find occasion for. ▶ *n* act of picking;
choicest part. **pick'ings** *pl n*
gleanings; odds and ends of profit.
pick-me-up *n inf* stimulating drink,
tonic. **pick'pock·et** *n* one who
steals from another's pocket.
pick'up *n* device for conversion of
mechanical energy into electric

signals, as in record player, etc.
pickup truck small truck with open body. **pick on** find fault with. **pick up** raise, lift; collect; improve, get better; accelerate.

pick² n tool with curved steel crossbar and wooden shaft, for breaking up hard ground or masonry. **pick'ax** n pick.

pick·er·el [PIK-ər-əl] n small pike.

pick·et [PIK-it] n prong, pointed stake; person, esp. striker, posted outside building, etc. to prevent use of facility, deter would-be workers during strike. ▶ vt post as picket; beset with pickets; tether to peg. **picket fence** fence of pickets. **picket line** line of pickets.

pick·le [PIK-əl] n food, esp. cucumber, preserved in brine, vinegar, etc.; liquid used for preserving; inf awkward situation. ▶ pl pickled vegetables. ▶ vt **-led, -ling.** preserve in pickle. **pickled** adj sl drunk.

pic·nic [PIK-nik] n pleasure outing including meal out of doors. ▶ vi **-nicked, -nick·ing.** take part in picnic.

Pict [pikt] n member of ancient people of NE Scotland.

pic·ture [PIK-chər] n drawing or painting; mental image; beautiful or picturesque object. ▶ pl inf movies. ▶ vt **-tured, -tur·ing.** represent in, or as in, a picture. **pic·to'ri·al** adj of, in, with, painting or pictures; graphic. **pic·tur·esque** [pik-chə-RESK] adj such as would be effective in picture; striking, vivid.

pidg·in [PIJ-ən] n language, not a mother tongue, made up of elements of two or more other languages.

pie [pī] n baked dish of fruit, meat, etc., usu. with pastry crust.

pie·bald [PĪ-bawld] adj irregularly marked with black and white; motley. ▶ n piebald horse or other animal.

piece [pees] n bit, part, fragment; single object; literary or musical composition, etc.; small object

used in checkers, chess, etc.; firearm. ▶ vt **pieced, piec·ing.** mend, put together. **piece'meal** adv by, in, or into pieces, a bit at a time. **piece'work** n work paid for according to quantity produced.

pièce de ré·sis·tance [pyes də ray-zee-STAHNS] Fr most impressive item.

pied [pīd] adj piebald; variegated.

pie-eyed [PĪ-īd] adj sl drunk.

pier [peer] n structure running into sea as landing stage; piece of solid upright masonry as foundation for building, etc.

pierce [peers] vt **pierced, pierc·ing.** make hole in; make a way through. **piercing** adj keen; penetrating.

pi·e·ty [PĪ-i-tee] n, pl **-ties.** godliness; devoutness; goodness; dutifulness.

pig n wild or domesticated mammal killed for pork, ham, bacon; inf greedy, dirty person; offens sl policeman; oblong mass of smelted metal. ▶ vi **pigged, pig·ging.** of sow, produce litter. **pig'gish** adj dirty; greedy; stubborn. **pig'head·ed** adj obstinate. **pig'skin** n (leather made from) the skin of a pig; inf a football. **pig'tail** n braid of hair hanging from back of head.

pi·geon [PIJ-ən] n bird of many wild and domesticated varieties, often trained to carry messages; sl dupe. **pi'geon·hole** [-hohl] n compartment for papers in desk, etc. ▶ vt **-holed, -hol·ing.** defer; classify. **pi'geon-toed** [-tohd] adj with feet, toes turned inward.

pig·ment [PIG-mənt] n coloring matter, paint or dye.

pigmy see PYGMY.

pike¹ [pīk] n various types of large, predatory freshwater fish.

pike² n spear formerly used by infantry.

pi·laf [PEE-lahf] n Middle Eastern dish of steamed rice with spices, sometimes with meat or fowl, etc.

pi·las·ter [pi-LAS-tər] n square column, usu. set in wall.

pile¹ [pīl] n heap; great mass of

building. ▶ *v* **piled, pil·ing.** ▶ *vt*
heap (up), stack load. ▶ *vi* (with *in*
or *out*) move in a group. **atomic
pile** nuclear reactor.

pile² *n* beam driven into the
ground, esp. as foundation for
building in water or wet ground.
pile driver *n* machine for driving
down piles; person who operates
this machine.

pile³ *n* nap of cloth, esp. of velvet,
carpet, etc.; down.

piles [pīlz] *pl n* tumors of veins of
rectum, hemorrhoids.

pil·fer [PIL-fər] *v* steal in small
quantities. **pil'fer·age** [-ij] *n*
pil'fer·er *n*

pil'grim *n* one who journeys to
sacred place; wanderer, wayfarer.
pil'grim·age [-ij] *n*

pill *n* small ball of medicine
swallowed whole; anything
disagreeable that has to be
endured. **the pill** oral
contraceptive. **pill'box** *n* small box
for pills; small concrete fort.

pil·lage [PIL-ij] *v* **-laged, -lag·ing.**
plunder, ravage, sack. ▶ *n* seizure of
goods, esp. in war; plunder.

pil·lar [PIL-ər] *n* slender, upright
structure, column; prominent
supporter.

pil·lo·ry [PIL-ə-ree] *n, pl* **-ries.** frame
with holes for head and hands in
which offender was confined and
exposed to public abuse and
ridicule. ▶ *vt* **-ried, -ry·ing.** expose
to ridicule and abuse; set in pillory.

pil·low [PIL-oh] *n* cushion for the
head, esp. in bed. ▶ *vt* lay on, or as
on, pillow.

pi·lot [PĪ-lət] *n* person qualified to
fly an aircraft or spacecraft; one
qualified to take charge of ship
entering or leaving harbor, or
where knowledge of local water is
needed; steersman; guide. ▶ *adj*
experimental and preliminary. ▶ *vt*
act as pilot to; steer. **pilot light**
small auxiliary flame lighting main
one in gas appliance, etc.

pi·mi·en·to [pi-MYEN-toh] *n, pl*
-tos. (fruit of the) sweet red pepper
(also **pi·men'to**).

pimp *n* one who solicits for
prostitute. ▶ *vi* act as pimp.

pim·ple [PIM-pəl] *n* small pus-filled
spot on the skin. **pim'ply** *adj*
-pli·er, -li·est.

pin *n* short thin piece of stiff wire
with point and head, for fastening;
wooden or metal peg or rivet. ▶ *vt*
pinned, pin·ning. fasten with pin;
seize and hold fast. **pin'ball** *n* table
game, where small ball is shot
through various hazards. **pin
money** trivial sum. **pin'point** *vt*
mark exactly.

pin·a·fore [PIN-ə-for] *n* child's
apron; woman's dress with a bib
top.

pince-nez [PANS-nay] *n, pl*
pince-nez. eyeglasses kept on nose
by spring.

pin·cers [PIN-sərz] *pl n* tool for
gripping, composed of two limbs
crossed and pivoted; claws of
lobster, etc. **pincers movement**
military maneuver in which both
flanks of a force are attacked
simultaneously.

pinch *vt* nip, squeeze; stint; *sl* steal;
sl arrest. ▶ *n* nip; as much as can be
taken up between finger and
thumb; stress; emergency.
pinch'bar *n* crowbar.

pine¹ [pīn] *n* evergreen coniferous
tree; its wood.

pine² *vi* **pined, pin·ing.** yearn; waste
away with grief, etc.

pin·e·al [PIN-ee-əl] *adj* shaped like
pine cone. **pineal gland** small
cone-shaped gland situated at base
of brain.

pine·ap·ple [PĪ-nap-əl] *n* tropical
plant with spiny leaves bearing
large edible fruit; the fruit; *sl* a
bomb.

ping *vi* produce brief ringing sound;
of engine, knock.

pin·guid [PING-gwid] *adj* oily; fat.

pin·ion¹ [PIN-yən] *n* bird's wing.
▶ *vt* disable or confine by binding
wings, arms, etc.

pinion² *n* small cogwheel.

pink [pingk] *n* pale red color;
garden plant; best condition,
fitness. ▶ *adj* of color pink. ▶ *vt*

pierce; finish edge (of fabric) with perforations or scallops.

pin·na·cle [PIN-ə-kəl] n highest pitch or point; mountain peak; pointed turret on buttress or roof.

pint [pīnt] n liquid measure, one eighth of gallon (.568 liter).

pin·tle [PIN-tl] n pivot pin.

pin'up n picture of sexually attractive person, esp. (partly) naked.

pi·o·neer [pī-ə-NEER] n explorer; early settler; originator; one of advance party preparing road, etc. for troops. ▶ vi act as pioneer or leader.

pi·ous [PĪ-əs] adj devout; righteous.

pip¹ n seed in fruit; inf something or someone outstanding.

pip² n spot on playing cards, dice, or dominoes; inf metal insigne on officer's shoulder showing rank.

pip³ n disease of poultry.

pipe [pīp] n tube of metal or other material; tube with small bowl at end for smoking tobacco; musical instrument, whistle. ▶ pl bagpipes. ▶ v **piped, pip·ing.** play on pipe; utter in shrill tone; convey by pipe; ornament with a piping or fancy edging. **pip'er** n player on pipe or bagpipes. **piping** n system of pipes; fancy edging or trimming on clothes; act or art of playing on pipe, esp. bagpipes. **pipe down** inf stop making noise; stop talking. **pipe dream** fanciful, impossible plan, etc. **pipe'line** n long pipe for transporting oil, water, etc.; means of communications. **pipe up** inf assert oneself by speaking; speak louder. **in the pipeline** yet to come; in process of completion, etc.

pi·pette [pī-PET] n slender glass tube to transfer fluids from one vessel to another.

pip'pin n kind of apple.

pi·quant [PEE-kənt] adj pungent; stimulating. **pi'quan·cy** n

pique [peek] n feeling of injury, baffled curiosity or resentment. ▶ vt **piqued, piqu·ing.** hurt pride of; irritate; stimulate.

pi·qué [pi-KAY] n stiff ribbed cotton fabric.

pi·ra·nha [pi-RAHN-yə] n, pl **-nhas.** small voracious freshwater fish of tropical Amer.

pi·rate [PĪ-rət] n sea robber; publisher, etc., who infringes copyright. ▶ n, adj (person) broadcasting illegally. ▶ vt **-rat·ed, -rat·ing.** use or reproduce (artistic work, etc.) illicitly. **pi'ra·cy** [-see] n, pl **-cies.**

pir·ou·ette [pir-oo-ET] n spinning around on the toe. ▶ vi **-et·ted, -et·ting.** do this.

pissed [pist] adj sl angry, annoyed, or disappointed.

pis·tach·i·o [pi-STASH-ee-oh] n, pl **-i·os.** small hard-shelled, sweet-tasting nut; tree producing it.

pis·til [PIS-tl] n seed-bearing organ of flower.

pis·tol [PIS-tl] n small firearm for one hand. ▶ vt **-toled, -tol·ing.** shoot with pistol.

pis·ton [PIS-tən] n in internal combustion engine, steam engine, etc., cylindrical part propelled to and fro in hollow cylinder by pressure of gas, etc. to convert reciprocating motion to rotation.

pit n deep hole in ground; mine or its shaft; depression; enclosure where cocks are set to fight; servicing, refueling area on automobile racetrack. ▶ vt **pit·ted, pit·ting.** set to fight, match; mark with small dents or scars. **pit'fall** n any hidden danger; covered pit for trapping animals or people.

pitch¹ [pich] vt cast or throw; set up; set the key of (a tune). ▶ vi fall headlong; of ship, plunge lengthwise. ▶ n act of pitching; degree, height, intensity; slope; distance propeller advances during one revolution; distance between threads of screw, teeth of saw, etc.; acuteness of tone; Baseball ball delivered by pitcher to batter; inf persuasive sales talk. **pitch'er** n Baseball player who delivers ball to batter. **pitch'fork** n fork for lifting hay, etc. ▶ vt throw with, as with, pitchfork. **pitch'out** n Baseball pitch thrown intentionally beyond batter's reach to improve catcher's chance of putting out base runner attempting to steal.

pitch² n dark sticky substance obtained from tar or turpentine. ▸ vt coat with this. **pitch'y** adj **pitch·i·er, pitch·i·est.** covered with pitch; black as pitch. **pitch-black, -dark** adj very dark.

pitch·blende [PICH-blend] n mineral composed largely of uranium oxide, yielding radium.

pitch·er [PICH-ər] n large jug; see also PITCH.

pith n tissue in stems and branches of certain plants; essential substance, most important part. **pith'i·ly** adv **pith'y** adj **pith·i·er, pith·i·est.** terse, cogent, concise; consisting of pith.

pi·ton [PEE-ton] n metal spike used in mountain climbing.

pit·tance [PIT-ns] n small allowance; inadequate wages.

pi·tu·i·tar·y [pi-TOO-i-ter-ee] adj of, pert. to, the endocrine gland at base of brain.

pit·y [PIT-ee] n, pl **pit·ies.** sympathy, sorrow for others' suffering; regrettable fact. ▸ vt **pit·ied, pit·y·ing.** feel pity for. **pit'e·ous** adj deserving pity; sad, wretched. **pit'i·a·ble** adj **pit'i·ful** [-i-fəl] adj woeful; contemptible. **pit'i·less** [-i-lis] adj feeling no pity; hard, merciless.

piv·ot [PIV-ət] n shaft or pin on which thing turns. ▸ vt furnish with pivot. ▸ vi hinge on one. **piv'ot·al** [-ət-əl] adj of, acting as, pivot; of crucial importance.

pix·ie [PIK-see] n fairy; mischievous person.

pi·zazz [pə-ZAZ] n inf sparkle, vitality, glamour.

piz·za [PEET-sə] n dish of baked disk of dough covered with cheese and tomato sauce and wide variety of garnishes. **piz·ze·ri'a** [-REE-ə] n place selling pizzas.

piz·zi·ca·to [pit-si-KAH-toh] adj Mus played by plucking string of violin, etc., with finger.

plac·ard [PLAK-ahrd] n paper or card with notice on one side for posting up or carrying, poster. ▸ vt post placards on; advertise, display on placards.

pla·cate [PLAY-klayt] vt **-cat·ed, -cat·ing.** conciliate, pacify, appease. **pla·ca·to'ry** [-kə-tor-ee] adj

place [plays] n locality, spot; position; stead; duty; town, village, residence, buildings; office, employment; seat, space. ▸ vt **placed, plac·ing.** put in particular place; set; identify; make (order, bet, etc.).

pla·ce·bo [plə-SEE-boh] n, pl **-bos.** sugar pill, etc. given to unsuspecting patient as active drug.

pla·cen·ta [plə-SEN-tə] n, pl **-tas.** organ formed in uterus during pregnancy, providing nutrients for fetus; afterbirth.

plac·id [PLAS-id] adj calm; equable. **pla·cid·i·ty** [plə-SID-i-tee] n mildness, quiet.

pla·gia·rism [PLAY-jə-riz-əm] n taking ideas, passages, etc. from an author and presenting them, unacknowledged, as one's own. **pla'gia·rize** [-rīz] v **-rized, -riz·ing.** **pla'gia·rist** n

plague [playg] n highly contagious disease, esp. bubonic plague; nuisance; affliction. ▸ vt **plagued, pla·guing.** trouble, annoy.

plaid [plad] n checked or tartan pattern; fabric made of this.

plain [playn] adj **-er, -est.** flat, level; unobstructed, not intricate; clear, obvious; easily understood; simple; ordinary; without decoration; not beautiful. ▸ n tract of level country. ▸ adv clearly. **plain'ly** [-lee] adv **plain'ness** [-nis] n **plain clothes** civilian dress, as opposed to uniform. **plain dealing** directness and honesty in transactions. **plain sailing** unobstructed course of action. **plain speaking** frankness, candor.

plain·tiff [PLAYN-tif] n Law one who sues in court.

plain·tive [PLAYN-tiv] *adj* sad, mournful, melancholy.

plait [playt] *n* braid of hair, straw, etc. ▸ *vt* form or weave into braids.

plan *n* scheme; way of proceeding; project, design; drawing of horizontal section; diagram, map. ▸ *vt* **planned, plan·ning.** make plan of; arrange beforehand.

planch·et [PLAN-chit] *n* flat sheet of metal; disk of metal from which coin is stamped.

plan·chette [plan-SHET] *n* small board used in spiritualism.

plane¹ [playn] *n* smooth surface; a level; carpenter's tool for smoothing wood. ▸ *vt* **planed, plan·ing.** make smooth with one. ▸ *adj* perfectly flat or level. **plan'er** *n* planing machine.

plane² *v* **planed, plan·ing.** of airplane, glide; of boat, rise and partly skim over water. ▸ *n* wing of airplane; airplane.

plan·et [PLAN-it] *n* heavenly body revolving around the sun. **plan'e·tar·y** [-i-ter-ee] *adj* of, like, planets.

plan·e·tar·i·um [plan-i-TAIR-ee-əm] *n* an apparatus that shows the movement of sun, moon, stars and planets by projecting lights on the inside of a dome; building in which the apparatus is housed.

plan·gent [PLAN-jənt] *adj* resounding.

plank [plangk] *n* long flat piece of sawn timber. ▸ *vt* cover with planks.

plank·ton [PLANGK-tən] *n* minute animal and vegetable organisms floating in ocean.

plant *n* living organism feeding on inorganic substances and without power of locomotion; such an organism that is smaller than tree or shrub; equipment or machinery needed for manufacture; building and equipment for manufacturing purposes; complete equipment used for heating, air conditioning, etc. ▸ *vt* set in ground, to grow; support, establish; stock with plants; *sl* hide, esp. to deceive or observe. **plant'er** *n* one who

plants; ornamental pot or stand for house plants.

plan·tain¹ [PLAN-tin] *n* low-growing weed with broad leaves.

plantain² *n* tropical plant like banana; its fruit.

plan·ta·tion [plan-TAY-shən] *n* estate or large farm for cultivation of tobacco, cotton, etc.; wood of planted trees; formerly, colony.

plaque [plak] *n* ornamental plate, tablet; plate of clasp or brooch; filmy deposit on surfaces of teeth, conducive to decay.

plas·ma [PLAZ-mə] *n* clear, fluid portion of blood.

plas·ter [PLAS-tər] *n* mixture of lime, sand, etc. for coating walls, etc.; piece of fabric spread with medicinal or adhesive substance. ▸ *vt* apply plaster to; apply like plaster; *inf* defeat soundly. **plas'tered** *adj sl* drunk.

plas·tic [PLAS-tik] *n* any of a group of synthetic products derived from casein, cellulose, etc. that can be readily molded into any form and are extremely durable. ▸ *adj* made of plastic; easily molded, pliant; capable of being molded; produced by molding. **plas·tic·i·ty** [pla-STIS-i-tee] *n* ability to be molded. **plastic surgery** repair or reconstruction of missing or malformed parts of the body for medical or cosmetic reasons.

plate [playt] *n* shallow round dish; flat thin sheet of metal, glass, etc.; household utensils of gold or silver; device for printing; illustration in book; set of false teeth, part of this that adheres to roof of mouth. ▸ *vt* **plat·ed, plat·ing.** cover with thin coating of gold, silver, or other metal. **plate'ful** [-fəl] *n, pl* **-fuls.** **plat'er** *n* person who plates; inferior race horse. **plate glass** kind of thick glass used for mirrors, windows, etc. **plate tec·ton'ics** *Geology* study of structure of Earth's crust, esp. movement of layers of rocks.

pla·teau [pla-TOH] *n, pl* **-teaus** [-TOHZ] tract of level high land, tableland; period of stability.

plat·en [PLAT-n] *n Printing* plate by which paper is pressed against type; roller in typewriter.

plat·form *n* raised level surface or floor, stage; raised area in station from which passengers board trains; political program.

plat·i·num [PLAT-n-əm] *n* white heavy malleable metal.

plat·i·tude [PLAT-i-tood] *n* commonplace remark. **plat·i·tu'di·nous** *adj*

Pla·ton·ic [plə-TON-ik] *adj* of Plato or his philosophy; (**p-**) (of love) purely spiritual, friendly.

pla·toon [plə-TOON] *n* two or more squads of soldiers employed as unit.

plat·ter [PLAT-ər] *n* flat dish.

plat·y·pus [PLAT-i-pəs] *n, pl* **-pus·es.** small Aust. egg-laying amphibious mammal, with dense fur, webbed feet and ducklike bill (also **duckbilled platypus**).

plau·dit [PLAW-dit] *n* act of applause, handclapping.

plau·si·ble [PLAW-zə-bəl] *adj* apparently fair or reasonable; fair-spoken. **plau·si·bil'i·ty** *n*

play *vi* amuse oneself; take part in game; behave carelessly; act a part on the stage; perform on musical instrument; move with light or irregular motion, flicker, etc. ▶ *vt* contend with in game; take part in (game); trifle; act the part of; perform (music); perform on (instrument); use, work (instrument). ▶ *n* dramatic piece or performance; sport; amusement; manner of action or conduct; activity; brisk or free movement; gambling. **play'boy** *n* rich man who lives only for pleasure.

play'ful [-fəl] *adj* lively. **play'group** [-groop] *n* group of young children playing regularly under adult supervision. **play'house** *n* theater; small house for children to play in. **playing card** one of set of usu. 52 cards used in card games. **playing field** extensive piece of ground for open-air games. **play'thing** *n* toy.

play'wright [-rīt] *n* author of plays.

pla·za [PLAH-zə] *n* open space or square; complex of retail stores, etc.

plea [plee] *n* entreaty; statement of prisoner or defendant; excuse. **plead** *v* **plead·ed** or **pled, plead·ing.** make earnest appeal; address court of law; bring forward as excuse or plea. **plea bargaining** procedure in which defendant agrees to plead guilty in return for leniency in sentencing, etc.

please [pleez] *v* **pleased, pleas·ing.** ▶ *vt* be agreeable to; gratify; delight. ▶ *vi* like; be willing. ▶ *adv* word of request. **pleas'ant** [PLEZ-ənt] *adj* pleasing, agreeable. **pleas'ant·ry** [-ən-tree] *n, pl* **-ries.** joke, humor. **pleas·ur·a·ble** [PLEZH-ər-ə-bəl] *adj* giving pleasure. **pleas'ure** *n* enjoyment; satisfaction, will, choice.

pleat [pleet] *n* any of various types of fold made by doubling material back on itself. ▶ *vi* make, gather into pleats.

plebe [pleeb] *n* at US military and naval academies, member of first-year class.

ple·be·ian [pli-BEE-ən] *adj* belonging to the common people; low or rough. ▶ *n* one of the common people.

pleb·i·scite [PLEB-ə-sīt] *n* decision by direct voting of the electorate.

plec·trum [PLEK-trəm] *n, pl* **-trums.** small implement for plucking strings of guitar, etc.

pledge [plej] *n* promise; thing given over as security; toast. ▶ *vt* **pledged, pledg·ing.** promise formally; bind or secure by pledge; give over as security.

Pleis·to·cene [PLĪ-stə-seen] *adj Geology* of the glacial period of formation.

ple·na·ry [PLEE-nə-ree] *adj* complete, without limitations, absolute; of meeting, etc., with all members present.

plen·i·po·ten·ti·ar·y [plen-ə-pə-TEN-shee-er-ee] *adj, n* (envoy) having full powers.

plen·i·tude [PLEN-i-tood] *n*

completeness, abundance, entirety.

plen·ty n, pl **-ties.** abundance; quite enough. **plen'te·ous** [-tee-əs] adj ample; rich; copious. **plen'ti·ful** [-ti-fəl] adj abundant.

ple·num [PLEE-nəm] n, pl **-nums.** space as considered to be full of matter (opposed to vacuum); condition of fullness; space above ceiling, etc. for receiving, storing heated or cooled air.

ple·o·nasm [PLEE-ə-naz-əm] n use of more words than necessary. **ple·o·nas'tic** [-NAS-tik] adj redundant.

pleth·o·ra [PLETH-ər-ə] n oversupply. **ple·thor·ic** [ple-THOR-ik] adj

pleu·ri·sy [PLUUR-ə-see] n inflammation of the pleura. **pleura** n membrane lining the chest and covering the lungs.

plex·us [PLEK-səs] n, pl **-us·es.** network of nerves, or fibers.

pli·a·ble [PLĪ-ə-bəl] adj easily bent or influenced. **pli·a·bil'i·ty** n **pli'an·cy** [-ən-see] n **pli'ant** adj pliable.

pli·ers [PLĪ-ərz] pl n tool with hinged arms and jaws for gripping.

plight[1] [plīt] n distressing state; predicament.

plight[2] vt promise, engage oneself to.

Plim·soll line [PLIM-səl] mark on ships indicating maximum displacement permitted when loaded.

Pli·o·cene [PLĪ-ə-seen] n Geology the most recent tertiary deposits.

plod vi **plod·ded, plod·ding.** walk or work doggedly.

plop n sound of object falling into water. ▶ vi **plopped, plop·ping.** fall with, as though with, such a sound; make the sound.

plot[1] n secret plan, conspiracy; essence of story, play, etc. ▶ v **plot·ted, plot·ting.** devise secretly; mark position of; make map of; conspire.

plot[2] n small piece of land.

plov·er [PLUV-ər] n one of various shore birds, typically with round

head, straight bill and long pointed wings.

plow n implement for turning up soil; similar implement for clearing snow, etc. ▶ vt turn up with plow, furrow. ▶ vi work at slowly. **plow'share** [-shair] n blade of plow. **plow under** bury beneath soil by plowing; overwhelm.

ploy [ploi] n stratagem; occupation; prank.

pluck [pluk] vt pull, pick off; strip from; sound strings of (guitar, etc.) with fingers, plectrum. ▶ n courage; sudden pull or tug. **pluck'y** adj **pluck·i·er, pluck·i·est.** courageous.

plug n thing fitting into and filling a hole; Electricity device connecting appliance to electricity supply; tobacco pressed hard; inf recommendation, advertisement; sl worn-out horse. ▶ vt **plugged, plug·ging.** stop with plug; inf advertise anything by constant repetition; sl punch; sl shoot. **plug away** work hard. **plug in** connect (electrical appliance) with power source by means of plug.

plum n stone fruit; tree bearing it; choicest part, piece, position, etc.; dark reddish-purple color. ▶ adj choice; plum-colored.

plumage see PLUME.

plumb [plum] n ball of lead attached to string used for sounding, finding the perpendicular, etc. ▶ adj perpendicular. ▶ adv perpendicularly; exactly; inf downright; honestly. ▶ vt set exactly upright; find depth of; reach, undergo; equip with, connect to plumbing system. **plumb'er** [PLUM-ər] n worker who attends to water and sewage systems. **plumb'ing** n trade of plumber; system of water and sewage pipes. **plumb'line** n cord with plumb attached.

plume [ploom] n feather; ornament of feathers, etc. ▶ vt **plumed, plum·ing.** furnish with plumes; pride oneself. **plum·age** [PLOO-mij] n bird's feathers collectively.

plum·met [PLUM-it] *vi* plunge headlong. ▶ *n* plumbline.

plump[1] *adj* **-er, -est.** of rounded form, moderately fat, chubby. ▶ *v* make, become plump.

plump[2] *vi* sit, fall abruptly; (with *for*) support enthusiastically. ▶ *vt* drop, throw abruptly. ▶ *adv* suddenly; heavily; directly.

plun·der [PLUN-dər] *vt* take by force; rob systematically. ▶ *vi* rob. ▶ *n* pillage; booty, spoils.

plunge [plunj] *v* **plunged, plung·ing.** ▶ *vt* put forcibly (into). ▶ *vi* throw oneself (into); enter, rush with violence; descend very suddenly. ▶ *n* dive. **plung'er** *n* rubber suction cap with handle to unblock drains. **take the plunge** *inf* embark on risky enterprise; get married.

plunk *v* pluck (string of banjo, etc.); drop, fall suddenly and heavily. ▶ *n*

plu·ral [PLUUR-əl] *adj* of, denoting more than one person or thing. ▶ *n* word in its plural form. **plu'ral·ism** *n* holding of more than one office at a time; coexistence of different social groups, etc., in one society. **plu·ral'i·ty** *n, pl* **-ties.** of three or more candidates, etc.; largest share of votes.

plus *prep* with addition of. ▶ *adj* to be added; positive. ▶ *n* sign (+) denoting addition; advantage.

plush *n* fabric with long nap, long-piled velvet. ▶ *adj* **-er, -est.** luxurious.

Plu·to [PLOO-toh] *n* Greek god of the underworld; farthest planet from the sun.

plu·toc·ra·cy [ploo-TOK-rə-see] *n, pl* **-cies.** government by the rich; state ruled thus; wealthy class. **plu'to·crat** [-tə-krat] *n* wealthy person.

plu·to·ni·um [ploo-TOH-nee-əm] *n* radioactive metallic element used esp. in nuclear reactors and weapons.

ply[1] [plī] *v* **plied, ply·ing.** wield; work at; supply pressingly; urge; keep busy; go to and fro, run

regularly.

ply[2] *n* fold or thickness; strand of yarn. **ply'wood** [-wuud] *n* board of thin layers of wood glued together with grains at right angles.

Pm *Chem* promethium.

pneu·mat·ic [nuu-MAT-ik] *adj* of, worked by, inflated with wind or air.

pneu·mo·nia [nuu-MOHN-yə] *n* inflammation of the lungs.

Po *Chem* polonium.

poach[1] [pohch] *vt* take (game) illegally; trample, make swampy or soft. ▶ *vi* trespass for this purpose; encroach. **poach'er** *n*

poach[2] *vt* simmer (eggs, fish, etc.) gently in water, etc. **poach'er** *n*

pock [pok] *n* pustule, as in smallpox, etc. **pock'marked** *adj*

pock·et [POK-it] *n* small bag inserted in garment; cavity filled with ore, etc.; socket, cavity, pouch or hollow; mass of water or air differing from that surrounding it; isolated group or area. ▶ *vt* put into one's pocket; appropriate, steal. ▶ *adj* small. **pocket money** small, regular allowance given to children by parents; allowance for small, occasional expenses. **pocket veto** indirect veto of bill by president, governor, who retains bill unsigned until legislative adjournment.

pod *n* long seed vessel, as of peas, beans, etc. ▶ *v* **pod·ded, pod·ding.** ▶ *vi* form pods. ▶ *vt* shell.

po·di·um [POH-dee-əm] *n* small raised platform.

po·em [POH-əm] *n* imaginative composition in rhythmic lines. **po'et** [-it] *n* writer of poems. **po'et·ry** *n* art or work of poet, verse. **po'e·sy** [-ə-see] *n* poetry. **po·et'ic** [-ET-ik] *adj* **po·et'i·cal·ly** *adv* **po'et·as·ter** [-as-tər] *n* would-be or inferior poet.

po·grom [pə-GRUM] *n* organized persecution and massacre, esp. of Jews.

poign·ant [POIN-yənt] *adj* moving; biting, stinging; vivid; pungent. **poign'an·cy** *n, pl* **-cies.**

poin·set·ti·a [poin-SET-ee-ə] *n* orig.

Amer. shrub, widely cultivated for its clusters of scarlet leaves, resembling petals.

point *n* dot, mark; punctuation mark; item, detail; unit of value; position, degree, stage; moment; gist of an argument; purpose; striking or effective part or quality; essential object or thing; sharp end; single unit in scoring; headland; one of direction marks of compass; fine kind of lace; act of pointing; printing unit, one-twelfth of a pica. ▶ *pl* electrical contacts in distributor of engine. ▶ *vi* show direction or position by extending finger; direct attention; (of dog) indicate position of game by standing facing it. ▶ *vt* aim, direct; sharpen; fill up joints with mortar; give value to (words, etc.).
point'ed *adj* sharp; direct, telling.
point'er *n* index; indicating rod, etc., used for pointing; indication; dog trained to point. **point'less** [-lis] *adj* blunt; futile, irrelevant.
point-blank *adj* aimed horizontally, plain, blunt. ▶ *adv* with level aim (there being no necessity to elevate for distance); at short range.
poise [poiz] *n* composure; self-possession; balance, equilibrium, carriage (of body, etc.). ▶ *v* **poised, pois·ing.** (cause to be) balanced or suspended. ▶ *vt* hold in readiness.
poi·son [POI-zən] *n* substance that kills or injures when introduced into living organism. ▶ *vt* give poison to; infect; pervert, spoil. **poi'son·ous** *adj* **poison-pen letter** malicious anonymous letter.
poke¹ [pohk] *v* **poked, pok·ing.** ▶ *vt* push, thrust with finger, stick, etc.; thrust forward. ▶ *vi* make thrusts; pry. ▶ *n* act of poking. **pok'er** *n* metal rod for poking fire. **pok'y** *adj* **pok·i·er, pok·i·est.** small, confined, cramped.
poke² *n* **pig in a poke** something bought, etc. without previous inspection.
pok·er [POHK-ər] *n* card game. **poker face** expressionless face;

person with this.
polar *adj* see POLE².
Po·lar·oid [POH-lə-roid] *n* ® type of plastic that polarizes light; camera that develops print very quickly inside itself.
pole¹ [pohl] *n* long rounded piece of wood, etc. ▶ *vt* **poled, pol·ing.** propel with pole.
pole² *n* each of the ends of axis of Earth or celestial sphere; each of opposite ends of magnet, electric battery, etc. **po·lar** [POH-lər] *adj* pert. to the N and S pole, or to magnetic poles; directly opposite in tendency, character, etc. **po·lar'i·ty** *n* **po·lar·i·za'tion** [-ZAY-shən] *n* **po'lar·ize** *vt* **-rized, -riz·ing.** give polarity to; affect light in order to restrict vibration of its waves to certain directions. **polar bear** white Arctic bear. **poles apart** having completely opposite interests, etc.
po·lem·ic [pə-LEM-ik] *adj* controversial. ▶ *n* war of words, argument. **po·lem'i·cal** *adj* **po·lem'i·cize** [-sīz] *vt* **-cized, -ciz·ing.**
po·lice [pə-LEES] *n* the civil force that maintains public order. ▶ *vt* **-liced, -lic·ing.** keep in order. **police officer** *n* member of police force.
pol·i·cy¹ [POL-ə-see] *n, pl* **-cies.** course of action adopted, esp. in state affairs; prudence.
policy² *n, pl* **-cies.** insurance contract.
po·li·o [poh-lee-oh] *n* (also **po·li·o·my·e·li·tis**) disease of spinal cord characterized by fever and possibly paralysis.
pol'ish *vt* make smooth and glossy; refine. ▶ *n* shine; polishing; substance for polishing; refinement.
po·lite [pə-LIT] *adj* **-lit·er, -lit·est.** showing regard for others in manners, speech, etc.; refined, cultured. **po·lite'ness** *n* courtesy.
pol·i·tic [POL-i-tik] *adj* wise, shrewd, expedient, cunning.
pol'i·tics *n* art of government; political affairs or life. **po·lit'i·cal**

adj of the state or its affairs.
pol·i·ti'cian [-TISH-ən] *n* one engaged in politics. **pol'i·ty** *n, pl* **-ties.** form of government; organized state; civil government. **politically correct** (esp. of language) intended to avoid any implied prejudice.
pol·ka [POHL-kə] *n, pl* **-kas.** lively 19th-century dance; music for it. **polka dot** one of pattern of bold spots on fabric, etc.
poll [pohl] *n* voting; counting of votes; number of votes recorded; canvassing of sample of population to determine general opinion; (top of) head. ▶ *pl* place where votes are cast. ▶ *vt* receive (votes); take votes of; lop, shear; cut horns from animals. ▶ *vi* vote. **polled** *adj* hornless. **poll'ster** *n* one who conducts polls. **poll tax** (esp. formerly) tax on each person.
pol·lard [POL-ərd] *n* hornless animal of normally horned variety; tree on which a close head of young branches has been made by polling. ▶ *vt* make a pollard of.
pol·len [POL-ən] *n* fertilizing dust of flower. **pol'li·nate** *vt* **-nat·ed, -nat·ing.**
pol·lute [pə-LOOT] *vt* **-lut·ed, -lut·ing.** make foul; corrupt; desecrate. **pol·lu'tant** [-tənt] *n* **pol·lu'tion** *n*
po·lo [POH-loh] *n* game like hockey played by teams of 4 players on horseback. **water polo** game played similarly by swimmers seven to a side.
pol·o·naise [pol-ə-NAYZ] *n* Polish dance; music for it.
pol·ter·geist [POHL-tər-gīst] *n* noisy mischievous spirit.
poly- *comb. form* many, e.g. *polysyllabic.*
pol·y·an·dry [POL-ee-an-dree] *n* polygamy in which woman has more than one husband. **pol·y·an'drous** *adj*
pol·y·chrome [POL-ee-krohm] *adj* many colored. ▶ *n* work of art in many colors. **pol·y·chro·mat'ic** *adj*
pol·y·es·ter [POL-ee-es-tər] *n* any

of large class of synthetic materials used as plastics, textile fibers, etc.
pol·y·eth·yl·ene [pol-ee-ETH-ə-leen] *n* tough thermoplastic material.
po·lyg·a·my [pə-LIG-ə-mee] *n* custom of being married to several persons at a time. **po·lyg'a·mist** *n*
pol·y·glot [POL-ee-glot] *adj* speaking, writing in several languages. ▶ *n* person who speaks, read and writes in many languages.
pol·y·gon [POL-ee-gon] *n* figure with many angles or sides.
po·lyg·y·ny [pə-LIJ-ə-nee] *n* polygamy in which one man has more than one wife.
pol·y·he·dron [pol-ee-HEE-drən] *n* solid figure contained by many faces.
pol·y·math [POL-ee-math] *n* learned person.
pol·y·mer [POL-ə-mər] *n* compound, as polystyrene, that has large molecules formed from repeated units. **po·lym·er·i·za·tion** [pə-lim-ər-ə-ZAY-shən] *n* **po·lym'er·ize** [-LIM-ər-īz] *vt* **-ized, -iz·ing.**
pol·yp [POL-ip] *n* sea anemone, or allied animal; tumor with branched roots.
pol·y·sty·rene [pol-ee-STĪ-reen] *n* synthetic material used esp. as white rigid foam for packing, etc.
pol·y·tech·nic [pol-ee-TEK-nik] *n* college dealing mainly with technical subjects. ▶ *adj*
pol·y·the·ism [POL-ee-thee-iz-əm] *n* belief in many gods. **pol·y·the·is'tic** *adj*
pol·y·un·sat·u·rat·ed [pol-ee-un-SACH-ə-ray-tid] *adj* of group of fats that do not form cholesterol in blood.
pol·y·u·re·thane [pol-ee-YUUR-ə-thayn] *n* class of synthetic materials, often in foam or flexible form.
po·made [po-MAYD] *n* scented ointment for hair.
po·me·gran·ate [POM-ə-gran-it] *n* tree; its fruit with thick rind containing many seeds in red pulp.

pom·mel [PUM-əl] n front of saddle; knob of sword hilt. ▶ vt -meled, -mel·ing. pummel.

pomp n splendid display or ceremony.

pom'pom n tuft of ribbon, wool, feathers, etc., decorating hat, shoe, etc.

pomp·ous [POM-pəs] adj self-important; ostentatious; of language, inflated, stilted. **pom·pos'i·ty** n, pl -ties.

pon·cho [PON-choh] n, pl -chos. loose circular cloak with hole for head.

pond n small body, pool or lake of still water.

pon·der [PON-dər] v muse, meditate, think over; consider, deliberate on.

pon·der·ous [PON-dər-əs] adj heavy, unwieldy; boring. **pon'der·a·ble** adj able to be evaluated or weighed.

pon'tiff n Pope; high priest; bishop. **pon·tif'i·cal** adj **pon·tif'i·cate** [-kit] n dignity or office of pontiff. **pon·tif'i·cate** [-kayt] vi -cat·ed, -cat·ing. speak bombastically; act as pontiff.

pon·toon' n flat-bottomed boat or metal drum for use in supporting temporary bridge.

po·ny [POH-nee] n, pl -nies. horse of small breed; small horse; very small glass. **po'ny·tail** n long hair tied in one bunch at back of head.

poo·dle [POOD-l] n pet dog with long curly hair often clipped fancifully.

pool¹ n small body of still water; deep place in river or stream; puddle; swimming pool.

pool² n common fund or resources; group of people, e.g. typists, any of whom can work for any of several employers; collective stakes in various games; cartel; variety of billiards. ▶ vt put in common fund.

poop¹ n ship's stern.

poop² vt exhaust (someone). **poop out** sl fail in something; cease functioning.

poop³ n children's sl excrement. ▶ vi defecate.

poop⁴ n sl pertinent information.

poor [puur] adj -er, -est. having little money; unproductive; inadequate, insignificant; needy; miserable, pitiable; feeble; not fertile. **poor'ly** adv, adj not in good health.

pop¹ v popped, pop·ping. ▶ vi make small explosive sound; inf go or come unexpectedly or suddenly. ▶ vt cause to make small explosive sound; put or place suddenly. ▶ n small explosive sound; inf nonalcoholic soda. **pop'corn** n any kind of corn with kernels that puff up when roasted; the roasted product.

pop² n inf father; old man.

pop³ n music of general appeal, esp. to young people. ▶ adj short for POPULAR.

Pope [pohp] n bishop of Rome and head of R.C. Church.

pop·lar [POP-lər] n tree noted for its slender tallness.

pop'lin n corded fabric usu. of cotton.

pop·pa·dom [POP-ə-dəm] n thin, round, crisp Indian bread.

pop·py [POP-ee] n, pl -pies. bright-flowered plant yielding opium.

pop·u·lace [POP-yə-ləs] n the common people; the masses.

pop·u·lar [POP-yə-lər] adj finding general favor; of, by the people. **pop·u·lar'i·ty** n state or quality of being generally liked. **pop'u·lar·ize** vt -ized, -iz·ing. make popular.

pop·u·late [POP-yə-layt] vt -lat·ed, -lat·ing. fill with inhabitants. **pop·u·la'tion** [-LAY-shən] n inhabitants; their number. **pop'u·lous** [-ləs] adj thickly populated or inhabited.

pop·u·list [POP-yə-list] adj claiming to represent the whole of the people. ▶ n **pop'u·lism** [-liz-əm] n

por·ce·lain [POR-sə-lin] n fine earthenware, china.

porch n covered approach to entrance of building; veranda.

por·cine [POR-sin] *adj* of, like a pig.

por·cu·pine [POR-kyə-pīn] *n* rodent covered with long, pointed quills.

pore[1] [por] *vi* **pored, por·ing.** fix eye or mind upon; study closely.

pore[2] *n* minute opening, esp. in skin. **po·ros·i·ty** [pə-ROS-i-tee] *n* **por·ous** [POR-əs] *adj* allowing liquid to soak through; full of pores.

pork *n* pig's flesh as food. **pork'er** *n* pig raised for food. **pork'y** *adj* **pork·i·er, pork·i·est.** fleshy, fat.

porn, por'no *n inf* short for PORNOGRAPHY.

por·nog·ra·phy [por-NOG-rə-fee] *n* indecent literature, films, etc. **por·nog'ra·pher** *n* **por'no·graph'ic** *adj*

por·phy·ry [POR-fə-ree] *n, pl* **-ries.** reddish stone with embedded crystals.

por·poise [POR-pəs] *n* blunt-nosed sea mammal like dolphin.

por·ridge [POR-ij] *n* soft food of oatmeal, etc. boiled in water.

port[1] *n* harbor, haven; town with harbor.

port[2] *n* larboard or left side of ship. ▶ *vt* turn to left side of a ship.

port[3] *n* strong sweet, usu. red, fortified wine from Portugal.

port[4] *n* opening in side of ship. **port'hole** *n* small opening or window in side of ship.

port[5] *vt Military* carry rifle, etc. diagonally across body. ▶ *n* this position.

port·a·ble [POR-tə-bəl] *n, adj* (something) easily carried.

por·tage [POR-tij] *n* (cost of) transport.

por·tal [POR-tl] *n* large doorway or imposing gate; *Computers* Internet site providing links to other sites. **portal-to-portal pay** payment to worker that includes pay for all time spent on employer's premises.

port·cul·lis [port-KUL-is] *n* defense grating to raise or lower in front of castle gateway.

por·tend' *vt* foretell; be an omen of. **por'tent** *n* omen, warning; marvel. **por·ten'tous** [-təs] *adj* ominous; threatening; pompous.

por·ter [POR-tər] *n* person employed to carry luggage; doorkeeper.

port·fo·li·o [port-FOH-lee-oh] *n, pl* **-li·os.** flat portable case for loose papers; office of minister of state, member of cabinet.

por·ti·co [POR-ti-koh] *n, pl* **-coes** or **-cos.** colonnade; covered walk.

por·tiere [por-TYAIR] *n* heavy door curtain.

por·tion [POR-shən] *n* part, share, helping; destiny, lot. ▶ *vt* divide into shares.

port·ly [PORT-lee] *adj* **-li·er, -li·est.** bulky, stout.

port·man·teau [port-MAN-toh] *n, pl* **-teaus.** leather suitcase, esp. one opening into two compartments. **portmanteau word** word made by putting together parts of other words, such as *motel* from *motor* and *hotel*.

por·tray' *vt* make pictures of, describe. **por'trait** [-trit] *n* likeness of (face of) person. **por'trai·ture** [-tri-chər] *n* **por·tray'al** [-əl] *n* act of portraying.

pose [pohz] *v* **posed, pos·ing.** ▶ *vt* place in attitude; put forward. ▶ *vi* assume attitude, affect or pretend to be a certain character. ▶ *n* attitude, esp. one assumed for effect. **po·seur** [poh-ZUR] *n* one who assumes affected attitude to create impression.

pos·er [POH-zər] *n* puzzling question.

posh *adj inf* smart, elegant, stylish.

pos·it [POZ-it] *vt* lay down as principle.

po·si·tion [pə-ZISH-ən] *n* place; situation; location, attitude; status; state of affairs; employment; strategic point. ▶ *vt* place in position.

pos·i·tive [POZ-i-tiv] *adj* certain; sure; definite, absolute, unquestionable; utter; downright; confident; not negative; greater than zero; *Electricity* having deficiency of electrons. ▶ *n* something positive; *Photography* print in which lights and shadows are not reversed. **pos'i·tiv·ism** n philosophy recognizing only matters of fact and experience. **pos'i·tiv·ist** n believer in this.

pos·i·tron [POZ-i-tron] n positive electron.

pos·se [POS-ee] n body of armed people, esp. for maintaining law and order.

pos·sess [pə-ZES] vt own; (of evil spirit, etc.) have mastery of. **pos·ses'sion** n act of possessing; thing possessed; ownership. **pos·ses'sive** adj of, indicating possession; with excessive desire to possess, control. ▶ n possessive case in grammar. **pos·ses'sor** n owner.

pos·si·ble [POS-ə-bəl] adj that can, or may, be, exist, happen or be done; worthy of consideration. ▶ n possible candidate. **pos·si·bil'i·ty** n, pl **-ties. pos'si·bly** adv perhaps.

pos·sum [POS-əm] n opossum. **play possum** pretend to be dead, asleep, etc. to deceive opponent.

post¹ [pohst] n upright pole of timber or metal fixed firmly, usu. to support or mark something. ▶ vt display; stick up (on notice board, etc.); *Computers* make (e-mail) publicly available. **post'er** n large advertising bill; one who posts bills. **poster paints, colors** flat paints suited for posters.

post² n mail; collection or delivery of this; office; situation; point, station, place of duty; place where soldier is stationed; place held by body of troops; fort. ▶ vt put into mailbox; supply with latest information; station (soldiers, etc.) in particular spot; transfer (entries) to ledger. ▶ adv with haste. **post·age** [POH-stij] n charge for carrying letter. **post'al** [-əl] adj **postal money order** written order, available at post office, for payment of sum of money. **post'card** n stamped card sent by mail. **post'man** [-mən] n, pl **-men.** postal employee who collects or delivers mail. **post'mark** n official mark with name of office, etc. stamped on letters. **post'mas·ter** n

official in charge of post office. **post'mis·tress** [-tris] n, fem **post office** place where postal business is conducted.

post- prefix after, behind, later than, e.g. postwar.

post·date [pohst-DAYT] vt **-dat·ed, -dat·ing.** give date later than actual date.

poste res·tante [pohst re-STAHNT] *Fr* direction on mail to indicate that post office should keep traveler's letters till called for.

pos·te·ri·or [po-STEER-ee-ər] adj later, hinder. ▶ n the buttocks.

pos·ter·i·ty [po-STER-i-tee] n later generations; descendants.

post·grad·u·ate [pohst-GRAJ-oo-it] adj carried on after graduation. ▶ n

post·hu·mous [POS-chə-məs] adj occurring after death; born after father's death; published after author's death. **post'hu·mous·ly** adv

post·mor·tem [pohst-MOR-təm] n medical examination of dead body; evaluation after event, etc. ends. ▶ adj taking place after death.

post·par·tum [pohst-PAHR-təm] adj occurring after childbirth.

post·pone [pohs-POHN] vt **-poned, -pon·ing.** put off to later time, defer.

post·pran·di·al [pohst-PRAN-dee-əl] adj after a meal, esp. dinner.

post·script [POHST-skript] n addition to letter, book, etc.

pos·tu·lant [POS-chə-lənt] n candidate for admission to religious order.

pos·tu·late [POS-chə-layt] vt **-lat·ed, -lat·ing.** take for granted; lay down as self-evident; stipulate. ▶ n [-lit] proposition assumed without proof; prerequisite.

pos·ture [POS-chər] n attitude, position of body. ▶ v **-tured, -tur·ing.** pose.

po·sy [POH-zee] n, pl **-sies.** flower; bunch of flowers.

pot n round vessel; cooking vessel; trap, esp. for crabs, lobsters; *sl* marijuana; *inf* a lot. ▶ vt **pot·ted,**

pot·ting. put into, preserve in pot. **potted** adj cooked, preserved, in a pot; sl drunk. **pot'hole** n pitlike cavity in rocks, usu. limestone, produced by faulting and water action; hole worn in road. **pot'luck** n whatever is to be had (to eat). **pot'sherd** [-shurd] n broken fragment of pottery. **pot shot** easy or random shot.

po·ta·ble [POH-tə-bəl] adj drinkable. **po·ta'tion** [-TAY-shən] n drink; drinking.

pot'ash n alkali used in soap, etc.; crude potassium carbonate.

po·tas·si·um [pə-TAS-ee-əm] n white metallic element.

po·ta·to [pə-TAY-toh] n, pl **-toes.** plant with tubers grown for food. **hot potato** topic, etc. too threatening to bring up. **sweet potato** trailing plant; its edible sweetish tubers.

po·tent [POH-nt] adj powerful, influential; (of male) capable of sexual intercourse. **po'ten·cy** n physical or moral power; efficacy. **po·ten·tate** [POHT-n-tayt] n ruler. **po·ten·tial** [pə-TEN-shəl] adj latent, that may or might but does not now exist or act. ▶ n possibility; amount of potential energy; Electricity level of electric pressure. **po·ten·ti·al'i·ty** [-shee-AL-i-tee] n

po·tion [POH-shən] n dose of medicine or poison.

pot·pour·ri [poh-puu-REE] n mixture of rose petals, spices, etc.; musical, literary medley.

pot·tage [POT-ij] n soup or stew.

pot·ter [POT-ər] n maker of earthenware vessels. **pot'ter·y** n, pl **-ter·ies.** earthenware; where it is made; art of making it.

pouch [powch] n small bag; pocket. ▶ vt put into one.

poul·tice [POHL-tis] n soft composition of cloth, bread, etc., applied hot to sore or inflamed parts of the body.

poul·try [POHL-tree] n domestic fowl collectively.

pounce¹ [powns] vi **pounced,** **pounc·ing.** spring upon suddenly, swoop (upon). ▶ n swoop or sudden descent.

pounce² n fine powder used to prevent ink from spreading on unsized paper or in pattern making.

pound¹ [pownd] vt beat, thump; crush to pieces or powder; walk, run heavily.

pound² n unit of troy weight; unit of avoirdupois weight equal to 0.453 kg; monetary unit in United Kingdom.

pound³ n enclosure for stray animals or officially removed vehicles; confined space.

pound·al [POWN-dl] n a unit of force in the foot-pound-second system.

pour [por] vi come out in a stream, crowd, etc.; flow freely; rain heavily. ▶ vt give out thus; cause to run out.

pout [powt] v thrust out (lips), look sulky. ▶ n act of pouting. **pout'er** n pigeon with power of inflating its crop.

pov·er·ty [POV-ər-tee] n state of being poor; poorness; lack of means; scarcity.

pow·der [POW-dər] n solid matter in fine dry particles; medicine in this form; gunpowder; face powder, etc. ▶ vt apply powder to; reduce to powder. **pow'der·y** adj

pow·er [POW-ər] n ability to do or act; strength; authority; control; person or thing having authority; mechanical energy; electricity supply; rate of doing work; product from continuous multiplication of number by itself. **pow'ered** adj having or operated by mechanical or electrical power. **pow'er·ful** [-fəl] adj **pow'er·less** [-lis] adj **pow·er·house, power station** n installation for generating and distributing electric power.

pow'wow n conference. ▶ vi confer.

pox [poks] n one of several diseases marked by pustular eruptions of skin; inf syphilis.

Pr Chem praseodymium.

prac·ti·cal [PRAK-ti-kəl] adj given to action rather than theory; relating

to action or real existence; useful; in effect though not in name; virtual. **prac·ti·cal·ly** adv
prac·ti·ca·ble [-kə-bəl] adj that can be done, used, etc. **prac·ti'tion·er** n one engaged in a profession.
prac·tice [PRAK-tis] v **-ticed, -tic·ing.** ▸ vt do repeatedly, work at to gain skill; do habitually; put into action. ▸ vi exercise oneself; exercise profession. **practice** n habit; mastery or skill; exercise of art or profession; action, not theory.
prag·mat·ic [prag-MAT-ik] adj concerned with practical consequence; of the affairs of state. **prag'ma·tism** [-mə-tiz-əm] n **prag'ma·tist** n
prair·ie [PRAIR-ee] n large mostly treeless tract of grassland. **prairie dog** small Amer. rodent allied to marmot. **prairie oyster** as remedy for hangover, a drink of raw egg usu. with seasonings; as food, testis of a calf.
praise [prayz] n commendation; fact, state of being praised. ▸ vt **praised, prais·ing.** express approval, admiration of; speak well of; glorify. **praise'wor·thy** [-wur-thee] adj
pra·line [PRAH-leen] n candy made of nuts with caramel covering.
prance [prans] vi **pranced, pranc·ing.** swagger; caper; walk with bounds. ▸ n prancing.
pran·di·al [PRAN-dee-əl] adj of a meal, esp. dinner.
prank [prangk] n mischievous trick or escapade, frolic.
pra·se·o·dym·i·um [pray-zee-oh-DIM-ee-əm] n rare-earth chemical element.
prate [prayt] vi **prat·ed, prat·ing.** talk idly, chatter. ▸ n idle chatter.
prat·tle [PRAT-l] vi **-tled, -tling.** talk like child. ▸ n trifling, childish talk. **prat'tler** n babbler.
prawn n edible sea crustacean like a shrimp.
pray vt ask earnestly; entreat. ▸ vi offer prayers, esp. to God. **prayer** [prair] n action, practice of praying to God; earnest entreaty. **pray'er**

n one who prays.
pre- prefix before, beforehand, e.g. prenatal; prerecord; preshrunk.
preach [preech] vi deliver sermon; give moral, religious advice. ▸ vt set forth in religious discourse; advocate. **preach'er** n
pre·am·ble [PREE-am-bəl] n introductory part of document, story, etc.
pre·car·i·ous [pri-KAIR-ee-əs] adj insecure, unstable, perilous.
pre·cau·tion [pri-KAW-shən] n previous care to prevent evil or secure good; preventive measure. **pre·cau'tion·ar·y** adj
pre·cede [pri-SEED] v **-ced·ed, -ced·ing.** go, come before in rank, order, time, etc. **prec·e·dence** [PRES-i-dəns] n priority in position, rank, time, etc. **prec'e·dent** n previous case or occurrence taken as rule.
pre·cept [PREE-sept] n rule for conduct, maxim. **pre·cep'tor** n instructor.
pre·ces·sion [pree-SESH-ən] n act of preceding; motion of spinning body, in which the axis of rotation sweeps out a cone.
pre·cinct [PREE-singkt] n enclosed, limited area; administrative area of city, esp. of police, board of elections. ▸ pl environs. **precinct house** police station.
pre·cious [PRE-shəs] adj beloved, cherished; of great value, highly valued; rare. **pre·ci·os·i·ty** [presh-ee-OS-i-tee] n overrefinement in art or literature. **prec'ious·ly** adv
prec·i·pice [PRES-ə-pis] n very steep cliff or rockface. **pre·cip'i·tous** adj sheer.
pre·cip·i·tant [prə-SIP-i-tənt] adj hasty, rash; abrupt. **pre·cip'i·tance, -tan·cy** n
pre·cip·i·tate [pri-SIP-i-tayt] vt **-tat·ed, -tat·ing.** hasten happening of; throw headlong; Chem cause to be deposited in solid form from solution. ▸ adj [-i-tit] too sudden; rash, impetuous. ▸ n [-i-tit] substance chemically precipitated.

pre·cip'i·tate·ly [-tit-lee] *adv*
pre·cip·i·ta·tion [-TAY-shən] *n* esp. rain, snow, etc.
pré·cis [PRAY-see] *n, pl* **pré·cis** [PRAY-seez] abstract, summary.
pre·cise [pri-SĪS] *adj* definite; particular; exact, strictly worded; careful in observance; punctilious, formal. **pre·cise'ly** *adv* **pre·ci·sion** [-SIZH-ən] *n* accuracy.
pre·clude [pri-KLOOD] *vt* **-clud·ed, -clud·ing.** prevent from happening; shut out.
pre·co·cious [pri-KOH-shəs] *adj* developed, matured early or too soon. **pre·coc'i·ty** [-KOS-i-tee], **pre·co'cious·ness** [-KOH-shəs-nis] *n*
pre·con·ceive [pree-kən-SEEV] *vt* **-ceived, -ceiv·ing.** form an idea beforehand. **pre·con·cep'tion** [-SEP-shən] *n*
pre·con·di·tion [pree-kən-DISH-ən] *n* necessary or required condition.
pre·cur·sor [pri-KUR-sər] *n* forerunner. **pre·cur'sive** *adj* **pre·cur'so·ry** *adj*
pred·a·to·ry [PRED-ə-tor-ee] *adj* hunting, killing other animals, etc. for food; plundering. **pred'a·tor** *n* predatory animal.
pred·e·ces·sor [PRED-ə-ses-ər] *n* one who precedes another in an office or position; ancestor.
pre·des·tine [pri-DES-tin] *vt* **-tined, -tin·ing.** decree beforehand, foreordain. **pre·des·ti·na'tion** *n*
pre·dic·a·ment [pri-DIK-ə-mənt] *n* perplexing, embarrassing or difficult situation.
pred·i·cate [PRED-i-kayt] *vt* **-cat·ed, -cat·ing.** affirm, assert; base (on or upon). ▶ *n* [-kit] that which is predicated; *Grammar* statement made about a subject.
pre·dict [pri-DIKT] *vt* foretell, prophesy. **pre·dict'a·ble** *adj*
pre·di·lec·tion [pred-l-EK-shən] *n* preference, liking, partiality.
pre·dis·pose [pree-dis-POHZ] *vt* **-posed, -pos·ing.** incline, influence someone (toward); make susceptible (to).
pre·dom·i·nate [pri-DOM-ə-nayt] *vi* **-nat·ed, -nat·ing.** be main or

controlling element. **pre·dom'i·nance** [-nəns] *n* **pre·dom'i·nant** *adj* chief.
pre·em·i·nent [pree-EM-ə-nənt] *adj* excelling all others, outstanding. **pre·em'i·nence** *n*
pre·empt [pree-EMPT] *vt* acquire in advance or act in advance of or to exclusion of others. **pre·emp'tive** *adj*
preen *vt* trim (feathers) with beak, plume; smarten oneself.
pre·fab·ri·cate [pree-FAB-ri-kayt] *vt* **-cat·ed, -cat·ing.** manufacture buildings, etc. in shaped sections, for rapid assembly on the site. **pre'fab** *n* building so made.
pref·ace [PREF-is] *n* introduction to book, etc. ▶ *vt* **-faced, -fac·ing.** introduce. **pref'a·to·ry** *adj*
pre·fect [PREE-fekt] *n* person put in authority. **pre·fec·ture** [PREE-fek-chər] *n* office, residence, jurisdiction of a prefect.
pre·fer [pri-FUR] *vt* **-ferred, -fer·ring.** like better; promote. **pref·er·a·ble** [PREF-ər-ə-bəl] *adj* more desirable. **pref'er·a·bly** *adv* **pref'er·ence** [-əns] *n* **pref·er·en'tial** [-EN-shəl] *adj* giving, receiving preference.
pre·fix [PREE-fiks] *n* preposition or particle put at beginning of word or title. ▶ *vt* put as introduction; put before word to make compound.
preg·nant [PREG-nənt] *adj* carrying fetus in womb; full of meaning, significance; inventive. **preg'nan·cy** *n*
pre·hen·sile [pri-HEN-sil] *adj* capable of grasping.
pre·his·tor·ic [pree-hi-STOR-ik] *adj* before period in which written history begins. **pre·his'to·ry** *n*
prej·u·dice [PREJ-ə-dis] *n* preconceived opinion; bias, partiality; damage or injury likely to happen to person or person's rights as a result of others' action or judgment. ▶ *vt* **-diced, -dic·ing.** influence; bias; injure. **prej·u·di'cial** [-DISH-əl] *adj* injurious; disadvantageous.
prel·ate [PREL-it] *n* bishop or other

church dignitary of equal or higher rank. **prel′a·cy** [-ə-see] n prelate's office.

pre·lim·i·nar·y [pri-LIM-ə-ner-ee] adj preparatory, introductory. ▶ n, pl **-ies.** introductory, preparatory statement, action.

prel·ude [PRAY-lood] n Mus introductory movement; performance, event, etc. serving as introduction. ▶ v **-ud·ed, -ud·ing.** serve as prelude, introduce.

pre·mar·i·tal [pree-MA-ri-təl] adj occurring before marriage.

pre·ma·ture [pree-mə-CHUUR] adj happening, done before proper time.

pre·med·i·tate [pri-MED-i-tayt] vt **-tat·ed, -tat·ing.** consider, plan beforehand. **pre·med·i·ta′tion** n

pre·mier [pri-MEER] n prime minister. ▶ adj chief, foremost; first. **pre·mier′ship** n office of premier.

pre·miere [pri-MEER] n first performance of a play, film, etc. ▶ vi **-miered, -mier·ing.** have first performance.

prem·ise [PREM-is] n Logic proposition from which inference is drawn. ▶ pl house, building with its belongings. **premise** vt **-mised, -mis·ing.** state by way of introduction.

pre·mi·um [PREE-mee-əm] n prize, bonus; sum paid for insurance; excess over nominal value; great value or regard.

pre·mo·ni·tion [pree-mə-NISH-ən] n presentiment, foreboding. **pre·mon·i·to·ry** [pri-MON-i-tor-ee] adj

pre·na·tal [pree-NAYT-l] adj occurring before birth.

pre·oc·cu·py [pree-OK-yə-pī] vt **-pied, -py·ing.** occupy to the exclusion of other things. **pre·oc·cu·pa′tion** n mental concentration or absorption.

prep [prep] n preppy.

pre·pare [pri-PAIR] v **-pared, -par·ing.** ▶ vt make ready; make. ▶ vi get ready. **prep·a·ra′tion** n making ready beforehand; something that is prepared, as a

medicine; at school, (time spent) preparing work for lesson. **pre·par′a·to·ry** [-PA-rə-tor-ee] adj serving to prepare; introductory. **pre·par′ed·ness** [-id-nis] n state of being prepared. **preparatory school** private school preparing students for college.

pre·pay [pree-PAY] vt **-paid, -pay·ing.** pay or pay for beforehand. **pre·paid′** adj

pre·pon·der·ate [pri-PON-də-rayt] vi **-at·ed, -at·ing.** be of greater weight or power. **pre·pon′der·ance** [-əns] n superiority of power, numbers, etc.

prep·o·si·tion [prep-ə-ZISH-ən] n word marking relation between noun or pronoun and other words. **prep·o·si′tion·al** adj

pre·pos·sess [pree-pə-ZES] vt impress, esp. favorably, beforehand; possess beforehand. **pre·pos·sess′ing** adj inviting favorable opinion, attractive, winning.

pre·pos·ter·ous [pri-POS-tər-əs] adj utterly absurd, foolish.

prep·py, prep·pie [PRE-pee] n **-ies.** inf (person who behaves like) student or former student of preparatory school. ▶ adj

pre·puce [PRE-pyoos] n retractable fold of skin covering tip of penis, foreskin.

pre·req·ui·site [pri-REK-wə-zit] n, adj (something) required as prior condition.

pre·rog·a·tive [pri-ROG-ə-tiv] n peculiar power or right, esp. as vested in ruler. ▶ adj privileged.

pres·age [PRES-ij] n omen, indication of something to come. ▶ vt **-aged, -ag·ing.** foretell.

pres·by·o·pi·a [prez-bee-OH-pee-ə] n progressively diminishing ability of the eye to focus, esp. on near objects, farsightedness.

pres·by·ter [PREZ-bi-tər] n elder in early Christian church; priest; member of a presbytery. **Pres·by·te′ri·an** adj, n (member) of Protestant church governed by lay elders. **pres′by·ter·y** n church court composed of all ministers within a certain district and one or two ruling elders from each church; R.C. Church rectory.

pre·science [PRESH-əns] n foreknowledge. **pres′cient** adj

pre·scribe [pri-SKRĪB] v **-scribed, -scrib·ing.** set out rules for; order; ordain; order use of (medicine). **pre·scrip′tion** n prescribing; thing prescribed; written statement of it. **pre·scrip′tive** adj

pres·ent¹ [PREZ-ənt] adj that is here; now existing or happening. ▶ n present time or tense. **pres′ence** n being present; appearance, bearing. **pres′ent·ly** adv soon; at present.

present² [pri-ZENT] vt introduce formally; show; give; offer; point, aim. **pres′ent** n gift. **pre·sent′a·ble** adj fit to be seen. **pres·en·ta′tion** [-TAY-shən] n **pre·sent′er** n person who presents, esp. an award.

pre·sen·ti·ment [pri-ZEN-tə-mənt] n sense of something (esp. evil) about to happen.

pre·serve [pri-ZURV] vt **-served, -serv·ing.** keep from harm, injury or decay; maintain; pickle, can. ▶ n special area; that which is preserved, as fruit, etc.; place where game is kept for private fishing, shooting. ▶ pl preserved vegetables, fruit, etc. **pres·er·va′tion** n **pre·serv′a·tive** n chemical put into perishable foods, drinks, etc. to keep them from going bad. ▶ adj tending to preserve; having quality of preserving.

pre·side [pri-ZĪD] vi **-sid·ed, -sid·ing.** be chairperson; superintend. **pres′i·dent** [-dənt] n head of organization, company, republic, etc. **pres′i·den·cy** n, pl **-cies. pres·i·den′tial** [-DEN-shəl] adj

press¹ vt subject to push or squeeze; smooth by pressure or heat; urge steadily, earnestly. ▶ vi bring weight to bear; throng; hasten. ▶ n a pressing; machine for pressing, esp. printing machine; printing house; its work or art; newspapers collectively; reporters, journalists; crowd; stress. **press′ing** adj urgent; persistent. **press agent** person employed to advertise and secure publicity for any person, enterprise, etc. **press′man** [-mən] n printer who attends to the press.

press² vt force to serve esp. in navy or army. **press gang** formerly, body of men employed to press men into naval service.

pres·sure [PRESH-ər] n act of pressing; influence; authority; difficulties; Physics thrust per unit area. **pres·sur·i·za′tion** [-ZAY-shən] n in aircraft, maintenance of normal atmospheric pressure at high altitudes. **pres′sur·ize** vt **-ized, -iz·ing. pressure cooker** reinforced pot that cooks food rapidly by steam under pressure. **pressure group** organized group that exerts influence on policies, public opinion, etc.

pres·ti·dig·i·ta′tion [pres-ti-dij-i-TAY-shən] n sleight of hand. **pres·ti·dig′i·ta·tor** n

pres·tige [pre-STEEZH] n reputation; influence depending on it. **pres·tig′i·ous** [-STIJ-əs] adj

pres·to [PRES-toh] adv Mus quickly.

pre·stressed [PREE-strest] adj (of concrete) containing stretched steel cables for strengthening.

pre·sume [pri-ZOOM] v **-sumed, -sum·ing.** ▶ vt take for granted. ▶ vi take liberties. **pre·sum′a·bly** adv probably; doubtlessly. **pre·sump′tion** [-ZUM-shən] n forward, arrogant opinion or conduct; strong probability. **pre·sump′tive** adj that may be assumed as true or valid until contrary is proved. **pre·sump′tu·ous** [-shoo-əs] adj forward, impudent, taking liberties.

pre·sup·pose [pree-sə-POHZ] vt **-posed, -pos·ing.** assume or take for granted beforehand. **pre·sup·po·si′tion** [-ZI-shən] n previous supposition.

pre·tend [pri-TEND] *vt* claim or allege (something untrue); make believe, as in play. ▶ *vi* lay claim (to). **pre·tense'** *n* simulation; pretext. **pre·tend'er** *n* claimant (to throne). **pre·ten'sion** *n*

pre·ten'tious [-shəs] *adj* making claim to special merit or importance; given to outward show.

pre·ter·nat·u·ral [pre-tər-NACH-ər-əl] *adj* out of ordinary way of nature; abnormal, supernatural.

pre·text [PREE-tekst] *n* excuse; pretense.

pret·ty [PRIT-ee] *adj* **-ti·er, -ti·est.** having beauty that is attractive rather than imposing; charming, etc. ▶ *adv* fairly, moderately. **pret'ti·ness** [-nis] *n*

pret·zel [PRET-səl] *n* crisp, dry biscuit usu. shaped as knot or stick.

pre·vail [pri-VAYL] *vi* gain mastery; triumph; be in fashion, generally established. **pre·vail'ing** *adj* widespread; predominant. **prev'a·lence** [-ləns] *n* **prev'a·lent** [-lənt] *adj* extensively existing, rife.

pre·var·i·cate [pri-VA-ri-kayt] *vi* **-cat·ed, -cat·ing.** make evasive or misleading statements; lie. **pre·var'i·ca·tor** *n*

pre·vent [pri-VENT] *vt* stop, hinder. **pre·vent'a·ble** *adj* **pre·ven'tion** [-shən] *n* **pre·ven'tive** *adj, n*

pre·view [PREE-vyoo] *n* advance showing; a showing of scenes from a forthcoming film, etc.

pre·vi·ous [PREE-vee-əs] *adj* earlier; preceding; happening before. **pre'vi·ous·ly** *adv* before.

prey [pray] *n* animal hunted and killed by carnivorous animals; victim. ▶ *vi* seize for food; treat as prey; (with *upon*) afflict, obsess.

price [prīs] *n* amount, etc. for which thing is bought or sold; cost; value; reward; odds in betting. ▶ *vt* **priced, pric·ing.** fix, ask price for. **price'less** [-lis] *adj* invaluable; very funny. **pric'ey** [-ee] *adj* **pric·i·er, pric·i·est.** expensive.

prick [prik] *vt* pierce slightly with sharp point; cause to feel mental pain; mark by prick; erect (ears). ▶ *n* slight hole made by pricking; pricking or being pricked; sting; remorse; that which pricks; sharp point. **prick'le** *n* thorn, spike. ▶ *vi* **-kled, -kling.** feel tingling or pricking sensation. **prick'ly** *adj* **-li·er, -li·est. prickly heat** inflammation of skin with stinging pains.

pride [prīd] *n* too high an opinion of oneself; worthy self-esteem; feeling of elation or great satisfaction; something causing this; group (of lions). ▶ *v refl* **prid·ed, prid·ing.** take pride.

priest [preest] *n* official minister of religion, member of clergy. **priest'ess** *n, fem* **priest'hood** [-huud] *n* **priest'ly** *adj* **-li·er, -li·est.**

prig *n* self-righteous person who professes superior culture, morality, etc. **prig'gish** *adj*

prim *adj* **prim·mer, prim·mest.** very restrained, formally prudish.

pri·ma·cy [PRĪ-me-see] *n* state of being first in rank, grade, etc.; office of PRIMATE[1].

pri·ma don·na [pree-mə DON-ə] *n, pl* **donnas.** principal female singer in opera; temperamental person.

pri·ma fa·ci·e [PRĪ-mə FAY-shee] *Lat* at first sight; obvious.

pri·mal [PRĪ-məl] *adj* of earliest age; first, original. **pri·ma'ri·ly** *adv* **pri'ma·ry** *adj* chief; of the first stage, decision, etc.; elementary.

pri·mate[1] [PRĪ-mit] *n* archbishop.

pri·mate[2] [PRĪ-mayt] *n* one of order of mammals including monkeys and man.

prime[1] [prīm] *adj* fundamental; original; chief; best. ▶ *n* first, best part of anything; youth; full health and vigor. ▶ *vt* **primed, prim·ing.** prepare (gun, engine, pump, etc.) for use; fill up, e.g. with information. **prime minister** leader of parliamentary government.

prime[2] *vt* **primed, prim·ing.** prepare for paint with preliminary coating of oil, etc. **prim'er**

[PRĪM-ər] *n* paint, etc. for priming.

prim·er [PRIM-ər] *n* elementary schoolbook or manual.

pri·me·val [prī-MEE-vəl] *adj* of the earliest age of the world.

prim·i·tive [PRIM-i-tiv] *adj* of an early undeveloped kind, ancient; crude, rough.

pri·mo·gen·i·ture [prī-mə-JEN-i-chər] *n* rule by which real estate passes to the first born son. **pri·mo·gen'i·tor** *n* earliest ancestor; forefather.

pri·mor·di·al [prī-MOR-dee-əl] *adj* existing at or from the beginning.

prince [prins] *n* son or (in some countries) grandson of king or queen; ruler, chief. **prin'cess** *n*, *fem* **prince'ly** *adj* -li·er, -li·est. generous, lavish; stately; magnificent.

prin·ci·pal [PRIN-sə-pəl] *adj* chief in importance. ▶ *n* person for whom another is agent; head of institution, esp. school; sum of money lent and yielding interest; chief actor. **prin·ci·pal'i·ty** *n* territory, dignity of prince.

prin·ci·ple [PRIN-sə-pəl] *n* moral rule; settled reason of action; uprightness; fundamental truth or element.

print *vt* reproduce (words, pictures, etc., by pressing inked plates, type, blocks, etc. to paper, etc.); produce thus; write in imitation of this; impress; *Photography* produce pictures from negatives; stamp (fabric) with colored design. ▶ *n* printed matter; printed lettering; written imitation of printed type; photograph; impression, mark left on surface by thing that has pressed against it; printed cotton fabric. **print'er** *n* person or device engaged in printing. **printed circuit** electronic circuit with wiring printed on an insulating base. **print'out** *n* printed information from computer, teleprinter, etc.

pri·or [PRĪ-ər] *adj* earlier. ▶ *n* chief of religious house or order. **pri·or·ess** *n*, *fem* **pri·or'i·ty** *n*, *pl* -ties. precedence; something given

special attention. **pri'o·ry** *n*, *pl* -ries. monastery, convent under prior, prioress. **prior to** before, earlier.

prise [prīz] *vt* **prised, pris·ing.** force open by levering; obtain (information, etc.) with difficulty.

prism [PRIZ-əm] *n* transparent solid usu. with triangular ends and rectangular sides, used to disperse light into spectrum or refract it in optical instruments, etc. **pris·mat'ic** *adj* of prism shape; (of color) such as is produced by refraction through prism, rainbowlike, brilliant.

pris·on [PRIZ-ən] *n* jail. **pris'on·er** *n* one kept in prison; captive.

pris·sy [PRIS-ee] *adj* -si·er, -si·est. fussy, prim.

pris·tine [pris-TEEN] *adj* original, primitive, unspoiled, good.

pri·vate [PRĪ-vit] *adj* secret, not public; reserved for, or belonging to, or concerning, an individual only; personal; secluded; denoting soldier or marine of lowest rank; not controlled by government. ▶ *n* private soldier or marine. **pri'va·cy** [-vi-see] *n* **pri·va·tize** *vt* -tized, -tiz·ing. transfer from government or public ownership to private enterprise.

pri·va·tion [prī-VAY-shən] *n* want of comforts or necessities; hardship; act of depriving. **priv·a·tive** [PRIV-ə-tiv] *adj* of privation or negation.

priv·et [PRIV-it] *n* bushy shrub used for hedges.

priv·i·lege [PRIV-ə-lij] *n* advantage or favor that only a few obtain; right, advantage belonging to person or class. **priv'i·leged** *adj* enjoying special right or immunity.

priv·y [PRIV-ee] *adj* admitted to knowledge of secret. ▶ *n*, *pl* **priv·ies.** outhouse; *Law* person having interest in an action.

prize¹ [prīz] *n* reward given for success in competition; thing striven for; thing won. ▶ *adj* winning or likely to win a prize. ▶ *vt* **prized, priz·ing.** value highly.

prize'fight *n* boxing match for money.

prize² *n* ship, property captured in (naval) warfare.

pro¹ [proh] *adj, adv* in favor of.

pro² *n* professional. ▶ *adj* professional.

pro- *prefix* for, instead of, before, in front, e.g. *proconsul; pronoun; project.*

pro·ac·tive [proh-AK-tiv] *adj* taking the initiative and acting in advance, rather than simply reacting to circumstances and events.

prob·a·ble [PROB-ə-bəl] *adj* likely. **prob·a·bil'i·ty** *n* likelihood; anything that has appearance of truth. **prob'a·bly** *adv*

pro·bate [PROH-bayt] *n* proving of authenticity of will; certificate of this. **probate court** court with power over administration of estates of dead persons.

pro·ba·tion [proh-BAY-shən] *n* system of releasing lawbreakers, but placing them under supervision for stated period; testing of candidate before admission to full membership.

probe [prohb] *vt* **probed, prob·ing.** search into, examine, question closely. ▶ *n* that which probes, or is used to probe; thorough inquiry.

pro·bi·ty [PROH-bi-tee] *n* honesty, uprightness, integrity.

prob·lem [PROB-ləm] *n* matter, etc. difficult to deal with or solve; question set for solution; puzzle. **prob·le·mat'ic** *adj* questionable; uncertain; disputable.

pro·bos·cis [proh-BOS-is] *n, pl* **-cis·es.** trunk or long snout; *inf* nose, esp. prominent one.

pro·ceed [prə-SEED] *vi* go forward, continue; be carried on; take legal action. **pro·ceeds** [PROH-seedz] *pl n* amount of money or profit received. **pro·ce'dur·al** [-SEE-jər-əl] *adj* **pro·ce'dure** *n* act, manner of proceeding; conduct. **pro·ceed'ing** *n* act or course of action; transaction. ▶ *pl* minutes of meeting; methods of prosecuting

charge, claim, etc.

proc·ess [PROS-es] *n* series of actions or changes; method of operation; state of going on; action of law; outgrowth. ▶ *vt* handle, treat, prepare by special method of manufacture, etc. **pro·ces·sion** [prə-SESH-ən] *n* regular, orderly progress; line of persons in formal order. **pro·ces'sion·al** *adj*

proc·es·sor *n* person or device that processes; *Computers* same as CENTRAL PROCESSING UNIT.

pro·claim [proh-KLAYM] *vt* announce publicly, declare. **proc·la·ma'tion** [prok-lə-MAY-shən] *n*

pro·cliv·i·ty [proh-KLIV-i-tee] *n, pl* **-ties.** inclination, tendency.

pro·cras·ti·nate [proh-KRAS-tə-nayt] *vi* **-nat·ed, -nat·ing.** put off, delay. **pro·cras·ti·na'tion** *n* **pro·cras'ti·na·tor** *n*

pro·cre·ate [PROH-kree-ayt] *vt* **-at·ed, -at·ing.** produce offspring, generate. **pro·cre·a'tion** *n*

Pro·crus·te·an [proh-KRUS-tee-ən] *adj* compelling uniformity by violence.

proc·tol·o·gy [prok-TOL-ə-jee] *n* medical specialty dealing with diseases of anus and rectum.

proc·tor [PROK-tər] *n* person appointed to supervise students during examinations; university official with administrative, esp. disciplinary, duties.

pro·cure [prə-KYUUR] *v* **-cured, -cur·ing.** ▶ *vt* obtain, acquire; provide; bring about. ▶ *vi* act as pimp. **pro·cure'ment** *n* **pro·cur'er** *n* one who procures; pimp. **pro·cur'ess** *n, fem*

prod *vt* **prod·ded, prod·ding.** poke with something pointed; stimulate to action. ▶ *n* prodding; goad; pointed instrument.

prod·i·gal [PROD-i-gəl] *adj* wasteful; extravagant. ▶ *n* spendthrift. **prod·i·gal'i·ty** *n* reckless extravagance.

prod·i·gy [PROD-i-jee] *n, pl* **-gies.** person esp. precocious child with some marvelous gift; thing causing wonder. **pro·di·gious** [prə-DIJ-əs] *adj* very great, immense; extraordinary. **pro·di'gious·ly** *adv*

pro·duce [prə-DOOS] *vt* **-duced, -duc·ing.** bring into existence; yield; make; bring forward; manufacture; exhibit; present on stage, film, TV; *Geometry* extend in length. ▶ *n* [PROD-oos] that which is yielded or made, esp. vegetables. **pro·duc'er** *n* person who produces, esp. play, film, etc. **prod'uct** [-əkt] *n* result of process of manufacture; number resulting from multiplication. **pro·duc'tion** *n* producing; things produced. **pro·duc'tive** *adj* fertile; creative; efficient. **pro·duc·tiv'i·ty** *n*

pro·fam·i·ly [proh-FAM-ə-lee] *adj* antiabortion; pro-life.

pro·fane [prə-FAYN] *adj* irreverent, blasphemous; not sacred. ▶ *vt* **-faned, -fan·ing.** pollute, desecrate. **prof·a·na·tion** [prof-ə-NAY-shən] *n* **pro·fan·i·ty** [prə-FAN-i-tee] *n* profane talk or behavior, blasphemy.

pro·fess [prə-FES] *vt* affirm belief in; confess publicly; assert; claim, pretend. **pro·fess'ed·ly** *adv* avowedly. **pro·fes'sion** *n* calling or occupation, esp. learned, scientific or artistic; a professing; vow of religious faith on entering religious order. **pro·fes'sion·al** *adj* engaged in a profession; engaged in a game or sport for money. ▶ *n* member of profession; paid player. **pro·fes'sor** *n* teacher of highest rank in college or university. **pro·fes·so'ri·al** *adj*

prof·fer *vt, n* offer.

pro·fi·cient [prə-FISH-ənt] *adj* skilled; expert. **pro·fi'cien·cy** *n*

pro·file [PROH-fil] *n* outline, esp. of face, as seen from side; brief biographical sketch.

prof·it *n* money gained; benefit obtained. ▶ *v* benefit. **prof'it·a·ble** *adj* yielding profit. **prof·it·eer'** *n* one who makes excessive profits at the expense of the public. ▶ *vi* do this.

prof·li·gate [PROF-li-git] *adj* dissolute; reckless, wasteful. ▶ *n* dissolute person. **prof'li·ga·cy** [-li-gi-see] *n*

pro for·ma [proh FOR-mə] *Lat* prescribing a set form; for the sake of form.

pro·found [prə-FOWND] *adj* **-er, -est.** very learned; deep. **pro·fun'di·ty** *n*

pro·fuse [prə-FYOOS] *adj* abundant, prodigal. **pro·fu·sion** [-FYOO-zhən] *n*

prog·e·ny [PROJ-ə-nee] *n* children. **pro·gen·i·tor** [proh-JEN-i-tər] *n* ancestor.

pro·ges·ter·one [proh-JES-tə-rohn] *n* hormone that prepares uterus for pregnancy and prevents further ovulation.

prog·na·thous [prog-NAY-thəs] *adj* with projecting lower jaw.

prog·no·sis [prog-NOH-sis] *n, pl* **-ses** [-seez] art of foretelling course of disease by symptoms; forecast. **prog·nos'tic** *adj* of, serving as prognosis. ▶ *n* **prog·nos'ti·cate** *vt* **-cat·ed, -cat·ing.** foretell.

pro·gram [PROH-gram] *n* plan, detailed notes of intended proceedings; broadcast on radio or television; detailed instructions for a computer. ▶ *vt* **-grammed, -gram·ming.** feed program into (computer); arrange detailed instructions for computer. **pro'gram·mer** *n*

prog·ress *n* onward movement; development. ▶ *vi* [prə-GRES] go forward; improve. **pro·gres'sion** *n* moving forward; advance, improvement; increase or decrease of numbers or magnitudes according to fixed law; *Mus* regular succession of chords. **pro·gres'sive** *adj* progressing by degrees; favoring political or social reform.

pro·hib·it [proh-HIB-it] *vt* forbid. **pro·hi·bi'tion** *n* act of forbidding; interdict; interdiction of supply and consumption of alcoholic drinks. **pro·hib'i·tive** *adj* tending to forbid or exclude; (of prices) very high.

pro·ject [PROJ-ekt] *n* plan, scheme; design. ▸ *v* [prə-JEKT] ▸ *vt* plan; throw; cause to appear on distant background. ▸ *vi* stick out, protrude. **pro·jec'tile** [-JEK-til] *n* heavy missile, esp. shell or ball. ▸ *adj* for throwing. **pro·jec'tion** *n* **pro·jec'tion·ist** *n* operator of film projector. **pro·jec'tor** *n* apparatus for projecting photographic images, films, slides on screen; one that forms scheme or design.

pro·lapse [proh-LAPS] *n* falling, slipping down of part of body from normal position. ▸ *vi* fall or slip down in this way.

pro·le·tar·i·at [proh-li-TAIR-ee-ət] *n* lowest class of community, working class. **pro·le·tar'i·an** *adj*, *n*

pro-life *adj* see PROFAMILY.

pro·lif·er·ate [prə-LIF-ə-rayt] *v* -at·ed, -at·ing. grow or reproduce rapidly. **pro·lif·er·a'tion** *n*

pro·li·fic [prə-LIF-ik] *adj* fruitful; producing much.

pro·lix [proh-LIKS] *adj* wordy, long-winded. **pro·lix'i·ty** *n*

pro·logue [PROH-lawg] *n* preface, esp. speech before a play.

pro·long [prə-LAWNG] *vt* lengthen; protract.

prom *n* school or college dance, esp. at end of school year.

prom·e·nade [prom-ə-NAYD] *n* leisurely walk; place made or used for this. ▸ *vi* -nad·ed, -nad·ing. take leisurely walk; go up and down.

prom·i·nent [PROM-ə-nənt] *adj* sticking out; conspicuous; distinguished. **prom'i·nence** *n*

pro·mis·cu·ous [prə-MIS-kyoo-əs] *adj* indiscriminate, esp. in sexual relations; mixed without distinction. **prom·is·cu'i·ty** [-KYOO-ə-tee] *n*

prom·ise [PROM-is] *v* -mised, -mis·ing. ▸ *vt* give assurance. ▸ *vi* be likely to. ▸ *n* undertaking to do or not to do something; potential. **prom'is·ing** *adj* showing good signs, hopeful. **prom'is·so·ry** *adj* containing promise. **promissory note** written promise to pay sum to person named, at specified time.

prom·on·to·ry [PROM-ən-tor-ee] *n*, *pl* **-ries.** point of high land jutting out into the sea, headland.

pro·mote [prə-MOHT] *vt* -mot·ed, -mot·ing. help forward; move up to higher rank or position; work for; encourage sale of. **pro·mot'er** *n* **pro·mo'tion** *n* advancement; preferment.

prompt *adj* -er, -est. done at once; acting with alacrity; punctual; ready. ▸ *v* urge, suggest; help out (actor or speaker) by reading or suggesting next words. **prompt'er** *n* **prompt'ness** [-nis] *n* **prompt'ly** *adv*

prom·ul·gate [PROM-əl-gayt] *vt* -gat·ed, -gat·ing. proclaim, publish. **prom·ul·ga'tion** *n*

prone [prohn] *adj* lying face or front downward; inclined (to). **prone'ness** [-nis] *n*

prong *n* one tine of fork or similar instrument.

pro·noun [PROH-nown] *n* word used to replace noun. **pro·nom'i·nal** *adj* pert. to, like pronoun.

pro·nounce [prə-NOWNS] *v* -nounced, -nounc·ing. ▸ *vt* utter formally; form with organs of speech; speak distinctly; declare. ▸ *vi* give opinion or decision. **pro·nounce'able** *adj* **pro·nounced'** *adj* strongly marked, decided. **pro·nounce'ment** *n* declaration. **pro·nun·ci·a'tion** *n* way word, etc. is pronounced; articulation.

pron·to [PRON-toh] *adv inf* at once, immediately, quickly.

proof *n* evidence; thing that proves; test, demonstration; trial impression from type or engraved plate; *Photography* print from a negative; standard of strength of alcoholic drink. ▸ *adj* giving impenetrable defense against; of proven strength. **proof'read** [-reed] *v* -read, -read·ing. read and correct proofs. **proof'read·er** *n*

prop[1] *vt* propped, prop·ping. support, sustain, hold up. ▸ *n* pole, beam, etc.; used as support.

prop² *n* short for PROPELLER.

prop³ *n* short for (THEATRICAL) PROPERTY.

prop·a·gan·da [prop-ə-GAN-də] *n* organized dissemination of information to assist or damage political cause, etc. **prop·a·gan'dist** *n* **prop·a·gan'dize** [-dīz] *vt* -dized, -diz·ing.

prop·a·gate [pro-pə-gayt] *v* -gat·ed, -gat·ing. ▶ *vt* reproduce, breed, spread by sowing, breeding, etc.; transmit. ▶ *vi* breed, multiply. **prop·a·ga'tion** *n*

pro·pane [PROH-payn] *n* colorless, flammable gas from petroleum.

pro·pel [prə-PEL] *vt* -pelled, -pel·ling. cause to move forward. **pro·pel'lant, -lent** *n* something causing propulsion, such as rocket fuel. **pro·pel'ler** *n* revolving shaft with blades for driving ship or aircraft. **pro·pul'sion** *n* act of, means of, driving forward. **pro·pul'sive, pro·pul'so·ry** *adj* tending, having power to propel; urging on.

pro·pen·si·ty [prə-PEN-si-tee] *n, pl* -ties. inclination or bent; tendency; disposition.

prop·er [PROP-ər] *adj* appropriate; correct; conforming to etiquette, decorous; strict; (of noun) denoting individual person or place.

prop·er·ty [PROP-ər-tee] *n, pl* -ties. that which is owned; estate whether in lands, goods, or money; quality, attribute of something; article used on stage in play, etc.

proph·et [PROF-it] *n* inspired teacher or revealer of divine will; foreteller of future. **proph'e·cy** [-ə-see] *n, pl* -cies. prediction, prophetic utterance. **proph'e·sy** [-ə-sī] *v* -sied, -sy·ing. foretell, predict; make predictions. **pro·phet'ic** *adj* **pro·phet'i·cal·ly** *adv*

pro·phy·lac·tic [prof-ə-LAK-tik] *n, adj* (something) done or used to ward off disease; condom. **pro·phy·lax'is** *n*

pro·pin·qui·ty [proh-PING-kwi-tee] *n* nearness, proximity, close kinship.

pro·pi·ti·ate [prə-PISH-ee-ayt] *vt* -at·ed, -at·ing. appease, gain favor of. **pro·pi'ti·a·to·ry** *adj*

pro·pi'tious *adj* favorable, auspicious.

pro·po·nent [prə-POH-nənt] *n* one who advocates something.

pro·por·tion [prə-POR-shən] *n* relative size or number; comparison; due relation between connected things or parts; share; relation. ▶ *pl* dimensions. ▶ *vt* arrange proportions of. **pro·por'tion·al, pro·por'tion·ate** *adj* having a due proportion; corresponding in size, number, etc. **pro·por'tion·al·ly** *adv*

pro·pose [prə-POHZ] *v* -posed, -pos·ing. ▶ *vt* put forward for consideration; nominate; intend. ▶ *vi* offer marriage. **pro·pos'al** *n* **prop·o·si'tion** *n* offer; statement, assertion; theorem; suggestion of terms; thing to be dealt with; proposal of illicit sexual relations.

pro·pound [prə-POWND] *vt* put forward for consideration or solution.

pro·pri·e·tor [prə-PRĪ-i-tər] *n* owner. **pro·pri'e·tar·y** [-ter-ee] *adj* belonging to owner; made by firm with exclusive rights of manufacture.

pro·pri·e·ty [prə-PRĪ-itee] *n, pl* -ties. properness, correct conduct, fitness.

propulsion see PROPEL.

pro ra·ta [proh RAY-tə] *Lat* in proportion.

pro·sa·ic [proh-ZAY-ik] *adj* commonplace, unromantic.

pro·sce·ni·um [proh-SEE-nee-əm] *n, pl* -ni·a [-nee-ə] arch or opening framing stage.

pro·scribe [proh-SKRĪB] *vt* -scribed, -scrib·ing. outlaw, condemn. **pro·scrip'tion** *n*

prose [prohz] *n* speech or writing not verse. **pros'y** *adj* **pros·i·er, pros·i·est.** tedious, dull.

pros·e·cute [PROS-i-kyoot] *vt* -cut·ed, -cut·ing. carry on, bring legal proceedings against. **pros·e·cu'tion** *n* **pros'e·cu·tor** *n*

pros·e·lyte [PROS-ə-līt] *n* convert.

pros·e·lyt·ize [li-tīz] *vt* **-ized,
-iz·ing.**

pros·o·dy [PROS-ə-dee] *n* system,
study of versification. **pros'o·dist** *n*

pros·pect [PROS-pekt] *n*
expectation, chance for success;
view, outlook; likely customer or
subscriber; mental view. ▶ *v*
explore, esp. for gold.
pro·spec'tive *adj* anticipated;
future. **pros·pec'tor** *n*

pro·spec·tus [prə-SPEK-təs] *n, pl*
-tus·es. document describing
company, school, etc.

pros·per [PROS-pər] *vi* do well.
pros·per'i·ty *n, pl* **-ties.** good
fortune, well-being. **pros'per·ous**
adj doing well, successful;
flourishing, rich, well-off.

pros·tate [PROS-tayt] *n* gland
accessory to male generative
organs.

pros·the·sis [pros-THEE-sis] *n, pl*
-ses [-seez] (replacement of part of
body with) artificial substitute.

pros·ti·tute [PROS-ti-toot] *n* one
who offers sexual intercourse in
return for payment. ▶ *vt* **-tut·ed,
-tut·ing.** make a prostitute of; put
to unworthy use. **pros·ti·tu'tion** *n*

pros·trate [PROS-trayt] *adj* lying
flat; crushed, submissive,
overcome. ▶ *vt* **-trat·ed, -trat·ing.**
throw flat on ground; reduce to
exhaustion. **pros·tra'tion** *n*

pro·tag·o·nist [proh-TAG-ə-nist] *n*
leading character; principal actor;
champion of a cause.

pro·te·an [PROH-tee-ən] *adj*
variable; versatile.

pro·tect [prə-TEKT] *vt* defend,
guard, keep from harm.
pro·tec'tion *n* **pro·tec'tion·ist** *n*
one who advocates protecting
industries by taxing competing
imports. **pro·tec'tive** *adj*
pro·tec'tor *n* one who protects;
regent. **pro·tec'tor·ate** [-tər-it] *n*
relation of country to territory it
protects and controls; such
territory; office, period of protector
of a country.

pro·té·gé [PROH-tə-*zhay*] *n* one
under another's care, protection or

patronage. **pro·té·gée** *n, fem*

pro·tein [PROH-teen] *n* any of kinds
of organic compounds that form
most essential part of food of living
creatures.

pro·test [PROH-test] *n* declaration
or demonstration of objection. ▶ *vi*
[prə-TEST] object; make
declaration against; assert formally.
prot·es·ta·tion [prot-ə-STAY-shən]
n strong declaration.

Prot·es·tant [PROT-ə-stənt] *adj*
belonging to any branch of the
Western Christian Church outside
the Roman Catholic Church. ▶ *n*
member of such church.
Prot'es·tant·ism *n*

proto-, prot- *comb. form* first, e.g.
prototype.

pro·to·col [PROH-tə-kawl] *n*
diplomatic etiquette; draft of terms
signed by parties as basis of formal
treaty; *Computers* standardized
format for exchanging data, esp.
between different computer
systems.

pro·ton [PROH-ton] *n* positively
charged particle in nucleus of atom.

pro·to·plasm [PROH-tə-plaz-əm] *n*
substance that is living matter of all
animal and plant cells.

pro·to·type [PROH-tə-tīp] *n*
original, or model, after which
thing is copied; pattern.

pro·to·zo·an [proh-tə-ZOH-ən] *n*
minute animal of lowest and
simplest class.

pro·tract [proh-TRAKT] *vt*
lengthen; prolong; delay; draw to
scale. **pro·tract'ed** *adj* long drawn
out; tedious. **pro·trac'tor** *n*
instrument for measuring angles on
paper.

pro·trude [proh-TROOD] *v*
-trud·ed, -trud·ing. stick out,
project. **pro·tru'sion** [-zhən] *n*
pro·tru'sive [-siv] *adj* thrusting
forward.

pro·tu·ber·ant
[proh-TOO-bər-ənt] *adj* bulging
out. **pro·tu'ber·ance** [-əns] *n*
bulge, swelling.

proud [prowd] *adj* **-er, -est.** feeling
or displaying pride; arrogant;

gratified; noble; self-respecting; stately. **proud·ly** adv **proud flesh** flesh growing around healing wound.

Prov. Proverbs.

prove [proov] v **proved** or **prov·en**, **prov·ing.** ▶ vt establish validity of; demonstrate, test. ▶ vi turn out (to be, etc.); (of dough) rise in warm place before baking. **proven** adj proved.

prov·e·nance [PROV-ə-nəns] n place of origin, source.

prov·en·der [PROV-ən-dər] n fodder.

prov·erb [PROV-ərb] n short, pithy, traditional saying in common use. **pro·ver'bi·al** [prə-VUR-bee-əl] adj

pro·vide [prə-VID] v **-vid·ed**, **-vid·ing.** ▶ vi make preparation. ▶ vt supply, equip, prepare, furnish, give. **pro·vid'er** n provided that; on condition that.

prov·i·dent [PROV-i-dənt] adj thrifty; showing foresight. **prov'i·dence** n kindly care of God or nature; foresight; economy. **prov·i·den'tial** [-DEN-shəl] adj strikingly fortunate, lucky.

prov·ince [PROV-əns] n division of a country, district; sphere of action. ▶ pl any part of country outside capital or largest cities. **pro·vin'cial** [prə-VIN-shəl] adj of a province; unsophisticated; narrow in outlook. ▶ n unsophisticated person; inhabitant of province. **pro·vin'cial·ism** n narrowness of outlook; lack of refinement; idiom peculiar to district.

pro·vi·sion [prə-VIZH-ən] n a providing, esp. for the future; thing provided; Law article of instrument or statute. ▶ pl food. ▶ vt supply with food. **pro·vi'sion·al** adj temporary; conditional.

pro·vi·so [prə-VI-zoh] n, pl **-sos** or **-soes.** condition.

pro·vo·ca·teur [prə-vok-ə-TUR] n one who causes dissension, makes trouble; agitator; see AGENT PROVOCATEUR.

pro·voke [prə-VOHK] vt **-voked**, **-vok·ing.** irritate; incense; arouse; excite; cause. **prov·o·ca'tion** [-ə-KAY-shən] n **pro·voc'a·tive** [-VOK-ə-tiv] adj

pro·vost [PROH-vohst] n one who superintends or presides; high administrative officer of university. **provost marshal** head of military police.

prow [rhymes with **cow**] n bow of vessel.

prow·ess [PROW-is] n skill; bravery, fighting capacity.

prowl vi roam stealthily, esp. in search of prey or booty. ▶ n **prowl'er** n **on the prowl** searching stealthily; seeking sexual partner.

prox·i·mate [PROK-sə-mit] adj nearest, next, immediate. **prox·im'i·ty** n

prox·y [PROK-see] n, pl **prox·ies.** authorized agent or substitute; writing authorizing one to act as this.

prude [prood] n one who affects excessive modesty or propriety. **prud'er·y** n, pl **-er·ies.** **prud'ish** adj

pru·dent [PROOD-nt] adj careful, discreet; sensible. **pru'dence** n habit of acting with careful deliberation; wisdom applied to practice. **pru·den'tial** adj

prune¹ [proon] n dried plum.

prune² vt **pruned**, **prun·ing.** cut out dead parts, excessive branches, etc.; shorten, reduce.

pru·ri·ent [PRUUR-ee-ənt] adj given to, springing from lewd thoughts; having unhealthy curiosity or desire. **pru'ri·ence** n

pry [pri] vi **pried**, **pry·ing.** make furtive or impertinent inquiries; look curiously; force open.

Ps. Psalm(s).

psalm [sahm] n sacred song; (**P-**) any of the sacred songs making up the Book of Psalms in the Bible. **psalm'ist** n writer of psalms. **psal·mo·dy** [SAHM-ə-dee] n art, act of singing sacred music. **psal·ter** [SAWL-tər] n book of psalms; (**P-**) copy of the Psalms as separate book. **psal'ter·y** [-tə-ree] n, pl **-ter·ies.** obsolete stringed instrument like lyre.

pseu·do [SOO-doh] *adj* sham, fake.

pseudo- *comb. form* false, sham, e.g. *pseudo-Gothic; pseudoscience.*

pseu·do·nym [SOOD-n-im] *n* false, fictitious name; pen name.

psit·ta·co·sis [sit-ə-KOH-sis] *n* dangerous infectious disease, germ of which is carried by parrots.

psy·che [SĪ-kee] *n* human mind or soul.

psych·e·del·ic [sī-ki-DEL-ik] *adj* of or causing hallucinations; like intense colors, etc. experienced during hallucinations.

psy·chic [SĪ-kik] *adj* sensitive to phenomena lying outside range of normal experience; of soul or mind; that appears to be outside region of physical law.

psy·chi·a·try [si-KĪ-ə-tree] *n* medical treatment of mental diseases. **psy·chi·a·trist** *n*

psy·cho·a·nal·y·sis [sī-koh-] *n* method of studying and treating mental disorders. **psy·cho·an'a·lyst** *n*

psy·cho·log·i·cal [sī-kə-LOJ-i-kəl] *adj* of psychology; of the mind. **psy·chol'o·gist** *n* **psy·chol'o·gy** *n* study of mind; person's mental makeup. **psy·chom'e·try** *n* measurement, testing of psychological processes; supposed ability to divine unknown persons' qualities by handling object used or worn by them. **psy'cho·path** *n* person afflicted with severe mental disorder causing him or her to commit antisocial, often violent acts. **psy·cho·path'ic** *adj*

psy·cho·sis *n, pl* **-ses** [-seez] severe mental disorder in which person's contact with reality becomes distorted. **psy·cho'tic** *adj, n*

psy·cho·so·mat'ic [-sə-MAT-ik] *adj* of physical disorders thought to have psychological causes.

psy·cho·ther'a·py *n* treatment of disease by psychological, not physical, means.

psych up [sīk] *vt* prepare (oneself or another) psychologically for action, performance, etc.

Pt *Chem* platinum.

ptar·mi·gan [TAHR-mi-gən] *n* bird of grouse family that turns white in winter.

PT boat small, fast naval vessel used primarily for torpedoing enemy shipping.

pter·o·dac·tyl [ter-ə-DAK-til] *n* extinct flying reptile with large batlike wings.

pto·maine [TOH-mayn] *n* any of kinds of poisonous alkaloid found in decaying matter.

Pu *Chem* plutonium.

pu·ber·ty [PYOO-bər-tee] *n* sexual maturity.

pubic [PYOO-bik] *adj* of the lower abdomen.

pub·lic [PUB-lik] *adj* of or concerning the public as a whole; not private; open to general observation or knowledge; accessible to all; serving the people. ▶ *n* the community or its members. **pub'lic·ly** *adv* public relations; promotion of good relations of an organization or business with the general public. **public school** local elementary school. **public service** government employment. **public spirit** interest in and devotion to welfare of community.

pub·li·cist [PUB-lə-sist] *n* press agent; writer on public concerns. **pub·lic'i·ty** *n* process of attracting public attention; attention thus gained. **pub'li·cize** *vt* **-cized, -ciz·ing.** give publicity to; bring to public notice.

pub·lish *vt* prepare and issue for sale (books, music, etc.); make generally known; proclaim. **pub·li·ca'tion** [-KAY-shən] *n* **pub'lish·er** *n*

puce [pyoos] *adj, n* purplish-brown (color).

puck[1] [puk] *n* hard rubber disk used instead of ball in ice hockey.

puck[2] *n* mischievous sprite. **puck'ish** *adj*

puck·er [PUK-ər] *v* gather into wrinkles. ▶ *n* crease, fold.

pud·ding [PUUD-ing] *n* thick, cooked dessert, often made from

flour, milk, eggs, flavoring, etc.
pud·dle [PUD-l] n small pool of
water; rough cement for lining
walls of canals, etc. ▶ vt **-dled,
-dling.** line with puddle; make
muddy. **puddling** n method of
converting pig iron to wrought
iron by oxidizing the carbon.
pu·den·dum [pyoo-DEN-dəm] n, pl
-da [-də] external genital organs,
esp. of a woman; vulva.
pu·er·ile [PYOO-ər-il] adj childish;
foolish; trivial.
puff n short blast of breath, wind,
etc.; its sound; type of pastry;
laudatory review or advertisement.
▶ vi blow abruptly; breathe hard.
▶ vt send out in a puff; blow out,
inflate; advertise; smoke hard.
puff'y adj **puff·i·er, puff·i·est.**
short-winded; swollen. **puff'ball** n
ball-shaped fungus.
puf'fin n sea bird with large
brightly-colored beak.
pug n small snub-nosed dog; sl
boxer. **pug nose** snub nose.
pu·gi·list [PYOO-jə-list] n boxer.
pu'gi·lism n **pu·gi·lis'tic** adj
pug·na·cious [pug-NAY-shəs] adj
given to fighting. **pug·nac'i·ty**
[-NAS-i-tee] n
puke [pyook] sl ▶ vi **puked,
puk·ing.** vomit. ▶ n vomit.
pul·chri·tude [PUL-kri-tood] n
beauty. **pul·chri·tu'di·nous** adj
pull [puul] vt exert force on object
to move it toward source of force;
strain or stretch; tear; propel by
rowing. ▶ n act of pulling; force
exerted by it; drink of liquor; inf
power, influence. **pull in** (of train)
arrive; attract; sl arrest. **pull off** inf
carry through to successful issue.
pull out withdraw; extract; (of
train) depart; (of car, etc.) move
away from side of road or move
out to overtake. **pull over** (of car,
etc.) drive to side of road and stop.
pull someone's leg make fun of.
pull up tear up; recover lost
ground; improve; come to a stop;
halt; reprimand.
pul·let [PUUL-it] n young hen.
pul·ley [PUUL-ee] n, pl **-leys.** wheel

with groove in rim for cord, used to
raise weights by downward pull.
Pull·man [PUUL-mən] ® ▶ n, pl
-mans. railroad sleeping car or
parlor car.
pull·o·ver [PUUL-oh-vər] n sweater
without fastening, to be pulled
over head.
pul·mo·nar·y [PUUL-mə-ner-ee] adj
of lungs.
pulp n soft, moist, vegetable or
animal matter; flesh of fruit; any
soft soggy mass. ▶ vt reduce to
pulp.
pul·pit [PUUL-pit] n (enclosed)
platform for preacher, minister,
rabbi, etc.
pul·sar [PUL-sahr] n small dense
star emitting radio waves.
pulse [puls] n movement of blood
in arteries corresponding to
heartbeat, discernible to touch, for
example in the wrist; any regular
beat or vibration. **pul·sate**
[PUL-sayt] vi **-sat·ed, -sat·ing.**
throb, quiver. **pul·sa'tion**
[-SAY-shən] n
pul·ver·ize [PUL-və-rīz] vt **-ized,
-iz·ing.** reduce to powder; smash or
demolish.
pu·ma [PYOO-mə] n large Amer.
feline carnivore, cougar.
pum·ice [PUM-is] n light porous
variety of lava.
pum·mel [PUM-əl] vt **-meled,
-mel·ing.** strike repeatedly with fists.
pump¹ n appliance in which piston
and handle are used for raising
water, or putting in or taking out
air or liquid, etc. ▶ vt raise, put in,
take out, etc. with pump; empty by
means of a pump; extract
information from. ▶ vi work pump;
work like pump. **pump iron** lift
weights as exercise.
pump² n light shoe.
pump'kin n any of varieties of
gourd, eaten esp. as vegetable, in
pie.
pun n play on words. ▶ vi **punned,
pun·ning.** make one. **pun'ster**
[-stər] n
punch¹ n tool for perforating or
stamping; blow with fist; vigor. ▶ vt

stamp, perforate with punch; strike with fist. **pull punches** punch lightly; *inf* lessen, withhold, criticism. **punch-drunk** *adj inf* dazed, as by repeated blows.

punch² *n* drink of spirits or wine with fruit juice, spice, etc.

punc·til·i·ous [pungk-TIL-ee-əs] *adj* making much of details of etiquette; very exact, particular. **punc·til'i·ous·ness** [-nis] *n*

punc·tu·al [PUNGK-choo-əl] *adj* in good time, not late, prompt. **punc·tu·al'i·ty** *n*

punc·tu·ate [PUNGK-choo-ayt] *vt* **-at·ed, -at·ing.** put in punctuation marks; interrupt at intervals; emphasize. **punc·tu·a'tion** *n* marks, such as commas and colons, put in writing to assist in making sense clear.

punc·ture [PUNGK-chər] *n* small hole made by sharp object, esp. in tire; act of puncturing. ▶ *vt* **-tured, -tur·ing.** prick hole in, perforate.

pun'dit *n* self-appointed expert.

pun·gent [PUN-jənt] *adj* biting; irritant; piercing; tart; caustic. **pun'gen·cy** *n*

pun·ish *vt* cause to suffer for offense; inflict penalty on; use or treat roughly. **pun'ish·a·ble** *adj* **pun·ish·ment** *n* **pu'ni·tive** [PYOO-ni-tiv] *adj* inflicting or intending to inflict punishment.

punk *adj, n* inferior, rotten, worthless (person or thing); petty (hoodlum); (of) style of rock music.

punt¹ *n* flat-bottomed square-ended boat, propelled by pushing with pole. ▶ *vt* propel thus.

punt² *vt* *Football* kick ball before it touches ground, when let fall from hands. ▶ *n* such a kick.

punt³ *vi* gamble, bet. **punt'er** *n* one who punts; gambler.

pu·ny [PYOO-nee] *adj* **-ni·er, -ni·est.** small and feeble.

pup *n* young of certain animals, such as dogs and seals.

pu·pa [PYOO-pə] *n, pl* **-pas.** stage between larva and adult in metamorphosis of insect, chrysalis. **pu'pal** *adj*

pu·pil [PYOO-pəl] *n* person being taught; opening in iris of eye.

pup·pet [PUP-it] *n* small doll or figure of person, etc. controlled by operator's hand. **pup·pet·eer'** *n* **puppet show** show with puppets worked by hidden performer.

pup·py [PUP-ee] *n, pl* **-pies.** young dog.

pur·chase [PUR-chəs] *vt* **-chased, -chas·ing.** buy. ▶ *n* buying; what is bought; leverage, grip.

pur·dah [PUR-də] *n* Muslim, Hindu custom of keeping women in seclusion; screen, veil to achieve this.

pure [pyuur] *adj* **pur·er, pur·est.** unmixed, untainted; simple; spotless; faultless; innocent; concerned with theory only. **pure'ly** *adv* **pu·ri·fi·ca'tion** *n* **pu'ri·fy** *vt* **-fied, -fy·ing.** make, become pure, clear or clean. **pur'ism** *n* excessive insistence on correctness of language. **pur'ist** *n* **pu'ri·ty** *n* state of being pure.

pu·rée [pyuu-RAY] *n* pulp, soup, of cooked fruit or vegetables put through sieve, etc. ▶ *vt* **-réed, -rée·ing.**

pur·ga·to·ry [PUR-gə-tor-ee] *n* **-ries.** place or state of torment, pain or distress, esp. temporary.

purge [purj] *vt* **purged, purg·ing.** make clean, purify; remove, get rid of; clear out. ▶ *n* act, process of purging; removal of undesirable members from political party, army, etc. **pur'ga·tive** [-gə-tiv] *adj, n*

Pu·ri·tan [PYUUR-i-tn] *n Hist* member of extreme Protestant party; (**p-**) person of extreme strictness in morals or religion. **pu·ri·tan'i·cal** *adj* strict in the observance of religious and moral duties; overscrupulous. **pu'ri·tan·ism** *n*

purl *n* stitch that forms ridge in knitting. ▶ *vi* knit in purl.

pur·loin [pər-LOIN] *vt* steal; pilfer.

pur·ple [PUR-pəl] *n, adj* **-pler, -plest.** (of) color between crimson and violet.

pur·port [pər-PORT] *vt* claim to be (true, etc.); signify, imply. ▶ *n* [PUR-port] meaning; apparent meaning; significance.

pur·pose [PUR-pəs] *n* reason, object; design; aim, intention. ▶ *vt* **-posed, -pos·ing.** intend. **pur'pose·ly** *adv* **on purpose** intentionally.

purr *n* pleased noise that cat makes. ▶ *vi* utter this.

purse [purs] *n* small bag for money; handbag; resources; money as prize. ▶ *v* **pursed, purs·ing.** ▶ *vt* pucker in wrinkles. ▶ *vi* become wrinkled and drawn in. **purs'er** *n* ship's officer who keeps accounts.

pur·sue [pər-SOO] *v* **-sued, -su·ing.** ▶ *vt* run after; chase; aim at; engage in; continue; follow. ▶ *vi* go in pursuit; continue. **pur·su'ance** [-əns] *n* carrying out. **pur·su'ant** [-ənt] *adv* accordingly. **pur·su'er** *n* **pur·suit'** [-SOOT] *n* running after; attempt to catch; occupation.

purulent *adj* see PUS.

pur·vey [pər-VAY] *vt* supply (provisions). **pur·vey'or** *n*

pur·view [PUR-vyoo] *n* scope, range.

pus *n* yellowish matter produced by suppuration. **pu·ru·lence** [PYUUR-ə-ləns] *n* **pu'ru·lent** *adj* forming, discharging pus; septic.

push [puush] *vt* move, try to move away by pressure; drive or impel; *sl* sell (esp. narcotic drugs) illegally. ▶ *vi* make thrust; advance with steady effort. ▶ *n* thrust; persevering self-assertion; big military advance. **push'er** *n* **push'y** *adj* **push·i·er, push·i·est.** given to pushing oneself.

pu·sil·lan·i·mous [pyoo-sə-LAN-ə-məs] *adj* cowardly. **pu·sil·la·nim'i·ty** [-lə-NIM-ə-tee] *n*

puss [puus], **pus'sy** *n, pl* **-ses, -sies.** *inf* cat.

puss·y·foot [PUUS-ee-fuut] *vi* move stealthily; act indecisively, procrastinate.

pus·tule [PUS-chuul] *n* pimple containing pus.

put [puut] *vt* **put, put·ting.** place;

set; express; throw (esp. shot). ▶ *n* throw. **put across** express, carry out successfully. **put off** postpone; disconcert; repel. **put up** erect; accommodate; nominate.

pu·ta·tive [PYOO-tə-tiv] *adj* reputed, supposed.

pu·trid [PYOO-trid] *adj* decomposed; rotten. **pu'tre·fy** [-trə-fī] *v* **-fied, -fy·ing.** make or become rotten. **pu·tre·fac'tion** *n* **pu·tres'cent** [-ənt] *adj* becoming rotten.

putsch [puuch] *n* surprise attempt to overthrow the existing power, political revolt.

putt [put] *vt* strike (golf ball) along ground in direction of hole. **putt'er** *n* golf club for putting; person who putts.

put·ter [PUT-ər] *vi* work, act in feeble, unsystematic way.

put·ty [PUT-ee] *n, pl* **-ties.** paste of ground chalk and oil as used by glaziers. ▶ *vt* **-tied, -ty·ing.** fix, fill with putty.

puz·zle [PUZ-əl] *v* **-zled, -zling.** perplex or be perplexed. ▶ *n* bewildering, perplexing question, problem or toy. **puz'zle·ment** *n*

pyg·my, pig·my [PIG-mee] *n, pl* **-mies.** abnormally undersized person; (P-) member of one of dwarf peoples of Equatorial Africa. ▶ *adj* undersized.

py·lon [PĪ-lon] *n* post, tower, esp. for guiding aviators; steel tower for supporting power lines.

py·or·rhe·a [pī-ə-REE-ə] *n* inflammation of the gums with discharge of pus and loosening of teeth.

pyr·a·mid [PIR-ə-mid] *n* solid figure with sloping sides meeting at apex; structure of this shape, esp. ancient Egyptian; group of persons or things arranged, organized, like pyramid. **py·ram'i·dal** *adj*

pyre [pīr] *n* pile of wood for burning a dead body.

py·ri·tes [pī-RĪ-teez] *n, pl* **py·ri·tes.** sulfide of a metal, esp. iron pyrites.

py·ro·ma·ni·ac [pī-rə-MAY-nee-ak] *n* person with uncontrollable desire to set things on fire.

py·rom·e·ter [pī-ROM-i-tər] *n* instrument for measuring very high temperature.

py·ro·tech·nics [pī-rə-TEK-niks] *n* manufacture, display of fireworks.

Pyr·rhic victory [PIR-ik] one won at too high cost.

py·thon [PĪ-thon] *n* large nonpoisonous snake that crushes its prey.

pyx [piks] *n* vessel in which consecrated Host is preserved.

Q q

Q.E.D. which was to be shown or proved.

qua [kway] *prep* in the capacity of.

quack [kwak] *n* harsh cry of duck; pretender to medical or other skill. ▶ *vi* (of duck) utter cry.

quadr-, quadri- *comb. form* four, e.g. *quadrilateral*.

quad·ran·gle [KWOD-rang-gəl] *n* four-sided figure; four-sided courtyard in a building. **quad·ran'gu·lar** [-gyə-lər] *adj*

quad·rant [KWOD-rənt] *n* quarter of circle; instrument for taking angular measurements.

quad·rat'ic *adj* of equation, involving square of unknown quantity.

quad·ra·phon·ic [kwod-rə-FON-ik] *adj* of a sound system using four independent speakers.

quad·ri·lat·er·al [kwod-rə-LAT-ər-əl] *adj* four-sided. ▶ *n* four-sided figure.

quad·rille [kwo-DRIL] *n* square dance; music played for it.

quad·ril·lion [kwo-DRIL-yən] *n* cardinal number of 1 followed by 15 zeros.

quad·ru·man·ous [kwo-DROO-mə-nəs] *adj* of apes, etc. having four feet that can be used as hands.

quad·ru·ped [KWOD-ruu-ped] *n* four-footed animal.

quad·ru·ple [kwo-DROO-pəl] *adj* fourfold. ▶ *v* **-pled, -pling.** make, become four times as much. **quad·ru'pli·cate** [-kit] *adj* fourfold.

quad·ru·plet [kwo-DRUP-lit] *n* one of four offspring born at one birth.

quaff [kwof] *v* drink heartily or in one swallow.

quag·mire [KWAG-mīr] *n* bog, swamp.

quail¹ [kwayl] *n* small bird of partridge family.

quail² *vi* flinch; cower.

quaint [kwaynt] *adj* **-er, -est.** interestingly old-fashioned or odd; curious; whimsical. **quaint'ness** [-nis] *n*

quake [kwayk] *vi* **quaked, quak·ing.** shake, tremble.

Quak·er [KWAY-kər] *n* member of Christian sect, the **Society of Friends**.

qual·i·fy [KWOL-ə-fī] *v* **-fied, -fy·ing.** make oneself competent; moderate; limit; make competent; ascribe quality to; describe. **qual·i·fi·ca'tion** *n* thing that qualifies, attribute; restriction; qualifying.

qual·i·ty [KWOL-i-tee] *n, pl* **-ties.** attribute, characteristic, property; degree of excellence; rank. **qual'i·ta·tive** *adj* depending on quality.

qualm [kwahm] *n* misgiving; sudden feeling of sickness, nausea.

quan·da·ry [KWAN-dree] *n, pl* **-ries.** state of perplexity, puzzling situation, dilemma.

quan·ti·ty [KWON-ti-tee] *n, pl* **-ties.** size, number, amount; specified or considerable amount. **quan'ti·fy** [-fī] *vt* **-fied, -fy·ing.** discover, express quantity of. **quan'ti·ta·tive** *adj* **quan'tum** [-təm] *n, pl* **-ta** [-tə] desired or required amount.

quantum leap, jump *inf* sudden large change, increase, or advance.

quantum theory theory that in radiation, energy of electrons is discharged not continuously but in discrete units, or quanta.

quar·an·tine [KWOR-ən-teen] *n* isolation to prevent spreading of infection. ▶ *vt* **-tined, -tin·ing.** put, keep in quarantine.

quark [kwork] *n Physics* any of several hypothetical particles thought to be fundamental units of matter.

quar·rel [KWOR-əl] *n* angry dispute; argument. ▶ *vi* **-reled, -rel·ing.** argue; find fault with. **quar'rel·some** [-səm] *adj*

quar·ry¹ [KWOR-ee] *n, pl* **-ries.**

object of hunt or pursuit; prey.

quarry² *n, pl* **-ries.** excavation where stone, etc. is obtained from ground for building, etc. ▶ *v* **-ried, -ry·ing.** get from quarry.

quart [kwort] *n* liquid measure, quarter of gallon or 2 pints (0.964 liter).

quar·ter [KWOR-tər] *n* fourth part; 25 cents; region, district; mercy. ▶ *pl* lodgings. ▶ *vt* divide into quarters; lodge. **quar'ter·ly** *adj* happening, due, etc. each quarter of year. ▶ *n, pl* **-lies.** quarterly periodical. **quar·tet'** *n* group of four musicians; music for four performers. **quar'to** *n, pl* **-tos.** size of book in which sheets are folded into four leaves. ▶ *adj* of this size. **quar'ter·deck** *n* after part of upper deck used esp. for official, ceremonial purposes. **quarter horse** small, powerful breed of horse bred for short races. **quar'ter·mas·ter** *n* officer responsible for quarters, clothing, etc.

quartz [kworts] *n* stone of pure crystalline silica. **quartz'ite** [-īt] *n* quartz rock. **quartz timepiece** watch or clock operated by a vibrating quartz crystal.

qua·sar [KWAY-zahr] *n* extremely distant starlike object emitting powerful radio waves.

quash [kwosh] *vt* annul; reject; subdue forcibly.

quasi- [KWAY-zī] *comb. form* seemingly, resembling but not actually being, e.g. *quasi-scientific.*

quat·er·nar·y [KWOT-ər-ner-ee] *adj* of the number four; having four parts; **(Q-)** *Geology* of most recent period after Tertiary.

quat·rain [KWO-trayn] *n* four-line stanza, esp. rhymed alternately.

qua·ver [KWAY-vər] *vt* say or sing in quavering tones. ▶ *vi* tremble, shake, vibrate. ▶ *n* musical note half length of crotchet; quavering trill.

quay [kee] *n* solid, fixed landing stage; wharf.

quea·sy [KWEE-zee] *adj* **-si·er, -si·est.** inclined to, or causing,

sickness.

queen [kween] *n* king's wife; female ruler; piece in chess; fertile female bee, wasp, etc.; playing card with picture of a queen, ranking between king and jack; *sl, offens* male homosexual. **queen'ly** *adj* **-li·er, -li·est.**

queer [kweer] *adj* **-er, -est.** odd, strange; *sl, usu offens* homosexual. ▶ *n sl, usu. offens* homosexual. ▶ *vt* spoil; interfere with.

quell [kwel] *vt* crush, put down; allay; pacify.

quench [kwench] *vt* slake; extinguish, put out, suppress.

quer·u·lous [KWER-ə-ləs] *adj* fretful, peevish, whining.

que·ry [KWEER-ee] *n, pl* **-ries.** question; mark of interrogation. ▶ *vt* **-ried, -ry·ing.** question, ask.

quest [kwest] *n, vi* search.

ques·tion [KWES-chən] *n* sentence seeking for answer; that which is asked; interrogation; inquiry; problem; point for debate; debate, strife. ▶ *vt* ask questions of, interrogate; dispute; doubt. **ques'tion·a·ble** *adj* doubtful, esp. not clearly true or honest. **ques·tion·naire'** *n* list of questions drawn up for formal answer.

queue [kyoo] *n* line of waiting persons, vehicles; sequence of computer tasks awaiting action. ▶ *vi* **queued, queu·ing.** (with *up*) wait in line; arrange computer tasks in queue.

quib·ble [KWIB-əl] *n* trivial objection. ▶ *v* **-bled, -bling.** make this.

quiche [keesh] *n* open pielike dish of cheese, etc. on light pastry shell.

quick [kwik] *adj* **-er, -est.** rapid, swift; keen; brisk; hasty. ▶ *n* part of body sensitive to pain; sensitive flesh. **the quick** *obs* living people. *adv* rapidly. **quick'en** *v* make, become faster or more lively.

quick'ie *n inf* a quick drink, etc.

quick'ly *adv* **quick'sand** *n* loose wet sand easily yielding to pressure and engulfing persons, animals, etc. **quick'silver** *n* mercury.

quick-tempered *adj* irascible.

quid pro quo [KWID proh KWOH] *Lat* something given in exchange.

qui·es·cent [kwee-ES-ənt] *adj* at rest, inactive, inert; silent. **qui·es'cence** *n*

qui·et [KWĪ-it] *adj* **-er, -est.** with little or no motion or noise; undisturbed; not showy or obtrusive. ▶ *n* state of peacefulness, absence of noise or disturbance. ▶ *v* make, become quiet. **qui'et·ly** *adv* **qui'e·tude** *n*

quill [kwil] *n* large feather; hollow stem of this; pen, plectrum made from feather; spine of porcupine.

quilt [kwilt] *n* padded coverlet. ▶ *vt* stitch (two pieces of cloth) with pad between.

quince [kwins] *n* acid pear-shaped fruit; tree bearing it.

qui·nine [KWĪ-nīn] *n* bitter drug made from bark of tree, used to treat fever, and as mixer.

quin·quen·ni·al [kwin-KWEN-ee-əl] *adj* occurring once in, or lasting, five years.

quin·sy [KWIN-zee] *n* inflammation of throat or tonsils.

quint [kwint] *n* short for QUINTUPLET.

quin·tes·sence [kwin-TES-əns] *n* purest form, essential feature; embodiment. **quin·tes·sen'tial** [-tə-SEN-shəl] *adj*

quin·tet [kwin-TET] *n* set of five singers or players; composition for five voices or instruments.

quin·tu·plet [kwin-TUP-lit] *n* one of five offspring born at one birth.

quip [kwip] *n, v* **quipped, quip·ping.** (utter) witty saying.

quire [kwīr] *n* 24 sheets of writing paper.

quirk [kwurk] *n* individual peculiarity of character; unexpected twist or turn.

quis·ling [KWIZ-ling] *n* traitor who aids occupying enemy force.

quit [kwit] *v* **quit** or **quit·ted, quit·ting.** stop doing a thing;

depart; leave, go away from; cease from. ▶ *adj* free, rid. **quits** *adj* on equal or even terms by repayment, etc. **quit'tance** [KWIT-ns] *n* discharge; receipt. **quit'ter** *n* one lacking perseverance.

quite [kwīt] *adv* wholly, completely; very considerably; somewhat, rather. ▶ *interj* exactly, just so.

quiv·er¹ [KWIV-ər] *vi* shake or tremble. ▶ *n* quivering; vibration.

quiver² *n* carrying case for arrows.

quix·ot·ic [kwik-SOT-ik] *adj* unrealistically and impractically optimistic, idealistic, chivalrous.

quiz [kwiz] *n, pl* **quiz·zes.** entertainment in which general or specific knowledge of players is tested by questions; examination, interrogation. ▶ *vt* **quizzed, quiz·zing.** question, interrogate. **quiz'zi·cal** *adj* questioning; mocking.

quoit [kwoit] *n* ring for throwing at peg as a game. ▶ *pl* the game in which quoits are tossed at a stake in the ground in attempts to encircle it.

quo·rum [KWOR-əm] *n* least number that must be present in meeting to make its transactions valid.

quo·ta [KWOH-tə] *n* share to be contributed or received; specified number, quantity, that may be imported or admitted.

quote [kwoht] *vt* **quot·ed, quot·ing.** copy or repeat passages from; refer to, esp. to confirm view; state price for. **quot'a·ble** *adj* **quo·ta'tion** *n*

quoth [kwohth] *v obs* said.

quo·tid·i·an [kwoh-TID-ee-ən] *adj* daily; everyday, commonplace.

quo·tient [KWOH-shənt] *n* number resulting from dividing one number by another.

q.v. which see: used to refer a reader to another item in the same book.

R r

Ra *Chem* radium.

rab·bet [RAB-it] *n* recess, groove cut into piece of timber to join with matching piece. ▶ *vt* **-bet·ed, -bet·ing.** cut rabbet in.

rab·bi [RAB-ī] *n, pl* **-bis.** Jewish learned man, spiritual leader, teacher. **rab·bin'i·cal** *adj*

rab'bit *n* small burrowing rodent like hare. ▶ *vi* hunt rabbits. **rabbit punch** sharp blow to back of neck; *see* RAREBIT.

rab·ble [RAB-əl] *n* crowd of vulgar, noisy people; mob.

rab'id *adj* relating to or having rabies; furious; mad; fanatical.

ra·bies [RAY-beez] *n* acute infectious viral disease transmitted by dogs, etc.

rac·coon [ra-KOON] *n* small N Amer. mammal.

race¹ [rays] *n* contest of speed, as in running, swimming, etc.; contest, rivalry; strong current of water, esp. leading to water wheel. ▶ *pl* meeting for horse racing. ▶ *v* **raced, rac·ing.** ▶ *vt* cause to run rapidly. ▶ *vi* run swiftly; of engine, pedal, etc., to move rapidly and erratically, esp. on removal of resistance. **rac'er** *n* person, vehicle, animal that races.

race² *n* group of people of common ancestry with distinguishing physical features (skin color, etc.); species; type. **ra·cial** [RAY-shəl] *adj* **rac'ism** *n* belief in innate superiority of particular race; antagonism toward members of different race based on this belief. **rac'ist** *adj, n*

rack¹ [rak] *n* framework for displaying or holding baggage, books, hats, bottles, etc.; *Mechanics* straight bar with teeth on its edge, to work with pinion; instrument of torture by stretching. ▶ *vt* stretch on rack or wheel; torture; stretch, strain. **rack'ing** *adj* agonizing (pain).

rack² *n* **rack and ruin** destruction.

rack³ *n* neck or rib section of mutton, lamb, pork.

rack·et¹ [RAK-it] *n* loud noise, uproar; occupation by which money is made illegally.

rack·et·eer [rak-i-TEER] *n* one making illegal profits. **rack'et·y** *adj* noisy.

racket², rac·quet [RAK-it] *n* bat used in tennis, etc. ▶ *pl* ball game played in paved, walled court.

rac·on·teur [rak-ən-TUR] *n* skilled storyteller.

racquet *see* RACKET².

rac·y [RAY-see] *adj* **rac·i·er, rac·i·est.** spirited; lively; having strong flavor; spicy; piquant. **rac'i·ly** *adv* **rac'i·ness** *n*

ra·dar [RAY-dahr] *n* device for finding range and direction by ultrahigh frequency point-to-point radio waves, which reflect back to their source and reveal position and nature of objects sought.

radial *see* RADIUS.

ra·di·ate [RAY-dee-ayt] *v* **-at·ed, -at·ing.** emit, be emitted in rays; spread out from center. **ra'di·ance** [-əns] *n* brightness; splendor. **ra'di·ant** [-ənt] *adj* beaming; shining; emitting rays. **ra·di·a'tion** *n* transmission of heat, light, etc. from one body to another; particles, rays, emitted in nuclear decay; act of radiating. **ra'di·a·tor** *n* that which radiates, esp. heating apparatus for rooms; cooling apparatus of automobile engine.

rad·i·cal [RAD-i-kəl] *adj* fundamental, thorough; extreme; of root. ▶ *n* person of extreme (political) views; number expressed as root of another; group of atoms of several elements that remain unchanged in a series of chemical compounds.

ra·di·o [RAY-dee-oh] *n, pl* **-di·os.** use of electromagnetic waves for broadcasting, communication,

etc.; device for receiving, amplifying radio signals; broadcasting, content of radio program. ▶ *vt* **-di·oed, -di·o·ing.** transmit message, etc. by radio.
radio- *comb. form* of rays, of radiation, of radium, e.g. *radiology.*
ra·di·o·ac·tive [ray-dee-oh-AK-tiv] *adj* emitting invisible rays that penetrate matter.
ra·di·o·ac·tiv·i·ty *n*
ra·di·o·gra·phy [ray-dee-OG-rə-fee] *n* production of image on film or plate by radiation.
ra·di·ol·o·gy [ray-dee-OL-ə-jee] *n* science of use of rays in medicine. **ra·di·ol·o·gist** *n*
ra·di·o·ther·a·py [ray-dee-oh-THER-ə-pee] *n* diagnosis and treatment of disease by x-rays.
rad'ish *n* pungent root vegetable.
ra·di·um [RAY-dee-əm] *n* radioactive metallic element.
ra·di·us [RAY-dee-əs] *n, pl* **-di·i** [-dee-ī] straight line from center to circumference of circle; outer of two bones in forearm. **ra'di·al** [-əl] *adj* arranged like radii of circle; of ray or rays; of radius.
ra·dome [RAY-dohm] *n* dome-shaped housing for radar.
ra·don [RAY-don] *n* radioactive gaseous element.
raf·fi·a [RAF-fee-ə] *n* prepared palm fiber for making mats, etc.
raff'ish *adj* disreputable.
raf·fle [RAF-əl] *n* lottery in which an article is assigned by lot to one of those buying tickets. ▶ *vt* **-fled, -fling.** dispose of by raffle.
raft *n* floating structure of logs, planks, etc.
raf·ter [RAF-tər] *n* one of the main beams of a roof.
raft·ing [RAF-ting] *n* sport of traveling on rivers by raft. **raft·er** *n* participant in this.
rag¹ *n* fragment of cloth; torn piece; *inf* newspaper, etc., esp. one considered worthless; piece of ragtime music. ▶ *pl* tattered clothing. **rag·ged** [RAG-id] *adj*

shaggy; torn; clothed in torn clothes; lacking smoothness.
rag'bag *n* confused assortment.
rag'time *n* style of jazz piano music.
rag² *vt* **ragged, rag·ging.** tease; torment; play practical jokes on.
rag·a·muf·fin [RAG-ə-muf-in] *n* ragged, dirty person or child.
rage [rayj] *n* violent anger or passion; fury; aggressive behavior associated with a certain activity, e.g., road rage. ▶ *vi* **raged, rag·ing.** speak, act with fury; proceed violently and without check (as storm, battle, etc.); be widely and violently prevalent. **all the rage** very popular.
rag·lan [RAG-lən] *adj* of sleeves that continue to the neck so that there are no shoulder seams.
ra·gout [ra-GOO] *n* highly seasoned stew of meat and vegetables.
raid [rayd] *n* rush, attack; foray. ▶ *vt* make raid on.
rail¹ [rayl] *n* horizontal bar, esp. as part of fence, track, etc.; *sl* line of cocaine for sniffing. **rail'ing** *n* fence, barrier made of rails supported by posts. **rail'head** [-hed] *n* farthest point to which railway line extends. **rail'road, rail'way** *n* track of steel rails on which trains run; company operating railroad.
rail² *vi* utter abuse; scoff; scold; reproach. **rail'ler·y** [-ə-ree] *n, pl* **-ler·ies.** banter.
rail³ *n* any of kinds of marsh birds.
rai·ment [RAY-mənt] *n* clothing.
rain [rayn] *n* moisture falling in drops from clouds; fall of such drops. ▶ *vi* fall as rain. ▶ *vt* pour down like rain. **rain'y** *adj* **rain·i·er, rain·i·est. rain'bow** [-boh] *n* arch of prismatic colors in sky. **rain'coat** *n* light water-resistant overcoat.
raise [rayz] *vt* **raised, rais·ing.** lift up; set up; build; increase; elevate; promote; heighten, as pitch of voice; breed into existence; levy, collect; end (siege). **raise Cain** [KAYN] be riotous, angry, etc.
rai·sin [RAY-zin] *n* dried grape.

rai·son d'ê·tre [RAY-zohn DE-trə] *Fr* reason or justification for existence.

raj [rahj] *n* rule, sway, esp. in India. **ra'jah** *n* Indian prince or ruler.

rake¹ [rayk] *n* tool with long handle and crosspiece with teeth for gathering hay, leaves, etc. ▶ *vt* **raked, rak·ing.** gather, smooth with rake; sweep, search over; sweep with shot. **rake-off** *n* monetary commission, esp. illegal.

rake² *n* dissolute or dissipated man.

rake³ *n* slope, esp. backward, of ship's funnel, etc. ▶ *v* **raked, rak·ing.** incline from perpendicular. **rak'ish** *adj* appearing dashing or speedy.

ral·ly [RAL-ee] *v* **-lied, -ly·ing.** bring together, esp. what has been scattered, as routed army or dispersed troops; come together; regain health or strength, revive. ▶ *n* act of rallying; assembly, esp. outdoor, of any organization; *Tennis* lively exchange of strokes.

ram *n* male sheep; hydraulic machine; battering engine. ▶ *vt* **rammed, ram·ming.** force, drive; strike against with force; stuff; strike with ram.

RAM [ram] *Computers* random-access memory (as on a hard disk).

ram·ble [RAM-bəl] *vi* **-bled, -bling.** walk without definite route; wander; talk incoherently; spread in random fashion. ▶ *n* rambling walk. **ram'bler** *n* climbing rose; one who rambles.

ram·e·kin [RAM-i-kin] *n* small fireproof dish; food baked in it.

ram·i·fy [RAM-ə-fī] *v* **-fied, -fy·ing.** spread in branches, subdivide; become complex. **ram·i·fi·ca'tion** *n* branch, subdivision; process of branching out; consequence.

ra·mose [RAY-məs] *adj* branching.

ramp *n* gradual slope joining two level surfaces.

ram·page [ram-PAYJ] *vi* **-paged, -pag·ing.** dash about violently. ▶ *n* [RAM-payj] angry or destructive behavior. **ram·pa'geous** [-jəs] *adj*

ramp·ant [RAM-pənt] *adj* violent; rife; rearing.

ram·part [RAM-pahrt] *n* mound, wall for defense.

ram·shack·le [RAM-shak-əl] *adj* tumble-down, rickety, makeshift.

ran pt. of RUN.

ranch *n* cattle farm. ▶ *vi* manage one. **ranch'er** *n*

ran·cid [RAN-sid] *adj* smelling or tasting offensive, like stale fat.

ran·cor [RANG-kər] *n* bitter, inveterate hate. **ran'cor·ous** *adj* malignant; virulent.

ran·dom [RAN-dəm] *adj* made or done by chance, without plan. **at random** haphazard(ly).

rang pt. of RING².

range [raynj] *n* limits; row; scope, sphere; distance missile can travel; distance of mark shot at; place for shooting practice or rocket testing; rank; kitchen stove. ▶ *v* **ranged, rang·ing.** ▶ *vt* set in row; classify; roam. ▶ *vi* extend; roam; pass from one point to another; fluctuate (as prices). **rang'er** *n* official in charge of or patrolling park, etc. **rang'y** *adj* **rang·i·er, rang·i·est.** with long, slender limbs; spacious.

range'find·er *n* instrument for finding distance away of given object.

rank¹ [rangk] *n* row, line; order; social class; status; relative place or position. ▶ *vt* draw up in rank, classify. ▶ *vi* have rank, place; have certain distinctions. **the ranks** common soldiers. **rank and file** (esp. in labor unions) great mass or majority of people.

rank² *adj* **-er, -est.** growing too thickly, coarse; offensively strong; rancid; vile; flagrant. **rank'ly** *adv*

ran·kle [RANG-kəl] *vi* **-kled, -kling.** fester, continue to cause anger, resentment or bitterness.

ran·sack [RAN-sak] *vt* search thoroughly; pillage, plunder.

ran·som [RAN-səm] *n* release from captivity by payment; amount paid. ▶ *vt* pay ransom for.

rant *vi* rave in violent, high-sounding language. ▶ *n* noisy, boisterous speech; wild gaiety.

rap[1] *n* smart slight blow; rhythmic monologue performed to music. ▶ *v* **rapped, rap·ping.** give rap to; utter abruptly; perform rhythmic monologue to music. **rap'per** *n* singer of rap; person or thing that raps. **take the rap** *sl* take blame, suffer punishment (for), whether guilty or not.

rap[2] *n* **not care a rap** not care at all.

ra·pa·cious [rə-PAY-shəs] *adj* greedy; grasping. **ra·pac'i·ty** [-PAS-i-tee] *n*

rape [rayp] *vt* **raped, rap·ing.** force (person) to submit unwillingly to sexual intercourse. ▶ *n* act of raping; any violation or abuse. **rap'ist** *n*

rap'id *adj* quick, swift. **rapids** *pl n* part of river with fast, turbulent current. **ra·pid'i·ty** *n*

ra·pi·er [RAY-pee-ər] *n* fine-bladed sword for thrusting only.

rap·ine [RAP-in] *n* plunder.

rap·port [ra-POR] *n* harmony, agreement.

rap·proche·ment [rap-rohsh-MAHN] *n* reestablishment of friendly relations, esp. between nations.

rapt *adj* engrossed, spellbound. **rap'ture** [-chər] *n* ecstasy. **rap'tur·ous** *adj*

rare[1] [rair] *adj* **rar·er, rar·est.** uncommon; infrequent; of uncommon quality; of atmosphere, having low density, thin. **rare'ly** *adv* seldom. **rar'i·ty** *n, pl* **-ties.** anything rare; rareness.

rare[2] *adj* **rar·er, rar·est.** (of meat) lightly cooked.

rare·bit [RAIR-bit] *n* see WELSH RABBIT.

rar·e·fy [RAIR-ə-fī] *v* **-fied, -fy·ing.** make, become thin, rare, or less dense; refine.

rar·ing [RAIR-ing] *adj inf* enthusiastically willing, ready.

ras·cal [RAS-kəl] *n* rogue; naughty (young) person. **ras·cal'i·ty** [-KAL-i-tee] *n* roguery, baseness. **ras'cal·ly** [-kəl-ee] *adj*

rash[1] *adj* **-er, -est.** hasty, reckless, incautious.

rash[2] *n* skin eruption; outbreak, series of (unpleasant) occurrences.

rash·er [RASH-ər] *n* serving of bacon, usu. three or four slices; thin slice of bacon or ham.

rasp *n* harsh, grating noise; coarse file. ▶ *v* scrape with rasp; make scraping noise; speak in grating voice; grate upon; irritate.

rasp·ber·ry [RAZ-ber-ee] *n* red, juicy edible berry; plant which bears it; *inf* spluttering noise with tongue and lips to show contempt.

Ras·ta·far·i·an [ras-tə-FAIR-ee-ən] *n, adj* (member) of Jamaican cult regarding Haile Selassie, late emperor of Ethiopia, as the messiah.

rat *n* small rodent; *sl* contemptible person, esp. deserter, informer, etc. ▶ *vi* **rat·ted, rat·ting.** *sl* inform (on), betray, desert, abandon; hunt rats. **rat'ty** *adj sl* **-ti·er, -ti·est.** mean, ill-tempered, irritable. **rat race** continual hectic competitive activity. **rat'trap** *n* device for catching rats; dilapidated dwelling.

ratch·et [RACH-it] *n* set of teeth on bar or wheel allowing motion in one direction only.

rate[1] [rayt] *n* proportion between two things; charge; degree of speed, etc. ▶ *vt* **rat·ed, rat·ing.** value; estimate value of. **rat'a·ble** *adj* that can be rated or appraised.

rate[2] *vt* **rat·ed, rat·ing.** scold, chide.

rath·er [RATH-ər] *adv* to some extent; preferably; more willingly.

rat·i·fy [RAT-ə-fī] *vt* **-fied, -fy·ing.** confirm. **rat·i·fi·ca'tion** [-fi-KAY-shən] *n*

rat·ing [RAY-ting] *n* credit standing; fixing a rate; classification, esp. of ship, enlisted member of armed forces; angry rebuke.

ra·tio [RAY-shoh] *n, pl* **-tios.** proportion; quantitative relation.

ra·ti·oc·i·nate [rash-ee-OS-ə-nayt] *vi* **-nat·ed, -nat·ing.** reason. **ra·ti·oc·i·na'tion** [-NAY-shən] *n*

ra·tion [RASH-ən] *n* fixed allowance of food, etc. ▶ *vt* supply with, limit to certain amount.

ra·tion·al [RASH-ə-nl] *adj* reasonable, sensible; capable of thinking, reasoning. **ra·tion·ale'**

[-NAL] *n* reasons given for actions, etc. **ra'tion·al·ism** *n* philosophy that regards reason as only guide or authority. **ra·tion·al'i·ty** *n* **ra·tion·al·i·za'tion** *n* **ra'tion·al·ize** *vt* **-ized, -iz·ing.** justify by plausible reasoning; reorganize to improve efficiency, etc.

rat·tan [ra-TAN] *n* climbing palm with jointed stems; cane of this oft. used for furniture.

rat·tle [RAT-l] *v* **-tled, -tling.** ▶ *vi* give out succession of short sharp sounds; clatter. ▶ *vt* shake briskly causing a sharp clatter of sounds; confuse, fluster. ▶ *n* such sound; instrument for making it; set of horny rings in rattlesnake's tail. **rat'tle·snake** *n* poisonous snake.

rau·cous [RAW-kəs] *adj* hoarse; harsh.

raun·chy [RAWN-chee] *adj inf* **-chi·er, -chi·est.** earthy, vulgar, sexy; slovenly.

rav·age [RAV-ij] *vt* **-aged, -ag·ing.** lay waste, plunder. ▶ *n* destruction.

rave [rayv] *vi* **raved, rav·ing.** talk wildly in delirium or enthusiastically. ▶ *n*

rav·el [RAV-əl] *vt* **-eled, -el·ing.** entangle; fray out; disentangle.

ra·ven¹ [RAY-vən] *n* black bird like crow. ▶ *adj* shiny black.

raven² *v* seek prey, plunder. **rav·en·ous** [RAV-ə-nəs] *adj* very hungry.

ra·vine [rə-VEEN] *n* narrow steep-sided valley worn by stream, gorge.

ra·vi·o·li [rav-ee-OH-lee] *pl n* small, thin pieces of dough filled with highly seasoned, chopped meat and cooked.

rav'ish *vt* enrapture; commit rape upon. **rav'ish·ing** *adj* lovely, entrancing.

raw *adj* **-er, -est.** uncooked; not manufactured or refined; skinned; inexperienced, unpracticed, as recruits; sensitive; chilly. **raw deal** unfair or dishonest treatment. **raw'hide** *n* untanned hide; whip of this.

ray¹ *n* single line or narrow beam of light, heat, etc.; any of set of radiating lines. ▶ *vi* come out in rays; radiate.

ray² *n* marine fish, often very large, with winglike pectoral fins and whiplike tail.

ray'on *n* (fabric of) synthetic fiber.

raze [rayz] *vt* **razed, raz·ing.** destroy completely; wipe out, delete; level.

ra·zor [RAY-zər] *n* sharp instrument for shaving or for cutting hair.

Rb *Chem* rubidium.

re¹ [ray] *n* second sol-fa note.

re² *prep* with reference to, concerning.

Re *Chem* rhenium.

re- *prefix* again, e.g. *re-enter*; *retrial*.

reach [reech] *vt* arrive at; extend; succeed in touching; attain to. ▶ *vi* stretch out hand; extend. ▶ *n* act of reaching; power of touching; grasp, scope; range; straight stretch of river between two bends.

re·act [ree-AKT] *vi* act in return, opposition or toward former state. **re·ac'tance** [-əns] *n Electricity* resistance in coil, apart from ohmic resistance, due to current reacting on itself. **re·ac'tion** [-AK-shən] *n* any action resisting another; counter or backward tendency; response; chemical or nuclear change, combination or decomposition. **re·ac'tion·ar·y** *n, adj, pl* **-ar·ies.** (person) opposed to change, esp. in politics, etc. **re·ac'tive** *adj* chemically active. **re·ac'tor** *n* apparatus in which nuclear reaction is maintained and controlled to produce nuclear energy.

read [reed] *v* **read** [red], **read·ing.** ▶ *vt* look at and understand written or printed matter; learn by reading; interpret mentally; read and utter; interpret; study; understand any indicating instrument; (of instrument) register. ▶ *vi* be occupied in reading; find mentioned in reading. **read'a·ble** *adj* that can be read, or read with pleasure. **read'er** *n* one who reads; university professor's assistant;

school textbook; one who reads manuscripts submitted to publisher.

re·ad·just' v adapt to a new situation. **re·ad·just'ment** n

re·ad·mit' vt **-mitting, -mitted.** let (person, country, etc.) back in to a place or organization.

read·y [RED-ee] adj **read·i·er, read·i·est.** prepared for use or action; willing, prompt. **read'i·ly** adv promptly; willingly. **read'i·ness** [-nis] n

re·a·gent [ree-AY-jənt] n chemical substance that reacts with another and is used to detect presence of the other.

re·al [REE-əl] adj existing in fact; happening; actual; genuine; (of property) consisting of land and houses. **re'al·ism** n regarding things as they are; artistic treatment with this outlook. **re·al·is'tic** adj **re·al'i·ty** n real existence. **re'al·ly** adv **re'al·ty** n real estate. **real estate** landed property.

re·al·ize [REE-ə-līz] vt **-ized, -iz·ing.** apprehend, grasp significance of; make real; convert into money. **re·al·i·za'tion** n

realm [relm] n kingdom, province, domain, sphere.

ream[1] [reem] n twenty quires or 500 sheets of paper. ▶ pl large quantity of written matter.

ream[2] vt enlarge, bevel out, as hole in metal. **ream'er** n tool for this.

reap [reep] v cut and gather harvest; receive as fruit of previous activity. **reap'er** n

re·ap·pear' vi appear again. **re·ap·pear'ance** n

rear[1] [reer] n back part; part of army, procession, etc. behind others. **rear admiral** lowest flag rank in certain navies. **rear'guard** n troops protecting rear of army. **rear'most** [-mohst] adj

rear[2] vt care for and educate (children); breed; erect. ▶ vi rise, esp. on hind feet.

re·arm' v arm again. ▶ vt equip (army, nation, etc.) with better weapons. **re·ar'ma·ment** n

re·ar·range' vt organize differently, alter. **rearrangement** n

rea·son [REE-zən] n ground, motive; faculty of thinking; sanity; sensible or logical thought or view. ▶ vi think logically in forming conclusions. ▶ vt (usu. with with) persuade by logical argument into doing, etc. **rea'son·a·ble** adj sensible, not excessive; suitable; logical.

re·as·sure [ree-ə-SHUUR] vt **-sured, -sur·ing.** restore confidence to.

re·bate [REE-bayt] n discount, refund. ▶ vt **-bat·ed, -bat·ing.** deduct.

re·bel [ri-BEL] vi **-belled, -bel·ling.** revolt, resist lawful authority, take arms against ruling power. ▶ n [REB-əl] one who rebels; insurgent. ▶ adj [REB-əl] in rebellion. **re·bel·lion** [ri-BEL-yən] n organized open resistance to authority, revolt. **re·bel'lious** adj

re·birth' n revival or renaissance. **re·born'** adj active again after a period of inactivity.

re·boot' v to shut down and then restart (a computer system).

re·bound [ri-BOWND] vi spring back; misfire, esp. so as to hurt perpetrator (of plan, deed, etc.). ▶ n [REE-bownd] act of springing back or recoiling; return.

re·buff [ri-BUF] n blunt refusal; check. ▶ vt repulse, snub.

re·build' vt **-build'ing, -built.** build (building, town) again, after severe damage; develop (business, relationship, etc.) again after destruction or damage.

re·buke [ri-BYOOK] vt **-buked, -buk·ing.** reprove, reprimand, find fault with. ▶ n

re·bus [REE-bəs] n, pl **-bus·es.** riddle in which names of things, etc. are represented by pictures standing for syllables, etc.

re·but [ri-BUT] vt **-but·ted, -but·ting.** refute, disprove. **re·but'tal** n

re·cal·ci·trant [ri-KAL-si-trənt] adj, n willfully disobedient (person).

re·call [ri-KAWL] vt recollect,

remember; call, summon, order back; annul, cancel; revive, restore. ▶ *n* [REE-kawl] summons to return; ability to remember.

re·cant [ri-KANT] *vt* withdraw statement, opinion, etc. **re·can·ta'tion** *n*

re·ca·pit·u·late [ree-kə-PICH-ə-layt] *vt* **-lat·ed, -lat·ing.** state again briefly; repeat.

re·cap'ture *vt* experience again; capture again.

re·cede [ri-SEED] *vi* **-ced·ed, -ced·ing.** go back; become distant; slope backward; begin balding.

re·ceipt [ri-SEET] *n* written acknowledgment of money received; receiving or being received. ▶ *vt* acknowledge payment of in writing.

re·ceive [ri-SEEV] *vt* **-ceived, -ceiv·ing.** take, accept, get; experience; greet (guests). **re·ceiv'a·ble** *adj* **re·ceiv'er** *n* official appointed to receive money; fence, one who takes stolen goods knowing them to have been stolen; equipment in telephone, radio or TV that converts electrical signals into sound, light.

re·cent [REE-sənt] *adj* that has lately happened; new. **re'cent·ly** *adv*

re·cep·ta·cle [ri-SEP-tə-kəl] *n* vessel, place or space, to contain anything.

re·cep·tion [ri-SEP-shən] *n* receiving; manner of receiving; welcome; formal party; in broadcasting, quality of signals received. **re·cep'tion·ist** *n* person who receives guests, clients, etc.

re·cep·tive [ri-SEP-tiv] *adj* able, quick, willing to receive new ideas, suggestions, etc. **re·cep·tiv'i·ty** *n*

re·cess [REE-ses] *n* niche, alcove; hollow; secret, hidden place; remission or suspension of business; vacation, holiday.

re·ces·sion [ri-SESH-ən] *n* period of reduction in economic activity; act of receding. **re·ces'sive** *adj* receding.

re·ces·sion·al [ri-SESH-ə-nl] *n*

hymn sung while clergy retire.

re·cher·ché [rə-SHAIR-shay] *adj* of studied elegance; exquisite; choice.

re·cid·i·vist [ri-SID-ə-vist] *n* one who relapses into crime.

rec·i·pe [RES-ə-pee] *n* directions for cooking a dish; prescription; expedient.

re·cip·i·ent [ri-SIP-ee-ənt] *adj* that can or does receive. ▶ *n* one who, that which receives.

re·cip·ro·cal [ri-SIP-rə-kəl] *adj* complementary; mutual; moving backward and forward; alternating. **re·cip'ro·cate** [-rə-kayt] *v* **-cat·ed, -cat·ing.** ▶ *vt* give and receive mutually; return. ▶ *vi* move backward and forward. **re·ci·proc·i·ty** [res-ə-PROS-i-tee] *n*

re·cite [ri-SĪT] *vt* **-cit·ed, -cit·ing.** repeat aloud, esp. to audience. **re·cit'al** [-əl] *n* musical performance, usu. by one person; act of reciting; narration of facts, etc.; story; public entertainment of recitations, etc. **rec·i·ta'tion** *n* recital, usu. from memory, of poetry or prose; recountal. **rec·i·ta·tive** [res-i-tə-TEEV] *n* musical declamation.

reck·less [REK-lis] *adj* heedless, incautious.

reck·on [REK-ən] *v* count; include; consider; *inf* think, deem; make calculations.

re·claim [ri-KLAYM] *vt* make fit for cultivation; bring back; reform; demand the return of. **rec·la·ma'tion** *n*

re·cline [ri-KLĪN] *vi* **-clined, -clin·ing.** sit or lie back on one's side.

rec·luse [REK-loos] *n* hermit. ▶ *adj* [ri-KLOOS] living in seclusion, shut off from the world. **re·clu'sive** *adj*

rec·og·nize [REK-əg-nīz] *vt* **-nized, -niz·ing.** know again; treat as valid; notice, show appreciation of. **rec·og·ni'tion** *n* **rec·og·niz'a·ble** *adj* **re·cog·ni·zance** [ri-KOG-nə-zəns] *n* avowal; bond by which person undertakes before court to observe some condition; *obs* recognition.

re·coil [ri-KOIL] vi draw back in horror, etc.; go wrong so as to hurt the perpetrator; rebound (esp. of gun when fired). ▶ n [REE-koil] backward spring; retreat; recoiling.

rec·ol·lect [rek-ə-LEKT] vt call back to mind, remember.

rec·om·mend [rek-ə-MEND] vt advise, counsel; praise, commend; make acceptable.
rec·om·men·da'tion n

rec·om·pense [REK-əm-pens] vt -pensed, -pens·ing. reward; compensate, make up for. ▶ n compensation; reward; requital.

rec·on·cile [REK-ən-sīl] vt -ciled, -cil·ing. bring back into friendship; adjust, settle, harmonize.
rec·on·cil'a·ble adj
rec·on·cil·i·a'tion n

rec·on·dite [REK-ən-dīt] adj obscure, abstruse, little known.

re·con·di·tion [ree-kən-DISH-ən] vt restore to good condition, working order.

re·con·noi·ter [ree-kə-NOI-tər] vt make preliminary survey of; survey position of enemy. ▶ vi make reconnaissance. **re·con·nais·sance** [ri-KON-ə-səns] n examination or survey for military or engineering purposes; scouting.

re·con·sid·er v think about again, consider changing.

re·con·sti·tute [ree-KON-sti-toot] vt -tut·ed, -tut·ing. restore (food) to former state esp. by addition of water to a concentrate.

re·con·struct' v rebuild; use evidence to re-create.
re·con·struc'tion n

re·cord [REK-ərd] n being recorded; document or other thing that records; disk with indentations that phonograph transforms into sound; best recorded achievement; known facts about person's past. ▶ v [ri-KORD] preserve (sound, TV programs, etc.) on plastic disk, magnetic tape, etc. for reproduction on playback device. ▶ vt put in writing; register.
re·cord'er n one who, that which records; type of flute. **re·cord'ing** n process of making records from sound; something recorded, e.g. radio or TV program. **record player** instrument for reproducing sound on disks. **off the record** not for publication.

re·count [ri-KOWNT] vt tell in detail.

re·coup [ri-KOOP] vt recompense, compensate; recover what has been expended or lost.

re·course [REE-kors] n (resorting to) source of help; Law right of action or appeal.

re·cov·er [ri-KUV-ər] vt regain, get back. ▶ vi get back health.
re·cov'er·y n, pl -er·ies.

re·cre·ate' v make happen or exist again.

rec·re·a·tion [rek-ree-AY-shən] n agreeable or refreshing occupation, relaxation, amusement.
rec·re·a'tion·al adj

recreational vehicle large vanlike vehicle equipped to be lived in.

re·crim·i·nate [ri-KRIM-ə-nayt] vi -nat·ed, -nat·ing. make countercharge or mutual accusation. **re·crim·i·na'tion** n mutual abuse and blame.

re·cru·desce [ree-kroo-DES] vi -desced, -desc·ing. break out again. **re·cru·des'cent** adj

re·cruit [ri-KROOT] n newly-enlisted soldier; one newly joining society, etc. ▶ vt enlist fresh soldiers, etc.

rec·tan·gle [REK-tang-gəl] n oblong four-sided figure with four right angles. **rec·tang'u·lar** adj shaped thus.

rec·ti·fy vt -fied, -fy·ing. put right, correct, remedy, purify.
rec·ti·fi·ca'tion n act of setting right; Electricity conversion of alternating current into direct current. **rec'ti·fi·er** [-fī-ər] n person or thing that rectifies.

rec·ti·lin·e·ar [rek-tl-IN-ee-ər] adj in straight line; characterized by straight lines.

rec·ti·tude [REK-ti-tood] n moral uprightness; honesty of purpose.

rec·to [REK-toh] n, pl -tos. right-hand page of book, front of leaf.

rec·tor [REK-tər] *n* member of clergy with care of parish; head of certain institutions, chiefly academic. **rec'to·ry** *n* rector's house.

rec·tum [REK-təm] *n* final section of large intestine. **rec'tal** [-tl] *adj*

re·cum·bent [ri-KUM-bənt] *adj* lying down. **re·cum'ben·cy** *n*

re·cu·per·ate [ri-KOO-pər-ayt] *v* **-at·ed, -at·ing.** restore, be restored from illness, losses, etc.; convalesce. **re·cu·per·a'tion** *n*

re·cur [ri-KUR] *vi* **-curred, -cur·ring.** happen again; return again and again; go or come back in mind. **re·cur'rence** [-əns] *n* repetition. **re·cur'rent** [-ənt] *adj*

re·cy·cle [ree-SĪ-kəl] *vt* **-cled, -cling.** reprocess a manufactured substance for use again; reuse.

red *adj* of color varying from crimson to orange and seen in blood, rubies, glowing fire, etc. ▶ *n* the color; communist. **red'den** *v* make red; become red; flush. **red'dish** *adj* **red-blood·ed** [-blud-id] *adj* vigorous; virile. **red'coat** *n* in American Revolution, a British soldier. **red flag** danger signal. **red-hand'ed** *adj* (caught) in the act. **red herring** topic introduced to divert attention from main issue. **red-hot** red with heat; creating excitement. **red tape** excessive adherence to official rules. **red'wood** [-wuud] *n* giant coniferous tree of California. **in the red** operating at loss; in debt. **see red** *inf* be very angry.

re·deem [ri-DEEM] *vt* buy back; set free; free from sin; make up for. **re·demp'tion** [-DEM-shən] *n* **re·deem'a·ble** *adj* **The Re·deem·er** Jesus Christ.

re·de·vel·op *v* rebuild or renovate (an area or building). **re·de·vel'op·ment** *n*

red·o·lent [RED-l-ənt] *adj* smelling strongly, fragrant; reminiscent (of). **red'o·lence** *n*

re·dou·ble [ree-DUB-əl] *v* **-bled, -bling.** increase, multiply, intensify; double a second time.

re·doubt [ri-DOWT] *n* detached outwork in fortifications.

re·doubt·a·ble [ri-DOWT-ə-bəl] *adj* dreaded, formidable.

re·dound [ri-DOWND] *vt* contribute (to); recoil.

re·dress [ri-DRES] *vt* set right; make amends for. ▶ *n* [REE-dres] compensation, amends.

re·duce [ri-DOOS] *vt* **-duced, -duc·ing.** bring down, lower; lessen, weaken; bring by force or necessity to some state or action; slim; simplify; dilute; *Chem* separate substance from others with which it is combined. **re·duc'i·ble** *adj* **re·duc'tion** [-DUK-shən] *n* **reducing agent** substance used to deoxidize or lessen density of another substance.

re·dun·dant [ri-DUN-dənt] *adj* superfluous. **re·dun'dan·cy** *n*

re·ech·o *v* **-ech·o·ing, -ech·oed.** echo over and over again, resound.

reed *n* various marsh or water plants; tall straight stem of one; *Mus* vibrating cane or metal strip of certain wind instruments. **reed'y** *adj* **reed·i·er, reed·i·est.** full of reeds; like reed instrument, harsh and thin in tone.

reef *n* ridge of rock or coral near surface of sea; vein of ore; part of sail that can be rolled up to reduce area. ▶ *vt* take in a reef of. **reef'er** *n* sailor's close-fitting jacket; *sl* marijuana cigarette.

reek *n* strong (unpleasant) smell. ▶ *vi* emit fumes; smell.

reel *n* spool on which film is wound; *Motion Pictures* portion of film; winding apparatus; bobbin; thread wound on this; lively dance; music for it; act of staggering. ▶ *vt* wind on reel; draw (in) by means of reel. ▶ *vi* stagger, sway, rock. **reel off** recite, write fluently, quickly.

re·fec·to·ry [ri-FEK-tə-ree] *n, pl* **-ries.** dining room in monastery, college, etc. **re·fec'tion** *n* a meal.

re·fer [ri-FUR] *v* **-ferred, -fer·ring.** ▶ *vi* relate (to), allude. ▶ *vt* send to for information; trace, ascribe to; submit for decision. **re·fer'ral** *n*

act, instance of referring.
ref·er·ee' n arbitrator; person willing to whom scientific paper, etc. is sent for judgment of its quality, etc.; umpire. ▶ v **-eed, -ee·ing.** act as referee. **ref'er·ence** [-ins] n act of referring; citation or direction in book; appeal to judgment of another; testimonial; one to whom inquiries as to character, etc. may be made. **ref·er·en'dum** n, pl **-da** [-də] submitting of question to electorate.
re·fill' v fill again. ▶ n second or subsequent filling; replacement supply of something in a permanent container.
re·fine [ri-FĪN] vt **-fined, -fin·ing.** purify. **re·fine'ment** n subtlety; improvement, elaboration; fineness of feeling, taste or manners.
re·fin'er·y n, pl **-er·ies.** place for refining sugar, oil, etc.
re·fla'tion [ri-FLAY-shən] n (steps taken to produce) increase in economic activity of country, etc.
re·flect [ri-FLEKT] vt throw back, esp. rays of light; cast (discredit, etc.) upon. ▶ vi meditate.
re·flec'tion [-FLEK-shən] n act of reflecting; return of rays of heat, light, or waves of sound, from surface; image of object given back by mirror, etc.; conscious thought; meditation; expression of thought. **re·flec'tive** adj meditative, quiet, contemplative; throwing back images. **re·flec'tor** n polished surface for reflecting light, etc.
re·flex [REE-fleks] n reflex action; reflected image; reflected light, color, etc. ▶ adj (of muscular action) involuntary; reflected; bent back. **re·flex·ive** [ri-FLEK-siv] adj Grammar describes verb denoting agent's action on self. **reflex action** involuntary response to (nerve) stimulation.
re·form [ri-FORM] v improve; abandon evil practices; reconstruct. ▶ n improvement. **ref·or·ma'tion** [ref-ər-MAY-shən] n
re·form'a·to·ry n, pl **-ries.**

institution for reforming juvenile offenders.
re·fract [ri-FRAKT] vi change course of light, etc. passing from one medium to another. **re·frac'tion** n
re·frac·to·ry [ri-FRAK-tə-ree] adj unmanageable; difficult to treat or work; Med resistant to treatment; resistant to heat.
re·frain¹ [ri-FRAYN] vi abstain (from).
re·frain² n phrase or verse repeated regularly esp. in song or poem; chorus.
re·fran·gi·ble [ri-FRAN-jə-bəl] adj that can be refracted.
re·fresh [ri-FRESH] vt give freshness to; revive; renew; brighten; provide with refreshment. **re·fresh'er** n that which refreshes.
re·fresh'ment n that which refreshes, esp. food, drink; restorative.
re·frig·er·ate [ri-FRIJ-ə-rayt] vt **-at·ed, -at·ing.** freeze; cool.
re·frig'er·ant n refrigerating substance. ▶ adj **re·frig'er·a·tor** n apparatus in which foods, drinks are kept cool.
ref·uge [REF-yooj] n shelter, protection, retreat, sanctuary. **ref·u·gee** [ref-yuu-JEE] n one who seeks refuge, esp. in foreign country.
re·ful·gent [ri-FUL-jənt] adj shining, radiant. **re·ful'gence** n **re·ful'gen·cy** n splendor.
re·fund [ri-FUND] vt pay back. ▶ n [REE-fund] return of money; amount returned.
re·fur·bish [ree-FUR-bish] vt furbish, furnish or brighten anew.
re·fuse¹ [ri-FYOOZ] v **-fused, -fus·ing.** decline, deny, reject. **re·fus'al** n denial of anything demanded or offered; option.
ref·use² [REF-yoos] n rubbish, useless matter.
re·fute [ri-FYOOT] vt **-fut·ed, -fut·ing.** disprove. **re·fut'a·ble** adj **ref·u·ta·tion** [ref-yuu-TAY-shən] n
re·gal [REE-gəl] adj of, like a king.
re·ga·li·a [ri-GAY-lee-ə] pl n insignia of royalty, as used at coronation, etc.; emblems of high office, an

order, etc. **re·gal·i·ty** [ri-GAL-i-tee] *n, pl* **-ties.**

re·gale [ri-GAYL] *vt* **-galed, -gal·ing.** give pleasure to; feast.

re·gard [ri-GAHRD] *vt* look at; consider; relate to; heed. ▶ *n* look; attention; particular respect; esteem. ▶ *pl* expression of good will. **re·gard'ful** *adj* heedful, careful. **re·gard'less** *adj* heedless. ▶ *adv* in spite of everything.

re·gat·ta [ri-GAT-ə] *n* meeting for yacht or boat races.

re·gen·er·ate [ri-JEN-ə-rayt] *v* **-at·ed, -at·ing.** cause spiritual rebirth; reform morally; reproduce, re-create; reorganize. ▶ *adj* [-ə-rit] born anew. **re·gen·er·a'tion** *n* **re·gen'er·a·tive** *adj*

re·gent [REE-jənt] *n* ruler of kingdom during absence, minority, etc., of its monarch. ▶ *adj* ruling. **re'gen·cy** *n* status, (period of) office of regent.

reg·gae [REG-ay] *n* style of popular West Indian music with strong beat.

reg·i·cide [REJ-ə-sīd] *n* one who kills a king; this crime.

re·gime [rə-ZHEEM] *n* system of government, administration.

reg·i·men [REJ-ə-mən] *n* prescribed system of diet, etc.; rule.

reg·i·ment [REJ-ə-mənt] *n* organized body of troops as unit of army. ▶ *vt* [REJ-ə-ment] discipline, organize rigidly or too strictly. **reg·i·men'tal** *adj* of regiment.

re·gion [REE-jən] *n* area, district; stretch of country; part of the body; sphere, realm; administrative division of a country. **re'gion·al** *adj*

reg·is·ter [REJ-ə-stər] *n* list; catalogue; roll; device for registering; written record; range of voice or instrument. ▶ *v* show, be shown on meter, face, etc. ▶ *vt* enter in register; record; show; set down in writing; *Printing, photography* cause to correspond precisely. **reg'is·trar** [-trahr] *n* keeper of a register esp. in college or university. **reg·is·tra'tion** *n* **reg'is·try** *n, pl* **-tries.** registering; place where registers are kept, esp.

of births, marriages, deaths.

re·gorge [ri-GORJ] *v* **-gorged, -gorg·ing.** vomit up.

re·gress [ri-GRES] *vi* return, revert to former place, condition, etc. ▶ *n* **re·gres'sion** [-shən] *n* act of returning; retrogression. **re·gres'sive** *adj* falling back.

re·gret [ri-GRET] *vt* **-gret·ted, -gret·ting.** feel sorry, distressed for loss of or on account of. ▶ *n* sorrow, distress for thing done or left undone or lost. **re·gret'ful** *adj* **re·gret'ta·ble** *adj*

reg·u·lar [REG-yə-lər] *adj* normal; habitual; done, occurring, according to rule; periodical; straight, level; living under rule; belonging to standing army. ▶ *n* regular soldier; regular customer. **reg·u·lar'i·ty** *n* **reg'u·lar·ize** *vt* **-ized, -iz·ing.**

reg·u·late [REG-yə-layt] *vt* **-lat·ed, -lat·ing.** adjust; arrange; direct; govern; put under rule. **reg·u·la'tion** *n* **reg'u·la·tor** *n* contrivance to produce uniformity of motion, as flywheel, governor, etc.

re·gur·gi·tate [ri-GUR-ji-tayt] *v* vomit; bring back (swallowed food) into mouth.

re·ha·bil·i·tate [ree-hə-BIL-i-tayt] *vt* **-tat·ed, -tat·ing.** help (person) to readjust to society after a period of illness, imprisonment, etc.; restore to reputation or former position; make fit again; reinstate.

re·hash [ree-HASH] *vt* rework, reuse. ▶ *n* [REE-hash] old materials presented in new form.

re·hearse [ri-HURS] *vt* **-hearsed, -hears·ing.** practice (play, etc.); repeat aloud; say over again; train, drill. **re·hears'al** *n*

reign [rayn] *n* period of sovereign's rule. ▶ *vi* be ruler; be supreme.

re·im·burse [ree-im-BURS] *vt* **-bursed, -burs·ing.** refund; pay back. **re·im·burse'ment** *n*

rein [rayn] *n* narrow strap attached to bit to guide horse; instrument for governing. ▶ *vt* check, manage with reins; control. **give free rein**

to remove restraints.

re·in·car·na·tion
[ree-in-kahr-NAY-shən] *n* rebirth of soul in successive bodies; one of series of such transmigrations. **re·in·car′nate** [-KAHR-nayt] *vt* **-nat·ed, -nat·ing.**

rein·deer [RAYN-deer] *n* deer, with large branched antlers, that lives in the arctic regions.

re·in·force [ree-in-FORS] *vt* **-forced, -forc·ing.** strengthen with new support, material, force; strengthen with additional troops, ships, etc. **re·in·force′ment** *n* **reinforced concrete** concrete strengthened internally by steel bars.

re·in·state [ree-in-STAYT] *vt* **-stat·ed, -stat·ing.** replace, restore, reestablish.

re·it·er·ate [ree-IT-ə-rayt] *vt* **-at·ed, -at·ing.** repeat again and again. **re·it·er·a′tion** *n* repetition. **re·it′er·a·tive** [-ər-ə-tiv] *adj*

re·ject [ri-JEKT] *vt* refuse to accept; put aside; discard; renounce. ▶ *n* [REE-jekt] person or thing rejected as not up to standard. **re·jec′tion** *n* refusal.

re·joice [ri-JOIS] *v* **-joiced, -joic·ing.** make or be joyful, merry; gladden; exult.

re·join [ree-JOIN] *vt* reply; join again. **re·join·der** [ri-JOIN-dər] *n* answer, retort.

re·ju·ve·nate [ri-JOO-və-nayt] *vt* **-nat·ed, -nat·ing.** restore to youth. **re·ju·ve·na′tion** *n*

re·ju·ve·nes·cence
[ri-joo-və-NES-əns] *n* process of growing young again.

re·lapse [ri-LAPS] *vi* **-lapsed, -laps·ing.** fall back into evil, illness, etc. ▶ *n* [REE-laps] return of bad habits, illness, etc.

re·late [ri-LAYT] *v* **-lat·ed, -lat·ing.** ▶ *vt* narrate, recount; establish relation between; have reference or relation to. ▶ *vi* (with *to*) form sympathetic relationship.

re·la·tion [ri-LAY-shən] *n* relative quality or condition; connection by blood or marriage; connection between things; act of relating;

narrative. **re·la′tion·ship** *n*

rel·a·tive [REL-ə-tiv] *adj* dependent on relation to something else, not absolute; having reference or relation (to). ▶ *n* one connected by blood or marriage; relative word or thing. **rel·a·tiv′i·ty** *n* state of being relative; subject of two theories of Albert Einstein, dealing with relationships of space, time and motion, and acceleration and gravity.

re·lax [ri-LAKS] *vt* make loose or slack. ▶ *vi* become loosened or slack; ease up from effort or attention; become more friendly, less strict. **re·lax·a′tion** [ree-] *n* relaxing recreation; alleviation; abatement.

re·lay [REE-lay] *n* fresh set of people or animals relieving others; *Electricity* device for making or breaking local circuit. ▶ *vt* **-layed, -laying.** pass on, as message. **relay race** race between teams of which each runner races part of distance.

re·lease [ri-LEES] *vt* **-leased, -leas·ing.** give up, surrender, set free; permit public showing of (movie, etc.). ▶ *n* setting free; releasing; written discharge; permission to show publicly; film, record, etc. newly issued.

rel·e·gate [REL-i-gayt] *vt* **-gat·ed, -gat·ing.** banish, consign; demote. **re·le·ga′tion** *n*

re·lent [ri-LENT] *vi* give up harsh intention, become less severe. **re·lent′less** [-lis] *adj* pitiless; merciless.

rel·e·vant [REL-ə-vənt] *adj* having to do with the matter in hand, to the point. **rel′e·vance** *n*

reliable, reliance see RELY.

rel·ic [REL-ik] *n* thing remaining, esp. as memorial of saint; memento. ▶ *pl* remains, traces.

re·lief [ri-LEEF] *n* alleviation, end of pain, distress, etc.; money, food given to victims of disaster, poverty, etc.; release from duty; one who relieves another; freeing of besieged city, etc.; projection of carved design from surface;

distinctness, prominence. **re·lieve** [ri-LEEV] vt **-lieved, -liev·ing.** bring or give relief to. **relief map** map showing elevations and depressions of country in relief.

re·li·gion [ri-LIJ-ən] n system of belief in, worship of a supernatural power or god. **re·li'gious** adj pert. to religion; pious; conscientious. **re·li'gious·ly** adv in religious manner; scrupulously; conscientiously.

re·lin·quish [ri-LING-kwish] vt give up, abandon.

rel·i·quar·y [REL-i-kwer-ee] n, pl **-quar·ies.** case or shrine for holy relics.

rel·ish [REL-ish] v enjoy, like. ▶ n liking, gusto; appetizing savory food, such as pickle; taste or flavor.

re·luc·tant [ri-LUK-tənt] adj unwilling, loath, disinclined. **re·luc'tance** n

re·ly [ri-LĪ] vi **-lied, -ly·ing.** depend (on); trust. **re·li·a·bil'i·ty** n **re·li'a·ble** adj trustworthy, dependable. **re·li·ance** [ri-LĪ-əns] n trust; confidence; dependence. **re·li'ant** [-ənt] adj confident; trustful.

re·main [ri-MAYN] vi stay, be left behind; continue; abide; last. **remains** pl n relics, esp. of ancient buildings; dead body. **re·main'der** n rest, what is left after subtraction. ▶ vt offer (end of consignment of goods, material, etc.) at reduced prices.

re·mand [ri-MAND] vt send back, esp. into custody.

re·mark [ri-MAHRK] vi make casual comment (on). ▶ vt comment, observe; say; take notice of. ▶ n observation, comment. **re·mark'a·ble** adj noteworthy, unusual. **re·mark'a·bly** adv exceedingly; unusually.

re·mar·ry v **-ry·ing, -ried.** marry again following a divorce or the death of one's previous husband or wife.

rem·e·dy [REM-i-dee] n, pl **-dies.** means of curing, counteracting or relieving disease, trouble, etc. ▶ vt

-died, -dy·ing. put right.

re·me'di·a·ble adj **re·me'di·al** adj designed, intended to correct specific disability, handicap, etc. **re·me·di·a'tion** n

re·mem·ber [ri-MEM-bər] vt retain in, recall to memory. ▶ vi have in mind. **re·mem'brance** [-brəns] n memory; token; souvenir; reminiscence.

re·mind [ri-MĪND] vt cause to remember; put in mind (of). **re·mind'er** n

rem·i·nisce [rem-ə-NIS] vi **-nisced, -nisc·ing.** talk, write of past times, experiences, etc. **rem·i·nis'cence** n remembering; thing recollected. ▶ pl memoirs. **rem·i·nis'cent** adj reminding or suggestive (of).

re·miss [ri-MIS] adj negligent, careless.

re·mit [ri-MIT] v **-mit·ted, -mit·ting.** send money for goods, services, etc., esp. by mail; refrain from exacting; give up; restore, return; slacken; forgive (sin, etc.). ▶ n Law transfer of court record to another court. **re·mis'sion** n abatement; reduction in length of prison term; pardon, forgiveness. **re·mit'tance** n sending of money; money sent.

rem·nant [REM-nənt] n fragment or small piece remaining; oddment.

re·mon·strate [ri-MON-strayt] vi **-strat·ed, -strat·ing.** protest, reason with, argue. **re·mon'strance** [-strəns] n

re·morse [ri-MORS] n regret and repentance. **re·morse'ful** [-fəl] adj **re·morse'less** [-lis] adj pitiless.

re·mote [ri-MOHT] adj **-mot·er, -mot·est.** far away, distant; aloof; slight. **re·mote'ly** adv **remote control** control of apparatus from a distance by electrical device.

re·move [ri-MOOV] v **-moved, -mov·ing.** ▶ vt take away or off; transfer; withdraw. ▶ vi go away, change residence. ▶ n degree of difference. **re·mov·a·ble** adj **re·mov'al** n

re·mu·ner·ate [ri-MYOO-nə-rayt] vt reward, pay. **re·mu·ner·a'tion** n **re·mu'ner·a·tive** adj

ren·ais·sance [ren-ə-SAHNS] *n* revival, rebirth, esp. revival of learning in 14th to 16th centuries.

re·nal [REEN-l] *adj* of the kidneys.

re·nas·cent [ri-NAS-ənt] *adj* springing up again into being.

rend *v* **rent, rend·ing.** tear, wrench apart; burst, break, split.

ren·der [REN-dər] *vt* submit, present; give in return, deliver up; cause to become; portray, represent; melt down; cover with plaster.

ren·dez·vous [RAHN-de-voo] *n, pl* **rendezvous** [-vooz] meeting place; appointment; haunt; assignation. ▶ *vi* **-voused** [-vood], **-vous·ing** [-voo-ing] meet, come together.

ren·di·tion [ren-DISH-ən] *n* performance; translation.

ren·e·gade [REN-i-gayd] *n* deserter; outlaw; rebel. ▶ *adj*

re·nege [ri-NIG] *vi* **-neged, -neg·ing.** (usu. with *on*) go back on (promise, etc.); in cards, break rule.

re·new [ri-NOO] *vt* begin again; reaffirm; make valid again; make new; revive; restore to former state; replenish. ▶ *vi* be made new; grow again. **re·new·a·bil·i·ty** *n* quality of being renewable. **re·new·a·ble** *adj* **re·new·al** *n* revival, restoration; regeneration.

ren·net [REN-it] *n* lining membrane of calf's fourth stomach; preparation from this membrane for curdling milk.

re·nounce [ri-NOWNS] *vt* **-nounced, -nounc·ing.** give up, cast off, disown; abjure; resign, as title or claim. **re·nun·ci·a·tion** *n*

ren·o·vate [REN-ə-vayt] *vt* restore, repair, renew, do up. **ren·o·va·tion** *n*

re·nown [ri-NOWN] *n* fame.

rent[1] *n* payment for use of land, buildings, machines, etc. ▶ *vt* hold by lease; hire; let. **rent·al** [RENT-əl] *n* sum payable as rent.

rent[2] *n* tear; fissure; pt./pp. of REND.

renunciation SEE RENOUNCE.

rep[1] *n* fabric with corded surface for upholstery, etc.

rep[2] *adj, n* short for REPERTORY (COMPANY).

rep[3] *n* short for REPRESENTATIVE.

re·paid [ri-PAYD] pt./pp. of REPAY.

re·pair[1] [ri-PAIR] *vt* make whole, sound again; mend; patch; restore. ▶ *n* **re·pair'a·ble** *adj* **rep·a·ra·tion** [rep-ə-RAY-shən] *n* repairing; amends, compensation.

repair[2] *vi* resort (to), go.

rep·ar·tee [rep-ər-TEE] *n* witty retort; interchange of reports.

re·past [ri-PAST] *n* a meal.

re·pa·tri·ate [ri-PAY-tree-ayt] *vt* **-at·ed, -at·ing.** send (someone) back to own country.

re·pay [ri-PAY] *vt* **-paid, -pay·ing.** pay back, refund; make return for. **re·pay'ment** *n*

re·peal [ri-PEEL] *vt* revoke, annul, cancel. ▶ *n* act of repealing.

re·peat [ri-PEET] *vt* say, do again; reproduce; recur. ▶ *vi* recur; of food, be tasted repeatedly for some time after being eaten. ▶ *n* act, instance of repeating, esp. TV show broadcast again. **re·peat'ed·ly** *adv* again and again; frequently.

re·peat'er *n* firearm that can be discharged many times without reloading; watch that strikes hours.

rep·e·ti·tion [rep-i-TISH-ən] *n* act of repeating; thing repeated; piece learned by heart and repeated. **rep·e·ti'tious** *adj* repeated unnecessarily. **re·pet'i·tive** *adj* repeated.

re·pel [ri-PEL] *vt* **-pelled, -pel·ling.** drive back, ward off, refuse; be repulsive to. **re·pel'lent** [-ənt] *adj* distasteful; resisting water, etc. ▶ *n* that which repels, esp. chemical to repel insects.

re·pent [ri-PENT] *vi* wish one had not done something; feel regret for deed or omission. ▶ *vt* feel regret for. **re·pent'ance** [-əns] *n* contrition. **re·pent'ant** [-ənt] *adj*

re·per·cus·sion [ree-pər-KUSH-ən] *n* indirect effect, oft. unpleasant; recoil; echo.

rep·er·to·ry [REP-ər-tor-ee] *n, pl* **-ries.** repertoire, collection; store.

rep'er·toire [-twahr] *n* stock of plays, songs, etc. that performer or company can give. **repertory theater** theater with permanent company producing succession of plays.

repetition, repetitious, repetitive see REPEAT.

re·pine [ri-PĪN] vi **-pined, -pin·ing.** fret, complain.

re·place [ri-PLAYS] vt **-placed, -plac·ing.** substitute for; put back.

re·play [REE-play] n (also **instant replay**) immediate reshowing on TV of incident in sport, esp. in slow motion; replaying of a match. ▶ vt [ree-PLAY]

re·plen·ish [ri-PLEN-ish] vt fill up again. **re·plen'ish·ment** n

re·plete [ri-PLEET] adj filled, gorged.

rep·li·ca [REP-li-kə] n exact copy; facsimile, duplicate. **rep·li·cate** [REP-li-kayt] vt **-cat·ed, -cat·ing.** make, be a copy of. **rep·li·ca'tion** n **rep'li·ca·ble** adj

re·ply [ri-PLĪ] v **-plied, -ply·ing.** answer or respond. ▶ n, pl **-lies.** answer or response.

re·port [ri-PORT] n account, statement; written statement of child's progress at school; rumor; repute; bang. ▶ vt announce, relate; make, give account of; take down in writing; complain about. ▶ vi make report; act as reporter; present oneself (to). **re·port'er** n one who reports, esp. for newspaper.

re·pose [ri-POHZ] n peace; composure; sleep. ▶ v **-posed, -pos·ing.** ▶ vi rest. ▶ vt lay to rest; place; rely, lean (on). **re·pos'i·tor·y** [-POZ-i-tor-ee] n, pl **-tor·ies.** place where valuables are deposited for safekeeping; store.

rep·re·hend [rep-ri-HEND] vt find fault with. **rep·re·hen'si·ble** adj deserving censure; unworthy. **rep·re·hen'sion** n censure.

rep·re·sent [rep-ri-ZENT] vt stand for; deputize for; act, play; symbolize; make out to be; call up by description or portrait. **rep·re·sen·ta'tion** n

rep·re·sent'a·tive n one chosen to stand for group; (traveling)

salesman. ▶ adj typical.

re·press [ri-PRES] vt keep down or under, quell, check. **re·pres'sion** [-PRESH-ən] n restraint. **re·pres'sive** adj

re·prieve [ri-PREEV] vt **-prieved, -priev·ing.** suspend execution of (condemned person); give temporary relief (to). ▶ n postponement or cancellation of punishment; respite; last-minute intervention.

rep·ri·mand [REP-rə-mand] n sharp rebuke. ▶ vt rebuke sharply.

re·print' vt print further copies of (a book). ▶ n reprinted copy.

re·pris·al [ri-PRĪ-zəl] n retaliation.

re·proach [ri-PROHCH] vt blame, rebuke. ▶ n scolding, upbraiding; expression of this; thing bringing discredit. **re·proach'ful** [-fəl] adj

rep·ro·bate [REP-rə-bayt] adj depraved; rejected by God. ▶ n depraved or disreputable person. ▶ vt **-bat·ed, -bat·ing.** disapprove of, reject.

re·pro·duce [ree-prə-DOOS] v **-duced, -duc·ing.** ▶ vt produce copy of; bring new individuals into existence; re-create, produce anew. ▶ vi propagate; generate. **re·pro·duc'i·ble** adj **re·pro·duc'tion** n process of reproducing; that which is reproduced; facsimile, as of painting, etc. **re·pro·duc'tive** adj

re·prove [ri-PROOV] vt **-proved, -prov·ing.** censure, rebuke. **re·proof'** n

rep·tile [REP-til or REP-tīl] n cold-blooded, air breathing vertebrate with horny scales or plates, as snake, tortoise, etc. **rep·til'i·an** adj

re·pub·lic [ri-PUB-lik] n country without monarch in which supremacy of people or their elected representatives is formally acknowledged. **re·pub'li·can** adj, n

re·pu·di·ate [ri-PYOO-dee-ayt] vt **-at·ed, -at·ing.** reject authority or validity of; cast off, disown. **re·pu·di·a'tion** n

re·pug·nant [ri-PUG-nənt] adj

offensive; distasteful; contrary.
re·pug'nance n dislike, aversion; incompatibility.
re·pulse [ri-PULS] vt **-pulsed, -puls·ing.** drive back; rebuff; repel. ▶ n driving back, rejection, rebuff.
re·pul'sion [-shən] n distaste, aversion; *Physics* force separating two objects. **re·pul'sive** adj loathsome, disgusting.
re·pute [ri-PYOOT] vt **-put·ed, -put·ing.** reckon, consider. ▶ n reputation, credit. **rep'u·ta·ble** adj of good repute; respectable. **rep·u·ta'tion** n estimation in which person is held; character; good name.
re·quest [ri-KWEST] n asking; thing asked for. ▶ vt ask.
Req·ui·em [REK-wee-əm] n Mass for the dead; (**r-**) music for this.
re·quire [ri-KWIR] vt **-quired, -quir·ing.** want, need; demand. **re·quire'ment** n essential condition; specific need; want.
req·ui·site [REK-wə-zit] adj necessary; essential. ▶ n
req·ui·si·tion [rek-wə-ZISH-ən] n formal demand, such as for materials or supplies. ▶ vt demand (supplies); press into service.
re·quite [ri-KWIT] vt **-quit·ed, -quit·ing.** repay.
re·scind [ri-SIND] vt cancel, annul. **re·scis'sion** [-SIZH-ən] n
res·cue [RES-kyoo] vt **-cued, -cu·ing.** save, deliver, extricate. ▶ n **res'cu·er** n
re·search [ri-SURCH] n investigation, esp. scientific study to discover facts. ▶ v carry out investigations (on, into).
re·sem·ble [ri-ZEM-bəl] vt **-bled, -bling.** be like; look like. **re·sem'blance** n
re·sent [ri-ZENT] vt show, feel indignation at; retain bitterness about. **re·sent'ful** [-fəl] adj **re·sent'ment** [-mənt] n
re·serve [ri-ZURV] vt **-served, -serv·ing.** hold back, set aside, keep for future use. ▶ n (also pl) something, esp. money, troops, etc. kept for emergencies; (also

reservation) area of land reserved for particular purpose or for use by particular group of people, etc.; reticence, concealment of feelings or friendliness. **re·ser·va'tion** n reserving; thing reserved; doubt; exception or limitation. **reserved** adj not showing feelings, lacking cordiality. **re·serv'ist** n one serving in reserve.
res·er·voir [REZ-ər-vwahr] n enclosed area for storage of water, esp. for community supplies; receptacle for liquid, gas, etc.; place where anything is kept in store.
re·shuf'fle n reorganization. ▶ v reorganize.
re·side [ri-ZID] vi **-sid·ed, -sid·ing.** dwell permanently. **res·i·dence** [REZ-i-dəns] n home; house. **res'i·den·cy** n dwelling; position or period of medical resident. **res'i·dent** [-dənt] adj, n **res·i·den'tial** adj (of part of town) consisting mainly of residences; of, connected with residence; providing living accommodation. **resident** physician in residence at hospital and serving on staff to obtain advanced training.
res·i·due [REZ-i-doo] n what is left, remainder. **re·sid'u·al** [ri-ZIJ-oo-əl] adj **residuals** pl n additional payments to performers for reruns of film, TV programs, etc. in which they appear.
re·sign [ri-ZIN] vt give up. ▶ vi give up office, employment, etc.; reconcile (oneself) to. **res·ig·na'tion** [-ig-NAY-shən] n resigning; being resigned; submission. **re·signed'** [-ZIND] adj content to endure.
re·sil·ient [ri-ZIL-yənt] adj capable of returning to normal after stretching, etc., elastic; (of person) recovering quickly from shock, etc. **re·sil'ience, -ien·cy** n
res·in [REZ-in] n sticky substance formed in and oozing from plants, esp. firs and pines. **res'in·ous** [-nəs] adj of, like resin.
re·sist [ri-ZIST] v withstand,

oppose. **re·sist'ance** [-əns] n act of resisting; opposition; hindrance; *Electricity* opposition offered by circuit to passage of current through it. **re·sist'ant** [-ənt] adj **re·sist'i·ble** adj **re·sis·tiv'i·ty** n measure of electrical resistance. **re·sist'or** n component of electrical circuit producing resistance.

res·o·lute [REZ-ə-loot] adj determined; resolving; firmness; purpose or thing resolved upon; decision or vote of assembly.

re·solve [ri-ZOLV] vt **-solved, -solv·ing.** make up one's mind; decide with effort of will; form by resolution of vote; separate component parts of; make clear. ▶ n resolution; fixed purpose.

res·o·nance [REZ-ə-nəns] n echoing, esp. in deep tone; sound produced by body vibrating in sympathy with neighboring source of sound. **res'o·nant** [-nənt] adj **res'o·nate** vi, vt **-nat·ed, -nat·ing.**

re·sort [ri-ZORT] vi have recourse; frequent. ▶ n place for vacations; recourse; frequented place; haunt.

re·sound [ri-ZOWND] vi echo, ring, go on sounding. **re·sound'ing** adj echoing; thorough.

re·source [ri-ZORS or ri-SORS] n capability, ingenuity; that to which one resorts for support; expedient. ▶ pl source of economic wealth; supply that can be drawn on; means of support, funds. **re·source'ful** [-fəl] adj

re·spect [ri-SPEKT] n deference, esteem; point or aspect; reference, relation. ▶ vt treat with esteem; show consideration for. **re·spect·a·bil'i·ty** n **re·spect'a·ble** adj worthy of respect, decent; fairly good. **re·spect'ful** adj **re·spect'ing** prep concerning. **re·spect'ive** adj relating separately to each of those in question; several, separate.

res·pi·ra·tion [res-pə-RAY-shən] n breathing. **res'pi·ra·tor** n apparatus worn over mouth and breathed through as protection

against dust, poison gas, etc. or to provide artificial respiration. **res'pi·ra·to·ry** [-rə-tor-ee] adj

res·pite [RES-pit] n pause; interval; suspension of labor; delay; reprieve.

re·splend·ent [ri-SPLEN-dənt] adj brilliant, splendid; shining. **re·splend'en·cy** [-ən-see] n

re·spond [ri-SPOND] vi answer; act in answer to stimulus; react. **re·spond'ent** adj replying. ▶ n one who answers; defendant. **re·sponse'** n answer. **re·spon'sive** adj readily reacting to some influence.

re·spon·si·ble [ri-SPON-sə-bəl] adj liable to answer for; accountable; dependable; involving responsibility; of good credit or position. **re·spon·si·bil'i·ty** n state of being answerable; duty; charge; obligation.

rest¹ n repose; freedom from exertion, etc.; that on which anything rests or leans; pause, esp. in music; support. ▶ vi take rest; be supported. ▶ vt give rest to; place on support. **rest'ful** [-fəl] adj **rest'less** [-lis] adj offering no rest; uneasy, impatient. **rest home** residential establishment providing care for aged, convalescent, etc.

rest² n remainder; others. ▶ vi remain; continue to be.

res·tau·rant [RES-tər-ənt] n commercial establishment serving food. **res·tau·ra·teur'** [-ə-TUR] n keeper of one.

res·ti·tu·tion [res-ti-TOO-shən] n giving back or making up; reparation, compensation.

res·tive [RES-tiv] adj restless; resisting control, impatient.

re·store [ri-STOR] vt **-stored, -stor·ing.** build up again, repair, renew; reestablish; give back. **res·to·ra'tion** n **re·stor'a·tive** adj restoring. ▶ n medicine to strengthen, etc. **re·stor'er** n

re·strain [ri-STRAYN] vt check, hold back; prevent; confine. **re·straint'** n restraining, control, esp. self-control.

re·strict [ri-STRIKT] vt limit, bound.

re·stric'tion *n* limitation; restraint; rule. **re·stric'tive** *adj* **re·stric'ted** *adj* denying residence, membership to persons of certain races, ethnic groups, etc.

re·sult [ri-ZULT] *vi* follow as consequence; happen; end. ▶ *n* effect, outcome. **re·sult'ant** [-ZUL-tnt] *adj* arising as result.

re·sume [ri-ZOOM] *vt* **-sumed, -sum·ing.** begin again. **ré·su·mé** [REZ-uu-may] *n* summary, abstract; brief statement of one's qualifications for employment, public office, etc. **re·sump'tion** [-shən] *n* resuming; fresh start.

re·sur·gence [ri-SUR-jəns] *n* rising again. **re·sur'gent** *adj*

res·ur·rect [rez-ə-REKT] *vt* restore to life, resuscitate; use once more (something discarded, etc.). **res·ur·rec'tion** *n* rising again (esp. from dead); revival.

re·sus·ci·tate [ri-SUS-i-tayt] *vt* **-tat·ed, -tat·ing.** revive to life, consciousness.

re·tail [REE-tayl] *n* sale in small quantities. ▶ *adv* at retail. ▶ *v* sell, be sold, retail; recount.

re·tain [ri-TAYN] *vt* keep; engage services of. **re·tain'er** *n* fee to retain professional adviser, esp. lawyer. **re·ten'tion** [-shən] *n* **re·ten'tive** *adj* capable of retaining, remembering.

re·tal·i·ate [ri-TAL-ee-ayt] *v* **-at·ed, at·ing.** repay in kind; revenge. **re·tal·i·a'tion** *n* **re·tal'i·a·to·ry** *adj*

re·tard [ri-TAHRD] *vt* make slow or late; keep back; impede development of. **re·tard'ed** *adj* underdeveloped, esp. mentally. **re·tar·da'tion** *n*

retch [rech] *vi* try to vomit.

ret·i·cent [RET-ə-sənt] *adj* reserved in speech; uncommunicative. **ret'i·cence** *n*

ret·i·na [RET-n-ə] *n, pl* **-nas.** light-sensitive membrane at back of eye. **ret'i·nal** *adj* **ret·i·ni'tis** [-NĪ-tis] *n* inflammation of retina.

ret·i·nue [RET-n-yoo] *n* band of followers or attendants.

re·tire [ri-TĪR] *v* **-tired, -tir·ing.** ▶ *vi*

give up office or work; go away; withdraw; go to bed. ▶ *vt* cause to retire. **retired** *adj* that has retired from office, etc. **re·tire'ment** [-mənt] *n* **re·tir'ing** *adj* unobtrusive, shy.

re·tort [ri-TORT] *vt* reply; repay in kind, retaliate; hurl back (charge, etc.). ▶ *vi* reply with countercharge. ▶ *n* vigorous reply or repartee; vessel with bent neck used for distilling.

re·touch [ree-TUCH] *vt* touch up, improve by new touches, esp. of paint, etc.

re·trace [ri-TRAYS] *vt* **-traced, -trac·ing.** go back over (a route, etc.) again.

re·tract [ri-TRAKT] *v* draw back, recant. **re·tract'a·ble** *adj* **re·trac'tion** *n* drawing or taking back, esp. of statement, etc. **re·trac'tor** *n* muscle; surgical instrument.

re·tread [ree-TRED] *vt* restore tread to worn rubber tire. ▶ *n* [REE-tred] retreaded tire; *sl* person returned to work after dismissal; person training for new type of work; *inf* reworked old idea, etc.

re·treat [ri-TREET] *vi* move back from any position; retire. ▶ *n* act of, or military signal for, retiring, withdrawal; place to which anyone retires esp. for meditation; refuge; sunset call on bugle.

re·trench [ri-TRENCH] *vt* reduce expenditure, esp. by dismissing staff; cut down.

ret·ri·bu·tion [re-trə-BYOO-shən] *n* recompense, esp. for evil deeds; vengeance.

re·trieve [ri-TREEV] *vt* **-trieved, -triev·ing.** fetch back again; restore; rescue from ruin; recover, esp. information from computer; regain. **re·triev'al** *n* **re·triev'er** *n* dog trained to retrieve game.

ret·ro·ac·tive [re-troh-AK-tiv] *adj* applying or referring to the past.

ret·ro·grade [RE-trə-grayd] *adj* going backward, reverting; reactionary. **ret·ro·gres'sion** [-GRE-shən] *n* **ret·ro·gres'sive** *adj*

ret·ro·spect [RE-trə-spekt] *n* looking back, survey of past. **ret·ro·spec'tion** [-SPEK-shən] *n* **ret·ro·spec'tive** *adj*

re·trous·sé [ri-troo-SAY] *adj* of nose, turned upward.

re·turn [ri-TURN] *vi* go, come back. ▶ *vt* give, send back; report officially; elect. ▶ *n* returning, being returned; profit; official report esp. tax return.

re·un·ion [ree-YOON-yən] *n* gathering of people who have been apart. **re·u·nite'** *v* bring or come together again after a separation.

Rev. Revelations.

rev *n inf* revolution (of engine). ▶ *v* **revved, rev·ving.** (oft. with *up*) increase speed of revolution (of engine).

re·val·ue [ree-VAL-yoo] *v* **-ued, -u·ing.** adjust exchange value of currency upward.

re·vamp [ree-VAMP] *vt* renovate, restore.

re·veal [ri-VEEL] *vt* make known; show. **rev·e·la'tion** *n*

rev·eil·le [REV-ə-lee] *n* morning bugle call, etc. to waken soldiers.

rev·el [REV-əl] *vi* **-eled, -el·ing.** take pleasure (in); make merry. ▶ *n* (usu pl) merrymaking. **rev'el·ry** *n* festivity.

re·venge [ri-VENJ] *n* retaliation for wrong done; act that satisfies this; desire for this. ▶ *v* **-venged, -veng·ing.** ▶ *vt* avenge; make retaliation for. ▶ *v refl* avenge oneself. **re·venge'ful** [-fəl] *adj* vindictive; resentful.

rev·e·nue [REV-ən-yoo] *n* income, esp. of nation, as taxes, etc.

re·ver·ber·ate [ri-VUR-bə-rayt] *v* **-at·ed, -at·ing.** echo, resound, throw back (sound, etc.).

re·vere [ri-VEER] *vt* **-vered, -ver·ing.** hold in great regard or religious respect. **rev'er·ence** [-əns] *n* revering; awe mingled with respect and esteem; veneration. **rev'er·end** [-ənd] *adj* (esp. as prefix to clergyman's name) worthy of reverence.

rev'er·ent [-ənt] *adj* showing reverence. **rev·er·en'tial** *adj* marked by reverence.

rev·er·ie [REV-ə-ree] *n* daydream, absent-minded state.

re·verse [ri-VURS] *v* **-versed, -vers·ing.** (of vehicle) (cause to) move backward. ▶ *vt* turn upside down or other way round; change completely. ▶ *n* opposite, contrary; side opposite, obverse; defeat; reverse gear. ▶ *adj* opposite, contrary. **re·ver'sal** [-səl] *n* **re·vers'i·ble** *adj* **reverse gear** mechanism enabling vehicle to move backward.

re·vert [ri-VURT] *vi* return to former state; come back to subject; refer to a second time; turn backward. **re·ver'sion** [-VUR-zhən] *n* (of property) rightful passing to owner or designated heir, etc.

re·vet·ment [ri-VET-mənt] *n* facing of stone, sandbags, etc. for wall.

re·view [ri-VYOO] *vt* examine; look back on; reconsider; hold, make, write review of. ▶ *n* general survey; critical notice of book, etc.; periodical with critical articles; inspection of troops; revue. **re·view'er** *n* writer of reviews.

re·vile [ri-VĪL] *vt* **-viled, -vil·ing.** be viciously scornful of, abuse.

re·vise [ri-VĪZ] *vt* **-vised, -vis·ing.** look over and correct; change, alter. **re·vi'sion** [-zhən] *n* reexamination for purpose of correcting; act of revising; revised copy. **re·vi'sion·ism** *n* departure from generally accepted theory, interpretation. **re·vi'sion·ist** *adj, n*

re·vive [ri-VĪV] *v* **-vived, -viv·ing.** bring, come back to life, vigor, use, etc. **re·viv'al** [-vəl] *n* reviving, esp. of religious fervor. **re·viv'al·ist** *n* organizer of religious revival.

re·voke [ri-VOHK] *vt* **-voked, -vok·ing.** take back, withdraw; cancel. **rev'o·ca·ble** [-ə-kə-bəl] *adj* **rev·o·ca'tion** *n* repeal.

re·volt [ri-VOHLT] *n* rebellion. ▶ *vi* rise in rebellion; feel disgust. ▶ *vt* affect with disgust. **re·volt'ing** *adj* disgusting, horrible.

re·volve [ri-VOLV] v **-volved,
-volv·ing.** ▶ vi turn around, rotate;
be centered on. ▶ vt rotate.

rev·o·lu'tion n violent overthrow of
government; great change;
complete rotation, turning or
spinning around.
rev·o·lu'tion·ar·y adj, n
rev·o·lu'tion·ize vt **-ized, -iz·ing.**
change considerably; bring about
revolution in.

re·volv·er [ri-VOL-vər] n repeating
pistol with revolving cylinder.

re·vue, re·view [ri-VYOO] n
theatrical entertainment with
topical sketches and songs.

re·vul·sion [ri-VUL-shən] n sudden
violent change of feeling; marked
repugnance or abhorrence.

re·ward [ri-WORD] vt pay, make
return for service, conduct, etc. ▶ n
re·ward'ing adj giving personal
satisfaction, worthwhile.

re·wind' v run (tape or film) back to
an earlier point in order to replay.

Rf Chem rutherfordium.

Rh Chem rhodium.

rhap·so·dy [RAP-sə-dee] n, pl **-dies.**
enthusiastic or high-flown
(musical) composition or utterance.
rhap'so·dic adj **rhap'so·dize**
[-sə-dīz] v **-dized, -diz·ing.**

rhe·o·stat [REE-ə-stat] n instrument
for regulating the value of the
resistance in an electric circuit.

rhe·sus [REE-səs] n small,
long-tailed monkey of S Asia.
rhesus factor, Rh factor feature
distinguishing different types of
human blood.

rhet·o·ric [RET-ər-ik] n art of
effective speaking or writing;
artificial or exaggerated language.
rhe·tor·i·cal [ri-TOR-i-kəl] adj (of
question) not requiring an answer.
rhet·o·ri'cian [-RISH-ən] n

rheu·ma·tism [ROO-mə-tiz-əm] n
painful inflammation of joints or
muscles. **rheu·mat·ic** [ruu-MAT-ik]
adj, n **rheu·ma·toid**
[ROO-mə-toid] adj of, like
rheumatism.

Rh factor see RHESUS.

rhi·no·cer·os [rī-NOS-ər-əs] n, pl

-os·es. large thick-skinned animal
with one or two horns on nose.

rho·di·um [ROH-dee-əm] n hard
metal like platinum.

rhom·bus [ROM-bəs] n, pl **-bus·es**
or **-bi** [-bī] equilateral but not
right-angled parallelogram,
diamond-shaped figure.

rhu·barb [ROO-bahrb] n garden
plant of which the fleshy stalks are
cooked and used as fruit; laxative
from root of allied Chinese plant; sl
argument, fight.

rhyme [rīm] n identity of sounds at
ends of lines of verse, or in words;
word or syllable identical in sound
to another; verse marked by
rhyme. ▶ vt **rhymed, rhym·ing.**
make rhymes.

rhythm [RITH-əm] n measured beat
or flow, esp. of words, music, etc.
rhyth'mic adj **rhyth'mi·cal·ly** adv

rib[1] n one of curved bones
springing from spine and forming
framework of upper part of body;
cut of meat including rib(s); curved
timber of framework of boat; raised
series of rows in knitting, etc. ▶ vt
ribbed, rib·bing. furnish, mark
with ribs; knit to form a rib pattern.
rib'bing n

rib[2] vt inf **ribbed, rib·bing.** tease,
ridicule. **rib'bing** n

rib·ald [RIB-əld] adj irreverent,
scurrilous; indecent. ▶ n ribald
person. **rib'ald·ry** n vulgar,
indecent talk.

rib·bon [RIB-ən] n narrow band of
fabric used for trimming, tying,
etc.; long strip or line of anything.
ribbon development building of
houses, etc. along main road
leading out of town, etc.

ri·bo·fla·vin [RĪ-boh-flay-vin] n form
of vitamin B.

rice [rīs] n cereal plant; its seeds as
food. **rice paper** fine (edible)
Chinese paper.

rich adj **-er, -est.** wealthy; fertile;
abounding; valuable; (of food)
containing much fat or sugar;
mellow; amusing. ▶ n the wealthy
classes. **rich·es** [RICH-iz] pl n
wealth. **rich'ly** adv

rick·ets [RIK-its] *n* disease of children marked by softening of bones, bow legs, etc., caused by vitamin D deficiency. **rick'et·y** *adj* **-et·i·er, -et·i·est.** shaky, insecure, unstable; suffering from rickets.

rick·shaw [RIK-shaw] *n* light two-wheeled man-drawn Asian vehicle.

ric·o·chet [rik-ə-SHAY] *vi* **-cheted** [-SHAYD], **-chet·ing** [-SHAY-ing] (of bullet) rebound or be deflected by solid surface or water. ▶ *n* bullet or shot to which this happens.

rid *vt* **rid** or **rid·ded, rid·ding.** clear, relieve of; free; deliver. **rid·dance** [RID-ns] *n* clearance; act of ridding; deliverance; relief.

rid·den [RID-n] pp. of RIDE. *adj* afflicted or affected by the thing specified, e.g. *disease-ridden.*

rid·dle¹ [RID-l] *n* question made puzzling to test one's ingenuity; enigma; puzzling thing, person. ▶ *vi* **-dled, -dling.** speak in, make riddles.

rid·dle² *vt* **-dled, -dling.** pierce with many holes. **riddled with** full of, esp. holes.

ride [rīd] *v* **rode, rid·den, rid·ing.** sit on and control or propel (horse, bicycle, etc.); be carried on or across. ▶ *vi* go on horseback or in vehicle; lie at anchor. ▶ *vt* travel over. ▶ *n* journey on horse, etc., or in any vehicle. **rid'er** *n* one who rides; supplementary clause; addition to a document.

ridge [rij] *n* long narrow hill; long, narrow elevation on surface; line of meeting of two sloping surfaces. ▶ *vt* **ridged, ridg·ing.** form into ridges.

ri·dic·u·lous [ri-DIK-yə-ləs] *adj* deserving to be laughed at, absurd, foolish. **rid·i·cule** [RID-i-kyool] *n* treatment of person or thing as ridiculous. ▶ *vt* **-culed, -cul·ing.** laugh at, deride.

rife [rīf] *adj* prevalent, common.

rif·fle [RIF-əl] *v* **-fled, -fling.** flick through (pages, etc.) quickly.

riff'raff *n* rabble, disreputable people.

ri·fle [RĪ-fəl] *vt* **-fled, -fling.** search and rob; ransack; make spiral grooves in (gun barrel, etc.). ▶ *n* firearm with long barrel. **rifling** *n* arrangement of grooves in gun barrel; pillaging.

rift *n* crack, split, cleft.

rig *vt* **rigged, rig·ging.** provide (ship) with spars, ropes, etc.; equip; set up, esp. as makeshift; arrange in dishonest way. ▶ *n* way ship's masts and sails are arranged; apparatus for drilling for oil and gas; tractor-trailer truck; style of dress. **rigging** *n* ship's spars and ropes; lifting tackle.

right [rīt] *adj* just; in accordance with truth and duty; true; correct; proper; of side that faces east when front is turned to north; *Politics* (also **right wing**) conservative or reactionary; straight; upright; of outer or more finished side of fabric. ▶ *vt* bring back to vertical position; do justice to. ▶ *vi* come back to vertical position. ▶ *n* claim, title, etc. allowed or due; what is right, just or due; conservative political party; punch, blow with right hand. ▶ *adv* straight; properly; very; on or to right side. **right'ful** [-fəl] *adj* **right'ly** *adv* right angle; angle of 90 degrees. **right of way** *Law* right to pass over someone's land; path used; right to driver to proceed.

right·eous [RĪ-chəs] *adj* just, upright; godly; virtuous; good; honest.

rig·id [RIJ-id] *adj* inflexible; harsh, stiff. **ri·gid'i·ty** *n*

rig·ma·role [RIG-mə-rohl] *n* meaningless string of words; long, complicated procedure.

rig·or¹ [RIG-ər] *n* sudden coldness attended by shivering. **rigor mor'tis** stiffening of body after death.

rigor² *n* harshness, severity, strictness; hardship. **rig'or·ous** *adj* stern, harsh, severe.

rile [rīl] *vt* **riled, ril·ing.** *inf* anger, annoy.

rill *n* small stream.

rim *n* edge, border, margin; outer ring of wheel. ▶ *vt* **rimmed, rim·ming.** furnish with rim; coat or encrust; *Basketball, golf* of ball, go around basket, hole, and not drop in. **rimmed** *adj* bordered, edged. **rim'less** *adj*

rime [rīm] *n* hoarfrost. **rim'y** *adj* **rim·i·er, rim·i·est.**

rind [rīnd] *n* outer coating of fruits, etc.

ring¹ *n* circle of gold, etc., esp. for finger; any circular band, coil, rim, etc.; circle of persons; enclosed area, esp. roped-in square for boxing. ▶ *vt* **ringed, ring·ing.** put ring round; mark (bird, etc.) with ring. **ring'er** *n* one who rings bells; *sl* student, athlete, racehorse, etc. participating in examination, sporting event, etc. under false pretenses or fraudulently in place of another. **dead ringer** *sl* person, thing apparently identical to another. **ring'lead·er** [-leed-ər] *n* instigator of mutiny, riot, etc. **ring'let** [-lit] *n* curly lock of hair. **ring'worm** [-wurm] *n* fungal skin disease in circular patches.

ring² *vi* **rang, rung, ring·ing.** give out clear resonant sound, as bell; resound; cause (bell) to sound; telephone. ▶ *n* a ringing; telephone call.

rink [ringk] *n* sheet of ice for skating or hockey; floor for roller skating.

rinse [rins] *vt* **rinsed, rins·ing.** remove soap (from washed clothes, hair, etc.) by applying clean water; wash lightly. ▶ *n* a rinsing; liquid to tint hair.

ri·ot [RĪ-ət] *n* tumult, disorder; loud revelry; disorderly, unrestrained disturbance; profusion. ▶ *vi* make, engage in riot. **ri'ot·ous** *adj* unruly, rebellious, wanton.

R.I.P. rest in peace.

rip¹ *vt* **ripped, rip·ping.** cut, tear away, slash, rend. ▶ *n* rent, tear. **rip'cord** *n* cord pulled to open parachute. **rip'saw** *n* saw with coarse teeth (used for cutting wood along grain). **rip off** *sl* steal, cheat, overcharge. **rip'off** *n sl* act

of stealing, overcharging, etc.

rip² *n* strong current, esp. one moving away from the shore.

ri·par·i·an [ri-PAIR-ee-ən] *adj* of, on banks of river.

ripe [rīp] *adj* **rip·er, rip·est.** ready to be reaped, eaten, etc.; matured; (of judgment, etc.) sound. **rip'en** *v* grow ripe; mature.

ri·poste [ri-POHST] *n* verbal retort; counterstroke; *Fencing* quick lunge after parry.

rip·ple [RIP-əl] *n* slight wave, ruffling of surface; anything like this; sound like ripples of water. ▶ *v* **-pled, -pling.** ▶ *vi* flow, form into little waves; (of sounds) rise and fall gently. ▶ *vt* form ripples on.

rise [rīz] *vi* **rose, ris·en, ris·ing.** get up; move upward; appear above horizon; reach higher level; increase in value or price; rebel; adjourn; have its source. ▶ *n* rising; upslope; increase, esp. of prices. **ris'er** *n* one who rises, esp. from bed; vertical part of stair step. **rising** *n* revolt. ▶ *adj* increasing in rank, maturity.

ris·i·ble [RIS-ə-bəl] *adj* inclined to laugh; laughable. **ris·i·bil'i·ty** *n, pl* **-ties.**

risk *n* chance of disaster or loss. ▶ *vt* venture; put in jeopardy; take chance of. **risk'y** *adj* **risk·i·er, risk·i·est.** dangerous; hazardous.

ri·sot·to [ri-SAW-toh] *n* dish of rice cooked in stock with various other ingredients.

ris·qué [ri-SKAY] *adj* suggestive of indecency.

rite [rīt] *n* formal practice or custom, esp. religious. **rit·u·al** [RICH-oo-əl] *n* prescribed order or book of rites; regular, stereotyped action or behavior. ▶ *adj* concerning rites. **rit'u·al·ism** *n* practice of ritual.

ri·val [RĪ-vəl] *n* one that competes with another for favor, success, etc. ▶ *vt* **-valed, -val·ing.** vie with. ▶ *adj* in position of rival. **ri'val·ry** *n* keen competition.

riv·er [RIV-ər] *n* large natural stream of water; copious flow.

riv·et [RIV-it] *n* bolt for fastening metal plates, the end being put through holes and then beaten flat. ▶ *vt* **-et·ed, -et·ing.** fasten with rivets; cause to be fixed or held firmly, esp. in surprise, horror, etc. **riv'et·er** *n*

riv·u·let [RIV-yə-lit] *n* small stream.

Rn *Chem* radon.

roach [rohch] *n* cockroach; *sl* butt of marijuana cigarette.

road [rohd] *n* track, way prepared for passengers, vehicles, etc.; direction, way; street. **road'block** *n* barricade across road to stop traffic for inspection, etc. **road hog** selfish, aggressive driver. **road'run·ner** *n* large cuckoo of W US, Mexico, C Amer. able to run quickly. **road'side** *n, adj* **road'ster** *n obs* touring car. **road'work** [-wurk] *n* repairs to road; running, jogging along country roads as exercise for boxers. **road'worth·y** [-wur-*thee*] *adj* (of vehicle) mechanically sound. **road warrior** *inf* frequent business traveler.

roam [rohm] *v* wander about, rove. **roam'er** *n*

roan [rohn] *adj* (of horses) having coat in which main color is thickly interspersed with another, esp. bay, sorrel or chestnut mixed with white or gray. ▶ *n* roan horse.

roar [ror] *v* make or utter loud deep hoarse sound as of lion, thunder, voice in anger, etc. ▶ *n* such a sound. **roar'ing** *adj* brisk and profitable. ▶ *adv* noisily.

roast [rohst] *v* bake, cook in closed oven; cook by exposure to open fire; make, be very hot. ▶ *n* piece of meat for roasting; *inf* roasting. ▶ *adj* roasted. **roast'ing** *n* severe criticism, scolding; session of good-natured scolding by way of tribute to honored person.

rob *vt* **robbed, rob·bing.** plunder, steal from; pillage, defraud. **rob'ber** *n* **rob'ber·y** *n, pl* **-ber·ies.**

robe [rohb] *n* long outer garment, often denoting rank or office. ▶ *v* **robed, rob·ing.** ▶ *vt* dress. ▶ *vi* put on robes, vestments.

rob'in *n* large thrush with red breast. **robin's-egg blue** pale green to light blue.

ro·bot [ROH-bət] *n* automated machine, esp. performing functions in human manner; person of machine-like efficiency. **ro·bot·ics** [roh-BOT-iks] *n* science of designing and using robots.

ro·bust [roh-BUST] *adj* sturdy, strong. **ro·bust'ness** [-nis] *n*

roc [rok] *n* monstrous bird of Arabian mythology.

rock¹ [rok] *n* stone; large rugged mass of stone; *sl* diamond, gem. **rock'er·y** *n, pl* **-er·ies.** mound or grotto of stones or rocks for plants in a garden. **rock'y** *adj* **rock·i·er, rock·i·est.** having many rocks; rugged, presenting difficulty. **rock bottom** lowest possible level. **between a rock and a hard place** between equally unattractive alternatives.

rock² *v* (cause to) sway to and fro. ▶ *n* style of pop music derived from rock-'n'-roll. **rock'er** *n* curved piece of wood, etc. on which thing may rock. **rocking chair** chair allowing the sitter to rock backwards and forwards. **rock-'n'-roll** *n* popular dance rhythm. **rock the boat** *inf* disrupt smooth routine of company, etc. **off one's rocker** *sl* insane.

rock·et [ROK-it] *n* self-propelling device powered by burning of explosive contents (used as firework, for display, signaling, line carrying, weapon, etc.); vehicle propelled by rocket engine, as weapon or carrying spacecraft. ▶ *vi* move fast, esp. upward, as rocket. **rock'et·ry** *n*

ro·co·co [rə-KOH-koh] *adj* of furniture, architecture, etc. having much conventional decoration in style of early 18th cent. work in France; tastelessly florid.

rod *n* slender straight bar, stick; cane; old unit of length equal to 5.5 yards.

rode pt. of RIDE.

ro·dent [ROHD-nt] *n* animal with

teeth specialized for gnawing, such as a rat or squirrel.

ro·de·o [ROH-dee-oh] *n* display of skills, competition, with bareback riding, cattle handling techniques, etc.

roe [roh] *n* mass of eggs in fish.

roent·gen [RENT-gən] *n* measuring unit of radiation dose.

rogue [rohg] *n* rascal, knave, scoundrel; mischief-loving person or child; wild beast of savage temper, living apart from herd. **ro'guish** *adj*

rois·ter [ROI-stər] *vi* be noisy, boisterous, bragging. **roist'er·er** *n* reveler.

role, rôle [rohl] *n* actor's part; specific task or function.

roll [rohl] *v* move by turning over and over. ▶ *vt* wind around; smooth out with roller. ▶ *vi* move, sweep along; undulate; of ship, swing from side to side; of aircraft, turn about a line from nose to tail in flight. ▶ *n* act of lying down and turning over and over or from side to side; piece of paper, etc. rolled up; any object thus shaped, e.g. jelly roll; list, catalogue; bread baked into small oval or round; continuous sound, as of drums, thunder, etc. **roll'er** *n* cylinder of wood, stone, metal, etc. used for pressing, crushing, smoothing, supporting thing to be moved, winding thing on, etc.; long wave of sea. **roll call** act, time of calling over list of names, as in schools or army. **roller bearings** bearings of hardened steel rollers.

Roll'er·blade *n* ® roller skate with the wheels set in a straight line, mounted on a boot. **roller coaster** small gravity railroad in amusement park with steep ascents and descents for frightening riders; any experience with similar ups and downs. **roller skate** skate with wheels instead of runner. **roller towel** loop of towel on roller. **rolling pin** cylindrical roller for pastry or dough. **rolling stock** locomotives, freight cars, etc. of

railroad. **roll top** *n* in desk, flexible lid sliding in grooves; such a desk. **roll up** appear, turn up; increase, accumulate.

rol·lick·ing [ROL-i-king] *adj* boisterously jovial and merry.

ro·ly-po·ly [ROH-lee-poh-lee] *adj* round, plump. ▶ *n* round, plump person or thing.

ROM [rom] *Computers* read-only memory (permanently recorded on a computer chip).

Rom. Romans.

Ro·man [ROH-mən] *adj* of Rome or Roman Catholic Church. **Roman Catholic** member of Roman Catholic Church. **Roman Catholic Church** the Christian church that acknowledges supremacy of the Pope. **Roman numerals** letters I, V, X, L, C, D, M used to represent numbers in manner of Romans. **roman type** plain upright letters, ordinary style of printing.

roman á clef [roh-mah-na-KLAY] *n*, *pl* **romans á clef** [roh-mah-na-KLAY] *Fr* novel that disguises real events and people.

ro·mance [roh-MANS] *n* love affair, esp. intense and happy one; mysterious or exciting quality; tale of chivalry; tale with scenes remote from ordinary life; literature like this; picturesque falsehood. ▶ *v* **-manced, -manc·ing.** ▶ *vi* exaggerate, fantasize. ▶ *vt inf* woo, court. **Romance language** any of vernacular languages of certain countries, developed from Latin, as French, Spanish, etc. **ro·man'tic** *adj* characterized by romance; of or dealing with love; of literature, etc., preferring passion and imagination to proportion and finish. ▶ *n* **ro·man'ti·cism** [-ti-sizm] *n* **ro·man'ti·cize** *vi* **-cized, -ciz·ing.** **Ro·man·esque** [rohm-ən-NESK] *adj, n* (in) style of round-arched vaulted architecture of period between Classical and Gothic.

romp *vi* run, play wildly, joyfully. ▶ *n* spell of romping; easy victory. **romp·ers** [-ərz] *pl n* child's loose one-piece garment. **romp home**

win easily.

ron·deau [ron-DOH] *n, pl* **-deaux** [-DOHZ] short poem with opening words used as refrain. **ron·del'** *n* extended rondeau. **ron·de·let** [ron-dl-ET] *n* short rondeau.

ron·do [RON-doh] *n, pl* **-dos.** piece of music with leading theme to which return is continually made.

roof *n, pl* **roofs.** outside upper covering of building; top, covering part of anything. ▶ *vt* put roof on, over.

rook[1] [ruuk] *n* bird of crow family. ▶ *vt* swindle, cheat. **rook'er·y** *n, pl* **-er·ies.** colony of rooks.

rook[2] *n* chess piece shaped like a castle.

rook·ie [RUUK-ee] *n* recruit, esp. in army; *Sports* professional athlete playing in first season.

room *n* space; space enough; division of house; scope, opportunity. ▶ *pl* lodgings. **room'y** *adj* **room·i·er, room·i·est.** spacious.

roost *n* perch for poultry. ▶ *vi* perch. **roost'er** *n* male of domestic fowl; cock.

root[1] *n* part of plant that grows down into earth and conveys nourishment to plant; plant with edible root, such as a carrot; vital part; (also **roots**) source, origin, original cause of anything; *Anatomy* embedded portion of tooth, nail, hair, etc.; primitive word from which other words are derived; factor of a quantity that, when multiplied by itself the number of times indicated, gives the quantity. ▶ *v* (cause to) take root; pull by roots; dig, burrow.

root[2] *vi* cheer; applaud; encourage. **root'er** *n*

rope [rohp] *n* thick cord. ▶ *vt* **roped, rop·ing.** secure, mark off with rope. **rope in** *inf* entice, lure by deception.

ro·sa·ry [ROH-zə-ree] *n, pl* **-ries.** series of prayers; string of beads for counting these prayers as they are recited; rose garden, bed of roses.

rose[1] [rohz] *n* shrub, climbing plant usu. with prickly stems and fragrant flowers; the flower; perforated flat nozzle for hose, watering can, etc.; pink color. ▶ *adj* of this color.

ro·se·ate [ROH-zee-it] *adj* rose-colored, rosy. **ro·sette** [roh-ZET] *n* rose-shaped bunch of ribbon; rose-shaped architectural ornament. **ros'y** *adj* **ros·i·er, ros·i·est.** flushed; hopeful, promising. **rose-colored** *adj* having color of rose; unwarrantably optimistic. **rose window** circular window with series of mullions branching from center. **rose of Sharon** [SHAR-ən] low, spreading small tree or shrub with white, purplish or red flowers.

rose[2] pt. of RISE.

ro·sé [roh-ZAY] *n* pink wine.

rose·mar·y [ROHZ-mair-ee] *n* evergreen fragrant flowering shrub; its leaves and flowers used as seasoning.

Ro·si·cru·cian [roh-zi-KROO-shən] *n* member of secret order devoted to occult law. ▶ *adj* **Ro·si·cru'cian·ism** *n*

ros·in [ROZ-in] *n* resin esp. used for rubbing on bows of violins, etc.

ros·ter [ROS-tər] *n* list or plan showing turns of duty.

ros·trum [ROS-trəm] *n, pl* **-tra** [-trə] *or* **-trums.** platform, stage, pulpit; beak or bill of a bird.

rot *v* **rot·ted, rot·ting.** decompose naturally; corrupt. ▶ *n* decay, putrefaction; any disease producing decomposition of tissue; nonsense. **rot'ten** *adj* decomposed, putrid; corrupt.

ro·ta·ry [ROH-tə-ree] *adj* (of movement) circular; operated by rotary movement. **ro·tate** [ROH-tayt] *v* **-tat·ed, -tat·ing.** (cause to) move around center or on pivot. **ro·ta'tion** *n* rotating; regular succession. **Rotary Club** one of international association of businessmen's clubs. **Ro·tar'i·an** *n* member of such.

rote [roht] *n* habitual, mechanical repetition. **by rote** by memory.

ro·tis·ser·ie [roh-TIS-ə-ree] *n* (electrically driven) rotating spit for cooking meat.

ro·tor [ROH-tər] *n* rotating portion of a dynamo motor or turbine.

rotten see ROT.

ro·tund [roh-TUND] *adj* round; plump; sonorous. **ro·tun′di·ty** *n*

rouble see RUBLE.

rou·é [roo-AY] *n* dissolute or dissipated man; rake.

rouge [rooʑh] *n* red powder, cream used to color cheeks. ▶ *v* **rouged, roug·ing.** color with rouge.

rough [ruf] *adj* **-er, -est.** not smooth, of irregular surface; violent, stormy, boisterous; rude; uncivil; lacking refinement; approximate; in preliminary form. ▶ *vt* make rough; plan out approximately; (with *it*) live without usual comforts, etc. ▶ *n* rough condition or area; sketch. **diamond in the rough** excellent, valuable but unsophisticated person. **rough′en** [-n] *vt*

rough·age [RUF-ij] *n* unassimilated portion of food promoting proper intestinal action. **rough′house** [-hows] *n, v* **-housed, -hous·ing.** fight, row.

rou·lette [roo-LET] *n* game of chance played with revolving dishlike wheel and ball.

round [rownd] *adj* **-er, -est.** spherical, cylindrical, circular, curved; full, complete; roughly correct; large, considerable; plump; unqualified, positive. ▶ *adv* with circular or circuitous course. ▶ *n* thing round in shape; recurrent duties; stage in competition; customary course, as of postman; game (of golf); one of several periods in boxing match, etc.; cartridge for firearm; rung; movement in circle. ▶ *prep* about; on all sides of. ▶ *v* make, become round. ▶ *vt* move around. **round′ers** *n* British ball game resembling baseball. **round′ly** *adv* plainly; thoroughly. **round·a·bout′** *adj* not straightforward. **round robin** sports tournament in which all contestants play one another. **round up** drive (cattle) together;

collect and arrest criminals.

roun·de·lay [ROWN-dl-ay] *n* simple song with refrain.

rouse [rowz] *v* **roused, rous·ing.** ▶ *vt* wake up, stir up, excite to action; cause to rise. ▶ *vi* waken.

roust·a·bout [ROWST-ə-bowt] *n* laborer working in circus, oil rig, etc.

rout [rowt] *n* overwhelming defeat, disorderly retreat; noisy rabble. ▶ *vt* scatter and put to flight.

route [root] *n* road, chosen way. **go the route** *inf* see through to the end; *Baseball* pitch complete game.

rou·tine [roo-TEEN] *n* regularity of procedure, unvarying round; regular course. ▶ *adj* ordinary, regular.

roux [roo] *n* fat and flour cooked together as thickener for sauces.

rove [rohv] *v* **roved, rov·ing.** wander, roam. **rov′er** *n* one who roves; pirate.

row¹ [roh] *n* number of things in a straight line; rank; file; line.

row² *v* propel boat by oars. ▶ *n* spell of rowing. **row′boat** *n*

row³ [rhymes with **cow**] *n* dispute; disturbance. ▶ *vi* quarrel noisily.

row·dy [ROW-dee] *adj* **-di·er, -di·est.** disorderly, noisy and rough. ▶ *n* person like this.

roy·al [ROI-əl] *adj* of, worthy of, befitting, patronized by, king or queen; splendid. **roy′al·ist** *n* supporter of monarchy. **roy′al·ty** *n* royal dignity or power; royal persons; payment to owner of land for right to work minerals, or to inventor for use of invention; payment to author depending on sales.

Ru *Chem* ruthenium.

rub *v* **rubbed, rub·bing.** ▶ *vt* apply pressure to with circular or backward and forward movement; clean, polish, dry, thus; pass hand over; abrade, chafe; remove by friction. ▶ *vi* come into contact accompanied by friction; become frayed or worn by friction. ▶ *n* rubbing; impediment.

rub·ber¹ [RUB-ər] *n* coagulated sap

of rough, elastic consistency, of certain tropical trees; piece of rubber, etc. used for erasing; thing for rubbing; person who rubs; *sl* condom. ▶ *adj* of rubber.

rub·ber·ize *vt* **-ized, -iz·ing.** coat, impregnate, treat with rubber. **rub'ber·y** *adj* **rub'ber·neck** *v* gawk at. **rubber stamp** device for imprinting dates, etc.; automatic authorization.

rubber² *n* series of odd number of games or contests at various games, such as bridge; two out of three games won. **rubber match** deciding contest between tied opponents.

rub·bish [RUB-ish] *n* refuse, waste material, garbage; anything worthless; trash, nonsense. **rub'bish·y** *adj* valueless.

rub·ble [RUB-əl] *n* fragments of stone, etc.; builders' rubbish.

ru·bel·la [roo-BEL-ə] *n* mild contagious viral disease, German measles.

ru·bi·cund [ROO-bi-kund] *adj* ruddy.

ru·ble, rou·ble [ROO-bəl] *n* unit of currency of Russia and Belarus.

ru·bric [ROO-brik] *n* title, heading; direction in liturgy; instruction.

ru·by [ROO-bee] *n* **-bies.** precious red gem; its color. ▶ *adj* of this color.

ruck·sack [RUK-sak] *n* pack carried on back, knapsack.

ruck·us [RUK-əs] *n* uproar, disturbance.

rud·der [RUD-ər] *n* flat piece hinged to boat's stern or rear of aircraft to steer by.

rud·dy [RUD-ee] *adj* **-di·er, -di·est.** of fresh or healthy red color; rosy; florid.

rude [rood] *adj* impolite; coarse; vulgar; primitive; roughly made; uneducated; sudden, violent. **rude'ly** *adv* **rude'ness** *n*

ru·di·ments [ROO-də-mənts] *pl n* elements, first principles. **ru·di·men'ta·ry** *adj*

rue¹ [roo] *v* **rued, ru·ing.** grieve for; regret; deplore; repent. ▶ *n* sorrow;

repentance. **rue'ful** [-fəl] *adj* sorry; regretful; dejected; deplorable.

rue² *n* plant with evergreen bitter leaves.

ruff¹ *n* starched and frilled collar; natural collar of feathers, fur, etc. on some birds and animals; type of shore bird. **ruf'fle** *vt* **-fled, -fling.** rumple, disorder; annoy, put out; frill, pleat. ▶ *n* frilled trimming.

ruff² *n, v* Cards trump.

ruf·fi·an [RUF-ee-ən] *n* violent, lawless person.

rug *n* small, oft. shaggy or thick-piled floor mat; thick woolen wrap, coverlet; *sl* toupee, hairpiece. **rug'rat** *n inf* small child.

rug·by [RUG-bee] *n* form of football with two teams of 15 players.

rug·ged [RUG-id] *adj* rough; broken; unpolished; harsh, austere.

ru·in [ROO-in] *n* decay, destruction; downfall; fallen or broken state; loss of wealth, position, etc. ▶ *pl* ruined buildings, etc. ▶ *vt* reduce to ruins; bring to decay or destruction; spoil; impoverish. **ru·in·a'tion** *n* **ru'in·ous** *adj* causing or characterized by ruin or destruction.

rule [rool] *n* principle; precept; authority; government; what is usual; control; measuring stick. ▶ *vt* **ruled, rul·ing.** govern; decide; mark with straight lines; draw (line). **rul'er** *n* one who governs; stick for measuring or ruling lines.

rum *n* liquor distilled from sugar cane.

rum·ba [RUM-bə] *n, pl* **-bas.** rhythmic dance, orig. Cuban; music for it.

rum·ble [RUM-bəl] *vi* **-bled, -bling.** make noise as of distant thunder, heavy vehicle, etc.; *sl* engage in gang street fight. ▶ *n* noise like thunder, etc.; gang street fight.

ru·mi·nate [ROO-mə-nayt] *vi* **-nat·ed, -nat·ing.** chew cud; ponder over; meditate. **ru'mi·nant** [-nənt] *adj, n* cud-chewing (animal). **ru·mi·na'tion** [-NAY-shən] *n* quiet meditation and reflection. **ru'mi·na·tive**

[-mə-nə-tiv] *adj*
rum·mage [RUM-ij] *v* **-maged,
-mag·ing.** search thoroughly. ▶ *n*
rummage sale sale of
miscellaneous, usu. secondhand,
items.
rum·my¹ [RUM-ee] *n* card game.
rum·my² [RUM-ee] *n, pl* **-mies.** *sl*
drunkard.
ru·mor [ROO-mər] *n* hearsay,
common talk, unproved statement.
▶ *vt* put out as, by way of, rumor.
rump *n* tail end; buttocks.
rum·ple [RUM-pəl] *v, n* **-pled,
-pling.** crease, wrinkle.
rum·pus [RUM-pəs] *n, pl* **-us·es.**
disturbance; noise and confusion.
run *v* **ran, run, run·ning.** ▶ *vi* move
with more rapid gait than walking;
go quickly; flow; flee; compete in
race, contest, election; revolve;
continue; function; travel
according to schedule; fuse; melt;
spread over; have certain meaning.
▶ *vt* cross by running; expose
oneself (to risk, etc.); cause to run;
(of newspaper) print, publish;
transport and dispose of (smuggled
goods); manage; operate. ▶ *n* act,
spell of running; rush; tendency;
course; period; sequence; heavy
demand; enclosure for domestic
poultry, animals; ride in car; series
of unraveled stitches, ladder; score
of one at baseball; steep
snow-covered course for skiing.
run'ner *n* racer; messenger; curved
piece of wood on which sleigh
slides; any similar appliance;
slender stem of plant running
along ground forming new roots at
intervals; strip of cloth, carpet.
running *adj* continuous;
consecutive; flowing; discharging;
effortless; entered for race; used for
running. ▶ *n* act of moving or
flowing quickly; management.
run'ny *adj* **-ni·er, -ni·est.** tending
to flow or exude moisture.
run'down *n* summary. **run-down**
adj exhausted. **run down** stop
working; reduce; exhaust;
denigrate. **run'way** *n* level stretch
where aircraft take off and land. **in**

the running having fair chance in
competition.
rung¹ *n* crossbar or spoke, esp. in
ladder.
rung² pp. of RING².
runt *n* small animal, below usual
size of species; *offens* undersized
person.
ru·pee [roo-PEE] *n* monetary unit of
India and Pakistan.
rup·ture [RUP-chər] *n* breaking,
breach; hernia. ▶ *v* **-tured, tur·ing.**
break; burst, sever.
ru·ral [RUUR-əl] *adj* of the country;
rustic.
ruse [rooz] *n* stratagem, trick.
rush¹ *vt* impel, carry along violently
and rapidly; take by sudden assault.
▶ *vi* cause to hurry; move violently
or rapidly. ▶ *n* rushing, charge;
hurry; eager demand for; heavy
current (of air, water, etc.). ▶ *adj*
done with speed; characterized by
speed. **rush hour** period at
beginning and end of day when
many people are traveling to and
from work.
rush² *n* marsh plant with slender
pithy stem; the stems as material
for baskets.
rusk *n* kind of sweet raised bread
esp. used for feeding babies.
rus·set [RUS-it] *adj* reddish-brown.
▶ *n* the color; apple with skin of this
color.
rust *n* reddish-brown coating
formed on iron by oxidation;
disease of plants. ▶ *v* contract,
affect with rust. **rust'y** *adj*
rust·i·er, rust·i·est. coated with
rust, of rust color; out of practice.
rust'proof *adj*
rus·tic [RUS-tik] *adj* of, or as of,
country people; rural; of rough
manufacture; made of untrimmed
tree limbs. ▶ *n* country person,
peasant. **rus'ti·cate** *v* **-cat·ed,
-cat·ing.** ▶ *vt* send to, house in,
country. ▶ *vi* live a country life.
rus·tle¹ [RUS-əl] *vi* **-tled, -tling.**
make sound as of blown dead
leaves, etc. ▶ *n* this sound.
rustle² *vt* **-tled, -tling.** steal (cattle).
rus'tler *n* cattle thief.

rut[1] *n* furrow made by wheel; settled habit or way of living; groove. **rut'ty** *adj* **-ti·er, -ti·est.**

rut[2] *n* periodic sexual excitement among animals. ▶ *vi* **rut·ted, rut·ting.** be under influence of this.

ruth·less [ROOTH-lis] *adj* pitiless, merciless.

RV *n* recreational vehicle.

rye [rī] *n* grain used for forage and bread; plant bearing it; whisky made from rye.

S s

S *Chem* sulfur.

Sab·bath [SAB-əth] *n* Saturday, devoted to worship and rest from work in Judaism and certain Christian churches; Sunday, observed by Christians as day of worship and rest. **sab·bat·i·cal** [sə-BAT-ə-kəl] *adj, n* (denoting) leave granted to university staff, etc. for study.

sa·ber [SAY-bər] *n* curved cavalry sword; fencing sword having two cutting edges and blunt point.

sa·ble [SAY-bəl] *n* small weasellike animal of cold regions; its fur; black. ▶ *adj* black.

sab·o·tage [SAB-ə-tahzh] *n* intentional damage done to roads, machines, etc., esp. secretly in war. ▶ *v* **-taged, -tag·ing. sab·o·teur** [sab-ə-TUR] *n*

sac [sak] *n* pouchlike structure in an animal or vegetable body.

sac·cha·rin [SAK-ər-in] *n* artificial sweetener. **sac'cha·rine** [-in] *adj* excessively sweet.

sac·er·do·tal [sas-ər-DOHT-l] *adj* of priests.

sa·chet [sa-SHAY] *n* small envelope or bag, esp. one holding scented powder.

sack [sak] *n* large bag, orig. of coarse material; pillaging; *sl* dismissal; *sl* bed. ▶ *vt* pillage (captured town); *sl* fire (person) from a job. **sack'ing** *n* material for sacks. **sack·cloth** [SAK-klawth] *n* coarse fabric used for sacks and worn as sign of mourning.

sac·ra·ment [SAK-rə-mənt] *n* one of certain ceremonies of Christian church esp. Eucharist. **sac·ra·men'tal** *adj*

sa·cred [SAY-krid] *adj* dedicated, regarded as holy; set apart, reserved; inviolable; connected with, intended for religious use.

sac·ri·fice [SAK-rə-fīs] *n* giving something up for sake of something else; act of giving up; thing so given up; making of offering to a god; thing offered. ▶ *vt* **-ficed, -fic·ing.** offer as sacrifice; give up; sell at very cheap price. **sac·ri·fi'cial** [-FISH-l] *adj*

sac·ri·lege [SAK-rə-lij] *n* misuse, desecration of something sacred. **sac·ri·leg'ious** [-LEEJ-əs] *adj* profane; desecrating.

sac·ro·sanct [SAK-roh-sangkt] *adj* preserved by religious fear against desecration or violence; inviolable.

sac·rum [SAK-rəm] *n, pl* **sac·ra** [SAK-rə] five vertebrae forming compound bone at base of spinal column.

sad *adj* **sad·der, sad·dest.** sorrowful; unsatisfactory, deplorable. **sad·den** [SAD-n] *vt* make sad.

sad·dle [SAD-l] *n* rider's seat to fasten on horse, bicycle, etc.; anything resembling a saddle; cut of mutton, venison, etc. for roasting; ridge of hill. ▶ *vt* **-dled, -dling.** put saddle on; lay burden, responsibility on.

sa·dism [SAY-diz-əm] *n* form of (sexual) perversion marked by love of inflicting pain. **sa'dist** *n* **sa·dis·tic** [sə-DIS-tik] *adj*

sa·fa·ri [sə-FAH-ree] *n* (party making) overland (hunting) journey, esp. in Africa. **safari park** park where lions, etc. may be viewed by public from automobiles.

safe [sayf] *adj* **saf·er, saf·est.** secure, protected; uninjured, out of danger; not involving risk; trustworthy; sure, reliable; cautious. ▶ *n* strong lockable container; structure for storing meat, etc. **safe'ly** *adv* **safe'ty** *n* **safe-conduct** [KON-dukt] *n* a permit to pass somewhere. **safe'guard** [-GAHRD] *n* protection. ▶ *vt* protect. **safety glass** glass resistant to fragmenting when broken.

saf·fron [SAF-rən] *n* crocus; orange

colored flavoring obtained from it; the color. ▶ *adj* orange.

sag *vi* **sagged, sagging.** sink in middle; hang sideways; curve downward under pressure; give way; tire; (of clothes) hang loosely. ▶ *n* droop.

sa·ga [SAH-gə] *n* legend of Norse heroes; any long (heroic) story.

sa·ga·cious [sə-GAY-shəs] *adj* wise. **sa·gac'i·ty** [-GAS-i-tee] *n*

sage[1] [sayj] *n* very wise person. ▶ *adj* **sag·er, sag·est.** wise.

sage[2] *n* aromatic herb.

said [sed] pt./pp. of SAY.

sail [sayl] *n* piece of fabric stretched to catch wind for propelling ship, etc.; act of sailing; journey upon the water; ships collectively; arm of windmill. ▶ *vi* travel by water; move smoothly; begin voyage. ▶ *vt* navigate. **sail'or** *n* seaman; one who sails. **sail'board** [-bord] *n* craft used for windsurfing like surfboard with mast and single sail.

saint [saynt] *n* (title of) person formally recognized (esp. by R.C. Church) after death, as having gained by holy deeds a special place in heaven; exceptionally good person. **saint'ed** [-id] *adj* canonized; sacred. **saint'li·ness** [-nis] *n* holiness. **saint'ly** *adj*

sake[1] [sayk] *n* cause, account; end, purpose. **for the sake of** on behalf of; to please or benefit.

sa·ke[2] [SAH-kee] *n* Japanese alcoholic drink made of fermented rice.

sa·laam [sə-LAHM] *n* bow of salutation, mark of respect in East. ▶ *vt* salute.

salable *adj* see SALE.

sa·la·cious [sə-LAY-shəs] *adj* excessively concerned with sex, lewd.

sal·ad [SAL-əd] *n* mixed vegetables, or fruit, used as food without cooking, oft. combined with fish, meat, etc. ▶ *adj* **salad days** period of youthful inexperience. **salad dressing** oil, vinegar, herbs, etc. mixed together as sauce for salad.

sal·a·man·der [SAL-ə-man-dər] *n*

variety of lizard; portable space heater.

sa·la·mi [sə-LAH-mee] *n* variety of highly-spiced sausage.

sal·a·ry [SAL-ə-ree] *n, pl* **-ries.** fixed regular payment to persons employed usu. in nonmanual work. **sal'a·ried** *adj*

sale [sayl] *n* selling; selling of goods at unusually low prices; auction. **sal'a·ble** *adj* capable of being sold. **sales'per·son** *n* one who sells goods, etc. in store; one traveling to sell goods, esp. as representative of firm. **sales'man·ship** *n* art of selling or presenting goods in most effective way.

sa·li·ent [SAY-lee-ənt] *adj* prominent, noticeable; jutting out. ▶ *n* salient angle, esp. in fortification or line of battle.

sa·line [SAY-leen] *adj* containing, consisting of a chemical salt, esp. common salt; salty. **sa·lin·i·ty** [sə-LIN-i-tee] *n*

sa·li·va [sə-LI-və] *n* liquid that forms in mouth, spittle. **sal·i·var·y** [SAL-ə-ver-ee] *adj* **sal'i·vate** *v* **-vat·ed, -vat·ing.**

sal·low [SAL-oh] *adj* of unhealthy pale or yellowish color.

sal·ly [SAL-ee] *n, pl* **-lies.** rushing out, esp. by troops; outburst; witty remark. ▶ *vi* **-lied, -ly·ing.** rush; set out.

salm·on [SAM-ən] *n* large silvery fish with orange-pink flesh valued as food; color of its flesh. ▶ *adj* of this color.

sal·mo·nel·la [sal-mə-NEL-ə] *n, pl* **-lae** [-nee] bacteria causing disease (esp. food poisoning).

sa·lon [sə-LON] *n* (reception room for) guests in fashionable household; commercial premises of hairdressers, beauticians, etc.

sa·loon [sə-LOON] *n* principal cabin or sitting room in passenger ship; bar; public room for specified use, e.g. billiards.

salt [sawlt] *n* white powdery or granular crystalline substance consisting mainly of sodium chloride, used to season or preserve food; chemical compound of acid and metal; wit. ▶ vt season, sprinkle with, spread, preserve with salt. **salt'y** adj **salt·i·er, salt·i·est.** of, like salt. **old salt** sailor. **salt'cel·lar** [-sel-ər] n salt shaker. **salt lick** deposit, block of salt licked by game, cattle, etc. **salt pan** n depression encrusted with salt after partial draining away of water. **salt·pe·ter** [sawlt-PEE-tər] n potassium nitrate used in gunpowder. **with a pinch of salt** allowing for exaggeration. **worth one's salt** efficient.

sa·lu·bri·ous [sə-LOO-bree-əs] adj favorable to health, beneficial.

Sa·lu·ki [sə-LOO-kee] n tall hound with silky coat.

sal·u·tar·y [SAL-yə-ter-ee] adj wholesome, resulting in good.

sa·lute [sə-LOOT] v **-lut·ed, -lut·ing.** ▶ vt greet with words or sign; acknowledge with praise. ▶ vi perform military salute. ▶ n word, sign by which one greets another; motion of arm as mark of respect to superior, etc. in military usage; firing of guns as military greeting of honor. **sal·u·ta'tion** [-yə-TAY-shən] n

sal·vage [SAL-vij] n act of saving ship or other property from danger of loss; property so saved. ▶ vt **-vaged, -vag·ing.**

sal·va·tion [sal-VAY-shən] n fact or state of being saved, esp. of soul.

salve [sav] n healing ointment. ▶ vt **salved, salv·ing.** anoint with such, soothe.

sal·ver [SAL-vər] n (silver) tray for presentation of food, letters, etc.

sal·vo [SAL-voh] n, pl **-vos** or **-voes.** simultaneous discharge of guns, etc.

Sam. Samuel.

Sa·mar·i·tan [sə-MAR-i-tn] n native of ancient Samaria; (**s-**) benevolent person.

sam·ba [SAM-bə] n dance of S Amer. origin; music for it.

same [saym] adj identical, not different, unchanged; uniform; just mentioned previously. **same'ness**

[-nis] n similarity; monotony.

sam·o·var [SAM-ə-vahr] n Russian tea urn.

Sam·o·yed [sam-ə-YED] n dog with thick white coat and tightly curled tail.

sam'pan n small oriental boat.

sam·ple [SAM-pəl] n specimen. ▶ vt **-pled, -pling.** take, give sample of; try; test; select; use part of (old sound recording) in new recording. **sam'pler** n beginner's exercise in embroidery. **sampling** n the taking of samples; sample.

sam·u·rai [SAM-uu-rī] n, pl **samurai.** member of ancient Japanese warrior caste.

san·a·to·ri·um [san-ə-TOR-ee-əm] n, pl **-ri·ums** or **-ri·a** [-ree-ə] hospital, esp. for chronically ill; health resort.

sanc·ti·fy [SANGK-tə-fī] vt **-fied, -fying.** set apart as holy; free from sin. **sanc·ti·fi·ca'tion** n **sanc'ti·ty** n, pl **-ti·ties.** saintliness; sacredness; inviolability. **sanc'tu·ar·y** [-choo-er-ee] n, pl **-ar·ies.** holy place; part of church nearest altar; place of special holiness in synagogue; place where fugitive was safe from arrest or violence; place protected by law where animals, etc. can live without interference. **sanc·tum** [SANGK-təm] n sacred place or shrine; person's private room. **sanctum sanc·to·rum** [sangk-TOR-əm] n holy of holies in Temple in Jerusalem; sanctum.

sanc·ti·mo·ni·ous [sangk-tə-MOH-nee-əs] adj making a show of piety, holiness. **sanc·ti·mo'ni·ous·ness** n

sanc·tion [SANGK-shən] n permission, authorization; penalty for breaking law. ▶ pl boycott or other coercive measure esp. by one country against another regarded as having violated a law, right, etc. ▶ vt allow, authorize, permit.

sand n substance consisting of small grains of rock or mineral, esp. on beach or in desert. ▶ pl stretches or banks of this, usually forming seashore. ▶ *vt* polish, smooth with sandpaper; cover, mix with sand. **sand'er** *n* (power) tool for smoothing surfaces. **sand'y** *adj* **sand·i·er, sand·i·est.** like sand; sand-colored; consisting of, covered with sand. **sand'bag** *n* bag filled with sand or soil, used as protection against gunfire, floodwater, etc. and as weapon. ▶ *vt* **-bagged, -bag·ging.** beat, hit with sandbag; *inf* in football, tackle passer as if from ambush.

sand'blast *n* jet of sand blown from a nozzle under pressure for cleaning, grinding, etc. ▶ *vt* **sand'pa·per** *n* paper with sand stuck on it for scraping or polishing wood, etc. **sand'pit, sand'box** *n* quantity of sand for children to play in. **sand'stone** *n* rock composed of sand.

san·dal [SAN-dl] *n* shoe consisting of sole attached by straps.

sand'wich *n* two slices of bread with meat or other food between; anything resembling this. ▶ *vt* insert between two other things.

sane [sayn] *adj* **san·er, san·est.** of sound mind, sensible, rational. **san·i·ty** [SAN-i-tee] *n*

sang pt. of SING.

sang-froid [sahn-FRWAH] *n Fr* composure; indifference; self-possession.

san·guine [SANG-gwin] *adj* cheerful, confident; ruddy in complexion. **san·gui·nar·y** [SANG-gwə-ner-ee] *adj* accompanied by bloodshed; bloodthirsty.

san·i·tar·y [SAN-i-ter-ee] *adj* helping protection of health against dirt, etc. **san·i·ta'tion** *n* measures, apparatus for preservation of public health.

sank pt. of SINK.

San'skrit *n* ancient language of India.

sap[1] *n* moisture that circulates in plants; energy. ▶ *v* **sapped, sap·ping.** drain off sap. **sap'ling** *n* young tree.

sap[2] *v* **sapped, sap·ping.**

undermine; destroy insidiously; weaken. ▶ *n* trench dug in order to approach or undermine enemy position. **sap'per** [-pər] *n* soldier doing this.

sap[3] *n sl* foolish, gullible person.

sa·pi·ent [SAY-pee-ənt] *adj usu. ironical* wise; discerning; shrewd; knowing. **sa'pi·ence** *n*

Sap·phic [SAF-ik] *adj* of Sappho, a Grecian poet; denoting a kind of verse. ▶ *n* Sapphic verse. **sap'phism** [SAF-iz-əm] *n* lesbianism.

sap·phire [SAF-īr] *n* (usu. blue) precious stone; deep blue. ▶ *adj*

sar·a·band [SAR-ə-band] *n* slow, stately Spanish dance; music for it.

sar·casm [SAHR-kaz-əm] *n* bitter or wounding ironic remark; such remarks; taunt; sneer; irony; use of such expressions. **sar·cas'tic** [-KAS-tik] *adj* **sar·cas'ti·cal·ly** *adv*

sar·coph·a·gous [sahr-KOF-ə-gəs] *adj* carnivorous.

sar·coph·a·gus [sahr-KOF-ə-gəs] *n, pl* **-gi** [-jī] stone coffin.

sar·dine [sahr-DEEN] *n* small fish of herring family, usu. preserved in oil.

sar·don·ic [sahr-DON-ik] *adj* characterized by irony, mockery or derision.

sar·don·yx [sahr-DON-iks] *n* gemstone, variety of chalcedony.

sar·gas·sum [sahr-GAS-əm], **sar·gas·so** [-GAS-oh] *n* gulfweed, type of floating seaweed.

sa·ri [SAHR-ee] *n, pl* **-ris.** Hindu woman's robe.

sa·rong [sə-RAWNG] *n* skirtlike garment worn in Asian and Pacific countries.

sar·sa·pa·ril·la [sas-pə-RIL-ə] *n* (flavor of) drink like root beer orig. made from root of plant.

sar·to·ri·al [sahr-TOR-ee-əl] *adj* of tailor, tailoring, or men's clothes.

sash[1] *n* decorative belt, ribbon, wound around the body.

sash[2] *n* window frame opened by moving up and down in grooves.

sas·sa·fras [SAS-ə-fras] *n* tree of laurel family with aromatic bark used medicinally.

sat pt./pp. of SIT.

Sa·tan [SAYT-n] *n* the devil.
sa·tan'ic [sə-TAN-ik], **sa·tan'i·cal** *adj* devilish, fiendish.

satch·el [SACH-əl] *n* small bag, oft. with shoulder strap.

sate [sayt] *vt* **sat·ed, sat·ing.** satisfy a desire or appetite fully or excessively.

sat·el·lite [SAT-l-īt] *n* celestial body or manmade projectile orbiting planet; person, country, etc. dependent on another.

sa·ti·ate [SAY-shee-ayt] *vt* **-at·ed, at·ing.** satisfy to the full; surfeit. **sa·ti·a'tion** *n* **sa·ti·e·ty** [sə-TĪ-i-tee] *n* feeling of having had too much.

sat·in [SAT-n] *n* fabric (of silk, nylon, etc.) with glossy surface on one side. **sat'in·y** *adj* of, like satin.

sat·ire [SAT-īr] *n* composition in which vice, folly or foolish person is held up to ridicule; use of ridicule or sarcasm to expose vice and folly. **sa·tir·i·cal** [sə-TIR-i-kəl] *adj* of nature of satire; sarcastic; bitter. **sat'i·rist** *n* **sat'i·rize** *vt* **-rized, -riz·ing.** make object of satire; censure thus.

sat·is·fy [SAT-is-fī] *vt* **-fied, -fy·ing.** content, meet wishes of; pay; fulfill, supply adequately; convince. **sat·is·fac'tion** *n* **sat·is·fac'to·ry** *adj*

sa·trap [SAY-trap] *n* provincial governor in ancient Persia; subordinate ruler, oft. despotic.

sat·u·rate [SACH-ə-rayt] *vt* **-rat·ed, -rat·ing.** soak thoroughly; cause to absorb maximum amount; *Chem* cause substance to combine to its full capacity with another; shell or bomb heavily. **sat·u·ra'tion** *n* act, result of saturating.

Sat·urn [SAT-ərn] *n* Roman god; one of planets. **sat·ur·nine** [SAT-ər-nīn] *adj* gloomy; sluggish in temperament, dull, morose. **Sat·ur·na'li·a** [-NAY-lee-ə] *n, pl* **-li·as.** ancient festival of Saturn; (**s-**) noisy revelry, orgy.

sa·tyr [SAY-tər] *n* woodland deity, part man, part goat; lustful man.

sauce [saws] *n* liquid added to food to enhance flavor; *inf* impudence; *sl* whiskey. ▶ *vt* **sauced, sauc·ing.** add

sauce to; *inf* be cheeky, impudent to. **sau'ci·ly** *adv* **sau'cy** *adj* **-ci·er, -ci·est.** impudent. **sauce'pan** *n* cooking pot with long handle.

sau·cer [SAW-sər] *n* curved plate put under cup; shallow depression.

sau·er·kraut [SOW-ər-krowt] *n* German dish of finely shredded and pickled cabbage.

sau·na [SAW-nə] *n* steam bath, orig. Finnish.

saun·ter [SAWN-tər] *vi* walk in leisurely manner, stroll. ▶ *n* leisurely walk or stroll.

sau·ri·an [SOR-ee-ən] *n* one of the order of reptiles including the alligator, lizard, etc.

sau·sage [SAW-sij] *n* chopped seasoned meat enclosed in thin tube of animal intestine or synthetic material. **sausage meat** meat prepared for this.

sau·té [soh-TAY] *adj* cooked or browned in pan with little butter, oil, etc. ▶ *vt* **-téed, -té·ing.** cook in this way.

Sau·ternes [soh-TURN] *n* sweet white wine from S Bordeaux, France; (**s-**) similar wine made elsewhere.

sav·age [SAV-ij] *adj* wild; ferocious; brutal; uncivilized, primitive. ▶ *n* member of savage tribe, barbarian. ▶ *vt* **-aged, -ag·ing.** attack ferociously. **sav'age·ry** *n*

sa·van·na, sa·van·nah (sə-VAN-ə). *n* extensive open grassy plain.

sa·vant [sa-VAHNT] *n* person of learning.

save [sayv] *v* **saved, sav·ing.** ▶ *vt* rescue, preserve; protect; secure; keep for future, lay by; prevent need of; spare; except; *Computers* keep (data) by moving to location for storage. ▶ *vi* lay by money. ▶ *prep* except. ▶ *conj* but. **saving** *adj* frugal; thrifty; delivering from sin; excepting; compensating. ▶ *prep* except. ▶ *n* economy. ▶ *pl* money, earnings put by for future use.

sav·ior [SAYV-yər] *n* person who rescues another; (**S-**) Christ.

sa·voir-faire [sav-wahr-FAIR] *n Fr*

ability to do, say, the right thing in any situation.

sa·vor [SAY-vər] n characteristic taste; flavor; odor; distinctive quality. ▶ vi have particular smell or taste; have suggestion (of). ▶ vt give flavor to; have flavor of; enjoy, appreciate. **sa'vor·y** adj attractive to taste or smell; not sweet.

sa·vor·y [SAY-və-ree] n, pl **-vor·ies.** aromatic herb used in cooking.

sav·vy [SAV-ee] vt inf **-vied, -vy·ing.** understand. ▶ n wits, intelligence.

saw¹ n tool for cutting wood, etc. by tearing it with toothed edge. ▶ v **sawed** or **sawn, saw·ing.** cut with saw; make movements of sawing. **saw'dust** n fine wood fragments made in sawing. **saw'mill** n mill where timber is sawed by machine into planks, etc.

saw² pt. of SEE.

saw³ n wise saying, proverb.

sax·i·frage [SAK-sə-frij] n alpine or rock plant.

Sax·on [SAK-sən] n member of West Germanic people who settled widely in Europe in the early Middle Ages. ▶ adj

sax·o·phone [SAK-sə-fohn] n keyed wind instrument.

say vt **said** [sed], **say·ing, says** [sez] speak; pronounce; state; express; take as example or as near enough; form and deliver opinion. ▶ n what one has to say; chance of saying it; share in decision. **saying** n maxim, proverb.

Sb Chem antimony.

Sc Chem scandium.

scab [skab] n crust formed over wound; skin disease; disease of plants; strikebreaker. **scab'by** adj **-bi·er, -bi·est.**

scab·bard [SKAB-ərd] n sheath for sword or dagger.

scab·rous [SKAYB-rəs] adj having rough surface; thorny; indecent; risky.

scaf·fold [SKAF-əld] n temporary platform for workmen; gallows. **scaf'fold·ing** n (material for building) scaffold.

sca·lar [SKAY-lər] n variable

quantity, e.g. time, having magnitude but no direction. ▶ adj

scald [skawld] vt burn with hot liquid or steam; clean, sterilize with boiling water; heat (liquid) almost to boiling point. ▶ n injury by scalding.

scale¹ [skayl] n one of the thin, overlapping plates covering fishes and reptiles; thin flake; incrustation that forms in boilers, etc. ▶ v **scaled, scal·ing.** ▶ vt remove scales from. ▶ vi come off in scales. **scal'y** adj **scal·i·er, scal·i·est.** resembling or covered in scales. **scale insect** plant pest covered by waxy secretion.

scale² n (chiefly in pl) weighing instrument. ▶ vt **scaled, scal·ing.** weigh in scales; have weight of.

scale³ n graduated table or sequence of marks at regular intervals used as reference or for fixing standards, as in making measurements, in music, etc.; ratio of size between a thing and a model or map of it; (relative) degree, extent. ▶ vt **scaled, scal·ing.** climb. ▶ adj proportionate. **scale up, down** increase or decrease proportionately in size.

sca·lene [SKAY-leen] adj (of triangle) with three unequal sides.

scal·lop [SKOL-əp] n edible shellfish; edging in small curves like edge of scallop shell. ▶ vt shape like scallop shell; cook in scallop shell or dish like one.

scalp [skalp] n skin and hair of top of head. ▶ vt cut off scalp of.

scal·pel [SKAL-pəl] n small surgical knife.

scam [skam] n inf a dishonest scheme.

scamp [skamp] n mischievous person or child. ▶ v do or make hastily or carelessly.

scamp·er [SKAM-pər] vi run about; run hastily from place to place. ▶ n

scam·pi [SKAM-pee] n, pl **scampi.** large shrimp; dish of these sautéed in oil or butter and garlic.

scan [skan] v **scanned, scan·ning.**

look at carefully, scrutinize; measure or read (verse) by metrical feet; examine, search by systematically varying the direction of a radar or sonar beam; glance over quickly; (of verse) conform to metrical rules. ▶ *n* scanning.
scan'ner *n* device, esp. electronic, that scans. **scan'sion** [-shən] *n*
scan·dal [SKAN-dl] *n* action, event generally considered disgraceful; malicious gossip. **scan'dal·ize** *vt* **-ized, -iz·ing.** shock. **scan'dal·ous** [-dl-əs] *adj* outrageous, disgraceful.
scant [skant] *adj* **-er, -est.** barely sufficient or not sufficient. **scant'i·ly** *adv* **scant'y** *adj* **scant·i·er, scant·i·est. scant·ies** [SKAN-teez] *n* very brief underpants.
scape·goat [SKAYP-goht] *n* person bearing blame due to others. **scape'grace** [-grays] *n* rascal; unscrupulous person.
scap·u·la [SKAP-yə-lə] *n, pl* **-las.** shoulder blade. **scap'u·lar** [-lər] *adj* of scapula. ▶ *n* loose sleeveless monastic garment.
scar [skar] *n* mark left by healed wound, burn or sore; change resulting from emotional distress. ▶ *v* **scarred, scar·ring.** mark, heal with scar.
scar·ab [SKA-rəb] *n* sacred beetle of ancient Egypt; gem cut in shape of this.
scarce [skairs] *adj* hard to find; existing or available in insufficient quantity; uncommon. **scarce'ly** *adv* only just; not quite; definitely or probably not. **scar'ci·ty** [-si-tee] *n*
scare [skair] *vt* **scared, scar·ing.** frighten. ▶ *n* fright, sudden panic. **scar'y** *adj* **scar·i·er, scar·i·est.**
scare'crow [-kroh] *n* thing set up to frighten birds from crops; badly dressed or miserable looking person. **scare·mon·ger** [-mung-gər] *n* one who spreads alarming rumors.
scarf[1] [skarf] *n, pl* **scarfs** or **scarves.** long narrow strip, large piece of material to put around neck, head,

etc.
scarf[2] *n, pl* **scarfs.** part cut away from each of two pieces of timber to be jointed longitudinally; joint so made. ▶ *vt* cut or join in this way.
scar·i·fy [SKA-rə-fī] *vt* **-fied, -fy·ing.** scratch, cut slightly all over; lacerate; stir surface soil of; criticize mercilessly.
scar·let [SKAHR-lit] *n* a brilliant red color; cloth or clothing of this color. ▶ *adj* of this color; immoral, esp. unchaste. **scarlet fever** infectious fever with scarlet rash.
scarp [skahrp] *n* steep slope; inside slope of ditch in fortifications.
scath·ing [SKAY*th*-ing] *adj* harshly critical; cutting; damaging.
scat·ter [SKAT-ər] *vt* throw in various directions; put here and there; sprinkle. ▶ *vi* disperse. ▶ *n* **scat'ter·brain** [-brayn] *n* silly, careless person.
scav·enge [SKAV-inj] *v* **-enged, -eng·ing.** search for (anything usable) usu. among discarded material. **scav'en·ger** *n* person who scavenges; animal, bird that feeds on refuse.
scene [seen] *n* place of action of novel, play, etc.; place of any action; subdivision of play; view; episode; display of strong emotion. **scen'er·y** *n, pl* **-er·ies.** natural features of area; constructions of wood, canvas, etc. used on stage to represent a place where action is happening. **sce'nic** *adj* picturesque; of or on the stage. **sce·nar·i·o** [si-NAIR-ee-oh] *n, pl* **-i·os.** summary of plot (of play, etc.) or plan.
scent [sent] *n* distinctive smell, esp. pleasant one; trail, clue; perfume. ▶ *vt* detect or track (by smell); suspect, sense; fill with fragrance.
scep·ter [SEP-tər] *n* ornamental staff as symbol of royal power; royal dignity.
sched·ule [SKEJ-uul] *n* plan of procedure for a project; list; timetable. ▶ *vt* **-uled, -ul·ing.** enter in schedule; plan to occur at certain time. **on schedule** on time.

sche·ma [SKEE-mə] *n, pl* **-ma·ta** [-mə-tə] *or* **-mas.** overall plan or diagram. **sche·mat·ic** *adj* presented as plan or diagram. **sche'ma·tize** [-tīz] *v* **-tized, -tiz·ing.**

scheme [skeem] *n* plan, design; project; outline. ▶ *v* **schemed, schem·ing.** devise, plan, esp. in underhand manner. **schem'er** *n*

scher·zo [SKERT-soh] *n Mus* light playful composition.

schism [SIZ-əm] *n* (group resulting from) division in political party, church, etc. **schis·mat'ic** *n, adj*

schist [shist] *n* crystalline rock that splits into layers.

schiz·o·phre·ni·a [skit-sə-FREE-nee-ə] *n* mental disorder involving deterioration of, confusion about personality. **schiz·o·phren'ic** [-FREN-ik] *adj, n* **schiz'oid** [-soid] *adj* relating to schizophrenia.

schmaltz [shmahlts] *n* excessive sentimentality. **schmaltz'y** *adj* **schmaltz·i·er, schmaltz·i·est.**

schnapps [shnops] *n* spirit distilled from potatoes; any strong spirit.

schnit·zel [SHNIT-səl] *n* thin slice of meat, esp. veal.

scholar *n* see SCHOOL¹.

school¹ [skool] *n* institution for teaching children or for giving instruction in any subject; buildings of such institution; group of thinkers, writers, artists, etc. with principles or methods in common. ▶ *vt* educate; bring under control, train. **school'man** *n* medieval philosopher. **schol'ar** [SKOL-ər] *n* learned person; one taught in school; one quick to learn. **schol'ar·ly** *adj* learned, erudite. **schol'ar·ship** *n* learning; prize, grant to student for payment of school or college fees. **scho·las·tic** [skə-LAS-tik] *adj* of schools or scholars, or education; pedantic.

school² *n* large number (of fish, whales, etc.).

schoon·er [SKOO-nər] *n* fore-and-aft rigged vessel with two or more masts; tall glass.

schot·tische [SHOT-ish] *n* kind of

dance; music for this.

sci·at·i·ca [sī-AT-i-kə] *n* neuralgia of hip and thigh; pain in sciatic nerve. **sci·at'ic** *adj* of the hip; of sciatica.

sci·ence [SĪ-əns] *n* systematic study and knowledge of natural or physical phenomena; any branch of study concerned with observed material facts. **sci·en·tif'ic** *adj* of the principles of science; systematic. **sci·en·tif'i·cal·ly** *adv* **sci'en·tist** *n* one versed in natural sciences. **science fiction** stories set in the future making imaginative use of scientific knowledge.

scim·i·tar [SIM-i-tər] *n* oriental curved sword.

scin·til·late [SIN-tl-ayt] *vi* **-lat·ed, -lat·ing.** sparkle; be animated, witty, clever. **scin·til·la'tion** *n*

sci·on [SĪ-ən] *n* descendant, heir; slip for grafting.

scis·sors [SIZ-ərs] *pl n* cutting instrument with two crossed pivoted blades.

scle·ro·sis [skli-ROH-sis] *n, pl* **-ses** [-seez] a hardening of bodily organs, tissues, etc. **scle·rot'ic** [-ROT-ik] *adj*

scoff [skof] *vt* express derision for. ▶ *n* derision; mocking words. **scoff'er** *n*

scold [skohld] *v* find fault; reprimand, be angry with. ▶ *n* someone who does this. **scold'ing** *n*

sconce [skons] *n* bracket candlestick on wall.

scone [skohn] *n* small plain biscuit baked on griddle or in oven.

scoop [skoop] *n* small shovel-like tool for ladling, hollowing out, etc.; *inf* exclusive news item; *inf* information. ▶ *vt* ladle out; hollow out, rake in with scoop; make sudden profit; beat (rival newspaper, etc.).

scoot [skoot] *vi inf* move off quickly. **scoot'er** *n* child's vehicle propelled by pushing on ground with one foot; light motorcycle (also **motor scooter**).

scope [skohp] *n* range of activity or application; room, opportunity.

scorch [skorch] *v* burn, be burned, on surface; parch; shrivel; wither. ▶ *n* slight burn. **scorch'er** *n inf* very hot day.

score [skor] *n* points gained in game, competition; group of 20; musical notation; mark or notch, esp. to keep tally; reason, account; grievance. ▶ *pl* lots. ▶ *v* **scored, scor·ing.** ▶ *vt* gain points in game; mark; cross out; arrange music (for). ▶ *vi* keep tally of points; succeed.

scorn [skorn] *n* contempt, derision. ▶ *vt* despise. **scorn'ful** [-fəl] *adj* derisive. **scorn'ful·ly** *adv*

scor·pi·on [SKOR-pee-ən] *n* small lobster-shaped animal with sting at end of jointed tail.

Scot [skot] *n* native of Scotland. **Scot'tish** *adj* **Scotch** *n* whisky distilled in Scotland. **Scots** *adj* Scottish. ▶ *n* English dialect spoken in Scotland. **Scots'man** [-mən], **Scots'wom·an** *n*

scotch [skoch] *vt* put an end to.

scot-free [skot-free] *adj* without harm or loss.

scoun·drel [SKOWN-drəl] *n* villain, blackguard. **scoun'drel·ly** *adj*

scour¹ [skowr] *vt* clean, polish by rubbing; clear or flush out.

scour² *v* move rapidly along or over (territory) in search of something.

scourge [skurj] *n* whip, lash; severe affliction; pest; calamity. ▶ *vt* **scourged, scourg·ing.** flog; punish severely.

scout [skowt] *n* one sent out to reconnoiter; (**S-**) member of organization for young people which aims to develop character and responsibility. ▶ *vi* go out, act as scout; reconnoiter. **scout'mas·ter** *n* leader of troop of Boy Scouts.

scow [skow] *n* unpowered barge.

scowl [skowl] *vi* frown gloomily or sullenly. ▶ *n* angry or gloomy expression.

scrab·ble [SKRAB-əl] *v* **-bled, -bling.** scrape at with hands, claws in disorderly manner. ▶ *n* (**S-**) ® board game in which words are

formed by letter tiles.

scrag [skrag] *n* lean person or animal; lean end of a neck of mutton. **scrag'gy** *adj* **-gi·er, -gi·est.** thin, bony.

scrag·gly [SKRAG-lee] *adj* **-gli·er, -gli·est.** untidy.

scram¹ [skram] *v* **scrammed, scram·ming.** *inf* go away hastily, get out.

scram² *n* emergency shutdown of nuclear reactor. ▶ *v* **scrammed, scram·ming.**

scram·ble [SKRAM-bəl] *v* **-bled, -bling.** ▶ *vi* move along or up by crawling, climbing, etc.; struggle with others (for); (of aircraft, aircrew) take off hurriedly. ▶ *vt* mix up; cook (eggs) beaten up with milk; render (speech) unintelligible by electronic device. ▶ *n* scrambling; rough climb; disorderly proceeding; emergency takeoff of military aircraft.

scrap [skrap] *n* small piece or fragment; leftover material; *inf* fight. ▶ *v* **scrapped, scrap·ping.** break up, discard as useless; fight. **scrap'py** *adj* **-pi·er, -pi·est.** unequal in quality; badly finished. **scrap'book** [-buuk] *n* book in which newspaper clippings, etc. are kept.

scrape [skrayp] *vt* **scraped, scrap·ing.** rub with something sharp; clean, smooth thus; grate; scratch; rub with harsh noise. ▶ *n* act, sound of scraping; awkward situation, esp. as result of escapade. **scrap'er** *n* instrument for scraping; contrivance on which mud, etc. is scraped from shoes.

scratch [skrach] *vt* score, make narrow surface wound with claws, nails, or anything pointed; make marks on with pointed instruments; scrape (skin) with nails to relieve itching; remove, withdraw from list, race, etc. ▶ *vi* use claws or nails, esp. to relieve itching. ▶ *n* wound, mark or sound made by scratching; line or starting point. ▶ *adj* got together at short notice; impromptu; *Golf* without any

allowance. **scratch'y** *adj*
**scratch·i·er, scratch·i·est. scratch
hit** *Baseball* weak hit barely
enabling batter to reach first base.

scrawl [skrawl] *vt* write, draw
untidily. ▶ *n* thing scrawled;
careless writing.

scrawn·y [SKRAW-nee] *adj*
scrawn·i·er, scrawn·i·est. thin,
bony.

scream [skreem] *vi* utter piercing
cry, esp. of fear, pain, etc.; be very
obvious. ▶ *vt* utter in a scream. ▶ *n*
shrill, piercing cry; *inf* very funny
person or thing.

scree [skree] *n* loose shifting stones;
slope covered with these.

screech [skreech] *vi, n* scream.

screed [skreed] *n* long (tedious)
letter, passage or speech; thin layer
of cement; in masonry, board used
to make level.

screen [skreen] *n* device to shelter
from heat, light, draft, observation,
etc.; anything used for such
purpose; mesh over doors,
windows to keep out insects; white
or silvered surface on which
photographic images are
projected; windscreen; wooden or
stone partition in church. ▶ *vt*
shelter, hide; protect from
detection; show (film); scrutinize;
examine (group of people) for
presence of disease, weapons, etc.;
examine for political motives;
Electricity protect from stray electric
or magnetic fields. **screen saver**
Computers software that produces
changing images on a monitor
when the computer is operating
but idle. **the screen** motion
pictures generally.

screw [skroo] *n* (nail-like device or
cylinder with) spiral thread cut to
engage similar thread or to bore
into material (wood, etc.) to pin or
fasten; anything resembling a
screw in shape, esp. in spiral form;
propeller; twist. ▶ *vt* fasten with
screw; twist around; extort.
screw'y *adj* **screw·i·er, screw·i·est.**
sl crazy, eccentric. **screw'driv·er** *n*
tool for turning screws; drink of

vodka and orange juice. **screw up**
sl bungle, distort.

scrib·ble [SKRIB-əl] *v* **-bled, -bling.**
write, draw carelessly; make
meaningless marks with pen or
pencil. ▶ *n* something scribbled.

scribe [skrīb] *n* writer; copyist. ▶ *v*
scribed, scrib·ing. scratch a line
with pointed instrument.

scrim·mage [SKRIM-ij] *n* scuffle;
Football a play. ▶ *v* **-maged,
-mag·ing.** engage in scrimmage.

scrimp [skrimp] *vt* make too small
or short; treat meanly. **scrimp'y**
adj **scrimp·i·er, scrimp·i·est.**

scrip [skrip] *n* written certificate
esp. of holding fractional share of
stock; paper certificates issued in
place of money.

script [skript] *n* (system or style of)
handwriting; written characters;
written text of film, play, radio or
television program. ▶ *vt* write a
script.

scrip·ture [SKRIP-chər] *n* sacred
writings; (**S-**) the Bible. **scrip'tur·al**
adj

scrof·u·la [SKROF-yə-lə] *n*
tuberculosis of lymphatic glands,
esp. of neck. **scrof'u·lous** [-ləs] *adj*

scroll [skrohl] *n* roll of parchment or
paper; list; ornament shaped thus.
▶ *v* *Computers* move (text) up or
down on a VDU screen.

scro·tum [SKROH-təm] *n, pl* **-tums.**
pouch containing testicles.

scrounge [skrownj] *v* **scrounged,
scroung·ing.** get without cost, by
begging. **scroung'er** *n*

scrub¹ [skrub] *vt* **scrubbed,
scrub·bing.** clean with hard brush
and water; scour; *sl* cancel, get rid
of. ▶ *n* scrubbing.

scrub² *n* stunted trees; brushwood.
scrub'by *adj* **-bi·er, -bi·est.**
covered with scrub; stunted;
shabby.

scruff [skruf] *n* nape (of neck).

scrum [skrum] *n* *Rugby* restarting of
play in which opposing packs of
forwards push against each other
to gain possession of the ball.

scrunch [skrunch] *v* crumple or
crunch or be crumpled or

crunched. ▶ *n* act or sound of scrunching. **scrun'chie** [SKRUNCH-ee] *n* loop of elastic covered loosely with fabric, used to hold the hair in a ponytail.

scru·ple [SKROO-pəl] *n* doubt or hesitation about what is morally right; weight of 20 grains. ▶ *vi* **-pled, -pling.** hesitate.

scru'pu·lous [-pyə-ləs] *adj* extremely conscientious; thorough, attentive to small points.

scru·ti·ny [SKROOT-n-ee] *n, pl* **-nies.** close examination; critical investigation; searching look. **scru'ti·nize** *vt* **-nized, -niz·ing.** examine closely.

scu·ba [SKOO-bə] *n, adj* (relating to) self-contained underwater breathing apparatus.

scud [skud] *vi* **scud·ded, scud·ding.** run fast; run before wind.

scuff [skuf] *vi* drag, scrape with feet in walking. ▶ *vt* scrape with feet; scratch (something) by scraping. ▶ *n* act, sound of scuffing. ▶ *pl* thong sandals. **scuffed** *adj* (of shoes) scraped or slightly grazed.

scuf·fle [SKUF-əl] *vi* **-fled, -fling.** fight in disorderly manner; shuffle. ▶ *n*

scull [skul] *n* oar used in stern of boat; short oar used in pairs. ▶ *v* propel, move by means of scull(s). **scul·ler·y** [SKUL-ə-ree] *n, pl* **-ler·ies.** place for washing dishes, etc. **scul·lion** [SKUL-yən] *n* despicable person; kitchen servant doing menial work.

sculp·ture [SKULP-chər] *n* art of forming figures in relief or solid; product of this art. ▶ *vt* **-tured, -tur·ing.** represent by sculpture. **sculpt** *v* **sculp'tur·al** *adj* with qualities proper to sculpture. **sculp·tor, sculp'tress** [-tris] *n*

scum [skum] *n* froth or other floating matter on liquid; waste part of anything; vile person(s) or thing(s). **scum'my** *adj* **-mi·er, -mi·est.**

scup·per [SKUP-ər] *n* hole in ship's side level with deck to carry off water.

scurf [skurf] *n* flaky matter on scalp, dandruff. **scurf'y** *adj* **scurf·i·er, scurf·i·est.**

scur·ri·lous [SKUR-ə-ləs] *adj* coarse, indecently abusive. **scur·ril·i·ty** [skə-RIL-i-tee] *n, pl* **-ties.**

scur·ry [SKUR-ee] *vi* **-ried, -ry·ing.** run hastily. ▶ *n, pl* **-ries.** bustling haste; flurry.

scur·vy [SKUR-vee] *n* disease caused by lack of vitamin C. ▶ *adj* **-vi·er, -vi·est.** afflicted with the disease; mean, contemptible.

scut·tle¹ [SKUT-l] *n* fireside container for coal.

scuttle² *vi* **-tled, -tling.** rush away; run hurriedly. ▶ *n*

scuttle³ *vt* **-tled, -tling.** make hole in ship to sink it; abandon, cause to be abandoned.

scut·work [SKUT-wurk] *n inf* menial work.

scythe [sīth] *n* manual implement with long curved blade for cutting grass, grain. ▶ *vt* **scythed, scyth·ing.** cut with scythe.

Se *Chem* selenium.

sea [see] *n* mass of salt water covering greater part of Earth; broad tract of this; waves; swell; large quantity; vast expanse. **sea'board** [-bord] *n* coast. **sea'far·ing** [-fair-ing] *adj* occupied in sea voyages. **sea horse** fish with bony plated body and horselike head. **sea lion** kind of large seal. **sea'man** [-mən] *n* sailor. **sea'sick·ness** *n* nausea caused by motion of ship. **sea'sick** *adj* **sea urchin** marine animal, echinus. **sea'weed** *n* plant growing in sea. **sea'wor·thy** [-wurth-ee] *adj* **-thi·er, -thi·est.** in fit condition to put to sea.

seal¹ [seel] *n* piece of metal or stone engraved with device for impression on wax, etc.; impression thus made (on letters, etc.); device, material preventing passage of water, air, oil, etc. (also **seal'er**) ▶ *vt* affix seal to ratify, authorize; mark with stamp as evidence of some quality; keep close or secret; settle; make

watertight, airtight, etc.
seal² n amphibious furred carnivorous mammal with flippers as limbs. ▶ vi hunt seals. **seal'er** n person or ship engaged in sealing.
seal'skin n skin, fur of seals.
seam [seem] n line of junction of two edges, e.g. of two pieces of cloth, or two planks; thin layer, stratum. ▶ vt mark with furrows or wrinkles. **seam'less** [-lis] adj
seam'y adj **seam·i·er, seam·i·est.** sordid; marked with seams.
seam'stress [-stris] n sewing woman.
sé·ance [SAY-ahns] n meeting at which spiritualists attempt to communicate with the dead.
sear [seer] vt scorch, brand with hot iron; deaden.
search [surch] v look over or through to find something; probe into, examine. ▶ n act of searching; quest. **search'ing** adj keen; thorough; severe. **search engine** *Computers* Internet service enabling users to search for items of interest online. **search'light** n powerful electric light with concentrated beam.
sea·son [SEE-zən] n one of four divisions of year associated with type of weather and stage of agriculture; period during which thing happens, grows, is active, etc.; proper time. ▶ vt flavor with salt, herbs, etc.; make reliable or ready for use; make experienced.
sea'son·a·ble adj appropriate for the season; opportune; fit.
sea'son·al [-əl] adj depending on, varying with seasons. **sea'son·ing** n flavoring. **in season** (of an animal) in heat. **season ticket** one for series of events within a certain time.
seat [seet] n thing for sitting on; buttocks; base; right to sit (e.g. in legislature, etc.); place where something is located, centered; locality of disease, trouble, etc.; country house. ▶ vt make to sit; provide sitting accommodation for; install firmly.

se·ba·ceous [si-BAY-shəs] adj of, pert. to fat; secreting fat, oil.
se·cant [SEE-kant] n *Math* (secant of an angle) reciprocal of its cosine; line that intersects a curve.
se·cede [si-SEED] vi **-ced·ed, -ced·ing.** withdraw formally from federation, union, etc. **se·ces'sion** [-SESH-ən] n
se·clude [si-KLOOD] vt **-clud·ed, -clud·ing.** guard from, remove from sight, view, contact with others. **secluded** adj remote; private. **se·clu'sion** [-KLOO-zhən] n
sec·ond [SEK-ənd] adj next after first; alternate, additional; of lower quality. ▶ n person or thing coming second; attendant; sixtieth part of minute; SI unit of time; moment. ▶ pl inferior goods. ▶ vt support; support (motion in meeting) so that discussion may be in order. **sec·ond·hand'** adj bought after use by another; not original. **second sight** faculty of seeing events before they occur.
sec·ond·ar·y [SEK-ən-der-ee] adj subsidiary, of less importance; developed from, or dependent on, something else; *Education* after primary stage. **sec'ond·ar·i·ly** adv
se·cret [SEE-krit] adj kept, meant to be kept from knowledge of others; hidden; private. ▶ n thing kept secret. **se'cre·cy** [-krə-see] n, pl **-cies.** keeping or being kept secret.
se'cre·tive adj given to having secrets; uncommunicative; reticent.
se'cre·tive·ness [-tiv-nis] n
sec·re·tar·y [SEK-ri-ter-ee] n, pl **-tar·ies.** one employed by individual or organization to deal with papers and correspondence, keep records, prepare business, etc.; member of presidential cabinet. **sec·re·tar'i·al** [-TAIR-ee-əl] adj **sec·re·tar'i·at** [-ət] n body of secretaries; building occupied by secretarial staff.
se·crete [si-KREET] vt **-cret·ed, -cret·ing.** hide; conceal; (of gland, etc.) collect and supply particular substance in body. **se·cre'tion** n
sect [sekt] n group of people

(within religious body, etc.) with common interest; faction.

sec·tar·i·an [-TAIR-ee-ən] adj of a sect; narrow-minded.

sec·tion [SEK-shən] n part cut off; division; portion; distinct part of city, country, people, etc.; cutting; drawing of anything as if cut through. **sec'tion·al** adj

sec·tor [SEK-tər] n part or subdivision; part of circle enclosed by two radii and the arc they cut off.

sec·u·lar [SEK-yə-lər] adj worldly; lay, not religious; not monastic; lasting for, or occurring once in, an age; centuries old. **sec'u·lar·ism** n **sec'u·lar·ist** n one who believes that religion should have no place in civil affairs. **sec·u·lar·i·za'tion** n **sec'u·lar·ize** vt **-ized, -iz·ing.** transfer from religious to lay possession or use.

se·cure [si-KYOOR] adj **-cur·er, -cur·est.** safe; free from fear, anxiety; firmly fixed; certain; sure, confident. ▶ vt **-cured, -cur·ing.** gain possession of; make safe; free (creditor) from risk of loss; make firm. **se·cur'i·ty** n, pl **-ties.** state of safety; protection; that which secures; assurance; anything given as bond, caution or pledge; one who becomes surety for another.

se·dan [si-DAN] n enclosed automobile body with two or four doors. **sedan chair** Hist closed chair for one person, carried on poles by bearers.

se·date¹ [si-DAYT] adj calm, collected, serious.

sedate² vt **-dat·ed, -dat·ing.** make calm by sedative. **se·da'tion** n **sed'a·tive** adj having soothing or calming effect. ▶ n sedative drug.

sed·en·ta·ry [SED-n-ter-ee] adj done sitting down; sitting much.

Se·der [SAY-dər] n ritual for the first or first two nights of Passover.

sed·i·ment [SED-ə-mənt] n matter that settles to the bottom of liquid; dregs, lees. **sed·i·men'ta·ry** adj

se·di·tion [si-DISH-ən] n speech or action threatening authority of a

state. **se·di'tious** [-shəs] adj

se·duce [si-doos] vt **-duced, -duc·ing.** persuade to commit some (wrong) deed, esp. sexual intercourse; tempt; attract. **se·duc'er, se·duc'tress** n **se·duc'tion** [-DUK-shən] n **se·duc'tive** adj alluring; winning.

sed·u·lous [SEJ-ə-ləs] adj diligent; industrious; persevering, persistent. **se·du·li·ty** [si-DOO-li-tee] n

see¹ v **saw, seen, see·ing.** perceive with eyes or mentally; observe; watch; find out; reflect; come to know; interview; make sure; accompany; perceive; consider; understand. **seeing** conj since; in view of the fact that.

see² n diocese, office, or jurisdiction of bishop.

seed n reproductive germs of plants; one grain of this; such grains saved or used for sowing; origin; sperm; offspring. ▶ vt sow with seed; arrange draw for tennis or other tournament, so that best players do not meet in early rounds. ▶ vi produce seed. **seed'ling** n young plant raised from seed. **seed'y** adj **seed·i·er, seed·i·est.** shabby; gone to seed; unwell, ill.

seek v **sought** [sawt], **seek·ing.** make search or inquiry for; search.

seem vi appear (to be or to do); look; appear to one's judgment. **seem'ing** adj apparent but not real. **seem'ing·ly** adv

seem·ly [SEEM-lee] adj **-li·er, -li·est.** becoming and proper. **seem'li·ness** [-nis] n

seen pp. of SEE.

seep vi trickle through slowly, as water, ooze.

seer n prophet.

seer·suck·er [SEER-suk-ər] n light cotton fabric with slightly crinkled surface.

see'saw n game in which children sit at opposite ends of plank supported in middle and swing up and down; plank used for this. ▶ vi move up and down.

seethe [seeth] vi **seethed,**

seeth·ing. boil, foam; be very agitated; be in constant movement (as large crowd, etc.).

seg·ment [SEG-mənt] *n* piece cut off; section. ▸ *v* [SEG-ment] to divide into segments. **seg·men·ta'tion** *n*

seg·re·gate [SEG-ri-gayt] *vt* **-gat·ed, -gat·ing.** set apart from rest; dissociate; separate; isolate. **seg·re·ga'tion** *n*

se·gue [SAY-gway] *vi* **-gued, -gue·ing.** proceed from one section or piece of music to another without break; make a transition smoothly e.g. from one topic of conversation to another. ▸ *n*

seis·mic [SĪZ-mik] *adj* pert. to earthquakes. **seis'mo·graph** [-mə-graf] *n* instrument to record earthquakes. **seis·mo·log'ic·al** *adj* pert. to seismology. **seis·mol'o·gist** [-MOL-ə-jist] *n* one versed in seismology. **seis·mol'o·gy** *n* science concerned with study of earthquakes.

seize [seez] *v* **seized, seiz·ing.** ▸ *vt* grasp; lay hold of; capture. ▸ *vi* in machine, of bearing or piston, to stick tightly through overheating. **seiz·ure** [SEE-zhər] *n* act of taking, esp. by legal writ, as goods; sudden onset of disease.

sel·dom [SEL-dəm] *adv* not often, rarely.

se·lect [si-LEKT] *vt* pick out, choose. ▸ *adj* choice, picked; exclusive. **se·lec'tion** *n* **se·lec'tive** *adj* **se·lec·tiv'i·ty** *n*

se·le·ni·um [si-LEE-nee-əm] *n* nonmetallic element with photoelectric properties.

sel·e·nog·ra·phy [sel-ə-NOG-rə-fee] *n* study of surface of moon.

self *pron, pl* **selves.** used reflexively or to express emphasis. ▸ *adj* (of color, etc.) same throughout, uniform. ▸ *n* one's own person or individuality. **self'ish** *adj* concerned unduly over personal profit or pleasure; lacking consideration for others; greedy. **self'ish·ly** *adv* **self'less** [-lis] *adj*

having no regard for self; unselfish.

self- *prefix* used with many main words to mean: of oneself or itself; by, to, in, due to, for, or from the self; automatic(ally).

self-ad·dressed' *adj* addressed to the sender. **self-as·sured'** *adj* confident. **self-cen'tered** *adj* totally preoccupied with one's own concerns. **self-con'fi·dent** *adj* **self-con·tained'** containing everything needed, complete; (of an apartment) having its own facilities. **self-con·trol'** *n* ability to control one's feelings and reactions. **self-de·fense'** *n* defending of oneself or one's property. **self-em·ployed'** *adj* earning a living from one's own business. **self-ev'i·dent** *adj* obvious without proof. **self-help'** *n* use of one's own abilities to solve problems; practice of solving one's problems within a group of people with similar problems.

self-in·dul'gent *adj* tending to indulge one's desires. **self-in'ter·est** *adj* one's own advantage. **self-rais'ing** *adj* (of flour) containing a raising agent. **self-sat'is·fied** *adj* conceited.

self-con'scious [-KON-shəs] *adj* unduly aware of oneself; conscious of one's acts or states.

self-de·ter·mi·na·tion [-di-tur-mə-NAY-shən] *n* the right of person or nation to decide for itself.

self-made [-mayd] *adj* having achieved wealth, status, etc. by one's own efforts.

self-pos·sessed [-pə-ZEST] *adj* calm, composed. **self-pos·ses'sion** [-pə-ZESH-ən] *n*

self-re·spect' [-ri-SPEKT] *n* proper sense of one's own dignity and integrity.

self-right'eous [-RĪ-chəs] *adj* smugly sure of one's own virtue.

self-same [-saym] *adj* very same.

self-seek'ing *adj, n* (having) preoccupation with one's own interests.

self-serv'ice [-SUR-vis] *adj, n* (of)

the serving of oneself in a store or restaurant.

self·suf·fi'cient [-sə-FISH-ənt] *adj* sufficient in itself; relying on one's own powers.

self·will' *n* obstinacy; willfulness. **self-willed'** *adj* headstrong.

sell *v* **sold, sell·ing.** hand over for a price; stock, have for sale; make someone accept; find purchasers; *inf* betray, cheat. ▶ *n inf* hoax. **sell'er** *n* **sell'out** *n* disposing of completely by selling; betrayal.

selt·zer (water) [SELT-sər] *n* effervescent (mineral) water.

sel·vage [SEL-vij] *n* finished, unfraying edge of cloth.

se·man·tic [si-MAN-tik] *adj* relating to meaning of words or symbols. **se·man'tics** *n* study of linguistic meaning.

sem·a·phore [SEM-ə-for] *n* post with movable arms for signaling; system of signaling by human or mechanical arms.

sem·blance [SEM-bləns] *n* (false) appearance; image, likeness.

se·men [SEE-mən] *n* fluid carrying sperm of male animals; sperm.

se·mes·ter [si-MES-tər] *n* (half-year) session of academic year in many universities, colleges.

sem·i [SEM-ī] *n inf* semitrailer.

semi- *comb. form* half, partly, not completely, e.g. *semicircle.*

sem·i·breve [SEM-ee-breev] *n* musical note half the length of a breve.

sem·i·cir·cle [SEM-i-sur-kəl] *n* half of circle. **sem·i·cir'cu·lar** [-SUR-kyə-lər] *adj*

sem·i·co·lon [SEM-i-koh-lən] *n* punctuation mark (;).

sem·i·con·duc·tor [sem-i-kən-DUK-tər] *n* Physics substance with an electrical conductivity that increases with temperature or voltage.

sem·i·de·tached [sem-ee-di-TACHT] *adj, n* (of) house joined to another on one side only.

sem·i·fi·nal [sem-ee-FĪN-l] *n* match, round, etc. before final.

sem·i·nal [SEM-ə-nl] *adj* capable of developing; influential, important; rudimentary; of semen or seed.

sem·i·nar [SEM-ə-nahr] *n* meeting of group (of students) for discussion.

sem·i·nar·y [SEM-ə-ner-ee] *n, pl* **-nar·ies.** college for priests. **sem·i·nar'i·an** *n* student at seminary.

sem·i·pre·cious [sem-ee-PRESH-əs] *adj* (of gemstones) having less value than precious stones.

sem·i·skilled [sem-ee-SKILD] *adj* partly skilled, trained but not for specialized work.

Sem·ite [SEM-īt] *n* member of ancient and modern peoples including Jews and Arabs; Jew. **Se·mit·ic** [sə-MIT-ik] *adj* denoting a Semite; Jewish.

sem·i·tone [SEM-ee-tohn] *n* musical half tone.

sem·i·trail·er [SEM-i-tray-lər] *n* trailer used for hauling freight, having wheels at back but supported by towing vehicle in front.

sem·o·li·na [sem-ə-LEE-nə] *n* milled product of durum wheat, used for pasta, etc.

sen·ate [SEN-it] *n* upper legislative body of country; upper council of university, etc. **sen'a·tor** [-ə-tər] *n* **sen·a·to'ri·al** [-TOR-ee-əl] *adj*

send *vt* **sent, send·ing.** cause to go or be conveyed; dispatch; transmit (by radio).

se·nile [SEE-nīl] *adj* showing weakness of old age. **se·nil·i·ty** [si-NIL-i-tee] *n*

sen·ior [SEEN-yər] *adj* superior in rank or standing; older. ▶ *n* superior; elder person. **sen·ior'i·ty** [-YOR-i-tee] *n*

se·ñor [sayn-YOR] *n Sp* title of respect, like Mr. **se·ñor'a** *n* Mrs. **se·ño·ri·ta** [-REE-tə] *n* Miss.

sen·sa·tion [sen-SAY-shən] *n* operation of sense, feeling, awareness; excited feeling, state of excitement; exciting event; strong impression; commotion.

sen·sa'tion·al *adj* producing great

excitement; melodramatic; of perception by senses.
sen·sa'tion·al·ism n use of sensational language, etc. to arouse intense emotional excitement; doctrine that sensations are basis of all knowledge.
sense [sens] n any of bodily faculties of perception or feeling; sensitiveness of any or all of these faculties; ability to perceive, mental alertness; consciousness; meaning; coherence, intelligible meaning; sound practical judgment. ▶ vt **sensed, sens·ing.** perceive; understand. **sense'less** [-lis] adj
sen·si·ble [SEN-sə-bəl] adj reasonable, wise; perceptible by senses; aware, mindful; considerable, appreciable. **sen·si·bil'i·ty** n ability to feel esp. emotional or moral feelings. **sen'si·bly** adv
sen·si·tive [SEN-si-tiv] adj open to, acutely affected by, external impressions; easily affected or altered; easily upset by criticism; responsive to slight changes. **sen·si·tiv'i·ty** n **sen'si·tize** [-tīz] vt **-tized, -tiz·ing.** make sensitive, esp. make (photographic film, etc.) sensitive to light.
sen·sor [SEN-sər] n device that responds to stimulus.
sen·so·ry [SEN-sə-ree] adj relating to organs, operation, of senses.
sen·su·al [SEN-shoo-əl] adj of senses only and not of mind; given to pursuit of pleasures of sense; self-indulgent; licentious. **sen'su·al·ist** n
sen·su·ous [SEN-shoo-əs] adj stimulating, or apprehended by, senses esp. in aesthetic manner.
sent pt./pp. of SEND.
sen·tence [SEN-tns] n combination of words that is complete as expressing a thought; judgment passed on criminal by court or judge. ▶ vt **-tenced, -tenc·ing.** pass sentence on, condemn.
sen·ten'tial [-TEN-shəl] adj of sentence. **sen·ten'tious** [-shəs] adj

full of axioms and maxims; pithy; pompously moralizing. **sen·ten'tious·ness** n
sen·tient [SEN-shənt] adj capable of feeling; feeling; thinking. **sen'tience** n
sen·ti·ment [SEN-tə-mənt] n tendency to be moved by feeling rather than reason; verbal expression of feeling; mental feeling, emotion; opinion. **sen·ti·men'tal** adj given to indulgence in sentiment and in its expression; weak; sloppy. **sen·ti·men·tal'i·ty** n
sen·ti·nel [SEN-tn-l] n sentry.
sen·try [SEN-tree] n, pl **-tries.** soldier on watch.
se·pal [SEE-pəl] n leaf or division of the calyx of a flower.
sep·a·rate [SEP-ə-rayt] v **-rat·ed, -rat·ing.** ▶ vt part; divide; sever; put apart; occupy place between. ▶ vi withdraw, become parted from. ▶ adj [SEP-ər-it] disconnected, apart, distinct, individual. **sep'a·ra·ble** adj **sep·a·ra'tion** [-RAY-shən] n disconnection; Law living apart of married people without divorce. **sep'a·ra·tor** n that which separates; apparatus for separating cream from milk.
se·pi·a [SEE-pee-ə] n reddish-brown pigment made from a fluid secreted by the cuttlefish. ▶ adj of this color.
sep'sis n presence of pus-forming bacteria in body.
sep·ten·ni·al [sep-TEN-ee-əl] adj lasting, occurring every seven years.
sep·tet' n music for seven instruments or voices; group of seven performers.
sep·tic [SEP-tik] adj of, caused by, sepsis; (of wound) infected. **sep·ti·ce'mi·a** [-SEE-mee-ə] n blood poisoning.
sep·tu·a·ge·nar·i·an [sep-choo-ə-jə-NAIR-ee-ən] adj aged between seventy and eighty. ▶ n
sep·ul·cher [SEP-əl-kər] n tomb; burial vault. **se·pul·chral** [sə-PUL-krəl] adj of burial, or the

grave; mournful; gloomy.

sep·ul·ture [-əl-chər] n burial.

se·quel [SEE-kwəl] n consequence; continuation, e.g. of story.

se·quence [SEE-kwəns] n arrangement of things in successive order; section, episode of motion picture. **se·quen·tial** [si-KWEN-shəl] adj

se·ques·ter [si-KWES-tər] vt separate; seclude; put aside.

se·ques'trate [-KWES-trayt] vt **-trat·ed, -trat·ing.** confiscate; divert or appropriate income of property to satisfy claims against its owner. **se·ques·tra'tion** [-TRAY-shən] n

se·quin [SEE-kwin] n small ornamental metal disk or spangle on dresses, etc.; orig. Venetian gold coin.

se·quoi·a [si-KWOI-ə] n giant Californian coniferous tree.

se·ragl·io [si-RAL-yoh] n, pl **-ragl·ios.** harem, palace, of Turkish sultan.

ser·aph [SER-əf] n, pl **-a·phim** [-ə-fim] member of highest order of angels.

ser·e·nade [ser-ə-NAYD] n sentimental piece of music or song of type addressed to woman by lover esp. at evening. ▶ v **-nad·ed, -nad·ing.** sing serenade (to someone).

ser·en·dip·i·ty [ser-ən-DIP-i-tee] n faculty of making fortunate discoveries by accident.

se·rene [sə-REEN] adj calm, tranquil; unclouded; quiet, placid. **se·ren'i·ty** [-REN-i-tee] n

serf [surf] n one of class of medieval laborers bound to, and transferred with, land. **serf'dom** [-dəm] n

serge [surj] n strong hard-wearing twilled worsted fabric.

ser·geant [SAHR-jənt] n noncommissioned officer in Army, Marine Corps, police department. **sergeant major** noncommissioned Army officer serving as chief administrative assistant; noncommissioned officer ranking above first sergeant in Marine Corps. **sergeant at arms** legislative, organizational officer assigned to keep order, etc.

se·ries [SEER-eez] n, pl **series.** sequence; succession, set (e.g. of radio, TV programs with same characters, setting, but different stories). **se·ri·al** [SEER-ee-əl] n story or play produced in successive episodes or installments; periodical publication. ▶ adj **se'ri·al·ize** v **-ized, -iz·ing.** publish, present as serial. **serial killer** murderer who commits series of murders in same pattern oft. in same locality.

ser'if n small line finishing off stroke of letter.

se·ri·ous [SEER-ee-əs] adj thoughtful, solemn; earnest, sincere; of importance; giving cause for concern.

ser·mon [SUR-mən] n discourse of religious instruction or exhortation spoken or read from pulpit; any similar discourse. **ser'mon·ize** vi **-ized, -iz·ing.** talk like preacher; compose sermons.

ser·pent [SUR-pənt] n snake. **serp'en·tine** [-teen] adj like, shaped like, serpent.

ser·rate [SER-ayt], **ser·rat·ed** [SER-ay-tid] adj having notched, sawlike edge. **ser·ra'tion** n

se·rum [SEER-əm] n, pl **-rums.** watery animal fluid, esp. thin part of blood as used for inoculation or vaccination.

serve [surv] v **served, serv·ing.** (mainly tr) work for, under, another; attend (to customers) in store, etc.; provide; help to (food, etc.); present (food, etc.) in particular way; provide with regular supply of; be member of military unit; pay homage to; spend time doing; be useful, suitable enough; Tennis, etc. put (ball) into play. ▶ n Tennis, etc. act of serving ball. **ser'vant** [-vənt] n personal or domestic attendant; **ser'ver** [-vər] n person who serves; Computers computer or program that supplies data to other machines on a

network. **serv'ice** [-vis] *n* the act of serving, helping, assisting; system organized to provide for needs of public; maintenance of vehicle; use; readiness, availability for use; set of dishes, etc.; form, session, of public worship. ▶ *pl* armed forces. ▶ *vt* **-iced, -ic·ing.** overhaul.
serv'ice·a·ble *adj* in working order, usable; durable. **service road** narrow road giving access to houses, stores, etc. **service station** place supplying fuel, oil, maintenance for motor vehicles.
ser·vile [SUR-vil] *adj* slavish, without independence; cringing; fawning; menial. **ser·vil'i·ty** *n*
ser·vi·tude [SUR-vi-tood] *n* bondage, slavery.
ser·vo·mech·an·ism [SUR-voh-mek-ə-niz-əm] *n* electronic device for converting small mechanical, hydraulic or other type of force into larger, esp. in steering mechanisms.
ses·a·me [SES-ə-mee] *n* plant with seeds used as herbs and for making oil.
ses·sion [SESH-ən] *n* meeting of court, etc.; assembly; continuous series of such meetings; any period devoted to an activity; school or university term, e.g. *summer session.*
set *v* set, set·ting. (mainly *tr*) put or place in specified position or condition; cause to sit; fix, point, put up; make ready; become firm or fixed; establish; prescribe, allot; put to music; of hair, arrange while wet, so that it dries in position; of sun, go down; have direction. ▶ *adj* fixed, established; deliberate; formal, arranged beforehand; unvarying. ▶ *n* act or state of being set; bearing, posture; *Radio, TV* complete apparatus for reception or transmission; *Theater, films* organized settings and equipment to form ensemble of scene; number of things, persons associated as being similar, complementary or used together; *Math* group of numbers, objects, etc. with at least one common

property. **set'back** *n* anything that hinders or impedes. **set'up** *n* position; organization. **set up** establish; *inf* treat, as to drinks; *inf* frame, entrap; *inf* lure into embarrassing, dangerous, situation. **set shot** *Basketball* shot at basket taken from standing position and relatively distant from basket.
set·tee' *n* couch.
set·ter [SET-ər] *n* various breeds of gun dog.
set·ting [SET-ing] *n* background; surroundings; scenery and other stage accessories; act of fixing; decorative metalwork holding precious stone, etc. in position; tableware and cutlery for (single place at) table; descending below horizon of sun; music for song.
set·tle [SET-l] *v* **-tled, -tling.** ▶ *vt* arrange, put in order; establish; make firm or secure or quiet; decide upon; end (dispute, etc.); pay; bestow (property) by legal deed. ▶ *vi* come to rest; subside; become clear; take up residence; subside, sink to bottom; come to agreement. **set'tle·ment** [-mənt] *n* act of settling; place newly inhabited; money bestowed legally; subsidence (of building).
set·tler [SET-lər] *n* colonist.
sev·en [SEV-ən] *adj, n* cardinal number, next after six. **sev'enth** *adj* the ordinal number.
sev'en·teen' *adj, n* ten and seven.
sev'en·ty *adj, n, pl* **-ties.** ten times seven.
sev·er [SEV-ər] *v* separate, divide; cut off. **sev·er·ance** [-əns] *n* **severance pay** compensation paid by a firm to an employee for loss of employment.
sev·er·al [SEV-ər-əl] *adj* some, a few; separate; individual; various; different. ▶ *pron* indefinite small number. **sev'er·al·ly** *adv* apart from others; singly.
se·vere [sə-VEER] *adj* **-ver·er, -ver·est.** strict; rigorous; hard to do; harsh; austere; extreme. **se·ver'i·ty** [-VER-i-tee] *n*

sew [soh] v **sewed, sewn** or **sewed, sew·ing.** join with needle and thread; make by sewing.

sew·age [SOO-ij] n refuse, waste matter, excrement conveyed in sewer. **sew'er** n underground drain to remove waste water and refuse. **sew'er·age** n arrangement of sewers; sewage.

sex [seks] n state of being male or female; males or females collectively; sexual intercourse. ▶ adj concerning sex. ▶ vt ascertain sex of. **sex'ism** n discrimination on basis of sex. **sex'ist** n, adj **sex·u·al** [SEK-shoo-əl] adj **sex'y** adj **sex·i·er, sex·i·est. sexual intercourse** act of procreation in which male's penis is inserted into female's vagina.

sex·a·ge·nar·i·an [sek-sə-jə-NAIR-ee-ən] adj, n (person) sixty to seventy years old.

sex·tant [SEK-stənt] n navigator's instrument for measuring elevations of heavenly body, etc.

sex·tet [seks-TET] n (composition for) six singers or players; group of six.

sex·ton [SEK-stən] n official who takes care of church building and its contents and sometimes assists in burial of dead; official who takes care of synagogue and sometimes assists cantor in conducting services.

Sg Chem seaborgium.

shab·by [SHAB-ee] adj **-bi·er, -bi·est.** faded, worn, ragged; poorly dressed; mean, dishonorable; stingy. **shab'bi·ly** adv **shab'bi·ness** [-nis] n

shack [shak] n rough hut. **shack up (with)** sl live (with) esp. as husband and wife without being legally married.

shack·le [SHAK-əl] n metal ring or fastening for prisoner's wrist or ankle; anything that confines. ▶ vt **-led, -ling.** fasten with shackles; hamper.

shade [shayd] n partial darkness; shelter, place sheltered from light, heat, etc.; darker part of anything; depth of color; tinge; ghost; screen; anything used to screen; window blind. ▶ pl sl sunglasses. ▶ vt **shad·ed, shad·ing.** screen from light, darken; represent shades in drawing. **shad'y** adj **shad·i·er, shad·i·est.** shielded from sun; dim; dubious; dishonest; dishonorable.

shad·ow [SHAD-oh] n dark figure projected by anything that intercepts rays of light; patch of shade; slight trace; indistinct image; gloom; inseparable companion. ▶ vt cast shadow over; follow and watch closely. **shad'ow·y** adj

shaft n straight rod, stem, handle; arrow; ray, beam (of light); revolving rod for transmitting power; one of the bars between which horse is harnessed; entrance boring of mine.

shag¹ n matted wool or hair; long-napped cloth; coarse shredded tobacco. **shag'gy** adj **-gi·er, -gi·est.** covered with rough hair or wool; tousled; unkempt.

shag² vt **shagged, shag·ging.** chase after; Baseball in practice, chase and catch fly balls.

shah n formerly, ruler of Iran.

shake [shayk] v **shook** [shuuk], **shak·en.** (cause to) move with quick vibrations; tremble; grasp the hand (of another) in greeting; upset; wave, brandish. ▶ n act of shaking; vibration; jolt; inf short period of time, jiffy. **shak'i·ly** adv **shak'y** adj **shak·i·er, shak·i·est.** unsteady, insecure.

shale [shayl] n flaky, sedimentary rock.

shall [shal] v, pt **should.** used as an auxiliary to make the future tense or to indicate intention, obligation, or inevitability.

shal·lot [SHAL-ət] n kind of small onion.

shal·low [SHAL-oh] adj **-er, -est.** not deep; having little depth of water; superficial; not sincere. ▶ n shallow place.

sham adj, n imitation, counterfeit. ▶ v **shammed, sham·ming.**

pretend, feign.

sham·ble [SHAM-bəl] *vi* **-bled, -bling.** walk in shuffling, awkward way.

sham·bles [SHAM-bəlz] *n* messy, disorderly thing or place.

shame [shaym] *n* emotion caused by consciousness of guilt or dishonor in one's conduct or state; cause of disgrace; ignominy; pity, hard luck. ▶ *vt* **shamed, sham·ing.** cause to feel shame; disgrace; force by shame (into). **shame'ful** [-fəl] *adj* disgraceful. **shame·less** [-lis] *adj* with no sense of shame; indecent. **shame'faced** [-faysd] *adj* ashamed.

sham·poo' *n* various preparations of liquid soap for washing hair, carpets, etc.; this process. ▶ *vt* **-pooed, -poo·ing.** use shampoo to wash.

sham·rock [SHAM-rok] *n* cloverlike plant with three leaves on each stem, esp. as Irish emblem.

shang·hai [SHANG-hī] *vt* **-haied, -hai·ing.** force, trick someone to do something.

shank *n* lower leg; shinbone; stem of thing. **shank of the evening** best or main part of the evening.

shan'tung *n* soft, natural Chinese silk.

shan·ty[1] [SHAN-tee] *n, pl* **-ties.** temporary wooden building; crude dwelling.

shanty[2] see CHANTEY.

shape [shayp] *n* external form or appearance, esp. of a woman; mold, pattern; condition, esp. of physical fitness. ▶ *v* **shaped, shap·ing.** ▶ *vt* form, mold, fashion, make. ▶ *vi* develop. **shape'less** [-lis] *adj* **shape'ly** *adj* **-li·er, -li·est.** well-proportioned.

shard [shahrd] *n* broken fragment, esp. of earthenware.

share[1] [shair] *n* portion; quota; lot; unit of ownership in corporation. ▶ *v* **shared, shar·ing.** give, take a share; join with others in doing, using, something. **share'hold·er** *n*

share[2] *n* blade of plow.

shark [shahrk] *n* large sometimes

predatory sea fish; person who cheats others; *inf* person of great ability in cards, etc.

sharp [shahrp] *adj* **-er, -est.** having keen cutting edge or fine point; keen; not gradual or gentle; brisk; clever; harsh; dealing cleverly but unfairly; shrill; strongly marked, esp. in outline. ▶ *adv* promptly. ▶ *n* *Mus* note half a tone above natural pitch; cheat, swindler (also **sharp'er**). **sharp'en** *vt* make sharp. **sharp'shoot·er** *n* marksman.

shat·ter [SHAT-ər] *v* break in pieces; ruin (plans, etc.); disturb (person) greatly.

shave [shayv] *v* **shaved** or **shav·en, shav·ing.** cut close, esp. hair of face or head; pare away; graze; reduce. ▶ *n* shaving. **shav'ings** *pl n* parings. **close shave** narrow escape.

shawl *n* piece of fabric to cover woman's shoulders or head.

she [shee] *pron* 3rd person singular feminine pronoun.

sheaf [sheef] *n, pl* **sheaves.** bundle, esp. corn; loose leaves of paper.

shear [sheer] *vt* **sheared** or **shorn, shear·ing.** clip hair, wool from; cut through; trim (e.g. hedge); fracture. **shears** *pl. n* large pair of scissors; mechanical shearing, cutting instrument.

sheath [sheeth] *n, pl* **sheaths** [sheethz] close-fitting cover, esp. for knife or sword; scabbard; condom. **sheathe** [sheeth] *vt* **sheathed, sheath·ing.** put into sheath.

she·bang [shə-BANG] *n inf* situation, matter, esp. whole shebang.

shed[1] *n* roofed shelter used for storage or as workshop.

shed[2] *vt* **shed, shed·ding.** (cause to) pour forth (e.g. tears, blood); cast off.

sheen *n* gloss.

sheep *n* ruminant animal bred for wool and meat. **sheep'ish** *adj* embarrassed, shy. **sheep-dip** *n* solution in which sheep are immersed to kill vermin and germs in fleece. **sheep'dog** n dog of various breeds orig. for herding sheep. **sheep'skin** n skin of sheep (with fleece) used for clothing, rug or without fleece for parchment; inf diploma.

sheer[1] adj **-er, -est.** perpendicular; of material, very fine, transparent; absolute, unmitigated.

sheer[2] vi deviate from course; swerve; turn aside.

sheet[1] n large piece of cotton, etc. to cover bed; broad piece of any thin material; large expanse. ▶ vt cover with sheet.

sheet[2] n rope fastened in corner of sail. **sheet anchor** large anchor for emergency.

sheik [shayk or sheek] n Arab chief.

shek·el [SHEK-əl] n monetary unit of Israel. ▶ pl inf money.

shelf n, pl **shelves.** board fixed horizontally (on wall, etc.) for holding things; ledge.

shell n hard outer case (esp. of egg, nut, etc.); husk; explosive projectile; outer part of structure left when interior is removed; racing shell. ▶ vt take shell from; take out of shell; fire at with shells. **racing shell** long light racing boat for rowing by crew of one or more. **shell'fish** n mollusk; crustacean. **shell shock** battle fatigue, nervous disorder caused by bursting of shells or bombs. **shell out** inf pay up.

shel·lac [shə-LAK] n varnish. ▶ vt **-lacked, -lack·ing.** coat with shellac.

shel·ter [SHEL-tər] n place, structure giving protection; protection; refuge; haven. ▶ vt give protection to; screen. ▶ vi take shelter.

shelve [shelv] v **shelved, shelv·ing.** ▶ vt put on a shelf; put off; cease to employ; defer indefinitely. ▶ vi slope gradually.

she·nan·i·gans [shə-NAN-i-gənz] pl n inf frolicking; playing tricks, etc.

shep·herd [SHEP-ərd] n person who tends sheep. ▶ vt guide, watch over. **shep'herd·ess** [-is] n, fem

sher·bet [SHUR-bit] n frozen fruit-flavored dessert like ices but with gelatin, etc. added.

sher·iff n law enforcement officer.

Sher·pa [SHUR-pə] n, pl **-pas** or **-pa.** member of a Tibetan people.

sher·ry [SHER-ee] n, pl **-ries.** fortified wine from S Spain.

shib·bo·leth [SHIB-ə-lith] n custom, word, etc. distinguishing people of particular class or group; test word, pet phrase of sect or party.

shield [sheeld] n piece of armor carried on arm; any protection used to stop blows, missiles, etc.; any protective device; sports trophy. ▶ vt cover, protect.

shift v (cause to) move, change position. ▶ n relay of workers; time of their working; evasion; expedient; removal; woman's underskirt or dress. **shift'i·ness** [-nis] n **shift'less** [-lis] adj lacking in resource or character. **shift'y** adj **shift·i·er, shift·i·est.** evasive, of dubious character.

shil·le·lagh [shə-LAY-lə] n (in Ireland) cudgel.

shil'ling n former Brit. coin, now 5 pence; monetary unit in various countries.

shil·ly-shal·ly [SHIL-ee-shal-ee] vi **-lied, -ly·ing.** waver. ▶ n wavering, indecision.

shim·mer [SHIM-ər] vi shine with quivering light. ▶ n such light; glimmer.

shin n front of lower leg. ▶ v **shinned, shin·ning.** climb with arms and legs. **shin'bone** [-bohn] n tibia.

shin'dig n inf elaborate party, dance, etc.

shine [shīn] v **shone, shin·ing.** give out, reflect light; perform very well, excel; cause to shine by polishing. ▶ n brightness, luster; polishing. **shin'y** adj **shin·i·er, shin·i·est.**

shin·gle[1] [SHIN-gəl] n wooden roof and wall tile. ▶ vt **-gled, -gling.** cover with shingles.

shingle[2] n mass of pebbles.

shin·gles [SHIN-gəlz] n disease causing inflammation along a nerve.

Shin·to [SHIN-toh] n native Japanese religion. **Shin'to·ism** n

ship n large seagoing vessel. ▶ v **shipped, ship·ping.** put on or send (esp. by ship); embark; take employment on ship. **ship'ment** [-mənt] n act of shipping; goods shipped. **shipping** n freight transport business; ships collectively. **ship'shape** [-shayp] adj orderly, trim. **ship'wreck** [-rek] n destruction of a ship through storm, collision, etc. ▶ vt cause to undergo shipwreck. **ship'yard** n place for building and repair of ships. **ship out** leave by ship; inf quit, resign, be fired.

shirk [shurk] vt evade, try to avoid (duty, etc.).

shirr [shur] vt gather (fabric) into parallel rows. ▶ n series of gathered rows decorating a dress, blouse, etc. (also **shir'ring**).

shirt [shurt] n garment for upper part of body.

shiv n sl knife.

shiv·er¹ [SHIV-ər] vi tremble, usu. with cold or fear; shudder; vibrate. ▶ n act, state, of shivering.

shiver² v splinter, break in pieces. ▶ n splinter.

shoal [shohl] n stretch of shallow water; sandbank or bar. ▶ v make, become, shallow.

shock¹ [shok] vt horrify, scandalize. ▶ n violent or damaging blow; emotional disturbance; state of weakness, illness, caused by physical or mental shock; paralytic stroke; collision; effect on sensory nerves of electric discharge. **shock'er** n person or thing that shocks or distresses. **shock absorber** device (esp. in automobiles) to absorb shocks.

shock² n group of corn sheaves placed together.

shock³ n mass of hair. ▶ adj shaggy. **shock'head·ed** [-hed-id] adj

shod·dy [SHOD-ee] adj **-di·er, -di·est.** worthless, trashy, second-rate, of poor material.

shoe [shoo] n, pl **shoes.** covering for foot, not enclosing ankle; metal rim or curved bar put on horse's hoof; various protective plates or undercoverings. ▶ vt **shod** or **shoed, shod** or **shoed, shoe·ing.** protect, furnish with shoe or shoes. **shoe'string** adj, n very small (amount of money, etc.).

shone pt./pp. of SHINE.

shoo interj go away! ▶ vt **shooed, shoo·ing.** drive away. **shoo'-in** n inf person or thing certain to win or succeed; match or contest that is easy to win.

shook [shuuk] pt. of SHAKE.

shoot v **shot, shoot·ing.** hit, wound, kill with missile fired from weapon; discharge weapon; send, slide, push rapidly; photograph, film; hunt; sprout. ▶ n young branch, sprout; shooting competition; hunting expedition.

shop n store, place for retail sale of goods and services; workshop, factory. ▶ vi **shopped, shop·ping.** visit stores to buy or examine. **shop'lift·er** n one who steals from store. **shop stew'ard** [STOO-ərd] n labor union representative of workers in factory, etc. **talk shop** talk of one's business, etc. at unsuitable moments.

shore¹ [shor] n edge of sea or lake.

shore² vt **shored, shor·ing.** prop (up).

shorn pp. of SHEAR.

short adj **-er, -est.** not long; not tall; brief, hasty; not reaching quantity or standard required; wanting, lacking; abrupt, rude; Stock Exchange not in possession of stock shares when selling them. ▶ adv suddenly, abruptly; without reaching end. ▶ n short film. ▶ pl short trousers. **short'age** [-ij] n deficiency. **short'en** v **short'ly** adv soon; briefly. **short'bread** [-bred] n butter cookie. **short'cake** [-kayk] n cake made of butter, flour and sugar; dessert of biscuit dough with fruit topping. **short circuit** Electricity connection, often accidental, of low resistance between two parts of circuit. **short'com·ing** [-kum-ing] n failing;

defect. **short'hand** n method of rapid writing by signs or contractions. **short'-hand·ed** adj lacking the usual or necessary number of workers, helpers. **short list** selected list of candidates (esp. for job) from which final selection will be made. **short shrift** summary treatment. **short ton** ton (2000 lbs.). **short wave** radio wave of frequency greater than 1600 kHz.

short·en·ing [SHORT-ning] n fat used to make cake, etc. rich and crumbly; pr. p. of SHORTEN.

shot n act of shooting; missile; lead in small pellets; marksman, shooter; try, attempt; photograph; short film sequence; dose; hypodermic injection. ▶ adj woven so that color is different, according to angle of light; pt./pp. of SHOOT.

should [shuud] v past tense of **shall** used as an auxiliary to make the subjunctive mood or to indicate obligation or possibility.

shoul·der [SHOHL-dər] n part of body to which arm or foreleg is attached; anything resembling shoulder; side of road. ▶ vt undertake; bear (burden); accept (responsibility); put on one's shoulder. ▶ vi make way by pushing. **shoulder blade** [blayd] shoulder bone.

shout [showt] n loud cry. ▶ v utter (cry, etc.) with loud voice.

shove [shuv] vt **shoved, shov·ing.** push. ▶ n push. **shove off** inf go away.

shovel [SHUV-əl] n instrument for scooping, lifting earth, etc. ▶ vt **-eled, -el·ing.** lift, move (as) with shovel.

show [shoh] v **showed, shown, show·ing.** expose to view; point out; display; exhibit; explain; prove; guide; accord (favor, etc.); appear; be noticeable. ▶ n display; exhibition; spectacle; theatrical or other entertainment; indication; competitive event; ostentation; semblance; pretense. **show'i·ly** adv **show'y** adj **show·i·er,**

show·i·est. gaudy; ostentatious. **show'down** n confrontation; final test. **show jump·ing** horse-riding competition to demonstrate skill in jumping obstacles. **show'man** [-mən] n, pl **-men.** organizer of theatrical events, circuses, etc.; one skilled at presenting anything in effective way. **show off** exhibit to invite admiration; behave in this way. **show-off** n ▶ **show up** reveal; expose; embarrass; arrive.

show·er [SHOW-ər] n short fall of rain; anything coming down like rain; kind of bath in which person stands while being sprayed with water; party to present gifts to a person, as a prospective bride. ▶ vt bestow liberally. ▶ vi take bath in shower. **show'er·y** adj

shrank pt. of SHRINK.

shrap·nel [SHRAP-nəl] n shell filled with pellets that scatter on bursting; shell splinters.

shred n fragment, torn strip; small amount. ▶ vt **shred** or **shred·ded, shred·ding.** cut, tear to shreds.

shrew [shroo] n animal like mouse; bad-tempered woman; scold. **shrew'ish** adj nagging.

shrewd [shrood] adj **-er, -est.** astute, intelligent; crafty. **shrewd'ness** [-nis] n

shriek [shreek] n shrill cry; piercing scream. ▶ v screech.

shrike [shrīk] n bird of prey with heavy hooked bill.

shrill adj piercing, sharp in tone. ▶ v utter in such tone. **shril'ly** adv

shrimp n, pl **shrimp** or **shrimps.** small edible crustacean; (pl **shrimps**) inf undersized person. ▶ vi go catching shrimps.

shrine [shrīn] n place (building, tomb, alcove) of worship, usu. associated with saint.

shrink [shreenk] v **shrank** or **shrunk, shrunk** or **shrunk·en, shrink·ing.** become smaller; retire, flinch, recoil; make smaller. ▶ n sl psychiatrist, psychotherapist. **shrink'age** [-ij] n

shrive [shrīv] vt **shrove** or **shrived, shriv·en** or **shrived, shriv·ing.** give

absolution to. **shrift** n obs
confession; absolution.

shriv·el [SHRIV-əl] vi **-eled, -el·ing.**
shrink and wither.

shroud [shrowd] n sheet, wrapping,
for corpse; anything that covers,
envelops like shroud. ▶ pl set of
ropes to masthead. ▶ vt put shroud
on; screen, veil; wrap up.

Shrove Tuesday [shrohv] day
before Ash Wednesday.

shrub n bushy plant; drink of fruit
juices, etc. oft. with alcohol.
shrub·ber·y [-ər-ee] n, pl **-ber·ies.**
planting of shrubs; shrubs
collectively.

shrug v **shrugged, shrug·ging.**
raise shoulders, as sign of
indifference, ignorance, etc.; move
(shoulders) thus; (with off) dismiss
as unimportant. ▶ n shrugging.

shrunk, shrunken pp. of SHRINK.

shuck [shuk] n shell, husk, pod. ▶ vt
remove husks, etc. from. **shucks**
interj inf used as mild expression of
regret.

shud·der [SHUD-ər] vi shake,
tremble violently, esp. with horror.
▶ n shuddering, tremor.

shuf·fle [SHUF-əl] vi **-fled, -fling.**
move feet without lifting them;
dance like this; act evasively. ▶ vt
mix (cards); (with off) evade, pass
to another. ▶ n shuffling;
rearrangement.

shun vt **shunned, shun·ning.** avoid;
keep away from.

shunt vt push aside; divert; move
(train) from one line to another.

shut v **shut, shut·ting.** close; bar;
forbid entrance to. **shut'ter** [-ər] n
movable window screen, usu.
hinged to frame; device in camera
admitting light as required to film
or plate. **shut down** close or stop
factory, machine, etc.

shut·tle [SHUT-l] n instrument that
threads weft between threads of
warp in weaving; similar appliance
in sewing machine; plane, bus, etc.
traveling to and fro over short
distance. ▶ v **-tled, -tling.** (cause to)
move back and forth.

shut'tle·cock n small, light cone

with cork stub and fan of feathers
used as a ball in badminton.

shy¹ [shī] adj **shy·er** or **shi·er,
shy·est** or **shi·est.** awkward in
company; timid; bashful; reluctant;
scarce, lacking (esp. in card games,
not having enough money for bet,
etc.). ▶ vi **shied, shy·ing.** start back
in fear; show sudden reluctance.
▶ n, pl **shies.** start of fear by horse.
shy'ly adv **shy'ness** [-nis] n

shy² vt, n shied, **shy·ing.** throw.

shy·ster [SHĪ-stər] n inf dishonest,
deceitful person, esp.
unprofessional lawyer.

SI Fr Système International
(d'Unités), international system of
units of measurement based on
units of ten.

Si Chem silicon.

Si·a·mese cat [SĪ-ə-MEEZ] breed of
cat with blue eyes.

Siamese twins nontechnical name
for CONJOINED TWINS.

sib·i·lant [SIB-ə-lənt] adj hissing.
▶ n speech sound with hissing
effect.

sib'ling n person's brother or sister.
▶ adj

sib·yl [SIB-əl] n woman endowed
with spirit of prophecy. **sib'yl·line**
[-een] adj occult.

sic [sik] Lat thus: oft. used to call
attention to a quoted mistake.

sick [sik] adj **-er, -est.** inclined to
vomit, vomiting; not well or
healthy, physically or mentally;
macabre, sadistic, morbid; bored,
tired; disgusted. **sick'en** [-ən] v
make, become, sick; disgust;
nauseate. **sick'ly** adj unhealthy,
weakly; inducing nausea. **sick'ness**
[-nis] n **sick bay** place set aside for
treating sick people, esp. aboard
ships.

sick·le [SIK-əl] n reaping hook.

side [sīd] n one of the surfaces of
object, esp. upright inner or outer
surface; either surface of thing
having only two; part of body that
is to right or left; region nearer or
farther than, or right or left of,
dividing line, etc.; region; aspect or
part; one of two parties or sets of

opponents; sect, faction; line of descent traced through one parent. ▶ *adj* at, in, the side; subordinate, incidental. ▶ *vi* **sid·ed, sid·ing.** (usu. with *with*) take up cause of. **siding** *n* short line of rails on which trains or wagons are shunted from main line. **side'board** [-bord] *n* piece of furniture for holding dishes, etc. in dining room. **side'burns** [-burnz] *pl n* man's side whiskers. **side'car** *n* small car attached to side of motorcycle; cocktail made with brandy, orange liqueur and lemon juice. **side'kick** *n* pal; assistant. **side'light** [-līt] *n* esp. either of two lights on vessel for use at night; item of incidental information. **side'line** *n Sports* boundary of playing area; subsidiary interest or activity. **side'long** [-lawng] *adj* lateral, not directly forward. ▶ *adv* obliquely. **side'man** *n, pl* **-men.** instrumentalist in band. **side'track** *v* deviate from main topic. ▶ *n* **side'walk** *n* footpath beside road. **side'ways** [-wayz] *adv* to or from the side; laterally.

si·de·re·al [sī-DEER-ee-əl] *adj* relating to, fixed by, stars.

si·dle [SĪD-l] *vi* **-dled, -dling.** move in furtive or stealthy manner; move sideways.

SIDS sudden infant death syndrome, unexplained death of baby while asleep.

siege [seej] *n* besieging of town or fortified place.

si·en·na [see-EN-ə] *n* (pigment of) brownish-yellow color.

si·er·ra [see-ER-ə] *n* range of mountains with jagged peaks.

si·es·ta [see-ES-tə] *n* rest, sleep in afternoon.

sieve [siv] *n* device with network or perforated bottom for sifting. ▶ *v* **sieved, siev·ing.** sift; strain.

sift *vt* separate (e.g. with sieve) coarser portion from finer; examine closely. **sift'er** *n*

sigh [sī] *v, n* (utter) long audible breath. **sigh for** yearn for, grieve for.

sight [sīt] *n* faculty of seeing; seeing; thing seen; view; glimpse; device for guiding eye; spectacle; *inf* pitiful or ridiculous or unusual object; *inf* large number, great deal. ▶ *vt* catch sight of; adjust sights of gun, etc. **sight for sore eyes** *inf* person or thing one is glad to see. **sight'less** [-lis] *adj* **sight-read** [-reed] *v* **-read** [-red], **-read·ing** [-reed-ing] play, sing music without previous preparation. **sight'see** *v* visit (place) to look at interesting sights.

sign [sīn] *n* mark, gesture, etc. to convey some meaning; (board, placard, bearing) notice, warning, etc.; symbol; omen; evidence. ▶ *vt* put one's signature to; ratify. ▶ *vi* make sign or gesture; affix signature; use symbols of sign language. **sign language** gestures used for communicating with deaf people.

sig·nal [SIG-nəl] *n* sign to convey order or information, esp. on railroads; that which in first place impels any action; sequence of electrical impulses or radio waves transmitted or received. ▶ *adj* remarkable, striking. ▶ *v* **-naled, -nal·ing.** make signals to; give orders, etc. by signals. **sig'nal·ize** *vt* **-ized, -iz·ing.** make notable.

sig·na·to·ry [SIG-nə-tor-ee] *n, pl* **-ries.** one of those who sign agreements, treaties.

sig·na·ture [SIG-nə-chər] *n* person's name written by self; act of writing it. **signature tune** theme song.

sig·net [SIG-nit] *n* small seal.

sig·nif·i·cant [sig-NIF-i-kənt] *adj* revealing; designed to make something known; important. **sig·nif'i·cance** [-kəns] *n* import, weight; meaning. **sig·ni·fi·ca'tion** *n* meaning.

sig·ni·fy [SIG-nə-fī] *v* **-fied, -fy·ing.** mean; indicate; denote; imply; be of importance.

si·gnor [SEEN-yor] *n* Italian title of respect, like Mr. **si·gno·ra** [sin-YOR-ə] *n* Mrs. **si·gno·ri'na**

[seen-yə-REEN-ə] *n* Miss.

Sikh [seek] *n* member of Hindu religious sect.

si·lage [SĪ-lij] *n* fodder crop harvested while green and stored in state of partial fermentation.

si·lence [SĪ-ləns] *n* absence of noise; refraining from speech. ▶ *vt* **-lenced, -lenc·ing.** make silent; put a stop to. **si'lenc·er** *n* device to reduce noise of firearm. **si'lent** *adj*

sil·hou·ette [sil-oo-ET] *n* outline of object seen against light background; profile portrait in black. ▶ *vt* **-et·ted, -et·ting.** show in or as if in silhouette.

sil·i·ca [SIL-i-kə] *n* naturally occurring dioxide of silicon. **si·li·ceous** [sə-LEE-shəs] *adj* **si·li·co·sis** [si-li-KOH-sis] *n* lung disease caused by inhaling silica dust over a long period.

sil·i·con [SIL-i-kən] *n* brittle metalloid element found in sand, clay, stone, widely used in chemistry, industry. **sil'i·cone** [-kohn] *n* large class of synthetic substances, related to silicon and used in chemistry, industry, medicine.

silk *n* fiber made by larvae (**silkworms**) of a certain moth; thread, fabric made from this. **silk'en** *adj* made of, like silk; soft; smooth; dressed in silk. **silk'i·ness** [-nis] *n*

sill *n* ledge beneath window; bottom part of door or window frame.

sil·ly [SIL-ee] *adj* **-li·er, -li·est.** foolish; trivial; feebleminded. **sil'li·ness** [-nis] *n*

si·lo [SĪ-loh] *n*, *pl* **-los.** pit, tower for storing fodder or grain; underground missile launching site.

silt *n* mud deposited by water. ▶ *v* fill, be choked with silt. **sil·ta'tion** *n*

sil·ver [SIL-vər] *n* white precious metal; things made of it; silver coins; cutlery. ▶ *adj* made of silver; resembling silver or its color; having pale luster, as moon; soft, melodious, as sound; bright. ▶ *vt* coat with silver. **sil'ver·y** *adj* **silver**

birch tree having silvery white peeling bark. **silver wedding** 25th wedding anniversary.

sim·i·an [SIM-ee-ən] *adj* of, like apes.

sim·i·lar [SIM-ə-lər] *adj* resembling, like. **sim·i·lar'i·ty** *n* likeness; close resemblance.

sim·i·le [SIM-ə-lee] *n* comparison of one thing with another, using *as* or *like*, esp. in poetry.

si·mil·i·tude [si-MIL-i-tood] *n* outward appearance, likeness; guise.

sim·mer [SIM-ər] *v* keep or be just bubbling or just below boiling point; to be in state of suppressed anger or laughter.

sim·per [SIM-pər] *vi* smile, utter in silly or affected way. ▶ *n*

sim·ple [SIM-pəl] *adj* **-pler, -plest.** not complicated; plain; not combined or complex; ordinary; mere; guileless; stupid. **sim'ple·ton** [-tən] *n* foolish person. **sim·plic'i·ty** [-PLIS-ə-tee] *n*, *pl* **-ties.** simpleness, clearness, artlessness. **sim·pli·fi·ca'tion** *n* **sim'pli·fy** *vt* **-fied, -fy·ing.** make simple, plain or easy. **sim·plis'tic** *adj* extremely simple, naive. **sim'ply** *adv* **simple fraction** one in which both the numerator and the denominator are whole numbers.

sim·u·late [SIM-yə-layt] *vt* **-lat·ed, -lat·ing.** make pretense of; reproduce, copy, esp. conditions of particular situation. **sim·u·la'tion** *n* **sim'u·la·tor** *n*

si·mul·ta·ne·ous [sī-məl-TAY-nee-əs] *adj* occurring at the same time. **si·mul·ta·ne'i·ty** [-tə-NEE-i-tee] *n* **simulta'ne·ous·ly** *adv*

sin *n* transgression of divine or moral law, esp. committed consciously; offense against principle or standard. ▶ *vi* **sinned, sin·ning.** commit sin. **sin'ful** [-fəl] *adj* of nature of sin; guilty of sin. **sin'ful·ly** *adv*

since [sins] *prep* during or throughout period of time after. ▶ *conj* from time when; because.

▶ *adv* from that time.

sin·cere [sin-SEER] *adj* not hypocritical, actually moved by or feeling apparent emotions; true, genuine; unaffected. **sin·cere'ly** *adv* **sin·cer'i·ty** [-SER-i-tee] *n*

sine [sīn] *n* mathematical function, esp. ratio of length of hypotenuse to opposite side in right triangle.

si·ne·cure [SĪ-ni-kyuur] *n* office with pay but minimal duties.

si·ne di·e [SĪ-nee DĪ-ee] *Lat* with no date, indefinitely postponed.

si·ne qua non [SĪ-nee kway non] *Lat* essential condition or requirement.

sin·ew [SIN-yoo] *n* tough, fibrous cord joining muscle to bone. ▶ *pl* muscles, strength. **sin'ew·y** *adj* stringy; muscular.

sing *v* **sang, sung, sing·ing.** utter musical sounds; hum, whistle, ring; utter (words) with musical modulation; celebrate in song or poetry. **sing'song** [-sawng] *adj* monotonously regular in tone, rhythm.

singe [sinj] *vt* **singed, singe·ing.** burn surface of. ▶ *n* act or effect of singeing.

sin·gle [SING-gəl] *adj* one only; alone, separate; unmarried; for one; formed of only one part, fold, etc.; wholehearted, straightforward. ▶ *n* single thing; phonograph record with one short item on each side; *Baseball* one-base hit. ▶ *vt* **-gled, -gling.** pick (out); make single. **sin'gly** *adv* **single file** persons, things arranged in one line. **single-hand·ed** *adj* without assistance. **singles bar** bar or club that is social meeting place esp. for single people.

sin·gu·lar [SING-gyə-lər] *adj* remarkable; unusual; unique; denoting one person or thing. **sin·gu·lar'i·ty** *n, pl* **-ties.** something unusual. **sin'gu·lar·ly** [-lər-lee] *adv* particularly; peculiarly.

sin·is·ter [SIN-ə-stər] *adj* threatening; evil-looking; wicked; unlucky; *Heraldry* on bearer's left-hand side. **sin'is·trous** [-trəs]

adj ill-omened.

sink [singk] *v* **sank** or **sunk, sunk** or **sunk·en, sink·ing.** become submerged (in water); drop, give way; decline in value, health, etc.; penetrate (into); cause to sink; make by digging out; invest. ▶ *n* receptacle with pipe for carrying away waste water; cesspool; place of corruption, vice. **sink'er** *n* weight for fishing line. **sink'hole** [-hohl] *n* low land where drainage collects; cavity formed in rock by water. **sinking fund** money set aside at intervals for payment of particular liability at fixed date.

Sino- *comb. form* Chinese, of China, e.g. *Sino-American relations.*

sin·u·ous [SIN-yoo-əs] *adj* curving, devious, lithe. **sin·u·os'i·ty** [-OS-i-tee] *n, pl* **-ties.**

si·nus [SĪ-nəs] *n, pl* **-nus·es.** cavity, esp. air passages in bones of skull. **si·nus·i'tis** [-SĪ-tis] *n* inflammation of sinus.

sip *v* **sipped, sip·ping.** drink in very small portions. ▶ *n*

si·phon [SĪ-fən] *n* device, esp. bent tube, that uses atmospheric or gaseous pressure to draw liquid from container. ▶ *v* draw off thus; draw off in small amounts.

sir [sur] *n* polite term of address for a man; (**S-**) title of knight or baronet.

sire [sīr] *n* male parent, esp. of horse or domestic animal; term of address to king. ▶ *v* **sired, sir·ing.** beget.

si·ren [SĪ-rən] *n* device making loud wailing noise, esp. giving warning of danger; legendary sea nymph who lured sailors to destruction; alluring woman.

sir·loin [SUR-loin] *n* prime cut of loin of beef.

si·sal [SĪ-səl] *n* (fiber of) plant used in making ropes.

sis·sy [SIS-ee] *adj, n, pl* **-sies.** weak, cowardly (person); effeminate boy or man.

sis·ter [SIS-tər] *n* daughter of same parents; woman fellow member esp. of religious body. ▶ *adj* closely related, similar. **sis'ter·hood** [-huud] *n* relation of sister; order, band of women. **sis'ter·ly** *adj* **sister-in-law** *n* sister of husband or wife; brother's wife.

sit *v* **sat, sit·ting.** (mainly intr) adopt posture or rest on buttocks, thighs; perch; incubate; pose for portrait; occupy official position; hold session; remain; take examination; keep watch over baby, etc. **sit in** protest by refusing to move from place. **sit-in** *n* such protest.

si·tar [si-TAHR] *n* stringed musical instrument, esp. of India. **si·tar'ist** *n*

site [sīt] *n* place, location; space for, with, a building; same as WEBSITE.

sit·u·ate [SICH-oo-ayt] *v* **-at·ed, -at·ing.** place, locate. **sit·u·a'tion** *n* place, position; state of affairs; employment, post.

six [siks] *adj, n* cardinal number one more than five. **sixth** *adj* ordinal number. ▶ *n* sixth part. **six'teen'** *n, adj* six and ten. **six'ty** *n, adj, pl* **-ties.** six times ten.

size[1] [sīz] *n* bigness, dimensions; one of series of standard measurements of clothes, etc.; *inf* state of affairs. ▶ *vt* **sized, siz·ing.** arrange according to size. **siz'a·ble, size'a·ble** *adj* quite large. **size up** *inf* assess (person, situation, etc.).

size[2] *n* gluelike sealer, filler. ▶ *vt* **sized, siz·ing.** coat, treat with size.

siz·zle [SIZ-l] *v, n* **-zled, -zling.** (make) hissing, spluttering sound as of frying. **siz'zler** [-lər] *n inf* hot day.

skate[1] [skayt] *n* steel blade attached to boot, for gliding over ice. ▶ *vi* **skat·ed, skat·ing.** glide as on skates. **skat'er** *n* **skate'board** *n* small board mounted on roller-skate wheels.

skate[2] *n* large marine ray.

ske·dad·dle [ski-DAD-l] *vi inf* **-dled, -dling.** flee; run away hurriedly.

skeet *n* shooting sport with clay target propelled from trap to simulate flying bird.

skein [skayn] *n* quantity of yarn, wool, etc. in loose knot; flight of wildfowl.

skel·e·ton [SKEL-i-tn] *n* bones of animal; bones separated from flesh and preserved in their natural position; very thin person; outline, draft, framework; nucleus. ▶ *adj* reduced to a minimum; drawn in outline; not in detail. **skel'e·tal** [-təl] *adj* **skeleton key** key filed down so as to open many different locks.

skep·tic [SKEP-tik] *n* one who maintains doubt or disbelief; agnostic; unbeliever. **skep'ti·cal** [-kəl] *adj* **skep'ti·cism** [-siz-əm] *n*

sketch [skech] *n* rough drawing; brief account; essay; short humorous play. ▶ *v* make sketch (of). **sketch'y** *adj* **sketch·i·er, sketch·i·est.** omitting detail; incomplete; inadequate.

skew [skyoo] *vi* move obliquely. ▶ *adj* slanting; crooked.

skew·er [SKYOO-ər] *n* pin to fasten (meat) together. ▶ *v* pierce or fasten (as though) with skewer.

ski [skee] *n, pl* **skis.** long runner fastened to boot for sliding over snow or water. ▶ *v* **skied, ski·ing.** slide on skis; go skiing.

skid *v* **skid·ded, skid·ding.** slide (sideways), esp. vehicle out of control with wheels not rotating. ▶ *n* instance of this; device to facilitate sliding, e.g. in moving heavy objects. **skid·dy** *adj* **-di·er, -di·est.**

skiff *n* small boat.

skill *n* practical ability, cleverness, dexterity. **skilled** *adj* having, requiring knowledge, united with readiness and dexterity. **skill'ful** [-fəl] *adj* expert, masterly; adroit.

skil·let [SKIL-it] *n* small frying pan.

skim *v* **skimmed, skim·ming.** remove floating matter from surface of liquid; glide over lightly and rapidly; read thus; move thus. **skim milk, skimmed milk** milk from which cream has been removed.

skimp *vt* give short measure; do

thing imperfectly. **skimp'y** *adj*
skimp·i·er, skimp·i·est. meager;
scanty.

skin *n* outer covering of vertebrate
body, lower animal or fruit; animal
skin used as material or container;
film on surface of cooling liquid,
etc.; complexion. ▶ *vt* **skinned,
skin·ning.** remove skin of. **skin'ny**
adj **-ni·er, -ni·est.** thin. **skin-deep**
adj superficial; slight. **skin diving**
underwater swimming using
breathing apparatus. **skin'flint** *n*
miser, niggard. **skin graft**
transplant of piece of healthy skin
to wound to form new skin.
skin·tight [-tīt] *adj* fitting close to
skin.

skip[1] *v* **skipped, skip·ping.** leap
lightly; jump a rope as it is swung
under one; pass over, omit. ▶ *n* act
of skipping.

skip[2] *n* large bucket, container for
transporting people, materials in
mines, etc.

skip·per [SKIP-ər] *n* captain of ship,
plane or team. ▶ *vt* captain.

skirl [skurl] *n* sound of bagpipes.

skir·mish [SKUR-mish] *n* fight
between small parties, small battle.
▶ *vi* fight briefly or irregularly.

skirt [skurt] *n* woman's garment
hanging from waist; lower part of
woman's dress, coat, etc.; outlying
part; *sl, offens* woman. ▶ *vi* border;
go around. **skirt'ing** *n* material for
women's skirts.

skit *n* short satirical piece, esp.
theatrical sketch.

skit'tish *adj* frisky, frivolous.

skit·tle [SKIT-l] *n* bottle-shaped
object used as a target in some
games. ▶ *pl* game in which players
try to knock over skittles by rolling
a ball at them.

skoal [skohl] *interj* (as a toast) to
your health.

skul·dug·ger·y [skul-DUG-ə-ree] *n,
pl* **-ger·ies.** trickery.

skulk *vi* sneak out of the way; lurk.
skulk'er *n*

skull *n* bony case that encloses
brain. **skull'cap** *n* close-fitting cap.

skunk *n* small N Amer. animal that

emits evil-smelling fluid; *inf* mean
person.

sky [skī] *n, pl* **skies.** apparently
dome-shaped expanse extending
upward from the horizon; outer
space; heavenly regions. ▶ *vt* **skied,
sky·ing.** *inf* hit, throw (ball) high.
sky'div·ing *n* parachute jumping
with delayed opening of
parachute. **sky'light** [-līt] *n*
window in roof or ceiling.
sky'scrap·er [-skrayp-ər] *n* very tall
building.

slab *n* thick, broad piece.

slack [slak] *adj* loose; sluggish;
careless, negligent; not busy. ▶ *n*
loose part, as of rope. ▶ *vi* be idle or
lazy. **slack'en** *v* become looser;
become slower, abate.

slacks [slaks] *pl n* informal trousers
worn by men or women.

slag *n* refuse of smelted metal.

slain pp. of SLAY.

slake [slayk] *vt* **slaked, slak·ing.**
satisfy (thirst, desire, etc.); combine
(lime) with water to produce
calcium hydroxide.

sla·lom [SLAH-ləm] *n, v* race over
winding course in skiing,
automobile racing, etc.

slam *v* **slammed, slam·ming.** shut
noisily; bang; hit; dash down; *inf*
criticize harshly. ▶ *n* (noise of) this
action. **slam dunk** *n Basketball*
forceful downward basket; *inf*
clearcut success. ▶ *vt*
slam-dunked', slam-dunk'ing.
Basketball shoot (ball) in a slam
dunk. **grand slam** *Cards* winning
of all tricks; *Sports* winning of
selected group of major
tournaments in one year.

slan·der [SLAN-dər] *n* false or
malicious statement about person.
▶ *v* utter such statement.
slan'der·ous *adj*

slang *n* words, etc. or meanings of
these used very informally for
novelty or vividness or for the sake
of unconventionality.

slant *v* slope; put at angle; write,
present (news, etc.) with bias. ▶ *n*
slope; point of view; idea. ▶ *adj*
sloping, oblique. **slant'wise** [-wīz]

adv

slap *n* blow with open hand or flat instrument. ▶ *vt* **slapped, slap·ping.** strike thus; put on, down carelessly or messily.

slap'dash *adj* careless and abrupt.

slap'stick *n* broad boisterous comedy.

slash *vt* gash; lash; cut, slit; criticize unmercifully. ▶ *n* gash; cutting stroke; sloping punctuation mark, either **/** or ****.

slat *n* narrow strip of wood or metal as in window blinds, etc.

slate [slayt] *n* kind of stone that splits easily in flat sheets; piece of this for covering roof or, formerly, for writing on. ▶ *vt* **slat·ed, slat·ing.** cover with slates.

slath·er [SLA*TH*-ər] *n inf* generous amount. ▶ *vt inf* **-ered, -er·ing.** spread, apply thickly.

slat·tern [SLAT-ərn] *n* slut. **slatt'ern·ly** *adj* slovenly, untidy.

slaugh·ter [SLAW-tər] *n* killing. ▶ *vt* kill. **slaugh'ter·ous** *adj* **slaugh'ter·house** [-hows] *n* place for butchering animals for food.

slave [slayv] *n* captive, person without freedom or personal rights; one dominated by another or by a habit, etc. ▶ *vi* **slaved, slav·ing.** work like slave. **slav'er** *n* person, ship engaged in slave traffic. **slav'er·y** *n* **slav'ish** *adj* servile.

slav·er [SLAV-ər] *vi* dribble saliva from mouth; fawn. ▶ *n* saliva running from mouth.

slay *vt* **slew, slain, slay·ing.** kill; *inf* impress, esp. by being very funny. **slay'er** *n* killer.

slea·zy [SLEE-zee] *adj* **-zi·er, -zi·est.** sordid. **sleaze** [sleez] *n sl* sordidness; contemptible person.

sled *n* carriage on runners for sliding on snow; toboggan. ▶ *v* **sled·ded, sled·ding.**

sledge [slej] *n* sledgehammer; sled.

sledge·ham·mer [SLEJ-ham-ər] *n* heavy hammer with long handle.

sleek *adj* **-er, -est.** glossy, smooth, shiny.

sleep *n* unconscious state regularly occurring in humans and animals; slumber, repose; *inf* dried particles oft. found in corners of eyes after sleeping. ▶ *v* **slept, sleep·ing.** take rest in sleep, slumber; accommodate for sleeping. **sleep'er** *n* one who sleeps; railroad sleeping car; *inf* person, firm, etc. that succeeds unexpectedly. **sleep'i·ly** *adv* **sleep'i·ness** [-nis] *n* **sleep'less** [-lis] *adj* **sleep'y** *adj* **sleep·i·er, -i·est. sleeping sickness** Afr. disease spread by tsetse fly. **sleep'o·ver** *n* instance of spending the night at another person's home.

sleet *n* rain and snow or hail falling together.

sleeve [sleev] *n* part of garment that covers arm; case surrounding shaft; phonograph record cover. ▶ *vt* **sleeved, sleev·ing.** furnish with sleeves. **sleeved** *adj* **sleeve'less** [-lis] *adj* **have up one's sleeve** have something prepared secretly for emergency or as trick.

sleigh [slay] *n* sled.

sleight [slīt] *n* dexterity; trickery; deviousness. **sleight of hand** (manual dexterity in) conjuring, juggling; legerdemain.

slen·der [SLEN-dər] *adj* slim, slight; feeble.

slept pt./pp. of SLEEP.

sleuth [slooth] *n* detective; bloodhound. ▶ *vt* track.

slew[1] [sloo] pt. of SLAY.

slew[2] *v* swing around.

slew[3] *n inf* large number or quantity.

slice [slīs] *n* thin flat piece cut off; share; spatula; slice of pizza. ▶ *vt* **sliced, slic·ing.** cut into slices; cut cleanly; hit with bat, club, etc. at angle.

slick [slik] *adj* smooth; smooth-tongued; flattering; superficially attractive; sly. ▶ *vt* make glossy, smooth. ▶ *n* slippery area; patch of oil on water.

slide [slīd] *v* **slid** or **slid·den, slid·ing.** slip smoothly along; glide, as over ice; pass imperceptibly; deteriorate morally. ▶ *n* sliding; surface, track for sliding; sliding part of mechanism; piece of glass holding object to be viewed under microscope; photographic transparency. **slide rule** mathematical instrument of two parts, one of which slides upon the other, for rapid calculations. **sliding scale** schedule for automatically varying one thing (e.g. wages) according to fluctuations of another (e.g. cost of living).

slight [slīt] *adj* small, trifling; not substantial, fragile; slim, slender. ▶ *vt* disregard; neglect. ▶ *n* indifference; act of discourtesy.

slim *adj* **slim·mer, slim·mest.** thin; slight. ▶ *v* **slimmed, slim·ming.** reduce person's weight by diet and exercise. **slim'ness** *n* **slim'line** *adj* appearing slim; pert. to slimness.

slime [slīm] *n* greasy, thick, liquid mud or similar substance. **slim'y** *adj* **slim·i·er, slim·i·est.** like slime; fawning.

sling *n* strap, loop with string attached at each end for hurling stone; bandage for supporting wounded limb; rope, belt, etc. for hoisting, carrying weights. ▶ *vt* **slung, sling·ing.** throw; hoist, swing by rope.

slink *vi* **slunk, slink·ing.** move stealthily, sneak. **slink'y** *adj* **slink·i·er, slink·i·est.** sinuously graceful; (of clothes, etc.) figure-hugging.

slip[1] *v* **slipped, slip·ping.** (cause to) move smoothly, easily, quietly; pass out of (mind, etc.); (of motor vehicle clutch) engage partially, fail. ▶ *vi* lose balance by sliding; fall from person's grasp; (usu. with *up*) make mistake; decline in health, morals. ▶ *vt* put on or take off easily, quickly; let go (anchor, etc.); dislocate (bone). ▶ *n* act or occasion of slipping; mistake; petticoat; small piece of paper; plant cutting; launching slope on which ships are built; covering for pillow; small child. **slip'shod** *adj* slovenly, careless. **slip'stream** *n* *Aviation* stream of air driven astern by engine.

slip[2] *n* clay mixed with water to creamy consistency, used for decorating ceramic ware.

slip·per [SLIP-ər] *n* light shoe for indoor use. **slip'pered** *adj*

slip·per·y [SLIP-ə-ree] *adj* so smooth as to cause slipping or to be difficult to hold or catch; changeable; unreliable; crafty; wily.

slit *vt* **slit, slit·ting.** make long straight cut in; cut in strips. ▶ *n*

slith·er [SLITH-ər] *vi* slide unsteadily (down slope, etc.).

sliv·er [SLIV-ər] *n* thin small piece torn off something; splinter.

slob *n* slovenly, coarse person.

slob·ber [SLOB-ər] *v* slaver; be weakly and excessively demonstrative. ▶ *n* running saliva; maudlin speech.

sloe [sloh] *n* blue-black, sour fruit of blackthorn. **sloe-eyed** *adj* dark-eyed; slanty-eyed. **sloe gin** [jin] liqueur of sloes steeped in gin.

slog *v* **slogged, slog·ging.** hit vigorously, esp. in boxing; work or study with dogged determination; move, work with difficulty. ▶ *n*

slo·gan [SLOH-gən] *n* distinctive phrase (in advertising, etc.).

sloop *n* small one-masted vessel; *Hist* small warship.

slop *v* **slopped, slop·ping.** spill; splash. ▶ *n* spilled liquid; watery food; dirty liquid. ▶ *pl* liquid refuse. **slop'py** *adj* **-pi·er, -pi·est.** careless, untidy; sentimental; wet, muddy.

slope [slohp] *v* **sloped, slop·ing.** ▶ *vt* place slanting. ▶ *vi* lie in, follow an inclined course; go furtively. ▶ *n* slant; upward, downward inclination.

slosh *n* watery mud, etc. ▶ *v* splash. **sloshed** *adj* *sl* drunk.

slot *n* narrow hole or depression; slit for coins. ▶ *vt* **slot·ted, slot·ting.** put in slot; sort; place in series, organization. **slot machine** automatic machine worked by insertion of coin.

sloth [slawth] *n* sluggish S Amer. animal; sluggishness. **sloth'ful** [-fəl] *adj* lazy, idle.

slouch [slowch] *vi* walk, sit, etc. in

lazy or ungainly, drooping manner.
▶ *n, adj* (of hat) with wide, flexible
brim.

slough¹ [rhymes with **cow**] *n* bog.

slough² [sluf] *n* skin shed by snake.
▶ *v* shed (skin); drop off.

slov·en [SLUV-ən] *n* dirty, untidy
person. **slov'en·ly** *adj* **-li·er, -li·est.**
untidy; careless; disorderly. ▶ *adv*

slow [sloh] *adj* **-er, -est.** lasting a
long time; moving at low speed;
behind the true time; dull. ▶ *v*
slacken speed (of). **slow motion**
motion picture showing movement
greatly slowed down. **slow'poke**
[-pohk] *n* person slow in moving,
acting, deciding, etc.

sludge [sluj] *n* slush, ooze; sewage.

slug¹ *n* land snail with no shell;
bullet. **slug'gard** [-ərd] *n* lazy, idle
person. **slug'gish** *adj* slow; lazy,
inert; not functioning well.
slug'gish·ness *n*

slug² *v* **slugged, slug·ging.** hit,
slog. ▶ *n inf* heavy blow; shot of
whiskey. **slug'ger** *n* hard-hitting
boxer, baseball batter.

sluice [sloos] *n* gate, door to control
flow of water. ▶ *vt* **sluiced,
sluic·ing.** pour water over, through.

slum *n* squalid street or
neighborhood. ▶ *vi* **slummed,
slum·ming.** visit slums. **slum'lord** *n*
landlord who owns buildings in
slums and neglects them.

slum·ber [SLUM-bər] *vi, n* sleep.
slum'ber·er *n*

slump *v* fall heavily; relax
ungracefully; decline suddenly in
value, volume or esteem. ▶ *n*
sudden decline; (of prices, etc.)
sharp fall; depression.

slung pt./pp. of SLING.

slunk pt./pp. of SLINK.

slur *vt* **slurred, slur·ring.** pass over
lightly; run together (words,
musical notes); disparage. ▶ *n*
slight, stigma; *Mus* curved line
above or below notes to be slurred.

slurp *v* eat, drink noisily.

slur·ry [SLUR-ee] *n, pl* **-ries.** muddy
liquid mixture as cement, mud, etc.

slush *n* watery, muddy substance;
excessive sentimentality. **slush'y**

adj **slush·i·er, slush·i·est. slush
fund** fund for financing bribery,
corruption.

slut *n offens* promiscuous woman.
slut'tish *adj*

sly [slī] *adj* **sly·er** or **sli·er, sly·est** or
sli·est. cunning, wily, knowing;
secret, deceitful. **sly'ly, sli'ly** *adv*
sly'ness [-nis] *n*

Sm *Chem* samarium.

smack¹ [smak] *n* taste, flavor; *sl*
heroin. ▶ *vi* taste (of); suggest.

smack² *vt* slap; open and close (lips)
with loud sound. ▶ *n* smacking
slap; crack; such sound; loud kiss.
▶ *adv inf* squarely; directly.
smack'dab' *adv inf* smack.

smack³ *n* small sailing vessel, usu.
for fishing.

small [smawl] *adj* **-er, -est.** little,
unimportant; petty; short; weak;
mean. ▶ *n* small slender part esp. of
the back. **small hours** hours just
after midnight. **small-mind·ed**
[-mīnd-id] *adj* having narrow views;
petty. **small'pox** *n* contagious
disease. **small talk** light, polite
conversation.

smarm·y [SMAHR-mee] *adj*
smarm·i·er, smarm·i·est.
unpleasantly suave; fawning.

smart [smahrt] *adj* **-er, -est.** astute;
brisk; clever, witty; impertinent;
trim, well dressed; fashionable;
causing stinging pain. ▶ *v* feel,
cause pain. ▶ *n* sharp pain.
smart'en *vt* **smart'ly** *adv*
smart'ness [-nis] *n* **smart al'eck**
conceited person, know-it-all.
smart ass *sl, offens* smart aleck.
smart card plastic card with
integrated circuit capable of storing
and processing data, used for
identification, bank and store
transactions, etc.

smash *vt* break violently; strike
hard; ruin; destroy. ▶ *vi* break; dash
violently against. ▶ *n* heavy blow;
collision (of vehicles, etc.); total
financial failure; *inf* popular success.

smashed *adj sl* very drunk or
affected by drugs. **smash'er** *n*
attractive person, thing.

smat·ter·ing [SMAT-ər-ing] *n* slight

superficial knowledge.

smear [smeer] *vt* rub with grease, etc.; smudge, spread with dirt, grease, etc. ▶ *n* mark made thus; sample of secretion for medical examination; slander.

smell *v* **smelled** *or* **smelt, smell·ing.** perceive by nose; suspect; give out odor; use nose. ▶ *n* faculty of perceiving odors by nose; anything detected by sense of smell. **smell'y** *adj* **smell·i·er, smell·i·est.** with strong (unpleasant) smell.

smelt[1] *vt* extract metal from ore. **smelt'er** *n*

smelt[2] *n* fish of salmon family.

smid·gen [SMIJ-ən] *n* very small amount.

smile [smīl] *n* curving or parting of lips in pleased or amused expression. ▶ *v* **smiled, smil·ing.** wear, assume a smile; approve, favor.

smirch [smurch] *vt* dirty, sully; disgrace, discredit. ▶ *n* stain; disgrace.

smirk [smurk] *n* smile expressing scorn, smugness. ▶ *v*

smite [smīt] *vt* **smote, smit'ten** *or* **smit, smit'ing.** strike; attack; afflict; affect, esp. with love or fear.

smith *n* worker in iron, gold, etc. **smith'y** *n, pl* **smith·ies.** blacksmith's workshop; blacksmith.

smith·er·eens [SMITH-ər-eenz] *pl n* small bits.

smock [smok] *n* loose outer garment. ▶ *vt* gather by sewing in honeycomb pattern. **smock'ing** *n*

smog *n* mixture of smoke and fog.

smoke [smohk] *n* cloudy mass of suspended particles that rises from fire or anything burning; spell of tobacco smoking. ▶ *v* **smoked, smok·ing.** ▶ *vi* give off smoke; inhale and expel tobacco smoke. ▶ *vt* use (tobacco) by smoking; expose to smoke (esp. in curing fish, etc.). **smok'er** *n* one who smokes; informal party.

smol·der [SMOHL-dər] *vi* burn slowly without flame; (of feelings) exist in suppressed state.

smooch *v, n inf* kiss, cuddle.

smooth [smooth] *adj* not rough, even of surface or texture; sinuous; flowing; calm, soft, soothing; suave, plausible; free from jolts. ▶ *vt* make smooth; quiet. **smooth'ly** *adv*

smor·gas·bord [SMOR-gəs-bord] *n* buffet meal of assorted dishes.

smote pt. of SMITE.

smoth·er [SMUTH-ər] *v* suffocate; envelop; suppress. ▶ *vi* be suffocated.

SMS Short Message Server, system for sending messages of no more than 160 characters to a cell phone.

smudge [smuj] *v* **smudged, smudg·ing.** make smear, stain, dirty mark (on). ▶ *n*

smug *adj* **smug·ger.** self-satisfied, complacent. **smug'ly** *adv*

smug·gle [SMUG-əl] *vt* **-gled, -gling.** import, export without paying customs duties; conceal, take secretly. **smug'gler** *n*

smut *n* piece of soot, particle of dirt; lewd or obscene talk, etc.; disease of grain. ▶ *vt* **smut·ted, smut·ting.** blacken, smudge. **smut'ty** *adj* **-ti·er, -ti·est.** soiled with smut, soot; obscene, lewd.

Sn *Chem* tin.

snack [snak] *n* light portion of food eaten hastily between meals. ▶ *vi* eat thus. **snack bar** lunchroom at which light meals are served.

snag *n* difficulty; sharp protuberance; hole, loop in fabric caused by sharp object; obstacle (e.g. tree branch, etc. in river bed). ▶ *vt* **snagged, snag'ging.** catch, damage on snag.

snail [snayl] *n* slow-moving mollusk with shell; slow, sluggish person. **snail'like** *adj* **snail mail** *n inf* conventional mail, as opposed to e-mail; the conventional postal system. **snail-mail** *vt* send by the conventional postal system, rather than by e-mail.

snake [snayk] *n* long scaly limbless reptile, serpent. ▶ *v* **snaked, snak·ing.** move like snake. **snak'y** *adj* **snak·i·er, snak·i·est.** twisted or winding. **snake in the grass**

hidden enemy.

snap v **snapped, snap·ping.** break suddenly; make cracking sound; bite (at) suddenly; speak suddenly, angrily. ▶ n act of snapping; fastener; snapshot; inf easy task; brief period, esp. of cold weather. ▶ adj sudden, unplanned, arranged quickly. **snap'py** adj **-pi·er, -pi·est.** irritable; inf quick; inf well-dressed, fashionable. **snap'drag·on** n plant with flowers that can be opened like a mouth. **snap'shot** n informal photograph.

snare [snair] n (noose used as) trap. ▶ vt **snared, snar·ing.** catch with one.

snarl [snahrl] n growl of angry dog; tangle, knot. ▶ vi utter snarl; grumble.

snatch [snach] v make quick grab or bite (at); seize, catch. ▶ n grab; fragment; short spell.

sneak [sneek] vi **sneaked, sneak·ing.** slink; move about furtively; act in mean, underhand manner. ▶ n mean, treacherous person. **sneak'ing** adj secret but persistent. **sneak pre'view** unannounced showing of movie before general release. ▶ n

sneak·ers [SNEEK-ərz] pl n flexible, informal sports shoes.

sneer n scornful, contemptuous expression or remark. ▶ v

sneeze [sneez] vi **sneezed, sneez·ing.** emit breath through nose with sudden involuntary spasm and noise. ▶ n

snick·er [SNIK-ər] n sly, disrespectful laugh, esp. partly stifled. ▶ v

snide [snīd] adj **snid·er, snid·est.** malicious; supercilious.

sniff vi inhale through nose with sharp hiss; (with at) express disapproval, etc. by sniffing. ▶ vt take up through nose, smell. ▶ n **snif'fle** vi **-fled, -fling.** sniff noisily through nose, esp. when suffering from a cold in the head; snuffle.

snig·ger [SNIG-ər] n snicker.

snip vt **snipped, snip·ping.** cut, cut bits off. ▶ n act, sound of snipping;

bit cut off; inf small, insignificant, impertinent person. **snip·pet** [SNIP-it] n shred, fragment, clipping. **snips** pl n tool for cutting.

snipe [snīp] n wading bird. ▶ v **sniped, snip·ing.** shoot at enemy from cover; (with at) criticize, attack (person) slyly. **snip'er** n

snit n irritated state of mind.

snitch [snich] vt inf steal. ▶ vi inform. ▶ n informer.

sniv·el [SNIV-əl] vi **-eled, -el·ing.** sniffle to show distress; whine.

snob n one who pretentiously judges others by social rank, etc. **snob'ber·y** n **snob'bish** adj of or like a snob.

snook·er [SNUUK-ər] n game like pool played with 21 balls. ▶ vt leave (opponent) in unfavorable position; place (someone) in difficult situation; sl cheat.

snoop v pry, meddle; peer into. ▶ n one who acts thus; snooping.

snoot·y [SNOOT-ee] adj **snoot·i·er, snoot·i·est.** inf haughty.

snooze [snooz] vi **snoozed, snooz·ing.** take short sleep. ▶ n nap.

snore [snor] vi **snored, snor·ing.** breathe noisily when asleep. ▶ n

snor·kel [SNOR-kəl] n tube for breathing underwater. ▶ vi swim, fish using this.

snort vi make (contemptuous) noise by driving breath through nostrils; sl inhale drug. ▶ n noise of snorting; sl shot of liquor; sl amount of drug inhaled.

snot n vulg mucus from nose. **snot·ty** [-tee] adj **-ti·er, -ti·est.** inf arrogant.

snout [snowt] n animal's nose.

snow [snoh] n frozen vapor that falls in flakes; sl cocaine. ▶ v fall, sprinkle as snow; let fall, throw down like snow; cover with snow; sl overwhelm; sl deceive. **snow'y** adj **snow·i·er, snow·i·est.** of, like snow; covered with snow; very white. **snow'ball** n snow pressed into hard ball for throwing. ▶ v increase rapidly; play, fight with snowballs. **snow blind·ness** temporary blindness due to brightness of snow. **snow'board** *n* board like surfboard for descending ski slopes. **snow'drift** *n* bank of deep snow. **snow fence** fence for erecting in winter beside exposed road. **snow job** *sl* attempt to deceive by flattery or exaggeration. **snow line** elevation above which snow does not melt. **snow'shoes** [-shooz] *pl n* shoes like rackets for traveling on snow. **snow under** cover and block with snow; *fig* overwhelm.

snub *vt* **snubbed, snub·bing.** insult (esp. by ignoring) intentionally. ▶ *n, adj* short and blunt. **snub-nosed** *adj*

snuff[1] *n* powdered tobacco for inhaling through nose. **up to snuff** *inf* up to a standard.

snuff[2] *v* extinguish (esp. candle, etc.).

snuf·fle [SNUF-əl] *vi* **-fled, -fling.** breathe noisily, with difficulty.

snug *adj* **-ger, -gest.** warm, comfortable. **snug'gle** *v* **-gled, -gling.** lie close to for warmth or affection. **snug'ly** *adv*

so[1] [soh] *adv* to such an extent; in such a manner; very; the case being such; accordingly. ▶ *conj* therefore; in order that; with the result that. ▶ *interj* well! **so-called** *adj* called by but doubtfully deserving that name. **so long** *inf* goodbye.

so[2] see SOL.

soak [sohk] *v* steep; absorb; drench; lie in liquid; *sl* overcharge (customer). ▶ *n* soaking; *sl* habitual drunkard.

soap [sohp] *n* compound of alkali and oil used in washing. ▶ *vt* apply soap to. **soap'y** *adj* **soap·i·er, soap·i·est. soap opera** radio or TV serial of domestic life.

soar [sor] *vi* fly high; increase, rise (in price, etc.).

sob *vi* **sobbed, sob·bing.** catch breath, esp. in weeping. ▶ *n* sobbing. **sob story** tale of personal distress told to arouse sympathy.

so·ber [SOH-bər] *adj* **-ber·er,**

-ber·est. not drunk; temperate; subdued; dull, plain; solemn. ▶ *v* make, become sober. **so·bri·e·ty** [sə-BRĪ-i-tee] *n* state of being sober.

so·bri·quet [SOH-brə-kay] *n* nickname; assumed name.

soc·cer [SOK-ər] *n* ball game played with feet and spherical ball.

so·cia·ble [SOH-shə-bəl] *adj* friendly; convivial. **so·cia·bil'i·ty** *n*

so·cial [SOH-shəl] *adj* living in communities; relating to society; sociable. ▶ *n* informal gathering. **so'cial·ite** *n* member of fashionable society. **so'cial·ize** *v* **-ized, -iz·ing.** **so'cial·ly** *adv* **social security** government-sponsored provision for the disabled, unemployed, aged, etc. **social work** work to improve welfare of others.

so·cial·ism [SOH-shə-liz-əm] *n* political system that advocates public ownership of means of production, distribution and exchange. **so'cial·ist** *n, adj*

so·ci·e·ty [sə-SĪ-i-tee] *n, pl* **-ties.** living associated with others; those so living; companionship; company; association; club; fashionable people collectively.

so·ci·ol·o·gy [soh-see-OL-ə-jee] *n* study of societies.

sock[1] [sok] *n* cloth covering for foot.

sock[2] *vt* hit. ▶ *n* blow.

sock·et [SOK-it] *n* hole or recess for something to fit into.

So·crat·ic [sə-KRAT-ik] *adj* of, like Greek philosopher Socrates.

sod *n* lump of earth with grass.

so·da [SOH-də] *n* compound of sodium; soda water. **soda water** water charged with carbon dioxide.

sod·den [SOD-n] *adj* soaked; drunk; heavy and lumpy.

so·di·um [SOD-dee-əm] *n* metallic alkaline element. **sodium bicarbonate** white crystalline soluble compound (also **bicarbonate of soda**).

sod·om·y [SOD-ə-mee] *n* anal intercourse. **sod'om·ite** *n*

so·fa [SOH-fə] *n* upholstered couch with back and arms, for two or more people.

soft [sawft] *adj* **-er, -est.** yielding easily to pressure, not hard; mild; easy; subdued; quiet, gentle; (too) lenient; oversentimental; foolish, stupid; (of water) containing few mineral salts; (of drugs) not liable to cause addiction. **soft'en** [SAWF-ən] *v* make, become soft or softer; mollify; lighten; mitigate; make less loud. ▶ **soft'ly** *adv* gently, quietly. **soft'ball** *n* (ball used in) variation of baseball using larger, softer ball. **soft drink** one that is nonalcoholic. **soft goods** nondurable goods, e.g. curtains, rugs. **soft soap** *inf* flattery. **soft'ware** *n* programs used with a computer. **soft'wood** [-wuud] *n* wood of coniferous tree.

sog·gy [SOG-ee] *adj* **-gi·er, -gi·est.** soaked with liquid; damp and heavy.

soil' *n* earth, ground; country, territory.

soil² *v* make, become dirty; tarnish, defile. ▶ *n* dirt; sewage; stain.

soir·ee [swah-RAY] *n* private evening party esp. with music.

so·journ [SOH-jurn] *vi* stay for a time. ▶ *n* short stay. **so'journ·er** *n*

sol, so *n* fifth sol-fa note.

sol·ace [SOL-is] *n, vt* **-aced, -ac·ing.** comfort in distress.

sol·ar [SOH-lər] *adj* of the sun. **solar plex'us** network of nerves at pit of stomach.

so·lar·i·um [sə-LAIR-ee-əm] *n, pl* **-i·ums.** room built mainly of glass to give exposure to sun.

sold pt./pp. of SELL.

sol·der [SOD-ər] *n* easily-melted alloy used for joining metal. ▶ *vt* join with it. **soldering iron** tool for melting and applying solder.

sol·dier [SOHL-jər] *n* one serving in army. ▶ *vi* serve in army; *inf* loaf; (with *on*) persist doggedly. **sol'dier·ly** *adj*

sole¹ [sohl] *adj* one and only, unique; solitary. **sole'ly** *adv* alone; only; entirely.

sole² *n* underside of foot; underpart of shoe, etc. ▶ *vt* **soled, sol·ing.** fit with sole.

sole³ *n* small edible flatfish.

sol·e·cism [SOL-ə-siz-əm] *n* breach of grammar or etiquette.

sol·emn [SOL-əm] *adj* serious; formal; impressive. **sol'emn·ly** *adv* **so·lem·ni·ty** [sə-LEM-ni-tee] *n* **sol·em·nize** [SOL-əm-nīz] *vt* **-nized, -niz·ing.** celebrate, perform; make solemn.

so·le·noid [SOH-lə-noid] *n* coil of wire as part of electrical apparatus.

sol-fa [sohl-FAH] *n Mus* system of syllables sol, fa, etc. sung in scale.

so·lic·it [sə-LIS-it] *vt* request; accost; urge; entice. **so·lic·i·ta'tion** *n* **so·lic'i·tor** *n* one who solicits. **so·lic'i·tous** *adj* anxious; eager; earnest. **so·lic'i·tude** *n*

sol'id *adj* not hollow; compact; composed of one substance; firm; massive; reliable, sound. ▶ *n* body of three dimensions; substance not liquid or gas. **sol·i·dar'i·ty** *n* unity of interests; united condition. **so·lid'i·fy** *v* **-fied, -fy·ing.** make, become solid or firm; harden. **so·lid'i·ty** *n*

so·lil·o·quy [sə-LIL-ə-kwee] *n, pl* **-quies.** (esp. in drama) thoughts spoken by person while alone. **so·lil'o·quize** *vi* **-quized, -quiz·ing.**

sol·ip·sism [SOL-ip-siz-əm] *n* doctrine that self is the only thing known to exist. **sol'ip·sist** *n*

sol·i·tar·y [SOL-i-ter-ee] *adj* alone, single. ▶ *n* hermit. **sol'i·taire** *n* game for one person played with cards or with pegs set in board; single precious stone set by itself. **sol'i·tude** *n* state of being alone; loneliness.

so·lo [SOH-loh] *n, pl* **-los.** music for one performer. ▶ *adj* not concerted; unaccompanied, alone; piloting airplane alone. **so'lo·ist** *n*

sol·stice [SOL-stis] *n* either shortest (winter) or longest (summer) day of year.

solve [solv] *vt* **solved, solv·ing.** work out, explain; find answer to. **sol·u·bil'i·ty** *n* **sol'u·ble** *adj* capable of being dissolved in liquid; able to be solved or explained. **so·lu'tion**

[sə-LOO-shən] *n* answer to problem; dissolving; liquid with something dissolved in it. **solv'a·ble** *adj* **sol'ven·cy** [-vən-see] *n* **sol'vent** *adj* able to meet financial obligations. ▶ *n* liquid with power of dissolving.

som·ber [SOM-bər] *adj* dark, gloomy.

som·bre·ro [som-BRAIR-oh] *n, pl* **-bre·ros.** wide-brimmed hat worn in Mexico, Spain, etc.

some [sum] *adj* denoting an indefinite number, amount or extent; one or other; amount of; certain; approximately. ▶ *pron* portion, quantity. **some'bod·y** *n* some person; important person. **some'how** *adv* by some means unknown. **some'thing** *n* thing not clearly defined; indefinite amount, quantity or degree. **-something** *comb. form* (person) of an age above a given figure, e.g. *thirtysomething.* **some'time** *adv* formerly; at some (past or future) time. ▶ *adj* former. **some'times** *adv* occasionally; now and then. **some'what** [-hwot] *adv* to some extent, rather. **some'where** [-hwair] *adv*

som·er·sault [SUM-ər-sawlt] *n* tumbling head over heels.

som·nam·bu·list [som-NAM-byə-list] *n* sleepwalker. **som·nam'bu·lism** *n*

som·no·lent [SOM-nə-lənt] *adj* drowsy; causing sleep. **som'no·lence** *n*

son [sun] *n* male child. **son-in-law** *n* daughter's husband.

so·nar [SOH-nahr] *n* device like echo sounder.

so·na·ta [sə-NAH-tə] *n* piece of music in several movements. **son·a·ti·na** [son-ə-TEE-nə] *n* short sonata.

son et lumière [saw-nay-luu-MYAIR] *Fr* entertainment staged at night in famous place, building, giving dramatic history of it with lighting and sound effects.

song [sawng] *n* singing; poem, etc.

for singing. **song'ster** *n* singer; songbird. **song'stress** [-stris] *n, fem*

sonic [SON-ik] *adj* pert. to sound waves. **sonic boom** explosive sound caused by aircraft traveling at supersonic speed.

son·net [SON-it] *n* fourteen-line poem with definite rhyme scheme. **son·net·eer** [son-i-TEER] *n* writer of this.

so·no·rous [sə-NOR-ees or SAHN-ər-us] *adj* giving out (deep) sound, resonant. **so·nor'i·ty** *n*

soon *adv* in a short time; before long; early, quickly.

soot [suut] *n* black powdery substance formed by burning of coal, etc. **soot'y** *adj* **soot·i·er, soot·i·est.** of, like soot.

sooth *n* truth. **sooth'say·er** *n* one who foretells future; diviner.

soothe [sooth] *vt* **soothed, sooth·ing.** make calm, tranquil; relieve (pain, etc.).

sop *n* piece of bread, etc. soaked in liquid; concession, bribe. ▶ *vt* **sopped, sop·ping.** steep in water, etc.; soak (up). **sopping** *adj* completely soaked.

soph·ist [SOF-ist] *n* fallacious reasoner, quibbler. **soph'ism** [-izm] *n* specious argument. **soph'ist·ry** *n*

so·phis·ti·cate [sə-FIS-ti-kayt] *vt* **-cat·ed, -cat·ing.** make artificial, spoil, falsify, corrupt. ▶ *n* [-kit] sophisticated person. **sophisticated** *adj* having refined or cultured tastes, habits; worldly wise; superficially clever; complex. **so·phis·ti·ca'tion** *n*

soph·o·more [SOF-ə-mor] *n* student in second year at high school or college. **soph·o·mor'ic** intellectually pretentious.

sop·o·rif·ic [sop-ə-RIF-ik] *adj* causing sleep (esp. by drugs).

so·pran·o [sə-PRAN-oh] *n, pl* **-pran·os.** highest voice in women and boys; singer with this voice; musical part for it.

sor·bet [sor-BAY] *n* sherbet.

sor·cer·er [SOR-sər-ər] *n* magician. **sor'cer·ess** [-ris] *n, fem* **sor'cer·y**

n, pl **-ies.** witchcraft, magic.

sor'did *adj* mean, squalid; ignoble, base. **sor'did·ly** *adv* **sor'did·ness** [-nis] *n*

sore [sor] *adj* **sor·er, sor·est.** painful; causing annoyance; severe; distressed; annoyed. ▶ *adv obs* grievously, intensely. ▶ *n* sore place, ulcer, boil, etc. **sore'ly** *adv* grievously; greatly.

sor·ghum [SOR-gəm] *n* kind of grass cultivated for grain.

sor·rel [SOR-əl] *n* plant; reddish-brown color; horse of this color. ▶ *adj* of this color.

sor·row [SOR-oh] *n* pain of mind, grief, sadness. ▶ *vi* grieve. **sor'row·ful** [-fəl] *adj*

sor·ry [SOR-ee] *adj* **-ri·er, -ri·est.** feeling pity or regret; distressed; miserable, wretched; mean, poor. **sor'ri·ly** *adv*

sort *n* kind or class. ▶ *vt* classify. **sort'er** *n*

sor·tie [SOR-tee] *n* sally by besieged forces.

SOS *n* international code signal of distress; call for help.

so-so [SOH-soh] *adj* mediocre. ▶ *adv* tolerably.

sot *n* habitual drunkard.

sot·to vo·ce [SOT-oh VOH-chee] *It* in an undertone.

souf·flé [soo-FLAY] *n* dish of eggs beaten to froth, flavored and baked; dessert like this of various ingredients.

sough [rhymes with **cow**] *n* low murmuring sound as of wind in trees.

sought [sawt] *pt./pp.* of SEEK.

soul [sohl] *n* spiritual and immortal part of human being; example, pattern; person; (also **soul music**) type of Black music combining urban blues with jazz, pop, etc. **soul'ful** [-fəl] *adj* full of emotion or sentiment. **soul'less** [-lis] *adj* mechanical; lacking sensitivity or nobility; heartless, cruel.

sound¹ [sownd] *n* what is heard; noise. ▶ *vi* make a sound; seem; give impression of. ▶ *vt* cause to sound; utter. **sound barrier**

hypothetical barrier to flight at speed of sound waves. **sound bite** short pithy statement extracted from a longer speech for use esp. in television or radio news reports. **sound track** recorded sound accompaniment of motion picture, etc.

sound² *adj* **-er, -est.** in good condition; solid; of good judgment; legal; solvent; thorough; effective; watertight; deep. **sound'ly** *adv* thoroughly.

sound³ *vt* find depth of, as water; ascertain views of; probe. **sound'ings** *pl n* measurements taken by sounding.

sound⁴ *n* channel; strait.

soup [soop] *n* liquid food made by boiling or simmering meat, vegetables, etc. **soup'y** *adj* **soup·i·er, soup·i·est.** like soup; murky; sentimental.

sour [sowr] *adj* acid; gone bad; rancid; peevish; disagreeable. ▶ *v* make, become sour. **sour'ness** [-nis] *n* **sour'puss** [-puus] *n inf* sullen, sour-faced person.

source [sors] *n* origin, starting point; spring.

souse [rhymes with **louse**] *v* **soused, sous·ing.** plunge, drench; pickle. ▶ *n* sousing; brine for pickling; *sl* drunkard. **soused** *adj sl* drunk.

south [sowth] *n* cardinal point opposite north; region, part of country, etc. lying to that side. ▶ *adj, adv* (that is) toward south. **south'ward** [-wərd] *adj, adv* **south'wards** [-wərdz] *adv* **south·er·ly** [SUTH-ər-lee] *adj* toward south. ▶ *n, pl* **-lies.** wind from the south. **south·ern** [SUTH-ərn] *adj* in south. **south·west·er** [sowth-WES-tər] *n* wind, storm from the southwest.

sou·ve·nir [soo-və-NEER] *n* keepsake, memento.

sov·er·eign [SOV-rin] *n* king, queen; former British gold coin worth 20 shillings. ▶ *adj* supreme; efficacious. **sov'er·eign·ty** *n, pl* **-ties.** supreme power and right to exercise it; dominion; independent state.

so·vi·et [SOH-vee-et] *n* formerly, elected council at various levels of government in USSR; (**S-**) official or citizen of the former USSR. ▸ *adj* of the former USSR.

sow¹ [soh] *v* **sowed, sown** or **sowed, sow·ing.** ▸ *vi* scatter, plant seed. ▸ *vt* scatter, deposit (seed); spread abroad.

sow² [rhymes with **cow**] *n* female adult pig.

soy·bean [SOI-been] *n* edible bean used as livestock feed, meat substitute, etc.

soy sauce [SOI saws] sauce made by fermenting soybeans in brine.

spa [spah] *n* medicinal spring; place, resort with one.

space [spays] *n* extent; room; period; empty place; area; expanse; region beyond Earth's atmosphere. ▸ *vt* **spaced, spac·ing.** place at intervals. **spa'cious** [-shəs] *adj* roomy, extensive. **space'craft, space'ship** *n* vehicle for travel beyond Earth's atmosphere. **space shuttle** vehicle for repeated space flights. **space'suit** *n* sealed, pressurized suit worn by astronaut.

spade¹ [spayd] *n* tool for digging. **spade·work** [SPAYD-wurk] *n* arduous preparatory work.

spade² *n* leaf-shaped black symbol on playing card.

spa·ghet·ti [spə-GET-ee] *n* pasta in form of long strings.

spake [spayk] *obs* pt. of SPEAK.

spam *v* **spam·ming, spammed.** *Computers, sl* send unsolicited e-mail simultaneously to a number of users on the Internet.

span *n* space from thumb to little finger as measure; extent; space; stretch of arch, etc. ▸ *vt* **spanned, span·ning.** stretch over; measure with hand.

span·gle [SPANG-gəl] *n* small shiny metallic ornament. ▸ *vt* **-gled, -gling.** decorate with spangles.

span·iel [SPAN-yəl] *n* breed of dog with long ears and silky hair.

spank [spangk] *vt* slap with flat of

hand, etc. esp. on buttocks. ▸ *n* **spank'ing** *n* series of spanks. ▸ *adj* quick, lively; large, fine.

spar¹ [spahr] *n* pole, beam, esp. as part of ship's rigging.

spar² *vi* **sparred, spar·ring.** box; dispute, esp. in fun. ▸ *n* sparring.

spar³ *n* any of kinds of crystalline mineral.

spare [spair] *vt* **spared, spar·ing.** leave unhurt; show mercy; abstain from using; do without; give away. ▸ *adj* additional; in reserve; thin; lean; scanty. ▸ *n* spare part (for machine). **sparing** *adj* economical, careful.

spark [spahrk] *n* small glowing or burning particle; flash of light produced by electrical discharge; vivacity, humor; trace; in internal-combustion engines, electric spark (in spark plug) that ignites explosive mixture in cylinder. ▸ *v* emit sparks; kindle, excite; *obs* woo.

spar·kle [SPAHR-kəl] *vi* **-kled, -kling.** glitter; effervesce; scintillate. ▸ *n* small spark; glitter; lustre. **sparkling** *adj* flashing; glittering; brilliant; lively; (of wines) effervescent.

spar·row [SPA-roh] *n* small finch.

sparse [spahrs] *adj* **spars·er, spars·est.** thinly scattered.

Spar·tan [SPAHR-tn] *adj* hardy; austere; frugal; undaunted.

spasm [SPAZ-əm] *n* sudden convulsive (muscular) contraction; sudden burst of activity, etc. **spas·mod·ic** [spaz-MOD-ik] *adj* occurring in spasms.

spas·tic [SPAS-tik] *n oft considered offens* person who has cerebral palsy. ▸ *adj* affected by involuntary muscle contractions, e.g. *spastic colon; oft considered offens* suffering from cerebral palsy.

spat¹ pt. of SPIT¹.

spat² *n* short gaiter.

spat³ *n* slight quarrel. ▸ *vi* **spat·ted, spat·ting.** quarrel.

spate [spayt] *n* rush, outpouring; flood.

spa·tial [SPAY-shəl] *adj* of, in space.

spat·ter [SPAT-ər] *vt* splash, cast drops over. ▶ *vi* be scattered in drops. ▶ *n* slight splash; sprinkling.

spat·u·la [SPACH-ə-lə] *n* utensil with broad, flat blade for various purposes.

spav'in *n* injury to, growth on horse's leg. **spav'ined** *adj* lame, decrepit.

spawn *n* eggs of fish, frog, etc. ▶ *vi* (of fish or frog) cast eggs; produce in great numbers.

spay *vt* remove ovaries from (animal).

speak [speek] *v* **spoke, spo·ken, speak·ing.** utter words; converse; deliver discourse; utter; pronounce; express; communicate in. **speak'er** *n* one who speaks; one who specializes in speechmaking; **(S-)** official chairman of US House of Representatives, other legislative bodies; loudspeaker.

spear [speer] *n* long pointed weapon; slender shoot, as of asparagus. ▶ *vt* transfix, pierce, wound with spear. **spear'head** [-hed] *n* leading force in attack, campaign. ▶ *vt*

spear·mint [SPEER-mint] *n* type of mint.

spec [spek] *n* **on spec** *inf* as a risk or gamble.

spe·cial [SPESH-əl] *adj* beyond the usual; particular, individual; distinct; limited. **spe'cial·ist** *n* one who devotes self to special subject or branch of subject. **spe'cial·ty** *n*, *pl* **-ties.** special product, skill, characteristic, etc. **spe'cial·ize** *v* **-ized, -iz·ing.** ▶ *vi* be specialist; be adapted to special function or environment. ▶ *vt* make special.

spe·cie [SPEE-shee] *n* coined, as distinct from paper, money.

spe·cies [SPEE-sheez] *n, pl* **species.** sort, kind, esp. animals, etc.; class; subdivision.

spe·cif·ic [spə-SIF-ik] *adj* definite; exact in detail; characteristic of a thing or kind. **spe·cif'i·cal·ly** *adv* **spec'i·fy** *vt* **-fied, -fy·ing.** state definitely or in detail. **spec·i·fi·ca'tion** [-KAY-shən] *n*

detailed description of something to be made, done. **specific gravity** ratio of density of substance to that of water.

spec·i·men [SPES-ə-mən] *n* part typifying whole; individual example.

spe·cious [SPEE-shəs] *adj* deceptively plausible, but false. **spe'cious·ly** *adv* **spe'cious·ness** [-nis] *n*

speck [spek] *n* small spot, particle. ▶ *vt* spot. **speck·le** [SPEK-l] *n, vt* **-led, -ling.** speck.

spec·ta·cle [SPEK-tə-kəl] *n* show; thing exhibited; ridiculous sight. **spectacles** *pl n* eyeglasses. **spec·tac'u·lar** *adj* impressive; showy; grand; magnificent. ▶ *n* lavishly produced performance. **spec·ta·tor** [SPEK-tay-tər] *n* one who looks on.

spec·ter [SPEK-tər] *n* ghost; image of something unpleasant. **spec'tral** [-trəl] *adj* ghostly.

spec·trum [SPEK-trəm] *n, pl* **-tra** [-trə] band of colors into which beam of light can be decomposed e.g. by prism; range (of e.g. opinions, occupations). **spec'tro·scope** [-trə-skohp] *n* instrument for producing, examining physical spectra.

spec·u·late [SPEK-yə-layt] *vi* **-lat·ed, -lat·ing.** guess, conjecture; engage in (risky) commercial transactions. **spec·u·la'tion** *n* **spec'u·la·tive** [-lə-tiv] *adj* given to, characterized by speculation. **spec'u·la·tor** *n*

spec·u·lum [SPEK-yə-ləm] *n, pl* **-lums.** mirror; reflector of polished metal, esp. in reflecting telescopes.

speech *n* act, faculty of speaking; words, language; conversation; discourse; (formal) talk given before audience. **speech'i·fy** *vi* **-fied, -fy·ing.** make speech, esp. long and tedious one. **speech'less** [-lis] *adj* mute; at a loss for words.

speed *n* swiftness; rate of progress; degree of sensitivity of photographic film; *sl* amphetamine. ▶ *v* **sped** or

speed·ed, speed·ing. move quickly; drive vehicle at high speed; further; expedite. **speed'ing** n driving (vehicle) at high speed, esp. over legal limit. **speed'i·ly** adv **speed'y** adj **speed·i·er, speed·i·est.** quick; rapid; nimble; prompt. **speed'boat** n light fast motorboat. **speed·om'e·ter** [-OM-ə-tər] n instrument to show speed of vehicle. **speed'way** n track for automobile or motorcycle racing.

spe·le·ol·o·gy [spee-lee-OL-ə-jee] n study, exploring of caves. **spe·le·ol'o·gist** n

spell¹ vt **spelled** or **spelt, spell·ing.** give letters of in order; read letter by letter; indicate, result in. **spelling** n Computers program that finds words in a document that are not recognized as being correctly spelled. **spell out** make explicit.

spell² n magic formula; enchantment. **spell'bound** [-bownd] adj enchanted; entranced.

spell³ n (short) period of time, work.

spend vt **spent, spend·ing.** pay out; pass (time) on activity, etc.; use up completely. **spend'thrift** n wasteful person.

sperm [spurm] n male reproductive cell; semen. **sper·mat'ic** adj of sperm. **sperm'i·cide** [-sīd] n drug, etc. that kills sperm.

sper·ma·cet·i [spur-mə-SET-ee] n white, waxy substance obtained from oil from head of sperm whale. **sperm whale** large, toothed whale.

spew [spyoo] v vomit; gush.

sphag·num [SFAG-nəm] n moss that grows in bogs.

sphere [sfeer] n ball, globe; range; field of action; status; position; province. **spher·i·cal** [SFER-i-kəl] adj

sphinc·ter [SFINGK-tər] n ring of muscle surrounding opening of hollow bodily organ.

sphinx [sfingks] n, pl **-es.** figure in Egypt with lion's body and human head; **(S-)** the great statue of this near the pyramids of Giza; monster, half woman, half lion; enigmatic person.

spice [spīs] n aromatic or pungent vegetable substance; spices collectively; anything that adds flavor, relish, piquancy, interest, etc. ▶ vt **spiced, spic·ing.** season with spices, flavor. **spic'y** adj **spic·i·er, spic·i·est.** flavored with spices; slightly indecent, risqué.

spick-and-span [SPIK-ən-SPAN] adj spotlessly clean; neat, smart, new-looking.

spi·der [SPĪ-dər] n small eight-legged creature that spins web to catch prey. **spi'der·y** adj

spiel [speel] n inf glib (sales) talk. ▶ vi deliver spiel, recite. **spiel'er** n

spig·ot [SPIG-ət] n peg or plug; faucet.

spike [spīk] n sharp point; sharp pointed object; long flower cluster with flowers attached directly to the stalk. ▶ vt **spiked, spik·ing.** pierce, fasten with spike; render ineffective; add alcohol to (drink).

spill v **spilled** or **spilt, spill·ing.** (cause to) pour from, flow over, fall out, esp. unintentionally; upset; be lost or wasted. ▶ n spillway; spillage. **spill'age** [-ij] n amount spilled. **spill'way** n passageway through which excess water spills.

spin v **spun, spin·ning.** (cause to) revolve rapidly; whirl; twist into thread; prolong; tell (a story); fish with lure. ▶ n spinning; (of aircraft) descent in dive with continued rotation; rapid run or ride; Politics interpretation (of event, speech, etc.) to gain partisan advantage. **spinning** n act, process of drawing out and twisting into threads, as wool, cotton, flax, etc. **spinning wheel** household machine with large wheel turned by treadle for spinning wool, etc. into thread. **spin doctor** inf person who provides a favourable slant to a news item or policy on behalf of a political personality or party. **spin-dry** vt **-dried, -dry·ing.** spin clothes in (washing) machine to remove excess water.

spin·ach [SPIN-ich] n dark green leafy vegetable.

spin·dle [SPIN-dl] n rod, axis for spinning. **spin′dly** adj **-dli·er, -dli·est.** long and slender; attenuated.

spin′drift n spray blown along surface of sea.

spine [spīn] n backbone; thin spike, esp. on fish, etc.; ridge; back of book. **spi′nal** [-əl] adj **spine′less** [-lis] adj lacking spine; cowardly.

spin·et [SPIN-it] n small piano; small harpsichord.

spin·na·ker [SPIN-ə-kər] n large yacht sail.

spin·ster [SPIN-stər] n unmarried woman.

spi·ral [SPĪ-rəl] n continuous curve drawn at ever increasing distance from fixed point; anything resembling this; *Football* kick or pass turning on longer axis. ▶ v **-raled, -ral·ing.** of e.g. football or inflation, (cause to) take spiral course. ▶ adj

spire [spīr] n pointed part of steeple; pointed stem of plant.

spir·it n life principle animating body; disposition; liveliness; courage; frame of mind; essential character or meaning; soul; ghost; liquid got by distillation, alcohol. ▶ pl emotional state; strong alcoholic drink e.g. whiskey. ▶ vt carry away mysteriously. **spir′it·ed** [-id] adj lively. **spir′it·less** [-lis] adj listless, apathetic. **spir·it·u·al** [-choo-əl] adj given to, interested in things of the spirit. ▶ n religious song, hymn. **spir′it·u·al·ism** n belief that spirits of the dead communicate with the living. **spir′it·u·al·ist** n **spir′it·u·ous** adj alcoholic. **spirit level** glass tube containing bubble in liquid, used to check horizontal, vertical surfaces.

spirt n see SPURT.

spit[1] v **spit** or **spat, spit·ting.** eject saliva; eject from mouth. ▶ n spitting, saliva. **spit·tle** [SPIT-l] n saliva. **spit′ball** n illegal pitch of baseball moistened with saliva by pitcher; ball of chewed paper used as missile. **spit·toon′** n vessel to spit into. **spit′fire** n person, esp. woman or girl, with fiery temper.

spit[2] n sharp rod to put through meat for roasting; sandy point projecting into the sea. ▶ vt **spit·ted, spit·ting.** thrust through.

spite [spīt] n malice. ▶ vt **spit·ed, spit·ing.** thwart spitefully. **spite′ful** [-fəl] adj **in spite of** prep regardless of; notwithstanding.

splash v scatter liquid about or on, over something; print, display prominently. ▶ n sound of this; patch, esp. of color; (effect of) extravagant display; small amount.

splat n wet, slapping sound.

splat·ter [SPLAT-ər] v, n spatter.

splay adj spread out; slanting; turned outward. ▶ vt spread out; twist outward. ▶ n slanted surface. **splay′foot·ed** [-fuut-id] adj flat and broad (of foot).

spleen n organ in the abdomen; anger; irritable or morose temper. **sple·net·ic** [splə-NET-ik] adj

splen′did adj magnificent, brilliant, excellent. **splen′did·ly** adv **splen′dor** [-dər] n

splice [splīs] vt **spliced, splic·ing.** join by interweaving strands; join (wood) by overlapping; *inf* join in marriage. ▶ n spliced joint.

spline [splīn] n narrow groove, ridge, strip, esp. joining wood, etc.

splint n rigid support for broken limb, etc.

splin·ter [SPLIN-tər] n thin fragment. ▶ vi break into fragments, shiver. **splinter group** group that separates from main party, organization, oft. after disagreement.

split v **split, split′ting.** break asunder; separate; divide; *sl* depart. ▶ n crack, fissure; dessert of fruit, usu. banana, and ice cream.

splotch [sploch] n, v splash, daub. **splotch′y** adj **splotch·i·er, splotch·i·est.**

splurge [splurj] v **splurged, splurg·ing.** spend money extravagantly. ▶ n

splut·ter [SPLUT-ər] v make hissing, spitting sounds; utter incoherently with spitting sounds. ▶ n

spoil v **spoiled** or **spoilt, spoil·ing.** damage, injure; damage manners or behavior of (esp. child) by indulgence; pillage; go bad. ▶ n booty; waste material, esp. in mining (also **spoil'age**). **spoil'er** n slowing device on aircraft wing, etc. **spoiling for** eager for.

spoke[1] [spohk] pt. of SPEAK. **spokes'per·son, -wo·man, -man** n one deputed to speak for others.

spoke[2] n radial bar of a wheel.

spoken pp. of SPEAK.

spo·li·a·tion [spoh-lee-AY-shən] n act of spoiling; robbery; destruction. **spo'li·ate** [-ayt] v **-at·ed, -at·ing.** despoil, plunder, pillage.

spon'dee n metrical foot consisting of two long syllables.

sponge [spunj] n marine animal; its skeleton, or a synthetic substance like it, used to absorb liquids; type of light cake. ▶ v **sponged, spong·ing.** ▶ vt wipe with sponge. ▶ vi live meanly at expense of others; cadge. **spong'er** n sl one who cadges, or lives at expense of others. **spon'gy** adj **-gi·er, -gi·est.** spongelike; wet and soft.

spon·sor [SPON-sər] n one promoting, advertising something; one who agrees to give money to a charity on completion of specified activity by another; one taking responsibility (esp. for welfare of child at baptism, i.e. godparent); guarantor. ▶ vt act as sponsor. **spon'sor·ship** n

spon·ta·ne·ous [spon-TAY-nee-əs] adj voluntary; natural; not forced; produced without external force. **spon·ta·ne'i·ty** [-tə-NEE-i-tee] n

spoof n mild satirical mockery; trick, hoax. ▶ v

spook n ghost. ▶ vt haunt. **spook'y** adj **spook·i·er, spook·i·est.**

spool n reel, bobbin.

spoon n implement with shallow bowl at end of handle for carrying food to mouth, etc. ▶ vt lift with

spoon. **spoon'ful** [-fəl] n, pl **-fuls** [-fəlz] **spoon'fed** adj fed (as if) with spoon; pampered.

spoon·er·ism [SPOO-nə-riz-əm] n amusing transposition of initial consonants, such as half-warmed fish for half-formed wish.

spoor [spuur] n trail of wild animals. ▶ v follow spoor.

spo·rad·ic [spə-RAD-ik] adj intermittent; scattered, single. **spo·rad'i·cal·ly** adv

spore [spor] n minute reproductive organism of some plants and protozoans.

sport n game, activity for pleasure, competition, exercise; enjoyment; mockery; cheerful person, good loser. ▶ vt wear (esp. ostentatiously). ▶ vi frolic; play (sport). **sport'ing** adj of sport; behaving with fairness, generosity. **sport'ive** adj playful. **sports car** fast (open) car. **sports jacket** man's casual jacket. **sports'man** [-mən] n, pl **-men.** one who engages in sport; good loser. **sports'man·ship** n **sport utility vehicle** powerful four-wheel drive vehicle for rough terrain.

spot n small mark, stain; blemish; pimple; place; (difficult) situation. ▶ vt **spot·ted, spot·ting.** mark with spots; detect; observe; blemish. **spot'less** [-lis] adj unblemished; pure. **spot'less·ly** adv **spot'ty** adj **-ti·er, -ti·est.** with spots; uneven. **spot check** random examination. **spot'light** n powerful light illuminating small area; center of attention.

spouse [spows] n husband or wife. **spous·al** [SPOWZ-əl] n, adj (of) marriage.

spout [spowt] v pour out; inf speechify. ▶ n projecting tube or lip for pouring liquids; copious discharge.

sprain n, vt wrench or twist (of muscle, etc.).

sprang pt. of SPRING.

sprat n small sea fish.

sprawl vi lie or sit about awkwardly; spread in rambling, unplanned way. ▶ *n* sprawling.

spray[1] *n* (device for producing) fine drops of liquid. ▶ *vt* sprinkle with shower of fine drops.

spray[2] *n* branch, twig with buds, flowers, etc.; floral ornament, brooch, etc. like this.

spread [spred] *v* **spread, spread'ing.** extend; stretch out; open out; scatter; distribute; unfold; cover. ▶ *n* extent; increase; ample meal; food that can be spread on bread, etc.
  spread'-ea·gle *adj* with arms and legs outstretched. **spread'sheet** *n* computer program for manipulating figures.

spree *n* session of overindulgence; romp.

sprig *n* small twig; ornamental design like this; small headless nail.

spright·ly [SPRĪT-lee] *adj* **-li·er, -li·est.** lively, brisk. **spright'li·ness** [-nis] *n*

spring *v* **sprang, sprung, spring·ing.** leap; shoot up or forth; come into being; appear; grow; become bent or split; produce unexpectedly; set off (trap). ▶ *n* leap; recoil; piece of coiled or bent metal with much resilience; flow of water from earth; first season of year. **spring'y** *adj* **spring·i·er, spring·i·est.** elastic. **spring'board** [-bord] *n* flexible board for diving; anything that supplies impetus for action.

sprin·kle [SPRING-kəl] *vt* **-kled, -kling.** scatter small drops on, strew. **sprin'kler** *n* **sprinkling** *n* small amount or number.

sprint *vt* run short distance at great speed. ▶ *n* such run, race. **sprint'er** *n* one who sprints.

sprit *n* small spar set diagonally across a fore-and-aft sail in order to extend it.

sprite [sprīt] *n* fairy, elf.

sprock·et [SPROK-it] *n* projection on wheel or capstan for engaging chain; wheel with these.

sprout [sprowt] *vi* put forth shoots, spring up. ▶ *n* shoot. **Brus'sels sprout** [-səlz] kind of miniature cabbage.

spruce[1] [sproos] *n* variety of fir.

spruce[2] *adj* **spruc·er, spruc·est.** neat in dress. ▶ *v* **spruced, spruc·ing.** (with *up*) make (oneself) spruce.

sprung pp. of SPRING.

spry [sprī] *adj* **spry·er** or **spri·er, spry·est** or **spri·est.** nimble, vigorous.

spud *n inf* potato.

spume [spyoom] *n, vi* **spumed, spum·ing.** foam, froth.

spun pt./pp. of SPIN.

spunk *n* courage, spirit.

spur *n* pricking instrument attached to horseman's heel; incitement; stimulus; projection on rooster's leg; projecting mountain range; branch (road, etc.). ▶ *vt* **spurred, spur·ring.** equip with spurs; urge on.

spu·ri·ous [SPYUUR-ee-əs] *adj* not genuine.

spurn *vt* reject with scorn, thrust aside.

spurt *v* send, come out in jet; rush suddenly. ▶ *n* jet; short sudden effort, esp. in race.

sput·nik [SPUUT-nik] *n* one of series of Russian satellites.

sput·ter [SPUT-ər] *v* splutter.

spu·tum [SPYOO-təm] *n, pl* **-ta** [-tə] spittle.

spy [spī] *n, pl* **spies.** one who watches (esp. in rival countries, companies, etc.) and reports secretly. ▶ *v* **spied, spy·ing.** act as spy; catch sight of. **spy'glass** *n* small telescope.

squab·ble [SKWOB-əl] *vi* **-bled, -bling.** engage in petty, noisy quarrel, bicker. ▶ *n*

squad [skwod] *n* small party, esp. of soldiers or police. **squad car** police patrol automobile (also **patrol car**). **squad·ron** [-rən] *n* division of an air force, fleet, or cavalry regiment.

squal·id [SKWOL-id] *adj* mean and dirty. **squal'or** [-ər] *n*

squall [skwawl] *n* harsh cry; sudden gust of wind; short storm. ▶ *vi* yell.

squan·der [SKWON-dər] *vt* spend wastefully, dissipate.

square [skwair] n equilateral rectangle; area of this shape; in town, open space (of this shape); product of a number multiplied by itself; instrument for drawing right angles; sl person behind the times. ▶ adj square in form; honest; straight, even; level, equal; denoting a measure of area; inf straightforward, honest; sl ignorant of current trends in dress, music, etc., conservative. ▶ v **squared, squar·ing.** ▶ vt make square; find square of; pay. ▶ vi fit, suit. **square′ly** adv **square off** get ready to dispute or fight. **square root** number that, multiplied by itself, gives number of which it is factor.

squash [skwosh] vt crush flat; pulp; suppress; humiliate (person). ▶ n act of squashing; (also **squash racquets**) game played with rackets and soft balls in walled court; plant bearing gourds used as a vegetable.

squat [skwot] vi **squat·ted** or **squat, squat·ting.** sit on heels; act as squatter. ▶ adj **squat·ter, squat·test.** short and thick. **squatter** n one who settles on land or occupies house without permission.

squaw [skwaw] n offens Amer. Indian woman; sl wife.

squawk [skwawk] n short harsh cry, esp. of bird. ▶ v utter this.

squeak [skweek] v, n (make) short shrill sound.

squeal [skweel] n long piercing squeak. ▶ vi make one; sl turn informer, supply information (about another). **squeal′er** n

squeam·ish [SKWEEM-ish] adj easily nauseated; easily shocked; overscrupulous.

squee·gee [SKWEE-jee] n tool with rubber blade for clearing water (from glass, etc., spreading wet paper, etc.). ▶ vt **-geed, -gee·ing.** press, smooth with a squeegee.

squeeze [skweez] vt **squeezed, squeez·ing.** press; wring; force; hug; subject to extortion. ▶ n act of squeezing; period of hardship,

difficulty caused by financial weakness.

squelch [skwelch] vt squash; silence with crushing rebuke, etc. ▶ vi make, walk with wet sucking sound, as in walking through mud. ▶ n

squib [skwib] n small (faulty) firework; short piece of writing; short news story.

squid [skwid] n type of cuttlefish.

squig·gle [SKWIG-əl] n wavy, wriggling mark. ▶ vi **-gled, -gling.** wriggle; draw squiggle.

squint [skwint] vi look with eyes partially closed; have the eyes turned in different directions; glance sideways; look askance. ▶ n partially closed eyes; crossed eyes; inf a glance.

squire [skwīr] n country gentleman.

squirm [skwurm] vi wriggle; be embarrassed. ▶ n

squir·rel [SKWUR-əl] n small graceful bushy-tailed tree animal. ▶ vt **-reled, -rel·ing.** store or hide (possession) for future use.

squirt [skwurt] v (of liquid) force, be forced through narrow opening. ▶ n jet; inf short or insignificant person; inf (impudent) youngster.

squish [skwish] v, n (make) soft splashing sound.

Sr Chem strontium.

stab v **stabbed, stab·bing.** pierce, strike (at) with pointed weapon. ▶ n blow, wound so inflicted; sudden unpleasant sensation; attempt.

sta·bi·lize [STAY-bə-līz] vt **-ized, -iz·ing.** make steady, restore to equilibrium, esp. of money values, prices and wages. **sta·bi·li·za′tion** n **sta′bi·liz·er** n device to maintain equilibrium of ship, aircraft, etc.

sta·ble¹ [STAY-bəl] n building for horses; racehorses of particular owner, establishment; such establishment. ▶ vt **-bled, -bling.** put into, lodge in, a stable.

stable² adj **-bler, -blest.** firmly fixed; steadfast, resolute. **sta·bil·i·ty** [stə-BIL-ə-tee] n steadiness; ability to resist change of any kind. **sta′bly** adv

stac·ca·to [stə-KAH-toh] *adj, adv*
Mus with notes sharply separated;
abrupt.

stack [stak] *n* ordered pile, heap;
chimney. ▶ *vt* pile in stack; control
aircraft waiting to land so that they
fly safely at different altitudes.

sta·di·um [STAY-dee-əm] *n, pl*
-di·ums. open-air or covered arena
for athletics, etc.

staff[1] *n, pl* **staffs.** body of officers or
workers; personnel; pole. ▶ *vt*
employ personnel; supply with
personnel.

staff[2] *n, pl* **staffs** *or* **staves.** five
lines on which music is written.

stag *n* adult male deer. ▶ *adj* for
men only, e.g. *stag party.*

stage [stayj] *n* period, division of
development; raised floor or
platform; (platform of) theater;
scene of action; stopping place of
stagecoach, etc. on road, distance
between two of them; separate
unit of space rocket, which can
usu. be jettisoned. ▶ *vt* **staged,**
stag·ing. put (play) on stage;
arrange, bring about. **stag′y** *adj*
stag·i·er, stag·i·est. theatrical. **by**
easy stages unhurriedly; gradually.
stage whisper loud whisper
intended to be heard by audience.

stag·ger [STAG-ər] *vi* walk
unsteadily. ▶ *vt* astound; arrange in
overlapping or alternating
positions, times; distribute over a
period. ▶ *n* act of staggering.
stag′gers *n* form of vertigo;
disease of horses. **stag′ger·ing** *adj*
astounding.

stag·nate [STAG-nayt] *vi* **-nat·ed,**
-nat·ing. cease to flow or develop.
stag·na′tion *n* **stag′nant** [-nənt]
adj sluggish; not flowing; foul,
impure.

staid [stayd] *adj* of sober and quiet
character, sedate. **staid′ly** *adv*
staid′ness [-nis] *n*

stain [stayn] *v* spot, mark; apply
liquid coloring to (wood, etc.);
bring disgrace upon. ▶ *n* **stain′less**
adj **stainless steel** rustless steel
alloy.

stairs [stairz] *pl n* set of steps, esp.

as part of house. **stair′case, -way**
n structure enclosing stairs; stairs.
stair′well *n* vertical opening
enclosing staircase.

stake [stayk] *n* sharpened stick or
post; money wagered or
contended for. ▶ *vt* **staked,**
stak·ing. secure, mark out with
stakes; wager, risk.

sta·lac·tite [stə-LAK-tīt] *n* lime
deposit like icicle on roof of cave.

sta·lag·mite [stə-LAG-mīt] *n* lime
deposit like pillar on floor of cave.

stale [stayl] *adj* **stal·er, stal·est.**
old, lacking freshness; hackneyed;
lacking energy, interest through
monotony. **stale′mate** *n Chess*
draw through one player being
unable to move; deadlock, impasse.

stalk[1] [stawk] *n* plant's stem;
anything like this.

stalk[2] *v* follow, approach stealthily;
walk in stiff and stately manner;
pursue persistently and,
sometimes, attack (a person with
whom one is obsessed). ▶ *n*
stalking. **stalk′er** *n*
stalk′ing-horse *n* pretext.

stall [stawl] *n* compartment in
stable, etc.; booth for display and
sale of goods; seat in choir or
chancel of church; slowdown. ▶ *v*
put in stall; stick fast; (motor
engine) unintentionally stop;
(aircraft) lose flying speed; delay;
hinder.

stal·lion [STAL-yən] *n* uncastrated
male horse, esp. for breeding.

stal·wart [STAWL-wərt] *adj* strong,
brave; staunch. ▶ *n* stalwart person.

sta·men [STAY-mən] *n* male organ
of a flowering plant.

stam·i·na [STAM-ə-nə] *n* power of
endurance, vitality.

stam·mer [STAM-ər] *v* speak, say
with repetition of syllables, stutter.
▶ *n* habit of so speaking.
stam′mer·er *n*

stamp *vi* put down foot with force.
▶ *vt* impress mark on; affix postage
stamp; fix in memory; reveal,
characterize. ▶ *n* stamping with
foot; imprinted mark; appliance for
marking; piece of gummed paper

printed with device as evidence of postage, etc.; character.

stam·pede [stam-PEED] *n* sudden frightened rush, esp. of herd of cattle, crowd. ▶ *v* **-ped·ed, -ped·ing.** cause, take part in stampede.

stance [stans] *n* manner, position of standing; attitude; point of view.

stanch [stawnch] *vt* stop flow (of blood) from.

stan·chion [STAN-shən] *n* upright bar, support. ▶ *vt* make secure with stanchion.

stand *v* **stood** [stuud], **stand·ing.** have, take, set in upright position; remain; be situated; remain firm or stationary; cease to move; endure; adhere to principles; offer oneself as a candidate; be symbol, etc. of; provide free treat to. ▶ *n* holding firm; position; halt; something on which thing can be placed; structure from which spectators watch sport, etc.; stop made by traveling entertainer, etc., e.g. *one-night stand.* **standing** *n* reputation, status; duration. ▶ *adj* erect; permanent, lasting; stagnant; performed from stationary position, e.g. *standing jump.* **stand'by** [-bī] *n, pl* **-bys** [-bīz] someone, something that can be relied on. **stand in** act as substitute (for). **stand-in** *n* substitute. **stand over** watch closely; postpone.

stand·ard [STAN-dərd] *n* accepted example of something against which others are judged; degree, quality; flag; weight or measure to which others must conform; post. ▶ *adj* usual, regular; average; of recognized authority, competence; accepted as correct. **stand'ard·ize** *vt* **-ized, -iz·ing.** regulate by a standard.

stand·off [STAND-awf] *n* (objectionable) aloofness; *Sports* a tie. ▶ *adj* (objectionably) aloof; reserved.

stand'point *n* point of view, opinion; mental attitude.

stank pt. of STINK.

stan·nous [STAN-əs] *adj* of, containing tin.

stan·za [STAN-zə] *n, pl* **-zas.** group of lines of verse.

sta·ple [STAY-pəl] *n* U-shaped piece of metal with pointed ends to drive into wood for use as ring; paper fastener; main product; fiber; pile of wool, etc. ▶ *adj* principal; regularly produced or made for market. ▶ *vt* **-pled, -pling.** fasten with staple; sort, classify (wool, etc.) according to length of fibre. **sta'pler** *n* small device for fastening papers together.

star [stahr] *n* celestial body, seen as twinkling point of light; asterisk; celebrated player, actor; medal, jewel, etc. of apparent shape of star. ▶ *v* **starred, star·ring.** adorn with stars; mark (with asterisk); feature as star performer; play leading role in film, etc. ▶ *adj* leading, most important, famous. **star'ry** *adj* **-ri·er, -ri·est.** covered with stars. **star'dom** [-dəm] *n* **star'fish** *n* small star-shaped sea creature.

star·board [STAHR-bərd] *n* right-hand side of ship, looking forward. ▶ *adj* of, on this side.

starch *n* substance forming the main food element in bread, potatoes, etc., and used mixed with water, for stiffening laundered fabrics; *inf* boldness; vigor; energy. ▶ *vt* stiffen thus. **starch'y** *adj* **starch·i·er, starch·i·est.** containing starch; stiff; formal; prim.

stare [stair] *vi* **stared, star·ing.** look fixedly at; gaze with eyes wide open; be obvious or visible to. ▶ *n* staring, fixed gaze. **stare down** abash by staring at; defeat by staring.

stark [stahrk] *adj* **-er, -est.** blunt, bare; desolate; absolute. ▶ *adv* completely.

start [stahrt] *vt* begin; set going. ▶ *vi* begin, esp. journey; make sudden movement. ▶ *n* beginning; abrupt movement; advantage of a lead in a race. **start'er** *n* electric motor starting car engine;

competitor in, supervisor of, start of race.

star·tle [STAHR-tl] vt **-tled, -tling.** give a fright to.

starve [stahrv] v **starved, starv·ing.** (cause to) suffer or die from hunger. **star·va'tion** [-VAY-shən] n

stash vt put away, store, hide. ▶ n anything stashed; place for this; sl supply of illicit drugs.

state [stayt] n condition; place, situation; politically organized people e.g. any of the fifty states of the USA; government; rank; pomp. ▶ vt **stat·ed, stat·ing.** express in words. **stated** adj fixed; regular; settled. **state'ly** adj **-li·er, -li·est.** dignified, lofty. **state'ment** [-mənt] n expression in words; account. **state'room** [-ruum] n private cabin on ship. **states'man** [-mən] n, pl **-men.** respected political leader. **states'man·ship** n statesman's art.

stat·ic [STAT-ik] adj motionless, inactive; pert. to bodies at rest, or in equilibrium. ▶ n electrical interference in radio reception. **stat'i·cal·ly** adv

sta·tion [STAY-shən] n place where thing stops or is placed; stopping place for railroad trains, buses; local office for police force, fire department, etc.; place equipped for radio or television transmission; post; status; position in life. ▶ vt put in position. **sta'tion·ar·y** [-er-ee] adj not moving, fixed; not changing.

sta·tion·er [STAY-shən-ər] n dealer in writing materials, etc. **sta'tion·er·y** n

sta·tis·tic [stə-TIS-tik] n numerical fact collected and classified systematically. **sta·tis·tics** n science of classifying and interpreting numerical information. **sta·tis'ti·cal** [-kəl] adj **stat·is·ti·cian** [stat-i-STISH-ən] n one who compiles and studies statistics.

stat·ue [STACH-oo] n solid carved or cast image of person, animal, etc. **stat'u·ar·y** [-er-ee] n statues

collectively. **stat·u·esque'** [-esk] adj like statue; dignified.

stat·ure [STACH-ər] n bodily height; greatness.

sta·tus [STAY-təs] n position, rank; prestige; relation to others. **status quo** [kwoh] existing state of affairs.

stat·ute [STACH-oot] n written law. **stat'u·to·ry** [-ə-tor-ee] adj enacted, defined or authorized by statute.

staunch [stawnch] adj **-er, -est.** trustworthy, loyal.

stave [stayv] n one of the pieces forming barrel; verse, stanza; Mus staff. ▶ vt **staved** or **stove, stav·ing.** break hole in; ward (off).

stay[1] v **stayed, stay·ing.** remain; sojourn; pause; wait; endure; stop; hinder; postpone. ▶ n remaining, sojourning; check; restraint; deterrent; postponement.

stay[2] n support, prop, rope supporting mast, etc. ▶ pl formerly, laced corsets.

stead [sted] n place. **in stead** in place (of). **in good stead** of service.

stead·y [STED-ee] adj **stead·i·er, stead·i·est.** firm; regular; temperate; industrious; reliable. ▶ vt **stead·ied, stead·y·ing.** make steady. **stead'i·ly** adv **stead'i·ness** [-nis] n **stead'fast** [-fast] adj firm, fixed, unyielding. **stead'fast·ly** adv

steak [stayk] n slice of meat, esp. beef; slice of fish.

steal [steel] v **stole, sto·len, steal·ing.** rob; move silently; take without right or leave.

stealth [stelth] n secret or underhanded procedure, behavior. **stealth'i·ly** adv **stealth'y** adj **stealth·i·er, stealth·i·est.**

steam [steem] n vapor of boiling water; inf power, energy. ▶ vi give off steam; rise in vapor; move by steam power. ▶ vt cook or treat with steam. **steam'er** n steam-propelled ship; vessel for cooking or treating with steam. **steam engine** engine worked or propelled by steam. **steam'roll·er** n large roller, orig. moved by steam, for leveling road surfaces, etc.; any great power used to crush opposition. ▶ *vt* crush.

steed *n Poet* horse.

steel *n* hard and malleable metal made by mixing carbon in iron; tool, weapon of steel. ▶ *vt* harden. **steel'y** *adj* **steel·i·er, steel·i·est.**

steep[1] *adj* **-er, -est.** rising, sloping abruptly; precipitous; (of prices) very high or exorbitant; unreasonable. **steep'en** *v* **steep'ly** *adv* **steep'ness** *n*

steep[2] *v* soak, saturate. ▶ *n* act or process of steeping; the liquid used.

stee·ple [STEE-pəl] *n* church tower with spire. **stee'ple·chase** *n* horse race with ditches and fences to jump; foot race with hurdles, etc. to jump. **stee'ple·jack** *n* one who builds, repairs chimneys, steeples, etc.

steer[1] *vt* guide, direct course of vessel, motor vehicle, etc. ▶ *vi* direct one's course. **steer'age** [-ij] *n* formerly, cheapest accommodation on ship. **steer'ing wheel** wheel turned by the driver of a vehicle in order to steer it.

steer[2] *n* castrated bull.

stein [stīn] *n* earthenware beer mug.

ste·le [STEE-lee] *n* ancient carved stone pillar or slab.

stel·lar [STEL-ər] *adj* of stars.

stem[1] *n* stalk, trunk; long slender part, as in tobacco pipe; part of word to which inflections are added; foremost part of ship. **stem cell** *Histology* undifferentiated embryonic cell that gives rise to specialized cells, such as blood, bone, etc.

stem[2] *vt* **stemmed, stem·ming.** check, stop, dam up.

stench *n* evil smell.

sten·cil [STEN-səl] *n* thin sheet pierced with pattern which is brushed over with paint or ink, leaving pattern on surface under it; the pattern; the plate; pattern made. ▶ *vt* **-ciled, -cil·ing.**

ste·nog·ra·phy [stə-NOG-rə-fee] *n* shorthand writing. **sten·og'ra·pher** *n* **sten·o·graph'ic** *adj*

stent *n* surgical implant to keep an artery open.

sten·to·ri·an [sten-TOR-ee-ən] *adj* (of voice) very loud.

step *v* **stepped, step·ping.** move and set down foot; proceed (in this way); measure in paces. ▶ *n* act of stepping; sound made by stepping; mark made by foot; manner of walking; series of foot movements forming part of dance; gait; pace; measure, act, stage in proceeding; board, rung, etc. to put foot on; degree in scale; mast socket; promotion. ▶ *pl* portable ladder with hinged prop attached, stepladder. **step'lad·der** *n* four-legged ladder having broad flat steps.

step·child [STEP-chīld] *n, pl* **-child·ren** [-CHIL-drən] child of husband or wife by former marriage; person, organization, idea, etc. treated improperly. **step'broth·er** *n* **step'fa·ther** *n* **step'moth·er** *n* **step'sis·ter** *n*

steppe [step] *n* extensive treeless plain in European and Asiatic Russia.

stere [steer] *n* cubic meter.

ster·e·o·phon·ic [ster-ee-ə-FON-ik] *adj* (of sound) giving effect of coming from many directions. **ster'e·o** *adj, n* (of, for) stereophonic record player, etc.

ster·e·o·scop·ic [ster-ee-ə-SKOP-ik] *adj* having three-dimensional effect.

ster·e·o·type [STER-ee-ə-tīp] *n* metal plate for printing cast from type; something (monotonously) familiar, conventional, predictable. ▶ *vt* **-typed, -typ·ing.** make stereotype of.

ster·ile [STER-əl] *adj* unable to produce fruit, crops, young, etc.; free from (harmful) germs. **ste·ril·i·ty** [stə-RIL-ə-tee] *n* **ster·i·li·za'tion** *n* process or act of making sterile. **ster'i·lize** *vt* **-lized, -liz·ing.** render sterile.

ster·ling [STUR-ling] *adj* genuine, true; of solid worth, dependable; in British money. ▶ *n* British money.

stern[1] [sturn] *adj* severe, strict. **stern'ly** *adv* **stern'ness** [-nis] *n*

stern² *n* rear part of ship.

ster·num [STUR-nəm] *n* the breast bone.

ster·to·rous [STUR-tər-əs] *adj* with sound of heavy breathing, hoarse snoring.

stet *Lat* let it stand (proofreader's direction to cancel alteration previously made).

steth·o·scope [STETH-ə-skohp] *n* instrument for listening to action of heart, lungs, etc.

Stet·son [STET-sən] *n* ® type of broad-brimmed felt hat esp. cowboy hat.

ste·ve·dore [STEE-vi-dor] *n* one who loads or unloads ships.

stew [stoo] *n* food cooked slowly in closed vessel; state of excitement, agitation or worry. ▶ *v* cook by stewing; worry. **stew in one's own juice** suffer consequences of one's own actions.

stew·ard [STOO-ərd] *n* one who manages another's property; official managing race meeting, assembly, etc.; attendant on ship's or aircraft's passengers.

stew'ard·ess [-is] *n, fem*

stick [stik] *n* long, thin piece of wood; anything shaped like a stick; *inf* uninteresting person. ▶ *v* **stuck, stick·ing.** ▶ *vt* pierce, stab; place, fasten, as by pins, glue; protrude; bewilder; *inf* impose disagreeable responsibility on (someone). ▶ *vi* adhere; come to stop, jam; remain; be fastened; protrude. **stick'er** *n* adhesive label, e.g. *bumper sticker.* **stick'y** *adj* **stick·i·er, stick·i·est.** covered with, like adhesive substance; (of weather) warm, humid; *inf* difficult, unpleasant. **stick shift** automobile transmission with manually operated shift lever. **stick·ler** [STIK-lər] *n* person who insists on something.

stiff *adj* **-er, -est.** not easily bent or moved; rigid; awkward; difficult; thick, not fluid; formal; stubborn; unnatural; strong or fresh, as breeze; *inf* excessive. ▶ *n sl* corpse; *sl* a drunk. ▶ *vt sl* fail to tip (waiter, etc.). **stiff'en** [-in] *v* **stiff'ly** *adv*

stiff-necked [-nekt] *adj* obstinate, stubborn; haughty.

sti·fle [STIF-əl] *vt* **-fled, -fling.** smother, suppress.

stig·ma [STIG-mə] *n, pl* **-mas** or **-ma·ta** [-MAH-tə] distinguishing mark esp. of disgrace. **stig'ma·tize** *vt* **-tized, -tiz·ing.** mark with stigma.

sti·let·to [sti-LET-oh] *n, pl* **-tos** or **-toes.** small dagger; small boring tool. ▶ *adj* thin, pointed like a stiletto.

still¹ *adj* **-er, -est.** motionless, noiseless, at rest. ▶ *vt* quiet. ▶ *adv* to this time; yet; even. ▶ *n* photograph esp. of motion picture scene. **still'born** *adj* born dead. **still life** a painting of inanimate objects.

still² *n* apparatus for distilling.

stilt *n* pole with footrests for walking raised from ground; long post supporting building, etc. **stilt'ed** [-id] *adj* stiff in manner, pompous.

stim·u·lus [STIM-yə-ləs] *n, pl* **-li** [-lī] something that rouses to activity; incentive. **stim'u·lant** [-lənt] *n* drug, etc. acting as a stimulus. **stim'u·late** *vt* **-lat·ed, -lat·ing.** rouse up, spur. **stim'u·lat·ing** *adj* acting as stimulus. **stim·u·la'tion** *n* **stim'u·la·tive** [-lə-tiv] *adj*

sting *v* **stung, sting·ing.** thrust sting into; cause sharp pain to; *sl* cheat, take advantage of, esp. by overcharging; feel sharp pain. ▶ *n* (wound, pain, caused by) sharp pointed organ, often poisonous, of certain insects and animals; *sl* illegal operation conducted by police, etc. to collect evidence against criminals.

stin·gy [STIN-jee] *adj* **-gi·er, -gi·est.** mean; avaricious; niggardly. **stin'gi·ness** [-nis] *n*

stink *vi* **stank** or **stunk, stunk, stink·ing.** give out strongly offensive smell; *inf* be markedly inferior. ▶ *n* such smell, stench; *inf* fuss, bother; scandal.

stint *vt* be frugal, miserly to (someone) or with (something). ▶ *n* allotted amount of work or time;

sti·pend [STI-pend] n payment, esp. scholarship or fellowship allowance given to student. **sti·pen′di·ar·y** [-dee-er-ee] adj receiving stipend.

stip·ple [STIP-əl] vt -pled, -pling. engrave, paint in dots. ▶ n this process.

stip·u·late [STIP-yə-layt] vi -lat·ed, -lat·ing. specify in making a bargain. **stip·u·la′tion** n proviso; condition.

stir [stur] v **stirred, stir·ring.** (begin to) move; rouse; cause trouble; set, keep in motion; excite. ▶ n commotion, disturbance.

stir·rup [STUR-əp] n metal loop hung from strap for supporting foot of rider on horse.

stitch [stich] n movement of needle in sewing, etc.; its result in the work; sharp pain in side; least fragment (of clothing). ▶ v sew.

stock [stok] n goods, material stored, esp. for sale or later use; reserve, fund; shares in, or capital of, company, etc.; standing, reputation; farm animals (livestock); plant, stem from which cuttings are taken; handle of gun, tool, etc.; liquid broth produced by boiling meat, etc.; flowering plant; lineage. ▶ pl Hist frame to secure feet, hands (of offender); frame to support ship during construction. ▶ adj kept in stock; standard, hackneyed. ▶ vt keep, store; supply with livestock, fish, etc. **stock′y** adj **stock·i·er, stock·i·est.** thickset. **stock′brok·er** [-brohk-ər] n agent for buying, selling stocks and bonds. **stock car** ordinary automobile strengthened and modified for a form of racing in which automobiles often collide. **stock ex·change** institution for buying and selling shares. **stock′pile** v acquire and store large quantity of (something). **stock-still** adj motionless. **stock′tak·ing** n examination, counting and valuing of goods in a store, etc. **put stock in** believe,

trust.

stock·ade [sto-KAYD] n enclosure of stakes, barrier.

stock·ing [STOK-ing] n close-fitting covering for leg and foot.

stodg·y [STOJ-ee] adj **stodg·i·er, stodg·i·est.** heavy, dull.

sto·gy [STOH-gee] n, pl **-gies.** cheap cigar.

sto·ic [STOH-ik] adj capable of much self-control, great endurance without complaint. ▶ n stoical person. **sto′i·cal** [-kəl] adj

stoke [stohk] v **stoked, stok·ing.** feed, tend fire or furnace. **stok′er** n

stole¹ [stohl] pt. of STEAL.

stole² n long scarf or shawl.

sto′len [stohl-ən] pp. of STEAL.

stol′id adj hard to excite; heavy, slow, apathetic.

stom·ach [STUM-ək] n sac forming chief digestive organ in any animal; appetite; desire, inclination. ▶ vt put up with.

stomp vi put down foot with force.

stone [stohn] n (piece of) rock; gem; hard seed of fruit; hard deposit formed in kidneys, bladder; British unit of weight, 14 lbs. ▶ vt **stoned, ston·ing.** throw stones at; free (fruit) from stones. **stoned** adj sl stupefied by alcohol or drugs. **ston′i·ly** adv **ston′y** adj **ston·i·er, ston·i·est.** of, like stone; hard; cold. **stone-broke** [-brohk] adj with no money left. **stone-dead** adj completely dead. **stone-deaf** adj completely deaf. **stone′wall** v stall; evade; filibuster. **stone′ware** [-wair] n heavy common pottery.

stood [stuud] pt./pp. of STAND.

stooge [stooj] n performer always the butt of another's jokes; anyone taken advantage of by another.

stool n backless chair; excrement.

stoop¹ [stoop] vi lean forward or down, bend; swoop; abase, degrade oneself. ▶ n stooping carriage of the body.

stoop² n steps or small porch in front of house.

stop v **stopped, stop·ping.** check, bring to halt; prevent; interrupt; suspend; desist from; fill up an opening; cease, come to a halt; stay. ▶ *n* stopping or becoming stopped; any device for altering or regulating pitch; set of pipes in organ having tones of a distinct quality. **stop'page** [-ij] *n* **stop'per** [-ər] *n* plug for closing bottle, etc. **stop'gap** *n* temporary substitute. **stop'off, stop'o·ver** *n* short break in journey. **stop'watch** *n* one that can be stopped for exact timing e.g. of race. **pull out all the stops** use all available means.

store [stor] *vt* **stored, stor·ing.** stock, furnish, keep; *Computers* enter or retain (data). ▶ *n* retail store; abundance; stock; place for keeping goods; warehouse. ▶ *pl* stocks of goods, provisions. **stor'age** *n* **in store** in readiness; imminent.

stork *n* large wading bird.

storm *n* violent weather with wind, rain, hail, sand, snow, etc.; assault on fortress; violent outbreak, discharge. ▶ *vt* assault; take by storm. ▶ *vi* rage. **storm'y** *adj* **storm·i·er, storm·i·est.** like storm; (emotionally) violent.

sto·ry¹ [STOR-ee] *n, pl* **-ries.** (book, piece of prose, etc.) telling about events, happenings; lie.

story² *n, pl* **-ries.** horizontal division of a building.

stoup [stoop] *n* small basin for holy water.

stout [stowt] *adj* **-er, -est.** fat; sturdy, resolute. ▶ *n* kind of beer. **stout'ly** *adv* **stout'ness** [-nis] *n*

stove¹ [stohv] *n* apparatus for cooking, heating, etc.

stove² pt./pp. of STAVE.

stow [stoh] *vt* pack away. **stow'age** [-ij] *n* **stow'a·way** *n* one who hides in ship to obtain free passage.

strad·dle [STRAD-l] *v* **-dled, -dling.** ▶ *vt* bestride. ▶ *vi* spread legs wide. ▶ *n*

strafe [strayf] *vt* **strafed, straf·ing.** attack (esp. with bullets, rockets) from air.

strag·gle [STRAG-əl] *vi* **-gled, -gling.** stray, get dispersed, linger.

strag'gler *n*

straight [strayt] *adj* **-er, -est.** without bend; honest; level; in order; (of whiskey) undiluted, neat; expressionless; (of drama, actor, etc.) serious; *sl* heterosexual. ▶ *n* straight condition or part. ▶ *adv* direct. **straight'en** [-in] *v*

straight'a·way *adv* immediately.

straight·for'ward [-wərd] *adj* open, frank; simple; honest.

strain¹ [strayn] *vt* stretch tightly; stretch to full or to excess; filter. ▶ *vi* make great effort. ▶ *n* stretching force; violent effort; injury from being strained; burst of music or poetry; great demand; (condition caused by) overwork, worry, etc.; tone of speaking or writing. **strain'er** [-ər] *n* filter, sieve.

strain² *n* breed or race; type (esp. in biology); trace, streak.

strait [strayt] *n* channel of water connecting two larger areas of water. ▶ *pl* position of difficulty or distress. ▶ *adj* narrow; strict. **strait'en** [-in] *vt* make strait, narrow; press with poverty. **strait'jack·et** *n* jacket to confine arms of violent person. **strait-laced** [-laysd] *adj* austere, strict; puritanical.

strand¹ *v* run aground; leave, be left in difficulties or helpless.

strand² *n* one single string or wire of rope, etc.

strange [straynj] *adj* **strang·er, strang·est.** odd; queer; unaccustomed; foreign; uncommon; wonderful; singular. **stran'ger** *n* unknown person; foreigner; one unaccustomed (to). **strange'ness** [-nis] *n*

stran·gle [STRANG-gəl] *vt* **-gled, -gling.** kill by squeezing windpipe; suppress. **stran·gu·la'tion** [-yə-LAY-shən] *n* strangling.

strap *n* strip, esp. of leather. ▶ *vt* **strapped, strap·ping.** fasten, beat with strap. **strap'ping** *adj* tall and powerful. **strap'hang·er** *n* in bus, subway car, one who has to stand, steadying self with strap provided for this purpose.

strat·a·gem [STRAT-ə-jəm] *n* plan, trick. **strat′e·gy** *n, pl* **-gies.** art of war; overall plan. **strat′e·gist** *n* **stra·te·gic** [strə-TEE-jik] *adj*

strat·o·sphere [STRAT-ə-sfeer] *n* upper part of the atmosphere from approx. 11 km to 50 km above Earth's surface.

stra·tum [STRAY-təm] *n, pl* **stra·ta** [-tə] layer, class of rock; class in society. **strat′i·fy** *v* **-fied, -fy·ing.** form, deposit in layers. **strat·i·fi·ca′tion** *n*

straw *n* stalks of grain; single stalk; long, narrow tube used to suck up liquid. **straw′ber·ry** *n* creeping plant producing a red, juicy fruit; the fruit.

stray *vi* wander; digress; get lost. ▶ *adj* strayed; occasional, scattered. ▶ *n* stray animal.

streak [streek] *n* long line or band; element, trace. ▶ *vt* mark with streaks. ▶ *vi* move fast; run naked in public. **streak′y** *adj* **streak·i·er, streak·i·est.** having streaks; striped.

stream [streem] *n* flowing body of water or other liquid; steady flow. ▶ *vi* flow; run with liquid; float, wave in the air. ▶ *vt* discharge, send in stream. **stream′er** [-ər] *n* (paper) ribbon, narrow flag.

stream·lined [STREEM-līnd] *adj* (of train, plane, etc.) built so as to offer least resistance to air.

street *n* road in town, etc. usu. lined with houses. **street′car** *n* vehicle (esp. electrically driven and for public transport) running usu. on rails laid on roadway. **street′walk·er** *n* prostitute. **street′wise, -smart** *adj inf* adept at surviving in urban, oft. criminal, environment.

strength [strengkth] *n* quality of being strong; power; capacity for exertion or endurance; vehemence; force; full or necessary number of people. **strength′en** *v* make stronger, reinforce. **on the strength of** relying on; because of.

stren·u·ous [STREN-yoo-əs] *adj* energetic; earnest.

strep·to·coc·cus [strep-tə-KOK-əs] *n, pl* **-coc·ci** [-KOK-sī] genus of bacteria.

strep·to·my·cin [strep-tə-MĪ-sin] *n* antibiotic drug.

stress *n* emphasis; strain; impelling force; effort; tension. ▶ *vt* emphasize; accent; put mechanical stress on.

stretch [strech] *vt* extend; exert to utmost; tighten, pull out; reach out. ▶ *vi* reach; have elasticity. ▶ *n* stretching, being stretched; expanse; spell. **stretch′er** *n* person, thing that stretches; appliance on which disabled person is carried; bar linking legs of chair.

strew [stroo] *vt* **strewed, strewn** or **strewed, strew·ing.** scatter over surface, spread.

stri·ate [STRĪ-ayt] *vt* **-at·ed, -at·ing.** mark with streaks; score. **stri·a′tion** *n* **striated** *adj* streaked, furrowed, grooved.

strick·en [STRIK-ən] *adj* seriously affected by disease, grief, famine; afflicted; pp. of STRIKE.

strict [strikt] *adj* **-er, -est.** stern, not lax or indulgent; defined; without exception.

stric·ture [STRIK-chər] *n* critical remark; constriction.

stride [strīd] *vi* **strode, strid·den, strid·ing.** walk with long steps. ▶ *n* single step; its length; regular pace. **hit one's stride** reach the level at which one consistently functions best.

stri·dent [STRĪD-nt] *adj* harsh in tone; loud; urgent.

strife [strīf] *n* conflict; quarreling.

strike [strīk] *v* **struck** or **strick·en, strik·ing.** hit (against); ignite; (of snake) bite; arrive at, come upon; of plants (cause to) take root; attack; hook (fish); assume (time) as bell in clock, etc.; *Baseball* swing and miss a pitch, etc. ▶ *vt* affect; enter mind of; discover (gold, oil, etc.); dismantle, remove; make (coin). ▶ *vi* cease work as protest or to make demands. ▶ *n* act of striking. **strik′er** *n* **striking** *adj* noteworthy, impressive. **strike it rich** meet unexpected financial success. **strike off** remove. **strike out** fail in a venture; *Baseball* make three strikes.

string *n* (length of) thin cord or other material; strand, row; series; fiber in plants. ▶ *pl* conditions. ▶ *vt* **strung, string·ing.** provide with, thread on string; form in line, series. **stringed** *adj* (of musical instruments) furnished with strings. **string'y** *adj* **string·i·er, string·i·est.** like string; fibrous.

strin·gent [STRIN-jənt] *adj* strict, rigid, binding. **strin'gen·cy** *n* severity.

strip *v* **stripped, strip·ping.** lay bare, take covering off; dismantle; deprive (of); undress. ▶ *n* long, narrow piece. **strip'per** *n* person who performs a striptease. **strip'tease** [-teez] *n* nightclub or theater act in which stripper undresses in time to music.

stripe [strīp] *n* narrow mark, band; chevron as symbol of military rank; style, kind.

strip'ling *n* a youth.

strive [strīv] *vi* **strove** *or* **strived, striv·en** *or* **strived, striv·ing.** try hard, struggle, contend.

strobe [strohb] *n* apparatus that produces high-intensity flashing light.

strode [strohd] pt. of STRIDE.

stroke [strohk] *n* blow; sudden action, occurrence; apoplexy; mark of pen, pencil, brush, etc.; chime of clock; completed movement in series; act, manner of striking (ball, etc.); style, method of swimming; rower sitting nearest stern setting the rate; act of stroking. ▶ *vt* **stroked, strok·ing.** set time in rowing; pass hand lightly over.

stroll [strohl] *vi* walk in leisurely or idle manner. ▶ *n*

strong [strawng] *adj* **-er, -est.** powerful, robust, healthy; difficult to break; noticeable; intense; emphatic; not diluted; having a certain number. **strong'hold** [-hohld] *n* fortress.

stron·ti·um [STRON-shee-əm] *n* silvery-white chemical element. **strontium 90** radioactive isotope of strontium present in fallout of nuclear explosions.

strop *n* leather for sharpening razors. ▶ *vt* **stropped, strop·ping.** sharpen on one.

strove [strohv] pt. of STRIVE.

struck pt./pp. of STRIKE.

struc·ture [STRUK-chər] *n* (arrangement of parts in) construction, building, etc.; form; organization. ▶ *vt* **-tured, -tur·ing.** give structure to. **struc'tur·al** [-chər-əl] *adj*

strug·gle [STRUG-əl] *vi* **-gled, -gling.** contend; fight; proceed, work, move with difficulty and effort. ▶ *n*

strum *v* **strummed, strum·ming.** strike notes of guitar, etc.

strum·pet [STRUM-pit] *n* promiscuous woman; prostitute.

strung pt./pp. of STRING.

strut *vi* **strut·ted, strut·ting.** walk affectedly or pompously. ▶ *n* brace; rigid support, usu. set obliquely; strutting gait.

strych·nine [STRIK-nin] *n* poison obtained from nux vomica seeds.

stub *n* remnant of anything, e.g. pencil, cigarette, etc.; retained portion of check, etc. ▶ *vt* **stubbed, stub·bing.** strike (e.g. toes) against fixed object; extinguish by pressing against surface. **stub'by** *adj* **-bi·er, -bi·est.** short, broad.

stub·ble [STUB-əl] *n* stumps of cut grain, etc. after cutting; short growth of beard.

stub·born [STUB-ərn] *adj* unyielding, obstinate. **stub'born·ness** [-nis] *n*

stuc·co [STUK-oh] *n, pl* **-coes** *or* **-cos.** plaster. ▶ *vt* **-coed, -co·ing.** apply stucco to (wall).

stuck pt./pp. of STICK.

stud¹ *n* nail with large head; type of button; vertical wall support. ▶ *vt* **stud'ded, stud'ding.** set with studs. **stud'ding** *n*

stud² *n* stallion, set of horses, kept for breeding; *sl* man known for sexual prowess. **stud'book** [-buuk] *n* book giving pedigree of noted or thoroughbred animals, esp. horses. **stud farm** establishment where horses are kept for breeding.

stu·di·o [STOO-dee-oh] *n, pl* **-di·os.** workroom of artist, photographer, etc.; building, room where motion pictures, TV or radio shows are made, broadcast; apartment of one main room.

stud·y [STUD-ee] *v* **stud·ied, stud·y·ing.** be engaged in learning; make study of; try constantly to do; consider; scrutinize. ▶ *n, pl* **stud·ies.** effort to acquire knowledge; subject of this; room to study in; book, report, etc. produced as result of study; sketch. **stu·dent** [STOOD-nt] *n* one who studies, esp. at college, etc. **studied** *adj* carefully designed, premeditated. **stu·di·ous** [STOO-dee-əs] *adj* fond of study; thoughtful; painstaking; deliberate. **stu·di·ous·ly** *adv*

stuff *v* pack, cram, fill (completely); eat large amount; fill with seasoned mixture; fill (animal's skin) with material to preserve lifelike form. ▶ *n* material, fabric; any substance. **stuff'ing** *n* material for stuffing, esp. seasoned mixture for inserting in poultry, etc. before cooking. **stuff'y** *adj* **stuff·i·er, stuff·i·est.** lacking fresh air; dull, conventional. **stuffed shirt** pompous person.

stul·ti·fy [STUL-tə-fī] *vt* **-fied, -fy·ing.** make ineffectual. **stul·ti·fi·ca'tion** *n*

stum·ble [STUM-bəl] *vi* **-bled, -bling.** trip and nearly fall; falter. ▶ *n* **stumbling block** obstacle.

stump *n* remnant of tree, tooth, etc., when main part has been cut away; part of leg or arm remaining after amputation. ▶ *vt* confuse, puzzle. ▶ *vi* walk heavily, noisily. **stump'y** *adj* **stump·i·er, stump·i·est.** short and thickset.

stun *vt* **stunned, stun·ning.** knock senseless; amaze.

stung pt./pp. of STING.

stunk pp. of STINK.

stunt¹ *vt* check growth of, dwarf. **stunt'ed** *adj* underdeveloped; undersized.

stunt² *n* feat of dexterity or daring; anything spectacular, unusual done to gain publicity.

stu·pe·fy [STOO-pə-fī] *vt* **-fied, -fy·ing.** make insensitive, lethargic; astound. **stu·pe·fac'tion** *n*

stu·pen·dous [stoo-PEN-dəs] *adj* astonishing; amazing; huge.

stu·pid [STOO-pid] *adj* **-er, -est.** slow-witted; silly; in a stupor. **stu·pid'i·ty** *n, pl* **-ties.**

stu·por [STOO-pər] *n* dazed state; insensibility. **stu'por·ous** *adj*

stur·dy [STUR-dee] *adj* **-di·er, -di·est.** robust, strongly built; vigorous. **stur'di·ly** *adv*

stur·geon [STUR-jən] *n* fish yielding caviar.

stut·ter [STUT-ər] *v* speak with difficulty; stammer. ▶ *n*

sty¹ [stī] *n, pl* **sties.** place to keep pigs in; hovel, dirty place.

sty² *n, pl* **sties.** inflammation on edge of eyelid.

Styg·i·an [STIJ-ee-ən] *adj* of river Styx in Hades; gloomy; infernal.

style [stīl] *n* manner of writing, doing, etc.; designation; sort; elegance, refinement; superior manner, quality; design. ▶ *vt* **styled, styl·ing.** shape, design; adapt; designate. **styl'ish** *adj* fashionable. **styl'ist** *n* one cultivating style in literary or other execution; designer; hairdresser. **styl·is'tic** *adj* **styl'ize** *vt* **-ized, -iz·ing.** give conventional stylistic form to.

sty·lus [STĪ-ləs] *n, pl* **-lus·es.** writing instrument; (in record player) tiny point running in groove of record.

sty·mie [STĪ-mee] *vt* **-mied, -my·ing.** hinder, thwart.

styp·tic [STIP-tik] *adj, n* (designating) a substance that stops bleeding.

suave [swahv] *adj* **suav·er, suav·est.** smoothly polite, affable, bland. **suav'i·ty** *n*

sub submarine; submarine sandwich; substitute. *vi inf* **subbed,**

sub·bing. serve as substitute.

sub- *prefix* under, less than, in lower position, subordinate, forming subdivision, etc., e.g. *subaquatic; subheading; subnormal; subsoil.*

sub·com·mit·tee [SUB-kə-mit-ee] *n* section of committee functioning separately from main body.

sub·con·scious [sub-KON-shəs] *adj* acting, existing without one's awareness. ▶ *n Psychology* that part of the human mind unknown, or only partly known to possessor.

sub·cu·ta·ne·ous [sub-kyoo-TAY-nee-əs] *adj* under the skin.

sub·di·vide [sub-di-VĪD] *vt* **-vid·ed, -vid·ing.** divide again. **sub'di·vi·sion** [-vizh-ən] *n*

sub·due [səb-DOO] *v* **-dued, -du·ing.** overcome. **subdued'** *adj* cowed, quiet; (of light) not bright or intense.

subject [SUB-jikt] *n* theme, topic; that about which something is predicated; conscious self; one under power of another. ▶ *adj* owing allegiance; subordinate; dependent; liable (to). ▶ *vt* [səb-JEKT] cause to undergo; make liable; subdue. **sub·jec'tion** [-JEK-shən] *n* act of bringing, or state of being, under control. **sub·jec'tive** *adj* based on personal feelings, not impartial; of the self; existing in the mind; displaying artist's individuality. **sub·jec·tiv'i·ty** *n*

sub ju·di·ce [sub JOO-di-see] *Lat* under judicial consideration.

sub·ju·gate [SUB-jə-gayt] *vt* **-gat·ed, -gat·ing.** force to submit; conquer. **sub·ju·ga'tion** *n*

sub·junc·tive [səb-JUNGK-tiv] *n* mood used mainly in subordinate clauses expressing wish, possibility. ▶ *adj* in, of, that mood.

sub·let' *vt* **-let, -let·ting.** (of tenant) let to another all or part of what tenant has rented.

sub·li·mate [SUB-lə-mayt] *vt* **-mat·ed, -mat·ing.** *Psychology* direct energy (esp. sexual) into activities considered more socially acceptable; refine. ▶ *n* [-mit] *Chem* material obtained when substance is sublimed. **sub·li·ma'tion** *n Psychology* unconscious diversion of sexual impulses towards new aim and activities; *Chem* process in which a solid changes directly into a vapor.

sub·lime [sə-BLĪM] *adj* elevated; eminent; majestic; inspiring awe; exalted. ▶ *v* **-limed, -lim·ing.** *Chem* change or cause to change from solid to vapor. **sub·lime'ly** *adv*

sub·lim·i·nal [sub-LIM-ə-nl] *adj* resulting from processes of which the individual is not aware.

sub·ma·rine [sub-mə-REEN] *n* ship that can travel below surface of sea and remain submerged for long periods. ▶ *adj* below surface of sea. **submarine sandwich** overstuffed sandwich of meats, cheese, etc. in long loaf of Italian bread.

sub·merge [səb-MURJ] *v* **-merged, -merg·ing.** place, go under water. **sub·mer'sion** [-MUR-zhən] *n*

sub·mit [səb-MIT] *v* **-mit·ted, -mit·ting.** surrender; put forward for consideration; surrender; defer. **sub·mis'sion** [-MISH-ən] *n* **sub·mis'sive** *adj* meek, obedient.

sub·or·di·nate [sə-BOR-dn-it] *adj* of lower rank or less importance. ▶ *n* inferior; one under order of another. ▶ *vt* [-dn-ayt] **-nat·ed, -nat·ing.** make, treat as subordinate. **sub·or·di·na'tion** [-NAY-shən] *n*

sub·orn [sə-BORN] *vt* bribe to do evil. **sub·or·na·tion** [sub-or-NAY-shən] *n*

sub·poe·na [sə-PEE-nə] *n* writ requiring attendance at court of law. ▶ *vt* **-naed, -na·ing.** summon by such order.

sub·scribe [səb-SKRĪB] *vt* **-scribed, -scrib·ing.** pay, promise to pay (contribution); write one's name at end of document. **sub·scrip'tion** *n* subscribing; money paid.

sub·se·quent [SUB-si-kwənt] *adj* later, following or coming after in time.

sub·ser·vi·ent [səb-SUR-vee-ənt]

adj submissive, servile.
sub·ser'vi·ence *n*

sub·side [səb-SĪD] *vi* **-sid·ed,
-sid·ing.** abate, come to an end;
sink; settle; collapse. **sub·sid'ence**
n

sub·sid·i·ar·y [səb-SID-ee-er-ee] *adj*
supplementing; secondary;
auxiliary. ▶ *n, pl* **-ar·ies.**

sub·si·dize [SUB-si-dīz] *vt* **-dized,
-diz·ing.** help financially; pay grant
to. **sub'si·dy** [-dee] *n, pl* **-dies.**
money granted.

sub·sist [səb-SIST] *vi* exist, sustain
life. **sub·sist'ence** [-əns] *n* the
means by which one supports life;
livelihood.

sub·son·ic [sub-SON-ik] *adj*
concerning speeds less than that of
sound.

sub·stance [SUB-stəns] *n* matter;
particular kind of matter; chief part,
essence; wealth. **sub·stan·tial**
[səb-STAN-shəl] *adj* considerable;
of real value; solid, big, important;
really existing. **sub·stan'ti·ate**
[-shee-ayt] *vt* **-at·ed, -at·ing.** bring
evidence for, confirm, prove.
sub·stan·ti·a'tion *n* **sub'stan·tive**
[-stən-tiv] *adj* having independent
existence; real, fixed. ▶ *n* noun.

sub·sti·tute [SUB-sti-toot] *v*
-tut·ed, -tut·ing. put, serve in
exchange (for). ▶ *n* thing, person
put in place of another; deputy.
sub·sti·tu'tion *n*

sub·sume [səb-SOOM] *vt* **-sumed,
-sum·ing.** incorporate (idea, case,
etc.) under comprehensive
heading, classification.

sub·tend [səb-TEND] *vt* be
opposite to and delimit.

sub·ter·fuge [SUB-tər-fyooj] *n*
trick, lying excuse used to evade
something.

sub·ter·ra·ne·an
[sub-tə-RAY-nee-ən] *adj*
underground; in concealment.

sub·ti·tle [SUB-tīt-l] *n* secondary
title of book; written translation of
film dialogue, superimposed on
film.

sub·tle [SUT-l] *adj* **-tler, -tlest.** not
immediately obvious; ingenious,

acute; crafty; intricate; delicate;
making fine distinctions. **sub'tle·ty**
[-tee] *n, pl* **-ties.**

sub·tract [səb-TRAKT] *vt* take away,
deduct. **sub·trac'tion**
[-TRAK-shən] *n*

sub·trop·i·cal [sub-TROP-i-kəl] *adj*
of regions bordering on the tropics.

sub'urb *n* residential area on
outskirts of city. **sub·ur·ban**
[sə-BUR-bən] *adj* **sub·ur'bi·a**
[-bee-ə] *n* suburbs of a city.

sub·ven·tion [səb-VEN-shən] *n*
subsidy.

sub·vert [səb-VURT] *vt* overthrow;
corrupt. **sub·ver'sion** [-zhən] *n*
sub·ver'sive [-siv] *adj*

sub'way *n* underground passage;
underground railroad.

suc·ceed [sək-SEED] *vi* accomplish
purpose; turn out satisfactorily;
follow. ▶ *vt* follow, take place of.
suc·cess' *n* favorable
accomplishment, attainment, issue
or outcome; successful person or
thing. **suc·cess'ful** [-fəl] *adj*
suc·ces'sion [-SESH-ən] *n*
following; series; succeeding.
suc·ces'sive *adj* following in order;
consecutive. **suc·ces'sor** [-ər] *n*

suc·cinct [sək-SINGKT] *adj* terse,
concise. **succinct'ly** *adv*
suc·cinct'ness [-nis] *n*

suc·cor [SUK-ər] *vt, n* help in
distress.

suc·cu·bus [SUK-yə-bəs] *n, pl* **-bi**
[-bī] female demon fabled to have
sexual intercourse with sleeping
men.

suc·cu·lent [SUK-yə-lənt] *adj* juicy,
full of juice; (of plant) having thick,
fleshy leaves. ▶ *n* such plant.
suc'cu·lence [-lins] *n*

suc·cumb [sə-KUM] *vi* yield, give
way; die.

such *adj* of the kind or degree
mentioned; so great, so much; so
made, etc.; of the same kind.
such'like *adj* such. ▶ *pron* other
such things.

suck [suk] *vt* draw into mouth; hold
(dissolve) in mouth; draw in. ▶ *n*
sucking. **suck'er** *n* person, thing
that sucks; organ, appliance that

adheres by suction; shoot coming from root or base of stem of plant; *inf* person easily deceived or taken in.

suck·le [SUK-əl] *v* **-led, -ling.** feed from the breast. **suck'ling** *n* unweaned infant.

suc·tion [SUK-shən] *n* drawing or sucking of air or fluid; force produced by difference in pressure.

sud·den [SUD-n] *adj* done, occurring unexpectedly; abrupt, hurried. **sud'den·ness** [-dən-is] *n*

su·dor·if·ic [soo-də-RIF-ik] *adj* causing perspiration. ▶ *n* medicine that produces sweat.

suds [sudz] *pl n* froth of soap and water, lather; *sl* beer.

sue [soo] *v* **sued, su·ing.** ▶ *vt* prosecute; seek justice from. ▶ *vi* make application or entreaty; beseech.

suede [swayd] *n* leather with soft, velvety finish.

su·et [SOO-it] *n* hard animal fat from sheep, cow, etc.

suf·fer [SUF-ər] *v* undergo, endure, experience (pain, etc.); allow. **suf'fer·a·ble** *adj* **suf'fer·ance** [-əns] *n* toleration.

suf·fice [sə-FĪS] *v* **-ficed, -fic·ing.** be adequate, satisfactory (for). **suf·fi·cien·cy** [sə-FISH-ən-see] *n* adequate amount. **suf·fi'cient** *adj* enough, adequate.

suf·fix [SUF-iks] *n* letter or word added to end of word. ▶ *vt* add, annex to the end.

suf·fo·cate [SUF-ə-kayt] *v* **-cat·ed, -cat·ing.** kill, be killed by deprivation of oxygen; smother.

suf·frage [SUF-rij] *n* vote or right of voting. **suf'fra·gist** *n* one claiming a right of voting. **suf·fra·gette'** *n, fem*

suf·fuse [sə-FYOOZ] *vt* **-fused, -fus·ing.** well up and spread over. **suf·fu'sion** [-FYOO-zhən] *n*

sug·ar [SHUUG-ər] *n* sweet crystalline vegetable substance. ▶ *vt* sweeten, make pleasant (with sugar). **sug'ar·y** *adj* **sugar cane** plant from whose juice sugar is obtained. **sugar daddy** *inf* wealthy

(elderly) man who pays for (esp. sexual) favors of younger woman.

sug·gest [səg-JEST] *vt* propose; call up the idea of. **sug·gest'i·ble** *adj* easily influenced. **sug·gest'ion** [-chən] *n* hint; proposal; insinuation of impression, belief, etc., into mind. **sug·gest'ive** *adj* containing, open to suggestion, esp. of something indecent.

su·i·cide [SOO-ə-sīd] *n* (act of) one who takes own life. **su·i·cid'al** [-əl] *adj*

suit [soot] *n* set of clothing; garment worn for particular event, purpose; one of four sets in pack of cards; action at law. ▶ *v* make, be fit or appropriate for; be acceptable to (someone). **suit'a·ble** *adj* fitting, proper, convenient; becoming. **suit'a·bly** *adv* **suit'case** [-kays] *n* flat rectangular traveling case.

suite [sweet] *n* matched set esp. furniture; set of rooms.

suit·or [SOOT-ər] *n* wooer; one who sues; petitioner.

sul·fate [SUL-fayt] *n* salt formed by sulfuric acid in combination with any base.

sul·fon·a·mides [sul-FON-ə-mīdz] *n* group of drugs used as internal germicides in treatment of many bacterial diseases.

sul·fur [SUL-fər] *n* pale yellow nonmetallic element. **sul·fur·ic** [sul-FYUUR-ik] *adj*

sulk *vi* be silent, resentful, esp. to draw attention to oneself. ▶ *n* this mood. **sulk'y** *adj* **sulk·i·er, sulk·i·est.**

sul·len [SUL-ən] *adj* unwilling to talk or be sociable, morose; dismal; dull.

sul·ly [SUL-ee] *vt* **-lied, -ly·ing.** stain, tarnish, disgrace.

sul·tan [SUL-tn] *n* ruler of Muslim country. **sul·tan'a** *n* sultan's wife or concubine; kind of raisin.

sul·try [SUL-tree] *adj* **-tri·er, -tri·est.** (of weather) hot, humid; (of person) looking sensual.

sum *n* amount, total; problem in arithmetic. ▶ *v* **summed, sum·ming.** add up; make summary of main parts.

sum·ma·ry [SUM-ə-ree] *n, pl* **-ries.** abridgment or statement of chief points of longer document, speech, etc.; abstract. ▸ *adj* done quickly. **sum·mar·i·ly** [sə-MAIR-ə-lee] *adv* speedily; abruptly. **sum'ma·rize** [-ə-rīz] *vt* **-rized, -riz·ing.** make summary of; present briefly and concisely.

sum·mer [SUM-ər] *n* second, warmest season. ▸ *vi* pass the summer. **sum'mer·y** *adj*

sum'mit *n* top, peak. **summit conference** meeting of heads of governments. **sum'mit·ry** [-mi-tree] *n* practice, art of holding summit conferences.

sum·mon [SUM-ən] *vt* demand attendance of; call on; bid witness appear in court; gather up (energies, etc.). **sum'mons** *n* call; authoritative demand.

sump *n* place or receptacle (esp. as oil reservoir in engine) where fluid collects.

sump·tu·ous [SUMP-choo-əs] *adj* lavish, magnificent; costly. **sump'tu·ous·ness** [-nis] *n* **sump'tu·ar·y** [-er-ee] *adj* pert. to or regulating expenditure.

sun *n* luminous body around which Earth and other planets revolve; its rays. ▸ *v* **sunned, sun·ning.** expose (self) to sun's rays. **sun'ny** *adj* **-ni·er, -ni·est.** like the sun; warm; cheerful. **sun'bath·ing** [-bayth-ing] *n* exposure of whole or part of body to sun's rays. **sun'beam** [-beem] *n* ray of sun. **sun'burn** *n* inflammation of skin due to excessive exposure to sun. **sun'down** *n* sunset. **sun'spot** *n* dark patch appearing temporarily on sun's surface. **sun'stroke** [-strohk] *n* illness caused by prolonged exposure to intensely hot sun. **sun'tan** *n* coloring of skin by exposure to sun.

sun·dae [SUN-day] *n* ice cream topped with fruit, etc.

sun·der [SUN-dər] *vt* separate, sever.

sun·dry [SUN-dree] *adj* several,

various. **sun'dries** *pl n* odd items not mentioned in detail.

sung pp. of SING.

sunk, sunk'en [-in] pp. of SINK.

sup *v* **supped, sup·ping.** take by sips; take supper. ▸ *n* mouthful of liquid.

su·per [SOO-pər] *adj* very good. ▸ *n* short for SUPERINTENDENT.

super- *prefix* above, greater, exceeding(ly), e.g. *superhuman; superman; supertanker.*

su·per·a·ble [SOO-pər-ə-bəl] *adj* capable of being overcome; surmountable.

su·per·an·nu·ate [soo-pər-AN-yoo-ayt] *vt* **-at·ed, -at·ing.** pension off; discharge or dismiss as too old.

su·perb [suu-PURB] *adj* splendid, grand, impressive.

su·per·charge [SOO-pər-chahrj] *vt* **-charged, -charg·ing.** charge, fill to excess. **su'per·charg·er** *n* (internal-combustion engine) device to ensure complete filling of cylinder with explosive mixture when running at high speed.

su·per·cil·i·ous [soo-pər-SIL-ee-əs] *adj* displaying arrogant pride, scorn, indifference. **su·per·cil'i·ous·ness** [-nis] *n*

su·per·fi·cial [soo-pər-FISH-əl] *adj* of or on surface; not careful or thorough; without depth, shallow.

su·per·flu·ous [suu-PUR-floo-əs] *adj* extra, unnecessary; excessive; left over. **su·per·flu'i·ty** [-FLOO-i-tee] *n, pl* **-ties.** superabundance; unnecessary amount.

su·per·high·way [soo-pər-HĪ-way] *n* broad multilane highway for travel at high speeds.

su·per·in·tend [soo-pər-in-TEND] *v* have charge of; overlook; supervise. **su·per·in·tend'ent** *n* esp. person in charge of building maintenance.

su·pe·ri·or [sə-PEER-ee-ər] *adj* greater in quality or quantity; upper, higher in position, rank or quality; showing consciousness of being so. **su·pe·ri·or'i·ty** *n* quality of being higher, greater, or more excellent.

su·per·la·tive [sə-PUR-lə-tiv] *adj* of, in highest degree or quality; surpassing; *Grammar* denoting form of adjective, adverb meaning *most.* ▶ *n Grammar* superlative degree of adjective or adverb.

su·per·mar·ket [SOO-pər-mahr-kit] *n* large self-service store selling chiefly food and household goods.

su·per·mod·el [SOO-pər-mod-l] *n* famous and highly-paid fashion model.

su·per·nal [suu-PUR-nl] *adj* celestial.

su·per·nat·u·ral [soo-pər-NACH-ər-əl] *adj* being beyond the powers or laws of nature; miraculous. ▶ *n* being, place, etc. of miraculous powers.

su·per·nu·mer·ar·y [soo-pər-NOO-mə-rer-ee] *adj* in excess of normal number, extra. ▶ *n, pl* **-ar·ies.** extra person or thing.

su·per·script [SOO-pər-skript] *n, adj* (character) printed, written above the line.

su·per·sede [soo-pər-SEED] *vt* **-sed·ed, -sed·ing.** take the place of; set aside, discard, supplant.

su·per·son·ic [soo-pər-SON-ik] *adj* denoting speed greater than that of sound.

su·per·sti·tion [soo-pər-STISH-ən] *n* religion, opinion or practice based on belief in luck or magic. **su·per·sti·tious** [-STI-shəs] *adj*

su·per·vene [soo-pər-VEEN] *vi* **-vened, -ven·ing.** happen, as an interruption or change. **su·per·ven·tion** [-shən] *n*

su·per·vise [SOO-pər-vīz] *vt* **-vised, -vis·ing.** oversee; direct; inspect and control; superintend. **su·per·vi·sion** [-VIZH-ən] *n* **su′per·vis·or** *n*

su·pine [soo-PĪN] *adj* lying on back with face upward; indolent. ▶ *n* [SOO-pīn] Latin verbal noun.

sup·per [SUP-ər] *n* (light) evening meal.

sup·plant [sə-PLANT] *vt* take the place of, esp. unfairly; oust.

sup·ple [SUP-əl] *adj* **-pler, -plest.**

pliable; flexible; compliant. **sup·ply** [SUP-lee] *adv*

sup·ple·ment [SUP-lə-mənt] *n* thing added to fill up, supply deficiency, esp. extra part added to book, etc.; additional number of periodical, usu. on special subject; separate, often illustrated section published periodically with newspaper. ▶ *vt* add to; supply deficiency. **sup·ple·men·ta·ry** [-tə-ree] *adj* additional.

sup·pli·ant [SUP-lee-ənt] *adj* petitioning. ▶ *n* petitioner.

sup·pli·cate [SUP-li-kayt] *v* **-cat·ed, -cat·ing.** beg humbly, entreat. **sup′pli·cant** [-pli-kənt] *n* **sup·pli·ca′tion** [-KAY-shən] *n* **sup′pli·ca·to·ry** [-kə-tor-ee] *adj*

sup·ply [sə-PLĪ] *vt* **-plied, -ply·ing.** furnish; make available; provide. ▶ *n, pl* **-plies.** supplying, substitute; stock, store.

sup·port [sə-PORT] *vt* hold up; sustain; assist. ▶ *n* supporting, being supported; means of support. **sup·port′a·ble** *adj* **sup·port′er** *n* adherent. **sup·port′ing** *adj* (of motion picture, etc. role) less important. **sup·port′ive** *adj*

sup·pose [sə-POHZ] *vt* **-posed, -pos·ing.** assume as theory; take for granted; accept as likely; (in passive) be expected, obliged; ought. **sup·posed′** *adj* **sup·pos·ed·ly** [sə-POH-zid-lee] *adv* **sup·po·si·tion** [-ZISH-ən] *n* assumption; belief without proof; conjecture. **sup·po·si′tious** *adj* **sup·pos·i·ti·tious** [sə-poz-i-TISH-əs] *adj* sham; spurious; counterfeit. **sup·pos·i·to·ry** [sə-POZ-i-tor-ee] *n, pl* **-ries.** medication (in capsule) for insertion in orifice of body.

sup·press [sə-PRES] *vt* put down; restrain; crush, stifle; keep or withdraw from publication. **sup·pres′sion** [-PRESH-ən] *n*

sup·pu·rate [SUP-yə-rayt] *vi* **-rat·ed, -rat·ing.** fester, form pus. **sup·pu·ra′tion** [-shən] *n*

supra- *prefix* above, over, e.g.

supranational.

su·preme [sə-PREEM] *adj* highest in authority or rank; utmost. **su·prem·a·cy** [-PREM-ə-see] *n* position of being supreme.

sur·cease [sur-SEES] *vi* **-ceased, -ceas·ing.** cease, desist. ▶ *n* cessation.

sur·charge [SUR-chahrj] *n* additional charge. ▶ *vt* [sur-CHAHRJ] **-charged, -charg·ing.** make additional charge.

sure [shuur] *adj* certain; trustworthy; without doubt. ▶ *adv inf* certainly. **sure'ly** *adv* **sur·e·ty** [SHUUR-i-tee] *n, pl* **-ties.** one who takes responsibility for another's obligations; security against damage, etc.; certainty.

surf *n* waves breaking on shore. ▶ *v* swim in, ride surf; move quickly through a medium such as the World Wide Web. **surf'ing** *n* this sport. **surf'er** *n* one who (often) goes surfing. **surf'board** *n* board used in surfing.

sur·face [SUR-fis] *n* outside face of body; exterior; plane; top, visible side; superficial appearance, outward impression. ▶ *adj* involving the surface only; going no deeper than surface. ▶ *v* **-faced, -fac·ing.** (cause to) come to surface; put a surface on.

sur·feit [SUR-fit] *n* excess; disgust caused by excess. ▶ *v* feed to excess; provide anything in excess.

surge [surj] *n* wave; sudden increase; *Electricity* sudden rush of current in circuit. ▶ *vi* **surged, surg·ing.** move in large waves; swell, billow; rise precipitately.

sur·geon [SUR-jən] *n* physician who performs operations. **sur'ger·y** *n* medical treatment by operation. **sur'gi·cal** [-kəl] *adj*

sur·ly [SUR-lee] *adj* **-li·er, -li·est.** gloomily morose; ill-natured; cross and rude. **sur'li·ness** [-nis] *n*

sur·mise [sər-MĪZ] *v, n* **-mised, -mis·ing.** guess, conjecture.

sur·mount [sər-MOWNT] *vt* get over, overcome. **sur·mount'a·ble** *adj*

sur·name [SUR-naym] *n* family name.

sur·pass [sər-PAS] *vt* go beyond; excel; outstrip. **sur·pass'a·ble** *adj* **sur·pass'ing** *adj* excellent; exceeding others.

sur·plice [SUR-plis] *n* loose white vestment worn by clergy and choir members.

sur'plus *n* what remains over in excess.

sur·prise [sər-PRĪZ] *vt* **-prised, -pris·ing.** cause surprise to; astonish; take, come upon unexpectedly; startle (someone) into action thus. ▶ *n* what takes unawares; something unexpected; emotion aroused by being taken unawares.

sur·re·al·ism [sə-REE-ə-liz-əm] *n* movement in art and literature emphasizing expression of the unconscious. **sur·re'al** *adj* **sur·re'al·ist** *n, adj*

sur·ren·der [sə-REN-dər] *vt* hand over, give up. ▶ *vi* yield; cease resistance; capitulate. ▶ *n* act of surrendering.

sur·rep·ti·tious [sur-əp-TISH-əs] *adj* done secretly or stealthily; furtive.

sur·ro·gate [SUR-ə-gayt *or* SUR-ə-git] *n* deputy, esp. of bishop; substitute; judicial officer supervising probate of wills. **surrogate mother** woman who bears child on behalf of childless woman.

sur·round [sə-ROWND] *vt* be, come all around, encompass; encircle; hem in. ▶ *n* border, edging. **sur·round'ings** *pl n* conditions, scenery, etc. around a person, place, environment.

sur·tax [SUR-taks] *n* additional tax.

sur·veil·lance [sər-VAY-ləns] *n* close watch, supervision. **sur·veil'lant** *adj, n*

sur·vey [sər-VAY] *vt* view, scrutinize; inspect, examine; measure, map (land). ▶ *n* [SUR-vay] *pl* **-veys.** a surveying; inspection; report incorporating results of survey. **sur·vey'or** *n*

sur·vive [sər-VĪV] v -**vived, -viv·ing.**
▸ vt outlive; come through alive.
▸ vi continue to live or exist.
sur·viv·al [-əl] n continuation of existence of persons, things, etc.
sur·viv·or [-ər] n one left alive when others have died; one who continues to function despite setbacks.
sus·cep·ti·ble [sə-SEP-tə-bəl] adj yielding readily (to); capable (of); impressionable. **sus·cep·ti·bil'i·ty** n
sus·pect [sə-SPEKT] vt doubt innocence of; have impression of existence or presence of; be inclined to believe that; mistrust.
▸ adj [SUS-pekt] of suspected character. ▸ n [SUS-pekt] suspected person.
sus·pend [sə-SPEND] vt hang up; cause to cease for a time; debar from an office or privilege; keep inoperative; sustain in fluid.
sus·pend'ers pl n straps for supporting trousers, etc.
sus·pense [sə-SPENS] n state of uncertainty, esp. while awaiting news, an event, etc.; anxiety, worry. **sus·pen'sion** [-shən] n state of being suspended; springs on axle of body of vehicle.
sus·pen'so·ry [-sə-ree] adj
sus·pi·cion [sə-SPISH-ən] n suspecting, being suspected; slight trace. **sus·pi'cious** adj
sus·tain [sə-STAYN] vt keep, hold up; endure; keep alive; confirm.
sus·tain'a·ble adj **sus'te·nance** [-nəns] n food.
su·ture [SOO-chər] n act of sewing; sewing up of a wound; material used for this; a joining of the bones of the skull. ▸ vt -**tured, -tur·ing.** join by suture.
SUV sport utility vehicle.
su·ze·rain [SOO-zə-rin] n sovereign with rights over autonomous state; feudal lord. **su'ze·rain·ty** [-tee] n
svelte [svelt] adj **svelt·er, svelt·est.** lightly built, slender; sophisticated.
swab [swob] n mop; pad of surgical cotton, etc. for cleaning, taking specimen, etc.; sl sailor, low or unmannerly fellow. ▸ vt **swabbed,**

swab'bing. clean with swab.
swad·dle [SWOD-l] vt -**dled, -dling.** swathe. **swaddling clothes** Hist long strips of cloth for wrapping infant.
swag n sl stolen property.
swag·ger [SWAG-ər] vi strut; boast.
▸ n strutting gait; boastful, overconfident manner.
swain [swayn] n rustic lover.
swal·low¹ [SWOL-oh] vt cause, allow to pass down gullet; engulf; suppress, keep back; believe gullibly. ▸ n act of swallowing.
swallow² n migratory bird with forked tail and skimming manner of flight.
swam pt. of SWIM.
swamp [swomp] n bog. ▸ vt entangle in swamp; overwhelm; flood. **swamp'y** adj **swamp·i·er, swamp·i·est.**
swan [swon] n large, web-footed water bird with graceful curved neck. **swan song** fabled song of a swan before death; last act, etc. before death.
swank [swangk] vi swagger; show off. ▸ n smartness; style. **swank'y** adj **swank·i·er, swank·i·est.** smart; showy.
swap [swop] n, v **swapped, swap·ping.** exchange; barter.
swarm [sworm] n large cluster of insects; vast crowd. ▸ vi (of bees) be on the move in swarm; gather in large numbers.
swarth·y [SWOR-thee] adj **swarth·i·er, swarth·i·est.** of dark complexion.
swash·buck·ler [SWOSH-buk-lər] n swaggering daredevil person.
swash'buck·ling adj
swas·ti·ka [SWOS-ti-kə] n form of cross with arms bent at right angles, used as emblem by Nazis.
swat [swot] vt **swat·ted, swat·ting.** hit smartly; kill, esp. insects.
swath [swoth] n line of grass or grain cut and thrown together by scythe or mower; whole sweep of scythe or mower.
swathe [swoth] vt **swathed, swath·ing.** cover with wraps or

bandages.

sway v swing unsteadily; (cause to) vacillate in opinion, etc.; influence opinion, etc. ▶ n control; power; swaying motion.

swear [swair] v **swore, sworn, swear·ing.** ▶ vt promise on oath; cause to take an oath. ▶ vi declare; use profanity.

sweat [swet] n moisture oozing from, forming on skin, esp. in humans. ▶ v **sweat** or **sweat·ed, sweat·ing.** (cause to) exude sweat; toil; employ at wrongfully low wages; worry; wait anxiously. **sweat'y** adj **sweat·i·er, sweat·i·est. sweat'shirt** [-shurt] n long-sleeved cotton pullover.

sweat·er [SWET-ər] n knitted pullover or cardigan with or without sleeves.

sweep v **swept, sweep·ing.** ▶ vi effect cleaning with broom; pass quickly or magnificently; extend in continuous curve. ▶ vt clean with broom; carry impetuously. ▶ n act of cleaning with broom; sweeping motion; wide curve; range; long oar; one who cleans chimneys. **sweeping** adj wide-ranging; without limitations, reservations. **sweep'stakes** n gamble in which winner takes stakes contributed by all; type of lottery; risky venture promising great return.

sweet adj **-er, -est.** tasting like sugar; agreeable; kind, charming; fresh, fragrant; in good condition; tuneful; gentle, dear, beloved. ▶ n small piece of sweet food; something pleasant. ▶ pl cake, etc. containing much sugar. **sweet'en** [-in] v **sweet'en·er** [-ən-ər] n **sweet'bread** [-bred] n animal's pancreas used as food. **sweet'heart** n lover. **sweetheart contract** collusive contract between labor union and company benefiting latter. **sweet'meat** n sweetened delicacy e.g. small cake, candy. **sweet potato** trailing plant; its edible, sweetish, starchy tubers. **sweet talk** inf flattery. **sweet-talk** v inf coax, flatter.

swell v **swelled, swol·len** [SWOHL-ən] or **swelled, swel·ling.** expand. ▶ vi be greatly filled with pride, emotion. ▶ n act of swelling or being swollen; wave of sea; mechanism in organ to vary volume of sound; inf person of high social standing. ▶ adj inf stylish, socially prominent; fine.

swel·ter [SWEL-tər] vi be oppressed with heat.

swept pt./pp. of SWEEP.

swerve [swurv] vi **swerved, swerv·ing.** swing around, change direction during motion; turn aside (from duty, etc.). ▶ n swerving.

swift adj **-er, -est.** rapid, quick, ready. ▶ n bird like a swallow.

swig n inf large swallow of drink. ▶ v inf **swigged, swig·ging.** drink thus.

swill v drink greedily; feed (pigs) with swill. ▶ n liquid or wet pig food; greedy drinking; kitchen refuse; drivel.

swim v **swam, swum, swim·ming.** ▶ vi support and move oneself in water; float; be flooded; have feeling of dizziness. ▶ vt cross by swimming; compete in by swimming. ▶ n spell of swimming. **swim'ming·ly** adv successfully, effortlessly.

swin·dle [SWIN-dl] n, v **-dled, -dling.** cheat. **swind'ler** [-lər] n **swind'ling** n

swine [swin] n, pl swine. pig; contemptible person. **swin'ish** adj

swing v **swung, swing·ing.** (cause to) move to and fro; (cause to) pivot, turn; hang; arrange, play music with (jazz) rhythm. ▶ vi be hanged; hit out (at). ▶ n act, instance of swinging; seat hung to swing on; fluctuation (esp. e.g. in voting pattern). **swing'er** n sl person regarded as modern and lively or sexually promiscuous.

swipe [swīp] v **swiped, swip·ing.** strike with wide, sweeping or glancing blow; inf steal; pass (a plastic card, such as a credit card) through a machine which electronically reads information on the card.

swirl [swurl] v (cause to) move with eddying motion. ▶ n such motion.

swish v (cause to) move with audible hissing sound. ▶ n the sound; sl effeminate homosexual male. ▶ adj sl effeminate.

switch [swich] n mechanism to complete or interrupt electric circuit, etc.; abrupt change; flexible stick or twig; tufted end of animal's tail; type of women's hairpiece. ▶ vi shift, change; swing. ▶ vt affect (current, etc.) with switch; change abruptly; strike with switch. **switch'back** n road, railway with steep rises and descents. **switch'board** [-bord] n installation for establishing or varying connections in telephone and electric circuits.

swiv·el [SWIV-əl] n mechanism of two parts that can revolve the one on the other. ▶ v -eled, -el·ing. turn (on swivel).

swollen [SWOH-lən] pp. of SWELL.

swoon vi, n faint.

swoop vi dive, as hawk. ▶ n act of swooping; sudden attack.

sword [sord] n weapon with long blade for cutting or thrusting.

swore v pt. of SWEAR.

sworn v pp. of SWEAR. ▶ adj bound by or as if by an oath, e.g. sworn enemies.

swum pp. of SWIM.

swung pt./pp. of SWING.

syb·a·rite [SIB-ə-rīt] n lover of luxury. **syb·a·rit'ic** [-RIT-ik] adj

syc·o·phant [SIK-ə-fənt] n one using flattery to gain favors. **syc·o·phan'tic** [-FAN-tik] adj **syc'o·phan·cy** [-fən-see] n

syl·la·ble [SIL-ə-bəl] n division of word as unit for pronunciation. **syl·lab'ic** adj **syl·lab'i·fy** vt -fied, -fy·ing.

syl·la·bus [SIL-ə-bəs] n, pl -bus·es, -bi [-bī] outline of a course of study; list of subjects studied in course.

syl·lo·gism [SIL-ə-jiz-əm] n form of logical reasoning consisting of two premises and conclusion. **syl·lo·gis'tic** adj

sylph [silf] n slender, graceful woman; sprite.

syl·van [SIL-vən] adj of forests, trees.

sym- see SYN-.

sym·bi·o·sis [sim-bee-OH-sis] n, pl -ses [-seez] living together of two organisms of different kinds, esp. to their mutual benefit; similar relationship involving people, etc. **sym·bi·ot'ic** [-OT-ik] adj

sym·bol [SIM-bəl] n sign; thing representing or typifying something. **sym·bol'ic** adj **sym·bol'i·cal·ly** adv **sym'bol·ism** n use of, representation by symbols; movement in art holding that work of art should express idea in symbolic form. **sym'bol·ist** n, adj **sym'bol·ize** vt -ized, -iz·ing.

sym·me·try [SIM-ə-tree] n, pl -tries. proportion between parts; balance of arrangement between two sides; order. **sym·met'ri·cal** adj having due proportion in its parts; harmonious; regular.

sym·pa·thy [SIM-pə-thee] n, pl -thies. feeling for another in pain, etc.; compassion, pity; sharing of emotion, interest, desire, etc.; fellow feeling. **sym·pa·thet'ic** adj **sym'pa·thize** [-thīz] vi -thized, -thiz·ing.

sym·pho·ny [SIM-fə-nee] n, pl -nies. composition for full orchestra; harmony of sounds. **sym·phon'ic** [-FON-ik] adj **sym·pho'ni·ous** [-FOH-nee-əs] adj harmonious.

sym·po·si·um [sim-POH-zee-əm] n, pl -si·a [-zee-ə] conference, meeting; discussion, writings on a given topic.

symp·tom [SIMP-təm] n change in body indicating its state of health or disease; sign, token. **symp·to·mat'ic** adj

syn- prefix with, together, alike, e.g. synchronize; syncopate.

syn·a·gogue [SIN-ə-gog] n (place of worship of) Jewish congregation.

syn·chro·nize [SING-krə-nīz] v -nized, -niz·ing. ▶ vt make agree in time. ▶ vi happen at same time. **syn·chro·ni·za'tion** n

syn'chro·nous [-nis] *adj*
simultaneous.
syn·co·pate [SING-kə-payt] *vt*
-pat·ed, -pat·ing. accentuate weak
beat in bar of music.
syn·co·pa'tion *n*
syn·di·cate [SIN-di-kit] *n* body of
people, delegates associated for
some enterprise. ▶ *v* [-kayt] **-cat·ed,
-cat·ing.** form syndicate. ▶ *vt*
publish in many newspapers at the
same time.
syn·drome [SIN-drohm] *n*
combination of several symptoms
in disease; symptom, set of
symptoms or characteristics.
syn·ec·do·che [si-NEK-də-kee] *n*
figure of speech by which whole of
thing is put for part or part for
whole, such as *sail* for *ship*.
syn·er·gy [SIN-ər-jee] *n* potential
ability for people or groups to be
more successful working together
than on their own.
syn·od [SIN-əd] *n* church council;
convention.
syn·o·nym [SIN-ə-nim] *n* word with
(nearly) same meaning as another.
syn·on·y·mous [si-NON-ə-məs] *adj*
syn·op·sis [si-NOP-sis] *n, pl* **-ses**
[-seez] summary, outline.
syn·op'tic *adj* of, like synopsis;
having same viewpoint.
syn·tax [SIN-taks] *n* part of
grammar treating of arrangement
of words in sentence. **syn·tac'tic**

adj
syn·the·sis [SIN-thə-sis] *n, pl* **-ses**
[-seez] putting together,
combination. **syn'the·size** *v*
-sized, -siz·ing. make artificially.
syn'the·siz·er [-sīz-ər] *n* electronic
keyboard instrument capable of
reproducing a wide range of
musical sounds. **syn·thet'ic** *adj*
artificial; of synthesis.
syph·i·lis [SIF-ə-lis] *n* contagious
venereal disease. **syph·i·lit'ic** *adj*
sy·ringe [sə-RINJ] *n* instrument for
drawing in liquid by piston and
forcing it out in fine stream or
spray; squirt. ▶ *vt* **-ringed,
-ring·ing.** spray, cleanse with
syringe.
syr·up [SIR-əp] *n* thick solution
obtained in process of refining
sugar, molasses, etc.; any liquid like
this, esp. in consistency. **syr'up·y**
adj
sys·tem [SIS-təm] *n* complex
whole, organization; method;
classification. **sys·tem·at'ic** *adj*
methodical. **sys'tem·a·tize** [-tīz] *vt*
-tized, -tiz·ing. reduce to system;
arrange methodically. **sys·tem'ic**
adj affecting entire body or
organism.
sys·to·le [SIS-tə-lee] *n* contraction
of heart and arteries for expelling
blood and carrying on circulation.
sys·tol·ic [sis-TOL-ik] *adj*
contracting; of systole.

T t

T *Chem* tritium. **to a T** precisely, to a nicety.

Ta *Chem* tantalum.

tab *n* tag, label, short strap. **keep tabs on** *inf* keep watchful eye on.

tab·er·na·cle [TAB-ər-nak-əl] *n* portable shrine of Israelites; receptacle containing reserved Eucharist; place of worship.

ta·ble [TAY-bəl] *n* piece of furniture consisting of flat board supported by legs; food; set of facts, figures arranged in lines or columns. ▸ *vt* **-bled, -bling.** lay on table; lay aside (motion, etc.) for possible but unlikely consideration in future. **ta′ble·land** *n* plateau, high flat area. **ta′ble·spoon** *n* spoon used for serving food, etc. **under the table** secretly; as bribe; drunk.

tab·leau [ta-BLOH] *n, pl* **-leaux** or **-leaus** [-BLOHZ] group of persons, silent and motionless, arranged to represent some scene; dramatic scene.

ta·ble d'hôte [TAH-bəl DOHT] *n, pl* **ta·bles d'hôte** [TAH-bəl DOHT] *Fr* meal, with limited choice of dishes, at a fixed price.

tab·let [TAB-lit] *n* pill of compressed powdered medicinal substance; writing pad; slab of stone, wood, etc., esp. used formerly for writing on.

tab′loid *n* (illustrated) popular small-sized newspaper usu. with terse, sensational headlines.

ta·boo [tə-BOO] *adj* forbidden or disapproved of. ▸ *n, pl* **-boos.** prohibition resulting from social conventions, etc.; thing prohibited. ▸ *vt* **-booed, -boo·ing.** place under taboo.

tab·u·lar [TAB-yə-lər] *adj* shaped, arranged like a table. **tab·u·late** [-layt] *vt* **-lat·ed, -lat·ing.** arrange (figures, facts, etc.) in tables.

tacho- *comb. form* speed, e.g. *tachometer.*

ta·chom·e·ter [ta-KOM-i-tər] *n*
device for measuring speed, esp. of revolving shaft (e.g. in automobile) and hence revolutions per minute.

tac·it [TAS-it] *adj* implied but not spoken; silent. **tac′it·ly** *adv* **tac′i·turn** *adj* talking little; habitually silent.

tack¹ [tak] *n* small nail; long loose stitch; *Nautical* course of ship obliquely to windward; course, direction. ▸ *vt* nail with tacks; stitch lightly; append, attach; sail to windward.

tack² *n* riding harness for horses.

tack·le [TAK-əl] *n* equipment, apparatus, esp. for fishing; lifting appliances with ropes; *Football* lineman between guard and end. ▸ *vt* **-led, -ling.** take in hand; grip, grapple with; undertake to cope with, master, etc.; *Football* seize, bring down (ball-carrier).

tack·y [TAK-ee] *adj* **tack·i·er, tack·i·est.** sticky; not quite dry; dowdy, shabby. **tack′i·ness** [-nis] *n*

ta·co [TAK-oh] *n* **-cos.** usu. fried tortilla folded or wrapped round filling.

tact [takt] *n* skill in dealing with people or situations; delicate perception of the feelings of others. **tact′ful** [-fəl] *adj* **tact′less** [-lis] *adj*

tac·tics [TAK-tiks] *n* art of handling troops, ships in battle; adroit management of a situation; plans for this. **tac·ti·cal** [TAK-ti-kəl] *adj* **tac·ti′cian** [-TISH-ən] *n*

tac·tile [TAK-til] *adj* of, relating to the sense of touch.

tad′pole [TAD-pohl] *n* immature frog, in its first state before gills and tail are absorbed.

taf·fe·ta [TAF-i-tə] *n* smooth, stiff fabric of silk, nylon, etc.

taf·fy [TAF-ee] *n, pl* **-fies.** candy of molasses and sugar.

tag¹ *n* label identifying or showing price of (something); ragged, hanging end; pointed end of shoelace, etc.; trite saying or

quotation; any appendage. ▶ *vt*
tagged, tag·ging. append, add
(on); trail (along) behind.

tag² *n* children's game where one
being chased becomes the chaser
upon being touched. ▶ *vt* **tagged,
tag·ging.** touch. **tag wrestling**
wrestling match for teams of two,
where one partner may replace the
other upon being touched on hand.

tail [tayl] *n* flexible prolongation of
animal's spine; lower or inferior
part of anything; appendage; rear
part of aircraft; *inf* person
employed to follow another. ▶ *pl*
reverse side of coin; tail coat. ▶ *vt*
remove tail of; *inf* follow closely,
trail. **tail'ings** *pl n* waste left over
from some (e.g. industrial) process.
tail'less [-lis] *adj* **tail'board** [-bord]
n removable or hinged rear board
on truck, etc. **tail end** last part.
tail'light *n* light carried at rear of
vehicle. **tail'spin** *n* spinning dive of
aircraft; sudden (e.g. emotional,
financial) collapse. **tail'wind** *n*
wind coming from behind. **tail off**
diminish gradually, dwindle. **turn
tail** run away.

tai·lor [TAY-lər] *n* maker of outer
clothing, esp. for men.
tailor-made *adj* made by tailor;
well-fitting; appropriate.

taint [taynt] *v* affect or be affected
by pollution, corruption, etc. ▶ *n*
defect, flaw; infection,
contamination.

take [tayk] *v* **took** [tuuk], **tak·en,
tak·ing.** ▶ *vt* grasp, get hold of; get;
receive, assume; adopt; accept;
understand; consider; carry,
conduct; use; capture; consume;
subtract; require. ▶ *vi* be effective;
please; go. ▶ *n Motion Pictures*
(recording of) scene, sequence
photographed without
interruption; *inf* earnings, receipts.
tak'ing *adj* charming. **take'off** *n*
instant at which aircraft becomes
airborne; commencement of flight.
take after resemble in face or
character. **take down** write down;
dismantle; humiliate. **take in**
understand; make (garment, etc.)

smaller; deceive. **take in vain**
blaspheme; be facetious. **take off**
(of aircraft) leave ground; *inf* go
away; *inf* mimic. **take to** become
fond of.

tal·cum pow·der [TAL-kəm]
powder, usu. scented, to absorb
body moisture, deodorize, etc.

tale [tayl] *n* story, narrative, report;
fictitious story.

tal·ent [TAL-ənt] *n* natural ability or
power; ancient weight or money.
tal'ent·ed [-id] *adj* gifted.

tal·is·man [TAL-is-mən] *n, pl* **-mans.**
object supposed to have magic
power; amulet. **tal·is·man'ic**
[-MAN-ik] *adj*

talk [tawk] *vi* express, exchange
ideas, etc. in words. ▶ *vt* express in
speech, utter; discuss. ▶ *n* speech,
lecture; conversation; rumor.
talk'a·tive *adj* fond of talking.
talking-to *n, pl* **-tos.** reproof. **talk
show** TV or radio program in
which guests are interviewed
informally.

tall [tawl] *adj* high; of great stature.
tall story unlikely and probably
untrue tale.

tal·low [TAL-oh] *n* melted and
clarified animal fat. ▶ *vt* smear with
this.

tal·ly [TAL-ee] *vi* **-lied, -ly·ing.**
correspond one with the other;
keep record. ▶ *n, pl* **-lies.** record,
account, total number.

Tal·mud [TAHL-muud] *n* body of
Jewish law. **Tal·mud'ic** [-MUUD-ik]
adj

tal·on [TAL-ən] *n* claw.

tam·bou·rine [tam-bə-REEN] *n* flat
half-drum with jingling disks of
metal attached.

tame [taym] *adj* **tam·er, tam·est.**
not wild, domesticated; subdued;
uninteresting. ▶ *vt* make tame.
tame'ly *adv* in a tame manner;
without resisting.

tamp *vt* pack, force down by
repeated blows.

tam·per [TAM-pər] *vi* interfere
(with) improperly; meddle.

tam'pon *n* plug of lint, cotton, etc.
inserted in wound, body cavity, to

stop flow of blood, absorb secretions, etc.

tan n, adj **tan·ner, tan·nest.** (of) brown color of skin after long exposure to rays of sun, etc. ▸ v **tanned, tan·ning.** (cause to) go brown; (of animal hide) convert to leather by chemical treatment. **tan'ner** n **tan'ner·y** n place where hides are tanned. **tan'nic** adj **tan'nin** n vegetable substance used as tanning agent. **tan'bark** n bark of certain trees, yielding tannin.

tang n strong pungent taste or smell; trace, hint; spike, barb. **tang'y** adj **tang·i·er, tang·i·est.**

tan·gent [TAN-jənt] n line that touches a curve without cutting; divergent course. ▸ adj touching, meeting without cutting. **tan·gen'tial** [-JEN-shəl] adj **tan·gen'tial·ly** adv

tan·ge·rine [tan-jə-REEN] n citrus tree; its fruit, a variety of orange.

tan·gi·ble [TAN-jə-bəl] adj that can be touched; definite; palpable; concrete.

tan·gle [TANG-gəl] n confused mass or situation. ▸ vt **-gled, -gling.** twist together in muddle; contend (with).

tan·go [TANG-goh] n, pl **-gos.** dance of S Amer. origin.

tank n storage vessel for liquids or gas; armored motor vehicle moving on tracks; cistern; reservoir. **tank'er** n ship, truck, etc. for carrying liquid in bulk.

tan·kard [TANG-kərd] n large drinking cup of metal or glass; its contents, esp. beer.

tannin see TAN.

tan·ta·lize [TAN-tə-līz] vt **-lized, -liz·ing.** torment by appearing to offer something desired; tease.

tan·ta·mount [TAN-tə-mownt] adj equivalent in value or signification; equal, amounting (to).

tan·trum [TAN-trəm] n childish outburst of temper.

tap¹ v **tapped, tap·ping.** strike lightly but with some noise. ▸ n slight blow, rap.

tap² n valve with handle to regulate or stop flow of fluid in pipe, etc.; stopper, plug permitting liquid to be drawn from cask, etc.; steel tool for forming internal screw threads. ▸ vt **tapped, tap·ping.** put tap in; draw off with or as with tap; make secret connection to telephone wire to overhear conversation on it; make connection for supply of electricity at intermediate point in supply line; form internal threads in.

tape [tayp] n narrow long strip of fabric, paper, etc.; magnetic recording of music, data, etc. ▸ vt **taped, tap·ing.** record (speech, music, etc.). **tape deck** device for playing magnetic tape recordings. **tape measure** tape of fabric, metal marked off in centimeters, inches, etc. **tape recorder** apparatus for recording sound on magnetized tape and playing it back.

tape'worm [-wurm] n long flat worm parasitic in animals and people.

ta·per [TAY-pər] vi become gradually thinner toward one end. ▸ n thin candle; long wick covered with wax; a narrowing.

tap·es·try [TAP-ə-stree] n, pl **-tries.** fabric decorated with designs in colors woven by needles. **tap'es·tried** adj

tap·i·o·ca [tap-ee-OH-kə] n beadlike starch made from cassava root, used esp. in puddings, as thickener, etc.

ta·pir [TAY-pər] n Amer. animal with elongated snout, allied to pig.

tap'root n large single root growing straight down.

tar¹ [tahr] n thick black liquid distilled from coal, etc. ▸ vt **tarred, tar·ring.** coat, treat (as though) with tar. **tarred with same brush** (made to appear) guilty of same misdeeds.

tar² n inf sailor.

tar·an·tel·la [ta-rən-TEL-ə] n lively Italian dance; music for it.

ta·ran·tu·la [tə-RAN-chuu-lə] n, pl **-las.** any of various large (poisonous) hairy spiders.

tar·dy [TAHR-dee] adj **-di·er,**

-di·est. slow, late. **tar'di·ly** *adv*

tare [tair] *n* weight of wrapping, container for goods; unladen weight of vehicle.

tar·get [TAHR-git] *n* mark to aim at in shooting; thing aimed at; object of criticism; butt.

tar·iff [TA-rif] *n* tax levied on imports, etc.; list of charges; bill.

tarn [tahrn] *n* small mountain lake.

tar·nish [TAHR-nish] *v* (cause to) become stained, lose shine or become dimmed or sullied. ▶ *n* discoloration, blemish.

ta·ro [TAHR-oh] *n, pl* **-ros.** plant of Pacific islands now cultivated widely; its edible tuber.

ta·rot [TA-roh] *n* one of special pack of cards now used mainly in fortunetelling.

tar·pau·lin [tahr-PAW-lin] *n* (sheet of) heavy hard-wearing waterproof fabric.

tar·ry *vi* **-ried, -ry·ing.** linger, delay; stay behind.

tart[1] [tahrt] *n* small pie filled with fruit, jam, etc.; *sl* promiscuous woman; prostitute.

tart[2] *adj* **-er, -est.** sour; sharp; bitter.

tar·tan [TAHR-tn] *n* woolen cloth woven in pattern of colored checks, esp. in colors, patterns associated with Scottish clans; such pattern.

tar·tar[1] [TAHR-tər] *n* crust deposited on teeth; deposit formed during fermentation of wine.

tartar[2] *n* ill-tempered person, difficult to deal with; (**T-**) member of group of peoples including Mongols and Turks.

task *n* piece of work (esp. unpleasant or difficult) set or undertaken. ▶ *vt* assign task to; exact. **task force** naval or military unit dispatched to carry out specific undertaking; any similar group in government, industry. **task'mas·ter** *n* (stern) overseer. **take to task** reprove.

tas·sel [TAS-əl] *n* ornament of fringed knot of threads, etc.; tuft. **tas'seled** *adj*

taste [tayst] *n* sense by which flavor, quality of substance is detected by the tongue; this act or sensation; (brief) experience of something; small amount; preference, liking; power of discerning, judging; discretion, delicacy. ▶ *v* **tast·ed, tast·ing.** observe or distinguish the taste of a substance; take small amount into mouth; experience. ▶ *vi* have specific flavor. **taste'ful** [-fəl] *adj* in good style; with, showing good taste. **taste'less** [-lis] *adj* **tast'y** *adj* **tast·i·er, tast·i·est.** pleasantly or highly flavored. **taste bud** small organ of taste on tongue.

tat *v* **tat·ted, tat·ting.** make by tatting. **tatting** *n* type of handmade lace.

tat·ter [TAT-ər] *v* make or become ragged, worn to shreds. ▶ *n* ragged piece.

tat·tle *vi, n, v* **-tled, -tling.** gossip, chatter.

tat·too[1] [ta-TOO] *n, pl* **-toos.** beat of drum and bugle call; military spectacle or pageant.

tattoo[2] *vt* **-tooed, -too·ing.** mark skin in patterns, etc. by pricking and filling punctures with indelible colored inks. ▶ *n, pl* **-toos.** mark so made.

tat·ty [TAT-ee] *adj* **-ti·er, -ti·est.** shabby, worn out.

taught [tawt] *pt./pp.* of TEACH.

taunt [tawnt] *vt* provoke, deride with insulting words, etc. ▶ *n* instance of this; words used for this.

taut [tawt] *adj* **-er, -est.** drawn tight; under strain.

tau·tol·o·gy [taw-TOL-ə-gee] *n, pl* **-gies.** needless repetition of same thing in other words in same sentence. **tau·to·log'i·cal** [-tə-LOJ-ə-kəl] *adj*

tav·ern [TAV-ərn] *n* bar; inn.

taw·dry [TAW-dree] *adj* **-dri·er, -dri·est.** showy, but cheap and without taste, flashy. **taw'dri·ness** [-nis] *n*

taw·ny [TAW-nee] *adj, n* **-ni·er, -ni·est.** (of) light (yellowish) brown.

tax [taks] *n* compulsory payments by wage earners, companies, etc.

imposed by government to raise revenue; heavy demand on something. ▸ *vt* impose tax on; strain; accuse, blame. **tax'a·ble** *adj* **tax·a'tion** *n* levying of taxes. **tax'pay·er** *n* **tax return** statement supplied to authorities of personal income and tax due.

tax·i [TAK-see] *n, pl* **tax·is.** (also **tax'i·cab**) motor vehicle for hire with driver. ▸ *vi* **tax·ied, tax·i·ing** *or* **tax·y·ing.** (of aircraft) run along ground under its own power; ride in taxi.

tax·i·der·my [TAK-si-dur-mee] *n* art of stuffing, mounting animal skins to give them lifelike appearance. **tax'i·der·mist** *n*

tax·on·o·my [tak-SON-ə-mee] *n* science, practice of classification, esp. of biological organisms.

Tb *Chem* terbium.

T-bone steak loin steak with T-shaped bone.

Tc *Chem* technetium.

te see ⊤ɪ.

Te *Chem* tellurium.

tea [tee] *n* dried leaves of plant cultivated esp. in (sub)tropical Asia; infusion of it as beverage; various herbal beverages; tea, cakes, etc. as light afternoon meal; *sl* marijuana. **tea bag** small porous bag of paper containing tea leaves. **tea'spoon** *n* small spoon for stirring tea, etc.

teach [teech] *v* **taught** [tawt], **teach·ing.** instruct; educate; train; impart knowledge of; act as teacher. **teach'er** *n*

teak [teek] *n* East Indian tree; very hard wood obtained from it.

teal [teel] *n* type of small duck; greenish-blue color.

team [teem] *n* set of animals, players of game, etc. associated in activity. ▸ *vi* (usu. with *up*) (cause to) make a team. **team'ster** *n* driver of truck or team of draft animals. **team spirit** subordination of individual desire for good of team. **team'work** *n* cooperative work by team acting as unit.

tear¹ [teer] *n* drop of fluid appearing in and falling from eye.

tear'ful [-fəl] *adj* inclined to weep; involving tears. **tear gas** irritant gas causing abnormal watering of eyes, and temporary blindness. **tear·jerk·er** [TEER-jur-kər] *n inf* excessively sentimental story, moving picture, etc.

tear² [tair] *v* **tore, torn, tear·ing.** pull apart, rend; become torn; rush. ▸ *n* hole, cut or split.

tease [teez] *vt* **teased, teas·ing.** tantalize, torment, irritate, bait; pull apart fibers of. ▸ *n* one who teases.

teat [teet] *n* nipple of female breast; rubber nipple of baby's feeding bottle.

tech·ni·cal [TEK-ni-kəl] *adj* of, specializing in industrial, practical or mechanical arts and applied sciences; skilled in practical and mechanical arts; belonging to particular art or science; according to letter of the law. **tech·ni·cal'i·ty** *n* point of procedure; state of being technical. **tech·ni'cian** [-NISH-ən] *n* one skilled in technique of an art. **tech·nique** [tek-NEEK] *n* method of performance in an art; skill required for mastery of subject. **technical college** higher educational institution specializing in mechanical and industrial arts and applied science, etc. **technical knockout** *Boxing* termination of bout by referee who judges that one boxer is not fit to continue.

tech·noc·ra·cy [tek-NOK-rə-see] *n* government by technical experts; example of this. **tech'no·crat** [-nə-krat] *n*

tech·nol·o·gy [tek-NOL-ə-gee] *n, pl* **-gies.** application of practical, mechanical sciences to industry, commerce; technical methods, skills, knowledge. **tech·no·log'i·cal** *adj*

tec·ton·ic [tek-TON-ik] *adj* of construction or building; *Geology* pert. to (forces or condition of) structure of Earth's crust. **tec·ton'ics** *n* art, science of building.

te·di·ous [TEE-dee-əs] *adj* causing

fatigue or boredom, monotonous. **te·di·um** [-əm] n monotony.

tee n Golf slightly raised ground from which first stroke of hole is made; small peg supporting ball for this stroke. **tee off** make first stroke of hole in golf; sl scold; sl irritate.

teem vi abound with; swarm; be prolific; pour, rain heavily.

teens [teenz] pl n years of life from 13 to 19. **teen'age** adj **teen'ag·er** n person in teens.

teepee n see TEPEE.

tee·ter [TEE-tər] vi seesaw or make similar movements; vacillate.

teeth pl. of TOOTH.

teethe [teeth] vi **teethed**, **teeth·ing.** (of baby) grow first teeth. **teething ring** ring on which baby can bite.

tee·to·tal [tee-TOHT-l] adj pledged to abstain from alcohol. **tee·to'tal·er** n

tele- comb. form at a distance, and from far off, e.g. telecommunications; by telephone, e.g. telebanking; of or involving television, e.g. telecast.

tel·e·cast [TEL-i-kast] v, n -cast or -cast·ed, -cast·ing. (broadcast) TV program.

tel·e·com·mu·ni·ca·tions [tel-i-kə-myoo-ni-KAY-shənz] n science and technology of communications by telephony, radio, TV, etc.

tel·e·gram [TEL-i-gram] n message sent by telegraph.

tel·e·graph [TEL-i-graf] n electrical apparatus for transmitting messages to a distance; any signaling device for transmitting messages. ▶ v communicate by telegraph. **tel·e·graph'ic** adj **te·leg'ra·pher** n one who works telegraph. **te·leg'ra·phy** n science of telegraph; use of telegraph.

tel·e·mar·ket·ing [tel-ə-MAHR-ki-ting] n selling or advertising by telephone, television.

tel·e·ol·o·gy [tel-ee-OL-ə-jee] n doctrine of final causes; belief that things happen because of the purpose or design that will be fulfilled by them.

te·lep·a·thy [tə-LEP-ə-thee] n action of one mind on another at a distance. **tel·e·path'ic** [-ə-PATH-ik] adj

tel·e·phone [tel-ə-FOHN] n apparatus for communicating sound to hearer at a distance. ▶ v -phoned, -phon·ing. communicate, speak by telephone. **tel·e·phon'ic** [-FON-ik] adj **te·leph·o·ny** [tə-LEF-ə-nee] n

tel·e·pho·to [TEL-ə-foh-toh] adj (of lens) producing magnified image of distant object.

Tel·e·Promp·Ter [TEL-ə-promp-tər] n ® off-camera device to enable TV performer to refer to magnified script out of sight of the cameras.

tel·e·scope [TEL-ə-skohp] n optical instrument for magnifying images of distant objects. ▶ v -scoped, -scop·ing. slide or drive together, esp. parts designed to fit one inside the other; make smaller, shorter. **tel·e·scop'ic** [-SKOP-ik] adj

tel·e·text [TEL-i-tekst] n electronic system that shows information, news, graphics on subscribers' TV screens.

tel·e·vi·sion [TEL-ə-vizh-ən] n system of producing on screen images of distant objects, events, etc. by electromagnetic radiation; device for receiving this transmission and converting it to optical images; programs, etc. viewed on TV set. **tel'e·vise** [-vīz] vt -vised, -vis·ing. transmit by TV; make, produce as TV program.

tel·e·work·ing [TEL-i-wurk-ing] n use of home computers, telephones, etc., to enable a person to work from home while maintaining contact with colleagues or customers. **tel'e·work·er** n

tell v told, tell·ing. ▶ vt let know; order, direct; narrate, make known; discern; distinguish; count. ▶ vi give account; be of weight, importance; reveal secrets. **tel'ler** n narrator; bank cashier. **telling** adj effective, striking. **tell'tale** n sneak; automatic indicator. ▸ adj revealing.

tel·lu'ri·um [te-LUUR-ee-əm] n nonmetallic bluish-white element. **tel·lu'ric** adj

tem·blor [TEM-blər] n earthquake.

te·mer'i·ty [tə-MER-i-tee] n boldness, audacity.

temp n inf one employed on temporary basis.

tem·per [TEM-pər] n frame of mind; anger, oft. noisy; mental constitution; degree of hardness of steel, etc. ▸ vt restrain, qualify, moderate; harden; bring to proper condition.

tem·per·a [TEM-pər-ə] n emulsion used as painting medium. ▸ n painting made with this.

tem·per·a·ment [TEM-pər-ə-mənt] n natural disposition; emotional mood; mental constitution. **tem·per·a·men'tal** adj given to extremes of temperament, moody; of, occasioned by temperament.

tem·per·ate [TEM-pər-it] adj not extreme; showing, practicing moderation. **tem'per·ance** [-əns] n moderation; abstinence, esp. from alcohol.

tem·per·a·ture [TEM-pər-ə-chər] n degree of heat or coldness; inf (abnormally) high body temperature.

tem·pest [TEM-pist] n violent storm. **tem·pes·tu·ous** [tem-PES-choo-əs] adj turbulent; violent, stormy.

tem·plate [TEM-plit] n mold, pattern to help shape something accurately.

tem·ple¹ [TEM-pəl] n building for worship; shrine.

temple² n flat part on either side of forehead.

tem·po [TEM-poh] n, pl **-pos.** rate, rhythm, esp. in music.

tem·po·ral [TEM-pə-rəl] adj of time; of this life or world; secular.

tem·po·rar·y [TEM-pə-rer-ee] adj lasting, used only for a time. ▸ n, pl **-ies.** person employed on temporary basis. **tem·po·rar'i·ly** adv

tem·po·rize [TEM-pə-rīz] vi **-ized, -iz·ing.** use evasive action; hedge; gain time by negotiation, etc.; conform to circumstances. **tem'po·riz·er** n

tempt vt try to persuade, entice, esp. to something wrong or unwise; dispose, cause to be inclined to. **temp·ta'tion** [-TAY-shən] n act of tempting; thing that tempts. **tempt'er, tempt'ress** n **tempt'ing** adj attractive, inviting.

ten n, adj cardinal number next after nine. **tenth** adj, n ordinal number.

ten·a·ble [TEN-ə-bəl] adj able to be held, defended, maintained.

te·na·cious [tə-NAY-shəs] adj holding fast; retentive; stubborn. **te·nac'i·ty** [-NAS-i-tee] n

ten·ant [TEN-ənt] n one who holds lands, house, etc. on rent or lease. **ten'an·cy** n, pl **-cies.**

tend¹ vi be inclined; be conducive; make in direction of. **ten'den·cy** [-dən-see] n, pl **-cies.** inclination, bent. **ten·den'tious** [-DEN-shəs] adj having, showing tendency or bias; controversial.

tend² vt take care of, watch over. **tend'er** n small boat carried by yacht or ship; carriage for fuel and water attached to steam locomotive; one who tends, e.g. bartender.

ten·der¹ [TEN-dər] adj not tough or hard; easily injured; gentle, loving, affectionate; delicate, soft. **ten'der·ness** [-nis] n **ten'der·ize** vt **-ized, -iz·ing.** soften (meat) by pounding or by treating (it) with substance made for this purpose. **ten'der·foot** [-fuut] n, pl **-feet** or **-foots.** newcomer, esp. to ranch, etc.

tender² vt offer. ▸ vi make offer or estimate. ▸ n offer; offer or estimate for contract to undertake specific work; what may legally be offered in payment.

ten·don [TEN-dən] n sinew attaching muscle to bone, etc. **ten·di·ni'tis** [-NĪ-tis] n inflammation of tendon.

ten'dril n slender curling stem by which climbing plant clings to anything; curl, as of hair.

ten·e·ment [TEN-ə-mənt] n run-down apartment house, esp. in slum.

ten·et [TEN-it] n doctrine, belief.

ten'nis n game in which ball is struck with racket by players on opposite sides of net, lawn tennis. **tennis elbow** strained muscle as a result of playing tennis.

ten·on [TEN-ən] n tongue put on end of piece of wood, etc., to fit into a mortise.

ten·or [TEN-ər] n male voice between alto and bass; music for, singer with this; general course, meaning.

tense¹ [tens] n modification of verb to show time of action.

tense² adj **tens·er, tens·est.** stretched tight; strained; taut; emotionally strained. ▶ v **tensed, tens·ing.** make, become tense. **ten'sile** [-səl] adj of, relating to tension; capable of being stretched. **ten'sion** [-shən] n stretching; strain when stretched; emotional strain or excitement; hostility, suspense; Electricity voltage.

tent n portable shelter of canvas, etc.

ten·ta·cle [TEN-tə-kəl] n elongated, flexible organ of some animals (e.g. octopus) used for grasping, feeding, etc.

ten·ta·tive [TEN-tə-tiv] adj done as a trial; experimental, cautious.

ten·ter·hooks [TEN-tər-huuks] pl n **on tenterhooks** in anxious suspense.

ten·u·ous [TEN-yoo-əs] adj flimsy, uncertain; thin, fine, slender.

ten·ure [TEN-yər] n (length of time of) possession, holding of office, position, etc.

te·pee, tee·pee [TEE-pee] n N Amer. Indian cone-shaped tent of animal skins.

tep'id adj moderately warm, lukewarm; half-hearted.

te·qui·la [tə-KEE-lə] n Mexican alcoholic liquor.

tera- comb. form denoting one million million (10^{12}), e.g. terameter.

ter·bi·um [TUR-bee-əm] n rare metallic element.

ter·cen·ten·ar·y [tur-sen-TEN-ə-ree] adj, n, pl **-nar·ies.** (of) three-hundredth anniversary.

term [turm] n word, expression; limited period of time; period during which courts sit, schools are open, etc.; limit, end. ▶ pl conditions; mutual relationship. ▶ vt name, designate.

ter·mi·nal [TUR-mə-nl] adj at, forming an end; pert. to, forming a terminus; (of disease) ending in death. ▶ n terminal part or structure; extremity; point where current enters, leaves electrical device (e.g. battery); device permitting operation of computer at some distance from it.

ter·mi·nate [TUR-mə-nayt] v **-nat·ed, -nat·ing.** bring, come to an end. **ter·mi·na'tion** [-shən] n

ter·mi·nol·o·gy [tur-mə-NOL-ə-jee] n, pl **-gies.** set of technical terms or vocabulary; study of terms.

ter·mi·nus [TUR-mə-nəs] n, pl **-ni** [-nī] finishing point; farthest limit; railroad station, bus station, etc. at end of long-distance line.

ter·mite [TUR-mīt] n insect, some species of which feed on and damage wood (also **white ant**).

ter·race [TER-əs] n raised level place; level cut out of hill; row, street of houses built as one block. ▶ vt **-raced, -rac·ing.** form into, furnish with terrace.

ter·ra cot·ta [TER-ə KOT-ə] hard unglazed pottery; its color, a brownish-red.

ter·ra fir·ma [FUR-mə] Lat firm ground; dry land.

ter·rain [tə-RAYN] n area of ground, esp. with reference to its physical character.

ter·ra·pin [TER-ə-pin] n type of aquatic tortoise.

ter·rar·i·um [tə-RAIR-ee-əm] *n, pl* **-i·ums.** enclosed container in which small plants, animals are kept.

ter·raz·zo [tə-RAZ-oh] *n* floor, wall finish of chips of stone set in mortar and polished.

ter·res·tri·al [tə-RES-tree-əl] *adj* of the earth; of, living on land.

ter·ri·ble [TER-ə-bəl] *adj* serious; dreadful, frightful; excessive; causing fear. **ter′ri·bly** *adv*

ter·ri·er [TER-ee-ər] *n* small dog of various breeds, orig. for following quarry into burrow.

ter·rif·ic [tə-RIF-ik] *adj* very great; *inf* good, excellent; terrible, awe-inspiring.

ter·ri·fy [TER-ə-fī] *vt* **-fied, -fy·ing.** fill with fear, dread.

ter·ri·to·ry [TER-i-tor-ee] *n, pl* **-ries.** region; geographical area under control of a political unit, esp. a sovereign state; area of knowledge. **ter·ri·to′ri·al** *adj*

ter·ror [TER-ər] *n* great fear; *inf* troublesome person or thing. **ter′ror·ism** *n* use of violence, intimidation to achieve ends; state of terror. **ter′ror·ist** *n, adj* **ter′ror·ize** *vt* **-ized, -iz·ing.** force, oppress by fear, violence.

terse [turs] *adj* **ters·er, ters·est.** expressed in few words, concise; abrupt.

ter·ti·ar·y [TUR-shee-er-ee] *adj* third in degree, order, etc. ▶ *n* (**T-**) geological period before Quaternary.

tes·sel·late [TES-ə-layt] *vt* **-lat·ed, -lat·ing.** make, pave, inlay with mosaic of small tiles; (of identical shapes) fit together exactly. **tes′ser·a** [-ər-ə] *n, pl* **-ae** [-ee] stone used in mosaic.

test *vt* try, put to the proof; carry out test(s) on. ▶ *n* (critical) examination; means of trial. **test′ing** *adj* difficult. **test case** lawsuit viewed as means of establishing precedent. **test tube** narrow cylindrical glass vessel used in scientific experiments. **test-tube baby** baby conceived in artificial womb.

tes·ta·ment [TES-tə-mənt] *n Law* will; declaration; (**T-**) one of the two main divisions of the Bible. **tes·ta·men′ta·ry** *adj*

tes·tate [TES-tayt] *adj* having left a valid will. **tes′ta·cy** *n* [-tə-see] state of being testate. **tes′ta·tor** [-tay-tər], (*fem*) **tes·ta·trix** [te-STAY-triks] *n* maker of will.

tes·ti·cle [TES-ti-kəl] *n* either of two male reproductive glands.

tes·ti·fy [TES-tə-fī] *v* **-fied, -fy·ing.** declare; bear witness (to).

tes·ti·mo·ny [TES-tə-moh-nee] *n, pl* **-nies.** affirmation; evidence. **tes·ti·mo′ni·al** [-əl] *n* certificate of character, ability, etc.; gift, reception, etc. by organization or person expressing regard for recipient. ▶ *adj*

tes·tis *n, pl* **-tes** [-teez] testicle.

tes′ty *adj* **-ti·er, -ti·est.** irritable, short-tempered. **tes′ti·ly** *adv*

tet·a·nus [TET-n-əs] *n* acute infectious disease producing muscular spasms, contractions (also **lockjaw**).

tête-à-tête [TAYT-ə-TAYT] *n, pl* **tête-à-têtes** [-tayts] *Fr* private conversation.

teth·er [TE*TH*-ər] *n* rope or chain for fastening (grazing) animal. ▶ *vt* tie up with rope. **be at the end of one's tether** have reached limit of one's endurance.

Teu·ton·ic [too-TON-ik] *adj* German; of ancient Teutons.

text [tekst] *n* (actual words of) book, passage, etc.; passage of Scriptures, etc., esp. as subject of discourse. ▶ *v* send text message (to). **tex′tu·al** [-choo-əl] *adj* of, in a text. **text′book** *n* book of instruction on particular subject. **text message** message, usu. in form of coded abbreviations, sent from cell phone to cell phone.

tex·tile [TEKS-tīl] *n* any fabric or cloth, esp. woven. ▶ *adj* of (the making of) fabrics.

tex·ture [TEKS-chər] *n* character, structure; consistency.

Th *Chem* thorium.

tha·lid·o·mide [thə-LID-ə-mīd] *n*

drug formerly used as sedative, but found to cause abnormalities in developing fetus.

thal·li·um [THAL-ee-əm] *n* highly toxic metallic element. **thal'lic** *adj*

than [*than*] *conj* introduces second part of comparison.

thank [thangk] *vt* express gratitude to; say thanks; hold responsible. **thanks** *pl n* words of gratitude. **thank'ful** [-fəl] *adj* grateful, appreciative. **thank'less** [-lis] *adj* having, bringing no thanks; unprofitable. **Thanks·giv'ing Day** public holiday in US, Canada.

that [*that*] *adj, pron* used to refer to something already mentioned or familiar, or further away. ▶ *conj* used to introduce a clause. ▶ *pron* used to introduce a relative clause.

thatch [thach] *n* reeds, straw, etc. used as roofing material. ▶ *vt* to roof (a house) with reeds, straw, etc. **thatch'er** *n*

thaw *v* melt; (cause to) unfreeze; defrost; become warmer, or more genial. ▶ *n* a melting (of frost, etc.).

the [thə or thee] *adj* the definite article.

the·a·ter [THEE-ə-tər] *n* place where plays, etc. are performed; drama, dramatic works generally; large room with (tiered) seats, used for lectures, etc.; surgical operating room. **the·at'ri·cal** *adj* of, for the theater; exaggerated, affected.

thee [thee] *pron obs* objective and dative of THOU.

theft *n* stealing.

their [thair] *adj* of or associated with them. **theirs** *pron* (thing or person) belonging to them.

the·ism [THEE-iz-əm] *n* belief in creation of universe by one god. **the'ist** *n*

them [them] *pron* refers to people or things other than the speaker or those addressed. **themselves** *pron* emphatic and reflexive form of THEY or THEM.

theme [theem] *n* main idea or topic of conversation, book, etc.; subject of composition; recurring melody in music. **the·mat·ic** [thə-MAT-ik]

adj **theme park** leisure area designed around one subject. **theme song** one associated with particular program, person, etc.

then [then] *adv* at that time; next; that being so.

thence [thens] *adv obs* from that place, point of reasoning, etc.

the·oc·ra·cy [thee-OK-rə-see] *n, pl* **-cies.** government by a deity or a priesthood. **the·o·crat'ic** [-ə-KRAT-ik] *adj*

the·od·o·lite [thee-OD-l-īt] *n* surveying instrument for measuring angles.

the·ol·o·gy [thee-OL-ə-jee] *n, pl* **-gies.** systematic study of religion(s) and religious belief(s). **the·o·lo·gian** [thee-ə-LOH-jən] *n*

the·o·rem [THEE-ər-əm or THEER-əm] *n* proposition that can be demonstrated by argument.

the·o·ry [THEE-ə-ree] *n, pl* **-ries.** supposition to account for something; system of rules and principles; rules and reasoning, etc. as distinguished from practice. **the·o·ret'i·cal** *adj* based on theory; speculative, as opposed to practical. **the'o·rize** *vi* **-rized, -riz·ing.** form theories, speculate.

the·os·o·phy [thee-OS-ə-fee] *n* any of various religious, philosophical systems claiming possibility of intuitive insight into divine nature.

ther·a·py [THER-ə-pee] *n, pl* **-pies.** healing treatment. **ther·a·peu'tic** [-PYOO-tik] *adj* of healing; serving to improve or maintain health. **ther·a·peu'tics** *n* art of healing. **ther'a·pist** *n* esp. psychotherapist.

there [thair] *adv* in that place; to that point. **there·by'** *adv* by that means. **there'fore** *adv* in consequence, that being so. **there·up·on** *conj* at that point, immediately afterward.

therm [thurm] *n* unit of measurement of heat. **ther'mal** [-əl] *adj* of, pert. to heat; hot, warm (esp. of a spring, etc.).

therm·i·on [THURM-ī-ən] *n* ion emitted by incandescent body. **therm·i·on·ic** [thur-mee-ON-ik] *adj* pert. to thermion.

thermo- *comb. form* related to, caused by or producing heat.

ther·mo·dy·nam·ics [thur-moh-dī-NAM-iks] *n* the science that deals with the interrelationship and interconversion of different forms of energy.

ther·mom·e·ter [thə-MOM-ə-tər] *n* instrument to measure temperature. **ther·mo·met·ric** [thur-mə-MET-rik] *adj*

ther·mo·nu·cle·ar [thur-moh-NOO-klee-ər] *adj* involving nuclear fusion.

ther·mo·plas·tic [thur-mə-PLAS-tik] *n* plastic that retains its properties after being melted and solidified. ▶ *adj*

ther·mos [THUR-məs] *n* double-walled flask with vacuum between walls, for keeping contents of inner flask at temperature at which they were inserted.

ther·mo·stat [THUR-mə-stat] *n* apparatus for automatically regulating temperature. **ther·mo·stat'ic** *adj*

the·sau·rus [thi-SOR-əs] *n* book containing lists of synonyms and antonyms; dictionary of selected words, topics.

these [theez] pl. of THIS.

the·sis [THEE-sis] *n, pl* **-ses** [-seez] written work submitted for degree, diploma; theory maintained in argument.

thes·pi·an [THES-pee-ən] *adj* theatrical. ▶ *n* actor, actress.

they [thay] *pron* the third person plural pronoun.

thick [thik] *adj* **-er, -est.** having great thickness, not thin; dense, crowded; viscous; (of voice) throaty; *inf* stupid, insensitive; *inf* friendly. ▶ *n* busiest, most intense part. **thick·en** [THIK-ən] *v* make, become thick; become more involved, complicated. **thick'ly** *adv* **thick'ness** [-nis] *n* dimensions of anything measured through it, at right angles to length and breadth;

state of being thick; layer. **thick·et** [THIK-it] *n* thick growth of small trees. **thick'set** *adj* sturdy and solid of body; set closely together.

thief [theef] *n, pl* **thieves.** one who steals. **thieve** [theev] *v* **thieved, thiev·ing.** steal. **thiev'ish** *adj*

thigh [thī] *n* upper part of leg.

thim·ble [THIM-bəl] *n* cap protecting end of finger when sewing.

thin *adj* **thin·ner, thin·nest.** of little thickness; slim; lean; of little density; sparse; fine; loose, not close-packed; *inf* unlikely. ▶ *v* **thinned, thin·ning.** make, become thin. **thin'ness** [-nis] *n*

thine [thīn] *pron, adj obs* belonging to thee.

thing *n* material object; any possible object of thought.

think [thingk] *v* **thought** [thawt], **think·ing.** ▶ *vi* have one's mind at work; reflect, meditate; reason; deliberate; imagine; hold opinion. ▶ *vt* conceive, consider in the mind; believe; esteem. **think'a·ble** *adj* able to be conceived, considered, possible, feasible. **thinking** *adj* reflecting. **think tank** group of experts studying specific problems.

third [thurd] *adj* ordinal number corresponding to three. ▶ *n* third part. **third degree** violent interrogation. **third party** *Law* person involved by chance or only incidentally in legal proceedings, etc. **Third World** developing countries of Africa, Asia, Latin Amer.

thirst [thurst] *n* desire to drink; feeling caused by lack of drink; craving; yearning. ▶ *v* feel lack of drink. **thirst'y** *adj* **thirst·i·er, thirst·i·est.**

thir·teen [thur-TEEN] *adj, n* three plus ten. **thir'ty** *n, adj, pl* **-ties.** three times ten.

this [this] *adj, pron* used to refer to a thing or person nearby, just mentioned, or about to be mentioned. ▶ *adj* used to refer to the present time, e.g. *this morning*.

this·tle [THIS-əl] *n* prickly plant with dense flower heads.

thong [thawng] *n* narrow strip of leather, strap; type of light sandal.

thor·ax [THOR-aks] *n* part of body between neck and belly. **tho·rac·ic** [thaw-RAS-ik] *adj*

tho·ri·um [THOR-ee-əm] *n* radioactive metallic element.

thorn *n* prickle on plant; spine; bush noted for its thorns; anything that causes trouble or annoyance. **thorn'y** *adj* **thorn·i·er, thorn·i·est.**

thor·ough [THUR-oh] *adj* careful, methodical; complete, entire. **thor'ough·ly** *adv* **thor'ough·bred** *adj* of pure breed. ▶ *n* purebred animal, esp. horse. **thor'ough·fare** [-fair] *n* road or passage open at both ends; right of way.

those [thohz] *adj, pron* pl. OF THAT.

thou [thow] *pron, pl* **ye** or **you.** *obs* the second person singular pronoun.

though [thoh] *conj* in spite of the fact that, even if. ▶ *adv* nevertheless.

thought [thawt] *n* process of thinking; what one thinks; product of thinking; meditation; pt./pp. of THINK. **thought'ful** [-fəl] *adj* considerate; showing careful thought; engaged in meditation; attentive. **thought'less** [-lis] *adj* inconsiderate, careless, heedless.

thou·sand [THOW-zənd] *n, adj* cardinal number, ten hundred.

thrall [thrawl] *n* slavery; slave, bondsman. **thrall'dom** [-dəm] *n* bondage.

thrash *vt* beat, whip soundly; defeat soundly; thresh. ▶ *vi* move, plunge (esp. arms, legs) in wild manner. **thrash out** argue about from every angle; solve by exhaustive discussion.

thread [thred] *n* fine cord; yarn; ridge cut spirally on screw; theme, meaning. ▶ *vt* put thread into; fit film, magnetic tape, etc. into machine; put on thread; pick (one's way, etc.). **thread'bare** [-bair] *adj* worn, with nap rubbed off; meager; shabby.

threat [thret] *n* declaration of intention to harm, injure, etc.; person or thing regarded as dangerous. **threat·en** [THRET-n] *vt* utter threats against; menace.

three *n, adj* cardinal number, one more than two. **three-ply** [-plī] *adj* having three layers (as wood) or strands (as wool). **three'some** [-səm] *n* group of three. **three-di·men'sion·al, 3-D** *adj* having three dimensions; simulating the effect of depth.

thresh *v* beat, rub (wheat, etc.) to separate grain from husks and straw; thrash.

thresh·old [THRESH-ohld] *n* bar of stone or wood forming bottom of doorway; entrance; starting point; point at which a stimulus is perceived, or produces a response.

threw [throo] pt. of THROW.

thrice [thrīs] *adv* three times.

thrift *n* saving, economy; savings organization; genus of plant, sea pink. **thrift'y** *adj* **thrift·i·er, thrift·i·est.** economical, frugal, sparing.

thrill *n* sudden sensation of excitement and pleasure. ▶ *v* (cause to) feel a thrill; vibrate, tremble. **thrill'er** *n* book, motion picture, etc. with story of mystery, suspense. **thrill'ing** *adj* exciting.

thrive [thrīv] *vi* **thrived** or **throve** [throhv] **thrived** or **thriv·en, thriv·ing.** grow well; flourish, prosper.

throat [throht] *n* front of neck; either or both of passages through it. **throat'y** *adj* **throat·i·er, throat·i·est.** (of voice) hoarse.

throb *vi* **throbbed, throb·bing.** beat, quiver strongly, pulsate. ▶ *n* pulsation, beat; vibration.

throes [throhz] *pl n* condition of violent pangs, pain, etc. **in the throes of** in the process of.

throm·bo·sis [throm-BOH-sis] *n* formation of clot of coagulated blood in blood vessel or heart.

throne [throhn] *n* ceremonial seat, powers and duties of king or queen. ▶ *vt* **throned, thron·ing.** place on throne, declare king, etc.

throng [thrawng] *n, v* crowd.

throt·tle [THROT-l] *n* device

controlling amount of fuel entering engine and thereby its speed. ▶ *vt* **-tled, -tling.** strangle; suppress; restrict (flow of liquid, etc.).

through [throo] *prep* from end to end, from side to side of; between the sides of; in consequence of; by means or fault of. ▶ *adv* from end to end; to the end. ▶ *adj* completed; finished; continuous; (of transport, traffic) not stopping. **through·out′** [-OWT] *adv, prep* in every part (of). **through′put** [-puut] *n* quantity of material processed, esp. by computer. **through train** train that travels whole (unbroken) length of long journey. **carry through** accomplish.

throve [throhv] pt. of THRIVE.

throw [throh] *vt* **threw** [throo], **thrown, throw·ing.** fling, cast; move, put abruptly, carelessly; give, hold (party, etc.); cause to fall; shape on potter's wheel; move (switch, lever, etc.); *inf* baffle, disconcert. ▶ *n* act or distance of throwing. **throw′back** *n* one who, that which reverts to character of an ancestor; this process.

thrush[1] *n* songbird.

thrush[2] *n* fungal disease of mouth, esp. in infants; foot disease of horses.

thrust *v* **thrust, thrust·ing.** push, drive; stab; push one's way. ▶ *n* lunge, stab with pointed weapon, etc.; cutting remark; propulsive force or power.

thud *n* dull heavy sound. ▶ *vi* **thud·ded, thud·ding.** make thud.

thug *n* brutal, violent person.

thumb [thum] *n* first, shortest, thickest finger of hand. ▶ *vt* handle, dirty with thumb; make hitchhiker's signal to give ride; flick through (pages of book, etc.).

thump *n* dull heavy blow; sound of one. ▶ *vt* strike heavily.

thun·der [THUN-dər] *n* loud noise accompanying lightning. ▶ *vi* rumble with thunder; make noise like thunder. ▶ *vt* utter loudly. **thun′der·ous** [-əs] *adj*

thun′der·bolt [-bohlt], **thun′der·clap** *n* lightning flash followed by peal of thunder; anything totally unexpected and unpleasant. **thun′der·struck** *adj* amazed.

thus [thus] *adv* in this way; therefore.

thwack [thwak] *vt, n* whack.

thwart [thwort] *vt* foil, frustrate, baffle. ▶ *adv obs* across. ▶ *n* seat across a boat.

thy [thī] *adj obs* belonging to thee. **thy·self′** *pron* emphasized form of THOU.

thyme [tīm] *n* aromatic herb.

thy·mus [THĪ-məs] *n* small ductless gland in upper part of chest.

thy·roid gland [THĪ-roid] endocrine gland controlling body growth, situated (in people) at base of neck.

ti, te [tee] *n* seventh sol-fa note.

Ti *Chem* titanium.

ti·ar·a [tee-AR-ə] *n* woman's jeweled head ornament, coronet.

tib·i·a [TIB-ee-ə] *n, pl* **-i·as.** thicker inner bone of lower leg.

tic [tik] *n* spasmodic twitch in muscles, esp. of face.

tick[1] [tik] *n* slight tapping sound, as of watch movement; small mark (✓). ▶ *vt* mark with tick. ▶ *vi* make the sound. **tick·er tape** continuous paper ribbon. **tick off** mark off; reprimand; make angry. **tick over** (of engine) idle; continue to function smoothly.

tick[2] *n* small insect-like parasite living on and sucking blood of warm-blooded animals.

tick[3] *n* mattress case. **tick′ing** *n* strong material for mattress covers.

tick·et [TIK-it] *n* card, paper entitling holder to admission, travel, etc.; list of candidates of one party for election. ▶ *vt* attach label to; issue tickets to.

tick·le [TIK-əl] *v* **-led, -ling.** ▶ *vt* touch, stroke, poke (person, part of body, etc.) to produce laughter, etc.; please, amuse. ▶ *vi* be irritated, itch. ▶ *n* act, instance of this. **tick′lish** *adj* sensitive to tickling; requiring care or tact.

tid′bit n tasty morsel of food; pleasing scrap (of scandal, etc.).

tide [tīd] n rise and fall of sea happening twice each lunar day; stream; season, time. **tid′al** [-əl] adj of, like tide. **tidal wave** great wave, esp. produced by earthquake. **tide over** help someone for a while, esp. by loan, etc.

ti·dings [TĪ-dingz] pl. n news.

ti·dy [TĪ-dee] adj -di·er, -di·est. orderly, neat; of fair size. ▶ vt -died, -dy·ing. put in order.

tie [tī] v tied, ty·ing. equal (score of). ▶ vt fasten, bind, secure; restrict. ▶ n that with which anything is bound; restriction, restraint; long, narrow piece of material worn knotted around neck; bond; connecting link; drawn game, contest; match, game in eliminating competition.

tie′-dye·ing n way of dyeing cloth in patterns by tying sections tightly so they will not absorb dye.

tier [teer] n row, rank, layer.

tiff n petty quarrel.

ti·ger [TĪ-gər] n large carnivorous feline animal.

tight [tīt] adj -er, -est. taut, tense; closely fitting; secure, firm; not allowing passage of water, etc.; cramped; inf mean, stingy; sl drunk. **tights** pl n one-piece clinging garment covering body from waist to feet. **tight′en** [-ən] v **tight′rope** n rope stretched taut above the ground, on which acrobats perform.

tile [tīl] n flat piece of ceramic, plastic, etc.; material used for roofs, walls, floors, fireplaces, etc. ▶ vt tiled, til·ing. cover with tiles.

till[1] prep up to the time of. ▶ conj to the time that.

till[2] vt cultivate. **till′er** n

till[3] n drawer for money in store; cash register.

til·ler [TĬL-ər] n lever to move rudder of boat.

tilt v incline, slope, slant; tip up. ▶ vi take part in medieval combat with lances; thrust, aim (at). ▶ n slope, incline; Hist combat for mounted men with lances, joust.

tim·ber [TIM-bər] n wood for building, etc.; trees suitable for the sawmill. **tim′bered** adj made of wood; covered with trees. **timber line** geographical limit beyond which trees will not grow.

tim·bre [TAM-bər] n quality of musical sound, or sound of human voice.

time [tīm] n existence as a succession of states; hour; duration; period; point in duration; opportunity; occasion; leisure; tempo. ▶ vt timed, tim·ing. choose time for; note time taken by. **time′ly** adj at opportune or appropriate time. **tim′er** [-ər] n person, device for recording or indicating time. **time bomb** bomb designed to explode at arranged time; situation resembling this. **time-honored** [-on-ərd] adj respectable because old. **time-lag** n period of time between cause and effect. **time′piece** [-pees] n watch, clock. **time share** n system of part ownership of vacation property for specified period each year. **time′ta·ble** n plan showing hours of work, times of arrival and departure, etc. **Greenwich Mean Time** [GREN-ich] world standard time, time as settled by passage of sun over the meridian at Greenwich, England.

tim′id adj easily frightened; lacking self-confidence. **ti·mid′i·ty** n **tim′or·ous** [-ər-əs] adj timid; indicating fear.

tim·pa·ni [TIM-pə-nee] pl n set of kettledrums. **tim′pa·nist** n

tin n malleable metal. ▶ vt tinned, tin·ning. coat with tin. **tin′ny** adj -ni·er, -ni·est. (of sound) thin, metallic; cheap, shoddy.

tinc·ture [TINGK-chər] n solution of medicinal substance in alcohol; color, stain. ▶ vt -tured, -tur·ing. color, tint.

tin·der [TIN-dər] n dry easily-burning material used to start fire.

tine [tīn] n tooth, spike of fork, antler, etc.

tinge [tinj] n slight trace, flavor. ▶ vt **tinged, tinge·ing.** color, flavor slightly.

tin·gle [TING-gəl] vi **-gled, -gling.** feel thrill or pricking sensation. ▶ n

tin·ker [TING-kər] n formerly, traveling mender of pots and pans. ▶ vi fiddle, meddle (e.g. with machinery) oft. inexpertly.

tin·kle [TING-kəl] v **-kled, -kling.** (cause to) give out series of light sounds like small bell. ▶ n this sound or action.

tin·sel [TIN-səl] n glittering metallic substance for decoration; anything sham and showy.

tint n color; shade of color; tinge. ▶ vt dye, give tint to.

ti·ny [TĪ-nee] adj **-ni·er, -ni·est.** very small, minute.

tip[1] n slender or pointed end of anything; piece of metal, leather, etc. protecting an extremity. ▶ vt **tipped, tip·ping.** put a tip on.

tip[2] n small present of money given for service rendered; helpful piece of information; warning, hint. ▶ vt **tipped, tip·ping.** give tip to.

tip'ster [-stər] n one who sells tips about races, etc.

tip[3] v **tipped, tip·ping.** ▶ vt tilt, upset; touch lightly. ▶ vi topple over.

tip·ple [TIP-əl] v **-pled, -pling.** drink (liquor) habitually, esp. in small quantities. ▶ n drink of liquor. **tip'pler** [-lər] n

tip·sy adj **-si·er, -si·est.** drunk, partly drunk.

tip·toe [-toed, -to·ing.] walk on ball of foot and toes; walk softly.

ti·rade [TĪ-rayd] n long speech, generally vigorous and hostile, denunciation.

tire[1] [tīr] v **tired, tir·ing.** ▶ vt reduce energy of, esp. by exertion; bore; irritate. ▶ vi become tired, wearied, bored. **tire'some** [-səm] adj wearisome, irritating, tedious.

tire[2] n (inflated) rubber or synthetic rubber ring over rim of road vehicle.

tis·sue [TISH-oo] n substance of animal body, plant, etc.; fine, soft paper, esp. used as handkerchief, etc.; fine woven fabric; interconnection e.g. of lies.

tit[1] n any of various small songbirds.

tit[2] n sl female breast.

ti·tan·ic [tī-TAN-ik] adj huge, epic.

ti·ta·ni·um [tī-TAY-nee-əm] n rare metal of great strength and rust-resisting qualities.

tit for tat blow for blow, retaliation.

tithe [tīth] n esp. formerly, one tenth part of agricultural produce paid for the upkeep of the clergy or as tax. ▶ v **tithed, tith·ing.** ▶ vt exact tithes from. ▶ vi give, pay tithe.

ti·tian [TISH-ən] adj (of hair) reddish-gold, auburn.

tit·il·late [TIT-l-ayt] vt **-lat·ed, -lat·ing.** tickle, stimulate agreeably.

ti·tle [TĪT-l] n name of book; heading; name; appellation denoting rank; legal right or document proving it; Sports championship. **title deed** legal document as proof of ownership.

tit·ter [TIT-ər] vi laugh in suppressed way. ▶ n such laugh.

tit·tle [TIT-l] n whit, detail.

tit·tle-tat·tle [TIT-l-tat-l] n, vi **-tled, -tling.** gossip.

tit·u·lar [TICH-ə-lər] adj pert. to title; nominal; held by virtue of a title.

tiz·zy [TIZ-ee] n sl pl **-zies.** state of confusion, anxiety.

Tl Chem thallium.

Tm Chem thulium.

to prep toward, in the direction of; as far as; used to introduce a comparison, ratio, indirect object, infinitive, etc. ▶ adv to the required or normal state or position.

toad [tohd] n animal like frog.

toad'y n, pl **toad·ies.** obsequious flatterer, sycophant. ▶ vi **toad·ied, toad·y·ing.** do this. **toad'stool** n fungus like mushroom, but usu. poisonous.

toast [tohst] n slice of bread crisped and browned on both sides by heat; tribute, proposal of health, success, etc. made by company of people and marked by drinking together; one toasted. ▶ *vt* crisp and brown (as bread); drink toast to; dry or warm at fire. **toast'er** *n* electrical device for toasting bread.

to·bac·co [tə-BAK-oh] *n, pl* **-cos** or **-coes**. plant with leaves used for smoking; the prepared leaves.

to·bog·gan [tə-BOG-ən] *n* sled for sliding down slope of snow. ▶ *vi* slide on one.

toc·ca·ta [tə-KAH-tə] *n* rapid piece of music for keyboard instrument.

toc·sin [TOK-sin] *n* alarm signal, bell.

to·day [tə-DAY] *n* this day. ▶ *adv* on this day; nowadays.

tod·dle [TOD-l] *vi* **-dled, -dling.** walk with unsteady short steps. ▶ *n* toddling. **tod'dler** [-lər] *n* child beginning to walk.

tod·dy [TOD-ee] *n, pl* **-dies.** sweetened mixture of alcoholic liquor, hot water, etc.

to·do [tə-DOO] *n inf pl* **-dos.** fuss, commotion.

toe [toh] *n* digit of foot; anything resembling toe in shape or position. ▶ *vt* **toed, toe·ing.** reach, touch with toe. **toe the line** conform.

tof·fee [TAW-fee] *n* brittle candy made of sugar and butter, etc.

to·ga [TOH-gə] *n, pl* **-gas.** loose outer garment worn by ancient Romans.

to·geth·er [tə-GETH-ər] *adv* in company, simultaneously. ▶ *adj sl* (well) organized.

tog·gle [TOG-əl] *n* small wooden, metal peg fixed crosswise on cord, wire, etc. and used for fastening as button; any similar device.

togs [togz] *pl n* clothes.

toil *n* heavy work or task. ▶ *vi* labor. **toil'worn** *adj* weary with toil; hard and lined.

toi·let [TOI-lit] *n* lavatory; ceramic toilet bowl; process of washing, dressing; articles used for this.

to·ken [TOH-kən] *n* sign or object used as evidence; symbol; disk used as money. ▶ *adj* nominal, slight.

told [tohld] pt./pp. of TELL.

tol·er·ate [TOL-ər-ayt] *vt* **-at·ed, -at·ing.** put up with; permit. **tol'er·a·ble** *adj* bearable; fair, moderate. **tol'er·ance** [-əns] *n* (degree of) ability to endure stress, pain, radiation, etc. **tol'er·ant** [-ənt] *adj* disinclined to interfere with others' ways or opinions; forbearing; broad-minded.

toll¹ [tohl] *vt* make (bell) ring slowly at regular intervals; announce death thus. ▶ *vi* ring thus. ▶ *n* tolling sound.

toll² *n* tax, esp. for the use of bridge or road; loss, damage incurred through accident, disaster, etc.

tom *n* male of some animals, esp. cat.

tom·a·hawk [TOM-ə-hawk] *n* formerly, fighting ax of N Amer. Indians. ▶ *vt* strike, kill with one.

to·ma·to [tə-MAY-toh] *n, pl* **-toes.** plant with red fruit; the fruit, used in salads, etc.

tomb [toom] *n* grave; monument over one. **tomb'stone** *n* gravestone.

tom·boy [TOM-boi] *n* girl who acts, dresses in boyish way.

tome [tohm] *n* large book or volume.

tom·fool·er·y [tom-FOO-lə-ree] *n, pl* **-er·ies.** nonsense, silly behavior.

to·mog·ra·phy [tə-MOG-rə-fee] *n* technique used to obtain an X-ray photograph of a plane section of the human body or some other object.

to·mor·row [tə-MOR-oh] *adv, n* (on) the day after today.

tom-tom *n* drum associated with N Amer. Indians or with Asia.

ton [tun] *n* measure of weight equal to 2000 pounds or 907 kilograms (short ton); measure of weight equal to 2240 pounds or 1016 kilograms (long ton). **ton·nage** [TUN-ij] *n* carrying capacity; charge per ton; ships collectively.

tone [tohn] *n* quality of musical sound; quality of voice, color, etc.; general character, style; healthy condition. ▶ *vt* **toned, ton·ing.** give

tone to; blend, harmonize (with).
ton'er [-ər] n substance that
modifies color or composition.
ton'al [-əl] adj **to·nal'i·ty** n, pl
-ties. tone poem orchestral work
based on story, legend, etc.
tongs [tongz] pl n large pincers,
esp. for handling coal, sugar.
tongue [tung] n muscular organ
inside mouth, used for speech,
taste, etc.; various things shaped
like this; language, speech, voice.
ton·ic [TON-ik] n medicine to
improve bodily tone or condition;
Mus keynote; Mus first note of
scale. ▶ adj invigorating,
restorative; of tone. **tonic (water)**
mineral water oft. containing
quinine.
to·night [tə-NIT] n this night; the
coming night. ▶ adv on this night.
ton·sil [TON-səl] n gland in throat.
ton·sil·li'tis [-LI-tis] n inflammation
of tonsils. **ton·sil·lec·to·my**
[-sə-LEK-tə-mee] n, pl -mies.
surgical removal of tonsil(s).
ton·sure [TON-shər] n shaving of
part of head as religious or
monastic practice; part shaved. ▶ vt
-sured, -sur·ing. shave thus.
too adv also, in addition; in excess,
overmuch.
took [tuuk] pt. of TAKE.
tool n implement or appliance for
mechanical operations; servile
helper; means to an end. ▶ vt work
on with tool, esp. chisel stone;
indent design on leather book
cover, etc. **tool'ing** n decorative
work; setting up, etc. of tools, esp.
for machine operation.
tooth n, pl **teeth.** bonelike
projection in gums of upper and
lower jaws of vertebrates; various
pointed things like this; prong, cog.
top[1] n highest part, summit; highest
rank; first in merit; garment for
upper part of body; lid, stopper of
bottle, etc. ▶ vt **topped, top'ping.**
cut off, pass, reach, surpass top;
provide top for. **top'less** [-lis] adj
(of costume, woman) with no
covering for breasts. **top'most**
[-mohst] adj supreme; highest. **top**

dressing layer of fertilizer spread
on the surface of land. **top hat**
man's hat with tall cylindrical
crown. **top-heavy** adj unbalanced;
with top too heavy for base.
top-notch adj excellent, first-class.
top-secret adj needing highest
level of secrecy, security. **top'soil** n
surface layer of soil; more fertile soil
spread on lawns, etc.
top[2] n toy that spins on tapering
point or ball bearing.
to·paz [TOH-paz] n precious stone
of various colors.
to·pee [toh-PEE] n lightweight hat
made of pith.
to·pi·ar·y [TOH-pee-er-ee] adj (of
shrubs) shaped by cutting or
pruning, made ornamental by
trimming or training. ▶ n
top·ic [TOP-ik] n subject of
discourse, conversation, etc.
top'i·cal [-ik-əl] adj up-to-date,
having news value; of topic.
to·pog·ra·phy [tə-POG-rə-fee] n, pl
-phies. (description of) surface
features of a place. **to·pog'ra·pher**
n
top·ple [TOP-əl] v **-pled, -ling.**
(cause to) fall over, collapse.
top·sy-tur·vy [TOP-see-TUR-vee]
adj, adv upside down, in confusion.
tor n high, rocky hill.
To·rah [TOH-rə] n parchment on
which is written the Pentateuch.
torch n portable hand light
containing electric battery and
bulb; burning brand, etc.; any
apparatus burning with hot flame,
e.g. for welding. **torch'bear·er**
[-bair-ər] n
tore pt. of TEAR[2].
tor·e·a·dor [TOR-ee-ə-dor] n
bullfighter.
tor·ment' v torture in body or
mind; afflict; tease. ▶ n [TOR-ment]
suffering, torture, agony of body or
mind.
torn pp. of TEAR[2].
tor·na·do [tor-NAY-doh] n, pl
-does. whirlwind; violent storm.
tor·pe·do [tor-PEE-doh] n, pl **-does.**
cylindrical self-propelled
underwater missile with explosive

warhead, fired esp. from submarine. ▶ *vt* **-doed, -do·ing.** strike, sink with, as with, torpedo.

tor·pid *adj* sluggish, apathetic. **tor·por** [TOR-pər] *n* torpid state.

torque [tork] *n* collar, similar ornament of twisted gold or other metal; *Mechanics* rotating or twisting force.

tor·rent [TOR-ənt] *n* a rushing stream; downpour. **tor·ren·tial** [tə-REN-shəl] *adj* resembling a torrent; overwhelming.

tor·rid [TOR-id] *adj* parched, dried with heat; highly emotional. **Torrid Zone** land between tropics.

tor·sion [TOR-shən] *n* twist, twisting.

tor·so [TOR-soh] *n, pl* **-sos.** (statue of) body without head or limbs; trunk.

tort *n Law* private or civil wrong.

tor·til·la [tor-TEE-yə] *n, pl* **-til·las.** thin Mexican pancake.

tor·toise [TOR-təs] *n* four-footed reptile covered with shell of horny plates. **tor·toise·shell** *n* mottled brown shell of hawksbill turtle used commercially. ▶ *adj*

tor·tu·ous [TOR-choo-əs] *adj* winding, twisting; involved, not straightforward.

tor·ture [TOR-chər] *n* infliction of severe pain. ▶ *vt* **-tured, -tur·ing.** subject to torture. **tor'tur·er** *n*

toss [taws] *vt* throw up, about. ▶ *vi* be thrown, fling oneself about. ▶ *n* act of tossing.

tot¹ *n* very small child.

tot² *v* **tot·ted, tot·ting.** (with *up*) add up; amount to.

to·tal [TOHT-l] *n* whole amount; sum, aggregate. ▶ *adj* complete, entire, full, absolute. ▶ *v* **-taled, -tal·ing.** amount to; add up.

to·tal'i·ty *n, pl* **-ties. to·tal·i·za·tor** [TOHT-l-ə-zay-tər] *n* machine to operate system of betting at racetrack in which money is paid out to winners in proportion to their bets.

to·tal·i·tar·i·an [toh-tal-i-TAIR-ee-ən] *adj* of dictatorial, one-party government.

tote¹ [toht] *n* short for TOTALIZATOR.

tote² *vt* **tot·ed, tot·ing.** haul, carry.

to·tem [TOH-təm] *n* tribal badge or emblem. **totem pole** post carved, painted with totems, esp. by Amer. Indians.

tot·ter [TOT-ər] *vi* walk unsteadily; begin to fall.

touch [tuch] *n* sense by which qualities of object, etc. are perceived by touching; characteristic manner or ability; touching; slight blow, stroke, contact, amount, etc. ▶ *vt* come into contact with; put hand on; reach; affect emotions of; deal with, handle; eat, drink; *sl* (try to) borrow from. ▶ *vi* be in contact; (with *on*) refer to. **touch'ing** *adj* emotionally moving. ▶ *prep* concerning. **touch'y** *adj* **touch·i·er, touch·i·est.** easily offended, sensitive. **touch'down** *n Football* crossing of goal line with football; act of, moment of, landing of aircraft. **touch'stone** *n* criterion. **touch and go** precarious (situation). **touch base** make contact, renew communication.

tou·ché [too-SHAY] *interj* acknowledgment that blow (orig. in fencing), remark, etc. has been successful.

tough [tuf] *adj* **-er, -est.** strong, resilient, not brittle; sturdy; able to bear hardship, strain; difficult; needing effort to chew; rough; uncivilized; violent; unlucky, unfair. ▶ *n* rough, violent person. **tough'en** [-ən] *v* **tough'ness** [-nis] *n*

tou·pee [too-PAY] *n* man's hairpiece, wig.

tour [toor] *n* traveling around; journey to one place after another; excursion. ▶ *v* make tour (of). **tour·ism** *n* tourist travel; this as an industry. **tour·ist** *n* one who travels for pleasure.

tour de force [toor də FORS] *Fr* brilliant stroke, achievement.

tour·ma·line [TUUR-mə-lin] *n* crystalline mineral used for optical instruments and as gem.

tour·na·ment [TUUR-nə-mənt] *n* competition, contest usu. with several stages to decide overall winner. **tour·ney** [TUUR-nee] *n, pl* **-neys.** tournament.

tour·ni·quet [TUR-ni-kit] *n* bandage, surgical instrument to constrict artery and stop bleeding.

tou·sle [TOW-zəl] *vt* **-sled, -sling.** tangle, ruffle; treat roughly.

tout [towt] *vi* solicit trade (usu. in undesirable fashion); obtain and sell information about racehorses, etc. ▶ *n* one who touts.

tow¹ [toh] *vt* drag along behind, esp. at end of rope. ▶ *n* towing or being towed; vessel, vehicle in tow. **tow'path** *n* path beside canal, river, orig. for towing.

tow² *n* fiber of hemp, flax. **tow-head·ed** [-hed-id] *adj* with pale-colored, or rumpled hair.

to·ward [tord], **to·wards** [tords] *prep* in direction of; with regard to; as contribution to.

tow·el [TOW-əl] *n* cloth for wiping off moisture after washing. **tow'el·ing** *n* material used for making towels.

tow·er [TOW-ər] *n* tall strong structure often forming part of church or other large building; fortress. ▶ *vi* stand very high; loom (over).

town *n* collection of dwellings, etc. larger than village and smaller than city. **town'ship** *n* small town. **towns'peo·ple** *n*

tox·ic [TOK-sik] *adj* poisonous; due to poison. **tox·e·mi·a** [tok-SEEM-ee-ə] *n* blood poisoning. **tox·ic'i·ty** [-IS-i-tee] *n* strength of a poison. **tox·i·col·o·gy** [tok-si-KOL-ə-jee] *n* study of poisons. **tox'in** *n* poison of bacterial origin.

toy [toi] *n* something designed to be played with; (miniature) replica. ▶ *adj* very small. ▶ *vi* act idly, trifle.

trace¹ [trays] *n* track left by anything; indication; minute quantity. ▶ *vt* **traced, trac·ing.** follow course, track of; find out; make plan of; draw or copy

exactly, esp. using tracing paper. **trace element** chemical element occurring in very small quantity in soil, etc. **tracer** bullet or shell that leaves visible trail so that aim can be checked. **tracing paper** transparent paper placed over drawing, map, etc. to enable exact copy to be taken.

trace² *n* chain, strap by which horse pulls vehicle. **kick over the traces** become defiant, independent.

tra·che·a [TRAY-kee-ə] *n, pl* **-che·as.** windpipe. **tra·che·al** [-əl] *adj* **tra·che·ot'o·my** [-OT-ə-mee] *n, pl* **-mies.** surgical incision into trachea.

tra·cho·ma [trə-KOH-mə] *n* contagious viral disease of eye.

track [trak] *n* mark, line of marks, left by passage of anything; path; rough road; course; railroad line; distance between two road wheels on one axle; circular jointed metal band driven by wheels as on tank, bulldozer, etc.; course for running or racing; separate section on phonograph record; class, division of schoolchildren grouped together because of similar ability. ▶ *vt* follow trail or path of; find thus. **track record** past accomplishments of person, company, etc.

tract¹ [trakt] *n* wide expanse, area; *Anatomy* system of organs, etc. with particular function.

tract² *n* treatise or pamphlet, esp. religious one. **trac'tate** [-tayt] *n* short tract.

trac·ta·ble [TRAK-tə-bəl] *adj* easy to manage, docile, amenable.

trac·tion [TRAK-shən] *n* action of drawing, pulling. **traction engine** locomotive running on surfaces other than tracks.

trac·tor [TRAK-tər] *n* motor vehicle for hauling, pulling, etc.

trade [trayd] *n* commerce, business; buying and selling; any profitable pursuit; those engaged in trade. ▶ *v* **trad·ed, trad·ing.** engage in trade; buy and sell; barter. **trade-in** *n* used article given in part payment for new.

trade′mark, -name *n* distinctive mark (secured by legal registration) on maker's goods. **trades′man** [-mən] *n, pl* **-men.** person engaged in trade; skilled worker. **trade union** society of workers for protection of their interests. **trade wind** wind blowing constantly toward equator in certain parts of globe.

tra·di·tion [trə-DISH-ən] *n* unwritten body of beliefs, facts, etc. handed down from generation to generation; custom, practice of long standing; process of handing down.

tra·duce [trə-DOOS] *vt* **-duced, -duc·ing.** slander.

traf·fic [TRAF-ik] *n* vehicles passing to and fro in street, town, etc.; (illicit) trade. ▶ *vi* **-ficked, -fick·ing.** trade, esp. in illicit goods, e.g. drugs. **traf′fick·er** *n* trader. **traffic lights** set of colored lights at road junctions, etc. to control flow of traffic.

trag·e·dy [TRAJ-i-dee] *n, pl* **-dies.** sad or calamitous event; dramatic, literary work dealing with serious, sad topic and with ending marked by (inevitable) disaster. **tra·ge·di·an** [trə-JEE-dee-ən] *n* actor in, writer of tragedies. **trag′ic** *adj* of, in manner of tragedy; disastrous; appalling. **trag′i·cal·ly** *adv*

trail [trayl] *vt* drag behind one. ▶ *vi* be drawn behind; hang; grow loosely. ▶ *n* track or trace; thing that trails; rough ill-defined track in wild country. **trail′er** *n* vehicle towed by another vehicle; trailing plant; *Motion Pictures* advertisement of forthcoming film. **trailer park** site for parking mobile homes, usu. providing facilities for trailer residents. **trailer trash** *offens* poor person or people living in trailer parks.

train [trayn] *vt* educate, instruct, exercise; cause to grow in particular way; aim (gun, etc.). ▶ *vi* follow course of training, esp. to achieve physical fitness for athletics. ▶ *n* line of railroad vehicles joined to locomotive; succession, esp. of thoughts, events, etc.; procession of animals, vehicles, etc. traveling together; trailing part of dress; body of attendants. **train·ee′** *n* one training to be skilled worker, esp. in industry.

traipse [trayps] *vi inf* **traipsed, traips·ing.** walk wearily.

trait [trayt] *n* characteristic feature.

trai·tor [TRAY-tər] *n* one who betrays or is guilty of treason. **trai′tor·ous** [-əs] *adj* disloyal; guilty of treachery.

tra·jec·to·ry [trə-JEK-tə-ree] *n, pl* **-ries.** line of flight, (curved) path of projectile.

tram·mel [TRAM-əl] *n* anything that restrains or holds captive; type of compasses. ▶ *vt* **-meled, -mel·ing.** restrain; hinder.

tramp *vi* travel on foot, esp. as vagabond or for pleasure; walk heavily. ▶ *n* homeless person who travels about on foot; walk; tramping; vessel that takes cargo wherever shippers desire.

tram·ple [TRAM-pəl] *vt* **-pled, -pling.** tread on and crush under foot.

tram·po·line [tram-pə-LEEN] *n* tough canvas sheet stretched horizontally with elastic cords, etc. to frame, for gymnastic, acrobatic use.

trance [trans] *n* unconscious or dazed state; state of ecstasy or total absorption.

tran·quil [TRANG-kwil] *adj* calm, quiet; serene. **tran·quil′li·ty** *n* **tran′quil·ize** *vt* **-ized, -iz·ing.** make calm. **tran′quil·iz·er** *n* drug that induces calm, tranquil state.

trans- *prefix* across, through, beyond, e.g. *transnational;* changing thoroughly, e.g. *transliterate.*

trans·act [tran-SAKT] *vt* carry through; negotiate; conduct (affair, etc.). **trans·ac′tion** *n* performing of any business; that which is performed; single sale or purchase.

▶ *pl* proceedings; reports of a society.

trans·ceiv·er [tran-SEE-vər] *n* combined radio transmitter and receiver.

tran·scend [tran-SEND] *vt* rise above; exceed, surpass. **tran·scend′ent** *adj* **tran·scen·den′tal** *adj* surpassing experience; supernatural; abstruse. **transcendental meditation** process seeking to induce detachment from problems, etc. by system of meditation.

tran·scribe [tran-SKRĪB] *vt* -**scribed**, -**scrib·ing**. copy out; record for later broadcast; arrange (music) for different instrument. **tran′script** *n* copy.

tran′sept *n* transverse part of cruciform church; either of its arms.

trans·fer [trans-FUR] *vt* -**ferred**, -**fer·ring**. move, send from one person, place, etc. to another. ▶ *n* [TRANS-fur] removal of person or thing from one place to another; design that can be transferred from one surface to another by pressure, heat, etc. **trans·fer′a·ble** *adj* **trans·fer′ence** *n* transfer.

trans·fig·ure [trans-FIG-yər] *vt* -**ured**, -**ur·ing**. alter appearance of.

trans·fix [trans-FIKS] *vt* astound, stun; pierce.

trans·form′ *vt* change shape, character of. **trans·for·ma′tion** *n* **trans·form′er** *n Electricity* apparatus for changing voltage of alternating current.

trans·fuse [trans-FYOOZ] *vt* -**fused**, -**fus·ing**. convey from one vessel to another, esp. blood from healthy person to one injured or ill. **trans·fu′sion** [-FYOO-zhən] *n*

trans·gress [trans-GRES] *vt* break (law); sin. **trans·gres′sion** [-GRESH-ən] *n* **trans·gres′sor** *n*

tran·sient [TRAN-shənt] *adj* fleeting, not permanent. **tran′sience** *n*

tran·sis·tor [tran-ZIS-tər] *n Electronics* small semiconducting device used to amplify electric currents; *inf* portable radio using

transistors.

tran·sit *n, v* -**sit·ed**, -**sit·ing**. (make) passage, crossing. **tran·si′tion** [-ZISH-ən] *n* change from one state to another. **tran·si′tion·al** *adj* **tran′si·tive** *adj* (of verb) requiring direct object. **tran′si·to·ry** *adj* not lasting long, transient.

trans·late [trans-LAYT] *vt* -**lat·ed**, -**lat·ing**. turn from one language into another; interpret. **trans·la′tion** *n* **trans·la′tor** *n*

trans·lit·er·ate [trans-LIT-ər-ayt] *vt* -**at·ed**, -**at·ing**. write in the letters of another alphabet. **trans·lit·er·a′tion** *n*

trans·lu·cent [trans-LOO-sənt] *adj* letting light pass through, semitransparent. **trans·lu′cence** *n*

trans·mi·grate [trans-MĪ-grayt] *vi* -**grat·ed**, -**grat·ing**. (of soul) pass into another body. **trans·mi·gra′tion** *n*

trans·mit [trans-MIT] *vt* -**mit·ted**, -**mit·ting**. send, cause to pass to another place, person, etc.; communicate; send out (signals) by means of radio waves; broadcast (radio, television program). **trans·mis′sion** *n* transference; gear by which power is communicated from engine to road wheels. **trans·mit′tal** *n* transmission.

trans·mog·ri·fy [trans-MOG-rə-fī] *vt inf* -**fied**, -**fy·ing**. change completely esp. into bizarre form.

trans·mute [trans-MYOOT] *vt* -**mut·ed**, -**mut·ing**. change in form, properties, or nature. **trans·mu·ta′tion** *n*

tran·som [TRAN-səm] *n* window above door; crosspiece separating the door and window.

trans·par·ent [trans-PA-rənt] *adj* letting light pass without distortion; that can be seen through distinctly; obvious. **trans·par′en·cy** *n, pl* -**cies**. quality of being transparent; photographic slide; picture made visible by light behind it.

tran·spire [tran-SPĪR] *vi* -**spired**, -**spir·ing**. become known; *inf* happen; (of plants) give off water vapor through leaves. **tran·spi·ra′tion** n

trans·plant [trans-PLANT] vt move and plant again in another place; transfer organ surgically from one body to another. ▶ n [TRANS-plant] surgical transplanting of organ; anything transplanted. **trans·plan·ta′tion** n

trans·port [trans-PORT] vt convey from one place to another; enrapture. ▶ n [TRANS-port] means of conveyance; ships, aircraft, etc. used in transporting supplies, troops, etc.; a ship, etc. so used.

trans·pose [trans-POHZ] vt -posed, -pos·ing. change order of; interchange; put music into different key. **trans·po·si′tion** [-pə-ZISH-ən] n

tran·sub·stan·ti·a·tion n [tran-səb-stan-shee-AY-shən] doctrine that substance of bread and wine changes into substance of Christ's body when consecrated in Eucharist.

trans·verse [trans-VURS] adj lying across; at right angles.

trans·ves·tite [trans-VES-tīt] n person seeking sexual pleasure by wearing clothes normally worn by opposite sex.

trap n snare, device for catching game, etc.; anything planned to deceive, betray, etc.; arrangement of pipes to prevent escape of gas; movable opening, esp. through ceiling, etc.; sl mouth. ▶ vt **trapped, trap·ping.** catch, ensnare. **trap′per** n one who traps animals for their fur. **trap′door** n door in floor or roof.

tra·peze [tra-PEEZ] n horizontal bar suspended from two ropes for use in gymnastics, acrobatic exhibitions, etc. **trapeze artist** one who performs on trapeze.

trap·e·zoid [TRAP-ə-zoid] n quadrilateral with two parallel sides.

trap·pings [TRAP-ingz] pl n equipment, ornaments.

trash n rubbish; nonsense. **trash′y** adj **trash·i·er, trash·i·est.**

worthless, cheap.

trau·ma [TROW-mə or TRAW-mə] n nervous shock; injury. **trau·mat′ic** adj of, causing, caused by trauma.

tra·vail [trə-VAYL] vi, n labor, toil.

trav·el [TRAV-əl] v -eled, -el·ing. go, move from one place to another. ▶ n act of traveling, esp. as tourist; Machinery distance component is allowed to move. ▶ pl (account of) traveling. **trav′el·er** n

trav·e·logue [TRAV-ə-log] n film, etc. about travels.

trav·erse [trə-VURS] vt -ersed, -ers·ing. cross, go through or over; (of gun) move laterally. ▶ n [TRA-vurs] anything set across; partition; Mountaineering face, steep slope to be crossed from side to side. ▶ adj being, lying across.

trav·es·ty [TRAV-ə-stee] n, pl -ties. farcical, grotesque imitation; mockery. ▶ vt -tied, -ty·ing. make, be a travesty of.

trawl n net dragged at deep levels behind special boat, to catch fish, shrimp, etc. ▶ vi fish with one. **trawl′er** n trawling vessel.

tray n flat board, usu. with rim, for carrying things; any similar utensil.

treach·er·y [TRECH-ə-ree] n, pl -er·ies. deceit, betrayal. **treach′er·ous** [-rəs] adj disloyal; unreliable, dangerous.

trea·cle [TREE-kəl] n cloying sentimentally; Brit molasses.

tread [tred] v trod, trod·den or trod, tread·ing. set foot on; trample; oppress; walk. ▶ n treading; fashion of walking; upper surface of step; part of motor vehicle tire in contact with ground. **tread′mill** n dreary routine, etc.

trea·dle [TRED-l] n lever worked by foot to turn wheel.

trea·son [TREE-zən] n violation by citizen of allegiance to country or ruler; treachery; disloyalty. **trea′son·a·ble** adj constituting treason. **trea′son·ous** adj

treas·ure [TREZH-ər] n riches; stored wealth or valuables. ▶ vt -ured, -ur·ing. prize, cherish; store up. **treas′ur·er** n official in charge of funds. **treas'ur·y** *n, pl* **-ur·ies.** place for treasure; government department in charge of finance. **treasure-trove** [-trohv] *n* treasure found hidden (with no evidence of ownership).

treat *n* (treet) pleasure, entertainment given. ▶ *vt* deal with, act toward; give medical treatment to; (with *of*) discourse on; entertain, esp. with food or drink. ▶ *vi* negotiate. **treat'ment** [-mənt] *n* method of counteracting a disease; act or mode of treating; manner of handling an artistic medium.

trea·tise [TREE-tis] *n* book discussing a subject, formal essay.

trea·ty [TREE-tee] *n, pl* **-ties.** signed contract between nations, etc.

tre·ble [TREB-l] *adj* threefold, triple; *Mus* high-pitched. ▶ *n* soprano voice; part of music for it; singer with such voice. ▶ *v* **-bled, -bling.** increase threefold. **tre'bly** [-blee] *adv*

tree *n* large perennial plant with woody trunk; beam; anything (e.g. genealogical chart) resembling tree, or tree's structure. ▶ *vt* **treed, tree·ing.** force, drive up tree; plant with trees.

tre·foil [TREE-foil] *n* plant with three-lobed leaf, clover; carved ornament like this.

trek *vi, n* **trekked, trek·king.** (make) long difficult journey.

trel·lis [TREL-is] *n* lattice or grating of light bars fixed crosswise. ▶ *vt* screen, supply with one.

trem·ble [TREM-bəl] *vi* **-bled, -bling.** quiver, shake; feel fear, anxiety. ▶ *n* involuntary shaking; quiver; tremor.

tre·men·dous [tri-MEN-dəs] *adj* vast, immense; exciting, unusual; excellent.

trem·o·lo [TREM-ə-loh] *n, pl* **-los.** quivering or vibrating effect in singing or playing.

trem·or [TREM-ər] *n* quiver; shaking; minor earthquake.

trem·u·lous [TREM-yə-ləs] *adj* quivering slightly; fearful, agitated.

trench *n* long narrow ditch, esp. as shelter in war. ▶ *vt* cut grooves or ditches in. **trench coat** double-breasted waterproof overcoat.

trench·ant [TRENCH-ənt] *adj* cutting, incisive, biting.

trend *n* direction, tendency, inclination, drift. **trend'y** *n, adj* **trend·i·er, trend·i·est.** consciously fashionable (person). **trend'i·ness** [-nis] *n*

tre·pan [tri-PAN] *n* instrument for cutting circular pieces, esp. from skull. ▶ *vt* **-panned, -pan·ning.**

trep·i·da·tion [trep-i-DAY-shən] *n* fear, anxiety.

tres·pass [TRES-pəs] *vi* intrude (on) property, etc. of another; transgress, sin. ▶ *n* wrongful entering on another's land; wrongdoing.

tress *n* long lock of hair.

tres·tle [TRES-l] *n* board fixed on pairs of spreading legs and used as support; structural member of bridge.

tri- *comb. form* three or thrice, e.g. *trilingual.* occurring every three, e.g. *triweekly.*

tri·ad [TRI-ad] *n* group of three; *Chem* element, radical with valence of three.

tri·al [TRI-əl] *n* act of trying, testing; experimental examination; *Law* conduct of case before judge, jury; thing, person that strains endurance or patience.

tri·an·gle [TRI-ang-gəl] *n* figure with three angles; percussion musical instrument. **tri·an'gu·lar** [-lər] *adj*

tribe [trīb] *n* subdivision of race of people. **trib'al** [-əl] *adj*

trib·u·la·tion [trib-yə-LAY-shən] *n* misery, trouble, affliction, distress; cause of this.

tri·bu·nal [trī-BYOON-l] *n* law court; body appointed to inquire into and decide specific matter; place, seat of judgment.

trib·u·tar·y [TRIB-yə-ter-ee] *n, pl* **-tar·ies.** stream flowing into another. ▶ *adj* auxiliary;

contributory; paying tribute.

trib·ute [TRIB-yoot] n sign of honor or recognition; tax paid by one country to another as sign of subjugation.

trice [trīs] n moment. **in a trice** instantly.

tri·chi·na [tri-KĪ-nə] n, pl **-nae** [-nee] minute parasitic worm.

trich·i·no·sis n [tri-kə-NOH-sis] disease caused by this.

trick [trik] n deception; prank; mannerism; illusion; feat of skill or cunning; knack; cards played in one round; spell of duty; sl prostitute's customer, sexual act. ▶ vt cheat; hoax; deceive.

trick'ster n **trick'y** adj **trick·i·er, trick·i·est.** difficult, needing careful handling; crafty.

trick·le [TRIK-l] v **-led, -ling.** (cause to) run, flow, move in thin stream or drops.

tri·col·or [TRĪ-kul-ər] adj three colored. ▶ n tricolor flag.

tri·cy·cle [TRĪ-si-kəl] n child's three-wheeled bike.

tri·dent [TRĪD-nt] n three-pronged fork or spear.

tri·en·ni·al [trī-EN-ee-əl] adj happening every, or lasting, three years.

tri·fle [TRĪ-fəl] n insignificant thing or matter; small amount. ▶ vi **-fled, -fling.** toy (with); act, speak idly. **tri'fler** [-flər] n

trig·ger [TRIG-ər] n catch that releases spring esp. to fire gun. ▶ vt (oft. with off) start, set in action, etc. **trigger-happy** adj tending to irresponsible, ill-considered behavior, esp. in use of firearms.

trig·o·nom·et·ry [trig-ə-NOM-i-tree] n branch of mathematics dealing with relations of sides and angles of triangles. **trig·o·no·met'ric** [-nə-MET-rik] adj

tri·lat·er·al [trī-LAT-ər-əl] adj having three sides.

trill vi sing with quavering voice; sing lightly; warble. ▶ n such singing or sound.

tril·lion [TRIL-yən] n number 1 followed by 12 zeroes.

tril·o·gy [TRIL-ə-jee] n, pl **-gies.** series of three related (literary) works.

trim adj **trim·mer, trim·mest.** neat, smart; slender; in good order. ▶ vt **trimmed, trim·ming.** shorten slightly by cutting; prune; decorate; adjust; put in good order; adjust balance of (ship, aircraft). ▶ n decoration; order, state of being trim; haircut that neatens existing style; upholstery, accessories in automobile; edging material, as inside woodwork around doors, windows, etc. **trimming** n (oft pl) decoration, addition; inf a defeat. ▶ pl garnish to main dish.

tri·ma·ran [TRĪ-mə-ran] n three-hulled vessel.

trin·i·ty [TRIN-i-tee] n the state of being threefold; (T-) the three persons of the Godhead.

trin·i·tar'i·an [-TAIR-ee-ən] n, adj

trin·ket [TRING-kit] n small ornament, trifle.

tri·o [TREE-oh] n, pl **tri·os.** group of three; music for three players.

tri·ode [TRĪ-ohd] n Electronics three-electrode vacuum tube.

trip n (short) journey for pleasure; stumble; switch; sl hallucinatory experience caused by drug. ▶ v **tripped, trip·ping.** (cause to) stumble; (cause to) make false step, mistake. ▶ vi run lightly; skip; dance; sl take hallucinatory drugs. ▶ vt operate (switch).

tri·par·tite [trī-PAHR-tīt] adj having, divided into three parts.

tripe [trīp] n stomach of cow, etc. prepared for food; sl nonsense.

tri·ple [TRIP-əl] adj threefold. ▶ v **-pled, -pling.** treble; hit triple. ▶ n Baseball three-base hit. **trip·let** [TRIP-lit] n three of a kind; one of three offspring born at one birth. **trip'lex** adj threefold; (of apartment) having three floors. **trip'ly** [-lee] adv

trip·li·cate [TRIP-li-kit] adj threefold. ▶ n state of being triplicate; one of set of three copies. ▶ vt [-kayt] **-cat·ed, -cat·ing.**

make threefold.

tri·pod [TRĪ-pod] *n* stool, stand, etc. with three feet.

trip·tych [TRIP-tik] *n* carving, set of pictures (esp. altarpiece) on three panels hinged side by side.

trite [trīt] *adj* hackneyed, banal.

trit·i·um [TRIT-ee-əm] *n* radioactive isotope of hydrogen.

tri·umph [TRĪ-əmf] *n* great success; victory; exultation. ▶ *vi* achieve great success or victory; prevail; exult. **tri·um′phal** [-UMF-əl] *adj* **tri·um′phant** [-fənt] *adj* victorious.

tri·um·vi·rate [trī-UM-vər-it] *n* joint rule by three persons.

triv·et [TRIV-it] *n* metal bracket or stand for pot or kettle.

triv·i·a [TRIV-ee-ə] *pl n* petty, unimportant things, details. **triv′i·al** *adj* of little consequence; commonplace. **triv·i·al′i·ty** *n*, *pl* **-ties.**

tro·chee [TROH-kee] *n* in verse, foot of two syllables, first long and second short. **tro·cha′ic** [-KAY-ik] *adj*

trod pt./pp. of TREAD. **trod′den** [TROD-ən] pp. of TREAD.

trog·lo·dyte [TROG-lə-dīt] *n* cave dweller.

Tro·jan [TROH-jən] *adj, n* (inhabitant) of ancient Troy; steadfast or persevering (person).

troll¹ [trohl] *vt* fish for by dragging baited hook or lure through water.

troll² *n* supernatural being in Scandinavian mythology and folklore.

trol·ley [TROL-ee] *n*, *pl* **-leys.** small wheeled table for food and drink; wheeled cart for moving goods; etc.; streetcar.

trol·lop [TROL-əp] *n* promiscuous or slovenly woman.

trom·bone [trom-BOHN] *n* deep-toned brass wind instrument with sliding tube. **trom·bon′ist** *n*

troop *n* group or crowd of persons or animals; unit of cavalry. ▶ *pl* soldiers. ▶ *vi* move in a troop, flock. **troop′er** *n* cavalry soldier; state police officer.

trope [trohp] *n* figure of speech.

tro·phy [TROH-fee] *n*, *pl* **-phies.** prize, award, as shield; cup; memorial of victory, hunt, etc. ▶ *adj inf* regraded as highly desirable symbol of wealth or success, e.g. *a trophy wife.*

trop·ic [TROP-ik] *n* either of two lines of latitude at 23½°N (**tropic of Cancer**) or 23½°S (**tropic of Capricorn**). ▶ *pl* area of Earth's surface between these lines. **trop′i·cal** [-kəl] *adj* pert. to, within tropics; (of climate) very hot.

trot *vi* **trot·ted, trot·ting.** (of horse) move at medium pace, lifting feet in diagonal pairs; (of person) run easily with short strides. ▶ *n* trotting, jog. **trot′ter** *n* horse trained to trot in race; foot of certain animals, esp. pig.

troth [trawth] *n* fidelity, truth.

trou·ba·dour [TROO-bə-dor] *n* one of school of early poets and singers.

trou·ble [TRUB-əl] *n* state or cause of mental distress, pain, inconvenience, etc.; care, effort. ▶ *v* **-bled, -bling.** ▶ *vt* be trouble to. ▶ *vi* be inconvenienced, concerned (about); be agitated; take pains, exert oneself. **trou′ble·some** [-səm] *adj*

trough [trawf] *n* long open vessel, esp. for animals' food or water; hollow between two waves; *Meteorology* area of low pressure.

trounce [trowns] *vt* **trounced, trounc·ing.** beat thoroughly, thrash.

troupe [troop] *n* company of performers. **troup′er** *n*

trou·sers [TROW-zərz] *pl n* two-legged outer garment with legs reaching to the ankles.

trous·seau [TROO-soh] *n*, *pl* **-seaux** [-sohz] bride's outfit of clothing.

trout [trowt] *n* freshwater sport and food fish.

trow·el [TROW-əl] *n* small tool like spade for spreading mortar, lifting plants, etc. ▶ *vt* **-eled, -el·ing.** work with or as if with trowel.

troy weight [troi] system of weights used for gold, silver and gems.

tru·ant [TROO-ənt] n one absent without leave, esp. child so absenting self from school. ▶ adj **tru'an·cy** [-ən-see] n, pl **-cies.**

truce [troos] n temporary cessation of fighting; respite, lull.

truck[1] [truk] n wheeled (motor) vehicle for moving goods.

truck[2] n **have no truck with** refuse to be involved with.

truck·le [TRUK-əl] vi **-led, -ling.** yield weakly (to).

truc·u·lent [TRUK-yə-lənt] adj aggressive, defiant. **truc·u·lence** [-ləns] n

trudge [truj] vi **trudged, trudg·ing.** walk laboriously. ▶ n laborious or wearisome walk.

true [troo] adj **tru·er, tru·est.** in accordance with facts; faithful; exact, correct; genuine. **tru·ism** [TROO-iz-əm] n self-evident truth. **tru'ly** adv exactly; really; sincerely. **truth** [trooth] n state of being true; something that is true. **truth'ful** [-fəl] adj accustomed to speak the truth; accurate, exact.

truf·fle [TRUF-əl] n edible fungus growing underground; candy resembling this.

truism [TROO-iz-əm] n see TRUE.

trump n card of suit temporarily ranking above others. ▶ vt take trick with a trump. **trump up** concoct, fabricate.

trump·er·y [TRUM-pə-ree] adj showy but worthless. ▶ n, pl **-er·ies.** worthless finery; trash; worthless stuff.

trum·pet [TRUM-pit] n metal wind instrument like horn. ▶ vi blow trumpet; make sound like one, as elephant. ▶ vt proclaim, make widely known.

trun·cate [TRUNG-kayt] vt **-cat·ed, -cat·ing.** cut short.

trun·cheon [TRUN-chən] n police officer's club; staff of office or authority; baton.

trun·dle [TRUN-dəl] vt **-dled, -dling.** roll, as a thing on little wheels.

trunk n main stem of tree; person's body without or excluding head and limbs; box for clothes, etc.; elephant's proboscis. ▶ pl man's bathing suit. **trunk line** main line of railroad, telephone, etc.

truss vt fasten up, tie up. ▶ n support; medical device of belt, etc. to hold hernia in place; pack, bundle; cluster of flowers at end of single stalk.

trust n confidence; firm belief; reliance; combination of producers to reduce competition and keep up prices; care, responsibility; property held for another. ▶ vt rely on; believe in; expect, hope; consign for care. **trust·ee'** n one legally holding property on another's behalf; trusty. **trust·ee'ship** n **trust'ful** [-fəl] adj inclined to trust; credulous. **trust'wor·thy** [-wur-thee] adj reliable; dependable; honest; safe. **trust'y** adj **trust·i·er, trust·i·est.** faithful; reliable. ▶ n, pl **trust·ies.** trustworthy convict with special privileges.

truth [trooth] see TRUE.

try [trī] v **tried, try·ing.** ▶ vi attempt, endeavor. ▶ vt attempt; test; make demands upon; investigate (case); examine (person) in court of law; purify or refine (as metals). ▶ n, pl **tries.** attempt, effort. **tried** adj proved; afflicted; **trying** adj upsetting, annoying; difficult.

tryst [trist] n appointment to meet; place appointed.

tsar [zahr] see CZAR.

tset·se [TSET-see] n Afr. bloodsucking fly whose bite transmits various diseases to man and animals.

T-shirt [TEE-shurt] n informal (short-sleeved) undershirt, sweater usu. of cotton.

T square n T-shaped ruler for drawing parallel lines, right angles, etc.

tsu·na·mi [tsuu-NAH-mee] n tidal wave, usu. caused by an earthquake under the sea.

tub n open wooden vessel like bottom half of barrel; small round container; bath; *inf* short, fat person; old, slow ship, etc.

tu·ba [TOO-bə] *n, pl* **-bas.** valved brass wind instrument of low pitch.

tube [toob] *n* long, narrow, hollow cylinder; flexible cylinder with cap to hold liquids, pastes. **tu'bu·lar** [-byə-lər] *adj* like tube.

tu·ber [TOO-bər] *n* fleshy underground stem of some plants, e.g. potato. **tu'ber·ous** [-əs] *adj*

tu·ber·cle [TOO-bər-kəl] *n* any small rounded nodule on skin, etc.; small lesion of tissue, esp. produced by tuberculosis. **tu·ber·cu·lar** *adj* (tuu-BUR-kyə-lər). **tu·ber'cu·lin** *n* extraction from bacillus used to test for and treat tuberculosis. **tu·ber·cu·lo'sis** *n* communicable disease, esp. of lungs.

tuck [tuk] *vt* push, fold into small space; gather, stitch in folds; draw, roll together. ▶ *n* stitched fold.

tuck'er *n* strip of linen or lace formerly worn across bosom by women. ▶ *vt inf* weary; tire.

tu·fa [TOO-fə] *n* porous rock formed as deposit from springs, etc.

tuf·fet [TUF-it] *n obs* small mound or seat.

tuft *n* bunch of feathers, threads, etc.

tug *vt* **tugged, tug·ging.** pull hard or violently; haul; jerk forward. ▶ *n* violent pull; ship used to tow other vessels. **tug of war** contest in which two teams pull against one another on a rope; hard-fought contest for supremacy.

tu·i·tion [too-ISH-ən] *n* teaching, instruction; fee for instruction.

tu·lip [TOO-lip] *n* plant with bright cup-shaped flowers.

tulle [tool] *n* kind of fine thin silk or lace.

tum·ble [TUM-bəl] *v* **-bled, -bling.** (cause to) fall or roll, twist, etc. (esp. in play); rumple, disturb. ▶ *n* fall; somersault. **tum'bler** *n* stemless drinking glass; acrobat; spring catch in lock.

tum'ble-down *adj* dilapidated.

tumble to *inf* realize, understand.

tu·me·fy [TOO-mə-fī] *v* **-fied, -fy·ing.** (cause to) swell. **tu·mes'cence** [too-MES-əns] *n* **tu·mes'cent** [-ənt] *adj* (becoming) swollen.

tu·mor [TOO-mər] *n* abnormal growth in or on body.

tu·mult [TOO-məlt] *n* violent uproar, commotion. **tu·mult'u·ous** [-MUL-choo-əs] *adj*

tu·na [TOO-nə] *n* large marine food and game fish.

tun·dra [TUN-drə] *n* vast treeless zone between ice cap and timber line of N America and Eurasia.

tune [toon] *n* melody; quality of being in pitch; adjustment of musical instrument; concord; frame of mind. ▶ *vt* **tuned, tun·ing.** put in tune; adjust machine to obtain most running efficient; adjust radio circuit. **tune'ful** [-fəl] *adj* **tun'er** [-ər] *n* **tune in** adjust (radio, TV) to receive (a station, program).

tung·sten [TUNG-stən] *n* grayish-white metal, used in lamp filaments, some steels, etc.

tu·nic [TOO-nik] *n* close-fitting jacket forming part of uniform; loose hip-length or knee-length garment.

tun·nel [TUN-l] *n* underground passage, esp. as track for railroad line; burrow of a mole, etc. ▶ *v* **-neled, -nel·ing.** make tunnel (through).

tur·ban [TUR-bən] *n* in certain countries, man's headdress, made by coiling length of cloth around head or a cap; woman's hat like this.

tur'bid *adj* muddy, not clear; disturbed. **tur·bid'i·ty** *n*

tur·bine [TUR-bin] *n* rotary engine driven by steam, gas, water or air playing on blades.

turbo- *comb. form* of, relating to, or driven by a turbine.

tur·bu·lent [TUR-byə-lənt] *adj* in commotion; swirling; riotous. **tur'bu·lence** [-ləns] *n* esp. instability of atmosphere causing gusty air currents, etc.

tu·reen [tuu-REEN] *n* serving dish

for soup.

turf *n, pl* **turfs.** short grass with earth bound to it by matted roots; grass, esp. as lawn; *sl* claimed territory of gang. ▶ *vt* lay with turf.

tur·gid [TUR-jid] *adj* swollen, inflated; bombastic. **tur·gid'i·ty** *n*

tur·key [TUR-kee] *n* large bird reared for food; *sl* loser, naive person; *sl* a flop.

Turk·ish [TUR-kish] *adj* of, pert. to Turkey, the Turks. **Turkish bath** steam bath. **Turkish delight** gelatin candy flavored and coated with powdered sugar.

tur'moil *n* confusion and bustle, commotion.

turn *v* move around, rotate; change, reverse, alter position or direction (of); (oft. with *into*) change in nature, character, etc. ▶ *vt* make, shape on lathe. ▶ *n* act of turning, inclination, etc.; period, spell; turning; short walk; (part of) rotation; performance. **turn'ing** *n* road, path leading off main route. **turn'coat** [-koht] *n* one who forsakes own party or principles. **turn'out** *n* number of people appearing for some purpose, occasion; way in which person is dressed, equipped. **turn'o·ver** *n* total sales made by business over certain period; rate at which employees leave and are replaced; small pastry; *Football, basketball* loss of ball to opponents through mistake. **turn'pike** *n Hist* (gate across) road where toll was paid; highway. **turn'stile** *n* revolving gate for controlling admission of people. **turn'ta·ble** *n* revolving platform. **turn down** refuse. **turn up** appear; be found; increase (flow, volume).

tur'nip *n* plant with globular root used as food.

tur·pen·tine [TUR-pən-tīn] *n* resin obtained from certain trees; oil made from this. **turps** *n* short for turpentine.

tur·pi·tude [TUR-pi-tood] *n* depravity.

tur·quoise [TUR-kwoiz] *n*

bluish-green precious stone; this color.

tur·ret [TUR-it] *n* small tower; revolving armored tower for guns on warship, tank, etc.

tur·tle [TUR-tl] *n* (esp. sea) tortoise.

tusk *n* long pointed side tooth of an elephant, walrus, etc.

tus·sle [TUS-əl] *n, v* **-sled, -sling.** fight, wrestle, struggle.

tu·te·lage [TOOT-l-ij] *n* act, office of tutor or guardian. **tu'te·lar·y** [-ler-ee] *adj*

tu·tor [TOO-tər] *n* one teaching individuals or small groups. ▶ *v* teach thus. **tu·to'ri·al** [-TOR-ee-əl] *n* period of instruction with tutor.

tu·tu [TOO-too] *n, pl* **-tus.** short, stiff skirt worn by ballerinas.

tux·e·do [tuk-SEE-doh] *n, pl* **-dos.** dinner jacket.

TV television. **TV dinner** frozen meal in tray for heating before serving. **TV game** game played on TV screen using special attachment.

twad·dle [TWOD-l] *n* silly talk.

twain [twayn] *n* two. **in twain** asunder.

twang *n* vibrating metallic sound; nasal speech. ▶ *v* (cause to) make such sounds.

tweak [tweek] *vt* pinch and twist or pull. ▶ *n*

tweed *n* rough-surfaced cloth used for clothing. ▶ *pl* suit of tweed.

tween *n* child of about 8 to 12 years of age.

tweet *n, vi* chirp. **tweet'er** *n* small loudspeaker reproducing high-frequency sounds.

tweez·ers [TWEE-zərz] *pl n* small forceps or tongs.

twelve [twelv] *n, adj* cardinal number two more than ten. **twelfth** *adj* the ordinal number. ▶ *n*

twen·ty [TWEN-tee] *n, adj, pl* **-ties.** cardinal number, twice ten. **twen'ti·eth** [-tee-ith] *adj* the ordinal number. ▶ *n*

twenty-four-seven, 24/7 *adj, adv inf* all the time.

twerp [twurp] *n sl* silly person.

twice [twīs] *adv* two times.

twid·dle [TWID-l] *v* **-dled, -dling.**

fiddle; twist.

twig *n* small branch, shoot.

twi·light [TWĪ-līt] *n* soft light after sunset.

twill *n* fabric woven so as to have surface of parallel ridges.

twin *n* one of pair, esp. of two children born together. ▸ *adj* being a twin. ▸ *v* **twinned, twin·ning.** pair, be paired.

twine [twīn] *v* **twined, twin·ing.** twist, coil around. ▸ *n* string, cord.

twinge [twinj] *n* momentary sharp, shooting pain; qualm.

twin·kle [TWING-kəl] *vi* **-kled, -kling.** shine with dancing or quivering light, sparkle. ▸ *n* twinkling; flash; gleam of amusement in eyes. **twinkling** *n* very brief time.

twirl [twurl] *vt* turn or twist round quickly; whirl; twiddle.

twist *v* make, become spiral, by turning with one end fast; distort, change; wind. ▸ *n* thing twisted. **twist'er** *n* person or thing that twists; *inf* tornado, whirlwind. **twist'y** *adj* **twist·i·er, twist·i·est.**

twit *n* *inf* foolish person. ▸ *vt* **twit·ted, twit·ting.** taunt.

twitch [twich] *v* give momentary sharp pull or jerk (to). ▸ *n* such pull or jerk; spasmodic jerk, spasm.

twit·ter [TWIT-ər] *vi* giggle; talk idly; (of birds) utter succession of tremulous sounds. ▸ *n* such succession of notes.

two [too] *n, adj* cardinal number, one more than one. **two'fold** *adj, adv* **two-faced** *adj* double-dealing, deceitful; with two faces.

two-stroke [-strohk] *adj* (of internal-combustion engine) making one explosion to every two strokes of piston.

ty·coon [tī-KOON] *n* powerful, influential businessperson.

tyke [tīk] *n* small, cheeky child; small (mongrel) dog.

tympani see TIMPANI.

type [tīp] *n* class; sort; model; pattern; characteristic build; specimen; block bearing letter used for printing; such pieces collectively. ▸ *vt* **typed, typ·ing.** print with typewriter; typify; classify. **type'script** *n* typewritten document or copy. **type'writ·er** *n* keyed writing machine. **typ'ist** *n* one who operates typewriter.

ty'po *n, pl* **ty·pos.** *inf* error in typing, printing.

ty·phoid [TĪ-foid] *n* acute infectious disease, affecting esp. intestines. ▸ *adj* **ty·phus** [TĪ-fəs] *n* infectious disease.

ty·phoon [tī-FOON] *n* violent tropical storm or cyclone.

typ·i·cal [TIP-i-kəl] *adj* true to type; characteristic. **typ'i·cal·ly** *adv*

typ·i·fy [TIP-i-fī] *vt* **-fied, -fy·ing.** serve as type or model of.

ty·pog·ra·phy [tī-POG-rə-fee] *n* art of printing; style of printing. **ty·po·graph'i·cal** *adj* **ty·pog'ra·pher** [-POG-rə-fər] *n*

ty·rant [TĪ-rənt] *n* oppressive or cruel ruler; one who forces own will on others cruelly and arbitrarily. **ty·ran·ni·cal** [ti-RAN-i-kəl] *adj* despotic; ruthless. **tyr·an·nize** [TIR-ə-nīz] *v* **-nized, -niz·ing.** exert ruthless or tyrannical authority (over). **tyr'an·nous** [-ə-nəs] *adj* **tyr'an·ny** *n* despotism.

ty·ro [tī-roh] *n, pl* **-ros.** novice, beginner.

U u

U *Chem* uranium.

u·biq·ui·tous [yoo-BIK-wi-təs] *adj* everywhere at once; omnipresent. **u·biq'ui·ty** *n*

ud·der [UD-ər] *n* milk-secreting organ of cow, etc.

ug·ly [UG-lee] *adj* **-li·er, -li·est.** unpleasing, repulsive to the sight, hideous; ill-omened; threatening. **ug'li·ness** [-nis] *n*

u·kase [yoo-KAYS] *n* an arbitrary command.

u·ku·le·le [yoo-kə-LAY-lee] *n* small four-stringed guitar, esp. of Hawaii.

ul·cer [UL-sər] *n* open sore on skin, mucous membrane that is slow to heal. **ul'cer·ate** *v* **-at·ed.** make, form ulcer(s). **ul·cer·a'tion** *n*

ul·lage [UL-ij] *n* quantity by which a container falls short of being full.

ul·na [UL-nə] *n, pl* **-nae** [-nee] longer of two bones of forearm.

ul·te·ri·or [ul-TEER-ee-ər] *adj* lying beneath, beyond what is revealed or evident (e.g. motives); situated beyond.

ul·ti·mate [UL-tə-mit] *adj* last; highest; most significant; fundamental. **ul·ti·ma'tum** [-MAY-təm] *n, pl* **-tums** or **-ta** [-tə] final proposition; final terms offered.

ultra- *prefix* beyond, excessively, e.g. *ultramodern.*

ul'tra·high frequency [UL-trə-hī] (band of) radio waves of very short wavelength.

ul·tra·ma·rine [ul-trə-mə-REEN] *n* blue pigment.

ul·tra·son·ic [ul-trə-SON-ik] *adj* of sound waves beyond the range of human ear.

ul·tra·vi·o·let [ul-trə-Vī-ə-lit] *adj* of electromagnetic radiation (e.g. of sun, etc.) beyond limit of visibility at violet end of spectrum.

um·bel [UM-bəl] *n* umbrella-like flower cluster with stalks springing from central point. **um·bel·lif·er·ous** [-LIF-ər-əs] *adj* bearing umbel(s).

um·ber [UM-bər] *n* dark brown pigment.

um·bil·i·cal [um-BIL-i-kəl] *adj* of (region of) navel. **umbilical cord** cordlike structure connecting fetus with placenta of mother; cord joining astronaut to spacecraft, etc.

um·brage [UM-brij] *n* offense, resentment.

um·brel·la [um-BREL-ə] *n* folding circular cover of nylon, etc. on stick, carried in hand to protect against rain, heat of sun; anything shaped or functioning like an umbrella.

um·pire [UM-pīr] *n* person chosen to decide question, or to decide disputes and enforce rules in a game. ▸ *v* **-pired, -pir·ing.** act as umpire (in).

un- *prefix* not, e.g. *unidentified;* denoting reversal of an action, e.g. *untie;* denoting removal from, e.g. *unthrone.*

un·ac·count·a·ble [un-ə-KOWNT-ə-bəl] *adj* that cannot be explained.

u·nan·i·mous [yoo-NAN-ə-məs] *adj* in complete agreement; agreed by all. **u·na·nim·i·ty** [yoo-nə-NIM-ə-tee] *n*

un·as·sum·ing [un-ə-SOO-ming] *adj* not pretentious, modest.

un·a·vail·ing [un-ə-VAY-ling] *adj* useless, futile.

un·a·ware [un-ə-WAIR] *adj* not aware, uninformed. **un·a·wares'** [-WAIRZ] *adv* without previous warning; unexpectedly.

un·bear'a·ble *adj* not able to be endured.

un·bos·om [un-BUUZ-əm] *vt* tell or reveal (one's secrets, etc.).

un·can·ny [un-KAN-ee] *adj* weird, mysterious; extraordinary.

un·cer·tain *adj* not able to be accurately known or predicted; not able to be depended upon; changeable.

un·cle [UNG-kəl] *n* brother of father or mother; husband of aunt.

un·com'fort·a·ble *adj* not physically relaxed; anxious or uneasy.

un·com'mon *adj* not happening or encountered often; in excess of what is normal.

un·com·pli·men·ta·ry [un-kom-plə-MEN-tə-ree] *adj* not complimentary; insulting, derogatory.

un·con·di'tion·al *adj* without conditions or limitations.

un·con·scion·a·ble [un-KON-shə-nə-bəl] *adj* unscrupulous, unprincipled; excessive.

un·con·scious [un-KON-shəs] *adj* insensible; not aware; not knowing; of thoughts, memories, etc. of which one is not normally aware. ▶ *n* these thoughts.

un·con'scious·ness [-nis] *n*

un·couth [un-KOOTH] *adj* clumsy, boorish; without ease or polish.

unc·tion [UNGK-shən] *n* anointing; excessive politeness; soothing words or thoughts. **unc'tu·ous** [-choo-əs] *adj* slippery, greasy; oily in manner, gushing.

un·de·cid'ed *adj* not having made up one's mind; (of an issue or problem) not agreed or decided upon.

un·der [UN-dər] *prep* below, beneath; bound by; included in; less than; subjected to; known by; in the time of. ▶ *adv* in lower place or condition. ▶ *adj* lower.

under- *prefix* beneath, below, lower, e.g. underground.

un·der·car·riage [UN-dər-ka-rij] *n* landing gear of vehicle esp. aircraft.

un·der·charge [un-dər-CHAHRJ] *vt* **-charged, -charg·ing.** charge less than proper amount. ▶ *n* [UN-dər-chahrj] too low a charge.

un·der·class [UN-dər-klas] *n* the most economically disadvantaged people, such as the long-term unemployed.

un·der·coat [UN-dər-koht] *n* coat of paint applied before top coat.

un·der·dog [un-dər-dawg] *n* person or team in a weak or underprivileged position.

un·der·go [un-dər-GOH] *vt* **-went, -gone, -go·ing.** experience, endure, sustain.

un·der·grad·u·ate [un-dər-GRAJ-oo-it] *n* student at college who has not received degree.

un·der·ground [UN-dər-grownd] *adj* under the ground; secret. ▶ *adv* secretly. ▶ *n* secret but organized resistance to government in power; subway.

un·der·hand [UN-dər-hand] *adj* secret, sly; *Sports* (of softball pitch, etc.) with hand swung below shoulder level.

un·der·lie [un-dər-LĪ] *vt* **-lay, -lain, -ly·ing.** be situated under, lie beneath.

un·der·line [UN-dər-līn] *vt* **-lined, -lin·ing.** put line under; emphasize.

un·der·ling [UN-dər-ling] *n* subordinate.

un·der·mine [un-dər-MĪN] *vt* **-mined, -min·ing.** wear away base, support of; weaken insidiously.

un·der·neath [un-dər-NEETH] *adv, prep* under or beneath. ▶ *adj, n* lower (part or surface).

un·der·pass [UN-dər-pas] *n* section of road passing under another road, railroad line, etc.

un·der·stand [un-dər-STAND] *v* **-stood** [-stuud], **-stand·ing.** know and comprehend; realize. ▶ *vt* infer; take for granted.

un·der·stand'a·ble *adj*

un·der·stand'ing *n* intelligence; opinion; agreement. ▶ *adj* sympathetic.

un·der·stud·y [UN-dər-stud-ee] *n, pl* **-stud·ies.** one prepared to take over theatrical part from performer if necessary. ▶ *vt* **-stud·ied, -stud·y·ing.** work as understudy to (performer).

un·der·take [un-dər-TAYK] *vt* **-took** [-tuuk], **-tak·en, -tak·ing.** make oneself responsible for; enter upon; promise. **un'der·tak·er** *n* one who arranges funerals. **un'der·tak·ing** *n* that which is undertaken; project; guarantee.

un·der·tone [UN-dər-tohn] *n* quiet, dropped tone of voice; underlying tone or suggestion.

un·der·tow [UN-dər-toh] *n* backwash of wave; current beneath surface moving in different direction from surface current.

un·der·wear [UN-dər-wair] *n* (also **un'der·clothes**) garments worn next to skin.

un·der·world [UN-dər-wurld] *n* criminals and their associates; *Mythology* abode of the dead.

un·der·write [un-dər-RĪT] *vt* **-wrote, -writ·ten, -writ·ing.** agree to pay; accept liability in insurance policy. **un'der·writ·er** *n* agent for insurance or stock issue.

un·do [un-DOO] *vt* **-did, -done, -do·ing.** untie, unfasten; reverse; cause downfall of. **un·do'ing** *n* **un·done** *adj* [un-DUN] ruined; not performed.

un·du·late [UN-jə-layt] *v* **-lat·ed, -lat·ing.** move up and down like waves. **un·du·la'tion** *n*

un·earth [un-URTH] *vt* dig up; discover.

un·eas·y [un-EE-zee] *adj* **-eas·i·er, -eas·i·est.** anxious; uncomfortable. **un·eas'i·ness** [-nis] *n*

un·em·ployed [un-im-PLOID] *adj* having no paid employment, out of work. **un·em·ploy'ment** [-mənt] *n*

un·e·quiv·o·cal *adj* completely clear in meaning.

un·err·ing [un-ER-ing] *adj* not missing the mark; consistently accurate.

un·fail'ing *adj* continuous or reliable.

un·fair' *adj* not right, fair, or just.

un·fit' *adj* unqualified or unsuitable; in poor physical condition.

un·fold' *v* open or spread out from a folded state; reveal or be revealed.

un·for·get'ta·ble *adj* impossible to forget, memorable.

un·for'tu·nate *adj* unlucky, unsuccessful, or unhappy; regrettable or unsuitable. ▶ *n* unlucky person.

un·gain·ly [un-GAYN-lee] *adj* **-li·er, -li·est.** awkward, clumsy. **un·gain'li·ness** [-nis] *n*

un·guent [UNG-gwənt] *n* ointment.

un·hap'py *adj* sad or depressed; unfortunate or wretched.

un·health'y *adj* likely to cause poor health; not fit or well; morbid, unnatural.

uni- *comb. form* one, e.g. unicorn; uniform.

u·ni·corn [YOO-ni-korn] *n* mythical horselike animal with single long horn.

u·ni·form [YOO-ni-form] *n* identifying clothes worn by members of same group e.g. soldiers, nurses, etc. ▶ *adj* not changing, unvarying; regular, consistent; conforming to same standard or rule. **u·ni·form'i·ty** *n* sameness. **u·ni·form'ly** *adv*

u·ni·fy [YOO-nə-fī] *v* **-fied, -fy·ing.** make or become one. **u·ni·fi·ca'tion** [-KAY-shən] *n*

u·ni·lat·er·al [yoo-nə-LAT-ər-əl] *adj* one-sided; (of contract) binding one party only.

un·ion [YOON-yən] *n* joining into one; state of being joined; result of being joined; federation, combination of states, etc.; labor union, trade union. **un'ion·ize** *v* **-ized, -iz·ing.** organize (workers) into labor union.

u·nique [yoo-NEEK] *adj* being only one of its kind; unparalleled.

u·ni·son [YOO-nə-sən] *n Mus* singing, etc. of same note as others; agreement, harmony, concord.

u·nit [YOO-nit] *n* single thing or person; standard quantity; group of people or things with one purpose.

u·nite [yoo-NĪT] *v* **u·nit·ed, u·nit·ing.** ▶ *vt* join into one, connect; associate; cause to adhere. ▶ *vi* become one; combine.

u·ni·ty [-nə-tee] *n* state of being one; harmony; agreement, uniformity; combination of separate parts into connected whole; *Mathematics* the number one.

u·ni·verse [YOO-nə-vurs] *n* all existing things considered as constituting systematic whole; the world. **u·ni·ver·sal** [-səl] *adj* relating to all things or all people; applying to all members of a community. **u·ni·ver·sal'i·ty** [-SAL-ə-tee] *n*

u·ni·ver·si·ty [yoo-nə-VUR-si-tee] *n, pl* **-ties.** educational institution for research, study, examination and award of degrees in various branches of learning.

un·kempt' *adj* of rough or uncared-for appearance.

un·less' *conj* if not, except.

un·men'tion·a·ble *adj* unsuitable as a topic of conversation.

un·moved' *adj* not affected by emotion, indifferent.

un·or'tho·dox *adj* (of ideas, methods, etc.) unconventional and not generally accepted; (of a person) having unusual opinions or methods.

un·pleas'ant *adj* not pleasant or agreeable.

un·rav·el [un-RAV-əl] *vt* **-eled, -el·ing.** undo, untangle.

un·re·mit·ting [un-ri-MIT-ing] *adj* never slackening or stopping.

un·re·quit'ed *adj* not returned, e.g. *unrequited love.*

un·roll' *v* open out or unwind (something rolled or coiled) or (of something rolled or coiled) become opened out or unwound.

un·ru·ly [un-ROO-lee] *adj* **-li·er, -li·est.** badly behaved, ungovernable, disorderly.

un·sa·vor·y [un-SAY-və-ree] *adj* distasteful, disagreeable.

un·sight·ly [un-SIT-lee] *adj* ugly.

un·suit'a·ble *adj* not right or appropriate for a particular purpose.

un·ten·a·ble [un-TEN-ə-bəl] *adj* (of theories, etc.) incapable of being maintained, defended.

un·think·a·ble [un-THING-kə-bəl] *adj* out of the question; inconceivable; unreasonable.

un·til' *conj* up to the time that. ▶ *prep* in or throughout the period

before.

un·to [UN-too] *prep* to.

un·touched [un-TUCHT] *adj* not touched; not harmed.

un·touch'a·ble *adj* not able to be touched. ▶ *n* esp. formerly, non-caste Hindu, forbidden to be touched by one of caste.

un·to·ward [un-TORD] *adj* awkward, inconvenient.

un·tram·meled [un-TRAM-əld] *adj* not confined, not constrained.

un·u'su·al *adj* uncommon or extraordinary.

un·wield·y [un-WEEL-dee] *adj* **-wield·i·er, -wield·i·est.** awkward, big, heavy to handle; clumsy.

un·wit'ting *adj* not knowing; not intentional.

un·wrap' *v* remove the wrapping from (something).

up *prep* from lower to higher position; along. ▶ *adv* in or to higher position, source, activity, etc.; indicating completion. **up'ward** *adj, adv* **up'wards** *adv* up against; confronted with.

up- *comb. form* up, upper, upwards, e.g. *uproot; upgrade.*

up·braid [up-BRAYD] *vt* scold, reproach.

up'bring·ing *n* rearing and education of children.

up·date [up-DAYT] *vt* **-dat·ed, -dat·ing.** bring up to date. ▶ *n*

up·front [up-frunt] *adj inf* open, frank. ▶ *adj, adv inf* (of money) paid out at beginning of business arrangement.

up·grade [up-GRAYD] *vt* **-grad·ed, -grad·ing.** promote to higher position; improve.

up·heav·al [up-HEE-vəl] *n* sudden or violent disturbance.

up·hold [up-HOHLD] *vt* **-held, -hold·ing.** maintain, support, etc.

up·hol·ster [up-HOHL-stər] *vt* fit springs, padding and coverings on chairs, etc. **up·hol'ster·er** *n* one who does this work. **up·hol'ster·y** *n*

up'keep *n* act, process or cost of keeping something in good repair.

up·lift' *vt* raise aloft. ▶ *n* [UP-lift] a

up·load *vt Computers* transfer data from a single computer to a server or host.

up·on [ə-PON] *prep* on.

up·per [UP-ər] *adj* higher, situated above; comp. of UP. ▶ *n* upper part of boot or shoe. **up'per·cut** *n* short-arm upward blow. **up'per·most** [-mohst] *adj* sup. of UP.

up·right [UP-rīt] *adj* erect; honest, just. ▶ *adv* vertically. ▶ *n* thing standing upright, e.g. post in framework.

up·ris·ing [UP-rī-zing] *n* rebellion, revolt.

up·roar [UP-ror] *n* tumult, disturbance. **up·roar'i·ous** [-ee-əs] *adj* rowdy.

up·set' *vt* **-set, -set·ting.** overturn; distress; disrupt; make ill. ▶ *n* [UP-set] unexpected defeat; confusion; trouble; overturning.

up'shot *n* outcome, end.

up·stage [up-stayj] *adj* of back of stage. ▶ *vt* **-staged, -stag·ing.** draw attention away from another to oneself.

up·start [UP-stahrt] *n* one suddenly raised to wealth, power, etc.

up·tight [up-tīt] *adj sl* displaying tense nervousness, irritability; repressed.

u·ra·ni·um [yuu-RAY-nee-əm] *n* white radioactive metallic element, used as chief source of nuclear energy.

U·ra·nus [YUUR-ə-nəs] *n* Greek god, personification of sky; seventh planet from the sun.

ur·ban [UR-bən] *adj* relating to town or city; describing modern pop music of African-American origin, such as hip-hop. **ur·ban·ize** *vt* **-ized, -iz·ing.** change countryside to residential or industrial area.

ur·bane [ur-BAIN] *adj* elegant, sophisticated. **ur·ban'i·ty** [-BAN-i-tee] *n*

ur'chin *n* mischievous, unkempt child.

u·re·a [yuu-REE-ə] *n* substance occurring in urine.

u·re·thra [yuu-REE-thrə] *n* canal conveying urine from bladder out of body.

urge [urj] *vt* **urged, urg·ing.** exhort earnestly; entreat; drive on. ▶ *n* strong desire. **ur'gen·cy** [-jən-see] *n, pl* **-cies. ur'gent** [-jənt] *adj* pressing; needing attention at once. **ur'gent·ly** *adv*

u·rine [YUUR-in] *n* fluid excreted by kidneys to bladder and passed as waste from body. **u'ric** *adj* **u·ri·nal** [YUUR-ə-nl] *n* (place with) sanitary fitting used by men for urination. **ur·i·nar·y** *adj* **u'ri·nate** *vi* **-nat·ed, -nat·ing.** discharge urine.

URL *Computers* uniform resource locator: standardized address of a location on the Internet.

urn *n* vessel like vase, esp. for ashes of the dead; large container with tap for making and dispensing tea, coffee, etc.

ur·sine [UR-sin] *adj* of, like a bear.

us *pron, pl* the objective case of the pronoun WE.

use [yooz] *vt* **used, us·ing.** employ, avail oneself of; exercise; exploit; consume. ▶ *n* [yoos] employment, application to a purpose; need to employ; serviceableness; profit; habit. **us·a·ble** [YOO-zə-bəl] *adj* fit for use. **us·age** [YOOS-ij] *n* act of using; custom; customary way of using. **used** [yoozd] *adj* secondhand, not new. **use·ful** [YOOS-fəl] *adj* of use; helpful; serviceable. **use'ful·ness** [-nis] *n* **use'less·ness** [-lis-nis] *n* **used to** [yoost] *adj* accustomed to. ▶ *vt* did so formerly. **us·er friendly** [YOO-zər] (of computer, etc.) easily understood and operated.

ush·er [USH-ər] *n* doorkeeper, one showing people to seats, etc. ▶ *vt* introduce, announce; inaugurate.

u·su·al [YOO-zhoo-əl] *adj* habitual, ordinary. **u'su·al·ly** *adv* as a rule; generally, commonly.

u·surp [yoo-SURP] *vt* seize wrongfully. **u·sur·pa·tion** [yoo-sər-PAY-shən] *n* violent or

unlawful seizing of power.
u·surp′er n
u·su·ry [YOO-zhə-ree] n lending of
money at excessive interest; such
interest. **u′su·rer** n money lender.
u·su′ri·ous [-ZHUUR-ee-əs] adj
u·ten·sil [yoo-TEN-səl] n vessel,
implement, esp. in domestic use.
u·ter·us [YOO-tər-əs] n, pl **-us·es.**
womb. **u·ter·ine** [-tər-in] adj
u·til·i·ty [yoo-TIL-i-tee] n, pl **-ties.**
usefulness; benefit; useful thing; a
public service, such as electricity.
▶ adj made for practical purposes.
u·til·i·tar′i·an [-TAIR-ee-ən] adj
useful rather than beautiful.
u·til·i·tar′i·an·ism n doctrine that
morality of actions is to be tested
by their utility, esp. that the
greatest good of the greatest
number should be the sole end of
public action. **u·ti·li·za′tion**
[-ZAY-shən] n **u′ti·lize** vt **-lized,**
-liz·ing. make use of.
ut·most [UT-mohst] adj to the

highest degree; extreme, furthest.
▶ n greatest possible amount.
u·to·pi·a [yoo-TOH-pee-ə] n
imaginary state with perfect
political and social conditions, or
constitution. **u·to′pi·an** [-pee-ən]
adj ideally perfect but
impracticable.
ut·ter¹ [UT-ər] vt express, emit
audibly, say; put in circulation
(forged bills, counterfeit coin).
ut′ter·ance [-əns] n act of
speaking; expression in words;
spoken words.
utter² adj complete, total, absolute.
ut′ter·ly adv
ut·ter·most [UT-ər-mohst] adj
farthest out; utmost. ▶ n highest
degree.
u·vu·la [YOO-vyə-lə] n, pl **-las** or
-lae [-lee] pendent fleshy part of
soft palate. **u′vu·lar** [-lər] adj
ux·o·ri·ous [uk-SOR-ee-əs] adj
excessively fond of one's wife.

V v

V *Chem* vanadium.

va·cant [VAY-kənt] *adj* without thought, empty; unoccupied. **va'can·cy** [-kən-see] *n, pl* **-cies.** state of being unoccupied; unfilled position, accommodation, etc.

va·cate [VAY-kayt] *vt* **-cat·ed, -cat·ing.** quit, leave empty. **va·ca'tion** [-KAY-shən] *n* act of vacating; holidays; time when schools and courts, etc. are closed.

vac·ci·nate [VAK-sə-nayt] *vt* **-nat·ed, -nat·ing.** inoculate with vaccine as protection against a specific disease. **vac·ci·na'tion** *n* **vac·cine** [vak-SEEN] *n* any substance used for inoculation against disease.

vac·il·late [VAS-ə-layt] *vi* **-lat·ed, -lat·ing.** fluctuate in opinion; waver; move to and fro. **vac·il·la'tion** *n* indecision; wavering; unsteadiness.

vac·u·um [VAK-yoom] *n, pl* **-u·ums.** place, region containing no matter and from which all or most air, gas has been removed. ▶ *v* clean with vacuum cleaner. **va·cu·i·ty** [va-KYOO-i-tee] *n* **vac·u·ous** [VA-kyoo-əs] *adj* vacant; expressionless; unintelligent. **vacuum cleaner** apparatus for removing dust by suction. **vac'uum-packed** *adj* contained in packaging from which air has been removed.

vag·a·bond [VAG-ə-bond] *n* person with no fixed home; wandering beggar or thief. ▶ *adj* like a vagabond.

va·gar·y [VAY-gə-ree] *n, pl* **-gar·ies.** something unusual, erratic; whim.

va·gi·na [və-JĪ-nə] *n, pl* **-nas.** passage from womb to exterior. **vag·i·nal** [VAJ-ə-nl] *adj*

va·grant [VAY-grənt] *n* vagabond, tramp. ▶ *adj* wandering, esp. without purpose. **va'gran·cy** *n, pl* **-cies.**

vague [vayg] *adj* **va·guer** [-gər],

va·guest [-gəst] indefinite or uncertain; indistinct; not clearly expressed; absent-minded.

vain [vayn] *adj* **-er, -est.** conceited; worthless, useless; unavailing; foolish. **vain'ly** *adv*

vain·glo·ry [VAYN-glor-ee] *n* boastfulness, vanity. **vain·glo'ri·ous** *adj*

val·ance [VAL-əns] *n* short curtain around base of bed, etc.

vale [vayl] *n* Poet valley.

val·e·dic·tion [val-i-DIK-shən] *n* farewell. **val·e·dic·to'ri·an** [-TOR-ee-ən] *n* **val·e·dic'to·ry** [-DIK-tə-ree] *n* farewell address. ▶ *adj*

va·lence [VAY-ləns], **va·len·cy** [-lən-see] *n* Chem combining power of element or atom.

val·en·tine [VAL-ən-tīn] *n* (one receiving) card, gift, expressing affection, on Saint Valentine's Day, Feb. 14th.

val·et [va-LAY] *n* gentleman's personal servant.

val·e·tu·di·nar·y [val-i-TOOD-n-er-ee] *adj* sickly; infirm. **val·e·tu·di·nar'i·an** [-NAIR-ee-ən] *n* person obliged or disposed to live the life of an invalid.

Val·hal·la [val-HAL-ə] *n* Norse mythology place of immortality for heroes slain in battle.

val·iant [VAL-yənt] *adj* brave, courageous.

val'id *adj* sound; capable of being justified; of binding force in law. **va·lid·i·ty** [və-LID-i-tee] *n* soundness; power to convince; legal force. **val'i·date** *vt* **-dat·ed, -dat·ing.** make valid.

va·lise [və-LEES] *n* traveling bag.

Val·kyr·ie [val-KEER-ee or VAL-ker-ee] *n* one of the Norse war goddesses who chose the slain and guided them to Valhalla.

val·ley [VAL-ee] *n, pl* **-leys.** low area between hills; river basin.

val·or [VAL-ər] n bravery.
val'or·ous [-əs] adj

val·ue [VAL-yoo] n worth; utility; equivalent; importance. ▶ pl principles, standards. ▶ vt **-ued, -u·ing.** estimate value of; hold in respect; prize. **val'u·a·ble** [-ə-bəl] adj precious; worthy; capable of being valued. ▶ n (usu pl) valuable thing. **val·u·a'tion** [-AY-shən] n estimated worth. **val'ue·less** [-lis] adj worthless. **value added tax** tax on difference between cost of basic materials and cost of article made from them.

valve [valv] n device to control passage of fluid, etc. through pipe; Anatomy part of body allowing one-way passage of fluids; any of separable parts of shell of mollusk; Mus device on brass instrument for lengthening tube.

va·moose [va-MOOS] v **-moosed, -moos·ing.** sl depart quickly.

vamp¹ n woman who deliberately allures men. ▶ v exploit (man) as vamp.

vamp² n something patched up; front part of shoe upper. ▶ vt patch up, rework; Jazz improvise.

vam·pire [VAM-pīr] n (in folklore) corpse that rises from dead to drink blood of the living. **vampire bat** one that sucks blood of animals.

van¹ n large covered truck, esp. for furniture; smaller such vehicle for camping; etc.

van² n short for VANGUARD.

va·na·di·um [və-NAY-dee-əm] n metallic element used in manufacture of hard steel.

van·dal [VAN-dl] n one who wantonly and deliberately damages or destroys. **van'dal·ism** n **van'dal·ize** vt **-ized, -iz·ing.**

vane [vayn] n weather vane; blade of propeller; fin on bomb, etc.; sight on quadrant.

van·guard [VAN-gahrd] n leading, foremost group, position, etc.

va·nil·la [və-NIL-ə] n tropical climbing orchid; its seed(pod); essence of this for flavoring.

van'ish vi disappear; fade away.

van·i·ty [VAN-i-tee] n, pl **-ties.** excessive pride or conceit; ostentation.

van·quish [VANG-kwish] vt subdue in battle; conquer, overcome.

vap'id adj flat, dull, insipid. **va·pid·i·ty** [və-PID-i-tee] n

va·por [VAY-pər] n gaseous form of a substance more familiar as liquid or solid; steam, mist; invisible moisture in air. **va'por·ize** [-pə-rīz] v **-ized, -iz·ing.** convert into, pass off in, vapor.

var·i·a·ble SEE VARY.

var·i·cose [VAR-i-kohs] adj of vein, swollen, twisted.

var·i·e·gate [VA-ree-i-gayt] vt **-gat·ed, -gat·ing.** diversify by patches of different colors. **var'i·e·gat·ed** adj streaked, spotted, dappled.

va·ri·e·ty [və-RĪ-i-tee] n, pl **-ties.** state of being varied or various; diversity; varied assortment; sort or kind.

var·i·o·rum [va-ree-OR-əm] adj, n (edition) with notes by various commentators.

var·i·ous [VA-ree-əs] adj manifold, diverse, of several kinds.

var·nish [VAHR-nish] n resinous solution put on a surface to make it hard and shiny. ▶ vt apply varnish to.

var·y [VAIR-ee] v **var·ied, var·y·ing.** (cause to) change, diversify, differ, deviate. **var·i·a·bil·i·ty** n **var'i·a·ble** adj changeable; unsteady or fickle. ▶ n something subject to variation. **var'i·ance** [-əns] n state of discord, discrepancy. **var'i·ant** [-ənt] adj different. ▶ n difference in form; alternative form or reading. **var·i·a'tion** [-AY-shən] n alteration; extent to which thing varies; modification. **var'ied** adj diverse; modified; variegated.

vas n, pl **va·sa** [VA-sə] vessel, tube carrying bodily fluid.

vas·cu·lar [VAS-kyə-lər] adj of, with vessels for conveying sap, blood, etc.

vase [vayz] n vessel, jar as ornament

or for holding flowers.

vas·ec·to·my [va-SEK-tə-mee] n, pl **-mies.** contraceptive measure of surgical removal of part of vas bearing sperm from testicle.

vas·sal [VAS-əl] n holder of land by feudal tenure; dependent.

vast adj **-er, -est.** very large. **vast'ly** [-lee] adv **vast'ness** [-nis] n

vat n large tub, tank.

Vat·i·can [VAT-i-kən] n Pope's palace; papal authority.

vaude·ville [VAWD-vil] n theatrical entertainment with songs, juggling acts, dance, etc.

vault¹ [vawlt] n arched roof; arched apartment; cellar; burial chamber; place for storing valuables. ▶ vt build with arched roof.

vault² v spring, jump over with the hands resting on something. ▶ n such jump. **vaulting horse** padded apparatus for support of hands in gymnastics.

vaunt [vawnt] v, n boast. **vaunt'ed** [-id] adj excessively praised.

VDU visual display unit, monitor.

veal [veel] n calf flesh as food.

vec·tor [VEK-tər] n quantity (e.g. force) having both magnitude and direction; disease-carrying organism, esp. insect; compass direction; course.

veer vi change direction; change one's mind.

veg·e·ta·ble [VEJ-tə-bəl] n plant, esp. edible one; inf person who has lost use of mental and physical faculties; dull person. ▶ adj of, from, concerned with plants.

veg·e·tar·i·an [vej-i-TAIR-ee-ən] n one who does not eat meat. ▶ adj **veg·e·tar'i·an·ism** n

veg·e·tate [VEJ-i-tayt] vi **-tat·ed, -tat·ing.** (of plants) grow, develop; (of person) live dull, unproductive life. **veg·e·ta'tion** n plants collectively; plants growing in a place; process of plant growth. **veg'e·ta·tive** [-tay-tiv] adj

ve·he·ment [VEE-ə-mənt] adj marked by intensity of feeling; vigorous; forcible. **ve'he·mence** [-məns] n

ve·hi·cle [VEE-i-kəl] n means of conveying; means of expression; medium. **ve·hic'u·lar** [-HIK-yə-lər] adj

veil [vayl] n light material to cover face or head; mask, cover. ▶ vt cover with, as with, veil. **veiled** adj disguised. **take the veil** become a nun.

vein [vayn] n tube in body taking blood to heart; rib of leaf or insect's wing; fissure in rock filled with ore; streak; distinctive trait, strain, etc.; mood. ▶ vt mark with streaks. **ve·nous** [VEE-nəs] adj of veins.

veld, veldt [velt] n elevated grassland in S Afr.

vel·lum [VEL-əm] n parchment of calf skin used for manuscripts or bindings; paper resembling this.

ve·loc·i·ty [və-LOS-i-tee] n, pl **-ties.** rate of motion in given direction, esp. of inanimate things; speed.

ve·lour [və-LUUR] n fabric with velvety finish.

ve·lum [VEE-ləm] n, pl **-la** [-lə] Zoology membranous covering or organ; soft palate.

vel·vet [VEL-vit] n silk or cotton fabric with thick, short pile. **vel·vet·een'** n cotton fabric resembling velvet. **vel'vet·y** adj of, like velvet; soft and smooth.

ve·nal [VEEN-l] adj guilty of taking, prepared to take, bribes; corrupt. **ve·nal'i·ty** n

vend vt sell. **ven·dor** [VEN-dər] n **vending machine** one that automatically dispenses goods when money is inserted.

ven·det·ta [ven-DET-ə] n bitter, prolonged feud.

ve·neer [və-NEER] n thin layer of fine wood; superficial appearance. ▶ vt cover with veneer.

ven·er·a·ble [VEN-ər-ə-bəl] adj worthy of reverence. **ven·er·ate** [VEN-ə-rayt] vt **-at·ed, -at·ing.** look up to, respect, revere. **ven·er·a'tion** n

ve·ne·re·al [və-NEER-ee-əl] adj (of disease) transmitted by sexual intercourse; infected with venereal disease; of, relating to genitals or sexual intercourse.

ven·er·y [VEN-ə-ree] n obs pursuit of sexual gratification.

Ve·ne·tian [və-NEE-shən] adj of Venice, port in NE Italy. ▶ n native or inhabitant of Venice. **Venetian blind** window blind made of thin horizontal slats that turn to let in more or less light.

ven·geance [VEN-jəns] n revenge; retribution for wrong done. **venge'ful** [-fəl] adj

ve·ni·al [VEE-nee-əl] adj pardonable.

ven·i·son [VEN-ə-sən] n flesh of deer as food.

ven·om [VEN-əm] n poison; spite. **ven'om·ous** [-əs] adj poisonous.

venous [VEE-nəs] see VEIN.

vent[1] n small hole or outlet. ▶ vt give outlet to; utter; pour forth.

vent[2] n vertical slit in garment esp. at back of jacket.

ven·ti·late [VEN-tl-ayt] vt **-lat·ed, -lat·ing.** supply with fresh air; bring into discussion. **ven'ti·la·tor** n

ven·tral [VEN-trəl] adj abdominal.

ven·tri·cle [VEN-tri-kəl] n cavity, hollow in body, esp. in heart or brain. **ven·tric'u·lar** [-TRIK-yə-lər] adj

ven·tril·o·quist [ven-TRIL-ə-kwist] n one who can so speak that the sounds seem to come from some other person or place. **ven·tril'o·quism** n

ven·ture [VEN-chər] v **-tured, -tur·ing.** ▶ vt expose to hazard; risk. ▶ vi dare; have courage to do something or go somewhere. ▶ n risky undertaking; speculative commercial undertaking. **ven'ture·some** [-səm] adj

ven·ue [VEN-yoo] n Law district in which case is tried; meeting place; location.

Ve·nus [VEE-nəs] n Roman goddess of love; planet between Earth and Mercury. **Venus's flytrap** insect-eating plant.

ve·ra·cious [və-RAY-shəs] adj truthful; true. **ve·rac'i·ty** [-RAS-i-tee] n

ve·ran·da, ve·ran·dah [və-RAN-də] n open or partly

enclosed porch on outside of house.

verb [vurb] n part of speech used to express action or being. **ver·bal** [VUR-bəl] adj of, by, or relating to words spoken rather than written; of, like a verb. **ver'bal·ize** v **-ized, -iz·ing.** put into words, speak. **ver'bal·ly** adv **ver·ba·tim** [vər-BAY-tim] adv, adj word for word, literal.

ver·bi·age [VUR-bee-ij] n excess of words. **ver·bose** [vər-BOHS] adj wordy, long-winded. **ver·bos'i·ty** [-BOS-i-tee] n

ver·dant [VUR-dnt] adj green and fresh. **ver·dure** [-jər] n greenery; freshness.

ver·dict [VUR-dikt] n decision of a jury; opinion reached after examination of facts.

ver·di·gris [VUR-di-grees] n green film on copper.

verdure [VUR-jər] see VERDANT.

verge [vurj] n edge; brink. ▶ vi **verged, verg·ing.** come close to; be on the border of.

ver·i·fy [VER-i-fī] vt **-fied, -fy·ing.** prove, confirm truth of; test accuracy of. **ver'i·fi·a·ble** adj

ver·i·si·mil·i·tude [ver-ə-si-MIL-i-tood] n appearance of truth; likelihood.

ver·i·ta·ble [VER-i-tə-bəl] adj actual, true, genuine. **ver'i·ta·bly** adv

ver·i·ty [VER-i-tee] n, pl **-ties.** truth; reality; true assertion.

ver·mi·cide [VUR-mə-sīd] n substance to destroy worms. **ver'mi·form** adj shaped like a worm, e.g. vermiform appendix.

ver·mil·ion [vər-MIL-yən] adj, n (of) bright red color or pigment.

ver·min [VUR-min] pl n injurious animals, parasites, etc.

ver·mouth [vər-MOOTH] n wine flavored with aromatic herbs, etc.

ver·nac·u·lar [vər-NAK-yə-lər] n commonly spoken language or dialect of particular country or place. ▶ adj of vernacular; native.

ver·nal [VUR-nl] adj of spring.

ver·ni·er [VUR-nee-ər] n sliding scale for obtaining fractional parts of subdivision of graduated scale.

ver·sa·tile [VUR-sə-tl] *adj* capable of or adapted to many different uses, skills, etc.; liable to change. **ver·sa·til'i·ty** *n*

verse [vurs] *n* stanza or short subdivision of poem or the Bible; poetry; line of poetry. **ver·si·fy** [VUR-sə-fī] *v* **-fied, -fy·ing.** turn into verse. **ver·si·fi·ca'tion** *n* **versed in** skilled.

ver·sion [VUR-zhən] *n* description from certain point of view; translation; adaptation.

ver·so [VUR-soh] *n* back of sheet of printed paper, left-hand page.

ver·sus [VUR-səs] *prep* against.

ver·te·bra [VUR-tə-brə] *n, pl* **-brae** [-bree] single section of backbone. **ver'te·bral** [-brəl] *adj* of the spine. **ver'te·brate** [-brit] *n* animal with backbone. ▶ *adj*

ver·tex [VUR-teks] *n, pl* **-ti·ces** [-tə-seez] summit.

ver·ti·cal [VUR-ti-kəl] *adj* at right angles to the horizon; upright; overhead.

ver·ti·go [VUR-ti-goh] *n; pl* **-goes.** giddiness. **ver·tig·i·nous** [vər-TIJ-ə-nəs] *adj* dizzy.

verve [vurv] *n* enthusiasm; spirit; energy, vigor.

ver·y [VER-ee] *adj* exact, ideal; same; complete; actual. ▶ *adv* extremely, to great extent.

ves·i·cle [VES-i-kəl] *n* small blister, bubble, or cavity. **ve·sic·u·lar** [və-SIK-yə-lər] *adj*

ves·pers [VES-pərz] *pl n* evening church service; evensong.

ves·sel [VES-əl] *n* any object used as a container, esp. for liquids; ship, large boat; tubular structure conveying liquids (e.g. blood) in body.

vest *n* sleeveless garment worn under jacket or coat. ▶ *vt* place; bestow; confer; clothe. **vest'ment** [-mənt] *n* robe or official garment. **vested interest** strong personal interest in particular state of affairs.

ves·tal [VES-tl] *adj* pure, chaste.

ves·ti·bule [VES-tə-byool] *n* entrance hall, lobby.

ves·tige [VES-tij] *n* small trace, amount. **ves·tig'i·al** [-TIJ-ee-əl] *adj*

ves·try [VES-tree] *n, pl* **-tries.** room in church for keeping vestments, holding meetings, etc.

vet *n* short for VETERAN; short for VETERINARIAN. ▶ *vt* **vet·ted, vet·ting.** examine; check.

vet·er·an [VET-ər-ən] *n* one who has served a long time, esp. in fighting services. ▶ *adj* long-serving.

vet·er·i·nar·i·an [vet-ər-ə-NAIR-ee-ən] *n* one qualified to treat animal ailments. **vet'er·i·nar·y** [-ner-ee] *adj* of, concerning the health of animals. ▶ *n* veterinarian.

ve·to [VEE-toh] *n, pl* **-toes.** power of rejecting piece of legislation, or preventing it from coming into effect; any prohibition. ▶ *vt* **-toed, -to·ing.** enforce veto against; forbid with authority.

vex [veks] *vt* annoy; distress. **vex·a'tion** *n* cause of irritation; state of distress. **vex·a'tious** *adj* **vexed** *adj* cross; annoyed; much discussed.

vi·a [VĪ-ə] *adv* by way of.

vi·a·ble [VĪ-ə-bəl] *adj* practicable; able to live and grow independently. **vi·a·bil'i·ty** *n*

vi·a·duct [VĪ-ə-dukt] *n* bridge over valley for a road or railroad.

Vi·ag·ra [vī-AG-rə] *n* ® drug used to treat impotence in men.

vi·al [VĪ-əl] *n* small bottle for medicine, etc.

vi·ands [VĪ-əndz] *pl n* food esp. delicacies.

vi·bra·harp [VĪ-brə-hahrp] *n* musical instrument like xylophone, but with electronic resonators, that produces a gentle vibrato (also **vi'bra·phone**).

vi·brate [VĪ-brayt] *v* **-brat·ed, -brat·ing.** (cause to) move to and fro rapidly and continuously; give off (light or sound) by vibration. ▶ *vi* oscillate; quiver. **vibes** *pl n inf* emotional reactions between people; atmosphere of a place. **vi'brant** [-brənt] *adj* throbbing; vibrating; appearing vigorous,

lively. **vi·bra′tion** n a vibrating.
vi·bra·to [vi-BRAH-toh] n, pl **-os.**
vibrating effect in music.
vic·ar [VIK-ər] n member of clergy
in charge of parish. **vic′ar·age** [-ij]
n vicar's house. **vi·car·i·al**
[vī-KAIR-ee-əl] adj of vicar.
vi·car·i·ous [vī-KAIR-ee-əs] adj
obtained, enjoyed or undergone
through sympathetic experience of
another's experiences; suffered,
done, etc. as substitute for another.
vice [vīs] n evil or immoral habit or
practice; criminal immorality esp.
prostitution; fault, imperfection.
vice- comb. form in place of, second
to, e.g. vice-chairman; viceroy.
vice·roy [VĪS-roi] n ruler acting for
king in province or dependency.
vice·re·gal adj
vi·ce ver·sa [VĪ-sə VUR-sə] Lat
conversely, the other way round.
vi·cin·i·ty [vi-SIN-i-tee] n, pl **-ties.**
neighborhood.
vi·cious [VISH-əs] adj wicked, cruel;
ferocious, dangerous; leading to
vice.
vi·cis·si·tude [vi-SIS-i-tood] n
change of fortune. ▶ pl ups and
downs of fortune.
vic·tim [VIK-tim] n person or thing
killed, injured, etc. as result of
another's deed, or accident,
circumstances, etc.; person
cheated; sacrifice. **vic·tim·i·za′tion**
[-ZAY-shən] n **vic′ti·mize** vt
-mized, -miz·ing. punish unfairly;
make victim of.
vic·tor [VIK-tər] n conqueror;
winner. **vic·to·ri·ous**
[vik-TOR-ee-əs] adj winning;
triumphant. **vic′to·ry** [-tə-ree] n, pl
-ries. winning of battle, etc.
vict·ual [VIT-l] n (usu in pl) food. ▶ v
-ualed, -ual·ing. supply with or
obtain food.
vi·cu·na [vī-KOO-nə] n S Amer.
animal like llama; fine, light cloth
made from its wool.
vi·de [VĪ-dee] Lat see. **vide in·fra**
[IN-frə] see below. **vide su·pra**
[SOO-prə] see above.
vi·de·li·cet [vi-DEL-ə-sit] Lat namely.
vid·e·o [VID-ee-oh] adj relating to

or used in transmission or
production of TV image. ▶ n
apparatus for recording TV
programs; film, etc. on
videocassette for viewing on this
apparatus. **vid′e·o·cas·sette**
cassette containing video tape.
videocassette recorder tape
recorder for vision and sound
signals, used for recording and
playing back TV programs and
films on cassette. **video game** any
of various games played on video
screen using electronic control.
videotape magnetic tape on which
to record TV program. **videotape
recorder** tape recorder for signals
for TV broadcast. **vid′e·o·tex** n
means of providing written or
graphical representation of
computerized information on TV
screen for information retrieval,
shopping at home, etc.
vie [vī] vi **vied, vy·ing.** (foll. by with
or for) contend, compete against or
for someone, something.
view [vyoo] n survey by eyes or
mind; range of vision; picture;
scene; opinion; purpose. ▶ vt look
at; survey; consider. **view′er** n one
who views; one who watches TV;
optical device to assist viewing of
photographic slides. **view′find·er**
n device on camera enabling user
to see what will be included in
photograph. **view′point** n way of
regarding a subject; position
commanding view of landscape.
vig·il [VIJ-əl] n a keeping awake,
watch; eve of church festival.
vig′i·lance [-ləns] n **vig′i·lant**
[-lənt] adj watchful, alert.
vig·i·lan·te [vij-ə-LAN-tee] n one
(esp. as member of group) who
unofficially takes on duty of
enforcing law.
vi·gnette [vin-YET] n short literary
essay, sketch; photograph or
portrait with the background
shaded off.
vig·or [VIG-ər] n force, strength;
energy, activity. **vig′or·ous** [-əs]
adj strong; energetic; flourishing.
Vi·king [VĪ-king] n medieval

Scandinavian seafarer, raider, settler.

vile [vīl] *adj* **vil·er, vil·est.** very wicked, shameful; disgusting; despicable. **vil·i·fy** [VIL-ə-fī] *vt* **-fied, -fy·ing.** speak ill of; slander. **vil·i·fi·ca'tion** [-fi-KAY-shən] *n*

vil·la [VIL-ə] *n* large, luxurious, country house.

vil·lage [VIL-ij] *n* small group of houses in country area.

vil·lain [VIL-ən] *n* wicked person; *inf* mischievous person. **vil'lain·ous** [-əs] *adj* wicked; vile. **vil'lain·y** *n, pl* **-lain·ies.**

vim *n* force, energy.

vin·ai·grette [vin-ə-GRET] *n* small bottle of smelling salts; type of salad dressing. ▶ *adj* (of food) served with vinaigrette.

vin·di·cate [VIN-di-kayt] *vt* **-cat·ed, -cat·ing.** clear of charges; justify; establish the truth or merit of. **vin·di·ca'tion** *n*

vin·dic·tive [vin-DIK-tiv] *adj* revengeful; inspired by resentment.

vine [vīn] *n* climbing plant bearing grapes. **vine·yard** [VIN-yərd] *n* plantation of vines. **vin'tage** [-tij] *n* gathering of the grapes; the yield; wine of particular year; time of origin. ▶ *adj* best and most typical. **vint'ner** [-nər] *n* dealer in wine.

vin·e·gar [VIN-i-gər] *n* acid liquid obtained from wine and other alcoholic liquors. **vin'e·gar·y** *adj* like vinegar; sour; bad-tempered.

vi·nyl [VĪN-l] *n* plastic material with variety of domestic and industrial uses.

vi·ol [VĪ-əl] *n* early stringed instrument preceding violin.

vi·o·la¹ [vee-OH-lə] *n* large violin with lower range.

vi·o·la² [vī-OH-lə] *n* single-colored variety of pansy.

vi·o·late [VĪ-ə-layt] *vt* **-lat·ed, -lat·ing.** break (law, agreement, etc.), infringe; rape; outrage; desecrate. **vi·o·la·ble** [-lə-bəl] *adj* **vi·o·la'tion** [-LAY-shən] *n*

vi·o·lent [VĪ-ə-lənt] *adj* marked by, due to, extreme force, passion or fierceness; of great force; intense.

vi·o·lence [-lins] *n*

vi·o·let [VĪ-ə-lit] *n* plant with small bluish-purple or white flowers; the flower; bluish-purple color. ▶ *adj* of this color.

vi·o·lin [vī-ə-LIN] *n* small four-stringed musical instrument. **vi·o·lin'ist** *n* **vi·o·lon·cel·lo** [vee-ə-lən-CHEL-oh] *n* see CELLO.

VIP very important person.

vi·per [VĪ-pər] *n* venomous snake.

vi·ra·go [vi-RAH-goh] *n, pl* **-goes** or **-gos.** abusive woman.

vir·gin [VUR-jin] *n* one who has not had sexual intercourse. ▶ *adj* without experience of sexual intercourse; unsullied, fresh; (of land) untilled. **vir·gin·al** [VUR-jə-nl] *adj* of, like virgin. ▶ *n* type of spinet. **vir·gin'i·ty** *n*

vir·ile [VIR-əl] *adj* (of male) capable of copulation or procreation; strong, forceful. **vi·ril'i·ty** [-RIL-i-tee] *n*

virology [vī-ROL-ə-jee] see VIRUS.

vir·tu·al [VUR-choo-əl] *adj* so in effect, though not in appearance or name. **vir'tu·al·ly** *adv* practically, almost. **virtual reality** computer-generated environment that seems real to the user.

vir·tue [VUR-choo] *n* moral goodness; good quality; merit; inherent power. **vir'tu·ous** [-əs] *adj* morally good; chaste.

vir·tu·o·so [vur-choo-OH-soh] *n, pl* **-sos** or **-si** [-see] one with special skill, esp. in a fine art. **vir·tu·os'i·ty** *n* great technical skill, esp. in a fine art as music.

vir·u·lent [VIR-yə-lənt] *adj* very infectious, poisonous, etc.; malicious.

vi·rus [VĪ-rəs] *n* any of various submicroscopic organisms, some causing disease; *Computers* program that propagates itself, via disks and electronic networks, to cause disruption. **vi·rol'o·gy** *n* study of viruses.

vi·sa [VEEZ-ə] *n, pl* **-sas.** endorsement on passport permitting the bearer to travel into country of issuing government.

visa *vt* **-saed, -sa·ing.** approve visa for (someone).

vis·age [VIZ-ij] *n* face.

vis-à-vis [vee-zə-VEE] *Fr* in relation to, regarding; opposite to.

vis·cer·a [VIS-ər-ə] *pl n* large internal organs of body, esp. of abdomen. **visc′er·al** [-əl] *adj*

vis·cid [VIS-id] *adj* sticky, of a consistency like molasses. **vis·cid′i·ty** *n*

vis·cous [VIS-kəs] *adj* thick and sticky. **vis·cos′i·ty** *n, pl* **-ties.**

vise [vīs] *n* appliance with screw jaw for holding things while working on them.

vis·i·ble [VIZ-ə-bəl] *adj* that can be seen. **vis·i·bil′i·ty** *n* degree of clarity of atmosphere, esp. for navigation. **vis′i·bly** *adv*

vi·sion [VIZH-ən] *n* sight; insight; dream; phantom; imagination.
vi′sion·ar·y [-er-ee] *adj* marked by vision; impractical. ▸ *n, pl* **-ar·ies.** mystic; impractical person.

vis·it [VIZ-it] *v* go, come and see, stay temporarily with (someone). ▸ *n* stay; call at person's home, etc.; official call. **vis·it·a′tion** [-ə-TAY-shən] *n* formal visit or inspection; affliction or plague. **vis′i·tor** *n*

vi·sor [VĪ-zər] *n* front part of helmet made to move up and down before the face; eyeshade, esp. on car; peak on cap.

vis·ta [VIS-tə] *n* view, esp. distant view.

vis·u·al [VIZH-oo-əl] *adj* of sight; visible. **vis′u·al·ize** *vt* **-ized, -iz·ing.** form mental image of. **vis·u·al·i·za′tion** *n*

vi·tal [VĪT-l] *adj* necessary to, affecting life; lively, animated; essential; highly important. **vi′tals** *pl n* vital organs of body. **vi·tal′i·ty** *n* life, vigor. **vi′tal·ize** [-tə-līz] *vt* **-ized, -iz·ing.** give life to; lend vigor to. **vi′tal·ly** *adv*

vi·ta·min [VĪ-tə-min] *n* any of group of substances occurring in foodstuffs and essential to health.

vi·ti·ate [VISH-ee-ayt] *vt* **-at·ed, -at·ing.** spoil; deprive of efficacy;

invalidate. **vi·ti·a′tion** *n*

vit·re·ous [VI-tree-əs] *adj* of glass; glassy. **vit·ri·fy** [VI-trə-fī] *v* **-fied, -fy·ing.** convert into glass, or glassy substance. **vit·ri·fi·ca′tion** *n*

vit·ri·ol [VI-tree-əl] *n* sulfuric acid; caustic speech. **vit·ri·ol′ic** *adj*

vi·tu·per·ate [vī-TOO-pə-rayt] *vt* **-at·ed, -at·ing.** abuse in words, revile. **vi·tu′per·a·tive** *adj*

vi·va·cious [vi-VAY-shəs] *adj* lively, gay, sprightly. **vi·vac′i·ty** [-VAS-i-tee] *n*

vi·va vo·ce [VĪ-və VOH-see] *Lat* ▸ *adj, adv* by word of mouth. ▸ *n* in European universities, oral examination.

viv′id *adj* bright, intense; clear; lively, animated; graphic. **viv′id·ly** *adv*

viv·i·fy [VIV-ə-fī] *vt* **-fied, -fy·ing.** animate, inspire.

vi·vip·a·rous [vī-VIP-ər-əs] *adj* bringing forth young alive.

viv·i·sec·tion [viv-ə-SEK-shən] *n* dissection of, or operating on, living animals. **viv·i·sec′tion·ist** *n*

vix·en [VIK-sən] *n* female fox; spiteful woman. **vix′en·ish** *adj*

viz. short for VIDELICET.

vi·zier [vi-ZEER] *n* (formerly) high official in some Muslim countries.

vo·cab·u·lar·y [voh-KAB-yə-ler-ee] *n, pl* **-lar·ies.** list of words, usu. in alphabetical order; stock of words used in particular language, etc.

vo·cal [VOH-kəl] *adj* of, with, or giving out voice; outspoken, articulate. ▸ *n* piece of popular music that is sung. **vo′cal·ist** *n* singer. **vo′cal·ize** *vt* **-ized, -iz·ing.** utter with voice.

vo·ca·tion [voh-KAY-shən] *n* (urge, inclination, predisposition to) particular career, profession, etc. **vo·ca′tion·al** [-əl] *adj*

voc·a·tive [VOK-ə-tiv] *n* in some languages, case of nouns used in addressing a person.

vo·cif·er·ate [voh-SIF-ə-rayt] *v* **-at·ed, -at·ing.** exclaim, cry out. **vo·cif′er·ous** [-əs] *adj* shouting, noisy.

vod·ka [VOD-kə] *n* Russian spirit

distilled from grain, potatoes, etc.
vogue [vohg] *n* fashion, style;
popularity.
voice [vois] *n* sound given out by
person in speaking, singing, etc.;
quality of the sound; expressed
opinion; (right to) share in
discussion; verbal forms proper to
relation of subject and action. ▶ *vt*
voiced, voic·ing. give utterance to,
express. **voice'less** [-lis] *adj* **voice
mail** electronic system for
recording and storage of telephone
messages, which can then be
checked later or accessed remotely.
void *adj* empty; destitute; not
legally binding. ▶ *n* empty space.
▶ *vt* make ineffectual or invalid;
empty out.
vol·a·tile [VOL-ə-tl] *adj* evaporating
quickly; lively; fickle, changeable.
vol·a·til·i·ty *n* **vol'a·ti·lize** *v* **-lized,
-liz·ing.** (cause to) evaporate.
vol·ca·no [vol-KAY-noh] *n, pl* **-noes,
-nos.** hole in Earth's crust through
which lava, ashes, smoke, etc. are
discharged; mountain so formed.
vol·can'ic *adj* **vol·can·ol'o·gy**
[-kə-NOL-ə-jee] *n* study of
volcanoes and volcanic
phenomena, vulcanology.
vole [vohl] *n* small rodent.
vo·li·tion [voh-LISH-ən] *n* act,
power of willing; exercise of the
will.
vol·ley [VOL-ee] *n, pl* **-leys.**
simultaneous discharge of weapons
or missiles; rush of oaths,
questions, etc.; *Tennis* flight, return
of moving ball before it touches
ground. ▶ *v* **-leyed, -ley·ing.**
discharge; utter; fly, strike, etc. in
volley. **vol'ley·ball** *n* team game
where large ball is hit by hand over
high net.
volt [vohlt] *n* unit of electric
potential. **volt'age** [-ij] *n* electric
potential difference expressed in
volts. **volt'me·ter** *n*
volte-face [vohlt-FAHS] *n, pl*
volte-face. *Fr* complete reversal of
opinion or direction.
vol·u·ble [VOL-yə-bəl] *adj* talking
easily, readily and at length.

vol'u·bly *adv* **vol·u·bil'i·ty** *n*
vol·ume [VOL-yəm] *n* space
occupied; bulk, mass; amount;
power, fullness of voice or sound;
control on radio, etc. for adjusting
this; book; part of book bound in
one cover. **vol·u·met'ric** *adj* pert.
to measurement by volume.
vo·lu·mi·nous [və-LOO-mə-nəs]
adj bulky, copious.
vol·un·tar·y [VOL-ən-ter-ee] *adj*
having, done by free will; done
without payment; supported by
freewill contributions;
spontaneous. ▶ *n, pl* **-tar·ies.** organ
solo in church service.
vol·un·tar'i·ly *adv* **vol·un·teer'** *n*
one who offers service, joins force,
etc. of own free will. ▶ *v* offer
oneself or one's services.
vol·up·tu·ous [və-LUP-choo-əs] *adj*
of, contributing to pleasures of the
senses. **vol·up'tu·ar·y** [-er-ee] *n, pl*
-ar·ies. one given to luxury and
sensual pleasures.
vo·lute [və-LOOT] *n* spiral or
twisting turn, form or object.
vom·it *v* eject (contents of
stomach) through mouth. ▶ *n*
matter vomited.
voo'doo *n, pl* **-doos.** practice of
black magic, esp. in W Indies,
witchcraft. ▶ *vt* **-dooed, -doo·ing.**
affect by voodoo.
vo·ra·cious [vaw-RAY-shəs] *adj*
greedy, ravenous. **vo·rac'i·ty**
[-RAS-i-tee] *n*
vor·tex [VOR-teks] *n, pl* **-ti·ces**
[-tə-seez] whirlpool; whirling mass
or motion.
vo·ta·ry [VOH-tə-ree] *n, pl* **-ta·ries.**
one vowed to service or pursuit.
vo'tive [-tiv] *adj* given, consecrated
by vow.
vote [voht] *n* formal expression of
choice; individual pronouncement;
right to give it, in question or
election; result of voting; that
which is given or allowed by vote.
▶ *v* **vot·ed, vot·ing.** express,
declare opinion, choice,
preference, etc. by vote; authorize,
enact, etc. by vote.
vouch [vowch] *vi* (usu. with *for*)

guarantee, make oneself responsible for. **vouch′er** *n* document proving correctness of item in accounts, or to establish facts; ticket as substitute for cash. **vouch·safe′** [-SAYF] *vt* **-safed, -saf·ing.** agree, condescend to grant or do something.

vow *n* solemn promise, esp. religious one. ▶ *vt* promise, threaten by vow.

vow·el [VOW-əl] *n* any speech sound pronounced without stoppage or friction of the breath; letter standing for such sound; e.g. *a, e, i, o, u.*

voy·age [VOI-ij] *n* journey, esp. long one, by sea or air. ▶ *vi* **-aged, -ag·ing.** make voyage. **voy′ag·er** *n*

vo·yeur [vwah-YUR] *n* one obtaining sexual pleasure by watching sexual activities of others.

vul·can·ize [VUL-kə-nīz] *vt* **-ized, -iz·ing.** treat (rubber) with sulfur at high temperature to increase its durability. **vul′can·ite** *n* rubber so hardened. **vul·can·i·za′tion** *n*

vul·can·ol·o·gy see VOLCANOLOGY.

vul·gar [VUL-gər] *adj* offending against good taste; coarse; common. **vul·gar′i·an** [-GAIR-ee-ən] *n* vulgar (rich) person. **vul′gar·ism** *n* coarse, obscene word, phrase. **vul·gar′i·ty** *n, pl* **-ties. vul·gar·i·za′tion** [-gə-ri-ZAY-shən] *n* **vul′gar·ize** *vt* **-ized, -iz·ing.** make vulgar or too common.

Vul·gate [VUL-gayt] *n* fourth-century Latin version of the Bible.

vul·ner·a·ble [VUL-nər-ə-bəl] *adj* capable of being physically or emotionally wounded or hurt; exposed, open to attack, persuasion, etc.

vul·pine [VUL-pin] *adj* of foxes; foxy.

vul·ture [VUL-chər] *n* large bird that feeds on carrion. **vul′tur·ous** [-əs] *adj* of vulture; rapacious.

vul·va [VUL-və] *n, pl* **-vas.** external genitals of human female.

vy·ing [Vī-ing] *pr. p.* of VIE.

W w

W *Chem* tungsten.

wack·y [WAK-ee] *adj* **wack·i·er,
wack·i·est.** *inf* eccentric or funny.
wack'i·ness [-nis] *n*

wad [wod] *n* small pad of fibrous
material; thick roll of paper money;
sum of money. ▶ *vt* **wad·ded,
wad·ding.** line, pad, stuff, etc. with
wad. **wadding** *n* stuffing.

wad·dle [WOD-l] *vi* **-dled, -dling.**
walk like duck. ▶ *n* this gait.

wade [wayd] *vi* **wad·ed, wad·ing.**
walk through something that
hampers movement, esp. water;
proceed with difficulty. **wad'er** *n*
person or bird that wades. ▶ *pl*
angler's high waterproof boots.

wa·di [WO-dee] *n, pl* **-dis.** in the
East, watercourse that is dry except
in wet season.

wa·fer [WAY-fər] *n* thin, crisp
biscuit; thin slice of anything; thin
disk of unleavened bread used in
the Eucharist.

waf·fle¹ [WOF-əl] *n* kind of batter
cake with gridlike design.

waf·fle² *inf* ▶ *vi* **-fled, -fling.** speak,
write in vague wordy manner. ▶ *n*
vague speech, etc.; nonsense.

waft [wahft] *vt* convey smoothly
through air or water. ▶ *n* breath of
wind; odor, whiff.

wag *v* **wagged, wag·ging.** (cause
to) move rapidly from side to side.
▶ *n* instance of wagging;
humorous, witty person. **wag'ish**
adj

wage [wayj] *n* (oft. in *pl*) payment
for work done. ▶ *vt* **waged,
wag·ing.** carry on.

wa·ger [WAY-jər] *n, vt* bet.

wag·on [WAG-ən] *n* four-wheeled
vehicle for heavy loads. **off the
wagon** *sl* drinking alcoholic
beverages again. **on the wagon** *sl*
abstaining from alcoholic
beverages.

waif [wayf] *n* homeless person, esp.
child.

wail [wayl] *v* cry out, lament. ▶ *n*
mournful cry.

wain·scot [WAYN-skət] *n* wooden
lining of walls of room. ▶ *vt*
-scot·ed, -scot·ting. line thus.

waist [wayst] *n* part of body
between hips and ribs; various
narrow central parts. **waist·coat**
[WES-kət] *n Brit* vest. **waist'line** *n*
line, size of waist (of person,
garment).

wait [wayt] *v* stay in one place,
remain inactive in expectation (of
something); be prepared (for
something); delay. ▶ *vi* serve in
restaurant, etc. ▶ *n* act or period of
waiting. **wait'er** *n* attendant
serving diners at hotel, restaurant,
etc.; one who waits. **wait·ress**
[WAY-tris] *n, fem*

waive [wayv] *vt* **waived, waiv·ing.**
forgo; not to insist on. **waiv'er** *n*
(written statement of) this act.

wake¹ [wayk] *v* **waked** or **woke,
waked** or **wok·en, wak·ing.** rouse
from sleep; stir up. ▶ *n* vigil; watch
beside corpse. **wak·en** [WAY-kən]
v wake. **wake·ful** [-fəl] *adj*

wake² *n* track or path left by
anything that has passed, as track
of turbulent water behind ship.

walk [wawk] *v* (cause, assist to)
move, travel on foot at ordinary
pace. ▶ *vt* cross, pass through by
walking; escort, conduct by
walking. ▶ *n* act, instance of
walking; path or other place or
route for walking; manner of
walking; occupation, career.
walk'er *n* one who walks;
framework of metal for support
while walking. **walk·ie-talk·ie**
[WAW-kee-TAW-kee] *n* portable
radio set containing both
transmission and receiver units.
walking stick stick, cane carried
while walking. **Walk·man**
[WAWK-man] *n* ® small portable
cassette player, radio, etc.
equipped with headphones.
walk'out *n* strike; act of leaving as

a protest. **walk'o·ver** n unopposed or easy victory.

wall [wawl] n structure of brick, stone, etc. serving as fence, side of building, etc.; surface of one; anything resembling this. ▶ vt enclose with wall; block up with wall. **wall'flow·er** n garden flower, often growing on walls; at dance, person who remains seated for lack of partner. **wall'pa·per** n paper, usu. patterned, to cover interior walls.

wal·la·by [WOL-ə-bee] n, pl -bies. Aust. marsupial similar to and smaller than kangaroo.

wal·let [WOL-it] n small folding case, esp. for paper money, documents, etc.

wall·eyed [WAWL-īd] adj having eyes turned outward in squint; having eyes with pale irises.

wal·lop [WOL-əp] inf ▶ vt beat soundly; strike hard. ▶ n stroke or blow. **wal'lop·er** n inf one who wallops. **wal'lop·ing** inf ▶ n thrashing. ▶ adj, adv very, great(ly).

wal·low [WOL-oh] vi roll (in liquid or mud); revel (in). ▶ n

wal·nut [WAWL-nut] n large nut with crinkled shell splitting easily into two halves; the tree; its wood.

wal·rus [WAWL-rəs] n large sea mammal with long tusks.

waltz [wawlts] n ballroom dance; music for it. ▶ v

wam·pum [WOM-pəm] n beads made of shells, formerly used by N Amer. Indians as money and for ornament.

wan [won] adj **wan·ner**, **wan·nest**. pale, sickly complexioned, pallid.

wand [wond] n stick, usu. straight and slender, esp. as carried by magician, etc.

wan·der [WON-dər] v roam, ramble. ▶ vi go astray, deviate. ▶ n **wan'der·er** n **wand'er·lust** n irrepressible urge to wander or travel.

wane [wayn] vi, n **waned**, **wan·ing**. decline; (of moon) decrease in size.

wan·gle [WANG-gəl] vt **-gled**, **-gling**. inf manipulate, manage in

skillful way.

want [wont] v desire; lack. ▶ n desire; need; deficiency. **want'ed** [-id] adj being sought, esp. by the police. **want'ing** adj lacking; below standard.

wan·ton [WON-tən] adj dissolute; without motive, thoughtless; unrestrained. ▶ n wanton person.

war [wor] n fighting between nations; state of hostility; conflict, contest. ▶ vi **warred**, **war·ring**. make war. **war'like** adj of, for war; fond of war. **war·ri·or** [WOR-ee-ər] n fighter. **war cry** cry used by attacking troops in war; distinctive word, phrase used by political party, etc. **war'fare** [-fair] n hostilities. **war'head** [-hed] n part of missile, etc. containing explosives. **war·mon·ger** [WOR-mung-gər] n one fostering, encouraging war. **war'ship** n vessel armed, armored for naval warfare.

war·ble [WOR-bəl] vi **-bled**, **-bling**. sing with trills. **war·bler** [-blər] n person or bird that warbles; any of various kinds of small songbirds.

ward [word] n division of city, hospital, etc.; minor under care of guardian; guardianship; curved bar in lock, groove in key that prevents incorrectly cut key opening lock. **ward'room** n officers' mess on warship. **ward off** avert, repel.

war·den [WOR-dn] n person, officer in charge of prison.

ward·robe [WOR-drohb] n piece of furniture for hanging clothes in; person's supply of clothes; costumes of theatrical company.

ware [wair] n goods; articles collectively. ▶ pl goods for sale; commodities; merchandise. **ware'house** n storehouse for goods prior to distribution and sale. ▶ vt store for future shipment or use.

war·lock [WOR-lok] n wizard, sorcerer.

warm [worm] adj moderately hot; serving to maintain heat; affectionate; ardent; earnest; hearty; (of color) having yellow or red for a basis. ▶ *v* make, become warm. **warm·ly** *adv* **warmth** *n* mild heat; cordiality; vehemence, anger.

warn [worn] *vt* put on guard; caution, admonish; give advance information to; notify authoritatively. **warn·ing** *n* hint of harm, etc.; admonition; advance notice of.

warp [worp] *v* (cause to) twist (out of shape); pervert or be perverted. ▶ *n* state, condition of being warped; lengthwise threads on loom.

war·rant [WOR-ənt] *n* authority; document giving authority. ▶ *vt* guarantee; authorize, justify. **war·ran·tee′** *n* person given warranty. **war′ran·tor** [-tər] *n* person, company giving warranty. **war′ran·ty** [-tee] *n, pl* **-ties.** guarantee of quality of goods; security. **warrant officer** officer in certain armed services holding rank between commissioned and noncommissioned officer.

war·ren [WOR-ən] *n* (burrows inhabited by) colony of rabbits.

warrior [WOR-ee-ər] *n* see WAR.

wart [wort] *n* small hard growth on skin. **wart hog** kind of Afr. wild pig.

war·y [WAIR-ee] *adj* **war·i·er, war·i·est.** watchful, cautious, alert. **war′i·ly** *adv*

was [wuz *or* woz] *v* first and third person sing. pt. of BE.

wash [wosh] *v* clean (oneself, clothes, etc.) esp. with water, soap, etc. ▶ *vi* be washable; *inf* be able to be proved true. ▶ *vt* move, be moved by water; flow, sweep over, against. ▶ *n* act of washing; clothes washed at one time; sweep of water, esp. set up by moving ship; thin coat of color. **wash′a·ble** *adj* capable of being washed without damage, etc. **wash′er** *n* one who, that which, washes; ring put under a nut. **wash′ing** *n* clothes to be washed. **wash′y** *adj* **wash·i·er, wash·i·est.** dilute; watery; insipid. **wash′out** *n* rainout; *inf* complete failure.

wasp [wosp] *n* striped stinging insect resembling bee. **wasp′ish** *adj* irritable, snappish. **wasp waist** very small waist.

waste [wayst] *v* **wast·ed, wast·ing.** ▶ *vt* expend uselessly, use extravagantly; fail to take advantage of; lay desolate. ▶ *vi* dwindle; pine away. ▶ *n* act of wasting; what is wasted; desert. ▶ *adj* worthless, useless; desert; wasted. **wast·age** [WAY-stij] *n* loss by use or decay; losses as result of wastefulness. **waste′ful** [-fəl] *adj* extravagant. **waste′ful·ness** [-nis] *n* **waste product** discarded material in manufacturing process; excreted urine, feces. **wast·rel** [WAY-strəl] *n* wasteful person, spendthrift.

watch [woch] *vt* observe closely; guard. ▶ *vi* wait expectantly (for); be on watch. ▶ *n* portable timepiece for wrist, pocket, etc.; state of being on the lookout; guard; spell of duty. **watch′ful** [-fəl] *adj* **watch′mak·er** *n* one skilled in making and repairing watches. **watch′man** [-mən] *n, pl* **-men.** person guarding building, etc., esp. at night. **watch′word** [-wurd] *n* password; rallying cry.

wa·ter [WAW-tər] *n* transparent, colorless, odorless, tasteless liquid, substance of rain, river, etc.; body of water; river; lake; sea; tear; urine. ▶ *vt* put water on or into; irrigate or provide with water. ▶ *vi* salivate; (of eyes) fill with tears; take in or obtain water. **wa′ter·y** *adj* **water buffalo** oxlike Asian animal. **water closet** [KLOZ-it] toilet. **wa′ter·col·or** *n* pigment mixed with water; painting in this. **wa′ter·course** *n* stream. **wa′ter·cress** *n* plant growing in clear ponds and streams. **wa′ter·fall** *n* perpendicular descent of waters of river, stream. **wa′ter·logged** *adj* saturated, filled with water. **wa′ter·mark** *n* faint translucent design stamped on substance of sheet of paper. **wa′ter·proof** *adj* not letting water

through. ▸ *v* make waterproof.
wa·ter·shed *n* area drained by a
river; important division between
conditions, phases. **water-ski·ing**
n sport of riding over water on ski
towed by speedboat. **water
sports** various sports, as
swimming, windsurfing, that take
place in or on water. **water·tight**
[-tīt] *adj* so fitted as to prevent
water entering or escaping; with
no loopholes or weak points.

watt [wot] *n* unit of electric power.
watt·age [-ij] *n* electric power
expressed in watts.

wat·tle [WOT-l] *n* fleshy pendent
lobe on head or neck of certain
birds, e.g. turkey.

wave [wayv] *v* **waved, wav·ing.**
move to and fro, as hand in
greeting or farewell; signal by
waving; give, take shape of waves
(as hair, etc.). ▸ *n* ridge and trough
on water, etc.; act, gesture of
waving; vibration, as in radio
waves, of electric and magnetic
forces alternating in direction;
prolonged spell of something;
upsurge; wavelike shapes in the
hair, etc. **wav'y** [-ee] *adj* **wav·i·er,
wav·i·est.** **wave'length** *n* distance
between same points of two
successive sound waves.

wav·er [WAY-vər] *n* hesitate, be
irresolute; be, become unsteady.

wax[1] [waks] *n* yellow, soft, pliable
material made by bees; this or
similar substance used for sealing,
making candles, etc.; waxy
secretion of ear. ▸ *vt* **waxed,
wax·ing.** put wax on. **wax'y** [-ee]
adj **wax·i·er, wax·i·est.** like wax.
wax'wing *n* small songbird.
wax'work [-wurk] *n* lifelike figure,
esp. of famous person, reproduced
in wax.

wax[2] *vi* **waxed, wax·ing.** grow,
increase.

way *n* manner; method, means;
track; direction; path; passage;
course; route; progress; state or
condition. **way'far·er** [-fair-ər] *n*
traveler, esp. on foot. **way'lay** *vt*
-laid, -lay·ing. lie in wait for and

accost, attack. **way'side** *n* side or
edge of a road. ▸ *adj* **way'ward**
[-wərd] *adj* capricious, perverse,
willful. **way'ward·ness** [-nis] *n*

we [wee] *pron* first person plural
pronoun.

weak [week] *adj* **-er, -est.** lacking
strength; feeble; fragile;
defenseless; easily influenced; faint.
weak·en [WEE-kən] *v* **weak'ling** *n*
feeble creature. **weak'ly** *adj* weak;
sickly. ▸ *adv*

wealth [welth] *n* riches; abundance.
wealth'y *adj* **wealth·i·er,
wealth·i·est.**

wean [ween] *vt* accustom to food
other than mother's milk; win over,
coax away from.

weap·on [WEP-ən] *n* implement to
fight with; anything used to get the
better of an opponent.
weap'on·ry [-ree] *n*

wear [wair] *v* **wore, worn,
wear·ing.** ▸ *vt* have on the body;
show; produce (hole, etc.) by
rubbing, etc.; harass or weaken.
▸ *vi* last; become impaired by use;
(of time) pass slowly. ▸ *n* act of
wearing; things to wear; damage
caused by use; ability to resist
effects of constant use.

wea·ry [WEER-ee] *adj* **-ri·er, -ri·est.**
tired, exhausted, jaded; tiring;
tedious. ▸ *v* **-ried, -ry·ing.** make,
become weary. **wea'ri·ness**
[-ree-nis] *n* **wea'ri·some**
[-ree-səm] *adj* causing weariness.

wea·sel [WEE-zəl] *n* small
carnivorous mammal with long
body and short legs.

weath·er [WE*TH*-ər] *n* day-to-day
meteorological conditions, esp.
temperature, cloudiness, etc. of a
place. ▸ *adj* toward the wind. ▸ *vt*
affect by weather; endure; resist;
come safely through; sail to
windward of. **weath'er·vane**
[-vain] *n* rotating vane to show
which way wind blows.

weave [weev] *v* **wove** or **weaved,
wo·ven** or **wove, weav·ing.** ▸ *vt*
form into texture or fabric by
interlacing, esp. on loom; fashion,
construct. ▸ *vi* become woven;

make one's way, esp. with side to side motion. **weav'er** [-ər] *n*

web *n* woven fabric; net spun by spider; membrane between toes of waterfowl, frogs, etc. **the Web** short for WORLD WIDE WEB. **web'bing** *n* strong fabric woven in strips. **web'cam** *n* camera that transmits images over the Internet. **web'cast** *n* broadcast of an event over the Internet. **web'site** *n* group of pages on the World Wide Web with a single address.

web·er [WEB-ər] *n* SI unit of magnetic flux.

wed *vt* **wed·ded, wed·ding.** marry; unite closely. **wedding** *n* act of marrying, nuptial ceremony. **wed'lock** *n* marriage.

wedge [wej] *n* piece of wood, metal, etc., thick at one end, tapering to a thin edge. ▶ *vt* **wedged, wedg·ing.** fasten, split with wedge; stick by compression or crowding.

weed *n* plant growing where undesired; *inf* tobacco; *sl* marijuana; thin, sickly person, animal. ▶ *vt* clear of weeds. **weed'y** *adj* **weed·i·er, weed·i·est.** full of weeds; thin, weakly. **weed out** remove, eliminate what is unwanted.

weeds [weedz] *pl n obs* (widow's) mourning clothes.

week *n* period of seven days, esp. one beginning on Sunday and ending on Saturday; hours, days of work in seven-day period. **week'ly** *adj, adv* happening, done, published, etc. once a week. ▶ *n* newspaper or magazine published once a week. **week'day** *n* any day of week except Sunday and usu. Saturday. **week'end** *n* (at least) Saturday and Sunday, esp. considered as rest period.

weep *v* **wept, weep·ing.** shed tears (for); grieve. **weep'y** *adj* **weep·i·er, weep·i·est. weeping willow** willow with drooping branches.

wee·vil [WEE-vəl] *n* small beetle harmful to cotton, etc.

weft *n* cross threads in weaving, woof.

weigh [way] *vt* find weight of; consider; raise (anchor). ▶ *vi* have weight; be burdensome. **weight** *n* measure of the heaviness of an object; quality of heaviness; heavy mass; object of known mass for weighing; unit of measurement of weight; importance, influence. ▶ *vt* add weight to. **weight'y** *adj* **weight·i·er, weight·i·est.** heavy; onerous; important; momentous.

weir [weer] *n* small dam in river or stream; fence or net in stream, etc. for catching fish.

weird [weerd] *adj* **-er, -est.** unearthly, uncanny; strange, bizarre.

wel·come [WEL-kəm] *adj* received gladly; freely permitted. ▶ *n, interj* kindly greeting. ▶ *vt* **-comed, -com·ing.** greet with pleasure; receive gladly.

weld *vt* unite metal by softening with heat; unite closely. ▶ *n* welded joint. **weld'er** *n* person who welds; machine used in welding. **weld'ment** [-mənt] *n* welded assembly.

wel·fare [WEL-fair] *n* well-being. **welfare state** system in which the government takes responsibility for the social, economic, etc. security of its citizens.

well¹ *adv* in good manner or degree; suitably; intimately; fully; favorably, kindly; to a considerable degree. ▶ *adj* **bet·ter, best.** in good health; suitable. ▶ *interj* exclamation of surprise, interrogation, etc. **well-being** *n* state of being well, happy, or prosperous. **well-disposed** *adj* inclined to be friendly, kindly (toward). **well-mannered** *adj* having good manners. **well-off** *adj* fairly rich. **well-read** [-red] *adj* having read much. **well-spoken** *adj* speaking fluently, graciously, aptly. **well-to-do** *adj* moderately wealthy.

well² *n* hole sunk into the earth to reach water, gas, oil, etc.; spring;

any shaft like a well. ▶ *vi* spring, gush.

Welsh *adj* of Wales. ▶ *n* language, people of Wales. **Welsh rabbit, rarebit** dish of melted cheese, beer, spices on toast.

welsh *vi inf* fail to pay debt or fulfill obligation (also **welch**). **welsh′er** [-ər], **welch·er** [WELCH-ər] *n*

welt *n* raised, strengthened seam; weal. ▶ *vt* provide with welt; thrash.

wel·ter [WEL-tər] *vi* roll or tumble. ▶ *n* turmoil, disorder.

wel·ter·weight [WEL-tər-wayt] *n Boxing* weight between light and middle; boxer of this weight.

wen *n* cyst, esp. on scalp.

wench *n obs.*, *now facetious* young woman.

wend *v* go, travel.

went pt. of GO.

wept pt./pp. of WEEP.

were [wur] past indicative, plural and subjunctive sing. and pl. of BE.

were·wolf [WAIR-wuulf] *n, pl* **-wolves.** (in folklore) human being turned into wolf.

west *n* part of sky where sun sets; part of country, etc. lying to this side; occident. ▶ *adj* that is toward or in this region. ▶ *adv* to the west. **west′er·ly** [-ər-lee] *adj* **west′ward** [-wərd] *adj, adv* **west′ward(s)** *adv* toward the west. **west′ern** [-ərn] *adj* of, in the west. ▶ *n* film, story, etc. about cowboys or frontiersmen in western US. **go west** *inf* die.

wet *adj* **wet·ter, wet·test.** having water or other liquid on a surface or being soaked in it; rainy; not yet dry (paint, ink, etc.). ▶ *vt* **wet** or **wet·ted, wet·ting.** make wet. ▶ *n* moisture, rain. **wet blanket** one depressing spirits of others. **wet′land** [-lənd] *n* area of swamp or marsh. **wet nurse** woman suckling another's child. **wet suit** close-fitting rubber suit worn by divers, etc.

whack [hwak] *vt* strike with sharp resounding blow. ▶ *n* such blow; *sl* share; *inf* attempt. **whack′ing** *adj inf* big, enormous.

whale [hwayl] *n* large fish-shaped

sea mammal. **whal′er** *n* person, ship employed in hunting whales. **whale′bone** *n* horny elastic substance from projections of upper jaw of certain whales. **whal′ing** *n* **a whale of a time** *inf* very enjoyable time.

wharf [hworf] *n* platform at harbor, on river, etc. for loading and unloading ships.

what [hwut *or* hwot] *pron* which thing; that which; request for statement to be repeated. ▶ *adj* which; as much as; how great, surprising, etc. ▶ *interj* exclamation of surprise, anger, etc. **what·ev′er** *pron* anything which; of what kind it may be. **what′not** *n* small stand with shelves; something, anything of same kind.

wheat [hweet] *n* cereal plant with thick four-sided seed spikes of which bread is chiefly made. **wheat′en** [-ən] *adj* **wheat germ** [-jurm] embryo of wheat kernel.

whee·dle [HWEED-l] *v* **-dled, -dling.** coax, cajole.

wheel [hweel] *n* circular frame or disk (with spokes) revolving on axle; anything like a wheel in shape or function; act of turning; steering wheel. ▶ *v* (cause to) turn as if on axis; (cause to) move on or as if on wheels; (cause to) change course, esp. in opposite direction. **wheel′bar·row** [-ba-roh] *n* barrow with one wheel. **wheel′base** [-bays] *n* distance between front and rear hubs of vehicle. **wheel′chair** *n* chair mounted on large wheels, used by people who cannot walk.

wheeze [hweez] *vi* **wheezed, wheez·ing.** breathe with difficulty and whistling noise. ▶ *n* this sound; story, etc.told too often. **wheez′y** [-ee] *adj* **wheez·i·er, wheez·i·est.**

whelp [hwelp] *n* pup, cub. ▶ *v* produce whelps.

when [hwen] *adv* at what time. ▶ *conj* at the time that; although; since. ▶ *pron* at which (time). **when·ev′er** *adv, conj* at whatever time.

whence [hwens] *adv, conj obs* from what place or source; how.

where [hwair] *adv, conj* at what place; at or to the place in which. **where'a·bouts** *adv, conj* in what, which place. ▶ *n* present position. **where·as'** *conj* considering that; while, on the contrary. **where·by'** [-BĪ] *conj* by which. **where'fore** *adv obs* why. ▶ *conj* consequently. **where·up·on'** *conj* at which point. **wher·ev'er** *adv* at whatever place. **where'with·al** [-with-awl] *n* necessary funds, resources, etc.

whet [hwet] *vt* **whet·ted, whetting.** sharpen; stimulate. **whet'stone** *n* stone for sharpening tools.

wheth·er [HWETH-ər] *conj* introduces the first of two alternatives, of which the second may be expressed or implied.

whey [hway] *n* watery part of milk left after separation of curd in cheese making.

which [hwich] *adj* used in requests for a selection from alternatives. ▶ *pron* which person or thing; the thing *who*. **which·ev'er** *pron*

whiff [hwif] *n* brief smell or suggestion of; puff of air. ▶ *v* smell.

while [hwīl] *conj* in the time that; in spite of the fact that, although; whereas. ▶ *vt* **whiled, whil·ing.** pass (time, usu. idly). ▶ *n* period of time.

whim [hwim] *n* sudden, passing fancy. **whim'si·cal** [-zi-kəl] *adj* fanciful; full of whims. **whim·si·cal'i·ty** [-zi-KAL-i-tee] *n, pl* **-ties.** **whim'sy** [-zee] *n, pl* **-sies.** whim; caprice.

whim·per [HWIM-pər] *vi* cry or whine softly; complain in this way. ▶ *n* such cry or complaint.

whine [hwīn] *n* high-pitched plaintive cry; peevish complaint. ▶ *vi* **whined, whin·ing.** utter this.

whin·ny [HWIN-ee] *vi* **-nied, -ny·ing.** neigh softly. ▶ *n*

whip [hwip] *v* **whipped, whip·ping.** ▶ *vt* strike with whip; thrash; beat (cream, eggs) to a froth; lash; pull, remove, quickly. ▶ *vi* dart. ▶ *n* lash attached to handle for urging or punishing; one who enforces attendance, voting, etc. of political party; elastic quality permitting bending in mast, fishing rod, etc.; whipped dessert. **whip'lash** *n* injury to neck as result of sudden jerking of unsupported head. **whipping boy** scapegoat.

whip·pet [HWIP-it] *n* racing dog like small greyhound.

whir [hwur] *v* **whirred, whir·ring.** (cause to) fly, spin, etc. with buzzing or whizzing sound; bustle. ▶ *n* this sound.

whirl [hwurl] *v* swing rapidly around; move rapidly in a circular course; drive at high speed. ▶ *n* whirling movement; confusion, bustle, giddiness. **whirl'pool** *n* circular current, eddy. **whirl'wind** *n* wind whirling around while moving forward. ▶ *adj*

whisk [hwisk] *v* brush, sweep, beat lightly; move, remove, quickly; beat to a froth. ▶ *n* light brush; eggbeating implement.

whisk·er [HWIS-kər] *n* any of the long stiff hairs at side of mouth of cat or other animal; any of hairs on a man's face. **by a whisker** only just.

whis·key [HWIS-kee] *n, pl* **-keys.** alcoholic liquor distilled from fermented cereals. **whis'ky** *n, pl* **-kies.** Scotch or Canadian whiskey.

whis·per [HWIS-pər] *v* speak in soft, hushed tones, without vibration of vocal cords; rustle. ▶ *n* such speech; trace or suspicion; rustle.

whist [hwist] *n* card game.

whis·tle [HWIS-əl] *v* **-tled, -tling.** ▶ *vi* produce shrill sound by forcing breath through rounded, nearly closed lips; make such a sound. ▶ *vt* utter, summon, etc. by whistle. ▶ *n* such sound; any similar sound; instrument to make it. **whis·tler** [HWIS-lər] *n* **whistle-blower** *n* person who informs on or puts stop to something.

whit [hwit] *n* **not a whit** not the slightest amount.

white [hwīt] *adj* **whit·er, whit·est.**

of the color of snow; pale; light in color; having a light-colored skin. ► *n* color of snow; white pigment; white part; clear fluid round yolk of egg; Caucasian person. **whi·ten** [-ən] *v* **white ant** termite.

white-collar *adj* denoting nonmanual salaried workers.

white elephant useless, unwanted, gift or possession. **white flag** white banner or cloth used as signal of surrender or truce. **white hope** one (formerly, a white person) expected to bring honor or glory to his group, team, etc. **white lie** minor, unimportant lie. **white paper** government report on matter recently investigated. **white slave** woman, child forced or enticed away for purposes of prostitution. **white·wash** [-wosh] *n* substance for whitening walls, etc. ► *vt* apply this; cover up, gloss over, suppress.

whith·er [HWIT*H*-ər] *adv* to what place; to which.

whit·tle [HWIT-l] *vt* **-tled, -tling.** cut, carve with knife; pare away. **whittle down** reduce gradually, wear (away).

whiz [hwiz] *n* loud hissing sound; *inf* person skillful at something. ► *v* **whizzed, whiz·zing.** move with such sound, or make it; *inf* move quickly. **take a whizz** *inf* urinate.

who [hoo] *pron* relative and interrogative pronoun, always referring to persons. **who·dun·it** *n* *inf* detective story. **who·ev'er** *pron* who, any one or every one that.

whole [hohl] *adj* complete; containing all elements or parts; entire; not defective or imperfect; healthy. ► *n* complete thing or system. **whol'ly** *adv* **whole·heart'ed** [-HART-id] *adj* sincere; enthusiastic. **whole'sale** [-sayl] *n* sale of goods in large quantities to retailers. ► *adj* dealing by wholesale; extensive. ► *vt* **-saled, -sal·ing. whole'sal·er** *n* **whole'some** [-səm] *adj* producing good effect, physically or morally. **whole·wheat** *adj* of, pert. to flour

that contains the complete wheat kernel. **on the whole** taking everything into consideration; in general.

whom [hoom] *pron* objective case of WHO.

whoop [hwuup] *n* shout or cry expressing excitement, etc.

whoop·ee [HWUUP-ee] *n* *inf* gay, riotous time. **make whoopee** participate in wild noisy party; go on spree.

whoop·ing cough [HUUP-ing] infectious disease of mucous membrane lining air passages, marked by convulsive coughing with loud whoop or indrawing of breath.

whop·per [HWOP-ər] *n* *inf* anything unusually large; monstrous lie. **whop'ping** *adj*

whore [hor] *n* prostitute.

whorl [hwurl] *n* ring of leaves or petals; turn of spiral; anything forming part of circular pattern, e.g. lines of human fingerprint.

whose [hooz] *pron* of whom or of which.

why [hwī] *adv* for what cause or reason.

wick [wik] *n* strip of thread feeding flame of lamp or candle with oil, grease, etc.

wick·ed [WIK-id] *adj* evil, sinful; very bad; mischievous. **wick'ed·ness** [-nis] *n*

wick·er [WIK-ər] *n* woven cane, etc. basketwork (also **wick·er·work**).

wick·et [WIK-it] *n* small window, gate; *Croquet* wire arch.

wide [wīd] *adj* **wid·er, wid·est.** having a great extent from side to side, broad; having considerable distance between; spacious; liberal; vast; far from the mark; opened fully. ► *adv* to the full extent; far from the intended target. **wi·den** [WĪD-n] *v* **width** *n* breadth. **wide'spread** [-spred] *adj* extending over a wide area.

wid·ow [WID-oh] *n* woman whose husband is dead and who has not married again. ► *vt* make a widow of. **wid'ow·er** *n* man whose wife is dead and who has not married again. **wid'ow·hood** [-huud] *n*

wield [weeld] *vt* hold and use; brandish; manage.

wife [wīf] *n, pl* **wives.** a man's partner in marriage, married woman. **wife'ly** *adj*

wig *n* artificial hair for the head. **wigged** *adj*

wig·gle [WIG-əl] *v* **-gled, -gling.** (cause to) move jerkily from side to side. ▶ *n*

wig·wam [WIG-wom] *n* Native American's tent.

wild [wīld] *adj* **-er, -est.** not tamed or domesticated; not cultivated; savage; stormy; uncontrolled; random; excited; rash; frantic; (of party, etc.) rowdy, unrestrained. **wild'ly** *adv* **wild'ness** [-nis] *n* **wild'cat** *n* any of various undomesticated feline animals; wild, savage person. ▶ *adj* unsound, irresponsible; sudden, unofficial, unauthorized. **wildcat strike** strike called without sanction of labor union. **wild-goose chase** futile pursuit. **wild'life** *n* wild animals and plants collectively.

wil·der·ness [WIL-dər-nis] *n* desert, waste place; state of desolation or confusion.

wild·fire [WĪLD-fīr] *n* raging, uncontrollable fire; anything spreading, moving fast.

wile [wīl] *n* trick. **wil'y** *adj* **wil·i·er, wil·i·est.** crafty, sly.

will *v aux, pt* **would** [wuud] forms moods and tenses indicating intention or conditional result. ▶ *vi* have a wish. ▶ *vt* wish; intend; leave as legacy. ▶ *n* faculty of deciding what one will do; purpose; volition; determination; wish; directions written for disposal of property after death. **will'ing** *adj* ready; given cheerfully. **will'ing·ly** *adv* **will'ing·ness** [-nis] *n* **will'pow·er** *n* ability to control oneself, one's actions, impulses.

will·ful [WIL-fəl] *adj* obstinate, self-willed; intentional. **will'ful·ness** [-nis] *n*

will-o'-the-wisp [WIL-ə-*thə*-WISP]

n brief pale flame or phosphorescence sometimes seen over marshes; elusive person or hope.

wil·low [WIL-oh] *n* tree, such as **weeping willow**, with long thin flexible branches; its wood. **wil'low·y** *adj* lithe, slender, supple.

wil·ly-nil·ly [WIL-ee-NIL-ee] *adv, adj* (occurring) whether desired or not.

wilt *v* (cause to) become limp, drooping or lose strength, etc.

wimp *n inf* feeble, ineffective person.

wim·ple [WIM-pəl] *n* garment worn by nun, around face.

win *v* won, win·ning. ▶ *vi* be successful, victorious. ▶ *vt* get by labor or effort; reach; lure; be successful in; gain the support, consent, etc. of. ▶ *n* victory, esp. in games. **winning** *adj* charming. **winnings** *pl n* sum won in game, betting, etc. **win-win** *adj* guaranteeing a favourable outcome for everyone involved.

wince [wins] *vi* **winced, winc·ing.** flinch, draw back, as from pain, etc. ▶ *n* this act.

winch *n* machine for hoisting or hauling using cable wound around drum. ▶ *vt* move (something) by using a winch.

wind[1] *n* air in motion; breath; flatulence; idle talk; hint or suggestion; scent borne by air. ▶ *vt* **wind·ed, wind·ing.** render short of breath, esp. by blow, etc.; get the scent of. **wind·ward** [-wərd] *n* side against which wind is blowing. **wind'y** *adj* **wind·i·er, wind·i·est.** exposed to wind; flatulent; talking too much. **wind'fall** *n* unexpected good luck; fallen fruit. **wind instrument** musical instrument played by blowing or air pressure. **wind'mill** *n* wind-driven apparatus with fanlike sails for raising water, crushing grain, etc. **wind'pipe** *n* passage from throat to lungs. **wind'shield** [-sheeld] *n* protective sheet of glass, etc. in front of driver or pilot. **wind'sock** *n* cone of material flown on mast at airfield to indicate wind direction.

wind'surf·ing *n* sport of sailing standing up on sailboard holding special boom to control sail.

wind² [wīnd] *v* **wound** [wownd], **wind·ing.** ▶ *vi* twine; meander. ▶ *vt* twist around, coil; wrap; make ready for working by tightening spring. ▶ *n* act of winding; single turn of something wound; a turn, curve.

wind·lass [WIND-ləs] *n* winch, esp. simple one worked by a crank.

win·dow [WIN-doh] *n* hole in wall (with glass) to admit light, air, etc.; anything similar in appearance or function; area for display of goods behind glass of store front.

window dressing arrangement of goods in a shop window; deceptive display.

wine [wīn] *n* fermented juice of grape, etc. **wine'press** *n* apparatus for extracting juice from grape.

wing *n* feathered limb a bird uses in flying; one of organs of flight of insect or some animals; main lifting surface of aircraft; lateral extension; side portion of building projecting from main central portion; one of sides of a stage; flank corps of army on either side; part of car body that surrounds wheels; administrative, tactical unit of air force; faction esp. of political party. ▶ *pl* insignia worn by qualified aircraft pilot; sides of stage. ▶ *vi* fly; move, go very fast. ▶ *vt* disable, wound slightly.

wing'span *n* distance between the wing tips of an aircraft, bird, or insect.

wink [wingk] *v* close and open (an eye) rapidly, esp. to indicate friendliness or as signal; twinkle. ▶ *n* act of winking.

win·now [WIN-oh] *vt* blow free of chaff; sift, examine.

win·some [WIN-səm] *adj* charming, winning. **win'some·ly** *adv*

win·ter [WIN-tər] *n* the coldest season. ▶ *vi* pass, spend the winter. **win'try** *adj* **-tri·er, -tri·est.** of, like winter; cold.

wipe [wīp] *vt* **wiped, wip·ing.** rub so as to clean. ▶ *n* wiping. **wi'per** *n* one that wipes; automatic wiping apparatus (esp. windshield wiper).

wipe out annihilate; *inf* kill; *sl* beat decisively. **wiped-out** *adj sl* exhausted; intoxicated. **wipe'out** *n inf* murder; decisive defeat.

wire [wīr] *n* metal drawn into thin, flexible strand; something made of wire, e.g. fence; telegram. ▶ *vt*

wired, wir·ing. provide, fasten with wire; send by telegraph.

wired *adj sl* excited or nervous; using computers and the Internet to send and receive information.

wiring *n* system of wires. **wir'y** *adj* **wir·i·er, wir·i·est.** like wire; lean and tough. **wire-haired** *adj* (of various breeds of dog) with short stiff hair.

wire·less [WIR-lis] *n obs.* term for RADIO or RADIO SET. ▶ *adj* not requiring wires.

wise¹ [wīz] *adj* having intelligence and knowledge; sensible. **wis·dom** [WIZ-dəm] *n* (accumulated) knowledge, learning; erudition. **wise'ly** *adv* **wise'a·cre** *n* one who wishes to seem wise. **wisdom tooth** third molar usually cut about 20th year.

wise² *n obs* manner.

wise·crack [WĪZ-krak] *n inf* flippant (would-be) clever remark.

wish *vi* have a desire. ▶ *vt* desire. ▶ *n* desire; thing desired. **wish'ful** [-fəl] *adj* desirous; too optimistic. **wish'bone** *n* V-shaped bone above breastbone of fowl.

wisp *n* light, delicate streak, as of smoke; twisted handful, usu. of straw, etc.; stray lock of hair. **wisp'y** *adj* **wisp·i·er, wisp·i·est.**

wist·ful [WIST-fəl] *adj* longing, yearning; sadly pensive. **wist'ful·ly** *adv*

wit *n* ingenuity in connecting amusingly incongruous ideas; person gifted with this power; sense; intellect; understanding; ingenuity; humor. **wit'ti·cism** [-ti-sizm] *n* witty remark. **wit'ti·ly** *adv* **wit'ting·ly** *adv* on purpose; knowingly. **wit'less** [-lis] *adj* foolish. **wit'ty** *adj* **-ti·er, -ti·est.**

witch [wich] *n* person, usu. female, believed to practice, practicing, or professing to practice (black) magic, sorcery; ugly, wicked woman; fascinating woman. **witch'craft** *n* **witch doctor** in certain societies, person appearing to cure or cause injury, disease by magic.

with [with] *prep* in company or possession of; against; in relation to; through; by means of. **with·al** [with-AWL] *adv* also, likewise. **with·in'** *prep, adv* in, inside. **with·out'** *prep* lacking; *obs* outside.

with·draw [with-DRAW] *v* **-drew, -drawn, -draw·ing.** draw back or out. **with·draw'al** *n* **with·drawn'** *adj* reserved, unsociable.

with·er [WITH-ər] *v* (cause to) wilt, dry up, decline. **with'er·ing** *adj* (of glance, etc.) scornful.

with·ers [WITH-ərz] *pl n* ridge between a horse's shoulder blades.

with·hold [with-HOHLD] *vt* **-held, -hold·ing.** restrain; keep back; refrain from giving.

with·stand' *vt* **-stood** [-stuud], **-stand·ing.** oppose, resist, esp. successfully.

wit·ness [WIT-nis] *n* one who sees something; testimony; one who gives testimony. ▶ *vi* give testimony. ▶ *vt* see; attest; see and sign as having seen.

wiz·ard [WIZ-ərd] *n* sorcerer, magician; conjurer. **wiz'ard·ry** *n*

wiz·ened [WIZ-ənd] *adj* shriveled, wrinkled.

wob·ble [WOB-əl] *vi* **-bled, -bling.** move unsteadily; sway. ▶ *n* an unsteady movement. **wob'bly** *adj* **-bli·er, -bli·est.**

woe [woh] *n* grief. **woe·be·gone** [WOH-bi-gawn] *adj* looking sorrowful. **woe'ful** [-fəl] *adj* sorrowful; pitiful; wretched. **woe'ful·ly** *adv*

wolf [wuulf] *n, pl* **wolves.** wild predatory doglike animal of northern countries; *inf* man who habitually tries to seduce women. ▶ *vt* eat ravenously. **wolf whistle**

whistle by man expressing admiration for a woman. **cry wolf** raise false alarm.

wolf·ram [WUUL-frəm] *n* tungsten.

wol·ver·ine [wuul-və-REEN] *n* carnivorous mammal inhabiting northern regions.

wom·an [WUUM-ən] *n, pl* **wom·en** [WIM-in] adult human female; women collectively. **wom'an·hood** [-huud] *n* **wom'an·ish** *adj* effeminate. **wom'an·ize** *vi* **-ized, -iz·ing.** (of man) indulge in many casual affairs with women. **wom'an·kind** [-kīnd] *n* **wom'an·ly** *adj* of, proper to woman.

women's liberation movement for removal of attitudes, practices that preserve social, economic, etc. inequalities between women and men (also **women's lib**).

womb [woom] *n* female organ of conception and gestation, uterus.

won [wun] pt./pp. of WIN.

won·der [WUN-dər] *n* emotion excited by amazing or unusual thing; marvel, miracle. ▶ *vi* be curious about; feel amazement. **won'der·ful** [-fəl] *adj* remarkable; very fine. **won'der·ment** [-mənt] *n* surprise. **won'drous** [-drəs] *adj* inspiring wonder; strange.

wont [wawnt] *n* custom. ▶ *adj* accustomed. **wont'ed** [-id] *adj* habitual, established.

woo *vt* court, seek to marry. **woo'er** [-ər] *n* suitor.

wood [wuud] *n* substance of trees, timber; firewood; tract of land with growing trees. **wood'ed** [-id] *adj* having (many) trees. **wood'en** [-n] *adj* made of wood; obstinate; without expression. **wood'y** *adj* **wood'chuck** *n* Amer. burrowing rodent. **wood'cut** *n* engraving on wood; impression from this. **wood'land** [-lənd] *n* woods, forest. **wood'peck·er** *n* bird that searches tree trunks for insects. **wood'wind** *adj, n* (of) wind instruments of orchestra, orig. made of wood.

woof [wuuf] *n* the threads that cross the warp in weaving.

woof·er [WUUF-ər] *n* loudspeaker

for reproducing low-frequency sounds.

wool [wuul] *n* soft hair of sheep, goat, etc.; yarn spun from this. **wool'en** [-in] *adj* **wool'ly** *adj* **-li·er**, **-li·est**. of wool; vague, muddled. ▶ *n* [-eez] (oft. pl) knitted woolen garment, esp. warm undergarment. **wool'gath·er·ing** *n* daydreaming.

word [wurd] *n* unit of speech or writing regarded by users of a language as the smallest separate meaningful unit; term; message; brief remark; information; promise; command. ▶ *vt* express in words, esp. in particular way. **word'ing** *n* choice and arrangement of words. **word'y** *adj* **word·i·er**, **word·i·est**. using more words than necessary, verbose. **word processor** keyboard, microprocessor and monitor for electronic organization and storage of written text.

wore pt. of WEAR.

work [wurk] *n* labor; employment; occupation; task; toil; something made or accomplished; production of art or science; book; needlework. ▶ *pl* factory; total of person's deeds, writings, etc.; *inf* everything, full or extreme treatment; mechanism of clock, etc. ▶ *vt* cause to operate; make, shape. ▶ *vi* apply effort; labor; operate; be engaged in trade, profession, etc.; turn out successfully; ferment. **work'a·ble** *adj* **work·a·hol·ic** [wur-kə-HAW-lik] *n* person addicted to work. **work·ing class** social class consisting of wage earners, esp. manual. **working-class** *adj* **work·man** [WURK-mən] *n*, *pl* **-men**. manual worker; male worker. **work'man·ship** *n* skill of workman; way thing is finished; style. **work'shop** *n* place where things are made; discussion group, seminar.

world [wurld] *n* the universe; Earth; sphere of existence; mankind, people generally; society. **world'ly** *adj* earthly; mundane; absorbed in the pursuit of material gain, advantage; carnal. **World Wide Web** global computer network sharing graphics, etc., via the Internet.

worm [wurm] *n* small limbless creeping snakelike creature; anything resembling worm in shape or movement; gear wheel with teeth forming part of screw threads; *inf* weak, despised person; *Computers* type of virus. ▶ *pl* (disorder caused by) infestation of worms, esp. in intestines. ▶ *vi* crawl. ▶ *vt* work (oneself) in insidiously; extract (secret) craftily; rid of worms. **worm'-eaten** *adj* full of holes gnawed by worms; old, antiquated. **worm'y** *adj* **worm·i·er**, **worm·i·est**.

worm·wood [WURM-wuud] *n* bitter herb; bitterness.

worn pp. of WEAR.

wor·ry [WUR-ee] *v* **-ried**, **-ry·ing**. ▶ *vi* be (unduly) concerned. ▶ *vt* trouble, pester, harass; (of dog) seize, shake with teeth. ▶ *n*, *pl* **-ries**. (cause of) anxiety, concern. **wor'ri·er** *n*

worse [wurs] *adj*, *adv* comp. of BAD, BADLY. ▶ *n* **worst** *adj*, *adv* sup. of BAD, BADLY. ▶ *n* **wors'en** [-in] *v* make, grow worse; impair; deteriorate.

wor·ship [WUR-ship] *vt* **-shiped**, **-ship·ing**. show religious devotion to; adore; love and admire. ▶ *n* act of worshiping. **wor'ship·er** *n*

wor·sted [WUUS-tid] *n* woolen yarn. ▶ *adj* made of woolen yarn; spun from wool.

worth [wurth] *adj* having or deserving to have value specified; meriting. ▶ *n* excellence; merit, value; virtue; usefulness; price; quantity to be had for a given sum. **wor·thy** [WUR-thee] *adj* **-thi·er**, **-thi·est**. virtuous; meriting. ▶ *n* one of eminent worth; celebrity. **wor'thi·ness** [-thee-nis] *n* **worth·less** [WURTH-lis] *adj* useless. **worth·while** [wurth-hwīl] *adj* worth the time, effort, etc. involved.

would [wuud] *v aux* expressing

wish, intention, probability; pt. of WILL. **would-be** [WUUD-bee] *adj* wishing, pretending to be.

wound¹ [woond] *n* injury, hurt from cut, stab, etc. ▶ *vt* inflict wound on; injure; pain.

wound² [rhymes with **sound**] pt./ pp. of WIND².

wove [wohv] pt. of WEAVE. **wo'ven** pp. of WEAVE.

wow *interj* of astonishment. ▶ *n inf* object of astonishment, admiration, etc.; variation, distortion in pitch in record player, etc.

wraith [rayth] *n* apparition of a person seen shortly before or after death; specter.

wran·gle [RANG-gəl] *vi* **-gled, -gling.** quarrel (noisily); dispute; herd cattle. ▶ *n* noisy quarrel; dispute. **wran'gler** [-glər] *n* cowboy; disputant.

wrap [rap] *v* **wrapped, wrap·ping.** cover, esp. by putting something around; put around. ▶ *n* sandwich made by wrapping filling in a tortilla, etc. **wrap'per** *n* loose garment; covering. **wrapping** *n* material used to wrap.

wrath [rath] *n* anger. **wrath'ful** [-fəl] *adj* **wrath'ful·ly** *adv*

wreak [reek] *vt* inflict (vengeance); cause.

wreath [reeth] *n* something twisted into ring form, esp. band of flowers, etc. as memorial or tribute on grave, etc. **wreathe** [reeth] *vt* **wreathed, wreath·ing.** form into wreath; surround; wind around.

wreck [rek] *n* destruction of ship; wrecked ship; ruin; something ruined. ▶ *vt* cause the wreck of. **wreck'age** [-ij] *n* **wreck'er** *n* person or thing that destroys, ruins; vehicle for towing disabled, wrecked, etc. automobiles, a tow truck.

wren [ren] *n* kind of small songbird.

wrench [rench] *vt* twist; distort; seize forcibly; sprain. ▶ *n* violent twist; tool for twisting or turning; tool for gripping nut or bolt head; sudden pain caused esp. by parting.

wrest [rest] *vt* take by force; twist violently.

wres·tle [RES-əl] *vi* **-tled, -tling.** fight (esp. as sport) by grappling and trying to throw down; strive (with); struggle. ▶ *n* **wrest'ler** [-lər] *n*

wretch [rech] *n* despicable person; miserable creature. **wretch'ed** [-id] *adj* **-ed·er, -ed·est.** miserable, unhappy; worthless. **wretch'ed·ly** *adv* **wretch'ed·ness** [-nis] *n*

wrig·gle [RIG-əl] *v* **-gled, -gling.** move with twisting action, as worm; squirm. ▶ *n* this action.

wring [ring] *vt* **wrung, wring·ing.** twist; extort; pain; squeeze out.

wrin·kle [RING-kəl] *n* slight ridge or furrow on surface; crease in the skin; fold; pucker; *inf* [useful] trick, hint] ▶ *v* **-kled, -kling.** make, become wrinkled, pucker.

wrist [rist] *n* joint between hand and arm. **wrist'let** [-lit] *n* band worn on wrist.

writ [rit] *n* written command from law court or other authority.

write [rīt] *v* **wrote, writ·ten, writ·ing.** ▶ *vi* mark paper, etc. with the symbols that are used to represent words or sounds; compose; send a letter. ▶ *vt* set down in words; compose; communicate in writing. **writ'er** *n* one who writes; author. **write-off** *n* cancellation from accounts as loss; *inf* person or thing considered hopeless. **write-up** *n* written (published) account of something.

writhe [rīth] *v* **writhed, writh·ing.** twist, squirm in or as in pain, etc. ▶ *vi* be acutely embarrassed, etc.

wrong [rawng] *adj* not right or good; not suitable; wicked; incorrect; mistaken; not functioning properly. ▶ *n* that which is wrong; harm; evil. ▶ *vt* do wrong to; think badly of without justification. **wrong'do·er** [-doo-ər] *n* one who acts immorally or illegally. **wrong'ful** [-fəl] *adj* **wrong'ful·ly** *adv*

wrote [roht] pt. of WRITE.

wrought [rawt] *adj* (of metals)

shaped by hammering or beating.
wrought iron pure form of iron
used esp. in decorative railings, etc.
wrung pt./pp. of WRING.
wry [rī] *adj* **wri·er, wri·est.** turned
to one side, contorted, askew;
sardonic, dryly humorous.
wuss [woos] *n, pl* **-us·ses.** *sl* feeble
person.
WWW World Wide Web.

X x

X Christ; Christian; cross; Roman numeral, 10; mark indicating something wrong, a choice, a kiss, signature, etc. *n* unknown, mysterious person, factor.

Xe *Chem* xenon.

xe·non [ZEE-non] *n* colorless, odorless gas occurring in very small quantities in air.

xen·o·pho·bi·a [zen-ə-FOH-bee-ə] *n* dislike, hatred, fear, of strangers or aliens. **xen·o·pho'bic** *adj*

xe·rog·ra·phy [zi-ROG-rə-fee] *n* photocopying process.

Xmas [EKS-məs] *n inf* Christmas.

x-rays [EKS-rayz] *pl n* radiation of very short wavelengths, capable of penetrating solid bodies, and printing on photographic plate shadow picture of objects not permeable by rays. **x-ray** *v* photograph by x-rays.

xy·lo·carp [ZĪ-lə-kahrp] *n* hard, woody fruit. **xy·lo·carp'ous** *adj* having fruit that becomes hard or woody.

xy·lo·graph [ZĪ-lə-graf] *n* wood engraving; impression from wood block.

xy·loid [ZĪ-loid] *adj* pert. to wood; woody, ligneous.

xy·lo·phone [ZĪ-lə-fohn] *n* musical instrument of wooden bars that sound when struck.

Y y

Y *Chem* yttrium.

Y2K *n inf* name for AD 2000 (esp. referring to the millennium bug).

yacht [yot] *n* vessel propelled by sail or power, used for racing, pleasure, etc. **yachts·man** [YOTS-mən] *n, pl* **-men**.

ya·hoo [YAH-hoo] *n, pl* **-hoos.** crude, coarse person.

Yah·weh [YAH-we] *n* Jehovah, God.

yak *n* shaggy-haired, long-horned ox of Central Asia.

yam *n* large edible tuber, sweet potato.

yank [yangk] *v* jerk, tug; pull quickly. ▶ *n* quick tug.

Yank [yangk], **Yank'ee** *adj, n inf* American.

yap *vi* **yapped, yap·ping.** bark (as small dog); *sl* talk shrilly, idly. ▶ *n* a bark; *sl* the mouth.

yard[1] [yahrd] *n* unit of length, 3 feet (36 inches, 0.9144 meter); spar slung across ship's mast to extend sails. **yard'stick** *n* 36-inch ruler; formula or standard of measurement or comparison. **yard'age** [-ij] *n* measurement of distance in yards; length in yards.

yard[2] *n* piece of enclosed ground adjoining building and used for some specific purpose, as garden, storage, holding livestock, etc. **yard'age** *n* use of yard; charge made for this.

yar·mul·ke [YAHR-məl-kə] *n* skullcap worn by Jewish men and boys, esp. in synagogue.

yarn [yahrn] *n* spun thread; *inf* long involved story.

yash·mak [yahsh-MAHK] *n* face veil worn by Muslim women.

yaw *vi* of aircraft, etc., turn about vertical axis; deviate temporarily from course.

yawl *n* two-masted sailing vessel.

yawn *vi* open mouth wide, esp. in sleepiness; gape. ▶ *n* a yawning.

yaws [yawz] *n* contagious tropical skin disease.

Yb *Chem* ytterbium.

ye [yee] *pron obs* you.

yea [yay] *interj* yes. ▶ *n* affirmative vote.

year [yeer] *n* time taken by one revolution of Earth around sun, about 365 days; twelve months. **year'ling** *n* animal one year old. **year'ly** *adv* every year, once a year. ▶ *adj* happening, etc. once a year.

yearn [yurn] *vi* feel longing, desire; be filled with pity, tenderness. **yearn'ing** *n*

yeast [yeest] *n* substance used as fermenting, leavening agent, esp. in brewing and in baking bread. **yeast'y** *adj* **yeast·i·er, yeast·i·est.** of, like yeast; frothy, fermenting; (of time) characterized by excitement, change, etc.

yell *v* cry out in loud shrill tone; speak in this way. ▶ *n* loud shrill cry; a cheer, shout.

yel·low [YEL-oh] *adj* **-er, -est.** of the color of lemons, gold, etc.; *inf* cowardly. ▶ *n* this color. **yel'low·bel·ly** *n, pl* **-lies.** *sl* coward. **yellow fever** acute infectious disease of (sub)tropical climates. **yellow jacket** type of wasp; *sl* yellow capsule of phenobarbital.

yelp *vi, n* (produce) quick, shrill cry.

yen[1] *n* Japanese monetary unit.

yen[2] *n inf* longing, craving.

yeo·man [YOH-mən] *n, pl* **-men.** petty officer in U.S. Navy having mainly clerical duties; *Brit. hist* farmer cultivating own land. ▶ *adj* performed in valiant, thorough manner.

yes *interj* affirms or consents, gives an affirmative answer. ▶ *n, pl* **yes·ses.** affirmative reply. **yes-man** *n, pl* **-men.** weak person willing to agree to anything.

yes·ter·day [YES-tər-day] *n* day before today; recent time. ▶ *adv, adj*

yet *adv* now, still, besides, hitherto; nevertheless. ▶ *conj* but, at the same time, nevertheless.

yet·i [YET-ee] n see ABOMINABLE SNOWMAN.

yew [yoo] n evergreen tree with dark leaves; its wood.

Yid·dish [YID-ish] adj, n (of, in) language used by many Jews in or from Europe, orig. a form of German written in Hebrew letters, with words from Hebrew and many other languages.

yield [yeeld] vt give or return as food; produce; provide; concede; give up, surrender. ▶ vi produce; submit; comply; surrender, give way. ▶ n amount produced, return, profit, result.

yo·del [YOHD-l] vi -deled, -del·ing. warble in falsetto tone. ▶ n falsetto warbling as practiced by Swiss mountaineers.

yo·ga [YOH-gə] n Hindu philosophical system aiming at spiritual, mental and physical well-being by means of certain physical and mental exercises. **yo·gi** [-gee] n, pl -gis. one who practices yoga.

yo·gurt [YOH-gərt] n thick, custard-like preparation of curdled milk.

yoke [yohk] n wooden bar put across the necks of two animals to hold them together and to which plow, etc. can be attached; various objects like a yoke in shape or use; fitted part of garment, esp. around neck, shoulders; bond or tie; domination. ▶ vt yoked, yok·ing. put a yoke on, couple, unite.

yo·kel [YOH-kəl] n offens person who lives in the country and is usu. simple and old-fashioned.

yolk [yohk] n yellow central part of egg; oily secretion of skin of sheep.

yon adj obs or dial that or those over there. **yon·der** [YON-dər] adj yon. ▶ adv over there, in that direction.

yore [yor] n Poet the distant past.

York·shire pudding [YORK-shər] baked batter eaten with roast beef.

you [yoo] pron referring to person(s) addressed, or to unspecified person(s).

young [yung] adj -er, -est. not far advanced in growth, life or existence; not yet old; immature; junior; recently formed; vigorous. ▶ n offspring. **young'ster** [-stər] n child.

your [yuur] adj of, belonging to, or associated with you; of, belonging to, or associated with an unspecified person or people in general. **yours** pron something belonging to you. **your·self'** pron, pl -selves.

youth [yooth] n state or time of being young; state before adult age; young man; young people. **youth'ful** [-fəl] adj

yowl v, n (produce) mournful cry.

yo-yo [YOH-yoh] n, pl -yos. toy consisting of a spool attached to a string, by which it can be spun out and reeled in while attached to the finger.

yuc·ca [YUK-ə] n tropical plant with stiff lancelike leaves.

Yule [yool] n the Christmas festival or season.

yup·pie [YUP-ee] n young urban professional. ▶ adj

Z z

za·ba·glio·ne [zah-bəl-YOH-nee] *n* Italian custardlike dessert of whipped and heated egg yolks, sugar and Marsala wine.

za·ny [ZAY-nee] *adj* **-ni·er, -ni·est.** comical, funny in unusual way. ▶ *n,* *pl* **-nies.** eccentric person; silly person.

zap *inf* ▶ *vt* **zapped, zap·ping.** attack, kill or destroy; *Computers* clear from screen, erase; change (TV channels) rapidly by remote control; skip over or delete sound of (commercials).

zeal [zeel] *n* fervor; keenness, enthusiasm. **zeal·ot** [ZEL-ət] *n* fanatic; enthusiast. **zeal·ous** [-əs] *adj* ardent; enthusiastic; earnest. **zeal·ous·ly** *adv*

ze·bra [ZEE-brə] *n, pl* **-bras.** striped Afr. animal like a horse.

ze·bu [ZEE-byoo] *n* humped Indian ox or cow.

Zen *n* Japanese school teaching contemplation, meditation.

ze·nith [ZEE-nith] *n* point of the heavens directly above an observer; point opposite nadir; summit, peak; climax.

zeph·yr [ZEF-ər] *n* soft, gentle breeze.

zep·pe·lin [ZEP-ə-lin] *n* large, cylindrical, rigid airship.

ze·ro [ZEER-oh] *n, pl* **-ros, -roes.** nothing; figure 0; point on graduated instrument from which positive and negative quantities are reckoned; the lowest point. ▶ *vt* **-roed, -ro·ing.** reduce to zero; adjust (instrument, etc.) to zero.

zest *n* enjoyment; excitement; interest, flavor; peel of orange or lemon. **zest'ful** [-fəl] *adj*

zig·zag *n* line or course characterized by sharp turns in alternating directions. ▶ *vi* **-zagged, -zag·ging.** move along in zigzag course.

zinc [zingk] *n* bluish-white metallic element with wide variety of uses,

esp. in alloys as brass, etc.

zin·ni·a [ZIN-ee-ə] *n* plant with daisylike, brightly colored flowers.

Zi·on [ZĪ-ən] *n* hill on which Jerusalem stands; modern Jewish nation; Israel; *Christian Church* heaven. **Zi'on·ism** *n* movement to found, support Jewish homeland in what now is state of Israel. **Zi'on·ist** *n, adj*

zip *n* short whizzing sound; energy, vigor. ▶ *v* **zipped, zip·ping.** move with zip.

zip code [kohd] system of numbers used to aid sorting of mail (also **ZIP code**).

zip·per [ZIP-ər] *n* device for fastening with two rows of flexible metal or plastic teeth, interlocked and opened by a sliding clip. ▶ *vt* fasten with zipper.

zir·con [ZUR-kon] *n* mineral used as gemstone and in industry.

zith·er [ZITH-ər] *n* flat stringed instrument.

Zn *Chem* zinc.

zo·di·ac [ZOH-dee-ak] *n* imaginary belt of the heavens along which the sun, moon, and chief planets appear to move, divided crosswise into twelve equal areas, called **signs of the zodiac,** each named after a constellation. **zo·di·a·cal** [zoh-DĪ-ə-kəl] *adj*

zom·bie [ZOM-bee] *n* person appearing lifeless, apathetic, etc.; corpse supposedly brought to life by supernatural spirit.

zone [zohn] *n* region with particular characteristics or use; any of the five belts into which tropics and arctic and antarctic circles divide Earth.

zoo *n* place where wild animals are kept, studied, bred and exhibited.

zo·og·ra·phy [zoh-OG-rə-fee] *n* descriptive zoology. **zo·og'ra·pher, zo·og'ra·phist** *n* **zo·o·graph'i·cal** *adj*

zo·ol·o·gy [zoh-OL-ə-jee] *n*

scientific study of animals; characteristics of particular animals or of fauna of particular area. **zo·o·log'i·cal** *adj* **zo·ol'o·gist** *n*
zoom *v* (cause to) make loud buzzing, humming sound; (cause to) go fast or rise, increase sharply. ▶ *vi* (of camera) use lens of adjustable focal length to make subject appear to move closer or farther away. **zoom lens** lens used in this way.
zo·o·phyte [ZOH-ə-fīt] *n* animal resembling a plant, such as a sea anemone. **zo·o·phyt'ic** [-FIT-ik] *adj*
Zr *Chem* zirconium.
zuc·chi·ni [zoo-KEEN-ee] *n, pl* **-ni** or **-nis.** green-skinned summer squash.
Zu·lu [ZOO-loo] *n* member, language of S Afr. Bantu tribes.
zy·gote [ZĪ-goht] *n* fertilized egg cell.
zy·mot·ic [zī-MOT-ik] *adj* of, or caused by fermentation; of, caused by infection.

Biographies

Abelson, Philip. born 1913, U.S. physical chemist. He created (with Edwin McMillan) the first transuranic element, neptunium (1940).

Acheson, Dean (Gooderham). 1893–1971, U.S. lawyer and statesman: secretary of state (1949–53) under President Truman.

Adams, Gerry, full name *Gerrard Adams.* born 1948, Northern Ireland politician; president of Sinn Féin from 1983: negotiated the Irish Republican Army ceasefires in 1994–96 and 1997; **Henry (Brooks).** 1838–1918, U.S. historian and writer. His works include *Mont Saint Michel et Chartres* (1913) and his autobiography *The Education of Henry Adams* (1918); **John.** 1735–1826, second president of the U.S. (1797–1801); U.S. ambassador to Great Britain (1785–88); helped draft the Declaration of Independence (1776); **John Couch.** 1819–92, British astronomer who deduced the existence and position of the planet Neptune; **John Quincey.** son of John Adams. 1767–1848, sixth president of the U.S. (1825–29); secretary of state (1817–25); **Richard.** born 1920, British author; his novels include *Watership Down* (1972), *The Plague Dogs* (1977), and *Traveller* (1988); **Samuel.** 1722–1803, U.S. revolutionary leader; one of the organizers of the Boston Tea Party; a signatory of the Declaration of Independence.

Addams, Jane. 1860–1935, U.S. social reformer, feminist, and pacifist, who founded Hull House, a social settlement in Chicago: Nobel peace prize 1931.

Adler, Alfred. 1870–1937, Austrian psychiatrist, noted for his descriptions of overcompensation and inferiority feelings; **Larry,** full name *Lawrence Cecil Adler.* born 1914, U.S. harmonica player.

Agassi, Andre. born 1970, U.S. tennis player: won the Wimbledon men's singles in 1992 and the U.S. Open in 1994 and 1999.

Agassiz, Jean Louis Rodolphe. 1807–73, Swiss natural historian and geologist, settled in the U.S. after 1846.

Agee, James. 1909–55, U.S. novelist, poet, and film critic. His works include the autobiographical novel *A Death in the Family* (1957).

Agnew, Spiro Theodore. 1918–96, U.S. Republican politician; vice president (1969–73).

Aiken, Conrad (Potter). 1889–1973, U.S. poet, short-story writer, and critic. His works include *Collected Poems* (1953) and the novel *Blue Voyage* (1927); **Howard Hathaway.** 1900–73, U.S. mathematician; pioneered the construction of electronic computers.

Aitken, Robert Grant. 1864–1951, U.S. astronomer who discovered over three thousand double stars; **William Maxwell;** See Beaverbrook.

Albee, Edward. born 1928, U.S. dramatist. His plays include *Who's Afraid of Virginia Woolf?* (1962), *Seascape* (1975), *Marriage Play* (1986), *Three Tall Women* (1990), and *The Play About the Baby* (1998).

Albers, Josef. 1888–1976, U.S. painter, designer, and poet, born in Germany. His works include a series of abstract paintings entitled *Homage to the Square.*

Alcott, Louisa May. 1832–88, U.S. novelist, noted for her children's books, esp. *Little Women* (1869).

Aldrin, Edwin Eugene Jr., known as *Buzz.* born 1930, U.S. astronaut; the second man to set foot on the moon on July 20, 1969, during the Apollo 11 flight.

Aleichem, Sholom, real name *Solomon Rabinowitz.* 1859–1916, U.S. Jewish writer, born in Russia. His works include *Tevye the Milkman*, which was adapted for the stage musical *Fiddler on the Roof*.

Alger, Horatio. 1834–99, U.S. author of adventure stories for boys, including *Ragged Dick* (1867).

Algren, Nelson. 1909–81, U.S. novelist. His novels, mostly set in Chicago, include *Never Come Morning* (1942) and *The Man with the Golden Arm* (1949).

Allen, Ethan. 1738–89, American soldier during the War of Independence who led the Green Mountain Boys of Vermont; **Woody.** real name *Allen Stewart Konigsberg.* born 1935, U.S. film comedian, screenwriter, and director. His films as an actor and director include *Annie Hall* (1977), *Manhattan* (1979), *Hannah and Her Sisters* (1986), and *Celebrity* (1998).

Allston, Washington. 1779–1843, U.S. painter and author, regarded as the earliest U.S. Romantic painter. His paintings include *Elijah in the Desert* (1818) and *Moonlit Landscape* (1819).

Altman, Robert. U.S. film director; his films include *M*A*S*H* (1970) and *The Gingerbread Man* (1998).

Alvarez, Luis Walter. 1911–88, U.S. physicist. He made (with Felix Bloch) the first measurement of the neutron's magnetic moment (1939). Nobel prize for physics 1968.

Anderson, Carl David. 1905–91, U.S. physicist, who discovered the positron in cosmic rays (1932): Nobel prize for physics 1936; **Elizabeth Garrett.** 1836–1917, English physician and feminist: a campaigner for the admission of women to the professions; **John.** 1893–1962, Australian philosopher, born in Scotland, whose theories are expounded in *Studies in Empirical Philosophy* (1962); Dame **Judith,** real name *Frances Margaret Anderson.* 1898– 1992, Australian stage and film actress; **Lindsay (Gordon)** 1923–94, British film and theatre director: his films include *This Sporting Life* (1963), *If* (1968), and *O Lucky Man!* (1973); **Marian.**

1902–93, U.S. contralto, the first Black permanent member of the Metropolitan Opera Company, New York; **Philip Warren.** 1923–96, U.S. physicist, noted for his work on solid-state physics. Nobel prize for physics 1977; **Sherwood.** 1874–1941, U.S. novelist and short-story writer, best known for *Winesburg Ohio* (1919), a collection of short stories illustrating small-town life.

Andretti, Mario. born 1940, U.S. racing driver: world champion (1978).

Anfinsen, Christian Boehmer. 1916–95, U.S. biochemist, noted for his research on the structure of enzymes. Nobel prize for chemistry 1972.

Angelou, Maya, real name *Marguerite Johnson.* born 1928, U.S. Black novelist, poet, and dramatist. Her works include the autobiographical novel *I Know Why the Caged Bird Sings* (1970) and its sequels, the collection of poetry *I Shall Not be Moved* (1990), and *Phenomenal Woman* (1995).

Antheil, George. 1900–59, U.S. composer. His best known work is the controversial *Le Ballet Méchanique* (1924) for motor horns, bells, and airplane propellers.

Arbus, Diane, original name *Diane Nemerov.* 1923–71, U.S. photographer, noted esp. for her portraits of vagrants, dwarfs, transvestites, etc.

Archipenko, Aleksandr Porfiryevich. 1887– 1964, Russian sculptor and painter, in the U.S. after 1923, whose work is characterized by economy of form.

Arendt, Hannah. 1906–75, U.S. political philosopher, born in Germany. Her publications include *The Origins of Totalitarianism* (1951) and *Eichmann in Jerusalem* (1961).

Armstrong, Edwin Howard. 1890–1954, U.S. electrical engineer; invented the superheterodyne radio receiver and the FM radio; **(Daniel) Louis,** known as *Satchmo.* 1900–71, U.S. jazz trumpeter, bandleader, and singer; **Gillian.** born 1950, Australian film director; her films include *My Brilliant Career* (1978); **Neil (Alden).** born 1930, U.S. astronaut; commanded Apollo 11 on the first manned lunar landing during which he became the first man to set foot on the moon on July 20, 1969.

Arthur, a legendary king of the Britons in the sixth century A.D., who led Celtic resistance against the Saxons: possibly based on a historical figure; represented as leader of the Knights of the Round Table at Camelot; **Chester Alan.** 1830–86, 21st president of the U.S. (1881–85). **not know whether one is Arthur or Martha** *Austral. and N.Z informal* to be in a state of confusion.

Asch, Sholem. 1880–1957, U.S. writer, born in Poland, who wrote in Yiddish. His works include biblical novels.

Ashe, Arthur (Robert). 1943–93, U.S. tennis player: U.S. champion 1968; Wimbledon champion 1975.

Asimov, Isaac. 1920–92, U.S. writer and biochemist, born in Russia. His science-fiction works include *Foundation Trilogy* (1951–53; sequel 1982) and the collection of stories *I, Robot* (1950).

Astaire, Fred, real name *Frederick Austerlitz*. 1899–1987, U.S. dancer, singer, and actor, whose films include *Top Hat* (1935), *Swing Time* (1936), and *The Band Wagon* (1953).

Astor, John Jacob, 1st Baron Astor of Hever. 1886–1971, British proprietor of *The Times* (1922–66); **Nancy (Witcher),** Viscountess, original name *Nancy Langhorne*. 1879–1964, British Conservative politician, born in the U.S.; the first woman to sit in the British House of Commons.

Auden, W(ystan) H(ugh). 1907–73, U.S. poet, dramatist, critic, and librettist, born in Britain; noted for his lyric and satirical poems and for plays written in collaboration with Christopher Isherwood.

Audubon, John James. 1785–1851, U.S. naturalist and artist, noted particularly for his paintings of birds in *Birds of America* (1827–38).

Axelrod, Julius. born 1912, U.S. neuropharmacologist, renowned for his work on catecholamines. Nobel prize for physiology or medicine (with von Euler and Bernard Katz) 1970.

Bacharach, Burt born 1928, U.S. composer of popular songs, usually with lyricist Hal David.

Baez, Joan. born 1941, U.S. rock and folk singer and songwriter, noted for the pure quality of her voice and for her committed pacifist and protest songs.

Balanchine, George. 1904–83, U.S. choreographer, born in Russia.

Baldwin, James Arthur. 1924–87, U.S. Black writer, whose works include the novel *Go Tell it on the Mountain* (1954); **Stanley,** 1st Earl Baldwin of Bewdley. 1867–1947, British Conservative statesman: prime minister (1923–24, 1924–29, 1935–37).

Baltimore, David. born 1938, U.S. molecular biologist: shared the Nobel prize for physiology or medicine (1975) for his discovery of reverse transcriptase; **Lord.** See (Sir George) **Calvert.**

Bankhead, Tallulah (Brockman). 1902–68, U.S. stage and film actress; her successes included the plays *The Little Foxes* (1939) and *The Skin of Our Teeth* (1942).

Barber, Samuel. 1910–81, U.S. composer: his works include an *Adagio for Strings*, adapted from the second movement of his string quartet No. 1 (1936) and the opera *Vanessa* (1958).

Bardeen, John. 1908–91, U.S. physicist and electrical engineer, noted for his research on electrical conduction in solids; shared Nobel prize for physics 1956 for research on semiconductors leading to the invention of the transistor; shared Nobel prize for physics 1972 for contributions to the theory of superconductivity.

Barnard, Christiaan (Neethling). born 1923, South African surgeon, who performed the first human heart transplant (1967); **Edward Emerson.**

1857–1923, U.S. astronomer: noted for his discovery of the fifth satellite of Jupiter and his discovery of comets, nebulae, and a red dwarf (1916).

Barnes, Djuna. 1892–1982, U.S. novelist, noted for *Nightwood* (1936); **William.** 1801–86, British poet, best known for *Poems of Rural Life in the Dorset Dialect* (1879).

Barnum, P(hineas) T(aylor). 1810–91, U.S. showman, who created The Greatest Show on Earth (1871) and, with J. A. Bailey, founded the Barnum and Bailey Circus (1881).

Barth, Heinrich. 1821–65, German explorer: author of *Travels and Discoveries in North and Central Africa* (1857–58); **John (Simmons).** born 1930, U.S. novelist; his novels include *The Sot-Weed Factor* (1960), *Giles Goat-Boy* (1966), and *Once Upon a Time* (1994); **Karl.** 1886–1968, Swiss Protestant theologian. He stressed man's dependence on divine grace in such works as *Commentary on Romans* (1919).

Baryshnikov, Mikhail. born 1948, Soviet-born ballet dancer, who defected (1974) to the West while on tour with the Kirov Ballet: director (1980–90) of the American Ballet Theatre.

Basie, William, known as *Count Basie.* 1904–84, U.S. jazz pianist, bandleader, and composer: associated particularly with the polished phrasing and style of big-band jazz.

Battle, Kathleen. born 1948, U.S. opera singer: a coloratura soprano, she made her professional debut in 1972 and sang with New York City's Metropolitan Opera (1977–94).

Baum, L(yman) Frank 1856–1919, U.S. novelist, author of *The Wonderful Wizard of Oz* (1900) and its sequels.

Beadle, George Wells. 1903–89, U.S. biologist, who shared the Nobel prize for physiology or medicine in 1958 for his work in genetics.

Bechet, Sidney (Joseph). 1897–1959, U.S. jazz soprano saxophonist and clarinettist.

Beecher, Henry Ward. 1813–87, U.S. clergyman: a leader in the movement for the abolition of slavery.

Beiderbecke, Leon Bismarcke, known as *Bix.* 1903–31, U.S. jazz cornettist, composer, and pianist.

Békésy, Georg von. 1899–1972, U.S. physicist, born in Hungary; noted for his work on the mechanism of hearing: Nobel prize for physiology or medicine 1961.

Bell, Acton, Currer, and **Ellis.** pen names of the sisters Anne, Charlotte, and Emily Brontë; **Alexander Graham.** 1847–1922, U.S. scientist, born in Scotland, who invented the telephone (1876); Sir **Francis Henry Dillon.** 1851–1936, New Zealand statesman; prime minister of New Zealand (1925); **Gertrude (Margaret Lowthian).** 1868–1926, British traveller, writer, and diplomat; secretary to the British High Commissioner in Baghdad (1917–26); **(Susan) Jocelyn**, married name *Jocelyn Burnell*, born 1943, British radio astronomer, who discovered the first pulsar; **Vanessa**, original name *Vanessa Stephen*. 1879–1961, British painter; a member of the Bloomsbury group, sister of Virginia Woolf and wife of the art critic Clive Bell (1881–1964).

Bellow, Saul. born 1915, U.S. novelist, born in Canada. His works include *Dangling Man* (1944), *Herzog* (1964), *Humboldt's Gift* (1975), *Him with his Foot in his Mouth* (1986), and *The Actual* (1997): Nobel prize for literature 1976.

Benacerraf, Baruj. U.S. immunologist: shared the Nobel prize for physiology or medicine (1980) for his work on histocompatibility antigens.

Benét, Stephen Vincent. 1898–1943, U.S. poet and novelist, best known for his poem on the American Civil War *John Brown's Body* (1928).

Bennett, Alan. born 1934, British actor playwright. His plays include *Forty Years On* (1968), *The Old Country* (1977), *The Madness of*

George III (1991), and many television productions; **(Enoch) Arnold.** 1867–1931, British novelist, noted for *The Old Wives' Tale* (1908), *Clayhanger* (1910), and other works set in the Staffordshire Potteries; **James Gordon.** 1837–1931, U.S. newspaper editor, born in Scotland. He founded (1835) the *New York Herald* and introduced techniques of modern news reporting; **Jill.** 1931–90, British actress; **Richard Bedford,** 1st Viscount. 1870–1947, Canadian Conservative statesman; prime minister (1930–35); Sir **Richard Rodney.** born 1936, British composer, noted for his operas *The Mines of Sulphur* (1965) and *Victory* (1970).

Benny, Jack, real name *Benjamin Kubelsky*. 1894–1974, U.S. comedian.

Benton, Thomas Hart. 1889–1975, U.S. painter of rural life; a leader of the American Regionalist painters in the 1930s.

Berenson, Bernard 1865–1959, U.S. art historian, born in Lithuania: an authority on art of the Italian Renaissance.

Berg, Alban (Maria Johannes). 1885–1935, Austrian composer: a pupil of Schoenberg. His works include the operas *Wozzeck* (1921) and *Lulu* (1935), a violin concerto (1935), chamber works, and songs; **Paul.** born 1926, U.S. molecular biologist, the first to identify transfer RNA (1956). Nobel prize for chemistry 1980.

Berkeley, Busby. real name *William Berkeley Enos.* 1895–1976, U.S. dance director, noted esp. for his elaborate choreography in film musicals; **George.** 1685–1753, Irish philosopher and Anglican bishop, whose system of subjective idealism was expounded in his works *A Treatise concerning the Principles of Human Knowledge* (1710) and *Three Dialogues between Hylas and Philonous* (1713). He also wrote *Essay towards a New Theory of Vision* (1709); Sir **Lennox (Randal Francis).** 1903–89, British composer; his works include four symphonies, four

operas, and the *Serenade for Strings* (1939).

Berlin, Irving. original name *Israel Baline,* 1888–1989, U.S. composer and writer of lyrics, born in Russia. His musical comedies include *Annie Get Your Gun* (1946); his most popular song is *White Christmas*; Sir **Isaiah.** 1909–97, British philosopher, born in Latvia, historian, and diplomat. His books include *Historical Inevitability* (1954) and *The Magus of the North* (1993).

Bernstein, Leonard. 1918–90, U.S. conductor and composer, whose works include *The Age of Anxiety* (1949), the score of the musical *West Side Story* (1957), and *Mass* (1971).

Berry, Chuck, full name *Charles Edward Berry.* born 1926, U.S. rock-and-roll guitarist, singer, and songwriter. His frequently covered songs include "Maybellene" (1955), "Roll over Beethoven" (1956), "Johnny B. Goode" (1958), "Memphis, Tennessee" (1959), and "Promised Land" (1964); **Jean de France,** Duc de. 1340–1416, French prince, son of King John II; coregent (1380–88) for Charles VI and a famous patron of the arts.

Berryman, John. 1914–72, U.S. poet and critic, author of *Homage to Mistress Bradstreet* (1956) and *Dream Songs* (1964–68).

Bethe, Hans Albrecht. born 1906, U.S. physicist, born in Germany; noted for his research on astrophysics and nuclear physics: Nobel prize for physics 1967.

Bethmann Hollweg, Theobald von. 1856–1921, chancellor of Germany (1909–17).

Billy the Kid, nickname of *William H. Bonney.* 1859–81, U.S. outlaw.

Bishop, Elizabeth. 1911–79, U.S. poet, who lived in Brazil. Her poetry reflects her travelling experience, esp. in the tropics.

Blakey, Art, full name *Arthur Blakey.* (1919–90), U.S. Black jazz drummer and leader of the Jazz Messengers band.

Bloch, Ernest. 1880–1959, U.S. composer, born in Switzerland, who found inspiration in Jewish liturgical and folk music: his works include the symphonies *Israel*(1916) and *America* (1926); **Felix.** 1905–83, U.S. physicist, born in Switzerland: Nobel prize for physics (1952) for his work on the magnetic moments of atomic particles; **Konrad Emil.** born 1912, U.S. biochemist, born in Germany: shared the Nobel prize for physiology or medicine in 1964 for his work on fatty-acid metabolism; **Marc.** 1886–1944, French historian and Resistance fighter; author of *Feudal Society* (1935) and *Strange Defeat* (1940), an essay on the fall of France: killed by the Nazis.

Bloomfield, Leonard. 1887–1949, U.S. linguist, influential for his strictly scientific and descriptive approach to comparative linguistics; author of *Language* (1933).

Blumberg, Baruch Samuel. born 1925, U.S. physician, noted for work on antigens: shared the Nobel prize for physiology or medicine 1976.

Boas, Franz. 1858–1942, U.S. anthropologist, born in Germany. He made major contributions to cultural and linguistic anthropology in studies of North American Indians, including *The Mind of Primitive Man* (1911; 1938).

Bogart, Humphrey (DeForest). nicknamed *Bogie*. 1899–1957, U.S. film actor: his films include *High Sierra* (1941), *Casablanca* (1942), *The Big Sleep* (1946), *The African Queen* (1951), and *The Caine Mutiny* (1954).

Bolden, Buddy, real name *Charles Bolden*. 1868–1931, U.S. Black jazz cornet player; a pioneer of the New Orleans style and a celebrated improviser.

Booth, Edwin Thomas, son of Junius Brutus Booth. 1833–93, U.S. actor; **John Wilkes,** son of Junius Brutus Booth. 1838–65, U.S. actor; assassin of Abraham Lincoln; **Junius Brutus.** 1796–1852, U.S. actor, born in England; **William.** 1829–1912, British religious leader; founder and first general of the Salvation Army (1878).

Borglum, (John) Gutzon.

1867–1941, U.S. sculptor, noted for his monumental busts of U.S. presidents carved in the mountainside of Mount Rushmore.

Borlaug, Norman (Ernest). born 1914, U.S. agronomist, who bred new strains of high-yielding cereal crops for use in developing countries. Nobel peace prize 1970.

Bourke-White, Margaret. 1906–71, U.S. photographer, a pioneer of modern photojournalism: noted esp. for her coverage of World War II.

Bow, Clara, known as the *It Girl*. 1905–65, U.S. film actress, noted for her vivacity and sex appeal.

Bowie, David, real name *David Jones*. born 1947, British rock singer, songwriter, and film actor. His recordings include "Space Oddity" (1969), *The Rise and Fall of Ziggy Stardust and the Spiders from Mars* (1972), *Heroes* (1977), *Let's Dance* (1983), and *Earthling* (1997); **James,** known as *Jim Bowie*. 1796–1836, U.S. frontiersman. A hero of the Texas Revolution against Mexico (1835–36), he died at the Battle of the Alamo.

Bowles, Paul. born 1910, U.S. novelist, short-story writer, and composer, living in Tangiers. His novels include *The Sheltering Sky* (1949) and *The Spider's House* (1955).

Bradbury, Malcolm (Stanley). born 1932, British novelist and critic. His novels include *The History Man* (1975), *Rates of Exchange* (1983), *Cuts* (1988), and *Doctor Criminale* (1992); **Ray.** born 1920, U.S. science-fiction writer. His novels include *Fahrenheit 451* (1953), *Death is a Lonely Business* (1986), and *A Graveyard for Lunatics* (1990).

Bradstreet, Anne (Dudley). ?1612–72, U.S. poet, born in England: regarded as the first significant U.S. poet.

Brando, Marlon. born 1924, U.S. actor; his films include *On the Waterfront* (1954) and *The Godfather* (1972), for both of which he won Oscars, *Last Tango in Paris* (1972), *Apocalypse Now* (1979), and *The Island of Doctor Moreau* (1996).

Brattain, Walter Houser. 1902–87, U.S. physicist, who shared the Nobel prize for physics (1956) with W. B. Shockley and John Bardeen for their invention of the transistor.

Breuer, Josef. 1842–1925, Austrian physician: treated the mentally ill by hypnosis; **Marcel Lajos.** 1902–81, U.S. architect and furniture designer, born in Hungary. He developed bent plywood and tubular metal furniture and designed the UNESCO building in Paris (1953–58).

Brice, Fanny, real name *Fannie Borach.* 1891–1951, U.S. actress and singer. The film *Funny Girl* was based on her life.

Bridgman, Percy Williams. 1882–1961, U.S. physicist: Nobel prize for physics (1946) for his work on high-pressure physics and thermodynamics.

Brodsky, Joseph, original name *Iosif Aleksandrovich Brodsky.* 1940–96, U.S. poet, born in the Soviet Union. His collections include *The End of a Beautiful Era* (1977). Nobel prize for literature 1987.

Brooks, Mel, real name *Melvyn Kaminsky.* born 1926, U.S. comedy writer, actor, and film director. His films include *The Producers* (1968), *Blazing Saddles* (1974), *High Anxiety* (1977), and *Dracula: Dead and Loving It* (1996).

Broonzy, William Lee Conley, called *Big Bill.* 1893–1958, U.S. blues singer and guitarist.

Brown, Sir **Arthur Whitten** 1886–1948, British aviator who with J. W. Alcock made the first flight across the Atlantic (1919); **Ford Madox.** 1821–93, British painter, associated with the Pre-Raphaelite Brotherhood. His paintings include *The Last of England* (1865) and *Work* (1865); **George (Alfred)**, Lord George-Brown. 1914–85, British Labour politician; vice-chairman and deputy leader of the Labour party (1960–70); foreign secretary 1966–68; **George Mackay.** 1921–96, Scottish poet, novelist, and short-story writer. His works, which include the novels *Greenvoe* (1972)

and *Magnus* (1973), reflect the history and culture of Orkney; **(James) Gordon.** born 1951, British Labour politician; Chancellor of the Exchequer from 1997; **Herbert Charles.** born 1912, U.S. chemist, who worked on the compounds of boron. Nobel prize for chemistry 1979; **James.** born 1928, U.S. soul singer and songwriter, noted for his dynamic stage performances and for his commitment to Black rights; **John.** 1800–59, U.S. abolitionist leader, hanged after leading an unsuccessful rebellion of slaves at Harper's Ferry, Virginia; **Lancelot**, called *Capability Brown.* 1716–83, British landscape gardener; **Michael (Stuart).** born 1941, U.S. physician: shared the Nobel prize for physiology or medicine (1985) for work on cholesterol; **Robert.** 1773–1858, Scottish botanist who was the first to observe the Brownian movement in fluids.

Brubeck, Dave. born 1920, U.S. modern jazz pianist and composer; formed his own quartet in 1951.

Bruce, James. 1730–94, British explorer, who discovered the source of the Blue Nile (1770); **Lenny.** 1925–66, U.S. comedian, whose satirical sketches, esp. of the sexual attitudes of his contemporaries, brought him prosecutions for obscenity, but are now regarded as full of insight as well as wit; **Robert the.** See **Robert I; Stanley Melbourne**, 1st Viscount Bruce of Melbourne. 1883–1967, Australian statesman; prime minister, in coalition with Sir Earle Page's Country Party, of Australia (1923–29).

Buchanan, George. 1506–82, Scottish historian, who was tutor to Mary, Queen of Scots and James VI; author of *History of Scotland* (1582); **James.** 1791–1868, 15th president of the U.S. (1857–61).

Buck, Pearl S(ydenstricker). 1892–1973, U.S. novelist, noted particularly for her novel of Chinese life *The Good Earth* (1931): Nobel prize for literature 1938.

Budge, Don(ald). born 1915, U.S.

tennis player, the first man to win the Grand Slam of singles championships (Australia, France, Wimbledon, and the U.S.) in one year (1938).

Buffalo Bill, nickname of *William Frederick Cody*. 1846–1917, U.S. showman who toured Europe and the U.S. with his famous *Wild West Show*.

Bumbry, Grace. born 1937, U.S. soprano and mezzo-soprano.

Bunche, Ralph Johnson. 1904–71, U.S. diplomat and United Nations official: awarded the Nobel peace prize in 1950 for his work as UN mediator in Palestine (1948–49); UN undersecretary (1954–71).

Burnett, Frances Hodgson. 1849–1924, U.S. novelist, born in England; author of *Little Lord Fauntleroy* (1886) and *The Secret Garden* (1911).

Burr, Aaron. 1756–1836, U.S. vice-president (1800–04), who fled after killing a political rival in a duel and plotted to create an independent empire in the western U.S.; acquitted (1807) of treason.

Burroughs, Edgar Rice. 1875–1950, U.S. novelist, author of the *Tarzan* stories; **William S(eward).** 1914–97, U.S. novelist, noted for his experimental works exploring themes of drug addiction, violence, and homosexuality. His novels include *Junkie* (1953), *The Naked Lunch* (1959), and *Interzone* (1989).

Bush, George. born 1924, U.S. Republican politician; vice president of the U.S. (1981–89): 41st president of the U.S. (1989–93).

Byrd, Richard Evelyn. 1888–1957, U.S. rear admiral, aviator, and polar explorer; **William.** 1543–1623, English composer and organist, noted for his madrigals, masses, and music for virginals.

Cage, John. 1912–92, U.S. composer of experimental music for a variety of conventional, modified, or invented instruments. He evolved a type of music apparently undetermined by the composer, such as in *Imaginary Landscape* (1951) for 12 radio sets. Other works include *Reunion* (1968),

Apartment Building 1776 (1976), and *Europeras 3 and 4* (1990).

Cagney, James. 1899–1986, U.S. film actor, esp. in gangster roles; his films include *The Public Enemy* (1931), *Angels with Dirty Faces* (1938), *The Roaring Twenties* (1939), and *Yankee Doodle Dandy* (1942) for which he won an Oscar.

Calamity Jane, real name **Martha Canary.** ?1852–1903, U.S. frontierswoman, noted for her skill at shooting and riding.

Calder, Alexander. 1898–1976, U.S. sculptor, who originated mobiles and stabiles (moving or static abstract sculptures, generally suspended from wire).

Caldwell, Erskine. 1903–87, U.S. novelist whose works include *Tobacco Road* (1933).

Callas, Maria, real name *Maria Anna Cecilia Kalageropoulos*. 1923– 77, Greek operatic soprano, born in the U.S.

Calvin, John, original name *Jean Cauvin, Caulvin,* or *Chauvin*. 1509–64, French theologian: a leader of the Protestant Reformation in France and Switzerland, establishing the first presbyterian government in Geneva. His theological system is described in his *Institutes of the Christian Religion* (1536); **Melvin.** 1911–97, U.S. chemist, noted particularly for his research on photosynthesis: Nobel prize for chemistry 1961.

Camp, Walter (Chauncey). 1859–1925, U.S. sportsman and administrator; he introduced new rules to American football, which distinguished it from rugby.

Capone, Al, Alphonse, called *Al*. 1899–1947, U.S. gangster in Chicago during Prohibition.

Capote, Truman. 1924–84, U.S. writer; his novels include *Other Voices, Other Rooms* (1948) and *In Cold Blood* (1964), based on an actual multiple murder.

Capp, Al, full name *Alfred Caplin*. 1909–79, U.S. cartoonist, famous for his comic strip *Li'l Abner*.

Capra, Frank. 1896–1992, U.S. film

director born in Italy. His films include *It Happened One Night* (1934), *It's a Wonderful Life* (1946), and several propaganda films during World War II.

Carmichael, Hoaglund Howard, known as *Hoagy*. 1899--1981, U.S. pianist, singer, and composer of such standards as "Star Dust" (1929).

Carnap, Rudolf. 1891–1970, U.S. logical positivist philosopher, born in Germany: attempted to construct a formal language for the empirical sciences that would eliminate ambiguity.

Carnegie, Andrew. 1835–1919, U.S. steel manufacturer and philanthropist, born in Scotland: endowed public libraries, education, and research trusts.

Carpenter, John Alden. 1876–1951, U.S. composer who used jazz rhythms in orchestral music: his works include the ballet *Skyscrapers* (1926) and the orchestral suite *Adventures in a Perambulator* (1915).

Carson, Christopher, known as *Kit Carson*. 1809–68, U.S. frontiersman, trapper, scout, and Indian agent; **Edward henry,** Baron. 1854–1935, Irish politician and lawyer; led northern Irish resistance to the British government's home rule for Ireland; **Rachel (Louise).** 1907–64, U.S. marine biologist and science writer; author of *Silent Spring* (1962); **Willie,** full name *William Hunter Fisher Carson*. born 1942, Scottish jockey; retired in 1997.

Carter, Angela. 1940–92, British novelist and writer; her novels include *The Magic Toyshop* (1967) and *Nights at the Circus* (1984); **Elliot (Cook).** born 1908, U.S. composer. His works include the *Piano Sonata* (1945–46), four string quartets, and other orchestral pieces: Pulitzer Prize 1960, 1973; **Howard.** 1873–1939, English Egyptologist: excavated the tomb of the Pharaoh Tutankhamen; **James Earl,** known as *Jimmy*. born 1924, U.S. Democratic statesman; 39th president of the U.S. (1977–81).

Carver, George Washington.

?1864–1943, U.S. agricultural chemist and botanist.

Cash, Johnny. born 1932, U.S. country-and-western singer, guitarist, and songwriter. His hits include "I Walk the Line" (1956), "Ring of Fire" (1963), and "A Boy named Sue" (1969).

Cassatt, Mary. 1845–1926, U.S. impressionist painter, who lived in France.

Castner, Hamilton Young. 1858–98, U.S. chemist, who devised the **Castner process** for extracting sodium from sodium hydroxide.

Cather, Willa (Sibert). 1873–1947, U.S. novelist, whose works include *O Pioneers!* (1913) and *My Ántonia* (1918).

Chamberlain, Sir **(Joseph) Austen.** 1863–1937, British Conservative statesman; foreign secretary (1924–29); awarded a Nobel peace prize for his negotiation of the Locarno Pact (1925); his father, **Joseph.** 1836–1914, British statesman; originally a Liberal, he resigned in 1886 over Home Rule for Ireland and became leader of the Liberal Unionists; a leading advocate of preferential trading agreements with members of the British Empire; his son, **(Arthur) Neville.** 1869–1940, British Conservative statesman; prime minister (1937–40): pursued a policy of appeasement towards Germany; following the German invasion of Poland, he declared war on Germany on Sept. 3, 1939; **Owen.** born 1920, U.S. physicist, who discovered the antiproton. Nobel prize for physics jointly with Emilio Segré 1959.

Chandler, Raymond (Thornton). 1888–1959, U.S. thriller writer: created Philip Marlowe, one of the first detective heroes in fiction.

Chandrasekhar, Subrahmanyan. 1910–95, U.S. astronomer born in Lahore, India (now Pakistan). His work on stellar evolution led to an understanding of white dwarfs: shared the Nobel prize for physics 1983.

Chargaff, Erwin. born 1905, U.S.

biochemist, born in Austria, noted esp. for his work on DNA.

Charles, *Prince of Wales.* born 1948, son of Elizabeth II; heir apparent to the throne of Great Britain and Northern Ireland. He married (1981) Lady Diana Spencer; they separated in 1992 and were divorced in 1996; their son, Prince William of Wales, was born in 1982 and their second son, Prince Henry, in 1984; **Ray** real name *Ray Charles Robinson.* born 1930, U.S. singer, pianist, and songwriter, whose work spans jazz, blues, gospel, pop, and country music.

Cheever, John. 1912–82, U.S. novelist and short-story writer. His novels include *The Wapshot Chronicle* (1957) and *Bullet Park* (1969).

Chomsky, (Avram) Noam. born 1928, U.S. linguist and political critic. His theory of language structure, transformational generative grammar, superseded the behaviorist view of Bloomfield. **'Chomskyan** or **'Chomsky"ite**

Christian, Charlie. 1919–42, U.S. jazz guitarist.

Clark, James, known as *Jim.* 1936–68, Scottish racing driver; World Champion (1963, 1965); **Kenneth,** Baron Clark of Saltwood. 1903–83, English art historian: his books include *Civilization* (1969), which he first presented as a television series; **William.** 1770–1838, U.S. explorer and frontiersman: best known for his expedition to the Pacific Northwest (1804–06) with Meriwether Lewis.

Claude, Albert. 1898–1983, U.S. cell biologist, born in Belgium: shared the Nobel prize for physiology or medicine (1974) for work on microsomes and mitochondria.

Clay, Cassius; See **Muhammad Ali. Henry.** 1777–1852, U.S. statesman and orator; secretary of state (1825–29).

Cleveland, Stephen Grover. 1837–1908, U.S. Democratic politician; the 22nd and 24th president of the U.S. (1885–89; 1893–97).

Clinton, Bill, full name *William Jefferson.* born 1946, U.S. Democrat politician; 42nd president of the U.S. from 1993; re-elected in 1996.

Cohen, Stanley. born 1922, U.S. biochemist: shared the Nobel prize for physiology or medicine 1986.

Colbert, Claudette. real name *Lily Claudette Chauchoin.* 1903–96, U.S. film actress, born in France. Her Hollywood comedies include *Three-Cornered Moon* (1933) and *It Happened One Night* (1934); **Jean Baptiste.** 1619–83, French statesman; chief minister to Louis XIV: reformed the taille and pursued a mercantilist policy, creating a powerful navy and merchant fleet and building roads and canals.

Cole, Nat 'King', real name *Nathaniel Adams Cole.* 1917–65, U.S. popular singer and jazz pianist.

Coleman, Ornette. born 1930, U.S. avant-garde jazz alto saxophonist and multi-instrumentalist.

Coltrane, John (William). 1926–67, U.S. jazz tenor and soprano saxophonist and composer.

Comaneci, Nadia. born 1961, Romanian gymnast; gold medal winner in the 1976 Olympic Games: defected to the U.S. in 1989.

Compton, Arthur Holly. 1892–1962, U.S. physicist, noted for his research on X-rays, gamma rays, and nuclear energy: Nobel prize for physics 1927; **Denis.** 1918–97, English cricketer, who played for Middlesex and England (1937–57); broke two records in 1947 scoring 3816 runs and 18 centuries in one season.

Connors, Jimmy. born 1952, U.S. tennis player: Wimbledon champion 1974 and 1982; U.S. champion 1974, 1976, 1978, 1982, and 1983.

Coolidge, (John) Calvin. 1872–1933, 30th president of the U.S. (1923–29).

Cooper, Anthony Ashley. See (Earl of) **Shaftesbury. Gary,** real name *Frank James Cooper.* 1901–61, U.S. film actor; his many films include *Sergeant York* (1941) and *High Noon* (1952), for both of which he won Oscars; **Henry.** born 1934, British boxer; European heavyweight champion (1964; 1968–71); **James Fenimore** 1789–1851, U.S. novelist, noted for his stories of American Indians, esp. *The Last of the Mohicans* (1826); **Leon Neil.** born 1930, U.S. physicist, noted for his work on the theory of superconductivity. He shared the Nobel prize for physics 1972; **Samuel** 1609–72, English miniaturist.

Copland, Aaron. 1900–90, U.S. composer of orchestral and chamber music, ballets, and film music.

Copley, John Singleton. 1738–1815, U.S. painter.

Coppola, Francis Ford. born 1939, U.S. film director. His films include *The Godfather* (1972), *Apocalypse Now* (1979), and *Tucker* (1988).

Cori, Carl Ferdinand. 1896–1984, U.S. biochemist, born in Bohemia; shared a Nobel prize for physiology or medicine (1947) with his wife **Gerty Theresa Radnitz Cori** (1896–1957) and Bernardo Houssay, for elucidating the stages of glycolysis.

Costner, Kevin. born 1955, U.S. film actor: his films include *Robin Hood: Prince of Thieves* (1990), *Dances with Wolves* (1990; also directed), *JFK* (1991), *Waterworld* (1995), and *Message in a Bottle* (1999).

Cournand, André (Frederic). 1895–1988, U.S. physician, born in France: shared the 1956 Nobel prize for physiology or medicine for his work on heart catheterization.

Crane, (Harold) Hart. 1899–1932, U.S. poet; author of *The Bridge* (1930); **Stephen.** 1871–1900, U.S. novelist and short-story writer, noted particularly for his novel *The Red Badge of Courage* (1895); **Walter.** 1845–1915, British painter, illustrator of children's books, and designer of textiles and wallpaper.

Crawford, Joan, real name *Lucille le Sueur*. 1908–77, U.S. film actress, who portrayed ambitious women in such films as *Mildred Pierce* (1945); **Michael,** real name *Michael Dumbell Smith*. born 1942, British actor.

Crippen, Hawley Harvey, known as *Doctor Crippen*. 1862–1910, U.S.

doctor living in England: executed for poisoning his wife; the first criminal to be apprehended by the use of radiotelegraphy.

Crockett, David, known as *Davy Crockett*. 1786–1836, U.S. frontiersman, politician, and soldier.

Cronin, A(rchibald) J(oseph). 1896–1981, British novelist and physician. His works include *Hatter's Castle* (1931), *The Judas Tree* (1961), and *Dr Finlay's Casebook*, a TV series based on his medical experiences; **James Watson.** born 1931, U.S. physicist; shared the Nobel prize for physics (1980) for his work on parity conservation in weak interactions.

Crosby, Bing, real name *Harry Lillis Crosby*. 1904–77, U.S. singer and film actor; famous for his style of crooning: best known for the song "White Christmas" from the film *Holiday Inn* (1942).

Culbertson, Ely. 1891–1955, U.S. authority on contract bridge.

Cummings, Edward Estlin, (preferred typographical representation of name **e. e. cummings**). 1894–1962, U.S. poet.

Cunningham, Merce. born 1919, U.S. dancer and choreographer. His experimental ballets include *Suit for Five* (1956) and *Travelogue* (1977).

Cushing, Harvey Williams. 1869–1939, U.S. neurosurgeon: identified a pituitary tumour as a cause of the disease named after him.

Custer, George Armstrong. 1839–76, U.S. cavalry general: Civil War hero, killed fighting the Sioux Indians at Little Bighorn, Montana.

Dana, James Dwight. 1813–95, American geologist; noted for his work *The System of Mineralogy* (1837).

Davis, Bette, real name *Ruth Elizabeth Davis*. 1908–89, U.S. film actress, whose films include *Of Human Bondage* (1934), *Jezebel* (1938) for which she won an Oscar, *Now Voyager* (1942), *Whatever Happened to Baby Jane?* (1962), *The Nanny* (1965), and *Death on the Nile* (1978); **Sir Colin (Rex).** born 1927, English conductor, noted for his interpretation of the music of Berlioz; **Jefferson.** 1808–89, president of the Confederate States of America during the Civil War (1861–65); **Joe.** 1901–78, English billiards and snooker player: world champion from 1927 to 1946; **John.** Also called: **John Davys.** ?1550–1605, English navigator: discovered the Falkland Islands (1592); searched for a Northwest Passage; **Miles (Dewey).** 1926–91, U.S. jazz trumpeter and composer; **Steve.** born 1957, English snooker player: world champion 1981, 1983–84, 1987–89.

Davisson, Clinton Joseph. 1881–1958, U.S. physicist, noted for his discovery of electron diffraction; shared the Nobel prize for physics in 1937.

Dawes, Charles Gates. 1865–1951, U.S. financier, diplomat, and statesman, who devised the Dawes Plan for German reparations payments after World War I; vice president of the U.S. (1925–29); Nobel peace prize 1925.

Dean, Christopher. See **Torvill and Dean. James (Byron).** 1931–55, U.S. film actor, who became a cult figure; his films include *East of Eden* and *Rebel Without a Cause* (both 1955). He died in a car crash.

Debs, Eugene Victor. 1855–1926, U.S. labor leader; five times Socialist presidential candidate (1900–20).

Decatur, Stephen. 1779–1820, U.S. naval officer, noted for his raid on Tripoli harbor (1804) and his role in the War of 1812.

De Forest, Lee. 1873–1961, U.S. inventor of telegraphic, telephonic, and radio equipment: patented the first triode valve (1907).

Delbrück, Max. 1906–81, U.S. molecular biologist, born in Germany. Noted for his work on bacteriophages, he shared the Nobel prize for physiology or medicine in 1969.

De Mille, Cecil B(lount). 1881–1959, U.S. film producer and director.

Dempsey, Jack. real name *William Harrison Dempsey.* 1895–1983, U.S.

boxer; world heavyweight champion (1919–26).

De Niro, Robert. born 1943, U.S. film actor. His films include *The Deer Hunter* (1978), *Raging Bull* (1980), *GoodFellas* (1990), *A Bronx Tale* (1993), which he directed, *Ronin* (1998), and *Analyze This* (1999).

Dewey, John. 1859–1952, U.S. pragmatist philosopher and educator: an exponent of progressivism in education, he formulated an instrumentalist theory of learning through experience. His works include *The School and Society* (1899), *Democracy and Education* (1916), and *Logic: the Theory of Inquiry* (1938).

Dickinson, Emily. 1830–86, U.S. poet, noted for her short mostly unrhymed mystical lyrics.

Dietrich, Marlene. real name *Maria Magdalene von Losch.* 1901–92, U.S. film actress and cabaret singer, born in Germany.

DiMaggio, Joe. 1914–99, U.S. baseball player.

Disney, Walt(er Elias). 1901–66, U.S. film producer, who pioneered animated cartoons: noted esp. for his creations *Mickey Mouse* and *Donald Duck* and films such as *Fantasia* (1940). **"Disney'esque**

Dobzhansky, Theodosius. 1900–75, U.S. biologist, born in Russia, noted for work on evolution and genetic variation.

Doisy, Edward Adelbert. 1893–1986, U.S. biochemist. He discovered (1939) the nature of vitamin K and shared a Nobel prize for medicine with Carl Dam (1943).

Domino, Fats. real name *Antoine Domino.* born 1928, U.S. rhythm-and- blues and rock-and-roll pianist, singer, and songwriter. His singles include "Ain't that a Shame" (1955) and "Blueberry Hill" (1956).

Donleavy, J(ames) P(atrick). born 1926, Irish-American novelist. His books include *The Ginger Man* (1956), *The Onion Eaters* (1971), *Are You Listening Rabbi Löw?* (1987), *That Darcy, That Dancer, That Gentleman* (1990), and *The Lady*

Who Liked Clean Rest Rooms (1995).

Doolittle, Hilda. known as *H.D.* 1886–1961, U.S. imagist poet and novelist, living in Europe.

Doráti, Antal. 1906–88, U.S. conductor and composer.

Dos Passos, John (Roderigo). 1896–1970, U.S. novelist of the Lost Generation; author of *Three Soldiers* (1921), *Manhattan Transfer* (1925), and the trilogy *U.S.A.* (1930–36).

Draper, Henry. 1837–82, U.S. astronomer, who contributed to stellar classification and spectroscopy; his father, **John William.** 1811–82, U.S. chemist and historian, born in England, made the first photograph of the moon.

Dreiser, Theodore (Herman Albert). 1871–1945, U.S. novelist; his works include *Sister Carrie* (1900) and *An American Tragedy* (1925).

Dubois, W(illiam) E(dward) B(urghardt). 1868–1963, U.S. Black sociologist, writer, and political activist; a founder of the National Association for the Advancement of Colored People (NAACP).

Duchamp, Marcel. 1887–1968, U.S. painter and sculptor, born in France; noted as a leading exponent of Dada. His best-known work is *Nude Descending a Staircase* (1912).

Dulbecco, Renato. born 1914, U.S. physician and molecular biologist, born in Italy: shared the Nobel prize for physiology or medicine (1975) for cancer research.

Dulles, John Foster. 1888–1959, U.S. statesman and lawyer; secretary of state (1953–59).

Du Mont, Allen Balcom. 1901–65, U.S. inventor and electronics manufacturer. He developed the cathode-ray tube used in television sets and oscilloscopes.

Duncan, Isadora. 1878–1927, U.S. dancer and choreographer, who influenced modern ballet by introducing greater freedom of movement.

Durante, Jimmy, known as *Schnozzle.* 1893–1980, U.S. comedian.

Dutton, Clarence Edward.

1841–1912, American geologist who first developed the theory of isostasy.

Du Vigneaud, Vincent. 1901–78, U.S. biochemist: Nobel prize for chemistry (1955) for his synthesis of the hormones oxytocin and vasopressin.

Dylan, Bob. real name *Robert Allen Zimmerman.* born 1941, U.S. rock singer and songwriter, also noted for his acoustic protest songs in the early 1960s. His albums include *The Freewheelin' Bob Dylan* (1963), *Highway 61 Revisited* (1965), *Blonde on Blonde* (1966), *John Wesley Harding* (1968), *Blood on the Tracks* (1974), *Oh Mercy* (1989), and *Time Out of Mind* (1997).

Eakins, Thomas. 1844–1916, U.S. painter of portraits and sporting life: a noted realist.

Earhart, Amelia. 1898–1937, U.S. aviator: the first woman to fly the Atlantic (1928). She disappeared on a Pacific flight (1937).

Eastman, George. 1854–1932, U.S. manufacturer of photographic equipment: noted for the introduction of roll film and developments in color photography.

Eastwood, Clint. born 1930, U.S. film actor and director. His films as an actor include *The Good The Bad and The Ugly* (1966), *Dirty Harry* (1971), and as actor and director *Play Misty for Me* (1971), *Unforgiven* (1993), and *True Crime* (1999). He was mayor of Carmel, California (1985–88).

Eckert, John Presper. 1919–95, U.S. electronics engineer: built the first electronic computer with John W. Mauchly in 1946.

Eddy, Mary Baker. 1821–1910, U.S. religious leader; founder of the Christian Science movement (1866).

Edelman, Gerald Maurice. born 1929, U.S. biochemist: he shared the Nobel prize for physiology or medicine (1972) with Rodney Porter for determining the structure of antibodies.

Edison, Thomas Alva. 1847–1931, U.S. inventor. He patented more than a thousand inventions, including the phonograph, the incandescent electric lamp, the microphone, and the kinetoscope.

Edwards, Gareth (Owen). born 1947, Welsh Rugby Union footballer: halfback for Wales (1967–78) and the British Lions (1968–74); **Jonathan.** 1703–58, American Calvinist theologian and metaphysician; author of *The Freedom of the Will* (1754).

Einstein, Albert. 1879–1955, U.S. physicist and mathematician, born in Germany. He formulated the special theory of relativity (1905) and the general theory of relativity (1916), and made major contributions to the quantum theory, for which he was awarded the Nobel prize for physics in 1921. He was noted also for his work for world peace. **Ein'steinian**

Eisenhower, Dwight David, known as *Ike.* 1890–1969, U.S. general and Republican statesman; Supreme Commander of the Allied Expeditionary Force (1943–45) and 34th president of the U.S. (1953–61). He commanded Allied forces in Europe and North Africa (1942), directed the invasion of Italy (1943), and was Supreme Commander of the combined land forces of NATO (1950–52).

Eisenstaedt, Alfred. 1898–1995, U.S. photographer, born in Germany.

Eliot, George, real name *Mary Ann Evans.* 1819–80, English novelist, noted for her analysis of provincial Victorian society. Her best-known novels include *Adam Bede* (1859), *The Mill on the Floss* (1860), *Silas Marner* (1861), and *Middlemarch* (1872); Sir **John.** 1592–1632, English statesman, a leader of parliamentary opposition to Charles I; **T(homas) S(tearns).** 1888–1965, British poet, dramatist, and critic, born in the U.S. His poetry includes *Prufrock and Other Observations* (1917), *The Waste Land* (1922), *Ash Wednesday* (1930), and *Four Quartets* (1943). Among his verse plays are *Murder in the Cathedral* (1935), *The Family Reunion* (1939), *The Cocktail Party* (1950), and *The Confidential Clerk*

(1954): Nobel prize for literature 1948.

Ellington, Duke, nickname of *Edward Kennedy Ellington.* 1899–1974, U.S. jazz composer, pianist, and conductor, famous for such works as "Mood Indigo" and "Creole Love Call".

Emerson, Ralph Waldo.. 1803–82, U.S. poet, essayist, and transcendentalist.

Enders, John Franklin. 1897–1985, U.S. microbiologist: shared the Nobel prize for physiology or medicine (1954) with Frederick Robbins and Thomas Weller for their work on viruses.

Epstein, Sir **Jacob.** 1880–1959, British sculptor, born in the U.S. of Russo-Polish parents.

Erlanger, Joseph. 1874–1965, U.S. physiologist. He shared a Nobel prize for physiology or medicine (1944) with Gasser for their work on the electrical signs of nervous activity.

Evans, Sir **Arthur (John).** 1851–1941, British archaeologist, whose excavations of the palace of Knossos in Crete provided evidence for the existence of the Minoan civilization; Dame **Edith (Mary Booth).** 1888–1976, British actress; Sir **Geraint (Llewellyn).** 1922–92, Welsh operatic baritone; **Herbert McLean.** 1882–1971, U.S. anatomist and embryologist; discoverer of vitamin E (1922); **Mary Ann.** real name of (George) **Eliot. Oliver.** 1755–1819, U.S. engineer: invented the continuous production line and a high-pressure steam engine; **Walker.** 1903–75, U.S. photographer, noted esp. for his studies of rural poverty in the Great Depression.

Evert, Chris(tine). born 1954, U.S. tennis player: Wimbledon champion 1974, 1976, and 1981; U.S. champion 1975–78, 1980, and 1982.

Fairbanks, Douglas (Elton), real name *Julius Ullman.* 1883–1939, U.S. film actor and producer; his son, **Douglas, Jnr.** born 1909, U.S. film actor.

Fargo, William. 1818–81, U.S. businessman: founded (1852) with

Henry Wells the express mail service Wells, Fargo and Company.

Farrell, J(ames) G(ordon) 1935–79, British novelist: author of *Troubles* (1970), *The Siege of Krishnapur* (1973), and *The Singapore Grip* (1978); **James T(homas)** 1904–79, U.S. writer. His works include the trilogy *Young* (1932), *The Young Manhood of Studs Lonigan* (1934), and *Judgment Day* (1935).

Faulkner or **Falkner. William.** 1897–1962, U.S. novelist and short-story writer. Most of his works portray the problems of the southern U.S., esp. the novels set in the imaginary county of Yoknapatawpha in Mississippi. Other novels include *The Sound and the Fury* (1929) and *Light in August* (1932): Nobel prize for literature 1949.

Feininger, Lyonel. 1871–1956, U.S. artist, who worked at the Bauhaus, noted for his use of superimposed translucent planes of color.

Ferlinghetti, Lawrence. born 1920, U.S. poet of the Beat Generation. His poetry includes the collections *Pictures of the Gone World* (1955) and *When I Look at Pictures* (1990).

Feynman, Richard. 1918–88, U.S. physicist, noted for his research on quantum electrodynamics; shared the Nobel prize for physics in 1965.

Fields, Dame **Gracie.** real name *Grace Stansfield*. 1898–1979, English popular singer and entertainer; **W. C.** real name *William Claude Dukenfield*. 1880–1946, U.S. film actor, noted for his portrayal of comic roles.

Fillmore, Millard. 1800–74, 13th president of the U.S. (1850-53); a leader of the Whig Party.

Fischer, Emil Hermann. 1852–1919, German chemist, noted particularly for his work on synthetic sugars and the purine group: Nobel prize for chemistry 1902; **Ernst Otto.** 1918–94, German chemist: shared the Nobel prize for chemistry in 1973 with Geoffrey Wilkinson for his work on inorganic complexes; **Hans.** 1881–1945, German chemist, noted particularly for his work on chlorophyll, haemin, and the

porphyrins: Nobel prize for chemistry 1930; **Robert James,** known as *Bobby.* born 1943, U.S. chess player; world champion 1972–75.

Fitzgerald, Edward. 1809–83, English poet, noted particularly for his free translation of the *Rubáiyát of Omar Khayyám* (1859); **Ella.** 1918–96, U.S. jazz singer, noted esp. for her vocal range and scat singing; **F(rancis) Scott (Key).** 1896–1940, U.S. novelist and short-story writer, noted particularly for his portrayal of the 1920s in *The Great Gatsby* (1925) and *Tender is the Night* (1934); **Garret.** born 1926, Irish politician; leader of Fine Gael Party (1977–87); prime minister of the Republic of Ireland (1981–82; and 1982–87).

Flaherty, Robert (Joseph). 1884–1951, U.S. film director, a pioneer of documentary film; his work includes *Nanook of the North* (1922) and *Elephant Boy* (1935).

Fokine, Michel. 1880–1942, U.S. choreographer, born in Russia, regarded as the creator of modern ballet. He worked with Diaghilev as director of the Ballet Russe (1909–15), producing works such as *Les Sylphides* and *Petrushka.*

Fonda, Henry. 1905–82, U.S. film actor. His many films include *Young Mr Lincoln* (1939), *The Grapes of Wrath* (1940), *Twelve Angry Men* (1957), and *On Golden Pond* (1981) for which he won an Oscar; his daughter **Jane.** born 1937, U.S. film actress. Her films include *Klute* (1971) for which she won an Oscar, *Julia* (1977), *The China Syndrome* (1979), *On Golden Pond* (1981), and *The Old Gringo* (1989); her brother, **Peter.** born 1939, U.S. film actor, who made his name in *Easy Rider* (1969).

Ford, Ford Maddox original name *Ford Madox Hueffer*. 1873–1939, English novelist, editor, and critic; works include *The Good Soldier* (1915) and the war tetralogy *Parade's End* (1924–28).; **Gerald R(udolph).** born 1913, U.S. politician; 38th president of the U.S.

(1974–77); **Harrison.** born 1942, U.S. film actor. His films include *Star Wars* (1977) and its sequels, *Raiders of the Lost Ark* (1981) and its sequels, *Bladerunner* (1982), *Clear and Present Danger* (1994), and *Air Force One* (1997); **Henry.** 1863–1947, U.S. car manufacturer, who pioneered mass production; **John.** 1586–?1639, English dramatist; author of revenge tragedies such as *'Tis Pity She's a Whore* (1633); **John,** real name *Sean O'Feeney.* 1895–1973, U.S. film director, esp. of Westerns such as *Stagecoach* (1939) and *She Wore a Yellow Ribbon* (1949).

Foreman, George. born 1949, U.S. boxer: WBA world heavyweight champion (1973–74); he regained the title in 1994 but refused to fight the WBA's top-ranked challenger and was stripped of the title in 1995; recognized as WBU champion until 1997.

Foster, Jodie. born 1962, U.S. film actress: her films include *Taxi Driver* (1976), *The Accused* (1988), *The Silence of the Lambs* (1990), *Little Man Tate* (1991; also directed), and *Contact* (1997); **Norman,** Baron. born 1935, British architect. His works include the Willis Faber building (1978) in Ipswich, Stansted Airport, Essex (1991), Chek Lap Kok Airport, Hong Kong (1998), and the renovation of the Reichstag, Berlin (1999); **Stephen Collins.** 1826–64, U.S. composer of songs such as *The Old Folks at Home* and *Oh Susanna.*

Franck, César (Auguste). 1822–90, French composer, organist, and teacher, born in Belgium. His works, some of which make use of cyclic form, include a violin sonata, a string quartet, the *Symphony in D Minor* (1888), and much organ music; **James.** 1882–1964, U.S. physicist, born in Germany: shared a Nobel prize for physics with Gustav Hertz (1925) for work on the quantum theory, particularly the effects of bombarding atoms with electrons.

Frank, Anne. 1929–45, German Jewess, whose *Diary* (1947) recorded the experiences of her family while in hiding from the Nazis in Amsterdam

(1942–44). They were betrayed and she died in a concentration camp; **Robert.** born 1924, U.S. photographer and film maker, born in Switzerland; best known for his photographic book *The Americans* (1959).

Franklin, Aretha born 1942, U.S. soul, pop, and gospel singer; **Benjamin** 1706–90, American statesman, scientist, and author. He helped draw up the Declaration of Independence (1776) and, as ambassador to France (1776–85), he negotiated an alliance with France and a peace settlement with Britain. As a scientist, he is noted particularly for his researches in electricity, esp. his invention of the lightning conductor; **Sir John.** 1786–1847, English explorer of the Arctic: lieutenant-governor of Van Diemen's Land (now Tasmania) (1836–43): died while on a voyage to discover the Northwest Passage; **Rosalind.** 1920–58, British x-ray crystallographer. She contributed to the discovery of the structure of DNA, before her premature death from cancer.

Frazier, Joe. born 1944, U.S. boxer: won the world heavyweight title in 1970 and was the first to beat Muhammad Ali professionally (1971).

Freneau, Philip. 1752–1832, U.S. poet, journalist, and patriot; editor of the *National Gazette* (1791–93).

Friedan, Betty. born 1921, U.S. feminist, founder and first president (1966–70) of the National Organization for Women. Her books include *The Feminine Mystique* (1963), *The Second Stage* (1982), and *The Fountain of Life* (1993).

Friedman, Milton. born 1912. U.S. economist, particularly associated with monetarism; a forceful advocate of free market capitalism. **'Friedman"ite**

Fromm, Erich. 1900–80, U.S. psychologist and philosopher, born in Germany. His works include *The Art of Loving* (1956) and *To Have and To Be* (1976).

Frost, Robert (Lee). 1874–1963,

U.S. poet, noted for his lyrical verse on country life in New England. His books include *A Boy's Will* (1913), *North of Boston* (1914), and *New Hampshire* (1923).

Fuller, (Richard) Buckminster. 1895–1983, U.S. architect and engineer: developed the geodesic dome; **Roy (Broadbent).** 1912–91, British poet and writer, whose collections include *The Middle of a War* (1942) and *A Lost Season* (1944), both of which are concerned with World War II, *Epitaphs and Occasions* (1949), and *Available for Dreams* (1989); **Thomas.** 1608–61, English clergyman and antiquarian; author of *The Worthies of England* (1662).

Fulton, Robert. 1765–1815, U.S. engineer: designed the first successful steamboat (1807) and steam warship (1814).

Funk, Casimir. 1884–1967, U.S. biochemist, born in Poland: studied and named vitamins.

Gable, (William) Clark. 1901–60, U.S. film actor. His films include *It Happened One Night* (1934), *San Francisco* (1936), *Gone with the Wind* (1939), *Mogambo* (1953), and *The Misfits* (1960).

Gabo, Naum, original name *Naum Neemia Pevsner.* 1890–1977, U.S. sculptor, born in Russia: a leading constructivist.

Galbraith, John Kenneth. born 1908, U.S. economist and diplomat born in Canada; author of *The Affluent Society* (1958) and *The New Industrial State* (1967). **Gal'braithian**

Gallup, George Horace. 1901–84, U.S. statistician: devised the Gallup Poll; founded the American Institute of Public Opinion (1935) and its British counterpart (1936).

Garbo, Greta, real name *Greta Lovisa Gustafson.* 1905–90, U.S. film actress, born in Sweden. Her films include *Grand Hotel* (1932), *Queen Christina* (1933), *Anna Karenina* (1935), *Camille* (1936), and *Ninotchka* (1939).

Gardner, Ava. 1922–90, U.S. film actress. Her films include *The Killers*

(1946), *The Sun also Rises* (1957), and *The Night of the Iguana* (1964).

Garfield, James Abram. 1831–81, 20th president of the U.S. (1881); assassinated in office.

Garland, Judy, real name *Frances Gumm.* 1922–69, U.S. singer and film actress. Already a child star, she achieved international fame with *The Wizard of Oz* (1939). Later films included *Meet Me in St Louis* (1944) and *A Star is Born* (1954).

Garner, Erroll. 1921–77, U.S. jazz pianist and composer.

Gasser, Herbert Spencer. 1888–1963, U.S. physiologist: shared a Nobel prize for physiology or medicine (1944) with Erlanger for work on electrical signs of nervous activity.

Gates, Bill, full name *William Henry Gates.* born 1955, U.S. computer-software executive; founder (1976) of Microsoft Corporation; **Horatio.** ?1728–1806, American Revolutionary general: defeated the British at Saratoga (1777).

Gell-Mann, Murray. born 1929, U.S. physicist, noted for his research on the interaction and classification of elementary particles: Nobel prize for physics in 1969.

George, David Lloyd. See **Lloyd George. Henry.** 1839–97, U.S. economist: advocated a single tax on land values, esp. in *Progress and Poverty* (1879); **Saint.** died ?303 A.D., Christian martyr, the patron saint of England; the hero of a legend in which he slew a dragon. Feast day: April 23; **Stefan (Anton).** 1868–1933, German poet and aesthete. Influenced by the French Symbolists, esp. Mallarmé and later by Nietzsche, he sought for an idealized purity of form in his verse. He refused Nazi honors and went into exile in 1933.

Gershwin, George, original name *Jacob Gershvin.* 1898–1937, U.S. composer: incorporated jazz into works such as *Rhapsody in Blue* (1924) for piano and jazz band and the opera *Porgy and Bess* (1935); his brother, **Ira,** original name *Israel Gershvin.* 1896–1983, U.S. song lyricist, noted esp. for his collaboration with George Gershwin.

Getty, J(ean) Paul. 1892–1976, U.S. oil executive, millionaire, and art collector.

Getz, Stanley, known as *Stan.* 1927–91, U.S. jazz saxophonist: leader of his own group from 1949.

Gibbs, James. 1682–1754, British architect; his buildings include St Martin's-in-the-Fields, London (1722–26), and the Radcliffe Camera, Oxford (1737–49); **Josiah Willard.** 1839–1903, U.S. physicist and mathematician: founder of chemical thermodynamics.

Gilbert, Grove Karl. 1843–1918, U.S. geologist who pioneered the study of river development and valley erosion; Sir **Humphrey.** ?1539–83, English navigator: founded the colony at St John's, Newfoundland (1583); **William.** 1540–1603, English physician and physicist, noted for his study of terrestrial magnetism in *De Magnete* (1600); Sir **W(illiam) S(chwenck).** 1836–1911, English dramatist, humorist, and librettist. He collaborated (1871–96) with Arthur Sullivan on the famous series of comic operettas, including *The Pirates of Penzance* (1879), *Iolanthe* (1882), and *The Mikado* (1885).

Gillespie, Dizzy, nickname of *John Birks Gillespie.* 1917–93, U.S. jazz trumpeter.

Ginsberg, Allen. 1926–97, U.S. poet of the Beat Generation. His poetry includes *Howl* (1956) and *Kaddish* (1960).

Gish, Dorothy. 1898–1968, U.S. film actress, chiefly in silent films; her sister, **Lillian.** 1896–1993, U.S. film and stage actress, noted esp. for her roles in such silent films as *The Birth of a Nation* (1915) and *Intolerance* (1916).

Glaser, Donald Arthur. born 1926, U.S. physicist: invented the bubble chamber; Nobel prize for physics 1960.

Glass, Philip. born 1937, U.S. avant-garde composer noted for his

minimalist style: his works include *Music in Fifths* (1970), *Akhnaten* (1984), *The Voyage* (1992), and *Monsters of Grace* (1998).

Glenn, John. born 1921, U.S. astronaut and politician. The first American to orbit the earth (Feb., 1962), he later became a senator.

Goddard, Robert Hutchings. 1882–1945, U.S. physicist. He made the first workable liquid-fuelled rocket.

Gödel, Kurt. 1906–78, U.S. logician and mathematician, born in Austria-Hungary. He showed (**Gödel's proof**) that in a formal axiomatic system, such as logic or mathematics, it is impossible to prove consistency without using methods from outside the system.

Goldschmidt, Richard Benedikt. 1878–1958, U.S. geneticist, born in Germany. He advanced the theory that heredity is determined by the chemical configuration of the chromosome molecule rather than by the qualities of the individual genes.

Gomberg, Moses. 1866–1947, U.S. chemist, born in Russia, noted for his work on free radicals.

Gompers, Samuel. 1850–1924, U.S. labor leader, born in England; a founder of the American Federation of Labor and its president (1886–94; 1896–1924).

Goodman, Benny, full name *Benjamin David Goodman.* 1909–86, U.S. jazz clarinetist and bandleader, whose treatment of popular songs created the jazz idiom known as swing.

Goodyear, Charles. 1800–60, U.S. inventor of vulcanized rubber.

Gore, Al(bert) Jr. born 1948, U.S. Democrat politician; vice president of the U.S. from 1993.

Gorky, Arshile. 1904–48, U.S. abstract expressionist painter, born in Armenia. Influenced by Picasso and Miró, his style is characterized by fluid lines and resonant colors.

Gould, Benjamin Apthorp. 1824–96, U.S. astronomer: the first to use the telegraph to determine longitudes;

founded the *Astronomical Journal* (1849); **Glenn.** 1932–82, Canadian pianist.

Graham, Martha. 1893–1991, U.S. dancer and choreographer; **Thomas.** 1805–69, British physicist: proposed **Graham's law** (1831) of gaseous diffusion and coined the terms osmosis, crystalloids, and colloids; **William Franklin,** known as *Billy Graham.* born 1918, U.S. evangelist.

Grant, Cary, real name *Alexander Archibald Leach.* 1904–86, U.S. film actor, born in England. His many films include *Bringing up Baby* (1938), *The Philadelphia Story* (1940), *Arsenic and Old Lace* (1944), and *Mr Blandings Builds his Dream House* (1948); **Duncan (James Corrowr).** 1885–1978, British painter and designer; **Ulysses S(impson),** real name *Hiram Ulysses Grant.* 1822–85, 18th president of the U.S. (1869–77); commander in chief of Union forces in the American Civil War (1864–65).

Greeley, Horace. 1811–72, U.S. journalist and political leader: founder (1841) and editor of the *New York Tribune,* which championed the abolition of slavery.

Grey, Charles, 2nd Earl Grey. 1764–1845, British statesman. As Whig prime minister (1830–34), he carried the Reform Bill of 1832 and the bill for the abolition of slavery throughout the British Empire (1833); Sir **Edward,** 1st Viscount Grey of Fallodon. 1862–1933, British statesman; foreign secretary (1905–16); Sir **George.** 1812–98, British statesman and colonial administrator; prime minister of New Zealand (1877–79); Lady **Jane.** 1537–54, queen of England (July 9–19, 1553); great-granddaughter of Henry VII. Her father-in-law, the Duke of Northumberland, persuaded Edward VI to alter the succession in her favor, but after ten days as queen she was imprisoned and later executed; **Zane.** 1875–1939, U.S. author of Westerns, including *Riders of the Purple Sage* (1912).

Griffith, Arthur. 1872–1922, Irish journalist and nationalist: founder of Sinn Féin (1905); president of the Irish Free State (1922); **D(avid Lewelyn) W(ark).** 1875–1948, U.S. film director and producer. He introduced several cinematic techniques, including the flashback and the fade-out, in his masterpiece *The Birth of a Nation* (1915).

Griffith-Joyner, Florence, known as *Flojo.* 1959–98, U.S. sprinter, winner of two gold medals at the 1988 Olympic Games.

Gropius, Walter. 1883–1969, U.S. architect, designer, and teacher, born in Germany. He founded (1919) and directed (1919–28) the Bauhaus in Germany. His influence stemmed from his adaptation of architecture to modern social needs and his pioneering use of industrial materials, such as concrete and steel. His buildings include the Fagus factory at Alfeld (1911) and the Bauhaus at Dessau (1926).

Guthrie, Samuel. 1782–1848, U.S. chemist: invented percussion priming powder and a punch lock for exploding it, and discovered chloroform (1831); Sir **(William) Tyrone.** 1900–71, English theatrical director; **Woody,** full name *Woodrow Wilson Guthrie.* 1912–67, U.S. folk singer and songwriter. His songs include "So Long, it's been Good to Know you" (1940) and "This Land is your Land" (1944).

Hagen, Walter. 1892–1969, U.S. golfer.

Hale, George Ellery. 1868–1938, U.S. astronomer: undertook research into sunspots and invented the spectroheliograph; Sir **Matthew.** 1609–76, English judge and scholar; Lord Chief Justice (1671–76).

Haley, Bill, full name *William John Clifton Haley.* 1925–81, U.S. rock and roll singer, best known for his recording of "Rock Around the Clock" (1955).

Hall, Charles Martin. 1863–1914, U.S. chemist: discovered the electrolytic process for producing aluminium; Sir **John.** 1824–1907, New Zealand statesman, born in

England: prime minister of New Zealand (1879–82); Sir **Peter.** born 1930, English stage director: director of the Royal Shakespeare Company (1960–73) and of the National Theatre (1973–88); **(Margueritte) Radclyffe.** 1883–1943, British novelist and poet. Her frank treatment of a lesbian theme in the novel *The Well of Loneliness* (1928) led to an obscenity trial.

Hamilton, Alexander. ?1757–1804, American statesman. He was a leader of the Federalists and as first secretary of the Treasury (1789–95) established a federal bank; Lady **Emma.** ?1765–1815, mistress of Nelson; **James,** 1st Duke of Hamilton. 1606–49, Scottish supporter of Charles I in the English Civil War: defeated by Cromwell at the Battle of Preston and executed; **Richard.** born 1922, British artist: a pioneer of the pop art style; Sir **William Rowan.** 1805–65, Irish mathematician: founded Hamiltonian mechanics and formulated the theory of quaternions.

Hamlisch, Marvin. born 1944, U.S. composer, best known for the musical *A Chorus Line* (1975).

Hammerstein II, Oscar. 1895–1960, U.S. librettist and songwriter: collaborated with the composer Richard Rodgers in musicals such as *South Pacific* (1949) and *The Sound of Music* (1959).

Hammett, Dashiell. 1894–1961, U.S. writer of detective novels. His books include *The Maltese Falcon* (1930) and *The Thin Man* (1932).

Hampton, Christopher James. born 1946, British playwright: his works include *When Did You Last See My Mother?* (1964) and the screenplays for the films *Dangerous Liaisons* (1988) and *Carrington* (1995); **Lionel.** 1913–96, U.S. jazz-band leader and vibraphone player.

Hancock, Anthony John, known as *Tony.* 1924–68, British comedian, noted for his radio series *Hancock's Half Hour*; **John.** 1737–93, American statesman; first signatory of the Declaration of Independence.

Handy, W(illiam) C(hristopher). 1873–1958, U.S. blues musician and songwriter, esp. noted for the song "St Louis Blues".

Hanks, Tom. born 1956, U.S. film actor: his films include *Splash* (1984), *Philadelphia* (1993), *Forrest Gump* (1994), and *Saving Private Ryan* (1998).

Harding, Warren G(amaliel). 1865–1923, 29th president of the U.S. (1921–23).

Harlow, Jean, real name *Harlean Carpentier.* 1911–37, U.S. film actress, whose films include *Hell's Angels* (1930), *Red Dust* (1932), and *Bombshell* (1933).

Harriman, W(illiam) Averell. 1891–1986, U.S. diplomat: negotiated the Nuclear Test Ban Treaty with the Soviet Union (1963); governor of New York (1955–58).

Harris, Sir **Arthur Travers,** known as *Bomber Harris.* 1892–1984, British air marshal. He was commander-in-chief of Bomber Command of the RAF (1942–45); **Frank.** 1856–1931, British writer and journalist; his books include his autobiography *My Life and Loves* (1923–27) and *Contemporary Portraits* (1915–30); **Joel Chandler.** 1848–1908, U.S. writer; creator of Uncle Remus; **Roy.** 1898–1979, U.S. composer, esp. of orchestral and choral music incorporating American folk tunes.

Harrison, Benjamin. 1833–1901, 23rd president of the U.S. (1889–93); **George.** born 1943, British rock singer, guitarist, and songwriter: a member of the Beatles (1962–70). His solo recordings include *All Things Must Pass* (1970) and *Cloud Nine* (1987); **Rex (Carey).** 1908–90, British actor. His many films include *Major Barbara* (1940), *Blithe Spirit* (1945), and *My Fair Lady* (1964); **Tony.** born 1937, British poet, dramatist, and translator: best known for his long poem *v.* (1985) and his translations for the stage; grandfather of Benjamin, **William Henry.** 1773–1841, 9th president of the U.S. (1841).

Hart, Lorenz. 1895–1943, U.S.

lyricist: collaborated with Richard Rodgers in writing musicals; **Moss.** 1904–61, U.S. dramatist: collaborated with George Kaufman on Broadway comedies and wrote libretti for musicals.

Harte, (Francis) Bret. 1836–1902, U.S. poet and short-story writer, noted for his sketches of Californian gold miners, such as *The Luck of Roaring Camp* (1870).

Hawkins, Coleman. 1904–69, U.S. pioneer of the tenor saxophone for jazz; **Sir John.** 1532–95, English naval commander and slave trader, treasurer of the navy (1577–89); commander of a squadron in the fleet that defeated the Spanish Armada (1588).

Hawks, Howard (Winchester). 1896–1977, U.S. film director. His films include *Sergeant York* (1941) and *The Big Sleep* (1946).

Hawthorne, Nathaniel. 1804–64, U.S. novelist and short-story writer: his works include the novels *The Scarlet Letter* (1850) and *The House of the Seven Gables* (1851) and the children's stories *Tanglewood Tales* (1853).

Hayes, Rutherford B(irchard). 1822–93, 19th president of the U.S. (1877–81).

Head, Edith. 1907–81, U.S. dress designer: won many Oscars for her Hollywood film costume designs.

Hearst, William Randolph. 1863–1951, U.S. newspaper publisher, whose newspapers were noted for their sensationalism.

Heifetz, Jascha. 1901–87, U.S. violinist, born in Russia.

Heller, Joseph. born 1923, U.S. novelist. His works include *Catch 22* (1961), *God Knows* (1984), *Picture This* (1988), and *Closing Time* (1994).

Hellman, Lillian. 1905–84, U.S. dramatist. Her works include the plays *The Little Foxes* (1939), *The Searching Wind* (1944), and the autobiographical *Scoundrel Time* (1976).

Hemingway, Ernest. 1899–1961, U.S. novelist and short-story writer. His novels include *The Sun Also Rises* (1926), *A Farewell to Arms* (1929), *For Whom the Bell Tolls* (1940), and *The Old Man and the Sea* (1952): Nobel prize for literature 1954.

Hendrix, Jimi, full name *James Marshall Hendrix.* 1942–70, U.S. rock guitarist, singer, and songwriter, noted for his innovative guitar technique. His recordings include "Purple Haze" (1967) and *Are you Experienced?* (1967).

Henry, Joseph. 1797–1878, U.S. physicist. He discovered the principle of electromagnetic induction independently of Faraday and constructed the first electromagnetic motor (1829). He also discovered self-induction and the oscillatory nature of electric discharges (1842); **O.** See **O. Henry.** **Patrick.** 1736–99, American statesman and orator, a leading opponent of British rule during the War of American Independence; **Prince.** born 1984, second son of Charles, Prince of Wales, and Diana, Princess of Wales.

Hepburn, Audrey. 1929–93, U.S. actress, born in Belgium. Her films include *Roman Holiday* (1955), *Funny Face* (1957), and *My Fair Lady* (1964); **Katharine.** born 1909, U.S. film actress, whose films include *The Philadelphia Story* (1940), *Adam's Rib* (1949), *The African Queen* (1951), *The Lion in Winter* (1968) for which she won an Oscar, and *On Golden Pond* (1981).

Hess, Dame **Myra.** 1890–1965, English pianist; **(Walther Richard) Rudolf.** 1894–1987, German Nazi leader. He made a secret flight to Scotland (1941) to negotiate peace with Britain but was held as a prisoner of war; later sentenced to life imprisonment at the Nuremberg trials (1946); committed suicide; **Victor Francis.** 1883–1964, U.S. physicist, born in Austria: pioneered the investigation of cosmic rays: shared the Nobel prize for physics (1936).

Hickok, James Butler, known as *Wild Bill Hickok.* 1837–76, U.S. frontiersman and marshal.

Highsmith, Patricia. 1921–95, U.S.

author of crime fiction. Her novels include *Strangers on a Train* (1950) and *Ripley's Game* (1974).

Hines, Earl, known as *Earl "Fatha" Hines*. 1905–83, U.S. jazz pianist, conductor, and songwriter.

Hiss, Alger. 1904–96, U.S. politician: imprisoned (1950–54) for perjury in connection with alleged espionage activities.

Hoffman, Dustin (Lee). born 1937, U.S. stage and film actor. His films include *The Graduate* (1967), *Midnight Cowboy* (1969), *All the President's Men* (1976), *Kramer vs Kramer* (1979), *Rain Man* (1989), *Accidental Hero* (1992), and *Wag the Dog* (1998).

Hofmann, Hans. 1880–1966, U.S. painter, born in Germany: a pioneer of the abstract expressionist style.

Holiday, Billie. real name *Eleanora Fagan*; known as *Lady Day*. 1915–59, U.S. jazz singer.

Holly, Buddy. real name *Charles Harden Holley*. 1936–59, U.S. rock-and-roll singer, guitarist, and songwriter. His hits (all 1956–59) include "That'll be the Day", "Maybe Baby", "Peggy Sue", "Oh, Boy", "Think it over", and "It doesn't Matter anymore".

Holmes, Oliver Wendell. 1809–94, U.S. author, esp. of humorous essays, such as *The Autocrat of the Breakfast Table* (1858) and its sequels; his son, **Oliver Wendell.** 1841–1935, U.S. jurist, noted for his liberal judgments.

Homer, c. 800 B.C., Greek poet to whom are attributed the *Iliad* and the *Odyssey*. Almost nothing is known of him, but it is thought that he was born on the island of Chios and was blind; **Winslow.** 1836–1910, U.S. painter, noted for his seascapes and scenes of working life.

Hoover, Herbert (Clark). 1874–1964, U.S. statesman; 31st president of the U.S. (1929–33). He organized relief for Europe during and after World War I, but as president he lost favor after his failure to alleviate the effects of the Depression; **J(ohn) Edgar.**

1895–1972, U.S. lawyer: director of the FBI (1924–72). He used new scientific methods to combat crime, including the first fingerprint file.

Hope, Anthony, real name *Sir Anthony Hope Hawkins*. 1863–1933, English novelist; author of *The Prisoner of Zenda* (1894); **Bob,** real name *Leslie Townes Hope*. born 1903, U.S. comedian and comic actor, born in England. His films include *The Cat and the Canary* (1939), *Road to Morocco* (1942), and *The Paleface* (1947). He was awarded an honorary knighthood in 1998.

Hopkins, Sir **Anthony.** born 1937, Welsh actor: his films include *The Silence of the Lambs* (1991), *Shadowlands* (1994), *Surviving Picasso* (1996), and *Meet Joe Black* (1999); Sir **Frederick Gowland.** 1861–1947, British biochemist, who pioneered research into what came to be called vitamins: shared the Nobel prize for physiology or medicine (1929); **Gerald Manley.** 1844–89, British poet and Jesuit priest, who experimented with sprung rhythm in his highly original poetry; **Harry L(loyd).** 1890–1946, U.S. administrator. During World War II he was a personal aide to President Roosevelt and administered the lend-lease programme.

Hopper, Edward. 1882–1967, U.S. painter, noted for his realistic depiction of everyday scenes.

Houdini, Harry, real name *Ehrich Weiss*. 1874–1926, U.S. magician and escapologist.

Howe, Elias. 1819–67, U.S. inventor of the sewing machine (1846); **Howe of Aberavon,** Baron, title of (*Richard Edward*) *Geoffrey Howe*. born 1926, British Conservative politician; Chancellor of the Exchequer (1979–83); foreign secretary (1983–89); deputy prime minister (1989–90); **Richard,** 4th Viscount Howe. 1726–99, British admiral: served (1776–78) in the War of American Independence and commanded the Channel fleet against France, winning the Battle of the Glorious First of June (1794); his brother, **William,** 5th Viscount Howe. 1729–1814, British general; commander in chief (1776–78) of British forces in the War of American Independence.

Howlin' Wolf, real name *Chester Burnett.* 1910–76, U.S. blues singer and songwriter.

Hubble, Edwin Powell. 1889–1953, U.S. astronomer, noted for his investigations of nebulae and the recession of the galaxies.

Hughes, Howard. 1905–76, U.S. industrialist, aviator, and film producer. He became a total recluse during the last years of his life; **(James Mercer) Langston.** 1902–67, U.S. Black poet and writer. His collections include *The Weary Blues* (1926) and *The Panther and the Lash* (1967); **Richard (Arthur Warren).** 1900–76, British novelist. He wrote *A High Wind in Jamaica* (1929), *In Hazard* (1938), and *The Fox in the Attic* (1961); **Ted,** full name *Edward James Hughes.* 1930–98, British poet: his works include *The Hawk in the Rain* (1957), *Crow* (1970), and *Birthday Letters* (1998). Poet laureate (1984–98); **Thomas.** 1822–96, British novelist; author of *Tom Brown's Schooldays* (1857); **William Morris.** 1864–1952, Australian statesman, born in England: prime minister of Australia (1915–23).

Hull, Cordell. 1871–1955, U.S. statesman; secretary of state (1933–44). He helped to found the U.N.: Nobel peace prize 1945.

Humphrey, Duke. See (Humphrey, Duke of) **Gloucester; Hubert Horatio.** 1911–78, U.S. statesman; vice-president of the U.S. under President Johnson (1965–69).

Huston, John. 1906–87, U.S. film director. His films include *The Treasure of the Sierra Madre* (1947), for which he won an Oscar, *The African Queen* (1951), *The Man Who Would Be King* (1975), *Prizzi's Honour* (1985), and *The Dead* (1987).

Illich, Ivan. born 1926. U.S. teacher and writer, born in Austria. His books include *Deschooling Society* (1971), *Medical Nemesis* (1975), and *In the*

Mirror of the Past (1991).

Ipatieff, Vladimir Nikolaievich. 1867–1952, U.S. physicist, born in Russia. He discovered the structure of isoprene (1897) and later developed high-octane fuels.

Irving, Sir Henry. real name *John Henry Brodribb.* 1838–1905, English actor and manager of the Lyceum Theatre in London (1878–1902); **Washington.** 1783–1859, U.S. essayist and short-story writer, noted for *The Sketch Book of Geoffrey Crayon* (1820), which contains the stories *Rip Van Winkle* and *The Legend of Sleepy Hollow.*

Isherwood, Christopher, full name *Christopher William Bradshaw-Isherwood.* 1904–86, U.S. novelist and dramatist, born in England. His works include the novel *Goodbye to Berlin* (1939) and three verse plays written in collaboration with W.H. Auden.

Ives, Charles Edward. 1874–1954, U.S. composer, noted for his innovative use of polytonality, polyrhythms, and quarter tones. His works include *Second Piano Sonata: Concord* (1915), five symphonies, chamber music, and songs; **Frederick Eugene.** 1856–1937, U.S. inventor of halftone photography.

Ivory, James. born 1928, U.S. film director. With the producer Ismael Merchant, his films include *Shakespeare Wallah* (1964), *Heat and Dust* (1983), *A Room With a view* (1986), and *A Soldier's Daughter Never Cries* (1998).

Jackson, Andrew. 1767–1845, U.S. statesman, general, and lawyer; seventh president of the U.S. (1829–37). He became a national hero after successfully defending New Orleans from the British (1815). During his administration the spoils system was introduced and the national debt was fully paid off; **Colin (Ray).** born 1967, British athlete, broke world record for 110 m hurdles in 1993 (12.91 seconds) and for the 60 m hurdles in 1994 (7.3 seconds); **Glenda.** born 1936, British stage, film, and television actress, and Labour politician. Her films include *Women in Love* (1969) for which she won an Oscar, *The Music Lovers* (1970), *Sunday Bloody Sunday* (1971), and *Turtle Diary* (1985); became a member of parliament in 1992; **Jesse (Louis).** born 1941, U.S. Democrat politician and clergyman; Black campaigner for minority rights; **Michael (Joe).** born 1958, U.S. pop singer, lead vocalist with the Jacksons (originally the Jackson 5) (1969–86). His solo albums include *Thriller* (1982) and *Bad* (1989); **Thomas Jonathan,** known as *Stonewall Jackson.* 1824–63, Confederate general in the American Civil War, noted particularly for his command at the first Battle of Bull Run (1861). **Jacksonian**

Jakobson, Roman (Osipovič). 1896–1982, U.S. linguist, born in Russia. His publications include *Children's Speech* (1941) and *Fundamentals of Language* (1956).

James, Henry 1843–1916, British novelist, short-story writer, and critic, born in the U.S. Among his novels are *Washington Square* (1880), *The Portrait of a Lady* (1881), *The Bostonians* (1886), *The Wings of the Dove* (1902), *The Ambassadors* (1903), and *The Golden Bowl* (1904); **Jesse (Woodson).** 1847–82, U.S. outlaw; **P(hyllis) D(orothy),** Baroness James of Holland Park. born 1920, British detective novelist. Her books include *Death of an Expert Witness* (1977), *Original Sin* (1994), and *A Certain Justice* (1997); **William,** brother of Henry James. 1842–1910, U.S. philosopher and psychologist, whose theory of pragmatism is expounded in *Essays in Radical Empiricism* (1912). His other works include *The Will to Believe* (1897), *The Principles of Psychology* (1890), and *The Varieties of Religious Experience* (1902); **New Testament a** known as *James the Great.* one of the twelve apostles, a son of Zebedee and brother to John the apostle (Matthew 4:21). Feast day: July 25 or April 30. **b** known as *James the Less.* one of the twelve apostles, son of Alphaeus (Matthew 10:3). Feast day:

May 3 or Oct. 9. **c** known as *James the brother of the Lord.* a brother or close relative of Jesus (Mark 6:3; Galatians 1:19). Feast day: Oct. 23. **d** the book ascribed to his authorship (in full **The Epistle of James**).

Jansky, Karl Guthe 1905–50, U.S. electrical engineer. He discovered a source of radio waves outside the solar system (1932) and pioneered radio astronomy.

Jarrett, Keith born 1945, U.S. jazz pianist and composer.

Jay, John 1745–1829, American statesman, jurist, and diplomat; first chief justice of the Supreme Court (1789–95). He negotiated the treaty with Great Britain (**Jay's treaty,** 1794), that settled outstanding disputes.

Jefferson, Thomas. 1743–1826, U.S. statesman: secretary of state (1790–93); third president (1801–09). He was the chief drafter of the Declaration of Independence (1776), the chief opponent of the centralizing policies of the Federalists under Hamilton, and effected the Louisiana Purchase (1803). **Jeffersonian**

Johns, Jasper. born 1930, U.S. artist, noted for his collages and constructions.

Johnson, Amy 1903–41, British aviator, who made several record flights, including those to Australia (1930) and to Cape Town and back (1936); **Andrew** 1808–75, U.S. Democrat statesman who was elected vice president under the Republican Abraham Lincoln; 17th president of the U.S. (1865–69); became president after Lincoln's assassination. His lenience towards the South after the American Civil War led to strong opposition from radical Republicans, who tried to impeach him; **Jack** 1878–1946, U.S. boxer; world heavyweight champion (1908–15); **Lionel (Pigot)** 1867–1902, British poet and critic, best known for his poems "Dark Angel" and "By the Statue of King Charles at Charing Cross"; **Lyndon Baines** known as *LBJ.* 1908–73, U.S.

Democrat statesman; 36th president of the U.S. (1963–69). His administration carried the Civil Rights Acts of 1964 and 1965, but he lost popularity by increasing U.S. involvement in the Vietnam war; **Michael (Duane)** born 1967, U.S. athlete: world (1995) and Olympic (1996) 200- and 400-metre gold medallist; **Robert** ?1898–1937, U.S. blues singer and guitarist; **Samuel** known as *Dr. Johnson*. 1709–84, British lexicographer, critic, and conversationalist, whose greatest works are his *Dictionary* (1755), his edition of Shakespeare (1765), and his *Lives of the Most Eminent English Poets* (1779–81). His fame, however, rests as much on his literary output.

Jolson, Al, real name *Asa Yoelson*. 1886–1950, U.S. singer and film actor, born in Russia; star of the first talking picture *The Jazz Singer* (1927).

Jones, Daniel. 1881–1967, British phonetician; **Daniel.** 1912–93, Welsh composer. He wrote nine symphonies and much chamber music; **David.** 1895–1974, British artist and writer: his literary works, which combine poetry and prose, include *In Parenthesis* (1937), an account of World War I, and *The Anathemata* (1952); **Inigo.** 1573–1652, English architect and theatrical designer, who introduced Palladianism to England. His buildings include the Banqueting Hall of Whitehall. He also designed the settings for court masques, being the first to use the proscenium arch and movable scenery in England; **John Paul,** original name *John Paul*. 1747–92, U.S. naval commander, born in Scotland: noted for his part in the War of American Independence; **(Everett) Le Roi,** Muslim name *Imanu Amiri Baraka*. born 1934, U.S. Black poet, dramatist, and political figure; **Robert Tyre,** known as *Bobby Jones*. 1902–71, U.S. golfer.

Joplin, Janis 1943–70, U.S. rock singer, noted for her hoarse and passionate style. Her albums include *Cheap Thrills* (1968) and *Pearl*

(1971); **Scott** 1868–1917, U.S. pianist and composer: creator of ragtime.

Jordan, Michael (Jeffrey). born 1963, U.S. basketball player.

Kahn, Herman. 1922–83, U.S. mathematician and futurologist; director of the Hudson Institute (1961–83); **Louis I(sadore).** 1901–74, U.S. architect, noted for his art museums at Yale (1951–53), Fort Worth (1966–72), and New Haven (1969–74).

Kaufman, George S(imon). 1889–1961, U.S. dramatist who, with Moss Hart, collaborated on many Broadway comedy hits.

Kazan, Elia, real name *Elia Kazanjoglous* born 1909, U.S. stage and film director and writer, born in Turkey. His films include *Gentleman's Agreement* (1947) and *On the Waterfront* (1954) for both of which he won Oscars, and *East of Eden* (1955).

Keaton, Buster, real name *Joseph Francis Keaton* 1895–1966, U.S. film comedian who starred in silent films such as *The Navigator* (1924), *The General* (1926), and *Steamboat Bill Junior* (1927).

Keller, Gottfried. 1819–90, Swiss novelist and short-story writer, who wrote in German: noted esp. for the novel *Der Grüne Heinrich* (1855, rewritten 1880); **Helen (Adams).** 1880–1968, U.S. author and lecturer. Blind and deaf from infancy, she was taught to read, write, and speak and became noted for her work for the handicapped.

Kelly, Gene, full name *Eugene Curran Kelly*. 1912–96, U.S. dancer, choreographer, film actor, and director. His many films include *An American in Paris* (1951) and *Singin' in the Rain* (1952); **Grace.** 1929–82, U.S. film actress. Her films included *High Noon* (1952) and *High Society* (1956). She married Prince Rainier III of Monaco in 1956 and died following a car crash; **Ned.** 1855–80, Australian horse and cattle thief and bushranger, active in Victoria: captured by the police and hanged.

(as) game as Ned Kelly See **game**[1] *(sense 25).*

Kendall, Edward Calvin. 1886–1972, U.S. biochemist, who isolated the hormone thyroxine (1916). He shared the Nobel prize for physiology or medicine (1950) with Phillip Hench and Tadeus Reichstein for their work on hormones.

Kennedy, Charles Peter. born 1959, British politician, leader of the Liberal Democrats from 1999; **Edward (Moore),** known as *Ted.* born 1932, U.S. Democrat politician; senator since 1962; his brother, **John (Fitzgerald),** known as *JFK.* 1917–63, U.S. Democrat statesman; 35th president of the U.S. (1961–63), the first Roman Catholic and the youngest man ever to be president. He demanded the withdrawal of Soviet missiles from Cuba (1962) and prepared civil rights reforms; assassinated; **Nigel (Paul).** born 1956, British violinist, noted for his flamboyant style; **Robert (Francis),** known as *Bobby,* brother of John Kennedy. 1925–68; U.S. Democrat statesman; attorney general (1961–64) and senator for New York (1965–68); assassinated.

Kennelly, Arthur Edwin. 1861–1939, U.S. electrical engineer: independently of Heaviside, he predicted the existence of an ionized layer in the upper atmosphere, known as the Kennelly-Heaviside layer or E region.

Kern, Jerome (David). 1885–1945, U.S. composer of musical comedies, esp. *Show Boat* (1927).

Kerouac, Jack, real name *Jean-Louis Lebris de Kérouac.* 1922–69, U.S. novelist and poet of the Beat Generation. His works include *On the Road* (1957) and *Big Sur* (1962).

Kesey, Ken. born 1935, U.S. novelist, best-known for *One Flew Over the Cuckoo's Nest* (1962).

King, B.B., real name *Riley B. King.* born 1925, U.S. blues singer and guitarist; **Billie Jean** (née*Moffitt*). born 1943, U.S. tennis player: Wimbledon champion 1966–68, 1972–73, and 1975; U.S. champion 1967, 1971–72, and 1974; **Martin Luther.** 1929–68, U.S. Baptist minister and civil-rights leader. He advocated nonviolence in his campaigns against the segregation of Blacks in the South: assassinated: Nobel Peace Prize 1964; **William Lyon Mackenzie.** 1874–1950, Canadian Liberal statesman; prime minister (1921–26; 1926–30; 1935–48).

Kinsey, Alfred Charles. 1894–1956, U.S. zoologist, who directed a survey of human sexual behavior.

Kissinger, Henry (Alfred). born 1923, U.S. academic and diplomat, born in Germany; assistant to President Nixon for national security affairs (1969–75); Secretary of State (1973–77): shared the Nobel peace prize 1973.

Kitaj, R. B. born 1932, U.S. painter working in Britain, noted for such large figurative works as *If Not, Not* (1976).

Klein, Calvin (Richard). born 1942, U.S. fashion designer; **Melanie.** 1882–1960, Austrian psychoanalyst resident in England (from 1926), noted for her work on child behavior.

Kline, Franz. 1910–62, U.S. abstract expressionist painter. His works are characterized by heavy black strokes on a white or grey background.

Kooning, Willem de. 1904–97, U.S. abstract expressionist painter, born in Holland.

Korzybski, Alfred (Habdank Skarbek). 1879–1950, U.S. originator of the theory and study of general semantics, born in Poland.

Kreisler, Fritz. 1875–1962, U.S. violinist, born in Austria.

Kubrick, Stanley. 1928–99, U.S. film writer, director, and producer. He directed *Lolita* (1962), *Dr Strangelove* (1963), *2001: A Space Odyssey* (1968), *A Clockwork Orange* (1971), *The Shining* (1980), *Full Metal Jacket* (1987), and *Eyes Wide Shut* (1999).

Kuznets, Simon. 1901–85, U.S. economist born in Russia. His books include *National Income and its Composition (1919–1938)* (1941) and *Economic Growth of Nations*

(1971). He was awarded the Nobel Prize for economics in 1971.

La Guardia, Fiorello H(enry). 1882–1947, U.S. politician. As mayor of New York (1933–45), he organized slum-clearance and labor safeguard schemes and suppressed racketeering.

Lamb, Charles, pen name *Elia*. 1775–1834, English essayist and critic. He collaborated with his sister Mary on *Tales from Shakespeare* (1807). His other works include *Specimens of English Dramatic Poets* (1808) and the largely autobiographical essays collected in *Essays of Elia* (1823; 1833); **William.** See (2nd Viscount) **Melbourne**. **Willis Eugene.** born 1913, U.S. physicist. He detected the small difference in energy between two states of the hydrogen atom (**Lamb shift**). Nobel prize for physics 1955.

Land, Edwin Herbert. 1909–91, U.S. inventor of the Polaroid Land camera.

Landowska, Wanda. 1877–1959, U.S. harpsichordist, born in Poland.

Langley, Samuel Pierpont. 1834–1906, U.S. astronomer and physicist: invented the bolometer (1878) and pioneered the construction of heavier-than-air flying machines.

Langmuir, Irving. 1881–1957, U.S. chemist. He developed the gas-filled tungsten lamp and the atomic hydrogen welding process: Nobel prize for chemistry 1932.

Lardner, Ring(old Wilmer). 1885–1933, U.S. short-story writer and journalist, whose best-known works are collected in *How to Write Short Stories* (1924) and *The Love Nest* (1926).

Laughton, Charles. 1899–1962, U.S. actor, born in England: noted esp. for his films of the 1930s, such as *The Private Life of Henry VIII* (1933), for which he won an Oscar, and *Mutiny on the Bounty* (1935).

Lawrence, Saint. died 258 A.D., Roman martyr: according to tradition he was roasted to death on a gridiron. Feast day: Aug. 10; **D(avid) H(erbert).** 1885–1930, British

novelist, poet, and short-story writer. Many of his works deal with the destructiveness of modern industrial society, contrasted with the beauty of nature and instinct, esp. the sexual impulse. His novels include *Sons and Lovers* (1913), *The Rainbow* (1915), *Women in Love* (1920), and *Lady Chatterley's Lover* (1928); **Ernest Orlando.** 1901–58, U.S. physicist, who invented the cyclotron (1931): Nobel prize for physics 1939; **Gertrude.** 1898–1952, British actress, noted esp. for her roles in comedies such as Noël Coward's *Private Lives* (1930); Sir **Thomas.** 1769–1830, British portrait painter; **T(homas) E(dward),** known as *Lawrence of Arabia.* 1888–1935, British soldier and writer. He took a major part in the Arab revolt against the Turks (1916–18), proving himself an outstanding guerrilla leader. He described his experiences in *The Seven Pillars of Wisdom* (1926).

Leadbelly, real name *Huddie Ledbetter.* 1888–1949, U.S. blues singer and guitarist.

Lederberg, Joshua. born 1925, U.S. geneticist, who discovered the phenomenon of transduction in bacteria. Nobel prize for physiology or medicine 1958 with George Beadle and Edward Tatum.

Lee, Bruce, original name *Lee Yuen Kam.* 1940–73, U.S. film actor and kung fu expert who starred in such films as *Enter the Dragon* (1973); **Gypsy Rose,** original name *Rose Louise Hovick.* 1914–70, U.S. striptease and burlesque artiste, who appeared in the Ziegfeld Follies (1936) and in films; **Laurie.** 1914–97, British poet and writer, best known for the autobiographical *Cider with Rosie* (1959); **Richard Henry.** 1732–94, American Revolutionary statesman, who moved the resolution in favor of American independence (1776); **Robert E(dward).** 1807–70, American general; commander-in-chief of the Confederate armies in the Civil War; **Spike,** real name *Shelton Jackson Lee.* born 1957, U.S. film director: his films include *She's*

Gotta Have It (1985), *Malcolm X* (1992), and *He Got Game* (1998); **T(sung)-D(ao).** born 1926, U.S. physicist, born in China. With Yang he disproved the principle that that parity is always conserved and shared the Nobel prize for physics in 1957.

Lehmann, Lilli. 1848–1929, German soprano; **Lotte.** 1888–1976, U.S. soprano, born in Germany; **Rosamond (Nina).** 1903–90, British novelist. Her books include *Dusty Answer* (1927), *Invitation to the Waltz* (1932), and *The Echoing Grove* (1953).

Leonard, Sugar Ray, real name *Ray Charles Leonard.* born 1956, U.S. boxer: the first man to have won world titles at five officially recognized weights.

Lerner, Alan Jay. 1914–86, U.S. songwriter and librettist. With Frederick Loewe he wrote *My Fair Lady* (1956) and *Camelot* (1960) as well as a number of film scripts, including *Gigi* (1958).

Lewis, Carl. full name *Frederick Carleton Lewis.* born 1961, U.S. athlete; winner of the long jump, 100 metres, 200 metres, and 4 metres relay at the 1984 Olympic Games; winner of the 100 metres in the 1988 Olympic Games; winner of the long jump in the 1992 and 1996 Olympic Games; See (Cecil) **Day-Lewis. C(live) S(taples).** 1898–1963, English novelist, critic, and Christian apologist, noted for his critical work, *Allegory of Love* (1936), his theological study, *The Screwtape Letters* (1942), and for his children's books chronicling the land of Narnia; **Matthew Gregory,** known as *Monk Lewis.* 1775–1818, English novelist and dramatist, noted for his Gothic horror story *The Monk* (1796); **Meriwether.** 1774–1807, American explorer who, with William Clark, led an overland expedition from St. Louis to the Pacific Ocean (1804–06); **(John) Saunders.** 1893–1985, Welsh poet, dramatist, critic, and politician: founder (1926) and president (1926–39) of the Welsh Nationalist Party; **(Harry) Sinclair.** 1885–1951, U.S. novelist. He satirized the complacency and philistinism of American small-town life, esp. in *Main Street* (1920) and *Babbitt* (1922): Nobel prize for literature 1930; **Wally.** born 1959, Australian rugby league player; **(Percy) Wyndham.** 1884–1957, British painter, novelist, and critic, born in the U.S.: a founder of vorticism. His writings include *Time and Western Man* (1927), *The Apes of God* (1930), and the trilogy *The Human Age* (1928–55).

Libby, Willard Frank. 1908–80, U.S. chemist, who devised the technique of radiocarbon dating: Nobel prize for chemistry 1960.

Lichtenstein, Roy. 1923–97, U.S. pop artist.

Lincoln, Abraham. 1809–65, U.S. Republican statesman; 16th president of the U.S. His fame rests on his success in saving the Union in the Civil War (1861– 65) and on his emancipation of slaves (1863); assassinated by Booth.

Lindbergh, Charles Augustus. 1902–74, U.S. aviator, who made the first solo nonstop flight across the Atlantic (1927).

Lindsay, See (Sir David) **Lyndsay. (Nicholas) Vachel.** 1879–1931, U.S. poet; best known for *General William Booth* (1913) and *The Congo* (1914); **Norman Alfred William.** 1879–1969, Australian artist and writer.

Lipchitz, Jacques. 1891–1973, U.S. sculptor, born in Lithuania: he pioneered cubist sculpture.

Liston, Sonny, real name *Charles.* 1922–70, U.S. boxer: former world heavyweight champion.

Lloyd, Clive (Hubert). born 1944, West Indian (Guyanese) cricketer; captained the West Indies (1974–88); **Harold (Clayton).** 1893–1971, U.S. comic film actor; **Marie,** real name *Matilda Alice Victoria Wood.* 1870–1922, English music-hall entertainer.

Loeb, Jacques. 1859–1924, U.S. physiologist, born in Germany, noted esp. for his pioneering work on artificial parthenogenesis.

Loewe, Frederick. 1904–88, U.S.

composer of such musical comedies as *Brigadoon* (1947), *My Fair Lady* (1956), and *Camelot* (1960), all with librettos by Alan Jay Lerner.

Loewi, Otto. 1873–1961, U.S. pharmacologist, born in Germany. He shared a Nobel prize for physiology or medicine (1936) with Dale for their work on the chemical transmission of nerve impulses.

Lomax, Alan. born 1915, and his father **John Avery** (1867–1948), U.S. folklorists.

Lombardi, Vincent Thomas. 1913–70, American football coach, whose team won the first two Superbowls, and after whom the Superbowl trophy is named.

London, Jack, full name *John Griffith London*. 1876–1916, U.S. novelist, short-story writer, and adventurer. His works include *Call of the Wild* (1903), *The Sea Wolf* (1904), *The Iron Heel* (1907), and the semiautobiographical *John Barleycorn* (1913).

Long, Crawford Williamson. 1815–78, U.S. surgeon. He was the first to use ether as an anaesthetic.

Longfellow, Henry Wadsworth. 1807–82, U.S. poet, noted particularly for his long narrative poems *Evangeline* (1847) and *The Song of Hiawatha* (1855).

Losey, Joseph. 1909–84, U.S. film director, in Britain from 1952. His films include *The Servant* (1963), *Accident* (1967), *Secret Ceremony* (1968), and *The Go-Between* (1971).

Louis, Joe, real name *Joseph Louis Barrow*, nicknamed *the Brown Bomber*. 1914–81, U.S. boxer; world heavyweight champion (1937–49).

Lowell, Amy (Lawrence). 1874–1925, U.S. imagist poet and critic; **James Russell.** 1819–91, U.S. poet, essayist, and diplomat, noted for his series of poems in Yankee dialect, *Biglow Papers* (1848; 1867); **Robert (Traill Spence).** 1917–77, U.S. poet. His volumes of verse include *Lord Weary's Castle* (1946), *Life Studies* (1959), *For the Union Dead* (1964), and a book of free translations of European poems,

Imitations (1961).

Lubitsch, Ernst. 1890–1947, U.S. film director, born in Germany; best known for such sophisticated comedies as *Forbidden Paradise* (1924) and *Ninotchka* (1939).

Lucas, George. born 1944, U.S. film director, producer, and writer of screenplays. Films include *American Graffiti* (1973) and *Star Wars* (1977) and its prequel *The Phantom Menace* (1999).

Lurie, Alison. born 1926, U.S. novelist. Her novels include *Imaginary Friends* (1967), *The War Between the Tates* (1974), and *Foreign Affairs* (1985).

Ma, Yo-Yo. born 1955, U.S. cellist, born in France to Chinese parents.

MacArthur, Douglas. 1880–1964, U.S. general. During World War II he became commanding general of U.S. armed forces in the Pacific (1944) and accepted the surrender of Japan, the Allied occupation of which he commanded (1945–51). He was commander in chief of United Nations forces in Korea (1950–51) until dismissed by President Truman.

McCarthy, Joseph R(aymond). 1908-57, U.S. Republican senator, who led (1950-54) the notorious investigations of alleged Communist infiltration into the U.S. government; **Mary (Therese).** 1912–89, U.S. novelist and critic; her works include *The Group* (1963).

McCormack, John. 1884–1945, Irish tenor: became U.S. citizen 1919.

McCormick, Cyrus Hall. 1809–84, U.S. inventor of the reaping machine (1831).

McCullers, Carson. 1917–67, U.S. writer, whose novels include *The Heart is a Lonely Hunter* (1940).

McEnroe, John (Patrick Jr). born 1959, U.S. tennis player: U.S. singles champion (1979–81; 1984) and doubles champion (1979; 1981; 1989): Wimbledon singles champion (1981; 1983; 1984) and doubles champion (1979; 1981; 1983; 1984; 1992).

McKinley, William. 1843–1901, 25th president of the U.S. (1897–1901).

His administration was marked by high tariffs and by expansionist policies. He was assassinated.

Macleish, Archibald. 1892–1982, U.S. poet and public official; his works include *Collected Poems* (1952) and *J.B.* (1958).

McMillan, Edwin M(attison). 1907–91, U.S. physicist; Nobel prize for chemistry 1951 (with Glenn Seaborg) for the discovery of transuranic elements.

McQueen, Steve. 1930–80, U.S. film actor, noted for his portrayal of tough characters.

Madison, James. 1751–1836, U.S. statesman; 4th president of the U.S. (1809–17). He helped to draft the U.S. Constitution and Bill of Rights. His presidency was dominated by the War of 1812.

Madonna, full name *Madonna Louise Veronica Ciccone.* born 1958, U.S. rock singer and film actress. Her hits include "Like a Virgin" (1985), "Into the Groove" (1985), and "Ray of Light" (1998). Her films include *Desperately Seeking Susan* (1985), and *Evita* (1996).

Mailer, Norman. born 1923, U.S. author. His works, which are frequently critical of modern American society, include the war novel *The Naked and the Dead* (1948), *An American Dream* (1965), his account of the 1967 peace march on Washington *The Armies of the Night* (1968), *Why Are We In Vietnam* (1967) and *Harlot's Ghost* (1991).

Malamud, Bernard. 1914–86, U.S. novelist and short-story writer. His works include *The Fixer* (1966) and *Dubin's Lives* (1979).

Malcolm X, original name *Malcolm Little.* 1925–65, U.S. Black civil-rights leader: assassinated.

Mamet, David. born 1947, U.S. dramatist and film director. His plays include *Sexual Perversity in Chicago* (1974), *American Buffalo* (1976), *Glengarry Glen Ross* (1983), and *The Spanish Prisoner* (1998).

Marciano, Rocky. original name *Rocco Francis Marchegiano.* 1923–69, U.S. heavyweight boxer; world

heavyweight champion, 1952–56.

Marcuse, Herbert. 1898–1979, U.S. philosopher, born in Germany. In his later works he analysed the situation of man under monopoly capitalism and the dehumanizing effects of modern technology. His works include *Eros and Civilization* (1958) and *One Dimensional Man* (1964).

Marin, John. 1870–1953, U.S. painter, noted esp. for his watercolor landscapes and seascapes.

Marquand, J(ohn) P(hillips). 1893–1960, U.S. novelist, noted for his stories featuring the Japanese detective Mr Moto and for his satirical comedies of New England life, such as *The Late George Apley* (1937).

Marquis, Don(ald Robert Perry). 1878–1937, U.S. humorist; author of archy and mehitabel (1927).

Marsalis, Wynton. born 1962, U.S. jazz and classical trumpeter.

Marshall, 1842–1924, English economist, author of *Principles of Economics* (1890); **George Catlett.** 1880–1959, U.S. general and statesman. He was chief of staff of the U.S. army (1939–45) and, as secretary of state (1947– 49), he proposed the Marshall Plan (1947), later called the European Recovery Programme: Nobel peace prize 1953; **John.** 1755–1835, U.S. jurist and statesman. As chief justice of the Supreme Court (1801–35), he established the principles of U.S. constitutional law; Sir **John Ross.** 1912–88, New Zealand politician; prime minister (1972).

Massine, Léonide. 1896–1979, U.S. ballet dancer and choreographer, born in Russia.

Masters, Edgar Lee. 1868–1950, U.S. poet; best known for *Spoon River Anthology* (1915).

Maury, Matthew Fontaine. 1806–73, U.S. pioneer hydrographer and oceanographer.

Maxim, Sir **Hiram Stevens.** 1840–1916, British inventor of the first automatic machine gun (1884), born in the U.S.

Mayer, Julius Robert von. 1814–78,

German physicist whose research in thermodynamics (1842) contributed to the discovery of the law of conservation of energy; **Louis B(urt).** 1885–1957, U.S. film producer, born in Russia; founder (with S. Goldwyn) and first head (1924–48) of the Metro-Goldwyn-Mayer (MGM) film company.

Mead, Margaret. 1901–78, U.S. anthropologist. Her works include *Coming of Age in Samoa* (1928) and *Male and Female* (1949).

Meade, George Gordon. 1815–72, Union general in the American Civil War. He commanded the Army of the Potomac, defeating the Confederates at Gettysburg (1863).

Melchior, (in Christian tradition) one of the Magi, the others being Balthazar and Caspar; **Lauritz.** 1890–1973, U.S. operatic tenor, born in Denmark.

Melville, Herman. 1819–91, U.S. novelist and short-story writer. Among his works, *Moby Dick* (1851) and *Billy Budd* (written 1891, published 1924) are outstanding.

Mencken, H(enry) L(ouis). 1880–1956, U.S. journalist and literary critic, noted for *The American Language* (1919): editor of the *Smart Set* and the *American Mercury*, which he founded (1924).

Menuhin, Yehudi, Baron. 1916–99, British violinist, born in the U.S.

Mercer, Johnny, full name *John Herndon Mercer.* 1909–76, U.S. popular songwriter and singer. His most popular songs include "Blues in the Night" (1941) and "Moon River" (1961).

Merton, Thomas (Feverel). 1915–68, U.S. writer, monk, and mystic; noted esp. for his autobiography *The Seven Storey Mountain* (1948).

Meštrović, Ivan. 1883–1962, U.S. sculptor, born in Austria: his works include portraits of Sir Thomas Beecham and Pope Pius XI.

Michelson, Albert Abraham. 1852–1931, U.S. physicist, born in Germany: noted for his part in the Michelson-Morley experiment: Nobel

prize for physics 1907.

Mies van der Rohe, Ludwig. 1886–1969, U.S. architect, born in Germany. He directed the Bauhaus (1929–33) and developed a functional style, characterized by geometrical design. His works include the Seagram building, New York (1958).

Millay, Edna St Vincent. 1892–1950, U.S. poet, noted esp. for her sonnets; her collections include *The Buck in the Snow* (1928) and *Fatal Interview* (1931).

Miller, Arthur. born 1915, U.S. dramatist. His plays include *Death of a Salesman* (1949), *The Crucible* (1953), *A View from the Bridge* (1955), and *Mr Peters' Connections* (1998); **Glenn.** 1904–44, U.S. composer, trombonist, and band leader. His popular compositions include "Moonlight Serenade". During World War II he was leader of the U.S. Air Force band in Europe. He disappeared without trace on a flight between England and France; **Henry.** 1891–1980, U.S. novelist, author of *Tropic of Cancer* (1934) and *Tropic of Capricorn* (1938); **Hugh** 1802–56, Scottish geologist and writer; **Jonathon (Wolfe).** born 1934, British doctor, actor, and theatre director. His productions include Shakespeare, Ibsen, and Chekhov as well as several operas. He has also presented many television medical programmes.

Millett, Kate. full name *Katherine Murray Millett.* born 1934, U.S. feminist writer and artist; books include *Sexual Politics* (1969) and *The Politics of Cruelty* (1994).

Millikan, Robert Andrews. 1868–1953, U.S. physicist. He measured the charge of an electron (1910), verified Einstein's equation for the photoelectric effect (1916), and studied cosmic rays; Nobel prize for physics 1923.

Miłosz, Czeslaw. born 1911, U.S. poet and writer, born in Lithuania, writing in Polish; author of *The Captive Mind* (1953). Nobel prize for literature 1980.

Milstein, Nathan. 1904–92, U.S.

violinist, born in the Ukraine.

Mingus, Charles, known as *Charlie Mingus.* 1922–79, U.S. jazz double bassist, composer, and band leader.

Minnelli, Liza. born 1946, U.S. actress and singer, daughter of Judy Garland. Her films include *Charlie Bubbles* (1968), *Cabaret* (1972), *Arthur* (1981), and *Stepping Out* (1991).

Mitchell, Joni, original name *Roberta Joan Anderson.* born 1943, Canadian folk-rock singer and songwriter. Her albums include *Blue* (1971), *Court and Spark* (1974), *Mingus* (1979), and *Turbulent Indigo* (1994); **Margaret.** 1900–49, U.S. novelist; author of *Gone with the Wind* (1936); **Reginald Joseph.** 1895–1937, British aeronautical engineer; designer of the Spitfire fighter; Sir **Thomas Livingstone,** known as *Major Mitchell.* 1792–1855, Australian explorer born in Scotland.

Mitchum, Robert. 1917–97, U.S. film actor. His many films include *Night of the Hunter* (1955) and *Farewell my Lovely* (1975).

Moholy-Nagy, Laszlo *or* **Ladislaus.** 1895–1946, U.S. painter and teacher, born in Hungary. He worked at the Bauhaus (1923–29).

Mondale, Walter (Frederick). born 1928, U.S. Democratic politician; vice president of the U.S. (1977–81).

Monk, Thelonious (Sphere). 1920–82, U.S. jazz pianist and composer; a variant spelling of (George) **Monck**.

Monroe, James. 1758–1831, U.S. statesman; fifth president of the U.S. (1817–25). He promulgated the Monroe Doctrine (1823); **Marilyn,** real name *Norma Jean Baker* or *Mortenson.* 1926–62, U.S. film actress. Her films include *Niagara* (1952), *Gentlemen Prefer Blondes* (1953), and *Some Like It Hot* (1959).

Montana, Joe. born 1958, American football quarterback.

Monteux, Pierre. 1875–1964, U.S. conductor, born in France.

Moody, Dwight Lyman. 1837–99, U.S. evangelist and hymnodist, noted for his revivalist campaigns in Britain

and the U.S. with I. D. Sankey.

Moore, Bobby. full name *Robert Frederick Moore.* 1941–93, British footballer captain of the England team that won the World Cup in 1966; **Dudley (Stuart John).** born 1935, British actor, comedian, and musician noted for his comedy partnership (1960–73) with Peter Cook and such films as *10* (1979) and *Arthur* (1981); **George.** 1852–1933, Irish novelist. His works include *Esther Waters* (1894) and *The Brook Kerith* (1916); **G(eorge) E(dward).** 1873–1958, British philosopher, noted esp. for his *Principia Ethica* (1903); **Gerald.** 1899–1987, British pianist, noted as an accompanist esp. to lieder singers; **Henry.** 1898–1986, British sculptor. His works are characterized by monumental organic forms and include the *Madonna and Child* (1943) at St Matthew's Church, Northampton; Sir **John.** 1761–1809, British general; commander of the British army (1808–09) in the Peninsular War: killed at Corunna; **Marianne (Craig).** 1887–1972, U.S. poet: her works include *Observations* (1924) and *Selected Poems* (1935); **Thomas.** 1779–1852, Irish poet, best known for *Irish Melodies* (1807–34).

Morgan, Sir **Henry.** 1635–88, Welsh buccaneer, who raided Spanish colonies in the West Indies for the English; **John Pierpont.** 1837–1913, U.S. financier, philanthropist, and art collector; **Thomas Hunt.** 1866–1945, U.S. biologist. He formulated the chromosome theory of heredity. Nobel prize for physiology or medicine 1933.

Morley, Edward Williams. 1838–1923, U.S. chemist who collaborated with A. A. Michelson in the Michelson-Morley experiment; **John,** Viscount Morley of Blackburn. 1838–1923, British Liberal statesman and writer; secretary of state for India (1905–10); **Robert.** 1908–92, British actor. His many films include *Major Barbara* (1940), *Oscar Wilde* (1960), and *The Blue Bird* (1976); **Thomas.** ?1557–?1603, English composer and organist, noted for his madrigals and his textbook on music, *A Plaine and Easie Introduction to Practicall Musicke* (1597).

Morphy, Paul. 1837–84, U.S. chess player, widely considered to have been the world's greatest player.

Morrison, Herbert Stanley, Baron Morrison of Lambeth. 1888–1965, British Labour statesman, Home Secretary and Minister for Home Security in Churchill's War Cabinet (1942–45); **Jim,** full name *James Douglas Morrison.* 1943–71, U.S. rock singer and songwriter, lead vocalist with the Doors; **Toni,** full name *Chloe Anthony Morrison.* born 1931, U.S. novelist, whose works include *Sula* (1974), *Song of Solomon* (1977), *Beloved* (1987), *Jazz* (1992), and *Paradise* (1998): awarded the Nobel Prize for literature in 1993; **Van,** full name *George Ivan Morrison.* born 1945, Northern Irish rock singer and songwriter. His albums include *Astral Weeks* (1968), *Moondance* (1970), and *Too Long in Exile* (1993).

Morse, Samuel Finley Breese. 1791–1872, U.S. inventor and painter. He invented the first electric telegraph and the Morse code.

Morton, 4th Earl of, title of *James Douglas.* 1516–81, regent of Scotland (1572–78) for the young James VI. He was implicated in the murders of Rizzio (1566) and Darnley (1567) and played a leading role in ousting Mary, Queen of Scots; executed; **Jelly Roll,** real name *Ferdinand Joseph La Menthe Morton.* 1885–1941, U.S. jazz pianist, singer, and songwriter; one of the creators of New Orleans jazz.

Moses, *Old Testament* the Hebrew prophet who led the Israelites out of Egypt to the Promised Land and gave them divinely revealed laws; **Ed.** born 1956, U.S. hurdler; winner of the 400 m hurdles in the 1976 and 1984 Olympic Games; **Grandma,** real name *Anna Mary Robertson Moses.* 1860–1961, U.S. painter of primitives, who began to paint at the age of 75.

Muhammad Ali *or* **Muhammed Ali** *or* **Mohammed Ali.** original name

Cassius (Marcellus) Clay. born 1942, U.S. boxer, who was world heavyweight champion three times (1964–67; 1974–78; 1978).

Muller, Hermann Joseph. 1890–1967, U.S. geneticist, noted for his work on the transmutation of genes by X-rays: Nobel prize for physiology or medicine 1946.

Mulliken, Robert Sanderson. 1896–1986, U.S. physicist and chemist, who won the Nobel prize for chemistry (1966) for his work on bonding and the electronic structure of molecules.

Mumford, Lewis. 1895–1990, U.S. sociologist, whose works are chiefly concerned with the relationship between man and his environment. They include *The City in History* (1962) and *Roots of Contemporary Architecture* (1972).

Murdoch, Dame (Jean) Iris. 1919–99, British writer. Her books include *The Bell* (1958), *A Severed Head* (1961), *The Sea, The Sea* (1978), which won the Booker Prize, *The Philosopher's Pupil* (1983), *Existentialists and Mystics* (1997); **(Keith) Rupert.** born 1931, U.S. publisher and media entrepreneur, born in Australia; chairman of News International Ltd. and Times Newspapers Ltd.

Murphy, Alex. born 1939, British rugby league player and coach; **William Parry.** 1892–1987, U.S. physician: with G. R. Minot, he discovered the liver treatment for anaemia and they shared, with G. H. Whipple, the Nobel prize for physiology or medicine in 1934.

Muskie, Edmund (Sixtus). 1914–96, U.S. Democratic politician: Governor of Maine (1955–59): senator for Maine (1959–80): Secretary of State (1980–81).

Muybridge, Eadweard, original name *Edward James Muggeridge.* 1830–1904, U.S. photographer, born in England; noted for his high-speed photographic studies of animals and people in motion.

Nabokov, Vladimir Vladimirovich. 1899–1977, U.S. novelist, born in

Russia. His works include *Lolita* (1955), *Pnin* (1957), *Pale Fire* (1962), and *Ada* (1969). **Nabokovian**

Nader, Ralph. born 1934, U.S. lawyer and campaigner for consumer rights.

Nash, John. 1752–1835, English town planner and architect. He designed Regent's Park, Regent Street, and the Marble Arch in London; **Ogden.** 1902–71, U.S. humorous poet; **Paul.** 1889–1946, English painter, noted esp. as a war artist in both World Wars and for his landscapes; **Richard,** known as *Beau Nash.* 1674–1762, English dandy; See (Thomas) **Nashe.** Sir **Walter.** 1882–1968, New Zealand Labour statesman, born in England: prime minister of New Zealand (1957–60).

Navratilova, Martina. born 1956, Czech-born U.S. tennis player: Wimbledon champion 1978, 1979, 1982–87, 1990; world champion 1980 and 1984.

Nelson, Horatio, Viscount Nelson. 1758–1805, British naval commander during the Revolutionary and Napoleonic Wars. He became rear admiral in 1797 after the battle of Cape St Vincent and in 1798 almost destroyed the French fleet at the battle of the Nile. He was killed at Trafalgar (1805) after defeating Villeneuve's fleet; **Willie.** born 1933, U.S. country singer and songwriter.

Newcomb, Simon. 1835–1909, U.S. astronomer, noted for his tables of celestial bodies and astronomical constants.

Newman, Barnet. 1905–70, U.S. painter, a founder of Abstract Expressionism: his paintings include the series *Stations of the Cross* (1965–66); **John Henry.** 1801–90, British theologian and writer. Originally an Anglican minister, he was a prominent figure in the Oxford Movement. He became a Roman Catholic (1845) and a priest (1847) and was made a cardinal (1879). His writings include the spiritual autobiography, *Apologia pro vita sua* (1864), a treatise on the nature of

belief, *The Grammar of Assent* (1870), and hymns; **Paul.** born 1925, U.S. film actor and director, who appeared in such films as *Hud* (1963), *Butch Cassidy and the Sundance Kid* (1969), *The Sting* (1973), *The Verdict* (1982), *Blaze* (1990), and *Twilight* (1998).

Nicholson, Ben. 1894–1982, English painter, noted esp. for his abstract geometrical works; **Jack.** born 1937, U.S. film actor. His films include *Easy Rider* (1969), *One Flew Over the Cuckoo's Nest* (1974), *Terms of Endearment* (1983), *Batman* (1989), and *As Good As It Gets* (1998); **John.** 1821–57, British general and administrator, born in Ireland: deputy commissioner in the Punjab (1851–56), where he became the object of hero-worship among the natives and kept the Punjab loyal during the Indian Mutiny: played a major role in the capture of Delhi.

Nicklaus, Jack. born 1940, U.S. professional golfer: won the British Open Championship (1966; 1970; 1978) and the U.S. Open Championship (1962; 1967; 1972; 1980).

Niebuhr, Barthold Georg. 1776–1831, German historian, noted for his critical approach to sources, esp. in *History of Rome* (1811–32); **Reinhold.** 1892–1971, U.S. Protestant theologian. His works include *Moral Man and Immoral Society* (1932) and *The Nature and Destiny of Man* (1941–43).

Nimitz, Chester William. 1885–1966, U.S. admiral; commander in chief of the U.S. Pacific fleet in World War II (1941–45).

Nirenberg, Marshall Warren. born 1927, U.S. biochemist; shared the Nobel prize for physiology or medicine (1968) for his role in deciphering the genetic code.

Nixon, Richard M(ilhous). 1913–94, U.S. Republican politician; 37th president from 1969 until he resigned in 1974.

Norman, Greg. born 1955, Australian golfer; **Jessye.** born 1945,

U.S. Black soprano.

Oakley, Annie, real name *Phoebe Anne Oakley Mozee.* 1860–1926, U.S. markswoman.

O'Connor, Feargus. 1794–1855, Irish politician and journalist, a leader of the Chartist movement; **(Mary) Flannery.** 1925–64, U.S. novelist and short-story writer, author of *Wise Blood* (1952) and *The Violent Bear it Away* (1960); **Frank,** real name *Michael O'Donovan.* 1903–66, Irish short- story writer and critic; **Thomas Power,** known as *Tay Pay.* 1848–1929, Irish journalist and nationalist leader.

Odets, Clifford. 1906–63, U.S. dramatist; founder member of the Group Theatre. His plays include *Waiting for Lefty* (1935) and *Golden Boy* (1937).

O. Henry, pen name of *William Sidney Porter.* 1862–1910, U.S. short-story writer. His collections of stories, characterized by his use of caricature and surprising endings, include *Cabbages and Kings* (1904) and *The Four Million* (1906).

O'Keeffe, Georgia. 1887–1986, U.S. painter, best known for her semiabstract still lifes, esp. of flowers: married the photographer Alfred Stieglitz.

Oldenburg, Claes. born 1929, U.S. pop sculptor and artist, born in Sweden.

Oliver, one of Charlemagne's 12 paladins; See also **Roland. Isaac.** ?1556–1617, English portrait miniaturist, born in France: he studied under Hilliard and worked at James I's court; **Joseph,** known as *King Oliver.* 1885–1938, U.S. pioneer jazz cornetist.

O'Neill, Eugene (Gladstone). 1888–1953, U.S. dramatist. His works, which are notable for their emotional power and psychological analysis, include *Desire under the Elms* (1924), *Strange Interlude* (1928), *Mourning becomes Elektra* (1931), *Long Day's Journey into Night* (1941), and *The Iceman Cometh* (1946): Nobel prize for literature 1936.

Oppenheimer, J(ulius) Robert. 1904–67, U.S. nuclear physicist. He was director of the Los Alamos laboratory (1943–45), which produced the first atomic bomb. He opposed the development of the hydrogen bomb (1949) and in 1953 was alleged to be a security risk. He was later exonerated.

Orbison, Roy (Kelton). 1936–89, U.S. pop singer and songwriter. His records include the singles "Only the Lonely" (1960) and "Oh Pretty Woman" (1964) and the album *Mystery Girl* (1989).

Ormandy, Eugene. 1899–1985, U.S. conductor, born in Hungary.

Oswald, Lee Harvey. 1939–63, presumed assassin (1963) of U.S. president John F. Kennedy; murdered by Jack Ruby two days later; **Saint.** ?605–41 A.D., king of Northumbria (634–41); with St Aidan he restored Christianity to the region. He was killed in battle by Penda of Mercia. Feast day: Aug. 5.

Owens, Jesse, real name *John Cleveland Owens.* 1913–80, U.S. Black athlete: won four gold medals at the Berlin Olympics (1936).

Pacino, Al, full name *Alfredo James Pacino.* born 1940, U.S. film actor; his films include *The Godfather* (1972), *Dog Day Afternoon* (1975), *Scent of a Woman* (1992), for which he won an Oscar, and *Heat* (1995).

Paine, Thomas. 1737–1809, American political pamphleteer, born in England. His works include the pamphlets *Common Sense* (1776) and *Crisis* (1776–83), supporting the American colonists' fight for independence; *The Rights of Man* (1791–92), a justification of the French Revolution; and *The Age of Reason* (1794–96), a defence of deism.

Palmer, Arnold. born 1929, U.S. professional golfer: won the U.S. Open Championship (1960) and the British Open Championship (1961; 1962); **Samuel.** 1805–81, English painter of visionary landscapes, influenced by William Blake.

Parker, Charlie. nickname *Bird* or

Yardbird. 1920–55, U.S. jazz alto saxophonist and composer; the leading exponent of early bop; **Dorothy (Rothschild).** 1893–1967, U.S. writer, noted esp. for the ironical humor of her short stories; **Matthew.** 1504–75, English prelate. As archbishop of Canterbury (1559–75), he supervised Elizabeth I's religious settlement.

Parsons, Sir **Charles Algernon.** 1854–1931, English engineer, who developed the steam turbine; **Talcott.** 1902–79, U.S. sociologist, author of *The Structure of Social Action* (1937) and *The Social System* (1951).

Parton, Dolly. born 1946, U.S. country and pop singer and songwriter.

Patton, George Smith. 1885–1945, U.S. general, who successfully developed tank warfare as an extension of cavalry tactics in World War II: captured Palermo, Sicily (1942) and much of France (1944).

Paul, Saint. Also called: **Paul the Apostle, Saul of Tarsus.** original name *Saul.* died ?67 A.D., one of the first Christian missionaries to the Gentiles, who died a martyr in Rome. Until his revelatory conversion he had assisted in persecuting the Christians. He wrote many of the Epistles in the New Testament. Feast day: June 29; Related adj **Pauline**; **Jean.** See **Jean Paul. Les,** real name *Lester Polfuss.* born 1915, U.S. guitarist: creator of the solid-body electric guitar and pioneer in multitrack recording.

Pauli, Wolfgang. 1900–58, U.S. physicist, born in Austria. He formulated the exclusion principle (1924) and postulated the existence of the neutrino (1931), later confirmed by Fermi: Nobel prize for physics 1945.

Pauling, Linus Carl. 1901–94, U.S. chemist, noted particularly for his work on the nature of the chemical bond and his opposition to nuclear tests: Nobel prize for chemistry 1954; Nobel peace prize 1962.

Payton, Walter. born 1954, American footballer and sports administrator.

Peabody, George. 1795–1869, U.S. merchant, banker, and philanthropist in the U.S. and England.

Peary, Robert Edwin. 1856–1920, U.S. arctic explorer, generally regarded as the first man to reach the North Pole (1909).

Peck, Gregory. born 1916, U.S. film actor; his films include *Keys of the Kingdom* (1944), *The Gunfighter* (1950), *The Big Country* (1958), *To Kill a Mockingbird* (1963), *The Omen* (1976), and *Other People's Money* (1991).

Peckinpah, Sam(uel David). 1926–84, U.S. film director, esp. of Westerns, such as *The Wild Bunch* (1969). Among his other films are *Straw Dogs* (1971), *Bring me the Head of Alfredo Garcia* (1974), and *Cross of Iron* (1977).

Pei, I(eoh) M(ing). born 1917, U.S. architect, born in China. His buildings include the E wing of the National Museum of Art, Washington DC (1978), a glass and steel pyramid at the Louvre, Paris (1989), and the Rock and Roll Hall of Fame, Cleveland, U.S.A. (1995).

Peirce, Charles Sanders. 1839–1914, U.S. logician, philosopher, and mathematician; pioneer of pragmatism.

Penn, Irving. born 1917, U.S. photographer, noted for his portraits and his innovations in color photography; **William.** 1644–1718, English Quaker and founder of Pennsylvania.

Penzias, Arno Allan. born 1933, U.S. astrophysicist, who shared the Nobel prize for physics (1978) with Robert W. Wilson for their discovery of cosmic microwave background radiation.

Perelman, S(idney) J(oseph). 1904–79, U.S. humorous writer. After scriptwriting for the Marx Brothers, he published many collections of articles, including *Crazy Like a Fox* (1944) and *Eastward, Hi!* (1977).

Perry, Fred(erick John). 1909–95,

English tennis and table-tennis player; world singles table-tennis champion (1929); Wimbledon singles champion (1934–36); **Matthew Calbraith.** 1794–1858, U.S. naval officer, who led a naval expedition to Japan that obtained a treaty (1854) opening up Japan to western trade; his brother, **Oliver Hazard.** 1785–1819, U.S. naval officer. His defeat of a British squadron on Lake Erie (1813) was the turning point in the War of 1812, leading to the recapture of Detroit.

Pershing, John Joseph, nickname *Black Jack.* 1860–1948, U.S. general. He was commander in chief of the American Expeditionary Force in Europe (1917–19).

Phyfe *or* **Fife. Duncan.** ?1768–1854, U.S. cabinet-maker, born in Scotland.

Piccard, Auguste. 1884–1962, Swiss physicist, whose study of cosmic rays led to his pioneer balloon ascents in the stratosphere (1931–32); his twin brother, **Jean Félix.** 1884–1963, U.S. chemist and aeronautical engineer, born in Switzerland, noted for his balloon ascent into the stratosphere (1934).

Pickering, Edward Charles. 1846–1919, U.S. astronomer, who invented the meridian photometer; his brother, **William Henry.** 1858–1938, U.S. astronomer, who discovered Phoebe, the ninth satellite of Saturn, and predicted (1919) the existence and position of Pluto.

Pickford, Mary, real name *Gladys Mary Smith.* 1893–1979, U.S. actress in silent films, born in Canada.

Pierce, Franklin. 1804–69, U.S. statesman; 14th president of the U.S. (1853–57).

Pinckney, Charles. 1757–1824, U.S. statesman, who was a leading member of the convention that framed the U.S. Constitution (1787); his cousin, **Charles Cotesworth.** 1746–1825, U.S. soldier, statesman, and diplomat, who also served at the Constitutional Convention; his brother, **Thomas.** 1750–1828, U.S. soldier and politician. He was U.S. minister to Britain (1792–96) and special envoy to Spain (1795–96).

Pincus, Gregory Goodwin. 1903–67, U.S. physiologist, whose work on steroid hormones led to the development of the first contraceptive pill.

Pinkerton, Allan. 1819–84, U.S. private detective, born in Scotland. He founded the first detective agency in the U.S. (1850) and organized an intelligence system for the Federal States of America (1861).

Plath, Sylvia. 1932–63, U.S. poet living in England. She wrote two volumes of verse, *The Colossus* (1960) and *Ariel* (1965), and a novel, *The Bell Jar* (1963).

Poe, Edgar Allan. 1809–49, U.S. short-story writer, poet, and critic. Most of his short stories, such as *The Fall of the House of Usher* (1839) and the *Tales of the Grotesque and Arabesque* (1840), are about death, decay, and madness. *The Murders in the Rue Morgue* (1841) is regarded as the first modern detective story.

Polk, James Knox. 1795–1849, U.S. statesman; 11th president of the U.S. (1845–49). During his administration, Texas and territory now included in New Mexico, Colorado, Utah, Nevada, Arizona, Oregon, and California were added to the Union.

Pollack, Sydney. born 1934, U.S. film director. His films include *Tootsie* (1982), *Out of Africa* (1986), and *The Firm* (1993).

Pollock, Sir **Frederick.** 1845–1937, English legal scholar: with Maitland, he wrote *History of English Law before the Time of Edward I* (1895); **Jackson.** 1912–56, U.S. abstract expressionist painter; chief exponent of action painting in the U.S.

Porter, Cole. 1893–1964, U.S. composer and lyricist of musical comedies. His most popular songs include *Night and Day* and *Let's do It*; **George,** Baron Porter of Luddenham. born 1920, British chemist, who shared a Nobel prize for chemistry in 1967 for his work on flash photolysis; **Katherine Anne.** 1890–1980, U.S. short-story writer and novelist. Her best-known collections of stories are *Flowering Judas* (1930) and *Pale Horse, Pale Rider* (1939); **Peter.** born 1929, Australian poet, living in Britain; **Rodney Robert.** 1917–85, British biochemist: shared the Nobel prize for physiology or medicine 1972 for determining the structure of an antibody; **William Sidney.** original name of **O. Henry.**

Pound, Ezra (Loomis). 1885–1972, U.S. poet, translator, and critic, living in Europe. Indicted for treason by the U.S. government (1945) for pro-Fascist broadcasts during World War II, he was committed to a mental hospital until 1958. He was a founder of imagism and championed the early work of such writers as T. S. Eliot, Joyce, and Hemingway. His life work, the *Cantos* (1925–70), is an unfinished sequence of poems, which incorporates mythological and historical materials in several languages as well as political, economic, and autobiographical elements.

Powell, Anthony (Dymoke). born 1905, British novelist, best known for his sequence of novels under the general title *A Dance to the Music of Time* (1951–75); **Cecil Frank.** 1903–69, British physicist, who was awarded the Nobel prize for physics in 1950 for his discovery of the pi-meson; **Earl,** known as **Bud Powell.** 1924–1966, U.S. modern-jazz pianist; **(John) Enoch.** 1912–98, British politician. An outspoken opponent of Commonwealth immigration into Britain and of British membership of the Common Market (now the European Union), in 1974 he resigned from the Conservative Party, returning to Parliament as a United Ulster Unionist Council member (1974–87); **Michael.** 1905–90, British film writer, producer, and director, best known for his collaboration (1942–57) with Emeric Pressburger. Films include *The Life and Death of Colonel Blimp* (1943), *A Matter of Life and Death* (1946), *The Red Shoes* (1948), and *Peeping Tom* (1960).

Preminger, Otto (Ludwig). 1906–86, U.S. film director, born in Austria. His films include *Carmen Jones* (1954) and *Anatomy of a Murder* (1959).

Prescott, John Leslie. born 1938, British politician: deputy leader of the Labour Party from 1994; deputy prime minister from 1997; **William Hickling.** 1796–1859, U.S. historian, noted for his work on the history of Spain and her colonies.

Presley, Elvis (Aaron *or* Aron). 1935–77, U.S. rock and roll singer. His recordings include "That's all Right (Mama)" (1954), "Heartbreak Hotel" (1956), "Hound Dog" (1956), numbers from the films *Loving You* and *Jailhouse Rock* (both 1957), and *Elvis is back* (1960).

Previn, André. born 1929, U.S. orchestral conductor, born in Germany; living in Britain.

Prince, full name *Prince Rogers Nelson.* born 1958, U.S. rock singer, songwriter, record producer, and multi-instrumentalist. His albums include *Dirty Mind* (1981), *Purple Rain* (1984), *Parade* (1986), and *Emancipation* (1996). He changed his stage name to a symbol and is often referred to as 'The Artist formerly known as Prince'.

Pulitzer, Joseph. 1847–1911, U.S. newspaper publisher, born in Hungary. He established the Pulitzer prizes.

Purcell, Edward Mills. 1912–97, U.S. physicist, noted for his work on the magnetic moments of atomic nuclei: shared the Nobel prize for physics (1952); **Henry.** ?1659–95, English composer, noted chiefly for his rhythmic and harmonic subtlety in setting words. His works include the opera *Dido and Aeneas* (1689), music for the theatrical pieces *King Arthur* (1691) and *The Fairy Queen* (1692), several choral odes, fantasias, sonatas, and church music.

Putnam, Israel. 1718–90, American general in the War of Independence; his cousin **Rufus.** 1738–1824, American soldier in the War of Independence; surveyor general of the U.S. (1796–1803).

Pynchon, Thomas. born 1937, U.S. novelist, author of *V* (1963), *The Crying of Lot 49* (1967), *Gravity's Rainbow* (1973), and *Mason and Dixon* (1997).

Quine, Willard van Orman. born 1908, U.S. philosopher. His works include *Word and Object* (1960), *Philosophy of Logic* (1970), *The Roots of Reference* (1973), and *The Logic of Sequences* (1990).

Quinn, Anthony. born 1915, U.S. film actor, born in Mexico: noted esp. for his performances in *La Strada* (1954) and *Zorba the Greek* (1964).

Rabi, Isidor Isaac. 1898–1988, U.S. physicist, born in Austria, who devised the atomic and molecular beam resonance method of observing atomic spectra. Nobel prize for physics 1944.

Randolph, Edmund Jennings, 1753–1813, U.S. politician. He was a member of the convention that framed the U.S. constitution (1787), attorney general (1789–94), and secretary of state (1794–95); **John,** called *Randolph of Roanoke.* 1773–1833, U.S. politician, noted for his eloquence: in 1820 he opposed the Missouri Compromise that outlawed slavery; Sir **Thomas,** 1st Earl of Moray. Died 1332, Scottish soldier: regent after the death of Robert the Bruce (1329).

Ransom, John Crowe. 1888–1974, U.S. poet and critic.

Rauschenberg, Robert. born 1925, U.S. artist; one of the foremost exponents of pop art.

Ray, John. 1627–1705, English naturalist. He originated natural botanical classification and the division of flowering plants into monocotyledons and dicotyledons; **Man,** real name *Emmanuel Rudnitsky.* 1890–1976, U.S. surrealist photographer; **Satyajit.** 1921–92, Indian film director.

Reagan, Ronald. born 1911, U.S. film actor and Republican statesman: Governor of California (1966–74): 40th president of the U.S. (1981–89).

Redding, Otis. 1941–67, U.S. soul singer and songwriter. His recordings include "Respect" (1965), *Dictionary of Soul* (1966), and "(Sittin' on) The Dock of the Bay" (1968).

Redford, Robert. born 1937, U.S. film actor and director. His films include (as actor) *The Chase* (1966), *Butch Cassidy and the Sundance Kid* (1969), *The Sting* (1973), *All the President's Men* (1976), *Up Close and Personal* (1996) and (as director) *Ordinary People* (1980), *A River Runs Through It* (1992), *Quiz Show* (1994), and *The Horse Whisperer* (1998).

Reed, Sir **Carol.** 1906–76, English film director. His films include *The Third Man* (1949), *An Outcast of the Islands* (1951), and *Oliver!* (1968), for which he won an Oscar; **Lou.** born 1942, U.S. rock singer, songwriter, and guitarist: member of the Velvet Underground (1965–70). His albums include *Transformer* (1972), *Berlin* (1973), *Street Hassle* (1978), *New York* (1989), and *Magic and Loss* (1992); **Walter.** 1851–1902, U.S. physician, who proved that yellow fever is transmitted by mosquitoes (1900).

Reich, Steve. born 1936, U.S. composer, whose works are characterized by the repetition and modification of small rhythmic motifs. His works include *Drumming* (1971), *Music for Large Ensemble* (1978), and *The Desert Music* (1984); **Wilhelm.** 1897–1957, Austrian psychologist, lived in the U.S. An ardent socialist and advocate of sexual freedom, he proclaimed a cosmic unity of all energy and built a machine (the orgone accumulator) to concentrate this energy on human beings. His books include *The Function of the Orgasm* (1927).

Remarque, Erich Maria. 1898–1970, U.S. novelist, born in Germany, noted for his novel of World War I, *All Quiet on the Western Front* (1929).

Revere, Paul. 1735–1818, American patriot and silversmith, best known for his night ride on April 18, 1775, to warn the Massachusetts colonists of the coming of the British troops.

Rice, Elmer, original name *Elmer*

Reizenstein. 1892–1967, U.S. dramatist. His plays include *The Adding Machine* (1923) and *Street Scene* (1929), which was made into a musical by Kurt Weill in 1947.

Rich, Buddy, real name *Bernard Rich.* 1917–87, U.S. jazz drummer and band leader.

Richter, Burton. born 1931, U.S. physicist: shared the 1976 Nobel prize for physics with Samuel Tring for discovering the subatomic particle known as the J/psi particle; **Johann Friedrich**, wrote under the name *Jean Paul.* 1763–1825, German romantic novelist. His works include *Hesperus* (1795) and *Titan* (1800–03); **Sviatoslav.** 1915–97, Ukrainian concert pianist.

Ripley, George. 1802–80, U.S. social reformer and transcendentalist: founder of the Brook Farm experiment in communal living in Massachusetts (1841).

Roach, Hal, full name *Harald Eugene Roach.* 1892–1992, U.S. film producer, whose company produced numerous comedy films in the 1920s and 1930s, including those featuring Harold Lloyd and Laurel and Hardy.

Robbins, Jerome. 1918–98, U.S. ballet dancer and choreographer. He choreographed the musicals *The King and I* (1951) and *West Side Story* (1957).

Robeson, Paul. 1898–1976, U.S. bass singer, actor, and leader in the Black civil rights movement.

Robinson, Edward G., real name *Emanuel Goldenberg.* 1893–1973, U.S. film actor, born in Romania, famous esp. for gangster roles. His films include *Little Caesar* (1930), *Brother Orchid* (1940), *Double Indemnity* (1944), and *All My Sons* (1948); **Edward Arlington.** 1869–1935, U.S. poet, author of narrative verse, often based on Arthurian legend. His works include *Collected Poems* (1922), *The Man Who Died Twice* (1924), and *Tristram* (1927); **(William) Heath.** 1872–1944, British cartoonist and book illustrator, best known for his comic drawings of fantastic

machines; **John (Arthur Thomas)**1919–83, British bishop and theologian, best known for his controversial *Honest to God* (1963), which popularized radical theological discussion. He was suffragan Bishop of Woolwich (1959–69); **Mary.** born 1944, Irish barrister and politician: president of Ireland 1990–97; **Smokey**, real name *William Robinson.* born 1940, U.S. Motown singer, songwriter, and producer. His hits include "The Tears of a Clown" (1970) (with the Miracles) and "Being with you" (1981); **"Sugar" Ray**, real name *Walker Smith.* 1921–89, U.S. boxer, winner of the world middleweight championship on five separate occasions.

Rockefeller, John D(avison). 1839–1937, U.S. industrialist and philanthropist; his son, **John D(avison).** 1874–1960, U.S. capitalist and philanthropist; his son, **Nelson (Aldrich).** 1908–79, U.S. politician: governor of New York State (1958–74); vice president (1974–76).

Rockwell, Norman. 1894–1978, U.S. illustrator, noted esp. for magazine covers.

Rodgers, Richard. 1902–79, U.S. composer of musical comedies. He collaborated with the librettist Lorenz Hart on such musicals as *A Connecticut Yankee* (1927), *On Your Toes* (1936), and *Pal Joey* (1940). After Hart's death his librettist was Oscar Hammerstein II. Two of their musicals, *Oklahoma!* (1943) and *South Pacific* (1949), received the Pulitzer Prize.

Roethke, Theodore. 1908–63, U.S. poet, whose books include *Words for the Wind* (1957) and *The Far Field* (1964).

Rogers, Ginger, real name *Virginia McMath.* 1911–95, U.S. dancer and film actress, who partnered Fred Astaire; **Richard**, Baron Rogers of Riverside. born 1933, British architect. His works include the Pompidou Centre in Paris (1971–77; with Renzo Piano), the Lloyd's building in London (1986), and the Millennium Dome in Greenwich,

London; **William Penn Adair**, known as *Will*. 1879–1935, U.S. actor, newspaper columnist, and humorist in the homespun tradition.

Rollins, Sonny, original name *Theodore Walter Rollins*. born 1930, U.S. jazz tenor saxophonist, noted for his improvisation.

Romberg, Sigmund. 1887–1951, U.S. composer of operettas, born in Hungary. He wrote *The Student Prince* (1924) and *The Desert Song* (1926).

Roosevelt, (Anna) Eleanor. 1884–1962, U.S. writer, diplomat, and advocate of liberal causes: delegate to the United Nations (1945–52); her husband, **Franklin Delano**, known as *FDR*. 1882–1945, 32nd president of the U.S. (1933–45); elected four times. He instituted major reforms (the **New Deal**) to counter the economic crisis of the 1930s and was a forceful leader during World War II; **Theodore**. 1858–1919, 26th president of the U.S. (1901–09). A proponent of extending military power, he won for the U.S. the right to build the Panama Canal (1903). He won the Nobel peace prize (1906), for mediating in the Russo-Japanese war.

Rosenberg, Alfred. 1893–1946, German Nazi politician and writer, who devised much of the racial ideology of Nazism: hanged for war crimes; **Isaac**. 1890–1918, British poet and painter, best known for his poems about life in the trenches during World War I: died in action; **Julius**. 1918–53, U.S. spy, who, with his wife **Ethel** (1914–53), was executed for passing information about nuclear weapons to the Russians.

Ross, Diana. born 1944, U.S. singer: lead vocalist (1961–69) with Motown group the Supremes, whose hits include "Baby Love" (1964). Her subsequent recordings include *Lady Sings the Blues* (film soundtrack, 1972); Sir **James Clark**. 1800–62, British naval officer; explorer of the Arctic and Antarctic. He located the

north magnetic pole (1831) and discovered the Ross Sea during an Antarctic voyage (1839–43); his uncle, Sir **John**. 1777–1856, Scottish naval officer and Arctic explorer; Sir **Ronald**. 1857–1932, English bacteriologist, who discovered the transmission of malaria by mosquitoes: Nobel prize for physiology or medicine 1902.

Roth, Philip. born 1933, U.S. novelist. His works include *Goodbye, Columbus* (1959), *Portnoy's Complaint* (1969), *My Life as a Man* (1974), *Sabbath's Theater* (1995), and *I Married a Communist* (1998).

Rothko, Mark. 1903–70, U.S. abstract expressionist painter, born in Russia.

Royce, Josiah. 1855–1916, U.S. philosopher of monistic idealism. In his ethical studies he emphasized the need for individual loyalty to the world community.

Rubinstein, Anton Grigorevich. 1829–94, Russian composer and pianist; **Artur**. 1886–1982, U.S. pianist, born in Poland.

Runyon, (Alfred) Damon. 1884–1946, U.S. short-story writer, best known for his humorous tales about racy Broadway characters. His story collections include *Guys and Dolls* (1932), which became the basis of a musical (1950).

Rusk, (David) Dean. 1909–94, U.S. statesman: secretary of state (1961–69). He defended U.S. military involvement in Vietnam and opposed recognition of communist China.

Russell, Bertrand (Arthur William), 3rd Earl. 1872–1970, British philosopher and mathematician. His books include *Principles of Mathematics* (1903), *Principia Mathematica* (1910–13) with A. N. Whitehead, *Introduction to Mathematical Philosophy* (1919), *The Problems of Philosophy* (1912), *The Analysis of Mind* (1921), and *An Enquiry into Meaning and Truth* (1940): Nobel prize for literature 1950; **George William** pen name æ. 1867–1935, Irish poet and journalist; **Henry Norris**. 1877–1957, U.S.

astronomer and astrophysicist, who originated one form of the Hertzsprung–Russell diagram; **John**, 1st Earl. 1792–1878, British statesman; prime minister (1846–52; 1865–66). He led the campaign to carry the 1832 Reform Act; **Ken.** born 1927, British film director. His films include *Women in Love* (1969), *The Music Lovers* (1970), *The Boy Friend* (1971), *Valentino* (1977), *Gothic* (1986), and *The Rainbow* (1989).

Ruth, *Old Testament* **a** a Moabite woman, who left her own people to remain with her mother-in-law Naomi, and became the wife of Boaz; an ancestress of David. **b** the book in which these events are recounted; **George Herman**, nicknamed *Babe*. 1895–1948, U.S. professional baseball player from 1914 to 1935.

Saarinen, Eero. 1910–61, U.S. architect, born in Finland. His works include the U.S. Embassy, London (1960).

Sabin, Albert Bruce. 1906–93, U.S. microbiologist, born in Poland. He developed the **Sabin vaccine** (1955), taken orally to immunize against poliomyelitis.

Sacco, Nicola. 1891–1927, U.S. radical agitator, born in Italy. With Bartolomeo Vanzetti, he was executed for murder (1927) despite suspicions that their political opinions influenced the verdict: the case caused international protests.

Salinger, J(erome) D(avid) born 1919, U.S. writer, noted particularly for his novel of adolescence *The Catcher in the Rye* (1951). His first novel for 34 years, *Hapworth 16, 1924* was published in 1997.

Salk, Jonas Edward. 1914–95, U.S. virologist: developed an injected vaccine against poliomyelitis (1954).

Sampras, Pete. born 1971, U.S. tennis player: U.S. singles champion (1990, 1993, 1995, 1996); Wimbledon singles champion (1993–95, 1997–99).

Sandage, Allan Rex. born 1926, U.S. astronomer, who discovered the first quasar (1961).

Sandburg, Carl. 1878–1967, U.S. writer, noted esp. for his poetry, often written in free verse.

Sanger, Frederick. born 1918, English biochemist, who determined the molecular structure of insulin: awarded two Nobel prizes for chemistry (1958; 1980); **Margaret (Higgins).** 1883–1966, U.S. leader of the birth- control movement.

Sankey, Ira David. 1840–1908, U.S. evangelist and hymnodist, noted for his revivalist campaigns in Britain and the U.S. with D. L. Moody.

Santayana, George. 1863–1952, U.S. philosopher, poet, and critic, born in Spain. His works include *The Life of Reason* (1905–06) and *The Realms of Being* (1927–40).

Sapir, Edward. 1884–1939, U.S. anthropologist and linguist, noted for his study of the ethnology and languages of North American Indians.

Sarandon, Susan Abigail. born 1946, U.S. film actress: her films include *Thelma and Louise* (1991), *Lorenzo's Oil* (1992), *The Client* (1994), and *Dead Man Walking* (1996).

Sargent, Sir **(Harold) Malcolm (Watts).** 1895–1967, English conductor; **John Singer.** 1856–1925, U.S. painter, esp. of society portraits; in London from 1885.

Schnabel, Artur. 1882–1951, U.S. pianist and composer, born in Austria.

Schuman, Robert. 1886–1963, French statesman; prime minister (1947–48). He proposed (1950) pooling the coal and steel resources of W Europe; **William (Howard).** 1910–91, U.S. composer.

Schwarzkopf, Elisabeth. born 1915, Austro-British operatic soprano, born in Germany; **Norman**, nicknamed *Stormin' Norman*. born 1934, U.S. general. As head of Central Command, the U.S. military district covering the Middle East, he became the victorious commander-in-chief of the U.S.-led UN forces in the Gulf War (1991).

Scorsese, Martin. born 1942, U.S. film director, whose films include *Taxi Driver* (1976), *Raging Bull*

(1980), *Casino* (1995), *Kundun* (1998), and the controversial *The Last Temptation of Christ* (1988).

Seaborg, Glenn Theodore. 1912–99, U.S. chemist and nuclear physicist. With E.M. McMillan, he discovered several transuranic elements, including plutonium (1940), curium, and americium (1944), and shared a Nobel prize for chemistry 1951.

Seeger, Pete. born 1919. U.S. folk singer and songwriter, noted for his protest songs, which include "We shall Overcome" (1960), "Where have all the Flowers gone?" (1961), "If I had a Hammer" (1962), and "Little Boxes" (1962).

Segrè, Emilio. 1905–89, U.S. physicist, born in Italy, who was the first to produce an artificial element. He shared the Nobel prize for physics (1959) with Owen Chamberlain for their discovery (1955) of the antiproton.

Seles, Monica. born 1973, U.S. tennis player, born in Yugoslavia: winner of the U.S. Open (1991, 1992); stabbed while on court in an unprovoked attack.

Selznick, David O(liver). 1902–62, U.S. film producer, who produced such films as *A Star is Born* (1937), *Gone with the Wind* (1939), and *A Farewell to Arms* (1957).

Sendak, Maurice (Bernard). born 1928, U.S. artist and set designer, best known as an illustrator of children's books, including *Where the Wild Things Are* (1963), *In the Night Kitchen* (1971), and *Nutcracker* (1984).

Sennett, Mack, original name *Michael Sinott.* 1884–1960, U.S. film producer and director, born in Canada, who produced many silent comedy films featuring the Keystone Kops, Charlie Chaplin, and Harold Lloyd, for the Keystone Company.

Sessions, Roger (Huntington). 1896–1985, U.S. composer.

Seton, Ernest Thompson. 1860–1946, U.S. author and illustrator of animal books, born in England.

Seward, William Henry. 1801–72, U.S. statesman; secretary of state (1861- -69). He was a leading opponent of slavery and was responsible for the purchase of Alaska (1867).

Shahn, Ben. 1898–1969, U.S. artist, born in Lithuania, best known as an exponent of social realism, especially in the series (1931–32) inspired by the executions of Sacco and Vanzetti.

Shannon, Claude (Elwood). born 1916, U.S. mathematician, who first developed information theory.

Shapley, Harlow. 1885–1972, U.S. astronomer, director of the Harvard College Observatory (1922–56): noted for his work on the size and structure of the galaxy.

Shaw, Artie, original name *Arthur Arshawsky.* born 1910, U.S. jazz clarinetist, band leader, and composer; **George Bernard,** often known as *GBS.* 1856–1950, Irish dramatist and critic, in England from 1876. He was an active socialist and became a member of the Fabian Society but his major works are effective as satiric attacks rather than political tracts. These include *Arms and the Man* (1894), *Candida* (1894), *Man and Superman* (1903), *Major Barbara* (1905), *Pygmalion* (1913), *Back to Methuselah* (1921), and *St. Joan* (1923): Nobel prize for literature 1925; **Richard Norman.** 1831–1912, English architect; **Thomas Edward.** the name assumed by (T. E.) **Lawrence** after 1927.

Shays, Daniel. ?1747–1825, American soldier and revolutionary leader of a rebellion of Massachusetts farmers against the U.S. government (1786–87).

Shepard, Alan Bartlett, Jr. 1923–98, U.S. naval officer; first U.S. astronaut in space (1961); **Sam,** original name *Samuel Shepard Rogers.* born 1943, U.S. dramatist, film actor, and director. His plays include *Chicago* (1966), *The Tooth of Crime* (1972), and *Buried Child* (1978): films as actor include *Days of Heaven* (1978) and *The Right Stuff* (1983); films as director include *Far North* (1989) and *Silent Tongue* (1994).

Sheridan, Philip Henry. 1831–88, American Union cavalry commander in the Civil War. He forced Lee's surrender to Grant (1865); **Richard Brinsley.** 1751–1816, Irish dramatist, politician, and orator, noted for his comedies of manners *The Rivals* (1775), *School for Scandal* (1777), and *The Critic* (1779).

Sherman, William Tecumseh. 1820–91, American Union commander during the Civil War. He led the victorious march through Georgia (1864), becoming commander of the army in 1869.

Sherwood, Robert Emmet. 1896–1955, U.S. dramatist. His plays include *The Petrified Forest* (1935), *Idiot's Delight* (1936), and *There shall be no Night* (1940).

Shockley, William Bradfield. 1910–89, U.S. physicist, born in Britain, who shared the Nobel prize for physics (1956) with John Bardeen and Walter Brattain for developing the transistor. He also held controversial views on the connection between race and intelligence.

Sholes, Christopher Latham. 1819–90, U.S. inventor, who invented (1868) the typewriter and sold the patent to the Remington company (1873).

Sikorsky, Igor. 1889–1972, U.S. aeronautical engineer, born in Russia. He designed and flew the first four-engined aircraft (1913) and designed the first successful helicopter (1939).

Sills, Beverley, original name *Belle Silverman.* born 1929, U.S. soprano: director of the New York City Opera (1979–89).

Simon, the original name of (Saint) **Peter;** *New Testament* **a** See **Simon Zelotes. b** a relative of Jesus, who may have been identical with Simon Zelotes (Matthew 13:55). **c** Also called: **Simon the Tanner.** a Christian of Joppa with whom Peter stayed (Acts of the Apostles 9:43); **John (Allsebrook),** 1st Viscount Simon. 1873–1954, British statesman and lawyer. He was Liberal home

secretary (1915–16) and, as a leader of the National Liberals, foreign secretary (1931–35), home secretary (1935–37), Chancellor of the Exchequer (1937–40), Lord Chancellor (1940–45); **(Marvin) Neil.** born 1927, U.S. dramatist and librettist, whose plays include *Barefoot in the Park* (1963), *California Suite* (1976), *Biloxi Blues* (1985), *Lost in Yonkers* (1990), and *London Suite* (1995): many have been made into films; **Paul.** born 1942, U.S. pop singer and songwriter. His albums include: with Art Garfunkel (born 1941), *The Sounds of Silence* (1966), and *Bridge over Troubled Water* (1970); and, solo, *Graceland* (1986), and *The Rhythm of the Saints* (1990).

Sinatra, Francis Albert, known as *Frank.* 1915–98, U.S. popular singer and film actor. His recordings include "One for My Baby (and One More for the Road)" (1955) and "My Way" (1969).

Sinclair, Sir **Clive (Marles).** born 1940, British electronics engineer, inventor, and entrepreneur, who produced such electronic goods as pocket calculators and some of the first home computers; however, the Sinclair C5, a small light electric vehicle for one person, proved a commercial failure; **Upton (Beall).** 1878–1968, U.S. novelist, whose *The Jungle* (1906) exposed the working and sanitary conditions of the Chicago meat-packing industry and prompted the passage of food inspection laws.

Singer, Isaac Bashevis. 1904–91, U.S. writer of Yiddish novels and short stories; born in Poland. His works include *Satan in Goray* (1935), *The Family Moscat* (1950), the autobiographical *In my Father's Court* (1966), and *The King of the Fields* (1989): Nobel prize for literature 1978; **Isaac Merrit.** 1811–75, U.S. inventor, who originated and developed an improved chain-stitch sewing machine (1852).

Skinner, B(urrhus) F(rederic). 1904–90, U.S. behavioral psychologist. His "laws of learning", derived from experiments with animals, have been widely applied to education and behavior therapy.

Sloan, John. 1871–1951, U.S. painter and etcher, a leading member of the group of realistic painters known as the Ash Can School. His pictures of city scenes include *McSorley's Bar* (1912) and *Backyards, Greenwich Village* (1914).

Smith, Adam. 1723–90, Scottish economist and philosopher, whose influential book *The Wealth of Nations* (1776) advocated free trade and private enterprise and opposed state interference; **Bessie,** known as *Empress of the Blues.* 1894–1937, U.S. blues singer and songwriter; **Delia.** born 1941, British cookery writer and broadcaster: her publications include *The Complete Cookery Course* (1982); **F.E.** See (1st Earl of) **Birkenhead**. **Harvey.** born 1938, British showjumper; **Ian (Douglas).** born 1919, Zimbabwean statesman; prime minister of Rhodesia (1964–79). He declared independence from Britain unilaterally (1965); **John.** ?1580–1631, English explorer and writer, who helped found the North American colony of Jamestown, Virginia. He was reputedly saved by the Indian chief's daughter Pocahontas from execution by her tribe. Among his works is a *Description of New England* (1616); **John.** 1938–94, British Labour politician; leader of the Labour Party 1992–94; **Joseph.** 1805–44, U.S. religious leader; founder of the Mormon Church; Dame **Maggie.** born 1934, British actress. Her films include *The VIPs* (1963), *The Prime of Miss Jean Brodie* (1969), *The Lonely Passion of Judith Hearne* (1988), and *The Secret Garden* (1993); **Stevie,** real name *Florence Margaret Smith.* 1902–71, British poet. Her works include *Novel on Yellow Paper* (1936), and the poems 'A Good Time was had by All' (1937) and 'Not Waving but Drowning' (1957); **Sydney.** 1771–1845, British clergyman and writer, noted for *The Letters of Peter Plymley* (1807–08), in which he advocated Catholic emancipation;

William. 1769–1839, English geologist, who founded the science of stratigraphy by proving that rock strata could be dated by the fossils they contained.

Sondheim, Stephen (Joshua). born 1930, U.S. songwriter. He wrote the lyrics for *West Side Story* (1957), the score for *Company* (1971), and both for *A Little Night Music* (1973) and *Into the Woods* (1987).

Sontag, Susan. born 1933, U.S. intellectual and essayist, noted esp. for her writings on modern culture. Her works include 'Notes on Camp' (1964), 'Against Interpretation' (1968), *On Photography* (1977), *Illness as Metaphor* (1978), and the novel *The Volcano Lover* (1992).

Sousa, John Philip. 1854–1932, U.S. bandmaster and composer of military marches, such as *The Stars and Stripes Forever* (1897) and *The Liberty Bell* (1893).

Spector, Phil. born 1940, U.S. record producer and songwriter, noted for the densely orchestrated "Wall of Sound" in his work with groups such as the Ronettes and the Crystals.

Spielberg, Steven. born 1947, U.S. film director, noted esp. for the commercial success of such films as *Jaws* (1975), *Close Encounters of the Third Kind* (1977), *Raiders of the Lost Ark* (1981) and its sequels, *E.T.* (1982), and *Jurassic Park* (1993). Other films include *The Color Purple* (1986), *Empire of the Sun* (1988), *Schindler's List* (1993), and *Saving Private Ryan* (1998).

Spillane, Mickey, original name *Frank Morrison Spillane.* born 1918, U.S. detective-story writer, best known for his books featuring the detective Mike Hammer, for example *I, the Jury* (1947) and *The Twisted Thing* (1966).

Spitz, Mark. born 1950, U.S. swimmer, who won seven gold medals at the 1972 Olympic Games.

Spock, Benjamin, known as *Dr Spock.* 1903–98, U.S. paediatrician, whose *The Common Sense Book of Baby and Child Care* (1946) has influenced the upbringing of children throughout the world.

Springsteen, Bruce. born 1949, U.S. rock singer, songwriter, and guitarist. His albums with the E Street Band include *Born to Run* (1975), *Darkness on the Edge of Town* (1978), and *Born in the U.S.A.* (1984).

Starr, (Myra) Belle. 1848–89, U.S. outlaw, a famous rustler of horses and cattle; **Ringo**, original name *Richard Starkey.* born 1940, British rock musician; drummer (1962–70) with the Beatles.

Steffens, (Joseph) Lincoln. 1866–1936, U.S. political analyst, known for his exposure of political corruption.

Stein, Gertrude. 1874–1946, U.S. writer, resident in Paris (1903–1946). Her works include *Three Lives* (1908) and *The Autobiography of Alice B. Toklas* (1933); **Heinrich Friedrich Carl**, Baron Stein. 1757–1831, Prussian statesman, who contributed greatly to the modernization of Prussia and played a major role in the European coalition against Napoleon (1813–15); **Jock**, real name *John.* 1922–85, Scottish footballer and manager: managed Celtic (1965–78) and Scotland (1978–85).

Steinbeck, John (Ernst). 1902–68, U.S. writer, noted for his novels about agricultural workers, esp. *The Grapes of Wrath* (1939): Nobel prize for literature 1962.

Steinitz, Wilhelm. 1836–1900, U.S. chess player, born in Prague; world champion (1866–94).

Steinway, Henry (Engelhard), original name *Heinrich Engelhardt Steinweg.* 1797–1871, U.S. piano maker, born in Germany.

Stern, Isaac. born 1920, U.S. concert violinist, born in Russia.

Stevens, Thaddeus. 1792–1868, U.S. Radical Republican politician. An opponent of slavery, he supported Reconstruction and entered the resolution calling for the impeachment of President Andrew Johnson; **Wallace.** 1879–1955, U.S. poet, whose books include the collections *Harmonium* (1923), *The Man with the Blue Guitar* (1937), and *Transport to Summer* (1947).

Stevenson, Adlai Ewing. 1900–68, U.S. statesman: twice defeated as Democratic presidential candidate (1952; 1956); U.S. delegate at the United Nations (1961–65); **Robert Louis (Balfour).** 1850–94, Scottish writer: his novels include *Treasure Island* (1883), *Kidnapped* (1886), and *The Master of Ballantrae* (1889).

Stewart, the usual spelling for the royal house of **Stuart** before the reign of Mary Queen of Scots (Mary Stuart); **Jackie,** full name *John Young Stewart.* born 1939, Scottish motor-racing driver: world champion 1969, 1971, and 1973; **James (Maitland).** 1908–97, U.S. film actor, known for his distinctive drawl; appeared in many films including *Destry Rides Again* (1939), *The Glenn Miller Story* (1953), *Shenandoah* (1965), and *Airport 77* (1977); **Rod.** born 1945, British rock singer: vocalist with the Faces (1969–75). His albums include *Gasoline Alley* (1970), *Every Picture Tells a Story* (1971), and *Atlantic Crossing* (1975).

Stieglitz, Alfred. 1864–1946, U.S. photographer, whose work helped to develop photography as an art: among his best photographs are those of his wife Georgia O'Keeffe. He was also well known as a promoter of modern art.

Stilwell, Joseph W(arren), known as *Vinegar Joe.* 1883–1946, U.S. general, who was (1941–44) Chiang Kai-shek's chief of staff and commander of all U.S. forces in China, Burma (Myanmar), and India.

Stokowski, Leopold. 1887–1977, U.S. conductor, born in Britain. He did much to popularize classical music with orchestral transcriptions and film appearances, esp. in *Fantasia* (1940).

Stone, Oliver. born 1946, U.S. film director and screenwriter: his films include *Platoon* (1986), *Born on the Fourth of July* (1989), *JFK* (1991), and *Nixon* (1995); **Sharon.** born 1958, U.S. film actress: her films include *Basic Instinct* (1991) and *Casino* (1995).

Stowe, Harriet Elizabeth Beecher.

1811–96, U.S. writer, whose bestselling novel *Uncle Tom's Cabin* (1852) contributed to the antislavery cause.

Stravinsky, Igor Fyodorovich. 1882–1971, U.S. composer, born in Russia. He created ballet scores, such as *The Firebird* (1910), *Petrushka* (1911), and *The Rite of Spring* (1913), for Diaghilev. These were followed by neoclassical works, including *Oedipus Rex* (1927) and the *Symphony of Psalms* (1930). The 1950s saw him reconciled to serial techniques, which he employed in such works as the *Canticum Sacrum* (1955), the ballet *Agon* (1957), and *Requiem Canticles* (1966).

Strayhorn, Billy, full name *William Strayhorn*. 1915–67, U.S. jazz composer and pianist, noted esp. for his association (1939–67) with Duke Ellington.

Streep, Meryl, original name *Mary Louise Streep*. born 1949, U.S. actress. Her films include *The Deerhunter* (1978), *Kramer vs Kramer* (1979), *The French Lieutenant's Woman* (1981), *Sophie's Choice* (1982), *Out of Africa* (1986), and *Dancing at Lughnasa* (1999).

Streisand, Barbra. born 1942, U.S. singer, actress, and film director: the films she has acted in include *Funny Girl* (1968) and *A Star is Born* (1976); her films as actress and director include *Yentl* (1983), *Prince of Tides* (1990), and *The Mirror has Two Faces* (1996).

Struve, Otto. 1897–1963, U.S. astronomer, born in Russia, noted for his work in stellar spectroscopy and his discovery (1937) of interstellar hydrogen.

Sullivan, Sir **Arthur (Seymour).** 1842–1900, English composer who wrote operettas, such as *H.M.S. Pinafore* (1878) and *The Mikado* (1885), with W. S. Gilbert as librettist; **Louis (Henri).** 1856–1924, U.S. pioneer of modern architecture: he coined the slogan "form follows function".

Szell, George. 1897–1970, U.S. conductor, born in Hungary.

Szent-Györgyi, Albert (von Nagyrapolt). 1893–1986, U.S. biochemist, born in Hungary, who isolated ascorbic acid and identified it as vitamin C. Nobel prize for physiology or medicine 1937.

Szilard, Leo. 1898–1964, U.S. physicist, born in Hungary, who originated the idea of a self-sustaining nuclear chain reaction (1934). He worked on the atomic bomb during World War II but later pressed for the international control of nuclear weapons.

Taft, William Howard. 1857–1930, U.S. statesman; 27th president of the U.S. (1909–13).

Tanguy, Yves. 1900–55, U.S. surrealist painter, born in France.

Tarkington, (Newton) Booth. 1869–1946, U.S. novelist. His works include the historical romance *Monsieur Beaucaire* (1900), tales of the Middle West, such as *The Magnificent Ambersons* (1918) and *Alice Adams* (1921), and the series featuring the character Penrod.

Tate, (John Orley) Allen. 1899–1979, U.S. poet and critic; Sir **Henry.** 1819–99, British sugar refiner and philanthropist; founder of the Tate Gallery; **Nahum.** 1652–1715, British poet, dramatist, and hymn-writer, born in Ireland: poet laureate (1692–1715). He is best known for writing a version of *King Lear* with a happy ending.

Tatum, Art, full name *Arthur Tatum*. 1910–56, U.S. jazz pianist; **Edward Lawrie.** 1909–75, U.S. biochemist, who showed how genes regulate biochemical processes in an organism and demonstrated that bacteria reproduce sexually; Nobel prize for physiology or medicine (1958) with Beadle and Lederberg.

Taylor, A(lan) J(ohn) P(ercivale). 1906–90, British historian whose many works include *The Origins of the Second World War* (1961); **Brook.** 1685–1731, English mathematician, who laid the foundations of differential calculus; **Elizabeth.** born 1932, U.S. film actress, born in England: films include *National Velvet*

(1944), *Cat on a Hot Tin Roof* (1958), *Suddenly Last Summer* (1959), and *Butterfield 8* (1960) and *Who's Afraid of Virginia Woolf?* (1966), for both of which she won Oscars; **Frederick Winslow.** 1856–1915, U.S. engineer, who pioneered the use of time and motion studies to increase efficiency in industry; **Jeremy.** 1613–67, English cleric, best known for his devotional manuals *Holy Living* (1650) and *Holy Dying* (1651); **Zachary.** 1784–1850, 12th president of the U.S. (1849–50); hero of the Mexican War.

Teller, Edward. born 1908, U.S. nuclear physicist, born in Hungary: a major contributor to the development of the hydrogen bomb (1952).

Temple, Shirley, married name *Shirley Temple Black.* born 1928, U.S. film actress and politician. Her films as a child star include *Little Miss Marker* (1934), *Wee Willie Winkie* (1937), and *Heidi* (1937). She was U.S. ambassador to Ghana (1974–76) and to Czechoslovakia (1989–92); Sir **William.** 1628–99, English diplomat and essayist. He negotiated the Triple Alliance (1668) and the marriage of William of Orange to Mary II; **William.** 1881–1944, English prelate and advocate of social reform; archbishop of Canterbury (1942–44).

Tesla, Nikola. 1857–1943, U.S. electrical engineer and inventor, born in Smiljan, now in Croatia. His inventions include a transformer, generators, and dynamos.

Theiler, Max. 1899–1972, U.S. virologist, born in South Africa, who developed a vaccine against yellow fever. Nobel prize for physiology or medicine 1951.

Theroux, Paul (Edward). born 1941, U.S. novelist and travel writer. His novels include *Picture Palace* (1978), *The Mosquito Coast* (1981), and *My Other Life* (1996); travel writings include *The Great Railway Bazaar* (1975).

Thomson, Sir **George Paget,** son of Joseph John Thomson. 1892–1975,

British physicist, who discovered (1927) the diffraction of electrons by crystals: shared the Nobel prize for physics 1937; **James.** 1700–48, Scottish poet. He anticipated the romantics' feeling for nature in *The Seasons* (1726–30); **James,** pen name *B.V.* 1834–82, British poet, born in Scotland, noted esp. for *The City of Dreadful Night* (1874), reflecting man's isolation and despair; Sir **Joseph John.** 1856–1940, British physicist. He discovered the electron (1897) and his work on the nature of positive rays led to the discovery of isotopes: Nobel prize for physics 1906; **Roy,** 1st Baron Thomson of Fleet. 1894–1976, British newspaper proprietor, born in Canada; **Virgil.** 1896–1989, U.S. composer, music critic, and conductor, whose works include two operas, *Four Saints in Three Acts* (1928) and *The Mother of Us All* (1947), piano sonatas, a cello concerto, songs, and film music; Sir **William.** See (1st Baron) **Kelvin.**

Thoreau, Henry David. 1817–62, U.S. writer, noted esp. for *Walden, or Life in the Woods* (1854), an account of his experiment in living in solitude. A powerful social critic, his essay *Civil Disobedience* (1849) influenced such dissenters as Gandhi.

Thorndike, Edward Lee. 1874–1949, U.S. psychologist, who worked on animals and proposed that all learnt behavior is regulated by rewards and punishments (**Thorndike's law** *or* **law of effect**); Dame (**Agnes**) **Sybil.** 1882–1976, British actress.

Thorpe, James Francis. 1888–1953, American football player and athlete: Olympic pentathlon and decathlon champion (1912); **Jeremy.** born 1929, British politician; leader of the Liberal party (1967–76).

Thurber, James (Grover). 1894–1961, U.S. humorist and illustrator. He contributed drawings and stories to the *New Yorker* and his books include *Is Sex Necessary?* (1929), written with E. B. White.

Tiffany, Louis Comfort. 1848–1933,

U.S. glass-maker and Art-Nouveau craftsman, best known for creating the Favrile style of stained glass.

Tilden, Bill, full name *William Tatem Tilden,* known as *Big Bill.* 1893–1953, U.S. tennis player: won the U.S. singles championship (1920–25, 1929) and the British singles championship (1920–21, 1930).

Tillich, Paul Johannes. 1886–1965, U.S. Protestant theologian and philosopher, born in Germany. His works include *The Courage to Be* (1952) and *Systematic Theology* (1951–63).

Ting, Samuel Chao Chung. U.S. physicist, who discovered the J/psi particle independently of Burton Richter, with whom he shared (1976) the Nobel prize for physics.

Tobey, Mark. 1890–1976, U.S. painter. Influenced by Chinese calligraphy, he devised a style of improvisatory abstract painting called "white writing".

Tombaugh, Clyde William. 1906–97, U.S. astronomer, who discovered (1930) the planet Pluto.

Tom Thumb, General, stage name of *Charles Stratton.* 1838–83, U.S. midget, exhibited in P. T. Barnum's circus; a dwarf; midget. [after *Tom Thumb,* the tiny hero of several English folk tales]

Townes, Charles Hard. born 1915, U.S. physicist, noted for his research in quantum electronics leading to the invention of the maser and the laser; shared the Nobel prize for physics in 1964.

Tracy, Spencer. 1900–67, U.S. film actor. His films include *The Power and the Glory* (1933), *Captains Courageous* (1937) and *Boys' Town* (1938), for both of which he won Oscars, *Adam's Rib* (1949), and *Bad Day at Black Rock* (1955).

Traven, B(en), original name *Albert Otto Max Feige.* ?1882–1969, U.S. novelist, born in Germany and living in Mexico from 1920, who kept his identity secret. His novels, originally written in German, include *The Treasure of Sierra Madre* (1934).

Trevino, Lee. born 1939, U.S.

professional golfer: winner of the U.S. Open Championship (1968; 1971) and the British Open Championship (1971; 1972).

Trilling, Lionel. 1905–75, U.S. literary critic, whose works include *The Liberal Imagination* (1950) and *Sincerity and Authenticity* (1974).

Truman, Harry S. 1884–1972, U.S. Democratic statesman; 33rd president of the U.S. (1945–53). He approved the dropping of the two atomic bombs on Japan (1945), advocated the postwar loan to Britain, and involved the U.S. in the Korean War.

Tunney, Gene, original name *James Joseph Tunney.* 1897–1978, U.S. boxer; world heavyweight champion (1926–28).

Turner, J(oseph) M(allord) W(illiam). 1775–1851, British landscape painter; a master of water colors. He sought to convey atmosphere by means of an innovative use of color and gradations of light; **Nat.** 1800–31, U.S. rebel slave, who led (1831) Turner's Insurrection, the only major slave revolt in U.S. history: executed; **Tina,** real name *Annie Mae Bullock.* born 1940, U.S. rock singer who performed (1958–75) with her then husband Ike Turner (born 1931) and later as a solo act. Her recordings include "River Deep, Mountain High" (1966) and Simply the Best (1991).

Twain, Mark, pen name of *Samuel Langhorne Clemens.* 1835–1910, U.S. novelist and humorist, famous for his classics *The Adventures of Tom Sawyer* (1876) and *The Adventures of Huckleberry Finn* (1885).

Tyler, John. 1790–1862, U.S. statesman; tenth president of the U.S. (1841–45); **Wat.** died 1381, English leader of the Peasants' Revolt (1381).

Tyson, Mike. born 1966, U.S. boxer. World heavyweight champion (1986–90, and 1996): jailed for rape (1992–95); banned from professional boxing in 1997 after biting off part of his opponent's ear.

Updike, John (Hoyer). born 1932,

U.S. writer. His novels include *Rabbit, Run* (1960), *Couples* (1968), *The Coup* (1979), *Brazil* (1993), *Toward the End of Time* (1998), and *Rabbit is Rich* (1982) and *Rabbit at Rest* (1990), both of which won Pulitzer prizes.

Urey, Harold Clayton. 1893–1981, U.S. chemist, who discovered the heavy isotope of hydrogen, deuterium (1932), and worked on methods of separating uranium isotopes: Nobel prize for chemistry 1934.

Valentino, Rudolph, original name *Rodolpho Guglielmi di Valentina d'Antonguolla.* 1895–1926, U.S. silent-film actor, born in Italy. He is famous for his romantic roles in such films as *The Sheik* (1921).

Van Allen, James Alfred. born 1914, U.S. physicist, noted for his use of satellites to investigate cosmic radiation in the upper atmosphere.

Van Buren, Martin. 1782–1862, U.S. Democratic statesman; 8th president of the U.S. (1837–41).

Vanderbilt, Cornelius, known as *Commodore Vanderbilt.* 1794–1877, U.S. steamship and railway magnate and philanthropist.

Vanzetti, Bartolomeo. 1888–1927, U.S. radical agitator, born in Italy: executed with Sacco in a case that had worldwide political repercussions.

Varèse, Edgar(d). 1883–1965, U.S. composer, born in France. His works, which combine extreme dissonance with complex rhythms and the use of electronic techniques, include *Ionisation* (1931) and *Poème électronique* (1958).

Vaughan, Henry. 1622–95, Welsh mystic poet, best known for his *Silex Scintillans* (1650; 1655); Dame **Janet (Maria).** 1899–1993, British physician and university official: helped set up Britain's first National Blood Transfusion Service (1939): after World War II, became Britain's expert on the effects of radiation on humans; Principal of Somerville College, Oxford (1945–67); **Sarah (Lois).** 1924–90, U.S. jazz vocalist and pianist, noted esp. for her skill in

vocal improvisation.

Veblen, Thorstein. 1857–1929, U.S. economist and social scientist, noted for his analysis of social and economic institutions. His works include *The Theory of the Leisure Class* (1899) and *The Theory of Business Enterprise* (1904).

Venturi, Robert. born 1925, U.S. architect, a pioneer of the postmodernist style. His writings include *Complexity and Contradiction in Architecture* (1966).

Vidal, Gore. born 1925, U.S. novelist and critic. His novels include *Burr* (1974), *Lincoln* (1984), and *The Season of Conflict* (1996).

von Braun, Wernher. 1912–77, U.S. rocket engineer, born in Germany, where he designed the V-2 missile used in World War II. In the U.S. he worked on the Apollo project.

Vonnegut, Kurt. born 1922, U.S. novelist. His works include *Cat's Cradle* (1963), *Slaughterhouse Five* (1969), *Galapagos* (1985), *Hocus Pocus* (1990), and *Timequake* (1997).

von Neumann, John. 1903–57, U.S. mathematician, born in Hungary. He formulated game theory and contributed to the development of the atomic bomb and to the development of the stored-program computer (**von Neumann machine**).

von Sternberg, Joseph, real name *Jonas Sternberg.* 1894–1969, U.S. film director, born in Austria, whose films include *The Blue Angel* (1930), *Blonde Venus* (1932), *The Scarlet Empress* (1934), and the unfinished *I, Claudius* (1937).

von Stroheim, Erich, real name *Hans Erich Maria Stroheim von Nordenwall.* 1885–1957, U.S. film director and actor, born in Austria, whose films include *Foolish Wives* (1921) and *Greed* (1923).

Waksman, Selman Abraham. 1888–1973, U.S. microbiologist, born in Russia. He discovered streptomycin: Nobel prize for physiology or medicine 1952.

Walcott, Derek (Alton). born 1930, St Lucian poet and playwright, whose works include the poetry collections *In a Green Night* (1962) and *The Bounty* (1997), the play *The Dream on Monkey Mountain* (1967), and the long poem *Omeros* (1990): awarded the Nobel prize for literature 1992; **Jersey Joe,** real name *Arnold Raymond Cream.* 1914–94, U.S. boxer: world heavyweight champion 1951–52.

Walker, Alice (Malsenior). born 1944, U.S. writer: her works include *In Love and Trouble: Stories of Black Women* (1973) and the novels *Meridian* (1976), *The Color Purple* (1982), and *Possessing the Secret of Joy* (1992); **John.** born 1952, New Zealand middle-distance runner, the first athlete to run one hundred sub-four-minute miles.

Waller, Edmund. 1606–87, English poet and politician, famous for his poem *Go, Lovely Rose;* **Fats,** real name *Thomas Waller.* 1904–43, U.S. jazz pianist and singer.

Walter, Bruno, real name *Bruno Walter Schlesinger.* 1876–1962, U.S. conductor, born in Germany: famous for his performances of Haydn, Mozart, and Mahler; **John.** 1739–1812, English publisher; founded *The Daily Universal Register* (1785), which in 1788 became *The Times.*

Warhol, Andy, real name *Andrew Warhola.* ?1926–87, U.S. artist and film maker; one of the foremost exponents of pop art.

Warren, Earl. 1891–1974, U.S. lawyer; chief justice of the U.S. (1953– 69). He chaired the commission that investigated the murder of President Kennedy.

Washington, Booker T(aliaferro). 1856–1915, U.S. Black educationalist and writer; **George.** 1732–99, U.S. general and statesman; first president of the U.S. (1789–97). He was appointed commander in chief of the Continental Army (1775) at the outbreak of the War of American Independence, which ended with his defeat of Cornwallis at Yorktown (1781). He presided over the convention at Philadelphia (1787) that formulated the constitution of

the U.S. and elected him president.

Waters, Muddy, real name *McKinley Morganfield.* 1915–83, U.S. blues guitarist, singer, and songwriter. His songs include "Rollin' Stone" (1948) and "Got my Mojo Working" (1954).

Watson, James Dewey. born 1928, U.S. biologist, whose contribution to the discovery of the helical structure of DNA won him a Nobel prize for physiology or medicine shared with Francis Crick and Maurice Wilkins in 1962; **John B(roadus).** 1878–1958, U.S. psychologist; a leading exponent of behaviorism; **John Christian.** 1867–1941, Australian statesman, born in Chile: prime minister of Australia (1904); **Tom,** full name *Thomas Sturges Watson.* born 1949, U.S. golfer: won the U.S. Open Championship (1982), the British Open Championship (1975, 1977, 1980, 1982, 1983), and the World Series (1975, 1977, 1980).

Wayne, John, real name *Marion Michael Morrison.* 1907–79, U.S. film actor, noted esp. for his many Westerns, which include *Stagecoach* (1939), *The Alamo* (1960), and *True Grit* (1969), for which he won an Oscar.

Webster, Daniel. 1782–1852, U.S. politician and orator; **John.** ?1580–?1625, English dramatist, noted for his revenge tragedies *The White Devil* (?1612) and *The Duchess of Malfi* (?1613); **Noah.** 1758–1843, U.S. lexicographer, famous for his *American Dictionary of the English Language* (1828).

Weinberg, Steven. born 1933, U.S. physicist, who shared the Nobel prize for physics (1979) with Sheldon Glashow and Abdus Salam for his role in formulating the electroweak theory.

Weissmuller, John Peter, known as *Johnny.* 1904–84, U.S. swimmer and film actor, who won Olympic gold medals in 1924 and 1928 and played the title role in the early Tarzan films.

Welles, (George) Orson 1915–85, U.S. film director, actor, producer, and screenwriter. His *Citizen Kane* (1941) and *The Magnificent*

Ambersons (1942) are regarded as film classics.

Wells, Henry. 1805–78, U.S. businessman, who founded (1852) with William Fargo the express mail service Wells, Fargo and Company;

H(erbert) G(eorge). 1866–1946, British writer. His science-fiction stories include *The Time Machine* (1895), *War of the Worlds* (1898), and *The Shape of Things to Come* (1933). His novels on contemporary social questions, such as *Kipps* (1905), *Tono-Bungay* (1909), and *Ann Veronica* (1909), affected the opinions of his day. His nonfiction works include *The Outline of History* (1920).

Welty, Eudora. born 1909, U.S. novelist and short-story writer, noted for her depiction of life in the Mississippi delta. Her novels include *Delta Wedding* (1946) and *The Optimist's Daughter* (1972).

West, Benjamin. 1738–1820, U.S. painter, in England from 1763; **Mae.** 1892–1980, U.S. film actress; **Nathanael,** real name *Nathan Weinstein.* 1903–40, U.S. novelist: author of *Miss Lonely-Hearts* (1933) and *The Day of the Locust* (1939); Dame **Rebecca,** real name *Cicily Isabel Andrews* (née *Fairfield*). 1892–1983, British journalist, novelist, and critic.

Weyl, Hermann. 1885–1955, U.S. mathematician, born in Germany; noted for his work on group theory and the mathematics of relativity.

Wharton, Edith (Newbold). 1862–1937, U.S. novelist; author of *The House of Mirth* (1905) and *Ethan Frome* (1911).

Wheeler, John Archibald. born 1911, U.S. physicist, noted for his work on nuclear fission and the development (1949–51) of the hydrogen bomb, also for his work on unified field theory; Sir (**Robert Eric**) **Mortimer.** 1890–1976, Scottish archaeologist, who did much to increase public interest in archaeology. He is noted esp. for his excavations at Mohenjo-Daro and Harappa in the Indus Valley and at

Maiden Castle in Dorset.

Whistler, James Abbott McNeill. 1834–1903, U.S. painter and etcher, living in Europe. He is best known for his sequence of nocturnes and his portraits.

Whitman, Walt(er). 1819–92, U.S. poet, whose life's work is collected in *Leaves of Grass* (1855 and subsequent enlarged editions). His poems celebrate existence and the multiple elements that make up a democratic society.

Whitney, Eli. 1765–1825, U.S. inventor of a mechanical cotton gin (1793) and pioneer manufacturer of interchangeable parts; **William Dwight.** 1827–94, U.S. philologist, noted esp. for his *Sanskrit Grammar* (1879).

Whittier, John Greenleaf. 1807–92, U.S. poet and humanitarian: a leading campaigner in the antislavery movement. His poems include *Snow-Bound* (1866).

Whorf, Benjamin Lee. 1897–1943, U.S. linguist, who argued that human language determines perception; See also **Sapir-Whorf hypothesis**.

Wiener, Norbert. 1894–1964, U.S. mathematician, who developed the concept of cybernetics.

Wiesel, Elie. born 1928, U.S. human rights campaigner: noted esp. for his documentaries of wartime atrocities against the Jews; Nobel peace prize 1986.

Wigner, Eugene Paul. 1902–95, U.S. physicist, born in Hungary. He is noted for his contributions to nuclear physics: shared the Nobel prize for physics 1963.

Wilder, Billy, real name *Samuel Wilder.* born 1906, U.S. film director and screenwriter, born in Austria. His films include *Double Indemnity* (1944), *The Lost Weekend* (1945), *Sunset Boulevard* (1950), *The Seven Year Itch* (1955), *Some Like it Hot* (1959), *The Apartment* (1960), and *Buddy Buddy* (1981); **Thornton.** 1897–1975 U.S. novelist and dramatist. His works include the novel *The Bridge of San Luis Rey*

(1927) and the play *The Skin of Our Teeth* (1942).

Wilkes, Charles. 1798–1877, U.S. explorer of Antarctica; **John.** 1727–97, English politician, who was expelled from the House of Commons and outlawed for writing scurrilous articles about the government. He became a champion of parliamentary reform.

Williams, Hank, real name *Hiram Williams.* 1923–53, U.S. country singer and songwriter. His songs (all 1948–52) include "Jambalaya", "Your Cheatin' Heart", and "Why Don't you Love me (like you Used to Do?)"; **John.** born 1941, Australian classical guitarist, living in Britain; **Ralph Vaughan.** See (Ralph) Vaughan Williams. **Raymond (Henry).** 1921–88, British literary critic and novelist, noted esp. for such works as *Culture and Society* (1958) and *The Long Revolution* (1961), which offer a socialist analysis of the relationship between society and culture; **Tennessee,** real name *Thomas Lanier Williams.* 1911–83, U.S. dramatist. His plays include *The Glass Menagerie* (1944), *A Streetcar Named Desire* (1947), *Cat on a Hot Tin Roof* (1955), and *Night of the Iguana* (1961); **William Carlos.** 1883–1963, U.S. poet, who formulated the poetic concept "no ideas but in things". His works include *Paterson* (1946–58), which explores the daily life of a man living in a modern city, and the prose work *In the American Grain* (1925).

Wills, Helen Newington, married name *Helen Wills Moody Roark.* 1905–98, U.S. tennis player. She was Wimbledon singles champion eight times between 1927 and 1938. She also won the U.S. title seven times and the French title four times; **William John.** 1834–61, English explorer: Robert Burke's deputy in an expedition on which both men died after crossing Australia from north to south for the first time.

Wilson, Alexander. 1766–1813, Scottish ornithologist in the U.S.; **Sir Angus (Frank Johnstone).** 1913–91, British writer, whose works include

the collection of short stories *The Wrong Set* (1949) and the novels *Anglo-Saxon Attitudes* (1956) and *No Laughing Matter* (1967); **Charles Thomson Rees.** 1869–1959, Scottish physicist, who invented the cloud chamber: shared the Nobel prize for physics 1927; **Edmund.** 1895–1972, U.S. critic, noted esp. for *Axel's Castle* (1931), a study of the symbolist movement; **(James) Harold,** Baron Wilson of Rievaulx. 1916–95, British Labour statesman; prime minister (1964–70; 1974–76); **Richard.** 1714–82, Welsh landscape painter; **(Thomas) Woodrow.** 1856–1924, U.S. Democratic statesman; 28th president of the U.S. (1913–21). He led the U.S. into World War I in 1917 and proposed the Fourteen Points (1918) as a basis for peace. Although he secured the formation of the League of Nations, the U.S. Senate refused to support it: Nobel peace prize 1919. **Wilsonian**

Wodehouse, Sir **P(elham) G(renville).** 1881–1975, U.S. author, born in England. His humorous novels of upper-class life in England include the *Psmith* and *Jeeves* series. **Wode'housian**

Wolfe, James. 1727–59, English soldier, who commanded the British capture of Quebec, in which he was killed; **Thomas (Clayton).** 1900–38, U.S. novelist, noted for his autobiographical fiction, esp. *Look Homeward, Angel* (1929).

Wonder, Stevie. real name *Steveland Judkins Morris.* born 1950, U.S. Motown singer, songwriter, and multi-instrumentalist. His recordings include *Up-Tight* (1966), "Superstition" (1972), *Innervisions* (1973), *Songs in the Key of Life* (1976), and "I Just Called to Say I Love You" (1985).

Woods, Tiger, real name *Eldrick Woods.* born 1975, U.S. golfer: youngest U.S. Masters champion (1997) and first Black golfer to win a major championship; also won USPGA in 1999.

Woodward, R(obert) B(urns). 1917–79, U.S. chemist. For his work on the synthesis of quinine, strychnine, cholesterol, and other organic compounds he won the Nobel prize for chemistry 1965.

Woollcott, Alexander. 1887–1943, U.S. writer and critic. His collected essays include *Shouts and Murmurs* (1922).

Woolworth, Frank Winfield. 1852–1919, U.S. merchant; founder of an international chain of department stores selling inexpensive goods.

Wright, Frank Lloyd. 1869–1959, U.S. architect, whose designs include the Imperial Hotel, Tokyo (1916), the Guggenheim Museum, New York (1943), and many private houses. His "organic architecture" sought a close relationship between buildings and their natural surroundings; **Joseph,** known as *Wright of Derby.* 1734–97, British painter, noted for his paintings of industrial and scientific subjects, esp. *The Orrery* (?1765) and *The Air Pump* (1768); **Joseph.** 1855–1930, British philologist; editor of *The English Dialect Dictionary* (1898–1905); **Judith (Arundel).** born 1915, Australian poet, critic, and conservationist. Her collections of poetry include *The Moving Image* (1946), *Woman to Man* (1949), and *A Human Pattern* (1990); **Richard.** 1908–60, U.S. Black novelist and short-story writer, best known for the novel *Native Son* (1940); **Wilbur** (1867–1912) and his brother, **Orville** (1871–1948), U.S. aviation pioneers, who designed and flew the first powered aircraft (1903); **William,** known as *Billy.* 1924–94, English footballer: winner of 105 caps.

Yamasaki, Minoru. 1912–86, U.S. architect. His buildings include St Louis Airport, Missouri (1953–55) and the World Trade Center, New York (1970–77).

York, the English royal house that reigned from 1461 to 1485 and was descended from Richard Plantagenet, **Duke of York** (1411–60), whose claim to the throne precipitated the Wars of the Roses. His sons reigned

as Edward IV and Richard III; **Alvin C(ullum).** 1887–1964, U.S. soldier and hero of World War I; **Duke of,** full name *Prince Frederick Augustus, Duke of York and Albany.* 1763–1827, second son of George III of Great Britain and Ireland. An undistinguished commander-in-chief of the British army (1798–1809), he is the "grand old Duke of York" of the nursery rhyme; **Prince Andrew, Duke of.** born 1960, second son of Elizabeth II of Great Britain and Northern Ireland. He married (1986) Miss Sarah Ferguson; they divorced in 1996; their first daughter, Princess Beatrice of York, was born in 1988 and their second, Princess Eugenie of York, in 1990.

Young, Brigham. 1801–77, U.S. Mormon leader, who led the Mormon migration to Utah and founded Salt Lake City (1847); **Edward.** 1683–1765, English poet and dramatist, noted for his *Night Thoughts on Life, Death, and Immortality* (1742–45); **Lester.** 1909–59, U.S. saxophonist and clarinetist. He was a leading early exponent of the tenor saxophone in jazz; **Neil (Percival).** born 1945, Canadian rock guitarist, singer, and songwriter. His albums include *Harvest* (1972), *Rust Never Sleeps* (1979), and *Sleeps with Angels* (1994); **Thomas.** 1773–1829, English physicist, physician, and Egyptologist. He helped to establish the wave theory of light by his experiments on optical interference and assisted in the decipherment of the Rosetta Stone.

Zappa, Frank. 1940–93, U.S. rock musician, songwriter, and producer: founder and only permanent member of the Mothers of Invention. His recordings include *Freak Out* (1966), *Hot Rats* (1969), and *Sheik Yerbouti* (1979).

Ziegfeld, Florenz. 1869–1932, U.S. theatrical producer, noted for his series of extravagant revues (1907–31), known as the Ziegfeld Follies.